W9-CHB-131

THE BANKERS' HANDBOOK

The Bankers' Handbook

Edited by

WILLIAM H. BAUGHN
Professor of Finance
University of Colorado
Boulder, Colorado
and
Director Emeritus
Stonier Graduate School of Banking

THOMAS I. STORRS
Retired Chairman, NCNB Corporation
Charlotte, North Carolina

CHARLS E. WALKER
President, Charls E. Walker Associates, Inc.
Washington, D.C.

THIRD EDITION

DOW JONES-IRWIN
Homewood, Illinois 60430

Dow Jones-Irwin is a trademark of Dow Jones & Company, Inc.

©DOW JONES-IRWIN 1966, 1978, and 1988

All rights reserved. No part of this publication may be
reproduced, stored in a retrieval system, or transmitted,
in any form or by any means, electronic, mechanical,
photocopying, recording, or otherwise, without the prior
written permission of the publisher.

This publication is designed to provide accurate and
authoritative information in regard to the subject matter
covered. It is sold with the understanding that the
publisher is not engaged in rendering legal, accounting, or
other professional service. If legal advice or other expert
assistance is required, the services of a competent
professional person should be sought.

*From a Declaration of Principles jointly adopted by a Committee
of the American Bar Association and a Committee of Publishers.*

Production editor: Margaret S. Haywood
Copyediting coordinator: Merrily D. Mazza
Production manager: Irene H. Sotiroff
Artist: Benoit Design
Compositor: Carlisle Communications Limited
Typeface: 10/12 Caledonia
Printer: Arcata Graphics/Kingsport

ISBN 1-55623-043-5

Library of Congress Catalog Card No. 87–73024

Printed in the United States of America

3 4 5 6 7 8 9 0 K 5 4 3 2 1 0 9 8

The preface to the 1978 revised edition of this book states, "In the decade since the publication of *The Bankers' Handbook*, the banking system of the nation has undergone substantial changes in size, structure, and function." This statement is as appropriate today as it was then.

Changes initiated by the bank holding company movement and competition from other financial institutions have accelerated during the past nine years. Interstate banking, sparked by state laws aimed at regional reciprocity, has become a major factor for change.

In addition, the impact of current technology and advanced information systems continues as a major element of change. Banking has been at the forefront in the application of electronics. It has maintained that position not only for operations but also for management information and sophisticated decision making.

The result is that this third edition is to a considerable degree a new volume. It draws on the earlier editions for its general organization, although even this has been modified. Very few of the chapters are simply revisions of earlier chapters. Most have been written anew—in most cases by new authors.

Even as it adjusts to change, the *Handbook* sticks to its original purpose—to provide a basic reference on the subjects that are currently most important to performance in banking. It draws on a panel of exceptionally talented authors, many of whom are at the forefront of thought in their respective fields. We appreciate their willingness to share their thoughts.

William H. Baughn
Thomas I. Storrs
Charls E. Walker

Willard Alexander Vice Chairman, The Citizens & Southern Corporation, Atlanta, Georgia

Paul Allen Principal, McKinsey & Company, Inc., New York, New York

Marilyn MacGruder Barnewall President, The MacGruder Agency, Inc., Aurora, Colorado

Paul R. Beares Vice President, The First National Bank of Maryland, Glen Burnie, Maryland

Steven J. Beck Vice President, Huntington National Bank of Indiana, Indianapolis, Indiana

Robert R. Bench Partner, Price Waterhouse, Washington, D.C.

Sandra A. Boone Vice President, Sovran Financial Corporation, Norfolk, Virginia

Fred M. Borchardt Partner, Peat Marwick Main & Co., New York, New York

William H. Bowen Chairman and Chief Executive Officer, First Commercial Bank, N.A., Little Rock, Arkansas

Richard S. Braddock Sector Executive, Citicorp/Citibank, New York, New York

Kenneth A. Bretthorst Chairman, First St. Louis Securities, St. Louis, Missouri

Jere J. Brommer Senior Vice President, Valley National Bank of Arizona, Phoenix, Arizona

Lowell Bryan Director, McKinsey & Company, Inc., New York, New York

Andre A. Cappon Partner, Oliver, Wyman & Company, New York, New York

David C. Cates   President, Cates Consulting Analysts, Inc., New York, New York

David R. Christenson   President, Farmers State Bank, Nerstrand, Minnesota

Robert F. Clodfelter   Lecturer in Law, School of Law, Wake Forest University, Winston-Salem, North Carolina

Dr. Robert E. Coffey   Professor of Management and Organization Behavior, Graduate School of Business, University of Southern California, Los Angeles, California

Sharli Colladay   Intern, Security Pacific National Bank, Los Angeles, California

George W. Cowles   Senior Vice President, Bankers Trust Company, New York, New York

Frederick Deane, Jr.   Chairman and CEO, Signet Banking Corporation, Richmond, Virginia

Walter A. Diaz   Principal, Booz Allen & Hamilton, Inc., New York, New York

Charles S. Dickerson   President, Crossing Financial Consultants, Princeton, New Jersey

Dr. Arnold A. Dill   Senior Vice President and Chief Economist, The Citizens & Southern Corporation, Atlanta, Georgia

Virgil M. Dissmeyer   D/R Management Services, Inc., Edina, Minnesota

Dr. John Dominick   Arkansas Bankers Association Chair of Banking and the J.W. Bellamy Chair of Banking and Finance, University of Arkansas, Fayetteville, Arkansas

Richard E. Dooley   President, The Dooley Group, Hopkins, Minnesota

Donald M. Douglas   Senior Vice President, Sovran Investment Corporation, Richmond, Virginia

Gerald R. Downey, Jr.   Executive Vice President, The Citizens & Southern Florida Corporation, Atlanta, Georgia

Thomas A. Farin   President, Farin, Parliment & Associates, Inc., Madison, Wisconsin

Jerry Goldstein   Senior Vice President, Mercantile Bank, St. Louis, Missouri

Dr. Carter H. Golembe   Chairman, Golembe Associates, Inc., Washington, D.C.

Dee Hamilton   Vice President, Hancock Bank, Gulfport, Mississippi

Dr. Frederick S. Hammer   Chairman and Chief Executive Officer, Meritor Financial Group, Philadelphia, Pennsylvania.

Jack L. Hancock Executive Vice President, Wells Fargo Bank, San Francisco, California

Milton M. Harris Chairman, Maryland National Leasing Corporation, Towson, Maryland

Timothy P. Hartman Corporate Executive Vice President and Chief Financial Officer, NCNB Corporation, Charlotte, North Carolina

Richard W. Heiss Senior Vice President and Senior Trust Officer, Manufacturers National Bank of Detroit, New York, New York

Robert Herrmann Senior Deputy Comptroller for Bank Supervision, Office of the Comptroller of the Currency, Washington, D.C.

Douglas G. Hoffman CPCU-ARM, Tillinghast, a Towers Perrin Company, Darien, Connecticut

Preston T. Holmes Formerly Executive Vice President, Credit Administration, United Virginia Bank (now CRESTAR Financial Corporation), Richmond, Virginia

Dr. Paul Horvitz James A. Elkins Professor of Banking and Finance, University of Houston, Houston, Texas

William M. Isaac Managing Director and Chief Executive Officer, The Secura Group, Washington, D.C.

Willis Johnson Vice President, SunTrust Banks, Inc., Atlanta, Georgia

Thomas F. Keaveney National Director - Banking, Peat Marwick Main & Co., New York, New York

Dr. Sydney J. Key Economist, Division of International Finance, Board of Governors of the Federal Reserve System, Washington, D.C.

Dr. Lawrence E. Kreider Executive Vice President and Economist, Conference of State Bank Supervisors, Washington, D.C.

James M. LaVier III First Vice President, Sovran Investment Corporation, Richmond, Virginia

R. C. Letson IBM, Charlotte, North Carolina

Peter C. Lincoln Vice President, Investments, United States Steel and Carnegie Pension Fund, Inc., New York, New York

Donald R. Lipkin Assistant Vice President, The First Boston Corporation, New York, New York

Richard D. Lodge Senior Vice President, Bank One Columbus, N.A., Columbus, Ohio

John B. Logan Senior Vice President, Barnett Bank, Jacksonville, Florida

John Ward Logan Executive Vice President, First American Corporation, Nashville, Tennessee

Leslie H. London Senior Vice President, First National Bank of Louisville, Louisville, Kentucky

John E. Mack Senior Vice President and Treasurer, NCNB Corporation, Charlotte, North Carolina

Margaret L. Maguire Managing Director, The Secura Group, Washington, D.C.

Donald R. Mandich Chairman and Chief Executive Officer, Comerica, Inc., Detroit, Michigan

Irving Margol Executive Vice President, Security Pacific National Bank, Los Angeles, California

Lazaros P. Mavrides Vice President, Investment Portfolio Management, Morgan Guaranty Trust Company, New York, New York

George J. McClaran President, Pittsburgh National Bank, Pittsburgh, Pennsylvania

Hugh L. McColl, Jr. Chairman and CEO, NCNB Corporation, Charlotte, North Carolina

David Melnicoff Senior Adjunct Professor of Finance, Temple University, Philadelphia, Pennsylvania

James C. Montague Chairman, Financial Information Products, Inc., Bethesda, Maryland

Thomas V. Moriarty II Senior Vice President, Shawmut Bank, N.A., Boston, Massachusetts

Denis C. Murphy Partner, Touche Ross & Co., Denver, Colorado

J. William Murray Senior Vice President, First National Bank of Maryland, Baltimore, Maryland

Dr. Paul Nadler Professor of Finance, Graduate School of Management, Rutgers University, Newark, New Jersey

Axel M. Neubohn Vice President, Citicorp, New York, New York

H. Richard Noon President, Bankers Mortgage and Investment Group, Inc., Overland Park, Kansas

Edward T. O'Leary Senior Vice President and Manager, Special Asset Group, Liberty National Bank, Oklahoma City, Oklahoma

Dr. Ronald L. Olson Chairman of the Board, Olson Research Associates, Inc., Greenbelt, Maryland

Rhoger H. Pugh Manager, Policy Development Section, Division of Bank Supervision and Regulation, Board of Governors of the Federal Reserve System, Washington, D.C.

Charles G. Reavis, Jr. Senior Vice President, Wachovia Bank and Trust Company, N.A., Winston-Salem, North Carolina

Donald S. Redding Senior Vice President, NCNB National Bank, Charlotte, North Carolina

Carl E. Reichardt Chairman and CEO, Wells Fargo Bank, San Francisco, California

Donald B. Riefler   Chairman, Sources and Uses of Funds Committee, Morgan Guaranty Trust Company, New York, New York

Dr. Peter S. Rose   Professor of Finance, College of Business Administration, Texas A&M University, College Station, Texas

Richard M. Rosenberg   Vice Chairman, Bank of America, San Francisco, California

Dorothy Sable   Formerly Director of Litigation and Special Assistant to the Chief Counsel, Office of the Comptroller of the Currency, Washington, D.C.

Sanford F. Sadler   Senior Vice President, First Interstate Bank of Nevada, Las Vegas, Nevada

Timothy K. Scanlan   Vice President, Security Pacific National Bank, Los Angeles, California

James B. Schmitt   Vice President - Retail Banking, Norwest Corporation, Minneapolis, Minnesota

Stuart A. Schweitzer   Vice President, Morgan Guaranty Trust Company, New York, New York

M. Carl Sneeden   Senior Vice President, Third National Bank, Nashville, Tennessee

Richard H. Snelsire   Group Vice President, First Wachovia Corporate Services, Winston-Salem, North Carolina

A.A. Sommer, Jr.   Morgan, Lewis & Bockius, Washington, D.C.

William J. Stallkamp   Executive Vice President, Mellon Bank, N.A., Pittsburgh, Pennsylvania

Gary H. Stern   President, Federal Reserve Bank of Minneapolis, Minneapolis, Minnesota

Dr. Thomas I. Storrs   Retired Chairman, NCNB Corporation, Charlotte, North Carolina

Frederick M. Struble   Associate Director, Division of Bank Supervision and Regulation, Board of Governors of the Federal Reserve System, Washington, D.C.

Donald J. Stuhldreher   President, The Huntington Company, Columbus, Ohio

Lynda Swenson   Formerly Investment Officer, Bank One, Columbus, N.A., Columbus, Ohio

Dr. Peter M. Tobia   Vice President, Kepner-Tregoe, Inc., Princeton, New Jersey

Dr. Benjamin B. Tregoe   Chairman and CEO, Kepner-Tregoe, Inc., Princeton, New Jersey

Terence J. Trsar   CBA, CPA, Director, Bank Audit Program, Bank Administration Institute, Rolling Meadows, Illinois

Edwin C. Wallace, Jr. National Accounts Manager, Security Pacific Organizational Consultants, Inc., Los Angeles, California

John R. Wells Senior Vice President, Boatmen's Bancshares, Inc., St. Louis, Missouri

Gary M. Welsh, Esq. Partner, Prather Seeger Doolittle and Farmer, Washington, D.C.

Diane White Vice President and Divisional Controller for Operations, First Wachovia Corporation, Atlanta, Georgia

Dr. Charles M. Williams George Gund Professor of Commercial Banking, Emeritus, Graduate School of Business, Harvard University, Soldiers Field, Boston, Massachusetts

Howard L. Wright Director of Bank Taxation, Office of Federal Services, Arthur Andersen & Co., Washington, D.C.

John W. Zimmerman Senior Vice President, Kepner-Tregoe, Inc., Princeton, New Jersey

John Zimmermann Executive Vice President and Chief Operating Officer, The Enterprise Bank Network, Inc., Atlanta, Georgia

CONTENTS

Metaphors and Supervision. Conclusion.

20. **Federal Regulations Affecting Bank Personnel**
    Management *by Edwin C. Wallace, Jr. and Sandra A.*
    Boone **263**

    Fair Labor Standards Act (Wage-Hour Law): *Minimum Wage*
    and Overtime Requirements. Fluctuating Workweek. Exempt
    Employees. Equal Pay. Child Labor. Age Discrimination in
    Employment Act. The Occupational Safety and Health Act
    (OSHA). Enforcement and Record Retention. National Labor
    Relations Act: *Rights of Employees. Unfair Labor Practices.*
    Collective Bargaining. Enforcement. Social Security Act.
    Federal Wage Garnishment Law. Universal Military Training
    and Service Act: *Executive Order 11701.* Other Federal
    Banking Regulations: *Regulations of the Comptroller of the*
    Currency. Rules and Regulations, Board of Governors of the
    Federal Reserve System. United States Code, Title 12.
    Fingerprinting. Polygraphing: *Usage. Legality.* The 1984 Tax
    Reform Act: *Computations under §§7872. Application.*
    Conclusion.

PART 4   Financial Management   285

21. **Funding Sources and Strategies for Banks of Various Sizes** *by*
    Donald B. Riefler and Lazaros P. Mavrides **287**

    Introduction. Deposits: *Demand Deposits. Savings Deposits.*
    Nonnegotiable Time Deposits. Negotiable Certificates of
    Deposit. Treasury Tax and Loan Deposits. Eurodollar
    Deposits. Borrowings: *Federal Funds. Repurchase Agreements.*
    Commercial Paper. Long-Term Debt. Borrowings from the
    Discount Window. Capital: *Mandatory Convertible Securities.*
    Variable Rate Preferred Stock. Funding Strategy: *Capital*
    Funds. Other Funds. Liquidity Management. Interest Rate
    Risk Management. Interest Rate Futures, Options, and Swaps.
    Appendix I. Appendix II.

22. **Bank/Investor Relationships** *by Peter C. Lincoln* **308**

    Introduction. Why Investor Relations? How to Build
    Credibility. Importance of Conciseness, Realism, and

Controls. Financial Statement Reporting Requirements.
Conclusion.

Audits. Single Audit Letters. Specialized Bank Experience:
Tax Services. Management Consulting Services. Conclusion.

Objectives of Tax Planning: *The Banks' Tax Burden.*
Compliance Considerations. Customer Considerations.
Employee Considerations. Financial Statement Implications.
Legislative Concerns. Implementing Tax Planning: *Keeping up*
to Date. Focusing on Specific Areas: *The Tax Plan Process.*
Concepts of Tax Planning for Specific Areas. Accounting
Methods. Securities. Loans. Loan Loss Reserves. Property and
Equipment. Other Assets. Intangible Assets. Deposits. Other
Liabilities. Capital Accounts. Income Accounts. Expenses. The
Computation of Tax. Summary.

The Risk Management Process and Discipline. Exposure
Identification. Risk Evaluation. Risk Control. The Risk
Assessment Matrix. Risk Finance and Insurance.
Administration. Conclusion.

The Math. Discount. Interest-Bearing. Federal Funds.
Repurchase Agreements. Eurodeposits. Negotiable Certificates
of Deposit: *Domestic. Eurodollar. Yankee. Floating Rate*
Certificates of Deposit. Bankers' Acceptances. Commercial
Paper. U.S. Treasury Securities: *U.S. Treasury Bills. U.S.*
Treasury Notes and Bonds. Federal Agency Securities.
Muncipal Securities. Futures. Options. Conclusion.

Introduction. Size of Debt. Structure of Debt. Breadth of
Acceptance of U.S. Government Securities. Market Operation.
United States Government Securities. U.S. Treasury Bills.
Treasury Notes and Bonds. The Markets for Treasury

Securities. Book Entry. U.S. Treasury Securities Yield Curve. Price Volatility.

Statement. Full Service versus Niche. Buy or Make. Defining
the Market. Distribution Facilities: The Technology Is the
Product. Execution: The People Problem. Conclusion: Use a
Blackboard.

Introduction. Retail Banking's Most Profitable Segments.
Defining Upscale. Category 1: *Private Banking/Trust
Customers (Affluent Passive Investors). Minimum Net Worth
and Income Requirements—Passive Affluent.* Category 2:
*Private Banking Active Investor Customers. Minimum Net
Worth and Income Requirements.* Junior Level Customers
(Active Investor): *Middle Level Customer (Active Investor).
Senior Level Customers (Active Investor).* Category 3: *Young
Upwardly Mobile Professionals in Economic* Stress (Yumpies).
Category 4: *Personal Banking Upscale Customers. Senior
Middle Market Upscale Personal Banking Customers. Mid-
Level Upscale Middle Market Personal Banking Customers.
Junior Middle Market Personal Banking Customers. Double-
Income Blue-Collar/Single-Income White-Collar Families.
Psychographics and Buying Motivations of Each Segment.*
How to Identify Existing Profitable Retail Customer Segments.
How to Identify Profitable Noncustomer Segments.
Conclusion.

Strategic Analysis. Product Analysis and Management.
Customer Characteristics. Distribution. Product. Delivery.
Product Enhancement/Development: *Phase 1—Product
Proposal—Evaluation. Phase 2—Executing the Action Plan.
Phase 3. Phase 4. Phase 5. Phase 6. Phase 7.* Product Cost
Analysis: *Concepts of Cost. Cost Factors.* Pricing Deposit
Products: *Pricing Philosophy. Pricing Objectives. Competitive
Pricing. Price Sensitivity. Pricing Strategies.* Conclusion.

Emerging Consumer Credit Product Line. Open-End/
Revolving Credit Products. Home Equity Lines of Credit.
Unsecured Lines of Credit. Credit Cards. Closed-End Loan
Products. Automobile Loans. Variable-Rate Loans. Summary.

Climate in the Years Ahead: Intensifying Pressures? The
Competition for Funding. The Bottom Line—Trends in
Industry Profitability. Burgeoning Loan Losses—Transitory
Phenomena or Continuing Challenge? The Structural Changes
Ahead: Some Management Implications. Will Merger Mania
Develop? The Ongoing Transition from Traditional Banking—
Key Implications for Senior/Top Management.

LIST OF EXHIBITS

PART ONE

Banking in the Overall Financial Structure

What's Happening to Banking?

Dr. Thomas I. Storrs

Retired Chairman
NCNB Corporation

Bankers' hopes and fears of 25 years became reality by the mid-1980s.

Those who had hoped to be more competitive found that they were—and so were other banks and many other financial companies. Those who had sought additional powers found them through revised corporate structures and through gradually broadening powers for banks. Those who had hoped for less regulation found it, and found their unregulated competitors pushing hard on every aspect of their businesses.

Many bankers had feared the changes in the markets and the laws which governed them. Events proved some of their concerns justified. More competition and less regulation resulted in lower earnings for many. In fact, all sizes of banks were under earnings pressures during the first half of the decade, and the prospect seems to be for more of the same.

The reasons for the changes are many.

Banking lived in a cage designed for another era—designed primarily by the facts of the 1930s and the theories as to how those facts came about. That cage became increasingly inconsistent with the real world about it, and bankers moved to free themselves of what they regarded as intolerable constraints.

The year 1961 saw an ingenious response to the regulation of rates paid on deposits, the issuance of large negotiable certificates of deposit, and the creation of a market to give them liquidity despite their extended maturities. Five years later, however, a credit crunch found banks virtually shut off from funds as market rates rose above the maximum permitted on CDs of any maturity.

The extensive spread of bank holding companies soon followed. The goals were freedom to compete for funds, freedom to offer a broader range of products, and freedom to operate beyond the geographic bounds imposed by state and federal laws. The move had many successes for individual banks, but the war was nearly lost in the Bank Holding Company Act amendments of 1970. Potential competitors, regulators, and congressmen who were openly suspicious of banks joined to severely restrict the new-found freedom.

Continuing upward pressure on interest rates led bank customers to look more closely at alternatives to bank deposits and their regulated rates. It also caused banks to look more closely at their own nonearning assets. For members of the Federal Reserve System, the largest category of nonearners was the reserve account at the Fed.

Fed membership came under study. Many of its privileges had been diluted. Liquidity problems of 1974 showed that savings and loans and nonmember banks could look to the Federal Reserve banks in time of need. Both groups had increasing access to the Fed payments system, and neither privilege carried the burdens of membership. Not surprisingly, there were significant defections from membership.

The Monetary Control Act of 1980 was the outcome. Fed membership became virtually irrelevant as reserve requirements were imposed on all depositories and access to the Fed was formally opened to them. This action solved the Fed's membership problems but raised broader issues as to what a bank is and how it is to be regulated.

The regulation of interest paid on bank deposits came under increasing attack during the 1970s as rates on comparable financial assets were consistently higher and bank customers used deposits to buy them. Despite strong pressure from housing, which had long been subsidized by the savers of the nation, the Depository Institutions Deregulatory Act of 1980 opened the door for interest rate deregulation. By 1986 banks and savings and loans were completely freed for price competition with other takers of funds and among themselves.

By the early 1980s yet another move toward greater freedom appeared. The New England states and the Southeastern states began serious consideration of what became regional compacts for interstate banking among the states in each region. Supported by a Supreme Court decision in 1985, these compacts became common and provided a path for the emergence of a group of larger regional banks. Such banks are much stronger competition for money center banks and give promise of a broad-based banking system when interstate banking becomes possible on a national basis.

Change has brought increased risk, and risk has brought adversity to some banks. Size has provided no protection. Decreased earnings and failures have struck banks of all sizes. The number of failures has been startling after decades of virtually no failures but quite small when compared with periods of recession and depression in the early part of this century. The deposit insurance program has been successful in protecting depositors and in preventing many bank runs. Bank shareholders have learned that the trade-off for earnings and dividends is the acceptance of risk.

Let's turn from history to look at what it is that banks do, the forces that have acted on these functions, and finally the forces that will shape banking in the future.

I.

Banking is a terribly complex business. How can we break it down into functions that are applicable to giants and to the small bank enjoying 100 percent of some small and remote banking market? If we had said "activities" instead of "functions," the answer would be that we can't. But functions are what you do rather than how you do it.

There are some peripheral operations banks have done so long as to make them seem essential elements of the business: safe deposit boxes, trust services, and letters of introduction for customers. But, dealing with basics, banking is indeed but three basic functions:

- Participating in the payments system.
- Getting money to lend.
- Lending money.

Historically the three functions have been closely interrelated. The nature of the payment process has forced customers—consumers, businesses, and governments—to carry funds on deposit to cover delays in payments and irregularities in the flows of their receipts and payments. During much of the time that federal law prohibited the payment of interest on checking account balances, the lack of return didn't seem a great burden to customers. It was simply a cost of maintaining adequate liquidity to meet needs for payments. Economists called it, like pocket money, the transactions use of money.

Until recent years banks had a virtual monopoly on the payments system other than cash. Banks' monopoly on cash had been eroded by the Federal Reserve Act in 1913 and finished off by the Banking Act of 1935. But only banks had direct access to the check payment system, which has for years accounted for a large proportion of all payments. If a customer wished to use this system, he had to maintain a checking relationship with a bank, and the price of entry was a deposit account with a balance.

The monopoly has been damaged in two ways: First, thrift institutions can now offer transaction accounts and are using NOW and other accounts en route to becoming consumer banks. They also have direct access to the Federal Reserve check-collection and funds-transfer systems, obviating their former need to go through commercial banks for Fed services. Second, other developing payment systems are expected to cut the importance of checks, reducing their growth and ultimately their absolute number. Let's look at the diversity of these other systems.

Many bankers are promoters of one of the competing payments systems: credit cards. They have provided a new product, a way to earn fees and to set up credit accounts that are attractive to consumers and merchants. The new product, however, has taken away the banker's face-to-face contact with his customers. A credit card holder no longer cares who issued it or where the issuer is located. He doesn't care what bank it is—or even whether the issuer is a bank. The same is true for the merchant who honors the card—so long as he can receive his funds as quickly from other issuers as he can from his local bank. Banks now dominate the field, but there's no natural monopoly for them.

Automated teller machines are generally operated with bank cards. Many bankers have regarded them simply as an extension of the bank's teller line. Increasingly, however, they handle transactions with a number—or a multitude—of banks. They also handle transactions with companies that operate a financial business without a bank charter. Originally adopted as a means of product differentiation, the machines are becoming common carriers. Soon customers will be unable to tell the difference in product delivered by a bank located behind the machine and one 3,000 miles away. Even worse for many bankers, the customers won't care.

Point-of-sale terminals are appearing in increasing numbers, reading credit and debit cards and charging transactions directly to credit card balances or to bank accounts. Many electronic cash registers can be adapted to capture and transmit charges and deposit data to a bank or another credit granter. Again the customer cannot distinguish the product's origin from his bank, the bank in a far-off state, or even a nonbank issuer of credit cards.

Much less widely used in number of transactions is the automated clearing house, a Federal Reserve facility that permits participants to enter batches of debits or credits to be posted to the bank accounts of debtors or creditors wherever located. Currently the process takes one or two days. Its proponents confidently talk about same-day completion of the transactions. Seepage has occurred here as well. These transactions can be originated through virtually any depository institution, and that statement should be understood literally. It means that many bank customers will go online with this payments system.

The list can get longer—and will.

What's happened to those nice free balances that bankers enjoyed and customers accepted as a necessary evil? They are well on their way to extinction. High interest rates and technological changes are the miscreants.

As interest rates rose from nominal levels and assistant treasurers were recruited from business schools, corporate customers became less willing to maintain balances that provided banks extra profits beyond the service charges on the accounts' activity. Customers became more knowledgeable about such matters as float and banking practices. They insisted on analysis statements, which gave them as much cost information as the banker had. Competitive pressures led bankers to be accomplices in their own downfall, and cash management services became—and are today—a major field of bank competition. They also enable even moderate-size corporate customers to end each day with no more than nominal balances in their checking accounts—and with their own books showing bank account overdrafts as the normal situation!

The consumer has joined the fight. He now receives competitive interest rates on his checking account, offset in some banks by the costs of providing services to him.

So bankers have two pieces of bad news so far:

- Banks face a continuing erosion of their former monopoly of the payments system.
- Bank customers no longer support their relationship with large amounts of free balances. Some even pay carefully negotiated service charges rather than maintaining balances.

II.

Speaking of free balances, what became of those low-cost savings accounts that consumers once carried in banks and thrift institutions? Surprisingly enough, they haven't disappeared—yet. In November 1982 such accounts reached a total of $165 billion in commercial banks; they were $135 billion in mid-1986. It's always been obvious that many such accounts were not very sensitive to interest rate differentials. Observant bankers say that those accounts are owned by older people who place a premium on safety and convenience as opposed to interest income. They confidently predict that in the future savings balances will become more interest-sensitive as that generation dies off! In any case, banks will pay market rates on these balances before long or risk their loss to other people who will.

For the present they have real significance for banks, as do consumer certificates and money market deposit accounts, which pay higher rates of interest. Given the ability to compete with money market accounts, banks have been able to achieve a good share of this market. Bankers should still be aware that Merrill Lynch's cash management account, which preempted this market, has maintained a large share of the market it created. Despite this fact, banks are able to use their branch systems to get access to consumer funds at rates below those paid on funds they raise in national markets.

This is a bright spot, but the use of funds purchased in indifferent markets has become increasingly important in the funding of bank balance sheets. We should expect that trend to continue.

"So," you might say, "what's so bad about that? Maybe it's even good. If you had been dependent on the growth of core deposits and the Fed were holding a tight rein on those, how would you have grown to your present size and profitability? God bless money brokers and negotiable CDs."

III.

Quite true, but it's not an unmixed blessing for banks. In the old days—which generally means more than 20 but less than 50 years ago—a bank's credit was presumed as above reproach short of overwhelming evidence to the contrary. Textbooks of those days stated as a key fact of banking that banks substituted their own creditworthiness for that of their borrowers. It went without saying that the banks' credit would be better.

Once banks entered arms-length markets, their creditworthiness no longer was taken for granted. By the early 1970s one of the major rating agencies proposed to rate the commercial paper of bank holding companies, a clear affront to the bankers who operated them.

Somewhat to bankers' surprise, they found that some of their customers were considered at least as good credit risks as some of the banks. Indeed!

The blue-chip customers—and some with lesser credentials—found that they could go directly to banks' sources of funds and obtain them at rates clearly competitive with bank money costs—and sometimes lower. With many of these customers, banks have been reduced to providing backup lines of credit and occasionally supplying funds at what are euphemistically called money market rates; that is, rates that provide a gross before-tax margin less than the after-tax return on assets necessary for a bank to achieve a reasonable return on equity.

So a third piece of bad news: Many bank customers are bypassing their banks to go directly to funds sources for their loans.

Other areas of lending have had different sets of problems, but problems nevertheless. Foreign lending, once the domain of money center banks which were later joined by ambitious regional banks, became a trap for loan dollars and executives' time. The final chapters have not yet been written on the foreign adventures of American bankers in the late 1970s and early 1980s, but there's no basis for expecting good news.

Domestically banks have turned increasingly to what are sometimes known as deal loans and to the old standby customer of the local bank, loans to the middle-market business concern. Some of the deal loans now fall into the category of bad deals, and the profitable middle market has become somewhat less profitable as the number and anxiety of lenders have increased.

Finally, banks as consumer lenders have always faced tough competition from nonbank lenders, many of whom have access to funds at bank rates—that is, the rates that banks pay—and operate outside the restrictive framework imposed on banks. Banks held 47 percent of total consumer installment loans in 1980 and 45 percent at year-end 1986. Not much change, but not a very long time either.

IV.

What of the years ahead?

For bankers the years ahead will be as much fun as you will find anywhere. Change fathers opportunity as well as danger. There are massive forces at work on banking, and the opportunities they create will be on a similar scale. They present a tremendous management challenge for they will require sweeping changes of attitudes, rewards, products, and delivery systems. The times will be made to order for people with ambition, judgment—and courage!

In the future the definition of the banking business may be a functional one. Should any one say to you 10 years hence, "Show me a bank," you might or might not pick a banking market player that had a bank charter. You would perhaps be just as likely to pick a company performing one or more banking functions. You might even pick a company performing most or all banking functions but still not having a bank charter.

Back to the three banking functions.

The payments system will not be cashless or checkless, as was so often forecast by futurists of the past. But convenience and economics will continue to drive it heavily towards electronics, and the overwhelming majority of the dollars will flow through electronic systems. The market action for the players will be to devise products for market segments that attract and hold customers. It's going to be a tough fight in which location—the only claim to uniqueness for many banks—loses ground as a competitive factor.

What will be the real product differentiation in such a market? For business customers it will be the information facet—which is just a fancy way of saying transaction data provided in forms that permit customers to post accounting ledgers, revise financial forecasts, drive treasury systems, and strengthen management control systems. Banks, using that term generically, may well provide the computer software for corporate customers. Preemptive strikes by large banks may establish system dominance that will lead to claims such as "X Bank-compatible" in describing the products of other banking companies.

It's hard to believe that the consumer will be left behind in this process. The top of the market for consumer deposit banking—which presently provides an overwhelming share of the profitability of the total market—will be mentally conditioned and adequately equipped for banking by personal computer.

The payments system will continue to lose importance as a source of funding of balance sheets. If you question this, consider the current turnover of demand deposits. Leaving out the major New York banks and their heavy flow of financial transactions, demand deposits in 1986 reached a turnover rate of 345 times per annum. That's more than $1\frac{1}{3}$ full turns per business day. "How can that increase?" you may ask. You might have asked the same question in 1980, when it was only (only!) 186 times per year.

Financial institutions, including what today are called banks, will continue to look to consumers as important sources of funds. All of today's efforts at market segmentation and product differentiation will continue. The odds are, however, that consumers are going to become more market-driven, more disposed to seek the high return wherever offered. In a system in Florida, consumers use home computers to shop five banks for rates and to move funds to the one offering the highest rate.

As an opposite force to unbundling bank services, many banks today are seeking to expand the scope of customer relationships to include peripheral services, generally to produce fee or commission income. Perhaps more important are the hoped-for results of:

- Solidifying the customer's relationship with one principal source of financial services.
- Making that company price-attractive and perceived as the source of services that are somehow "better" than those competitors offer.

Branch systems, maligned by those who lack them, offer a necessary element in the delivery system for these additional services as well as providing face-to-face sales opportunities.

What about banks as lenders? The basic question is whether banks as an industry operating with the constraints and burdens of regulation can compete effectively with other lenders not so blessed. They will do so, but in a substantially different fashion from what they do today. Their role as arranger of credit will, for some banks, eclipse their participation in the credits. Their commitment to specialized fields of credit may make them fully competitive even with the unregulated lenders. The payments-system players will be in a position to provide payments-related credit services such as overdraft banking. Nevertheless, if present trends continue, banks will be less distinctive players in virtually all the lending markets.

A future with these characteristics will raise a host of questions.

Banks will need to make decisions as to the markets in which they will operate and the products they will bring to those markets. Not every bank will be able to be all things to all people as most have tried to be in the past. The important strategic decision for each financial company will be the range of products to be offered, and the day-to-day challenges will be the pricing, marketing, and delivery of those services.

It will be a far cry from what has been described as menu banking, the practice of yesteryear that offered a short list of deposits a bank would accept and loans it would make, all priced at rates set by law and regulation.

The structure of the industry will change dramatically. There's little gain in forecasting that 15,000 banks will become 10,000 or 2,000 or whatever. There are important consequences, however, in the structure that evolves and the way it evolves.

Finally, bankers have been forced to think the unthinkable: What would it be like to trade in the bank charter for a less regulated position in the market? The CitiCorp chairman of 1980 spoke of an apocryphal dream, one might suppose, in which his predecessor appeared and when asked for advice, said, "Sell CitiBank! Buy Merrill Lynch!" More recently the president of The Chase Manhattan Bank was quoted in the newspaper as saying that his company was giving serious consideration to changing to a nonbank charter.

Unthinkable or not, the facts of the mid-1980s support such speculation.

Those facts point to a time when nonbank competitors may have all the aspects of a bank except the burdens of bank regulation and the not always enviable role of being the medium of monetary policy.

Those and other concerns—some rational—worry the people who must make the laws and regulations fit a new world and help to mold it. Their answer for many years has been to lag the market and sometimes to solve the problems of yesteryear. In the mid-1980s they frequently seemed unable to agree on a course of action even to do this. Over time, however, the laws and regulations *will* change to accommodate changes driven by the market.

Or at least they always have.

CHAPTER TWO

The Broad Segments of Financial Markets

Dr. Paul Horvitz

*James A. Elkins Professor
of Banking and Finance
University of Houston*

The United States has a complex financial system comprising different types of institutions and markets. Commercial banks play an important role in this system—they are not simply one of many institutions. Virtually all aspects of the operations of commercial banks are discussed in this book, but the purpose of this chapter is to describe where banks fit in the overall financial system, while describing the role of the financial system in the economy.

The function of the financial system in the economy is to facilitate the process of saving and investment. An economy cannot grow without new investment. Real investment is the acquisition of new productive capacity—equipment, buildings, and inventories.[1] This represents an addition to the capital stock or productive capacity of the economy only to the extent that these assets are not used for consumption purposes. Real investment can only take place when someone in the economy abstains from consumption ("saves"). The decision to save—to postpone consumption—is not primarily a financial one, though the availability of financial assets in which one can hold savings may encourage the act of saving.

Saving and investment take place even in simple economies. The farmer who reserves some of his harvest to use as seed for the next

---

[1]We must distinguish investment in this sense—the acquisition of real assets—from the acquisition of financial assets, such as stocks, bonds, loans, etc. Financial investment, in which ownership of a financial instrument is transferred from one party to another, does not directly represent a real increase in the capital stock of the society. However, financial investment facilitates real investment. Without financing, the real investment may not be possible.

year is simultaneously saving and investing. In a developed economy, saving and investment are carried out by different parties. The role of the financial system is to facilitate the transfer of funds from the savers to those who need funds for investment.

Some funds may flow directly from saver to investor in an efficient manner. The new small business may be financed by loans from relatives or friends, and AT&T may raise new funds by selling securities directly to existing stockholders. In most cases, however, *indirect* finance, whereby funds move from savers to investors through an intermediary, is more efficient. Borrowers want funds for risky projects in large amounts and for fixed periods of time; savers often have small amounts that they wish to keep in liquid form and with a high degree of safety. The bank or thrift institution can offer liabilities in any denomination that are more liquid and safer than the liabilities of the firm needing funds for investment. The borrower reduces his cost of searching for funds by dealing with an institutional lender rather than seeking out individual savers. The efficiency of financial intermediation is that the borrower gets funds at lower cost (considering search costs) while the saver can simultaneously earn a higher return (adjusted for risk, liquidity, and costs) than if he had to find a borrower to lend to directly.

The remainder of this chapter considers the various types of financial intermediaries in the economy and their different specialties.

TYPES OF FINANCIAL INSTITUTIONS

Commercial Banks

It is logical to begin this discussion by considering commercial banks. There are three good reasons to do so. First, commercial banks, with total assets of over $2 trillion, are the largest component of the financial system. Second, commercial banks engage in a wider range of financial activities than any other type of institution. While some institutions specialize in consumer lending, farm lending, housing finance, or lending on certain types of business collateral, commercial banks engage in a wide range of financing activities.[2] Third, commercial banks have primary responsibility for the payments system, the most basic and crucial financial service, without which other financial institutions could not function. This means that banks become the focus of mon-

---

[2]There are some conglomerate firms that own several different financial institutions and may include a wider range of activities than is allowed to commercial banks. Sears owns a savings and loan association, a brokerage firm, and an insurance company as well as a commercial bank and a chain of department stores.

etary policy and of governmental regulation aimed at protecting the money supply and the payments system.

Commercial banks are stockholder-owned, as are most financial firms, though, as we shall see, mutual institutions are important in the thrift industry and the insurance business. Commercial banks can obtain a charter from either their state banking regulatory agency or from the Comptroller of the Currency. Nearly all state-chartered banks are members of the FDIC, and hence are subject to some federal supervision, and national banks are subject to many state laws (perhaps most importantly, those regarding branching).

The importance of the payments system role of commercial banks suggests that demand deposits are the distinctive source of funds for commercial banks. That is still true, though demand deposits no longer represent the bulk of deposits of the typical commercial bank, and other institutions now handle deposits on which checks can be written. While household checking accounts can be based on a savings account (NOW accounts), corporate checking accounts require a demand deposit. Demand deposits, on which interest payments are prohibited by law, are now the only type of deposit subject to regulatory restrictions on interest rates. With this exception, banks are free to design deposit instruments with maturities, payments powers, and other features as needed to meet market preferences. Depending on their size and location, banks emphasize somewhat different types of deposits. Large banks have access to funds generated in foreign branches as well as in the United States, and a well-developed market in negotiable certificates allows banks to tap the national money market for funds. Smaller banks can tap a broker-based market in $100,000 (federally insured) CDs. Banks in need of funds beyond their ability to generate can also make use of the federal funds market. The ability of banks to borrow from the Federal Reserve is an important safety valve for the system even though amounts borrowed at any one time are rarely a major source of funds.[3]

Commercial banks are required to maintain reserves, in the form of cash or deposits with the Federal Reserve, equal to a fraction of transaction deposits and nonpersonal time deposits. These requirements, which once applied only to members of the Federal Reserve System, now apply to thrift institutions as well as to all commercial banks. Reserve requirements represent a more significant burden for commercial banks, since demand deposits and corporate time deposits represent more important sources of funds for them as compared with

---

[3]In contrast, borrowings by savings and loans from the Federal Home Loan Banks represent a continual and important source of funds.

thrift institutions. Moreover, for most of the latter, their normal holdings of vault cash are sufficient to meet their reserve needs.

Banks invest in government securities both for income and to meet liquidity needs. Traditionally, banks have been the largest institutional holders of tax-exempt securities issued by state and local governments. Such securities are likely to play a smaller role in bank portfolios in the future as recent changes in the tax law make such investments less attractive.

Loans are the most important asset for commercial banks. As noted above, banks make a wide variety of loans. (Bank lending is discussed in detail in Parts 8 and 9 of this book.) Lending is the most profitable activity of commercial banks, and also the activity that they can do better than any other institution. They are located close to the business and household borrower, maintain long-term deposit relationships with them, and are in a good position to assess creditworthiness and service the loans.

The banking industry is characterized by a low profit margin on a large volume of business per dollar of equity capital. In the first half of the 1980s, net income averaged less than .75 percent of assets, though return on equity averaged over 12 percent. The major source of net income is the spread between interest paid on deposits and interest received on loans and securities. Over the past five years this spread has averaged slightly over 3 percent. Banks also receive non-interest income, such as service charges on deposits and credit cards. This noninterest income has been growing as banks have expanded their activities and increased their service charges, partly as a result of paying interest on checking accounts. Noninterest income now represents about 1.5 percent of assets, compared with under 1 percent in 1980.

Thrift Institutions

Savings banks, savings and loan associations, and credit unions are frequently designated as thrift institutions or nonbank depository institutions. At one time it was possible to make a sharp distinction between the operations of these types of institutions and commercial banks, but now there are many savings banks or savings and loans that would be indistinguishable from many commercial banks. The customers of thrift institutions are primarily households rather than businesses, their deposits are primarily savings and time deposits rather than transaction accounts (in most states they did not have authority to offer checking accounts until 1980), and many are mutual institutions rather than stockholder-owned (all credit unions are mutual). The principal asset of savings banks and savings and loans has traditionally been home mortgage loans, while credit unions specialize in consumer loans.

These institutions, like commercial banks, have charters available from either federal or state authorities (though federal savings bank charters are a relatively new development). Like commercial banks, thrift institutions must meet Federal Reserve reserve requirements, though the burden of such requirements is relatively low since transaction accounts represent a minor portion of their liabilities, and personal time deposits currently have a zero reserve requirement. Deposits in savings and loan associations are insured by the Federal Savings and Loan Insurance Corporation (FSLIC), and a separate deposit insurance fund (the National Credit Union Share Insurance Fund) insures deposits of credit unions. Most savings banks are insured by FDIC. Savings and loans and savings banks may be members of the Federal Home Loan Bank System. The Federal Home Loan Banks function as a sort of central bank for thrift institutions, providing correspondent banking services and serving as a source of credit. Advances from Home Loan Banks are available as a regular source of funds to members, as distinct from commercial bank borrowing from the Federal Reserve. Home Loan Bank advances totaled about $100 billion in 1987.

Mortgage-oriented thrift institutions suffered severe losses in the early 1980s when interest rates (and their cost of funds) reached record levels while earnings on fixed-rate mortgages did not increase. In the face of this problem, many institutions adopted riskier portfolio policies that resulted in serious credit losses, particularly in those parts of the country where the energy business and farming are most important. While the majority of thrift institutions earned record profits in 1986, a significant minority of the industry suffered large losses. These problems were severe enough to become a threat to the soundness of the FSLIC, which was urgently in need of recapitalization by 1986.

The combination of serious savings and loan problems, and the broadening of powers granted in the legislation of the 1980s led the Comptroller of the Currency, in a December 1986 speech, to question the need for, and viability of, a separate savings and loan industry.[4]

---

[4]In a speech to the 12th Annual Conference of the Federal Home Loan Bank of San Francisco, Comptroller Robert L. Clarke said: "I can envision a day in the not too distant future when the distinctions between [savings institutions] and commercial banks might no longer exist in law and regulation. ... [T]he providers of finance for ... housing have become so diverse, and sources of finance are available from so many different places that it does not seem ... that you necessarily need to have a separate, specialized [business].

Savings and loans are no longer single-purpose, home mortgage lenders, but compete across the board with commercial banks. A restructuring of the system of depository institutions, including both commercial banks and thrift institutions, is a possibility for the future.

Insurance

Life Insurance Companies.   Most life insurance policies represent a combination of protection and savings. Because of the savings element, life insurance companies accumulate funds that must be invested. The growth of the life insurance industry has been steady, but its share of the financial business of the country has tended to decline. Personal savings made through insurance companies represented more than 2 percent of disposable personal income in the 1940s, and is now less than 1 percent. This trend reflects, on the one hand, the growing role of Social Security and private pensions in the long-run financial planning of consumers, and, on the other hand, the growing proportion of insurance policies that are pure protection rather than including a savings element (term insurance). This trend has not all been negative from the point of view of the insurance companies, since they have played an important role as managers of pension funds.

Life insurance companies are chartered by the various states, and may be either stock or mutual in form. Although more than 90 percent of the 1,800 companies are stock companies, the mutuals are much larger, accounting for more than 50 percent of the life insurance in force. As distinct from the depository institutions, there is no provision for federal chartering of insurance companies and no system of federal regulation or supervision.

Life insurance companies need little liquidity since their cash needs are easy to predict. Because they operate with relatively low capital, safety of assets is important, and, since their liabilities are fixed in dollar terms, they have a preference for fixed-rate assets. Bonds and mortgages comprise the bulk of life insurance company assets.

Nonlife Insurance Companies.   Nonlife or casualty insurance companies sell protection against loss of property from various disasters and from obligations incurred because of damage done by the insured to third parties. They are not savings institutions in the same sense that life insurance companies are because the insurance premium is a payment only for protection—there is no savings element. But because premiums are paid in advance, the companies accumulate large sums which are invested until needed to settle claims.

The majority of casualty insurance companies are mutual companies though, in contrast to the life insurance industry, the stock companies are larger, accounting for more than 75 percent of the total assets of the industry. Their investment policy is different than the life companies. While death is certain, fires, tornadoes, and hurricanes are not. The possibility of having to make large payments to policyholders on short notice requires holding larger amounts of liquid assets. Most companies have capital ratios considerably higher than the life companies, and this allows them to invest a portion of their assets in a less defensive manner. Common and preferred stocks are attractive not only because of the possibility of appreciation, but because dividends receive favorable tax treatment.

Pension Funds.   The total of private and public retirement funds exceeded $1.25 trillion at the end of 1986. These funds are accumulated out of the contributions of employers and employees, and are invested to provide an income at retirement. For many people, their pension represents the major share of their wealth. Since payments are on a definite contractual basis, retirement funds need little liquidity. Most of the assets are invested in stocks and corporate bonds.

The conduct of pension plans is governed by the Employee Retirement Income Security Act (ERISA), enacted in 1974. The act established minimum standards of funding of programs by employers and minimum requirements for vesting. Retirement plans may be established on a "defined contribution" basis whereby a specified amount is contributed periodically and the employee has a claim on the accumulated earnings, or on a defined benefit basis whereby the employee is entitled to a specific benefit and contributions must be sufficient to generate that benefit. The Pension Benefits Guaranty Corporation provides federal insurance for employee retirement benefits. Life insurance companies are the principal institutions administering pension plans, particularly defined benefit plans, but commercial banks are also active through their trust departments.

Finance Companies

Finance companies are financial intermediaries that raise funds in the market or by borrowing from banks, and make loans to consumers or businesses. At one time most firms specialized in either consumer lending (personal finance companies) or business lending (commercial finance companies), but now the major companies provide credit to both types of borrower.

Prominent in the industry are the "captive" companies that are subsidiaries of large manufacturers. All the major automobile companies have finance company subsidiaries that finance sales to their dealers ("floor plan loans") and sales by dealers to consumers. Consumer finance companies make loans on a secured or unsecured basis, generally at rates higher than those charged by commercial banks. A large proportion of those consumers borrowing from finance companies could not meet the generally higher credit standards of the banks.

Commercial finance companies specialize in "asset-based lending" to business firms—lending secured by such assets as inventories or accounts receivable. Many banks prefer not to engage in this lending, viewed as higher cost and riskier than traditional bank lending, and some do it through holding company affiliates. (Asset-based lending by commercial banks is discussed in Part 9.)

Small finance companies raise their funds primarily by borrowing from banks, while the large companies depend almost entirely on open market paper—that is, long-term bonds or commercial paper. Some companies issue small-denomination paper to the public in a form similar to deposits (though these obligations, of course, do not carry federal deposit insurance).

While there are several thousand finance companies in operation, most are quite small. The giant firms are active in a range of financial activities. General Motors Acceptance Corporation is the largest mortgage servicer in the country, and Ford Financial has a large savings and loan subsidiary. The finance companies are both competitors and customers of commercial banks. Not only do they borrow from commercial banks, but much of the commercial paper issued by medium-sized finance companies is backed by commercial bank letters of credit.

Brokers and Dealers

The U.S. financial system is rich in entities designed to facilitate the flow of funds from one sector to another. These include stockbrokers, dealers, and investment bankers. While some large firms, such as Merrill Lynch and Salomon Brothers, may function in all three capacities, the activities are different. A broker facilitates a transaction by bringing buyer and seller together but without ever owning the asset being exchanged. He earns a commission for his efforts, but his risk is less than that of the dealer who owns an inventory and profits by selling at a markup over his cost. Dealers play an important role in trading bonds and over-the-counter stocks. A number of banks operate as dealers in government securities. Investment bankers serve as underwriters of securities issues and as advisors in deals involving mergers and acquisitions.

Many of these functions involve activities in which commercial banks have considerable expertise. Existing law and regulation severely limits the extent to which banks can participate in the securities business. Banks can offer discount brokerage services (and perhaps be in the full-service brokerage business) and be dealers and underwriters of government securities, but not municipal revenue bonds or corporate securities (except perhaps for commercial paper). Rationalization of these rules has long been needed.

Mortgage bankers play a role in the mortgage market analogous to that played by brokers, dealers, and investment bankers in the securities markets. Mortgage bankers originate mortgage loans with borrowers, complete the loan documentation, and pay the seller of the property. The mortgages are then accumulated in large blocks and sold to institutional investors directly or in the form of mortgage-backed securities. The mortgage banker may service the loan for the investor for a fee.

Commercial banks and thrift institutions have long been active in mortgage banking, and several bank holding companies have mortgage banking subsidiaries. Mortgage bankers obviously need large amounts of funds to enable them to extend mortgage loans and hold them until they have accumulated a salable package and found a buyer. They obtain funds from commercial banks, with their holdings of mortgages as collateral for the loan. This practice is referred to as "warehousing" of mortgages.

Investment Companies

Most of the institutions described so far operate with equity funds supplied by stockholders and a larger component of funds in debt form supplied by individual and institutional investors. For banks and thrift institutions, of course, the principal source of funds is deposits, and depositors are creditors of the institution. The U.S. financial system also includes a type of intermediary that sells equity shares to the public and invests the proceeds in financial assets, the return on which is directly passed on to shareholders (after deducting operating expenses).

The most common form of this type of entity is a "mutual fund." The mutual fund typically stands ready to sell additional shares at the per-share net asset value (plus, in some cases, a selling commission or "loading charge") and to redeem shares of owners who wish to sell. There are many different types of mutual funds with differing investment objectives. Some may invest in a broad range of securities, while others limit their portfolio to holdings of common stocks or stocks in particular industries. Some seek income maximization, while others pursue growth. Many funds are oriented toward nonequity investments, such as tax-free municipal bonds, government securities, or mortgage instruments.

The major service provided by the investment company approach is diversification, though many companies emphasize their management expertise. The individual of modest wealth cannot easily accumulate a diversified portfolio of securities. The commission costs of buying a few shares of many common stocks would be prohibitive. Bonds are generally sold in minimum denominations of $1,000 (though the minimum denomination of Treasury bills is $10,000), and the costs of buying bonds in small lots are high. Diversification is a valuable means of reducing investment risk, and the investment company device is an efficient means of making diversification available to the small investor.

The money market mutual fund is a relative newcomer to the financial marketplace. These institutions came into existence in 1974, but their growth began with rising interest rates in the late 1970s. From total assets of under $4 billion in 1977, they grew to over $40 billion in 1979 and $200 billion in 1982. Money market mutual funds invest only in safe, liquid, money market instruments, such as commercial paper, bank CDs, and short-term government securities (some funds invest *only* in government securities). The investor in such a fund holds a relatively safe, liquid asset similar to a deposit, but he is actually a shareholder and not a creditor. The value of a share is not fixed as is a deposit, but fluctuates with the value of the funds assets (though for convenience most funds keep the per-share value fixed and charge changes in value to income—this works if such changes in value are small).

Money market mutual funds got their start when depository institutions were restricted in the rates they could pay on deposits. Since interest rate ceilings on deposits have been removed, the money market funds have not grown. For most investors the insured deposit is a superior instrument, and the growth or shrinkage of the money market funds depends on bank pricing of deposits and the spread between returns offered by banks and the funds. The growth of the funds in the period of Regulation Q rate ceilings, which prevented savers from earning market returns on their funds, illustrates the ability of the financial system to find new ways of delivering financial services.

Government Lending Agencies

The federal government is a major source of credit in the economy. While most of the lending is oriented toward housing and farming, other credit programs are designed to assist small businesses, exporters, and students. These programs involve both the direct advance of funds and the guarantee of loans made by private sector lenders.

Given the variety of private financial institutions in the economy, it may seem peculiar that the government has found it necessary to become a major lending institution. Most government lending programs originated with a perception that some deserving sector of the economy was not receiving credit from private financial markets on terms that Congress believed were "fair" or appropriate, given the importance of the potential borrowers. It is possible, of course, that market imperfections of various sorts lead to a situation in which some sectors do not receive credit that their objective economic circumstances warrant. Lending by the government may eliminate or break down such market imperfections. In many cases, of course, the motivation for government involvement is to provide a subsidy through the credit mechanism.

Housing Finance.   The United States has long viewed home ownership as an important social goal and has developed a number of government programs designed to facilitate home ownership and to cure perceived imperfections in the mortgage market. The Federal Housing Administration and the Veterans Administration provide insurance or guarantees of privately financed mortgage loans. Such a guarantee obviously improves the credit quality of the loans and makes lenders more willing to fund them. Government backing also facilitates development of a secondary market in mortgage loans since the buyer no longer has to be concerned with the creditworthiness of the individual borrower or the condition of the property securing the loan. The existence of a secondary market means that mortgage loans are more liquid, and this, in turn, makes lenders more willing to hold such assets. In fact, the contribution that a secondary market can make to expansion of the primary market is so great that the government initiated other programs to foster the secondary market. The Federal National Mortgage Association (FNMA or Fannie Mae) and the Government National Mortgage Association (GNMA or Ginnie Mae) were created to buy and sell federally guaranteed mortgage loans and to facilitate the workings of a market in mortgage-backed securities. Actually, Fannie Mae has become an important source of funds to the mortgage market as a long-term investor in such loans. Its holdings are more than needed to carry out a secondary market operation.

The Federal Home Loan Mortgage Corporation (FHLMC or Freddie Mac) was created in 1970 to buy conventional mortgages from private lenders. (Fannie Mae and Ginnie Mae deal in FHA- and VA-guaranteed mortgages and deal primarily with mortgage bankers, while Freddie Mac's major customers are savings and loan associations.) Freddie Mac is in effect a subsidiary of the Federal Home Loan Bank Board whose members serve as the Board of Directors of Freddie Mac.

Freddie Mac and Fannie Mae are so-called federally sponsored agencies. They are financed primarily by selling their own securities in the market. Because of their close connection with the federal government as well as their own earnings capability, their securities sell at relatively small spreads above Treasury securities though they do not carry an explicit government guarantee.

While these agencies have unquestionably stimulated growth of the mortgage market, some now question whether they play too large a role in the market. In early 1987 a task force appointed by the Federal Home Loan Bank Board to study Freddie Mac's operations recommended that they be curtailed or that Freddie Mac be privatized.

Farm Credit System.   The Farm Credit System consists of the Federal Land Banks, the Federal Intermediate Credit Banks, and the Banks for Cooperatives. These institutions operate primarily by making loans to cooperatives (federal land bank associations or production credit associations) formed by farmers. These cooperatives then make loans to their members. Borrowing members must buy stock in the association, which, in turn, buys stock in the Federal Bank. The Farm Credit System, is owned by its members, in a manner analogous to savings and loan ownership of the Federal Home Loan Bank System and commercial bank ownership of the Federal Reserve System. Ownership rights are limited by the significant federal sponsorship and interest in the system. It is this federal relationship, of course, that allows the Farm Credit System to sell its securities in the market at relatively low cost.

The Farm Credit System, dating back to 1916, was the first federal venture into the lending business. The system has grown tremendously and is now the largest source of financing for farmers and a direct competitor of the commercial banks. The decline in the prices of farm products and farm land in the mid-1980s resulted in severe stress for the Farm Credit System just as it did for commercial banks active in lending to farmers. The system came close to collapse in 1985, and support from Congress was necessary to keep it going. As the crisis came to a head, securities issued by the Farm Credit System sold at greatly increased yields. After Congress acted, yields fell, reflecting market expectations that, one way or another, the federal government would stand behind the obligations of the system. However, the spreads on these securities over Treasury securities remain higher than in the past, indicating some recognition of increased risk.

Credit Guarantors

We have noted the role of the FHA and VA as guarantors of mortgage credit and the boost such guarantees provide to the market for that type of credit. Other government agencies provide similar guarantees, including such programs as the Small Business Administration's guarantees of loans to small firms, the Import-Export Bank's guarantees of export financing, and federally guaranteed loans to college students. All such programs work in the sense that they enhance the quality of the credit and make private lenders more willing to make loans to the sector favored by the availability of the government guarantees. If the total volume of credit is limited, however, that benefit comes at the expense of those borrowers or would-be borrowers whose credit applications are not accompanied by such enhancement. Further, while such programs seem to be of little cost to the government since it does not directly fund the loans, the losses on many of these programs have been large (one study of an SBA program found that over 40 percent of the loans resulted in loss to the government).[5]

The apparent success of the federal government's guarantee of mortgage credit attracted some private firms to the loan guarantee business. There is now an active private market in guarantees of mortgage loans and municipal securities.

The use of credit guarantees has become important in several markets in which commercial banks are active. The trend toward securitization, whereby banks sell loans to pools that issue securities backed by the loans, often depends on a third-party guarantee of the loans in the pool. Commercial banks have become an important source of the credit enhancement needed to make some financing feasible. The great expansion of the commercial paper market in the 1980s resulted as firms with less than premier credit standing were able to issue paper backed by a commercial bank letter of credit. Commercial banks have been able to earn fees from exercise of their credit expertise without the need to actually advance funds and hold assets. Some have chosen this type of off-balance sheet activity as a means of minimizing the need for additional capital, but in 1987 the regulatory agencies indicated their intent to apply capital requirements against such contingent liabilities. This will not eliminate the activity because credit guarantees have now found a permanent role in the financial system.

CONCLUSION

This chapter has attempted to describe the variety of financial institutions operating in the U.S. financial system and the role of com-

---

[5]See Timothy Bates, "A Review of the Small Business Administrations's Major Loan Programs," in *Sources of Financing for Small Business*, ed. Paul M. Horvitz and R. Richardson Pettit (Greenwich, Conn.: JAI Press, 1984), p. 223.

mercial banks in that system. Commercial banks are active in virtually all segments of the financial system, and those in which bank participation is limited, such as insurance and securities, are precisely those in which commercial banks have been seeking expanded powers.

Any description of the structure of the financial system at a point in time becomes dated rather rapidly. The most important characteristic of the financial system in recent years has been change. The system has had the flexibility to innovate and fill any gaps that might exist or that might be created by changes in economic conditions. Money market mutual funds did not exist 15 years ago; neither did options on financial futures (or financial futures for that matter) nor securities backed by automobile loans or credit card receivables. The trend toward the creation of financial conglomerates, represented by combinations of firms specializing in the securities business, insurance, credit cards, and other financial (and nonfinancial) products, may tend to blur the lines between the types of institutions described here. One of the pressing issues of public policy that remains to be resolved is the appropriate role for commercial banks (and bank holding companies) in the broad financial services business and the extent to which banking (or, more generally, financial activities) should be kept separate from other commercial activity.

CHAPTER THREE

Geographic Strategies for the 1990s: Preparing for a Smart Endgame

Lowell Bryan

Director
McKinsey & Company, Inc.

Paul Allen

Principal
McKinsey & Company, Inc.

Many U.S. banks—even at the community bank level—have a surfeit of options for competition for the 1990s. They can choose among numerous market segments, deciding whether to compete broadscale (selling all products to all customer segments) or selectively in product and customer niches. They can also choose among several approaches to their chosen segments. Many will be geographic competitors, seeking to gain a disproportionately high share of their community, regional, or national market. Others will be product players, leveraging national processing and advertising economies. Others will be customer relationship banks, building on the franchise value of attractive customers' inertia.

This chapter focuses on the geographic approach to competition. It summarizes the findings of a recent internal McKinsey R&D project in which we analyzed how players in personal financial service markets can become winners in the 1990s.[1] Here, we first outline how geographic competition is evolving. Then, we describe the most viable endgames for the 1990s. Finally, we summarize our thoughts about the practical steps that smart players are taking today to ensure that they are among the endgame winners five years from now.

---

[1] We would like to thank Peter Walker and our other colleagues who have contributed to McKinsey's Personal Financial Services Project. This chapter was written with data available from the project as of October 1986.

WHERE ARE WE TODAY?

There have been three distinct phases of geographic competition that can be characterized as:

- Era I, 1960–1981: Regulated oligarchies
- Era II, 1981–1985: Deposit price deregulation
- Era III, 1985–1990s: Geographic deregulation.

Era I, 1960–1981: Planting Local Branch Flags

Geographic and price regulation in the 1960s and 1970s led to a fragmented, geographically dispersed, and localized banking industry. The top five competitors controlled only about 5 percent of both consumer deposits and consumer credit and mortgages. Even for larger corporate customers, where competition did become national, they controlled only about a fifth of the total of C&I loans and commercial paper. In contrast, the top five car manufacturers, for example, controlled over 95 percent of their market.

Regulation constraints led to oligarchic, cartel-like pricing. Competition was often fierce (particularly in the Southeast and California), but it was generally based on "giveaway" services that bankers and customers alike saw and priced as "bundled." Both knew that when interest rates were high, the wide spreads from deposits would compensate for, or subsidize, thinner credit returns (or even negative net interest margins due to usury law rate ceilings). Conversely, when interest rates were low, wide credit spreads would offset the reduced deposit subsidy. (Exhibit 1 illustrates the contracyclical operating income of deposit and credit products from the branch-based retail and commercial markets.) Overall, returns were attractive, and bankers were prepared to accept these cross-subsidies between the two sides of the balance sheet over the course of the interest rate cycle. Indeed, the general trend of total earnings was upward through 1981 as interest rates rose. The deposit subsidy from individuals and small commercial customers increased from $12.4 billion in 1977 to $63.1 billion in 1981. The 1981 subsidy allowed bankers to absorb the negative credit spread of $9 billion for retail loans that usury laws caused that year. Moreover, given the size of the deposit subsidy, the total operating expense base of the branches seemed insignificant then, at about $38 billion.

One key feature of branch-based bank economics was the fact that affluent and elderly consumers subsidized the transaction accounts of low-income customers (a bottom-line subsidy of over $4 billion in 1981) because the more attractive customers valued the geographic convenience of local, personalized service enough to accept this subsidy. To lock in these customers, banks expanded their networks, plant-

EXHIBIT 1   The Contracyclical Returns of Retail Deposits and Credits 1970–1986—Operating Income

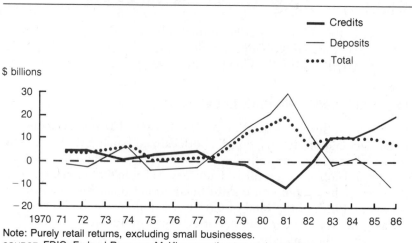

Note: Purely retail returns, excluding small businesses.
SOURCE: FDIC; Federal Reserve; McKinsey estimates and analysis.

ing the flags of an additional 16,800 branches between 1960 and 1980 for a total of 41,900 branches. This expansion greatly enlarged the shared-cost base of geographic competitors. Exhibit 2 illustrates the typical cost structure for branch-based banks. Less than 30 percent of costs are unique to specific products. From 70 to 85 percent are shared costs, which relate to multiple product or market segments and do not disappear when a business or product is discontinued or a branch closed. The shared cost base can be thought of as a ticking bomb during the second competitive era. As the third era plays out over the next 10 years, optimizing it will be central to winning or losing.

Era II, 1981–1985: Unwinding the Deposit Subsidy

Beginning in 1981, the banking industry experienced a fundamental repricing and a radical change in the competitive dynamics for core deposit products. We estimate that the net interest margin from retail and commercial deposits declined from $63 billion in 1981 to about $27 billion in 1986 as average spreads on consumer deposits declined from 750 to 180 basis points. Reflecting this change, operating income from consumer and small commercial liabilities declined from $39.8 billion to a loss of $3.6 billion. Obviously this was partly because we had reached the bottom of the interest rate cycle. But it was also caused by a basic shift from interest rate insensitive to interest rate sensitive products, with the latter increasing from 37 percent to 57 percent of consumer bank deposits during the second era.

EXHIBIT 2   Shared Operating Costs in a Typical Bank (illustrative)

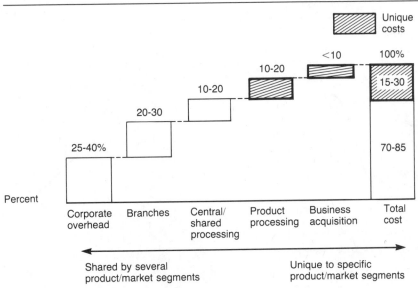

SOURCE: FDIC; McKinsey estimates and analysis.

Many banks managed extremely effectively through this economic reconfiguration, thanks partly to improved credit returns. Those banks with sufficient scale in credit to obtain operating economies enjoyed net interest margins on consumer debt that increased from a negative 1 percent to a 9 to 10 percent positive spread between 1981 and 1986, enabling the industry to handle deposit repricing. On the other hand, smaller banks, without consumer credit portfolios to fall back on, have suffered. Other larger banks took excessive credit risk and found loan losses mounting. As Exhibit 3 shows, the range of performance among banks has widened considerably between 1979 and 1985. In 1985, nearly 30 percent of banks were earning under 4 percent return on equity. As a result, the number of banks actually losing money increased from 681 in 1981 to 3,100 in 1986.

It will be more difficult in the future for even those banks with credit economies of scale to justify their large shared cost structures (particularly branches) because credit returns are becoming disassociated from the branch system. In 1975, about 44 percent of non-mortgage debt origination was branch-based; we estimate that this declined to about 32 percent by 1985 as consumer asset origination shifted to point-of-purchase or direct response. Therefore, branch-related costs must be justified primarily by deposit products whose revenues do not now, and may never again, reach levels capable of

EXHIBIT 3   Distribution of Return on Equity of U.S. Commercial Banks, 1979 and 1985

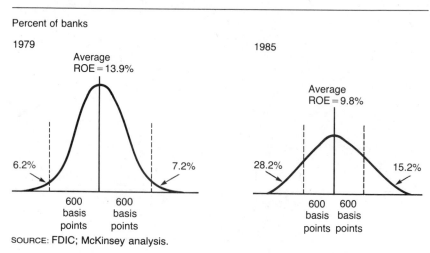

SOURCE: FDIC; McKinsey analysis.

supporting all of these costs for all players—particularly if funding mismatching gains and losses are excluded from the income calculation. And all this is true at a time when the elderly and upscale are still subsidizing the transaction accounts and branch access of low-income customers to the tune of about $4 billion.

As branch-based revenues have declined, shared costs have mushroomed. Investments in new channel technology have failed to substitute for, and have merely supplemented, traditional shared costs. For example, bankers have invested over $2.5 billion in the capital costs alone of the 68,000 ATMs now installed while checks per household have continued to rise, branch numbers have grown to record heights, and teller efficiency has worsened. Real deposits per teller (deflated to 1974 dollars by the CPI) have declined from about $1.8 million to $1.6 million between 1974 and 1985 while the average number of tellers per branch has remained flat at about six. As Exhibit 4 illustrates, the work of a New York McKinsey principal, Tom Steiner, has shown that increased credit earnings and fees between 1981 and 1986 were not enough to offset a reduced deposit spread, increased loan losses, and especially the burgeoning operating expenses of the branch network. These expenses may well reflect duplicate branch channel costs that can be managed out in the future or spread across a broader product base, but today they are a clear drag on returns.

EXHIBIT 4   Source of Change in Retail Branch Economics, 1982–1986

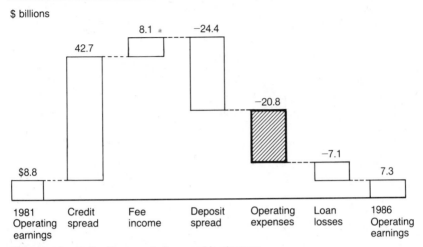

$ billions

	42.7	8.1	−24.4	−20.8	−7.1	
$8.8						7.3
1981 Operating earnings	Credit spread	Fee income	Deposit spread	Operating expenses	Loan losses	1986 Operating earnings

Note: Purely retail returns, excluding small businesses.
SOURCE: FDIC; McKinsey analysis.

Era III, 1985–1990s: Meeting the Challenge of Geographic Deregulation

As bankers face the new era of geographic deregulation, pressure on branch-based economics may increase further. In addition to being decoupled from the branch system, credit revenues may actually drop for two reasons. First, credit spreads could drop as interest rates rise, particularly if nonbanks like Sears can securitize their credit card receivables. Securitization would remove the cost of capital advantage that banks have had through higher allowed debt to equity levels in the past, and encourage price competition by nonbank competitors to gain share. Second, credit volume itself could decline. While not rate sensitive, consumers probably are sensitive to the absolute cash flow associated with their debt. Therefore, they may well reduce volumes to keep cash flow fairly flat if suppliers increase rates much above current levels to sustain today's spreads during the interest rate cycle's upturn. Moreover, while some improvements in deposit spreads will occur to offset any credit squeeze as interest rates rise, consumers have become educated to expect high real returns and are unlikely to accept the deposit spreads of the past. Exhibit 5 shows the potential impact on 1986 corporate earnings of an unmanaged result for large scale consumer lenders. This is not a projection. As we have seen,

EXHIBIT 5   Consumer Credit in Relation to Corporate Earnings

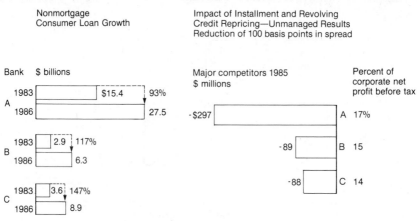

SOURCE: Annual reports; 10-Ks; McKinsey analysis.

retail bankers have been adept at protecting their income streams. Nonetheless, a clear vulnerability exists.

One way of combating such pressures is, of course, to seek economies of scale through geographic expansion, which has only recently become possible. While the era of consolidation has only just begun, we can already see that for some it is the key to a winning strategy.

The table below illustrates that geographic consolidation has barely begun:

Number of Acquisitions

Year	Total	Across State Lines	Assets Involved ($ billions)
1980	130	6	13
1981	167	16	29
1982	233	31	47
1983	187	30	37
1984	176	15	31
1985	191	33	30
1986*	108	21	17

*First two quarters.
SOURCE: "Mergers and Acquisitions," McKinsey analysis.

Still, the potential for efficiencies—at least at the regional level—has already been illustrated. NCNB, for example, has acquired eight banks between 1982 and 1985 that had assets of $6.4 billion and average preacquisition operating costs/assets of about 350 basis points. Before the acquisitions began, NCNB had a ratio of 260 basis points: It now has a ratio of about 270 basis points. We estimate that the efficiencies NCNB has achieved are worth approximately $18 million incrementally to the bottom line of the acquired banks, 9 percent of NCNB's 1985 income before taxes. Moreover, some of the acquisitions are recent, and since it takes time to ring out efficiencies, we suspect that NCNB has the potential to gain even more benefits.

Building on the work of our colleague, George Feiger, in McKinsey's San Francisco office, we show in Exhibit 6 the scale economies that can be achieved *within* five classes of U.S. banks: small community, large community, small regional, large regional, and the top 20 banks in the United States. Exhibit 7 indicates that these savings are achieved by gaining corporate overhead, branch, and operations economies of scale. They reflect moving from an inefficient to an efficient paper-handling job shop for community banks, moving from an inefficient to an efficient midtechnology batch processor for regional banks, and moving from there to the technologically state-of-the-art processing and funding efficiency (given higher leverage and therefore lower intermediation costs of capital) of a top 20 bank. We

EXHIBIT 6   Operating Cost Economies of Community Banks, Adjusted Business Mix

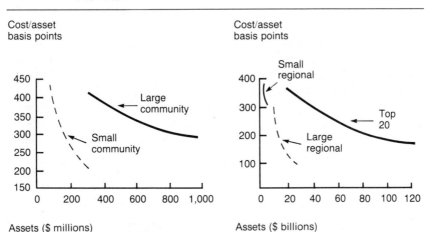

Cost/asset basis points

Cost/asset basis points

Assets ($ millions)

Assets ($ billions)

SOURCE: FDIC; McKinsey estimates and analysis.

EXHIBIT 7   Shared Cost Economies of Larger Scale Banks

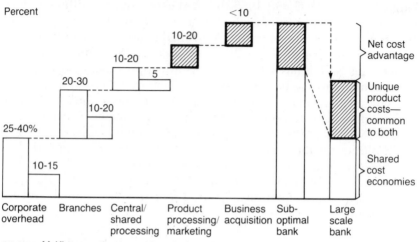

SOURCE: McKinsey estimates and analysis.

should emphasize that these are scale curves for mix-adjusted players; differences have been factored out in mix of retail versus wholesale and fee-based and nonfee-based business, which also have a huge impact on costs.

While in some cases size means economy, Exhibit 6 shows that there are often step function *increases* in costs as one moves *between* categories because of major changes in overhead and other shared costs required to move from one category of bank to the next—for example, from a large regional to a top 20 bank. Because of these increases, a very efficient small community bank can match the cost ratios of a midscale large regional bank and even a $50 billion top 20 bank. Moreover, community banks may also be providing higher perceived value to customers at this cost level (through better local knowledge and community identification, better service quality control, and so on). Thus, while a geographic entry by a midscale regional bank, for example, might make a small community bank uneconomic, there remains a clear basis for cost and value competitiveness for a large number of scale-efficient community banks.

Also, it is not clear whether the current cost curve for the top 20 banks represents the last step function increase. The top 20 are still essentially one-state banks with major international capabilities. If national geographic competition became possible, further scale potential may be realizable (for example, in advertising). Of course, this might also require managing through a further step function increase in costs.

Even at the beginning of Era III for geographic competition, we already know that there is potential for smart moves as in the NCNB example. Using a chess analogy, we are only beginning the midgame of geographic competition. What are the viable roles for a winning endgame as the process of geographic deregulation accelerates towards the 1990s?

HOW CAN WE WIN IN THE FUTURE?

The three *geographic* winning roles as we approach the 1990s will be: (1) community, (2) regional, and (3) national. We will discuss only these roles in this chapter. There are already national *product* competitors; large bank credit card players like Chase, Citibank, and Bank of America are clear examples. Similarly, there may be national *customer group* opportunities that are not dependent on any local physical presences (for example, discount brokerage). The interaction between national players across these three "how to compete" approaches is covered in later chapters. Here we will only evaluate the potential for and characteristics of winners among community, regional, and national geographic competitors.

We should also stress immediately that, while we will distinguish three classes of future geographic winners, we believe *all* geographic competition is essentially local. Customers in Manhattan do not have the same value perceptions as customers in Savannah; their price/ service trade-offs vary markedly. Indeed, this is true even between blocks in Chicago or Los Angeles, and among counties or even districts in small towns. Bankers can learn a lot from retailers, such as Benetton, who locate stores and adjust inventory according to customer demographics and behavior patterns on a microgeographic basis (for example, block-by-block in a large city).

Let us now look at the three winning geographic roles:

1. *Effective community banks.* A winning niche strategy will leverage local physical distribution costs by pushing more products through local channels. This will mean developing portfolios of products that can be effectively cross-sold (home equity loans are a clear example; insurance is more doubtful). The future winners here will have branches staffed with people who know how to cross-sell. They will have transferred all facilities where they have insufficient scale to service bureaus and will have stripped out all unproductive spending. On the market site, they will have maintained and enhanced their strong local reputation and their sales and service skills, and thus will have strengthened their existing customer franchise. They may even be able to charge a premium for the value added of distinctive, local service. There will be thousands of such winners.

2. *Dominant superregional banks.* Perhaps 15 to 25 regional banks will become dominant superregionals. They will have strong franchises, like community banks, across multiple towns and states, and will also enjoy the scale economies of regional operations. Future winners here have already evaluated potential acquisition candidates and are acting now to preempt future national competitors in capturing the prize targets.

3. *Truly "national" banks.* There will probably be two or three large national banks who add a national brand franchise to local service and regional operating efficiencies, leveraging overhead costs through national scale. Future winners will have used a strong return on equity and thus share price to fund an effective acquisition strategy. Our colleagues, Joel Bleeke, Laura Daniels, and Richard Gridley from McKinsey's Chicago and Cleveland offices, have described in detail how to develop an acquisitions strategy in the work sponsored by the Bank Administration Institute and summarized in *The American Banker* in September 1985.

Future geographic winners are working intelligently and creatively today with a long-term perspective. They know they must use today's midgame as a time for focused preparation for tomorrow's consolidation, so they are choosing their role now based on a realistic view of their potential. In contrast, future losers are working hard but focusing on the short term. They are pricing deposits below cost to retain balances and spending most of their time working out loan loss problems. This may help for a while. However, without a clear vision of their future role, this kind of hard work is guaranteed to have disappointing results.

HOW SHOULD WE PREPARE FOR THE FUTURE?

Having chosen a future role that they can realistically hope to play, the smart competitors are taking three key steps now. They are:

1. Learning to manage the true dynamics of shared and unique revenues and costs.
2. Optimizing existing and acquired networks.
3. Building product, service, and geographic management skills.

We will outline each of these programs below and show their four phases in the Appendix.

Learning to Manage Economics

Winners will understand the true economics and cost/revenue dynamics of their business and take strategic decisions that will optimize them. The first step—developing the needed understanding—takes considerable effort for two reasons. First, the transfer pricing systems for cost of funds used today often obscure true product and branch economics by confusing gains and losses from maturity mismatching decisions by Treasury or line-of-business managers with underlying product and customer segment returns. Moreover, transfer pricing rarely takes into account fluctuating returns over the interest rate cycle—encouraging, for example, the sales of credit card businesses in 1981 that look questionable with hindsight.

The second reason why economics are difficult to understand is that the basis by which shared costs are usually allocated down to the level of individual product/market segments (for example, pro rata to assets, floor space, usage, or profits) often has little or no real economic significance. Thus, although allocation may motivate line managers to attempt to recover shared costs fully, it does not help bank managers forecast the economic consequences of strategic actions. For example, while closing a particular branch would certainly result in a loss of marginal revenue, it might not make costs go away. This may have been the case with many branch rationalization or branch sales programs in the past. Our experience is that it takes several years to realize most of the cost savings that can be expected from either divestments of activities or from rationalizing acquisitions.

We have found that the true economics of a geographic competitor's business can best be understood through a strategic cost/revenue diagnostic. This approach avoids the difficulties associated with normal cost allocation methods and analyzes the businesses in terms of their unique and shared revenues and costs. The steps of this process are illustrated in Exhibit 8 and consist of:

1. Identification of the accounting costs and revenues at each level of the current organizational "tree." Significant cost/revenue areas are categorized by major activities or functions, such as processing, marketing, and so on. Then, if cost/revenue items are *substantially* unique (for example, more than 75 percent attributable to the activities of a given unit, such as a sales force for a particular customer group in a branch), they are attributed to the relevant unit, and returns on spending and equity are calculated. Revenues are determined using the market rate for risk-free securities with the same interest rate maturity to avoid including any mismatching gains or losses.

2. Detailed categorization of the shared costs that are not attributable to customer/product areas, and assessment of any step function increases or decreases in these costs that would result from changes in business volumes or mix. This procedure gives the bank a good sense of an activity's true economics and thus a good basis for generating strategic options for entering or exiting product/market seg-

---

EXHIBIT 8   Key Elements of Cost/Revenue Diagnostic

---

1. Cost Revenue Tree—
   Today

2. Options

3. Cost Revenue Tree—
   3-Year Target

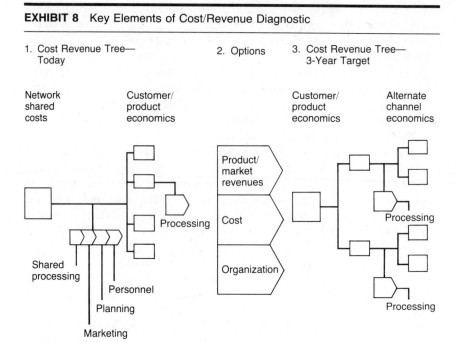

SOURCE: McKinsey practice development.

ments or spreading shared costs across different distribution channels for current businesses. The advantage of this approach is that it is top-down. In other words, it is driven primarily by the needs of strategic decision making and strategic management, not by particular theories of allocation methodologies or a management commitment to one particular dimension, such as product-line profitability over customer returns.

3. Development of cost/revenue targets. Having understood the economic dynamics of their business, future winners choose the end-game role most appropriate for them, and then design a target cost/revenue tree for, say, three years out, that will best leverage the scale economies of the chosen geographic role. These targets are pursued vigorously through management of the revenue or cost levers where they are actually controllable in the organization. This will often result in a fundamental economic reconfiguration of the bank.

Optimizing Network Scale Advantages

Again building on George Feiger's work in McKinsey's San Francisco office, we have repeatedly seen that the geographic competitors with the best results are those that have both a higher *share* of channel locations and the *right type* of channels (for example, branch, ATM, and so on) in the *right place*. This is illustrated in Exhibit 9 for three residential boroughs of New York City. Competitor A controls 30 percent, 32 percent, and 39 percent of deposits for 20 percent, 23 percent, and 33 percent of network share in Queens, the Bronx, and Staten Island. Furthermore, in total, the top four banks take over 80 percent of deposits for 70 percent of branch network share. Competitors E, F, and G are illustrative of likely future losers, whose scale disadvantage is evident.

Both share and location are critical to a winning formula. Time and again we have seen clients with branch and other channel loca-

---

EXHIBIT 9   New York City: Scale Impact of Branch Coverage, 1986

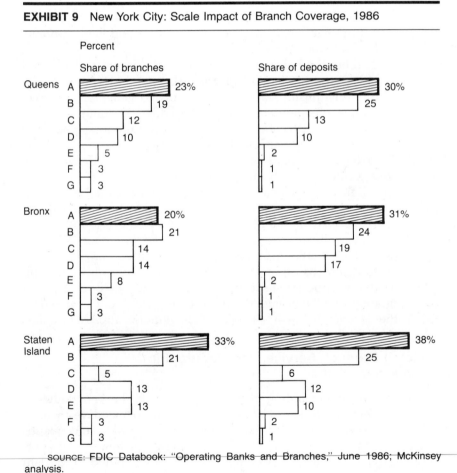

SOURCE: FDIC Databook: "Operating Banks and Branches," June 1986; McKinsey analysis.

tions that bear little correlation to the relative attractiveness of customers banking in those locations or to relative competitive share.

Future geographic winners are linking their strategic cost/revenue diagnostic work with three programs to optimize existing and acquired branch networks:

1. *Evaluation of location potential.* Winners prepare to respond to differentiated customer demand by developing a detailed understanding of their specific geographic locations. This involves understanding:
   a. Customer needs—to determine which are not met adequately by the bank or its competitors.
   b. The demographics of attractive consumer, commercial, and, to the extent relevant, corporate customer segments for each microgeographic area.
   c. The concentrations of attractive segments and definition of natural markets through commuter flow and bank-at-home/bank-at-work analysis.
   d. The buying behavior of each segment in terms of who decides on a particular purchase, the purchase process, and the relationship of demand to price, geographic convenience, channel, and other value-added attributes.
   e. The competitive environment—that is, numbers, types, and effectiveness of alternative suppliers.
2. *Tailoring of channels to each retained location.* To avoid creating technological channels where consumers do not want them and high-cost personalized approaches where they cannot afford them, winners weigh customer value perceptions with alternative distribution channel costs in each location.
3. *Optimization of throughput in retained branches.* Winners establish specific cross-sales programs with clear quotas and performance-based incentives. Simply, this boils down to competitively superior execution that maximizes the flow of appropriate products through the shared-cost pipeline. It is based on the economic insights and management approaches just described.

Building Product, Service, and Geographic Management Skills

Linked to an understanding of true economics is the knowledge of the key levers for improved performance. Many banks have focused too heavily on cost alone without understanding fully—and quantifying through effective use of market research—customer value perceptions. Thus, in many banks, tellers were downgraded in the late

1970s and early 1980s. Lines lengthened, and the quality of personal service declined. Some banks, like Wells Fargo, realized that their customers valued the contact of a smiling, attentive, intelligent banker and that it took high-quality staff supported by sophisticated management systems to be capable of effective cross-selling.

The future winners have been, and are now during the competitive midgame, investing heavily in three new or upgraded functions that add value to customers:

1. *A strong and innovative product function.* While basic product development (for example, for bankwide mortgage products) may rest with product-driven organizations within a bank, the geographic competitor needs to develop the responsive local merchandising skills that will enable it to tailor generic products to local conditions. To develop the product function they need, winning banks are creating:

   a. A product strategy that maximizes the impact of new product technologies. Building a clear role with regard to the profound effects of credit securitization is a good example. Most bankers will need to re-engineer their loan products so that the loans can be sold off to investors rather than retained. Our analysis indicates that the value added of credit origination probably can be retained by a geographic competitor maintaining the profits from distribution; the value added of holding assets on the balance sheet will probably be lost.

   b. The necessary organization and skills to tailor generic products to meet geographic variations.

   c. An evaluation process for product suppliers both within and outside the bank to enable the geographic sector to obtain the highest returns consistent with quality and supply assurance.

   d. Methods for educating network staff on product attributes and sales techniques to ensure timely distribution.

   e. Monitoring criteria and processes for tracking planned performance.

2. *A flexible, cost-conscious "store management" function.* We have found that branch managers often pay ample attention to increasing efficiency in the pure processing and delivery functions in their branches. However, sales and marketing initiatives tend to be rudimentary and are often sacrificed for incremental operations streamlining without regard to the resulting impact on flexibility and value added in customer service. Winners will work to develop a store management function that focuses on sales and marketing with programs to:

      a. Improve local information gathering to identify target customers and new customer needs in the future and thus understand the relative attractiveness of locations and channels to serve them.

      b. Refocus branch staff time and other selling resources (such as ATMs, videos, "take-ones," and the like) to meet the customer needs of a particular location.

      c. Streamline nonsales resources through adjustments of operations and delivery systems while increasing cost-effective sales efforts.

3. A *geographic management function.* Managing multiple-channel types with different objectives and priorities will require a far more demanding leadership and coordination function than most banks have today. Future winners are trying to create this without causing excessive organizational layering and overhead expense. Specifically, they are developing skills in:

      a. How to manage discrete forms of channels with differing product and customer priorities (and the resulting differences in staff skill requirements).

      b. How to coordinate product initiatives throughout the network.

      c. How to motivate and monitor performance against sharply differentiated targets.

The crux of each of the three programs is superiority in basic blocking and tackling—the often hard-to-emulate competitive edge of: a smiling, friendly staff; tellers who are listening for the clues to cross-sales opportunities that customers provide ("My grandson's off to school—I do hope he can afford to look after himself."); branch layouts that encourage, not discourage, ATM usage and browsing through product take-ones; and sales and marketing managers that listen to customer focus groups for service improvements, not to their instincts for what customers want. These advantages are, in fact, all the characteristics that add so much value to the shopping experience at Neiman Marcus or Saks Fifth Avenue that customers flock there even though they know prices are higher than in the nearby discount stores. These institutional skills can be systematically developed and nurtured. However, they require both time and investment to create and constant daily attention to sustain. Winners are willing to pay this price.

The pace of geographic deregulation has been fairly pedestrian to date. This has been a clear advantage for the banks emerging as likely geographic winners who have been using the midgame to maneuver for the best position, skills, and return on equity from which to strike as the endgame is played out. Future losers have been competing harder and harder and head-to-head but without the focus of a clear, realistic vision of their future role and without investment in the institutional skills and systems we have described that will underlie future success.

Many geographic bankers have weathered the first batterings of deregulation well. The potential returns of the next era will be high for those who are smart and are prepared; the pain of being shaken-out will be difficult to bear for those who are not. Competing harder will not suffice . . . as we have shown, only the smarter competitors will win.

APPENDIX
PREPARING A SMART ENDGAME

Phase 1 Identifying Key Improvement Levers		Phase 2 Specifying Strategic Opportunities	
Key Activities	*End Products*	*Key Activities*	*End Products*
Understand current stock price and levers to improve it		Produce strategic options by geographic area and the required investment/ resources, risks, returns, and skills	Choice of strategic thrusts and commitment of resources
Agree on approach to product/ customer economics (transfer pricing, costs, and diagnostic steps)	Consensus on scope and content of economic fact base	Design product approaches by identifying attributes for cost or value advantage	Variations of product by type of geographic location
Prepare initial diagnostic trees • Identify appropriate customer/ product groups • Distinguish unique and shared costs	Understanding of "true" economics of bank; and categories and variability of shared costs	Produce branch "models"	Detailed "models" for 3 or 4 different branch/other channel approaches fitting different geographic and product profiles
Develop product profiles	Detailed business approach for each element of product marketing, processing, and support	Assess channel alternatives	Channel strategies by product and type of location and acquisition or de novo strategies to achieve them
Develop geographic profiles	Detailed profile of customer demographics, needs, values, buying behavior, and servicing economics by location	Develop target cost/ revenue trees • Establish future economic potential • Identify responsibilities for shared costs	Clear objectives and responsibilities for revenue and cost management at both product/ market and shared cost levels
Assess internal capabilities	"Gap analysis" of relative strengths and weaknesses of staff skills and comparisons with best practices of competitors		

Phase 3 **Creating the Future Bank**		Phase 4 **Designing an Implementation Road Map**	
Key Activities	*End Products*	*Key Activities*	*End Products*
Design the product function	Structure, staffing, and processes for product management for local tailoring	Assign specific responsibilities for defined actions in agreed time frames	Detailed road map and plan for executing change program; and recommendation for rollout phasing
Design the store management function	Structure, staffing, and processes for optimizing contribution to shared cost base	Develop approach for subsequent expansion opportunities	Target regional bank evaluation systems and models (manual and electronic) and processes for evaluating subsequent geographic opportunities.
Design the geographic management function	Structure, staffing, and processes to coordinate multiple channels and manage differentiated targets by channel		
Establish interbank cooperation • Identify interfaces (e.g., with credit card in product management sector) • Design cooperation approaches and processes	Processes and systems for planning, monitoring, reporting, and rewarding cross-sector initiatives		

SOURCE: McKinsey practice development.

CHAPTER FOUR

Competition in Banking

Richard M. Rosenberg

Vice Chairman
Bank of America

The nature of bank competition has changed dramatically in the past five years. This chapter will explore the nature of the new competition and some of the reasons for that explosive change. However, it is clear that pre-1980 analyses of bank competition are totally obsolete, and every financial institution must adapt to the new realities of competition in the 80s in an environment that has virtually no historical precedent.

From the end of World War II to 1980, a period of more than 35 years, almost all banks looked on the savings and loan and savings bank industries and credit unions as their primary competitors. For example, in certain banking trade associations, the proposal to allow a savings and loan officer to attend a seminar or a school under a nonmember fee schedule evoked incredible emotional response to the extent that such proposals were always tabled.

Certainly, in a few specialized banking areas, there was additional and recognized competition from nonbanks, such as automobile financing by the captive finance subsidiaries of the automobile manufacturers or, in investment management, by specialty firms established exclusively to perform that service. There were, of course, also areas of concern relative to the government's role in financial services competition fostered by agricultural banks who often faced difficult competition from quasi-government agencies, such as the Production Credit Associations.

Obviously, with access to the financial markets far beyond the reach of the typical farm bank, the PCA system was a formidable competitor despite such inhibiting regulations as the necessity of the borrower to purchase stock in the PCA.

But, for most of the nations 14,000 banks, the local savings and loan association and the credit unions represented the most visible

and most formidable competition—especially for deposits and consumer loans, the most basic product lines of the commercial banking
system.

Although industry studies urged banks to understand the nature
of other competitors from manufacturers to securities brokers, the industry's focus was riveted on interstate banking and the thrift industry.

It is difficult to pinpoint the exact date when the potential profit
in the business of banking was "discovered" by those outside the
industry. Some industry analysts believe it occurred in the inflation-
rampant period of the late 1970s when money market funds began
their surge because the real value of savings was vastly higher than
the interest rate the banking industry could pay as a result of Regulation Q. Others marked the day of the new competition as that day
when Merrill Lynch announced its now famous cash management
account (CMA), which offered checking, savings, and credit features
from a securities broker. Still other observers believed the day of the
new beginning for bank competition was the day that Sears Roebuck
announced that it was buying Dean Witter and would marry that securities firm with its Coldwell Banker and Allstate Insurance operations to create consumer financial centers.

Regardless of the specific event that marked the beginning of the
new competition, it is now clear that by 1980, manufacturers who coul·¹·¹
no longer compete effectively in their chosen field, retailers who were
struggling in their basic business against new competition from bou-
tiques to off-price chains, and securities and insurance firms who were
facing shrinking margins and acceptability of bread-and-butter products, all turned to the "business of banking" for new profitable ventures.

This change was, of course, natural and inevitable. Unlike their own
industries where success went to competitors who executed well, were
innovative in marketing and production, and responsive to customer
needs, banking did not have those characteristics because it was ham-
pered by laws and regulations spawned by anticompetitive special-
interest groups and depression-era fears. Virtually every classic competitive foray in the banking industry by a bank, from more realistic
interest rates to greater customer convenience, was either challenged
by regulators or the courts, and banking lost in almost every case. To a
competitor outside the industry, banking represented the proverbial
gold mine since banks could *not* be truly innovative and could *not* be
truly customer responsive because of regulations.

In the aggregate, the industry of 14,000 institutions represented
billions of dollars of profit even though returns on capital for most
institutions were not spectacular and, in fact, were below overall industry averages. If a competitor could only ensure that it was not faced
with banking's archaic regulation and laws, it would be like shooting

fish in a barrel to generate profits that would be taken from banks. For many new competitors, this was true.

Some of the factors that made banking so noncompetitive in the early 1980s have changed, but many have not. Yet because much has not changed and what has changed has changed so recently, it is now necessary to analyze competition—not just from savings and loans and from a few isolated competitors in narrow product lines, but from new rivals in each of the product lines or services a bank offers. In this chapter, only a broad overview can be given, but it will suggest each market and each product line has its own unique competitive characteristics and to succeed a bank must understand *who* the real competitor is and what that competitor's strengths are.

COMPETITION IN THE WHOLESALE MARKETS

Competitive analysis in wholesale or in the medium or large business markets can be divided into three broad categories: (1) competition in asset origination and extension of credit, (2) competition in non-credit or operational services, and (3) competition in investment banking services.

Competition in asset origination and credit extension in the wholesale market has been, perhaps, the least affected by the number of new competitors. Of course, there is a fundamental reason for the relative lack of new competitors for this function in this market: this market segment and product line have suffered from relatively low margins in the past decade. In fact, on a risk-adjusted and capital-required basis, many banks engaged in corporate business lending experience virtually no margin.

Although, relatively few new competitors have entered this field, it does not mean that there is a lack of competition in corporate wholesale lending. To the contrary, competition is fierce since traditional asset origination is a commodity business; that is, competition has not been characterized by such factors as innovation, service quality, or delivery systems but rather by *price*.

If price becomes the major competitive factor, the low-cost producer will win the battle, and here is where banks have a distinct disadvantage. Banks cannot become the low-cost producer because of regulations, and therefore the banking industry will always be at a competitive disadvantage to two significant competitors—the commercial paper market and foreign banks.

Unlike the banking system—whose Federal Reserve requirements represent a hidden tax on funds raised by banks, thus increasing their cost—the commercial paper market has no such reserve requirements. As a result, banks have to face the fact that more and more borrowers are turning to the commercial paper market. For an increasing number of companies, the commercial paper market is simply a less expensive means of borrowing because the hidden tax called reserves is not a factor in the cost of such borrowings.

In all fairness, it must also be pointed out that the commercial banking system has also been unable to compete with the commercial paper market because the credit rating of many borrowers in this market has been better than the banks who formerly served as an intermediary between those who provided funds and those who wished to use them. When the intermediary's credit rating is weaker in the eyes of those providing funds than the ultimate borrower, there is no value added by the intermediary, which in the past was most often a bank.

Of greater concern to those engaged in lending in the wholesale market is the increasing market penetration of foreign banks, especially the Japanese. Unlike many other industries who were simply outmanufactured or outmarketed by the Japanese and other foreign competitors, the banking industry was a victim of its own regulators, who established one standard for U.S. banks and a less stringent standard for foreign banks competing for the same U.S. customers.

Therefore, it should be no surprise that each year an increasing percentage of C&I loans in the major federal reserve districts are made by foreign banks. It should be no surprise that the L/C requirements of U.S. municipalities increasingly are being provided by the Japanese. It should be no surprise that, while much asset origination is a matter of price, the federal regulators have virtually guaranteed that a U.S. bank cannot compete with banks from certain nations on the basis of price.

This is a very harsh statement, but let's examine it further. The economics of banking are quite simple. Return on assets times leverage equals return on equity (ROA $\times$ L = ROE). If an institution wishes to achieve an improved or competitive return on equity, it can improve its return on assets or increase its leverage or both. Unfortunately, the regulators have determined that leverage must decrease, and therefore to achieve the same return on equity, the institution must increase its ROA using the formula. Although operational efficiencies do enter to some extent into the determination of ROA, the ROA in the wholesale asset origination market is much more sensitive to price as the most significant factor.

For example, a Japanese bank is allowed to leverage at a far greater level than its U.S. competitor. Therefore, simply take debt in Japan, send it to a subsidiary bank in the United States, and call it equity (thus reducing the leverage of the U.S. subsidiary bank in the mind of the U.S. regulator). To gain the business of U.S. public and private sector operations while keeping ROE high, a foreign, highly leveraged competitor can cut the price of a product whether it's a commercial loan or an L/C. However, because the leverage or L factor is higher than a U.S. competitor, it can obtain an equal or better ROE while gaining market share with a reduced price. The U.S. competitor must, of course, raise its price and ROA to gain an equal ROE.

This extensive discussion of competition in the wholesale markets sets the stage for the methodology that every financial institution should use when evaluating competition whether in the wholesale market or consumer market. The institution must ask:

1. What are the critical competitive components?
2. Who is the competitor in this market?
3. Can our institution meet or exceed our competitor's advantage in the critical competitive areas?
4. Can we change the nature of the competitive struggle by changing those factors that are considered critical by the ultimate purchaser?

To use the commercial loan product as an example of how to evaluate competition, let's answer the four questions. If one honestly answers the four critical questions in the wholesale asset origination market, I believe the following. (1) The critical competitive component is price. Relationship banking is becoming less of a factor as more and more loan transactions are put out to bid or "shopped." (2) The banking industry's competitors are commercial paper, foreign competition, and, increasingly, private placements. (3) These competitors enjoy a cost advantage that cannot be overcome. (4) The nature of the competition cannot be changed in the immediate future, and for many institutions, especially large ones, the traditional commercial loan on a risk-adjusted basis with the proper allocation of capital becomes the least profitable service in the portfolio.

Because this is a one-chapter overview of competition, space does not permit extensive discussion of all of the subareas of commercial lending, such as real estate construction lending, where the answers to these four questions are radically different.

For example, price often is not the most critical variable in construction lending. Many foreign competitors are reluctant to compete in this market because of lack of expertise, perception of risk, or both. As a result, banks with the expertise (and banks who understand that with expertise the perception of risk is not the same as risk) can often compete effectively and profitably in this subsection of the wholesale commercial lending area. Again, this example points up the necessity to segment product lines and markets when evaluating an institution's competition and its ability to compete.

NONCREDIT SERVICES—WHOLESALE MARKETS

Noncredit services are often considered synonymous with operational services that are provided by banks to both large and small businesses. Technically, noncredit services encompass more than operational services. Noncredit services include such services as financial forecasting, economic advisory services, and others, but the overwhelming amount of revenue being generated by banks today and in the foreseeable future from noncredit services will come from operational services.

Banks entered this competitive arena at an early stage and have done a reasonably commendable job in maintaining their overwhelming market share. It is believed that the first significant noncredit service offered was account reconcilement, introduced by the National Bank of Detroit in 1933. Although banks had prepared payrolls for business customers for many years, Bank of America is generally given credit for offering this service on an exclusively fee-oriented basis beginning in 1960. For many years, the noncredit services were relatively static in most banks, and their use among customers was also reasonably stable. Account reconcilement, lockbox, and payroll were the three principal noncredit services. Again, with each general statement one makes about an industry with 14,000 participants and hundreds of thousands of business customers, there are caveats that must be raised. Certain banks found certain niches in the noncredit service area that were not widespread in the industry. For example, the Bank of Boston managed a freight payment service with several other banks throughout the United States. But in general, product innovation and development was limited until the mid-1970s. With the advent of new, more powerful, and less costly computers and a recognition that lending to business was becoming ever less profitable, an explosion of noncredit services burst on the banking industry. Initially these new services were developed only for larger business customers.

These services ranged from balance reporting to treasury work stations to remote disbursing, a service designed to gain advantage from the float inherent in the banking system. Gradually all of these operational services and others are becoming available to smaller companies, and it is rare today that a major middle-market company has not been exposed to most of these noncredit services that were once exclusively reserved for major corporations. Since many of these services are costly to develop and still represent a limited market for most banks, the prudent bank should closely evaluate the market for these services, the competition, and the potential for offering such services.

The strategies for offering these services differ greatly by service and by market and require bankers in the 1980s to explore delivery opportunities vastly different than in the past.

Two examples can be cited to illustrate the wide range of alternatives that are available.

Chemical Bank has given many banks throughout the United States the ability to offer many of its cash management services under a franchise-type arrangement. Chemical's family of ChemLink products are thus given wider distribution than if Chemical were to directly market these services itself. This plan obviously has made development costs more reasonable for Chemical and its franchisee banks and has made the offering of many of these sophisticated services feasible.

An example of cooperation with nonbank competition in the noncredit services area is the arrangement that ADP has entered into with scores of banks throughout the United States. In many cases, ADP has purchased the payroll service of the bank but has committed to producing checks for payroll customers on the acount of the selling bank. In addition, ADP has offered to pay a fee for customers of the bank that are referred to ADP for payroll services in the future.

It is clear that to compete for noncredit services in the future, it will be necessary to offer increasingly sophisticated products to business customers of any significant size. How a bank chooses to compete in offering these services is an important strategic decision, but it is critical that the basis for that decision be broadened to include the feasibility of establishing organizational and marketing structures that have not been common in most banks in the past. These structures may range from franchises to sales agents to joint ventures. All of these new arrangements must be considered in reviewing the competition for noncredit services and the response to these competitors.

INVESTMENT BANKING

The enormous fees that have been enjoyed by investment banking firms for services provided to corporations in the United States have come about, in the eyes of many U.S. commercial bankers, only because the investment banking industry is a oligarchy as a result of the Glass-Steagall Act.

With commercial lending declining in profitability, which was the major source of income to the largest banks in the United States, it is only natural that there have been widespread attempts by these banks to move into the investment banking arena on a broader basis in recent years.

While still operating under archaic regulations, a handful of banks have enjoyed considerable success in investment banking in recent years. Since the ability to offer a broad range of investment banking services directly to business customers will be confined to relatively few banks, space will not be devoted in this chapter to extensive discussion of the competitive factors involved in the nature of competition.

However, one strategic issue should be reviewed by all banks serving the business market. That critical issue is whether a banking institution can truly serve as a banker to business without offering some fundamental investment banking products such as interest rate swaps.

If the institution obviously cannot afford the expertise required to offer investment banking products, it must consider how it can offer these products through some other means while still maintaining its basic relationship with the business customer. Again, this is an area where new affiliations must be considered.

Similar to noncredit services, investment banking may be offered on a referral or a private label business. Nevertheless, it is apparent that the future will require every bank serving businesses with sales in excess of $10 million to provide at least "plain vanilla" investment banking services or the overall profitability of its relationship with the customer will suffer. Competition will force this arrangement because those firms now offering investment banking will broaden their product lines to include traditional commercial banking products, including a wide variety of loan services.

CONSUMER MARKETS

Although bank competitors in the consumer market area are offering a wide array of new services from financial planning to limited insurance packages, the overwhelming percentage of income in consumer banking still results from net interest spread. Therefore, the discussion of competition in the consumer market area will be confined to the two components of net interest spread—consumer loans and deposits.

The competition banks face for these consumer banking services is so broad and pervasive that a banker faced with a competitive analysis for these products is often overwhelmed by the sheer number of competitors to be analyzed.

Traditional competitors, such as independent and captive consumer finance companies competing for loans and savings and loans competing for deposits, have been augmented by a host of new competitors ranging from automobile manufacturers competing for mortgages to retailers offering savings deposits to securities firms competing for checking accounts.

Given the enormous number of competitors, a very focused competitive analysis must be developed if one is to gain any value from evaluating the competition for consumer banking services.

CONSUMER LOANS

Although consumer loans is the broad overview heading under which a competitive analysis may be performed, every banker knows that there is a wide range of products and services under this heading, all of which have different competitive characteristics. The list of consumer loan types include automobile loans, boat loans, mortgages (both first and second), credit cards, mobile homes or manufactured housing, and aircraft. This list is merely representative of loan categories that are discrete and large enough to warrant unique competitive analysis; it is by no means inclusive. Further complicating consumer loan competitive analysis is the fact that consumer loans should be additionally characterized as direct or indirect (dealer participation), secured or unsecured, and as a revolving line of credit or under a fixed repayment schedule. To add to the complexities of competitive loan product analysis, the 1980s saw the advent of the variable rate consumer loan with variable or fixed monthly payments.

With this menu, it is obvious that few banks can profitably engage in an in-depth competitive analysis for every consumer loan category that the bank offers. Instead, the bank must focus on those categories that have the most impact on its overall loan portfolio and ask the same questions (with some minor modifications) as those that were asked in conducting a corporate or business loan competitive analysis.

These questions are:

1. What are the critical competitive components?
2. Who are my principal competitors for this category of loan service?
3. Can our institution meet or exceed our principal competitors in the critical competitive areas?
4. Can we change the nature of the competitive struggle by changing the factors that are considered critical by the ultimate purchaser?

However, every institution must understand four additional basic aspects relative to the consumer market and their importance in the buying decision and in the ability to compete for consumer banking business.

To some extent, these basic issues are present in competing in the wholesale or large business market, but with the exception of pricing, these factors are much less critical in the wholesale area.

These factors and an example of some of the competitive issues that must be analyzed in connection with each of these factors is as follows:

1. *Pricing.* How sensitive is price in gaining market share for this loan product? For some consumer loans, especially for costly items, pricing may be critical. However, research suggests that for consumer loans price (rate) within a certain range may be a minimal factor in the competitive situation.
2. *Delivery system.* How important is a physical location to increasing market share? Credit cards are a classic example of a consumer loan that has been sold by mail without a physical presence.
3. *Service quality.* Is higher quality service an important factor in gaining market share? Research has established that quality of service in terms of rapid response has been a factor in some cases of increasing market share. The quality of service for other aspects of the transaction may be less of a factor in influencing the buying decision.
4. *Product innovation.* How necessary is it to generate a stream of new products in order to meet both market share and profitability targets? Mixed results have been reported from consumer research in this area. As a new product, variable rates with fixed payments was a success. However, first mortgages and revolving credit second mortgages combined into one package have met with limited success according to many banks.

In summary, the number and diversity of competitors for each consumer loan product and market make it extremely difficult to conduct useful competitive analysis, but the discipline and time invested in answering the four key questions may lead to better decision making. For example, although the new Sears Discover Card is receiving enormous media attention, the local savings and loan that is offering a credit card with a 500 basis point interest differential with no fee may represent substantially greater competition than a nationally publicized marketing effort. Thus, determining *who* the *primary* competitor is must always be a major part of any competitive analysis.

CONSUMER DEPOSITS

In the field of consumer deposits, we are again faced with a myriad of competitors. The traditional competitors such as savings and loans and credit unions have long been supplemented by money market funds and the cash management accounts of the major securities brokers. In addition, the banking industry's consumer deposits have always competed with instruments of the U.S. government, ranging from Treasury bills to savings bonds.

However, any competitive analysis relative to savings deposits emanating from the consumer sector must consider a factor that is not as critical in competitive analyses for most other major banking services. This additional competitive factor is the external rate environment.

The external rate environment has a vastly different impact on consumer deposits than it has for other banking services. A particular rate environment may shrink or expand a market for a product such as commercial loans, but it may expand the total market for consumer deposits while creating a substitute product for those deposits outside of the banking industry.

In the high rate environment of the early 1980s, millions of bank customers left the banking system to deposit more than $220 billion in money market funds. It is true that this phenomenon was fostered in large part by Regulation Q. But even after the demise of Q, the funds fell only to $165 billion and have now returned to well over $200 billion. This situation illustrates that a market lost is rarely, if ever, regained except at a prohibitive cost—an important lesson for the future of banking.

As we enter the late 1980s, deposit customers are again turning away from banks for substitute products. Ironically, this results from a low rate environment. Customers who have been accustomed to 10 percent interest for their CDs (despite a 12 percent inflationary environment) are less content to accept 6 percent interest in a 4 percent inflationary environment.

This situation is not mitigated by the fact that consumer lending rates are low. The significant consumer saver is rarely the significant consumer installment loan borrower.

As a result, the industry has seen billions flow from bank deposits to any alternative competitive instrument that provides a higher return. If we accept the premise of a customer once lost rarely returns, the banking industry must determine what product lines it will substitute for consumer deposits. This will be especially critical when the industry is again faced with robust loan demand. In addition, the industry must determine how the interest spread on consumer deposits will be replaced in order to maintain the profitability of a retail banking system. The issue of a deposit market lost initially to competitors in a high-rate environment and now being further lost in a low-rate environment is one of the most important competitive issues that the industry must address. This issue ranks on a priority list with issues such as how the industry will compete with the vast array of new competitors, most of whom enjoy major advantages resulting from less regulation and more legislative freedom.

It should be obvious by now that just *identifying* bank competitors could fill a book and not a chapter, but there are certain fundamentals that can and must be analyzed in evaluating the competition for any banking product in any market. Rationally answering and analyzing the four fundamental questions posed in this chapter are the basic steps that can lead to well reasoned anticipatory actions and effective competitive responses that will result in greater market share and increased profitability.

Foreign Banks in the United States

Dr. Sydney J. Key*

Economist
Division of International Finance
Board of Governors of the Federal Reserve System

Gary M. Welsh

Partner
Prather Seeger Doolittle and Farmer

During the past three decades a dramatic expansion of multinational banking has accompanied the increasing interdependence of national economies and the rapid growth of world trade. Since the early 1960s, U.S. banks have been expanding their foreign operations significantly; in the 1970s, foreign banks began a similar expansion of their activities in the United States. (See Chart 1.) The growth of U.S. activities of foreign banks has continued, although at a more moderate pace, in the 1980s. By the end of 1986, 257 foreign banks from 57 countries operated 643 banking offices in the United States. Total assets of these offices as of December 1986 amounted to more than $525 billion; in 1972, the comparable figure was less than $25 billion.

By the mid-1970s, the size and growth of foreign bank activities in the United States and the competitive impact on the domestic banking industry had focused attention on the absence of both a federal regulatory framework and any governmental overview of the multistate activities of foreign banks.[1] The International Banking Act of 1978 (IBA) was enacted to remedy these problems and to promote competitive equality between domestic and foreign banking institutions in the United States. The basic policy embodied in the IBA was

---

*The views expressed in this chapter are those of the authors and should not be interpreted as representing the views of the Federal Reserve System.

[1]At that time, unlike virtually all domestic banks, U.S. agencies and branches were supervised only by the licensing state. Moreover, agencies and branches were not required to hold reserves with the Federal Reserve System, a situation that tended to complicate monetary management.

CHART 1   U.S. Activities of Foreign Banks, 1972–1986

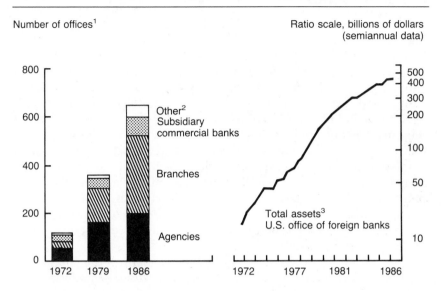

Number of offices[1]

Ratio scale, billions of dollars
(semiannual data)

1. As of December of each year.
2. New York investment companies, Agreement corporations, and, after enactment of the International Banking Act of 1978, Edge corporations.
3. "Total assets" includes assets on the books of International Banking Facilities.

one of national treatment, which attempts to give foreign enterprises operating in a host country the same powers and to subject them to the same obligations as their domestic counterparts. In adopting this policy, the U.S. Congress specifically rejected a policy of reciprocity at the federal level. Congress was, however, desirous that such an approach would promote similar attitudes on the part of foreign governments. In recent years, there has been increasing congressional concern about the treatment of U.S. banks abroad, but national treatment as opposed to reciprocity remains the basic U.S. policy toward foreign banks.[2]

This chapter first describes the institutional structure and the activities of U.S. offices of foreign banks. It then summarizes the legal and regulatory framework affecting U.S. operations of foreign banks. The final section of the chapter discusses policy issues affecting future entry and expansion by foreign banks in the U.S. market.

---

[2]See Department of Treasury, *National Treatment Study: 1986 Update*, pp. 16–17.

STRUCTURE AND ACTIVITIES OF U.S. OFFICES OF FOREIGN BANKS

Foreign banks operate in the United States through five types of banking offices: agencies, branches, commercial banks, New York State investment companies, and Edge or Agreement corporations.[3] Unlike the other types of U.S. offices, which are separately incorporated institutions, agencies and branches are integral parts of their parent banks. Both agencies and branches may conduct full-scale lending operations, but in general agencies may not accept deposits (although they may accept credit balances in connection with the exercise of their other banking powers).[4] Agencies and branches generally are wholesale banking offices; that is, their customers are chiefly banks and other nonbank businesses rather than individuals, and they compete primarily with large U.S. banks.[5] Nearly half of the credit extended by the agencies and branches is in the form of commercial and industrial loans; about one-quarter of these loans represents lending to non-U.S. residents.

In contrast to the agencies and branches, many of the commercial bank subsidiaries are retail banks whose customers include many individuals and smaller businesses. Unlike agencies and branches, these banks are engaged in consumer and real estate lending in about the same proportions as domestically owned commercial banks. In California in particular, foreign banks have acquired subsidiary commercial banks with large retail branch networks. Most of the 79 U.S.-chartered banks that are now owned by foreign banks are very small, although 26 have assets at their U.S. offices in excess of $1 billion; these 26 banks account for 90 percent of the $124 billion in assets at

---

[3]Edge corporations are chartered by the Federal Reserve Board to engage in international banking and financial operations and may be established in locations outside the state in which their owner operates. Agreement corporations are state-chartered corporations that have entered into an agreement with the Federal Reserve Board to limit their activities to those of an Edge corporation. Until enactment of the IBA, foreign banks were not permitted to own Edge corporations.

Article XII investment companies are New York State-chartered corporations that may not accept deposits but may engage in other banking activities. Like agencies, these companies may accept credit balances in connection with the exercise of their other banking powers.

[4]Federally licensed agencies may not accept deposits of either U.S. or foreign residents. However, if state law permits them to do so (as in New York, for example), state-licensed agencies may accept deposits of foreign residents.

[5]At the end of 1986, only 39 of the 324 U.S. branches of foreign banks were "retail" branches with deposits insured by the Federal Deposit Insurance Corporation.

U.S. commercial banks owned by foreign banks. Large U.S. banks acquired by banks from other industrial countries in the late 1970s and early 1980s include Bank of California, Harris Trust and Savings Bank, LaSalle National Bank, Marine Midland Bank, National Bank of North America, and Union Bank; Crocker National Bank and Long Island Trust Company were also acquired by banks from industrial countries, but were later sold to domestic banking organizations. More recently, a number of banks from developing countries have sought to acquire or establish banks in the United States.

Foreign banks may open agencies and limited branches in more than one state with relative ease,[6] and nearly half of the foreign banks with U.S. offices have established multistate banking facilities. For ease of access to the major U.S. financial markets, most foreign banks initially opened offices in New York City; offices were then opened in other parts of the country, particularly in those places where the bank's home-country customers had trade or financial relationships. Although foreign banks now operate in 16 states and the District of Columbia, New York accounts for 70 percent of the assets of all types of U.S. offices of foreign banks; California accounts for an additional 19 percent. (See Table 1.)

Banks from G-10 countries operate about half of the U.S. offices of foreign banks but account for more than 80 percent of the assets.[7] Japanese banks alone account for more than 45 percent of the assets. The size of the Japanese banks' U.S. activities reflects in part their role in financing the increasing trade between the United States and Japan and in servicing the growing number of U.S. subsidiaries of Japanese corporations; it may also reflect the fact that historically the Japanese banks have not used Caribbean offices to the extent that banks from other countries have used such offices. Although banks from non-G-10 countries, particularly in Latin America and Asia, have opened U.S. offices in large numbers during the 1980s, the share of total assets of U.S. offices of foreign banks accounted for by banks from the G-10 countries has increased somewhat during this period.

After the introduction of International Banking Facilities (IBFs) in the United States in December 1981, foreign banks established

---

[6]The IBA required that branches established outside a foreign bank's home state after July 27, 1978, must limit their deposit-taking powers to those of an Edge corporation.

[7]The G–10 (Group of 10) countries are the 11 participants in the General Arrangements to Borrow of the International Monetary Fund; namely Belgium–Luxembourg, Canada, France, Germany, Italy, Japan, the Netherlands, Sweden, Switzerland, the United Kingdom, and the United States. (Switzerland officially became a participant in 1984, but the countries are still referred to as the G–10.)

TABLE 1   Total Assets of U.S. Offices of Foreign Banks, by Type of Office and by State, as of December 1986* (in billions of dollars)

Type of Office	All States[†]	New York	California	Illinois	Florida
Agencies	79.2	9.1	57.7	—[‡]	5.8
Branches	317.6	284.6	4.8	21.9	—[§]
Commercial banks	123.9	69.3	36.4	10.9	0.4
New York investment companies	3.9	3.9	—	—	—
Edge corporations	2.3	0.5	0.2	[#]	1.5
All types of offices	526.9	367.4	99.1	32.8	7.7

*"Total assets" includes assets on the books of International Banking Facilities. Details may not add to totals due to rounding.

[†]Includes offices located in California, Delaware, Florida, Georgia, Hawaii, Illinois, Louisiana, Maryland, Massachusetts, Michigan, New Mexico, New York, Oregon, Pennsylvania, Texas, Washington, and the District of Columbia.

[‡]Illinois law does not permit the establishment of state-licensed agencies; therefore, under the IBA (see text below), federally licensed agencies are not permitted.

[§]Florida law does not permit the establishment of state-licensed branches; therefore, under the IBA, federally licensed branches are not permitted.

[#]Less than $50 million.

IBFs at many of their U.S. offices.[8] At the end of 1986, about half of the total assets of U.S. agencies and branches of foreign banks were booked at their IBFs. The agencies and branches accounted for more than two-thirds of IBF activity.

Foreign banks have typically established offices in the United States for several reasons: to conduct trade financing activities, to service U.S. activities of home-country corporations, to participate in the U.S. interbank market, to manage the dollar assets and liabilities of their parent banking organizations, to engage in foreign exchange trading, and in some cases to develop a retail banking business. A number of the larger foreign banking institutions used the contacts and expertise developed through their initial presence here to compete for the business of large U.S. companies.

---

[8]An IBF is a segregated set of asset and liability accounts that may be established at a banking office located in the United States for the purpose of conducting transactions with foreign residents without being subject to Federal reserve requirements or to deposit insurance coverage and assessments. In addition, some states have granted tax relief under state or local law for IBF operations.

By the 1980s, however, many of these banks had already captured their most natural U.S. business from large national and international companies, and they found that establishing a credit business with medium-sized U.S. companies was more difficult. As a result, a number of U.S. offices of foreign banks have become actively engaged in new areas, such as merger-related lending and off-balance sheet activities (for example, standby letters of credit for municipal bonds), or have begun to place more emphasis on specialized areas in which they have expertise, such as forfaiting.[9]

The activities of the U.S. offices of foreign banks grew dramatically in the 1970s as they tried to establish a foothold in the U.S. market through aggressive price competition. The early 1980s was a period of slower growth although in the past year or two the pace of activity has picked up again. A rough indication of the foreign banks' success in establishing a significant presence in the U.S. market is given by their share of total assets booked at banking offices in the United States: 17 percent as of year-end 1986, up from less than 4 percent in the early 1970s.[10] As noted, the agencies and branches of foreign banks have been particularly active participants in the commercial and industrial loan market, and by December 1986 they had captured nearly 17 percent of the market for such loans booked at banking offices in the United States. (If subsidiary commercial banks are included, the foreign banks' share of the commercial and industrial loan market is 23 percent.)

LEGAL AND REGULATORY FRAMEWORK FOR U.S. OPERATIONS OF FOREIGN BANKS

Bank regulation in the United States can be viewed on three levels. The first level involves examination and supervision of individual banking institutions and rules designed to ensure that each banking organization is being operated in a safe and sound manner. The second

---

[9]"Forfaiting" involves nonrecourse financing of receivables similar to factoring; however, a factor usually purchases a company's short-term receivables while a forfaiter purchases notes that are medium- or long-term receivables with maximum maturities of eight years.

[10]The foreign banks' "share" can be calculated in various ways. The measure used here is based on a comparison of assets booked at U.S. offices (including IBFs) of foreign and domestic banks; assets booked at offices of domestic and foreign banks located outside the United States are not included in the calculation. International Monetary Fund data suggest that the volume of loans to nonbank U.S. residents booked at overseas offices of foreign banks may be equal to the $90 billion in business loans booked at the foreign banks' U.S. agencies and branches as of year-end 1986.

level of regulation is concerned with competitive conditions and expansion within the banking industry. Its focus is on maintaining not only soundly operated banks but also a competitive banking system that balances economic efficiency with certain political and economic goals. These concerns are reflected in legislation governing bank mergers and acquisitions, intrastate and interstate expansion of banking organizations, and monetary control. The third level of regulation involves ownership and other relationships between banking organizations and other financial, commercial, industrial, and service enterprises operating in the United States. While this level of regulation includes elements of bank safety and soundness and competitive concerns, its primary focus is on broader policy objectives such as maintaining a separation between banking and commerce. This type of regulation is embodied in the Bank Holding Company Act (BHCA) and the Glass-Steagall Act.

Examination and Supervision

State and federally chartered banks that are subsidiaries of foreign banks are supervised and examined by appropriate federal and state banking authorities and in virtually all respects are treated the same as other state or federally chartered banks.

Examination and supervision of U.S. agencies and branches of foreign banks differs in many respects from that of subsidiary banks because, as noted, these offices are not separately incorporated legal entities but rather are integral parts of their foreign parent banks. As a result, examination and supervision of a U.S. agency or branch of a foreign bank is generally aimed at ensuring that the office is operated in a safe and sound manner and that local depositors and creditors are protected in case of a problem with the parent banking institution. Because an agency or branch must rely for support on the resources of its parent bank, lending limits and similar prudential controls applied to branches and agencies are generally based on the capital and surplus of the foreign parent bank.

Regulation of U.S. Banking Activities of Foreign Banks

To open an agency or branch in New York City, for example, a foreign bank must obtain approval either from the New York State banking authorities to establish a state-licensed office or from the Comptroller of the Currency to establish a federally licensed office. The same situation would apply in other states, except that some states permit only agencies, some permit only branches, and some permit neither. While the IBA gave foreign banks the option of establishing federal agencies or branches, the IBA also defers to the states by allowing the Comptroller to approve the establishment of a branch or agency by a foreign bank only where such an office is not prohibited under state law. However, if a state does not prohibit foreign bank agencies or branches but merely sets conditions for their establishment (such as requiring that state banks have reciprocal privileges in the foreign bank's home country), the Comptroller may approve the establishment of a federal branch or agency in that state without regard to such requirements. Thus, as long as there is not an outright prohibition in state law, a foreign bank has the dual-banking system option of proceeding under the more favorable regulatory climate.

Until enactment of the IBA, foreign banks were free to establish deposit-taking operations in more than one state so long as state laws permitted such operations. Because Congress determined that this gave foreign banks a competitive advantage in the United States that was inconsistent with national treatment, the IBA subjected foreign banks to interstate banking prohibitions on deposit taking designed to parallel those applied to domestic banks. However, Congress provided foreign banks with liberal grandfather treatment and permitted the establishment of "limited" interstate branches; these branches may accept only deposits that are permissible for an Edge corporation, that is, deposits that are incidental to international or foreign banking activities.

As a result of enactment of the IBA, foreign banks have been required to designate a home state; under Federal Reserve Board regulations, a foreign bank may change its home state only one time, subject to certain conditions. A foreign bank may not establish outside its home state a branch that takes domestic deposits and may not acquire more than 5 percent of the voting shares of a domestic bank outside its home state if such an acquisition would be prohibited under Section 3(d) of the BHCA if the foreign bank were a bank holding company with banking subsidiaries whose operations were conducted principally in the home state.[11] Section 3(d) of the BHCA generally prohibits the Federal Reserve Board from approving interstate bank acquisitions by bank holding companies unless such acquisitions are permitted by the law of the state in which the acquired bank is located. Although state laws are increasingly being amended to permit bank holding company acquisitions across state lines on a regional and even

---

[11]The interstate banking restrictions of the IBA do not apply to state- or federally licensed agencies, to "limited" branches, or to New York investment company subsidiaries of foreign banks because these operations do not accept domestic deposits.

national basis, foreign banks are not always able to take full advantage of these opportunities.

A foreign bank seeking to expand in the United States by establishing a *de novo* bank subsidiary or by acquiring an existing bank must obtain the prior approval of the Federal Reserve Board to become a bank holding company. Like any other bank holding company, a foreign bank's acquisitions must be consistent with interstate banking restrictions, with restrictions on nonbanking activities, and with competitive, safety and soundness, and other public interest criteria.

In addition to placing restrictions on the geographic expansion of deposit-taking activities of foreign banks, Congress also decided to subject such deposit-taking activities to federal reserve requirements. The purpose was to promote competitive equality between domestic and foreign banking institutions in the United States and to ensure that the effectiveness of monetary policy would not be impaired by the existence of a rapidly growing segment of the banking industry not subject to federal reserve requirements. Subsequent to enactment of the IBA, Congress extended federal reserve requirements to all depository institutions in the United States in the Monetary Control Act of 1980.

Regulation of Nonbanking Activities of Foreign Banks

A foreign bank that has a controlling interest in a U.S. bank, whether state- or federally chartered, is a bank holding company under U.S. law and subject to both the banking and nonbanking prohibitions of the BHCA with regard to its activities in the United States. Foreign banks that have established branches, agencies, or New York investment company subsidiaries in the United States but do not control a domestic bank are not bank holding companies; however, under the IBA, they are subject to the nonbanking prohibitions of the BHCA and are thereby subject to regulation by the Federal Reserve Board with regard to their nonbanking activities and investments in the United States.

In general, consistent with the principle of national treatment, foreign banks with a branch, agency, commercial bank, or New York investment company subsidiary in the United States must comply with the same prohibitions and limitations that domestic bank holding companies face in attempting to diversify into nonbanking activities. However, many foreign banks enjoy grandfather privileges with respect to activities or investments in the United States that the banks had commenced before enactment of the IBA. For example, some European banks have grandfathered investment banking subsidiaries in the United States that would otherwise be prohibited under the BHCA.

In addition, at the time of the IBA, Congress was also faced with the problem that many foreign banks were linked through stock ownership in their home or other markets with foreign nonbanking companies that were expanding into the United States. Strict application of BHCA rules in such situations would have either required foreign banks with U.S. banking operations to divest themselves of many non-U.S. stockholdings or blocked investment in the United States by foreign companies in which foreign banks have substantial ownership interests.

Congress decided that neither of these options was in the political or economic interests of the United States and thus granted certain exemptions in the IBA. In general, foreign banks that are principally engaged in the banking business outside the United States are permitted to maintain both their banking operations in the United States and certain investments in foreign nonbanking enterprises that also conduct activities in the United States. The exemption permits foreign banking organizations to own a foreign nonbank company that engages in the same commercial nonbanking activities in the United States that it conducts abroad. Financial nonbanking activities in the United States require prior approval by the Federal Reserve Board and are generally permitted only to the extent that U.S. bank holding companies may engage in the activities.

POLICY ISSUES AFFECTING FUTURE ENTRY AND EXPANSION

Despite enactment of the IBA in 1978, the role of foreign banks in the U.S. banking system continues to be the subject of much attention and debate. Three issues in particular could have a significant impact on future foreign bank entry and expansion in the United States.

National Treatment versus Reciprocity

In late 1983, legislation was proposed in the U.S. Senate that would have required the Comptroller to consider "whether or not United States banks are permitted to conduct business in the home country of the applicant" before approving the establishment of a federal agency or branch.[12] This proposal reflected a judgment that, at least in some countries, U.S. banks were not being given equal competitive opportunities with local banks and that reciprocity would be a useful means for opening banking markets abroad to U.S. banks. Although limited in scope and ultimately never enacted, the bill became the focus of

---

[12]Senate Bill No. 2193, 98th Congress, 1st Session (1983).

considerable debate as to whether reciprocity should be a consideration in U.S. policy toward foreign bank entry and expansion.[13]

Reciprocity is typically used to refer to efforts to assure a precise balancing of the treatment countries that are trading partners accord to each other. For example, under a policy of reciprocity, if a foreign country limited the presence of U.S. banks to agencies, banks from that country would be able to establish only agencies in the United States. Such "mirror image" reciprocity has been consistently opposed by the U.S. government on the grounds that it would be almost impossible to administer in the United States, would remove flexibility, and would interfere with the role of the United States as a major international financial center.[14] Instead, in order to attack the problem of discrimination against U.S. banks abroad, the U.S. government has used both bilateral and multinational channels to promote greater liberalization and equality of competitive opportunity in banking markets abroad. These efforts are likely to continue in the years ahead, especially in such multinational fora as the General Agreement on Tariffs and Trade (GATT).

Capital Adequacy

In addition to establishing various prudential standards for international lending, the International Lending Supervision Act of 1983 (ILSA) required U.S. bank regulatory authorities to establish minimum capital ratios for U.S. banking institutions. The establishment of such ratios focused increased attention on perceived disparities between U.S. and foreign bank capital requirements, with the larger U.S. banks claiming that many foreign banks enjoy competitive advantages due to lower capital ratios.

The Federal Reserve Board addressed these concerns in a 1984 order concerning Mitsubishi Bank Ltd.'s acquisition of BanCal Tri-State Corporation:

> Section 3(c) of the [BHCA] requires in every case that the Board consider the financial resources of the applicant organization and the bank or bank holding company to be acquired. As the Board has previously stated, the Board believes that the principles of national treatment and competitive equity require that, in general, foreign banks seeking to es-

---

[13]See Department of Treasury, *National Treatment Study: 1986 Update,* pp. 16–21.

[14]See testimony of Secretary of the Treasury Donald Regan before the Committee on Banking, Housing, and Urban Affairs, U.S. Senate, September 26, 1984, quoted in Department of Treasury, *National Treatment Study: 1986 Update,* p. 18.

tablish or acquire banking operations in the United States should meet the same general standards of strength, experience, and reputation as are required of domestic banking organizations and should be able to serve on a continuing basis as a source of strength to their banking operations in the United States. On the other hand, the Board is aware that foreign banks operate outside the United States in accordance with different regulatory and supervisory requirements, accounting principles, asset quality standards, and banking practices and traditions, all of which makes difficult comparisons of the capital positions of foreign and domestic banks.

The appropriate balancing of these concerns raises a number of complex issues that the Board believes require careful consideration and that the Board has currently under review. In this regard, the Board has initiated consultations with appropriate foreign bank supervisors and notes that work is currently in progress among foreign and domestic bank supervisory officials to develop more fully the concept of functional equivalency of capital ratios for banks of different countries. Pending the outcome of these consultations and deliberations, the Board has determined to consider the issue raised by applications by foreign banks to acquire domestic banks on a case-by-case basis.[15]

One outcome of ongoing discussions with foreign bank supervisors regarding capital adequacy has been the recent issuance of a proposed risk-based capital framework for banks and bank holding companies that was developed jointly by U.S. bank regulatory authorities and the Bank of England.[16] This proposal represents an important step toward achieving broader international comparability of capital standards and suggests that the U.S. authorities may increasingly try to assess foreign banks' capital adequacy according to functionally equivalent international standards.

Interstate Expansion

Interstate banking in the United States has been moving forward at a rapid pace as a result of the enactment of laws by a number of states to permit acquisitions of in-state banks by bank holding companies in other states. However, many of these state laws permit interstate acquisitions only among states with regional or historical ties; for example, laws in many Southeastern states restrict acquisitions to bank holding companies headquartered in those states.

Under the principle of national treatment embodied in the IBA, it would seem that a foreign bank might be treated as if it were a local

---

[15]*Federal Reserve Bulletin*, Volume 70, p. 519 (1984).

[16]See Comptroller of the Currency, Federal Reserve Board, and Federal Deposit Insurance Corporation, Joint News Release, January 8, 1987.

bank headquartered in the state the foreign bank has chosen as its home state.[17] For example, a Canadian bank with Georgia as its home state could be treated as a Georgia bank for purposes of regional interstate banking statutes. However, in some states, regional interstate banking laws have either expressly or implicitly excluded foreign banks or their U.S. bank subsidiaries from taking advantage of regional acquisition opportunities. Foreign banks have expressed the view that such state laws deny them equal competitive opportunities and are thus inconsistent with national treatment. However, Congress has largely deferred to the states in the area of interstate banking and to date has not addressed this issue of possible discrimination against foreign banks.

CONCLUSION

Foreign banks have become a significant and well-accepted part of the U.S. banking system. They have brought increased competition, new financing techniques, and specialized expertise to the U.S. market, and have played an important role in facilitating foreign investment in the United States. In general, the policy of national treatment has worked well and has fully integrated foreign banks into the U.S. bank supervisory and regulatory structure. It is hoped that other countries will continue to move toward this principle as the fairest and most workable policy toward the entry and operation of nonlocal banks.

BIBLIOGRAPHY

Andrews, Suzanna. "Foreign Banks Take Aim at the Middle Market." *Institutional Investor,* March 1984, pp. 277–84.

"Assets and Liabilities of U.S. Branches and Agencies of Foreign Banks." *Federal Reserve Bulletin,* special tables for end-of-quarter report dates, published periodically.

Bellanger, Serge. "Foreign Banking in America." *The Bankers' Magazine,* May–June 1986, pp. 18–22.

Blanden, Michael. "Foreign Banks: The Impetus Slackens." *The Banker,* February 1984, pp. 89–93.

Board of Governors of the Federal Reserve System. Regulation K, 12 C.F.R. 211 (1986).

Comptroller of the Currency. Regulations for Federal Branches and Agencies of Foreign Banks, 12 C.F.R. 28 (1986).

Department of the Treasury. *National Treatment Study: 1986 Update.*

---

[17]See Department of Treasury, *National Treatment Study: 1986 Update,* p. 21.

Report submitted to the Committee on Banking, Housing, and Urban Affairs, U.S. Senate, December 18, 1986.

Fairlamb, David. "Foreign Banks Take an Increasing Share of the Cake." *The Banker*, March 1986, pp. 87–90.

"Foreign Banking in the U.S.: Annual Statistics Review." *American Banker*, February 16, 1986, pp. 1A–24A.

Goldberg, Lawrence G., and Anthony Saunders. "The Determinants of Foreign Banking Activity in the United States." *Journal of Banking and Finance*, March 1981, pp. 17–32.

Heller, Pauline. *Federal Bank Holding Company Law*, Chapter 5 (Regulation of Foreign Bank Nonbank Activities), 1986, pp. 137–57.

Holden, Dennis W. "Asian Banks in New York." *United States Banker*, July 1984, pp. 37–41.

Hook, Andrew T., and M. Alberto Alvarez. "Competition from Foreign Banks." *Recent Trends in Commercial Bank Profitability*, Staff Study, Federal Reserve Bank of New York, 1986.

Houpt, James V. "Foreign Ownership of U.S. Banks: Trends and Effects." *Journal of Bank Research*, Summer 1983, pp. 144–56.

The International Banking Act of 1978. Pub. L. No. 95–369, 92 Stat. 607 (1978).

The International Lending Supervision Act of 1983. Title IX of Pub. L. No. 98–181, 97 Stat. 1278 (1983).

Key, Sydney J. "International Banking Facilities." *Federal Reserve Bulletin*, October 1982, pp. 565–77.

Key, Sydney J., and James M. Brundy. "Implementation of the International Banking Act of 1978." *Federal Reserve Bulletin*, October 1979, pp. 785–96.

Miller, Stephen W., and Seung H. Kim. "Marketing International Banking Services in the United States." *The Bankers Magazine*, March–April 1984, pp. 62–69.

Peter Merrill Associates. "The Future Development of Foreign Banking Organizations in the U.S." Study for the American Bankers Association, January 1981.

Wallich, Henry C. "Perspectives on Foreign Banking in the United States." *Northwestern Journal of International Law and Business*, Winter 1983–84, pp. 711–21.

Welsh, Gary. "The Case for Federal Regulation of Foreign Banks." *The Columbia Journal of World Business*, Winter 1975, pp. 98–108.

Welsh, Gary, and D. Yellon. "Counseling Foreign Banks on United States Bank Acquisitions: The Foreign Banker Meets His U.S. Lawyer." *Journal of Comparative, Corporate Law and Securities Regulation* 2 (1979), pp. 303–33.

White, Betsy Buttrill. "Foreign Banking in the United States: A Regulatory and Supervisory Perspective." *Federal Reserve Bank of New York Quarterly Review*, December 1982, pp. 48–58.

CHAPTER SIX

Special Constraints on Commercial Banks—Line of Business Limitations

Dr. Carter H. Golembe

Chairman
Golembe Associates, Inc.

What constitutes the business of banking and what should not be a part of that business has been a subject of debate from the time that banking first appeared on the North American continent. Analysis is complicated by the fact that regardless of what was intended by legislators, commercial banking in the United States continually adapted itself to the changing requirements of a developing and expanding economic system. Moreover, there has never been in this nation a single grantor of banking powers; the 50 states and the federal government establish the rules under which banks may do business so that a line of business available to banks in a particular jurisdiction may be expressly banned in another.

For roughly the first 175 years of banking in the United States, the question of permissible and impermissible banking activities turned on the powers of individual banks. Since about 1970, the debate has largely shifted to what a bank holding company may do rather than what a bank may do. Accordingly, the discussion below is divided into two major parts—line-of-business limitations on banks and line-of-business limitations on corporations owning or controlling banks.

LIMITATIONS ON BANKS

It would be pleasant if somewhere in the law there could be found a clear, unambiguous statement as to what constitutes the business of banking so that one might be able to decide immediately whether a particular line of business falls inside or outside of that definition. No such legal formulation exists, nor is there any firm consensus as to what that business might be.

If there is a common understanding as to what constitutes the business of commercial banking it would likely be the offering of demand deposit facilities (particularly checking accounts) to the general public; around this core activity is a cluster of traditional and related lending and financial services. This is essentially how the U.S. Supreme Court described commercial banking in the course of deciding that commercial banking itself is a distinct line of commerce (*United States* v. *Philadelphia Nat. Bank,* 374 U.S. 356, 1963).

If the foregoing is an acceptable or at least workable definition of the banking business, then the line-of-business limitations on banking (with one major exception to be discussed later) are those activities that are not incidental to the conduct of that business. Put differently, for any corporation chartered to do only a banking business, a court will generally hold it to be *ultra vires* if that corporation engages in any activity that is not either implied by or incidental to the business of banking unless the activity is specifically permitted by law.

The question therefore becomes: What is incidental to the banking business? To that question, definitive answers cannot be given. This does not mean, however, that the record is devoid of a wide variety of views.

Early in U.S. banking history it was generally understood by legislators who looked to British experience for guidance that commercial banks should not engage in "trade." Indeed, there was a belief in some quarters, drawn from Adam Smith's *The Wealth of Nations,* that a bank should engage only in the making of short-term, self-liquidating loans to those engaged in the distribution of "real" goods, and that virtually any other activity was not permissible. This so-called real bills doctrine never took hold in the United States although, curiously, it survives even to the present day in certain discussions of the business of banking.

Probably a more useful way of approaching this subject is to begin by focusing on Section 24(7) of the National Bank Act. In 1864, Congress attempted to describe the powers of the new national institutions, drawing for guidance on state law and experience. Specifically, the new national banks were authorized to exercise:

> all such incidental powers as shall be necessary to carry on the business of banking by discounting and negotiating promissory notes, drafts, bills of exchange, and other evidences of debt; by receiving deposits; by buying and selling exchange, coin, and bullion; by loaning money on personal security; by obtaining, issuing, and circulating notes according to the provisions of this act . . .

The section quoted, still in the law and essentially unchanged, has been the subject of continuing controversy even to the present day. There is, for example, a so-called narrow view, holding that the authority to engage in the business of banking grants no specific powers to national banks other than those listed together with such incidental powers as relate to each of the listed specific powers.

This view of what constitutes the business of banking—and therefore what lines of business cannot be conducted—is regarded by most authorities as inaccurate or unrealistic (though as late as 1986 a Federal Reserve Board staff paper, titled "The Separation of Banking and Commerce in American Banking History," seemingly endorsed the narrow view). For one thing, banks have long been engaged in lines of business not mentioned in the section quoted and have rarely been challenged for doing so—for example, providing safe deposit facilities, offering letters of credit, or making consumer loans.

Commentators taking the broad view of the business of banking argue that the specific enumerated powers were simply illustrations of the kinds of activities in which banks were engaging in the early 1860s, useful to the courts only as a means of deciding when non-banking corporations were straying into the business of banking. They argue that the phrase *the business of banking* is a separate and distinct grant of power by the Congress, that the incidental or implied powers of a bank will necessarily change over time, and, in the more extreme views, that any financial activity is potentially a part of the business of banking. (See Edward L. Symons, "The Business of Banking in Historical Perspective," *The George Washington Law Review*, August 1983, for a recent discussion of the various viewpoints.)

One of many possible illustrations of the way that a line of business precluded to banks may become permissible involves the leasing business. For many decades it was believed that commercial banks could not take title to personal property (airplanes, railroad cars, and the like) in order to lease such properties to business firms. To the consternation of some observers in 1963, Comptroller of the Currency James Saxon ruled that such a business was incidental to the business of banking. It has since become a major line of business for national as well as state-chartered banks.

The courts for the most part have relied in part on intuition and in part on the assumption that banks, with liabilities that serve as circulating medium, were not intended to engage in activities that involved undue risk taking. Thus many opinions can be found to the effect that it is *ultra vires* for a bank to engage in mining or manufacturing or agriculture. Still there are those who argue (see, for example, Henry Harfield's "Sermon on Genesis . . ." *The Banking Law Journal*, July 1968) that even the operation of a merchandise mart—a Sears Roebuck type business—can conceivably be viewed as properly incidental to the banking business.

In my view, perhaps the most perceptive comment on what constitutes the business of banking was made well over a century ago in a famous New York State decision. In 1857, the New York Court of Appeals was called on to interpret a provision of New York's Free Banking Act (from which the section of the National Bank Act quoted earlier had been drawn) and concluded (in *Curtis* v. *Leavitt*):

> The implied powers [of a bank] exist by virtue of the grant [to do the business of banking], and are not enumerated and defined; because no human sagacity can foresee what implied powers may in the progress of time, the discovery and perfection of better methods of business, and the ever-varying attitude of human relations, be required to give effect to the express powers. They are, therefore, left to implication.

In the history of banking legislation, at least at the federal level, there has been only one significant departure from the general proposition that an institution with authority to conduct a banking business may do such business as is implied thereby, subject to review by the courts. That exception was the enactment in 1933 of the Glass-Steagall Act, where the U.S. Congress specifically separated certain types of investment banking from commercial banking. The key section, copied by a number of states incidentally, reads as follows:

> . . . any person [or business activity] . . . engaged in the business of issuing, underwriting, selling, or distributing at wholesale or retail or through syndicate participation, stocks, bonds, debentures, notes, or other securities [may not] . . . engage at the same time to any extent whatever in the business of receiving deposits . . . [Section 21(5)]

This particular limitation, directed, it might be noted, at all deposit-taking institutions rather than just at commercial banks, represented a significant break from the past. One of the more fascinating aspects of the evolution of commercial banking in the United States was the early joining in the same institutions of investment banking and commercial banking.

In current debates over the Glass-Steagall Act, it is a favorite ploy of the securities industry to argue that commercial banks only entered into the securities business during the 1920s through the use of securities affiliates, an activity that led to all kinds of difficulties and was put to an end by the Glass-Steagall Act. In fact, it was commercial banks who were the pioneer investment bankers in the United States, and the joining of commercial banking and investment banking in the same or affiliated institutions dated back more than a century prior to 1933. Readers interested in this history might consult, among others, the towering study of American banking by Fritz Redlich (*Molding of American Banking*, Hafner Publishing Co., 1951).

The separation of the line of business that might be described as investment banking from commercial banking was not water-tight. In fact, the Glass-Steagall Act provided that commercial banks could continue to underwrite and distribute certain kinds of securities—the most important of which are U.S. government obligations and the general obligations of states and their political subdivisions. Since then Congress has added to the list of securities that may be underwritten and distributed by commercial banks (primarily the issues of various governmental and international agencies).

Moreover, national banks and state bank members of the Federal Reserve System were specifically authorized to purchase and sell "securities and stock without recourse, solely upon the order and for the account of customers" but "in no case for (their) own account." As a result a new line of business for commercial banks has been discount brokerage.

An important aspect of the Glass-Steagall limitations on the banking business is that they do not apply to activities of commercial banks outside of the United States. In other words, U.S. commmercial banks may, and many do, conduct a full range of investment banking activities in those foreign financial centers which permit them to do so.

Another important aspect of the Glass-Steagall prohibition set forth in Section 21 is that underwriting is not really defined. As a result, even domestically, U.S. commercial banks may engage in a broad range of activities usually associated with investment banking, such as providing merger and acquisition services or arranging for the private placement of debt obligations of American firms.

The principal businesses from which commercial banks are precluded because of the Glass-Steagall Act are underwriting or dealing in revenue bonds issued by states and their political subdivisions and in most corporate debt and equity issues. The direct provision of mutual funds (although advisory services may be provided) is also seemingly prohibited. However, as this is being written, some of these activities may be made permissible under certain restrictions for bank holding companies.

In summary, line-of-business limitations on banks are not usually set forth by statute, although individual states may have red-lined certain specific activities for their banks. Basically, however, line-of-business restrictions are comprised of those businesses or activities that are not implied by or are not incidental to the conduct of a banking business. As a result, one does not have for banks a handy list of line-of-business limitations, and while such a list possibly could be culled from a review of 50 state banking codes and decisions, it would not reflect much more than local, special interest factors.

The weight of opinion today would hold that the implied or incidental powers of banks should be liberally construed so as to reflect changing financial needs. At the same time, however, weight is usually given to the need to preserve a sound banking system.

Specific statutory limitations on the lines of business in which banks may engage, while not common, do exist. The most important, at least at the federal level, is the Glass-Steagall Act, separating commercial banking and investment banking. Other express limitations, including replicas of the Glass-Steagall Act, can be found in some state codes or state court decisions. More often than not these will reflect the interests of strong competitor industries, such as the insurance industry.

CORPORATIONS OWNING BANKS

Controversy over line-of-business limitations on commercial banks switched during the late 1960s from a focus on the banks themselves to a focus on bank holding companies. During the earlier part of the decade, the Comptroller of the Currency, relying primarily on the incidental powers clause of the National Bank Act, had moved vigorously to expand the businesses in which national banks could engage. As a result, major banks across the nation began to desert the state banking systems and convert to national charters. However, by the middle of the decade, the Comptroller's liberal policies were under strong attack from competitor industries, and the courts were beginning to nullify many of the Comptroller's most innovative actions. To cite one of a number of illustrations, an effort by the Comptroller to permit banks to enter the mutual fund business was defeated when the Supreme Court concluded that the Comptroller had exceeded his authority (*Investment Company Institute v. Camp*, 401 U.S. 617 (1971)).

By the second half of the 1960s, the organization of one-bank holding companies appeared to be a way of avoiding suits that had been brought against national banks or the comptroller of the Currency for the purpose of limiting the business activities of national banks. Multibank holding companies had been made subject to federal regulation in 1956, but one-bank companies remained exempt from such regulation. Accordingly, major commercial banks began to organize one-bank holding companies, beginning about 1967.

Although the data are not precise, it appears that by the end of 1969 some 120 major banks had organized one-bank holding companies. Although the banks involved comprised less than 1 percent of all commercial banks, their deposits accounted at the time for roughly one-third of all commercial bank deposits. Not surprisingly, Congress became concerned about the possibility of expansion by commercial banking organizations into new kinds of businesses and sought to extend federal control to the one-bank holding company. The result was adoption of the Bank Holding Company Act amendments of 1970, signed into law by the president on the last day of the year.

The solution adopted by the Congress to control line-of-business expansion through one-bank holding companies organized by commercial banks was to amend Section 4(c)(8) of the Bank Holding Company Act to provide that bank holding companies, in addition to permission to own the stock of banking organizations, could hold:

> shares of any company the activities of which the Board after due notice and opportunity for hearing has determined (by order or regulation) to be so closely related to banking or managing or controlling banks as to be a proper incident thereto. In determining whether a particular activity is a proper incident to banking or managing or controlling banks the Board shall consider whether its performance by an affiliate of a holding company can reasonably be expected to produce benefits to the public, such as greater convenience, increased competition, or gains in efficiency that outweigh possible adverse effects, such as undue concentration of resources, decreased or unfair competition, conflicts of interest, or unsound banking practices.

By the adoption of the amended Section 4(c)(8), which remains as stated in present law, the federal government injected itself in significant fashion into the matter of determining line-of-business limitations for commercial banking organizations. With the exception of the Glass-Steagall Act of 1933, which separated the banking business from certain aspects of the securities business, there is no comparable situation to be found in American banking history.

Since adoption of the 1970 legislation, the Board of Governors, by order or regulation, has determined (as of January 31, 1987) that 47 activities by bank holding companies meet both the closely related and proper incident tests of Section 4(c)(8) (see the Appendix). With respect to the closely related test, the courts have instructed the Federal Reserve Board to examine certain criteria, and these for the most part are used by the board in making that determination. The criteria are:

1. Banks generally have in fact provided the proposed services.
2. Banks generally provide services that are operationally or functionally so similar to the proposed services as to equip them particularly well to provide the proposed services.
3. Banks generally provide services that are so integrally related to the proposed services as to require their provision in a specialized form. (*National Courier Association* v. *Board of Governors*, 516 F2 d1229, 1975).

A bank holding company may in seeking to expand its activities, meet the closely related test but fail to meet the proper incident test set forth in Section 4(c)(8). The criteria for the latter test are included in Section 4(c)(8). Probably the best known illustration of an activity which the board has determined meets the first but not the second test is the acquisition of sound savings and loan associations by bank holding companies. As a result, this particular line of business remains (as of January 31, 1987) unavailable to bank holding companies (see item 9 under "Activities Prohibited" in the Appendix to this chapter, as well as item 9 under "Activities Permitted—by Order").

Line-of-business expansion by bank holding companies under Section 4(c)(8) has been challenged by competitor industries in the courts and the legislature. For the most part, challenge in the courts has been unsuccessful. Such challenges appear to come most frequently from the securities industry, and generally the courts tend to give considerable weight to the experience and expertise of the Federal Reserve Board. For example, in 1981 the U.S. Supreme Court upheld a Federal Reserve Board regulation permitting bank holding companies to sponsor closed-end investment companies (*Board of Governors* v. *Investment Company Institute,* 450 U.S. 46). On the other hand, competitor industries have had somewhat more success in the Congress. For example, in 1982, Congress, as part of the Garn-St. Germain Act, severely restricted insurance activities of bank holding companies.

When consulting the Appendix to this chapter, it should be kept in mind that the list of 23 prohibited activities does not constitute a comprehensive list of line-of-business limitations on bank holding companies. The list is derived from decisions by the Federal Reserve Board with respect to specific applications made by bank holding companies. Thus, for example, engaging in the manufacture of automobiles is not listed as a prohibited activity because no bank holding company has ever asked for or is likely to ask for such authority.

UNRESOLVED ISSUES

For banks and bank holding companies, line-of-business limitations continue to be actively debated, in part because market pressures and changes in technology continue to throw up questions which had not been contemplated in earlier and calmer times. A few of these current issues, as of the beginning of 1987, follow.

Each state of course retains the right to determine the kinds of activities in which its chartered banks may engage. In recent years, partly in response to a perceived conservative approach by the Federal Reserve Board, states have begun to liberalize their laws. The question that immediately arises, of course, is whether or to what extent the Federal Reserve Board will accept such liberalization when the bank is part of a bank holding company and the activity is one that is not permissible for subsidiaries of bank holding companies. Certain kinds of real estate development or insurance activities are recent illustrations.

Efforts by Congress and the Federal Reserve Board to draw a line between commerce and banking when it comes to bank holding companies have been threatened, in the view of some, by the fact that nonbank institutions, such as merchandising firms or insurance companies, have been able to acquire banks even though bank holding companies cannot engage fully in those particular businesses. These acquisitions have been made possible by reason of the fact that the banks acquired by the nonbank firms conduct their business in such fashion as to avoid being classified as banks under terms of the Bank Holding Company Act. That is, a bank is not a bank under that act unless it engages both in the making of commercial loans and in the acceptance of demand deposits. Engaging in only one of these activities does not make it a bank for purposes of bank holding company regulation—hence the development of the term *nonbank bank*. Whether this so-called loophole in the Bank Holding Company Act will be allowed to remain is a matter of current debate in the Congress.

Probably the most significant line-of-business limitation on banks and bank holding companies is that imposed by the Glass-Steagall Act having to do with investment banking activities. As this chapter is being written, the Federal Reserve Board is giving serious consideration to permitting substantial entry by bank holding companies into heretofore impermissible underwriting and dealing activities. This may be possible, should the board so decide, because the Glass-Steagall Act does not prohibit impermissible underwriting activities in affiliates of commercial banks where such affiliates are not "engaged principally" in underwriting, dealing in, and distributing securities.

It is possible, though not likely, that each of the issues mentioned will have been resolved by the time that this book reaches the reader. Even so, it is certain to be the case that new issues revolving around line-of-business limitations for commercial banking organizations will have arisen.

APPENDIX
SUMMARY OF ACTIVITIES THE FEDERAL RESERVE BOARD HAS PERMITTED AS "CLOSELY RELATED" UNDER SECTION 4(c)(8) AND THOSE PROHIBITED AS "NOT CLOSELY RELATED" OR "NOT A PROPER INCIDENT", AS OF JANUARY 31, 1987

Activities Permitted as "Closely Related to Banking"

By Regulation

1. Making or acquiring loans or other extensions of credit for own account or account of others, such as would be made by mortgage, finance, credit card, or factoring companies [§ 225.25(b)(1); 57 FRB 512 (June 1971)].

2. Operating as an industrial bank or industrial loan company [§ 225.25(b)(2); 57 FRB 513 (June 1971)].

3. Servicing loans or other extensions of credit [§ 225.25(b)(1); 57 FRB 513 (June 1971)].

4. Conducting trust or fiduciary activities [§ 225.25(b)(3); 57 FRB 513 (June 1971); 60 FRB 447 (June 1974); 71 FRB 168 (March 1985)].

5. Acting as investment or financial adviser to the extent of (1) serving as advisory company to a mortgage or real estate investment trust, (2) serving as investment adviser to mutual funds, (3) providing portfolio investment advice to other persons, (4) furnishing general economic information, general statistical forecasting, and industry studies, and (5) providing financial advice to state and local governments on matters such as issuing securities and financing real estate projects [§ 225.25(b)(4); 57 FRB 513 (June 1971); 58 FRB 149 (February 1972); 58 FRB 571 (June 1972); 59 FRB 701 (September 1973); 66 FRB 984 (December 1980); *Board of Governors* v. *Investment Company Institute*, 450 U.S. 46 (1981); 70 FRB 661 (August 1984); 71 FRB 168 (March 1985)].

6. Leasing personal and real property provided the transaction is the functional equivalent of an extension of credit, i.e., a full payout lease [§ 225.25(b)(5); 57 FRB 513 (June 1971); 57 FRB 725 (September 1971); 62 FRB 930 (November 1976)].

7. Making equity or debt investments in corporations designed to promote community welfare or rehabilitation [§ 225.25(b)(6); 57 FRB 513, 515 (June 1971); 58 FRB 572, 595 (June 1972); 62 FRB 639 (July 1976); 64 FRB 45 (January 1978); Board staff letter BHC-180 (June 25, 1979)].

8. Providing data processing and data transmission services, data bases, or facilities (including data processing and data transmission

hardware, software, documentation, and operating personnel), or access to such services, data bases, or facilities by any technologically feasible means, where the data to be processed are financial, banking, or economic [§ 225.25(b)(7) and § 225.123(e); 57 FRB 513, 515 (June 1971); 61 FRB 245 (April 1975); 68 FRB 505 (August 1982); 68 FRB 552 (September 1982); *ADAPSO v. Board of Governors*, 745 F2d 677 (D.C. Cir. 1984)].

9. Engaging in the following insurance agency and underwriting activities: (1) credit insurance—acting as principal, agent, or broker for credit-related insurance, including home mortgage redemption insurance; (2) finance company subsidiary—acting as agent or broker for insurance directly related to an extension of credit by a finance company that is a subsidiary of a bank holding company, if, among other conditions, the extension of credit is not more than $10,000, or $25,000 if it is to finance the purchase of a residential manufactured home; (3) insurance in small towns—engaging in any insurance agency activity in a place where the bank holding company or a subsidiary of the bank holding company has a lending office and that has a population not exceeding 5,000 or has inadequate insurance agency facilities; (4) insurance agency activities conducted on May 1, 1982—engaging in any specific insurance agency activity if the bank holding company, or subsidiary conducting the specific activity, conducted such activity on May 1, 1982, or received Board approval to conduct such activity on or before May 1, 1982; (5) supervision of real estate agents—supervising on behalf of insurance underwriters the activities of retail insurance agents who sell fidelity insurance, property and casualty insurance, and group insurance pertaining to the property and employees of the bank holding company or its subsidiaries; (6) small bank holding companies—engaging in any insurance agency activity if the bank holding company has total consolidated assets of $50 million or less; (7) insurance agency activities conducted before 1971—engaging in any insurance agency activity performed at any location in the United States directly or indirectly by a bank holding company that was engaged in insurance agency activities prior to January 1, 1971, as a consequence of approval by the Board prior to January 1, 1971 [§ 225.25(b)(8), 72 FRB 833 (December 1986); 57 FRB 674 (August 1971); 58 FRB 800 (September 1972); *Alabama Association of Insurance Agents v. Board of Governors*, 533 F2d 224 (5th Cir. 1976), rehearing denied 558 F2d 729, cert. den. 435 U.S. 904; 65 FRB 924 (November 1979); 59 FRB 20 (January 1973); 62 FRB 537 (June 1976); 66 FRB 987 (December 1980); 67 FRB 629 (August 1981); 69 FRB 815 (October 1983); 72 FRB 339 (May 1986) and 72 FRB 671 (September 1986) for home mortgage redemption insurance underwriting; § 601 of the Garn–St Germain Act of 1982 (Pub. L. No. 97-320)].

10. Operating courier services for time-critical bank or financially-related instruments, documents, records, and processing media [§ 225.25(b)(10); 59 FRB 892 (December 1973); *National Courier Association* v. *Board of Governors*, 516 F2d 1229 (D.C. Cir. 1975); 61 FRB 588 (September 1975)].

11. Providing management consulting advice to nonaffiliated banks and nonbank depository institutions [§ 225.25(b)(11); 60 FRB 223 (March 1974); 60 FRB 446, 470 (June 1974); 68 FRB 237, 248 (April 1982); 69 FRB 926 (December 1983)].

12. Issuance and sale of travelers checks [§ 225.25(b)(12); 65 FRB 250 (March 1979); 67 FRB 912 (December 1981)].

13. Issuance and sale at retail of money orders and similar consumer-type payment instruments ($1,000 maximum face value), and sale of U.S. savings bonds [§ 225.25(b)(12); 63 FRB 414, 416 (April 1977); 65 FRB 250 (March 1979); 67 FRB 912 (December 1981)].

14. Performing real estate and personal property appraisals [§ 225.25(b)(13), 72 FRB 833 (December 1986); 66 FRB 975, 984 (December 1980)].

15. Arranging equity financing, which involves arranging for the financing of commercial or industrial income-producing real estate through the transfer of the title, control, and risk of the project from the owner/developer to one or more investors [§ 225.25(b)(14); 68 FRB 647 (October 1982); 69 FRB 34 (January 1983); 69 FRB 225 (March 1983); 69 FRB 646, 651 (August 1983)].

16. Conducting securities brokerage and margin lending activities [§ 225.25(b)(15); 69 FRB 105 (February 1983); 69 FRB 718 (September 1983); *Securities Industry Association* v. *Board of Governors ("Bank America–Schwab")*, 104 S.Ct. 3003 (1984)]. Offering securities brokerage services and unrelated investment advice within the same entity [71 FRB 662 (August 1985); 72 FRB 146 (February 1986)].

17. Underwriting and dealing in obligations of the United States, general obligations of states and their political subdivisions, and other obligations eligible for that purpose to member banks, including certain money market instruments such as bankers acceptances and certificates of deposit [§ 225.25(b)(16); 62 FRB 928 (November 1976); 64 FRB 222, 223 (March 1978); 65 FRB 363 (April 1979); 68 FRB 249 (April 1982); 69 FRB 465 (June 1983)].

18. Providing advice concerning foreign exchange operations, policies, and procedures and arranging for the execution of foreign exchange transactions [§ 225.25(b)(17); 69 FRB 221 (March 1983)].

19. Acting as futures commission merchant for futures contracts covering bullion, foreign exchange, U.S. government securities, negotiable U.S. money market instruments, and certain other money market instruments (futures commission merchant activities also cover

the provision of options on certain futures contracts) [§ 225.25(b)(18); 63 FRB 951 (October 1977); 68 FRB 514 (August 1982); 68 FRB 651 (October 1982); 68 FRB 776 (December 1982); 69 FRB 216, 220 (March 1983); 69 FRB 733 (September 1983); 69 FRB 871 (November 1983); 70 FRB 53 (January 1984)].

20. Providing futures advisory services on a fee basis as a futures commission merchant ("FCM") or a commodity trading advisor ("CTA") [70 FRB 369 (April 1984); 70 FRB 780 (October 1984); 70 FRB 885 (December 1984); 71 FRB 650 (August 1985); 71 FRB 803 72 FRB 833 (December 1986)].

21. Providing consumer financial counseling services, including advice, educational courses, and instructional materials [65 FRB 265 (March 1979); 71 FRB 253 (April 1985); 71 FRB 662 (August 1985); § 225.25(b)(20), 72 FRB 833 (December 1986)].

22. Providing tax planning and preparation services [71 FRB 168 (March 1985); § 225.25(b)(21), 72 FRB 833 (December 1986)].

23. Providing check authorization, verification, or guarantee services for subscribing merchants [65 FRB 263 (March 1979); 66 FRB 64 (January 1980); 67 FRB 740 (September 1981); § 225.25(b)(22), 72 FRB 833 (December 1986)].

24. Engaging in collection agency activities [72 FRB 669 (September 1986); § 225.25(b)(23), 72 FRB 833 (December 1986)].

25. Engaging in credit bureau activities [72 FRB 669 (September 1986); § 225.25(b)(24), 72 FRB 833 (December 1986)].

By Order

1. Operating a "pool-reserve plan" for the pooling of loss reserves of banks with respect to their loans to small business [57 FRB 1037 (December 1971)].

2. Operating a savings and loan type business in Rhode Island [58 FRB 313 (March 1972); 58 FRB 417 (April 1972); 66 FRB 665 (August 1980); 71 FRB 473 (June 1985); see also entry No. 9].

3. Operating certain state stock savings banks [61 FRB 901 (December 1975); 66 FRB 590, 594 (July 1980); 66 FRB 917 (November 1980); 69 FRB 860 (November 1983); 69 FRB 874 (November 1983); 70 FRB 359 (April 1984); 70 FRB 654 (August 1984); 70 FRB 829 (November 1984); 72 FRB 487 (July 1986); 72 FRB 731 (October 1986)].

4. Buying and selling gold and silver bullion and silver coin; dealing in exchange and silver futures and arbitraging gold and silver internationally [Board Order September 27, 1973, re Standard and Chartered Banking Group, Ltd., 38 Federal Register 27552, October 4, 1973; 67 FRB 635 (August 1981); 71 FRB 467 (June 1985); Board Order, April 30, 1985, re PNC Financial Corp.; 72 FRB 146 (February 1986); 72 FRB 345 (May 1986); 72 FRB 501 (July 1986); 72 FRB 840 (December 1986); 73 FRB 61 (January 1986)].

5. Operating an Article XII New York Investment Company [63 FRB 595 (June 1977); 69 FRB 42 (January 1983); 72 FRB 71 (January 1986); 72 FRB 200 (March 1986)].

6. Executing unsolicited purchases and sales of securities as agent solely on the order and for the account of customers [67 FRB 635 (August 1981)].

7. Performing commercial banking functions at offshore locations; such functions include funding domestic operations through the offshore wholesale money market [68 FRB 251 (April 1982); 69 FRB 36 (January 1983)].

8. Offering NOW accounts, provided they are subject to the same federal interest rate limitations and reserve requirements that apply to a federally insured depository institution [68 FRB 253 (April 1982); See *First Bancorporation v. Board of Governors*, 728 F2d 434 (10th Cir. 1984)].

9. Operating a savings and loan association, provided the powers of the S&L are no broader than the powers of bank holding companies and the S&L acquired is threatened with financial harm [68 FRB 316 (May 1982); 68 FRB 382 (June 1982); 68 FRB 656 (October 1982); 69 FRB 554 (July 1983); 69 FRB 812 (October 1983); 70 FRB 149, 157 (February 1984); 70 FRB 593 (July 1984); 71 FRB 340 (May 1985); 71 FRB 462 (June 1985); 71 FRB 901 (November 1985); 72 FRB 342 (May 1986); 72 FRB 666 (September 1986); 72 FRB 724 (October 1986)].

10. Issuance and sale of variably denominated payment instruments with a maximum face value of $10,000 [70 FRB 364 (April 1984); 71 FRB 58 (January 1985); 71 FRB 724 (September 1985); 71 FRB 905 (November 1985); 72 FRB 148 (February 1986); 72 FRB 662 (September 1986)] and with no maximum face value, but subject to conditions [72 FRB 148 (February 1986); 72 FRB 662 (September 1986)].

11. Brokering options on securities issued or guaranteed by the U.S. government and its agencies and on money market instruments; brokering options in foreign currency on exchanges regulated by the SEC [70 FRB 53 (January 1984); 70 FRB 238 (March 1984); 70 FRB 368 (April 1984); 72 FRB 146 (February 1986)].

12. Operating a chartered bank that does not both take demand deposits and make commercial loans [69 FRB 556 (July 1983); 69 FRB 923 (December 1983); 70 FRB 371 (April 1984); 70 FRB 660 (August 1984); 71 FRB 51, 55, 61 (January 1985); 71 FRB 115 (February 1985); 71 FRB 173 (March 1985); 71 FRB 249, 253, 256 (April 1985)].

13. Executing and clearing options on bullion and foreign exchange on commodity exchanges regulated by the CFTC [70 FRB 591 (July 1984)].

14. Executing and clearing futures contracts on a municipal bond index [71 FRB 111 (February 1985); 71 FRB 650 (August 1985); 71

FRB 803 (October 1985); 71 FRB 970 (December 1985); 72 FRB 144 (February 1986)].

15. Providing: (1) financial feasibility studies for specific projects of private corporations; (2) valuations of companies and large blocks of stock for a variety of purposes; (3) expert witness testimony on behalf of utility companies in rate cases [71 FRB 118 (February 1985)]. Providing: (1) advice regarding the structuring of and arranging for loan syndications and interest rate swap, interest rate cap, and similar transactions; (2) advice in connection with merger, acquisition/divestiture, and financing transactions for nonaffiliated financial and nonfinancial institutions; (3) valuations for nonaffiliated financial and nonfinancial institutions; (4) fairness opinions in connection with merger, acquisition, and similar transactions for nonaffiliated financial and nonfinancial institutions [73 FRB 59 (January 1987)].

16. Executing and clearing futures contracts on stock indexes, and options on such futures contracts [71 FRB 251 (April 1985); 71 FRB 801 (October 1985); 71 FRB 970 (December 1985); 72 FRB 144 (February 1986); 72 FRB 203 (March 1986)].

17. Providing credit card authorization services and lost or stolen credit card reporting services [71 FRB 648 (August 1985)].

18. Acting as a brokers' broker of municipal securities [71 FRB 651 (August 1985)].

19. Acting as an employee benefits consultant by providing a full range of services with regard to employee benefits plans [71 FRB 656 (August 1985); 72 FRB 337 (May 1986); 72 FRB 729 (October 1986)].

20. Providing a variety of student loan servicing activities [71 FRB 725 (September 1985)].

21. Offering securities brokerage services and unrelated investment advice within the same entity [71 FRB 662 (August 1985); 72 FRB 146 (February 1986)]. Offering the combination of securities brokerage services and related investment advice to institutional customers [72 FRB 584 (August 1986)].

22. Printing and selling checks and related documents that require MICR–encoded information [72 FRB 794 (November 1986)].

Activities Prohibited Under Section 4(c)(8)

1. Insurance premium [equity] funding—that is, the combined sale of mutual funds and insurance [58 FRB 905 (October 1972)].

2. Underwriting life insurance that is not sold in connection with a credit transaction by a bank holding company or a subsidiary thereof [58 FRB 905 (October 1972)].

3. Real estate brokerage [58 FRB 427 (April 1972); 58 FRB 905 (October 1972)].

4. Land investment or development [58 FRB 428 (April 1972); 58 FRB 905 (October 1972); 61 FRB 325 (May 1975)].

5. Real estate syndication [58 FRB 905 (October 1972); Board letter re BankAmerica Corp., April 4, 1972)].

6. Management consulting [58 FRB 674, 676 (July 1972); 58 FRB 905 (October 1972)].

7. Property management services generally [58 FRB 652 (July 1972); 58 FRB 905 (October 1972); 64 FRB 415 (May 1978); 71 FRB 168 (March 1985)].

8. Underwriting mortgage guaranty insurance [60 FRB 681 (September 1974); 60 FRB 727 (October 1974)].

9. Operation of a travel agency [62 FRB 148 (February 1976); *Association of Bank Travel Bureaus* v. *Board of Governors*, 568 F2d 549 (7th Cir. 1978)].

10. Operation of a savings and loan association [63 FRB 280 (March 1977); Board letter March 16, 1981, re National Detroit Corporation/ Landmark Savings & Loan; 68 FRB 316 (May 1982); 68 FRB 382 (June 1982); 68 FRB 656 (October 1982); 70 FRB 593 (July 1984)].

11. Underwriting home loan life mortgage insurance [66 FRB 660 (August 1980); *but see* 72 FRB 339 (May 1986)].

12. Contract key entry services [66 FRB 666 (August 1980)].

13. Underwriting property and casualty insurance, and adjusting claims and making appraisals relative thereto [64 FRB 506 (June 1978); *NCNB Corp.* v. *Board of Governors*, 599 F2d 609 (4th Cir. 1979)].

14. Dealing in platinum and palladium and other commodities [Board Order, September 27, 1973, re Standard and Chartered Banking Group, Ltd., 38 Federal Register 27552, October 14, 1973; 71 FRB 467 (June 1985); Board Order, April 30, 1985, re PNC Financial Corp.].

15. Issuance of market rate intrastate notes [68 FRB 198 (March 1982); *see also* 12 C.F.R. § 217.156, § 250.221].

16. Underwriting group mortgage life insurance (credit life insurance directly related to real estate loans) [68 FRB 319 (May 1982); *but see* 72 FRB 339 (May 1986)].

17. Pit arbitrage (an activity conducted in connection with futures commission merchant functions) [68 FRB 776 (December 1982)].

18. Issuance and sale of money orders with a face value of $50,000 or higher [Board letter dated April 28, 1983].

19. The publication and sale of personnel tests and related materials [70 FRB 462 (May 1984)].

20. Providing public credit ratings on bonds, preferred stock, and commercial paper [71 FRB 118 (February 1985)].

21. Providing independent actuarial services [71 FRB 656 (August 1985)].

22. Acting as a specialist in French franc options on the Philadelphia Stock Exchange [72 FRB 141 (February 1986)].

23. Selling title insurance [Board letter re Independence Bancorp, Inc., March 17, 1986].

Note: Unless otherwise indicated, citations are to the Board's Regulation Y and to the volume number, page number, month, and year of the *Federal Reserve Bulletin (FRB)*; the Reg Y citation is to the revision that became effective February 6, 1983.

Source: Golembe Associates Inc., Washington D.C.

CHAPTER SEVEN

Special Constraints on Commercial Banks—Geographical Limitations

Dr. Carter H. Golembe
Chairman
Golembe Associates, Inc.

It is possible that this will be the last time that the *Bankers' Handbook* carries a full chapter on geographical limitations on banking organizations. So rapidly are the traditional barriers to geographic expansion disappearing that future editions are likely to incorporate the subject in broader chapters or perhaps even relegate it to an historical appendix. Still, the dismantling process has a way to go. Not all geographical limitations are gone, and the ways in which most of those that remain will fall, and the timing of their fall, can be of considerable importance to individual banking organizations.

In general, geographical limitations on banks can be regarded as a rudimentary and somewhat illogical form of size control. For reasons that have never been entirely clear, there has always existed within the American public a deeply ingrained fear of banking power. Power, inevitably, was viewed as a concomitant of size, and size in turn was likely to be the result of permitting relatively few institutions to engage in banking.

As a result, the so-called free banking laws were enacted early in American history, first by the states (beginning in 1837–38) and finally by the federal government with passage of the National Bank Act (1863–64). These kinds of statutes, largely still in place, were revolutionary for their time, throwing open the business of banking to all citizens able to supply the necessary capital and willing to accept government regulation. They are, of course, responsible for the fact that the United States has a commercial banking system composed of some 14,000 banks, the large majority of which are quite small.

Multioffice banking over broad geographic areas was not a matter of particular interest or concern during most of the 19th century. Communication and transportation facilities made it difficult to conduct such operations although in a few instances (Wells Fargo, for example) banks operated over many states. In general, however, it was not until the early part of the present century that technological change (the automobile was probably the single most important development) made it feasible for the banking business to be conducted over broader geographic areas than could be served by the head-office bank. At that point, the interest of independent bankers in protecting themselves against competition from (or absorption by) larger banking organizations coincided with the general public's fear of bank size to result in the adoption by many state legislatures of geographical limitations on multioffice banking—indeed limitations on any kind of multioffice banking in some instances.

Multioffice banking is generally conducted directly by a bank through branches, or by a bank holding company through banks and nonbank affiliates, or by both means in the same organization. There have been various reasons for the formation of bank holding companies but one certainly was as a reaction to multioffice limitations on individual banks (that is, branch limitations), with the bank holding company serving as an alternative means of accomplishing geographic expansion. Accordingly, geographical limitations are discussed first as they apply to banks and next as they apply to bank holding companies.

GEOGRAPHICAL LIMITATIONS ON BANKS

Federal policy with respect to geographical limitations on bank expansion has largely deferred to the states. As a result, banks chartered by the federal government—national banks—are generally held to the provisions of state law with respect to intrastate branching. Interstate branching, even today, is virtually unknown.

Following a ruling in 1911 by the U.S. attorney general to the effect that branching was not a power contained in the National Bank Act, various Comptrollers of the Currency sought to provide such power through regulation or sought legislative relief for national banks, at least to the same extent that states permitted their banks to branch. The result was passage of the McFadden Act in 1927, permitting national banks to establish full-service branches within the cities in which they were located if state banks possessed similar authority. Later, in 1933, national banks were permitted to branch throughout entire states, but only in those states in which state-chartered banks had the same authority.

Passage of the McFadden Act had the result of stimulating individual state laws that restricted branching. However, during the Depression of the early 1930s, when many communities were left without banking facilities because of the large number of bank failures, many states began to permit wider branching privileges. With the end of the Depression and the establishment of federal deposit insurance, the move to liberalize state branching laws came to an end, not to reappear until recent years.

For several decades following the banking crisis of the early 1930s, the distribution of states by type of geographical restriction on branching showed little change. The typical distribution displayed the states in three groups, each with about the same numbers. One-third of the states permitted branching statewide; one-third imposed various area limitations, for example, home-office city or county, or groups of counties; and about one-third prohibited or so severely restricted branching as to be designated as unit banking states.

Within the current decade, many states have liberalized their banking laws. The result, as shown in Appendix A, is that today about half of the states permit branching on a statewide basis. In some instances, however, this authority is not unrestricted since some states have so-called home-office protection statutes, which restrict or prohibit branching into communities in which there is a head office (or sometimes any office) of another bank.

A slightly smaller group of states permit branching only within specified geographic areas within the states, typically the county or groups of counties. Here too, home-office protection statutes are often found.

Only a handful of states still maintain rather strict limitations on geographic expansion within their borders. In most such instances, some kinds of limited service facilities are available to the banks. Also, as will be pointed out later, most states with strict branching limitations nevertheless permit multioffice banking through bank holding companies.

Interstate branching, while theoretically possible for state-chartered banks (other than members of the Federal Reserve System), under mutual agreement among the states has never been of much significance. There are a few grandfathered situations, such as the Bank of California, and some states have tinkered with reciprocal laws. However, the McFadden Act prohibits, at least implicitly, national banks and state banks that are members of the Federal Reserve System from interstate branching by authorizing such banks to branch within the states in which they are located to the same extent as the state permits state-chartered banks to branch within those states. The Comptroller of the Currency is given no authority by the McFadden Act to permit national banks to branch outside of the state of their location. Thus one important geographical limitation on banks—the right to branch interstate—still remains largely in place, and there is little present agitation for any significant change. The reason, of course, is the growing ability of banking organizations to operate interstate through the bank holding company vehicle, a subject to be considered later.

The number of banks operating branches and the number of branches have increased significantly during recent decades. In 1960, for example, there were only 2,386 banks operating more than one office; today, approximately half of all insured commercial banks are operating branch offices. It was not until 1963 that the number of branch offices exceeded the number of main banking offices in the United States. Today, the number of branches far exceeds the number of banks; as of December 31, 1986, there were 14,603 insured commercial banks operating 46,406 branches.

No survey of geographical limitations on banks should fail to note the vast literature, much of it in the form of court opinions, dealing with what constitutes a branch office and whether a particular office or activity is a branch by definition and therefore subject to restriction on branching. For the purposes of this chapter, however, it is only necssary to alert readers to the fact that such controversies are becoming less significant today as the nation moves toward a system in which banking services are increasingly becoming available through offices of banks and nonbank firms on an interstate basis. Nonetheless, so long as the McFadden Act remains law, there will be efforts to use that act to block expansion by banking organizations. A recent case involving both geographical and product expansion is illustrative.

A branch is defined in the McFadden Act as any office of a bank that performs at least one of three functions: receives deposits, pays checks, or makes loans. In 1982 the Securities Industry Association (SIA) brought an action against the Comptroller of the Currency, who had authorized national banks to provide discount brokerage services at places where branches might not have been permissible. The SIA, joined in this instance by the Independent Bankers Association of America, argued that these offices were in fact branches. On January 14, 1987, the U.S. Supreme Court held that the offices in question did not offer "core" banking services and held in favor of the Comptroller. (*Clarke* v. *Securities Industry Association*, Doc. No. 85-971 and *Security Pacific National Bank* v. *Securities Industry Association*, Doc. No. 85-972.)

The same kind of issue has arisen in the past with respect to other types of banking offices. For example, so-called loan production offices of national banks were alleged to be branches, but the courts eventually disagreed. Such offices therefore may be operated by banks over broad geographical areas. A 1981 White House study (*Geographical Restrictions on Commercial Banking in the United States*) estimated that at the time there were at least 350 loan production offices doing business in 20 states.

GEOGRAPHICAL LIMITATIONS ON
BANK HOLDING COMPANIES

Bank holding companies provide a vehicle for conducting a banking business over broad geographic areas. One might quarrel with whether such companies are more efficient in this respect than banks operating through branch offices. The fact is, however, that the American banking and regulatory structures are such as to accommodate more readily the bank holding company than the individual bank when it comes to geographical expansion.

Until 1970, multibank holding companies were largely to be found in states which prohibited or rather severely restricted branch banking. Interstate banking by bank holding companies was prohibited by federal law (again reflecting a deference to state interests), exept for six institutions which had conducted an interstate business prior to adoption of the Bank Holding Company Act of 1956. The prohibition took the rather curious form of leaving it up to each state to decide whether to permit acquisitions of its banks by out-of-state bank holding companies, and for a long time no state adopted such a law.

It should also be noted that the operation of multibank holding companies within states where branching was prohibited was not universal. A number of states prohibited or severely restricted multioffice banking by either form, that is, by branches or by subsidiary banks of bank holding companies. Today, in marked contrast to the situation of just a few years ago, there is no state in the union which does not permit at least one form of multioffice banking, and many states now permit entry by out-of-state bank holding companies.

Intrastate geographical limitations on bank holding companies still exist in a number of instances, and more or less follow the pattern of intrastate limitations on branching. For example, in the state of Illinois, bank holding company acquisitions are restricted to certain designated areas and are not permitted statewide. Another form of limitation found in many states, not directly related to geography but nonetheless having a bearing on it, relates to size. That is, a bank holding company may not hold more than X percent of banking assets in a given state.

A most significant but often overlooked relaxation of geographical limitations on bank holding company activities occurred in 1971 when in the course of announcing the first set of permissible activities under the recently enacted Section 4 (c) (8) of the Bank Holding Company Act, the Federal Reserve Board stated:

> The regulation as proposed does not limit the location at which permissible activities may be conducted to any state of other geographical area. Such limitations might be imposed by regulation or by order in particular cases.

By this single statement, the board removed bank-related activities of bank holding companies from interstate restrictions. The result was that since 1971 bank holding companies have been able to conduct virtually any type of banking business across state lines, with the exception of the acceptance of demand deposits. Readers might wish to consult the list of permissible activities for bank holding companies, listed in the Appendix to Chapter 6, to obtain a better understanding of the significance of the Federal Reserve Board's 1971 action.

Not all states were particularly happy with this result: the ability of bank holding companies to do an interstate bank business through nonbank subsidiaries. However, so long as the business conducted was not done through a bank subsidiary, there was generally little that could be done by the states to stop it. A key U.S. Supreme Court decision in this instance was *Lewis* v. *B. T. Investment Managers, Inc.,* (447 U.S. 27) where the court struck down a Florida statute that attempted to prohibit out-of-state bank holding companies from doing an investment advisory business in Florida. The court held that the state could not discriminate with respect to kind of business between out-of-state and in-state banking organizations.

In recent years, the most dramatic change in geographical limitations on bank holding companies has resulted from new authority by such companies to do a banking business through bank subsidiaries on an interstate basis. As mentioned earlier, the Bank Holding Company Act of 1956 provided, in Section 3(d), the so-called Douglas Amendment, that the Federal Reserve Board could not approve an application by a bank holding company to acquire a bank in another state "unless the acquisition of such shares or assets of a state bank by an out-of-state bank holding company is specifically authorized by the statute laws of the state in which such bank is located, by language to that effect and not merely by implication."

Until the early 1980s, Section 3(d) constituted a nationwide ban on interstate bank acquisitions by bank holding companies. Only one state (Maine) had enacted legislation offering to accept out-of-state bank holding companies on a reciprocal basis, and no other state accepted the invitation. However, after 1980 various groups of states began to enact reciprocal interstate legislation intended to promote regional banking, that is, permitting entry by bank holding companies in certain states while prohibiting companies in other states from entering the proposed region. Bank holding companies in excluded states challenged the constitutionality of such selective relaxation of interstate banking restrictions. In June 1985, the Supreme Court removed the constitutional cloud which hovered over laws of this kind in *Northeast Bancorp* v. *Board of Governors* (105 S.Ct. 2545, 1985). As a result, many states hastened to adopt regional reciprocal interstate banking statutes, and there have since occurred numerous combinations of banking organizations operating across state lines.

The trend in state legislation is clearly toward nationwide banking. As shown in Appendix B to this chapter, as of the end of 1986, regional reciprocal interstate laws had been enacted by 27 states. However, in nine of these cases, the statute provides for abandonment of the regional concept at a particular future date, that is, the state generally would accept entry on a reciprocal basis by bank holding companies in any state whether or not it was in the region. Moreover, there are already five states which provide now for nationwide entry on a reciprocal basis, and another seven states that permit entry by bank holding companies located in other states, whether or not those states are willing to reciprocate.

It is safe to say that in most of the states which do not now have interstate banking laws of one kind or another or which presently have regional restrictions on interstate banking, there is some activity underway to significantly broaden the scope of existing law. Accordingly, the tabulation presented in Appendix B is best viewed as a snapshot of interstate banking at a point in time during which the nation was moving rapidly toward nationwide banking. Such a tabulation, if made just three years ago, would have included only a handful of states, and only one or two in 1980.

While the federal government has refrained from directing the course of interstate banking, it can play a limited role in the case of failed insured banks. The Garn-St Germain Act in 1982 provided that the FDIC, as receiver of a failed bank, could, under certain restrictions, arrange for purchase of the failed bank by an out-of-state bank holding company. At this writing, Congress is considering extending that authority.

Mention should also be made of the traditional role played by the federal government affecting interstate banking as well as intrastate banking. This role is determined most importantly by the basic antitrust provisions of the 1966 Bank Merger Act, which were added by amendment in the same year to the Bank Holding Company Act. While the federal government has left it to the states to decide on the nature and timing of interstate banking, the Federal Reserve Board still plays its usual role in approving or denying holding company applications, based on a variety of statutory criteria, including antitrust criteria.

CURRENT ISSUES AND TRENDS

In future years the matter of geographical limitations on commercial bank expansion is not likely to occupy a prominent position in a book of this kind. The reason, of course, is that the nation is moving rapidly toward nationwide banking although rather surprisingly this is being accomplished under state rather than federal aegis. At the same time, laws restricting multioffice banking on an intrastate basis have been liberalized throughout the nation so that there is no state today in which multioffice banking is not permissible.

The issue that is likely to arise in the future will not be whether banking organizations may do business over broad geographic areas or where they may be precluded from doing so, but whether banking organizations are becoming too large. Inevitably, changes in multioffice banking laws, whether intrastate or interstate, will lead to combinations of banks that may be larger than some would like to see. It is often argued that the antitrust laws are not capable of preventing such combinations. Whether the antitrust laws will be changed or whether absolute size caps will be placed on banking organizations (as is already true in a number of states) is likely to be a matter of considerable debate in future years.

APPENDIX A
STATE BRANCHING LAWS
AS OF JUNE 30, 1986

Statewide (22)	Limited (20)	Unit (9)
Alaska	Alabama	Colorado
Arizona	Arkansas	Illinois
California	Florida*	Kansas†
Connecticut	Georgia	Minnesota
Delaware	Indiana	Missouri
District of Columbia	Iowa	Montana
Hawaii	Kentucky	North Dakota
Idaho	Louisiana	Texas
Maine	Massachusetts	Wyoming
Maryland	Michigan*	
Nevada	Mississippi (Statewide 1989)*	
New Hampshire	Nebraska*	
New Jersey	New Mexico	
New York	Ohio (Statewide 1989)	
North Carolina	Oklahoma†	
Oregon	Pennsylvania (Statewide 1990)	
Rhode Island	Tennessee	
South Carolina	Virginia*	
South Dakota	West Virginia (Statewide 1987)	
Utah	Wisconsin	
Vermont		
Washington		

*Statewide branching by mergers permitted. Mississippi currently permits statewide branching by mergers. A 100-mile limitation on de novo branching will be phased out by 1989. See the accompanying state bank holding company laws table for "caps" that may apply to bank mergers.

†More liberal branching through the acquisition of failing institutions pemitted.

SOURCE: Golembe Associates Inc., *Bank Expansion Quarterly* 36, 2 (1986).

APPENDIX B
INTERSTATE BANKING LAWS
AS OF OCTOBER 1986

	Grandfather Laws	Limited Purpose Laws	Reciprocity Laws*	Regional Reciprocity Laws*	Regional Laws	Troubled Institution Laws	Unrestricted and Semirestricted Laws
Alabama	—	—	—	X	—	—	X
Alaska	—	—	—	—	—	—	X
Arizona	—	—	—	—	—	—	—
California	—	—	—	X(1/1/91)	—	—	—
Connecticut	—	—	—	X	—	—	—
Delaware	—	X	—	X	—	—	X
D.C.	—	—	—	X	—	—	—
Florida	X	—	—	X	—	—	—
Georgia	—	—	—	X	—	—	—
Idaho	—	—	—	X	—	X	—
Illinois	X	—	—	X	—	—	—
Indiana	—	—	—	—	—	—	—
Iowa	X	—	—	—	—	—	—
Kentucky	—	—	X(7/15/86)	—	—	—	—
Louisiana	—	—	—	X(1/1/89)	—	—	—
Maine	—	X	—	X	—	X	X
Maryland	—	—	—	X	—	—	X
Massachusetts	—	—	—	X(10/10/88)	—	—	—
Michigan	—	—	—	X	—	—	—
Minnesota	—	—	—	X	—	—	—
Mississippi	—	—	—	X	—	—	—
Missouri	—	—	—	—	—	—	—
Nebraska	X	X	—	—	—	—	—
Nevada	—	X	—	X(1/1/89)	—	—	—
New Jersey	—	—	—	X(?)†	—	—	—

97

APPENDIX B (continued)
INTERSTATE BANKING LAWS
AS OF OCTOBER 1986

	Grandfather Laws	Limited Purpose Laws	Regional Laws	Troubled Institution Laws	Regional Laws	Troubled Institution Laws	Unrestricted and Semirestricted Laws
New Mexico	—	—	—	—	—	X	X
New York	—	—	X	—	—	—	—
North Carolina	—	—	—	X	—	X	—
Ohio	—	—	X	X(10/16/88)	—	X	—
Oklahoma	—	—	—	—	—	X	X
Oregon	—	—	—	—	X	X	—
Pennsylvania	—	—	—	X(3/4/90)	—	—	—
Rhode Island	—	—	—	X(7/1/88)	—	—	—
South Carolina	—	X	—	—	—	—	—
South Dakota	—	—	—	X	—	—	—
Tennessee	—	—	—	X	—	X	X
Texas	—	—	—	—	—	—	—
Utah	—	X	—	X(12/31/87)‡	—	X	—
Virginia	—	—	—	X	—	—	—
Washington	—	—	X	—	—	X	—
West Virginia	—	X	X	—	—	—	—
Wisconsin	—	—	—	X	—	—	—
Totals	4	7	5	27	1	8	7

*Nationwide trigger dates are given for states that plan to drop or have dropped the regional requirement in their regional reciprocity laws.

†New Jersey's nationwide trigger is dependent on the passage of reciprocal legislation by 13 other states, at least four of which are among the 10 states with the largest amount of commercial bank deposits.

‡On Utah's nationwide trigger date, both the regional and reciprocity requirements will be dropped.

SOURCE: Banking Expansion Reporter 5, no. 20 (October 20, 1986).

CHAPTER EIGHT

The Special Role of Banks in the Economic System

Dr. Paul Nadler

Professor of Finance
Graduate School of Management
Rutgers University

There was a time when it was easy to pinpoint the special role of banks in the economic system.

Every student of money and banking was taught right from the start that financial intermediaries, such as savings banks, savings and loan associations, credit unions, and the like, were merely conduits of money. They accepted savings deposits and placed them as demand deposits in their commercial bank. And when they paid out funds they wrote checks on their banks just as individuals do.

What was the role of the commercial banks? They accepted demand deposits and created money. This made them the sole intermediary between the Federal Reserve and the economy. When a bank made a loan or bought an investment, it created a new demand deposit which in turn meant that it was expanding the money supply through this procedure. The Federal Reserve thus had to regulate the banking system's reserves to control this deposit creation operation, for only through this means could we control the money supply and make monetary policy a basic weapon for economic stability and growth under conditions of free markets.

What else did banks do that made them special?

Banks were not only the only providers of demand deposit or checking account services (with a few exceptions allowed by state laws for some state-chartered savings institutions in some states), but they were also the kingpin in the provision of commercial loans. A company that wanted a loan went to its bank for credit accommodation. Sure there was Wall Street and investment banking operations available as a source of credit, but this was for large companies and governmental units only. The typical business in need of funds went to the bank.

These two areas of banking were held to be so unique that our legal definitions of what a bank is usually included the mention that a bank accepted demand deposits and made commercial loans. This description also became the key to freedom from the rules and regulations that apply to banks when companies, both operated by banks and nonbanks, tried to get around the laws that limit a commercial bank's geographical expansion and operational authority. By eliminating either commercial loan granting or acceptance of demand deposits, a group was able to establish a so-called nonbank bank—an institution that, until 1987 legislation, was allowed to expand into other states, combine banking with nonbanking operations, and in other ways expand its scope of operations without the restraints that full-service commercial banks face. Those established before the law change have been allowed to remain in business.

To be sure, banks engaged in operations that were similar to those of other financial institutions. Banks have accepted savings deposits (although for some time they legally had to be called thrift deposits in some jurisdictions because of a savings institution monopoly on the word *savings!*). Banks have made consumer loans in competition against the finance companies; they have been in the mortgage market, and some banks have also engaged in the trust business in head-to-head competition against specialized trust companies.

Following the passage of the Glass-Steagall Act in 1933, bank operations in investment banking have been strictly limited, with underwriting restricted to Treasury securities and general obligations of state and local government units, although this limitation is slowly being eroded by legal changes and more liberal regulatory interpretations.

But when it came to the special role of commercial banks in the economic system, it was demand deposits—the power to create money—and commercial loans that differentiated the bank from all other financial institutions. But with these powers over demand deposit solicitation and commercial lending came an equally significant role of bankers—that of the financial counselor and friend of the community. And, as we will see in this chapter, it is this role that still differentiates banks most sharply from their competitors and gives banking its most significant exclusive role in most communities today.

THE CHANGES

How are we to differentiate a bank from a nonbank organization today? Changing legislation has given savings banks, savings and loans, credit unions, and other deposit-taking institutions the same powers banks have to accept checking account deposits, negotiable orders of withdrawal, and every other type of payment account. With these powers have come similar reserve requirements and other restraints—restraints banks asked to be imposed in their search for a "level playing field" so that their competitors no longer would gain the benefits of powers formerly belonging exclusively to the banks but without the restraints banks faced.

There are some differences between banks and thrifts, notably different tax structures and different requirements for loan loss reserves. Thrifts retain these benefits as long as they place a certain minimum percentage of their funds into home mortgage lending. Credit unions, for their part, have the added advantage of extreme freedom from taxes, despite their growing size and the continual erosion of the "common bond" requirement that formerly limited them to serving people with ties to the same factory or church.

But in basic ways the differences between banks and thrifts are eroding rapidly. Thrifts can make loans by adding funds to a borrower's checking account, which of course means that they can create money in the same way banks can. Some thrifts have not joined clearing houses yet and still operate as conduits to their own correspondent commercial bank. This eliminates their ability to create deposit money since they hold their funds in the correspondent bank's account instead of placing receipts and making payments out of their own balances at a branch of the Federal Reserve.

But in most ways banks and thrifts are becoming more and more alike. Many people do all their banking with a thrift, or with a money fund for that matter, with the money fund piggy backing on its account at an accommodating commercial bank.

What is the difference between a bank and a thrift today? Some observers say "it is merely a matter of tradition". Some thrifts feel they are thrifts and concentrate on home loans and thrift business fairly exclusively although they have the right to adopt full bank powers.

And when others are asked about the difference between a bank and a thrift, they answer with a twinkle in the eye "about three years."

What about commercial lending? Has that gone the way of the demand deposit as a service that formerly was an exclusive bank offering? Again, the answer is yes. Thrifts have received commercial lending authority, and some investment bankers are also trying to win the small company's business in competition against the banks. Commercial finance companies are expanding their asset-based lending operations to make themselves more competitive with commercial bank lending operations too.

So what is left of the special role of commercial banks in the economic system? It all boils down to the type of people and the special way of dealing with individuals, business firms, and the community.

This is the special strength and secret weapon that has kept community banking alive and kept all commercial banks in the forefront in our economic environment despite the steady erosion of banking's powers and the growing similarity in function of all financial institutions.

PEOPLE

What is it about bank people that makes them such an important resource for the industry? How have bankers themselves been a force that kept alive banking's special role in the economic system?

Largely it has been because most bankers who have had contact with members of the business community have felt that their contact was a continuing relationship rather than a one-time sale of a service.

What does such a relationship involve?

Maybe the best way to answer this is to repeat the comments of the treasurer of a major American company to a group of his bank relationship officers about what the company expects to give and to receive from its banks:

> Our company keeps generous balances in your banks and pays fees for credit facilities. It has given each bank what it feels is a decent return which rises to 2 percent on assets whenever we borrow (a rather generous amount to be sure).
>
> What do we want in return?
>
> - A superior contact officer
> - First access to the bank's best ideas
> - Assured credit availability at market prices
> - Rapid turnover time on inquiries
> - Efficient cash management and operating services
> - Ability to tap the large store of information available in the bank
> - A financially strong and well run bank.

This treasurer concluded that the optimum relationship should include interlocking directorships, large holdings of the company's stock in some of the bank's trust accounts, pension management services, and investment banking relationships.

This is the type of special relationship that acute treasurers would like from their banks—a relationship that does not price each individual service used on a profit center basis but rather looks at a long-range relationship in which not every service must be analyzed on a stand alone basis. It should also be a relationship in which officers have long tenure with the customer and are not replaced so frequently that the treasurer has to explain his operations, needs, and special problems to a new bank officer on a periodic basis.

How close to this treasurer's ideal relationship are bank-customer ties today?

Certainly they have weakened. Some banks have been guilty of rotating officers far too quickly and making the corporate treasurer feel that his operation is merely a training ground for bankers on their way up the ladder. Other corporate treasurers report that banks are looking at each service provided as a separate profit center and are violating the relationship the treasurer wants. And still others report that the traditional ties of banker with borrower that would allow the borrowing customer to obtain unusual credits or relaxed terms in special situations because of a sound relationship are being replaced by strict evaluation of each request. Loans are now made by syndicates, and the lead bankers report they must please each and every member of the bank syndicate before the loan is granted. In the past the banker could be more relaxed because the loan was made completely by his institution and was granted to a customer the bank knew well and had worked with profitably for many years.

But on the whole, bank-customer relationships remain closer to this treasurer's ideal.

1. Bankers do know their people. The typical community banker sits at his desk, and as he waves to every passing customer in the lobby, he can recite the basics of the customer's balance sheet, needs, problems, and potential. When the customer comes in for a request, the good community banker usually has learned that he is coming in and has prepared for the visit, so he is just as likely as not to say: "The answer is yes, now what do you want?"

2. Bankers are not revolving doors. When people come to the bank, they are likely to have the same contact officer they have had for years. When this changes, the result is often the loss of the business. Community bankers report that when the bank across the street is sold and new faces appear on the platform and even in the tellers' windows, people frequently move to the bank that still offers familiar local people.

3. Bankers are prepared to give advice, and in virtually all cases this advice is free. Bankers report that frequently they feel they are financial therapists rather than bank officers as they sit and help people structure their financial affairs so that they can keep their families and business ventures viable. Although some bankers are talking about charging for providing advice in the way that attorneys do, the banker is the special individual who helps you with your financial affairs. This in turn makes the bank special in our economic system.

4. Bankers offer loyalty. They know their customers and try their best to make borrowing proposals "bankable" in any manner possible.

Bankers report that they lend looking at the eyeballs more than they lend looking at the financial statement—something no other industry offers its customers. Of the four Cs of credit—character, capacity, collateral, and conditions—one must conclude that to most bankers character is the most important (again a trait that makes the industry have an especially vital role in our economy).

5. Bankers play a role in the community. Every public drive has a banker involved. Every good cause, whether charity or rebuilding the community, has bankers in the forefront. Every community function has bankers on the dias, providing talent and financial support to make the community and its important ventures prosper.

These are the special roles of the banking industry in today's era of deregulation.

And while financial journalists may report on the new services some banks are providing (such as interest rate swaps, merger and acquisition assistance, and other capital market type programs that are more of an investment banking than commercial banking nature), in actuality most banks do not enter these areas. Most remain as in the past, offering traditional services—taking deposits and making loans, handling trust business, and helping with public finance through the purchase of bond issues offered by the public bodies of the communities they serve.

International banking and its problem loans get national attention, yet only a hundred or so of our 14,000 banks are really involved in the field. The vast majority of commercial banks concentrate on serving their own communities in traditional ways with traditional service. They recognize that by being good community citizens and friends of the people their unique role can be maintained despite the new competition that deregulation has brought.

STRUCTURE

But is this picture of the bank as the community's friend likely to remain a force in the American economy?

Deregulation involves not only an expansion of services of each of the various types of financial institutions so that each now competes with the offerings of the others, it also involves geographical expansion and the new concepts of regional and nationwide banking.

Will this territorial growth end the uniqueness of commercial banking in our economic system as banks become giants and bump head to head with the large investment bankers and the nonfinancial firms encroaching on banking such as Sears Roebuck and American Express?

Again from the vantage point of the mid-1980s it still looks as if the answer is no.

One can look at this question from two viewpoints: from the viewpoint of the large bank expanding its territories and from the viewpoint of the community bank that has always been in the local community and wants to remain there.

The large commercial banking organizations are not stupid. They are trying to go national in scope or at least to develop regional scope. But they also recognize that the real power of the bank in each of the communities it serves is its personal nature. Thus, despite the fact that regionalism and potential nationwide banking may place the logo of one institution over offices through several states or throughout the nation, astute bankers are trying to leave the individual offices alone to serve their communities as they have always served them and with the local flavor remaining.

To be sure, this goal has not always been achieved. And one of the greatest strengths of the community bank has been its consistency in policy, personnel, and attitude in the face of the changes often imposed on the competing banks that have been taken over by holding companies and branch networks. But to the greatest extent possible, most major banking organizations have tried to keep the community flavor and autonomy in granting credit in the institutions they have purchased, recognizing that this is one of the great strengths of the organization they paid to obtain.

What about the apparent contradiction of trying to gain state-of-the-art efficiency while at the same time still trying to keep the public's feeling that the bank is a local, personal organization that values its relationship in the community?

How can a bank keep its personal touch while it gains acceptance of automated teller machines, point-of-sale terminals, banking by phone and in the home, and other programs that remove the customer more and more from personal contact with bank personnel?

To answer this question consider an analogy—the approach taken by the telephone companies. AT&T and other phone companies have developed two-tier pricing—a low rate for automated nonoperator-handled calls and a higher rate for assisted calls. Similarly banks are slowly accepting the idea that personal service does not necessarily mean having a human being handle cash inflow and outflow and the routine deposit of checks. This can be handled automatically just as direct-dial phone calls are routed. But banking must concentrate its efforts and attention on providing the special personal service that customers want at the infrequent times they want and need it—and with superb delivery. This is truly personal service; bankers feel customers will accept routine handling of routine transactions if the bank is really able to deliver special service and attention when needed.

Thus the smart banks that are trying to grow will do their best to carry water on both shoulders—to maintain their personal touch while they grow and try to obtain the economies of scale that they feel they can glean from a large-scale regional or nationwide operation.

COMMUNITY BANKS

What about the community banks? Are their days numbered in a world of ever-growing banking giants? Evidence up to the mid-1980s indicates that the answer is a resounding no.

Despite the prediction that community banks would die and despite failures of banks in large numbers due to the agricultural and energy problems of the mid-1980s, the number of commercial banks actually has increased over the past decade from 13,500 to around 14,000.

The reason is obvious. New banks are continually being formed to meet the public's need for personal banking service and the type of financial advice, local interest, and informal way of doing business that has made the commercial bank unique in our economic system.

Will these banks survive? Up to now it appears that most have done so. The ones that want to be sold have found buyers except when the territory has been unattractive or the asking price too high. The demise of banks through unfriendly takeovers has also been infrequent. The reasons for this involve understanding what one obtains when he buys a bank: He gets the buildings (in most instances a dubious asset because they could be replaced by newer, more efficient structures). He gets the old fixed-rate loans, many of which are worth considerably less than their book value because of rising interest rates. And he gets the few remaining core deposits—a vanishing breed of liability in today's highly competitive banking game.

So the most important asset he gets is the loyalty of the officers and the staff of the bank and of the bank's board. And since an unfriendly takeover deprives the bank of this talent or at least of its loyalty, most buyers of banks find that a takeover is not worth it. The exception is when the bank is treating its shareholders so poorly and doing so little to keep its stock price in a fair range that it is worth making a tender offer at the risk of alienating the staff and board because the bank's shares are available so cheap.

Will the community bank be killed by the greater efficiency of the giant institution? Again it appears that this is not likely. Larger banks do gain large-scale marketing efficiency, equipment consolidation, and other benefits of size. But community banks usually have lower personnel costs, fewer highly paid specialists, and benefits of control that keep the costs of operation down. The result is that the community bank generally has a higher return on assets and capital than its larger competitor. It does business simply and can obtain many needed complex services from vendors, correspondent banks, and facilities managers without having to invest great sums in providing these complex operations for itself.

How about the nonbank competitors (such as Sears Roebuck and American Express)—companies that want to get into the banking market and be the individual's banker? And what about the credit unions that are growing in importance and expanding their concept of common bond to include whole regions and states instead of limiting their membership to those who belong to the same church or company? Will they be the death of America's commercial banks?

Again present evidence indicates that they will continue to grow in importance but that the commercial bank will retain its unique role and viability despite their growth. Reasons for this stability are that the commercial bank provides available financial talent, a friendly long-term relationship, and a full gamut of financial resources to the public.

Certainly the Sears Roebuck approach of convenience with one-stop shopping and banking has appeal. But as we automate the routine bank functions, we find less need for this locational convenience. So the talent of the people on board and the quality of the services offered when unusual expertise or accommodation is needed will play a more important role in determining where people bank then will closeness of location and the ability to obtain stocks, CDs, mortgages, and socks as well from one company in one location.

CONCLUSION

To say that commercial banking can retain a unique role in an ever-changing financial environment and that it can continue to play an important role in our economy does not mean to imply that banks will not have to change.

Banks will change. They will provide more services either directly through their own personnel or through service companies and correspondent banks. Our bank structure may well be layered with a handful of nationwide giants operating everywhere, a group of regionals blanketing a state or several neighboring states, and a full layer of independent community banks each serving a small region or town. But when it is remembered that to the majority of the public the bank service required is a simple one of taking deposits and making loans with friendly service, quick response, and competitive rates being the only criteria of importance, the three types of banks can survive in competition with one another and with the nonbank institutions offering similar services.

As has been stressed in this chapter, however, the great strength that separates the commercial banks from all the other contenders for the public's financial business is the talent, friendliness, and continuing presence of the individual banker who has learned that in our complex society he or she must be a counselor and friend as much as a purveyor of money.

It is this closeness with the borrower and depositor—be he rich or poor, public body corporation or individual, professional or laborer—that has made the difference between individual banks and the difference between the banking industry and its nonbank competitors on the financial scene.

As long as bankers remember this difference and stress its importance in their day-to-day operation, no matter how much deregulation we may see, no matter how much innovation we may witness, and no matter how our financial world may change, there will continue to be a major special role for the commercial bank in our economic system.

PART TWO

Organization and Management of the Banking Corporation

CHAPTER NINE

Corporate Organization Structures to Manage Banks and Bank Holding Companies

Carl E. Reichardt

Chairman and CEO
Wells Fargo Bank

Jack L. Hancock

Executive Vice President
Wells Fargo Bank

A large U.S. university, like many other such institutions, undertook a major new construction program soon after World War II. This particular university had no space for expansion on its existing campus and had to build on a nearby site. A number of new classroom buildings, dormitories, and administrative facilities were built. One unique aspect of this program was that after construction was completed and the lawns were planted and landscaped, very few sidewalks were installed. Students were permitted to walk from building to building in any pattern they chose. It was only after the travel patterns were established that a complete set of sidewalks was created. Thus, today one sees a campus with an efficient transit pattern between buildings. Although the pattern is not an aesthetically pleasing one, there are few if any worn spots in the grass.

Does the solution to this specific problem have any application to organizational theory? Perhaps it does if one is not too rigorous in rendering a judgment. First, it can be argued that formal organizational structures like sidewalks are created to facilitate the objectives and goals of an enterprise; they are not created as an end unto themselves. We need organizational structures just as we need sidewalks—to get where we are going as effectively and as efficiently as possible.

Second, it really does not matter whether the setting we have described is a university, an office park, or a large hospital; the methodology applies. What is important is the purpose for which the buildings are used and the interaction between the functions performed in the buildings. Likewise, sound organizational concepts apply to all enterprises—governmental units, manufacturing organizations, banks, and the like.

Third, if for whatever reason the university management should redesignate the functions performed in the buildings, it might find it necessary either to enlarge certain sidewalks and build new ones, or watch others become less heavily traveled and see grass become worn in new locations. So it is with business enterprises. As the functions within the enterprise change, the formal organizational structure may well require modification. The extent of the modification will depend on the extent of the functional changes which have taken place within and between the various elements.

Fourth, the success of a university basically depends on its programs, its people (faculty, students, staff, and so forth), and its relationships with the external world (parents, politicians, the community, sources of funding, and the like) rather than the ease and speed with which people move within and between the facilities. The latter, of course, speaks to such issues as efficiency, stress or lack thereof, and responsiveness. Formal organization is much the same. The success of an enterprise is largely determined by its purpose, its goals, its people, its capital, its markets, and so forth. Its formal organizational structure, like sidewalks at the university, albeit important, is simply a facilitator of the process.

Finally, the sidewalk pattern at the university is not symmetrical or aesthetically pleasing, but it works efficiently. So too, well-designed organizational patterns are not necessarily symmetrical or aesthetically pleasing, but they work for a specific enterprise and perhaps for that enterprise only. No two businesses require the same formal organizational structure and that structure does not need to present a "pretty picture" when documented by an organizational chart.

Let's not pursue the analogy further, but we hope that some points have been made:

1. Organizational design should not be thought of as an end product but rather as a means to an end. Organizational structure is a means of helping an enterprise achieve its goals and objectives as efficiently and effectively as possible.
2. Organizational concepts are not industry specific. Furthermore, an organizational design that perfectly fits one organization would rarely fit another even one in the same industry.
3. An organizational design should never be cast in stone. An enterprise should be willing to make organizational changes freely in answer to changing objectives and goals and to the strengths and weaknesses of the people who are employed by it.

4. The organizational arrangement for any enterprise should be the one that fits the organization without regard to the way it might appear when committed to a chart on a piece of paper.

There is a large body of literature on organizational theory and design. Most of the readers of this handbook are undoubtedly familiar with much of it as a result of previous academic and professional pursuits. We will not attempt a duplication of the formal, more traditional literature. Instead, we will present some thoughts on organizational concepts and alternative designs and discuss how senior managers, particularly managers in commercial banking, might deal with issues concerning the subject.

WHY WORRY ABOUT ORGANIZATIONAL STRUCTURE?

A basic question that must be addressed is: Why does the organizational structure of a particular enterprise really matter? On the one hand, the answer is as simple but as sterile as that found in many basic textbooks on management: Only by providing for an effective organizational structure within an enterprise is it possible to establish the proper relationship between the activities to be performed, the people who are to perform them, and the physical factors which are required. On the other hand, while this answer is certainly accurate, it belies the real importance of an organizational structure.

The question is better answered by saying that the organizational structure of a given enterprise is critical because it largely dictates how the enterprise will be managed on a day-to-day, week-by-week, and year-by-year basis. An organizational structure explicitly imposes on the enterprise the management systems the people in the enterprise use to plan, lead, operate, control, evaluate, and correct the functions performed within it. It follows that the issue of organizational structures is preceded in importance only by the very basic and primary questions for the enterprise: What is the business? What are its basic goals and objectives? What underlying strategy will it follow? What are the personalities, the capabilities, and strengths and weaknesses of the people?

The answers to these questions lead to the beginning of the organizational design process because they provide the specifications that outline what is expected of the organizational structure. Put another way, they stipulate what the organizational structure is suppose to accomplish. We believe that the establishment of clear-cut goals, objectives, and supporting strategies is paramount for any successful enterprise. However, it is not our purpose to describe the processes by which they are established. Rather, we assume for the moment the reader's agreement with the primacy of goals and objectives, and we

further assume that they will have been clearly articulated as a pre-
condition to the consideration of organizational alternatives. We will
subsequently return to the subject of the importance of goals and
objectives as they relate to structure.

ORGANIZATIONAL DESIGN ALTERNATIVES

As we previously indicated, organization theory is not industry or
enterprise specific. Thus, the basics apply equally to manufacturing
firms, retailers, banks, and so forth. However, each industry has its
peculiarities, and this fact will often result in different applications of
organizational theory. In the remainder of this chapter, we will concern
ourselves with organizational issues as they relate to banks and bank
holding companies.

But first a caveat to which we will return: Managers in an enterprise often make the mistake of looking almost exclusively at others
in their own industry for answers to perplexing questions, including
questions on organizational issues. How frequently has the reader
heard such questions as: How is the First National Bank of _____
organized? Where do our peer group banks have their marketing department? To whom does the Wire Transfer Department report in Jim's
bank? Would it not be at least as constructive to have answers to
questions such as: How is the _____retailing chain organized? Where does the _____stock brokerage firm have its
marketing department? To whom does the Wire Transfer Department
in Bob's Insurance Company report? Simply stated, bankers can learn
much by examining the basic business strategies followed by their
manager colleagues in nonbank enterprises—McDonalds, Nordstrom,
Merrill Lynch, Digital Equipment, and Tiffany & Co., to name a few.

There are three discrete alternative organizational structures which
can be employed by an enterprise.[1]

1. Centralized.
2. Divisional.
3. Matrix.

Of course, there is a mixture or hybrid arrangement in which two
or even all three arrangements are intermixed. In fact, the hybrid
arrangement is probably the most common form, but the issue then

---

[1]Much of the discussion in this section has been taken from treatment of
organizational structures by the staff of the Management Analysis Center, Inc.,
in *Implementing Strategy*, edited by Paul J. Stonich, Ballinger Publishing,
1982.

becomes one of how heavily weighted the hybrid is in favor of one or the other organizational structures.

The Centralized Structure

Under a purely centralized arrangement, a bank organizes its specialized functions (Personnel, Finance, Real Property Management, Marketing, Credit Administration, and the like) into separate departments and places them in staff units at the top reporting to senior bank managers. The line, or operating functions, are likewise grouped in some logical manner, normally into a set of functional structures such as Retail Branch Management, Operations, Corporate Banking, Consumer Credit, and the like.

Control is centralized and exercised through a well-defined chain of command. Requests and recommendations are forwarded up the chain for approval. Approval of the requests and bank policies, and approved procedures are passed down the chain. In a pure centralized structure, delegation of authority is minimal and responsibility for the performance at the line level is generally limited to correctly implementing approved procedures and keeping management informed on all aspects of the business.

In the centralized structure, the role of the staff departments is integral to the management process. Most requests and recommendations flow through the various staff groups which have responsibility for analyzing and then either providing management with a recommendation or, in fact, acting for management under clearly defined rules. The staff departments, rather than line groups, are generally responsible for coordinating line group requests. The staff groups frequently serve senior management as its alter ego. The staff units in many centralized business units assume a dominance over the line units. Line group personnel are normally thought of as implementors and operators.

Communication is critical in a centralized structure since the specialization that exists requires much coordination to ensure that knowledge and expertise of the various specialists are brought to bear on the subject at hand and that all of those who should do so have the opportunity to review and comment on a particular subject. The same requirement makes committees, task forces, and special project officers important as integrating vehicles.

The Divisional Structure

The second organizational arrangement is often called a decentralized structure, but we think the term divisional as used in *Implementing Strategy* is more descriptive. This approach stresses the decentralization of responsibility and places authority on a much lower level than in the centralized mode. Here markets are emphasized. Defined markets are appropriately aggregated, and the responsibility for serving them is assigned to a set of divisional managers. The divisional managers are then given the specialized staff resources necessary to afford them a great deal of control over their respective divisions.

Staff units in a divisional structure are much smaller than their counterparts in the banks of the same size organized in a centralized structure. Certain staff and support units may even be eliminated altogether when the responsibilities for the functions which they perform are dispersed throughout the divisions of the bank. For example, the credit approval process may be delegated to those divisions having credit serving responsibility rather than maintained as a central credit approval authority.

Staff sections in this structure most frequently assume an advisory role serving both senior management and the managers of the divisional units.

If likened to a conduit, the chain of command in the divisional structure is of a much smaller diameter than is the case in the centralized structure. This is because, in concept, only policies and *major* decisions move down the pipe; and only requests for approval of major actions, decisions already taken at the division level and communicated for information only, and performance reporting moves upward. Under this arrangement, the divisions tend to be self-contained and have both the responsibility and resources to control their own destinies within constraints set by basic bank policy.

Because divisions are self-contained and are exclusively responsible for specific markets, the process of allocating corporate resources is different in a very significant way from the process followed in centralized organizations. The division managers can be expected to justify resources through the submission of complete "business cases," which present market-oriented financial data. This is contrasted to the resource allocation system generally used within most centralized structures. The latter focuses on line item expenses and revenue (for example, expenses associated with personnel, telecommunications, supplies, data processing, and so forth) and the *revenue* associated with such functions as branch operations, consumer lending, corporate credit, and trust fees.

In a divisional structure, the various divisions within the bank normally compete among themselves for resources to serve their markets. Put another way, markets and products compete for resources in the divisional structure, whereas in the centralized mode the line managers compete for resources on the basis of the staff required to serve x number of customers, the amount of travel required for y number to make customer calls, the amount of training required for a staff of a certain size, and so forth.

Communications within the divisional structure is more difficult because competition between divisions is greater and because barriers tend to develop between divisions which make it difficult to process actions which cross divisional lines. Also, the staff sections play a much smaller coordinating role which places greater responsibility for coordination on the line groups.

The Matrix Structure

The matrix arrangement is less common in banks than in other types of enterprises, but has application in certain banking situations. In the purest sense, the matrix structure provides that certain functions must serve two "masters" in order to be effectively accomplished. Thus, the individuals performing those functions have two bosses. We sometimes hear this described as a solid and a dotted line relationship. Functions that lend themselves to this arrangement include personnel, financial control, and project management. In larger banks, there is application of the matrix in which certain branches in the bank are oriented as consumer branches and others in the same bank as corporate or commercial branches. Both type of branches look alike and must have the same basic procedures, services, and products, yet they serve different markets. In this case, a matrix arrangement may be used in which the manager of the branches have two bosses—the retail banking manager and the corporate or commercial banking manager.

The staff groups in a matrix arrangement may also be placed in the two-boss role. For example, certain members of staff groups may report to both the head of a line unit and the head of their own staff unit. For example, each line unit in a given bank may have a personnel officer who reports both to a line manager and the manager of the personnel department. Certain professionals in the data processing organization in a bank often operate in a matrix mode, reporting to both the head of data processing and to the head of the line group which they are serving.

The matrix organization places a heavy burden on those individuals who have two bosses and makes frequent interpersonal communications as necessary as it is difficult. Further, personnel policies and procedures must be tuned to accommodate the matrix lest the employees affected have careers based on performance that can rarely be satisfactory to all bosses.

As we indicated, few if any banks are likely to have pure organizational structures. This reality dictates that a combination of two, perhaps all three, of the alternative structures may be appropriate.

A common hybrid arrangement is one in which the basic divisional structure is employed and divisional managers are given responsibility for designated markets such as consumer, commercial, and real estate. They have most of the resources required to service those markets except that certain functions are performed for them on a centralized utility basis and others on a matrixed basis. For example, legal, purchasing, and real property management might continue to be provided centrally while data processing and personnel support are provided under a matrix arrangement with those providing the support reporting to both the appropriate line group managers and the heads of data processing and personnel.

ORGANIZATIONAL DESIGN CONSIDERATIONS

What major factors should be considered in developing the organizational structure for a bank? Six key factors should exercise significant influence over the development of an organizational structure:

1. Basic goals, objectives, and strategy.
2. Competitive and regulatory environment.
3. Size.
4. Culture.
5. Use and comfort with electronic technology.
6. The management team.

Obviously, we are not discussing organizational issues for a startup bank. We are presenting considerations for managers of banks that are ongoing concerns. Thus our discussion of the factors that should be considered in developing an organizational design are not presented as factors to be considered in sequence. Instead the individual factors tend to influence each other in a mutual cause-and-effect relationship; that is, the bank's goals, objectives, and strategy both affect and are affected by the competitive and regulatory environment. To a lesser extent but still true to the point, the competitive and regulatory environment both influences and is influenced by the size of the bank and the resources available to it. However, for presentation purposes, we will discuss each of the factors separately and share our views on the influence they have or should have on the bank's organizational structure.

Basic Goals, Objectives, and Strategy

In the era before deregulation of the financial industry in the United States, bank management had little reason to concern itself with goals, objectives, and strategy, particularly with respect to domestic banking. In fact, it was often said that all banks look, act, and smell the same.

A customer selected his or her bank based largely on location, personality fit, or historical family or business ties. The goals, objectives, and strategies that were articulated were aimed at internal concerns rather than the marketplace.

It is clear that this situation has changed. The need for clearly articulated goals and objectives and a supporting strategy is well understood by bank chief executive officers today. It is also true that many different combinations of goals and objectives will result in a successful bank. The corollary of this is that two banks of approximately the same size with the same resources in similar geographical areas can have different goals and objectives an still be equally profitable.

The specific goals and objectives developed by management must be permitted to influence the organizational structure significantly. A set of goals and a supporting strategy aimed at making the bank a competitor in a broad range of diverse markets should cause the management to consider a divisional type of organizational structure. This tends to assure that there is a designated manager with relative freedom and with the resources under his or her direct control to address each marketplace. Likewise, this arrangement forces the managers of the various divisions to compete for resources on the basis of the contribution they forecast they will make to the bank's profits. The staffs should play a supporting rather than a coordinative and supervisory role. This divisional structure permits the bank having a strategy aimed at diverse markets to move more quickly within a given market area.

However, if the goals and strategy of the bank are aimed at a limited number of markets, a centralized approach may be best. Under these circumstances the bank can concentrate its resources by placing them in specialized functional units whose management can be expert in the few markets of concern. Staff groups should play a more significant role because of this concentration. There are fewer diverse possibilities for the uses of resources so the allocation algorithm can concentrate on line items rather than on market and products. Finally, by having a narrow focus of attention, the top management team will itself become much more expert in all aspects of the bank and will be in a better position to direct on a more centralized basis the details of the operation.

Obviously the choices of goals and strategies is not limited to the two extremes. There are numerous combinations, and each will influence the organizational structure differently. For example, the organizational structure most appropriate to the bank with many closely related markets may be a centralized one because it is possible to concentrate expertise. The geographic dispersion of the markets being served should serve to influence the organizational pattern; that is, if a market is located near the headquarters and the top management of the bank, a centralized structure is more appropriate and less costly than if the markets are greatly dispersed geographically.

Competitive and Regulatory Environment

The deregulation of the financial industry means that senior managers of banks must be more aware of the competitive and regulatory environment in which they operate.

As banks have been able to compete in an increasing number of markets, both geographical as well as functional, they have had to adjust their organizational structure accordingly. When states moved from unit to regional or statewide banking, banks that successfully took advantage of the change made significant adjustments to their organization. Most frequently they moved from a centralized to a more divisional structure. Typically, the more governmental units having influence in the areas where a bank is located, the more decentralized or divisional its organizational structure should become. As a bank enters new businesses, (for example, discount brokerage), it normally becomes necessary to employ individuals with skills not found elsewhere in the bank. This lends itself to further divisional moves. Divisional structures also become more desirable as a bank expands from its home states to other states. Parenthetically, at the extreme, as a bank moves into the international environment, it will also ordinarily find it mandatory to adopt a divisional structure at least with its international commitments.

Size and Available Resources

Should size have a major influence over the organizational structure the bank adopts? We have heard it said that specific banks are such slow movers and such ineffective competitors because they're so big. This is tantamount to saying that because a bank is large it will be a slow mover and a less then effective competitor. We do not agree with this logic.

We do not believe that a large bank has to be bureaucratic. To the contrary, size gives a bank potential competitive advantage if the bank is organized to capitalize on its size.

It is generally but not always the case that the larger the bank, the more it should bend toward a decentralized organizational structure. However, the goals, objectives, and strategy factor is an ever-present offset to this. Even those few larger banks that limit their markets and choose to compete in a narrow range will find that their size is not a deterrent to adopting a centralized structure. However, as a bank grows in size, it will find it increasingly difficult to manage in a centralized structure. Interpersonal communication becomes very difficult, and the timely analysis of data at the top can truly preclude the bank from making decisions rapidly enough to be competitive. Decision by committee becomes a way of life. Ultimately, as a colleague once observed, "These banks tend to reach organizational grid-lock"—a situation in which nothing moves. As that condition occurs, individuals who are expected to deal with customers begin to shortcut the policies and procedures and cut corners in order to meet their responsibilities as they see them. This erodes the control mechanisms in place, and the outcome may be financial losses and loss of customers.

As we will point out subsequently, a successful bank that employs a divisional structure has a greater obligation to ensure that its officers in the divisions are trained and otherwise qualified to operate reasonably independently. Banks with a more centralized structure have less need to do so. Thus banks whose centralized structures become so bureaucratic that business is transacted only with great effort may find themselves beginning to operate in a de facto decentralized mode without the qualified people necessary to do so.

Culture

Periodically in the business world certain words and phrases come into vogue, are used and misused with increasing frequency, and then, largely as a result of inappropriate application and general overuse, pass from the scene as quickly as they arrived. For example, remember interface, zero-based budgeting, perameters, and synergism? A word that has burst on to the business community with a vengeance is culture. Unfortunately, the word culture will likely suffer the same fate as the words and phrases just mentioned. However, the concept of corporate culture is powerful and provides a very useful way of thinking about a particular enterprise and how and why it functions as it does. As Deal and Kennedy point out in their excellent treatment of the subject, "Every business—in fact every organization—has a culture."[2] We believe that it could not be otherwise.

Some cultures are more clearly defined than others, and the effectively organized enterprise has most likely given thoughtful attention to defining and understanding its own unique culture. We believe that generally the solidity and effectiveness of the organizational structure within a bank is directly proportionate to the strength of its culture. That is, a bank with a strong, well-defined, and understood culture will be more successful in developing a well-defined, broadly understood organizational structure; whereas banks with weak or amorphous cultures will tend to have a "soft," not well understood, and therefore ineffective organizational structure.

Any discussion of corporate culture is difficult because the descriptions tend to be laced with value-laden words—innovative, customer-

---

[2]Terrence E. Deal and Allen A. Kennedy, *Corporate Cultures* (Reading, Mass.: Addison-Wesley, 1984), p. 4.

oriented, shared values, resistant to change, heroes, customers, rituals, and so forth. However, when considering alternative organizational structures, one must be objective in understanding the culture of his or her bank in order not to be swayed by what sounds desirable with respect to cultural characteristics as opposed to those characteristics that really define the enterprise. Furthermore, one should not be apologetic if, for substantial reasons, one elects a strategy for his or her bank that does not require a high degree of some of the characteristics with such positive sounds and meanings—for example, innovation, hero, and the like.

It is generally the cultural component that renders the "people" issues so important in organizational design. Regardless of the other factors (for example, goals, objectives and strategies, the competitive environment, size, and so forth), the cultural component can make or break a given organizational arrangement.

A bank whose culture generally encourages and rewards innovation, tolerates errors in judgment, accepts the notion that results rather than longevity should dictate compensation of employees, and is comfortable with the periodic entry of outsiders at all levels will be more comfortable with a fully divisional structure. At the other end of the spectrum, a bank that is more comfortable with proven products and services, is generally risk averse, and is quite comfortable with and confident in its longer term employees will be most apt to function better in a centralized environment. As with most other contrasting pictures painted in this chapter, there are rarely such clear-cut distinctions. However, as the reader is aware, distinct variations in culture seem to have a natural affinity for a specific organizational structure. All other things being equal, our experience shows that when the culture of an organization is either weak or is in a state of change, a centralized structure is more effective. On the other hand, a strong culture that has existed for a long time tends to find its fullest expression in a divisional structure. The matrix, not surprisingly, is often effectively employed as a transitional structure as business enterprises cross from one to the other of the two more extreme organizational forms.

Use and Comfort with Electronic Technology

This factor over a relatively short time has greatly increased in importance as an influence over the organizational structure a bank adopts.

As a general rule and as anomalous as it may seem, the more *decentralized* or *divisional* an enterprise, the more it requires a *highly centralized* information control and reporting system. This results from the fact that when operations and decision making are centralized a small group of managers are involved and they take action as the need arises and accept responsibility for the results. The outcome of decisions made centrally may not, of course, be immediately known; but the fact that the action or decisions have been taken *is* known, and the results are amenable to monitoring by the decision maker.

This cannot occur in a divisional structure. Under the divisional structure, decisions are made throughout the enterprise. Although decisions are made *within* guidelines, the existence of the decisions and the resulting actions cannot be generally known at higher levels unless reported by the decision makers. Therefore, without a centralized information control and reporting system, management above that level at which the decisions are made must be quickly and accurately aware of the actions and likely results, and be in a position to ensure that the enterprise is able to cope with results that may arise from the decentralized decision making.

While it is true that management reporting systems need not be based on electronic technology, in today's environment they usually are.

It is also clear that as organizations become more expert in and more comfortable with electronic technology, they can be in a better position to "push" the decision-making responsibility down through the organization. Further, with today's technology, data and information can be entered into, stored, processed, and extracted from the system at many points. This facilitates and even encourages a divisional structure. If a bank is in the early stages of the introduction of electronic technology or if its management is uncomfortable with the technology, it should be justifiably wary of decentralizing its decision making and management in general.

The Management Team

We have not discussed the six primary factors that influence organizational structures in any order of importance because we do not believe that there is a universal order of importance. However, we debated at length whether this factor—the skill, experience, and capability of the management team—should be listed first or last. The management team may be viewed as either the capstone or the base on which an organizational structure exists. From either perspective, the management team—with its unique combination of skills, values, fears, "hot buttons," aspirations, mutual trust among members, and length of time the team has been together—should have a significant influence in determining the organizational design.

Before proceeding, let's take a moment to define what we refer to as the management team. In every enterprise a relatively small group of key executives form the management team. Typically, banks have a formal management structure consisting of a group of individuals sometimes called the Office of the Chairman, the Executive Office, the Senior Management Committee, or the Management Group. These groups, regardless of the name, ostensibly manage the bank. However, when we speak of the management team, we are not talking about these formal structures. We are referring to the key individuals who make the decisions, take the actions, and assume the responsibility for setting the course of the bank, both long term and day-to-day. Rarely are the formally designated group and the less well-defined one the same.

For example, an examination of a cross section of banks will show such situations as:

1. An Executive Office whose members include one or more individuals from a previous management era who are no longer active in day-to-day events.
2. A Senior Management Committee that includes all officers from the rank of executive vice president and above or all senior vice presidents and above who get together periodically to exchange views and "hear the latest."
3. A formal Office of the Chairman, whose members neither meet regularly nor discuss significant events concerning the bank's future.

None of the above should be thought of as the management team of the bank. We further caution that neither the "executives" typically listed in the front of an annual report nor the "senior management" listed at the rear of an annual report necessarily represents the real management team. It is impossible to discern the management team from an organization chart, but the members of the real management team are aware of their role, and other employees know who they are. The real management team is composed of those who make the decisions, take the actions, and directly influence the bank's day-to-day operations.

It is not important for our discussions that we know who composes the management team of a given organization. It will vary greatly in both composition and size. It is important for those who develop the organizational structure to understand such variables as:

1. How long the team has been together.
2. Whether the team is large enough to cover most areas of the bank.
3. The extent of mutual confidence and trust the members have in each other.
4. The expertise and skills of the management team.
5. The raw intelligence of the team member.

Centralized structure is frequently necessary if the management team is somewhat weak, has not been together long enough to have developed mutual confidence and trust, or is simply not large enough to cover most of the bank's business areas. Likewise if the members of the team lack skills or experience in certain functional areas (for example, data processing), it may be necessary to maintain a central data processing operation even while decentralizing the other functions.

A divisional structure is more appropriate when the team is large enough to cover most areas of the bank and its members have worked together long enough to understand each other.

One cannot provide a training program to improve mutual trust among members of any team. However, it *is* possible to provide training and support to improve the expertise and skills of any individual. Therefore it is important to understand that if changes in an organizational structure are dictated by factors such as changes in the bank's goals and objectives or changes in the competitive environment, the skills of the management team can be improved and honed so that members are capable of taking on larger and more important roles.

We have all seen situations in which a strong CEO has built a bank and has either failed to develop a team or has put together a team consisting of only two or three trusted individuals. Organizations in which this condition exists invariably are highly centralized. As the bank grows in size or as the competitive environment changes, it is frequently desirable to begin to move away from such a centralized mode. However, such a move without developing a larger, more effective management team is certainly doomed to fail. In the absence of an effective broad-based management team, the bank would be better off remaining centralized and moving toward a decentralized mode only as the team develops.

As with the cultural component, the management team component is susceptible to change, and changes probably can be made fairly quickly. As with culture, the management team factor can certainly be understood, but it cannot be easily quantified. Yet it is important, and it is one factor top management must always contend with as it develops the organizational structure.

SUMMARY

We have not discussed formal organizational theory or tried to duplicate textbook discussions on the subject of organizational structures. Instead we have explored the more subjective side of organizational design. We recognize the importance of understanding such technical issues as span of control, reporting relationships, relational analysis, and the like. However, we are convinced that no organization can be effective if its structure has not been developed with heavy, perhaps predominant, consideration to the six soft factors discussed.

CHAPTER TEN

The Changing Environment of Bank Management

Frederick Deane, Jr.

Chairman and CEO
Signet Banking Corporation

Welcome to the new world! Bank managers today may feel a little bit like Columbus setting out to explore the unknown beyond the edge of the "flat" ocean. The deregulation of the banking industry, the shifts in the economy, and our changing society as a whole have put bank managers face-to-face with a business environment unlike any they have seen before.

The deregulation of banking has spurred a flurry of mergers and acquisitions creating bedfellows where there was once opposition. The competition may not come from the institution across town but from the big, out-of-state holding company that has decided it wants a piece of your economic pie.

The massive fluctuations of the economy have made strategic placement of banking funds critical to the survival of the firm. The old 3-6-3 logic of borrowing at 3 percent, lending it out at 6 percent, and being on the golf course by 3 P.M. is just as outdated. Those were the days when interest rates might have shifted a point in a year or two; now they do that in a month or a week.

The new economy, deregulation, and competition make the job of bank management a game with a whole new set of rules. Moreover, those rules continue to change, creating different roles for bank managers and their employees. Successful bank managers of today have to be flexible in responding to these changes if they and the banks are to survive.

In the following pages we will discuss the changes in the banking environment, the impact those changes have had on bank management, and the best characteristics of the professional bank manager of today and tomorrow.

ENVIRONMENTAL CHANGES

Deregulation

The greatest impact on the banking manager has come from the loosening of the regulatory process. In the days of the more regulated environment, most decisions made by bank management were limited by numerous controlling regulations. Bank management now has a litany of decisions to make such as: What are the products going to look like? How are they going to be produced? What segments of the market will they appeal to? And, most importantly, what about price?

If you are trying to maintain a small simple bank, and are not anxious to be aggressive in the marketplace, then you don't like these changes. They do complicate banking. The additional costs for software, hardware, and people are substantial.

If you have an aggressive management, however, you will see this as an opportunity to develop segments of the market not previously accessible or expand segments of the market to a greater degree than you ever had before.

The most important judgments a bank manager has to make these days probably concern pricing decisions. In the past, a bank was told it could pay X percent on a deposit and charge Y percent on a loan. Now, with the exception of a few minor disclosure rules, there are no regulations regarding this area.

Many bankers are intimidated by this new responsibility, but to many others it is a welcome change to the real business world. Banks are now more a part of the free enterprise system of supply and demand. Instead of being in a protected cocoon, bankers are out in the real world making tough business decisions that directly affect financial performance.

Essentially, every aspect of the product side of banking has been affected by deregulation, with the exception of the restrictions between commercial and investment banking. There are still only limited ways that banks can be in the business of underwriting and distributing securities. Nevertheless, banks are creating investment banking functions that are technically legal but are in fact pushing against the barriers all of the time.

Deposit products have seen most of the changes during deregulation. We now pay interest on demand deposits through interest checking accounts. We also offer products that compete with the money market funds. These two product changes represent landmark advances for banks.

The phase out of regulations on interest rates paid on different types of deposits has obviously turned the pricing picture upside down.

Pricing is a complicated business because of the need to define the shapes of demand curves for specific products. At the same time knowledge of your own cost structure is important, not because cost drives prices, but because you're in big trouble if you price below cost. Costs determine the minimum price. Then you have to figure out what value the customer places on that product and the resulting demand at various prices.

Banks can develop the expertise to make these pricing decisions either through the people they hire or by purchasing the knowledge. In either case it is not cheap and makes running a bank, particularly a smaller one, a lot tougher.

On the loan side of the pricing picture, usury laws are now the exception. There are hardly any usury laws affecting banks today. There are a few in some states, but none at the federal level.

Geographic changes in the banking world can be seen from two perspectives: the changes within a state and the change across state lines.

Over the past 10 years, most states have dramatically liberalized the ability of a bank to branch and have locations within the state— only a few states resist this trend. Statewide banking is becoming the norm and not the exception.

The farthest reaching changes in geographic deregulation have come from the regional, reciprocal, interstate compacts. These agreements allow a bank holding company to own a bank in another state. This change has allowed the creation of huge regional institutions with thousands of branches and assets that have doubled or tripled.

Despite all of the deregulation and liberalization of banking, one area is actually more regulated. Perhaps this could best be described as the "how to" and "how not to" area. Included here are truth in lending practices, fair credit reporting, the pension laws, and equal lending practices. These regulations are extremely difficult to manage. To deal with these areas, it seems that some bureaucracy needs to be maintained within your organization. In other words, you are going to need some lawyers, compliance officers, policies, and reporting. There is no way around the fact that this complicates the business of banking.

These changes in the environment of banking have also placed a greater burden on the training departments in banks. It doesn't take much imagination to understand that the training needed today with the extended list of products and services is much more extensive than the training needed when all that was offered was checking accounts, savings accounts, and installment loans.

Economy

Just as more attention needs to be given to coping with deregulation, more attention needs to be given to economic factors in the marketplace today. The long-term, essentially steady economic trends of the 1950s have given way to the roller coaster rides of the 1960s, 1970s, and 1980s.

A good example of how swiftly these changes can impact a bank occurred in the mortgage market during the spring of 1987. With the booming housing market, some banks began to do mortgage business in mass volume, committing to a loan rate on day 1 for a closing date on day 60 or day 90. By the time the loan closed and the bank wanted to sell the loan into the secondary market, interest rates had gone up. A lot of bankers had to scramble to figure out how to cover that interest rate change.

Understanding today's economic developments requires bankers to look beyond the back door. Movements in many U.S. economic variables are affected more by the international scene than ever before. Not everyone can be an international expert, but bankers must expand their view of the economy to remain competitive. In the past, you might have been able to get away without a clear understanding of the dynamics of the domestic and international economies—but not anymore. Today a bank manager should have some idea of how the economies in Europe, South America, and the Far East are faring and what interest rates in those areas are doing. Knowing what is happening to the value of the dollar along with import and export figures is a necessity.

The result of this international understanding of the economy is not so bank managers can make economic forecasts, but so they have some appreciation of the forces that can affect their bank business. Although there is no set formula for gaining that broader understanding, a bank manager ought to review the available publications and discuss the issues often to gain insight into these areas.

Competition

Some of these external changes are not caused by the economy but by the competition across the street. What used to be the local competition is now the local flagship for a huge regional firm that merged with your former competitor. This new player has more assets, services, and high-tech equipment.

With the creation of these huge regionals an opening has been created that is sprouting numerous smaller institutions. These smaller banks are stressing personal service with a hometown flavor. They tend to depict the regional banks, rightly or wrongly, as impersonal and unfeeling toward the smaller customer. The competition doesn't stop there.

Just as banks are standing on a fine line between themselves and investment banking, those investment banking firms are doing the same thing in reverse. These nonbank financial institutions offer money market funds that put them in the deposit-taking business. They may call it something else, but in reality they are taking business that used to be the sole domain of the banks.

The competition doesn't stop there. Down the block there's Sears, Kmart, insurance companies, credit card firms, and automobile companies. These firms offer a wide array of financial services that compete head to head with established bank services.

It is not hard to see how all of the competition brought on by other financial institutions, the economy, and deregulation have created a new world in which the bank manager must operate. These changes strongly suggest that to survive the bank manager should evolve into a more aggressive, dynamic leader.

IMPACT ON BANK MANAGEMENT

Changes in the banking environment can be viewed in terms of their impact on bank managers. In considering how they are affected it makes sense to think about decision making, people issues, and complexity. The scope of decision making now is broader than ever. In addition, bank managers no longer have regulations to use as a guide as they had in the past. Coping with these increased demands requires a mix of technical and managerial expertise.

Bank managers need to be able to think strategically. They must understand and think about the dynamics of their own institution and how it is affected by the external forces in the marketplace. Whether it is the economy, regulations, or competition, bank managers must be able to see how such forces will affect their business and be prepared to formulate responses that will produce quality performance. A largely internal view of the business will miss the most important determinants of performance.

The interaction of these various segments of the marketplace must also be understood. To look at only one aspect of the picture and leave out the other factors would be too narrow a view. For example, much of the deregulation of banks has been driven by technology and economic volatility. In turn, capitalizing on newly available technology is one response to managing interest rate volatility. The better these interactions are understood, the better a bank manager can anticipate and avoid a competitive disadvantage.

Bank managers are also learning how better to view the quantitative side of their business. For years we thought of banking as a quantitative or numbers business; in the last few years we have just begun to learn how it all works. Figuring out how your balance sheet will be affected by movements in interest rates and translating that into an income number is extraordinarily complex. For the most part, understanding interest rate sensitivity requires computer models with in-depth software and someone with a pretty good head to get the right data into the program and interpret what is going on.

Another side of the quantitative dimension is understanding your costs better. Traditionally noninterest expense (people, facilities, equipment, and the like) has been a small part of banking costs. It is becoming a larger part, however, as products and services become more complicated and more people and hardware are needed to offer them. In the 1970s inflation escalated these costs further.

Greatly complicating the business is the phenomenon of shared customers and shared costs. Think about a branch for a minute. A teller handles a full range of products: demand deposits, commercial loans, installment loans, consumer certificates, and more. Not only do the tellers deal with a variety of products, but they also deal with a wide variety of customers. People with lots of money, people with a little money, large businesses, small businesses, and so forth all deal with the same teller. The problem is to determine how much it costs for each transaction for the various customers. Obviously, it is a complicated quantitative task.

More and more people are needed to offer products and services, and increased efficiency required from these skills is put to greater tests. One of the best ways to contain costs is with increased productivity. Improving individual productivity is important; it is equally important that everyone in the organization be heading in the same direction. The bank manager is responsible for keeping all employees focused on the goals of the institution. Because people approach the same topic with a variety of perspectives and personality styles, getting them focused on the same goals is a challenging task.

As a manager, you must find that unifying thread that brings the whole organization together. Then once you've identified that binding formula, you must apply it in a meaningful way. The result will have managers at all levels feeling a part of the overall plan and having an important role to play in achieving the organization's goals. There is no magic formula for the thread that pulls the bank team together. It traditionally involves, however, a combination of financial performance, growth, market share, and both internal and external image.

Accurately assessing the bank's situation in the mix of economic and competitive terms is often the hardest task for a bank manager. The picture has become so complicated. To be a good manager, at some point, you must roll up your sleeves and get into the thick of things. It is essential to stand back and view the whole picture and determine how to pull the various components of the figure together while maintaining the individual management of each part.

There is no formula for this balancing act; it is a personal decision made by each bank manager, with each approaching the situation a little differently.

CHARACTERISTICS OF PROFESSIONAL BANK MANAGERS

The complexity of the banking business, both externally and internally, requires that these individuals develop into professional managers as well as traditional good bankers. Strategic thinking combined with appreciating the interaction of market forces and quantitative aspects of the business are key tools for the successful bank managers. Knowing how these processes function will help bank managers run their institutions, but they still must have the substantive understanding of the industry.

There is a breadth and depth of leadership qualities to be learned by the bank manager. Some of these can be taught in the classroom. Many of these attributes can only be acquired in the banking environment with hands-on experience. The proper balance of intelligence, people skills, and working knowledge of the institution is critical for a successful bank manager.

Putting these talents to work while building your own managerial style is the final test for the bank manager. Deciding how to pull the organization together and keep it that way is something only a good manager can do. The decisions are not always easy. You often have more demands placed on you than you have resources to respond to those demands.

One of the ways a successful bank manager can meet the needs of employees and customers is by remaining flexible. The dramatic changes in the banking environment in the past few years highlight the need for flexibility in an accomplished manager. Being able to adapt to changes in the marketplace is a key. Managers who have the most success see change as a new challenge for growth instead of a burden. When managers stay set in their ways and unwilling to adapt, they are placing their feet in cement, which may take themselves and their institution below the waterline.

NEW RULES FOR CORPORATIONS AND DIRECTORS

The public is becoming more demanding in what they expect from their financial institutions. They are getting accustomed to the increased products and services and are more sensitive than ever to their costs.

The public is also beginning to insist that they receive more personalized service. They do not want to be caught up in corporate anonymity. Banks must find ways to meet these demands.

Amid all these changes directors and corporations must maintain their community leadership role. Customers want their bank to be supportive of community causes, and the institution must be responsive to the community needs. This is particularly important when a bank is involved in a merger and the community is faced with a player operating under a new name.

The possibility of an acquisition or merger places more demands on the director and corporation. The key to success in the merger arena is to have a sound, profitable institution. This guarantees your stockholders of getting the best value whether your institution is for or against the merger. The worst thing you can do is stumble because that means your bank may be picked off at less than its underlying value.

More mergers and acquisitions are a foregone conclusion. The institutions with the best looking financial statements and market positions cannot lose in this corporate game—they can only win.

CONCLUSION

The keys to succeeding in the ever-changing banking environment are to remain flexible and aggressive. Being able to adapt to changes in the marketplace and take on those changes as an opportunity to expand your business are crucial aspects in this new marketplace. The competition is coming from more sides every time you turn around. Only innovative, forward-thinking bank managers will rise to the top, and their firms will rise with them.

CHAPTER ELEVEN

Organization and Functioning of the Board of Directors

Hugh L. McColl, Jr.

Chairman and CEO
NCNB Corporation

By the rule of law, a corporation must have a board of directors. Within the law, however, there is a very wide range of functions that a board may perform as well as several organizational structures it may have. At one extreme, all of us know of directors who believe their only duty should be to vote yes or no on a motion to remove the current president of the bank. There are also directors who express opinions not only on the company's policies but also on virtually every decision the president makes. This chapter is designed to help you find some middle ground that is appropriate for you, your company, your directors, and most importantly your stockholders.

At bedrock, the directors represent owners. They may be significant owners themselves, as several of my directors are. Alternatively, they may have been selected as directors specifically because they represent some broad community interest or have some needed insight into running a company. In any case, their clear fiduciary duty is to the shareholders at large. In the case of a bank there is also a clear duty to the depositors.

Fortunately, the long-run best interest of the shareholders at large usually coincides with the long-run best interest of major shareholders, depositors, and various other constituencies the bank serves. It is in instances in which interests diverge or, more often, are not clear that the role of the board becomes most critical in corporate life.

DUTIES AND RESPONSIBILITIES OF BANK DIRECTORS

With respect to the shareholders, directors should keep in mind that they are expected to safeguard the bank's assets in the shareholders' long-term interest. Those long-term interests include the expectation of an overall return on their investment through the receipt of dividends and capital appreciation. In addition, the stockholders need assurance and confidence that policies of the bank are sound and provide for long-range growth and stability.

With respect to the depositors, both corporate and individual, directors should keep in mind that they are expected to provide for the safety of deposits. Depositors must also have assurance that policies of the bank are sound and provide for stability as well as long-range growth.

Directors should recognize that their obligations to the bank fall into two broad categories, a duty of loyalty and a duty of care. With respect to the duty of loyalty, directors commit allegiance to the bank and acknowledge that the best interest of the bank and its shareholders must prevail over any individual interest of their own. A basic principle to be observed is that a director should not use the position to make a personal profit or to gain other personal advantage. The duty of loyalty is manifested by certain detailed legal concepts that include the disclosure of and abstention from acting on any matter in which the director has a personal interest, and the adherence to a strict practice of treating all matters involving the bank in confidence until such time as there has been general public disclosure. With respect to the duty of care, a director assumes a duty to act carefully in fulfilling the important tasks of monitoring and directing the activities of management. This duty of care requires directors to act in good faith and with the degree of diligence, care, and skill that ordinary prudence would require under similar circumstances—the "prudent man" rule.

In addition to the traditional responsibilities of a bank director to provide assistance to the bank in its overall efforts to obtain new business and increase existing business and to offer personal prestige and economic influence in the community to enhance the image of the bank, there are some functional responsibilities that bank directors must discharge.

One section of the national banking laws provide in part that "the affairs of each association should be managed by . . . directors, who shall be elected by the shareholders." Various attempts by executives, business associations, lawyers, and scholars have been made over the years to describe just what directors can and should do in managing the affairs of a national bank or a corporation. The consensus seems to be that the operations of the business and the handling of the day-to-day affairs of the bank or corporation are functions of management and that, rather than becoming involved in those day-to-day affairs, the board should provide the general direction to management in its handling of those affairs. In other words, the consensus seems to be that the statutory language should be interpreted broadly to require that the affairs of the corporation or bank are managed "under the direction of" the board of directors.

It is also generally recognized that a board of directors can fulfill its responsibility to provide direction to management through board committees and that duties and responsibilities of the board can be handled through authority delegated to those committees.

While there is no direct statutory provision permitting delegation of authority in the national banking laws, the Comptroller of the Currency has stated in an interpretive ruling (No. 7.4425) that the board of directors of a national bank can "assign the performance" of its duties. That interpretation, however, contains a provision that makes it clear that the board "may not delegate responsibility for its duties." Thus it is both permissible and expected that the corporate director will delegate to others some functions traditionally associated with board activities. Board members, however, have a responsibility to keep informed of the activities delegated. The extent of this monitoring function will vary depending on the nature and importance of the delegation and usually will be satisfied by the receipt of periodic reports concerning those activities.

At NCNB we expect the board to use committees and to assign the performance of some duties to those committees. There are five standing committees: the Asset Quality Review Committee, the Examining Committee, the Executive Committee, the Finance Committee, and the Trust Committee. Each has a specific "charter" that contains a description of duties and of the specific roles assigned. Each of these committees is directly responsible to the board, acts for the board, and reports on its actions to the board at the next succeeding board meeting. While different situations may require different committees, some committee system is essential for all but the smallest banks.

Generally, the executive committee will have the authority and the responsibility to act for the board on matters that need attention between meetings of the board. It will have full power of the board, except for the power to take action on those matters that by law must be handled by the full board such as merger, dissolution, sale of substantially all of the assets, filling vacancies on the board or committees, fixing compensation of the board or committees, and amending bylaws. The executive committee may consider those issues that are appropriate only for board action and may make recommendations to the board with respect to them.

With respect to lending, directors should see that a loan policy has been established and that its implementation is adequately monitored. In addition, they should periodically to determine whether the policy is adequately meeting the credit requirements of the community or bank trading area. The board should also be satisfied that there is an adequate diversity in loans reflected in the loan policy, that the lending officers are competent in administering the loan policy, and that an effective credit department is maintained with sufficient authority to ask questions and secure pertinent information needed to satisfy internal requirements and requirements of outside supervisory agencies. At NCNB we expect the board to use the Asset Quality Review Committee in carrying out this responsibility.

With respect to investments, the board must be assured that management has full knowledge of the various qualitative and quantitative constraints of regulatory agencies. It should also be aware of the various sources of a bank's funds (capital funds, demand, time and savings deposits, and borrowed funds) and its liquidity requirements, and should be satisfied that the bank can shift funds rapidly with a minimum risk of loss. The board should also concern itself with capital adequacy and thoroughly understand the relationship of the bank's capital to its total assets and deposits. At NCNB we expect the board to use the Asset Quality Review Committee and the Finance Committee in carrying out this responsibility.

With respect to internal controls, each director should be satisfied that the necessary controls are in place and that periodic independent reviews are made to determine the effectiveness of those controls. Each member of the board should be familiar with the reasons for internal audits and should be satisfied that those audits are adequate for the size and complexity of the bank. In addition to the internal audit, an independent external audit should be made. At NCNB we expect the board to use the Examining Committee to assist it in carrying out its responsibilities in this area. In organizations with smaller boards, this function can be combined with the asset review functions in one committee.

With respect to trust and fiduciary matters, the board should be satisfied that they are being handled in accordance with appropriate policies and fiduciary principles. These matters include the development of policies, the investment and disposition of property held in a fiduciary capacity, and the review of the actions of all officers and employees used by the bank in the exercise of its fiduciary powers. At NCNB we expect the board to use the Trust Committee to assist it in carrying out this responsibility.

Supervision is another basic functional responsibility of directors. Since the board of directors is charged with the overall responsibility of seeing that the business and affairs of the corporation are being managed, it must exercise reasonable supervision through an effective reporting system. The board should expect to hear reports from man-

agement on the implementation of and compliance with various policies, and should receive periodic summaries of progress toward long-
range objectives and of comparisons of actual results against short-
range forecasts. The reporting system should also include information
and data which legally must be presented to the directors.

SELECTION AND RECRUITMENT OF DIRECTORS

Perhaps the most obvious duty of a board of directors is the selection
of management, especially the chief executive officer of the bank.
Ironically, the chief executive officer, given enough time in office, has
the opportunity to strongly influence the makeup of the board and in
some cases can practically pick his own board. In such cases, it is
sorely tempting to shape a board that is certain to approve all management proposals. The idea is tempting but inconsistent with the
proper role of a board and ultimately not in the best interest of the
CEO. A properly constructed board can be a great help in decision
making; a group of "yes men" cannot.

Remembering that directors represent owners, it is a good idea to
place significant shareholders on the board. Not only can they be
counted on to take the point of view of owners, they are far less likely
to become disaffected if they participate directly in policy making.
Two cautions are in order. First, representatives of significant shareholders are rarely a satisfactory substitute for owners on a board. They
often act as filters of communications between managers and owners.
Second, major shareholders should be balanced on a board by directors
who are primarily concerned about the interests of minor holders.
Issues will arise in which major and minor holders have different
concerns.

At NCNB we have always valued the input of our directors who
are top managers of publicly traded corporations outside the banking
industry. Their insights into the economic and political climates have
been helpful. They face many of the same management problems that
banks do in cost control, personnel policy, and other issues. We would
clearly recommend that your board include managers drawn from nonbanking firms that are as large or larger than your bank. In the special
case of bank management, no more than 20 percent of the board should
be drawn from active management. Boards of wholly owned subsidiaries by contrast can and in many instances should be dominated by
insiders.

Another group usually considered for board seats are representatives of the community. We at NCNB agree. We actively seek board
members who can provide unique insights into community needs.
Finding the people who can responsibly represent both shareholders

and a broader constituency is not easy but worth doing. Too many companies, in an effort to diversify the board, have named someone with no particular qualifications as director. We strongly believe that all directors must be sensitive to community needs and that individuals who are not should not be considered for a board seat. Likewise, all directors must discharge their fiduciary duties to shareholders, and there is no room on a board for anyone who cannot accept that role. The challenge is to recruit those who can do both.

In this era of frequent litigation and large judgments against directors, it is more difficult to recruit and retain a quality board. However difficult, we must do it, and I recommend that you pay particular attention to the problem. Adequate liability insurance for directors is important, but full and open communication with your directors is the first line of defense.

TO MERGE OR NOT—THE DIRECTORS' ULTIMATE DECISION

As the banking industry responds to deregulation, there has been and will continue to be consolidation within the industry. For the most part, the consolidation is taking place through mergers and acquisitions. Almost inevitably a bank board will face a decision to buy, sell, or merge. How they respond depends a great deal on the performance of management. There is an old saying: Managements never want to sell the company, owners often do. The board of a bank or other public company represents owners not management, and thus plays the key role in deciding to sell. Likewise, they must play a key role in the decision to buy if they are to protect the shareholder wealth measured by the company's market valuation.

The only reason that a board of directors should recommend a merger is to enhance the wealth of the shareholders.

I am quite confident that should you go to a witness stand in defense of your actions on a merger, most lawyers would tell you to adopt that answer and to stick to it. That is the prime responsibility of directors—and that includes members of management who serve on the board.

There's a one-word question that complicates that answer; the word is "When?" It has many answers. Let's look at some.

Ask an institutional portfolio manager, and here's what he says: "I'll take my wealth enhancement in nice, even amounts. How about annual increases in per share earnings that are above what most other companies are doing but are still credible and put each quarter above the same quarter of last year? Or, if you can't do that, give me a mammoth increase so that I can sell out and move to the next stock." The daughter of a former president of the bank may say, "I'm in for

the long run. I'll take lower earnings now for higher earnings later."
Many people will fall somewhere between these two extremes.

I'm not sure that many boards do in fact think along these lines.
What are likely to be uppermost in their thoughts are the factors that
will affect future earnings and perhaps are affecting today's earnings:
management, competence, and succession; changing competitive
forces; changing laws and regulations; and past mistakes in policy.

The future effects of these factors are not readily quantifiable.
They don't lend themselves to a calculation that assumes x, y, and z
to be equal to a_1, a_2, and a_3, the present value of the next five years
earnings will be \$D." Instead they require a vision of the future, a vision
that assigns some order of magnitude to each factor in its effects on
earnings and reaches a conclusion as to what the overall result will be.

That's hard work—and these are hard times. The very factors that
I listed are the dominant forces in today's banking world: management, competition, regulation, past mistakes, and so on. They are causing managements and boards to consider more seriously than ever
before these questions: What does the future hold for our bank? How
can we best turn it to the advantage of our stockholders?

You noticed perhaps that nothing I have said applies solely to
acquiring banks or to banks being acquired. The enhancement of
shareholder wealth is a universal responsibility for directors. It needs
to be the linchpin for any board in decisions to merge or not to merge.

That's not to say that other considerations never influence or dominate these decisions. Managements sometimes push through acquisitions because they want to run a bigger company. Banks sometimes
are acquired because a major stockholder who is face to face with
mortality needs greater liquidity in his estate. However pressing these
issues may be, in none of these instances are directors relieved of
their responsibility to all the shareholders to act in their interest.

With management's recommendations in hand, the board will decide. The decision either way and on either side of the deal will change
the bank's future dramatically. If both management and the board have
done their jobs, it will be the right decision.

CONCLUSION

Shareholders look to directors to safeguard their interests. In very
small firms they can do this by making all the important decisions.
However, in practically all cases they must delegate the decision-
making power to management and committees of the board. This delegation in no way relieves the directors of their responsibility for the
results, a lesson that some have learned in the courts.

Since directors can delegate power to management but cannot avoid responsibility, it is incumbent on both management and the board to be sure that there is adequate and timely information available as well as a two-way flow of ideas and opinion. A well structured committee system, directors who are competent and involved, and a management who looks on the board as a source of strength rather than a problem to be managed will go a long way toward insuring the success of the firm. It is worth the time it takes to build the system.

CHAPTER TWELVE

Strategy and Resource Allocation*

Dr. Benjamin B. Tregoe
Chairman and CEO
Kepner-Tregoe, Inc.

Dr. Peter M. Tobia
Vice President
Kepner-Tregoe, Inc.

John W. Zimmerman
Senior Vice President
Kepner-Tregoe, Inc.

Recent banking history can be divided into two great periods: B.D. and A.D., Before Deregulation and After Deregulation. Since the government loosened its grip on banking, old rules no longer apply. Changes abound, such as growing product proliferation on the part of many banks, increased competition from nonbank financial institutions, and the rise of interstate banking.

"All of these factors," a chief operating officer of a sizable regional bank stated recently, "make it imperative for a bank and indeed any financial institution to take stock of where it is going. What kind of bank will it be? What products or services will it offer? What markets will it serve? What kind of customers would it like to emphasize or de-emphasize? What resources will it need to support its efforts?"

These are the really tough questions. They cut to the very nature and direction of any business enterprise. They are questions of strategy.

Turbulent times such as the banking industry is experiencing demand that such questions be raised and answered. "For a ship without a port," Seneca somewhere observed, "any wind is the right wind." And, Murphy would add, the wrong one as well.

Without a clear strategic direction, managing change becomes difficult. Organizations tend to drift toward this or that opportunity or

---

*Copyright © 1987 by Kepner-Tregoe, Inc. All rights reserved.

away from some perceived threat. But which product or market opportunity should be pursued and exploited and with what competitive advantage? Organizations cannot be all things to all people. How, then, should scarce resources be allocated? Given the changing banking context, few banks could afford the luxury of avoiding answers.

This chapter outlines the fundamental of strategic thinking and traces the implications of such thinking on the important question of resource allocation. Our thoughts are based on 15 years of practical consulting experience in the field of strategy. During that time we have worked with the top teams of over 250 organizations, including many banks and financial institutions. Let us begin with the question, what is strategy?

STRATEGY DEFINED

The word *strategy* has been used rather loosely in the marketplace. Managers talk about marketing strategy, human resources strategy, and pricing strategy. Such "strategies" typically are major operational decision points that presume an understanding of what the organization wants to be. They are related to how an organization will achieve its overall mission.

Strategy is vision. *It is a framework which guides those choices that determine the nature and direction of an organization.* Strategy is *what* an organization wants to be, and operations relate to *how* it will get there. Strategy should precede long-range and operational planning. Today's organizations must formulate a clear strategy from which flows effective operations. We must do things right; that is always an operational given. But we must also do the right things; that is the strategic dimension.

If strategy is the "what" and operation the "how," then the relationship between the two can be represented by the illustration on the following page.

Organizations require clear strategic direction and effective operations (Quadrant I). At the opposite end, Quadrant IV, organizations have neither clear strategies nor are they effective operationally. These are the losers who either improve and progress to one of the other quadrants, get acquired, or fade from the scene. W. T. Grant and International Harvester, now Navistar, are examples. The long-term survival and success of organizations in Quadrants II and III is iffy. Even in the short run, survival is in some doubt, especially where organizations are buffeted by the kinds of turmoil and change facing financial institutions.

There are some very hard-nosed, pragmatic reasons for creating and implementing strategic vision. Every organization is headed somewhere. Top managers who do not consciously set strategy risk

The Strategy/Operations Relationship

		Strategy	
What / How		**Clear**	**Unclear**
Operations — Effective		**I** Clear strategy and effective operations have equaled success in the past and will in the future	**II** Unclear strategy but effective operations have equaled success in the past, but success is doubtful in the future
Operations — Ineffective		**III** Clear strategy but ineffective operations have sometimes worked in the past in the short run, but increasing competition makes success doubtful in the future	**IV** Unclear strategy and ineffective operations have equaled failure in the past and will in the future

having their organization's direction set elsewhere by others inside or outside the organization. "It's really a matter of controlling your own destiny," the president of a consumer goods company recently commented. "The importance of vision is to have that control."

Strategy also reduces decision-making time in an organization. Once the top team articulates its vision, shares it with key managers and contributors throughout the organization, and gains their commitment, there is little need to explain continually the rationale for decisions and to argue over what direction is best. As one CEO put it, "Strategy creates a oneness of mind about where we want to go." It becomes the basic premise of all decisions.

The sense of focus that strategy gives to decision making is critically important for organizations undergoing strategic change. A bank we work with decided to significantly expand its product offerings to meet a wider range of client needs. Here is what the executive vice president observed about a change in strategy and organization structure:

> We decided to become much more market oriented, and as a result we are changing the way decisions get made. We were a highly centralized

organization. Now we are moving in the direction of being a market-driven, much more decentralized organization. In the centralized hierarchical structure we had, the formal control system was essential to the way we managed. But this impedes the flexibility and responsiveness to the marketplace demanded by our new strategy. If you have a vision that is internalized by all our people at the various decision-making points, then you simply don't need the hierarchical control system.

Earlier we defined strategy as a framework for the key choices confronting an organization regarding its strategy or vision. What are the strategic choices? What is the nature of that framework? What is the impact on the allocation of resources?

THE ANATOMY OF STRATEGIC VISION

For a strategy to be clear and useful, it must address the following questions:

- What are the organization's basic beliefs?
- What is the driving force?
- What is the thrust for new business development?
- What is future product scope and market scope, emphasis, and mix?
- What key capabilities are required?
- What are the future growth and return guidelines?

Every organization faces these strategic choices. Assuming these choices are properly made, an organization will have a well-defined framework or vision to guide long- and short-range planning and day-to-day decision making.

Basic Beliefs

Basic beliefs are the underlying values, assumptions, and norms held about what should and should not be done. Often an organization's basic beliefs are implicitly held and lodged in the viscera of key personnel. Yet they can exercise a kind of gravitational pull on decision making. A company we know manufactures electronic components and prided itself on its high-quality products. It spent considerable R&D money to engineer its products and to differentiate them from the competition. Top management decided that it would change its direction dramatically and became a commodity-type organization producing "no-frills" products for the low end of the market. This was fine, but R&D continued in its leading-edge research for a premium product line. The staff was not being deliberately subversive. Engineers found it tough to shake off the belief in state-of-the-art quality that had been the hallmark of the organization.

The first task in formulating strategy is to make basic beliefs explicit. Here is one CEO's comment on the subject:

> Basic beliefs can be motherhood and apple pie. You have to live them to make them meaningful. The most difficult part of setting strategy was putting our basic beliefs down on paper. They are very deeply felt, and we wanted to be sure to dot every I and cross every T. The essence of what we believe was not too difficult to identify, but codifying them in a single document was a real challenge.

Basic beliefs are of two types: strategic and operational. Strategic beliefs are those relating to directional issues; operational beliefs relate to how you get there. For example, typical strategic beliefs relate to such issues as remaining independent as an organization, product quality, and the like. Examples of operational beliefs include values around how employees are treated, customer service, and business ethics.

Whether strategic or operational, basic beliefs must be made explicit so they can be critically examined and, if need be, modified or set aside, depending on their fit with the overall strategy.

Driving Force: Shaping Your Vision

With the exception of the concept of *driving force*, the elements that form the strategic anatomy or framework may seem an obvious part of the prevailing wisdom on strategy. But determining how an organization should shape or determine its vision around these elements is less obvious. Ask yourself:

- How do you focus your organization's thrust for new business development?
- What should determine your future product/market scope, emphasis, and mix?
- What will your organization "look like" in terms of physical and human resources as you implement your vision?

The driving force concept is the basis for answering these questions and for defining each element of the strategic framework.

We define driving force as *the primary determiner of the scope of future products and markets*. The driving force and the product and market scope it suggests provide the basis for defining the other choices in the strategic framework.

Our research and work with clients suggest there are nine basic strategic areas that serve as sources for the driving force. These can be grouped in three categories:

Category	Strategic Areas
Products/markets	Products offered Market needs
Capabilities	Technology Production capability Method of sale Method of distribution Natural resources
Results	Size/growth Return/profit

All nine areas are critically important to every company. However, in every one of the organizations with which we have worked, we have found that *one and only one* of the above nine areas should be the driving force for the entire organization. Likewise, for any business unit within that organization there should be only one driving force, though not necessarily the same as the driving force of the entire organization. This is not to say that one or two of these key strategic areas might not be very close to the driving force as secondary screens for product and market choices. But the ultimate question is: When the final decision about a product or a market is made, which of these strategic areas proved to be most decisive? This is the driving force!

Here are the basic definitions for each strategic area:

1. *Products/services offered*—This organization has a concept of its products or services that is key to the future markets it serves and to the ways in which it will meet the needs of those markets. The organization driven by this criteria will continue to produce and deliver products similar to those it has and will constantly be looking for ways to improve or extend these products. This organization will seek new geographic markets and market segments where there is a need for its product.

2. *Market needs*—This organization will provide a range of products to fill current and emerging needs in the market segments or customer groups it serves. It will be constantly looking for alternative ways to fill the needs it is currently filling and searching for new or emerging needs in the market segments it serves. The market needs-driven organization develops or acquires new and different products to meet needs in its market segments.

3. Technology—This organization offers only products or services that emanate from or capitalize on its technological capability. In such

an organization, technology determines the scope of products offered and markets served rather than the products and market determining the technology. The technology-driven organization seeks a variety of applications for its technology. It does this through the products or services it develops from this technology or by selling the output of its technology to those who would develop further products or services.

4. *Production/operation capability*—This organization offers only those products that can be made or developed using its production know-how, processes, systems, and equipment.

There are two very different forms of production/operations capability as a driving force—the commodity type of business and the job shop type of business (machine shop).

5. *Method of sale*—This organization will determine the products it provides, the markets it enters, and its geographic scope on the basis of the capabilities and limitations of that primary method of sale.

6. *Method of distribution*—This organization will determine the products it sells, the customers it sells them to, and its geographic scope on the basis of those kinds of products or services and customers that can be handled through its established distribution channels. It may seek other distribution channels that are similar to its current method of distribution.

7. *Natural resources*—This organization would develop its products and markets through the use or conservation of its natural resources. It would concentrate on control of those resources as a means of increasing their value.

8. *Return/profit*—This organization will determine the scope of its products and markets by its desire for specific levels of return/profit. Return/profit is the driving force only if a change is made in the product or market scope in order to achieve its return/profit requirements. An organization that wants to increase its return and profit and yet stay within its current product scope and market scope is not return/profit-driven. To be return/profit-driven these return and profit targets must be used to determine the scope of future products or markets and not as a screen for particular products and markets to select within that product scope. This driving force may lead an organization to seek a variety of unrelated products over time.

9. *Size/growth*—This organization determines the scope of the products it offers, the markets it serves, and its geographic scope from its desire to become larger or smaller. Size/growth is the driving force only if the desire to grow leads to a change in the product and market scope. An organization that wants rapid growth, but within its current product and market scope, is not size/growth-driven. Organizations typically remain size/growth-driven for a limited period of time as a transition to another driving force.

To quickly illustrate the driving force concept, let us take a large savings bank that happens to be one of our clients. The top team met to set strategy and decided to shift the organization's direction from a products offered to a market needs driving force. As a products offered organization this bank had a relatively narrow scope of products characterized by high quality, differentiated product offerings, each of which enjoyed brand name recognition. This fits squarely with the products offered characteristics previously defined. "When we stepped back and looked at our company as a whole," commented the vice president for operations, "we realized our greatest asset was our customer base and that future growth would come from penetrating that customer base with a broad range of financial services."

With a market needs approach, this bank capitalized on its strong reputation with its current customers by expanding current loan and deposit business to such new areas as securities, insurance, and travel service.

How does top management determine its future driving force? How does the CEO get his "gut feelings" out so the top team can understand, refine, and use it to guide the business?

First, top management must pull together a rich information base from which to consider possible future driving forces and then narrow these to the one that has the best fit and feel for the future. This information base includes an analysis of external factors such as competition and environmental opportunities and threats, as well as internal factors such as basic beliefs, unique strengths, and vulnerabilities.

Once the future driving force has been determined, it provides the basis for defining the future product and market scope, and the future product/market, emphasis, and mix. With this accomplished, the top team can identify the key capability requirements and the growth and return guidelines that are possible.

FOCUSED THRUST FOR NEW BUSINESS DEVELOPMENT

There are a wide variety of opportunities for new business development facing just about every organization. Such development can take a variety of directions: deeper penetration of current markets with existing products; penetration of new markets with current product offerings; developing new products for current markets; and developing new products for new markets. While the directions for new business development are many, so are the risks. What strategic guidance should top management provide for new business development whether that development is internal or by acquisition?

In the diagram, we illustrate the relationship between that future driving force and the primary thrust for new business development.

The Driving Force/New Business Development Relationship

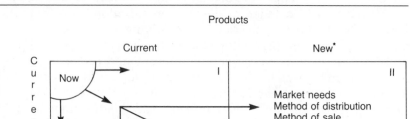

*NEW means new to the organization.

Every organization operates in Quadrant I, the section labelled "Now." It has current customers to whom it offers existing products. As the arrows indicate, in any organization there is a push to expand the perimeter of its operations within Quadrant I.

But as an organization thinks more strategically and looks to future product/market outcomes, it is likely to cross over the lines from Quadrant I. As it does so, risk becomes greater. The key question becomes: In what primary direction should we head?

Most organizations can ill afford a shot-gun approach. The driving force helps top management fire a rifle. It allows the top team to provide focus for new product, market or business development, or acquisition; that is, to direct the organization's energies and creativity toward the kinds of new business opportunities that will optimize the strategy top management has set. In our experience there is ample room for creativity within whatever thrust for new business development top management determines.

Thus one client organization developed a future strategy centered around a products offered driving force. This organization continues to fulfill a basic long-term need satisfied by its current products. It puts considerable emphasis on making sure that its products are unique and supported with latest leading-edge features and benefits to meet the customer need. New products have characteristics similar to those it currently offers. The primary thrust for new business development for this products offered organization is from Quadrant I to Quadrant III. It will look to new customer groups in current or new geographic areas in order to exploit its product advantage.

Significant improvements will come both from new features and functions of current products for current customers and from the slightly different application requirements of any new customer groups with the same basic need. Thus, while the products offered organization may push out the "new need" line between Quadrants I and II, it would not cross that line without reconsidering its driving force.

If a products offered company finds itself pursuing significant new business development opportunities in Quadrants II and IV, then top management must redirect that activity to keep it in line with the thrust of the driving force and the primary new business development it suggests. Experiments in Quadrants II and IV should be noted as exceptions to the primary thrust. They should be justified as intelligent approaches to exploring a possible longer term future driving force and resulting strategy for the organization.

Earlier we mentioned a bank that moved from a products offered to a market needs driving force for the future. This organization had an exceptionally strong franchise with a definable customer group to which it currently offered a limited line of products. With its new market needs driving force, top management focused on filling an increasingly broader range of needs for that customer group.

The primary thrust for new business development for this organization is from Quadrant I to Quadrant II. The mind set of a market needs organization is to provide new products to fill a wider range of needs for the customer group it serves. Such an organization will not fill any or all needs for that group. It may put a boundary around the scope of needs it will fill. However, that boundary will be considerably wider than the current products it offers.

In a third organization, top management at corporate level wanted to take advantage of its holding company structure, given a number of governmental restrictions that just had been lifted. Top management moved quickly to exploit its return/profit driving force for the future.

Specific new and expanded future return targets were set. Other business characteristics such as the degree of concentration and diversification were included in the statement of future driving force. It would develop or acquire new businesses that had the potential to meet these targets, regardless of the particular products they offered or the customers they served. Current businesses that did not meet these new revenue and return expectations became candidates for the corporate axe.

Given its return/profit driving force, the thrust for new business development was primarily from Quadrant I to Quadrant IV.

Each of the other driving forces provides its own thrust for new business development.

Once top management has defined the basic thrust for new business development, factors such as the direction, extent, and limits of that thrust—and why—must be clearly communicated to all managers down the line who are responsible for new products and/or market development, both internal or through acquisition. Their plans and resulting actions can then be monitored to ensure that the creativity they apply to exploiting new opportunities is in line with the thrust for new business development suggested by the strategy that top management has set.

FUTURE PRODUCT AND MARKET SCOPE, EMPHASIS, AND MIX

It might be said without much oversimplification that an organization is the sum total of the products it offers and customer groups and geographic markets it serves. Indeed, much of an organization's resources and capabilities, plans and structure, and decision making and problem solving—in short all of its important activities—are ultimately directed toward its products and markets. What guidance should top management provide on future product/market scope, emphasis, and mix?

Perhaps no area of strategy has received more attention than this question. Almost all strategy consultants have their favorite variation of a product/market matrix. We therefore will not go through all the detail of our alternative. Rather, in the remarks that follow, we will focus on a few basic principles and explore their implications.

Our first principle is that as part of its strategy formulation and implementation responsibilities, top management must provide guidance on the organization's future product and market scopes, emphasis, and mix. All too often the top team shies away from this effort or is pushed and dragged into it because prevailing portfolio techniques rapidly become an exercise in numbers crunching and tedious detail. Responsibility for product and market planning then devolves to planners or line managers two or three levels down. In the absence of clear guidance from the top, analyses are conducted and decisions are made that have decisive impact on the organization's future product and market scope. The top team loses control of the organization's future.

Second, the top team must segment products and markets at the level of specificity with which it tends to review the business. There are no formulas or hard and fast rules. Finding the right level at which top management should segment is crucial.

Third, in meeting its responsibility to provide guidance for products and markets, the top team has a powerful *strategic* tool at its disposal. That tool is the driving force.

Let us take a quick look at the relationship between driving force and product and market scope, emphasis, and mix.

We define scope as a set of common characteristics that describe the extent or boundary within which future product, geographic market, and market segment choices are made. These characteristics serve as a standard by which to test future product and market decisions. When these characteristics are clearly defined, managers can separate specific product and market choices that fall outside the organization's strategy from those that fall within it.

An organization's driving force is the basis for defining its future product and market scope. For example, we worked with a company that provided various products for the electrical energy field. It developed a production capability driving force and redefined and broadened its product characteristics to reflect that driving force. These product characteristics included:

- Industrial product.
- Electrical, mechanical, and metallurgical properties.
- High quality/reliability requirements.
- After-sale service requirements.
- Compatible with high-technology inputs.
- Low content of ferrous metals.

In addition, several of the organization's market characteristics significantly changed. It shifted its focus to industries with a few large customers. It also sought specific customers who could not supply their own after-sale service and who required a system versus just a single product. Geographically, it would no longer cover the entire country but would concentrate on major industrial areas.

Regarding the issue we raised about how specific top management's segmentation of the organization's products and markets should be, several years ago we worked with a company in the textile business that produced more than 4,000 end products.

The key to top management's segmentation was to use the driving force to identify the primary variable that would help to sort products into distinguishable groups for the top team's degree of detail and interest. Top management found that an end-use variable was primary in categorizing such a wide number of products. That end-use variable suggested primary differentiation around textile fabrics used for apparel, industrial, and home furnishings. Apparels was concerned with fashion, industrial with meeting specifications and consistency, and home furnishing with room coordination.

The next most important variable coming from the driving force related to function. Therefore the top team further sorted apparel into underwear, outerwear, sportswear, and so on. This segmentation continued until top management ended up with 13 major product categories within which it felt comfortable to review product strategy. It followed a similar process for customer segmentation.

Top management arrayed those product and customer groups on a matrix. This segmentation helped them indicate future product and market emphasis and mix, given the driving force they had set.

The product and customer groups included both current and new opportunities that fit the intent of the future driving force.

Once top management segments its products and markets or customer groups, it must assess the future emphasis to be given product/market combinations or pairs within the matrix. Once again, the future driving force, along with the other elements of the strategic framework and the information base from which the strategy was developed, provide the basis for top management to develop a set of criteria from which to assess the future emphasis.

Using these criteria, top management indicates future emphasis for product/market combinations or pairs within each of the matrices it develops as "high," "medium," "low," or "zero." This emphasis is an assessment of the amount of time, energy, and resources that should be allocated. This same segmentation and emphasis process is repeated at levels down through the organization for business units, product/market groups, and the like.

The emphasis for products or customer groups or product/market cells in the matrix can be expressed in the following categories:

- *Maintenance* of past levels and type of emphasis.
- *Phase-down* from past levels and type of emphasis.
- *Phase-up* of increased or changing levels and type of emphasis.
- *Exploration* to test future levels of effort and support.
- *Monitoring* of key assumptions for low or zero emphasis cells.

Depending on the category, the organization's strategic efforts will be directed accordingly.

With the analysis of emphasis completed, top management must see that the future product and market mix is determined. Given the strategy and future product/market emphasis, future revenue and return expectations must be distributed among product categories and customer segments.

When top management completes its analysis of future product and market scope, emphasis, and mix, it has presented a clear picture of the intent of the future driving force.

Next, top management must see that the current product and market emphasis and mix are added to its future work. Now top management draws strategic conclusions regarding major shifts in future product and market emphasis and mix among current and new product and customer groups, and specific product/market pairs in the matrix.

The future product/market scope, emphasis, and mix provided by top management becomes the basis for much more specific and detailed product, and market planning and decision making down through the organization. This ensures that top management's strategic vision will be translated into product/market action wherever such action is taken.

KEY CAPABILITY REQUIREMENTS

Every organization has capabilities such as production, marketing, distribution, and sales which support its product and market choices.

A certain level of quantity and proficiency in each of these capabilities is required before any organization can function effectively. The driving force and the future product and market scope give priority to these capabilities and determine precisely how each one will support the driving force. Given a particular driving force, product scope, and market scope, some of these capabilities will require a much higher level of quantity or proficiency than others. For example, if your future driving force is different from your current driving force or if your future driving force is a significant modification of your current driving force, certain capabilities may require major change to support the new driving force and the resulting product and market scope. Capabilities that have been critical in the past may diminish in importance. Others may require significant changes in scope, limit, or level of proficiency to support that future driving force.

A company we know was founded on the strength of a technological breakthrough. Its initial products were quite unique. While this company enjoyed a strong market position, its unique advantage was rapidly evaporating. Larger competitors were planning to muscle into the lucrative market this organization had built. In addition, proprietary technological breakthroughs became increasingly tough to make. In sizing up the situation, the top team opted to change the organization's driving force from technology to products offered.

Given the new products offered thrust, technology became a key capability but with a very different focus than it previously had as the driving force. The bulk of the organization's technological strength would now be directed toward making product improvements in its current product line. Frontier technological research would be replaced by efforts to keep these products up-to-date and in the forefront. In addition, given the new products offered driving force, production and sales became critically important key capabilities as the company searched to keep its main products ahead of the well-heeled competition.

SIZE/GROWTH AND RETURN/PROFIT GUIDELINES

Just about every organization uses financial and growth targets as a basis to plan and judge its results. However, such targets tend to be operational in nature. They presume a scope of products and a customer base. In addition, these targets are derived not from the possibilities and constraints implied by the organization's driving force, but rather are built up from a historical database. They are then projected forward along with certain economic, technological, and sociopolitical assumptions. These targets may result in giving current product and market "winners" the bulk of the organization's resources whether or not that makes strategic sense. Or it may mean that some of the "losers" are getting more of the corporate resources than they deserve, given the tendency for making overly optimistic projections. Conversely, newer or more experimental products or markets may get short-changed in spite of their long-term strategic significance. In the absence of a clear strategic framework, such operational targets guide major decisions regardless of strategic considerations or consequences.

It is critical for an organization to have operational growth and return targets to guide day-by-day decision making. However, they in no way replace or can be equated with strategic growth and return guidelines. Such guidelines answer the questions: Given the future driving force, product/market scope, emphasis, and mix, and the key capabilities required, how much growth is suggested and is feasible over the next few years and what should its trend be? How much return is possible and what is its likely trend over the time frame of our future strategy?

Strategically-set size/growth and return/profit guidelines are statements about how quickly or slowly an organization should grow and about its return, given the intent of the driving force and the other elements of the strategic framework. For example, an organization that changes from a production capability to a market needs driving force typically must make substantial resource commitments to its marketing and sales capabilities in the early stage of the implementation of its strategy. The intent of the strategy and these commitments is to produce a range of products that will better ensure the organization's growth and survival as the strategy matures. This organization therefore must establish its strategic size/growth and return/profit guidelines with this new emphasis and resource commitment in mind.

STRATEGY AND RESOURCE ALLOCATION

When a clear strategy has been set, whether at corporate, divisional, business unit, or major product/market group level, the issue of resource allocation is put in sharp, strategic perspective. This is in contrast to many organizations, which allocate resources solely on the basis of long-range plans and operational requirements.

As we have said throughout, the essence of strategy is to provide definition and guidance around the scope of products the organization will and will not offer and the markets it will and will not serve, along with the future strategic emphasis and mix.

The driving force gives focus to vision. Defining the thrust for new business development is top management's first step in providing such definition and guidance. It tells the organization what the primary direction will be for future expansion and growth through new product or market development or acquisition and therefore where resources will be allocated. That gives focus to anyone in the organization who touches product or market development in any way. A lot of folks, indeed!

The future product and market scope, emphasis, and mix really frames the strategic resource allocation issue. Thus the future strategy may suggest that some current business units or product/market groups fall outside the intent of the new strategy. Top management must make some tough phase-out decisions.

Or the intent of the future strategy may suggest that the organization needs to develop or acquire new products/markets/businesses. Here, top management may be required to shift resources from existing businesses to new business units. This too is tough decision making.

Every organization has developed some way of allocating resources against current and new product/market priorities. Often this is done through the mechanism of long-range planning. This is not the place to discuss the inadequacies of long-range planning as a strategy setting tool.[1] Here we simply observe that the projective nature of long-range planning, its tendency to optimize from current operations, and its bottoms-up approach pose serious difficulties for resource allocation that proceeds without a strategic focus.

Once future strategy is clearly set, it will seal top management's perspective on how time, energy, and resources will be allocated between current and new products and markets and then among current product and market groups.

The future strategy may suggest that some current products and market pairs currently receiving high emphasis may receive less future emphasis in terms of management time, attention, and allocation of resources.

---

[1] For a detailed discussion, see Benjamin B. Tregoe and John W. Zimmerman, *Top Management Strategy* (New York: Simon & Schuster, 1980), pp. 23–27.

On the other hand, some current product/market groups may require a greater allocation of resources, given the future strategy. Organizations significantly modifying their future driving force tend to be in somewhat embryonic form and are not the current "biggies."

Still other products and market groups become the "cash cows" that require maintenance but no new resources.

The new strategy that is set may also require a shift in the revenue and profit mix coming from the different product/market combinations in top management's broad product/market matrix. For example, in the textile company mentioned earlier, we said that the top team separated its markets into three broad categories: apparel, home furnishings, and industrial. All three segments used fabric as the base material. In the apparel segment, it was hard to add value and obtain any significant competitive advantage. On the other hand, the organization produced branded products in the home furnishings segment, and it produced fabric to customer specifications in the industrial segment. There were real possibilities for obtaining a competitive advantage. Both these segments commanded premium prices because of the high value-added component. The products offered driving force this organization adopted suggested that a high proportion of future business should come from these two high value-added segments versus apparel. Given the greater revenue and profit expectations from these segments, resources had to be shifted accordingly.

In another example, a bank shifted from a traditional products offered to a market needs strategy. Top management found that its real competitive advantage in filling a broader range of needs could be exploited much more from its upper-income, adult market segment than its traditional lower-income, adult group. Top management shifted resources from lower- and middle-income adults to the upper-income population as the organization moved to meet a broad set of needs within the upper-income segment.

In addition to the driving force, the thrust for new business development, and the product/market scope, emphasis, and mix, the key capabilities element of the strategic framework has an obvious bearing on the resource allocation issue. As we have seen, the statement of key capabilities specifies the quality and type of capabilities required by the strategy and therefore where capabilities should be added or trimmed.

Adding or eliminating capabilities, whether physical or human, is no easy task. There is considerable inertia from current operations to keep capabilities as is. Therefore, management at every level must spend time and resources—and put the mechanisms in place—to ensure that those responsible for bringing on or developing new capabilities to support the strategy are doing their job.

One other important dimension of resource allocation should not be taken lightly. Setting strategy is only half the battle. Implementing the strategy is where the payoff is. To make strategic vision take hold requires the time and energy not only of top management but of key managers and contributors throughout the organization.

Implementation begins with formulation. The thrust for new business development and the product/market scope, emphasis, and mix are two important bridges to implementation. In many organizations in which we have worked, task forces of senior and middle managers have labored mightily to refine the strategic vision top management has set, so it is relevant to their part of the business.

There are resource allocation needs in virtually every facet of the strategy. In one bank, the top team put their views of basic beliefs in writing. This had never been done before. Next it wanted to know how well or poorly those beliefs squared with reality. It appointed a committee on values staffed by middle managers with authority to roam through the organization to find answers and then report conclusions directly to top management.

The product/market work accomplished by the top team during the strategy formulation process is just the beginning. The top team's segmentation must be refined further, assumptions must be tested, areas of threats and opportunities within product/market grouping must be evaluated, and more detailed product and market plans must be developed. This takes people and money. Many of our client organizations have organized product/market teams of middle managers to take the necessary next steps. Here is real strategic participation and involvement!

When strategy is formulated and implementation begins, critical issues emerge. Critical issues are those major changes, modifications, and additions to the organization's structure and systems, to its capabilities and resources, and to its information needs and management that result from setting strategy. Resolving these critical issues presents great involvement opportunities.

A large manufacturer of farm equipment significantly altered its products offered strategy. This changed its product and market segmentation. It went from strict geography with all products to farming worldwide and only relevant products. This dramatically changed the marketing and product development functions. While its management structure and MIS system were geographically oriented, it developed a management structure and information system to support its new product and market segmentation. The organization had to devote high-powered senior and junior managers to resolve this critical issue.

As one CEO commented about critical issues:

Managing our critical issues is really at the heart of implementing our strategy. Our operational plans and budgeting told us where we were going to be in three to five years if we maintained our current direction. Our strategic plan told us what we really should look like and the changes to be made. And there was a disjunction between the strategic plan and current operations. The critical issues are those issues that have to be addressed if we are to remove this disjunction and become what we envisioned.

We formed an executive committee of eight managers and have a one day business meeting each month. The agenda is strictly on critical issues, and we assess how we are addressing them and what progress is being made. That keeps our focus squarely on the strategy.

The final step in measuring the allocation of resources against the strategic direction is to set in place appropriate review procedures. This allows top and divisional management to take stock frequently of the strategic allocation of resources against the vision of the corporation.

SUMMARY

The driving force is critical to setting clear strategy. That clear strategy includes the basic beliefs, the thrust for new business development, the product and market scope, emphasis, and mix, the key capabilities required, and size/growth and return/profit guidelines. As the corporate strategic process is repeated at business unit and product and market group levels, broad participation is required.

Major resource allocation decisions flow from the formulation and implementation of strategy. When strategy is clearly formulated and effectively implemented and guides operations, resources will be optimally allocated to protect the long-term health and growth of the business.

CHAPTER THIRTEEN

Effective Communication of Corporate Policies*

William H. Bowen

Chairman and Chief Executive Officer
First Commercial Bank, N. A.

Dr. John Dominick

Arkansas Bankers Association Chair of Banking and
the J. W. Bellamy Chair of Banking and Finance
University of Arkansas

Socrates is supposed to have said: "If a man does not know to what port he is sailing, no wind is favorable." This quotation has direct application to strategic planning and to effective communication of corporate policies.

The strategic plan begins with a statement of the firm's mission and its related objectives. Next, strategies and policies are formulated to help the firm accomplish its goals. The mission statement and corporate objectives supply a port for Socrates' ship. Strategies and policies supply the favorable wind.

An organization may have an excellent strategic plan, but few benefits will flow from it unless it is implemented. Successful implementation depends on a number of factors. Here are three:

First, the plan has little chance of succeeding without the commitment of executive management to its development and implementation. Second, the employees of the organization must be committed to the plan. This is best accomplished by having broad-based employee participation in its development. People who participate in the decision-making process feel they have a greater stake in making the

*The authors express appreciation to Dr. Robert D. Hay, Professor of Management, University of Arkansas, for his invaluable assistance in the preparation of this article.

final plan work. Third, the plan must be communicated effectively throughout the organization.

This chapter is concerned with effective communication of corporate policies, not the communication of the entire strategic plan. But all policies have their basis in some plan regardless of whether the firm employs strategic planning.

The policy itself constitutes the "message" that is transmitted in the communications process. Effective communication requires that both the sender and the receiver of the message have a good understanding of the meaning of policy. They also should have a basic understanding of the communications process, so a brief review of communications theory is presented in this chapter. Finally, a firm communicates with various publics or constituencies: shareholders, board of directors, employees, customers, the general public, government, the news media, vendors, and others. A firm may desire to communicate a particular policy to several of its publics. Departmental meetings may be well suited to communicate the policy to employees, but a public meeting probably would not be effective in communicating the policy to customers. Communication with the firm's various publics is addressed in this chapter though only a limited number of examples will be used. However, a basic understanding of communications theory will enable the firm to use the communications process effectively with each of its publics.

WHAT IS POLICY?

Policies are frequently difficult to communicate effectively because many people make no distinctions among these terms: policies, procedures, rules, and strategies. What is policy to one individual may be a rule or a procedure to another. A review of management textbooks reveals there is no uniform definition of policy. But a close look at the various definitions found in the literature uncovers four elements stated or implied in most of the definitions: a principle, a recurring situation, a guide to action, and a reference to the achievement of an objective. A synthesis of these four elements provides a good definition of a business policy: A policy is a general statement of a principle or a group of related principles that serve as a guide to action in a recurring situation and that facilitates the achievement of a goal.[1]

Statement of Principle.   A principle is a general or fundamental truth. It is reflected in a company's policy and philosophy of management. It shows the "reasons why" of a policy.

[1]Robert D. Hay, *Written Communications For Business Administrators* (New York: Holt, Rinehart & Winston, 1965), p. 442.

General Guide to Action. A policy is a general guide to action. It is a general outline of the path to be followed, and it sets the general limits of action or establishes a standard. A policy is broader than a rule, which is a specific guide to action (for example: Don't smoke in the elevators). It is more general than a procedure, which is a series of sequential steps (for example, steps involved in processing a loan).

Recurring Situations. Policies are established to ensure consistency of action, which suggests that policies are established on matters that recur or that are likely to recur.

Achievement of an Objective. The purpose of establishing a policy is to reach a goal. A policy statement either sets forth or implies the goal and then gives the general path that is to be followed in order to attain the goal.

THE COMMUNICATIONS PROCESS

Probably no skill is more important to a manager than the ability to communicate effectively. But communication is a means, not an end, in the management process. Communications is the means through which planning is performed, organization is carried out, and management direction and control are achieved. Effective communication fosters better job performance, it gains acceptance of policies, and it brings about desired changes. It is obvious that faulty communication is costly and impedes the business process. What is not so obvious is its frequency. One study found that in no more than about 50 percent of the incidents examined was the message received by a subordinate congruent with the message sent by a superior.[2]

Communication is not the message itself, nor is it the transmission of a message. Communication is the interchange of thoughts or opinion; it is the mutual exchange of understanding. "Interchange," "mutual exchange," and "understanding" are emphasized because communication actually occurs when a message is received and understood.

This definition indicates the importance of feedback or interchange in the communications process. Feedback between the receiver and sender is often required to determine whether mutual understanding exists. Feedback serves as a motivator to the receiver and enables the sender to obtain the views and opinions of the receiver.

---

[2]T. Burns, "The Directions of Activity and Communication in a Departmental Executive Group," *Human Relations,* July 1954.

The communication process consists of eight factors:

1. Sender.	5. Receiver.
2. Message.	6. Some effect.
3. Method.	7. Feedback.
4. Channel.	8. Frame of reference.

These factors must exist in order to have an exchange of information that is meaningful to both sender and receiver. A diagram of the communication process is presented in Figure 1.

The sender and the receiver must have a common frame of reference if the communication process is to work effectively. The message must be conveyed by some method (written, oral, or graphic) to the receiver by some channel (telephone, mail, or meetings) for a purpose. Feedback between the sender and the receiver also have to take place in order to assess the effect of the communication.

The communication process may break down for a number of reasons: The message is unclear, the purpose is unclear, a common frame of reference does not exist between the sender and receiver, words meaningful to the sender may have a different meaning to the receiver, the message is too complex, the method or the channel selected is inappropriate for the message, inadequate feedback, negative attitudes, and so on.

FIGURE 1 The Process of Communication

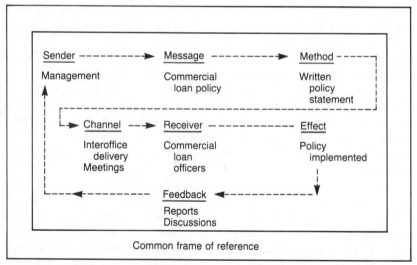

SOURCE: Adapted from Robert D. Hay, *Written Communications For Administrators* (New York: Holt, Rinehart & Winston, 1965), p. 4.

The sender can improve communication by carefully applying the principles of the process of effective communication outlined in Figure 1. The sender should focus on the receiver and emphasize the purpose of communication: to elicit a desired response or action from the receiver. The latter must understand the message for this to occur. The message should be tailored to specific recipients. For example, suppose bank management desires to communicate a revised residential lending policy to its loan officers and to the public. The content and wording of the message appropriate for a loan officer probably would be inappropriate for the public. Selecting the proper method and channel for transmitting a specific message facilitates understanding. Television and newspaper advertising may be effective in announcing a new deposit account to the public though the bank would not communicate the message to bank personnel in this manner. Finally, feedback should be emphasized because it facilitates understanding and involvement by the receiver.

COMMUNICATION OF CORPORATE POLICIES

A policy is ineffective unless it is implemented. Successful implementation cannot occur until the policy is communicated to the individual or individuals for whom the policy prescribes action. The question thus arises concerning the most effective and efficient method of communicating policy. This depends on several factors, including:

- Scope of the policy. Does it apply to the organization as a whole or to a particular event or activity?
- Length of the policy.
- Complexity of the policy.
- The receiver of the message: shareholders, board of directors, employees, customers, the general public, government, the news media, vendors, and so on.

Each of these should be considered in communicating policy. The process can be simplified somewhat by applying the principles of the process of effective communication (see Figure 1) to each communication. The examples used here apply to banking though they apply equally to any industry.

The sender of the communication is bank management. The message is bank policy. Should management communicate the entire policy or only part of it? This largely depends on the nature of the policy, its length and complexity, and the receiver of the message. Suppose the message consists of the bank's loan policy. Management probably would communicate the entire policy if the receiver is the Comptroller of the Currency or the bank's loan officers. But sometimes the most complete information is not the best information to communicate. Assume the receiver is the bank's customers. It would not be efficient or effective to supply each customer with a copy of the policy. It would be too expensive, and few customers would read, much less understand, it. Communicate the specific topic(s) of interest to them. The conclusion drawn is this: Tailor the message to the receiver of the communication.

The method of communication is next. As a general rule, policies should be in writing, especially when they are lengthy or complex. The human memory is fallible. Both the sender and receiver will have a written record for future reference. Verbal communication leaves no permanent record unless recorded. A written policy also promotes consistency and reduces misunderstanding.

The only effective way of communicating a bank's loan policy to its loan officers or board of directors is in writing. But a written policy cannot cover every situation, and some points that are covered require elaboration and further clarification. Communication of written policy is made more effective when it is followed up with a verbal presentation and discussion. This illustrates the significance of two-way communication and feedback between the sender and the receiver of a message.

There are instances when verbal communication may be the preferred way to communicate policy. Suppose a customer inquires about the bank's policy of financing used automobiles. The customer probably prefers a brief, verbal response.

What is the most appropriate channel to use in communicating loan policy? Again, the specifics should be tailored to the situation. The written policy would be distributed to loan officers by some method of in-house delivery. The response to a customer inquiry could be in the form of a letter delivered by mail, a telephone call, or face-to-face verbal discussion.

The sender may believe the communication is complete when the message (policy) is delivered to the receiver. This is a common mistake and a frequent cause of breakdown in communication. Communication is the mutual exchange of understanding, and there is no assurance at this point that the receiver understands the message. Feedback between the receiver and the sender should be used to make sure the message is understood and also carried out. This is two-way communication.

Two-way communication is the most effective way to communicate corporate policy. This illustration points out the distinction between one-way and two-way communication. The newscaster on the evening news is an example of one-way communication. No matter how carefully the message is planned, the newscaster cannot be sure whether his listeners understood or took action because of what he said. Put this same speaker before a noon meeting of a Rotary Club, and the audience may raise questions. This is two-way communication.

One-way communication is easier on the sender. But the sender actually may not be communicating but rather merely expressing himself. Two-way communication requires greater involvement by the participants but is more likely to accomplish the intended result.

Communication with Management and Employees

Policy has never been more important in banking than it is today, and the communication of policy has never been more complex. The historical dominance of the unit banking system has given way to branching systems, multibank holding companies, and interstate banking. Decentralization and delegation of authority has increased the number of decision-making points in a bank and thereby put even more emphasis on the formulation of sound bank policy. The post-Depression stability of the banking system has been shaken by economic uncertainty, deregulation, and intense competition.

The ultimate purpose of any bank policy is to help the bank accomplish one or more goals. A given policy may be directed to individuals, a department, a division, an affiliate, or to the bank or bank holding company as a whole. Through policy, management provides the receiver with a guide for action or decision making in a recurring situation. Management should establish definite channels or procedures to ensure that policy is communicated to the intended receiver, including definite procedures for feedback. The procedure (or procedures) should reflect the organizational structure of the institution.

An example of a written communications program for management and employees is shown in Figure 2. This program uses so-called downward channels of communication and consequently is weak in some areas.

The program is essentially one-way in nature and violates the concept of feedback. It makes no provision for mutual discussion or participation, which are so important for understanding. The media themselves offer little opportunity for personal points of view except in some bulletins, handbooks, and letters. The program is strengthened considerably when it is supplemented by verbal media and some sort of personal feedback. Management meetings, committee meetings, departmental meetings, staff meetings, and an employee meeting with a supervisor—all can be used for this purpose.

A bank's policies should be kept in one or more ring-binder manuals. This allows management to add, delete, or change statements as the situation demands. This also provides a central location where

FIGURE 2   Downward Written Communications for Management and Employees

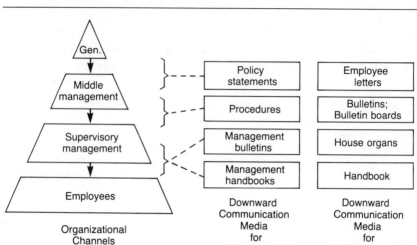

SOURCE: Robert D. Hay, *Written Communications For Business Administrators* (New York: Holt, Rinehart & Winston, 1965), p. 423.

policies can be found. Employees often lose or misplace policies when they are transmitted in letters, bulletins, and in-house newsletters. Policies posted on bulletin boards are frequently overlooked by employees and lack permanence. An employee who is subject to a policy should have access to that policy in a policy manual kept in the individual's department.

A bank expects its employees to know the duties and responsibilities of the positions for which they were hired. Employees are also expected to follow bank policies. Yet management often does not expect employees to know the bank's objectives. This is self-defeating at best. It seems obvious that a bank is more likely to accomplish its objectives when its employees know what those objectives are. The failure to communicate objectives also undermines the communication and the implementation of bank policies since the purpose of a policy is to help the bank accomplish its objectives. It behooves management to communicate both policies and objectives.

Communication with Directors

The role of the board of directors is explicit in the title: to direct or provide direction. The board is responsible for the overall operations of a bank. The terms *board* and *policy* are inseparable from a functional and a legal point of view.

The board of directors plays a vital role in policy formulation, and its members approve the major policies of the organization. Such policies should be reviewed, revised when appropriate, and approved on a regular basis.

The board should also monitor compliance with major policies. Board policy should determine the information required for this purpose.

Communication with Shareholders

Annual stockholders' meetings are used to communicate policy to the bank's owners, but only a few shareholders are reached if the bank's stock is widely held. Policy is therefore communicated in writing, usually in the form of quarterly and annual reports. The bank can supplement these reports with letters and bulletins mailed to shareholders.

Communication with Customers

Verbal communication between a bank and a customer is usually initiated by the customer: The customer goes to the bank or telephones the bank at his discretion. Verbal communication is not an effective way to communicate policy to customers as a group though it is effective on an individual basis. Written communication is better since action is initiated by the bank. Letters, statement stuffers, and advertisements are used for this purpose. The first two are delivered directly to the customer and are more likely to receive attention though there is no assurance the message will be read.

Communication with the Public

Generally, the most efficient way to communicate policy to this constituency is to use channels that convey information to the general public: newspapers, radio, and television. The message should be brief, direct, and clear. Repetition is necessary to reach a larger audience.

CONCLUDING REMARKS

Many objectives by their very nature are difficult to accomplish. Thus there is no assurance a bank will achieve all of its goals even if it has good policies that are communicated effectively and implemented. But the existence of all three facilitates this end.

No new information is presented in this chapter. Management is well aware that policies will not be effective unless they are communicated and implemented. Effective communication is often a weak link in the process because not enough time and effort are devoted to it. This chapter has presented a general framework that management can use to communicate policies more effectively.

CHAPTER FOURTEEN

The Essential Use or Value of Data, Information, and Systems in Banking Organization and Management

Richard E. Dooley

The Dooley Group

PHILOSOPHICAL BACKGROUND

The idea of information in systems has been and still is a topic of broad confusion in management circles. Some confusion is a result of the elusive connection between information systems and the management process. Both are more art than science and therefore may always be somewhat subjective in practice. Still more uncertainty comes from seeing information systems as a "high form" of data processing. The latter is a science (though relatively new and not yet certified) with jargon, products, and applications that seem removed from the urgent interests of many managers.

Furthermore, "computerese" and the normal ambiguity of the English language often obstruct management's ability to deal with these concepts. This problem with words is common in any technology. Unfortunately, this field is burdened. Some phrases can mean almost anything, and others are too general to carry much meaning for the uninitiated. Managers are swamped in alphabet soup and buzz words.

However, it is important to get some basic concepts down clearly in order to understand information systems and implement them effectively. It is an absolute must (not just ideal) to have this philosophical foundation in place.

Let's strike right to the heart of this matter with basic definitions of data and information.

THE RELATIONSHIP BETWEEN DATA AND INFORMATION

We have widespread lack of clarity in the use of the words data and information. The words do overlap in meaning, but they are used interchangeably by many technicians and managers.

If you were thoughtfully to review your use of each word, describing what comes to mind with each, a list like the following might be constructed.

Data	Information
Raw facts or statistics	Formatted or analyzed
Digital or alphanumeric	Analog or graphic
Unrelated	Related or comparative
Too much	Incomplete
Creates confusion	Reduces uncertainty
Neutral or objective	Often subjective
Yet to be processed	In a useful or relevant state
Hard	Soft
Oriented to the past	Oriented to the future
Used by machines	Used by humans
Is known or available	Contains new insight
	Connected to decision making
	Helps control change
	Need to reach objectives
	Need to solve problems
	Connected to risk taking

With this list, you may set some groundrules about the use of the two words:

1. Data and information do overlap in practical day-to-day business use. Very often, one element can be both. For example, customer balances might be simply stored in a file (as data) or used (as information) to help a lending officer make a decision about a rate charge.

2. One person's data is sometimes another person's information, and vice versa. For instance, a marketing executive may find certain statistics useful in establishing new customer services. That's information. But the comptroller might consider the same statistics unrelated, valueless, or simply raw data.

3. The crucial test of information is simply: Is it useful in some managerial activity, especially those in the right column of the list?

4. Information is not all data originated. Though there is a process of transformation that often moves or changes data to information, all information is not "data based." Some information comes as rumors, dreams, hunches, gossip, corridor conversation, and so on. In fact, many executives rely more on this kind of information, or at least feel

more comfortable with it, than with information derived from data records.

Interestingly enough, many data processing professionals have been reluctant to admit this. They have pushed the idea that better or more computers equals better or more data, and that better or more data equals better or more information, and that better or more information equals better or more management. Of course, we know that the value transferred (that is, from computers to data to information to management) is not direct or simple. Often the result is below expectations and/or less than promised.

5. Primarily because of the phenomena mentioned in (2), data and information change back and forth as they move vertically or horizontally in a business enterprise, that is, up or down through responsibility levels or across functional lines. Your boss might feel what you are dealing with is useless data when you feel it is relevant information. This is a very difficult design constraint for the developers of information systems. Imagine saying to the engineers of a new production assembly line: "Look, first, we'll be building and moving cars, but then as we get over that, our product must change into a boat, and around the corner it shifts into airplanes." That would be equally as difficult an engineering design request as some information systems designs have been (albeit unknowingly by either bank management or computer technicians).

6. People other than just managers require management information. Anyone in the management process needs useful data or information.

IMPLICATIONS FOR DATA PROCESSING AND INFORMATION SYSTEMS

This exercise can now be expanded to define and differentiate between data processing and information systems. After some consideration of our actual use of these two phrases as labels for organizational units, a list like the following might be made.

Data Processing	Information Systems
Tools/techniques	Problems/objectives
Technicians/specialists	Users/managers
Production/operations	Management/marketplace
Provide stability	Bring about change
Transactions	Models
Routine or known calculations	New equations which lack precedence
Structured problems	Unstructured problems
Machine/computer	Human
Efficiency	Effectiveness

In most banks the same set of workers or specialists are charged with accomplishing both. The organizational label today is often information services, implying a yet broader responsibility.

We have slowly learned that we cannot obtain the conditions or actions listed in the right-hand column by simply changing the department name. In fact, changing the formal label to information systems when what is really going on is data processing work is extremely misleading and results in unrealistic expectations. But this has been done repeatedly.

There is, of course, an inherent relationship between these two pairs, data versus information, and data processing versus information systems. They are really more like opposite ends or different directions in a continuum.

| ← —————Data —————→ Information —————→ |

Data	Information	
← ——	——→	——→
processing	systems	

HOW HUMANS FIT IN—COMMUNICATING AND COOPERATING EFFICIENTLY AND EFFECTIVELY

One thing we are tying to do in data processing/information systems is communicate. Professionals in the field of data processing/information systems may not always perceive this, nor do they always practice it successfully. And other groups (for example, bank managers) do not perceive or practice it to any greater extent in their duties.

We communicate to facilitate getting something done. This always involves people, a fundamental factor that is not clearly perceived nor successfully practiced where technology is concerned. Communication is needed so people can act as teams or task forces or organizational units in the process of carrying through the production or work function.

It is that simple. We want to communicate in data processing so people can work more efficiently or, as Peter Drucker says, "do things right."

If we move from data processing to information systems, the same conceptual framework holds. We have simply shifted to a different set of people, this time workers in the management process. We want to communicate, and we want as managers to work together. In addition, we have added another goal. We want to be effective, that is, do right things. Thus information systems conceptually are aimed at helping managers be efficient and effective in the management process, and hopefully this causes the "worker" to be more efficient in the work process—where data processing takes place.

The shift is signified by the change in focus from data to information. Once we are in the topical arena of information, we have moved (conceptually) from the production function to the management function, information potentially being one of a manager's main tools. In practice, we all know that many managers successfully use other tools like luck, inaction, other people's decisions, or the economy.

Thus as we move to the right in the continuum, we require more communication, and we begin to establish the need for "linking" of people in teams or units. We are into a completely human or behavioral dimension. An organization can have the best data and lots of it, and it can provide useful information to the right person, and still not be successful. There is a third dimension or column shown in the following list. It represents how people do in their management processes, and it involves both efficiency and effectiveness, timing, action in the right marketplace, and so on. It is completely outside of the realm of data/information.

A *Data*	B *Information*	C *Use-Value*
Raw facts or statistics	Formulated or analyzed	Communication/message
Unrelated	Related or comparative	Fits
Too much	Not enough	Significant
Creates confusion	Contains new insight	Reduces uncertainty
Yet to be processed	In a useful or relevant state	Applied
Neutral or objective	Often subjective	Better decisions
Hard	Soft	Intangible
Oriented to the past	Oriented to the future	Oriented to the present
Used by machines	Used by humans in the management process	Effective and efficient management
		Connected to risk taking, problem solving, objective achievement
		Mix with other human processes

EVOLUTION AND MERGER OF THREE SEPARATE DISCIPLINES IN THE CURRENT BODY OF PROFESSIONAL KNOWLEDGE: A NEW AWARENESS

As further background to understanding information systems in banking, consider what are generally thought of as three separate academic disciplines.

A	B	C
Industrial management	Computer sciences	Decision support systems

Let Column A represent the production function or the classic assembly line. In banking we usually call this operations. Let Column B represent the use of computer technology in a business. In banking this is often referred to as data processing. Let Column C represent the various skills, techniques, or theories that high-level technicians, mathematicians, economists, and analysts (they think of themselves in different categories) try to apply in business. In banking this was sometimes the operations research or management sciences and now the information services department. Some trends or relationships here are worth studying:

1. Column A is perhaps 75 years old, well thought out in theory, and applied in practical business situations. The manufacturing, processing, and engineering industries practice its principles by second nature. Schools turn out well-prepared graduates for entry into these fields. The service industries such as banking or insurance have only recently begun to accept the fact that production management or industrial engineering is relevant to their work processes. Some bankers in recent years have accepted the idea that their operations department is a "factory." Though the field is old, its appreciation in banking is still new.

2. Column B is perhaps 40 years old; it has been applied to banking for about 30 years.

3. The age of Column C is more arbitrary. In its mature form, information services are only 5 to 10 years old and for some banks are yet unborn.

4. Increasingly, all three are becoming connected or merging. There are many common techniques or ideas. Theories from one can be applied in another. For example, floor layout, a body of knowledge in classical industrial management, has been recently applied to the computer rooms of most large organizations. Furthermore, it is being used for the conceptual flow of data in an organization of knowledge workers, that is, to understand the work flow in relation to machine placement and human work stations.

5. Service industries that often emphasized Columns B or C in their hiring of technically trained people are now consciously seeking graduates with industrial engineering backgrounds. Some banks, for instance, have recognized that their check clearing system or deposit handling activities are basically horizontal work flows like an assembly line. They just are moving paper (or data really) instead of physical

products. However, since most of this work is done in data processing, this assembly line is often invisible because it is moving at the speed of light. The media is the electronic process. So banks do not see it as a production line. And for years, banks did not intensely apply lessons, ideas, and rules from basic industrial management. For instance, many banks have organized their check clearing production function in horizontal pieces to fit their departmental structure, which is vertical for other reasons. How many factories have you seen where the planning, controlling, and operating of the assembly line was not one unit, matching the whole horizontal flow? In my opinion, there is an accelerating movement toward recognizing the applicability of Column A ideas/people in service business and in banking in particular.

6. Increasingly, all three columns are being grouped at the top into a confederation of departments called "the administration department" or something similar. Of course, the senior management involved is often more experienced with Columns A, B or even C.

7. While the production function or assembly line was being automated over the last 25 years, much of Column A was taken over by Column B people. These computer specialists often knew little or nothing about classical production management. Banking to a considerable extent moved right into Column B without evolving through Column A, and our systems often reflect this abortive growth path.

8. As Column B took over many production-like work processes, some traditional management controls or information flows were lost. After automation these controls or data elements weren't available to the right people because they were not programmed into the computer system.

9. As all three columns merge organizationally, any manager responsible for them will have to have or must quickly acquire strong conceptual foundations or practical understanding of what is involved in each. As they merge, it becomes more difficult for an executive whose viewpoint by education and/or experience is, let's say, only marketing or only finance to relate to this new larger body of knowledge.

10. Unfortunately, this new larger body of knowledge has sometimes been represented by a large centralized staff of technically oriented personnel. They were surrounded by communication barriers and unsympathetic users of the services. There was an ineffective use of the three sets of skills, ideas, and theories for the "nonprofessional" who might be, let's say, a loan officer or branch manager. It is not just painful; it is maddening. In some firms, the "heat" generated between these two organizational areas is "incandescent." So organizational responsibility was often disbursed.

11. A dual education, cross-training or personnel transfers, help to relax the heat. Team management, which spans organizational bar-

riers or combines appropriate skills in new working groups, also facilitates. A basic conceptual grasp of what has happened these last few years would also help immensely.

HARNESSING THIS NEW AWARENESS

Some managers, particularly in banking, are not fully aware of the inherent connection between their management process and the disciplines covered in the columns. Below is another graphic representation of the idea.

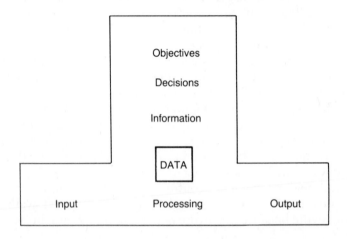

Let the bottom bar of the inverted T represent the production function or assembly line in its simplest form. Using the traditional "black box analysis" model of input, output, and some processing in between, we can relate to most of banking's normal work flows such as check clearing, deposit handling, and loan payments. These are banking's assembly lines, done at electronic speeds in the data processing department. This is what we "process" in banking.

Now going back to our examination of the difference between data and information, we can state that the only reason managers need data is because they have information requirements. And the only reason managers have information requirements is because they have decisions to make. And, again, the only reason that managers make decisions is to reach certain goals or objectives. That is the management process.

Management simulation games like BANKSIM follow this conceptual model rather well. Students input sets of decisions, which are processed by some data processing shop and result in output (printed sheets) being returned to each team. This output is data. Of course, the team's job is to use that data (useful data = information) as information in chosen areas of activity (decisions) to bring about certain changes or levels in their balance sheet or income statement (objectives). Obviously, the whole process—of defining and agreeing on objectives, choosing decisions or actions to reach those objectives, and finding the required useful data, in time to make the decision, and using a team approach—is a very provocative, relevant exercise in teaching banking management. It has been used successfully for years in the banking schools.

A serious problem in many organizations is that the two functions are not so well integrated as the first symbolic representation implies. In fact, they are often completely separate, looking more like this:

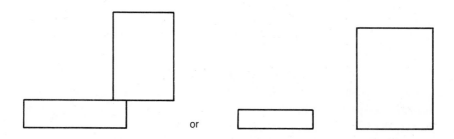

When we think about this partial connection or separation between the management process and the production process, the negative impact is primarily in the management process because a great deal of the data that is needed to help satisfy managers' information requirements is in the production function. Any poor connection in these processes lessens the effectiveness of the remaining management functions at all levels. With management being largely an information business and information being largely data originated, this poor connection gets much more burdensome when we focus only on data processing systems or certain functional areas that are highly computerized.

To overcome this situation, many firms have tried to link up with their production systems (management information system) after the production system was in place. Symbolically, they try to jam the top part of the inverted T down into the bottom bar. It does not work well. And what makes the situation worse is that most production systems (all the early ones) were designed and implemented with the objective of moving the work and with little attention given to the need to support the attached management process. For example, demand deposit systems (DDAs) were first built years ago just to post the checks and deposits, print the statements, list some work exceptions like overdrafts, and not much more. That was okay then. It was a big accomplishment just to do that, and we were not yet skilled at understanding either the philosophy or the engineering implied by the full connection.

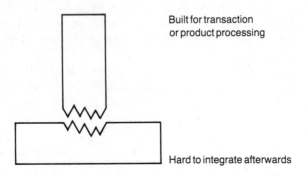

Built for transaction
or product processing

Hard to integrate afterwards

But in the late 1980s there is no defense for building any system just to do production work. All systems should be built with both objectives—production efficiency and management effectiveness—as design goals.

The schematic used in the beginning to help construct these ideas implies that all management information comes from the production system. But, as we reviewed earlier, all information is not "data" based. It can be and often is derived from other sources, such as the rumor mill. So even the best designed, perfectly implemented system will only partially satisfy the needed flow through production of data, to information, to decisions, to objectives. This realization will help avoid unrealistic expectations by management, a prevalent problem with which many system engineers have been saddled.

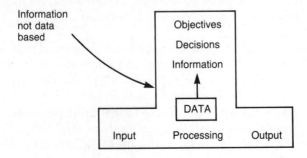

Information
not data
based

Objectives

Decisions

Information

DATA

Input   Processing   Output

Unfortunately, the kind of people who like to work in one part of our inverted T often do not like the other area. Not only are they not educated for it, but they feel emotionally unrelated, perhaps even alienated. Universities have not helped much because their past curricula produced people tending one way or the other (a business degree or an engineering degree or a computer science degree) although this has shifted, and newer graduates often have had a blend of course coverage. People are needed who can work well in either function, and are comfortable with the ambiguity and multidimensional aspects involved in management, but also at peace with the logic, sequence, and detail predominant in production. Most especially, those people who are in charge of building systems (project leaders, user representatives, systems managers, and the like) should understand each bar and the need for and the limited potential of the connection. They should be able to identify and communicate the ever-present trade-offs implicit in the modern twin goals of production efficiency and management effectiveness, such as the need for precision in complete accounting records versus the need for quick trend information in marketing plans.

Acquiring this "bridged vision" is crucial for optimizing the interrelationship between data processing, information systems, and management. We need bilingual professionals.

THE CONTRIBUTION OF DATA PROCESSING AND COMPUTER TECHNOLOGY

Technology in general has advanced much faster than most banks were capable of absorbing it. In fact, to be more realistic, the advancement has been much faster than they needed or wanted. Without trying to summarize completely the current state-of-the-art, let us simply review a few key conditions:

1. Our ability to store, manipulate, and access data in computer hardware of various kinds has multiplied at a high rate.
2. The sophistication of available software and available programming skills has improved significantly.
3. Our experience in planning, organizing, controlling, and leading efforts to link the accomplishments described in (1) and (2) in business systems is considerably better than even a few years ago.

The area that requires our most focused attention today is the "bridging" or supporting of the management process. Progress here must come equally from the information services world and from the line or executive manager who has new awareness of this knowledge. The data processing industry has done about all it can. In its own way, it was always ready but perhaps not able to support the management process. What can be done much better is to supply business design perspective and a continuous communication link to the management processes. This work is behavioral in nature. In a very real way, the baton for leadership has passed to the personnel, education, or management function because the main obstacles left to progress today are in this area, not within the technology itself.

SOME INFORMATION SYSTEMS GENERALIZATIONS

1. Information and data are corporate resources, and they must be managed as such. Organizational or personality barriers that may have existed between the storage and use of data need to be dissolved. But systems should not be designed with the naive assumption that this will be the case. People tend to personalize ownership of data. Security, customer privacy, and data integrity are three major issues that highlight the required corporate perspective.

2. Information systems are an investment, not an expense. The investment mentality (longer term, multiple pieces) is necessary to optimize the use of information. The classical 12-month budget cycle and its inherent expansions and contractions is a troublesome tool for appropriately managing information systems. Such systems may take longer and require consistent funding over several budget cycles. Actually, an appropriate set of information systems is much like a portfolio. There are some risky systems, some routine ones, some small ones, and some very large ones. It takes the same portfolio management mentality to run such a system set.

3. Sharing and prioritizing are always required. There is never enough test time, or good project leaders, or computer capacity, or work stations, or programming skills. Data processing/information systems managers, just like any line manager, never have enough authority, time, or resources. Both groups need to be realistic when making requests of the other. Classic resource allocation and priority setting between line and staff are processses yet to be well practiced in the banking business.

4. Technological change is more difficult in the user area. The effect of technological change can often be handled more easily inside a data processing/information services shop than in the line or user area. Thus, a technician often underestimates the amount of total change required by a shift in some hardware or software or in the network. The "ripple effect" goes much further out and lasts longer in the work place than just the immediate change itself. Most of the real work or

change is always in the client's area or in the individual workers themselves.

5. Leapfrogging is dangerous. Catching up by skipping a phase or some basic steps in the usual evolutionary process is extremely risky and usually disastrous. For example, moving to distributed processing directly from centralized batch processing without evolving through a centralized online environment is a highly risky leap to make. So is going right into design without enough time in definition. We should have an existing manual system before automating anything.

6. Systems work is management work. The very process of designing and implementing systems requires a high degree of planning, organizing, leading, controlling, communicating, and closing. Yet we seldom train systems people extensively in these processes. They often concentrate on the technology of the components to the detriment of the final outcome.

7. Computer systems are inflexible; humans are elastic. Employees often make up for inadequacies in a work flow, say, when someone is absent or a procedure manual is out of date. But computer system programs must be completely up to date and run the same way every day. Thus, in the shift from human control to equipment, we give up certain useful flexibilities.

8. Computerizing poor management will make it worse. Our aim, of course, in information systems is to support good management. We may or may not succeed; that is the risk. But if management talent is absent or poor, success is not probable. A system will only make it worse.

These ideas are themselves a necessary link between banking organizational units, bank management processes, and the specific application of an overall technical or systems architecture for survival and success in the financial services industry.

PART THREE

Managing Human Resources

CHAPTER FIFTEEN

The Economics of the Banking Firm

Dr. Peter S. Rose

Professor of Finance
College of Business Administration
Texas A & M University

INTRODUCTION

Every banking organization, regardless of its size or location, is a business firm striving for improved earnings, sustainable growth, and a stable or increasing share of the markets it chooses to serve. But the achievement of those objectives is a difficult task in today's banking environment. A volatile economy, increasingly linked to global markets rather than just local or regional markets, has resulted in increased operating and financial risks for banks of all sizes and in all situations. Interest costs on borrowed funds have soared over the past two decades, while employee compensation has been one of the fastest growing of all industry operating costs over the past decade. Banking organizations and bank employees must work harder and more efficiently today to earn the same rate of return and protect their profit margins from progressive erosion. More than ever before, earning a satisfactory rate of return for the bank's stockholders demands:

　　a. Managing and controlling banking risk in all forms (credit, interest-rate, liquidity, political, and so on).
　　b. Managing and controlling costs in the pricing, hiring, and deployment of bank employees and other resources.

But the management and control of both banking costs and risks today requires effective *tools* for understanding bank operating problems and for formulating strategies to deal with those problems. It is here that the economist and the banker can find common ground. Each has an important contribution to make in analyzing and coming to grips with management challenges posed by the modern bank.

ALTERNATIVE VIEWS OF THE BANK AS A FIRM

Managerial economists find it useful to view the banking firm from several vantage points. Each viewpoint highlights key issues and problems that must be addressed by bank management in reaching important and recurring decisions. The two most prominent economic models of the banking firm today are:

1. The *financial intermediary model,* which views the bank simply as a business firm selling funds-raising and funds-using services in an efficient market system.
2. The *economic unit model,* which views the bank as an organizational actor in the economic system, attracting and organizing scarce resources (land, labor, and capital) as efficiently as possible in order to generate those banking services the public demands.

Next we examine each of these views of the banking firm for the essential clues they provide to bank managers today.

The Bank as a Financial Intermediary

As a financial intermediary the individual banking firm focuses its resources and managerial skills, first of all, on the task of raising adequate debt and equity funds (that is, a sufficient supply of loanable funds) to support the bank's revenue-generating activities. These loanable funds flow through the organization to be allocated and focused by management toward those funds-using services—loans, lease receivables, security holdings, and the like—that propel the bank toward its earnings, growth, and capitalization goals. Under this view of the banking firm, the bank's *output* is the *credit* it supplies to businesses, consumers, and governments. Its *inputs* are the deposits, money market borrowings, and equity capital it has managed to raise by selling IOUs and stock to the public.

This familiar view of the bank as a financial intermediary—simultaneously borrowing and lending funds—helps to focus our attention on the key financial management issues that must be faced in running *any* bank. These include:

1. *Funds-source issues*—Is the mix of funds raised by the bank (through deposits, nondeposit borrowings, and long-term debt and equity capital) optimal in terms of achieving the *lowest* possible overall funding cost at a level of risk (especially liquidity, interest rate, and default risk) acceptable to management and to the stockholders?

EXHIBIT 1   The Bank as a Financial Intermediary

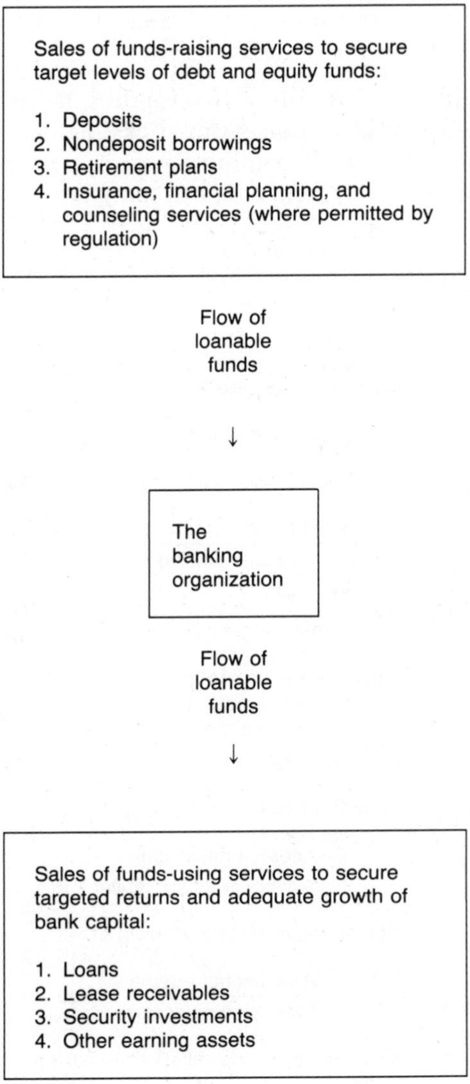

Sales of funds-raising services to secure
target levels of debt and equity funds:

1. Deposits
2. Nondeposit borrowings
3. Retirement plans
4. Insurance, financial planning, and
   counseling services (where permitted by
   regulation)

Flow of
loanable
funds

↓

The
banking
organization

Flow of
loanable
funds

↓

Sales of funds-using services to secure
targeted returns and adequate growth of
bank capital:

1. Loans
2. Lease receivables
3. Security investments
4. Other earning assets

2. *Funds-use issues*—Is the mix of funds uses made by the bank (in the form of loans, leases, security investments, and the like) optimal in terms of achieving the *highest* possible return at a level of risk (especially loan, interest rate, and bankruptcy risk) acceptable to management and the stockholders?

Each bank's effectiveness in resolving these two funding issues can be measured by several different indicators—yardsticks management can use to determine if the bank could be doing a more adequate job in raising and using scarce loanable funds. These *management effectiveness indicators* include:

Measures of the bank's effectiveness in securing an optimal mix of funds sources at the lowest possible cost

Funds-cost indicators:

Average historical cost of bank funds(%) =

$$\frac{\text{Total interest paid} + \text{Total noninterest cost of fund-raising}}{\text{Average total funds raised}} \times 100$$

Pooled marginal cost of bank funds(%) =

$$\frac{\text{Total interest paid on \textit{new} funds} + \text{Total noninterest cost of raising \textit{new} funds}}{\text{Total \textit{new} funds raised less required reserves and unutilized lending capacity}} \times 100$$

Break-even yield to cover the bank's funding costs (%) =

$$\frac{\text{Total interest costs}}{\text{Total average earning assets}} \times 100$$

Measures of the risk attached to bank funds sources:

Core deposit ratio (%) =

$$\frac{\text{Average total deposits less average large time deposits (over \$100,000) and foreign deposits}}{\text{Total assets}} \times 100$$

Volatile liability ratio (%) =

Measures of the bank's effectiveness in achieving an optimal mix of funds uses with the highest possible return

Rate of return indicators:

Gross yield on the bank's earning assets (%) =

$$\frac{\text{Income from earning assets}}{\text{Average total earning assets}} \times 100$$

Net interest margin (%) =

$$\frac{\text{Total interest income from earning assets minus total interest expense on deposits and other borrowed funds}}{\text{Average total earning assets}} \times 100$$

Rate of return on equity capital (%) =

$$\frac{\text{After-tax net income}}{\text{Total average equity capital}} \times 100$$

Rate of return on total assets (%) =

$$\frac{\text{After-tax net income}}{\text{Total average assets}} \times 100$$

Measures of the risk attached to bank funds uses:

Nonperforming assets ratio (%) =

$$\frac{\text{Total loans and leases 90 days or more past due}}{\text{Primary capital}} \times 100$$

Average total large time deposits (over $100,000) + Foreign-office deposits + Federal funds purchases and security RPs + Other borrowings

$$\frac{\text{Average total large time deposits (over \$100,000) + Foreign-office deposits + Federal funds purchases and security RPs + Other borrowings}}{\text{Average balances due from depository institutions + Federal funds sold and RPs + Trading account and investment securities one year or less to maturity}} \times 100$$

Brokered funds ratio (%) =

$$\frac{\text{Deposits placed with the bank by security brokers}}{\text{Total deposits}} \times 100$$

Credit capacity ratio (%) =

$$\frac{\text{Average total loans and leases}}{\text{Average total assets}} \times 100$$

Security valuation ratio (%) =

$$\frac{\text{Market value of all investment securities held}}{\text{Book value of all investment securities held}} \times 100$$

Total capitalization ratio (%) =

$$\frac{\text{Total equity capital}}{\text{Average total assets}} \times 100$$

Primary capital ratio (%) =

$$\frac{\text{Primary capital}}{\text{Average total assets}} \times 100$$

Management would want to detect adverse trends as quickly as possible in *any* of the above cost, return, and risk ratios (when compared with other banks of comparable size and market location) to formulate a strategic plan and to move quickly to implement that plan.

The Bank as an Economic Unit: Organizing and Managing Employees and Other Scarce Real Resources

There is another way to view a bank with its challenges and problems today—from the economist's perspective as a manager and organizer of real (as opposed to financial) resources. From an economist's viewpoint a bank is really no different from any other business firm producing several different product lines. It must attract productive factors—skilled management and employees, land and other natural resources, and plant and equipment (capital goods)—by paying competitive salaries and wage rates and competitive rates of return to owners of capital and other resources. Those productive factors must be combined under the roof of one organization, producing an identifiable package of services that the public will buy. Thus the bank as a firm brings *organization* to the financial-services production process, combining productive factors and technology in a mix effective and efficient enough to generate salable output at a competitive price.

EXHIBIT 2   The Bank as an Economic Unit—Organizing and Directing Real
Resources in the Production of Financial Services

> Hiring factors of production—
> land or natural resources,
> employee time and skill, and
> capital goods—through
> written and unwritten
> contracts

Factor inputs ↓	Factor payments ↑

> The banking organization,
> providing a framework for the
> application of technology in
> order to combine productive
> factors and generate the
> desired level of bank output

Financial services ↓	Sales revenue ↑

> Pricing and distributing
> financial services—selecting
> target markets, choosing
> pricing schedules, delivering
> services efficiently, and
> collecting revenues

The amount of output of financial services that can be produced will be defined by each bank's *production function:*

$$\text{Output of banking services} = f[\overbrace{\text{land, employee time and managerial skills, and capital goods}}^{\text{Banking inputs}}]$$

The inputs of employee time and management skill, land (natural resources), and capital equipment are transformed into bank outputs by applying any technology currently available to management and capable of cost-efficient production.

The behavior of a bank's service output *over time* is a critical factor to be reviewed by management. From an economic and effective management perspective, the bank's officers and policymakers must distinguish between *short-run* and *long-run* time periods in their decision making.

Bank Production in the Short Run.   In the *short run* some of the inputs into the bank's service production process are *fixed* in amount (for example, the number of branch offices, the capacity of the bank's mainframe computer, and so on) while other inputs are *variable*—they can be changed in amount with little advance notice or planning (for example, the size of the clerical staff). Once a bank's service output reaches the capacity of its fixed inputs in the short run, there is little or nothing that management can do to further increase the bank's output of loans, deposits, and other services. Fixed resources have simply been stretched to their limit and the application of additional variable inputs (such as employee time and managerial talent) will *not* increase output.

In the short run, then, each bank is limited by its currently available resources. As the economist sees it, the bank is subject to the *law of diminishing returns* in the short-run period. As variable inputs of employee time and natural resources are added to the bank's fixed resources (typically its land and capital equipment), the bank's total output of services will increase at an increasing rate at first until the *optimum* combination of all inputs is reached. However, if service output is pressed beyond the optimum production point, output will grow at a decreasing rate, meaning that diminishing returns from employee and managerial effort and other resources have set in. Eventually, if more personnel and other resources continue to be crowded onto the bank's existing fixed assets, its total output of services will actually fall.

To illustrate these points we might imagine a bank operating with 120 full-time employees. This institution finds that it can process about 12,000 loan and deposit accounts (total service output) or about 100 accounts per employee (average service output). Adding employees, of course, will increase the bank's capacity to attract and process more accounts, thereby accommodating more customers. Suppose the bank's management decides to double its staff size, from 120 to 240 employees and managers. If the bank after this strategic move still remains in the stage economists calls *increasing returns*, its service output may *more* than double, perhaps climbing to 27,000 or 28,000 loan and deposit accounts. The *average* number of accounts handled by each employee will rise as well because total service output is growing faster than the bank's staff. The increase in total output—marginal output—from doubling employment from 120 to 240 people will be substantial in this stage of increasing returns, rising by perhaps 15,000 or 16,000 accounts serviced.

Now suppose that management, impressed by these early "victories" in getting greater marginal gains in service output than its additions to staff, decides to push its luck. It adds still more employees and management talent to its staff; perhaps it balloons up to a staff of 550 or 650 full-time employees. The economist reminds us that, at some service output level in the short run, the bank will enter the stage of *diminishing returns*. In this case the addition of more management and staff will *not* yield greater gains in *marginal* output of loans and deposits (though total bank output may increase for a time). Indeed, marginal service output from adding more people to the payroll will begin to fall as employee productivity decreases due to overcrowding of the bank's fixed facilities. Eventually declining marginal service output pulls average output per employee down as well. This bank has passed the point of optimal efficiency. And should it continue to press onward, adding still more personnel to perhaps 800 or 850 full-time management and staff, even the total number of accounts serviced—its total output will decline as well. The bank will have reached the economist's stage of *negative returns* and face a serious shortfall in employee productivity.

We must hasten to add that determining the stages of increasing, diminishing, and negative returns for any particular bank is no easy task. In this case there is no substitute for management experience and careful monitoring of the behavior of bank service output as the bank's staff expands and contracts. Moreover, these output states will be heavily influenced by the particular services each bank offers. For example, banks that tend to emphasize retail or consumer-oriented services will require a larger staff per customer account to efficiently service their credit and deposit accounts than a bank emphasizing wholesale or business-oriented services.

Knowledge of the behavior of the bank's output as the size of its management and staff (and of other inputs) is varied can be highly useful, but it becomes even more valuable if we can apply some dollar amounts (prices and costs) to the output figures. If management knows the size of its annual fixed costs, the average costs of hiring each employee, and can estimate the average net revenue from the sale of each loan and deposit account, it will be able to derive a rough picture of how the bank's revenues and costs will vary with the level of its service output. And for each bank there will emerge at least two critical levels of service output:

1. The *break-even output* level at which total operating costs and total operating revenues are equal.
2. The *maximum profitability output* level.

Maximum profitability for an individual bank must occur at the point at which marginal revenue from the *last* financial-service unit sold equals the marginal cost of producing that *last* service unit. This point may be found by determining the bank output level at which the positive dollar gap between total operating revenues and total operating costs is the greatest. In the short run the bank would want to push its service output to the marginal-revenue-equal-to-marginal-cost point in order to maximize its profitability, but *no further.* Trying to expand beyond that point in the short run, given the bank's fixed resources, will actually *reduce* its profitability.

This analysis clearly emphasizes the importance of controlling bank costs and of controlling growth in the bank's scale of operations. In the short run management must ask and answer the critical question: *how many accounts can the bank accept if costs are to be held sufficiently in check to achieve the maximum possible profit?* Adding too many employees to existing facilities in the short run damages productivity and may ultimately drive some customers away due to inefficiency and poor service.

Bank Production in the Long Run.   Clearly, in the short run, management's flexibility is limited by certain fixed resources. In the *long run*, however, there are *no* fixed resources. *Every* resource used by the bank to produce its services can be expanded or reduced in amount, including the bank's buildings and equipment, ATM locations, and computer facilities. Thus management has far greater flexibility in the long run. It has the freedom (and the associated risk) to change any or all of the following key elements:

1. The *size* (scale) of bank operations—how many service units will be produced each year, month, and so on, and how many and what type of employees will be added? Is there an optimum size for the bank that will keep its costs low and competitive, and contribute to maximum employee productivity?
2. The *technology* that will be used to produce those services—what techniques (electronic and otherwise) for combining staff and management, capital equipment, and natural resources will be employed in order to generate the amount of service units desired?

3. The *organizational form* of the bank—should the bank be a unit or branch organization, affiliated with a holding company or independent, a conglomerate with the widest range of financial services or a narrowly focused company with only a few service specialities?

The first of these elements—the size of bank operations—is a particularly critical issue for management. Does management want to control a larger banking organization or a smaller one? Many bank managers would scoff at such a question. After all, isn't a larger banking organization always to be preferred to a smaller one? The answer to that question depends heavily on the particular services the bank plans to offer and the technology it will use to produce and deliver those services.

For some mixes of services and banking technologies, the bank will experience *increasing returns to scale* (that is, positive scale economies). In this case *service output will grow faster in percentage terms than the rate of growth of inputs of personnel and other productive resources.* If the prices of bank services and the cost of inputs are fixed and the spread between them is positive, the bank's profitability will increase as its service output grows because total operating revenues will increase faster than total operating costs. Clearly, in the case of increasing returns to scale, it pays to grow.

EXHIBIT 3   The Key Management Issues that All Banks Face and All Must Solve

Funds-mix issues: Where can loanable funds be raised at the *lowest* possible cost and at risk levels acceptable to management and the stockholders?

Scale issues: How large a banking organization (in terms of total resources employed and total service output) do we need?

Organizational issues: What type of banking organization (branch or unit bank, one-bank or multibank holding company, widely diversified conglomerate or narrowly focused financial service firm, and so on) do we want?

Technological issues: What methods should be used to produce and distribute banking services as efficiently as possible?

Funds-use issues: Is the bank making optimal use of its funds in terms of the *highest* possible returns at a level of risk acceptable to management and the stockholders?

Pricing issues: How much should the factors of production be paid and how should the services we offer be priced to generate adequate demand and revenue growth?

Marketing issues: How can the financial-service needs of our customers be identified and changes in those service needs detected and responded to? What processes exist within the bank to develop and test new services?

Resource issues: What combination of employees and managerial talent, natural resources, and capital goods will be needed to achieve the size (scale) desired, given the technology and organization of the bank?

Are there any bank services that display increasing returns to scale? Not many, and the behavior of costs is sensitive to local and regional market conditions and state regulations. There is some evidence, however, that under favorable conditions the production of demand deposits and real estate loans, investments in securities, and the use of cash-dispensing machines are subject to increasing returns to scale over a modest range of output levels. However, banking as a whole is *not* an increasing-returns-to-scale industry over a broad range of output. If it were, there would be very few banks to be found anywhere.

Suppose, however, that management chooses a mix of banking services and a technology for which there are *decreasing returns to scale* (that is, negative scale economies or diseconomies). Then service output will grow more slowly in percentage terms than inputs of employees, natural resources, and capital as the bank's output grows. With fixed prices and costs, the bank's profitability will decline as its output grows because total operating revenues will grow more slowly than total operating costs. Beyond a certain critical level of output, many banking services display decreasing returns to scale. This appears to be especially true of business development activities and safe-deposit services. Beyond a critical level of output, it usually does not pay to grow.

Finally, there is a middle ground here. Given the state of current banking technology and the services the bank wishes to offer, the growth of bank output and inputs may be closely correlated with each other. Bank output and resource inputs will expand at the same pace. In this case the bank experiences *constant returns to scale*. Growth in service output will have *neutral* effects on bank profitability—all other factors held constant. Some bank services (such as time and savings accounts) appear to come very close to the case of constant returns to scale.

STRATEGIES FOR INCREASING PROFITABILITY IN THE SHORT RUN AND THE LONG RUN

No matter how we view the banking firm—as a financial intermediary selling funds-raising and funds-using services or as an economic unit managing employees and other scarce real resources—the individual bank's primary goal must be to achieve a competitive rate of return on its capital. In order to retain its deposits and owners' capital and attract nondeposit borrowings, the bank must aim toward a profit level sufficient to keep both its creditors and its stockholders sufficiently satisfied with their returns from committed funds so that the bank has enough debt and equity capital to operate efficiently.

How can the bank achieve and maintain *competitive profitability?* Bankers know there are no easy answers to that question and indeed with deregulation and rapidly changing technology today, the answers to that key question seem to be harder to find. Fortunately, the two models of the banking firm discussed earlier point us in the direction we need to look to find helpful guidelines in achieving and maintaining competitive profitability. Those models of the banking firm point us toward such factors as: (1) the size of banking organization (to take advantage of any economies of scale), (2) the mix of funds sources, (3) the mix of funds uses, (4) service pricing, (5) technology, (6) expense control, and (7) organizational type.

Size of Banking Organization

Are there significant economies of scale in banking today? Does it pay for *all* banks to grow in size (output) if their goal is to reduce operating costs as much as possible?

While research in this field is limited and the methods still crude, we have evidence that it does *not* pay in terms of conventional measures of cost and return for *all* banks to grow in size. In recent years the most profitable banks in the nation have generally been of moderate size. For example, a recent study by Wall (1986) finds that the banks with the *highest* returns on assets (ROA) in 1984 and 1985 were those with consolidated assets of $100 million to $500 million, closely followed by banks in the $50 to $100 million asset-size range. The *least* profitable banks in terms of ROA were those with total assets of $0 to $25 million. Next to last place was reported by $1 billion-plus institutions though their average ROA was again half as large, on average, as the smallest banks in the industry.

While we are not sure that the minimum-cost point for banks today also lies in the $100 to $500 million asset-size range, other evidence suggests that the low-cost point probably lies close to that asset-size category. Examples include a recent study by Benston, Hanweck, and Murphy (1982), which finds the low-cost point for banks operating in unit and branching states in or near the $50 to $75 million deposit-size range. Branch offices appeared to reach minimum cost in the $10 to $25 million deposit-size range. These authors conclude that smaller banks today are "not at an operational disadvantage" relative to larger banking institutions and that mergers are not likely to yield cost savings in bank operations (p. 21).

Yet the profitability-size relationship in banking may be changing. For example, Wall's (1986) study of bank profits found that in 1985 only the largest banks in the nation ($1 billion and over in total assets) experienced improvements in their return on assets (ROA) and return on equity capital (ROE). In contrast, the smallest banks with assets below $25 million experienced a decline in both ROA and ROE, which left them with about one-third the profit levels they had reached earlier in the decade. One reason was continuing pressures on key industries in many local communities, especially agriculture and energy. Another factor has been the potent impact of deregulation on bank interest expenses on deposits, especially for smaller banks holding substantial proportions of savings and checkable deposits. As smaller institutions have been forced to pay market-sensitive interest rates even on their core deposits, the historic funding-rate gap between large and small banks, which in the past heavily favored the smallest institutions, has narrowed significantly. Moreover, with automation becoming increasingly important, the optimal size bank in the future may of necessity be far larger than the average-size bank today.

Mix of Funds Sources

Research evidence suggests the top-performing banks tend to have higher ratios of core deposits (that is, relatively small denomination checkable and savings accounts), lower ratios of large CDs and money-market borrowings relative to their total liabilities, and lower ratios of time deposits to total time and savings deposits than other banks (Rose 1977). The higher the ratio of "hot money" to total assets, the greater the chances of lower profitability (Haslem, Bedingfield, and Stagliano 1985). However, the larger the bank, the less important (in general) is funding mix in separating profitable from unprofitable banks.

Mix of Funds Uses

The top-performing banks in recent years have tended to emphasize certain kinds of loans and security investments in their asset portfolios. Generally those banks with greater proportions of municipal notes and bonds and installment credit have outperformed the average bank in profitability by a significant margin, while low proportions of bank assets invested in premises and real estate seem to be favorable to bank profits. However, the larger the bank, the less important is the portfolio mix factor in shaping relative profit performance.

High-profit banks have tended to have *smaller* proportions of their total assets devoted to loans and *more* to security investments (especially municipals and U.S. government securities). These security investments have held two important advantages over loans in recent years: (1) their default rate has been extremely low to nonexistent so that actual and expected returns have coincided in many instances, and (2) emphasizing security purchases over loans tends to reduce bank operating costs (Wall 1985).

Service Pricing

In an era of deregulation and market-determined deposit and loan rates, pricing techniques have become critical to successful bank performance. Banks must pass more of their costs of service production and delivery on to the customer who uses those services. Employing pricing schedules that encourage customers to hold higher deposit balances and minimize account activity benefits the bank's profit performance from two directions: (1) operating costs are reduced, and (2) a greater volume of loanable funds flows through to the credit side of the bank where it can be profitably invested. Full-cost pricing of noncredit and nondeposit services is also important because the size of fee income is a key factor today in differentiating deposit-type institutions with above-average profitability from those with below-average profitability.

Technology

One of the great debates in banking today is whether the changing technology of information and automation has fundamentally altered the optimal (low-cost) production point and profit potential for various sizes and types of banks. Because ATMs, for example, require a relatively high volume of transactions to be profitable, larger banks would appear to have a significant advantage as automation takes over a larger and larger proportion of bank service output and delivery.

Could it be true that smaller banks in the future will literally be squeezed out of the industry by automation because they cannot afford to take advantage of new technology? The argument sounds persuasive, but thus far at least the evidence doesn't provide much support for it.

For one thing, the cost of automated equipment has experienced a long-term decline due to improvements in circuitry, in production methods, and in competition. Moreover, smaller banks with limited capital have found new ways to finance technological updating, such as through networking agreements, group purchases, bankers' bank organizations, and loans from correspondents. And many customers still seem to prefer the *personal* approach to banking, suggesting a continuing significant role for human as well as machine service delivery. Finally, a number of studies of the behavior of automated service production costs find scant evidence of substantial scale economies with electronics-oriented mechanisms such as transfers of funds by wire and paper-check processing (Humphrey 1982).

Expense Control

High-profit banks display significantly better control over their operating and interest expenses than average and low-profit banks (Wall, 1985). In fact, the top-performing banks differ more from the "also rans" in expense control than they do in operating revenues, suggesting that putting a lid on operating costs accomplishes far more in terms of profit performance than trying to achieve superior profitability by focusing principally on revenues.

Organizational Type

There is little convincing evidence that the way a bank is organized—whether a large branching system, holding company, financial conglomerate, or unit bank—significantly affects its profitability, productivity, or efficiency. However, we have learned through numerous research studies that branch banking is an expensive way for a bank to grow, adding significantly to operating costs each time a new full-service branch office is added (Nelson 1985). And there is evidence

---

EXHIBIT 4   Future Improvements in Bank Performance Will Depend on Multiple Factors

More complete and aggressive use of automated processing techniques and electronic circuitry for producing and delivering financial services, including significant economic incentives to encourage customer use of automated facilities.

Formalized market-research programs that continually monitor changing customer needs and assess the appropriateness of the bank's service menu.

Continuing adult education programs for current employees to upgrade and broaden their skills and more effectively cross-sell services along with training programs for new employees that include awareness of the bank's plan and long-range goals.

Performance-oriented employee and officer reward systems that are also related to the bank's planning goals and objectives.

Formalized cash and capital budgeting systems, profit-planning and strategic-planning programs that are more closely linked to operations and influence both short-range and long-range management decisions.

Continuing assessment of employee compensation programs, wage and salary schedules to promote retention of the most productive employees and to attract well-qualified professionals in an increasingly technical and high-performance environment.

Improved programs and methods for assessing and controlling bank risk exposure in all its forms (credit, interest-rate, liquidity, currency, solvency, and so on) along with cooperative efforts with other bankers and banking organizations to promote legislation and regulatory change that allows greater freedom of private decision making for both customers and the banks that serve them.

---

that independent banks are on average at least as profitable as comparable-size holding-company affiliated banks and often more so (Rose and Scott 1984). Finally, retail-oriented banks typically outperform wholesale-oriented banks and emphasize personal service and accessibility in their dealings with customers (Holt and Walewski 1985).

Other Profitability Factors

In addition to the foregoing factors it now seems clear that several other factors contribute to superior bank profit performance. These include:

a. *Employee productivity*—High-profit banks usually report higher ratios of net income, assets, and revenues than low-profit banks, and pay their employees correspondingly higher salaries and other bonus incentives as well. Improving bank employee productivity in the future will require better analysis and knowledge of bank costs and more effective use of both long- and short-range planning. Productivity gains will also require openness to change, more aggressive use of automation, continuing market research, performance-oriented management, career counseling, and improved training programs (Metzger 1982–83).

b. *Tax management efficiency*—Control over tax exposure and effective management of taxable and nontaxable earnings is usually superior among high-profit banks. This factor is likely to be even more important in the future due to the increase in bank tax exposure brought about by the 1986 Tax Reform Law.

c. *Growth management*—Top-earning banks generally grow faster than banks with average earnings; however, they carefully manage their growth to hold down potential increases in operating expenses. As we might expect, the faster a market area grows, the more profitable banks in that market tend to be. And market share has been shown in several recent studies to be *positively* related to bank profitability though there is conflicting evidence here with some authorities. For example, Schuster (1984) finds no significant correlation between profitability and market share among banks operating in London, New York, Switzerland, and West Germany.

d. *Interest-rate risk exposure*—Top-earning banks make effective use of interest-rate hedging tools such as GAP Management, duration analysis, financial futures, and options. If used skillfully, these tools can make two important contributions to bank profitability: (1) countering the damage to operating margins from rising deposit interest costs, and (2) offsetting losses on securities and loans due to adverse changes in market interest rates.

Larger banks' *net interest margins* are often the key factor in determining annual profitability and typically are more sensitive to interest-rate changes than the net margins of smaller banks (though some authorities, such as Hanweck and Kilcollin, 1984, disagree). However, small banks appear to be especially vulnerable to protracted downturns in interest rates. Overall, the *margin* between interest rates on assets and interest rates on liabilities is far more important than the *direction* of interest-rate changes in determining what happens to bank profits (Flannery 1982a).

SUMMARY

All banks today, regardless of their location or size, must be operated aggressively if they are to survive and grow. At the top of their list of goals and objectives must be the pursuit of profitability levels that are competitive enough to retain existing capital and attract new capital funds for financial strength and to provide a base for future growth. But competitive returns today require that all banks learn how to manage and control risk in all its forms and how to control their resource costs.

If banking risk and resource costs are to be controlled, management will need more effective *tools* for analyzing banking problems and strategies. The economist's models of the banking firm can contribute significantly to understanding what management tools are needed and how they can be used. This chapter looks at the operations and activities of a bank from two prominent viewpoints used by economists: (1) the *financial intermediary model*, and (2) the *economic unit model*.

Banks viewed as *financial intermediaries* are analyzed simply as firms selling funds-raising and funds-using services in an efficient financial marketplace. Bank *output*, in this view, consists of credit supplied to businesses, consumers, and governments, while bank *inputs* consist of deposits, money market borrowings, and equity capital. From this perspective management's principal tasks are: (1) to raise funds at the *lowest* possible funding costs at an acceptable level of funding risk, and (2) to make an optimal use of the funds raised in order to achieve the *highest* possible returns at a level of risk acceptable to management and the stockholders. Several indicators of how effectively bank management is pursuing these essential tasks are presented in this chapter.

Banks viewed as *economic units* are really managers and users of real resources—land and other natural resources, labor time, management skill, and plant and equipment (capital goods) which they must hire at competitive wages and rates of return. The amount of banking services produced from each institution is a function of the quantities of land, labor, capital, and other inputs employed by each bank and the technological methods of service production and delivery it employs.

The maximum-potential output and the most-profitable output of services banks can produce are affected by *time*. In the *short run* some bank inputs are fixed, and diminishing returns will set in beyond the point of maximum efficiency. For maximum profitability in the short run, the individual bank should press its production of services to the point at which the revenue generated by the last unit sold equals the additional cost of producing one more service unit. In the *long run*, on the other hand, *all* bank inputs may be increased or decreased in amount and management has greater flexibility. It must, however, make a number of critical decisions in the long run concerning: (1) the size or scale of bank operations, (2) the technology available to produce services, and (3) the prices to be posted for both inputs employed and services offered to the public.

These economic models of the banking firm emphasize the important factors that determine whether any particular bank is profitable, including the size of the banking organization, the mix of funds sources and uses, service pricing, technological methods adopted, and organizational type. Research evidence suggests that the most efficient banks in terms of production costs are medium-sized institutions, perhaps in the $50 or $100 to $500 million asset-size range with larger size banks closing the profit-margin gap on smaller-size banks in recent years. The most profitable banks in recent years tend to hold higher ratios of core deposits, depend less heavily on the money market to supplement deposits, save on operating costs with above-average proportions of assets in securities as opposed to loans, make greater use of fee income, and avoid excessive use of full-service branching as a vehicle to reach their customers. Top-performing banks also have exceptional employee productivity, grow faster than average, and make effective use of hedging techniques to minimize their interest-rate risk exposure. Thus superior performance in banking today depends on a number of crucial long-run and short-run decisions that shape bank output levels, risk exposure, and the efficiency with which each institution responds to the changing needs of its customers.

SELECTED REFERENCES

Benston, George J.; Gerald A. Hanweck; and David B. Humphrey. "Operating Costs in Commercial Banking." *Economic Review,* Federal Reserve Bank of Atlanta, November 1982, pp. 6–21.

Bryan, William R. *The Determinants of Bank Profits.* Research paper prepared for the Department of Research and Planning, American Bankers Association, Washington, D.C., 1972.

Cole, David W. "Return on Equity Model for Banks." *The Bankers Magazine* 155, no. 3 (Summer 1972).

G. Davis, Richard. "The Recent Performance of the Commerical Banking Industry." *Quarterly Review,* Federal Reserve Bank of New York, Summer 1986, pp. 1–11.

Flannery, Mark J. "Market Interest and Commercial Bank Profitability: An Empirical Investigation." *Research Papers,* Federal Reserve Bank of Philadelphia, no. 53, 1982a.

————. "Retail Bank Deposits as Quasi-Fixed Factors of Production." *American Economic Review,* June 1982b, pp. 527–536.

Fraser, Donald R. "The Determinants of Bank Profits: An Analysis of Extremes." *Financial Review,* 1976, pp. 69–87.

Hanweck, Gerald A., and Thomas Eric Kilcollin. "Bank Profitability and Interest Rate Risk." *Journal of Economics and Business* 36 (1984), pp. 77–84.

Haslem, John A.; James P. Bedingfield; and A. J. Stagliano. "An Analysis of Liquidity Measures and Relative Bank Profitability." *Akron Business and Economic Review,* Winter 1985, pp. 38–43.

Holt, Robert N., and Karl S. Walewski. "Why do Some Banks Outperform Others?" *Magazine of Bank Administration,* April 1985, pp. 34, 36, 38, and 40.

Humphrey, David B. *Cost, Scale Economies, Competition, and Product Mix in the U.S. Payments Mechanism.* Staff Study No. 115, Board of Governors of the Federal Reserve System, April 1982.

Metzger, Robert O. "Banking in the 1980s: Productivity Improvement on an Exponential Curve." *National Productivity Review,* Winter 1982–83, pp. 22–28.

Nelson, Richard W. "Branching, Scale Economies, and Banking Costs." *Journal of Banking and Finance* 9, pp. 177–91.

Olson, Ronald L., and Donald G. Simonson. "Goal Management and Market Rate Sensitivity in Banks." *Journal of Bank Research,* Spring 1981, pp. 53–58.

Rhoades, Stephen A. *Structure-Performance Studies in Banking: An Updated Summary and Evaluation.* Staff Study No. 119, Board of Governors of the Federal Reserve System, Washington, D.C., 1982.

Rose, Peter S. "What Makes a Bank Profitable?" *Canadian Banker,* January–February 1977, pp. 55–58.

Rose, Peter S., and William L. Scott. "Heterogeneity in the Bank Holding Company Sector." *Journal of Economics and Business,* Winter 1984.

Schuster, Leo. "Profitability and Market Share of Banks." *Journal of Bank Research,* Spring 1984, pp. 56–61.

Wall, Larry D. "Largest Banks Lead in Profits." *Insight,* Federal Reserve Bank of Atlanta 6, no. 12 (September 15, 1986), pp. 1, 2, and 4.

————. "Why Are Some Banks More Profitable Than Others?" *Journal of Bank Research,* Winter 1985, pp. 240–56.

Wallich, Henry C. "Bank Profits and Inflation." *Economic Review,* Federal Reserve Bank of Richmond, May–June 1980.

CHAPTER SIXTEEN

Effective People Management for the 1980s and Beyond

Irving Margol

Executive Vice President
Security Pacific National Bank

Timothy K. Scanlan

Vice President
Security Pacific National Bank

Sharli Colladay

Intern
Security Pacific National Bank

Human resource departments of the past took reactionary responses to environmental situations because the traditional worker/manager relationship was adversarial. Now and in the future, the human resource function will focus on effectiveness and productivity (as well as long-term profitability) as opposed to control and procedures. The field has matured to include not only selection, compensation, training, employee relations, and the like, but strategic planning, vulnerability analysis, succession ladders, and support systems integration (hiring, paying, and training). This change has caused convenience and flexibility for customers. However, geographic location and wide distribution are no longer sufficient for convenience. Convenience is now measured in new terms: speed, accessibility, acceptability (lifestyle compatibility), and high-quality, flexible service. The information society we are a part of has caused a shift from financial capital to human capital, which will be the key strategic resource in the future. According to *Megatrends* (John Naisbitt 1982), people are now considered the competitive edge on the path to profits. Some of Naisbitt's forces for change which will transform our lives include:

1. Industrialized society to an information society.
2. Forced technology to high tech/high touch.
3. National economy to world economy.
4. Short term to long term.
5. Centralization to decentralization.
6. Institutional help to self help.
7. Representative democracy to a participatory democracy.
8. Hierarchies to networking.
9. North to South.
10. Either/or to multiple option.

These basic trends can also cause other related changes to occur. For example, the decline in middle management seen recently can be attributed to (2) the rise in high technology as well as (7) increased participation among employees.

Human resource issues in the future will be thought of in more general, more global terms, with an increased emphasis on long-term considerations. Human resource executives will function not as support staff but participants in the making of business decisions. The workplace of the future will be one with flexible schedules, decentralization of authority, cafeteria-style benefits, changed corporate culture to a more participatory one, recognition of merit, and a spirit of equality among employees. There is a need for an increased link between day-to-day business decisions and strategic planning. Other concerns for the future include control of benefit costs, especially health care costs, and productivity.

FIGURE 1 The Human Resource Planning Process

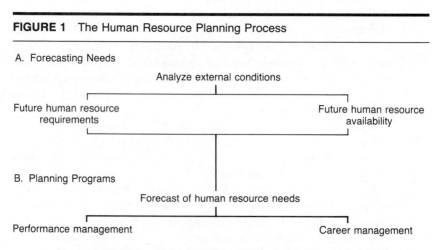

A. Forecasting Needs

Analyze external conditions

Future human resource requirements

Future human resource availability

B. Planning Programs

Forecast of human resource needs

Performance management

Career management

SOURCE: James W. Walker, *Human Resources Planning* (New York: McGraw-Hill, 1980).

The past 10 years have been characterized by change. Changes in demographics, in social attitudes, in lifestyles, in technology—all have had an impact on the human resource function. Because of this changing environment, workers must be managed differently in a business transformed by deregulation. Banks are people serving people; therefore they should be in close touch with this change happening among employees and customers. In the future banks will have to take greater care to ensure the hiring and development of the right type of people to succeed in this changing environment.

DEMOGRAPHIC CHANGES

One factor affecting this change is demographics. In the future, there will be an enormous change in the work force. The youth of the 1960s and 70s is becoming the mainstream of adult society in the 1980s and 90s. There will also be increasing opportunities for women and minorities. Because of the increase in career and education opportunities for women, more are staying single. For example, 22 percent of college-educated white women born in the 1950s are likely to stay single as compared to 9 percent in the previous generation. An increase in the median age, from 28 in 1970, to 30 in 1980, to 35 by 2000 will result from falling fertility. Because of this, we are becoming an aging population, a middle-aged society. By 1990 we will see a decline in the number of 18 to 24-year-olds entering the labor force, a surplus of white-collar professionals age 25 to 44, and a large number of over-55-year-olds. The perception of the middle aged is changing also from comfortable, settled, and conformist to dynamic, prosperous, and diverse (see Figure 2).

In the future we may be faced with a labor shortage as the new economy creates millions of jobs and the number of people entering the work force declines dramatically. Between the years 2010 and 2030, the baby boomers will reach retirement age. Today the percentage of the population over age 65 is 11 percent—it will be 21

FIGURE 2 Projection of the Percent Distribution of the Total Population by Age (1982, 2000, and 2030)

Age	1982	2000	2030
0–17	27.0%	25.1%	21.6%
18–39	36.9	30.9	27.4
40–64	24.5	30.9	29.9
65+	11.6	13.1	21.1

SOURCE: U.S. Bureau of the Census, Current Population Reports, Series P-25, No. 922 (October 1982), and unpublished data.

percent in 2030. Retirement will be looked at in new ways. Firms may be forced to encourage delayed retirement, which is the antithesis of the early retirement trend seen in America since the end of World War II. Retiring early has caused a gradual decline in the number of men working, while the number of women working is increasing rapidly. Delayed retirement will alleviate future pressure on Social Security at a time when fewer younger workers will be supporting a larger retired population. In the future retired people may work in some form of flexible employment.

The new white-collar workers are better educated and have higher job expectations than their predecessors. This widespread expectation that work should be fulfilling and fun is strong among baby boomers and a natural outgrowth of an affluent society.

Many women and men have higher education levels than did their counterparts of decades ago. The work force in fact is becoming overeducated; workers are overqualified for their positions because more of them are getting advanced degrees. This overeducation, combined with higher expectations for meaningful work, is presenting organizations with a serious human resource problem. Another change to consider is the shift in the work force from blue collar to white collar, which calls for recruitment strategies more closely tied to the collegiate educational system. These demographic changes put pressure on the effective use of the human resource function.

SOCIAL CHANGES

Social changes will go along with the demographic factor. Two-income households have proliferated, and the number will grow in the future. The increase in divorce will cause more single-parent families. Usually the woman retains custody of the children and being the sole support of the children, most likely gets a job if she doesn't have one already.

As costs of interviewing, recruiting, relocating, training, and compensation increase, managers are compelled to do a better job of human resource planning. Another increasing cost to be accounted for in the future is the rising salaries of MBAs entering the work force. Also a change in the inflation rate or the unemployment rate could affect labor force participation of married women and the retirement decisions of those 55 years old and over.

LEGISLATION AND REGULATION

Changes in legislation and regulation have also greatly affected the human resource function. Union membership has dropped because of the increasing amounts of white-collar and female workers, and will

FIGURE 3 Percentage of Nonfarm Work Force Organized in the United States

Percentage

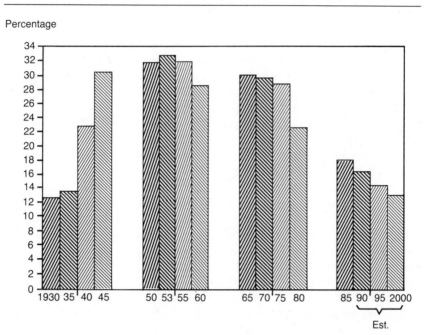

Est.

most likely continue to do so (see Figure 3). Unions are making little headway in organizing such growth industries as financial services and high technology, but these are unions' number 1 target for the future. This decline in union membership is stimulating an employee rights movement in the courts and state legislatures; instead of unions, laws and court rulings will protect workers. The increased likelihood of litigation and the potential for large damage awards have forced employers to be especially cautious about decisions to dismiss or demote employees. An overall deeper government involvement is expected in the work place, and proliferation of new laws will be seen (such as preventing firing except for just cause, preventing forced retirement at a certain age, and protecting employee privacy). Other concerns have been with plant closure laws and child care as well as implied contractual terms. In many cases, it has been necessary for the employer to review all forms of communication (especially the policy handbook) and modify any statement that might imply unintended rights or obligations.

There is more regulatory control, especially in the areas of health, safety, and affirmative action. The push for equal opportunity employment and affirmative action has lead to workshops for women and minorities, adjustments in pay, and more concern with the promotion of women and minorities.

TECHNOLOGICAL CHANGES

During the past 10 years, information technology has expanded tremendously. There is an emphasis on information, communications, and knowledge industries as well as service, professional, and technical or managerial fields. Banking is a knowledge-intensive, human resource based service industry dependent on information, communications, and technology.

Technology is a tool used to enhance the capacity and possibilities of humans. The human factor is made more important by technology. From the narrow perspective of bank productivity, the purpose of technology is to reduce or eliminate unwanted and unnecessary human contact. It is important to keep track of technological developments, not so much for capabilities as for implications—especially implications that affect or change societal interaction and communication, economic markets, and the organization itself.

The advent of the personal computer and the miniaturization of hardware has caused the ability to collect, analyze, and produce information of all sorts to expand exponentially. Major technological change in the use of computers and communications has increased the productivity of financial services manyfold. Customers' demands for more and new services continue to increase employment. By reducing unwanted and unnecessary human contact, technology facilitates an expansion of the variety of quality services offered by the financial industry. Therefore more customer-contact workers will be needed in these necessary areas. Future technological changes will pose challenges for futher adaptation. New opportunities in technology mean new product knowledge training. Unless we keep up with technological changes, workers will be left behind.

INTERNATIONAL COMPETITION

Other factors of change in the future are international economic and political affairs. There will be intense competition in the future on an international scale as well as the domestic level, which already has created enormous pressure for companies to change. This greater degree of competition within the United States and worldwide has caused corporations to reorganize and realign industry structures to become more effective in the world market. The economic development by Third World nations could drain off high-talent manpower from this country's labor pool. Many developing countries have substantial raw materials and offer potentially large, mostly untapped markets. They also have a lower wage rate, and because of this they can attract industries to their countries. These countries have become increasingly sophisticated competitors for the United States.

NEW ATTITUDES AND VALUES

A significant change affecting the human resource function in the future is the values system change. Values, attitudes, and lifestyles are more individually oriented. Individuals are more optimistic, risk taking, and self-determined. As a result, we will see more cohabitation, later marriages, fewer children, and smaller families. These values and attitudes are inner directed (not as influenced by society's traditional standards but one's own inner standards) and post materialistic (material things are not enough without fulfilling human relationships).

Increased participation by women has caused a change in management because of dual careers. Women are working not only to fulfill career aspirations and for self-fulfillment, but also because of economic conditions and a desire to increase family income.

Changing attitudes about relocations and transfers are creating new patterns of worker mobility. In the past it was not uncommon to be transferred, and it was readily accepted. Today, with the two-career family, a transfer may mean uprooting not one but two careers. There are also high housing costs with which to contend. Therefore job hopping is less common today than in the past. Because of this reluctance to transfer, there is an increasing career rigidity among dual-career-family employees. This reluctance may cause career path blockages, and slow down productivity for the employer. We may see special inducements given by the employer for the employee to relocate.

However, we are also seeing a conflict in the desires to increase income. Changes in individual work values and career attitudes create strong pressure on the work ethic and on management efforts to improve productivity and work satisfaction. People are more interested in "life values" and activities rather than income and opportunities. Nonwork activities are beginning to increase in importance. Therefore, it is important for the manager to employ a system of job enrichment to keep workers on the job.

There are social and economic problems related to the commitment gap of today's worker—and this lack of productivity must be addressed. Job security is not the motivator it was in the past; money is not the only incentive; fear of dismissal is not as great a threat as it once was. Today's worker still wants pay, benefits, and job security—but in addition, he is interested in participating in the destiny of the company, the public responsibility of the firm, quality of management,

---

FIGURE 4 What Workers Want from Their Jobs

Q. If you had to choose, which two or three of these are most important to you on the job?

A. A good salary   63%

   Job security   53

   Appreciation for a job well done   40

   A chance to use your mind and abilities   39

   Medical and other benefits   36

   Being able to retire early with a good pension   20

   A clean, quiet, comfortable place to work   19

Note: Survey of 967 employed adults conducted May 30–June 2, 1985. Overall results should be accurate to within 4 percentage points either way.
SOURCE: *Business Week,* July 8, 1985.

and job content. He wants control of his own destiny as well as the company's. This means reorganizing work and giving workers more control over their jobs (see Figure 4).

The work ethic is not dead, but it has changed. Workers will expend effort for something they own or belong to. The participatory ethic—that people must be part of the process of decision making that affects their lives—has seeped into the core of our value system. Authority will not be accepted if not first granted by those who agree to follow. This ethic will create new demands on businesses in the decade ahead, forcing a change in the corporate culture (basic attitudes, values, and ways of doing things), and emphasizing the importance of being able to communicate and produce well-informed people. It is important to keep people involved, emphasizing participation, discussion, and communication, giving workers information about competitive conditions, and encouraging formal complaint/grievance systems and employee participation programs such as quality circles.

Quality circles, only one example of the application of the participatory ethic, are small groups of staff members who work together to identify, analyze, and solve job-related problems. Resulting benefits may include increased employee motivation, increased productivity, increased staff and leadership development, and improved customer service. The participatory ethic itself will be the basis of the expansion of the quality circle and other movements as well as leading to increased productivity, higher quality, and reduced costs—signaling a return to the time when the spirit and satisfaction of the worker mattered.

IMPACT ON HUMAN RESOURCE MANAGEMENT

In order to cope with these new changes, personnel practices, policies, and people relations must become more individualized. The workplace should be reorganized away from the notion that everyone should be treated the same, and toward individualized work contracts emphasizing financial incentives and opportunities for personal growth. Workers should be viewed as the most important component in any business strategy. In the future, the role of management will change from one of authorization to one of collaboration, which will increase the importance of the individual worker. A need is evident for human resource functions designed to evoke high performance from individuals in the organization. This type of "morale management" is good for the future because it is the worker's performance and productivity that help to then create lower costs and higher quality essential for profitability. We will examine the effects of these changes on several human resource functions—planning, training and development, recruiting, compensation, and performance appraisal—and offer strategies to compensate for these changes.

HUMAN RESOURCES AND PLANNING

An important concern for future human resource management is the need to link human resources to long-range strategic planning. The long-run competitiveness of American industry will require considerably more sophisticated approaches to the human resource input that deal with its strategic role in organizational performance. It is necessary to plan for the long-term future—identifying the type of people needed to run the company—to guide current selection, placement, and training practices. It is not adequate to assume that the needed personnel can always be recruited in the marketplace to meet future needs. Business planners in the future will have to acknowledge the growing link between strategic planning and human resources, and not focus only on financial and marketing aspects of planning. It is important for an organization to remain competitive in the complex environment we are living in. Therefore the organization must have the right mix of people to get a profitable return on its human resources investment (see Figure 5).

Strategic planning is more complex, more conceptual, and less precise than shorter range planning. This is because assumptions must be made about an unpredictable future; this constitutes a significant amount of risk. Strategic planning involves consideration of several possible scenarios about the future business environment and consid-

---

FIGURE 5   Three Levels of Planning

Strategic

- Corporate philosophy
- Environmental conditions
- Strengths/weaknesses
- Goals/objectives
- Strategies

(Issues analysis)

Managerial

- Availability of resources
- Allocation of resources
- Planned programs
- Plans for entry into new businesses, acquisitions, and divestures

(Forecasting requirements)

Operational

- Budgets
- Staffing plans
- Unit/individual performance goals
- Production plans
- Production efficiency

(Action plans)

---

eration of several alternative courses of action for the business. The essence of this planning is knowing what the business is involved in now and deciding what the business will be involved in in the future. After this, it must be determined what is needed to bridge the gap between the two as far as staffing, hiring, training, and the like, and plan accordingly.

This planning does not have to be formal, just effective. It can be a highly individualistic, creative step in which the company's circumstances and people are dominant. For an effective plan, business executives must address company strengths and weaknesses, business and personal objectives, and implementation approaches. The planning process is one in which future resource allocation decisions (human resources being an important part of this process) are made on the basis of an informed analysis of the environment. This is why it is important to know the business now in order to plan for the future.

Planning at the strategic level deals with policy formation and overall goal setting. First, it is important to define the corporate philosophy—why the business exists and the contribution it makes. Next, the environmental conditions should be considered by recognizing opportunities and threats as well as competition. After this, the corporation's strengths and weaknesses should be evaluated—what factors limit or enhance the choice of future actions. Goals should be set, then specific objectives set to indicate what must be done to achieve these goals. Lastly, strategies should be developed that help the corporation to achieve its objectives while meeting specific operational goals along the way. This may require changes in organization, structure, management, and processes as well as personnel. An important step is to determine the kind of people needed to run the business long-term, and choose specific policies and programs for long-term development of these people, fitting to world conditions and the structure of the organization itself.

At the managerial level, it is necessary to have efficient human resource functions for acquisition, retention, and development of personnel under the strategic plan. At this level there is an emphasis on the availability and allocation of resources needed to carry out the strategic plan. The managerial-level issues are developing an effective and efficient human resource system for acquiring, appraising, rewarding, and developing human resources in order to achieve strategic goals.

Planning at the operational level emphasizes carrying out the day-to-day management of the organization under the umbrella of managerial plans. Therefore annual budgets, staffing plans, production plans, and central systems should be directly linked to medium-term managerial plans. Operational planning involves ensuring that people come to work, perform, get evaluated and rewarded, and have the necessary job skills or are trained in acquiring them. This type of planning assumes a fairly constant business environment and considers changes concerning short-term factors such as immediate tactics, production efficiency, adjustment of levels of business activity, and modification of products.

There are changes in operations expected in the future which will have an effect on human resources, especially in the area of financial services. Increasing mergers, acquisitions, and divestures are some of these. Human resource departments must be able to manage the integration of separate cultures into new systems. In the area of increasing diversification, a continuing human resource effort must be made to develop entrepreneurial managers as companies seek new market advantages. The human resource function, following the trend of decentralization, will consist of operating units.

TRAINING AND DEVELOPMENT

Training and development is the main vehicle for developing skills and abilities of employees other than through job assignments. It can be a major area of expenditure, both in dollars and in hours. It is an important means of influencing management values, attitudes, and practices in human resource management. The principal issue is assessing what type of training and development is needed by the organization for maximum employee productivity. This should be related to the needs for (1) improving performance on the current job (training), (2) preparing the individual for the next (target) job, and (3) allowing the individual to consider alternate career choices (development). Basically, training involves more tangible aspects of the job while development relates to the "big picture"—that is, long-term improvement. The job requirements, based on worked activities actually performed, should be used as the basis for identifying skill and knowledge gaps—thus identifying training and development needs. Through this analysis, one can identify the sequences of experiences necessary to equip an individual for assignment to specified types of positions, and enhance capabilities to better meet changing needs.

The best training starts with good hiring so that building on strengths is emphasized rather than correcting weaknesses. The best training will be learner controlled, which is where the computer becomes an important factor. The worker's boss is the best training instructor.

With the change in technologies, it will become increasingly important to keep workers up-to-date. One way to do this is to sponsor seminars and retraining programs. By bringing in instructors and trainers, workers are kept abreast of current technological changes. Another way to keep workers current is professional activities such as membership in professional associations and attending professional meetings. Other training incentives are in-house degree programs (staffed by visiting faculty and funded by the company) and tuition refund programs.

In the future an important change will be flexible work scheduling. This will be especially cost effective as well as keeping or getting older workers back into the work force. Some possible implementations may include permanent part-time jobs, phased-in retirement, flexible benefits, temporary employees, and job sharing, which is also a good method for working single parents. Other ideas are the encouragement of lateral and downward moves, job redesign, specialized training and retraining programs, and if necessary bringing back retirees when the need arises.

RECRUITING/EMPLOYMENT

In the past recruiting strategies were much more rigid than they are today. Job standards were black and white; requirements were set and narrow. Because of changes in the banking and service industries, today's requirements for a successful job candidate are different. Job requirements are broader and less precisely designed. Also new attitudes of the work force—such as the "self-expressionism" legacy of the 1970s—and higher education have led to the proliferation of entrepreneurs and more flexible views of work.

Because of a more competitive environment, it is becoming increasingly more important to hire the right people in order to increase productivity. Knowing before hiring the type of personnel needed (including duties, knowledge, and ability) can help avoid human resource backlog in the future. It is important to integrate needed skills with personal factors and unit needs to get the right match. By making this ideal match, workers will get more satisfaction out of their jobs, and there will be fewer under- and over-qualified people on the job. Also, with increased flexibility of employment and individual decision making, the worker has more control over the direction his career takes and what he is looking for. However, even when the right people are hired, there is the chance that they may be incorrectly promoted. This may increase the amount of over- and under-qualified employees unless promotions are carefully monitored.

Making the right match will also produce the most productive mix of skills as well as saving on payroll costs, enhancing the quality of work life, and providing management with a comprehensive yet focused approach to human resource planning. Another way of making the right match is outplacement. When an employee is no longer a good "fit" for the job, he can be assisted in finding other employment.

To match the job with the worker, it is necessary to measure input—what it takes in human terms to get the job done—then determine the correct skill level for each job. By aggregating this information, the right skills mix for the entire organization can be set. To forecast the future skills mix needed, it is necessary to combine those figures with business and personnel flow projections.

The most important issue to a recruiting executive is to know how the business operates. The recruiting executive should be familiar with the business strategy (for example, goals, objectives, and expectations) of each unit and work closely with unit managers and strategic planners to anticipate future needs. Line management should be able to assess the knowledge needed and be willing to pay for it.

In banking's future, there will be an ongoing need for a wide variety of personnel. With information technology changing, needed skills will change as well. There will always be a need for computer literacy, but not everyone will need to know four languages to be competitive or productive. The need for managers with a "personal touch" won't decline; as the importance of the individual worker grows, so will that of the "people" managers. Not everyone has to be a specialist—it's okay to be a generalist too. There will always be a need for entry-level programs although in the future many of these entry-level personnel may come from another job or returned to work from retirement rather than from traditional sources.

COMPENSATION/JOB EVALUATION

Financial institutions are in a new, highly competitive environment. They must contend with innovative new products, revolutionary new ways of selling them, and unrestricted competition. Many forces of change will cause us to re-evaluate our compensation practices in the future. For example, because there will be an increased number of 25- to 44-year-old white-collar workers and a decline in middle management, there will be increased competition for promotions of fewer jobs. Because of the changing needs of today's worker, employer, and customer, new ways of compensation should be implemented.

Financial institutions' response to competitive environments is to upgrade compensation systems so that real producers can be attracted and retained. For example, we may see more compensation payouts for proven managerial talent even at the higher levels as long as the person has been a productive worker. Therefore we will see more emphasis on providing competitive salaries and incentives. There is a change in the manager's expectation of the employee. In the past, it was loyalty: today it is excellence. Because of this, employers will compete more aggressively for the most skilled members of the available work force. In banking, skills in operations have become more important as have finding appropriate levels and forms of compensation to attract and hold key people in "relationships management" and "product development" positions, as well as in investment and trading positions.

Traditional merit salary programs don't motivate enough for the lower levels of management in the increasingly decentralized environment. This has opened doors for new methods. Motives are needed for workers who aren't accustomed to operating in a relatively free and very competitive marketplace. Incentives are also moving down to lower levels to hold down costs; these incentives may be awarded instead of merit salary increases. This can decrease the cost of fixed compensation over time and make the variable cost more closely tied to profits or production rather than inflation and cost of living adjustments (COLAs). Variable compensation is driven by deregulation and increased competitive pressure to control cost. Lower levels of management will have larger proportions of their total cash opportunities placed at risk through variable compensation approaches. Payouts will be based not only on competitive market pricing but also on business or human resource strategy and the attainment of performance goals.

Traditional compensation has been based on profit sharing or after-the-fact bonuses; the emphasis is now on gain sharing (a gain must be realized before the payout). In the future, we will also see the opening up of incentives to more people, especially to a shrinking middle management. Profit generating (or gain sharing) will be more prevalent (a certain percentage of the profits will be set aside to pay out). There will be trends toward performance-based incentives, annual incentives based on attainment of short-term business goals, team incentives, and especially individual contributor incentives, which relate payouts to individual production. The proportion of total compensation earned as an annual incentive will increase over the short term as employers attempt to preserve margins by shifting from fixed compensation costs (or salaries) to variable costs (or incentives).

In some cases compensation in the future may be based on an effort to treat the workers as sales people, paying them a low base salary but offering them the chance to make more money on "commission," measuring their contribution. This means an increased risk for the worker—he will forego a high base salary (or fixed cost) to have the opportunity to earn more (or variable cost). The change in responsibility from production to sales will necessitate a change in compensation practices. There will be other emerging roles in compensation in the future. There will be a more objective measurement and decentralized approach to job evaluations, originating from the emphasis of decentralization in the organization itself. There will also be more specific pricing to type of company, location, and job. Because of more linkages between human resource planning and strategic planning, there will be more linkages between compensation and strategic planning since it is necessary to produce compensation plans to meet future needs. We may also see an increase in the giving out of stock, rather than cash, as compensation practice in order to increase a feeling of "ownership." A way to attract more of the highly qualified people is to offer or sign up bonuses. And, with the advent of the importance of the part-time worker, we may see more bonuses to attract them.

Paying for worker's performance assures the worker that the system is fair and responsive to his efforts. Frequent recognition and awards are also key motivational tools. The payouts should be based on standards set in advance and should not be seen as an economic adjustment or an annual raise. To compensate workers fairly, an appropriate performance appraisal program must be set up, including proper job evaluation and fair systems of appraising performance.

Job evaluation is closely related to compensation in that it provides a rational, justifiable explanation for the pay levels assigned to each position in the organization. It is an approach to thinking about work and people's relationships to their organizations. Job evaluations are used to determine the relative worth within an organization. Before effective pricing of the structure can be accomplished, there needs to be an internal relationship between the value of the jobs within the organization. This ensures a feeling of fairness to the employees as well. Job evaluation is a systematic approach to measure each position against a standard of the main elements common to all jobs. The total of values resulting from the comparison of each of the common elements to all jobs determines the value relationship of one job to another.

The standards used when evaluating jobs include the experience and educational level required, complexity, initiative, responsibility, and working conditions encountered. The job description is the key when evaluating jobs; it is used to classify the employees into groups. After determining their internal value, the jobs are then ranked in order from high to low. This involves *judgmental* decisions made by management. No matter how quantitative the method, *all* job evaluation systems require some application of personal judgment. After this, the market should be surveyed so that pay levels involve external and internal factors in tandem. This is important because if pay levels are too low (because of lack of market surveying), the organization will lose its competitiveness, causing high turnover costs. If pay levels are too high, excessive compensation costs can result, and internal equity may be compromised when jobs are incorrectly classified.

One solution to this problem is the use of computers in job evaluation. This can save time, reducing the amount of paperwork and manual processing. It also increases accuracy and creates a more detailed database on which better compensation decisions can be made. However, it is important to keep in mind that a job description is just a photograph in time and can change daily. Therefore it is necessary to remain flexible in the evaluation program to allow for job flexibility. This requires more subjectivity, allowing for management flexibility. This becomes important, especially because of the increasing amounts of change taking place in the environment.

PERFORMANCE APPRAISAL

In appraising performance, the achievement of specified goals on the job behavior, general management or professional skills, and promotion potential should be measured. Before performance can be judged, job behaviors must be categorized and evaluated as to degree of performance necessary to fulfill these behaviors. Performance appraisal systems are used to determine pay increases and to identify training and development needs. They are also used to justify personnel actions such as promotions, transfers, terminations, and planning performance improvement and salary changes as well as providing specific feedback to employees as to their performance.

The performance appraisal system used is very important. A common one is MBO (management by objectives), which relates to goal setting. It emphasizes results or outcomes of job behaviors. MBO involves comparing the results and achievements with the preset objectives. Other methods used include essay or open-ended questions, ratings scales, checklists, and ranking or comparison of jobs within the organization, as well as absolute standards (that is, BARS or behaviorally anchored rating scales) where the ratee is rated against predetermined standards (see Figure 6).

When evaluating performance appraisal, specific program standards should be applied. Actual job requirements and on-the-job performance should be examined and analyzed, instead of the personality of the employee. The rational design of the program should be evident—it should be clearly designed for specific purposes. The evaluations should be documented to provide the company with a written record of judgments underlying personnel actions. A systematic approach should be taken with regular schedules for evaluations at least once a year. The evaluations should be clearly organized with nothing spontaneous or haphazard about them. It is also crucial that the appraisers are well trained in administering the program because when appraisers aren't trained correctly, a faulty program results. Appraisers need to understand the objectives, problems, and behavioral aspects of performance evaluation.

FIGURE 6   MBO versus BARS

MBO

(management by objectives)
- "Goal setting" type system
- Ratee rated according to the degree to which he or she attains predetermined job goals
- Measures employee effectiveness or contribution to the organization's success and goal attainment
- Goals/objectives are jointly set by superiors and subordinates at the beginning of a predetermined time period (for example, once a year)
- At the end of the time period, superiors and subordinates meet to evaluate results

BARS
(behaviorally anchored rating scales)
- "Absolute standard" type system
- Ratee rated against aspects of job performance
- Measures job behavior—what the employee actually does on the job
- Statements of behavioral standards are placed on scales, one scale for each performance area
- Each scale is "anchored" at each of several points with the behavioral standards

The future of performance appraisal may go two ways or combine both of the following. One emphasis may be on specific standards with specific objectives such as the MBO approach, involving quantifiable methods. The other direction performance appraisal may go toward a more judgmental method, assessing the leadership capacity of the employee. Even with a change in the direction of performance appraisal systems, the purpose will remain the same—to give performance and behavior feedback to the employee.

CONCLUSION

In the face of these ongoing changes, it is important to be aware of the external environment—be in tune with occurrences affected by change, and respond, not react, to these changes. By failing to realize opportunities (and threats) that change can bring, many organizations may be left behind. A successful organization is one which can recognize and acknowledge change and manipulate change to its advantage. Because of this, it is important to continually evaluate personnel policies and practices, and ensure that they are meeting today's needs as well as the strategic needs of the future.

BIBLIOGRAPHY

Books

Bernardin, H. John, and Richard W. Beatty. *Performance Appraisal: Assessing Human Behavior at Work.* Boston: Kent Publishing Company, 1984.

Naisbitt, John. *Megatrends.* New York: Warner Books, 1982.

Walker, James W. *Human Resource Planning.* New York: McGraw-Hill Book Company, 1980.

Magazines

Allen, Pat. "Human Resource Management Develops a New Role." *Savings Institutions,* August 1985, pp. 62–69.

Cassell, Frank H.; Hervey A. Juris; and Myron J. Roomkin. "Strategic Human Resource Planning: an Orientation to the Bottom Line." *Management Decision* 23, no. 3 (1985), pp. 16–28.

Devanna, Mary Anne; Charles Fombrun; and Noel Tichy. "Human Resource Management: A Strategic Perspective." *Organizational Dynamics,* Winter 1981, pp. 51–67.

Hoerr, John, et al. "Beyond Unions." *Business Week,* July 8, 1985, pp. 72–77.

Kien, Julian M. "Human Resource Management in Transition." *Pulp and Paper,* August 1985, p. 41.

Latham, Gary P.; Edwin A. Locke; and David M. Schweiger. "Participation in Decision Making: When Should It Be Used?" *Organizational Dynamics*, Winter 1986, pp. 65–79.

Odiorne, George S. "The Great American Brain Drain." *Personnel Journal*, August 1985, pp. 10–13.

Reports

Freedman, Audrey. "Perspectives on Employment." *The Conference Board Research Bulletin, No. 194*, 1986.

Peck, Charles. "Pay and Performance: The Interaction of Compensation and Performance Appraisal." *The Conference Board Research Bulletin, No. 155*, 1984.

Schein, Lawrence. "Current Issues in Human Resource Management." *The Conference Board Research Bulletin, No. 190*, 1986.

Interviews

Carson, Leslie Barnes. Vice President, Employment. Security Pacific National Bank, Los Angeles, California. June 13, 1986.

Eggleton, C. Harry. Vice President, Organizational Development. Security Pacific National Bank, Los Angeles, California. May 30, 1986.

Melinat, R. William. Vice President, Compensation. Security Pacific National Bank, Los Angeles, California. May 27, 1986.

Oblinger, Susan. Vice President, Training. Security Pacific National Bank, Los Angeles, California. May 22, 1986.

Selbert, Roger. Vice President, Futures Research. Security Pacific National Bank, Los Angeles, California. May 15, 1986.

CHAPTER SEVENTEEN

Selecting and Training Bank Personnel

John R. Wells

Senior Vice President
Boatmen's Bancshares, Inc.

OVERVIEW

The ebb and flow of American banking has resulted in major advances and setbacks during the last decade. However, regardless of the current situation, some banking institutions continue to avoid catastrophe and tend to always prosper in the long term. Most chief executive officers of these successful organizations decline to accept personal credit and will attribute success to the people throughout their organization "who make it happen."

Labor intensive organizations, such as banking, have no choice but to accept the fact that they are no better than the overall quality of the staff that runs them. Having the right person in the right spot at the right time can make the winning difference, and dependence on the wrong people can create critical losses.

Bank managers will spend most of their time making decisions on people issues, yet they tend to ignore good decision-making techniques by deferring to "gut feel" as their alternative. Peter Drucker recently characterized management's staffing decisions by stating that managers have a .333 batting average with one-third of their decisions being right, one-third being partially effective, and one-third being complete failures.[1] One would imagine that a loan officer with the same batting average would not last very long in any bank.

Selecting people that are wrong for a position or ignoring their development is similar to purchasing the wrong computer equipment

---

[1] Peter E. Drucker, "How To Make People Decisions," *Harvard Business Review,* July–August 1985, p. 22.

or not maintaining it properly. Both would be a waste of money and would hinder the productivity of the organization. Unfortunately, we tend to ignore the people side of our businesses while we are much more diligent in formalizing the decision-making process for a major expenditure for computer hardware. Cost-benefit analysis is a common term used for examining major capital expenditures in a banking organization, and the same type of analysis can be used when selecting or training bank personnel.

In the banking industry, staffing costs are usually the second largest expense following the cost of funds used to generate loans and investments. Most consider staffing to be the largest controllable expense in the bank, yet we tend to ignore ways to enhance our control of the quality of individuals we select for positions and the development needed to improve performance. Selecting the best person for a job is selecting the *right* person. Someone who has been very successful as a credit analyst is not necessarily the right person to be promoted to a business development role or to take over a complex managerial assignment. If people are to go through transitions in their career, they must be contemplated carefully, and such transitions can be much more successful if they are intertwined with well thought-out development techniques.

The material below will explore cost-effective selection techniques for both internal and external job candidates as well as discuss the proper application of training and development methodology to increase the chances for success.

EFFECTIVE SELECTION TECHNIQUES

Many believe that human resource management is a "touchy-feely" type of business that does not allow for the use of proven business procedures. Others take the alternate extreme by thinking that personnel management is best managed through strict rules and rigidity. Both positions are extremes, and neither can substitute for an effective human resource management function built on a disciplined management approach and supported by good individual judgment. Selection of personnel requires both discipline and judgment and, when used effectively, can create a good solution to an ongoing business problem.

The following describes the decision-making discipline needed to fill open positions. The difficulty of each step will depend on the complexity of the position being filled; for example, filling a position for an entry-level clerical position will be less difficult than filling a position for a chief financial officer. One must remember that the problem is getting the *right* person in the job, and regardless of the complexity of the open job, filling all job openings still requires an effective process of decision making.

Define the Opening

Before filling a job opening, an analysis should be made of the job itself. Job content is usually found in a formal job description, which depicts the major tasks that need to be performed by the incumbent. Without a job description, a list of these tasks should be developed.

Required knowledge and skills are the definable skills and knowledge that would be required for an individual to fill the open position. Examples would include such things as typing proficiency, computer knowledge, managerial skills, investment ability, familiarity with certain type of loans, and the like.

Pricing the job is important to locating the right person. One must remember that when going outside the organization for a candidate it may cost more than promoting a successor who has been developed to fill an opening. If a bank has been paying a competitive market rate for a position, it usually will have to pay more than market to attract a quality candidate to leave a current job which is also paying market.

Define Candidate Requirements

Once the job has been defined, one should develop a list of optimum requirements for potential candidates. If customer service is a major priority for a company, it will want to hire tellers who demonstrate appropriate abilities. Managing a turnaround situation can require a totally different approach than managing an area with aggressive growth objectives. Developing a greater market share in a highly competitive market requires different experiences than developing business in a captive market. Therefore, a well-thought-out list of requirements will help maximize the effectiveness of the search process by eliminating candidates with low potential for success.

Conduct the Search

Searching for internal candidates is an important step. Internal selections provide good continuity and give the employees a sense of career potential within the bank. Job posting programs are good sources of candidates and, when used effectively, minimize the need to "go outside." However, one should not select an internal candidate just for the sake of promoting from within. If the individual selected is not qualified for the position, a poor decision has been made that will stifle bank productivity and frustrate the individual's ability to continue their career.

Searching for external candidates requires a number of approaches that, when used together effectively, will provide good candidates. Reviewing past applications can provide a number of candidates as long as those records are readily available and informative. The combination of good record-keeping and well-documented screening interviews can provide a viable source of future candidates.

Advertising will usually generate a large volume of applicants who are not qualified along with a few strong candidates. Therefore a screening step is required to pinpoint those who are appropriate for consideration. Advertising also limits your audience to those looking for employment at the time.

Soliciting referrals can be effective as long as the source is reliable. Good "sourcing" is a very effective way to locate individuals, especially for finding candidates for higher level management jobs. The most effective sources are individuals in similar positions as potential candidates who have contact with a group of their peers in other organizations. Most people will recommend individuals if the approach is professional and provides a well-organized description of the opportunity.

Contacting a possible candidate from a referral requires tact and professionalism. Especially important is the confidentiality of the interaction and the ability to create interest while soliciting further information from the individual. Integrity is paramount since you are potentially creating a major change in someone's life, and a good initial contact should determine whether both parties are interested in further discussions.

Using a recruiting agency or executive search firm is a viable alternative when it is determined that other alternatives are not effective or efficient. This approach can add significant costs to the search, so a cost-benefit analysis should be made to determine if an external agency should be used.

Evaluate the Candidate

Once candidates are found, a formal evaluation should be followed to effectively determine if and to whom an offer should be made. The evaluation process, if handled well, will increase the quality of the final decision and should include:

1. Reviewing the Application or Resume.   Does the individual really have the background to fulfill the requirements of the job? Are their skills at an acceptable level, and do they possess the proper characteristics for the work environment? Are there unexplained gaps in employment or unusual circumstances surrounding their past job progression? Remember that a resume should be treated as an advertisement for an individual and should not totally be relied on as a screening tool.

2. Conducting an Effective Job Interview.   Interviewing is not just a friendly chat but should be a well organized forum for sharing significant information about the job and the candidate. All those interviewing the candidate should be given a briefing on the job definition and defined candidate requirements.

The interviewer should take control of the interview by setting a friendly but businesslike environment. Rapport should be established early to allow an easy flowing discussion throughout the interview. After an initial get-acquainted period, the interviewer should be prepared to ask cogent questions about the individual's background as it relates to the job opening. Tactful probing is appropriate, and a well-prepared candidate will expect and respond well to professional questioning.

The candidate should be given the opportunity to solicit information from the interviewer. In fact, the type of questions asked by candidates are good evaluators of their ability to focus on the important factors of the job.

Ending the interview is the interviewer's responsibility. The interviewers should summarize some of their observations about the applicability of the candidate's background to the job and some follow-up steps. Follow-up usually describes what type of future interaction the candidate should expect and when to expect it.

Timely follow-up is important. As soon as a candidate is determined to be *not* qualified, they should be told. Those who are still being considered should be given periodic information about where they stand and what will happen in the future. The longer the period between the initial interview of a candidate and the decision to make an offer, the greater the chance for the candidate to lose interest in the position. Therefore the organization should be prepared to respond in a timely manner.

3. Checking References.   References are an important method of obtaining relevant information about the candidate. Good reference checking will validate the individual's ability to actually handle the job now and in the future.

A candidate should be told that the bank is going to check references and asked to present a list of appropriate individuals. It is extremely important that the reference checker does not create any embarrassment for candidates or jeopardize their current employment.

When talking to a respondent, a description of the job should be given and followed by specific questions about the candidate's ability to handle the position. Asking for actual examples or experience can help formulate a more complete evaluation of the candidate. After the reference check, the interviewer should summarize the candidate's strengths and weaknesses and summarize the quality and objectivity of the respondent's reference.

Select the Best Candidate

After a number of candidates (usually three to five) have been interviewed, objectivity seems to suffer. It is important to review the original definitions for the job and the important requirements for candidates. When taking into account the results of reference checking, one can usually rank a first and second choice. Most important, this should not be an emotional decision, but an objective one based on the decision-making criteria determined initially.

Make an Offer

Offering a candidate a job is an important matter and should be done well. It is best to tell a candidate that you are going to present them with an offer and ask them to review a few items that you are going to present. Once they are composed and in a position to discuss the matter, the offer should be outlined in detail. An offer should include (1) the specific job title (and official title if appropriate), (2) the compensation (base salary and if appropriate bonus and any other compensatory items), (3) the starting date, and (4) any other pertinent items such as paying moving expenses, parking, and the like.

It is normal for a candidate to ask for some time to make a decision. Depending on the level of the job, decision time could be overnight to a few weeks. It is important that the time be defined in order to protect the bank from losing the opportunity to approach an alternate candidate.

Some negotiations usually take place. It is important for the company to be straightforward but not too rigid concerning all aspects of the offer. The original offer should always be realistic as to the requirements of the individual (which should have surfaced during the interview stage), but the company should also be receptive to some minor modifications.

Once the offer has been finalized and accepted, the employer should extend a written letter outlining the terms of the agreement. This does not represent a formal contract, but does document the items agreed to by both parties. Such documentation is helpful if any questions arise at a later date.

Orientation

New employees' initial contact with their employer is extremely important. The bank should be well organized to handle all administrative procedures for placing employees on the payroll and enrolling them in benefit programs. Any defined work rules and employment policies should be distributed and an informal tour of the work area should be conducted.

Supervisors should be especially sensitive to a new employee on their first day of employment. Introducing them to fellow workers, explaining procedures, and providing a place to get questions answered without embarrassment is critical. Without good orientation procedures, the work of finding the right employee for the job may not pay off as well as it should.

TRAINING AND DEVELOPMENT

Training for "trainings sake" is a costly error that can easily happen in a company. Most everyone will agree that training is important, but, without using training as a solution to a specific problem, one can waste time and money. For example, if tellers are trained to cross-sell products even though it is not an important part of the teller job, the training is unproductive. To provide customer service people with sales training when they are recognized and rewarded for increased sales can be quite productive.

In order for training to add to the profitability of an organization, one must require a specific return on the training investment. Business decision making must be used in order to ensure that training in solving real problems that can contribute to an improved bottom line. As with the selection of people, a decision-making process should be implemented in order to provide the bank with an adequate return the use of its resources.

A five-step process can be used to help an organization use training properly:

Determine Real Needs.   Formal business planning is the best time to formulate training needs. Usually during the business planning process, an organization evaluates what is and what is not going well and makes strategic changes for the upcoming year. Improving sales, decreasing expenses, introducing new products, and implementing different processes all suggest a bona fide need for training. Training designed to make people "feel better" or to keep a trainer busy can be wasteful and unproductive.

Define Optimum Behavior. By definition, training is designed to influence behavior. Whenever possible, the behavior that a specific training program is designed to influence should be defined in both qualitative and quantitative terms. To "sell more" is not as definitive as to increase consumer loans by 15 percent. To make operating supervisors "more productive" is not as definitive as to process the same check volume with a 12 percent reduction in expenses. When training is delivered to participants whom, as part of their job, have been given defined behavior expectations, it can be a powerful tool for management to use in achieving its goals.

Select the Best Approach. This step is the test of a good trainer. Finding alternatives to training programs is important instead of just buying canned products that are readily available. When possible, a cost-benefit analysis should be used to evaluate the applicability of each approach by using predetermined standards. There are many sales training programs available on the market, however, so finding one that meets the specific needs of the corporate trust business development department may take some work.

Implement. Implementing a training program is not just putting participants in front of a trainer. It is important for participants to know what organizational goals the program is designed to address, what they specifically can expect from the program, and the format being used to accomplish the program objectives.

Solicit Feedback. Training is a dynamic process that requires fine tuning to meet the ongoing needs of the organization. Feedback should be solicited from all participants, and measures should be implemented to see if participant performance has been enhanced. When needed, modifications should be made to address deficiencies or react to a significant change in organizational goals. It is also important to discard outdated programs no matter how successful they have been in the past.

Developing people to meet succession needs is also a critical human resource function. As discussed earlier, going outside the organization for new employees is disrupting to the company as well as to the existing employees. It is therefore important for banks to formally look at their ongoing staffing needs and prepare internal candidates to fill a majority of all openings.

One must continue to take inventory of its current staff to determine not only the quantity but also the quality of people who can fill potential openings. Quality can also be considered the *value* of a current employee expressed as some definition of current performance in conjunction with the employee's potential for advancement.

Once an inventory has been prepared, the organization needs to develop a replacement plan taking into account regular turnover as well as addressing any expansion or reorganization plans. Reorganization is the most common way to provide new opportunities for existing employees; but to be successful, the employee must be prepared to respond to the demands of the position opening.

Selective development is an important part of any "manpower plan." Employees with good potential need to be identified and should receive training and development experiences to help them fulfill that potential. A good commercial lender may need managerial training before being promoted to manage a national accounts group. An outstanding clerk typist may need secretarial training before becoming the secretary to a division manager.

SUMMARY

Human resource management must become a viable part of an organization's profitability plan, or it becomes an expense without sufficient return. Any staff must provide the services, as would an internal consultant, that enhances the operating unit's ability to be productive. When done well, the selection and training of employees can become an integral part of the organization's processes leading to success. When done poorly, selection and training can be a drain on profits and perpetuate mediocre performance.

CHAPTER EIGHTEEN

Productivity Is Vital

Dr. Robert E. Coffey

Professor of Management and Organization Behavior
University of Southern California

Productivity is a vital, complex, and challenging issue confronting many industries in the United States today. Newspapers, magazines, and professional journals continue to focus on and report the decline of American productivity. Many factors are blamed for the productivity problems: government regulations, lack of research investment by business, lazy workers, inept managers, and a tax system fostering consumption and discouraging savings. These and other factors are contributing to a decline in productivity, but the single-most critical factor is often invisible as a result of its all-pervasive and powerful impact. We are once again faced with a situation in which one cannot see the forest for the trees. The U.S. economy has matured and is continuing a 30-year change from an industrial to a service economy. Productivity gains are now much harder to achieve and measure. Government regulations, inept managers, and less-committed workers are "trees." The issue of understanding, measuring, and improving productivity within the context of a service economy is the "forest."

It is within this context that productivity becomes a critical concept to be understood by those directing and leading financial services institutions, particularly banking. Banking is a service industry with a critical interest in understanding how to *manage* productivity. This chapter will present a definition of productivity, a brief conceptual discussion of the concept, and a model for the management of productivity in banking.

THE PRODUCTIVITY CONCEPT

Why Measure Productivity?

Productivity has been defined traditionally as the ratio of the physical quantity of inputs consumed in production to the physical quantity of outputs produced. Interest in productivity in the past was found mainly in manufacturing, but deregulation and other economic forces have led to increased attention to productivity in banks and other parts of the service economy. Many bank managers focused primarily on the productivity of people in the lobby and operations areas, but some are now realizing the importance of the productivity of both labor and nonlabor resources in all parts of the bank.

A primary reason for focusing on productivity is that insights are gained about the effectiveness of an organization that may be missed by using only the traditional financial data and ratios commonly used by managers. Productivity measures can provide a basis for measuring progress that financial measures may obscure. For example, relatively noncompetitive markets and soft prices might blur the fact that a given number of human and/or nonhuman resources are turning out less product. Measuring physical units of inputs and their associated outputs provides a constant base for comparison of intrabank productivity over the years. Comparisons can also be made to other banks if they measure productivity using physical units.

In 1981 the Bank Administration Institute (BAI), in conjunction with the American Productivity Center, developed an important report titled "Total Bank Productivity Measurement." In this report it is pointed out (p. 5) that economic income results if the current value of resources received from customers in exchange for products and services is greater than the present value of resources used in production, including the costs of staying in business. The BAI report also uses the concept "price recovery," which is defined as the relationship between the selling price of output units and the purchase price of input units. Profitability is defined as productivity times price recovery.

A significant point of this analysis is that profitability is divided into two components, a productivity component and a price recovery component. Generally, of these two, productivity is more subject to managerial control. The reason is that to the extent output and input markets are competitive, bank managers have little significant influence over market prices. If this is the case, the importance of managing the relationship of the physical inputs to physical outputs (productivity) is critically important in maintaining a competitive edge.

Productivity, simply stated, means getting more for less. Productivity improvement involves being creative and innovative in managing the relationship between inputs and outputs to get more. Measuring productivity helps to focus on the efficiency of using inputs to produce outputs, an insight that might be obscured by looking only at dollar values. This way of thinking and measuring can be a stimulus to productivity improvement efforts over the long term. Managers at all levels and in all functions can benefit from understanding what is behind productivity measurement by looking for new and better ways to use inputs efficiently.

Problems of Productivity Measurement

Many readily agree that measuring productivity is important. However, the actual measuring can be difficult and causes many managers to turn away from the process. It is beyond the scope of this chapter to discuss in detail how to measure productivity. Rather, here a few key problems will be pointed out. Those who want to pursue the subject further can refer to the BAI report.

One key problem is that of clearly identifying outputs, or products. A second problem is identifying and measuring specific inputs associated with the various outputs. A third problem is how to collect productivity data without impacting negatively on the organization and its members.

For many years banks did not clearly identify their products. Many services and products were given away or intertwined with other products such that the costs associated with each were obscured. Most bankers today are well aware of this problem and are actively working to change it. The BAI report is helpful in identifying typical bank products and product lines.

A second problem is that of relating inputs to associated outputs or products. One reason is that many products flow through different parts of the bank organization and are handled by a variety of people. Costs are often collected by functional areas rather than by product lines. Thus it is difficult, if not impossible, to relate inputs and their costs directly to associated outputs and their revenues. For this reason, it is difficult to measure both productivity and price recovery (or profitability) by product or product line. Some inputs are difficult to isolate, and they influence several products. Examples include physical premises, members of the executive office, data and word processing, and various staff functions. The challenge of productivity measurement is to clearly identify the outputs (products) and their associated inputs, and then to measure each in physical units.

A third problem with measurement is that it sometimes can take the time and effort of people who see little immediate personal value in the process. In fact, some people fear that such measurement may be detrimental to them by leading to increased work loads, higher standards of output, or failure to meet standards. One reason that some of the work measurement programs in banks have failed is that people have resisted them as being either too complicated and time consuming or too threatening.

Productivity Improvement

Those leading and managing banking organizations need to understand that productivity improvement must be distinguished from productivity measurement. Productivity measurement is a quantitative function: Management keeps a count of checks processed, customers served, or ATM transactions. Productivity improvement is both a quantitative and qualitative function. Bank management and employees are involved in creating cost-reducing innovations. They introduce new ideas or methods that favorably affect the ratio of inputs to outputs. While this presentation is somewhat abstract, the important thing to remember is that productivity measurement in and of itself will not improve productivity. Measurement will inform management of current levels of production at any single point in time. It provides a baseline, a starting point, for managers to use in designing programs for improving productivity. Once the baseline is established, bank management can become involved in improving the production or service delivery process. After improvement programs have been implemented for a period of time, additional measurements can provide a means of assessing the efficiency and effectiveness of the changes.

Productivity improvement by definition has quantitative and qualitative dimensions. Using Peter Drucker's familair notions, the activity includes both doing things right and doing the right things. Doing things right is efficiency; getting the most output for the least input. Doing the right things leads to the achievement of desired results. Designing better methods for measuring productivity may provide a more efficient means of monitoring productivity, but if the desired result is improved productivity, such activity alone will not be effective. It is quite possible to be efficient without being effective, just as it is to be effective without being efficient.

Approaches to Productivity Improvement

Managers in both the manufacturing and service industries have tried many different approaches to improving productivity. Indeed, Frederick Taylor and his followers, who emphasized "scientific management" in the early 1900s, started a long and successful quest for improved productivity. During the first six decades of this century the United States represented the hallmark of high productivity in manufacturing. Industrial engineering techniques such as time and motion studies, production planning, and job analysis did much to advance productivity. Incentive pay, attention to work groups, and improvement of working conditions also became common approaches used primarily in manufacturing before the 1950s.

During the last half of this century several factors caused the need for new and improved techniques. One important factor is that the nature of the workforce has changed. For example, the values, expectations, and educational levels of people have changed importantly during the past 40 years. Also, the rapid rise in the size and significance of the service industries has created the necessity for using management techniques to foster productivity that were not used before. Today it is generally accepted that the service industries must find ways to enhance the productivity of both human and nonhuman resources.

Numerous programs and approaches have been tried. Some of these are old and some new. They include, among others, incentive pay, goal setting and management by objectives (MBO), work measurement programs, selection and training, employee surveys, job design, job enrichment, autonomous work teams, alternative work schedules, quality circles, and quality-of-life programs.

Although this chapter does not assess each of these approaches, each has some merit, and research indicates that when tried each produces reasonably favorable results. However, many of them have in common the fact that the positive results tend to diminish with time. A major thesis here is that banks will succeed most in improving productivity if they emphasize building productivity improvement into their culture as a normal and continuous part of work for managers and nonmanagers at all levels. This would be in contrast to short bursts of enthusiasm for special programs such as work measurement, job enrichment, or quality circles.

In 1985 the author conducted an informal survey of middle managers in 51 banks of various sizes. The banks are located throughout the United States although most were east of the Mississippi. The respondents were asked whether various programs had been used in their banks during the past five years and to what degree they had been successful. The latter question was answered using a scale of one to five—one being not at all successful, three being successful, and five being highly successful. The results are shown in Table 1, going from the most frequently used approach at the top to the least frequently used at the bottom. The number in the right-hand column is the average rating of success for all who indicated the approach had been used.

TABLE 1   Approaches to Productivity Improvements*

Approach	Use		Success of Program†					Average
	Yes	No	1	2	3	4	5	
Cross-training	92%	8%	2	19	58	15	6	3.04
In-house training	90	10	3	13	47	30	6	3.22
Salary increase tied to performance	88	12	0	13	51	27	9	3.31
Individual bonuses	84	16	7	16	26	33	18	3.40
ATM	76	24	0	15	23	39	23	3.69
Office automation	67	33	3	9	41	41	6	3.38
Outside consultants	67	33	6	38	29	24	3	2.79
Structural changes	63	37	6	19	47	19	9	3.06
Communication programs	59	41	0	20	43	30	7	3.33
Profit sharing	55	45	11	14	39	14	22	3.21
Personnel scheduling (to eliminate work flow problems)	53	47	0	19	44	33	4	3.22
"Other" technological changes	47	53	0	17	58	17	8	3.17
Customer education	43	57	0	18	55	27	0	3.09
PMS (Productivity Measurement System)	35	65	6	33	39	22	0	2.78
Job rotation	35	65	0	17	61	11	11	3.17
Ergonomics (or improved physical work environment)	35	65	0	17	39	27	17	3.44
Hiring programs	33	67	0	18	59	24	0	3.06
Job redesign/enrichment	29	71	0	20	47	20	13	3.27
Quality circles (or variations)	27	73	7	43	29	21	0	2.64
Group bonuses	22	78	0	36	46	9	9	2.91
Organizationwide gain sharing	22	78	9	18	46	9	18	3.09
Autonomous work groups (self-managing teams)	20	80	0	10	40	50	0	3.40

* Sample size is 51; all numbers show percent except the "Average" column.
†1 = no success; 3 = successful; 5 = highly successful.

FACTORS AFFECTING WORKER PRODUCTIVITY

Productivity is a complex challenge for bank management. Its measurement is useful yet difficult. Productivity measurement is essential for monitoring productivity improvement but not sufficient to cause it. Some traditional approaches to productivity improvement have worked, some have not. A review of the major factors affecting bank productivity may provide information useful in designing improvement programs.

The National Science Foundation sponsored a major research program focused on productivity in 57 large organizations, mostly Fortune 500 companies. The research identified nine major factors affecting worker productivity:[1]

- Pay, recognition, and reward systems.
- Worker autonomy and discretion.
- Task variety.
- Training leading to all workers being able to perform every task in a department or work unit.
- Support services available on demand by technical support groups.
- Organizational structure with very few hierarchical levels.
- The technical/physical layout.
- Information and feedback from user departments.
- The interpersonal/group process focusing on the amount and kind of interaction among group members.

Wherever the researchers found significant evidence of these nine factors, they found high productivity. Their conclusions were that by making improvements in these nine areas, the organization would experience the following benefits:

- A reduction in direct labor costs.
- Lower average error rates.
- Decreased turnover and absenteeism.
- Increased job satisfaction.
- Increased productivity per worker.

These nine factors and the above consequences of their presence in an organization provide information vital to the design of productivity improvement programs. These programs (for example, incentive pay for performance, quality circles and other participating efforts, flexible work schedules, and the like) have been successful in some instances, but are often short-lived in their effectiveness. Those designing productivity improvement programs often overlook a significant result of the research reported earlier. *All nine factors have to be present.*

All nine factors used as a system affect worker productivity. Reward systems, worker autonomy, task variety, comprehensive task

---

[1]Robert O. Metzger, "Productivity in Banking—And How To Improve It," *The Bankers Magazine*, May-June, 1981.

training, technical support, simplified organizational structures, appropriate physical plant, feedback from users and interpersonal relationships—all interact with each other to contribute to overall productivity. Most programs are directed at only one or two of the factors and either ignore or diminish the importance of the others.

Banking organizations are composites of many activities. These various activities are the functioning parts of an organizational system. The loan department, the data processing unit, the customer service group, front office and back office operations of all kinds, and the human resources management group interact to produce the services available through a banking system. Change any one of these "parts" and its impact will eventually be felt by the "whole" organization. If the human resources group suggests a job enrichment program that allows employees to learn all the tasks performed by their respective functions and if managers in the various functions fail to allow employees to change tasks, then the enrichment effort will not be effective. Customer service personnel are often provided with interpersonal competency training to enhance their face-to-face customer interactions. Such training will have limited value if interpersonal competency is not valued in all organizational relationships or if technical support is not adequate. Implementing a participative management program can significantly increase productivity, but not if the bank's hierarchy is complex and convoluted. Complex hierarchies are usually designed to limit and control decision-making authority, not to share decision-making responsibility.

These examples are intended to communicate the *systems* nature of organizational behavior and organizational productivity. Improvement programs which are focused only on parts of the banking system will have limited effectiveness. High-productivity banking organizations create an organizational "state-of-mind" that focuses on total organizational productivity. These banks have historically attended to all nine of the factors listed or they have redesigned their system to take advantage of the interactive power inherent in the combined factors.[2]

A SYSTEMS APPROACH

This section presents a total organizational productivity model (see Figure 1) which takes into consideration the systematic nature of organizations while it helps identify the variables which can be managed to achieve improved productivity. The nine factors have been sub-

[2]See Edward Lawler III, *High Involvement Management* (San Francisco: Jossey-Bass, 1986).

FIGURE 1   Total Organization Productivity Model

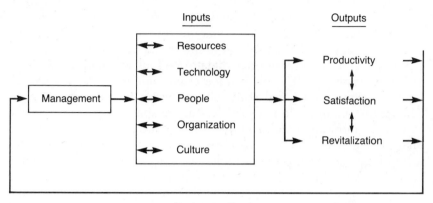

System feedback

sumed under five variables: technology, people, organization, resources, and culture. These variables, considered inputs, are coordinated by management to achieve desired results in an optimum fashion. The desired results are shown as model outputs and are listed as improved productivity, job satisfaction, and organizational revitalization.

The model reflects the management of the five variables. This management of productivity improvement activities and programs generates outputs which can be measured. These measures would include employee productivity, equipment productivity, and assets productivity. Employee job satisfaction levels can be assessed through a traditional questionnaire and by data on grievances, absenteeism, and turnover. Revitalization is measured by the condition of financial and physical resources, the condition of human resources, and the overall standing in the industry and society. The measurement results complete a feedback loop to managers that allows for program fine tuning or redesign. Without the feedback loop, management activities would be linear and undirectional. It would be like shooting in the dark. The target might be hit and, then again, it might not.

Model Inputs

Resources.   As used here, resources is a broad concept that includes nonhuman tangible assets such as land, buildings, furniture, equipment, and money. The management of tangible assets is a traditional managerial responsibility. These resources affect the technical and physical layout in any organization. They have a direct impact on the quality of the work environment as well as on the bottom line. Buildings appreciate and furniture depreciates, but they both add to or detract from the quality of the bank work environment.

Banks have often spent large amounts of money on designing the front-office operation. Considerable funds are used to buy furniture, paintings, and plants. Esthetics dictate the look and feel of the front-office environment. The back-office environment can be a very different situation. Functional utility often dictates the environment here. The environment is often less pleasing, the space more crowded, the furniture more functional, and the noise greater. Such conditions can take a toll on worker productivity. Such use of resources communicates a set of management values which may not be conducive to productivity. The value set implies that customers are valued and to be treated in a "first class" way and employees are not valued and deserve only "second class" treatment.

Technology. This variable refers to the methods and processes used in accomplishing work. An ATM is a resource but represents a certain technology for helping customers deposit and withdraw funds. A contrasting technology for helping customers is the use of tellers. Technology is how resources and people are used to get work done. Each of the two variables can be altered to affect service delivery and the way work gets done.

Job enrichment and job enlargement programs are examples of improvement programs focused on the technology variable. Job enrichment often consists of increasing the task variety in an employee's job responsibilities. Job enlargement can involve training workers to perform several or all of the tasks in their work unit or department.

The traditional tellers job involves the use of all resources—online teller machines, cash drawers, and teller windows—to control cash, make merchant deposits, to enter data, and balance, receive, and disburse customer funds. The technology involved is reflected in the way the teller incorporates and uses the resources to accomplish the task of servicing customer needs.

If the job of the teller is enriched and enlarged, the technology will change. If the teller were to keep responsibility for the previously listed tasks and also assume responsibility for acknowledging customers, identifying customer needs, problem solving, and selling services, the teller is now performing as a customer service representative and a teller. The teller is incorporating and using assigned resources to provide a quality service interaction at the teller windows. His or her tasks now involve monitoring and addressing the needs of the customer as well as responding to the more mundane functional requirements of the service transaction. The technology has changed in that the teller is now using additional skills and providing additional services using the same resources.

People. Productivity improvement starts with people. The human factor in productivity is subtle and often misunderstood. Studies done in the early 1980s indicate that more effective management of human resources might add from 10 to 25 percent in productivity growth in some organizations. It is difficult to estimate in dollars or percentages the possible improvements due to human factors such as skill, effort, ideas, imagination, and commitment. While these factors are difficult to measure, the most promising avenues available to bank management in productivity improvement efforts appear to be in the areas of selection, placement, training, appraisal, and compensation of staff. Dealing effectively with staff may be particularly rewarding in banking because it is a labor-intensive industry.

Management efforts focused on the people variable of this model must consider the interaction between training, recognition, and the reward system. While selection is critical, these three factors can determine the success or failure of productivity programs. Interpersonal skills training for front-office personnel can improve the quality of service provided to customers. Tellers and customer service representatives who receive such training report increased levels of job satisfaction due to an improvement in their ability to interact with customers in face-to-face transactions. They also frequently report a significant level of frustration because management often does not seem to notice the improved service delivery or to reward the use of learned skills. This is an example of trying to "fix a part" and not address the whole. Training employees to perform better in face-to-face transactions without designing recognition and reward systems to acknowledge and reinforce the use of the skills is an exercise in futility. In fact, productivity could suffer from an employee backlash of resentment due to managerial inattention to and lack of appreciation for the newly learned skills.

Organization. The variable organization includes both structures and processes. Structure refers to those things that give direction to and constrain peoples' behavior. Many managers think of structure mainly as a description of authority and reporting relationships as pictured on the bank's organizational chart. Structure is used here to include such things as objectives, plans, policies, procedures, rules, regulations, and methods. All of these factors give "structure" to peoples' behavior at work. Processes here give life and energy to structure. Such processes include patterns for decision making, information dissemination, control, hiring, developing the organization, rewarding performance, and improving productivity.

The following quote from Robert Metzger, a well-known bank consultant, presents a view of the problems inherent in the typical bank's organization of structure and processes:[3]

> Bankers now have tellers reporting to service tellers reporting to head tellers reporting to operations officers reporting to assistant branch managers reporting to branch managers reporting to regional vice-presidents reporting to division senior vice-presidents reporting to senior executive vice-presidents reporting to presidents reporting to deputy chairmen reporting to the chairman and chief executive officer.
>
> The six- and eight-tier reporting relationships, then, have been put in to horseshoe-shaped communication channels, thus doubling the organizational filters which seriously demoralize line and branch personnel. Communications (processes) have totally broken down, especially from the branches and operations upward toward senior management.

Such convoluted and complex hierarchical design does not provide a very fertile ground for the planting of productivity improvement programs. Participative management techniques are generally recognized by academic researchers and practitioners alike to contribute to productivity enhancement. Participative management, when applied effectively, creates an environment in which decision making, problem solving, action implementation, and recognition and reward activities are decentralized throughout the organization. Metzger's description of a bank's structure presents an environment in which the hierarchies have evolved to force the centralization of managerial authority and responsibility at higher levels.

Participative techniques applied at only one level of the organization may enhance the productivity of the unit or group temporarily, but the processes associated with the balance of the bank's organizational structure will eventually erode the gains. The traditional decision-making processes and control patterns will continue to be rewarded by those in authority. Unless the participative management program is instituted organizationwide, the effort will have only limited and temporary success.

Culture.　Culture is both one of the most important and most elusive of the model variables. It embodies the values, assumptions, beliefs, and philosophy that underlie the thinking, behaviors, and practices that make up the total organization. These underlying factors are often so deeply embedded in the fabric of the organization that they go

---

[3]Metzger, op. cit., p. 55.

unstated and even exist out of the awareness of people. Certain ways of doing things come to be taken for granted without the realization that such ways may be peculiar to only that organization. This is analogous to social cultures in which people assume their way of doing things is the right way. It is only when one encounters another culture that one realizes there are other ways of doing the same thing.

Culture deeply influences such things as who gets hired, who gets ahead, how people are rewarded, how conflict is handled, how decisions are made, how power and status are distributed, and how people relate and are organized. Culture develops over time and is often difficult to recognize. Because it is complex and elusive, it is the most difficult variable to change.

Organizational culture is frequently most observable in the group processes and interdepartmental interactions typical of organizational activity. Do departments support or compete with each other? Do departments share or hoard information? Do they protect their departmental "vested interests" or do they work together to advance the best interest of the bank? Are group meetings characterized by individuals exerting or sharing control? Do group leaders evaluate and judge people openly in public? Is performance in the unit judged on the basis of who one knows or on what one does? Is conflict in groups surfaced and addressed, or ignored and left to escalate?

Interdepartmental interactions and group processes internal to departments often reflect the cultural characteristics of the whole organization. If competition, political use of influence, and information hoarding characterize a culture, productivity programs will rarely be effective. On the other hand, if the culture can be characterized as cooperative, information and power sharing, and human resources oriented, then productivity improvement activities have an opportunity for success.

Organizational culture is pervasive and evasive. It offers barriers and facilitators to a total organization productivity program. The barriers have to be identified and modified. The facilitators must be surfaced and reinforced. This activity can be time-consuming and complex, but it is helpful to the success of improvement programs.

Management. The final variable in our model is management. The functions of management are to set goals and objectives and develop strategies, plans, policies, procedures, and programs that help achieve the bank's purposes. The job of management is to develop and coordinate a total system made up of resources, technology, people, organization, and culture that can produce the desired outputs. The concept of system is critical. How each of the variables fit together influences the productivity of the system. Because the variables are highly interdependent, a change in one leads to changes in the other variables, and the sum of the changes produces a new system. For example, the introduction of computers (resources and technology) led to changes in the skills and knowledge required of people as well as the need for new organizational relationships (a new department and new information flows—structure and process factors of the organization variable). These changes in turn are likely to influence changes in the culture of the total system.

Management's responsibility is to direct and coordinate action designed to integrate and influence productivity improvement activities in each of the variable areas. The responsibility includes monitoring changes for unintended consequences. If bank management decides to implement a performance-based compensation and reward system in their branch banks which only rewards the branch managers, some unintended consequences could be a work slow-down, absenteeism, and decreased job satisfaction at the branch.

Banking is no longer a one-person job, and the reward system should not reward just the branch manager. Eventually compensation for the entire branch team will have to become performance-based with bonus pools formed from the branch's profits. Monitoring a total productivity program entails looking for expected and unexpected outcomes.

Model Outputs

Productivity. This is the key result for most organizations. It includes both the concepts of efficiency and effectiveness. Producing the most outputs with the least inputs is the goal. However, productivity is not the only output that we should consider. Two others include satisfaction and revitalization.

Satisfaction. This is how people feel about their total work situation. It is important because it often influences productivity. However, the relationship between productivity and satisfaction is complex. Many people used to assume that if employees were satisfied they would be productive. But it is easy to think of situations in which satisfied people are not productive. More recently, some have concluded that productivity is what causes satisfaction. The fact is that there are four possible relationships between productivity and satisfaction: (1) high satisfaction/high productivity, (2) high satisfaction/low productivity, (3) low satisfaction/high productivity, and (4) low satisfaction/low productivity. Our purpose here is not to delve into these complexities other than to suggest that in any situation one of the key management decisions is to determine what is the right balance between productivity and satisfaction. One cannot safely assume that they go together easily. At times they may work against each other. Overemphasizing or underemphasizing one or the other may lead to reduced productivity. For example, pushing too hard for productivity may lead to dissatisfaction, which in turn may have adverse effects on productivity. Similarly, achieving high satisfaction may be gained at the expense of reduced productivity. The key is to find the right balance in a given situation. There are no magical formulas to follow in determining the right balance.

Revitalization. Here is another useful output concept. It means the regeneration of the system so that it is able to take care of future challenges as well as current ones. High productivity may be achieved in the short run at the expense of the organization in the long run. This concept signals management of the development and revitalization of the total system so that it will be strong over time. Again, management's job is to maintain the right balance between the three output variables—productivity, satisfaction, and revitalization.

CLOSING THE FEEDBACK LOOP

Measuring productivity, satisfaction, and revitalization is a challenging and necessary but not sufficient productivity improvement activity. Measurements in each area can be problematic as mentioned earlier. Productivity can be measured using a variety of broad-gauge financial and operating analyses and ratios available to bankers today from regulatory organizations and private sources. These measures can be valuable and provide insights into bank productivity, but they are overall indicators and do not reflect unique characteristics or differences among banks caused by the variety of markets they serve. While such broad-gauge measures offer usable information, they should be complemented by in-house productivity measurement programs designed by the employees whose performance will be subject to the measures. Bank personnel will be aware of the limitations and opportunities unique to individual banks and their respective market environments.

The most successful bank productivity improvement programs have been designed by those whose productivity is directly affected by the program. Employee activities which generate productivity programs and measures emphasize the importance of using the first-hand knowledge, skills, and experiences embedded in the people variable of the model. It also offers a testament to the value and worth of bank employees and can profoundly affect a bank's culture, particularly if the design and control of such programs has rested with top management historically.

Job satisfaction measures can be obtained through the use of employee attitude assessment surveys. These surveys assess employee perceptions of the bank environment and their personal responses to it. Such surveys can offer management valuable information in striking the necessary balance between productivity and job satisfaction. These surveys can also provide information contributing to turnover, absenteeism, and error rate situations which need managerial attention. They are only three of the many factors which contribute to low-productivity figures, but at times survey data can help managers identify and respond to problem areas before they seriously affect departmental or organizational productivity.

Finally, revitalization assessment activities are usually more qualitative than quantitative in nature. Creating a flexible organization capable of responding to change in a productive way is a process that takes place over time. The success of efforts to create such an organization are only visible over time and frequently only visible as cultural characteristics. Cultural assessment methods are time consuming and intricate but offer a necessary means of understanding the most complex of the model variables.

The feedback loop closed by the information and data revealed in output measurement methods provides management with the means for monitoring and modifying total productivity improvement activities in the bank. Productivity improvement is an ongoing management activity. It does not just begin and end. It continues as a process which becomes integrated into the organizational structural variable in the model. Once it becomes an integral part of the organization structure and process, it is part of the bank system and institutionalized in the bank's culture. This situation is the ultimate goal of all total organization productivity improvement programs.

CHAPTER NINETEEN

Effective Supervision

Dr. Robert E. Coffey

Professor of Management and Organization Behavior
University of Southern California

Most organizational charts picture a chief executive officer at the top of a pyramid. The pyramid expands with each successive layer of management descending in the following order: executive vice presidents, senior vice presidents, vice presidents, junior vice presidents, division managers, managers, assistant managers, and (near the base of the pyramid) supervisors. These individuals are most frequently called first-line supervisors because they supervise a bank's rank-and-file employees.

Too often people tend to think of supervision as a managerial function limited to first-line supervisors. This understanding of supervision is narrow and constraining. Supervision is a managerial function of every individual in the banking organization who has direct line reporting relationships with subordinate employees. This approach to supervision includes the CEO, the executive vice presidents, and each succeeding level of managers as supervisors.

The purpose of this chapter is to identify those characteristics of "effective" supervision that appear to be common to all levels of supervisors regardless of location in the bank's hierarchy. These characteristics are as important to the effectiveness of the CEO's supervisory performance as they are to the supervisory performance of each first-line supervisor. In fact, they are more critical to the CEO and his immediate reports—the executive vice presidents. It is CEOs and their top management team who set the tone and character of supervisory behavior throughout a bank. These supervisors are at the top of the banking organization and serve as models for all those aspiring to positions in higher levels of management. Top managers serve as successful models. After all, what they are doing and have done in supervising others facilitated their promotions into positions of responsibility and power.

Supervision involves directing and helping people accomplish desired objectives. This simple and straightforward definition applies to supervisory behavior at any level of bank management. The CEO directs and helps executive vice presidents who in turn direct and help vice presidents. This directing and helping behavior cascades until it eventually affects the interactions between those on the front line—a loan officer, a teller, or any person interfacing with the bank customer. If the desired objectives of a bank include the delivery of quality service to bank customers, then the directing and helping behavior will enhance customer satisfaction with the delivery of service. This model of effective supervision asserts that the CEO is more responsible for customer perceptions of service quality than the teller on the front line.

Functions of Supervision

Effective supervision is the combined management of people, work, technology, and resources to achieve desired results. Supervisors at all levels usually perform certain basic functions, including setting objectives, planning, organizing, staffing, directing, controlling, and coordinating. However, the emphasis on each of these functions varies with level. Top-level managers spend much more time understanding the environment and developing objectives, strategies, plans, and overall structures and systems designed to meet desired goals. Middle-level managers spend more time in designing, fine tuning, and implementing strategies, systems, and programs. First-line supervisors put more emphasis on directing people at work and troubleshooting within existing work systems.

Banks will not be successful unless they have efficient and effective technical systems, procedures, methods, and work flows. Modern technology, including both software and hardware, is essential for most institutions in the highly competitive environment of banking. Essential functions of managers and supervisors include the development and continual refinement of these important elements of success. These aspects of management and supervision are generally well recognized. Therefore this chapter assumes the importance of managing and supervising work systems, technology, and resources. Further, it assumes the traditional emphasis on the functional responsibilities of the supervisor (that is, planning, organizing, staffing, controlling, and coordinating) are important and necessary, but not sufficient for effective supervision. With this in mind, the emphasis here will be on managing social rather than technical processes. This approach will focus on a set of social processes often ignored in traditional discussions of supervision. An integration of functional responsibilities with the supervision of social processes will provide insight into the skills necessary *and* sufficient for those seeking to become effective supervisors, regardless of their position in the bank's managerial hierarchy.

MANAGING SOCIAL PROCESS

Banks are service organizations providing a variety of financial services to a diverse set of customers. The service provided may be the processing of a loan application, a transaction at a teller window, or the financing of a business venture. These services and numerous others involve an interaction between a bank employee and a customer. This interaction is a *social process,* an event that takes place between people. Since service delivery is a social process, it follows that effective supervision in a bank necessitates the supervision of social processes occurring among employees and consumers.

Earlier, we defined supervision as directing and helping others to accomplish desired objectives. The supervisor interacts with the employee in a manner that facilitates the employee's accomplishment of assigned tasks. The above definition implies that supervision is a one-way event—the supervisor directs and helps the employee. In reality, it is a two-way event. While the supervisor directs (communicates what is expected of the employee) and helps (provides the necessary information and resources), the employee also directs (lets the supervisor know what resources are needed to accomplish the task) and helps (provides suggestions for improving the task "product"). The quality of the interaction—the social process occurring between the supervisor and the employee—contributes to the effectiveness of the supervision. It becomes the responsibility of the supervisors to manage the quality of social processes within their work group.

The responsibility for managing social processes is an organizational responsibility for all those supervising in a bank. The cascading effect described earlier creates a situation in which each level of management from the CEO on down must manage social processes. Five critical social process areas will be presented. These areas are generic in that they need to be managed by all bank supervisors.

Knowledge and Information Sharing

Effective supervisors "know" their organization; they understand the reporting relationships outlined on the organization chart. They also understand the formal policies and procedures, and rules and regulations guiding the way work gets done in their bank. Effective supervisors have taken the time to understand functional relationships between departments and how each impacts the work of the others. They understand how problems in operations affect the quality of customer service. They know the services provided by the human resource department and other staff units and how those services can be accessed.

These organizationally smart supervisors share this knowledge with those they supervise. They become teachers by passing on organizational knowledge as they direct and help employees to achieve goals. Employees learn from the supervisor how their work contributes to the achievement of the bank's corporate goals and how their mistakes can slow down (or completely stop) work in other functional areas. Supervisors also help them understand how to pinpoint the source of problems (from other functions) impacting the quality of their work. Supervisors communicate procedural changes as they occur and make sure employees understand the implications and consequences of the changes.

In order to effectively supervise, supervisors must understand why their bank is organized as it is and how it goes about getting the job of banking done. This knowledge has to be shared through information directing and helping employees get their jobs done.

Socialization Agent

The effective supervisor helps new employees to understand their bank's culture. All organizations have unwritten rules and regulations about "the way things are done around here" that never show up in policy manuals. The bank's formal structure depicted on the organizational chart rarely explains much about the informal structure and the bank's culture.

An analogy might be drawn between an individual entering a new country and a new bank. Any time an individual moves from one country to another, a period of socialization becomes necessary. During this period the individual must learn a new language, new norms, and maybe even a new religion. The individual must also come to understand the values guiding behavior, the myths and stories which determine cultural heroes, and what behavior will be actually rewarded (as opposed to what others *say* will be rewarded). Much the same process occurs when an individual enters a new organization with its own culture.

It is the responsibility of the supervisor to help socialize the new employee. This social process requires that supervisors understand and communicate their understanding of the culture to new people.

The new employee should be helped to understand which rules and regulations can be flexibly applied and which ones cannot. The new employee should be told how to identify problems which must have managerial attention and which ones need not. New employees should quickly learn how to access communication channels that might be denied them on the organizational chart. For example, if rules and regulations state that employees must take interdepartmental conflicts to their respective managers before attempting resolution, lapsed time and inattention might escalate the conflict. Employees should be informed of the informal yet legitimate ways they can resolve interdepartment conflicts with each other, rather than risk conflict escalation. It may be that "Call 'em up and talk it over!" is the unwritten rule, but unless employees know this, they might stick to the policy manual, which allows associated unintended consequences to follow.

The CEO and his top management team share the responsibility of creating as well as maintaining a bank's culture. If this top management team launches a cost-effectiveness program designed to reduce costs bankwide without a careful consideration of potential unintended consequences, the bank's culture could be significantly altered. If the performance appraisal system becomes tied to cost-reduction program activities, the system could become an accounting function rather than a performance reward function. Employees with budgetary responsibility who are rewarded for reducing the costs eventually learn that numbers—low numbers—equal organizational rewards. The performance appraisal becomes a means for monitoring cost-reduction activity in the bank. The bank's values that once focused on quality performance may shift to a focus on cost control. The service provided by a cost-control culture is qualitatively different from the culture focused on quality performance in the delivery of service.

Monitoring bank culture is a top management responsibility. Communicating culture is a supervisory responsibility of all who supervise. Monitoring culture and socializing new employees are critical social process skills necessary for effective supervision.

Interpersonal Communication Model

The most important social process skill a supervisor can possess is that of interpersonal competency. The effective supervisor models interpersonal competency when they direct and help employees achieve goals. Interpersonal competency can be defined in many ways. Here it is used to communicate an attitude of respect and genuine concern for the employee. It means the ability to get intended results from social interactions, and it includes consideration of the needs of both parties in the interaction. It means much more than simply being a nice, pleasant person. It may include, for example, confronting difficult situations openly and assertively. The supervisor can "direct and help" in many ways. Interpersonally competent supervisors never forget that they are directing and helping another human being develop and achieve goals.

Effective supervisors communicate respect by managing social interactions with employees. They do this by giving them their undivided attention during conversation. They remove distractions (put down papers, phone, pencils, and the like) and make eye contact as they listen and respond to employees. They listen to what the employee has to say and try to see the issue or problem from the employee's vantage point. They reflect on what has been said to verify the meaning in the employee's words, not just the "sound" of the words.

They then share any and all information or organizational knowledge that might be related to the employee's issue. If the employee is expressing a need for personal development, the supervisor explores the organizational resources available to help. If the employee seeks help in resolving an interpersonal conflict with another employee, the supervisor listens and explores the conflict with the employee. The two together create an agenda for addressing the issue. Supervisors not only manage their social processes with individual employees, they also manage the social processes between employees. At all times, they model the interpersonal competency they expect employees to demonstrate with each other.

Such an attitude about and approach to the social process of interpersonal competency becomes an organizational asset to a service organization. Interpersonal competency becomes a quality of the bank's culture which carries over into interactions with customers. Employees supervised by interpersonally competent managers interact with each other and those they serve with respect and genuine concern. This expression of respect and concern is a critical characteristic of quality service and acts as a competitive edge in financial service markets.

Understanding Employee and Organization Needs

Successful supervision requires knowledge of what the organization expects from employees and knowledge of what employees expect from work. Aligning organizational and employee needs may be one of the most difficult tasks facing a supervisor. The bank requires that tasks be accomplished in a manner that facilitates overall organizational goals. The work—of whatever variety—must be of a quality that meets organizational standards. It should be accomplished in a timely fashion. Work should also conform to policy and procedure guidelines without violating bank rules and regulations.

Recognizing, understanding, and responding to employee work needs offers the supervisor a difficult challenge. Organizational requirements are often explicit. They can be verbalized and measured. Employee needs are frequently implicit, qualitative in nature, and value-based. Only the employee knows when his or her needs are truly met.

The supervisor's task in this social process area is to interact with employees in a way that their work needs are verbalized and become explicit. Only then can work be designed to meet employee needs. The work force in today's bank is well educated, ethnically diverse, increasingly more female than male, and imbued with an entrepreneurial spirit. The needs of such a work force place considerable demand on supervisors and organizations in general. People no longer work for work's sake alone. Their needs can be as diverse as they are, and their expectations are high that work will provide satisfaction.

A study conducted by Yankelovich, Skelly, and White for the 1983 Public Agenda Foundation gives supervisors many valuable insights into the work needs of the modern worker. The study reported that half of the people interviewed said they worked just hard enough to avoid getting fired. Seventy-five percent said they could be significantly more effective on the job.

When asked why they do not work hard, a frequent response was that managers provide little incentive to work hard. The study reported that people want the satisfaction of knowing that through their work they will feel competent, respected, and effective. It becomes obvious that the supervisor's task is to structure jobs in a way that allows employees to experience job satisfaction. The 1983 Public Agenda Foundation study reported the following top 10 qualities employees want in a job today:

1. To work with people who treat me with respect.
2. To do interesting work.
3. To be recognized for doing good work.
4. To have the opportunity to develop skills.
5. To work for people who listen if you have ideas about how to do things better.
6. To have the chance to think for myself rather than just carry out instructions.
7. To see the end results of my work.
8. To work for efficient managers.

9. To have a job that is not too easy.
10. To feel well-informed about what is going on.

Security, high pay, and good benefits were not in the top 10. Those issues that made the top 10 are, for the most part, *social process* issues. The effective supervisor recognizes and addresses the social nature of work and the critical need to create a work environment in which respect, interpersonal competency, and challenging work are integrated into organizational goal achievement efforts.

Service Orientation

Banks are service organizations and are personality intensive in the sense that the quality of the service supplied to the customer is a result of the way people perform in the provision of service. Earlier we asserted that service is a social process and that management in service organizations is concerned with the ability to direct social processes. Quality and economic performance in service organizations are highly dependent on the social performance of individuals or small groups who may have a high degree of freedom to influence the provision of service. This point has important implications for those supervising service delivery employees.

Effective supervision of service delivery personnel requires that supervisors imbue their work groups with a service orientation. Service orientations are often the primary factor contributing to customer perceptions of excellent service. Such an orientation becomes a characteristic of the culture of service work groups and organizations. Banks enjoy thousands of customer contacts (moments of truth) every day, most involving employees working on the front line. The only way to achieve high quality in every single contact is to create and nourish a pervasive service-oriented culture. Supervisors must manage the social processes which ensure that every employee possesses the appropriate skills and is guided by the appropriate cultural principles.

A service orientation rests on the three following principles. When these principles operate as the foundation of a service group's values and culture, a special kind of atmosphere arises in the bank. Bank employees help create and communicate this atmosphere and customers recognize and respond to it.

Principle 1: Service Is Our Primary Product. Service is a nonpatentable, subjective phenomenon. When an employee services a customer's needs at the new accounts desk, the customer judges the service event on the basis of the *interaction* that occurs, not on the stack of brochures or forms to be signed or the speed of the new accounts representative. Customers respond to the manner in which the new accounts representative shares information, explains bank services, and seeks to understand their banking needs.

Does the employee smile, listen, and treat the customer with respect and consideration? Is the employee technically knowledgeable and competent? Is the employee sensitive to hearing and sensing the customer's needs and preferences, including knowing when to suggest and "sell" and when not to press but to do just what the customer wants? All too frequently new account representatives are busy meeting the needs of management (sell more services) or their own needs (the more I sell the larger the bonus I'll receive) rather than those of the customer.

Service is a social process occurring between an employee and a customer. The minute that employees begin to impose their needs on the service event, the customer's needs become secondary. Effective supervision in such a situation requires that the supervisor emphasize that the customer's needs come first and selling is secondary. The product mix of the bank will sell itself if the service interactions presented to the customer possess high quality.

One very important consideration is that employees cannot be expected to give high-quality service if they themselves are feeling pressured and stressed. Nor can they give the desired level of service if the technical systems on which they must rely are inadequate. The supervisor's job is to monitor and ensure that the appropriate conditions, resources, and knowledge necessary for high-quality service are available. If these essential service elements are available, the supervisor can then focus on helping each employee develop the technical competence and interpersonal skills that lead to extraordinary service.

High-quality service should be an inseparable part of each bank product. Service might even be considered the primary "product," the foundation of the product mix. The supervisor's task is to establish and reinforce this approach to service delivery.

Principle 2: The Customer Is the Best Judge of Quality Service. Managerial and customer definitions of service quality may not coincide. Bank management frequently defines quality service from a "numbers" perspective. The number of minutes of contact per customer, the number of customer contacts per employee, and the number of bank products sold per contact may equal quality service from a cost-effective managerial perspective. Such an approach to defining quality service may satisfy "return on investment" criteria established by a bank's board of directors, but it may also contribute significantly to customer dissatisfaction.

Customers have a subjective set of criteria they use to assess quality service that has little to do with numbers. The customer is buying the interaction first and the product mix second. Even if timely service is a major consideration to customers, they usually want speedy, *considerate*, and competent service. Most customers do not want mechanically efficient, impersonal service in their face-to-face contacts with bank personnel. They get that from ATMs, car washes, and vending machines. The numbers approach to quality service often "automates" service. While this may appeal to some service users, it will not appeal to the majority.

A service orientation requires that knowledge of customer definitions of quality service guide service delivery. Customers know what they want and are very good about telling people, if asked. The supervisor should interact with consumers as often as possible. Personal attention to consumer service needs does not require a great deal of time. Simple questions such as "How was the service you received today?" can elicit a wealth of information useful to supervisors. They may hear a dozen complaints or a dozen compliments. Both sets of responses contain valuable information supervisors can use to fine tune service delivery.

The information can be shared with employees. They can help redesign service delivery problem areas to reduce complaints or ensure the behavior that gave rise to the compliments. Such activity guided by the supervisor can facilitate both *customer and employee participation* in improving service.

Principle 3: We Serve Each Other as Well as the Customers. A service orientation, when embedded in a bank's culture, becomes a way of working together, not just a way of working with the customer. Back-office and front-office operations serve each other, so do managers and employees, and so do functional departments.

A bank's product mix (that is, loans, demand and savings accounts, portfolio management, and so on) are delivered to the consuming public as a result of many interactions between departments, managerial hierarchies, and individuals inside the bank. The "product" may travel through several departments and across many desks in each department. As the product moves, it becomes an "opportunity to serve." Each person involved serves the needs of all others included . in finalizing product delivery. This internal service demands the same attention to quality as service provided to the consumer.

Supervisors managing employees whose work will be used by others should emphasize this principle of internal service orientation. They can do this by managing the quality of the social processes occurring between employees and those with whom they interact.

The management of social processes is as important as managing the quality of the actual work done. Supervision is the management of social processes within and between work groups as well as managing the social processes between customer contact employees and the customer. An internal service orientation facilitates service by implying that all participants in the service event—service designers, providers, and consumers—are deserving of equal respect and consideration. Where such orientations exist, a special service environment emerges that enhances the self-respect of all those involved.

METAPHORS AND SUPERVISION

Many people find it useful to get the "right" metaphor for understanding what makes a good supervisor. Of course, there is no single right metaphor, but several different ones are usually most helpful. Traditionally, the metaphors frequently used were those of overseer, director, driver, and boss. It is easy to see that these communicate rather different connotations than those of coach, teambuilder, teacher, and facilitator. A useful exercise can be to brainstorm a list of metaphors for supervisors. Once the list is developed, discussion and evaluation of each can help give useful insights. Those that are judged inappropriate can be as revealing as those deemed most suitable. The value of thinking about and choosing appropriate metaphors is that mental pictures of the functions, behaviors, and roles are stimulated. Sometimes identifying and talking about a single powerful metaphor can communicate more than pages of words.

CONCLUSION

Supervisors, whether CEO or manager of rank-and-file employees, must manage social processes in the areas of knowledge and information sharing, employee socialization, interpersonal competency, understanding the needs of employees, and in instilling a service orientation in their work group. The bank supervisor, while directing and helping employees achieve organizational goals, must at the same time recognize the importance of developing and educating people who will be providing service to each other as well as to the ultimate service consumer. Managing social processes in work groups helps in the developmental and educational efforts which will eventually result in the delivery of quality service.

While employees must learn the technical skills necessary to do their jobs, it is the interactive social process skills which will determine excellent service. These interactive skills are often taught in training and development programs designed to help customer contact employees deal with customers (particularly problem customers) in face-to-face situations. Such programs will have limited value if the superiors of the participants have not also received the training. If supervisors do not understand or share the values on which the training is based, then it will be difficult for them to recognize and reinforce the behavior in their employees.

If the purpose of this training is to develop a service-oriented culture in the bank, other problems arise. Many studies have shown that it is almost impossible to develop and maintain a service-oriented culture between bank employees and between customer contact employees and customers unless the same culture and basic values exist in the relationships between front-line employees and their supervisors. If one behavioral code and one set of values exists inside the bank and another in external contacts with customers, the contact employees will find themselves in a difficult double bind. The lack of clarity in the situation will reduce the quality of the service as well as work motivation and customer satisfaction. This situation will ultimately affect the bottom line. If supervisors treat employees one way and expect employees to treat customers in another, contact employees will be confused and unintentionally communicate their confusion to the customer.

Common characteristics do determine the effectiveness of supervision whether at the top or bottom of a bank's hierarchy. Throughout a bank organization, supervisors at all levels must manage the social processes as well as their functional responsibilities. One can organize and plan and delegate and control and still not supervise effectively. The service organization requires attention to social as well as functional responsibilities. Only when the two are integrated in supervisory activity will the necessary and sufficient characteristics of effective supervision exist.

CHAPTER TWENTY

Federal Regulations Affecting Bank Personnel Management

Edwin C. Wallace, Jr.

National Accounts Manager
Security Pacific Organizational Consultants, Inc.

Sandra A. Boone

Vice President
Sovran Financial Corporation

A number of laws and regulations governing the employment relationship between banks and bank employees were discussed in previous chapters. This chapter will highlight additional government requirements which must be observed in managing human resources.

Neither the list of laws nor the treatment of many of the individual laws covered is exhaustive, so one caveat is in order: just as any provision of law may be subject to different interpretations, so may any generalized statement regarding such a provision be subject to different interpretations or be contradicted by citing an exception or a special qualification to the rule. This is true of much that follows. The intent is to provide a broad overview of the laws and regulations, not a detailed guide to legal compliance.

FAIR LABOR STANDARDS ACT (WAGE-HOUR LAW)

The Fair Labor Standards Act, commonly known as the Wage-Hour Law, was enacted in 1938 to establish fair pay standards for covered employees. Specifically, the law sets requirements for the payment of minimum wages and overtime pay, establishes special restrictions on the employment of children, and prohibits discrimination in pay rates on the basis of sex.

Bank employees are covered under the act because banks regularly use the channels of interstate commerce in the course of operations. Such interstate activity includes the preparation of documents which cross state lines—the handling, receiving, or transmitting of money or documents across state lines and the interstate use of communications channels such as telephones, telegraph, and the mails. Employees may be covered even though they do not directly participate in these interstate activities.

Minimum Wage and Overtime Requirements

Simply stated, employers are required to pay each covered employee at least the *minimum wage* for each *hour worked* and 1½ times the employee's *regular rate of pay* for each hour worked over 40 hours in each *work week*. This statement becomes a little more complicated with closer examination of the italicized phrases which are defined as follows:

1. Hours worked is all time during which an employee is required or permitted to work at the bank, at home, or any other place. Questions frequently arise about the following areas:
   a. Short breaks or rest periods count as work time.
   b. Meal periods of approximately 30 minutes or longer during which an employee is completely relieved from all work duties do not count as work time.
   c. Required attendance at lectures, meetings, and training programs is work time.
   d. Normal commuting to and from work does not count as work time.
   e. Travel time involved in answering an "emergency" call to work and travel time between work sites that is all in a day's work count as work time.
   f. Travel time involved in out-of-town travel that does not keep the employee away from home overnight counts as work time. Normal home to office commuting time and normal meal periods may be deducted from total out-of-town travel time.
   g. Travel as a passenger that keeps an employee away from home overnight is generally counted as work time only to the extent that the travel time coincides with the employee's normally scheduled work hours (or on corresponding hours on Saturdays or Sundays). If the employee is required to drive on such trips because public transportation is unavailable, all driving time counts as work time.
   h. Work for charitable or civic organizations counts as work time only if it is performed (1) at the request or under the

direction or control of the employer or (2) while the employee is required to be on the employer's premises.

2. Regular rate of pay is defined to include all remuneration for employment paid to, or on behalf of, the employee. There are several specific types of payments that are excluded from this definition:

   a. Gifts that are not given on the basis of hours worked, production, or efficiency.

   b. Payments made for holidays, vacation, illness, and so on, and payments made to reimburse an employee for expenses incurred on behalf of the employer (such as travel expenses).

   c. Discretionary bonuses and payments under a bona fide profit sharing, thrift, or savings plan.

   d. Payments made to a trustee or a third party to provide benefits under a bona fide employee benefit plan.

   e. Certain overtime premiums.

3. A work week is defined as a regularly recurring period of 168 consecutive hours (seven days). It may begin and end on any day of the week and any hour of the day.

Fluctuating Workweek

An alternative method of calculating overtime is allowed under certain conditions. This method is referred to as the "fluctuating workweek" method. Under permissible circumstances, an employer and employee may enter into an agreement in which the employee's weekly salary is straight-time compensation for all hours worked, including those beyond 40, plus one-half time [$\frac{1}{2} \times$ (salary $\div$ hours worked)] for the hours in excess of 40.

To illustrate the regular method of overtime calculation versus the fluctuating workweek method, assume an employee is paid a salary of $240 per week works 48 hours during one workweek.

Regular method

Regular pay... $240.00

Overtime pay

$240 (regular pay) $\div$ 40 (hours per week) = $6.00 (hourly rate)

$6.00 (hourly rate) $\times$ $1\frac{1}{2}$ = $9.00 (overtime rate)

$9.00 $\times$ 8 (overtime hours)................................. $ 72.00

Total pay for week... $312.00

Fluctuating workweek method

Regular pay.. $240.00

Overtime Pay

    $240 (regular pay) ÷ 48 (hours worked) = $5.00 (hourly rate)

    $5.00 (hourly rate) × ½ = $2.50 (overtime rate)

    $2.50 × 8 (overtime hours)..................................... $ 20.00

Total pay for week.. $260.00

Although significant savings may be derived using this method, it may also have a negative impact on the morale of employees.

Exempt Employees

Exemption from the minimum wage and overtime provisions of the act is provided for some white-collar employees. Exemption depends on employee duties, responsibilities, and salary level; title is not a determining factor. Following are various categories of exempt employees and the criteria used to determine whether an employee falls into each category:

1. Executives
   a. Primary duty must be management of the establishment or a recognized department.
   b. Must regularly direct the work of at least two full-time employees.
   c. Must have the authority to hire and fire, or so recommend.
   d. Must regularly exercise discretionary powers.
   e. Must devote no more than 20 percent of the workweek to nonexempt work.
   f. Must earn a salary of at least $155 per week.
      Note. The 20 percent test need not be met if (1) the employee is in sole charge of the establishment where employed, or (2) owns at least 20 percent of the establishment. Also, an employee who earns at least $250 per week need only meet the first two tests to be exempt.
2. Administrative employees. There are three types of administrative employees: (1) executive and administrative assistants such as executive secretaries, assistants to the general manager, and confidential assistants; (2) staff employees who are advisory specialists for management; and (3) those who perform special assignments, often away from their employer's workplace.

    a. Primary duty must be responsible, office or nonmanual work of substantial importance to management or operation of the business.

    b. Must customarily and regularly exercise discretion and independent judgment as distinguished from using skills and following established procedures, including power to make important decisions.

    c. Must spend no more than 20 percent of workweek on nonexempt work—that is, work not closely related to administrative duties.

    d. Must be paid at least $155 per week.

        Note. Only the first two tests must be met by employees earning at least $250 per week.

3. Professional employees

    a. Work must require advanced knowledge in a field of science or learning usually obtained by a long course of specialized intellectual instruction at a college or university, or must be original and creative, and results must depend mainly on invention, imagination, and talent.

    b. Must consistently exercise discretion and judgment.

    c. Must do work that is mainly intellectual and varied as distinguished from routine or mechanical duties.

    d. Must spend no more than 20 percent of the workweek on activities not closely related to professional duties.

    e. Must be paid at least $170 per week.

        Note. Only the first test must be met if the employee earns at least $250 per week.

4. Outside salesmen

    a. Must normally work away from the employer's place of business in making sales or obtaining orders or contracts for services.

    b. Time spent on nonexempt work may not exceed 20 percent of the workweek of nonexempt employees of the same employer.

Equal Pay

The Fair Labor Standards Act was amended in 1963 by the Equal Pay Act. This amendment prohibits discrimination in pay between covered employees on the basis of sex. It applies to employees of the same establishment who perform work that requires equal skill, effort, and responsibility, and that is performed under similar working conditions. The act does not prohibit discrimination on the basis of bona fide seniority systems, merit systems, or systems that measure earnings by quality or quantity of production or any other factor other than sex. An employer may not reduce the wages of any employee in order to comply.

Any wage difference approved under the Equal Pay Act is valid under the subsequently enacted Civil Rights Act of 1964.

Child Labor

The child labor provisions of the Fair Labor Standards Act were designed to protect minor employees between the ages of 14 and 18 from "oppressive child labor" practices. Special provisions are provided for the employment of individuals in certain age brackets:

A. Over age 18—no restrictions.
B. Ages 16 to 18—employees between ages 16 and 18 may be employed in any occupation except those declared hazardous.
C. Ages 14 to 16—employment of individuals between the ages of 14 and 15 is allowed only under the following conditions:
   a. The employer must obtain and maintain on file an unexpired certificate of age issued by appropriate federal or state authorities.
   b. Employment must be confined to the following periods:
      (1) When school is in session.
          i. Outside school hours except if enrolled in a school administered work experience or career exploration program
          ii. more than three hours in any one day.
          iii. Between 7 A.M. and 7 P.M.
      (2) When school is not in session.
          i. Not more than 40 hours in any one week.
          ii. Between 7 A.M. and 9 P.M.
   c. The work must be in nonhazardous occupations.

Whenever state law establishes stricter restrictions, state law prevails.

AGE DISCRIMINATION IN EMPLOYMENT ACT

The Age Discrimination in Employment Act of 1967 imposes requirements on employers, labor organizations, and employment agencies in order to protect individuals who are at least 40 years of age. Employers with 20 or more employees and who are engaged in commerce are covered.

Under the act it is illegal for an employer:

1. To fail or refuse to hire or to discharge any individual or otherwise discriminate against any individual with respect to com-

pensation, terms, conditions, or privileges of employment because of the individual's age.
2. To limit, segregate, or classify employees in any way which would deprive or tend to deprive any individual of employment opportunities or otherwise adversely affect their status as an employee because of the individual's age.
3. To reduce the wage rate of any employee in order to comply with the act.
4. To retaliate against employees or applicants for asserting their rights under the act.
5. To indicate any preference, limitation, specification, or discrimination based on age in its employment advertising.

It is not illegal under the act for an employer:

1. To discriminate where age is a bona fide occupational qualification or where differentiation is made on some basis other than age.
2. To observe the terms of bona fide seniority system or benefit plan which is not a subterfuge to the act.
3. To discharge or otherwise discipline an individual for a good cause.

While the act prohibits mandatory retirement, an employee who is 65 years of age with a retirement package totaling at least $44,000 and is employed in a policy-making position may be retired.

THE OCCUPATIONAL SAFETY AND HEALTH ACT (OSHA)

OSHA covers virtually every employer in the United States. Basically, the law requires employers to maintain workplaces free from recognized hazards and to meet certain minimum safety standards for specific hazards. The law sets standards, provides for inspections, imposes severe penalties for repeated serious violations, and requires mandatory reporting and disclosure to both the Department of Labor and employees.

While the law is addressed principally to manufacturing and construction industries, many of the safety standards and requirements, such as those related to electricity and provisions of toilet facilities, apply to all industries. Banks which have warehouses, print shops, courier services, and the like should insure that the work areas meet specific OSHA requirements and that workers follow prescribed OSHA rules.

If a violation is found, the Department of Labor issues a citation. The employer has 15 working days to contest. If the citation is not contested, it becomes final and binding. Contested violations are heard by the OSHA Review Commission. Findings may be appealed through the U.S. Court of Appeals. In the case of repeated violations, penalties may be up to $10,000 or six months in prison or both.

Detailed records must be kept of all occupational injuries, and any serious accidents or deaths must be reported to the area OSHA director within 48 hours. An annual summary of all occupational injuries must be posted in each work location. Forms for maintaining the records are available from local area offices.

ENFORCEMENT AND RECORD RETENTION

The Equal Pay Act and the Age Discrimination Act are enforced and administered by the Equal Employment Opportunity Commission.

The Fair Labor Standards Act is administered by the U.S. Department of Labor. The administrator of the Wage and Hour Division, through compliance officers, may make necessary inspections and investigations to determine compliance with the law.

Enforcement of OSHA is also through the Department of Labor. Violations of safety regulations are detected through on-site inspections or through employee complaints to the Department of Labor.

Exhibit 1 indicates the required records under these acts and the period of time over which these records must be retained.[1]

NATIONAL LABOR RELATIONS ACT

The purpose of the act is to define and protect the rights of employees and employers, to encourage collective bargaining, and to eliminate certain practices on the part of labor and management that are harmful to the general welfare. Primarily, the act governs labor and management actions in unionized organizations.

Although attempts to organize banks have increased in recent years, there are currently few unionized banks. Because of this and because of the complexity of the law, the following is a very "broadbrush" description. Perhaps of equal value to the layman's knowledge of the law is the advice to seek competent legal advice from a labor specialist at the first sign of any union-organizing activity.

Rights of Employees

Under the provisions of the National Labor Relations Act (NLRA), employees are guaranteed the right:

---

[1]*Federal Wage Hour Handbook for Banks* (American Bankers Association-Bank Personnel Division, 1975) p. 31.

EXHIBIT 1   Record Requirements

Authority (Federal)	Records to be Retained	Time Period Required
Fair Labor Standards Act 1938 **Nonexempt requirements**	**A.** Employee's name, address, birthdate (if under age 19), sex, occupation, hour, and day when employee's workweek begins, hours worked each day and each workweek. Basis on which wages are paid, regular hourly rate for any overtime, weekly amount and nature of payment excluded from the regular rate, total daily or weekly straight-time earnings, total overtime earnings for workweek, all wage additions or deductions and total wages paid each pay period, dates of payment and of pay period.	**A. For three years:** Basic payroll records, relevant union or individual employment contracts, applicable certificates and notices of wage-hour administrator, sales and purchase records. **For two years:** Basic time and earnings cards, wage rate tables worktime schedules, shipping and billing records, records of additions to or deductions from wages.
Exempt requirements (executive, administrative, professional and outside salesman)	**B.** Employee's name, address, birthdate (if under 19), sex, occupation, time of day, and day of week on which the employee's workweek begins, total wages paid each pay period, date of payment and the pay period, date of payment and the pay period covered by payment.	
Equal Pay Law (Section 11C of Wage-Hour Law of 1962)	**A.** Employee's name in full, home address, date of birth (if under 19), sex and occupation in which employed; time of day and day of week in which workweek begins; regular rate of pay for any week when overtime pay is due; hours worked each workday and total hours worked each week, total daily or weekly straight-time earnings; total overtime pay in excess of straight-time; total additions or deductions from wages for each pay period; total wages paid each pay period; date of payment and pay period covered.	**A.** Not specified.

EXHIBIT 1   (*continued*)

Authority (Federal)	Records to be Retained	Time Period Required
	B. Additionally, employers must keep any records they normally retain of: wage payments, wage rate, job evaluations, job descriptions, merit systems, seniority systems, collective bargaining agreements, descriptions of pay practices or other matters explaining basis for payment of wage differentials which might be pertinent in determining whether they are based on a factor other than sex.	**B.** Two years.
Age Discrimination Act 1967	**A.** Payroll records containing each employee's name, address, date of birth, occupation, rate of pay, and compensation earned each week.	**A.** Three years.
	B. Personnel records relating to (1) job applications, resumes, or other replies to job advertisements, including records pertaining to failure to hire; (2) promotion, demotion, transfer, selection for training, layoff, recall or discharge; (3) job orders submitted to employment agency or union; (4) test papers in connection with employment— administered aptitude or other employment tests; (5) physical examination results; (6) job advertisements or notices to employers regarding openings, promotions, training programs or opportunities for overtime work.	**B.** One year from date of personnel action to which record relates, except 90 days for application forms and other preemployment records for temporary jobs.
	C. Employee benefit plans, written seniority or merit rating systems.	**C.** Period plan or system is in one year.

EXHIBIT 1 (*concluded*)

Authority (Federal)	Records to be Retained	Time Period Required
Occupational Safety and Health Act of 1970	A. OSHA No. 200 - Log and Summary. The log is a mandatory means for classifying injury and illness cases and for noting the extent of and outcome of each.	A. Five years.
	B. OSHA No. 101 - The Supplementary Record. For every recordable injury or illness, it is necessary to record additional information requested on the OSHA No. 101 form. However, the OSHA No. 101 form itself does not have to be used. Worker's compensation, insurance or other reports are acceptable supplementary records if they contain all items found on the OSHA No. 101 form.	B. Five years.

- To self-organization.
- To form, join, or assist labor organizations.
- To bargain collectively through representatives of their own choosing.
- To engage in other concerted activities for the purpose of collective bargaining or other mutual aid or protection.
- To refrain from any or all of such activities except to the extent that such right may be affected by an agreement requiring membership in a labor organization as a condition of employment.

It should be noted that these rights are guaranteed to employees whether or not they are unionized. Consequently, nonunionized employees also enjoy the protection of the law when undertaking a "concerted action"—an action taken by two or more employees for their mutual aid or protection.

Unfair Labor Practices

The law enumerates unfair labor practices on the part of both employers and labor organizations:

1. Employers may not:
   a. Interfere with, restrain, or coerce employees exercising their rights under the act.
   b. Dominate or support a labor organization.
   c. Encourage or discourage membership in a labor organization by discriminating in hiring or in tenure, terms, or conditions of employment.
   d. Discriminate against employees for filing charges or testifying with the National Labor Relations Board.
   e. Refuse to bargain in good faith about wages, hours, and other conditions of employment with a duly selected bargaining representative.

2. Labor organizations may not:
   a. Restrain or coerce employees in the exercise of their rights under the act.
   b. Cause an employer to discriminate against an employee in regard to wages, hours, and other conditions of employment for the purpose of encouraging or discouraging membership in a labor organization.
   c. Refuse to bargain in good faith with an employer about wages, hours, and other conditions of employment.
   d. Engage in strikes and boycotts or take other specified actions to accomplish illegal purposes.
   e. Charge excessive or discriminatory membership fees where union membership is required as a condition of employment.
   f. Featherbed.
   g. Use picketing as a device to organize employees or gain recognition as an employee representative.

Collective Bargaining

Employers are required to bargain with duly designated or selected employee representatives of employees in an appropriate bargaining unit. An "appropriate bargaining unit" is a group of two or more employees who share common employment interests and conditions and may reasonably be grouped together for purposes of collective bargaining.

The National Labor Relations Board (NLRB) determines whether an employee group constitutes an appropriate bargaining unit by examining the circumstances of each situation. Consequently, there is no clear-cut guideline as to what group may or may not be determined to be an appropriate bargaining unit. However, in determining an appropriate bargaining unit, the NLRB considers such criteria as geographic proximity, commonality of personnel policies and pay practices, and transfers into and out of the unit.

Enforcement

Responsibility for enforcing the act has been delegated by Congress to the National Labor Relations Board. To assist in administering the law, the NLRB has established regional and field offices throughout the states.

The three main functions of the NLRB are (1) to interpret the act, (2) to conduct representative elections and certify results, and (3) to prevent employers and unions from engaging in unfair labor practices. The NLRB acts only on requests in the form of "petitions" requesting elections and "charges" of unfair labor practices.

Although the National Labor Relations Board could exercise its powers to enforce the NLRA in all cases involving enterprises whose operations affect commerce, the board does not act in all such cases. In its discretion it limits the exercise of its powers to cases involving enterprises whose effect on commerce is "substantial." Substantial effect is determined by the yearly amount of business done by the bank or company.

SOCIAL SECURITY ACT

The Social Security Act is one of the most far-reaching pieces of social welfare legislation in the United States. The act covers every private employer and 9 out of 10 workers. Social security was originally established on the principle of employers and employees sharing the cost of providing old age and unemployment benefits. The original concept of shared cost has been maintained—but the level of benefits, the types of benefits, and the number of people covered have increased dramatically over the years. Amendments to the Social Security Act tying increases in benefit levels to the consumer price index practically ensure increases in future benefit levels and taxes. These future increases must be considered in projecting employee salary costs and planning employee benefits.

The social security system is financed through taxes paid by employers, employees, and self-employed individuals under the Federal Insurance Contributions Act (FICA) and the Self-Employed Contributions Act. The taxes must be paid by both the employer and the employee on all taxable wages up to the annual maximum. Determination of an employer's liability for taxes depends largely on whether employees meet the definition of "employee" under the act and the amount of taxable "wages." As a practical matter, almost every employee is covered. The basic test is whether the employee is subject to the will and control of an employer with regard to what and how the work is to be done. Whether the employer exercises this right does not matter. Exceptions exist for certain classes of employees.

The wages subject to FICA taxes include cash wages, tips, bonuses, commissions, and the value of any remuneration paid in other than cash. Payments generally not subject to taxes include sick pay and retirement payments. The amount of tax is determined by applying a FICA tax rate to the taxable wages which are less than the current maximum social security wage base in any calendar year. Both the tax rate and the maximum wage base are subject to annual increases. The Internal Revenue Service collects the taxes from employers who are required to withhold the employee portion. Every employer liable for FICA taxes must submit a quarterly return reporting income tax withheld from wages, and the employer FICA tax and employee FICA taxes withheld from wages. The frequency of payment is at least quarterly, with more frequent payments required for higher tax liabilities.

Benefits provided to participants by the amended Social Security Act cover a wide variety of social, welfare, and public assistance programs. The social security system covers 11 major programs in three major categories:

1. Social insurance.
   a. Old age, survivors, and disability income.
   b. Unemployment insurance.
   c. Health insurance for aged (Medicare).
2. Public assistance and welfare assistance.
   a. Supplemental security income for the aged, blind, and disabled.
   b. Medicaid.
   c. Aid to families with dependent children.
   d. Grants to states for services to aged, blind, and disabled.
3. Children's services.
   a. Maternal and child health services.
   b. Services for crippled children.
   c. Child welfare services.
   d. Mental retardation services.

Some of these programs are administered in conjunction with state governments with federal subsidies from the social security system. Consideration should be given to such benefits as retirement income, disability income, Medicare, and Medicaid in developing benefit programs to ensure that benefits already provided under these programs are not duplicated.

FEDERAL WAGE GARNISHMENT LAW

Title III of the Consumer Credit Protection Act contains provisions governing the garnishment of employee wages. A garnishment is any legal or equitable procedure through which earnings of any individual are required to be withheld for payment of any debt.

Only a portion of an employee's disposable earnings are subject to garnishment. Disposable earnings are earnings remaining after legally required withholdings. The maximum amount of an employee's disposable earnings which is subject to garnishment in any workweek may not exceed the lessor of:

a. Twenty-five percent of disposable earnings for that week.
b. The amount by which disposable earnings for that week exceeds 30 times the federal minimum hourly wage in effect at the time that earnings are payable.

Discharging of employees because their earnings have been subject to garnishment for any one indebtedness is prohibited. "One indebtedness" refers to a single debt, regardless of the number of levies made or number of proceedings brought for its collection.

State laws governing garnishment may set more liberal standards regarding the number of indebtedness which would subject an individual to discharge. In addition, the wording of certain state statutes may require that banks withhold all funds in an employee's bank account as well as withholding the prescribed percentage of his disposable earnings.

UNIVERSAL MILITARY TRAINING AND SERVICE ACT

This act protects the reemployment rights of veterans returning from the satisfactory performance of military service. Basically, the law provides that if veterans apply for reemployment within a certain period after discharge, they must be reemployed in the same position or one of the same seniority status, and pay.

Veterans must apply within 90 days after release from active duty and must still be qualified to perform their previous job. Seniority must be adjusted to reflect military service and the employer cannot discharge the employee for one year without sufficient cause.

The reemployment rights apply to both inductees and voluntary enlistees. The rights apply for employees who voluntarily extend their period of service provided the total period is not more than four years.

Special provisions are made for Ready Reserve trainees. Ready reservists who undergo three to six months' training must reapply within 31 days of separation.

Employees who receive discharges under "undesirable," "bad conduct," "dishonorable," or "conditions other than honorable" are not entitled to reemployment rights.

Executive Order 11701

Executive Order 11701 directed the Secretary of Labor to issue regulations requiring federal contractors to list job openings with appropriate government employment agencies in order to aid the employment of Vietnam veterans. The regulations themselves require each contractor to list all appropriate job openings with the state employment system. Each contractor must file quarterly reports providing (1) the number of people hired, (2) the number of disabled veterans hired, (3) the number of Vietnam-era veterans hired, and (4) maintain an affirmative action program for Vietnam-era veterans.

OTHER FEDERAL BANKING REGULATIONS

Regulations of the Comptroller of the Currency

The regulations contained in this section apply to employees of national banks.

Sec. 4.18(c)	Prohibits disclosure of information contained in a report of examination to any person or organization not officially connected with the bank.
Sec. 7.4020	Prohibits officers, clerks, tellers, and bookkeepers from being designated to act as proxy.
Sec. 7.4205	Prohibits, without the written consent of the FDIC, persons who have been convicted of any criminal offense involving dishonesty or breach of trust from serving as a director, officer, or employee.
Sec. 7.4415	Prohibits an officer from administering the oath to be taken by directors.
Sec. 7.5000	Permits a bank to adopt reasonable bonus or sharing plans.
Sec. 7.5010	Encourages banks to adopt qualified pension plans.
Sec. 7.5015	Permits the provision of employee stock purchase and stock option plans.
Sec. 7.5215	Requires adequate fidelity coverage for officers and employees.
Sec. 7.5217	Permits banks to provide indemnification coverage for directors, officers, and other employees.
Sec. 7.5220	Permits a board of directors to enter into reasonable employment contracts with officers and employees.

Sec. 7.5225	Establishes reporting requirements for known or suspected defalcations involving bank personnel and any mysterious disappearances of $1,000 or more.
Sec. 7.5230	Permits banks to purchase homes of transferred employees. Requires early divestment of title to such property.
Sec. 7.7115	Permits banks to purchase keyman insurance.
Sec. 9.7	Permits the board of directors to delegate fiduciary powers to officers, employees, and committees. Requires bonding of trust department employees.
Sec. 9.12	Limits self-dealing transactions involving fiduciary accounts.
Sec. 9.15	Requires board of director approval to permit any officer or employee to retain any compensation for acting as co-fiduciary with the bank in the administration of a fiduciary account.
Sec. 21.2	Requires the board of directors to designate an officer or other employee to be responsible for meeting prescribed security standards.
Sec. 23	Requires each director and principal officer to file a Statement of Interest, Form CC–3030–29, which is to be kept at the bank's main office and revised as significant changes occur.

Rules and Regulations, Board of Governors of the Federal Reserve System

These rules and regulations apply to employees of Federal Reserve System member banks:

Sec. 212	Regulation L provides that only under certain exceptions may directors, officers, and employees of member banks serve simultaneously as a director, officer, or employee of any other bank, banking association, savings bank, or trust company organized under the National Bank Act or the laws of any state or the District of Columbia.
Sec. 215	Regulation O limits loans which may be made to executive officers of member banks.
Sec. 216	Regulation P requires the board of directors of Federal Reserve banks and state member banks to designate an officer or other employee to be responsible for meeting prescribed security standards.
Sec. 218	Regulation R prohibits directors, officers, and employees of member banks from serving as an em-

ployee, officer, or director of certain organizations that deal with securities.

United States Code, Title 12

Sec. 375(a)   Limits loans which may be made to executive officers of member banks.

Sec. 376   Limits interest rates which may be paid by member banks on deposits of directors, officers, attorneys, and employees to the interest rates paid to other depositors.

Sec. 503   Imposes personal liability on directors and officers of member banks who knowingly violate or permit others to violate certain sections of Title 12 and Title 18 of the U.S. code.

FINGERPRINTING

Section 19 of the Federal Depositor's Insurance Corporation Act authorizes a penalty of not more than $100.00 a day for employing persons convicted of any criminal offense involving dishonesty or a breach of trust.

The significance of this legislation is twofold for financial institutions. First, it places the primary responsibility of ensuring the integrity of employees with the employing institution. Second, in order to ascertain the previous criminal histories of applicants, the legislation affords financial institutions access to the fingerprint records of the Federal Bureau of Investigations. However, the use of fingerprinting in the employment process is still voluntary.

The decision to implement an applicant fingerprinting program should involve a detailed study that considers (1) the increased expenses to be incurred in submitting the prints to the FBI. It should be noted that the process can be facilitated through the use of certain professional banking associations or a local enforcement agency, (2) the availability of trained in-house personnel to fingerprint applicants, (3) the value to smaller community banks of instituting fingerprinting procedures versus the possible loss of goodwill from future applicants, which may occur when organizations are known to require mandatory fingerprinting, and (4) the feasibility of alternate methods to obtain past criminal records.

Finally, in order to avoid any potential liability under certain employment discrimination laws, applicant fingerprinting should always be done on a uniform basis. The single exception to this caveat would be a program instituted pursuant to the Securities Exchange Commission Regulations, which require that only those employees handling certain stocks and trust instruments be fingerprinted.

POLYGRAPHING

Polygraphing is gaining greater acceptance as a screening device for applicants, as well as an effective part of a total in-house investigative system in many financial institutions.

A polygraph in its simplest form is an instrument that records changes in blood pressure, pulse, respiration, and galvanic skin responses. The monitoring of the changes in these areas induced by asking relevant questions is believed to be able to allow an expert to determine truth or deception on the part of the individual being tested. Most authorities in the use of polygraphs agree that the critical elements in the polygraphing process are the skill and integrity of the examiner. Consequently, it is imperative that all examiners used by a bank are licensed and have the optimum level of experience, qualifications, and credibility. Currently, several states have established minimum standards for polygraph examiners. Exhibit 2 provides a listing of those states.

Usage

Polygraphs may be used both as an investigative aid and as an applicant screening tool. When used in the screening process, it is important that its usage does not have an adverse impact on minorities and other protective classes under federal employment discrimination laws.

The use of polygraphs in the investigative process should be controlled by structured in-house policies, which at the minimum should include:

1. A requirement that employees who submit to polygraphs, sign a waiver prepared by the bank's legal counsel.
2. That all employees, where permissible by state law, sign an employment application agreeing to submit to a polygraph as a condition of employment, if requested.
3. That polygraphing will only be administered after a bank review board determines the appropriateness of the test.
4. That polygraphing be used only after all investigative methods have reached a stalemate.

Legality

Perhaps the major factor to be considered in the use of the polygraph is the varying degrees of state restrictions governing its use. These

---

EXHIBIT 2 Polygraphing

State	Sets Mimimum Standards for Polygraph Operators	Law Governing the Use of Polygraph
Alabama	Yes	Yes
Alaska		Yes
Arizona	Yes	
Arkansas	Yes	
California		Yes
Colorado		
Connecticut		Yes
Delaware		Yes
District of Columbia		Yes
Florida	Yes	
Georgia	Yes	
Hawaii		Yes
Idaho		Yes
Illinois	Yes	Yes
Indiana		
Iowa		Yes
Kansas		
Kentucky	Yes	
Louisiana		
Maine	Yes	Yes
Maryland		Yes
Massachusetts	Yes	Yes
Michigan	Yes	Yes
Minnesota		Yes
Mississippi	Yes	
Missouri		Yes
Montana		Yes
Nebraska		Yes
Nevada	Yes	
New Hampshire		Yes
New Jersey		
New Mexico	Yes	Yes
New York		
North Carolina	Yes	
North Dakota		
Ohio		
Oklahoma	Yes	
Oregon	Yes	Yes
Pennsylvania		Yes
Puerto Rico		
Rhode Island		Yes
South Carolina	Yes	
South Dakota		
Tennessee		
Texas	Yes	
Utah	Yes	Yes
Vermont	Yes	Yes
Virginia	Yes	Yes
Virgin Islands		
Washington		Yes
West Virginia		Yes
Wisconsin		Yes
Wyoming		

restrictions range from a total state ban on the use of polygraphs as a condition of employment to limitations on the form and types of questions which may be asked. Exhibit 2 provides a listing of states which have laws that address the use of polygraphs.

THE 1984 TAX REFORM ACT

The enactment of §§ 7872 of the 1984 Tax Reform Act has resulted in a comprehensive review of the practice of extending interest free or "below market loans" to bank employees.

Prior to the passage of this legislation, banks and other private employers were given considerable latitude in the extension of loans to employees at rates well below the prevailing market level. While such practices are not prohibited under §§ 7872, it does make such extensions less desirable by imputing to the participants stronger tax consequences.

Simply stated, the act attributes the difference in the lowered interest rate received by the employee and the higher prevailing "federal rate" of interest to be imputed income or compensation and thereby taxable as such to the employee.

For the employer it is necessary to note that imputed payments will not be subject to wage withholding, but that FICA and FUTA are still required. Many authorities agree that the burden of withholding FICA and FUTA may be reduced on demand loans since all the imputed payments under such loans are deemed to occur only on the last day of the calendar year. By this time, FICA and FUTA limits generally have been exceeded and no withholding should be required.[2]

Computations under §§ 7872

The act requires that a determination be made by the employer regarding the actual amount of imputed income and expense which has resulted from any loans covered by §§ 7872.

This amount is determined by comparing the interest rate charged to the employee on the loan to the federal rate of interest. The federal rate of interest is computed on a six-month period by the Internal Revenue Service.

The amount by which the federal rates exceeds the rate extended to the employee is considered "foregone interest" and will be subject to the provisions of §§ 7872.

---

[2]Howard McCue and Patricia Brosterhous, "Interest-Free and Below Market Loans after Dickman and the Tax Reform Act," *The Tax Magazine* 1010 (December 1984).

Application

§§ 7872 generally applies to demand loans outstanding after June 6, 1984, and to loans other than demand loans made after that date.

Loans between an employer and employee which is conditioned on the employee's continued service is considered a demand loan.

The legislation allows an exception to its application if the aggregate outstanding loans between the employer and the employee does not exceed $10,000.

CONCLUSION

Government regulation of the conditions of employment is here to stay. The changes imposed by new laws and government regulatory agencies will undoubtedly continue to increase. As regulation restricts management choices in the human resource management field, banks and other employers will have to ensure both legal compliance and imaginative use of the options available. The banking industry itself is one of the most regulated industries—and the burden of complying with multiple and sometimes conflicting government agencies, laws, and regulations can be a difficult one. The record-keeping and reporting requirements, the continual threat of lawsuit, and the constantly changing regulations all contribute to the complexity of personnel administration.

PART FOUR

Financial Management

CHAPTER TWENTY-ONE

Funding Sources and Strategies for Banks of Various Sizes

Donald B. Riefler

Chairman, Sources and Uses of Funds Committee
Morgan Guaranty Trust Company

Lazaros P. Mavrides

Vice President, Investment Portfolio Management
Morgan Guaranty Trust Company

INTRODUCTION

Sources of bank funds can be classified into three broad categories: deposits, borrowings, and capital. The level and composition of capital funds is governed by regulatory and tax considerations as well as by management's preferences. Other funds are chosen depending on relative cost, subject to considerations of liquidity and interest rate risk. Interest rate futures, options, and swaps can be used as alternative instruments in adjusting interest rate risk. This chapter discusses the funding instruments used by various-sized banking organizations and the issues that influence funding strategy.

Data on funding sources by bank size are provided in Appendix I, both in dollar amounts and as percent of assets. Similar data on bank holding companies (BHCs) are provided in Appendix II. For this purpose, banks and BHCs were classified into four categories: Category 1, multinational organizations; Category 2, assets over $10 billion (excluding multinational organizations, all of which have assets over $10 billion); Category 3, assets of $1–10 billion; and Category 4, assets under $1 billion. The bank data were derived from the March 31, 1986, "Consolidated Reports of Condition and Income" (call reports) filed quarterly by all FDIC-insured banks (there were 14,338 such banks as of this reporting date). The BHC data were derived from the December 31, 1985, "Bank Holding Company Financial Supple-

ments" (FR Y–9 reports), which included 877 BHCs with assets over
$150 million.

The multinational BHC group includes the following 18 institutions which the Office of the Comptroller of the Currency has defined
as such as of March 1986: Citicorp, BankAmerica Corp., Chase Manhattan Corp., Manufacturers Hanover Corp., J.P. Morgan & Co., Chemical New York Corp., Bankers Trust New York Corp., Security Pacific
Corp., First Interstate Bancorp., First Chicago Corp., Mellon Bank
Corp., Continental Illinois Corp., Wells Fargo & Co., Bank of Boston
Corp., Marine Midland Banks, Irving Bank Corp., Crocker National
Corp. (since merged into Wells Fargo), and Interfirst Corp. The multinational bank group includes the lead banks of these BHCs.

DEPOSITS

Deposits can be classified into six categories: (*a*) demand deposits, (*b*)
savings deposits, (*c*) nonnegotiable time deposits, (*d*) negotiable certificates of deposit, (*e*) Treasury tax and loan (TT&L) deposits, and (*f*)
Eurodollar deposits.

Demand Deposits

Demand deposits are funds that can be withdrawn or transferred to a
third party at any time without advance notice. Such deposits are kept
in a bank by individuals and corporations for transaction purposes,
and by the latter also as required balances in connection wih credit
facilities and operations services. In recent years demand deposits
held in payment for operations services in many cases have been
converted to direct fees. The payment of interest on domestic demand
deposits was disallowed by the Federal Reserve in 1933 through Regulation Q.

Domestic demand deposits are subject to a reserve requirement
of 12 percent. For FDIC-insured banks, they are also subject to an
annualized FDIC fee of 1/12 of 1 percent, levied semiannually against
83 1/3 percent of the average of the ending demand deposits in the
previous two quarters (reduced from 100 percent to account for float),
which is equivalent to $694 per $1 million of the unadjusted balance
or about seven basis points (hundredths of 1%). The FDIC fee is
applicable to total balances although each account is insured only up
to $100,000. FDIC fees can be partly rebated if the accumulated amount
is judged to be more than sufficient to meet future obligations, but no
such rebates occurred during the past two years, and none are anticipated for the near future.

In 1976 savings and loan associations and mutual savings banks as well as commercial banks in the New England states were authorized to introduce negotiable orders of withdrawal (NOW) accounts, which allowed an unlimited number of checks and the payment of interest at the passbook rate (then 5.50 percent for thrifts and 5.25 percent for commercial banks). The Depository Institutions Deregulation and Monetary Control Act of 1980 extended this authority to all states.

Banks introduced automatic transfer service (ATS) accounts in 1978, allowing natural persons and government and nonprofit organizations to transfer funds automatically from a savings to a checking account. Thus funds could continue earning interest in a savings account until needed in the checking account.

The "super NOW" account was introduced in early 1983, allowing the payment of market interest rates as well as the use of an unlimited number of checks, but requiring a minimum average balance of $2,500.

The NOW, ATS, and super NOW accounts are all classified as transaction accounts. As such, they are subject to the above reserve requirements and FDIC fees for demand deposits.

Domestic, noninterest-bearing (demand) deposits constitute a major source of funds for banks of all sizes. As of March 31, 1986, such deposits funded 12.9, 14.4, 18.9, and 15.4 percent of the assets of banks in Categories 1, 2, 3, and 4 respectively (see line 1, Appendix I). The corresponding relative sizes of foreign, noninterest-bearing deposits at the same time were 1.2, 0.1, 0.1, and 0.0 percent, respectively (see line 3, Appendix I).

NOW, ATS, and super NOW accounts, which are all interest-paying domestic transaction accounts, are important sources for consumer-oriented banks. As of March 31, 1986, super NOW accounts, which are the most important of the three, funded 1.5, 2.6, 4.3, and 7.2 percent of the assets of banks in Categories 1, 2, 3, and 4 respectively (see line 15, Appendix I).

Savings Deposits

Savings accounts pay interest, have no fixed maturity, and offer no check privileges. Banks have the right to require seven-day advance notice for withdrawal but generally do not. Such accounts may be held by individuals and certain nonprofit organizations. Since 1975 savings accounts of up to $150,000 may be held by partnerships and corporations as well.

The sharp rise in interest rates in the late 1970s and early 1980s encouraged the formation of money market mutual funds, which were not subject to Regulation Q interest rate ceilings. Over $200 billion were attracted into such funds by 1982. Seeking to reverse this disintermediation, the Garn-St. Germain Act in late 1982 authorized bank regulators to introduce an instrument that would allow banks to compete with the money funds. As a result, the money market deposit account (MMDA) was introduced in December 1982, allowing the payment of market rates and up to six transfers to third parties (no more than three by check). The payment of a high interest rate was conditional on a minimum average balance of $2,500 (otherwise the rate would drop to the 5.25–5.50 percent of the NOW accounts).

By January 1, 1986, all minimum balance requirements and interest rate ceilings on deposit accounts were eliminated, as provided by the Depository Institutions Deregulation and Monetary Control Act of 1980.

Domestic savings accounts (including MMDAs) are now subject to a reserve requirement of 3 percent. For FDIC-insured banks they are also subject to an annualized FDIC fee of 1/12 of 1 percent, levied semiannually as in the case of demand deposits, but against 99 percent of the computed balance (the float reduction in this case is 1 percent, as opposed to 16 2/3 percent for demand deposits), which is equivalent to $825 per $1 million of the unadjusted balance or about 8 basis points. Again, the FDIC fee is applicable to total balances although the accounts are insured only up to $100,000.

Savings accounts constitute an important source of funds for consumer-oriented banks. As of March 31, 1986, such accounts (including MMDAs) funded 10.3, 12.3, 18.8, and 22.3 percent of the assets of banks in Categories 1, 2, 3, and 4 respectively (see line 16, Appendix I). MMDAs comprise the most important component of savings accounts. The corresponding relative sizes for MMDAs were 8.3, 9.6, 14.1, and 15.3 percent, respectively (see line 17, Appendix I).

Nonnegotiable Time Deposits

Nonnegotiable time deposits, which pay a fixed rate over a specified period, are usually held by consumers (individuals or small organizations). Their maturities vary from seven days (the minimum required by regulators) to around eight years. They can be redeemed before maturity at a penalty. They generally pay higher rates than savings accounts.

In 1974 banks introduced individual retirement accounts (IRAs), which are not subject to taxation until withdrawal after the depositor becomes 59 1/2 years old. Funds can be withdrawn earlier at a penalty. This account was made possible by the Employee Retirement Income Security Act (ERISA) of 1974, which initially applied only to individuals with no employer-sponsored pension plans but in 1981 was extended to almost all employees. As of 1986, employees could place up to $2,000 annually in these accounts. Self-employed individuals could place up to $15,000 annually in similar accounts called Keogh plan accounts. As of March 31, 1986, IRA and Keogh plan accounts amounted to 1.2, 1.6, 2.6, and 3.5 percent of the assets of banks in Categories 1, 2, 3, and 4 respectively (see line 18, Appendix I). However, the Tax Reform Act of 1986 drastically reduced the number of employees that could continue to add tax-deferred funds to their IRA accounts after 1986.

Nonnegotiable time deposits are particularly important sources of funds for consumer-oriented banks. As of March 31, 1986, small time deposits (up to $100,000, which are generally nonnegotiable), funded 4.9, 8.3, 15.1, and 28.7 pecent of the assets of banks in Categories 1, 2, 3, and 4 respectively (see line 19, Appendix I).

Demand, savings, and nonnegotiable time deposits constitute the main sources of funds for smaller banks. As of March 31, 1986, these sources together funded 57.1 percent and 73.6 percent of the assets of banks in Categories 3 and 4, as opposed to 29.6 percent and 37.6 percent for Categories 1 and 2 respectively (derived by adding lines 1, 15, 16, and 19 in Appendix I).

Negotiable Certificates of Deposit

The first negotiable CD was issued in 1961 by Citibank (then First National City Bank). Negotiable CDs are usually issued in maturities of 30, 90, and 180 days. The minimum denomination is $100,000, but they are usually issued with a face value of $1 million. They are traded in a secondary market made by securities dealers.

Negotiable CDs over the years increased in importance as a source of bank funds, particularly for large banks. Regulation Q ceilings on large domestic time deposits (over $100,000, negotiable as well as nonnegotiable) were eliminated in 1973. Although at the same time they became subject to an 8 percent reserve requirement, the importance of negotiable CDs increased further as banks could depend on them for liquidity.

Time deposits (negotiable and nonnegotiable) are subject to the same FDIC fee as savings deposits (equivalent to about eight basis points) and to a reserve requirement of 3 percent on maturities up to 18 months (longer maturities are now free of reserve requirements).

Variable rate CDs were introduced in the late 1970s. The interest rate on these is typically adjustable every one, two, or three months while their final maturity is six months or longer. Reserve requirements for CDs longer than 18 months have been eliminated, so 18-

month variable rate CDs have become particularly attractive for banks. Thus, when a bank expects rates to drop and prefers short-term CDs but is concerned about its liquidity position, 18-month variable rate CDs achieve both objectives and by avoiding reserve requirements are generally less expensive than consecutive short-term CDs.

All money center and large regional banks participate in the national CD market. Smaller banks effectively lack access to this market, but they issue nonnegotiable and also some negotiable CDs to local customers. As of March 31, 1986, CDs over $100,000 (negotiable and nonnegotiable) funded 6.3, 10.5, 12.1, and 12.0 percent of the assets of banks in Categories 1, 2, 3, and 4 respectively (see line 20, Appendix I).

Treasury Tax and Loan Deposits

Treasury tax and loan (TT&L) accounts were established at banks in 1917 for deposits of income and social security taxes. In order for a bank to qualify for TT&L accounts, it must pledge qualified securities against the deposits.

During the first day TT&L deposits earn no interest and are treated as transactions balances with respect to reserve requirements and FDIC fees. If the funds are not transferred to the Treasury's accounts at the Federal Reserve within one day, they become interest-paying at a rate set by the Treasury (generally 25 basis points below the Federal funds rate) but cease to be subject to reserve requirements and FDIC fees (they become reclassified as "other liabilities for borrowed money"). As of March 31, 1986, notes issued to the Treasury amounted to around 0.4 percent of the assets of banks in all four categories under consideration (see line 6, Appendix I).

Eurodollar Deposits

Eurodollars are U.S. dollar-denominated deposits held overseas by foreign banks and branches of U.S. banks. Deposits outside their country of origin in other currencies are named accordingly. Their maturities typically range from one day to six months although they can be as long as several years. Eurocurrencies held by a bank at another bank are commonly called redeposits by the former. Although the term Eurodollars is used almost exclusively in this chapter, the discussion applies in general to all currencies outside their country of origin.

Eurodollar deposits are generally free of U.S. regulatory restrictions. They are also generally free of regulations by the host country. Thus they are not subject to reserve requirements and FDIC fees (a proposal to subject Eurodollar deposits to FDIC fees was recently passed by the Senate but was excluded by the House). However, net domestic borrowings from the Eurodollar market (borrowings less re-deposits and loans, if positive) are now subject to a 3 percent domestic reserve requirement (under Regulation D, which also treats Euro-dollar loans to U.S. residents as reservable if funded from the Euro-dollar market).

The Eurocurrency market is predominantly an interbank market and is largely dollar-denominated. According to statistics compiled by Morgan Guaranty Trust, gross liabilities in the Eurocurrency market as of March 31, 1986, were $3.4 trillion, of which $2.3 trillion were dollar-denominated and $2.6 trillion were interbank liabilities.[1]

Negotiable Eurodollar CDs were introduced in London by Citi-bank in 1966. They are usually sold in denominations larger than $250,000, but some large CDs are parcelled and sold to smaller inves-tors in certificates of as little as $10,000. Eurodollar CDs are much less liquid than domestic CDs. Nonnegotiable time deposits continue to be the predominant type in the Eurodollar market.

While domestic CDs are subject to a 3 percent reserve requirement and an FDIC fee of about 8 basis points, Eurodollar CDs are free of both provided that the bank's domestic offices do not borrow more than they lend in the Eurodollar market. As a result, Eurodollar CD rates are approximately equal to domestic CD rates plus the combined cost of the reserve requirement and the FDIC fee (about 25 basis points presently). Nonnegotiable Eurodollar deposit rates are gener-ally 1/16 to 1/8 percent higher than negotiable Eurodollar CD rates for similar maturities.

Floating rate Eurodollar CDs were introduced recently. They are priced at a spread off LIBOR (the London interbank offered rate) about every three or six months and have maturities as long as several years. Floating rate notes priced off LIBOR and ranging in maturity from a few years to around 20 years have become an important factor in the Eurodollar market in recent years. Many foreign corporations, gov-ernments, and banks have raised sizable quantities of the latter (some issues have exceeded $1 billion).

International banking facilities (IBFs) were authorized in the United States in December 1981. IBF deposits are considered Eu-rodeposits and therefore are free of reserve requirements and FDIC fees. IBFs are prohibited from engaging in such activities as accepting deposits from or making loans to U.S. residents or to non-U.S. residents for U.S. purposes, issuing negotiable instruments, offering demand deposit accounts, and accepting overnight deposits from nonbank cus-tomers. IBF earnings are not subject to state and local taxes. Although

---

[1]See Morgan Guaranty Trust Company, *World Financial Markets*, Sep-tember 1986, p. 15.

a lot of Eurodeposits and loans were transferred from Nassau and other offshore locations into the IBFs, as it was hoped, offshore locations continue to function because they can at least carry out the activities that are not available to the IBFs.

All money market banks and large regional banks participate in the Eurodollar market, generally as both borrowers and lenders. Some smaller banks have entered this market in recent years, primarily as lenders of funds attracted by the relatively higher rates available in this market. Eurodollar deposits are a very important source of funds for large banks, particularly the 17 multinational banks of Category 1. As of March 31, 1986, foreign interest-bearing deposits (largely Eurodollar deposits) funded 31.3 percent, 15.2 percent, 4.8 percent, and 0.3 percent of the assets of banks in Categories 1, 2, 3, and 4 respectively (see line 4, Appendix I).

BORROWINGS

There are five principal types of borrowings available to banks or bank holding companies: (*a*) Federal funds, (*b*) repurchase agreements, (*c*) commercial paper, (*d*) long-term debt, and (*e*) borrowings from the discount window.

Federal Funds

Federal funds are balances at the Federal Reserve that banks lend to one another. In addition to domestic and foreign commercial banks, this market includes as participants the World Bank, savings and loan associations, mutual savings banks, and other depository institutions. Securities dealers and securities clearing corporations can also participate as sellers of funds in this market when they are left with excess funds due to delivery fails. Federal funds are not subject to reserve requirements or FDIC fees. Term Federal funds are Federal funds transacted at a fixed rate for a period longer than one day. Typical maturities are 30, 60, and 90 days, and occasionally 180 days.

The Federal funds rate can be very volatile on reserve settlement days (every other Wednesday), depending on the relative reserve positions of banks and on quarter-end days due to "window dressing" of balance sheets. The Federal funds rate is very sensitive to the open market operations of the Federal Reserve (and their interpretations by the market). Nonetheless, these operations generally serve to prevent undue fluctuations in the Federal funds rate over time.

Money center banks are usually net buyers and small regional banks are usually net sellers of Federal funds. Large regional banks are both buyers and sellers, often buying from the smaller banks and selling to their correspondent money center banks. The latter often take the funds even when they do not need them (for relationship purposes, in which case they sell them in the open market).

Repurchase Agreements

Repurchase agreements (RPs or repos) are essentially borrowings collateralized by securities. The borrower sells securities and simultaneously contracts to buy them back later at the same price plus accrued interest (at the agreed rate). Term RPs are fixed RPs with a maturity longer than one day. RPs are not subject to reserve requirements or FDIC fees. RPs from the lender's perspective are called reverse RPs.

Treasury securities provide the most desirable collateral for RPs. Government agency securities are sometimes acceptable as collateral. In early 1969 banks started using loans as collateral, but the Federal Reserve effectively stopped this practice later that year by subjecting such RPs to reserve requirements and Regulation Q ceilings.

The RP rate is usually 1/8 to 1/4 percent lower than the Federal funds rate, depending on market conditions, particularly on the amount of securities that can be offered as collateral. The spread practically disappears when there is an abundant supply of such securities, and may even become negative on occasion because nonbank government dealers do not have an alternative source of funds to finance their holdings. On the other hand, it can increase substantially above 25 basis points when there is a shortage of collateral because some short-term investors are obligated by indentures to invest only in instruments collateralized by Treasury securities.

Commercial banks and government dealers are natural borrowers in the RP market since they usually maintain sizable inventories of Treasury securities. They also lend in this market through reverse RPs in order to obtain specific securities to sell short. When scarce securities are demanded in connection with short selling, the RP rates with such securities as collateral may go down to 200 basis points (eight below the Federal funds rate or lower) at a time when RP rates with other securities as collateral may be close to the Federal funds rate.

Other participants in the RP market are the Federal Reserve, state and local governments, insurance companies, and other corporations. The Federal Reserve participates through its open market operations, temporarily supplying or absorbing reserves to the banking system through RPs and reverse RPs respectively. State and local governments generally invest in the RP market short-term funds that require collateralization. Corporations generally use this market as an alternative to investing in the commercial paper market for funds that they might wish to withdraw in less than seven days and that therefore cannot be invested in the CD market.

RPs constitute an important source of funds for banks that have sizable investment and trading accounts of U.S. government securities. Many banks routinely repo their entire holdings of such securities. As of March 31, 1986, RPs and Federal funds together funded 9.1 percent, 19.6 percent, 12.4 percent, and 2.8 percent of the assets of banks in Categories 1, 2, 3, and 4 respectively (see line 5, Appendix I).

Commercial Paper

Commercial paper is unsecured short-term debt sold by a corporation to money market investors without the intermediation of a commercial bank. The maturity of such paper can be as short as one day and as long as 270 days.

Commercial paper is not subject to reserve requirements and FDIC fees if issued by a BHC. In 1966 the Federal Reserve ruled that commercial paper obligations issued by banks are time deposits and therefore are subject to reserve requirements and FDIC fees.

Commercial paper rates are comparable to CD rates but are effectively less costly to the issuer because they are not subject to reserve requirements and FDIC fees. BHCs issue commercial paper for their short-term funding needs. Pursuant to Federal Reserve regulations issued in 1970, the proceeds of commercial paper issued by a BHC and channeled to a domestic bank subsidiary are considered time deposits and therefore are subject to reserve requirements and FDIC fees. As a result, such proceeds are being directed to nonbank subsidiaries or to overseas bank entities. With the growth of such qualifying subsidiaries in recent years, commercial paper has become a sizable source of funds for BHCs. However, only money center and large regional BHCs have access to the national commercial paper market. As of December 31, 1985, commercial paper funded 3.7 percent, 1.8 percent, 1.2 percent, and 0.1 percent of the assets of BHCs in Categories 1, 2, 3, and 4 respectively (see line 3, Appendix II).

Savings and loan associations and mutual savings banks began issuing commercial paper following enabling regulations in 1979 and 1980 respectively. The former have issued sizable quantities of commercial paper backed by mortgage loans while the latter are still relatively inactive in this market.

Foreign banks have become active participants in the commercial paper market in recent years, both as borrowers and guarantors of their clients' commercial paper issues through letters of credit.

Long-Term Debt

Banks as well as other corporations raise long-term funds at fixed interest rates. Whereas a long-term fixed rate corporate bond market does not exist in many countries, it is highly developed in the United States and is becoming increasingly so in Europe. Unlike government securities, corporate securities are generally callable after a number of years. Original maturities can be 30 years or longer. A banking organization's long-term fixed rate funding decision is part of its overall asset-liability strategy, which will be discussed later in this chapter.

Recently, the U.S. and Eurobond markets have absorbed a variety of fixed rate instruments such as convertible bonds (convertible to common stock at some premium above the current market price) and bonds with detachable stock or bond warrants. The yields on such instruments are lower, reflecting the conversion values to the investor. In addition, several long-term instruments floating with various indices were issued, mainly in the Eurodollar market. Many other innovations may be introduced in coming years since the number of possible combinations is practically infinite.[2]

Borrowings from the Discount Window

Borrowings from the Federal Reserve's discount window can be obtained either in the form of discounts or as advances. In the former case the bank offers eligible assets to the Federal Reserve for discount. In the latter an advance is obtained from the Federal Reserve by pledging eligible collateral. Advances are generally simpler and preferable to discounts.

Borrowings from the discount window are granted as a privilege rather than a right, and are intended for the following two cases:

a. As "adjustment credit" for brief periods when alternative sources of funds are not available at reasonable cost. Large banks in this case are expected to borrow to the next business day while smaller banks at times borrow for longer periods.

b. As "extended credit" in special situations when other sources are not available at reasonable cost. Extended credits longer than 60 days are subject to surcharges.

Banks generally try to manage their funding sources in such a way as to avoid having to borrow from the discount window. However, such borrowings tend to increase at times when the discount rate is substantially lower than alternative funding rates.[3]

---

[2]See Bank for International Settlements, *Recent Innovations in International Banking*, April 1986.

[3]For historical and other details on the various funding sources see E.N. Roussakis, *Commercial Banking in an Era of Deregulation*, Praeger, New York, 1984.

CAPITAL

In December 1981, bank regulators introduced two concepts of capital, primary and secondary. After several revisions, primary capital is now composed of common stock, perpetual preferred stock, capital surplus, undivided profits, contingency and other capital reserves, mandatory convertible securities, perpetual debt securities, allowance for possible credit losses, and minority interest in equity accounts of consolidated subsidiaries. Mandatory convertible securities are subject to a limitation of 20 percent of other primary capital, together with perpetual debt securities they are subject to a combined limitation of 20 percent of total primary capital, and together with perpetual preferred stock to an overall limitation of 33 1/3 percent of total primary capital. Secondary capital includes limited life preferred stock and unsecured long-term debt up to 50 percent of primary capital in the case of banks (no such limitation applies to bank holding companies). Total capital includes the components of both.

The minimum acceptable capital ratios in relation to adjusted assets (total assets plus the allowance for possible credit losses) are now 5 1/2 percent for primary capital and 6 percent for total capital for banks with adjusted assets larger than $150 million (smaller banks are regulated on a case-by-case basis). The minimum capital ratios apply to banking organizations having "average" risk. Institutions with higher than average risk are expected to maintain higher capital ratios. Thus institutions with a total capital ratio of over 7 percent (Zone 1) are considered adequately capitalized, with 6 to 7 percent (Zone 2) marginally capitalized and subject to regulatory scrutiny, and with 6 percent and lower (Zone 3) inadequately capitalized and subject to disciplinary action.

Mandatory Convertible Securities

Mandatory convertible securities, which were introduced in 1982, are qualifying debt instruments mandatorily redeemable within 12 years with proceeds from the issuance of common or perpetual preferred stock. There are two types of such instruments, equity commitment notes and equity contract notes.

In the case of equity commitment notes, the issuer commits to the regulators to redeem the securities with the proceeds of common or perpetual preferred stock, but has no contractual obligation with the holder to do so. On the other hand, the equity contract note issuer does have such a contractual obligation and can give equity securities to the holder for redemption if it becomes impossible to issue such securities in the market.

All the major money center banks raised capital through mandatory convertible securities, predominantly as floating rate notes in the Eurodollar market. The cost of such capital has been only slightly higher than the cost of comparable ordinary debt. Equity contract notes are subject to fewer restrictions than equity commitment notes and are generally preferred by both the banks and the Federal Reserve. As of March 31, 1986, only a few banks in Category 1 had equity commitment notes while equity contract notes amounted to 0.6 percent, 0.2 percent, 0.1 percent, and 0.0 percent of the assets of banks in Categories 1, 2, 3, and 4 respectively (see lines 7 and 8, Appendix I). Equity commitment notes were somewhat more significant for BHCs than for banks while equity contract notes had about the same importance for both (see lines 4 and 5, Appendix II).

Variable Rate Preferred Stock

The variable rate preferred stock market came into existence in 1982, primarily as a source of low-cost primary capital for banks. A fixed rate preferred stock market existed previously, but it was rarely used by banks because of its high cost and the absence of specific capital adequacy guidelines.

Preferred as well as common stock dividends are largely tax exempt to the corporate investor (80 percent for federal tax purposes and in varying amounts for state and local tax purposes) and are not tax deductible by the issuer.

When bank regulators established their capital adequacy guidelines in December 1981, many banks came under pressure to issue additional primary capital. Fixed rate perpetual preferred stock was less expensive than common stock, but it was still very expensive in relation to debt (after taxes). A perpetual but variable rate preferred stock instrument had the potential to achieve a substantially lower rate by reducing or eliminating the interest rate risk of fixed rate instruments, and would still qualify as primary capital. This realization prompted the development of the variable rate preferred stock market in 1982.

The adjustable rate preferred (ARP) was the first preferred stock instrument with a variable rate. The ARP has a perpetual maturity and a dividend rate that is adjusted within a designated range every three months at a fixed spread off the highest of three Treasury rates. In 1983, after nine successful months, the ARP market suddenly collapsed under the weight of a heavy supply of new issues, coupled with the realization that this was an instrument subject to substantial price risk. Very few ARP issues have come to market since then.

After the collapse of the ARP market, there have been several attempts to design a preferred stock instrument that would trade close to par. The money market preferred (MMP), which came into existence in 1984, has clearly dominated this market. The rate on the MMP is reset every 49 days through a Dutch auction. At each auction, current and potential new holders can bid the lowest dividend rate they would accept for the next 49 days. The minimum rate at which all shares are allocated becomes the new dividend rate. A large number of MMP-type issues have been brought to market already (some underwriters have used other names such as DARTS, STARS, and the like).

As of December 31, 1985, preferred stock funded 0.7 percent, 0.3 percent, 0.2 percent, and 0.1 percent of the assets of BHCs in Categories 1, 2, 3, and 4 respectively (see line 10, Appendix II). Apparently only a small portion of these funds were passed through to bank subsidiaries in the form of preferred stock (see line 12, Appendix I).

FUNDING STRATEGY

Capital Funds

A banking organization must have at least the minimum amounts of primary and total capital to comply with the capital adequacy guidelines discussed earlier. In addition, management may wish to consistently maintain some amount in excess of the minimum required. This additional amount may depend on the organization's position relative to peers and its perception of the trade-offs between the costs and benefits of doing so.

Once the decision on the level of capital funds has been made by management, the optimal composition of such funds depends largely on market and tax considerations. To a banking organization in a positive tax position (having positive current earnings for Federal tax purposes or past Federal taxes available for sheltering), the cost of debt capital such as mandatory convertible and perpetual debt securities is significantly lower than the cost of preferred and common stock. On the other hand, to a banking organization in a negative tax position (having negative current earnings for Federal tax purposes and no past Federal taxes available for sheltering), preferred stock is generally the least expensive form of capital. Common stock is generally by far the most expensive form of capital but may have to be issued at times since it is the only one with no regulatory restrictions. Moreover, management may wish to issue common stock for strategic reasons as it is generally perceived to be the purest and strongest form of capital. If management decides to issue preferred stock, MMP is generally the least expensive form that it can issue; however, only money center and large regional banks have access to this market.

Other Funds

In the short run, the level and composition of capital funds is fixed. The other funds are chosen depending on relative cost, subject to management's preferences regarding liquidity and interest rate risks. In general, money center banks buy most of their funds in the money market (Federal funds, RPs, CDs, Eurodollars, and so on), small banks depend almost exclusively on demand and nonmarketable domestic time and savings deposits, and regional banks depend on both types of sources.

At The Morgan Bank, the sources and uses of funds committee (S/U Committee) is the central body controlling the worldwide liquidity and interest rate exposures of the organization. Most large commercial banks now have such a committee (also called Asset and Liability Committee), which often includes the chief executive officer and other members of senior management and meets on a regular basis.

The various Morgan offices and subsidiaries are generally allowed to manage their own liquidity and interest rate exposures independently, subject to certain position limits. The S/U Committee reviews the combined positions on a weekly basis and, to the extent it decides to change them, instructs the New York office to take appropriate action to achieve the desired exposures. The establishment of a central decision-making body at the head office actually makes it possible to give greater freedom to the other offices; if the independent decisions of the various offices lead to excessive or insufficient exposures, the central body can take corrective action. The alternative would be to set narrow exposure limits so that the combined exposures can never become too large. Some banking organizations are similar to Morgan in this respect while others follow an approach closer to the latter.

Large regional banks usually have a lead bank which functions much like the head office of a money center bank. The lead bank generally monitors and adjusts the overall interest rate exposure of the organization. Regional banks generally have good access to local funds. Large regional banks do extensive correspondent business with local banks, particularly buying Federal funds which they in turn sell to money center banks.

Liquidity Management

Liquidity risk usually refers to the possibility of not being able to renew or replace maturing liabilities at a reasonable cost. A basic rule of liquidity management is diversification of sources of funds and of suppliers within each source. Many banks also monitor liquidity risk by using various liquidity measures.

At The Morgan Bank, the S/U Committee uses two measures of liquidity. The first is the difference between liquid assets and short-term liabilities. Liquid assets include government securities of all maturities and all other assets that mature within five weeks and can be discontinued without adverse implications. Short-term liabilities refer to all liabilities maturing within five weeks, excluding demand deposits and Federal funds coming from regular suppliers of such funds. If the value of this liquidity measure is nonnegative, the implication is that the bank could retire the liquid assets if it suddenly became impossible to renew or replace the short-term liabilities.

The second liquidity measure shows the portions of the liability book that are expected to be replaced within 5, 13, and 27 weeks, based on forecasts for loans and demand deposits. The values of these ratios are displayed on a chart going back two and one-half years. Whenever the present figure is out of line with past experience, this triggers a discussion on whether corrective action is indicated.

Liquidity management is important to banks of all sizes. Liquidity comfort is a prerequisite before engaging in interest rate risk management. Liquidity management has become significantly easier since 1960 due to the development of many new and highly liquid domestic and foreign markets for funds. Nonetheless, it requires constant monitoring because these markets become practically closed to a bank perceived to be in danger of being unable to meet its commitments. Furthermore, liquidity management is considered highly important by bank regulators.

For consumer-oriented banks, which are generally net sellers of funds obtained from local suppliers, another form of liquidity management is also very important: finding liquid assets at a positive spread. In order to maintain good relations with their customers, such banks must offer competitive rates and accept all funds offered to them at all times. Thus it is important that they have readily available uses for different types of funds. Floating rate notes at a fixed spread over Treasury bills and Eurodollar instruments are such uses. Their larger correspondent banks also provide such banks with substantial liquidity comfort by standing ready to accept their funds at market rates.

Interest Rate Risk Management[4]

The sensitivity of bank earnings to changes in interest rates depends on the maturity structure of the balance sheet. A bank of course has control over its balance sheet but almost no control over interest rates.

---

[4]For an extensive discussion of this subject, see M.L. Stigum and R.O. Branch, Jr., *Managing Risk Assets and Liabilities*, Dow Jones-Irwin, Homewood, Illinois, 1983. For a bibliography, see American Bankers Association, "A Selective Bibliography on Asset-Liability Management," February 1986.

The first step in measuring the interest rate exposure of a bank is to divide the balance sheet into repricing time intervals (for instance, 0 to 1 month, 1 to 3 months, 3 to 6 months, 6 to 12 months, 1 to 2 years, and so on) and to compute the difference between the assets and liabilities that mature or are subject to a rate adjustment within each such interval (the "gap"). A positive gap in a particular time interval means that more existing assets than liabilities would be repriced within that interval. Therefore a positive gap should cause earnings to benefit from increasing interest rates, assuming that interest rates on both assets and liabilities increase by similar amounts. The opposite holds for negative gaps. The earnings effect of a 1 percent change in rates over a time interval is approximately equal to 1 percent of the average cumulative gap over the interval times the length of the interval (assuming that market rates on all assets and liabilities move by 1 percent).

A more precise estimate of the sensitivity of earnings to interest rates can be obtained by constructing a bank model. Many banks use such models. The majority of these are "simulation models," which estimate future income statements on the basis of certain assumptions about the future economic environment and specific asset and liability decisions to be implemented. Some bank models seek to estimate the optimal size and composition of the balance sheet.[5]

The sensitivity of earnings to interest rates can be reduced (possibly eliminated) by matching maturities on opposite sides of the balance sheet. However, if expectations are strong that interest rates will move in a particular direction, a bank may be willing to mismatch its balance sheet in order to profit from such a development. Thus forecasting interest rates is of central importance to asset-liability management.

There are econometric models that forecast interest rates on the basis of factors such as inflation, economic growth, internal generation of funds, government deficit, and the like. In general, such models contain equations that tie together the important factors affecting interest rates and, given forecasted changes in the factors, estimate the combined effect on interest rates. Such models can be useful in understanding the processes shaping interest rate developments over time. However, interest rates in the short run are affected by a multitude of political as well as economic perceptions that cannot possibly be incorporated into an econometric model. At The Morgan Bank, asset-liability decisions are based on a subjective interest rate fore-

---

[5]For a review of the various types of bank models, see K.J. Cohen, S.F. Maier, and J.H. Vander Weide, "Recent Developments in Management Science in Banking," *Management Science* 27, No. 10, October 1981, pp. 1,097–1,119.

casting process.[6] Some banks use econometric models to forecast interest rates, some use subjective processes, and some refuse to forecast rates altogether. Banks in this third group should theoretically match maturities in all cases, but it is doubtful that they always do so in practice.

Another measure of interest rate risk that is becoming increasingly accepted is "net worth duration." The duration of a bond is approximately equal to the percentage change in its market value caused by a 1 percent change in rates. Similarly, net worth duration is approximately the percentage change in the net worth of the balance sheet caused by a 1 percent change in rates, and can be derived from the individual durations of the bank's assets and liabilities.

According to the duration method, eliminating interest rate risk is maintaining a net worth duration of zero. Such a policy would result in investing the organization's capital (net worth) in short-term instruments and matching all other assets and liabilities so that the net market value of the balance sheet would be insensitive to changes in interest rates. Of course, in that event earnings would vary directly with interest rates. When a bank feels strongly that interest rates are to move in a particular direction by a greater amount than implied by the market yield curve, a nonzero net worth duration would usually be consistent with its forecast. Some amount of positive duration would usually be called for since the market yield curve presumably reflects a risk premium in addition to interest rate expectations.

Interest Rate Futures, Options, and Swaps

Banks that base their asset-liability decisions on interest rate forecasts adjust their interest rate exposure as their interest rate outlook changes. Exposure to rising interest rates can be reduced by selling fixed rate assets and/or replacing Federal funds and other maturing liabilities with longer term borrowings. Alternatively, this can be done by selling futures, buying puts, or entering into an interest rate swap as the fixed rate payer. Similarly, exposure to falling interest rates can be reduced by acquiring fixed rate assets, buying back fixed rate liabilities to the extent this is feasible, buying futures, buying calls, or entering into an interest rate swap as the fixed rate receiver.

A futures contract for a security is a commitment to buy or sell that security at a specified future time at a specified price. A bank can hedge a portfolio security by selling a future in that security if a market for such a future exists. If interest rates then go up, the price of the

---

[6]For a description of this process, see I.K. Kabus, "You Can Bank on Uncertainty," *Harvard Business Review*, May–June 1976, pp. 95–105.

portfolio security will go down, but the loss will be offset by delivering the security at the price specified in the futures contract or by buying back the future at a lower price (the latter can be done prior to the specified delivery date). Similarly, if interest rates go down, the price of the portfolio security will go up, but the gain will be eliminated by a loss on the futures. Fixed rate liabilities can be hedged by buying futures. Thus a six-month CD can be effectively turned into a three-month CD by buying a three-month CD future. If a futures market for a particular security does not exist, a future for another security can be used for hedging, provided that the price volatilities of the two securities are similar. The historical relationship between the price movements of the two securities must be ascertained in order to determine what amount of the existing future is needed to hedge the security in question. However, such indirect hedging is subject to some basis risk as interest rates for different financial instruments do not always move in the same manner relative to one another.

A call (put) option gives to its holder the right to buy (sell) the underlying security within a specified time interval at a specified price. Hedging with puts and calls is essentially buying insurance to protect the bank against movements of interest rates in a particular direction, but leaving unrestrained the potential benefit from the other direction.

An interest rate swap is a contract between two parties obligating the one to pay a fixed rate to the other over a specified period in exchange for a floating rate based on some short-term instrument. A bank that enters into an interest rate swap as the fixed rate payer adjusts its balance sheet exposure to interest rates in a way similar to borrowing funds at a fixed rate. On the other hand, entering into an interest rate swap as the fixed rate receiver is similar to buying fixed rate assets in terms of their effects on balance sheet interest rate exposure.

Banks may find it attractive at times to adjust their interest rate exposure by using interest rate futures, options, or swaps for one or more of the following reasons: (a) as a way to generate profits (for example, it may be possible to generate an attractive spread by borrowing fixed rate funds and entering into an interest rate swap as the fixed rate receiver), (b) as an alternative to selling appreciated assets in order to avoid realizing gains and paying taxes on them, (c) as an alternative to adding assets in order to avoid increasing the size of the balance sheet.

Money center banks make extensive use of interest rates futures, options, and swaps. Regional banks generally use interest rate swaps and occasionally futures. Smaller banks do not generally use options and futures but are increasingly entering into interest rate swaps with their larger correspondent banks or with investment banking firms.

APPENDIX I

Funding Sources by Bank Size, as of March 31, 1986 (in $ billions and as percent of assets, the latter in parentheses below the former)

Funding Sources	Multinational	Assets over $10 Billion*	Assets $1– $10 Billion	Assets under $1 Billion
1. Domestic, noninterest-bearing deposits	107.7 (12.9)	18.6 (14.4)	155.0 (18.9)	145.9 (15.4)
2. Domestic, interest-bearing deposits	208.4 (25.0)	44.9 (34.8)	423.4 (51.8)	675.0 (71.3)
3. Foreign, noninterest-bearing deposits	9.9 (1.2)	0.1 (0.1)	0.8 (0.1)	0.2 (0.0)
4. Foreign, interest-bearing deposits	260.8 31.3	19.7 (15.2)	39.4 (4.8)	2.4 (0.3)
5. Federal funds and RPs	76.0 (9.1)	25.3 (19.6)	101.4 (12.4)	26.8 (2.8)
6. Notes issued to U.S. Treasury	3.2 (0.4)	0.5 (0.4)	2.9 (0.4)	2.4 (0.3)
7. Equity commitment notes	0.5 (0.1)	0.0 (0.0)	0.0 (0.0)	0.0 (0.0)
8. Equity contract notes	4.8 (0.6)	0.3 (0.2)	0.7 (0.1)	0.1 (0.0)
9. Other subordinated notes	4.0 (0.4)	0.4 (0.3)	3.3 (0.4)	1.3 (0.2)
10. Other liabilities	118.1 (14.2)	11.8 (9.2)	40.7 (5.0)	17.9 (1.9)
11. Total liabilities	793.5 (95.1)	121.5 (94.2)	767.6 (93.9)	871.9 (92.1)
12. Perpetual preferred stock	0.4 (0.1)	0.0 (0.0)	0.3 (0.0)	0.3 (0.0)
13. Common equity	40.4 (4.8)	7.5 (5.8)	50.0 (6.1)	74.2 (7.9)
14. Total liabilities and equity	834.3	129.0	817.9	946.4
15. Super NOW accounts	12.2 (1.5)	3.4 (2.6)	35.4 (4.3)	68.3 (7.2)
16. Saving deposits (including MMDAs)	85.7 (10.3)	15.9 (12.3)	153.5 (18.8)	210.6 (22.3)
17. Money market deposit accounts	6.9 (8.3)	12.4 (9.6)	114.9 (14.1)	145.1 (15.3)
18. IRA and Keogh plan accounts	9.6 (1.2)	2.1 (1.6)	21.1 (2.6)	33.3 (3.5)
19. Time deposits up to $100,000	41.2 (4.9)	10.7 (8.3)	123.7 (15.1)	271.7 (28.7)
20. Certificates of deposit over $100,000	52.3 (6.3)	13.5 (10.5)	98.7 (12.1)	113.2 (12.0)

*Excluding the 18 multinational banks (all having assets over $10 billion).

SOURCE: Compiled from the Federal Reserve System's "Consolidated Reports of Condition and Income."

APPENDIX II

Funding Sources by Bank Holding Company Size, as of December 31, 1985 (in $ billions and as percent of assets, the latter in parentheses below the former)

Funding Sources	Multinational	Assets over $10 Billion*	Assets $1–$10 Billion	Assets under $1 Billion
1. Total deposits	643.9	307.7	525.1	182.4
	(65.5)	(72.0)	(77.4)	(85.5)
2. Federal funds and RPs	73.8	47.8	60.2	7.2
	(7.5)	(11.2)	(8.9)	(3.4)
3. Commercial paper	36.7	7.7	8.1	0.2
	(3.7)	(1.8)	(1.2)	(0.1)
4. Equity commitment notes (net)	1.9	0.9	0.7	0.0
	(0.2)	(0.2)	(0.1)	(0.0)
5. Equity contract notes (net)	5.9	0.8	0.6	0.2
	(0.6)	(0.2)	(0.1)	(0.0)
6. Other subordinated notes	9.8	2.6	4.4	0.8
	(1.0)	(0.6)	(0.7)	(0.4)
7. Other liabilities	162.5	36.2	36.3	7.6
	(16.5)	(8.5)	(5.4)	(3.6)
8. Total liabilities	934.4	403.7	635.4	198.3
	(95.1)	(94.5)	(93.7)	(92.9)
9. Minority interest in consolidated subsidiaries	0.1	0.3	0.2	0.3
	(0.0)	(0.1)	(0.0)	(0.1)
10. Preferred stock	6.6	1.2	1.4	0.3
	(0.7)	(0.3)	(0.2)	(0.1)
11. Common equity	41.5	22.0	41.5	14.5
	(4.2)	(5.2)	(6.1)	(6.8)
12. Total liabilities and equity	982.7	427.2	678.5	213.4
13. Total primary capital	66.0	29.0	49.4	16.7
	(6.7)	(6.8)	(7.3)	(7.8)
14. Total secondary capital	21.5	7.1	8.9	1.1
	(2.2)	(1.7)	(1.3)	(0.5)

*Excluding the 18 multinational banks (all having assets over $10 billion).

SOURCE: Compiled from the Federal Reserve System's "Bank Holding Company Financial Supplement" reports.

CHAPTER TWENTY-TWO

Bank/Investor Relationships

Peter C. Lincoln

Vice President, Investments
United States Steel and Carnegie Pension Fund, Inc.

INTRODUCTION

This chapter first discusses why investor relations is important and at times critical to the success of a banking enterprise. The elements that should be included in the structure of a corporate information program are outlined, and the value of conciseness, realism, and consistency in producing a credible and successful program are stressed. The CEO as well as members of senior management must play a key role if a program is to be effective. Finally, commentary is provided on the elements of an integrated investor relations program including written reports, public presentations, visits with individual investors and analysts, and the nature of the investor relations position.

WHY INVESTOR RELATIONS?

The broad purpose of an investor relations program should be to ensure that a company's securities achieve realistic recognition and valuation in the financial markets, and that potential investors and the general public can have confidence in and an understanding of a company's ability to perform effectively in a variety of economic circumstances. If confidence and credibility are gained, the reward can be a more appropriate or favorable cost of capital and a greater availability of outside funds during difficult times.

On an operational level, the investor relations person serves at the focal point for questions about the company from investors and security analysts.

Banks and financial institutions, more than most industry groups, should appreciate the need for an effective investor relations program. First, the cost of new equity and debt securities issued to meet enhanced regulatory capital standards, and more recently involving the huge rush of interstate acquisitions and mergers, can be critical in determining whether a company can grow or be a survivor in the years ahead. More broadly, though, with something like 90 percent of all liabilities consisting of deposits or short-term borrowed funds, credibility and confidence are essential for the continued existence of a banking institution. While experience until now has suggested that the retail depositor will tend to keep his funds in a troubled institution due presumably to the presence of government insurance programs, such is not true for wholesale funds. Holders of large-denomination CDs, commercial paper, and Eurocurrencies are often very sensitive to adverse news, and in the absence of effective communications, will move funds with little regard to actual circumstances. Rating agencies are another critical investor relations audience.

Enhancement of employee morale and customer relationships are two important indirect targets for an investor relations program. Employees participating in company savings plans or holding options will obviously be happy if the common stock is selling at relatively favorable levels, and prospective employees can also be attracted by such success. But there can be some more intangible advantages as well. As will be discussed more fully, an effective investor relations program involves a clear statement of trends in the business and management goals and objectives. This type of discussion in the stockholder reports can enhance the awareness of employees of the broader direction of the organization, producing a greater sense of participation and responsiveness.

Finally, current and potential customers are also important indirect audiences for the investor relations program. Not only will corporate treasurers on occasion read stockholder reports when investing funds in banks, but potential loan and noncredit service customers will also want to have confidence in and an understanding of the institution's general health and direction.

HOW TO BUILD CREDIBILITY

Credibility and understanding are built over time only through a consistent information program that provides a realistic analysis of a company's business and management goals, and expectations for the future. With this framework, investors should be able to price a company's securities at fair values and to absorb adverse or unexpected news in a context of the longer term values and strengths of the organization.

The education effort should embrace the following four subjects:

    a. Nature of operations—Outline the basic structural and business segments of the company—geographical, product such as consumer, trust, mortgage banking, and so on. Discuss the relevant business environments such as profitability and growth trends of important products, changes in branching or interstate banking legislation, and important internal structural or management transitions.

b. Past performance—Analyze the important elements that contributed to recent results as well as those of the past five or 10 years. The focus should always be on basic trends and not simply be a repetition of the recent numbers presented in the financial statements.

c. Financial and strategic business objectives of management— Include return-on-asset and return-on-equity targets, dividend payout objectives, and capital ratio policies in light of Federal standards, acquisition policies, and the like. These should be discussed in terms of how the performance objectives will be met in specific terms, not just as hopes and wishes. Business strategies should be discussed both in terms of new directions as well as areas of de-emphasis or divestiture.

d. Potential results—Look ahead, especially at the variables that will be important in affecting these results such as the economy, interest rates, or competitive challenges. How might the company address such contingencies? The effort here should not so much be to produce specific earnings forecasts but to give some general sense of the direction or outlook in a framework of potential economic or industry change.

IMPORTANCE OF CONCISENESS, REALISM, AND CONSISTENCY

An investor relations program will be successful over time only if it is concise, discusses results realistically, and is carried out on a consistent basis.

The need for concise shareholder communications does not seem to be too surprising an objective. After all, one would always hope that written and oral reports would come to important points quickly and not get bogged down in minor detail or in the boilerplate of SEC documents. However, there is a special reason for raising this issue when discussing effective investor relations today. To put it bluntly, there is a dwindling number of experienced investment analysts who have the time to study each company carefully, and more and more investment decisions are being made by general portfolio managers who are unfamiliar with the inner workings of the banking industry and do not use much input from sell-side Wall Street analysts. If any kind of message is to be given in stockholder reports, it must be clear, concise, and upfront, not buried in the management discussion. The buyers of large CDs and commercial paper also need as concise a statement as possible that differentiates the company from its peers in the industry.

Realism is another objective that sounds like motherhood, but is crucial for an effective investor relations program. Part of the reason again is the need for conciseness and the wasted effort in reading platitudes and generalities. Another reason, though, is credibility. If page after page of the annual report contains "good-times," self-congratulatory praise from management, and no explanation for flat or down earnings, readers will recognize rather quickly that management is being evasive and perhaps worse. No trust or credibility will have been built.

The purpose of introducing realism with investor relations is to build an audience over time that has an understanding of the fundamental strengths and weaknesses of the institution. As this occurs, the securities can be fairly and properly valued in the market, and if adverse news develops, it can be assessed fairly in a solid framework and not on the basis of an uninformed, short-term, knee-jerk reaction.

It should be stated explicitly that the purpose of investor relations should not be to raise the stock price per se, or overpromote the company based on unrealistic promises. After a time, events will overtake rash or false expectations. If investors find they have been misled, the company will pay with several years of market distrust and downgrading.

Finally, on the issue of realism, it is clear that investors do not like surprises and can be very unforgiving about them. To the extent that the investor relations program has given a realistic picture of some of the risks involved in the company's business operations, and is forthright about problems as they emerge, investors can be much more understanding about such developments, and company stock and bond prices can evidence greater stability.

Consistency is another goal for investor relations that follows naturally from the previous comments. Managements must be candid and available for questioning in bad times as well as good. In fact, the worst thing that can occur in bad times is to cut back established disclosure patterns, outside meetings, and the analytical sections of published reports. Only the worst can be assumed when this occurs.

CRITICAL ROLE OF THE CEO

The CEO must play a critical role in the investor relations program if it is to be effective. There are two reasons for this—one external and the other internal.

The importance of the CEO relative to external communication starts with the fact that it is the CEO who is directly responsible for the establishment of objectives and policies and for the levels of performance. Investors naturally must be able to communicate with the

CEO to understand these objectives and to assess, however subjectively, the ability of this individual to carry out these responsibilities. No matter how well-informed the investor relations person may be, this assessment cannot be carried out on a second-hand basis.

The role of the CEO is just as critical for internal reasons. Only the CEO is in a position to set the tone for a realistic and forthright discussion of performance and prospects, especially in adverse times. Division managers will tend to say little if they are worried about top-level reactions. Public relations departments will sometimes stifle realistic assessments of performance, controllers may complain about the time and effort needed to produce new data, and legal counsel may advise silence based on a narrow or technical reading of law or regulations, unless there is CEO intervention and understanding of the need for forthright communications.

STRUCTURE OF AN INVESTOR RELATIONS PROGRAM

The structure of an effective investor relations program will vary depending on the size and nature of the institution. Essentially, such a program should consist of a coordinated communications effort through written reports to shareholders, public presentations, and personal visits with investors and analysts.

Written Reports. The annual report to stockholders is clearly the most important written document available to investors. There is a considerable amount of information that must be disclosed by public companies, and bank holding companies must meet additional standards under the SEC's Guide 61 supplemental data rules. However, within these requirements, bank managements have considerable flexibility to produce such disclosure material in an organized and well-written manner rather than following rigid and legalistic rules or patterns.

The chairman's letter is one of the weakest sections of many annual reports, but its improvement can make a dramatic difference in the effectiveness of the communications program. A good chairman's letter will focus on the basic business and performance trends and management's financial and strategic goals, setting a framework for the more detailed management discussion and analysis. By providing this framework and sense of direction up front, the small investor who may not have the background to understand the more esoteric aspects of banking can gain some sense of what is happening, and professional investors and potential customers who are faced with the task of absorbing large numbers of company reports can gain a basic understanding of company operations and read further if they so desire. So often, the typical letter implies that all is well (even if this is not the case) and then comments on the quality of the efforts of directors and employees. Apart from a missed communications opportunity, this only encourages feelings of confusion, frustration, and distrust.

Beyond the general principles of establishing structure and clarity, some companies with unusual business profiles can make a real contribution to investor understanding of operations by organizing the statistical data and the management discussion along lines of business. Large international banks are already required to report certain information in this manner. More recently, companies with important nonbank operations, such as Security Pacific and Norwest, have provided supplemental material to highlight performance in these areas. Another approach is to segment the data by customer group (large corporate, consumer, and so on) such as seen with Citicorp, First Chicago, and RepublicBank of Texas. Further, a geographic breakdown can be useful, and some of the newer super-regionals can give some vital understanding of results through this approach. In all of these instances, the operations are managed as distinct business units, and investors gain a much better understanding of the company in specific areas rather than consolidated results.

Data presented on a more traditional basis should also be structured to reflect the nature of the institution. For example, a retail bank should provide good breakdowns of average loan and deposit balances and yields as well as period-end data in the balance sheet, while international banks should give net interest margin breakdowns and some sense of the trends by geographic and product lines of loans, revenues, and earnings. The regulatory reporting requirements at times can obscure rather than illuminate these patterns.

Preparers of financial reports must be wary of two types of circumstances that can easily cause reports to be misleading if not addressed properly—unusual gains or losses in the income statement, and purchase accounting acquisitions. With unusual gains or losses, current accounting practice has called for many of these items to be included in the income statement even though they are not part of the basic ongoing operations of the company. Some of the more frequent items include realized securities gains or losses, gains on sales of buildings, and gains on pension fund reversions. These gains or losses should always be noted before and after tax in the management discussion and in the income statement. Moreover, if gains or losses are at all meaningful, they must also be mentioned in the chairman's letter when recent results are discussed. The reports should give an understanding of what ongoing or normal earnings might be, and gains certainly should not be used to obscure real operating problems.

Purchase accounting acquisitions can also lead to distortions in reported results, and special care is needed so that changes in income statement and balance sheet numbers are discussed excluding the acquired operation as well as including it so that the underlying trends of the existing company can be understood.

Preparers of financial reports should also be sensitive to current investor concerns, and address these promptly and forthrightly rather than waiting for a new regulation to require such disclosure. Credibility can often be damaged more badly when certain data are unknown than when the information is disclosed. Also, managements often assume that outsiders know when the company has little or no exposure to a problem situation so that there is no need to discuss the subject. The assumption is false; in times of stress and crisis, outsiders can react poorly to uncertainty, and a company would do well to indicate its lack of exposure in a problem area so as to allay investor concerns in advance. While additional disclosure may be a nuisance, the advantage to be gained from credibility in the securities markets is far greater than the cost of one more sentence in the report. Disclosure should be as specific as possible; the "not material" comment would not be believable or responsive.

While the annual report is the most important written document, the quarterly reports for bank holding companies have great importance for professional investors and analysts. Considerable attention should be paid to the quality and substance of the chairman's letter and management discussion text, and the statistical tables should be in the same format and detail as in the annuals.

Every effort should be made to have written reports in the hands of investors and analysts as promptly as possible.

Other written reports, such as postannual meeting reports, proxy statements, and the text of public presentations, should also be available to analysts and other interested parties. Larger banks make press releases available, often on the same day as the earnings release, and detailed financial data should be in hand when earnings are reported. In the annual report, 11 years of summary performance information should be provided so that longer term trends over varying economic circumstances can be observed. Historical per share earnings should be given when pooling acquisitions have occurred.

Public Presentations.   It is important for senior managements of bank holding companies to make public presentations to investor groups on a periodic and reasonably consistent basis. No matter how well the written reports may discuss a company's performance and plans for the future, many analysts will absorb the information more readily on an aural basis. By attending a meeting, analysts are making a much greater commitment of time and concentration than when reading the financials. Investors are interested in judging the character and depth of management, particularly how they handle questions and answers, and the opportunity to ask questions can induce a much greater understanding of a company. Many investors do not have the time or ability to travel to company offices, so these meetings provide the best way to become well-acquainted with a particular operation.

There are a variety of approaches that can be taken to public presentations depending on the nature and size of the bank. The most obvious approach is to address member societies of the Financial Analysts Federation, either in regional cities or in areas such as Boston, Chicago, and New York where large numbers of institutional investors and brokers are concentrated. Medium-sized and larger companies can appear at the monthly meetings of the Bank and Financial Analysts Association in New York. Companies themselves often sponsor meetings, or cosponsor them with their investment bankers. Finally, thorough presentations can be made at the annual stockholders meeting, and for regional banks this can also provide a good opportunity to communicate with important customer groups. Some regional banks have organized stockholder information meetings in key cities in their territory to reach a larger audience of investors and customers.

Personal Visits with Investors and Analysts.   The nature of a personal visitation program will vary with the institution, but for many it can involve a mixture of addressing the needs of analysts and investors for "maintenance" information and a more activist program of seeking out potential investors. Some brokerage house specialists and institutional investors with internal analytical staffs need to maintain a level of knowledge about many companies, and will speak with management by phone, invite management to their offices, or visit management at the company headquarters. Increasingly though, as confirmed by Ashley Weare, senior vice president of Bankers Trust, in a survey in 1985, investment decisions relating to bank securities increasingly are being made by portfolio managers rather than industry security analysts. These individuals must be contacted separately because they rarely join specialty analyst groups or attend these meetings. The investor relations contact and key management persons must take the initiative to visit with portfolio managers rather than assuming that they are well informed through the written materials or analyst presentations.

THE INVESTOR RELATIONS POSITION

The investor relations position can often be one of the most interesting staff functions in a bank holding company. In small institutions this function may be handled by the CEO or chief financial officer, and if this role is delegated to an investor relations person, this function is one of the few in the organization below the top management level whose scope embraces the entire organization rather than specific line departments. The nature of the responsibility means that the individual chosen must have some knowledge of accounting, finance, and banking, but must also possess general intelligence and a conceptual sense of how the organization operates and its place in the broader business and financial community.

The mandate for the investor relations person should be to organize a broad and integrated corporate communications program for the company, not simply to play a passive role reacting only to questions from outside. This would involve a direct role in shaping the content of the written reports and organizing an appropriate program of public presentations as well as meeting alone or with key executives with investors. While many other departments would also be involved in these tasks, these participants must be made aware of the existence of an organized and intelligent program, and the reasons why such a program is important to the success of the company. A further mandate for the investor relations person is to be sensitive to investor concerns about the company and to ensure that senior management promptly is made aware of such concerns and is responsive to the issues raised.

As suggested before, the participation by the CEO and senior department heads in the investor relations effort is quite important. While many questions can be addressed directly by an informed investor relations person, there are many subjects that can only be discussed by specific managers, and investor relations persons should never respond to questions that are beyond their area of knowledge or expertise. Just as a company must establish credibility, so must the investor contact. Analysts can quickly become disenchanted if they are given poor answers or are prevented from speaking directly with knowledgeable executives.

In responding to questions, promptness is essential. Analysts have little time to focus on one company in small chapters or over several days, and unexpected news or false rumors need to be addressed quickly before damage is done because of poor information in the market.

The investor relations person can obtain plentiful advice about how to improve this function from investment banking and public relations firms. In addition, the rapidly growing professional organization called the National Investor Relations Institute sponsors many conferences and seminars on how to perform this function. The Bank Investor Relations Association is a thriving organization whose members specialize in the banking area, and they too sponsor seminars. The Corporate Information Committee of the Financial Analysts Federation publishes guidelines for improved investor relations as part of its annual program of making awards of excellence in corporate reporting to banks and companies in other industries.

CHAPTER TWENTY-THREE

How Financial Markets Evaluate Banks and Bank Holding Companies

David C. Cates

President
Cates Consulting Analysts, Inc.

The "market acceptance" of bank paper, letters of credit, and securities has become one of the hotter buttons that larger banking companies must cope with. It was not always so. Prior to the first ratings of bank holding company (BHC) commercial paper and term debt (in 1973 by Moody's Investors Service and soon after by Standard & Poor's), the credit standing of banks and BHCs was unquestioned. Moreover, their investment qualities were perceived to be a simple function of their earnings and dividend outlook, not of their riskiness. Even after ratings became common in the late 1970s, there was still much banker indifference to the evaluation process. After all, the ratings—with very few exceptions—were all in the upper range of "investment grade." Downgrades were infrequent, usually matched by other upgrades.

In the 1980s all this changed. Starting with Moody's famous publication in 1982 of its bearish outlook for bank riskiness (domestic loan quality, LDC debt, eroding capital adequacy, and so on), downgrades became more frequent than upgrades. Today only one domestic BHC (J. P. Morgan) sports a triple-A compared to 12 in 1977. Meanwhile the same rating agencies appear to favor the credit of large foreign banks; 11 of these (for example, Industrial Bank of Japan, Union Bank of Switzerland, and National Westminster) enjoy triple-A ratings compared to none in 1977. This citation of ratings is not meant to defend them but to show the downtrend and the current low estate of the perceived credit standing of the domestic banking industry. This matters because large banks, more than any other kinds of business, depend for their very raw material on their perceived creditworthiness. In other words, how the financial markets evaluate these companies is not an idle topic.

Nor is it a simple topic. What, for instance, do we mean by "financial markets"? Is it just a handful of rating agencies and well-known securities analysts, or are banks evaluated within a more complex network of counterparties? Is the process of "evaluation" itself a mindless quantitative routine that ignores the true soul of a company in favor of a few pet ratios, or is it—at the other extreme—so qualitative that it fails to read the objective signals of financial soundness? What is it that the markets evaluate? Banks? Bank holding companies? Both? Is the evaluation done for credit and investment reasons only, or are there perhaps other needs as well? Do analysts differ in their views and methods from regulators? Finally, what can managements do about this evaluative process? Ignore it? Understand and adapt to it? Attempt to shape the process? In a single chapter it isn't possible to address all these questions in full. Our emphasis then will be on the *evaluative process*—at its best and worst—and on the *management response* to the process. We will approach these themes through a series of nine questions as follows:

1. Why are banks/BHCs evaluated?
2. Which banking companies are evaluated?
3. Who contributes to the evaluation process?
4. What is the training and competence of bank analysts?
5. Can the job be done at all?
6. How do good analysts think?
7. Is there any quality check on the work of analysts?
8. Do regulators and market-based analysts think alike?
9. Can bank managements influence the evaluation process?

WHY ARE BANKS/BHCs EVALUATED?

The overwhelming motive in *credit analysis* is to judge the creditworthiness of issuers of commercial paper, term debt, Fed funds, large-dollar CDs, loan commitments, and standby letters of credit. In fact, the growth of capital markets products serves to bring new legions of bank credit analysts into play, some of whom have not the slightest idea what they're doing.

There is also *investment analysis*, by which we mean the interests of equity investors and potential acquirors (whose orientation is quite similar). Moreover, emerging from the liability insurance crisis of 1984–85, is a new interest in *insurability analysis*, by which we mean that large brokers and carriers are paying more attention to financial performance as a condition of insurance than they used to.

WHICH BANKING COMPANIES ARE EVALUATED?

Understandably, the intensity of study is a function of size. Money center giants are exposed to more uninsured funds-providers and other counterparties than are large regional banks, which in turn are more exposed than smaller regionals. Any bank/BHC, however, which is "market dependent," relying on impersonal, uninsured funding (or on third-party acceptance of its LCs), must consider itself to be a target of evaluation. Any bank, moreover, which is acquirable (willingly or not) is also a target of evaluation, as is any bank or BHC whose stock is dealer-traded.

WHO CONTRIBUTES TO THE EVALUATION PROCESS?

The easy answer to this question is that only "analysts" evaluate banks, but this is wrong. Nor is the definition of "analysts" a clear one. To be sure, at the start of the evaluation process, someone has to pull financial data together into ratios, histories, and comparisons for interpretation leading to credit and investment decisions. This technical work, however necessary, merely supports decisions and rarely makes them. The decision makers tend to be generalists—credit policy officers and stock portfolio managers—whose information comes not just from specialist analysts but also from opinion leaders who frame so many of our ideas and from regulators who frame policy toward banks. Thus the matrix of evaluation is extremely diffuse, becoming even more so with the internationalization of financial markets. This is fortunate in one sense because the training and competence of specialist analysts is questionable.

Who are these analysts? Let's assume there are at least several thousand large-dollar creditors of large banks (including several hundred other banks, both foreign and domestic) who are committed to evaluation. Let's also assume there are perhaps two thousand institutional portfolios (including bank trust departments) with marketable bank stock positions. Does it follow that there are as many analysts? The answer is no. Most "downstream" institutions rely heavily on a small number of "upstream" analysts for data, for methodology and training, and for interpretation (or for any one or two of these functions). Though many large investors and funds-providers do employ full-time bank analysts, they recognize that this can be very expensive, especially if their professional standards are high.

The upstream analysts therefore exercise a disproportionate influence on the evaluation process. These are of several sorts. The oldest type is the bank stock analyst at those securities firms who choose to support such a costly individual or group (Salomon, First Boston, Merrill Lynch, Alex Brown, and Keefe among perhaps 20 others). These analysts concentrate on serving institutional stock investors, not creditors. A more recent type is the analytically experienced firm whose work is in part oriented to support credit decisions about banking companies but whose fees do not come from the rated institution (Keefe and Cates are two examples). A third type is the analytically experienced firm whose credit analytic work is paid for by the banks themselves (Duff & Phelps, Fitch, Moody's, and S&P). The most recent type is the firm supplying data and perhaps even credit ratings on banks/BHCs, whose experience is deeper in data processing than in bank analysis.

WHAT IS THE TRAINING AND COMPETENCE OF BANK ANALYSTS?

This is rather a central question that deserves more attention than it gets. Bank managements frequently complain that rating agency analysts seem insensitive, dogmatic, and unresponsive; that stock analysts are too often unprepared or ill-informed; that credit analysts are quite invisible; and that some credit ratings on their banks (and on others) seem to bear no relation to reality. More than a few managements believe that understanding a complex bank reaches so far beyond the resources of analysts that the whole group is either endured or courted, but rarely respected.

Is this dismay justified? Is it even possible to be objective about the professional skills and standards of analysts who look at banking companies? Part of the answer lies in the nature of the analytic target: If banks were simple and stable, adequate standards of training and competence can be more easily met. On the contrary, if the target of analysis (especially large banks) is complex and shifting, the training-and-competence issue is a more serious one. We will return to this shortly.

Here are some points to consider in framing an opinion about the range of competence among bank analysts:

- Banking is a sufficiently unique industry that the universal "categories of analysis" useful in most other industries just don't apply to banks (as they don't apply to insurance companies either).
- Though credit analysis and investment analysis are regularly taught in colleges, business schools, and employer training programs, the specific application of these skills to banks is rarely attempted.

- Trade books and publications are pathetically short on bank/BHC analytic principles and techniques; the few that exist were written before the formation of leveraged holding companies, the leveraging of banks with purchased funds, the deregulation and reregulation of banks, and the recent proliferation of capital markets activities.
- The novice bank analyst therefore comes to the job unprepared by specific academic work and can find little or nothing of a systematic nature to read or study.
- Though there are associations of bank analysts in New York and Boston, these are entirely for the purpose of hearing company presentations and occasional lectures on legislation, taxation, and the like. There is never any discussion of method, nor are there any training seminars for junior analysts.
- Most analyst training consists of oral guidance from upstream analysts, prior job incumbents, and a few bankers (usually CFOs) who may take the time to offer some methodological hints.
- Where there is only one bank analyst employed (surely the overwhelming majority of bank-watching institutions), there is no possibility of peer comparison and mutual influence, nor does a nonspecialist supervisor have adequate means to undertake professional guidance, informed review, and quality control.
- The situation is better in those rare situations where there is a group of bank analysts working together, but the "oral tradition" still governs. In other words, new analysts learn their craft through an apprenticeship not unlike that which produces boatswains and tea-tasters.

Compared to other professional endeavors (lending officer, tax attorney, and CPA), the developing bank analyst has no body of literature to turn to for guidance and standards, no hierarchy of experienced seniors to learn from, and no significant peer associations devoted to skill enhancement. In fact, the process of becoming a bank analyst is so unguided and uncertain that it is bound to produce counterfeits alongside truly conscientious and professional analysts. The problem is how to tell the difference. The problem is intensified by the rising demand for bank credit analysis.

CAN THE JOB BE DONE AT ALL?

The challenge to any outside analyst of banks is daunting. Recall that the external analysis of most companies is largely limited to the study of published financial disclosure supplemented at best by occasional interviews with company officers and discussions with competitors, suppliers, customers, employees, and the like. Limited to these resources, analysts must frame a documented view of the risk profile of given banks. This should take them through the analysis of several complex modules of performance: asset quality, liquidity, earnings, capital, and management (note the slightly rearranged appearance of CAMEL). Asset quality, for example, is itself not a unitary concept but needs to be examined under subheads like credit policy, review systems, charge-off policy, and reserve adequacy, all in the context of balance sheet and "off-balance-sheet" exposure. Liquidity is also a complex concept, one that includes study of liquid and marketable assets, off-balance-sheet contingencies, funding capacity under various possible conditions, and the cash-flow capacity of a BHC parent to service its debt.

These illustrations are not to show what analysts do but rather what they should be trying to do working from limited data and even more limited access to the real policies and concerns of managements. At face value, there is much to justify the occasional contention of bank managements that "you can't understand a bank from the outside." Does this mean that analysts are just spinning their wheels? Is the whole credit/investment evaluation process built on sand? We will now address this challenging question.

HOW DO GOOD ANALYSTS THINK?

It may be rash to characterize the work of a "good" bank analyst since we have already argued that there is no explicit body of common practice that lets us define craft standards. It is also well known that the only thing two analysts can agree on is why a third is wrong. Yet some fundamentals of method are self-evident, and from these we can reconstruct what the techniques, standards, and quality checks should be. It is these quality checks, finally, that will allow us to answer the question, Does it work?

Let's start with four unassailable axioms. First, analysts are limited to the published financial reports produced by banks/BHCs whether in response to regulators or to shareholders and the SEC. Our second axiom is that this data, however frequent and voluminous, is inevitably superficial, incomplete, ambiguous, and potentially misleading. Anyone who doubts this point runs the risk of confusing the "bank" with its "record," which is as diagnostically perilous as confusing the patient with medical test results, the student with exams, or the player with his stats.

Our third axiom—a controversial one—is that "meeting management" adds relatively little to the main analytic thrust, namely, careful study of the data, annual reports, and news events. There are at least four reasons for this caution. First, the financial record is in fact the only documented record of management; properly understood, it is the most objective commentary available. Second, the typical face-to-face contact with management (visits to banks or attendance at analyst presentations) is so brief and superficial that its only value to a professional should be to confirm a conviction or illuminate a doubt. Third, the cards are unfairly stacked in favor of management during these sessions. It is not that managements deliberately deceive (though this happens too); it is more likely that they have so persuaded themselves of the rightness of their strategies and policies that they simply overwhelm most analysts. A shocking example is the forceful and articulate story put forth by Continental Bank in the late 1970s and early 1980s. Other stories also sounded good (in retrospect, too good): First Pennsylvania, SeaFirst, and Texas Commerce come to mind. Fourth, let us not forget that managements are limited in what they can tell analysts about material information not yet publicly disclosed. A final point is that the overwhelming majority of working bank analysts (for example, those in bank credit departments) are not even invited to meet managements, nor do their budgets permit this costly luxury.

Our fourth and final axiom is that good analysts supplement their technical work with a well-developed and worldly sense of the environment: competitive, regulatory, and monetary. Without this sense, in fact, all the data in the world is without meaning. To put it another way, mere technical competence has to be buttressed with wordly understanding if an analyst's summary evaluation of a bank is to be taken seriously.

With these four axioms in place, it is now possible to characterize how the best analysts go about their work. At the center of the process is *comparative ratio analysis,* illuminated by a *sense of the environment* and perhaps (but not necessarily) by the *comments of management.*

The comparative process itself deserves some discussion. Because of the superficiality and inadequacy of data to represent the "real" bank, a good analyst uses ratios the way a medical diagnostician uses tests. Since each one is potentially misleading (that is, has a reliability factor well below 100 percent), the solution lies in using a cluster of tests (the more the better) and in interpreting the cluster rather than the single observation. Applied to bank analysis, this means, for example, that high apparent loan losses may be the end or the beginning of a crisis, that low apparent loan losses may or may not be a valid signal, that a high ROA may or may not be sustainable, that a high level of BHC parent debt may be appropriate, and so forth. It all depends on context and on the interpretation of the whole ratio context in the light of the analyst's other knowledge. If this sounds ultimately like a semiquantitative judgmental art, it is!

IS THERE ANY QUALITY CHECK ON THE WORK OF ANALYSTS?

Because analysts exercise so much influence on the perceived credit standing and investment worthiness of banks, there should exist (but does not) a recognized set of tests which can be applied by bank managements interacting with analysts, by nonspecialist supervisors hiring or reviewing bank analysts, and by downstream institutions assessing the work of upstream vendors. Fortunately, it is not hard to design such a set of questions.

- How would you have documented a precrisis analysis of Continental, First Oklahoma Bancorp, and other real and de facto failures, showing your view of the bank and the holding company? Did you in fact have any such analysis in place before the event? What did you miss? What did you learn?
- How do you document your current view of the creditworthiness of _____(any well-known bank/BHC that you and the analyst can agree to discuss)?
- What is your view of the overall condition of the banking industry today, subdivided by region or by size groups? What are the causes and the available remedies for the problems you see?

The first question explores whether the analyst has taken the trouble to study bank failure as a clue to its opposite, namely, health. The second question explores the quality and texture of an analyst's thinking about a bank not unlike your own. The third question focuses on the analyst's practical understanding of the industry as it exists today. If an analyst can satisfy reasonable professionals that he/she meets these tests, it should then be recognized that the power of the analyst to discern creditworthiness is real. To put it another way, at least a few analysts, after all that work, should be able to describe and predict bank performance with reasonable accuracy. If we can't do this, then bank analysts should fold their tents and silently steal away.

DOES THE THINKING OF MARKET-BASED ANALYSTS DIFFER FROM THAT OF REGULATORS?

Both groups are outsiders, both are paid to be objective, and both hold "safety and soundness" to be desirable standards. Shouldn't their methods be very similar? They are—up to a point. Much of the similarity results from an increasing interpenetration of technique. To illustrate, the Uniform Bank Performance Report and the Bank Holding Company Performance Report are full of ratios that originated with analysts. It is even safe to say that good examiners and good analysts do not differ materially in their working definitions of profitability, liquidity, asset quality, and management. True, examiners have an edge because of their access to loan files and the like, but a good analyst can compensate through superior skill and experience in comparative ratio analysis.

The two chief differences between the methods of the regulator and the market-based analyst concern *capital* and the *holding company*. Let's look first at the capital question. Regulatory policy toward bank capital tends to be both political and routine, the former because Congress must be placated and the latter because "fairness" must prevail (14,000 bank CEOs are each a phone call away from a congressman). One result is that the regulators have come to define as "equity equivalent capital" elements which no financial analyst should as easily accept: auction-rate permanent preferred, equity contract notes, and loan loss allowance. In the hands of weak issuers, these cannot be considered "permanent." Market-based analysts go a step further in their definition of capital. Because of the impact of securitization, they are increasingly attempting to estimate the market value of assets. As they do this, they also adjust their estimate of the true value of capital. Meanwhile the regulators remain committed to the nominal value of bank capital, a theoretically obsolete concept.

So much for the very definition of capital. There is also a profound difference of viewpoint toward determining its adequacy. Analysts, it is to be hoped, unlike regulators, have not institutionalized a formula approach to capital adequacy. Rather a good analyst always looks at the context: Does *this* bank/BHC have appropriate capital for *its* risk profile? Just as important, can it get more capital? By contrast, the regulatory formula for capital adequacy (even the "risk-adjusted" version) is an arbitrary cookie cutter that does not take into account, for example, differences among banks in risk management.

The other main difference between the market-based analyst and the regulator is their respective attitudes toward the holding company, or rather the relation between a bank and its holding company. The root of this difference is historic: The *bank* regulators are charged with the safety and soundness of *banks*. To a bank examiner, the BHC is just another type of ownership. True, the Federal Reserve System is charged with the inspection of *holding companies*, but this inspection effort is departmentally distinct from *bank* supervision. Thus jurisdictional history stands in the way of integrated analysis.

To illustrate the importance of this issue, many large banks conduct their capital markets activities partly through the bank and partly through other BHC subsidiaries. Unless the entire off-balance-sheet activity is viewed globally, the examination of just one piece is bound to be misleading. Another example is balance-sheet management which is typically conducted globally at the BHC level. This often means that a given *bank* affiliate will appear to be unbalanced with respect to its interest rate risk. Only an integrated view of the bank and the BHC can discern and solve this analytic problem. *Bank* equity capital—a third example—is often financed with BHC *parent* debt. To analyze the capital structure of a bank—and the debt quality of a BHC parent—therefore requires an integrated view of the bank and its BHC.

The private analyst has the freedom to look at banks in the context of their BHC and vice versa. The trouble is that this double (or integrated) perspective is rare since most analysts still tend to focus on one or the other according to their assignment. This analytic myopia may be due in part to the newness of BHC data. To illustrate, the Federal Reserve has published a BHC data "tape" (fully consolidated and parent only) only since 1980, and this information was relatively superficial until the large-scale revisions culminating in the tape of June 30, 1986.

Some examples of the value of this integrated perspective are as follows:

- Continental Bank in the early 1980s was chronically undercapitalized, retaining net income rather than paying a dividend to its parent. The parent, meanwhile, was passing an unsustainably high dividend to the shareholders, a dividend which it was not "earning" internally. This issue contributed to the financial instability of Continental.
- Penn Square Bank, on superficial analysis, did not look doomed to failure even after the charge-offs of 1981. The BHC parent, however, had issued debt which it passed to the bank as "equity capital." Thus the enterprise was drastically undercapitalized despite the false appearance of capital in the bank. This did not cause the failure but did give an important insight into management imprudence.

CAN BANK MANAGEMENTS INFLUENCE THE EVALUATION PROCESS?

The customary approach of bankers toward analysts (as toward regulators) alternates between persuasion and conciliation. It does not typically include confrontation. Whatever you think of analysts, you keep it to yourselves; you could be penalized for your criticism or blacklisted as a hard case. It also takes time to figure out where analysts are coming from and what their qualifications are. Finally, it is easy for analysts to view the complaining bank as wishful or self-serving. Yet the analytic process suffers from this absence of communication on methods and credentials—the tendency not to challenge technique and interpretation. As we have suggested, there are some loose cannons out there generating analyses that are poorly grounded, both quantitatively and qualitatively. To the extent that undisciplined analysts are influential, their work helps to distort the "public intelligibility" of banking, that is, how people generally think about banks. An industry challenge could serve to keep all analysts more attentive, informed, responsive, and responsible.

Such a challenge would have little visibility or impact if it occurred only at the level of individual banks, though eventually it can operate there. What should happen is that an appropriate group of banks (New York Clearing House, Robert Morris Associates, Association of Bank Holding Companies, Association of Reserve City Bankers, and the Chief Financial Officers Division of the ABA are all plausible candidates) should enter into systematic dialogue with the rating agencies, with other credit rating bodies, and with stock analysts. It is in such a visible forum, sponsored perhaps by the Financial Analysts Federation, that banker skepticism about analytic method can be aired, and analyst approaches and credentials justified.

What is sure to happen if the meetings are well planned and guided is that both sides will learn much from one another. Furthermore, if these meetings can generate publishable material, the value of the sessions will extend beyond the immediate audience and serve as guidance material for bankers and bank analysts everywhere. The credit and investment standing of the banking industry is too important to leave to the often haphazard and ill-considered process that shapes financial evaluation.

Whether this dialogue takes place, there is an important step which each market-dependent bank/BHC ought to take on its own. What we have in mind is a self-evaluation of the credit/investment qualities of the company, perceived deliberately from an *analyst* perspective as compared to a *regulatory* or *strategic/managerial* one. This "audit" (and audit is a good word because it connotes relentless objectivity toward facts) offers the possibility of a more constructive relation with analysts because you will have thought through your bank/BHC from their perspective, perhaps with greater care toward fundamentals than most analysts supply. This self-evaluation would be quite different, moreover, from the typical "presentation" to analysts, which too often is a barrage of favorable data convincing to its author, not necessarily to others.

The challenge in building this audit is that the mindset of analysts is very different from the management mindset, if only because the methodology and available information resources are so different. To "gear down" to what analysts do (or should do) takes training and experience that is not ordinarily included in the skill repertory of bankers, even of CFOs who deal with analysts. After all, the financial analysis of banks, at its best, was not invented within any of the banking professions, but within the investment profession. Its methods therefore can initially seem alien to managements, yet it is out of this tradition that banks get analyzed. No one has a greater interest in understanding how this process works than bankers themselves. One way to understand it, perhaps even to influence it, is to practice it yourselves.

CHAPTER TWENTY-FOUR

Capital Planning and Management

Timothy P. Hartman
Corporate Executive Vice President and
Chief Financial Officer
NCNB Corporation

John E. Mack
Senior Vice President and Treasurer
NCNB Corporation

INTRODUCTION

Banking begins only when an institution has established a capital base. This capital base is an institution's basic resource, which allows it to function as a financial intermediary. It represents the permanent commitment by investors to the business of banking and thereby generates a level of confidence for the institution which allows the gathering of deposits.

The permanent characteristics of capital are evident in the instruments which comprise an institution's capital base. Common stock, preferred stock, long-term debt, and loan loss reserve represent the principal components of any capital structure. Short-term liabilities—regardless of their source—are not considered as capital instruments.

A capital base which provides for the absorption of unexpected losses will support a level of public confidence and help overcome any concern regarding liquidity, thereby enabling an institution to gather deposits and function as a financial intermediary.

Capital planning and management represents the art or discipline of forecasting the adequate level of capital for an individual institution in a particular economic environment.

This task of capital planning takes place in an ever-changing economic environment and calls for a level of capital adequacy that is acceptable to a variety of publics—retail and wholesale liability markets, investors, rating agencies, and regulators.

Every institution has unique characteristics that determine its level of capital adequacy. This level of capital adequacy, as determined by bank management with considerable deference to various publics, represents a base from which most performance statistics evolve. Quality of earnings and capacity for growth, as well as a need for new capital, are but a few of the major business decisions which are closely tied to the determination of a bank's own level of capital adequacy.

The need for management to actively plan and manage its capital base cannot be overemphasized. To allow an institution's capital base to evolve as a result of the interaction of the balance sheet represents a missed opportunity. Bank capital includes common and preferred stock, long-term debt, and the reserve for loan losses.

The central importance of capital in the life cycle of a bank can be seen in Exhibit 1. Initially, capital, as shown on the balance sheet, allows a newly chartered bank to open an office and to begin accepting deposit liabilities. The acquired funds are then converted into loans and other earning assets that generate income. The resulting flow of income is shown on the statement of income. Net income is available either for distribution in the form of dividends to shareholders or for earnings retention. Retained earnings serve to replenish the stock of capital, and the process continues. Thus capital is the basic resource of a bank. It is the resource that allows a bank to acquire assets and to operate over time.

The regulatory view of an institution's capital base rightfully takes precedent over other statistical or market evaluations of capital adequacy. Regulatory standards for capital adequacy have been changed over time in order to accommodate the evolution of the banking industry. Regulators have used capital standards as a lever to encourage or discourage internal and external growth within the banking system. Regulatory standards of capital adequacy are an outgrowth of the regulatory mission to maintain a stable banking system and to safeguard the interests of depositors. However, such regulatory standards are basically static in nature and fail to consider adequately the importance of current earnings in the determination of capital adequacy.

The income statement exhibit illustrates the importance of earnings in the determination of capital adequacy. The flow of current earnings into retained earnings is the most dependable and recurring source of net additions to capital. A high and sustainable level of current earnings provides a significant cushion against unexpected loss and represents a significant source of financial strength.

While the primary determinant of capital adequacy is centered on a regulatory standard that is static in nature, it is necessary to temper this statistical result with an evaluation of the level and sustainability of current earnings. Implicit in this approach to capital adequacy is the importance of earnings quality and earnings sustainability, both

EXHIBIT 1   Balance Sheet and Income Statement Interrelationships

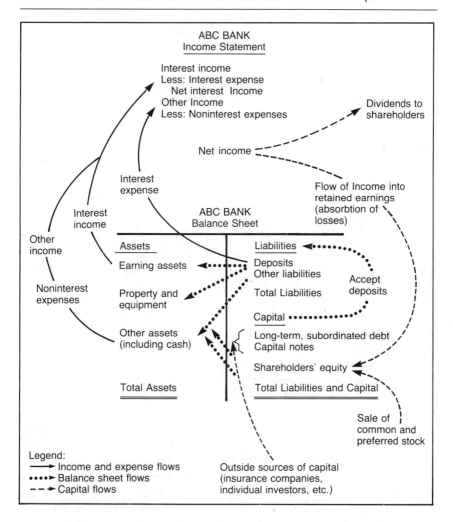

of which lead back to balance sheet considerations. The importance of this approach, as opposed to the more static regulatory approach to examining bank capital adequacy, is in its emphasis on the dynamic flow of earnings in a banking organization.

CAPITAL PLANNING

Prior to the 1970s, capital planning in the banking industry was largely reserved for either newly chartered or troubled banks. In both cases regulators primarily concerned with safety and soundness of the banking system dictated appropriate capital levels. Healthy banking companies generated sufficient capital primarily from internal sources such as retained earnings and the occasional offering of either equity or capital notes. Bank management justified capital adequacy without excessive external regulation.

During the 1970s banks responded to the increasingly competitive economic environment and growth opportunities by increased leverage on the capital base to improve investor returns. Bank regulators responded by imposing formal minimum capital ratios, first on community and regional banking companies and finally on all banking companies. As a result, formal capital planning programs are being adopted throughout the industry.

Capital planning is a process of determining the appropriate components and level of capital in an environment consistent with the assumptions of the bank's strategic business plan. The objective of capital planning is to ensure adequate capital to support the bank as it pursues its strategic business plan. Capital is an economically scarce and strategic resource, and thus the capital plan is a key component of the bank's overall planning effort. The nature of the strategic planning process, the limited availability of capital, and the necessity to ration scarce resources all dictate that capital planning be centralized within the organization.

The essence of capital planning is one of balancing the cost of the components of capital from internal and external sources with the interests of the various audiences. The components of capital are considered to be equity, reserves, and long-term debt. Equity consists of common and preferred stock as well as retained earnings. The audiences include customers, investors, rating agencies, and regulators. Each audience has its own particular, though not unique, interest. Customers are primarily interested in a bank's liquidity in order to fund loan and deposit obligations. Investors are seeking the highest return consistent with perceived risk. Rating agencies seek to provide information to debt holders. Regulators are influenced by their occupational goal, which is to protect the safety and soundness of the banking system.

The complexity of the capital plan can be largely based on the size of the bank. Small banks have more limited sources of external capital and fewer audiences with vested interests in the company. Raising capital in the marketplace is not generally an option. Debt capital is usually limited to capital notes which have to be subordinated to the claims of depositors. The capital plan generally shows the internally generated capital as the primary capital source to fund the ongoing growth of the business. Without an adequate level of retained profit, asset growth will be constrained.

Large banks generally have more complex capital structures. They blend different sources of capital within the framework dictated by the market and regulators to produce the appropriate mix at the lowest overall cost. Mandatory capital notes can be an especially attractive form of debt if it meets the standards set by the regulators for primary capital while at the same time leveraging the equity capital to provide a high return to the shareholder.

The process of capital planning begins with a review of the economic environment and the earnings prospects of the bank. The importance of internally generated capital and the capacity to provide adequate return to current and prospective investors cannot be overemphasized. Above average earnings give management additional flexibility in capital planning.

Management also reviews the existing capital structure given the capital requirements imposed by the regulators and the marketplace. Regulators prefer banks add common equity capital as opposed to qualifying long-term debt; however, management must be aware that additional common equity can be the most costly form of new capital. New common equity initially reduces leverage ratios, which reduces returns available to common shareholders and represent a continuing claim to the future earnings stream of the company. On the other hand, the marketplace will effectively limit the bank's proportion of debt capital.

Effective capital planning should anticipate future capital requirements that result from technological changes or an increased level of business activity. Small banks in particular may need additional capital to acquire the technology to serve their communities. Large banks are likely to enter a new geographic market or line of business that could require additional capital. Anticipating the need for additional capital can allow management to take advantage of a market opportunity in acquiring additional capital.

DYNAMICS OF CAPITAL FLOWS

The banking industry is in a competitive struggle to retain its position as the principal financial intermediary of our economic system. Increased business activity, as well as the emergence of new financial instruments, have proliferated at such a pace that the banking industry can no longer look to retained earnings as its only source of new capital.

Capital growth beyond the traditional retained earnings source is dependent on current returns on existing capital. This return on capital is the fundamental barometer which will determine the banking industry's success in competing with nonbank entities for external capital sources from the investment community. Nonbank entities now offer banking customers traditional bank financial services at an ever-increasing rate. To remain competitive the banking industry must reach out for new capital sources to secure its traditional financial intermediary role. The opportunity to access new sources of capital is dependent on current returns on capital. Adequate returns can be achieved by combining the sale of competitively priced financial services with the retention of an adequate level of business activity and the maintenance of an appropriate service level.

The need for new capital in order to remain competitive in the industry must be balanced against the necessity to maximize current returns on existing capital. This dichotomy forces banks to ration their financial and managerial resources to areas of business that produce the best returns on capital. The strategic flexibility of the banking industry and, for that matter, of each individual bank depends on current returns on capital. Only those institutions with above-average returns on capital will remain in a position to be masters of their own destiny.

Earning asset growth, whether it results from internal development or external expansion, is limited to a bank's ability to grow its capital base. No other source of funding is more determinative as to the success of the institution than its ability to secure new capital sources.

Bank regulators employ a carrot-and-stick approach in the enforcement of capital standards, which are more specific and far more restrictive than other market evaluations of capital adequacy. The historical approach adopted by the regulators as to specific and restrictive definitions for capital instruments has been relaxed and will be further modified in the future. In addition, the adoption of risk-based guidelines that assign weighted values to both on- and off-balance sheet relationships reflects the use of the carrot to facilitate the expansion of the industry's capital base. On the other hand, regulatory attitudes toward external expansion through mergers have become more restrictive. Regulators have placed increased emphasis on the level of capital remaining in the banking industry post mergers, and require that minimum standards of capital adequacy, adjusted for intangibles, are sustained post merger in the combined institution.

Capital constraints levied by the regulators on the banking industry are in many instances more restrictive than the market constraints that apply to many nonbank entities currently offering traditional banking services. The banking industry must assume an active posture regarding the management of its capital base in order to maintain its position as the principal financial intermediary of our economic system.

SOURCES OF CAPITAL

Capital sources may be divided into two major categories: internal sources and external sources. While both of these sources are important, internal sources provide bank management with alternatives that are less dependent on the vagaries of the marketplace than are external sources. Consequently, constant attention should be focused on internal sources since the decision process involved is for the most part unilateral. The primary internal source of capital is retained earnings (or net income less dividends paid to shareholders). Retained earnings must be the most regular and most significant source of new capital, or it is unlikely that any external source for new capital will be available due to an inadequate return on existing capital. Shareholder, management, and employee stock award or purchase programs represent unique capital sources that usually develop significant ancillary benefits as well as generate a recurring flow of new capital. The sale or exchange of existing assets or liabilities, including a product line, a division, or a subsidiary, in a transaction that generates new capital is often an overlooked source.

The achievement of an above-average return on capital requires a constant rationing of financial and managerial resources. A willingness to sell or liquidate operations that are not earning a reasonable return represents a capital source in that existing capital becomes available to support more profitable and faster growing activities.

External sources of capital include the sale of common stock, preferred stock, and long-term debt. In addition, the sophistication of the financial markets has produced a multitude of capital instruments that combine the permanent characteristics of these three principal capital instruments. The availability of these capital resources is dependent on the institution's return on capital and the condition of the market into which the particular capital issue will be sold.

External capital sources are best secured over a long planning period that enables the issuer to take advantage of the cyclical nature of the economic environment. A bank should avail itself of any or all of the new sophisticated financial instruments available in the marketplace. If, for instance, mandatory equity commitment notes qualify as capital, by all means take advantage of such an instrument at the time when the market offers it at an attractive price.

The sale of common equity is generally the most expensive form of capital since it represents a permanent allocation of future earnings to the new shareholders.

The sale of preferred stock is less expensive than the sale of common equity over the long term provided the dividend rate is not participating. Dividends on common and preferred stock are usually after-tax distributions of earnings since no significant tax benefit accrues to the paying institution. As a result, debt capital has become a major component of bank capital since interest payments on debt are tax deductible and therefore the lesser expensive form of capital. Debt capital is quite different than common and preferred stock and is not considered part of the bank's equity base. Since debt capital must be repaid at a future date, it is included in bank capital only to the extent that the repayment requirement is sufficiently distant to provide for a degree of permanence.

Common equity is the most important form of bank capital and represents the foundation for the institution's well-being. The financial markets will not provide economically priced alternative forms of capital unless a bank's existing capital base includes a large component of common equity.

CAPITAL ADEQUACY

In 1983 bank regulators were instructed by Congress to establish minimum capital standards for the banking industry. Such legislation further provided that whatever standards were established would be correct—or at least enforceable. Prior to this action regulators administered capital supervision on a case-by-case basis through the use of capital guidelines versus minimum standards. With the establishment of a minimum primary capital percent of 5.5 and a minimum total capital percent of 6.0, the banking industry now has a definition of what constitutes a minimum level of bank capital. With this floor for minimum capital requirements clearly in view, banks are challenged to determine what level of capital will be considered to be adequate for each individual institution.

Capital adequacy is essentially a matter of judgment for any institution at any point in time. While the judgment of bank management may be better informed as to an individual institution, it is no better or worse than the judgment of the variety of publics who, because of their interests in the institution, must play a vital role in the determination of capital adequacy. Competitive liability markets, rating agencies, regulators, and investors in capital instruments develop individual perceptions about the adequacy of a bank's level of capital. The external perception of capital adequacy for the banking industry has become increasingly more important as the industry experiences continued deregulation of the financial markets.

The convergence of legislative, economic, and technological changes is responsible for altering the manner in which financial services are delivered. Deposit deregulation, loan spread contraction, excessive charge-off ratios, changing delivery systems, and the loss of uniqueness in terms of services which banks offer have contributed to the public's perception that banking has become a more volatile and changing business. As a result, the marketplace requires enhanced levels of capital and more information about the measurement of bank capital.

It is important to note that while this chapter has attempted to discuss the relative standards of capital adequacy for banks and by inference for bank holding companies, it has not attempted to define capital adequacy in any explicit fashion. The omission of an explicit definition is intentional since capital adequacy is a relative concept in the viewpoint of various external publics as well as individual banks.

However, certain issues relative to capital adequacy are very relevant in the evaluation of an individual bank's capital ratio. Beyond the interpretation and determination of current regulatory standards that prescribe the numerator and denominator of a particular capital ratio is a more detailed examination of the particular institution under review. A complicating factor in this capital adequacy exercise is the lack of consistency in the application of specific formulas. Inconsistency has and is likely to continue among banking's principal regulators.

The numerator (or capital component) of a capital ratio calculation should reflect any significant variance between balance sheet carrying values and current market values. In particular, an assessment of loan quality that relates nonperforming loans to loan loss reserves needs to be performed to determine whether any adjustment of capital is necessary.

Particular attention needs to be focused on intangible assets to determine what regulatory standard has been applied in the computation of a bank's regulatory capital ratios. The underlying value of the net assets associated with intangible values and the regulatory treatment accorded such intangibles will determine whether any adjustment is needed in this area.

The denominator (or asset component) of the capital ratio calculation includes total or average assets (depending on the regulator) and the loan loss reserve.

Bank regulators have recently introduced supplemental guidelines which will affect the asset component of the capital ratio calculation. These risk-based capital guidelines assign varying degrees of risk to assets and certain off-balance sheet exposures through the application of a weighted value formula. These guidelines also provide an adjustment to the regulatory capital ratio computation and reduce the capital requirement for investment in low-risk relatively liquid assets. In addition the guidelines require a capital allocation for off-balance sheet exposures that have expanded rapidly over the last several years.

The use of the static regulatory capital ratios is necessary but by no means conclusive in the determination of capital adequacy. Many other factors need be considered—management, geographical market, funding sources, asset mix, stage of historical development, and others influence the evaluation of an individual bank's capital adequacy. And finally, the flow of current earnings into capital at a high and sustainable level must be considered as the key determinant in any capital adequacy evaluation. A strong earnings performance contributes more to the maintenance of a level of investor confidence than any other single component considered in the evaluation process.

BANKS—LARGE, SMALL, AND HOLDING COMPANIES

Capital planning and management is a necessary function for both large and small banking institutions. Both must aggressively seek out sources of new capital in order to remain competitive in their marketplace. Improved earnings, issuance of capital instruments in local markets, introduction of shareholder and/or employee stock plans, and consideration of merger opportunities are all viable sources of new capital available to each and every banking institution regardless of size. The inherent trade-off among depositors, employees, management, and shareholders must be addressed and resolved. Lack of attention in the pursuit of new capital sources will result in a loss of operational flexibility, in a decline of competitive power in the marketplace, and in an erosion of acceptable returns on existing capital, thereby eliminating many growth opportunities.

The bank holding company form of organization facilitates the accessing of new capital sources and provides for the allocation of capital among affiliated banks and nonbank affiliates. Capital flows are more easily managed in a holding company environment which provides for the raising and warehousing of capital when it is most favorably priced as well as available in the marketplace, and the subsequent allocation of new capital to the faster growing affiliates in the group. It further provides for the redeployment of existing capital among affiliates where dividends from mature operations can be invested in more rapidly growing markets.

Bank regulators have established minimum capital ratios for bank holding companies that are similar to those established for individual banks. These minimum standards are applied on a consolidated basis for the holding company as well as for each individual affiliated bank. In addition, the level of capital for nonbank subsidiaries is monitored by bank regulators to determine compliance with the appropriate industry norm.

SUMMARY

Banks require capital to maintain public confidence, to offer protection for depositors, to absorb losses, and to support growth.

Capital planning and management is an ongoing process that, more than any other management function, will determine the ultimate success or failure of the banking industry.

It represents the decision process which reconciles the allocation of financial and managerial resources between short- and long-term objectives.

It represents the resolution of the inherent conflicts that exist regarding a multitude of perceptions about an appropriate level of capital adequacy. Shareholders, management, employees, regulators, rating agencies, and creditors all view capital adequacy from a different perspective and all need to be satisfied.

It represents a resolution of the dichotomy that occurs when the need for new capital to fund the opportunities of the future must be postponed to assure an adequate return to investors on existing capital.

It represents an identification of individual lines of business or market segments that produce the best returns on capital, thereby maximizing a bank's return on existing capital.

The real issue surrounding the topic of capital planning and management is whether the banking industry will continue to be viewed by the financial markets as an attractive long-term investment and thereby retain its position as the principal financial intermediary of the economy.

CHAPTER TWENTY-FIVE

Legal and Regulatory Constraints Affecting Bank Financial Management

Dorothy Sable

Formerly Director of Litigation and Special Assistant to the Chief Counsel, Comptroller of the Currency.

The primary function of banks is to act as financial intermediaries—drawing funds from various sources for varying time periods and in turn investing those funds in different types of assets with different maturities. As if the process already was not sufficiently complicated by economic and market conditions, an ever-changing and growing body of laws, rules, and supervisory policies combine to make the role of a financial intermediary a constant challenge.

This chapter will discuss capital requirements because capital itself is a source of funds and because capital plays a crucial role in determining a bank's asset structure. Subsequently, the chapter will focus on other sources of funding and on the use of those funds.

STATUTORY AND REGULATORY MINIMUM CAPITAL REQUIREMENTS

The statutory requirements for capital, generally set years ago, are fairly low. The National Bank Act, for example, only requires capitalization of $200,000 for a national bank in a large city. However, regulators traditionally have placed great importance on capitalization appropriate to a bank's level of assets, liquidity, condition, and management. Normally, $1 million is the minimum capital required for a newly chartered bank, and capital is expected to increase thereafter proportionately with the asset size of the bank.

In 1983 Congress passed legislation applicable to all federally regulated banks and bank holding companies; it required the federal banking agencies to establish minimum adequate levels of capital for the institutions they supervise and to cause banks to achieve and maintain those capital levels. In response to this legislation, the three federal banking agencies issued rules in 1985 requiring banks to maintain capital at least at the level of 5 1/2 percent primary capital (essentially equity capital, loan loss reserves, and undivided profits) to total assets and 6 percent total capital (primary capital plus debt capital) to total assets. The agencies reserved the right to require an individual bank or bank holding company to increase its capital above the minimum requirements when its condition warrants a higher level. Therefore banks must now assure that any growth in assets is supported by at least the minimum required level of capital.

Current regulatory proposals would supplement or replace the straight capital-to-assets requirement with a risk-adjusted capital requirement; namely, one in which assets, including off-balance sheet assets, would be assigned to specific risk-weighted categories for the purpose of formulating a new sum of total assets adjusted for risk against which a bank's level of capital would be measured. Thus, in the future, management may have to consider not merely whether the bank's capital is sufficient to support a given amount of assets, but also whether a proposed asset will require more or less capital than an alternative.

CONSTRAINTS AFFECTING FUNDING

What Types of Funding Also Serve the Function of Capital?

Since capital can serve as a source of funding and is a necessity for growth in assets, management must be aware of what types of funding will also serve the function of capital. Currently, the regulatory definition of capital includes common and perpetual preferred stock and surplus, retained earnings, the allowance for loan and lease losses (ALLL), minority interests in consolidated subsidiaries, mandatory convertible debentures, and mortgage servicing rights. All of these are considered primary capital. Mandatory convertible debentures, however, are limited to 20 percent of the total of primary capital exclusive of such debentures. Remaining mandatory convertible debt, if any, is considered secondary capital along with limited life preferred stock and subordinated debt. Total secondary capital in turn is limited to 50 percent of primary capital.

Future regulatory changes, however, may eliminate new mandatory convertible debt and intangible assets from the primary capital category and limit perpetual preferred stock, while adding, with limits, perpetual debt and limited life preferred. Therefore management should determine in light of the regulatory definitions of capital current at the time whether a particular capital instrument, such as subordinated debt, can serve the dual function of a source of funds and a part of the bank's required capital base—whether primary or secondary.

In addition to the determination of what is capital, it is also necessary to consider how that capital will be raised. Public offerings of stock or debentures, for example, are subject to registration and other requirements under the securities laws applicable to banks. Moreover, certain types of capital or increases in capital may require prior regulatory approval.

What Sources of Funds Are Subject to Reserve Requirements?

The rules in this area are quite complex, but domestic funds and certain Eurocurrency liabilities generally will be subject to reserve requirements. The percentage requirement in turn is based primarily on the maturity of the funds. Traditional deposits, as well as nearly all types of bank borrowings, will be subject to reserve requirements as will funds raised by bank affiliates intended for the bank's use. Major exceptions are debt instruments counted as capital, trust funds, and bankers' acceptances.

What Sources of Funding Are Subject to Other Requirements or Limitations?

Interest rate controls essentially have been phased out like restrictions on bank borrowings, but in addition to reserve requirements, various sources or types of funding may be subject to other requirements or limitations that must be considered. For example, deposits will be subject to assessments for federal deposit insurance, government deposits usually must be secured, and asset sales with recourse require that the assets sold remain on the books of the selling bank.

Supervisory Liquidity Requirements

While there are no specific rules on liquidity, the bank examination process places considerable emphasis on liquidity, and supervisory analysis of each bank measures its liquidity in light of its overall condition. Bank supervisors may require that an individual bank take action to increase the liquidity of its portfolio if the bank's liquidity position is considered unsatisfactory. Accordingly, sources of funding always must be evaluated in terms of their impact on the bank's liquidity position.

CONSTRAINTS AFFECTING ASSETS

Now that funding has been obtained, what can management do with it? Here also are a host of regulatory requirements to be considered.

Restrictions as to Type

Some assets are not permissible for banks to invest in. Others are permitted with restrictions. Examples include:

Securities.   The Glass-Steagall Act, applicable to national banks and state member banks, prohibits nearly all bank investments in equity securities. By regulation, limited exceptions are provided for investments in subsidiaries performing bank functions and by statute, exceptions are provided for equity investments in Edge corporations (engaged in foreign banking), foreign banks, bank service corporations, bankers banks, small business investment companies, and several other types of organizations. Banks may invest in U.S. Treasury issued or guaranteed securities, and general obligations of state and municipal governments. The purchase of other investment grade debt securities is permitted, but investments in such securities are subject to a limit of 10 percent of the bank's capital and surplus per issuer.

Real Estate.   National banks may not invest in real estate except to the extent that it is used or intended for the bank's current and reasonable future requirements. Even so, total investment in bank premises is limited to the amount of the bank's capital stock unless specific permission is received from the comptroller. Many states also impose restrictions on state banks' holdings or investments in real estate.

Restrictions on real estate lending by national banks were repealed in 1982, and such loans now are subject only to the restrictions applicable to other types of extensions of credit.

Other Lines of Business.   This is covered in more detail in Part I, Chapter 6, but in general banks may not invest in nonfinancial sectors of the economy such as manufacturing or transportation. Even in the financial services sector, most banks are barred from such key industries as insurance and securities underwriting.

Assets Related to Insiders.   Both federal and state laws limit or impose requirements on the types and amounts of loans banks can make to their own executive officers, directors, or controlling shareholders. The least restrictive federal law limits apply to loans to executive officers secured by personal residences and loans for other personal uses such as medical or educational expenses. Overall limits apply to the aggregate amount of loans to member banks' executive officers, directors, and controlling shareholders, their business interests, and political campaign committees for their benefit. In some cases, the consent of other directors is required. Member banks may not pay any overdrafts on the accounts of their executive officers, directors, and controlling shareholders. Various reporting requirements also apply. Finally, purchases and sales of assets between a member bank and its "insiders," as well as lease and service agreements, also are subject to various statutory or regulatory restrictions to insure fairness to the bank.

Foreign Assets.   Special rules, generally more liberal than those for domestic investments, govern the types of investments banks and bank holding companies can make, and the activities they can engage in overseas. However, loans or other extensions of credit to or investments in certain foreign countries may be prohibited or restricted by statute or regulation. Restrictions on transactions with the government of South Africa and its entities are the most recent example of this type of prohibition.

Restrictions as to Amount

Even if a particular asset is a permissible investment, it may be subject to limitations on the amount that can be invested. Examples include:

Lending Limits.   A national bank's total loans and other extensions of credit to any one obligor are limited to 15 percent of the bank's capital and surplus. Exceptions are made for various types of secured loans such as loans secured by deposits or Treasury securities or guaranteed by the U.S. government. State banks are subject to lending limits imposed under state law.

Investment Security Limits.   National banks and state member banks are subject to a limit of 10 percent of capital and surplus on investments in the debt securities of any one issuer. The primary exceptions concern U.S. government securities and state and municipal government general obligations.

Limits on Investments in Premises.   National banks may not invest more than 100 percent of the amount of their capital stock in bank premises or in the stock of a company owning the bank premises without permission from the comptroller's office. Similar state bank investments usually also are subject to limitations under state law.

Limits on Bankers Acceptances. The aggregate of all outstanding acceptances or obligations for a participation share in acceptances is limited to a maximum of 150 percent of a bank's capital stock and surplus although the Federal Reserve Board may extend this limit to 200 percent. Unsecured acceptances are subject to a 10 percent of capital and surplus limit for any one entity.

Limits on Transactions with Affiliates. A member bank's covered transactions with its affiliates are subject to a statutory limit of 10 percent of the bank's capital and surplus per affiliate and an aggregate limit of 20 percent of capital and surplus for covered transactions with all affiliates. In addition to the limits, certain transactions, such as loans to affiliates, must be secured by collateral of the types and in the amounts specified in the statute. The purchase of "low quality assets" as defined in the statute is prohibited. "Covered transactions" are broadly defined and include extensions of credit to the affiliate, investments in the affiliate's securities, and loans to others secured by stock of the affiliate. Affiliates include the bank's parent holding company but not subsidiaries of the bank itself. Here too are exceptions, primarily for transactions between affiliated banks 80 percent or more owned by the same holding company.

Other Limits. Other types of assets also are subject to limits, for example, deposits in financial institutions not authorized to have access to Federal Reserve advances, and loans for the purchase of securities.

Capital Requirements for Particular Types of Assets under a Risk-Based Capital Ratio

The federal banking agencies are considering and may adopt a capital standard relating capital to the degree of risk inherent in various assets. Such a standard may supplement or replace the straight capital-to-assets gearing ratio now used. It would, of course, be impossible to determine the degree of risk posed by each individual asset. Therefore assets are likely to be grouped into broad risk categories. For example, cash and short-term U.S. Treasury securities would be placed in the lowest risk category, and short-term interbank transactions and U.S. government guaranteed loans might be placed in intermediate categories while most loans would go into the highest risk category. Assets in the lowest risk category might be given a zero percent weighting, meaning that no capital would be required to support such assets. Assets in the highest risk category, on the other hand, would be weighted at 100 percent for purposes of applying the capital gearing ratio. In addition, off-balance sheet items, such as standby letters of credit, would be counted as assets for the purpose of a capital requirement and would be placed in the appropriate category although they would be discounted to some extent, depending on the degree of contingency they represent.

If adopted, a risk-adjusted capital standard will require management to monitor the composition of the bank's asset portfolio, including off-balance sheet assets, in relation to the bank's capital. The capital required for assets falling into one of the specific categories will then be a factor to be weighed against the likely return on the assets, among other considerations.

It is also reasonable to expect that, as systems become more sophisticated for both bank management and bank supervisors, a risk-adjusted capital standard eventually may include factors such as liquidity, interest rate risk, and credit concentrations.

In conclusion, both funding and investment decisions must take into consideration the numerous, and often very complex, legal and regulatory constraints affecting these decisions. But then, bank management is no longer, if it ever was, a simple matter.

CHAPTER TWENTY-SIX

Tools and Techniques to Implement Asset/Liability Management

Dr. Arnold A. Dill

Senior Vice President and Chief Economist
The Citizens & Southern Corporation

Asset and liability management (ALM) is the strategic planning, implementation, and control processes that affect the volume, mix, maturity, rate sensitivity, quality, and liquidity of a bank's assets and liabilities. Since ALM involves the basic raising and employment of funds, it is the financial heart of a bank.

The goal of ALM is to produce a stable, large, and growing flow of net interest income. This goal is accomplished by achieving the optimum combination and level of assets and liabilities and financial risk.

A bank earns rewards by taking risk. Risk-taking capacity is limited by capital, depositors, regulators, and credit rating agencies. Because it is limited, risk capacity must be allocated among its various uses in a way that maximizes expected reward. Types of risk include capital expenditure risk (acquisitions, branching, and the like), service production risk (discount brokerage, trust, and the like), and financial risk (interest rate, credit, and funding). Once the CEO decides how much risk capacity to devote to financial risk, the ALM committee (ALCO) is usually responsible for managing that financial risk (see Figure 1). Once ALCO has been organized, it can decide what staff and computer software support it needs to be effective.

ALCO should measure and manage interest rate risk (mismatches in the interest sensitivity—repricing characteristics—of assets and liabilities), credit risk (default risk on loans or investments), and liquidity or funding risk (mismatches in cash inflows and outflows or in maturities of assets and liabilities).

Based on the bank's opportunities, the economic outlook, and estimated risk-reward relationships, ALCO determines its basic ALM

FIGURE 1 Risk Measurement and Allocation System (management committee)

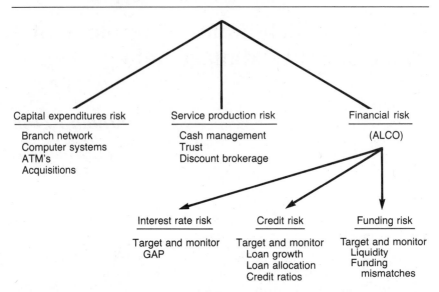

strategy and how to allocate available risk capacity. Should the bank concentrate on building market share of loans and increasing credit risk or on building share of deposits and decreasing funding risk? If a bank is blessed with ample loan demand and excess balance sheet capacity, it will probably decide to concentrate on increasing loans and credit risk while minimizing rate and liquidity risk.

ALCO's rate, credit, and liquidity risk policies must be coordinated. For instance, a decision to make long-term fixed rate loans affects credit, rate, and liquidity risk. If a bank's financial risk capacity is fully committed, it shouldn't take on additional credit risk unless it can manage to decrease either rate or liquidity risk exposure.

ALCO must have tools and techniques for measuring and managing rate, credit, and funding risk, including a managerial accounting system that rewards or punishes those who profitably or unprofitably take rate, credit, and funding risk.

Rate risk exposure can be measured either by the rate sensitivity GAP or by computer model simulations using various rate and balance sheet scenarios. Interest sensitivity refers to the repricing interval of an asset or liability. In the case of a fixed rate instrument, the repricing interval and maturity are identical. In the case of instruments whose rates float or change, the repricing period is less than the maturity.

The GAP is the difference between rate sensitive assets and liabilities. A bank with more rate sensitive assets than liabilities has a positive GAP and generally benefits from an increase in rates. Conversely, a bank with a surplus of rate sensitive liabilities has a negative GAP and generally benefits from a decline in rates. Theoretically, the greater the GAP, the greater the change in net interest margin resulting from changes in interest rates and the greater the rate risk exposure.

The GAP can either be based on assets and liabilities currently on the books (static GAP) or on a forecast of the balance sheet (dynamic GAP). Static GAPS include the cumulative, discrete, and duration GAPS. The *cumulative* GAP is the difference between assets and liabilities repricing *within* a given time interval such as within six months or within one year. The cumulative GAP indicates how a change in interest rates will likely affect net interest margin over an entire interval such as six months or one year. For instance, a bank with a cumulative positive GAP of 10 percent of earning assets at two years would likely experience and increase in net interest margin if interest rate rise over the next two years.

The *discrete* GAP measures the difference between assets and liabilities repricing during a time interval, such as *from* zero *to* 90 days or *from* 91 *to* 180 days. The discrete GAP indicates the timing of changes in the net interest margin due to changes in interest rates. For instance, if a bank has a positive discrete GAP from zero to 90 days but a negative discrete GAP from 91 to 180 days, a rise in rate would tend to positively impact the bank's net interest margin for 90 days before having a negative impact in the following 90 days.

The *duration* GAP is the difference between the interest sensitivity of a bank's entire portfolio of assets and the sensitivity of its entire portfolio of liabilities. Duration is a time statistic—in years or months—that is the weighted average of the present values of cash flows. The shorter the duration, the more rate sensitive the instrument. The duration GAP measures the sensitivity of a bank's *net worth* to changes in interest rates. If the duration of a bank's assets exceeds the duration of its liabilities, the bank's net worth would typically increase if interest rates fell. Through 1986 duration has proved more useful in decisions on how to fund a specific asset or homogeneous portfolio than in measuring the duration of a bank's entire asset or liability portfolio.

The *dynamic* GAP is a forecast of the GAP. Based on repricing schedules and forecasts of asset and liability categories, computer ALM models can forecast the GAP. The accuracy of that forecast will obviously depend on the accuracy of the assumptions programmed into the computer. The course of future interest rates will impact the composition of the forecasted balance sheet and the dynamic GAP. If interest rates decline sharply, for example, some borrowers may refinance high-cost, fixed rate loans. Thus what appeared to be fixed rate assets may not really be if rates decline—hence the importance of rigorous prepayment penalties. The benefit of the dynamic GAP is that it gives ALCO an early action to offset that development.

Simulating various rate scenarios with a computer ALM model can be an effective way to measure interest rate risk exposure. Such models are constantly being improved and are available from numerous vendors. ALCO might design and test three rate scenarios—a most likely, a high-rate, and a low-rate scenario. The impact of these scenarios on net interest margin is tested. The biggest problem is designing scenarios that are internally consistent. For instance, under a high-rate scenario, loan growth may be higher and core deposit growth lower than under a low-rate scenario. If ALCO is uncomfortable with the net interest margin variability indicated by various scenarios, it can take actions to reduce the bank's exposure to rate risk. The model is also helpful in designing the most effective strategy to adjust rate risk exposure.

ALCO should adopt a written policy on interest rate risk that states a tolerance range in which the GAP can vary as a percent of earning assets, that is, the six-month cumulative GAP can vary between a positive six and a negative one percent of earning assets. If the policy is based on model simulations, it would state that changes in interest rates should not be allowed to have more than a certain percentage of impact on the bank's net interest margin, that is, changes in interest rates should not impact the annual net interest margin by more than a plus or minus one-half of a percentage point.

The greater (less) the GAP tolerance range, the greater (less) a bank's expected return from taking interest rate risk. While a bank may choose to minimize interest rate risk exposure (aim at a GAP level that is expected to minimize interest rate risk), it does not follow that all banks should attempt to minimize their interest rate risk.

After the board of directors has approved the bank's rate risk policy and the CEO has determined how much financial risk the bank should take, ALCO should set target levels for the GAP. For instance, if ALCO concludes that interest rates will be rising in the future, it may target a positive one-year cumulative GAP of five percent of earning assets.

A bank needs to measure the GAP over enough time intervals to measure the bank's entire range of assets and liabilities. It does a bank little good to measure the GAP at six months if a bank has significant quantities of assets and liabilities repricing in one, two, or five years.

A bank can adjust its rate risk by changing the maturity of its assets or liabilities, the volume of its rate sensitive assets or liabilities, its pricing policies, or by off-balance-sheet techniques such as futures, options, and swaps. It is important for ALCO to develop *contingency plans to quickly alter rate risk* exposure if desired. Obviously, the more options a bank has to adjust its rate risk, the better.

It must be warned that the rate sensitivity GAP or simulations with an ALM model are only crude measures of interest rate risk that require careful analysis. Generally speaking, the smaller the GAP, the smaller the fluctuation in the net interest margin resulting from changes in interest rates. However, even with a zero GAP at all relevant intervals, a bank may experience fluctuations in its net interest margin due to changes in market spreads between various rates such as prime-Fed funds spread; changes in the composition of assets and liabilities such as substitution of NOW accounts for demand deposits; or different rate adjustments on maturing assets and liabilities such as occur when long-term instruments (like mortgages or long-term debt) mature and are subject to large yield adjustments. Static GAP measures typically ignore reinvestment of cash flows and practical repricing patterns. In the final analysis, all that can be said is that a positively (negatively) GAPped bank's net interest margin will be higher than it otherwise would be if rates rise (fall) by more than implied in the current structure of interest rates.

Regarding liquidity or funding risk, ALCO should also specify a tolerance range for a measure(s) of liquidity. Depending on its appetite for funding risk, ALCO would then set an aggressive or conservative liquidity target. The liquidity measure should be monitored at least monthly to check compliance with target.

Liquidity is the ability to meet maturing liabilities and customer demands for cash. Liquidity exists in assets that mature or can be sold and in liabilities that can be issued at the bank's discretion. While asset liquidity is the most secure, it is useful mainly in emergency situations since a bank would obviously go out of business if it had to continually deplete assets to meet cash demands. While some banks, mainly smaller ones, manage liquidity primarily by adjusting the quantity of Fed funds sold, most large banks manage liquidity by adjusting the quantity of their discretionary liabilities (Fed funds purchased, large CDs, etc.).

Liquidity is difficult to measure because it involves such intangibles as customer loyalty and the ability to borrow under possibly adverse conditions. Nevertheless, it would seem that an adequate liquidity measure would include at least the following ingredients: the volume of readily salable and soon maturing assets, forecasts of liability inflows and net loan growth, and an estimate of unused capacity to borrow or issue discretionary liabilities. These ingredients can be combined in a formula that would yield a net liquid asset total which can then be divided by earning assets to yield a liquidity ratio. For instance, the liquidity ratio might be defined as:

(Assets maturing within 90 days + Readily salable assets
+ Deposit inflows expected in the next 90 days
+ Unused capacity to borrow − Net loan growth expected in the
next 90 days) ÷ Earning assets

Once such a definition has been developed, ALCO would set a tolerance range in which the ratio could vary. Depending on ALCO's appetite for funding risk, it would set an aggressive or conservative liquidity ratio target within that tolerance range. However, no one formula will be adequate for all banks or for all times. Therefore a bank needs to periodically examine its liquidity measures and alter them to reflect changes in the bank and in financial markets.

If the liquidity ratio is off target, it can be managed by adjusting the maturity of assets and liabilities or diversifying and broadening sources of funds. Contingency plans for raising funds during possibly adverse conditions are even more important than contingency plans for quickly adjusting interest rate risk exposure.

Once ALCO has decided how much risk capacity to devote to *credit risk*, that risk can be managed either by ALCO or a credit policy subcommittee. Credit risk management involves targeting the growth and diversification of loans and the setting of tolerance ranges for credit ratios such as the loan-loss allowance to total loans. Credit criteria should also be set for the investment portfolio.

Depending on ALCO's appetite for credit risk, it can set aggressive or conservative loan growth and credit ratio targets that would be monitored monthly or quarterly. Successful implementation of credit policy requires effective communication with lending staff, perhaps in the form of a periodic credit policy publication. The more specific the lending and pricing criteria and the clearer the communication to staff, the better. Loan pricing policies, of course, must be coordinated with ALCO's interest rate risk policy.

If ALCO is to effectively measure and manage rate, credit, and funding risk, it must have an accounting system that segregates earnings resulting from these types of risk. Such a system could be used to reward those who profitably take financial risks and punish those who do not. The current "state of the art" accounting tool that so segregates earnings is the matched marginal funds transfer pricing system.

Under the pure form of this system, each profit center "sells" its liabilities to a Treasury function and "buys" funds from the Treasury to finance its assets. Users of funds, such as loan functions, are match funded. For instance, if a profit center adds a five-year fixed rate loan, the loan is match funded—locked in against—the bank's cost of raising five-year fixed rate funds. The lender is responsible for pricing the loan to cover that cost of funds plus credit risk and ROA. Suppliers of funds receive a rate equal to the bank's cost of acquiring alternative funds of comparable maturity and rate sensitivity. For instance, a retail branch providing fixed rate three-year CDs would earn a rate equal to the bank's alternative cost of raising three-year fixed rate funds.

Under this system, the most efficient users and providers of funds earn the highest spreads from Treasury transfer rates. Profit centers are motivated to add assets or liabilities only if they are profitable at current marginal interest rates which are continuously updated by the Treasury function. Also, ALCO can motivate users and providers of funds by the way it prices various pools of funds. For instance, if ALCO thought that interest rates were peaking, it might wish to set the price of longer term funds lower than the rate currently prevailing in the market. This would encourage the bank's users of funds to employ longer term funds and discourage suppliers from raising long-term liabilities as a cyclical peak in rates. The disadvantages of such a system are its complexity, cost, and potential conflicts over the prices of funds charged and paid by Treasury.

The management of rate and liquidity risk is centralized at the Treasury level in this system. While profit centers are match funded, ALCO may direct Treasury to mismatch rate sensitivities and maturities of assets and liabilities based on analyses of the economic outlook and financial markets. Any profits or losses from taking this rate and liquidity risk would accrue to the Treasury function, which gives ALCO an incentive to take such risks profitably. For instance, if ALCO is convinced that interest rates will fall by more than implied in the current structure of interest rates, it may direct Treasury to short fund the bank's assets (have a negative GAP). If rates decline as expected, the profits would accrue to Treasury when the actual cost of funds falls below that quoted and billed to profit centers.

In conclusion, new and more sophisticated ALM tools will evolve. Good ALM requires keeping up with technology, but it must be emphasized that the tools and techniques described here are only as good as the managers who use them. Sophisticated tools are of little use if their output is poorly understood or communicated. Despite all the sophisticated tools and techniques that have been created in recent years, ALM is still more an art than a science.

PART FIVE

Accounting and Control

CHAPTER TWENTY-SEVEN

General Accounting Systems Necessary to Produce Essential Financial Data

Denis C. Murphy

Partner
Touche Ross & Co.

INTRODUCTION

An accounting system must record, assemble, and produce accurate financial data whether in a community bank, an oil and gas conglomerate, or a real estate development company. Such data translate into the information needed by company management to make sound business decisions at any time. All accounting systems rely on inherent internal controls, which are simply the policies, procedures, and subsystems with which management safeguards assets and develops financial information for decision making.

Although this chapter deals in particular with the general accounting system of a bank, these statements are relevant to any business. This means that, when extending credit or making an investment decision, a banker must consider the accounting system of the prospective customer because it may have a significant impact on the performance of the credit or investment.

The bank's own accounting system provides financial information not only to the board of directors and management personnel, but also to a variety of users: governmental regulatory agencies, investors, depositors, borrowers, and the public. Regulators require information to be organized in a standard format for comparison with that of other banks, investors are concerned with the accounting system's accuracy and the reliability of the information it generates, and bank customers and the public focus on the bank's financial information to evaluate the bank's stability and liquidity. Such financial information, when presented to these users, must conform to generally accepted accounting principles, which prescribe the acceptable ways of handling accounting transactions.

A bank accounting system and the various subsystems which support it are unique in that they are balanced daily with one another. That is, a bank prepares a daily statement of condition (balance sheet) which will verify that its books are in balance each day. The statement is prepared from the general ledger control accounts after all debit and credit activities for the day have been posted and proved. It indicates the financial position of the bank at the close of each business day. This is in marked contrast to other business accounting systems where books usually are closed only on a monthly or other periodic basis.

ACCOUNTING SYSTEMS

A bank's accounting system can be broken down into three major areas:

- Proof and transit system.
- General ledger system.
- Subsidiary systems.

The proof system balances all the bank's financial transactions daily. It also captures critical processing data for both the general ledger system and the subsidiary systems. All balancing in a bank uses this data.

The general ledger system summarizes the bank's subsidiary systems into a format that can be used by management for planning, control, and review. This format is similar to that of a statement of condition and a statement of operations, but includes much more detail.

The subsidiary systems, many unique to the banking industry, are designed to account for the bank's assets and liabilities and to generate data for related income and expenses. These systems range from the simplest manual procedures and records to the most sophisticated electronic data processing and information storage systems.

The following discussion will focus on each accounting system in detail and its role in the rapidly changing banking industry.

Proof and Transit System

The focal point of the bank accounting system is the proof and transit department. Proof and transit refer to two separate functions: the proving of work (proof) and the sending of cash items (transit) for collection.

The objectives of a proof and transit system are:

- To accomplish the necessary activities in the most efficient manner.

- To segregate all incoming checks for proper distribution.
- To forward items (checks) for collection so the funds are available as soon as possible.
- To determine that deposit and loan payment totals balance with the totals shown on deposit tickets or loan payment coupons.
- To collect data for general ledger and subsystem posting.

The proof department receives batches of checks, deposit tickets, loan payments, and the like from other departments or branches of the bank. It also receives checks drawn by customers, outside sources such as clearing houses and correspondent banks, proves the accuracy of batch totals, and re-sorts the items for delivery to other departments for further processing, posting to subsidiary records, and reconciliation of totals to the general ledger.

Through this processing the teller's daily work is proved and summarized for posting to the general ledger and subsidiary systems. The proof department has only temporary custody of these items as everything it receives is delivered to other areas by the end of each day.

With the ever-increasing volume of checks and the need for operational efficiencies, most banks have a central department to perform the proof function. While a majority of banks use an encoding proof machine system, which encodes the dollar amount and other information on each document processed through use of magnetic ink character recognition (MICR) identifiers, the use of computers for proofing is becoming more practical and increasingly important. A computer system can more closely control financial matters such as prompt auditing of cash letters, maximum use of the short-term money market funds, accurate drawing against uncollected funds as soon as they are available, reducing float time, calculating reserve repayments, and providing for more complete analysis of demand deposit accounts.

In summary, the proof and transit department is the heart of a bank's internal operations as well as a strong internal control. As technology advances, more transactions are being summarized and transmitted between banks via telecommunications or magnetic tape. These state-of-the-art technologies expedite the transfer of funds and decrease the volume of paper transactions throughout the banking system. Computer use decreases costs and enhances benefits.

General Ledger

The bank's general ledger is one of the most important systems to senior management and the board of directors. It generates information and reports that enable management to make timely decisions on investment of bank capital.

A bank's existence flows from its ability to invest its assets at a greater return than its cost of funds. The investment margin, that is, the difference between investment income and cost of funds, is the most significant source of bank profit. Equally important is management's ability to control operating costs which eat away at the investment margin. Today the ability to manage the bank's assets and liabilities and the volatile interest rates associated with the portfolios of each one is critical in maintaining this interest margin.

Management of the bank should review the general ledger statements daily to determine whether any unusual or significant transactions or fluctuations in account balances have occurred, and should respond positively.

Specifically, the general ledger systems report income in a two-part format: interest income against interest expense, and other income against operational expense. Information produced by this format enables management to implement profitability in both areas.

In contrast to the condensed statement of condition, the general ledger system accumulates detailed data for numerous account types. Management determines the extent of detail required according to its needs for regulatory reporting, taxes, and internal control.

Large, medium, and some small banks use the cost center or profitability center feature of most computerized general ledger packages. This feature enables management to review each area of a bank separately. For example, senior management may want to analyze the profitability of a particular service. To accomplish this, a unique cost center number would be assigned to the general ledger accounts related to that service. Management can then request a cost center report of only the related account totals. Such a report is an excellent tool for managing a specific area of banking activities.

Again, the general ledger system is the key to financial management of a bank. Many general ledger systems are now integrated with proof and transit and major subsystems to improve both the accuracy and the timely updating of the general ledger.

Subsidiary Systems

Banks, like other companies, have subsystems that account for and control assets and liabilities on the balance sheet. The systems may be manual or computerized. This section deals with the major subsystems in a bank and gives brief coverage of the smaller systems.

Investment Securities and Trading.   The function of investing in marketable securities may be performed by many people in a large bank operating a sophisticated investment department, or by a single officer, usually the president or chief financial officer, in a small bank.

Most banks purchase securities exclusively for investment. The objectives of such investments are two-fold: to maintain liquidity and, simultaneously, to maximize investment income.

Investment securities most commonly found in banks are as follows:

- United States Treasury.
- Agencies of the U.S. government.
- Municipal bonds and obligations of states and political subdivisions.
- Other securities; for example, Federal Reserve Bank stock.

Banks usually use these classifications to group securities according to the logic of the inherent differences in risk, maturity, tax treatment, and so on. The income attributable to each class of investment is recorded and presented separately in the financial statements. (Note: The taxable status of security income has significantly changed under the Tax Reform Act of 1986.)

Depending on the size of the bank, information and computations on its securities may be computerized. If the bank does not maintain this activity on a computer system, it usually uses some type of manual system which specifically accounts for each single security and provides for entries to the related revenue, amortization, and accretion accounts. Service bureaus are readily available at nominal fees for securities accounting. Accordingly, most smaller banks use service bureaus in lieu of manual in-house systems.

Loans. Loans are usually divided into three categories—commercial, real estate, and consumer. In today's automated environment, each loan is set up on a subsidiary system. This subsystem is designed to monitor and process critical information on each loan such as, account number, original amount, current balance, payment due date, interest rate, accrued interest receivable, and collateral and loan documentation. These systems calculate income earned on each loan daily, and summarize the loan portfolio's principal balances and related accrued interest receivable balances.

By processing all loan transactions through the proof system, all data required to apply a customer payment or to record a new loan properly are interfaced with the loan system. This ensures that all transactions are processed and accounted for. The loan system in turn processes the transactions to the appropriate loan account and adjusts the loan balance and accrued interest accordingly.

All loan systems generate summary accounting data for the loan portfolio which is used to generate appropriate general ledger entries and balance the subsidiary systems to the general ledger control accounts. More sophisticated loan systems are integrated with the general ledger which eliminates the need for making manual entries.

Large banks today usually have their own in-house computer subsidiary systems while smaller banks use service bureaus for loan transactions and recording. These subsidiary systems can process loan transactions in seconds, which saves significant personnel costs as well as eliminating potential human error.

Fixed Assets. The components of this category of assets are land, buildings, and equipment used in conducting the bank's business as well as certain real estate that may be held for future expansion. Not included in this category are land and buildings acquired through foreclosures on bank loans. These assets are classified under the category of "other real estate owned."

The accounting systems for fixed assets may be manual or computerized, depending on the size of the bank and the number of assets to be accounted for. The entries to the general ledger, such as recording depreciation expense, purchases, and sales of assets, are usually done manually. The Accounting Department typically balances the fixed asset subsidiary ledger to the general ledger at month's end.

Demand, Savings, and Certificate of Deposit Accounts. *Demand deposits* generally include checking accounts, official checks, matured certificates of deposit, and escrow deposits. Checking accounts are the major component of the demand deposit group and consist of deposits subject to withdrawal on demand by check or electronic transfer. For control purposes, checking accounts are grouped as to deposits of individuals, partnerships, corporations, interest-bearing accounts such as NOW, super NOW, money markets, and all others. These accounts, involving a large volume of transactions, are accounted for by sophisticated data processing systems.

As deregulation continues and innovative services such as lines of credit, automated teller machines, debit cards, and automated clearing house services are offered to customers, control of the demand deposit system becomes more difficult and complex, and the subsystems will become even more valuable.

The demand deposit subsystems accrue interest expense daily for interest-bearing accounts, automatically calculate service charges on each account monthly, produce customer statements, and summarize the necessary accounting information to be posted to the general ledger. The more advanced systems are integrated with the general ledger, eliminating the need for manual entries.

The subsidiary ledger, including interest receivable and interest expense, is balanced to the general ledger daily.

The *savings systems,* which handle a moderate volume of transactions, are usually independent of the demand and certificate of deposit systems. They have similar reporting capabilities and accrue interest monthly, daily, or as bank policies require. Because of recent changes in the banking industry, customers are moving away from savings accounts and toward the interest-bearing demand accounts which are more versatile and offer higher interest rates.

Certificates of deposit are evidenced by negotiable or nonnegotiable instruments with a due date of 30 days or greater at a stated interest rate. The certificates are classified as time certificates until maturity date when interest ceases and the certificates, if not paid, are reclassified as demand deposits. Most certificates of deposit have a definite maturity date, but banks are permitted to issue automatically renewable certificates. The customer is given a set time for renewal or redemption on these certificates. Most banks will disburse the interest earned in the manner the customer desires.

A separate subsidiary system is used by most banks for certificates of deposit as the transaction volume is low and the reporting requirements for management control are different from those of demand deposits. However, the certificates of deposit subsystem accrues interest daily as well as produces the necessary accounting summaries in a manner similar to that for other demand deposits. Similarly, the certificate of deposit subsystem is balanced to the general ledger daily.

Manual Systems.   Like most other industries, banks monitor some of their low-volume asset and liability accounts manually. These are balanced periodically, at least monthly and more often if activity warrants. Examples of these accounts are cash, due from banks, allowance for loan losses, other real estate owned, and miscellaneous asset and liability accounts.

However, banks are getting away from the total manual system and using personal computers to account for assets. It would be very difficult and costly to process some accounts using a computerized subsystem as clearing reconciling items requires human judgment. Therefore these accounts are prime candidates for personal computer use.

INTERNAL ACCOUNTING CONTROLS

In each bank accounting system and its subsystems, numerous policies and procedures ensure that daily transactions are processed accurately. These policies and procedures, commonly referred to as internal accounting controls, are of great importance to any banking operation. The nature of banking operations involves daily processing of a significant volume of customer transactions dealing with the most liquid of assets—cash. Because of the asset's liquidity, the emotional over-tones associated with all monetary matters, and the importance of financial reliability, any number of errors would seriously disturb both management and the other users of the financial information, most particularly the public.

There are numerous accounting controls which are common to any industry such as segregation of duties, timely approval and review procedures, and establishment of monetary limits on transactions by employees. But most important in today's banking environment are the internal controls a bank has over its own computer and processing capabilities.

The more a bank uses and relies on computers, the greater are the risks associated with inadequate controls. Specifically, the risks of business interruption, fraud, unacceptable or inaccurate accounting, and competitive disadvantages prevail heavily in the banking industry. Periodic tests should be made of all computerized applications that directly affect the financial statements. These system tests should include the computer operations which affect all applications, the application controls, and all other key controls in the individual applications. Even in banks that do not have in-house computers but use service bureaus instead, designated personnel should test the systems output from time to time to ensure both the accuracy and the validity of the service bureau's operations.

Controlling the assets and transactions of a bank is the responsibility of management and the board of directors. To develop an effective system, assessing the risk of error is of primary concern to any business. But, when a business operates in the public eye and deals extensively in cash transactions as banks do, any conceivable risk could become reality at any moment.

FINANCIAL STATEMENT REPORTING REQUIREMENTS

As stated before, financial data produced by a bank's accounting system and reported on by management must conform to generally accepted accounting principles. Bank financial statements are prepared on the basis of accrual accounting whereby all revenues and all expenses are recognized when earned or incurred, regardless of the time received or paid. The only exceptions permitted by bank regulators are instances where one of the following is true:

1. The results of accounting on a cash basis would be only slightly different.
2. Accrual accounting is not feasible.

Generally, only the smallest of banks meet these criteria.

Bank financial statements include the following:

1. Statement of condition.
2. Statement of operations.
3. Statement of changes in stockholders' equity.
4. Statement of changes in financial position.
5. Notes to the financial statements.

The specific details of each statement, that is, the format, presentation requirements and information to be contained, are prescribed by the numerous rule-making authorities who regulate the banking industry. Most important is the fact that the majority of the accounting regulations and reporting requirements prescribed by these authorities are similar and conform to generally accepted accounting principles. The most important rule-making bodies are as follows:

1. Office of Comptroller of the Currency (OCC). Under Regulation 11, the comptroller sets the standard for the form and content of financial statements for national banks. From time to time, the comptroller will also issue releases on accounting principles and practices to be followed in specific areas.

2. Federal Deposit Insurance Corporation (FDIC). Regulation 335 prescribes the disclosure items and reporting requirements for an FDIC-insured member bank. The FDIC's manual of examination policies also provides guidance and information on a bank's financial statements. Like the OCC, the FDIC issues banking regulations and interpretations.

3. Board of Governors—Federal Reserve System. Form F–9 of Regulation F applies to all national banks and state member banks which meet certain criteria. This form outlines the format and content of bank financial statements. These rules are substantially like those of the FDIC.

4. Securities and Exchange Commission (SEC). This rule-making authority regulates banking entities in which the vast majority of stock owned is or will be publicly traded through the filing of registration statements. The general requirements to be followed in filings with the commission are contained under Article 9 of Regulation S–X. These requirements closely follow the regulations prescribed by the OCC and FDIC; the regulators have attempted to standardize reporting and disclosure requirements. From time to time, the SEC will issue either staff accounting bulletins or financial reporting releases which deal directly with specific accounting issues.

5. American Institute of Certified Public Accountants (AICPA). In 1983 the AICPA published its own industry guide, *Audits of Banks*, which discusses both the procedures used in bank auditing and the accounting principles to be followed by banks. The guide includes the accounting pronouncements of the Financial Accounting Standards Board (FASB) and its predecessor organization, the Accounting Principles Board (APB), as they relate to the banking industry. Both the AICPA and the FASB continually issue accounting statements and interpretations which affect the banking industry.

CONCLUSION

Today's banking environment is continually changing, not only its competition, regulation, and legal issues, but also its accounting systems and related regulations. It is extremely important for bank management to stay abreast of current accounting issues and changes as well as the technological advances in the industry and their effect on banks' accounting systems and internal controls. Now, more than ever, competition and the public demand that the banking industry bring sophistication, accuracy, and reliable information to its business endeavors.

CHAPTER TWENTY-EIGHT

Profitability Analysis, Cost Systems, and Pricing Policies

John Zimmermann

Executive Vice President and Chief Operating Officer
The Enterprise Bank Network, Inc.

Diane White

Vice President and Divisional Controller for Operations
First Wachovia Corporation

Deregulation has radically altered the product lines, market segments, and geographical constraints of all financial institutions. Currently, bank management is facing unprecedented changes. Competitive pressures on regional and money center banks have prompted the development of many new products offering sophisticated money management techniques. At the same time, technological advances have broadened the horizons of both customers and financial institutions with regard to access to financial services. All of these factors require bank management to know more about the sources of their profitability.

In addition, internal changes caused by rapid expansion have accelerated the need for better decision-making processes. However, frequent internal reorganizations caused by the changing and highly competitive marketplace make the gathering of pertinent and timely information about organizational unit or product line profitability both difficult and costly.

Proper accounting techniques allow bank management to determine profitability by product, department, and location. Although cost accounting is still not as well established in the financial services industry as in manufacturing, its importance and acceptability is growing significantly. Most, if not all, large financial institutions regard it as an essential tool to maximize profits.

Not only does the intangible nature of banking services present a challenge in analyzing costs, but a financial institution's information reporting structure is geared toward the requirements of regulatory agencies rather than costing. The prescribed accounting classifications of various regulators limit the usefulness of conventional bank accounting statement formats as a basis for costing and pricing decisions. However, it is certainly possible for a financial institution to build a comprehensive management accounting system that not only meets external requirements, but also addresses internal reporting, costing, and pricing needs.

The following material covers the nature of a financial institution's costs, cost allocations, organizational profitability, product profitability, customer profitability, pricing policies, and cost accounting software.

NATURE OF COSTS

The noninterest operating costs of financial institutions can be classified into direct production, selling, and overhead.

Direct production costs are costs of production that can be directly attributed to a function or unit of output. Included in these costs are personnel (for example, direct supervision and operations employees), occupancy, and supplies. It should be understood that direct production costs can have both fixed and variable components depending on capacity constraints. When considered over a sufficient range of volume, direct production costs are usually variable. For example, a department may have one supervisor and 10 employees. If volume increases sufficiently to require 20 employees, it may be necessary to add a second supervisor and acquire additional space.

Given that all costs do vary with sufficient changes in volume, it is usually necessary to specify a time frame, as well as a volume range, to identify a cost as fixed or variable. Over the short term, many production costs would be classified as fixed because volume would not vary sufficiently within that time frame to trigger a change in the amount of the cost.

Selling costs include costs of account representatives, product advertising, travel, transportation and entertainment, and the like. Because most of these costs are classified as account administration or customer service expenses, they are often omitted from product cost analysis.

Overhead costs are those costs not directly assignable to a given activity or function. Overhead costs can be classified as direct support, indirect support or general and administrative.

Direct support overhead includes all production management above the direct supervisory position, with any costs incurred in service support departments or other expenses directly associated with supporting a production area (for example, department managers, their secretaries, and other support personnel).

Indirect support overhead costs are further removed from the actual production, but are traceable to the production unit. Examples are costs of the personnel department that can be related to headcount, costs of building, security to occupied facilities, and the costs of the purchasing department that trace to purchase orders submitted. In most cases a good deal of judgment must be used to associate these costs with the production unit.

General and administrative overhead costs are mostly bankwide in nature and cannot be distributed directly. These costs are generally related to the total bank and its products (for example, institutional advertising, executive salaries, and regulatory reporting costs). These costs are usually allocated pro rata using total income, total other expenses, or some other acceptable measure of relative size.

FIXED AND VARIABLE CLASSIFICATION

Costs can be classified by volume sensitivity into variable and fixed costs. *Variable costs* occur immediately with and in direct proportion to activity. There are degrees of variability in all costs; however, the factor that determines variable costs is the range of volume during the time frame being considered. A good example of variable cost is computer paper, which is only used if activity is occurring. The total cost of computer paper used will vary directly with the extent of the activity.

Fixed costs do not change at the same time as, nor in direct proportion to, volume changes. For example, the number of employees in the purchasing department does not increase in direct proportion to a change in the volume of units produced. Given a sufficiently large change in the scope of production activity, the purchasing department may experience a similar need to increase its activity; however, the time lag is usually such that purchasing costs could not be said to vary concurrently with production volume.

INTEREST COSTS

Interest costs are not covered in the previous definitions; however, its allocation is of major importance. A bank's interest expense can be equated to a manufacturing company's cost of raw materials, except a bank has more difficulty in identifying the specific uses of its major raw material to a specific unit of output. The source of funds for a particular loan, and consequently the interest cost for that loan, is usually difficult to identify.

There is no one correct method for allocating funds. Concepts often used are a single pool rate, a marginal rate, and multiple pool rates. Still it is important that interest costs be allocated in a well thought-out and consistent manner. The method selected will depend on the objectives of bank management. The importance of management's understanding of the effect of the allocation decision cannot be over emphasized. Organization, product, and customer profitability will differ greatly if a single pool of funds rate is used rather than, for example, a marginal rate of funds. The usual intention is to be equitable in transferring the cost of funds from one organizational unit to another while compensating the provider to cover the costs of gathering the funds, plus what could be called a "return on internal equity."

COST ALLOCATION

Cost allocation can be defined as the process of transferring cost data from one responsibility center to another, based on benefits received. To simplify the cost allocation process and make it more meaningful, responsibility centers should be assigned on the basis of functional areas. For example, the assignment of responsibility centers in the bookkeeping department might be as follows:

Department
    Bookkeeping
Responsibility centers
    Bookkeeping administration
    Personal account processing
    Company account processing
    Return item processing
    Customer service

After the responsibility centers have been established, costs can be assigned to each center on a specific basis.

The next step is the determination of the transfer basis that reflects the best measure of service provided from one center to other centers. The effort applied to this determination depends on the accuracy desired and the cost of developing and maintaining the data.

The following procedures may be used to allocate costs to responsibility centers receiving the benefits of work performed by another center.

Standard costs are predetermined target costs requiring development of cost standards of each transfer unit. This concept of standard costs is used to indicate what costs "should be." This method enables actual costs incurred to be compared to standard costs, with emphasis placed on understanding the variance.

Average item costs are used where activity data can be collected. The dollars allocated are a function of the recipient responsibility center's percentage of total activities. This method is an alternate to the use of standards.

Fixed dollar costs are used where it is unlikely that the degree of effort will change from period to period, and is often based on a budgeted amount.

Fixed percentage costs are used where statistical data cannot be collected economically by the service providing responsibility center, or where sampling has been used to approximate the level of service. It may be appropriate to simply use percentages developed by management in lieu of engineered allocations.

Transfer prices are used when there is a desire for a responsibility center to be evaluated on its financial performance. The transfer price may be market equivalent, cost defined, or even negotiated between the service rendering and receiving units. The use of standards or of average item costs in determining the transfer price is sometimes helpful in this procedure.

Once a basis for allocating costs has been established, it is necessary to decide how to handle the allocations. Three common methods used are the direct, step, and reciprocal methods.

Under the *direct method,* all allocations are made directly to the responsibility centers that are the ultimate users. Responsibility centers that do not provide a service to the ultimate user are treated as overhead and may be allocated on the basis of direct labor hours, salary dollars or total direct costs.

The *step method* allows the recognition of services rendered from one service department to another. This recognition is accomplished through levels of sequences of allocations in which a responsibility center or group of responsibility centers are allocated to the other centers. A weakness of this method is that after a cost center is allocated, or closed, no subsequent allocations can be made to that center. The inaccuracies caused by this limitation can be minimized if those responsibility centers affecting the greatest number of other centers or those allocating the largest dollars are placed early in the sequence.

The *reciprocal method* is a complex modification of the step method in that service departments can be closed into each other. This can be done using a series of simultaneous equations, iterative allocation with a specified residual factor, matrix algebra, or trial and error.

ORGANIZATIONAL, PRODUCT, AND CUSTOMER PROFITABILITY

The size of many banking institutions requires extensive delegation of authority and responsibility, creating a commitment to internal management accounting systems and organizational profitability reporting. The three distinct types of bank profitability presentations are organizational, customer, and product. Although these presentations differ in output, they are actually only different perspectives or arrangements of the same underlying accounting and operating data. In fact, for a cost system to have credibility, each of the three systems must stay in balance.

Organizational Profitability

Management accounting is basically the coordination and distribution of accounting information into individual organizational units. The objective of the management accounting system is not only to provide management with accurate and timely information but also to provide control at the supervisory level. The role played by the individual organizational units in management accounting is vital because the organizational unit is the most effective point at which costs can be controlled. Allocations of cost from one unit to another can enhance cost control in those cases where the recipient unit can either accept the allocation and services or reject them.

Before designing a system of organizational profitability, management must thoroughly appraise the organizational structure. To be effective, the structure of the organization should reflect a hierarchy of reporting with well-defined spheres of responsibility and authority. The profitability system must then operate in conformity with the organizational structure.

The reporting system must be designed so that information pyramids upward to each consecutive managerial level. An example of this structure is illustrated below:

President
Summary of division reports
Division Head
Summary of department reports
Department Head
Summary of detailed responsibility center reports
Responsibility unit
Detailed reports

The direct accumulation of income and expense by responsibility center and their pyramiding in the organization is the simplest type of profitability system. Expanding this concept into a refined measure of organizational profitability requires development of a sophisticated intrabank cost allocation system.

The initial phase of determining organizational profitability is to examine the responsibility centers and to classify them as a direct profit center, a direct production center, or an overhead center. Generally, the classification is made according to the nature of costs to be assigned. Direct sales expense, for example, should be accumulated in units designated as direct profit centers; direct production expense should be accumulated in direct production centers; and costs not directly related to production processing, marketing, or sales should be accumulated in overhead centers. However, some units may fit into more than one of the three categories. A branch is an example since it has characteristics of both a direct profit center and a direct production center. In these cases responsibility classification should be consistent with the primary purpose of the center.

Direct profit centers are the sales areas of the organization which are primarily responsible for generating income. Direct sales expense, as well as income, should be assigned to these centers. Direct profit centers are assigned balance sheet items such as deposits, loans, float, and required reserves in order to properly reflect the assets and liabilities controlled by the center's manager. Direct profit centers are given credit for funds provided or charged for funds used based on a predetermined transfer rate. In addition, credit loss provisions are charged to these centers. In a refined cost allocation system, direct profit centers are also charged with an allocation of production and overhead expense.

Direct production centers are the units used to accumulate expenses directly associated with a production process. A production center is generally responsible for providing processing steps for a limited number of products, such as central proof encoding. Production centers are also identifiable with one or more statistics related to each product, for example, the number of deposited items on corporate demand deposits. An effective cost system must provide the means for collecting appropriate statistics. The product/statistic relationship facilitates allocation of the costs of production centers to direct profit centers.

Overhead centers are areas that are charged with costs that cannot be directly associated with either the production or marketing of a product. Generally, allocation of these costs is less specific and more arbitrary than the allocation of direct production costs. There are three types of overhead centers which are distinguished by their degree of direct relationship to a product. These centers can be defined as direct support, indirect support, and general and administrative.

Direct and indirect support centers are areas that provide centralized operations for the total organization. Organizational areas such as a printing department, a word processing center, or a division manager's cost center are good examples of direct support. Because these centers support a limited and definable segment of the business, cost allocations can usually be performed with high precision. Organizational units such as personnel and building services are indirect support centers and their cost should be distributed to other areas on a systematic basis, for example, by allocating costs based on the number of employees and square footage, respectively.

General and administrative centers are used to collect the cost of staff services provided to the overall organization, such as the controller and executive functions. Costs assigned to these centers are not directly associated with any particular product nor are they readily allocable. These costs must be absorbed at the total organization level or may be allocated to direct profit centers on an arbitrary basis.

Once the various types of responsibility units are identified and appropriate allocations are established for the production and overhead centers, organizational profit contribution can be measured. There are several levels of profit contribution that can be defined for a responsibility unit.

Exhibit 1 illustrates a profit center report produced by the system described. The four levels measuring profit contribution are described below:

Profit Level I Contribution represents revenue after direct operating expenses. This is the most basic reporting of profit contribution, and provides a comparison of direct income and expense recorded in that unit prior to any allocation of production and overhead. Direct revenues and expenses are usually those for which the unit manager has a direct decision-making responsibility.

Profit Level II Contribution represents Level I contribution after allocation of direct production expenses. This level includes all the direct processing costs of the products being managed in the profit center.

Profit Level III Contribution represents Level II contribution after direct and indirect support expenses. This level additionally reflects the costs of internal bank services.

Profit Level IV Contribution represents Level III contribution after general and administrative overhead. This level of profitability reflects full absorption of all the bank's costs. To maintain credibility in the system, the sum of Level IV profitability for all responsibility centers must equal the total bank pretax income.

Customer Profitability

Customer profitability is a natural extension of the concepts employed to derive organizational profitability and addresses the analysis of individual customer relationships as opposed to organizational areas. Since the cost to review the profitability of every customer relationship is unjustifiable, the value of this system is best realized in the review

EXHIBIT 1   Profit Contribution for National Accounts Profit Center

		Actual	Budget Variance	Prior Period Variance
Revenue from funds.............		$8,482	$371 −	$814
Charge for net funds used		(325)	31 −	79 −
Provision for credit losses.........		(300)	0	42
Net margin...................		7,857	340 −	851
Other income.................		362	35	17
Direct sales expense				
Staff.........................	$ 525			
Occupancy...................	64			
Equipment	23			
Advertising	89			
Other.......................	278	(979)	133 −	72 −
Profit Level I...............		7,240	172 −	940
Direct production expense				
Data processing	343			
Bookkeeping	190			
Proof and transit..............	901			
Reconcilement................	83			
Loan processing	31			
Other production centers........	1,189	(2,737)	22 −	15
Profit Level II...............		4,503	105 −	925
Direct and indirect support expense				
Personnel....................	33			
Building services..............	5			
Other service center...........	197	(235)	11 −	7
Profit Level III		4,268	139 −	918
General and administrative overhead expense				
Executive	121			
Controller	95			
Other overhead centers........	186	(402)	24	1
Profit Level IV		$3,866	$163 −	$917

Note: − indicates down from budget or prior period.

and evaluation of large corporate and correspondent bank customers. The profitability of individual consumers and small companies is best reflected through a product profitability system.

Identifying the total relationship of a given customer can be a difficult task. Some organizations include such items as trust fees, interest-bearing deposits, international banking services, data processing services, and money market transactions in their analyses, while other organizations may feel that some or all of these items should be treated individually.

For each customer relationship under review, a source and use of funds statement (see *Exhibit 2*) should be produced. The information contained in this exhibit is normally available from various accounting

---

EXHIBIT 2 ABC Corporation—Source and Use Statement

Uses	
Demand loans	$127,212
Term loans—net of unearned	2,966
Earning assets	130,178
Float...	143,146
Reserves.....................................	20,927
Nonearning assets...........................	164,073
Total funds used...........................	294,251
Sources	
Demand deposits..............................	298,612
Noninterest bearing CDs	15,380
Total fund sources	313,992
Net funds used (provided)	$(19,741)

---

systems, with the possible exception of float which may require a sampling of the activities in the customer's account.

The summation of direct income and expense for the corporate customer relationship corresponds to the accumulation of income and expense in an organizational profit center. Direct production costs are allocated to the customer center in the same manner used to transfer costs to the direct profit center. There should also be a charge for funds used or a credit for funds provided in accordance with the bank's transfer policy.

Since an officer normally services many accounts, the assignment of selling expense to individual customers can become complex, but can be accomplished with percentage allocations.

Overhead cost can be allocated; however, the marginal profitability (defined as Profit Level II contribution) of the customer relationship often is sufficient to make appropriate management decisions.

As with organizational profit centers, a profit goal should be established for the customer relationship which is consistent with the profit goal of the organization. In our example, if the organization's goal is a 1-percent return on assets after income tax, the customer's marginal profit goal must exceed a 2-percent return on total funds used so that the pricing structure will cover overhead and carrying costs of unallocated nonearning assets on a pretax basis.

Exhibit 3 illustrates a profit contribution statement for a corporate customer which meets this criteria. After allowing 30 percent of direct and production costs to cover overhead and carrying cost of nonearning assets, the return on total funds used exceeds the 2-percent goal.

EXHIBIT 3   ABC Corporation—Profit Contribution Statement

Interest on demand loans		$10,042	
Interest on term loans		360	
Fees on loans		378	
Revenue from funds			$10,780
Net funds credit (cost)			(1,184)
Provision for credit losses			(752)
Net margin			8,844
Service charges			1,074
Selling costs			(1,165)
Checking account services		(379)	
Teleconcentration		(190)	
Lockbox		(651)	
Accounts reconcilement		(81)	
Loan processing		(61)	
Direct production costs			(1,362)
Profit Level II contribution			7,391
Profit Level II return on assets	2.51%		
Overhead (30% of selling and direct production costs)			(706)
Profit Level IV contribution			$ 6,685
Profit Level IV return on assets	2.27%		

Product Profitability

Product profitability is a method of accumulating financial data relating to the bank's products and structuring this data in a format consistent with the management decision process. This information enables management to assess each product according to overall profitability goals. The knowledge that a particular product is unprofitable does not necessarily allow a bank to discontinue the product; however, it does provide a basis for an informed decision as to the degree to which a product is offered. The knowledge of which products are more profitable enables the bank to optimize its product mix.

The bank's general ledger is already classified by product, with the exception of operating and interest expenses, and in presenting product profitability analyses these expenses must be assigned to specific products. As with organizational profitability, the operating expenses must first be accumulated in responsibility centers, and then these centers must be classified as direct profit, direct production, and overhead centers.

The costs of direct and indirect overhead support centers should be allocated to responsibility centers for which internal service is provided, using the same methods and techniques as applied in developing organizational profitability. After this is accomplished, all operating costs will be in either a direct profit or a production center, with the exception of general and administrative. Each profit and production center can then be examined to determine the proper assignment of costs to specific products. In some profit and production centers, costs can be easily identified with a very limited number of products (for example, a credit card operation). In contrast, a full-service branch approximates a total bank with costs being assigned to many products.

Costs of general and administrative centers are accumulated and assigned on an arbitrary basis across all product lines. After all components have been classified in each center, they can be aggregated into fixed and variable operating costs by product. In addition, interest expense must also be assigned by product.

Exhibits 4 through 6 provide examples of profitability analyses of the various products of a bank. Exhibits 7 and 8 provide a more detailed example of the elements which must be considered in determining the profitability of a particular product. For illustrated purposes these examples use the "pool of funds" approach.

PRICING POLICIES

Until recently, price adjustments have not been a significant alternative for improving a bank's profitability. The great majority of revenue has been provided from loans and investments, and the price on these products is largely uncontrollable. Rates are determined by national money markets, or are limited by competition or local usury law. The only true pricing flexibility allowed by the marketplace generally has been a function of credit risk. Historically, banks have directed their profit improvement efforts at expanding the deposit base, controlling costs and reducing credit losses. Pricing considerations have normally dealt with temporary price reduction promotions to improve market share.

In recent years bank pricing policy has become a critical issue because of rising competition. This growing competition for funds has required development of fee income alternatives, and a wide variety of innovative services has been introduced to attract corporate and consumer deposits. In these areas a formal pricing policy which is based on sound cost accounting knowledge is essential.

As in other industries, the price of bank services is a function of cost, sales volume, and required profit margin. As discussed throughout this chapter, costs must be classified as production, selling, overhead, interest and credit loss. After performing the basic cost identification, the next step is to segregate costs into fixed and variable components. The need for this step is obvious. Pricing policy should

EXHIBIT 4 Product Profitability Analysis—Funds-Providing Functions—Year Ending December 31,19—

	Gross Balance	Deductions	Invest-able Balance	Interest Expense	Variable Handling Expense	Income	Credit for funds Provided	Marginal Profit-ability	Fixed Expenses	Net Contri-bution
Demand deposits										
Commercial	$ 32,863	$ 9,817*	$ 23,046	$ —	$ 521	$ 71	$ 1,382	$ 932	$ 299	$ 633
Personal	29,516	7,201	22,315	—	626	165	1,338	877	306	571
Special	5,168	851	4,317	—	278	209	259	190	124	66
Public	8,246	9,167	(921)	—	64	507	(55)	388	25	363
Trust	1,600	1,779	(179)	—	—	108	(10)	96	—	96
Total demand deposits	77,393	28,815	48,578	—	1,489	1,060	2,914	2,485	754	1,731
Time deposits										
Certificates of deposit										
Consumer	12,318	579	11,739	851	16	—	704	(163)	18	(181)
Corporate trust	89,876	92,571	(2,695)	5,198	4	5,547	(161)	184	1	183
Money market	17,267	845	16,422	1,069	19	—	985	(103)	17	(120)
Long term	40,927	1,228	39,699	2,974	50	—	2,381	(643)	43	(686)
Public funds	11,328	11,621	(293)	567	16	687	(17)	87	13	74
Total certificates of deposit	171,716	106,844	64,372	10,659	105	6,234	3,892	(638)	92	(730)
Regular savings	65,067	1,789	63,278	2,851	269	—	3,796	676	183	493
First choice	31,539	1,535	30,004	1,609	72	—	1,800	119	46	73
Christmas Club	1,273	55	1,218	45	27	—	73	1	12	(11)
Trust (Interest bearing)	900	939	(39)	55	2	60	(2)	1	—	1
Trust (Noninterest bearing)	1,500	1,571	(71)	—	2	101	(4)	95	—	95
Total other time deposits	100,279	5,889	94,390	4,560	372	161	5,663	892	241	651
Total time deposits	271,995	112,733	159,262	15,219	477	6,395	9,555	254	333	(79)
Equity capital and unassigned	19,567	—	19,567	622	938	1,406	1,167	1,013	2,896	(1,663)
Total funds providing functions	$368,955	$141,548	$227,407	$15,841	$2,904	$8,861	$13,636	$3,752	$3,983	$ (231)

*See Exhibit 7 for details.

EXHIBIT 5 Product Profitability Analysis—Funds-Using Functions—Year Ending December 31, 19—

	Gross Balance	Deductions	Invested Balance	Percent of Total Gross Balances	Interest Income	Other Income	Cost of Funds Used	Variable Handling Cost	Risk Cost	Marginal Profitability	Fixed Cost	Net Contribution
Commercial loans												
Business, commercial and industrial	$ 45,708	$ 9,943	$ 35,765	18.92%	$ 4,004	$ 22	$ 2,146	$ 3	$ 421	$1,334	$ 248	$1,086
Individual	11,276	1,185	10,091	4.67	971	—	605	4	36	272	162	110
Agricultural	876	88	788	0.36	78	—	47	14	—	28	5	23
Financial institutions	1,736	347	1,389	0.72	135	—	83	5	—	48	6	42
Tax exempt	6,496	—	6,496	2.69	365	—	389	209	—	(38)	24	(62)
Other	2,157	216	1,941	0.89	170	—	116	288	—	49	7	42
Total commercial loan	68,249	11,779	56,470	28.25	5,723	22	3,386		457	1,693	452	1,241
Direct lease financing	5,808	228	5,580	2.40	706	35	335		141	(23)	101	(124)
Installment loans												
Direct												
Automobile	4,017	57	3,960	1.66	453	8	237	98	35	91	112	(21)
Personal	8,275	285	7,990	3.43	972	16	479	224	178	107	174	(67)
Home improvement	712	6	706	0.29	82	9	42	21	4	24	40	(16)
Other	2,720	57	2,663	1.13	276	5	159	40	37	45	37	8
Total direct	15,724	405	15,319	6.51	1,783	38	917	383	254	267	363	(96)
Indirect												
Automobile	15,115	628	14,487	6.26	1,565	27	869	209	289	225	98	127
Home improvement	2,787	70	2,717	1.15	257	20	163	40	20	54	16	38
Other	851	7	844	0.35	100	2	50	36	5	11	12	(1)
Mobile home	4,926	67	4,859	2.04	395	7	291	16	4	91	12	79
Total indirect	23,679	772	22,907	9.80	2,317	56	1,373	301	318	381	138	243
Total installment loans	39,403	1,177	38,226	16.31	4,100	94	2,290	684	572	648	501	147

Floor plan												
Direct	6,225	772	5,453	2.58	549	20	327	26	—	216	35	181
Lease	2,078	208	1,870	0.86	182	—	112	5	—	65	10	55
Total floor plan	8,303	980	7,323	3.44	731	20	439	31	—	281	45	236
Mortgage loans												
Commercial	20,536	—	20,536	8.50	1,594	10	1,232	20	—	352	41	311
Residential	38,389	—	38,389	15.89	2,813	24	2,303	76	—	458	86	372
Agricultural	1,138	—	1,138	0.47	94	—	68	2	—	24	3	21
Tax exempt	6,288	—	6,288	2.61	352	—	377	4	—	(29)	7	(36)
Other	535	—	535	0.22	45	—	32	1	—	12	2	10
Total mortgage loans	66,886	—	66,886	27.69	4,898	34	4,012	103	—	817	139	678
Investments												
Taxable	40,728	—	40,728	16.86	2,764	—	2,443	3	—	318	5	313
Nontaxable	9,657	—	9,657	4.00	398	—	579	1	—	(182)	2	(184)
Trading	2,537	—	2,537	1.05	867	—	152	17	—	698	30	668
Total investments	52,922	—	52,922	21.91	4,029	—	3,174	21	—	834	37	797
Total fund using functions	$241,571	$14,164	$227,407	100.00%	$20,187	$205	$13,636	$1,336	$1,170	$4,250	$1,275	$2,975

EXHIBIT 6 Product Profitability Analysis—Nonfund Functions—Year Ending December 31, 19—

	Fee Income	Credit (charge) for Funds Provided or Used	Variable Handling Cost	Marginal Profitability	Fixed Cost	Net Contribution
Trust services						
Estates	$244	—	$ 75	$169	$128	$ 41
Personal	377	—	142	235	164	71
Employee benefits	44	—	52	(8)	74	(82)
Total trust services	665	—	269	396	366	30
Municipal and corporate services	84	—	99	(15)	73	(88)
Money market—customer	11	—	17	(6)	21	(27)
EDP services	183	—	80	103	78	25
Credit card—merchant	24	—	8	16	6	10
Safe deposit	85	—	41	44	33	11
Utility payment	21	—	44	(23)	17	(40)
Special customer service	120	—	149	(29)	67	(96)
One account	20	—	104	(84)	20	(104)
Total nonfund functions	$548	—	$542	$ 6	$315	($309)

EXHIBIT 7 Product Profitability Analysis—Commercial Demand Deposits—
Year Ending December 31, 19—

	Amount	Percent of Gross Balance
Balances:		
General ledger	$32,863	100.00%
Deductions:		
Float/pledge	5,429	16.52
Reserves	3,063	9.32
Overdrafts/cash items	1,249	3.80
Due from banks	76	0.23
Total deductions	9,817	29.87%
Investable	23,046	70.13%
Net credit for funds provided at 6%:		
Credit for funds provided	1,971	6.00%
Value of funds used	(589)	(1.79)
Net credit for funds provided	1,382	4.21%
Variable handling costs:		
Interest	0	0.00
Processing	(521)	1.59)
Total variable costs	(521)	(1.59)
Other income:		
Service charges and fees	71	0.22
Marginal profitability	932	2.84
Fixed costs	(299)	(0.91)
Net contribution	$ 633	1.93%

maximize revenue increases. Simply illustrated, basic cost identification may show a product to be currently generating inadequate profits. In this case there are two available pricing decisions—raise prices and risk lower sales volume, or lower prices in anticipation of stimulating sales to the point of increasing total revenues. Even with an accurate prediction of customer reaction to new prices, the decision can be made only with knowledge of what volume changes will do to overall expense levels.

SOFTWARE FOR BANK COST ACCOUNTING

One of the most encouraging developments in bank cost accounting during the last decade has been the availability of user-oriented software tailored to the needs of financial institutions. The power of automated computing for cost accounting is now a viable option for all banks, regardless of size, due to the expanding library of application programs written for personal as well as for mainframe computers.

Generic spreadsheet software is being used by countless bank cost analysts because of its flexibility and ease of use. These programs are

EXHIBIT 8 Product Profitability Analysis—Commercial Loans—Year Ending December 31, 19—

	Amount	Percent of Gross Balance
Balances:		
General ledger.	$45,708	100.00%
Deductions:		
Compensating balances	9,258	20.25
Reserve for loan losses	685	1.50
Total deductions	9,943	21.75
Invested	35,765	78.25
Interest and other income		
Interest	4,004	8.76
Other	22	0.05
Total interest and other income	4,026	8.81
Net charges for funds used at 6%		
Charge for funds used	2,742	6.00
Value of funds provided	(596)	(1.31)
Net charge for funds used	2,146	4.69
Variable handling costs	125	0.28
Risk costs	421	0.92
Marginal profitability	1,334	2.92
Fixed costs	248	0.54
Net contribution	$ 1,086	2.38%

especially useful for providing different scenarios and various analytical formats. Spreadsheet programs can be used for cost reporting systems; however, the more extensive the desired information, the less useful a generic spreadsheet will be.

For more sophisticated cost analysis and reporting needs, personal computer software of a more specialized nature is needed. PC-based cost accounting software is attractive for several reasons. It offers more flexibility of use than its mainframe counterpart, with essentially the same logic capabilities. It eliminates the traditional lag time required to obtain information and thereby increases productivity. It generally provides adequate and uniform reporting formats without additional user programming. Many of these programs can accept data downloaded from mainframe files, and ongoing vendor support is typically available.

Despite the growing availability of PC-based software the majority of large banks performing extensive cost accounting analysis rely on mainframe cost allocation software. The cost system is usually a module of the institution's general ledger. This software is generally run once a month as a part of the normal reporting cycle, and is usually not available for online, interactive use between month endings.

CONCLUSION

In conclusion, there has never been a time of greater need for financial management information in the financial services industry. However, to be useful, the information must be clearly understood by the management team. A well-conceived, well-implemented, and well-understood management information system will give a financial institution a competitive edge in a very competitive marketplace.

Evaluation of Financial Performance

Dr. Ronald L. Olson

Chairman of the Board
Olson Research Associates, Inc.

Should I buy stock in J. P. Morgan & Co. of New York? Should I sell Federal Funds to Old Kent Bank and Trust Company of Grand Rapids, Michigan? Should I place $250,000 on deposit with Penn Square National Bank of Oklahoma City? Do I manage a good bank? Should I approve next year's budget which has been proposed by my staff?

Questions such as these require an evaluation of bank financial performance. Answers to the questions are easier when information on bank size, levels of risk, and rates of return is developed. These perspectives are provided by financial data, relationship computations, and judgment benchmarks. These three criteria are presented and explained in this chapter.

WHO IS INTERESTED AND WHY?

The objectives of the individual who needs an evaluation of financial performance will determine what data to collect and what analyses to perform. Hundreds of ratios and growth rates can be computed from bank financial data, but collecting the data and performing the calculations must have a specific end-purpose to justify the time and expense. Five different groups can benefit from the evaluation of financial performance: bank management, investors, customers, regulators, and students.

Bank Management. Financial benchmarks of performance (for example, return on assets or return on equity) determine bonuses and other compensation. Comparisons of proposed budget amounts with the trend projections of prior periods help managers understand the relevancy of budget requests. Evaluation of financial performance can produce specific targets for rates of return and control points for risks (for example, liquidity and interest rate exposure).

Bank managers also evaluate banks other than their own. A review of peer group averages helps to assess internal performance. Evaluation of model banks or evaluation of specific competitors can help a manager decide how and whether to react to events in the marketplace. Minimizing the risk of possible loss associated with dealing in the funds market requires a knowledge of the character and quality of other banks.

Investors.   Evaluation of a bank's financial performance can help to determine whether a specific security in a specific banking company is likely to meet the investment objective. High dividend payout ratios will provide current investment income. Good growth and high equity retention should provide good investment appreciation. A low-risk philosophy of bank management should provide safety of debt principal. Since many investments in securities take place through the impersonal money and capital markets, evaluation of financial performance is a primary technique for understanding and judging performance.

Customers.   The business of banking is money—money placed on deposit for safekeeping or transfer, and money borrowed with the promise to pay rent (interest) and to return the principal at a future time. Evaluation of financial performance has become an important activity for both deposit and loan customers.

Depositors must believe that funds are deposited in a safe place. Although deposit insurance has been designed to assure customers that the risk of loss is small, some depositors may keep amounts in excess of insurance limits. Depositors need to evaluate a bank's liquidity to determine if transfers and withdrawals of deposited funds can be accomplished on a timely basis. Banks pay for deposits as well as interest and services, and these prices are negotiable. An evaluation of a bank's financial performance by a customer can provide information to use in the negotiation process.

Borrowers or loan customers can also make use of financial evaluation for price negotiations (that is, rate, collateral, and term). In addition, loan customers are very much concerned about credit availability. Will the bank be a survivor? Will credit lines be open for withdrawal? Will letters of credit be honored?

Regulators.   Federal and state banking regulators are charged with the responsibilities of assuring the safety and soundness of the banking industry, protecting the bank customers (up to a point), and seeing that bankers comply with the law. Evaluation of financial performance provides information that helps bank examiners and regulators carry out their responsibilities.

During the 1970s, federal regulators implemented the CAMEL ratings to help with their examination process. The acronym is derived from the first letters of capital adequacy, asset quality, management, earnings, and liquidity. The rating is expressed as a single number from one to five. Although professional judgment is the key to the successful development and interpretation of the CAMEL ratings, four of the five factors are based on the evaluation of financial performance. Financial data and relationships are the primary factors for scoring capital, asset quality, earnings, and liquidity.

The Federal Financial Institutions Examinations Council has designed and produces the Uniform Bank Performance Report. This report provides current financial information, historical performance information, and peer group data for every insured reporting bank. The analyst's capacity for inexpensive and early evaluation of financial performance has been greatly enhanced by this report.

Students. Banking is studied in university classes, banking school classes, internal training programs, and other places where understanding banking is required. Banking research is conducted by academics, practicing bankers, consultants, and regulators among others. Both the learning process and the research process are heavily dependent on financial data collection, analysis, and evaluation. Organized financial data can help to explain past events and current conditions. Case studies bring the real world into the classroom. Experimentation with simulation provides insight for future possibilities and answers to "what if" questions.

SOURCES OF INFORMATION

Evaluation of financial performance is totally dependent on the availability of financial data. The usefulness of the evaluation process and its result are determined by the timeliness, quality, and quantity of the underlying data. Fortunately, within the banking industry, financial data is reasonably available. The analyst must decide whether raw data is desired or whether analytical results prepared by someone else would provide the most efficient first step in the evaluation process.

Federal Banking Regulators.   One source of data is information gathered by the federal banking regulators. The Federal Deposit Insurance Corporation collects a call report from each insured domestic bank as of the last day of each calendar quarter. (Approximately 96 percent of all commercial banks carry FDIC deposit insurance.) The data from the call reports are computerized and "Fed tapes" are available approximately six months after each quarter-end. If the objective is to examine only one or a few banks over a short period of time, an analyst can request paper copies of actual call reports directly from the FDIC at a minimal cost. If the analysis is to include many banks, many time periods, or the examination of industrywide facts and trends, the analyst will probably need Fed tapes and computers to handle the masses of data.

The FDIC call reports provide data on individual banks. Bank holding companies that may own one or more commercial banks are required to report financial data to the Federal Reserve Board. If an analyst is studying investment opportunities, operating efficiencies, or the concentration of financial resources, bank holding company data will provide the most relevant information.

The Securities Exchange Commission. Information collected by the SEC is a second major source of data. The SEC is the federal regulator interested in the investing public. To this end, the SEC collects data from all corporations, including banks and bank holding companies, which have publicly traded securities.

When a banking corporation plans to issue securities to the public, it must register with the SEC. Subsequently, each corporation must file annual (10K) and quarterly (10Q) reports with the SEC. Copies of these reports are made available to the public. The initial registration and the subsequent reports include reasonably detailed financial statements and related supporting schedules which provide excellent raw data for analysis. Although the SEC reporting requirements are well defined, careful attention must be given to an individual bank's descriptive words, cross references, and footnotes. Most bank data reported to the SEC is from bank holding companies.

Internal Bank Records. A third source of financial data is the internal records of a bank. In today's electronic world, bank's usually have good internal information systems that provide data for evaluation purposes on either a routine or special-request basis. The bank's general ledger system yields financial statement (accounting) data. Transaction processing systems produce data on maturities, incremental cash flows, customer transaction accounts, and other operational information. Various "expert" systems will produce analytical byproducts of primary data.

Annual Reports. The banking company's annual report is another source of financial data. SEC rules require that banks with publicly traded securities furnish an annual report to stockholders. Some annual reports are more comprehensive than others. Some are prepared in a format which is acceptable by the SEC as the required 10K form. Banks which are not required to produce an annual report for stockholders often publish an annual report anyway for the benefit of customers and other interested parties.

The annual reports of banking companies usually contain the following: a message by the chief executive; financial statements; footnotes to financial statements; an accountant's opinion; exhibits that provide detailed information about facts summarized in the financial statements; and an analytical discussion by the bank's management. Usually, large banks disclose more information than small banks, but there are many exceptions.

Surveys.   Data may also be collected by requesting bankers to participate in a survey. This technique gives the analyst control of the definitions, data organization, and time schedule if the providers of the data obey the instructions. For a survey to generate sufficient response, however, the benefits to the banker must clearly be seen to offset the time and expense of returning a completed questionnaire.

Other Sources of Information.   All of these sources are primary sources of raw data (that is, data to be used in analysis and comparison). An alternative to collecting raw data is to use analyses and comparisons which have been performed by others. Another option is to acquire the end-result of someone else's evaluation.

Newspapers, such as *American Banker* and the *The Wall Street Journal*, collect and publish bank financial data, analytical comparisons, and rankings. Journals, such as *ABA Banking Journal* (published by the American Bankers Association) and *Bank Administration* (published by the Bank Administration Institute), also publish articles containing bank financial data, analysis, and comparisons.

Many commercial firms collect financial data from one of the primary sources and sell it in a changed format: tabular or analytical publications or electronic media for computers. Several firms provide security ratings and performance scores which represent their evaluations of financial performance. In many cases a subscription to an evaluation service may be more cost efficient than performing an evaluation from raw data.

BENCHMARKS FOR EVALUATING BANK PERFORMANCE

After bank data is collected, the analyst evaluates it by constructing analytical reports, computing ratios, making comparisons, and drawing conclusions. The analytical reports and ratios supply information on bank size, levels of risk, and rates of return. A bank's data is compared with its historical data and data on other banks. Conclusions can be drawn only when benchmarks are available for making judgments about good, bad, or acceptable performance.

Analysts use various benchmarks derived from practical experience and academic debates. As stated previously, the specific standards of performance used depend on the objectives of the evaluator. There are, however, some general benchmarks which are commonly used by experienced analysts. The benchmarks presented in this chapter are general and deliberately are not attributed to any source. The values used for illustration are subject to interpretation but will provide a basis for the process of evaluation.

Size

A bank's size is the financial measure which occurs first to many people when evaluating a bank. How large is the bank? What are the bank's total assets? What are the total deposits? How big is the loan portfolio? Answers to these questions place the bank in perspective for the experienced analyst.

With total assets of $196 billion at year-end 1986, Citicorp of New York was the largest U.S. banking company and, with total assets of $104 billion, BankAmerica of San Francisco was the second largest. A size perspective for the entire industry is shown in Table 1.

Bank size is an important base for evaluation. Larger assets mean a bank needs more capital, and a larger amount of capital means a larger lending limit. (Bank regulators permit national banks to make individual loans of up to 15 percent of capital). In principle, economies of scale come with larger size: one corporate headquarters, one executive team, more cost-effective computers for processing large volumes of transactions, and so on. And finally, size determines economic power. Large size means more flexibility, more knowledge, and more market opportunities for managing day-to-day financial risks.

TABLE 1 An Overview of Bank Size (estimates for December 31, 1986)

Size Group	Total Assets	Number of Banks	Percent of Total Banking Assets
Money center	$50 billion and over	10	34%
Regional	$5 to $50 billion	100	42
Mid-Size	$1 to $5 billion	150	16
Large community	$100 million to $1 billion	2,500	5
Community	Under $100 million	12,000	3

Bank size alone is not an adequate measure of financial performance. Size does, however, two things: It gives a perspective on complexity, and it allows the best interpretation of risk and return. Most of the benchmarks for risk and return in the following discussion will be presented with different expectations for large and small banks.

Financial Risks

The level of financial risk assumed by a bank should be consistent with the bank's ability to absorb losses and generate acceptable rates of returns. During the 1950s, 1960s, and early 1970s, the banking industry operated at low levels of risk and produced low rates of return. During the past 10 years, many banks have accepted higher degrees of financial risk with an eye toward greater financial rewards. Some have been more successful than others.

Risks in banking can be categorized in different ways. Financial risk is only one of many kinds (for example, location, security, and natural hazards). Furthermore, financial risks can be subcategorized into asset quality, liquidity, interest rate sensitivity, and capital adequacy. Benchmarks within each of these subcategories allows the analyst to draw conclusions and evaluate financial performance.

Asset Quality. Asset quality risk is the possibility that an asset currently shown on the books may become a future financial loss. Asset quality has several dimensions. The most important is loan quality. The obvious risk is that the borrower will not repay the loan according to the original terms and conditions.

Problem loans are classified in several ways. Nonperforming assets include loans with terms which have been renegotiated, loans on which the bank has stopped accruing interest, and real estate acquired by foreclosure (called other real estate owned or OREO). Regulators define classified assets as those just described, plus loans that are 90 days past due but still accruing interest. Large banks may have about 3 percent of their total loan portfolio shown in nonperforming loans while small banks tend to have 2 percent or less. Total classified assets of large banks represent about 30 percent of the bank's equity and about 15 percent of equity for small banks.

Another aspect of asset quality is the degree of diversification or concentration. Good asset quality as regards diversification is best illustrated by the axiom "don't put all your eggs in one basket." This component of risk is evaluated by observing the relationship of large blocks of loans to the total loan portfolio and relative to the bank's capital. SEC rules require that banks report on concentrations which exceed 10 percent of loans to one industry or in any foreign geographic area. Most banks report loan concentrations when the amount exceeds 50 percent of equity.

Current asset market values represent what the free market thinks of the bank's assets. Traditional accounting treatment of assets does not recognize the importance of asset market value risk, but evaluating market value is gaining in popularity with investors, analysts, and regulators. As a result, the market value of the security investments portfolio is often reported. Generally, the market-to-book percentage is in the range of 95 to 105 percent.

Earning asset efficiency is a measure popular among analysts. It is the percentage of earning assets to total assets. Large banks average 87 percent, and small banks average 92 percent. One component of earning asset efficiency is the total amount of cash, reserves, and float (that is, cash items in the process of collection). Total cash as a percentage of total deposits for large banks is about 9 percent and about 6 percent for small banks. Another component of earning asset efficiency is the investment in fixed assets. A regulatory rule is that banks should not invest more than 50 percent of their equity in brick and mortar.

Liquidity.   Liquidity is a bank's ability to meet anticipated demand for funds from both depositors and borrowers. Liquidity can be provided by selling existing assets or buying new liabilities. More specifically, commercial bank liquidity is measured by the ability to liquidate assets, to increase funding sources, to manage the asset/liability mix, and to draw from contingency sources.

Asset liquidity is defined as the amount of cash readily available from the bank's assets. Short-term earning assets in large banks are about 14 percent and about 18 percent in small banks. Investment securities are sometimes pledged against public deposits and repurchase transactions. A measure of liquidity is the percentage of the security portfolio which has been pledged. In large banks pledged securities are about 35 percent of total investments and in small banks the percentage of pledged securities is about 25 percent. Long-term investment securities and long-term loans (such as real estate mortgage loans) curtail liquidity. The percentage of long-term assets to total assets for large banks is about 25 percent while the percentage of long-term assets for small banks is 45 percent.

Funding position represents the bank's ability to attract sources of funds for liquidity purposes. Funding liquidity is measured by the extent to which a bank has already used purchased funds (that is, short-term borrowings plus large CDs) to fund the balance sheet. The amount of purchased funds as a percentage of earning assets for large banks is greater than 40 percent for most, and at times as high as 85 percent in some well-managed companies. For small banks, the percentage of purchased funds is 15 percent. Another often used measure of a bank's funding position is short-term borrowings net of short-term investments as a percentage of equity. In large banks the net borrowed funds percentage is greater than 50 percent with some banks approaching 100 percent. In small banks, net short-term borrowings is often negative (that is, a net sold position) but a net short-borrowed position of 20 percent could be easily managed.

The asset/liability mix concept of liquidity examines the relationship of loans to deposit balances in total, as well as by market segment (for example, retail, business, foreign, or money market instruments). A bank cannot loan every dollar of deposits received. Some of the deposit balances must be held in cash reserves; some will be operationally tied up in the process of collection; and some deposit funds are forced into investment securities due to pledging requirements. By subtracting cash, reserves, float, and public deposit balances from total deposits, the amount of available deposits is determined. Because large banks rely on purchased funds, the percentage of loans to available deposits will exceed 100 percent, but for small banks the percentage will be about 80 percent. Regardless of the size of the bank, bankers tend to run retail loans as a percentage of retail deposits between 50 percent and 70 percent and business loans as a percentage of deposits between 110 percent and 150 percent. Foreign assets tend to be funded 100 percent by foreign deposits or borrowings. The money market funding position net of the investment portfolio is the shock absorber for balancing the balance sheet daily.

Interest Rate Sensitivity.   Interest rate risk in a bank is the possibility that interest rates will change in the future and that these changes will cause the bank to incur an economic loss that it had not expected. It is important to emphasize that the risk occurs because interest rates may move differently from what management expected, and this results in less interest income or more interest expense than anticipated. The resulting loss is reflected in a lower interest margin, lower asset values, or both.

Concepts for measuring interest rate sensitivity are evolving, and no simple, single measurement has evolved for evaluation purposes. Interest variance analysis, gap reports, duration analysis, and simulation are the four computational techniques currently used to help bankers understand and manage interest rate exposure. Simulation and duration analysis generally require extensive data and are primarily useful for a bank's internal analysis. An interest variance analysis and the information necessary for a simple gap report are requirements of the SEC and, to a lesser degree, of the FDIC.

Many analysts have referred to a gap position of zero (that is, interest sensitive assets less interest sensitive liabilities equals zero) as a balanced position and a desirable goal. However, efforts to validate this concept have not yet produced evidence to support it. When attempting to evaluate the interest rate exposure risk, the analyst should computationally isolate the causes of interest variance, compute a gap position, and then explore other matters. These other matters include such things as managerial knowledge and understanding, market growth opportunities, and bank access to the money and capital markets. Another important consideration is how the bank uses sophisticated tools such as interest rate futures, option contracts, rate-swap contracts, or variable rate loan and deposit instruments.

Capital Adequacy.   Two approaches to determining capital adequacy have evolved: a market approach and a regulatory approach. In a world without bank regulators, the level of capital would be determined by the market. However, the reality is that bank regulators determine the minimum levels of capital. Two concepts of regulatory capital exist: primary capital and risk-based capital. These concepts are routinely changed to meet new conditions.

Primary capital is defined as all equity, plus the reserve for loan losses, plus certain qualifying subordinated debt and preferred-stock issues. The current regulatory requirement establishes a minimum ratio of 5½ percent for capital to adjusted total assets for well-managed banks of all sizes. In practice, many community banks maintain a ratio of 8 percent or higher.

Recently proposed by federal regulators, risk-based capital is a concept which adjusts the asset base and certain off-balance-sheet items by weightings according to one of five assigned-risk indexes. Primary capital is then divided by the weighted asset base to determine a risk-based capital ratio. If implemented as proposed, this concept will require banks to maintain higher capital levels when they allocate assets to risky categories.

Financial Returns

Profits and growth over time provide compensation to bankers and investors who have successfully managed banking risks. The larger the risk exposure, the larger should be the return, and vice versa. Evaluation of financial performance in banking seeks to determine if the risks have produced acceptable returns and if the returns are sustainable into the future.

Profitability.   Overall profitability is generally measured by the return on assets, return on equity, and other measurements which include the market value of the outstanding stock. A more detailed profitability analysis examines interest margin, net overhead, and loan-loss experience.

For stockholders the return on equity is a valuable measure since it relates net income to the book value of shareholder's equity. This ratio ranges from 12 percent to 15 percent for most banks, regardless of size. Return on equity is impacted by return on assets and leverage (that is, assets per dollar of equity). Large banks generally report a return on assets of .60 percent, and small banks generally report a return on assets of more than one percent. Large banks usually report a leverage factor higher than that for small banks, and therefore both large and small banks report similar returns on equity.

The market value of the outstanding stock is of great importance to a stockholder. The price-earnings (P/E) multiple, defined as the market price per share divided by earnings per share, indicates what the market thinks about the bank's risk position and future earnings prospects. Although the P/E multiple is somewhat dependent on over-all stock market performance, it is primarily driven by individual bank performance. A P/E of between 10 and 12 during December 1986 was considered good.

Market value compared to book value of the equity also is an important ratio for measurement. In small banks that have stock which is not actively traded, a market-to-book ratio of 1 is acceptable. In some areas where mergers and acquisitions have been frequent, a market-to-book ratio of 1.75 to 2 percent is common. Triple and qua-druple multiples to book have occurred in unique situations.

The major profit-producing factor in a bank is net interest income (that is, interest margin). The dollar amount of net interest margin is computed by subtracting interest expense from interest income; the net interest margin percentage is computed by dividing the net in-terest margin dollars by average earning assets. The interest margin percentage in large banks is about 3 percent and in small banks the percentage is greater than 5 percent. A good margin ratio is reflective of good yields, lower cost rates, effective use of earning assets, and a sensible mix of interest-bearing liabilities. A low margin reflects weak-nesses in one or more of these components.

Another key component in a bank's profitability is the net overhead burden. The convention for computing net overhead burden is to subtract noninterest income from gross noninterest operating expense (excluding the provision for loan losses). The net overhead burden is often expressed as a percentage of earning assets to provide compar-ability with the net interest margin percentage. For large banks the net overhead percentage ranges from 1.75 to 2.25 percent and for small banks, the percentage ranges from 2.75 percent to 3.25 percent.

A major component of overhead expense is the cost of salaries and benefits. Large banks have an average cost per employee higher than that of small banks, but the large banks also tend to have higher asset dollars per employee. The average annual sum of salaries and benefits per employee is $30,000 or more for large banks and $22,000 or less for small banks. Average assets per employee are approximately $2 million for large banks and $1 million for small banks.

Loan losses (or a lack of such losses) are also a major determinant of profitability. Commercial banks maintain a reserve for loan losses that reflects managements' estimate of potential future losses. The reserve balance is decreased by actual loans charged off, and it is replenished and increased (to adjust for loan growth) by an expense charge against earnings (that is, the provision for loan losses). Loan chargeoffs (net of recoveries) are between 0.6 and 0.9 percent of loans, regardless of bank size, and the expense provision is between 0.8 and 1.1 percent. The amount by which the provision percentage exceeds the chargeoff percentage is the amount which provides for growth in the loan portfolio.

Growth.   Growth in balance sheet size is necessary in commercial banks to meet the growing needs of customers, to offset inflationary pressures on operating costs, and to increase the returns to investors. Evaluation of growth has several components.

First, asset growth compared with the rate of inflation indicates whether the bank is growing in real terms or slipping in relation to changes in the economy. Second, asset growth compared to that of other banks indicates how well the management team can do in the same environment in which other banks are operating. Third, net income growth compared to asset growth indicates whether the bank is sacrificing profitability to achieve rapid asset growth. And fourth, consistency among the growth rates of loans, deposits, assets, and equity indicates how well management has balanced diverse pressures.

If assets grow more rapidly than capital, the bank's leverage is increased but increased leverage is a two-edged sword. Shareholders are interested in increased leverage to increase their return per dollar invested. Regulators, however, are critical of asset growth which increases leverage above a conservative level. Balanced growth rates between assets and capital will hold leverage constant. Evaluation of growth should take into consideration how the bank's performance is accepted by opposing interest groups.

CAVEATS AND SUMMARY

Caveats

This chapter outlines a process for evaluation of financial performance. An analyst should procede carefully to assure that no single piece of financial data or ratio is overly relied on. In addition, many nonfinancial items of information may be significant in the overall evaluation of performance.

Comparisons of current financial data with historical data and with the financial results of other banks can be revealing. Errors in the raw financial data also can cause erroneous conclusions. Also, if the underlying data or the computed ratios have not been consistently defined, the conclusions may be misleading.

Some analysts have redefined ratios in order to exclude unwelcome negative results. With the exception of illegal activities, research on bank failures over the past 10 years shows that traditional evaluation of each bank's performance (using simple techniques such as those presented here) would have revealed the specific problems which eventually led to the bank's collapse. Analytical bias and rationalization of deficiencies is somewhat natural but should be avoided. Evaluation of financial performance by means of a structured computational approach should enhance objectivity.

Summary

Evaluation of financial performance is a process which includes data collection, data analysis, and judgments on the results. This chapter identified five groups which can benefit from the evaluation of commercial bank performance: management, investors, customers, regulators, and students. The chapter also identifies the primary sources of raw data: federal bank regulators, the SEC, internal bank records, published annual reports, and surveys.

The bulk of the chapter presents specific benchmarks for judging bank performance. These benchmarks are general, debatable, and not cross-referenced to other material, but they do provide specific values for both large and small banks and can serve as a foundation for further analyses. The benchmarks are presented in the context of a logical framework of analysis of which size, risk, and return are the major elements. The financial risk element includes the issues of asset quality, liquidity, interest rate sensitivity, and capital adequacy. The financial return element includes the issues of profitability and growth.

CHAPTER THIRTY

Internal Auditing

Terence J. Trsar

CBA, CPA
Director Audit Programs
Bank Administration Institute

The internal audit function in banks has grown in recognized importance as banking itself has increasingly become a business of risk management. New legislation and increased competition have impacted the way banks conduct business and have certainly changed the role of the internal auditor. Today's audit department must have the capability of protecting a bank's assets, identifying risk, and readily assessing that risk decisions are made at the appropriate management level.

The audit function has undergone substantial change as it adjusts to the new way it must serve banking and to the new technologies it uses. Today's internal auditors must be proactive and action-oriented, and must possess the skill and knowledge to anticipate and assess risk.

But let us not forget the auditing fundamentals that have remained essentially the same over the past 50 years: the need of the institution for internal controls, a clear view of the internal auditor's role and responsibility, and professional competence among the auditing staff.

ACCOUNTABILITY

Accountability refers to the measures of effective audit performance.

Only the board of directors can protect the auditor's need for independence; consequently, the board should be the final judge of the auditor's performance. The fact that the process of measurement may be done through an audit committee does not alter the auditor's ultimate accountability to the board.

Both the auditor and executive management have received a delegation of authority from the board—management to design and maintain systems of control, and the auditor to evaluate these systems of control. Because the evaluation process exists to serve the design and maintenance responsibility, the auditor must also be accountable to executive management. This accountability, however, does not create the usual corollary right of the executive to directly apply sanctions or to otherwise restrict the auditor's functional independence. Such action, if necessary, must be decided by the board.

The auditor should be mindful that the audit function serves many users. The auditor has an obligation, if not accountability, to those users. The auditor's personal relationship with others should be characterized by integrity, open communication, and mutual respect. User satisfaction should be an important consideration in the board's evaluation of audit performance.

Independence is a matter of personal quality rather than of rules. The auditor's relationships, as indicated by the plan of organization and by the way in which the work is conducted, must always be such that a presumption of independence logically follows in the mind of the observer.[1]

Internal auditors receive their mandate from the board of directors. This mandate is to evaluate systems of control designed and maintained by management. Internal auditors must help management identify significant risks while the potential consequences are still avoidable, thereby preserving both the fact and appearance of integrity in financial institutions. The audit department's success at anticipating potential problems will depend on whether line managers are aware of audit's role and the support of senior management. A process to continually monitor risk areas must be established, and proactive auditing techniques must be adopted. Along with these elements, the audit department must be staffed by individuals who have a good working knowledge of banking. Further, bank management must be committed to the idea of notifying audit of all new products and systems.[2]

The board, usually through an audit committee, expects and receives reports from the internal audit department that educates them on the activities of the institution. This education is critical to the performance of the duties of the director. The director must (1) know what is going on in the institution, (2) be familiar with the laws that affect the institution, (3) ensure that the institution has policies and procedures so that bank activity can be tracked, (4) ensure that the bank has competent senior management and supervise that manage-

---

[1]*Statement of Principle and Standards for Internal Auditing in the Banking Industry* (Rolling Meadows, Illinois: Bank Administration Institute, 1977), pp. 12–13.

[2]Douglas E. Van Scoy and Richard L. Haug, "Auditing Takes on Strategic Dimensions," *The Magazine of Bank Administration*, March 1986, p. 49.

ment, and (5) take decisive action when necessary to prevent and correct violations.[3]

THE IMPORTANCE OF INTERNAL CONTROLS AND THE INTERNAL AUDITOR'S REVIEW RESPONSIBILITY

The main challenge in banking is to run a good bank—emphasizing loan, investment, and service quality, systems and technology, and profitable business activities. A good bank is also a balanced bank with no big concentration in any lending or business area—a bank that uses internal controls to ensure safety and soundness.[4]

Inadequate internal controls can create financial loss that can be devastating. Many of the recent bank failures can be specifically traced to internal control failures regarding brokered deposits, repo agreements, and faulty mortgage pools. Internal controls promoting regulatory compliance have also proved lacking recently with Bank Secrecy Act requirements that have led to financial loss and embarrassment. Members of management responsible for policy implementation are also responsible for the design and the maintenance of the internal control systems.

Internal control systems exist to aid in the achievement of desired business results as well as to provide reasonable assurance that assets are properly safeguarded, to promote operational efficiency to encourage compliance with managerial policies, laws, regulations, and sound fiduciary principles. Unlike the external auditors whose role is to verify the results of business activities, the responsibility of the internal auditor is to assess the continuing effectiveness of the systems of control that ultimately influences the achievement of desired business plans. The important qualities that must be evaluated are adequacy, effectiveness, and efficiency.

In evaluating adequacy, the internal auditor determines that systems include the proper features reasonably sufficient to effect control. This evaluation includes comparing the existing control design to other designs that will properly mitigate risk.

In evaluating effectiveness, the internal auditor measures the extent of compliance with control features. That is, are the control systems operating as designed?

---

[3]Robert L. Clarke, "Remarks Before the Annual Convention of the Pennsylvania Bankers Association," *Quarterly Journal* 5, no. 3 (September 1986), p. 46.

[4]*Audit: New Perspectives on Enduring Basics* (Rolling Meadows, Illinois: Bank Administration Institute, 1987), p. 5.

In evaluating efficiency, the internal auditor must determine the practicality of the control and the benefit derived relative to the cost of implementing the control. This evaluation includes reviewing the controls themselves and should be extended to operating performance associated with their functioning.

Internal controls must be established, maintained, and monitored for every business activity. These controls can act as a positive force to facilitate successful operations as well as a negative one that restricts activities. An internal auditor must keep this in mind when recommending new controls or changes to existing controls.

The system of control must detect material errors and irregularities when preventive controls fail. Sound control systems contain safeguards that identify failures in other controls. The control environment should also promote operational efficiency by establishing hiring and training practices, performance requirements, incentives, and measurement systems. And finally, control systems must encourage compliance with managerial policies, laws, and regulations through separation of duties, authority limits, mandatory vacations, and codes of conduct.

Audit Standards

The standards by which the banking industry measures success have changed considerably from a few years ago. The traditional measure of total assets to gauge the success, strength, and future viability of an institution has been replaced by measures, such as return on assets and return on equity, that more accurately monitor the ability to increase productivity and manage resources. This importance on productivity has arisen from pressures to create new products, conduct more business, control noninterest expense, and counter the effects of shrinking interest margins brought on by deregulation and resulting in increased competition.

Internal auditors can and should play a significant role in helping their institution survive and thrive. Internal auditors should be more aware of and involved in current events and new products, services, and technology. Success in the future will be tied to auditors' ability to deliver their products and services in a more timely, more efficient, and more effective manner. Auditors must recognize that the activities and scope of their work have evolved over the years as business has changed and the social attitudes toward it have changed.[5]

---

[5]Cameron V. Jarrett, "The Future Mission of Audit," *The Magazine of Bank Administration*, August 1983, p. 28.

Professional performance by internal auditors will work to achieve desired business results. This professional performance can best be measured through compliance with prescribed standards regarding the responsibility and objectives of internal auditors. Bank Administration Institute's Statement of Principle and Standards for Internal Auditing in the Banking Industry has been the hallmark for evaluating the professional performance of internal auditors in the banking industry.

Standards are essential to professional performance. They derive authoritative support from the organization's responsibility and commitment to provide for the internal audit function.

Organization Standards

1. The organization will have an internal audit function responsible for evaluating the adequacy, effectiveness, and efficiency of its system of control and the quality of ongoing operations.
2. The organization will maintain an environment within which the auditor has the freedom to act.
3. The organization will maintain an environment within which the audit function can conform to the standards of internal auditing.
4. The organization will require management to respond formally to adverse audit findings and to take appropriate corrective action.
5. The organization's systems of control will include measurement of audit effectiveness and efficiency.

Personal Standards

1. An internal auditor will have adequate technical training and proficiency.
2. An internal auditor will maintain a sufficiently independent state of mind to clearly demonstrate objectivity in matters affecting audit conclusions.
3. An internal auditor will respect the confidentiality of information acquired while performing the audit function.
4. An internal auditor will engage only in activities that do not conflict with the interest of the organization.
5. An internal auditor will adhere to conduct that enhances the professional stature of internal auditing.
6. An internal auditor will exercise due professional care in the performance of all duties and the fulfillment of all responsibilities.

Performance Standards

1. The internal auditor will prepare a formal audit plan that covers all significant organizational activities over an appropriate cycle of time.
2. The audit plan will include an evaluation of controls within new systems and significant modifications to existing systems before they become operational.
3. Audit procedures will provide sufficient and competent evidential matter to support conclusions regarding the adequacy, effectiveness, and efficiency of the systems of control and the quality of ongoing operations.
4. The organization of the audit function and related administrative practice will provide for the proper supervision of persons performing audits and for the proper review of work performed.

Communication Standards

1. The auditor will prepare a formal report on the scope and results of each audit performed.
2. Each audit report will contain an opinion on the adequacy, effectiveness, and efficiency of the systems of control and the quality of ongoing operations, the degree of compliance with previously evaluated systems of control, or an explanation of why an opinion cannot be expressed. When an adverse opinion is expressed, the report will contain a statement about the exposures that may exist if corrective action is not taken.
3. The auditor will communicate audit findings in a timely manner to the managers responsible for corrective action.
4. At least once each year the auditor shall make a summary report of audit activities to the board of directors and executive management. The report shall include an opinion on the overall condition of the organization's controls and operations.[6]

ORGANIZATION OF THE AUDIT DEPARTMENT

The board of directors/audit committee clearly communicate the perceptions and expectations of the internal audit department through a charter. This charter sets forth the purpose and objectives of the audit department as well as its authority and responsibility. From this charter auditors must effectively develop comprehensive audit plans to pro-

---

[6]*Internal Auditing in the Banking Industry* (Rolling Meadows, Illinois: Bank Administration Institute, 1984) pp. 2–4.

vide adequate audit coverage of the bank each year. These plans should detail the areas to be audited, staff assignments, and estimated hours to complete. Areas to be audited should be chosen based on risk assessments and regulatory requirements. In addition, audit work should be coordinated with external auditors to avoid duplication, but not at the expense of either party's independence.

CONDUCTING THE AUDIT

Work Program Development

After completion of a comprehensive audit plan, internal auditors must be prepared to develop, adopt, or revise an audit work program. This program should be prepared to include an analysis of the basic exposures present in the area being audited as well as adherence to general control objectives.

The first step in preparing the audit work program is to review the continuing audit file. From this file the internal auditor can better understand the business being conducted by the auditee. This review and knowledge of the business of the auditee is vital to the planning and execution of any audit. Typical contents of a continuous audit file include basic historical data such as an organizational chart and list of key personnel, internal control information such as flowcharts and risk identification, contracts and long-term documents, and significant prior audit findings.

A well prepared audit work program serves as a guideline to the completion of audit procedures and provides a consistent audit approach from audit to audit. An audit work program should emphasize procedures that are directed at areas of risk and test the existence and performance of internal control systems to reduce this risk.

As previously mentioned, the internal auditor must also coordinate the audit with reviews being conducted by external auditors. Duplication of effort should be held to a minimum and as with comments generated internally, significant comments made in externally generated reports should be followed up for compliance.

Preaudit Planning

Preaudit planning may be the single most important part of conducting any audit. However, this is often the part of the audit that is overlooked. At this stage, audit objectives are defined, the audit program is developed or revised, the audit scope is adjusted, and staff assignments are made. Here too it is critical that the auditor understand the business of the auditee, understand the audit objectives, and understand how each step in the audit program is designed to meet these objectives. In addition, the internal auditor should meet with the auditee prior to performing audit fieldwork to discuss the objectives and scope of the audit. This early communication sets the groundwork for the review and should continue throughout the audit. If this planning process is not well thought-out and documented, it is likely that the desired audit results will not be obtained.

Audit Fieldwork

Completion of the audit work program and appropriate internal control questionnaires takes place during the audit fieldwork stage. Properly completed work programs serve as a guideline to audit procedures and ensure a consistent audit approach. Audit procedures identified in the work program should be developed to accomplish the audit objectives. Completion of the procedures as evidenced in the audit workpapers serve to support the reviews and tests conducted to meet these objectives. In applying the programs during the audit, the auditor should keep in mind that the program is meant to be a guide and it is not intended to restrict the auditor from applying other audit procedures and tests or from modifying the scope of the audit, if deemed necessary.

Audit Report

The development of a clear and concise audit report is essential to the success of any audit. The primary objective of this report is to accurately inform management of the audit findings and provide a measure on which to evaluate the effectiveness of control systems and management support.

The audit report should include the objectives and scope of the audit performed, material audit findings and their control significance, recommended corrective action to be taken, and a statement or opinion as to the overall effectiveness of management in meeting control and business objectives.

Draft report findings and audit recommendations should be discussed with the auditee and corrective action taken prior to the final written report to demonstrate agreement to each finding and facilitate corrective action. Audit reports should be written in the active language, be impersonal, and be written in a positive fashion. In addition, in order for audit reports to be effective, they should be written and issued in a timely manner. All findings, including those not resolved as of the issuance of the report, should be followed up to ensure that corrective action has been taken.

THE EFFECTS OF TECHNOLOGY ON AUDITING

Controls

Banking has changed dramatically over the past decade. Virtually every operation that was once done manually is now automated or done with automated assistance. The internal auditor must understand how a transaction is processed through a computer, the controls that must be present, and methods to evaluate these controls. These controls can be identified as input, processing, or output.

Input controls are designed to provide reasonable assurance that authorized data is properly entered into the system. These input controls may be part of the system's software such as control totals on input reports, or may be generated externally such as a batch-control log. For online systems the input control often consists of a password restriction which allows only authorized individuals to access the system.

Processing controls are designed to provide reasonable assurance that authorized transactions are correctly processed and data files are properly updated and protected. Typical processing controls are application edit procedures that verify the accuracy of data.

Output controls are designed to provide assurance that output is reasonable and only made available to authorized users. Typical output controls include reconciliation by authorized users with input and processing control totals.

It is the responsibility of the internal auditor to test transactions to verify that control systems are designed and are functioning properly. This verification includes identifying transaction types, identifying methods of input, identifying master and transaction files used during the processing, and testing the validity and integrity of the transaction either by using normal system outputs or computer-assisted auditing techniques (CAATS).

Separation of Duties

The organization structure for computer-processed activities is similar to manual processed activities in that there should be separate functions for initiating and authorizing transactions, recording transactions, and maintaining custody of the assets.

Responsibility and duties for computer processing should be separate from systems development and maintenance activities, the responsibilities and duties related to reconciling computer input with output, and the control of computer files.

Disaster Recovery

The need for recovery capabilities to maintain the bank's day-to-day operations is critically important in the event of a disaster or disruption from normal operations. Management should be aware and convinced of the need for recovery capabilities and should allocate sufficient resources to develop and maintain a plan.

The responsibilities of the internal auditor depend on whether a plan exists and a judgment of its effectiveness. If a plan does exist, the auditor must be familiar with its objectives and how it works. The plan must not only be tested to see that the objectives are met, but also evaluated to see that the objectives themselves are adequate and effective. If a plan does not exist, the auditor must convince management of the importance of developing a plan.

The evaluation of the plan must at a minimum include a review of:

- The resource commitment from top management.
- The resource assignments for the development, maintenance, and testing/execution of the plan.
- Periodic reports made to a steering committee on the plans' development/maintenance.
- The resource requirements for each system.
- The DP file retention and rotation process to ensure compatibility with system requirements.

Use of Microcomputers

The use of microcomputers by bank internal auditors has grown dramatically over the past three years. In 1983, only 11 percent of banks were using the microcomputer as an audit tool. Today nearly half of all banks use the microcomputer to perform administrative and analytical audit tasks.

In addition, many banks are now beginning to down load information from the mainframe to the microcomputer to perform detail tests. Lap-top (light-weight portable) computers are also being used in the field to perform various audit tests and as a means of communicating findings and audit progress back to the home office.

AUDIT INVOLVEMENT IN SYSTEMS DEVELOPMENT AND NEW PRODUCTS

Regardless of size or complexity, development of new products and systems presents potential risks to an institution. It is important that these risks be controlled and minimized and that adequate internal controls be developed and evaluated prior to product offering or system use.

The internal auditor should be a part of the product/systems development team. It is the auditor's responsibility to identify and document material control points, ensure that the designed and implemented controls are adequate and effective, and ensure compliance with the development process.

AUDITOR TRAINING AND CERTIFICATION

The professional internal auditor is a key resource for planning a bank's future course by controlling expenses, improving opportunities and profits, identifying existing and potential problems, and building a more competitive bank.

Internal auditors must not only possess technical audit skills and knowledge but also supervisory and communication skills to provide an efficient and effective audit program. In addition, significant knowledge of EDP systems, the use of microcomputers, and analytical ability is also important.

Proper training is an essential element to the development of a professional internal auditor. Training can be on-the-job, self-administered, or acquired through schools, seminars, and conferences. In addition, internal auditor certification programs exist to train and attest to a level of professional skill and knowledge.

On-the-job training is primarily used to train new staff members on the objectives of audit work associated with a specific assignment. On-the-job training is facilitated by high-quality audit programs and workpapers.

Self-administered training is an important part of an auditor's development. This training consists of keeping informed on current banking and audit topics by reading trade journals and periodicals. Technical publications also provide information that is critical to providing a high-quality audit product. In addition, self-administered microcomputer and video assisted training programs are now available to meet specific educational needs.

Schools, seminars, and conferences provide internal auditors with a forum to share ideas with peers and to learn state-of-the-art audit techniques and practices as well as sharpen specific technical and managerial skills. These programs are available locally and nationally from the Bank Administration Institute, the Institute of Internal Auditors, and others.

Professional certification is an important part of an auditor's development. Certification indicates that the auditor has undergone an intense preparation period and has demonstrated technical knowledge and skill and professional conduct. Auditors may choose from several excellent certification programs such as the Chartered Bank Auditor (CBA), Certified Public Accountant (CPA), Certified Internal Auditor (CIA), or Certified Information Systems Auditor (CISA). The Chartered Bank Auditor program, sponsored by Bank Administration Institute, is a certification program that has been designed exclusively for measuring competence in the practice of *bank* auditing.

INTERNAL AUDITORS' RESPONSIBILITY FOR FRAUD DETECTION

The systems of control, not the internal auditor, provide the primary assurance against fraud. The internal auditor, however, must evaluate the systems' capability to achieve this end. Internal auditors represent the front line of defense against fraud, insider abuse, and unwise financial practices within the nation's corporations. Independence is critically important. Auditors need the power to delve into all of the bank's affairs, including those of the bank management. Without this independence, the internal auditor will lack effectiveness and be of little or no real value to the bank. Senior management must demonstrate, by the nature of its relationship with the internal auditors, that they are key players in the organization.[7]

SUMMARY

The importance of the internal audit department in banks cannot be overstated. Through the implementation of sound internal control systems and the internal auditors' continuous evaluation of these controls, it is a good bet that banks will be healthy and profitable.

---

[7]L. William Seidman, "FDIC Chairman Stresses Importance of Internal Auditors in Fraud Detection," FDIC news release, PR–98–86 (June 24, 1986), p. 1.

CHAPTER THIRTY-ONE

The Independent Accountant

Thomas F. Keaveney

National Director—Banking
Peat Marwick Main & Co.

Fred M. Borchardt

Partner
Peat Marwick Main & Co.

INTRODUCTION

One of the most significant professional relationships that bank management and the bank's board of directors can have is the relationship with its independent accountant. Historically, the most common professional relationship derives from the requirement that the independent accountant audit the bank's financial statements. Often, however, the concept of the audit may not be completely understood by its users, and may be viewed only as a time-consuming burden of little business value. This chapter deals with the concept of the audit in relationship to the independent accountants' professional responsibilities, breadth of audit services, and specialized bank experience. All of these will ensure a value-added business relationship.

RESPONSIBILITIES OF MANAGEMENT AND THE BOARD OF DIRECTORS

A bank's management and board of directors has the responsibility to determine the need for an independent accountant. This responsibility stems from the bank's moral and legal obligations to disclose and report accurate and reliable financial data to interested parties.

Bank shareholders, depositors, and lenders look to management and the board of directors to ensure that the maximum return on invested capital is obtained by the bank while at the same time providing the necessary safeguards over community funds. Banks invest billions of dollars each year by lending, by investing in securities, and by investing trust funds in the bank's fiduciary capacity. In order to meet

411

these responsibilities and compete successfully in the marketplace, banks must instill public confidence, both in their financial performance and the financial information they report. Such confidence can be earned by a record of stability and growth as evidenced by competent investment and lending policies, and by long-term profitability resulting in adequate liquidity and capital. The independent accountant can reinforce the level of public confidence in the bank by examining and reporting on the bank's financial statements.

RESPONSIBILITIES OF THE INDEPENDENT ACCOUNTANT

Bank management and directors who engage independent accountants should expect those accountants to demonstrate their competence and integrity during the engagement. This expectation has been acknowledged by independent accountants through the ethical code of the American Institute of Certified Public Accountants. The ethical code to which members of the institute must subscribe contains principles to be followed by the accountant.

These principles include independence, adherence to general and technical standards, due professional care, responsibility to clients, and responsibility to the profession and the public.

Independence

Independence has always been the cornerstone of the profession. The accountant's services would otherwise be of little use to third parties and to the public in general, and would be of less value to the client. Independence is related to actual as well as perceived independence. For example, accountants cannot both keep books and records and also audit such books and records. On the other hand, provided the accountant possesses the necessary skills, clients can and should expect the independent accountant to provide management advisory services, tax planning, and consultation.

Adherence to General and Technical Standards

The observance of general and technical standards is the means by which the independent accountant demonstrates continued professional competence. The license to practice as a certified public accountant is proof of competence in the general and technical aspect of the profession.

However, obtaining a license to practice as an accountant and keeping current with changes in auditing or accounting standards is not sufficient by itself to obtain an adequate understanding of the banking industry. Professional competence in the field of banking requires the independent accountant to be committed to his continued professional development. This should include the pursuit of courses sponsored by the accounting profession, academia, and the banking industry.

Due Professional Care

The exercise of due professional care is a natural extension of professional competence. Due care requires careful planning of audit engagements, a critical review of the work performed by subordinates, and the appropriate consideration of all relevant matters to form judgments on the appropriateness of audit procedures performed and the results of those audit procedures.

Successful planning of an audit engagement requires the accountant first know his client's business. In the bank audit the independent accountant should understand and assess such matters as the credit evaluation process, overall loan portfolio risk, asset/liability management, negotiability of assets, and internal controls over banking transactions and accounts. This knowledge is extremely important in preparing an appropriate audit plan, and allows accountants to use their experience in the industry to provide critical and constructive comments to management and boards of directors on both operational and control matters.

Responsibilities to Clients

Responsibilities to clients focus on the requirement for confidentiality of information. Independent accountants must hold all information about client's activities in strict confidence. Such matters as sensitive customer information, management compensation, mergers or acquisition plans, and marketing schemes all come to the accountants' attention during the performance of their professional duties. Obviously, disclosure of such information could be detrimental to customer relations and to a bank's competitive position.

Responsibility to Profession and Public

Responsibility to profession and public is of significant importance to the independent accountant; it enhances the stature of the profession of public accounting, and it promotes the ability to serve clients and the public. Over the past decade, there has been growing concern within the accounting profession about how well the role of the independent accountant is understood and how effectively the public perceives the profession to be discharging its responsibilities. Accordingly, in all dealings with bank clients, it is important that management and the bank's board of directors have a complete understanding and agreement with the independent accountant about the scope of the audit work and the responsibilities of the accountant.

AUDITS BY INDEPENDENT ACCOUNTANTS

As indicated earlier, the most common practice of the independent accountant is to provide some form of audit services. These may vary from full opinion audits to director's examinations. Whatever the source of the involvement, audit services provided by the independent accountant can and should be of great value to the client.

Opinion Audits

One of the most important services provided by the independent accountant is the expression of an opinion on the bank's financial statements. This opinion will either confirm that the financial statements are presented fairly in accordance with generally accepted accounting principles or will explain why not.

In arriving at opinions and in performing audits, independent accountants must follow generally accepted auditing standards. Fundamentally, these standards involve selected tests of transactions and accounts. The concept of testing is essential since verification of all transactions and accounts would be economically impractical.

Since the concept of testing is an essential aspect of the audit process, independent accountants must design audit procedures that reduce the probability of undetected material error. If a material error were to exist and go undetected in the course of an audit, the independent accountants' opinion would be incorrect. While an audit performed in accordance with generally accepted auditing standards seeks to reduce this risk to an acceptable minimum, it does not eliminate the risk completely.

In performing an audit, independent accountants first make a professional judgment as to what constitutes a material error. The accountants' consideration of materiality is influenced by their experience and the needs of those who will rely on the report. Materiality, as defined by the accounting profession, is "the magnitude of an omission or misstatement of accounting information that in light of surrounding circumstance makes it probable that the judgment of a reasonable person relying on the information would have been changed or influenced by the omission or misstatement." After initially determining what constitutes a material error, the accountant evaluates the risk that such an error may go undetected. This risk, which is referred to as audit risk, requires the independent accountant to assess the individual components of the risk: inherent risk, control risk, and detection risk.

Inherent risk and control risk are both subject to a bank's control. Inherent risk represents the susceptibility of an account or transaction to contain error. Control risk represents the probability that errors or irregularities may occur and not be detected by the internal control system. Evaluation of inherent risk is accomplished by an understanding of banking's economic conditions, loan demand, investment strategy, and products or services offered. Some banking activities are subject to greater inherent risk than others. For example, the allowance for loan losses, due to the judgmental nature of the balance, has a high potential for error. Additionally, transactions or accounts relating to new products, services, or unusual accounting transactions are often considered to have a high inherent risk if for no other reason than the lack of understanding on the part of bank employees of the proper accounting for these transactions. Control risk is evaluated through understanding of the control procedures performed by bank personnel. Control procedures are designed to ensure that transactions are properly controlled, recorded, and reported in the bank's financial records and that assets are properly controlled. These control procedures include timely reconciliations of general and subsidiary records, safeguards for negotiable assets, and other independent check-and-balance routines.

A principal purpose of the assessment of control risk is for the independent accountant to identify strong control procedures. The independent accountant then completes appropriate tests to obtain assurances that such procedures are being properly performed. If this were found to be the case, the independent accountant would then conclude that control risk is low, and therefore the lower the need for other audit procedures. The second principal purpose of the assessment of control risk is to identify gaps or weaknesses in a bank's control system that have come to the independent accountant's attention during the assessment. Such gaps increase the risk of errors or irregularities occurring and not being detected (the control risk), and thus require the independent accountant to perform those audit procedures designed to determine if such errors or irregularities do exist. A valuable by-product of the independent accountant's assessment of gaps or weaknesses in control procedures is that the bank will get a report of such gaps. The customary communication of such report to management and the bank's board of directors usually takes the form of a "management letter," (discussed in more detail later in this chapter).

The last component of audit risk is detection risk. This represents the risk that audit procedures will lead to a conclusion that a material error does not exist when in fact it does. Detection risk is a function of inherent and control risk. Since inherent and control risks usually exist in banks, especially with respect to loan losses and weaknesses often identified in control systems (not to mention that even strong control systems cannot be fully relied on), independent accountants are normally required to perform substantive audit procedures to determine whether material errors exist so that detection risk can be reduced to acceptable levels. The extent of these substantive audit procedures should vary based on the assessment of inherent and control risks. Where such risks are low, the audit procedures will usually be less extensive than would be the case otherwise. Such audit procedures would include confirmation with customers of selected accounts, examinations of negotiable collateral and other assets, and a review of selected banks' credit files on loans and other credit extensions.

The independent accountant, in performing an audit in accordance with generally accepted auditing standards, follows a careful, logical process in the course of conducting an audit, one that is designed to render his opinion on the financial statements of a bank. This process is designed to minimize the risk that a material error may exist in the financial statements and has not been detected. In addition to the increased creditability now attached to such financial statements, the independent accountant also provides management and directors with valuable insights into gaps or weaknesses in the banks' internal control system.

Allowance for Loan Losses

The audit for the allowance of loan losses is an example of the independent accountant's evaluation of inherent and control risk and its resulting benefit to the bank. To begin, an understanding of the bank's economic environment is essential to the audit of the allowance for loan losses. Several factors will be addressed by the independent accountant in analyzing the composition of the loan portfolio including:

- Primary lending markets and their position within the national and local economy.
- Portfolio trends and analysis of past and current performance.
- Composition of borrowers.
- Growth and disperson of loan risk.
- Current outlook for various industries and sectors to which loans are made.

After examining the economic conditions and the composition of the loan portfolio for its inherent risk, the independent accountant must then perform a review of the bank's lending process in order to assess the control risk. This review leads to an understanding of the bank's internal policies and practices when they concern the control of granting loans and other credits and managing the credit risk in the existing loan portfolio. Areas the accountant will address in the review include:

- Loan approval procedures, including approval of participation loans purchased and sold, lending credit limits, and levels of secured and unsecured lending.
- Required information before loans are approved and ongoing information requirements.
- Loan collection responsibilities and functions.
- Experience of lending personnel.
- Identification and reporting of problem loans.
- Segregation of duties.
- Present methods to measure and document loan risk and the related level of allowance for loan losses.
- Recent reports by bank regulatory authorities.

An understanding of all the areas discussed will not only provide a basis for establishing the extent of audit procedures, but should also place independent accountants in a knowledgeable position as to the effectiveness of the lending process. Their professional competence, often based on specialized banking experience, provides a ready comparison of the lending procedures being followed with those of other successful banking institutions.

Once independent accountants have developed an understanding of the lending process, they will often identify control strengths. These strengths will then be subject to audit test to ensure that the controls are functioning as intended. To the extent that strong controls exist, they influence the design of audit procedures. Where controls are found to be strong, audit procedures to detect material error will usually be reduced.

After evaluating inherent and control risk and testing strong control procedures to ensure that they are functioning as intended, independent accountants must design audit procedures for detection risk. These procedures usually include a detailed review of bank credit files for:

- Identified problem loans.
- Selected loans to borrowers in industries experiencing economic problems.
- Selected loans to other borrowers.

Often this detailed review identifies missing, stale, or inadequate information preventing the accountant from forming a judgment on the collectibility of the loans reviewed. In such cases, especially where the condition is other than isolated or involves small loan balances, the independent accountant may require the bank to obtain the missing information before concluding on the adequacy of the bank's allowance for loan losses. In addition, when the independent accountant finds troublesome conditions or identifies problem loans not previously recognized by the bank, the accountant will usually extend the scope of detailed review of the bank credit files to be sure that testing has disclosed all potential material errors. Through this process and in conjunction with the roles and responsibilities of regulatory authorities, independent accountants reach conclusions on the adequacy of the allowance for loan losses, and comment on the adequacy of lending and collection procedures and other internal control procedures.

OTHER AUDIT CONSIDERATIONS

Directors' Examinations

Sometimes banks' boards of directors request the independent accountant to assist it in performing an annual director's examination. Directors' examinations are often used at small- to moderate-sized banks to satisfy regulatory and/or bonding company requirements. Directors' examinations may consist of a balance sheet audit usually at a surprise date, or the application of agreed on audit procedures on specific elements, accounts, or items of a financial statement at a surprise date. This is often referred to as an accountability audit, the procedures of which are directed by the board of directors.

Balance sheet audits will encompass essentially the same consideration of audit risk and materiality as opinion audits. As their name implies, however, balance sheet audits will only focus on the balance sheet and will not address nor will they be associated with the income statement, the statement of changes in shareholders' equity, or the statement of changes in financial position. Balance sheet audits are generally desirable in situations in which the bank requires a verification of net worth in either an acquisition sale or as a result of borrowing agreements secured by bank stock.

Accountability audits include procedures that are similar to auditing procedures performed in connection with an opinion audit. However, these audits generally do not encompass such procedures as an evaluation of the allowance for losses and testing of internal control procedures. Furthermore, since the date of these surprise examinations normally do not correspond with the end of an accounting period, financial statements are not usually prepared. Accountability audits are desirable in situations in which full opinion audits are not required by regulatory guidelines or requested by management and directors, but where a certain degree of independent review is necessary because of bonding requirements or the delegation of fiduciary responsibilities.

It is important to note that the need for balance sheet audits versus accountability audits should be decided on a cost benefit basis determined by the needs of the management, the bank's board of directors, and applicable regulatory banking and bonding requirements. Accordingly, it is important that management and the directors have an active role in directing, reviewing, and approving the exact scope and resulting limitations of accountability audits. It would normally be appropriate to have such audit arrangements confirmed in writing by the independent accountant and the bank's board of directors, or its audit and examining committee.

Internal Audit Function

One of the most effective ways for management and boards of directors to supervise and maintain an adequate system of internal controls is through a strong internal audit function.

The internal audit function is viewed by the independent accountant as a separate, higher level of internal control that provides additional assurance that internal control procedures are operating effectively. The work of the internal auditor is frequently oriented toward organizational and operational matters as well as routine auditing procedures. The fact that the internal auditor can devote a substantial amount of effort to the monitoring of controls is an important aspect of the assessment of the level of detection risk to the bank and the independent accountant's reporting on the bank's financial statements.

An important service that the independent accountant performs is the evaluation of the internal audit function. In the case of an opinion audit, the accountant must evaluate the effectiveness of the internal auditors if their work will be relied on to determine the necessary level of audit procedures. Accordingly, the accountant must evaluate such matters as the internal auditor's qualifications, objectivity, documentation, and performance. A strong internal audit function usually enables the independent accountant to reduce the extent of the audit procedures that would otherwise be required.

In addition, for banks that do not require an opinion audit, the independent accountant can, as a separate service or as part of an accountability audit, evaluate the internal audit function to assess the adequacy of this function and to identify areas of improvement. The resulting effect of such a review can be directed toward improving the overall internal controls of the bank.

Management Letters

After performing audit services, the independent accountant will be in a position to present to management and the board of directors a letter stating suggested improvements in internal accounting controls and other operational matters. It is the accountant's experience that clients consider a well-written, comprehensive management letter to be one of the most valuable services an accountant can provide. Experience and insight place the accountant in an excellent position to provide management with constructive ideas that are responsive to the bank's needs.

Independent accountants should report to management on matters of particular importance such as the results of the review of lending and collection procedures, overall and specific risk considerations in the loan portfolio, and ineffective or nonexistent internal control procedures. Typically, independent accountants will not only identify potential or actual control problems but will also make recommendations about corrective action that can be taken.

In addition to the benefits derived from a well-written management letter, regulatory authorities and fidelity bond insurers are often interested in significant audit findings and the accountant's suggestions for strengthening internal control and improving accounting procedures.

Cooperation with Regulatory Authorities

The independent accountant recognizes the importance of cooperating with regulatory authorities in performing an efficient audit and providing valuable services to the bank.

Recent regulatory examinations can be of significant benefit to the independent accountant when designing audit procedures. In many instances, the independent accountant's review of areas subject to regulatory criticism serves to measure management's success in resolving the cause of criticism, or even aid in the design of procedures directed toward eliminating such criticism. Additionally, whenever possible, the independent accountant consults with regulatory agencies about the timing of examinations, the status of examinations under progress, and regulatory issues either under proposal or recently enacted. The independent accountant can in this manner provide timely information to the client on regulatory issues that may have a significant impact on the bank.

In dealing with regulatory authorities, the independent accountant recognizes the importance of maintaining client confidentially. Thus accountants will discuss client-specific matters with regulatory authorities only with the client's prior approval, and usually the client will be directly involved in such discussions.

Computers in Bank Audits

Since the banking industry itself has been a prime user of advanced computer technology, independent accountants serving bank clients have usually developed their own computer audit expertise. In order to establish an effective and efficient audit process, accountants will be able to access mainframe computer systems with their own audit software and have developed methodologies to effectively evaluate computer controls and security. Accountant's software not only allows for verification of computer-based accounting data, but can provide valuable assistance in preparing customer confirmations and providing additional information needed for an effective and efficient audit.

As a further step in computer audit expertise and the continued evaluation of audit efficiency, microcomputers are taking a prominent role in the auditing process. Microcomputer-based systems are increasingly being used by the independent accountant in automating much of the mechanical, nonjudgmental audit functions.

This, however, is only the beginning. The microcomputer is one of the greatest technological innovations to affect professional services. Independent accountants who use it are limited only by their imagination. The fact that all kinds of data can be analyzed in a matter of seconds may soon make yesterday's method of auditing obsolete.

Single Audit Letters

Single audit letters, particularly as they relate to trust departments and computer servicing operations, provide a significant service. The Employee Retirement Income Security Act (ERISA) of 1974 requires an independent accountant to perform an examination of the financial statements of certain employee benefit plans. As a result, banks may engage an independent accountant to review and report on the internal controls over its trust function. This single audit may be distributed to and relied on by other independent accountants in their examination of employee benefit plans of a bank's corporate clients, for which the bank acts as plan trustee.

The single audit approach under ERISA is basically two-fold:

1. The review testing and evaluation of the trust department's system of internal controls.

2. The issuance of a report on the system of internal controls that may be used by the plan auditor to document the nature of the auditing procedures with respect to the plan's financial statements.

The single audit approach has a number of obvious benefits:

- For the various pension plans, the bank's trust department will deal with one auditing firm and its personnel rather than with numerous auditing firms.
- Interruptions of the bank's trust department operations are kept to a minimum, and the confidentiality of the bank's trust function is maintained.
- Audit procedures will be more efficient because duplicative reviews and tests of the system of internal controls (security counts, examination of security transactions, and documentation) will be avoided.
- The responsibilities of the plan's administrator under the provisions of ERISA will be accomplished in a more efficient and reliable manner.

The single audit approach extends beyond that of the trust department. A single audit may also be performed for electronic data processing services bureaus, internal control reports for transfer and registrar agents, and serviced mortgaged loans and escrowed securities.

SPECIALIZED BANK EXPERIENCE

The concept of a value-added professional relationship is a natural extension of the independent accountant's client responsibilities. The specialized bank experience that the accountant has developed should provide the basis for serving the client beyond that of the customary audit. The majority of accounting firms today provide varying forms of valuable services through their tax and management consulting practice groups.

Tax Services

Tax services fall into three broad categories: tax compliance, tax planning, and specific transaction analysis. Tax compliance entails the completion of the various tax returns. In many cases the tax return process is integrated with the year-end audit process. The significance of tax legislation changes combined with the independent accountants' specialized banking experience often provides a cost-effective means of meeting the periodic filing requirements.

Tax planning and specific transaction reviews are without question the most significant aspect of the tax service. For example, the planning considerations relating to tax exempt securities, bad debt reserves, and the generation or use of tax loss carryforwards can dramatically affect the cash flow of a bank. In addition, specific transaction reviews will consider the tax treatment on new money market investments and off-balance-sheet instruments, the structuring of mergers and acquisitions, and the recognition of trading profits and tax treatment for debt and equity investments.

Management Consulting Services

As banks have demanded increasingly sophisticated services to support their strategy in an increasingly complex and competitive environment, management consulting services have become critical as value-added services to banks.

Management consulting practices encompass a broad spectrum of disciplines and services. Strategic management, credit management, employee and management compensation services, and information systems services are four of the more significant forms of consulting services.

Strategic management services entail assisting bank management in evaluating, choosing, and implementing corporate strategy. This strategy must consider such issues as the evaluation of financial products, the availability of the marketplace, profitability alternatives, delivery of products to the marketplace, and mergers and acquisitions.

Credit management provides an independent, critical evaluation of the bank's credit control process in order to improve the quality of the loan portfolio and to increase the return on assets. In credit management the approach is to assist the bank in resolving the issues of effective selection/marketing of credit to customers and managing the credits once they are booked.

Employee and management compensation services provided by the independent accountant must address such areas as the development of incentive performance plans and employee benefit plans, including pension and cafeteria plans and industry compensation analysis. The importance of an effective employee and management compensation program for qualified personnel at all levels of a banking organization cannot be underestimated in the present competitive climate.

Information systems services are critical to customer service and bank profitability in today's world of high technology. Management consulting practices must provide banking industry specialists with extensive data processing skills and experience. These services must focus on senior business management and their need for customer service, bank profitability, and management information.

CONCLUSION

The need for a professional relationship with independent accountants is in most cases obvious. Their audit services benefit both the institution and the public it serves. In order to provide an effective and cost-efficient audit, the accountant must be knowledgeable about the business affairs of the bank, including such matters as the bank's investment strategy, composition of its loan portfolio, and its strategic goals and objectives. The audit service extends, however, beyond the accountant's opinion on the financial statements of a bank. The bank's understanding of the audit process, combined with the benefits derived from the independent accountant's specialized banking experience, and the breadth of the audit will result in a satisfying professional relationship.

CHAPTER THIRTY-TWO

Tax Planning for Banks

Howard L. Wright

Director of Bank Taxation
Office of Federal Services
Arthur Andersen & Co.

Effective tax planning for banks demands a solid understanding of the web of tax provisions applied to banks as well as a clear grasp of the bank management's objectives. Historically, bankers have focused on reducing tax burdens, and several special provisions of the Internal Revenue Code have offered tax advantages to banks. Recent tax changes, however, including the Tax Reform Act of 1986, have changed the ground rules so much that comprehensive tax planning is even more complex and critical. This discussion highlights areas that offer tax planning opportunities and provides a framework for evaluating planning ideas. All banks will find tax planning activity very important due to the complexity of the rules applied to most banks. Banks with multinational activities or significant foreign loans must also deal with even more intricate tax rules governing cross-border activity.

OBJECTIVES OF TAX PLANNING

The Banks' Tax Burden

In the past, when doing tax planning, bank managements primarily concentrated on taking advantage of the benefits of tax-exempt income, income taxed at capital gains rates or tax deferral to obtain the time value of using the deferral benefit. Investment credits were also important to banking institutions involved in leasing. Many managements aimed to minimize taxes by these legitimate means. The structure of the banking organization also figured in tax planning since the bank holding company was frequently useful in minimizing taxes and maintaining capital. In the broad sense, as financial intermediaries, banks were passing to their customers the economic benefits of the tax law.

The 1986 tax law significantly changed the ground rules for tax planning. Many banks' tax planning objectives are greatly altered by the new provisions. Benefits of tax-exempt income have been reduced and capital gains eliminated. For larger banks, bad debt reserves will be phased out. Cash method accounting will be eliminated for all but relatively small banks while the capital gains tax and the investment credit have been deleted. Despite lower tax rates on corporations, most banks will face higher Federal income taxes over the next few years. This heavier tax burden need not affect bank earnings if it is wisely considered in evaluating bank investments and loans as well as other products and services. The new law does demand close attention to these areas, and bank decision makers must clearly grasp the impact of the changes on the bank's tax situation.

Banks also face a broad array of state taxes that need review in any tax planning activity. Because tax implications vary greatly from state to state, no effort is made here to analyze them individually. It may be observed that banks in high-tax states such as New York carefully scrutinize state tax burdens in deciding where to locate their facilities or holding company affiliates. For example, Delaware has attracted much activity from New York banks because of favorable state tax laws. Under lower Federal tax rates, the cost of state taxes will effectively rise as the benefit of the deduction for Federal taxes falls. Today state taxes will thus be even more carefully considered in a bank's tax planning process.

Compliance Considerations

Properly filing tax returns requires banks to monitor due dates to avoid penalties. In addition, elections for certain items must be made on the returns. If the bank chooses to take a position on an item of income or deduction that does not agree with the IRS position, it may be necessary to disclose that item on its tax return. Compliance problems also include filing a multitude of tax forms concerning transactions. The familiar 1099s sent to depositors and shareholders, the reports on cash transactions, and applicable payroll tax filings all require following proper procedures to avoid penalties the Internal Revenue Code imposes for late or erroneous filing. Recently the IRS has stepped up enforcement activity and is now more aggressively assessing penalties for noncompliance.

Customer Considerations

Tax planning should be an integral part of the bank's overall product and service development. Recent changes in the tax law directly influence a bank's customers as they face reduced or eliminated tax deductions for interest on personal borrowing. Likewise, the new rules for IRAs will influence customer decisions to increase or to establish these accounts. Corporate customers will also be affected by the tax changes because the revisions will influence their cash flow to repay borrowings.

The tax law thus carries multiple implications for banks in relation to their customers. A bank with the proper focus on tax planning will be alert to the opportunities as well as the problems the new law creates. Educating customers, as well as employees, about the consequences of change offers an opportunity to increase good will as well as to avoid problems.

Employee Considerations

The take-home pay of bank employees is closely tied to the tax laws. Employees' concern about after-tax income has prompted many companies to maximize fringe benefit and incentive compensation plans, programs generally established with two objectives. The first goal has been to provide an economic benefit to the employee without adding taxable income. The second objective has generally been to defer receipt of a benefit until the employee enters a lower tax bracket or to provide the benefit so as to create a capital gain. The new law's changed rate structure for individuals and the elimination of the capital gains rate differential call for review of bank employee plans to determine if they remain tax efficient in reducing employees' tax burden. Alert management will consider the tax implications of current and proposed employee compensation and fringe benefit programs for maximizing the plans' value to the bank and its employees alike.

Financial Statement Implications

The complexity of the tax law also is entwined with the financial statements' reporting of taxes. In many areas, determining taxable income may require different accounting methods than those used for financial accounting. These differences fall into two broad categories—timing and permanent differences. Timing differences are generally created by differences in the accounting methods used to report income or deductions. Under current generally accepted accounting principles (GAAP), accounting for timing differences requires the use of deferred or prepaid tax accounts to reflect the taxes in the financial statements applicable to the income and expenses reported for the accounting period. These accounting rules are currently being reviewed by the Financial Accounting Standards Board

(FASB), which may revise them for 1988 financial statements. Accounting for taxes is complicated by changing tax rates, the complexities of using tax benefits arising from net operating losses, the treatment of subsidiaries' income, and the like. The bank's internal accounting department must be especially alert and fully trained in these matters. The disclosure of taxes in the bank's annual report requires analysis of the components of the tax expense, the related liability accounts, and the effective tax rates compared to the statutory tax rate.

Legislative Concerns

The changing nature of the tax law and its interpretation by both the Internal Revenue Service and the courts frequently lead to legislative proposals to assuage the concerns of Congress. As noted, the 1986 Tax Reform Act made sweeping changes in the tax structure. The banking industry, like others, was heavily affected; individual banks as well as trade associations actively pressed on Congress their views of proposed changes as they were being enacted. From a tax planning standpoint, alert bankers were keeping up to date as best they could in order to minimize disadvantages arising from the changes and to capitalize on the opportunities provided.

While many smaller banks depend on trade organizations to speak up for them with Congress, they can generally keep abreast of changes through contact with their outside tax advisors, trade publications, and general news reports. The implications of all changes are not always immediately clear, and many will also require elaboration through regulations issued by the Internal Revenue Service. Some organizations approach this regulation-drafting process in an active way by directly lobbying the agency.

IMPLEMENTING TAX PLANNING

Given the complexity of the tax laws and their broad impact on the bank, its employees, and customers, many alert banks devote considerable effort to tax planning. Many first focused on year-end tax planning, and under the old law it was possible to put primary emphasis on such activity. From now on, year-end activity is likely only to refine a well-organized tax plan. Recent changes in the tax laws have significantly limited the means of reducing or deferring tax payments through year-end transactions.

To meet the bank's tax planning objective now, it is essential that the tax planning people have a role in shaping the bank's profit plan. The tax plan's purpose is to minimize adverse tax impacts of a profit plan; thus tax planning should be thoroughly integrated with the profit planning activity. As banks have grown and tax laws have become more complex, many banks have employed tax-trained people as inside tax consultants. In larger banks several people may perform the tax planning function while major banks with international activity may actually assign hundreds of employees to the tax function. What is right for the specific situation depends on bank size, the relative emphasis management places on tax minimization, and the complexity of the bank's tax position. The in-house tax group often reports directly to the bank president. In other cases, the group may be housed in the bank's accounting or legal group. A successful tax planning function depends less on how it is organized than on whether the tax people have access to senior management to ensure that tax issues are included in management's consideration of all significant business issues.

Some banks formalize a tax policy group as part of their asset/liability management process. This group is responsible for coordinating implementation of the bank's tax plan; it often includes members with responsibility for securities, loans, leasing, international activity, strategic planning, accounting, and financial reporting. Such groups also frequently seat an outside CPA or counsel to the bank as an advisory member. The purpose of tax policy groups is to plan investment in tax-sensitive assets to maximize earnings while assuring that tax benefits are currently used and that tax-motivated transactions stay within the scope of the organization's sound banking objectives. Since reporting taxes in the financial statements is important, the impact of tax decisions on both the tax return and the financial statements becomes significant. As issues arise on examination of the tax returns, they may be reviewed by the tax policy group to determine appropriate action.

Keeping up to Date

Changing tax laws and regulations require monitoring to avoid unpleasant surprises while taking advantage of favorable changes. This means banks must devote significant effort to monitoring developments. In banks with in-house tax groups, it is necessary to furnish a tax library and periodicals that will alert the group to changes. Smaller banks more often seek information from outside advisors, trade publications, and trade associations—information is also offered in seminars and on videotape. While the 1986 Tax Reform Act modified many provisions that directly affect bank taxation, it also made sweeping changes that touch both individuals and business. Because these changes carry many implications for the bank's future products and services, alertness to change may provide a competitive advantage to the bank.

FOCUSING ON SPECIFIC AREAS

The Tax Plan Process

Specific tax planning advice involves reviewing the overall situation of the bank and its affiliates. Such advice is also frequently transaction-oriented, using different legal forms of transactions to accomplish essentially the same results from a business viewpoint. Accounting methods particularly concern the tax planner. Historically, many banks used the cash method of accounting for Federal income tax purposes while using the accrual method for financial reporting. The 1986 tax act requires that all banks with gross receipts in excess of $5 million adopt the accrual method for tax purposes beginning in 1987.

Typically, the tax planning process should start with a determination of the expected level of taxable income based on the bank's anticipated earnings. The book earnings should be reconciled to taxable income, taking into account the permanent and timing differences between book and taxable income. Once these numbers have been established and tentative tax calculations made, the bank has built a secure base for further planning. An effective plan may then change the mix of investments, recognize gains or losses by selling securities, and accelerate or defer certain planned programs.

Many other factors must be taken into account in effective tax planning. If the bank is expecting a net operating loss for tax purposes, the possibility of obtaining a tax refund for taxes paid in a prior year should be determined. Use of foreign tax or other credits may also become important to the bank.

The tax plan must be updated periodically, perhaps at the end of each month or quarter. The periodic update is also useful in preparing estimates of taxes that must be paid quarterly. Major events will prompt interim updates, of course—events such as unanticipated gains or losses, changes in tax rates, tax cases with potential impact on the bank, and the like. Because they are easy to use, microcomputers now run the forecasting systems many banks have installed for updating their tax plans.

Concepts of Tax Planning for Specific Areas

Details of specific tax planning alternatives will vary from bank to bank and will require specific attention to the tax law, regulations, rulings, and cases governing the particular area of concern. This chapter obviously cannot cover such specifics. The intention here is to offer a general view of the complexity and opportunities for tax planning in specific areas—and to help managements focus on areas where both problems and opportunities for tax planning arise.

The review of specific transactions should involve competent professional advice, and management should be alert to this need for technical assistance. Generally, significant transactions involving the purchase or sale of assets, the establishment of new products and services, and any changes in the organization's capital planning or structure will require detailed tax analysis.

The following discussion of significant balance sheet and income statement accounts should be viewed as providing only a general understanding of the tax significance of each area discussed.

Accounting Methods

The 1986 tax act requires all banks with gross receipts over $5 million to use the accrual method for tax purposes beginning in 1987. For banks in holding companies, the $5 million threshold is determined on a consolidated basis. The transition rules provide for spreading the effect of this change over the next four years. Tax plans of banks that use the cash method of accounting will have to be revised, and they will require calculations to determine the best way of treating affected areas.

While both financial and tax accounting will in the future use the accrual basis, methods of determining accruals may differ. Estimates of accrued items, or the method of amortizing certain items, will often create differences between accounting practice and tax law requirements. Banks therefore should require that any changes in the method of determining accrued amounts be checked for their tax implications. Generally, changes in accounting methods require prior permission of the IRS. When they install more sophisticated computer systems, banks often make changes in the determination of income or expense items that may require IRS approval (unless the bank wants to keep duplicate records of these items).

Securities

In the past, securities transactions often created timing differences for tax purposes. Book and tax accounting are now generally the same. When gains and losses are recognized, the treatment of dividends or interest, cost of acquisition, and the like are normally the same for book and tax purposes. The key issue for many banks is how to treat income from municipal securities. The tax law still provides that most municipal securities generate tax-exempt interest income. The problem lies in the disallowance of all or a portion of the cost of the interest associated with carrying these securities. After the 1982, 1984, and 1986 tax law changes, increasing percentages of the interest cost to carry municipal securities are disallowed as Federal income tax deductions, changing the effective yield of these securities on a tax-equivalent basis. Bankers should consider the impact of these provisions when considering whether to sell or purchase municipal securities. For many banks the new provisions will make the securities acquired prior to the new law more valuable to hold to maturity than to sell or exchange.

Loans

Tax accounting for loans also involves understanding the financial accounting methods and analyzing the tax methods. Particular concerns include the proper timing of the recognition of fees and points charged to the customer as well as the methods used to calculate interest. The IRS' original-issue discount regulations require specific methods to be used in recognizing income on discounted loans. Historically, many banks have used various methods of accounting, and they may have to consider changing accounting methods if these do not comply with the tax accounting rules. The concept of original-issue discount is to recognize the income on the asset on a level-yield basis over the life of that asset.

Accounting for long-term loans such as mortgages raises special problems. Industry experience usually indicates that few mortgages run their full life. Thus many banks have used accounting methods that recognize the discount on mortgages and related points and fees as income over the expected life of the portfolio. This method, while generally acceptable for accounting purposes, may not be acceptable for tax purposes. For tax purposes the original-issue discount rules imply a mortgage-by-mortgage accounting for these items and recognition of unamortized balances if the mortgage is paid off early. Fortunately, these calculations may be made by many computerized accounting systems. From a planning viewpoint, this area requires tax knowledge to be applied in determining appropriate accounting and system practices.

Another loan area involves recognizing income on past-due loans. Many bank policies provide that loans beyond a certain past-due period will be placed in a nonaccrual status. When the loans are determined to be on nonaccrual, the bank should review the tax rules for determining nonaccrual status. The tax rules, while not altogether clear, generally require that income should be accrued as long as there is a reasonable prospect of collection (considering the borrower's capacity to repay). For tax purposes temporary liquidity problems of the borrower may not meet the test of nonaccrual.

Loan Loss Reserves

Banks have long covered expected loan losses through providing a loan loss reserve. This is appropriate for both financial statement and regulatory purposes. Because Congress apparently believed the loan loss reserve was an unwarranted income tax deduction, they discontinued the availability of the loan loss reserve for banks with over $500 million in assets beginning in 1987. The new law will also require the recapture of existing reserves of those banks over the next four years under certain optional methods. This action will create differences between the financial and tax reporting requirements. It will also shift the IRS' focus from determining the bad debt reserve based on a formula to reviewing the validity of a bank's loan chargeoffs. While many bankers, regulators, and accountants view this rule change as unwarranted, an effective bank tax plan will nevertheless have to accommodate it.

Banks must now focus on the proper time for charging off problem loans, too. Generally, it will be most beneficial to maximize chargeoffs in the earliest possible tax year. If recoveries of some magnitude are received in a subsequent year, the IRS may attempt to apply hindsight to the chargeoffs. (Chargeoffs may be expected to be the subject of future contention.) What further action Congress may take in the reserve area may depend on the scope and magnitude of problem loans.

Property and Equipment

For tax purposes, capital cost recovery on bank buildings and equipment must be determined on the basis of recovery periods and methods established by the Internal Revenue Code. Frequently, these methods differ from those used for financial accounting purposes, and thus they require separate calculations. The tax planning process should note and track these differences accurately.

Other Assets

Frequently, the other asset accounts contain many areas where tax planning and tax accounting must be reconciled. Accounting methods required for tax purposes may vary from those used for financial accounting purposes. The recognition of income and expense items related to workouts of loans and repossessed property requires careful analysis to determine their tax status. Foreclosures in particular should be reviewed.

The treatment of prepaid accounts generally follows financial accounting standards when applied to expense items. Some banks have been required to capitalize operating supplies as an inventory item for tax purposes while the items are expensed as received for accounting purposes.

The most important planning objective here is to understand the timing differences between financial and tax accounting—and to predict the effect of timing differences on the current year's taxable income. This entails making an inventory of the accounts and comparing the accounting methods. As new accounts are established, the accounting methods should be established with an understanding of any differences between financial and accounting practices.

Intangible Assets

In many bank acquisitions, a premium price is paid either for the bank or for the assets acquired. Depending on the form of the transaction, the tax accounting rules may offer an opportunity to assign some or all of the premium paid to amortizable intangible assets. Because this area is quite complex, banks involved in acquisitions should carefully review these transactions to determine the range of alternatives. In recent years, intangible values have been assigned to core deposits, favorable leases, values of credit card portfolios, work-force-in-place, and other items. The attitude of the IRS generally has been to challenge these assigned values. From a conceptual standpoint, it is proper to determine intangible values and their amortization over an expected useful life. The controversial issues are raised by methods of establishing value, of determining useful life, and of distinguishing intangibles from nonamortizable good will. Several cases are pending in this area, so banks involved should carefully plan transactions to maximize their potential tax benefits, preferably by planning before closing any acquisition arrangement.

Deposits

Dealing with deposit accounts involves understanding the tax accounting methods used to compute interest and any service charges or fees associated with the accounts. Generally, the interest will be treated as taxable to the depositor and deductible to the bank in the year in which it accrues. Recent changes in the tax law have virtually eliminated the ability to shift income or deductions between taxable years.

The treatment of service charges or fees generally provides that they should be recognized as income in the earlier of whichever year they are earned or received.

Tax planning in this area essentially involves a review of accounting methods and a review of methods for computing income and fees. There are significant compliance issues associated with deposit accounts, in particular the required reporting of interest on 1099s. Penalties for noncompliance in these areas may be substantial.

Other Liabilities

The bank's tax planning for other liabilities is likewise related to its tax accounting methods. Generally, the rules for accrual of liabilities and related expenses require that all events necessary to establish the amount and certainty of the liability must be established. This prohibits reserves for estimated expenses where the liability is uncertain. When unusual situations arise in determining a liability, it is appropriate to question the timing of its recognition for tax purposes. Matters related to disputed claims frequently require tax analysis. For those banks that can retain the cash method of accounting for tax purposes, determination of liabilities will be less important, but it may also result in deferring the tax recognition of expenses.

Capital Accounts

All transactions involving the bank's capital accounts may have tax significance. The form of new capital that qualifies for regulatory purposes may be either stock or certain types of long-term debt instruments. Many banks prefer to maximize long-term debt because interest on their debt is deductible while dividends on stock are not. The use of preferred stock has also been popular since the dividends received by corporate shareholders may in certain circumstances benefit from the dividends-received deduction. This may effectively lower the bank's cost of new capital. The determination of the taxability of dividends paid on bank stock will depend on the tax concept of "earnings and profits" that defines the status of distributions made with respect to stock. This analysis should be an ongoing part of the bank's tax records. For most banks, dividend distributions will be taxable, but for banks that have experienced significant losses or for those that have been involved in corporate reorganizations or acquisitions, the determination of earnings and profits is likely to change the tax character of certain dividends to their shareholders.

Income Accounts

Recognition of income, for most banks, will be computed using the accrual basis of accounting, and tax planning opportunities will open up in regard to the income. As discussed earlier, the new tax laws are less flexible in this area. Nonetheless, the changing rate structure will make it more attractive to postpone the recognition of income into later years when it may be taxed at lower rates. The planning objectives of many banks to maintain a significant investment in tax-exempt municipal securities will continue to tax shelter those banks to the extent that income on grandfathered bonds (those not subject to a full disallowance of related interest expense) continues. Thus decisions to liquidate particular securities holdings to recognize income for financial accounting purposes should be reviewed for tax consequences. Sale of other assets such as portions of loan portfolios or branch buildings should also be planned to take advantage of opportunities to defer income. The structuring of the transaction for tax purposes and the timing of the sale are usually what demands attention.

Expenses

Primary concerns in determining the tax status of expenses likewise relate to their timing. Issues frequently arise around the timing of expense amounts and their current deductibility. Generally, interest is required to be deducted on the cash or accrual method depending on the bank's tax accounting method. Most bank operating cost represent proper tax deductions in the year incurred although certain amounts may not be deducted. For example, fines and penalties are nondeductible as is interest related to carrying certain tax-exempt securities. Beginning in 1987, 20 percent of the cost of business meals will likewise be nondeductible. The record-keeping requirements to track nondeductible items should also be considered. Other areas where frequent timing differences exist between financial and tax accounting include employee benefit plans and stock option arrangements with executives. Each such arrangement should be reviewed for tax consequences.

The Computation of Tax

Historically, the tax computation for most banks was relatively simple—a matter of applying the tax rates to the taxable income and reducing the computed tax by allowable credits. In the future, as a result of the Tax Reform Act of 1986, many banks will have to be concerned with the corporate Alternative Minimum Tax. This tax will cause many banks to pay tax currently because its computation is more nearly focused on the economic income of the bank rather than the traditional method of computing taxable income. A new preference, representing one-half of the difference between financial statement income and income reported under regular tax accounting rules, will be a factor in determining the alternative minimum tax. The alternative minimum tax will be computed at a rate of 20 percent, and if the amount of the tax is larger than the regular tax, the bank will be required to pay the higher amount. Certain carryover and credit provisions of the law are designed to avoid taxing the same income twice under these rules. The focus of banks in future tax planning will absolutely require an understanding of this complex area of taxation.

SUMMARY

This discussion constructs a framework for understanding the fundamentals of tax planning for banks. Steady management attention to tax planning may save the bank many dollars in taxes while increasing its shareholders' capital and return on investment. Careful analysis is the first step toward reaping the full range of these benefits. Inattention to tax planning can cause banks to let opportunity slip away—with a corresponding negative effect on earnings. Staying up-to-date on tax matters becomes more important as our tax system continues to evolve and develop greater intricacy in most areas.

CHAPTER THIRTY-THREE

Risk Management

Douglas G. Hoffman

CPCU—ARM
Tillinghast, a Towers Perrin Company

Bank risk management has been defined in various ways. In perhaps its narrowest and least correct sense, it is applied to the bank insurance purchasing function. In a broader, more correct sense, it is used in the overall assessment, control, and funding of accidental loss exposures. In an even broader and equally correct context, it refers to the management of dynamic risks surrounding lending and deposit-taking activities where interest rate hedging is applied as one management technique.

Although these definitions have emerged from different perspectives, their objectives are clearly not incompatible. Each has developed as a means of conserving the banking institution's assets in the face of risk or loss potential. In fact, bank risk management in the near future may encompass all three definitions under a single organizational structure.

In this chapter we will focus primarily on the predominant definition, which gives the purpose for "state of the art" risk management techniques. That is, conservation of the bank's resources, earnings, and services against the effects of accidental loss or destruction at a minimum reasonable "cost of risk." Cost of risk is generally defined as the sum of:

- *Retained losses*—losses that are self-insured, uninsured, or retained within insurance policy deductibles.
- *Insurance premiums*—funds paid to the bank's insurers for services and financial protection against catastrophic loss and risks that the bank cannot afford to bear without such protection.
- *Risk control expenses*—funds used for the control of risk (loss prevention) and the reduction of accidental loss.

- *Administrative expenses*—costs for administering the bank's risk and insurance management function.

This chapter focuses on the process of risk management, including the key elements and recent developments in the field as well as trends and expectations for the future.

THE RISK MANAGEMENT PROCESS AND DISCIPLINE

The risk management process involves five interrelated elements:

- Exposure identification.
- Risk evaluation.
- Risk control.
- Risk Finance.
- Administration.

Banking activities are continually evolving in response to changing markets. The societal and legal environment in which banks operate is also constantly changing. As a result, new loss exposures emerge and must be continually evaluated, controlled, and financed. The overall risk management process and its administration therefore must be applied continuously. Exhibit 1 illustrates the continuity of the process.

As a discipline, risk management is relatively new. It evolved from the insurance industry after it was recognized that the traditional insurance process could no longer solve problems of risk effectively and economically in all situations.

As a reflection of this evolution, the organization representing corporate professionals in the field changed its name from the National Insurance Buyers Council in 1955 to the American Society of Insurance Management, and in 1975 to the Risk & Insurance Management Society (RIMS). The recognized professional designation—the associate in risk management (ARM)—was established in 1972 by the Insurance Institute of America. Prior to this time, the ARM program existed only as continuing education and resulted in a certificate of course completion.

Specific to bank risk management, the American Bankers Association (ABA) recognized the evolution of risk management by renaming its insurance and protection division the security and risk management division in 1983. From an educational standpoint, the ABA began its sponsorship of a national conference on financial institution risk management in 1982. Tillinghast/Towers Perrin began publishing *BankRisk—The Bank Risk Management Quarterly* in 1983.

Because of its relative youth, the risk management discipline has not yet developed generally accepted principles similar to those of

EXHIBIT 1   Risk Management Continuum

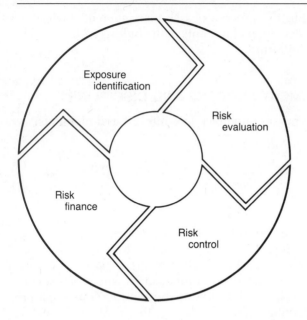

the accounting profession although some informal principles are beginning to emerge. Table 1 outlines 15 such principles and their relation to each element in the process.

These guiding principles have emerged from risk management practices applied to banks as well as other industries and organizations. With these principles any banking organization can evaluate the relative effectiveness of its risk management efforts.

EXPOSURE IDENTIFICATION

The first and most logical step in the risk management process is a thorough identification of important bank resources and the major loss exposures that can affect them. Initially, this step should include a systematic and continuing inventory of bank resources (Principle 1). In general, bank resources can be classified as:

- Physical resources—This category includes resources such as bank buildings, furniture, fixtures, data processing equipment, critical records, credit card blanks, vehicles, and (in some cases) fine arts. Aircraft, railroad cars, trucks, and ships may be resources under certain types of leasing agreements. The key to

TABLE 1   Emerging Risk Management Principles

Element	Guiding Principle
Exposure identification	1. Complete knowledge of resources.
	2. Complete knowledge of major accidental loss exposures.
Risk evaluation	3. Knowledge of the "values" of resources.
	4. Measurement of "current" risk.
	5. Forecasting of "future" risk and losses.
Risk control	6. Coordination of risk control within organizational objectives.
	7. Creation of incentives for reducing risk and potential or actual loss costs.
	8. Maintenance of systematic monitoring of the effectiveness of various risk control programs.
Risk financing	9. Application of a broad approach to risk financing using all available financial resources.
	10. Maintenance of appropriate financial protection for "catastrophes."
	11. Allocation of risk financing costs among operating units on equitable, understood, and acceptable bases.
Administration	12. Senior management commitment.
	13. A clearly designed risk management structure.
	14. Clearly targeted annual objectives.
	15. Sound communications with all affected levels of management.

the identification of physical resources is financial responsibility, which can take the form of direct ownership through purchases, foreclosures or repossessions, legal responsibility through leases and other contracts, or professional responsibility as in the trust area.

- Human resources—A bank's most critical resource is its people. Here the process should involve the identification of key directors, officers, and specialists inside the organization, and important customers and service providers outside the organization.
- Financial resources—These resources consist of capital, deposits, and collateral in the form of cash, securities, and precious metals. They should be identified by source, and will usually involve some combination of customers, shareholders, and government agencies.
- Natural resources—These include the availability of water and energy, and are most critical to banks with respect to uninterrupted operation of data processing facilities.

- Intangible resources—While difficult to identify in many cases, the effect of intangible resources can be very real. The dependence on swift, efficient, and reliable telecommunications services may be one of the most critical for banks today. Skilled police and fire protection is another intangible resource. Others include an adequate base of conscientious and in many cases skilled labor at reasonable wage levels and, perhaps most important, customer and public confidence in the bank and the banking system.

The resource identification process can be initiated through the use of universal bank resource checklists and personnel information already on file. The process should be maintained, however, through the application of identification techniques such as a systematic review of major capital expenditures, long-range plans, new merger or acquisition candidates, and marketing research studies for customer information. Many banking institutions have found themselves facing major unfunded loss exposures unexpectedly because they had not considered risk management part of the long-range planning or merger and acquisition processes. Consider the case of the regional bank that acquired a small community bank only to discover after the acquisition was consummated that in addition to assets it had also just acquired $1.2 million of underreserved pension liabilities.

The exposure identification process does not end with an inventory of bank resources. The second step consists of the identification of major loss exposures that can adversely affect those resources (Principle 2). In general terms, those loss exposures can be classified under four major headings:

1. Direct exposures—This category includes all direct physical damage exposures that may result in partial or total loss to bank resources as caused by perils under human control such as fire, explosion, transportation risks, vandalism, and both internal and external crime. Direct exposures can also include natural perils such as earthquake, flood, and windstorm.

When considering human resources, these exposures can also include death, disability, and accidental injury. In recognition of exposures to human resources, many banks have implemented wellness programs to combat specific exposures of illness, obesity, and addictions to drugs, alcohol, and smoking. Another important human resource exposure includes kidnap and hostage as well as injury from terrorism.

2. Indirect exposures—Because many direct exposures can have equally or more important secondary consequences, risk management professionals usually cite the latter separately. These indirect expo-

sures include the potential for loss of earnings or extra expense to continue operations following a direct physical damage loss. In most cases, the extra expense exposure is usually emphasized to a greater extent because banks generally cannot afford a protracted shutdown. They are therefore forced to incur nearly any cost necessary to continue operations. And almost without exception, the exposure is greatest at a bank's data processing center where the need to implement backup contingency plans can cost anywhere from $500,000 to several million dollars depending on the volume of processing.

On the earnings side, several types of contingent loss are possible. One bank operating in a remote offshore location recently identified major loss exposures involving the potential loss of interest income on investments should its telecommunications with mainland locations be interrupted. Another in a less exotic location viewed the loss of its check processing capabilities and inability to process its daily cash letters as its most severe earnings exposure.

3. Third-party liability exposures—A third major category of loss exposures involves the area of third-party legal liability. This area can consist of unintentional or intentional tort (a wrong against an individual or specific members of the public as opposed to criminal wrongs against society), contractual, or statutory liability. Given the current litigiousness of today's society and the potential severity of these exposures, third-party liabilities may represent the most critical risk problem for banks and all organizations operating in the United States today.

The most common types of liability exposures that banks face include advertising, automobile/vehicular, contractual, directors' and officers', discrimination, employee benefit plan and fiduciary (employee and customer) risks, employer's (including workers' compensation), liquor (incidental), personal injury, premises, and products (incidental related to bonus and premium programs) liability.

In addition to these more common exposures, some banks have exposures to aircraft and watercraft liability, particularly when bank staff use their own aircraft or watercraft on bank business. Other exposures have emerged in the U.S. court system in recent years such as a host of risks surrounding lending or mortgage activities, including products and environmental impairment liabilities. As an example, several banks have been found legally responsible for environmental impairment and clean-up costs in excess of $1 million associated with commercial properties on which they have foreclosed loans. Another bank recently settled out of court for $250,000 on an environmental impairment suit for a property on which it still held the mortgage!

Another major emerging problem area of bank liability exposure involves the broad classification of *professional* liability. Here suits have involved errors and omissions with regard to improper investment or legal advice, release of information (correct or incorrect), negligent repossessions, incorrect data processing for third parties, electronic funds transfer errors, or failure to perform banking activities on a timely basis. And, in addition to the contingent loan exposures cited above, some banks have found themselves the subject of lender liability suits, involving misrepresentations of rates, imprudent or unfair lending practices, or actual conspiracies to cause the borrower's demise!

4. Speculative, market and other exposures—A fourth, and potentially catastrophic exposure classification includes speculative, market, and other "nonaccidental" loss exposures. The speculative category includes three principal financial business risks. These include credit, liquidity, and interest rate exposures. In short, credit exposures are the basic risk of loan nonrepayments. They can have organizational, national, and international consequences based on the bank's geographic scope of operations. Liquidity exposures involve the inability to obtain funds in the money markets at all or at a reasonable cost, thereby being exposed to asset and liability mismatches. Interest rate exposures involve the effect of inflation.

Market exposures are sometimes differentiated from interest rate exposures. The former usually occurs when a bank is forced to sell a long-term fixed rate instrument, such as a bond, at a price below face value. Other exposures can include strategy risk, involving decisions related to the entry into specific lines of business; capital risk exposures or earnings risk; and overhead exposures, the risk of uncontrolled bureaucracy and mismanagement.

Traditionally these speculative, market, and other risks have been managed by senior management, independent of a formal risk management function. Nevertheless, they should all be recognized as major loss exposures, and appropriate subjects for the risk management process.

Methods for the identification of major loss exposures are clearly more subjective than those applied in the case of resource identification. From the perspective of Principle 2—a complete knowledge of major accidental loss exposures—the base of information should not be gathered in a central location and then left to stagnate. Instead, this portion of the exposure identification effort should be undertaken with *two* key objectives in mind: to gather exposure information on a systematic basis for the later application of risk treatment measures *and* to create an awareness of major loss exposures on the part of all operating personnel.

The following tools and techniques can be applied as part of the information gathering effort:

- Annual or more frequent risk assessment interviews with key bank officers.
- Review of major contracts and legal agreements for loss exposures accepted through these documents.
- Physical inspections and/or surveys at key bank locations (for example, data processing facilities, vault locations, wire transfer locations).
- Review of world banking and insurance literature for new and unusual loss occurrences.

Portions of these techniques, such as the risk assessment interviews, will naturally serve to create an awareness for exposures among operating personnel. Others can include:

- Preparation of annual risk assessment documentation for operating units.
- Special evaluation of data processing and other key operations along with an assessment of interdependencies and shared exposures.
- An annual "futurist" review of emerging loss exposures.

The distinguishing aspect of this second set of techniques is the active communication of the results back to key personnel within individual departments, affiliates, and operating units.

RISK EVALUATION

The second step in the risk management process is the evaluation of risk inherent in each of the loss exposures that the bank has identified. It involves the application of a combination of probability, financial loss severity, and numeric loss frequency values to each exposure. Drawing from the guiding principles for risk evaluation, this implies (Principle 3) a sound valuation of resources, (Principle 4) a complete measure of current risk through loss histories and probable loss estimates, and (Principle 5) forecasts of future risks and losses.

More often than not, banks have a reasonably good understanding of most of their major loss exposures. They tend to fall short, however, on the thorough evaluation of those exposures.

The valuation of resources requires a continuous system of determining changing values for each of the major resource categories identified (Principle 3). Some banks approach this task by reviewing physical property inventories maintained in their accounting departments. Others conduct periodic property appraisals using resident expertise or professional appraisers. Some have even drawn on student resources from local engineering colleges and universities to conduct appraisals. In any case, the values should be based on replacement cost values, as opposed to original acquisition costs or market values, as the preferred valuation technique for insurance and other risk funding techniques. And, to keep values current between appraisals, they should be indexed upward using local cost of construction factors.

Other "resources" such as earnings streams can be evaluated using business interruption calculations along with estimates of potential losses of markets. Human resources can be valued to some degree by reviewing payroll records and source data from placement service firms for specialist "searches."

Once resources have been valued, the bank should make an attempt to measure its "current" risk (Principle 4). This concept requires both a qualitative and quantitative analysis of exposure and past loss data.

On the qualitative side, some banks have developed, with or without the assistance of their insurers, "maximum foreseeable loss" and "maximum probable loss" estimates for the total losses that can arise from a single occurrence. These terms are generally defined as follows:

- Maximum foreseeable loss (MFL) is greatest total loss that might be suffered assuming the "worst" scenario where property and safety protection systems fail to operate.
- Maximum probable loss (MPL) is the worst loss case that could occur under expected conditions, assuming that the loss is controlled to some degree by effective protection and recovery systems.

Other subjective or qualitative risk evaluation measures can entail an extension of the key officer interviews identified earlier, whereby the discussion extends beyond the simple identification of loss exposures to include risk estimates based on probable and maximum cost estimates for a single occurrence and in the aggregate for a single year.

No single technological advancement has done more for quantitative risk evaluation analyses than the advent of the personal computer (PC). With the aid of a PC, a risk manager can and should maintain a minimum of the following reports as a foundation for the evaluation process:

- A database of incident reports with descriptions of causal factors.
- A complete five-year (or greater) loss history for both insured and self-insured losses. The latter should include a record of self-insured accidental operational losses, including credit card

fraud, check losses, net teller differences, counterfeit money, defalcation, forgery, and mysterious disappearance as well as other such losses.
• A summary report of losses by "class" and/or by cause.

As an extension of these data, the bank can draw on the resources and expertise of professional actuaries to trend and develop past losses, calculate an indication of incurred but not reported (IBNR) liability losses, and review or develop liability reserves. At the very least, where a reasonable correlation to assets, deposits, revenues, or some other base can be found, a bank can and should develop loss forecasts using simple regression analyses performed on a calculator or personal computer. Needless to say, however, these analyses will only be as accurate as the data supplied by the bank. Accurate records are therefore critical for this and other risk management exercises.

Last, the bank should make an attempt at forecasting "future" risk and losses (Principle 5) in an effort to avoid the "rear-view mirror" fallacy of expecting the future simply to replicate the past. As an integral part of their planning processes, some organizations have applied a subjective form of scenario analysis similar to a Delphi technique. This approach need not be any more complex than a brainstorming session in which key managers, officers, and specialists focus on potential risk related to future banking activities. When coupled with loss forecasts based on the bank's own loss data, as well as industry losses, the resulting view of the future can be very instructive for current risk planning efforts. Most specifically, the exercise can be instrumental in determining catastrophic risk funding levels.

Similar to the exposure identification process, risk evaluation efforts should be ongoing and their results continually revised and refined to maintain a current picture of potential for loss frequencies and severities by exposure type.

RISK CONTROL

Risk control has often been referred to as the heart of the risk management process. In fact, it is the key element that differentiates risk management from insurance management. Its objective—the elimination of risk of loss or at least the reduction of the financial impact of any loss—and its place in the risk management continuum are founded on the belief that it is far better to mitigate potential losses than simply to fund their cost.

Returning to our guiding principles, the initial thesis supporting an effective risk control effort calls for (Principle 6) the coordination of control measures within overall organizational objectives. In banking institutions, this is often easier said than done. The facts of the situation are that risk control efforts in many banks are often fragmented and administratively controlled by different areas of management. While this situation is not universally disastrous from a risk management standpoint, its inherent weakness is that, without some central coordination, it may result in omissions and/or redundancies in effort throughout the bank.

Because of the spread of involvement in these cases, the mandate for coordination of risk control efforts must come from the top. A written corporate risk control policy accepted by the board of directors and communicated to all staff can serve as the foundation for coordinated efforts. Armed with such a policy, some banks have formed effective risk control or risk management working committees chaired by a risk management officer.

In most banks, an effectively coordinated risk control program would address the following areas:

- Bank protection and security—Activities in this area are governed in large part by the Bank Protection Act of 1968 and Regulation P of the Federal Reserve System. Useful guidance in these efforts is provided by the *Bank Protection Manual*, published by the ABA. It is the area in which banks traditionally have devoted the most time and expense.
- Human safety—Some banks have fully developed safety programs in place, which target both injury patterns or potential loss, and spearhead efforts to reduce the future frequency of incidents. It is advisable for these efforts also to include the development of kidnap and ransom procedures and travel policies as well as driver education programs for users of bank vehicles.
- Property conservation—Many banks have property managers dedicated to planning, construction, and maintenance activities involving bank properties. Because protection of these properties from fire and other direct physical damage perils is an integral part of both property and risk management, the individuals responsible for these functions should maintain a close working relationship. Effective guidance for property conservation activities can be found in the publications distributed by the National Fire Protection Association and other specialty organizations.
- Data processing/operations center controls—Risk controls for data processing (DP) and the bank operations center are often treated separately from other property conservation efforts and may be handled on a decentralized basis by DP management. Here the risk management officer can operate as the common thread in

bankwide control efforts by serving as a sounding board for needed DP controls and funding and by representing a fresh, disassociated view for new ideas.

At a minimum, proper DP controls should include fire detection and extinguishment measures, data and physical security measures, and some treatment of equipment, software, telecommunications, and power backups.

- Audit department—The bank auditing effort should be viewed as an integral part of the organization's overall risk control program, especially in the areas of internal and external crime exposures. Audit and security functions in banks can be referred to as the "eyes and ears" of the risk management effort. The need for a close working relationship between risk management and both of these areas is essential.

- Contractual liability controls—Contracts and agreements can harbor significant liability problems. For this reason, the risk manager should also maintain a productive working relationship with the bank's internal or external legal counsel for the review of indemnification, insurance, and other key provisions of important legal documents.

- Contingency and disaster planning—Because banks cannot afford protracted interruptions of operations, they should maintain current *and tested* contingency and disaster plans for all critical operations, including the data processing area. Norwest Bancorporation's impressive recovery from the Thanksgiving Day fire in 1982 that nearly swept away its headquarters location, will long stand as the model example for other banks in the contingency planning area. We could devote an entire chapter to the subject of contingency planning, but suffice it to state that effective contingency plans must include:

  Management commitment.
  Departmental involvement.
  Central coordination and administration.
  Written documentation.
  Testing and update phases.
  An audit function.
  Flexibility (to accommodate change).

- Other risk control efforts—Other areas of risk control are sometimes decentralized and given only partial attention or overlooked altogether. These include control of accidental loss exposures in operations of automotive vehicles, lending activities, charge card security, electronic funds transfer (EFT) security, and product liability controls for products distributed in connection with retail bonus and premium programs.

Omissions in all of the above areas can be corrected through a coordinated risk control effort. One such coordinated approach can involve a risk control committee. Where a risk control committee is formed, however, it should be kept to a manageable size and should avoid unnecessary meetings to reduce the risk of uncontrolled bureaucracy and stifled productivity and creativity.

Sound risk control principles call for a maximum incentive for reducing risk and potential or actual loss costs (Principle 7). Any incentive system must be based on useful information. This might include loss and claim reports, loss cause and accident report analyses, both for internal losses, and those incurred by peer banks. Based on reliable information, a penalty/reward system can be developed that will reduce or increase insurance and risk funding charges to individual units such as specific branches, divisions, or affiliate banks.

Last, a prudent risk control effort should include a systematic monitoring of the effectiveness of the various risk control programs in place (Principle 8). In short, this will involve the development and application of performance measurement standards for the various control programs (for example, contingency planning and testing). It also implies the need to monitor compliance through inspections of operating locations and analysis of ongoing incident and accident data.

THE RISK ASSESSMENT MATRIX.

Many professional risk managers have found that it is more meaningful to map the exposure identification, risk evaluation, and risk control elements concurrently than to view each in isolation. The consolidated approach forces the user to consider a logical progression from identification through control, rather than fall into the fallacy of focusing on risk finance and insurance as the "ultimate solutions" to all exposures identified.

This consolidated approach can be illustrated in matrix form as presented in Exhibit 2. The hypothetical bank considers its exposure to the risk of extra expense at its operations center. The matrix gives a description of the exposure, the user's evaluation in view of past loss experience, and future expectations through a potential loss scenario as well as both current and planned risk control measures.

Matrices similar to Exhibit 2 are a useful approach for summarizing the results of the risk assessment effort. They should be maintained on a word processing or personal computer system so that periodic review and update is easy. The review process should be undertaken *at least* annually, and the matrices shared with the affected operating unit and/or senior management, as appropriate.

EXHIBIT 2 Sample Risk Assessment Matrix

Loss Exposure	Risk Evaluation	Risk Control Measures
Extra Expense at Operations Center Expenses incurred to continue operations at the bank's data processing (DP)/operations center in the face of a direct physical damage loss.	**Loss Exposure** The bank has never suffered a major data processing loss. A major fire in the center's telecommunications room was reported in 1985, however, and resulted in property damage amounting to $7,500 (no data processing interruption). **Maximum Probable Loss** Data processing management and risk management staff have constructed a loss scenario that would entail 4–6 months of processing at an alternative site. Extra expenses costs have been estimated at $2.25 million.	**Major Activities in Place** *Hardware backup:* Informal agreement in place with a friendly competitor. *Software backup:* Applications are backed up weekly; data files are backed up daily. All duplicates are stored offsite. *Power backup:* An isoregulation generator was installed in 1981. *Environmental control backup:* An auxiliary air conditioner was installed in DP room in 1986. **Activities Scheduled for Next Two Years** *Hardware backup:* Bank will subscribe to a hot site service for backup of both processing applications and proof and transit. *Contingency plan:* In conjunction with bank-wide planning efforts, a DP plan will be developed. An annual testing schedule will be included.

451

In short, the risk assessment matrix can be a dynamic working tool for risk management. It forces a formal review of risk assessment and control efforts for each major loss exposure with a particular focus on available risk control tactics.

RISK FINANCE AND INSURANCE

As the first line of defense in risk treatment, risk control activities must be applied within the reasonable parameters of a cost/benefit analysis. That is, because risk of loss cannot be completely eliminated (in the absence of a total shutdown of operations), the bank must determine the point of diminishing marginal returns for risk control expenditures. Beyond this point, management must accept the fact that some level of risk will remain, and in most cases its cost must be financed.

The primary objective of risk finance is to provide sufficient funds to meet loss situations as they occur. A bank's risk financing program should be designed to provide the highest degree of cost and coverage stability while maintaining the lowest overall direct cost from year to year in view of its needs for protection against catastrophic loss. This objective implies the need for:

- Retention of risk within the financial capacity of the bank, determined by studying its current financial resources and management's level of risk aversion.
- Use of outside risk funding resources (such as insurance) on the lowest cost basis for protection against catastrophe.
- Creation of maximum stability for the bank's long-term cost of risk.

Note that insurance only represents one portion of this overall risk financing objective. Clearly, the insurance mechanism can serve as a reasonably good tool for financing certain types of catastrophic loss. The cyclical nature of the insurance market, however, makes insurance an unreliable tool in view of the bank's need for cost stability at the lowest reasonable level.

To carry out our risk management principles, banks should take a broad approach to risk financing by using all available financial resources (Principle 9). The first step in this approach should be to develop an organizational guideline, or policy, on risk retention. That is, the bank should determine its annual threshold of "pain," or its "ouch point" for self-insurance of loss. This level will usually be based on a combination of factors, including bank earnings, equity, and debt levels; on "normal loss"—the loss level that is expected to occur from year to year; and on management's level of risk aversion. It should be stated in terms of per loss and annual aggregate levels and reviewed annually in light of changing conditions.

A risk retention guideline should be organizationally-based, not viewed in terms of insurance or risk classifications. Once developed, however, individual risks should be considered for funding with the guideline in mind, not in the reverse order. All too often banks make the mistake of setting their retention guideline at the level of the lowest financial institution bond deductible they can obtain in the marketplace. Thus their risk financing program is dictated by the whims of bond underwriters, not by rational bank-based decision making.

One can make an analogy between a risk retention guideline and a lending limit. In essence, bank officers responsible for risk management should have the latitude to make risk retention decisions within their guideline similar to the authorized limits granted to lending officers. Within the guideline, officers could opt for full retention in certain risks, partial retention of others, and limited retention of certain cases where they judge appropriate insurance premium and administrative savings may not be available.

With the risk retention guideline as a threshold for decision making, the bank should consider internal methods below, and external sources of funding above, that level. Internal methods can include one or more alternatives such as direct expensing, funded or book reserves for losses, or variations of cash flow or retrospectively rated plans. External options can include, but are not limited to, conventional insurance arrangements. Others may involve credit lines, debt, governmental funding or indemnification, post-loss funding, or risk sharing arrangements through captive insurance companies.

It is clear that the insurance market has traditionally played a very important role in the external funding programs of banks. Whether the importance of that role has been overstated is debatable. What is critical, however, is that bankers responsible for risk management must have a working knowledge of the strengths and limitations of insurance and the insurance market. Because usually only larger banks can justify employing a full-time risk and insurance management specialist or consultants, most others will be forced to rely heavily on the services of their insurance agents and brokers. This naturally implies a need to limit the number of agents or brokers servicing an individual bank's account in order to avoid confusion. In the absence of very specialized banking operations such as precious metals services or unique professional services that might require the service of a specialty broker, most banks only need one qualified insurance agent or broker. If more than one is used, each should be assigned a specific area of responsibility.

It is most often the banks unsophisticated in the insurance market that make the near fatal error of selecting their agent or broker on the basis of reciprocity for deposit relationships or least-cost insurance, rather than on the basis of the agent or broker's experience and expertise in bank insurance and risk management. In the view of many professionals, there are only two valid methods of selecting an insurance agent or broker:

- Selective bidding—This approach begins with the design of specifications for one or more forms of insurance. The specifications are then distributed to a prequalified group of agents or brokers, selected on the basis of their experience and expertise in bank insurance. Each agent or broker is assigned specific insurance markets from which they can solicit bids for coverage. The ultimate selection is made on a combination of agent/broker qualifications and low bid. In general, this process should not be repeated more frequently than every four to six years. More frequent bidding has been known to cause disinterest on the part of underwriters.
- Agent/broker presentation—In this case prequalified agents or brokers are requested to make both written and oral presentations to the bank. The chosen firm is selected on the basis of the experience, expertise, presentation, and references of the proposed account team as well as the firm it represents.

The second alternative is generally considered more professional because it separates the selection of agents and brokers from the selection of underwriters. And, in essence, this recognizes the different and independent roles of these parties.

In many cases, a combination of the selective bidding and presentation approaches has been used successfully over time. That is, initially, a bank may select its agent/brokers and underwriters using a selective bidding approach. This approach is not then repeated for four to six years. In the interim, if the bank becomes discontented with its insurance program, it can "test" its choice of agent/broker through a presentation approach. (This test will either result in a replacement of the agent/brokers or a reconfirmation of the choice.)

During restricted insurance market conditions, an agent/broker selection process should avoid insurance bidding if at all possible. Inherent during these conditions is an insufficient number of insurance carriers participating in coverage lines (or insufficient competition). Under these conditions, a bidding process cannot be successful.

Last, *open* bidding situations and decision making based solely on the low bid should be avoided at all times. Open bidding implies a "free for all" in the market in the absence of insurance specifications or designated markets. It has resulted in several agents or brokers approaching the same market, withdrawing from the process, and inconsistent coverage quotations. Decision making based on low bid ignores the value of differences in coverage from underwriters and the availability of services and expertise from agents and brokers.

The most important forms of insurance coverages for banks include:

- Financial institution bond or bankers blanket bond (in essence, internal and external crime coverage).
- Computer crime insurance.
- Safe depository liability insurance.
- Registered and first-class mail insurance.
- Property insurance for buildings and contents (preferably "all risk").
- Boiler and machinery insurance.
- Electronic data processing insurance.
- Extra expense insurance.
- Commercial (or comprehensive) general liability insurance.
- Automobile liability insurance.
- Workers' compensation (and employer's liability).
- Directors' and officers' liability insurance.
- Employee benefit and fiduciary liability insurance.
- Broad form bankers' professional liability insurance (usually only available in soft insurance market conditions).
- Trust liability insurance.
- Umbrella liability insurance.

The American Bankers Association includes in-depth details on these coverages in its publication, the *Digest of Bank Insurance*. In addition, specific bank risk management periodicals provide ongoing information about the best possible coverage terms and conditions available in the marketplace.

Although still used widely as an external risk financing tool, conventional insurance coverage may be losing its sparkle for a number of banks. Extremes in the underwriting cycle from 1984 to 1986, resulting in steep premium increases and coverage restrictions, caused banks to investigate alternatives to traditional commercial insurance programs, particularly in the area of financial institutions (bankers' blanket) bond and directors' and officers' liability coverages.

As of January 1987, *BankRisk: The Bank Risk Management Quarterly* had reported on the formation of a number of single-parent bank captive insurance companies and six group captives. In combination, within their first year of operation these ventures are expected to serve over 500 financial institutions' risk financing needs, ranging from some of the smallest to the largest institutions in the United States. *BankRisk* also reported on *possible* formation of over 10 other such group captives under consideration by financial institution groups such as state banking and savings associations as well as the Securities Industry Association in cooperation with New York Stock Exchange.

Although the formation of captives probably receives greater visibility in the trade press than other financing options, banks have clearly not limited their sights to captives alone. For instance, there are numerous cases of banks and savings institutions alike that have been driven from the conventional market to full self-insurance of their directors' and officers' liability (D&O) exposures, whether on a funded or unfunded basis. (In fact, in 1986 states like Delaware began passage of specific legislation enabling self-insurance of D&O risks by resident corporations.) Similarly, because bankers' professional liability coverage is rare in both hard and soft insurance markets, many organizations remain uninsured in this area. In addition, many have employed retrospectively-rated insurance programs, essentially a form of self-insurance, on their general, automobile liability and/or workers' compensation programs for years. There are numerous permutations on all of these concepts. Perhaps some of the most intriguing, however, are those beginning to emerge in the form of the letter of credit and capital market risk financing applications underwritten by commercial and investment bankers.

Regardless of the financing technique, maintenance of appropriate catastrophe protection (Principle 10) is critical. Catastrophe is a relative term. It requires definition by the bank itself, including some consensus on the issue of "how much is enough?" This process should involve a number of activities, including several or all of the following: review of maximum foreseeable loss (MFL) and maximum probable loss (MPL) estimates, review of the bank's own financial resources and liquidity, review of limits carried by peer banks (The *Cost-of-Risk Survey* published by the Risk and Insurance Management Society and Tillinghast, the *Bank Insurance Survey* published by the ABA, and the Wyatt Comprehensive Report on Directors and Officers and Fiduciary Liability are three good sources of this information), review of insurance market availability and costs, and advice of intermediaries and consultants.

From an organizational perspective, a sound risk financing program should also provide for an allocation of costs among operating units whether they are branches or entire subsidiaries on an equitable, understood, and accepted basis (Principle 11). This system, in and of itself, may be the most effective means of creating organizational awareness for the risk management process. Make no mistake that if operating units know nothing else about the bank's risk management program, they will be well aware of its associated costs, especially those costs allocated to them! That allocation system can either make or break the unit's participation in other risk management activities. Success factors include:

- Risk costs (or "premiums") based on an equitable exposure base such as revenues, assets, deposits, payroll, person-hours, area, and the like, as well as a risk assessment modifier.
- Sharing of low or intermediate levels of loss with the units that were involved below a clearly defined level.
- Absorption of shock or random loss at the bankwide or holding company level.

In summary, risk financing has evolved well beyond its origins in the simple purchase of insurance, to fuse an entire spectrum of financial resources, services, and relations—some of which are completely independent of the insurance industry. The key to future risk financing techniques will rest on creativity and fiscal conservatism not tradition.

ADMINISTRATION

Proper administration is vital to the success of any risk management program. Its importance cannot be overstated. In fact, some might argue that any valid treatment of the risk management process should address administration first and foremost. The simple reason for not taking that approach here is that a solid description of the "working elements" of the process is necessary to serve as the foundation for administration. Without that description, it is often difficult to make any case for administration principles and strategies.

The first and essential prerequisite for an effective program is a firmly based senior management commitment to the function (Principle 12). One means of establishing this commitment is through the design and discussion of program objectives along with a plan for accomplishing those objectives. This is often done by developing a clear and simple policy statement on risk management, formally accepted by bank senior management and the bank's board of directors. The statement should be communicated to all staff and, at the least, contain (1) an objective, (2) the bank's definition of the risk management process, (3) some indication of risk retention guidelines (as discussed under risk financing) and perhaps catastrophe limit requirements, (4) designation of staff responsibility for the program, and (5) a statement on a review process by the board of directors.

It is important to recognize that a bank risk management program must be organizationally based, not wholly based on the individuals with responsibility for its administration. From the policies on which it is founded to techniques applied in exposure identification (risk evaluation, control, and finance), the job cannot be left to one or even a handful of people—staff throughout the bank must all play a part. That is not to say, however, that a completely decentralized program is implied. In all practicality, there needs to be a reasonable combination of central and decentralized staff, and this ultimate structure must clearly be defined and understood (Principle 13).

The ultimate central responsibility should reside with one person. The role may be either full- or part-time, depending on the size and complexity of the bank. Although there are no hard and fast rules, there is some precedent for maintaining a full-time risk management function with clerical support once a bank represents $1 billion or more of corporate assets. More complex financial institution operations, from a risk or exposure perspective, would warrant a lower threshold and vice versa. If the position is part-time, it is usually combined with related functions such as finance, security, property management, or legal.

The function must be visible enough to accomplish its objectives, particularly in view of the need for constant communications throughout the bank. One means of achieving visibility is to set the coordinator's position at a vice president level or higher. Where the position is only part-time, some banks have established a vice president position but highlighted risk management in the title for visibility—that is, the formal title might be vice president of risk management and bank properties.

Responsibilities of the risk management staff must be defined along with clear reporting relationships. Often banks fail in their risk management efforts because of a lack of clear direction for the staff. This is particularly true where the broad concept of risk management is new to both the bank and those charged with responsibility.

Position responsibilities and objectives should dovetail neatly with clearly defined annual objectives for the program overall (Principle 14). In practice the program objectives should set the stage for individual objectives. One reliable means of setting risk management objectives for banks has been through the use of an annual statement on cost of risk (COR)—a barometer of risk management expenses. Using consistent components from year to year, COR can be a meaningful tool for monitoring risk management performance. All components can be maintained on a personal computer-based risk management information system.

Because external factors, such as extreme industrywide premium increases or savings in the insurance market, can wreak havoc with cost-based objectives, COR should not be applied in a vacuum. Other program objectives should include nonfinancial goals and reviews. For instance these can include risk assessments in a designated number of operating units each year (similar to the objectives of an audit department), implementation of specific risk control programs, or implementation of new computer applications for the bank's risk management information system. From an independent perspective, the bank can also undertake periodic audits of its risk management program either with an in-house staff or an outside firm.

Last, a sound risk management effort requires open and two-way communications with all affected levels of management (Principle 15). At the highest level, risk management staff should interact with senior management and the board. One clear opportunity for this interaction is the Federal Reserve requirement of an annual review of insurance coverages by the board. The risk manager should seize this opportunity to make annual reports on the state of the program, focusing on major loss exposures, new risk control efforts, COR, the status and outlook for the bank insurance market, its impact on the bank and its program, and major unfunded loss exposures self-insured voluntarily or involuntarily.

At another level, risk management staff should interact with operating management. One technique is the formation of a working risk management or risk control committee. In addition, some risk managers have been very successful at coordinating seminar or conference programs with key departments such as lending, audit, or legal. Interaction might also consist of facility surveys, brief written risk management bulletins or manuscripts, interviews, or cost allocation systems.

CONCLUSION

The risk management process is dynamic and broad-based. To be effective, it should never be allowed to stagnate. It should be as flexible and active as the organization itself. If run in this fashion, it can help banking institutions anticipate more effectively the risks of the future.

PART SIX

Investment Instruments and Markets

CHAPTER THIRTY-FOUR

Market Instruments and Market Structure for Short-Term Liquid Investments

Lynda Swenson

Formerly Investment Officer
Bank One, Columbus, N.A.

Richard D. Lodge

Senior Vice President
Bank One, Columbus, N.A.

The market for short-term liquid investments is more commonly referred to as the money market. It is a wholesale market for high-quality, short-term instruments. The instruments of the money market are constantly evolving and developing as the needs of issuers and investors change. It is a market where innovation flourishes. Other salient features of the money market include numerous and diverse participants, large dollar value trades, the importance of the telephone in connecting participants on a worldwide basis, and the lack of a central marketplace. The money market is not just one market but instead is a collection of markets that service distinct and different participants.

Money market instruments are diverse; in general they are one year or less in maturity. A list of money market instruments would generally include Federal funds (Fed funds), repurchase agreements (repos), Eurodeposits, all types of certificates of deposit (CDs)—domestic, Euro, Yankee, floating rate—bankers' acceptances (BAs), commercial paper, some U.S. Treasury securities, and the related futures and options.

Money market participants will vary from instrument to instrument. Often an issuer of an instrument will also be an investor in that particular market as well as others. In general, investors include commercial banks, savings and loans, corporations, state and local governments, various funds, and individuals. The money market brings together investors with surplus funds and qualified borrowers who need funds. The participants are aided by brokers and dealers; brokers functioning strictly to make deals between participants and collect a fee for the service; dealers who more broadly are making markets (buying and selling) as well as owning instruments that they may follow. It should be noted that one of the most important market participants is the Federal Reserve Bank.

Commercial banks are important players in the money market. Banks use the markets for funding their activities—issuing CDs, entering repo agreements, or selling BAs. Banks also use the market for investments, holding money market instruments as a form of secondary reserves. These secondary reserves are near-cash assets which can be converted into cash quickly at or near cost, thereby avoiding serious loss of principal. Money market instruments are held more for liquidity than yield in many banks; the bank will look to its liquid assets to meet potential deposit withdrawals and to meet potential increases in the demand for loans. This emphasis is in contrast to the investment portfolio which generally represents the more permanent investment of surplus funds for income.

THE MATH[1]

One of the challenges of the money market is to compare the returns or yields on various instruments. To analyze a Treasury bill discount with a EuroCD interest rate requires the computation of equivalency— to make apples and oranges into peaches. Inexperienced investors have made many decisions that were based on incorrect mathematics.

Two fundamental relationships are at the beginning of mathematical analysis for money market instruments: the relationship of risk and return, and the relationship of price and yield. The risk/return relationship is very simple: As the perceived level of risk increases, the return will increase. Perceived risk can include many factors: credit risk, interest rate risk, market risk, and sovereign risk. As the market evaluates various alternatives, those with a higher risk in any or all areas will have to pay up and provide a greater return in order to be accepted by the buyer.

The second fundamental relationship is between price and yield. As interest rates in the market rise (fall), the market price of outstanding fixed income securities will fall (rise). Price and yield move inversely. For example, a $1,000 bond with an 8 percent coupon produces $80 per year in interest. If interest rates on similar instruments are

---

[1]A definitive work in the area is Marcia Stigum's *Money Market Calculations: Yields, Break-Evens, and Arbitrage* (Homewood, Ill.: Dow Jones-Irwin, 1981).

now 9 percent in the market, the price of the 8 percent coupon bond must fall to achieve the current market yield. The yield/price relationship has some interesting characteristics. When prevailing interest rates change, the prices of longer term coupon bonds will change more dramatically than shorter term coupon bonds. Also, the prices of lower coupon bonds will have a greater percentage change than higher coupon bonds.

Money market instruments are of two essential types—discount and interest-bearing. Within each type are more categories based on the method of accrual of interest. The value of mathematical analysis is to make the various instruments' yields comparable so as to make the most rational investment decision.

DISCOUNT

Examples are U.S. Treasury bills, bankers' acceptances, and commercial paper. These instruments are issued at a price less than face value and mature at face value. The interest is the difference between cost and face value. Discount yield is recalculated into equivalent bond yield to facilitate the comparison with U.S. Treasury coupon securities. To calculate the equivalent bond yield for discount instruments with 182 days or less to maturity:

$$\frac{\text{Equivalent}}{\text{bond yield}} = \frac{365 \text{ (Rate of discount)}}{360 - [(\text{Rate of discount}) \text{ (Number of days)}]}$$

For discount instruments with more than 182 days to maturity, the formula is much more complex due to the compounding element. Fortunately, this calculation's results appear on daily quote sheets in various publications, and are easily computed on investment calculators.

INTEREST-BEARING

Examples of this include municipal notes and certificates of deposit. Normally these are issued at face value, mature on some specified date, and pay coupon interest. Interest-bearing instruments are compared on the basis of yield to maturity. This calculation takes into account not only the coupon interest but also any capital gain (loss) that the investor might realize based on the purchase price and the maturity value. The calculation of the yield to maturity is complicated as it represents a present value for future principal and interest payments as well as the present value for any capital gain or loss.

The basis for accrual of interest for money market instruments must also be considered in any evaluation. Accrual basis has two com-

TABLE 1   Number of Days in a Month/Year for Money Market Instruments

30/360	*Actual/360*	*Actual/365(366)*
Fed agency notes	Certificates of deposit	U.S. Treasury notes
Municipal bonds	Fed funds	and bonds
Municipal notes	Repos	Municipal notes
	Eurodeposits	
	Municipal notes	
	Discount securities	
	U.S. Treasury bills	
	Bankers' acceptances	
	Commercial paper	

ponents: how many days in each "monthly" period and how many days in the "year." This is especially important as it is advantageous to get a year's worth of interest in 360 days rather than 365 or 366 days. Table 1 shows money market and security instruments, and the basis of number of days in a month / number of days in a year.

A note of caution in using this list. A particular issuance of a security may have an accrual basis that is different from what is listed.

FEDERAL FUNDS

Federal funds (or Fed funds) are excess reserves of banks. A primary banking equation is that depositors' monies minus required reserves equals lendable and/or investable funds. Large money center banks traditionally find a shortage of depositors' funds relative to loan and investment needs; country banks are more generally deposit rich. Bringing these parties together through the exchange of excess reserves is the function of the Fed funds market.

The Fed funds market has its roots in interbank trades beginning in the 1920s; it became a very active market in the 1950s when brokering of one-day money was pegged to the discount rate. Money center banks were active buyers from downstream country bank correspondents in the 1960s until high interest rates prompted those downstream correspondents to look for investment opportunities with higher rates of return. The disparity between an artificially low discount rate (which was the pegged Fed funds rate) and other investment rates prompted money center banks to begin to buy Fed funds above the discount rate in 1964, and the market pricing of Fed funds began.

The Fed funds rate and activity is a closely watched and analyzed indicator of the short-term market. Until October 6, 1979, the Federal Reserve Board was extremely concerned about the day-to-day fluctuations in the Fed funds rate and would take appropriate action to peg the rate within a narrow and predetermined range. Since October 6, 1979, however, the Fed has monitored reserves and pays less attention to daily fluctuations in the Fed funds rate.

The majority of Fed funds transactions are for overnight or over-weekends (Friday, Saturday, and Sunday). Term Fed funds are for trades longer than one business day. Term Fed funds sold are considered a loan by Federal Reserve regulation and therefore are subject to a bank's legal lending limit to any particular bank. Fed funds purchased and term Fed funds purchased are classified as a borrowing (not a deposit) and as such are not subject to reserve requirements or FDIC insurance.

The typical Fed funds transaction is, in essence, an unsecured loan agreement; the seller loans (sells) excess reserves to the borrower (purchaser). Most banks therefore sell only to those banks which are considered good credit risks and are on an approved credit list.

The Fed funds desk at most banks has two major functions: to maintain required reserves and to manage reserves so that the bank does not hold excess reserves that can't be carried over to the next settlement period. Accomplishing these objectives requires the Fed funds market. A bank may be a buyer and seller of funds in the same day; buying from downstream correspondents and selling in the open market as an example. Some Fed funds desks are aggressive traders of Fed funds, buying from one broker to sell to another for a 1/16 percent pick up. The Fed funds desk uses brokers to handle most transactions. The Fed funds market is frantically paced, especially on settlement day as banks attempt to buy and sell funds to bring reserve positions into line.

Fed funds income (expense) is calculated as:

$$\text{Rate} \times \text{Principal} \times \frac{\text{Number of days}}{360}$$

REPURCHASE AGREEMENTS

Repurchase agreements are more commonly called repos or RPs. A repo is the acquisition of funds through the sale of securities with a simultaneous agreement by the seller of the securities to repurchase them at a specified price on a specified date. The near effect of the two simultaneous transactions is to create a secured loan with a guaranteed buy back of the collateral supporting that loan. A reverse repurchase agreement (reverse) is the same transaction when viewed as searching for a security rather than funds.

Repos began after World War II when security dealers used them to finance security holdings. The Federal Reserve amended Reg D in

1969 and exempted repos done by banks against the U.S. Treasury and Federal agency issues from reserve requirements which made repos a desirable source of funding. In 1974 banks' holdings of U.S. government securities that had been pledged to support Treasury tax and loan balances were freed when the Treasury moved TT&L to the Federal Reserve Banks; this allowed banks to use their security holdings as collateral for repos. Repos have increased as corporate treasurers, state and local governments, and investors have found them to be a flexible and secure investment instrument. Banks have used repos as a cheaper source of funding that is not subject to Reg Q ceilings or reserve requirements; most banks finance their U.S. government security positions with repo funds.

Although a repo can be tailored to meet the exact requirements of the two parties involved, most repos have some general characteristics. A repo is priced at the market including the accrued interest on the underlying collateral security. The repo's principal will be based on the value assigned to the collateral security, which is usually at a discount from the current market price of that security. The amount of discount (called margin or haircut) is a negotiable part of the transaction. The lender of funds seeks greater margin to insulate him from a rise in market interest rates and the corresponding fall in the collateral security's price and value; the borrower of funds seeks a smaller margin to protect against a fall in market interest rates which might result in the collateral's value exceeding the funds borrowed.

Most repos are overnight transactions though term repos are not uncommon. Open-ended or "continuing contract" repos are a convenience to both parties and often allow collateral substitutions. Many banks use repos to meet customer requests in addition to funding the bank's security holdings. A bank can run a book in repos and reverses: repoing securities to bank customers and reversing securities from dealers.

The Federal Reserve uses repos and reverses as a means to affect member bank reserves. When the Fed does repos with security dealers, reserves are added to the monetary system. Reverses take away reserves.

Repos have gotten bad publicity in the last several years. The collapse of some security dealers has had devastating effects on municipalities and financial institutions who had repo agreements with those dealers. In some cases, the lender of funds did not have a "perfected" interest in the collateral and so ended up with an unsecured borrowing. In other cases, the volatility of interest rates and the amount of margin given created a collateral value different than the funds lent. Despite these problems, repos are still widely used throughout the country.

The income or expense on a repo/reverse transaction is calculated as:

$$\text{Rate} \times \text{Repo value} \times \frac{\text{Number of days}}{360}$$

EURODEPOSITS

Although an Eurodeposit doesn't technically fit in this chapter as it is not a liquid instrument, Eurodeposits form such an integral part of the money market that to exclude them would be unthinkable. An Eurodeposit is the placement of a deposit denominated in one currency in a bank or branch of a bank which normally operates in another currency. The majority of Eurodeposits are dollar-denominated in banks and bank branches outside of the United States.

Eurodollar banking began after World War II when the British government restricted the use of the British pound sterling to Commonwealth nations' trades; U.S. dollars then became more widely used to settle international trade agreements. However, the Russian government and its allies who held dollars felt more secure with London rather than U.S. banks during the Cold War of the 1950s. Banks in London, including the U.S. bank branches, began accepting dollar-denominated deposits and making dollar-denominated loans. Eurodollar banking was further stimulated by the tight money conditions in the United States during the late 1960s. Foreign branches of U.S. banks could take deposits and therefore obtain funding that was not subject to Reg Q restrictions or reserve requirements in force at that time. Since then, Eurodollar banking has continued to flourish as the U.S. trade deficit has increased.

Eurodeposits are called placements if the bank is depositing funds; a bank "takes" funds when it receives them. Eurodeposits are nonmarketable and have a fixed maturity date, fixed rate, and other specifics agreed to at the onset of the transaction. Most Eurodeposits are for one year or less, with most occurring in three- and six-month maturities. However, some Eurodeposits may be negotiated for longer or shorter periods depending on the needs of the two parties.

Brokers are an integral part of the Eurodeposit market as participants are numerous and widely dispersed throughout the world. This is a 24-hour market as business is transacted in London, New York, Singapore, Bahrain, and other booking centers. Brokers will contact clients with the day's "run"; these are LIBOR (London interbank offered rate) rates from overnight to "spot" to "the week" and various months' maturity dates. Offers are quoted to settle spot (in two days) in clearinghouse funds. Clearinghouse funds become immediately available funds on the day after the delivery of the funds, so a banker must be cognizant of weekends and holidays. Brokers will be looking for money as well as looking for someone to take money. The smallest Eurodeposit is usually $1 million.

Like Fed funds lines, a bank will have a credit line for each bank with which it intends to place Eurodeposits. Credit analysis is complicated by sovereign risk. Sovereign risk may include such factors as the threat of nationalization of the foreign bank, the nonrepatriation of interest or principal, or the relative soundness of the foreign bank involved. Most U.S. banks will limit the amount of funds placed in a particular foreign bank and will also limit the exposure to all banks in a particular country. A "difficult lender" is a bank with very restrictive lines; a "difficult borrower" is a bank who will have to pay above LIBOR to obtain funds.

Eurodeposit expense or income is calculated as:

$$\text{Principal} \times \text{Rate} \times \frac{\text{Number of days}}{360}$$

NEGOTIABLE CERTIFICATES OF DEPOSIT

Domestic

Negotiable certificates of deposit (CDs) originated in the early 1960s in response to the needs of banks for funding and the needs of cash-rich investors for negotiable alternatives to U.S. Treasury bills. CDs are issued domestically by U.S. banks to attract deposits. The minimum denomination is usually $100,000; however, a minimum of $1 million is necessary for marketability in the secondary market. Most CDs have a maturity of one to three months with some extending six months or longer. The short maturity may reflect the need of the individual investor for liquidity or the corporation for an investment until tax or dividend dates. The short maturity benefits the issuing bank in a positive yield curve scenario as the bank can fund more cheaply by rolling three-month CDs rather than issuing six-month CDs if the level of interest rates remains the same. Some banks will issue longer CDs; these generally do not trade as well.

CDs are issued in New York, and most purchases and settlements occur in New York. This is due in part to the large role which the money center banks play. Although regional banks issue CDs, they often have to pay more interest (pay up) in the market. This can be explained by a scarce supply of CDs outstanding for most regionals which creates less trading activity. The rates that major CD issuers will pay will depend on the market's perception of the financial strengths and weaknesses of the issuing bank. CDs are sold by the issuing bank directly to investors and also to dealers. Dealers operate in several ways: positioning CDs in their own portfolio, trading with other dealers, and buying and selling to investors. Brokers are not as important to this market as they are to others.

It is important to note that the "all-in cost" of a CD to the issuing bank should include an analysis of the effect of reserve requirements and FDIC premium.

If a CD has an original maturity of one year or less, interest is paid at maturity and is calculated as:

$$\text{Principal} \times \text{Rate} \times \frac{\text{Number of days}}{360}$$

If a CD has an original maturity of greater than one year, interest is paid semiannually or annually.

Eurodollar

Eurodollar certificates of deposit (EuroCD) are dollar-denominated CDs issued by foreign banks and foreign branches of U.S. banks. Introduced in 1966 as a negotiable alternative to Eurodeposits, EuroCDs became more important in the tight money periods of the 1970s. For the issuer, EuroCDs like Eurodeposits are currently subject to reserve requirements.

EuroCDs are usually issued in a minimum denomination of $1 million from one month to one year or longer. Most have an original maturity of less than six months with three and six months the most common issuance periods. EuroCDs trade at a higher yield than U.S. domestic CDs due to the perception of sovereign risk and somewhat less liquidity in the secondary market. The EuroCD rate will usually be less than a Eurodeposit rate for the same issuing bank as the EuroCD has liquidity. The EuroCD secondary market is active, and both dealers and brokers are involved with issuing banks and investors. Like Eurodeposits, settlement is two business days forward in clearinghouse funds.

EuroCD interest is calculated in the same way as domestic CDs.

Yankee

Yankee CDs are U.S. dollar-denominated CDs issued by foreign banks through their U.S. branches. Because these branches are domiciled in the United States, Yankee CDs are subject to Federal Reserve regulation like domestic CDs. Most Yankee CDs are issued with original maturities of less than one year; these CDs are subject to reserve requirements.

Yankee CDs are issued to fund dollar-denominated loans made in the United States. Issuing banks use dealers and brokers to place Yankee CDs and make a secondary market in them. Yankee CDs issued by top banks trade at higher rates than similar EuroCDs due to a thinness in the secondary market; Yankee CDs trade higher than domestic CDs due to perceived sovereign risk. Most investors look to the creditworthiness of the parent foreign bank when evaluating Yankee CDs. The typical investor in Yankee CDs is a buyer who assumes some limitation of liquidity and some increased perception of risk in exchange for a higher yield.

Yankee CD interest is calculated on the same basis as interest on EuroCDs and domestic CDs.

Floating Rate

FRCDs were first issued in the late 1970s. These are term CDs with a maturity greater than 18 months and generally less than five years. The rate of interest is adjusted periodically.

FRCDs have been issued by domestic U.S. banks, in the EuroCD market, and as Yankee CDs. The coupon adjustment can be every month, semi-annually, or other time period; the adjustment can be tied to a variety of indexes, such as LIBOR, U.S. Treasury bills, or the CD composite rate. A secondary market is made by dealers and brokers.

BANKERS' ACCEPTANCES

"Bankers' acceptances represent one type of a broad class of credit instruments known as bills of exchange. Bills of exchange are drafts, or orders to pay a specified amount at a specified time, drawn on individuals, business firms, or financial institutions. When the drawee formally acknowledges his obligation to honor such a draft, usually by stamping 'accepted' on the face of the draft, it becomes an acceptance. When a bank accepts such a draft, it becomes a banker's acceptance."[2]

The formal use of BAs by the U.S. banking system began with the Federal Reserve Act of 1913 which allowed national banks to accept

---

[2]*Instruments of the Money Market* Federal Reserve Bank of Richmond, 1981, p. 114.

time drafts. During subsequent decades the Federal Reserve encouraged the holdings of BAs by member banks by rediscounting BAs, by holding BAs for its own account (discontinued March 1977), and by buying BAs for system repos (discontinued July 1984). The Federal Reserve System has maintained the exemption of "eligible" BAs from reserve requirements for the accepting bank.

BA eligibility is determined by Fed regulations. In a simplistic analysis, an eligible BA must (1) grow out of transactions involving the import/export of goods or the domestic shipment of goods or the storage of readily marketable staples, (2) be secured by documents conveying or securing title, (3) be no longer than six months and be self-liquidating in the same time period as the underlying transaction, and (4) be marked by a stamp on the face of the BA. Finance BAs, which had no underlying collateral and generally provided working capital to businesses, were declared ineligible by the Fed in 1973. BAs are issued by banks all over the world. Eligibility is an important factor to U.S. banks who create the BA and then want to sell it in the open market. However, eligibility is not as important in the secondary market activity of foreign banks' BAs.

BAs are discount notes with maturities from 30 days to 180 days, though 90 days is most common. BAs are available in a wide variety of principal amounts and are issued in bearer form. All documentation which relates to the underlying transaction is held by the accepting bank; the BA which is delivered to investors is a simply drawn discount note.

BAs are advantageous to both the accepting bank and any later investors. The accepting bank can hold the BA in its own loan portfolio or can sell it if the bank needs funds for other asset opportunities. The investor in a BA has a money market instrument with two ultimate sources of repayment—the accepting bank and the bank's commercial customer. The market also sees "three-name" BAs when a foreign accepting bank asks a top U.S. bank to endorse its BAs. BAs are perceived by the market as a very safe and liquid instrument.

Dealers and brokers make an active secondary market in BAs. Yields are quoted as a run from one to six months for the "tops"— nine top U.S. banks, second-tier banks' BAs, Edge act banks' BAs, and foreign BAs trade "off the run" (at higher rates). Principal investors of BAs are institutions such as money market mutual funds, trust departments, state and local governments, insurance companies and other corporations, pension funds, and commercial banks.

BAs are quoted, bought, and sold on a discount basis like Treasury bills and commercial paper.

COMMERCIAL PAPER

Commercial paper is a short-term unsecured promissory note issued by various types of economic entities to finance short-term credit needs. It is one of the oldest money market instruments in America. Commercial paper began in colonial times as domestic bills of exchange which were orders written by a seller requiring a buyer to pay the seller a sum of money at some future date. Bills of exchange were the primary means of financing trade prior to the advent of a strong banking system. Throughout the 19th and into the 20th century, commercial paper was issued and sold in ways which exploited the interest rate differentials that existed between various regions of the country. In the 1920s finance companies became important issuers of commercial paper. During the 1950s and 1960s strong consumer demand for durable goods fueled the issuance of commercial paper by manufacturers. In the tight money period of the late 1960s and the early 1970s, commercial paper was the replacement for high-cost or unavailable bank loans. Commercial paper continues to be a lower cost alternative to bank loans for high credit quality companies.

It is estimated that 1,500 economic entities issue rated commercial paper. The largest type of issuer is finance companies. Finance companies use commercial paper as their primary source of funding. Non-financial entities such as major corporations and state and local governmental units use commercial paper on a more seasonable basis to bridge gaps in longer term funding. Bank holding companies are another type of issuer and use proceeds from commercial paper sales to finance subsidiaries like leasing, factoring, and so on. Foreign companies have begun to issue commercial paper in the United States; the rate they pay is generally higher than U.S. companies as investors perceive an element of sovereign risk. Investors in commercial paper are as diverse as the issuers: money center banks, state and local governments, investment firms, pension funds, money market funds, and individuals.

Commercial paper is usually issued at a discount with a minimum denomination of $100,000. The maturity must be less than 271 days to avoid SEC registration requirements; the average maturity is 30 days. Commercial paper is issued in bearer form. Due to the heterogeneity of commercial paper issuers, the shortness in maturity, and the "hold to maturity" attitude of most commercial paper investors, there is no active secondary market. Commercial paper can be issued directly to investors by in-house sales departments (finance companies) or through dealers. Many dealers who sell commercial paper stand ready to buy it back from investors.

Since commercial paper is an unsecured promissory note, only the most creditworthy institutions can issue in the marketplace. Commercial paper is rated by Moody's, Standard & Poor's, and Fitch's; criteria includes strong management, good position in well-established industry, upward trend in earnings, adequate liquidity, and the ability to borrow to pay off the commercial paper issue. Commercial paper issues have bank lines of credit backing them in the event that new commercial paper cannot be sold to pay off the maturing issue. Companies whose own credit rating is low may obtain a bank letter of credit. This unconditional pledge by the bank to redeem the commercial paper will allow the company's paper to be sold with the bank's credit rating; this will reduce the interest cost to the company and increase the marketability of the issue.

One of the more recent developments in the commercial paper area is the issuance of tax-exempt commercial paper by state and local governmental units. TXCP provides cheaper funds to the governmental unit and gives investors tax-exempt income. In other respects it is similar to taxable commercial paper.

Commercial paper is quoted, bought, and sold on a discount basis like U.S. Treasury bills and bankers' acceptances.

The next three types of money market instruments—U.S. Treasury securities, Federal agency securities, and municipal securities—will be covered in subsequent chapters, so this chapter will take only a brief look at each.

U.S. TREASURY SECURITIES

U.S. Treasury Bills

U.S. Treasury bills (T bills) are perhaps the most important instruments of the money market. Due to the high volume of Treasury debt which is outstanding, the market watches the yields and prices of Treasury securities very carefully.

T bills are issued on a regular basis in maturities of three months, six months, and one year. The minimum denomination is $10,000 with subsequent $5,000 increments. T bills are issued only in book entry form, not physical form. A T bill is a discount security sold at a price less than maturity value. The discount on a particular T bill is based on the competitive tenders submitted by investors; smaller individual investors submit a noncompetitive tender and therefore receive the average yield of all competitive bids accepted.

T bills have four characteristics which make them desirable to investors. First, the minimum denomination of $10,000 is substantially lower than other money market instruments; this increases the number of individuals who are investors in the market. Second, favorable tax treatment. T bill income is exempt from state and local taxes. Third, lack of credit risk. T bills are direct obligations of the U.S. Treasury. Fourth, their liquidity is high, so T bills can be converted into cash quickly. The liquidity is created by the large dollar amount of T bills outstanding, short maturity, and an active secondary market.

T bills are an actively traded money market instrument. Investors range from individuals to money market funds to commercial and foreign banks as well as the Federal Reserve Bank. Dealers are an important factor before the auction, at auction time, and in the secondary market as they take positions in particular issues.

U.S. Treasury Notes and Bonds

Although U.S. Treasury notes and bonds are, at original issue, not technically part of the money market due to the length of maturity, issues enter the money market when they have one or less years remaining to maturity. "Short coupons," as they are called, are not as actively traded as U.S. Treasury bills, however.

U.S. Treasury notes are issued in various denominations in maturities from one to 10 years. U.S. Treasury bonds are issued for periods greater than 10 years. Notes and bonds are sold on an interest-bearing basis with semiannual interest payments. The secondary market for notes and bonds is usually most active in the "current" issues, which are the most recently issued securities.

FEDERAL AGENCY SECURITIES

The term *agency* covers a number of U.S. government credit institutions. In general, these agencies were created by Congress to act as financial intermediaries by borrowing money in the marketplace and channeling the proceeds to specified individuals, institutions, and areas of the economy that were felt to have restricted (or expensive) access to the credit markets.

Agencies are generally (1) sponsored by the U.S. government—some are explicitly backed like U.S. Treasury issues, (2) exempt from state and local taxes, (3) considered eligible investments for national banks and state member banks, (4) acceptable as collateral for borrowing at the Fed, (5) eligible for purchase and sale by the FOMC (Federal Open Market Committee), (6) higher in yields than similar Treasury issues due to an increase in perceived credit risk and a less liquid secondary market.

Most agency debt is sold at original issue through a fiscal agent and a selling group. Most debt is sold on an interest-bearing basis though shorter term issues are often sold on a discount basis. The secondary market is well-established though not as liquid as the Treasury markets. The Federal Financing Bank (FFB) acts as a financial intermediary for some agencies which do not issue debt directly. The FFB does not include the Farm Credit System, the Federal Home Loan Banks, the Federal Home Loan Mortgage Corporation, the Federal National Mortgage Association, or the Student Loan Marketing Association.

The Farm Credit System includes the 12 Federal Land Banks, the 12 Federal Intermediate Credit Banks, the 12 Banks for Cooperatives, and the Central Bank of Cooperatives. Several of these issue money market instruments—short-term discount notes and short-term collateralized trust debentures. Most debt is in bearer form and in book entry with relatively low minimum denominations. The purpose of the Farm Credit System is to provide lower cost financing to various agricultural entities.

The Federal Home Loan Bank System is 12 regional banks which provide a credit reserve system for the thrift industry. Short-term debt issued includes consolidated discount notes and consolidated bonds. Most are issued in book entry form. The purpose is to stabilize the flow of mortgage credit to the public.

The Federal National Mortgage Association (Fannie Mae) was created to make a secondary market in FHA mortgages; this was expanded to conventional mortgages in 1970. It issues short-term notes on a discount basis; these notes are similar to commercial paper in that they can be tailored to a buyer's needs. Fannie Mae buys mortgages when mortgage money is tight and sells when demand is lessened.

Government National Mortgage Association (Ginnie Mae) was a spin off from Fannie Mae. Ginnie Mae is a government corporation under HUD and is backed by the full faith and credit of the U.S. government; it administers mortgage support programs which cannot be carried out in the private markets. It has designed mortgage-backed securities, creating pools and selling participations in those pools to investors. Most pools have original maturities greater than one year.

Federal Home Loan Mortgage Corporation (Freddie Mac) was set up to develop, maintain, and promote a secondary market in conventional residential mortgages. Its function is similar to Fannie Mae. Freddie Mac issues several types of securities that are longer than one year in original maturity. It also offers discount notes which are short-term, book entry obligations.

Federal Home Loan Bank System, Fannie Mae, Ginnie Mae, and Freddie Mac all act as financial intermediaries for the housing industry. The Student Loan Marketing Association (Sallie Mae) provides liquidity for banks, savings and loan associations, educational institutions, agencies, and others who are involved in granting loans for educational purposes. In addition to longer term issues, Sallie Mae issues nonguaranteed discount notes and nonguaranteed short term floating rate notes.

MUNICIPAL SECURITIES

Municipal securities (Munis) are debt securities issued by state and local governments and their agencies. Most Munis are long-term and do not fall into the money market arena; these are bonds issued to finance capital projects and may be "GO" (general obligation) or "revenue" (revenue-based). Short-term municipal notes are money market instruments and are generally sold to bridge a timing gap in anticipation of the receipt of other funds, such as tax payments or proceeds from a bond issue.

In general, Muni notes have similar characteristics. Maturity ranges from one month to a year with minimum denominations from $5,000 to $5 million. Most are GO and therefore have the issuer's pledge of full faith, credit, and taxing power. Most are issued in bearer form. Interest income earned by the investor is exempt from Federal taxes and is usually exempt from taxes levied by the state where the Muni note is issued. Muni notes can be rated by either Moody's or Standard & Poor's.

There are many types of Muni notes including TANs (tax anticipation notes), RANs (revenue anticipation notes), and PNs (project notes which are backed by the full faith and credit of the U.S. government). In addition, municipalities issue TXCP (tax-exempt commercial paper), and one- or seven-day demand notes or "put" notes.

Investors in short-term municipal securities include high tax bracket individuals, tax-exempt money market funds, commercial banks, casualty insurance companies, and corporations. Most investors trade Muni less often than taxable issues. This is partially due to the taxability of capital gains which might be realized versus the tax exemption of the interest income. Additionally, the secondary market is much more complex than the government or Euro market as the Muni issues are more heterogeneous.

Muni notes can be interest-bearing or discount securities; they can accrue interest in many ways. In any case, the yield should be converted to a taxable basis for comparison with other money market instruments:

$$\text{Taxable yield} = \frac{\text{Tax-exempt yield}}{(1 - \text{Marginal tax rate})}$$

The last two items which will be covered are the newest and most exciting to some traders. The serious investor should consult other sources of information about these instruments; various commodity exchanges provide a variety of free pamphlets.

FUTURES

A futures contract is a legally binding agreement to make or accept delivery of a standardized commodity through stipulated delivery procedures at a specified date. Commodity futures have existed for agricultural products for decades. Futures contracts in money market instruments began in 1976 when the IMM (International Monetary Market) of the Chicago Mercantile Exchange began trading contracts on three-month Treasury bills. Since that time a number of money market contracts have been introduced, including 90-day commercial paper, 30-day commercial paper, domestic certificates of deposit, and Eurodollar futures. However, only three money market contracts trade currently: three-month T bill, domestic bank CDs, and Eurodollar.

There are two types of participants in the futures market. Hedgers want to minimize risk; they initiate positions in the futures market which act as a temporary substitute for some position in the cash market. A futures contract is therefore opposite to a cash position. For example, a bank investment portfolio manager who owns U.S. Treasury bills can protect against a rise in interest rates and the corresponding decrease in the value of the portfolio by selling T bill futures. Hedgers include banks, thrifts, pension funds, insurance companies, corporate treasurers, and state and local governments.

Speculators use the futures market to make money; they are willing to assume more risk for the possibility of more return. Speculators will buy or sell contracts on the basis of their opinion about the future price movements.

Summary of Money Market Futures Contract Specifications

	Treasury Bill	Domestic CD	Eurodollar
Size	$1,000,000	$1,000,000	$1,000,000
Method of quotation	100 minus T bill discount rate	100 minus CD yield (add on basis)	100 minus Eurodollar yield (add on basis)
Min. price fluctuation ($ value)	0.01 ($25)	0.01 ($25)	0.01 ($25)
Price Limits ($ value)	60 pts ($1,500)	80 pts ($2,000)	100 pts ($2,500)
Trading months	March, June, September, December		

Less than 3 percent of futures contracts are settled by the actual delivery of the underlying commodity. Futures contracts are usually offset by an opposite contract prior to settlement. However, actual delivery can occur.

OPTIONS

Holding an option gives the right to buy or sell a specific commodity at a specified price (strike price) anytime during a specific time period (before the expiration date). A call is the right to buy, and a put is the right to sell. Since holding an option gives a right, the option may expire and may never be exercised or used. The writer of a call or put is paid money (premium) and is obligated to perform if the holder exercises the option.

Call and Put Options

	BUY (Holder)	:	SELL (Writer)
CALL	Right to buy Wants prices to go up (Interest rates down)	: : : :	Obligation to sell Wants prices to stay the same or go down (Interest rates same or up)
PUT	Right to sell Wants prices to go down (Interest rates up)	: : : :	Obligation to buy Wants prices to stay the same or go up (Interest rates same or down)

The premium paid for an option will vary depending on several factors: (1) price of the underlying commodity, (2) volatility of the price of the underlying commodity, (3) the market's tone (bearish or bullish) regarding the underlying commodity, (4) the strike price of the option, and (5) the time remaining until the option expires. An option is a "wasting asset"; its value declines as time passes and the expiration date nears.

Options on money market instruments began in 1982 with options on three-month Treasury bills. Other options have been written in the over-the-counter market which allowed the tailoring of characteristics to the writer's and holder's requirements. The newest type of option is on futures contracts. The Chicago Mercantile Exchange has options on the 90-day Eurodollar futures contract as well as options on the three-month Treasury bill futures contracts. These represent the right to buy or sell one futures contract at a specified strike price during a specific time period (prior to the expiration date). Options on futures allow an opportunity for those seeking to protect against or profit from changes in interest rates. These perspectives are similar to the hedgers and speculators in futures.

The holder of a call or put option has limited his risk to the loss of the premium paid if the option is not exercised. The writer of a call or put may be exposed to unlimited risk if the option is exercised and the writer does not have a related offsetting position.

CONCLUSION

The money market is one of the most complex and challenging markets that a banker will encounter. It is constantly changing due to the creativity of the participants involved and their changing needs.

REFERENCES

Darst, D. M. *The Handbook of the Bond and Money Markets.* New York: McGraw-Hill, 1981.

Freund, W. C. *Investment Fundamentals.* Washington, D.C.: American Bankers Association, 1981.

Handbook of Securities of the United States Government and Federal Agencies. The First Boston Corporation, 1986.

Instruments of the Money Market. Federal Reserve Bank of Richmond, 1981.

Money Market Handbook. New York: Goldman, Sachs & Co., 1985.

Rebell, A. L., and G. Gordon. *Financial Futures and Investment Strategy.* Homewood, Ill.: Dow Jones-Irwin, 1984.

Stigum, M. *The Money Market. Myth, Reality, and Practice.* Homewood, Ill.: Dow Jones-Irwin, 1978.

————. *Money Market Calculations. Yields, Break-Evens, and Arbitrage.* Homewood, Ill.: Dow Jones-Irwin, 1981.

Stigum, M., and F. J. Fabozzi. *Bond and Money Market Investments.* Homewood, Ill.: Dow Jones-Irwin, 1987.

CHAPTER THIRTY-FIVE

Instruments and Markets for Government Securities

Donald J. Stuhldreher

President
The Huntington Company

INTRODUCTION

U.S. government securities constitute the largest and most widely accepted debt issued by any single obligor in the world. These securities have the broadest base of investors, are considered to have the greatest credit worthiness of any debt instruments, and enjoy the highest degree of liquidity of any class of securities.

U.S. government securities are backed by the full faith and credit of the United States government. This is very significant in that these securities are deemed to be free from credit risk. The United States constitution gives the U.S. Treasury the ability to levy taxes, collect fees, and print money which ensures the government will always have the ability to pay off maturing debt. Additionally, the political system within the United States enjoys a stability second to no other country in the world. Because of this, domestic investors in the United States and investors outside of the United States believe U.S. government securities provide the safest haven for investable funds. It is this world-wide acceptance in the credit quality of U.S. government securities that makes these instruments unique in international capital markets.

SIZE OF DEBT

As of June 30, 1986, the total U.S. government direct and guaranteed debt exceeded $2 trillion. It is estimated $558 trillion was held by official U.S. government agencies, trust funds, and the Federal Reserve

CHART 1   Holders of Total Public Debt

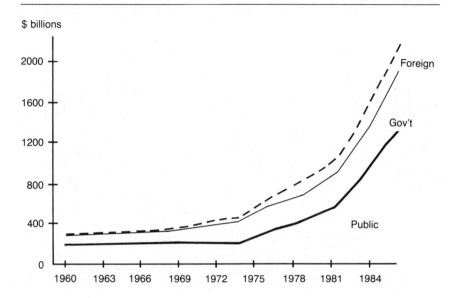

System; $1,264.8 billion was held by the public in the United States, and $237.9 billion was held by foreign investors (see Chart 1).

Of the amount held by the public in the United States, it is estimated $157 billion was held by individuals, $197 billion by commercial banks, roughly $250 billion by state and local governments, $60 billion by corporations, and the remaining $600 billion by insurance companies, mutual savings banks, and other investors. As of June 30, 1986, 10.6 percent of the assets of U.S. commercial banks were invested in U.S. government securities. Chart 2 gives the breakdown of private domestic holders.

STRUCTURE OF THE DEBT

U.S. government securities are issued in two broad categories: marketable and nonmarketable. Marketable securities constitute about 73 percent of the government debt outstanding. These securities are traded worldwide 24-hours a day in over-the-counter markets. An extremely active market exists for these securities, and billions of dollars are bought and sold each day. The nonmarketable securities are primarily savings bonds and special issues to state and local governments and to federal governmental agencies and funds (see Chart 3).

CHART 2   Private Domestic Holders

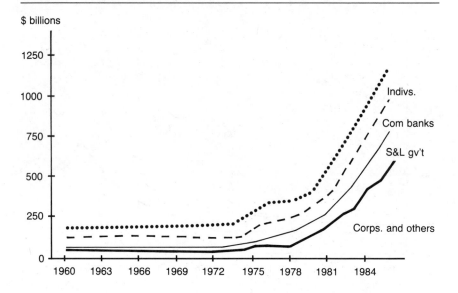

CHART 3   Nonmarketable Debt

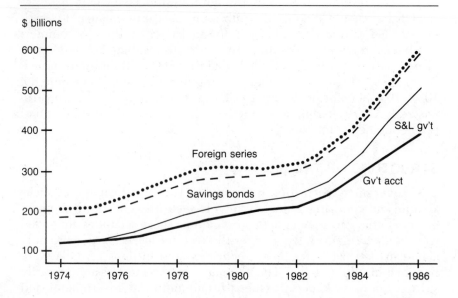

CHART 4   Public Debt Holders

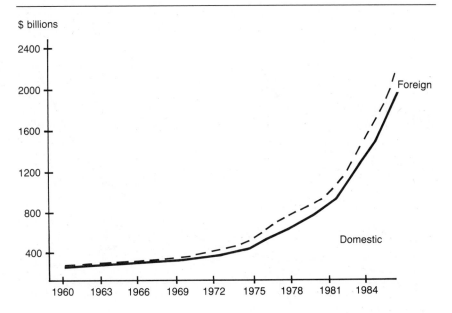

BREADTH OF ACCEPTANCE OF U.S. GOVERNMENT SECURITIES

U.S. government securities are held by investors worldwide. The unique credit aspect of the securities makes them the universal risk-less, interest-bearing investment. Not only are there no geographical bounds to the investors, but conversely all investors worldwide are potential investors in U.S. government securities (see Chart 4). This is so because of the unique credit quality of the securities. As a result, these securities provide the bench mark from which all other investments are compared.

The size, number of participants, credit quality, international acceptance, and relatively finite number of issues allows the U.S. government securities market to provide the ultimate in liquidity. Additionally, the active role played by a large number of securities dealers enhances the liquidity. These securities are traded every hour of the day in some part of the world (see Chart 5).

Liquidity of the U.S. government securities has been further enhanced by the development of futures and forward trading. Futures

CHART 5   Average Daily Trading Volume

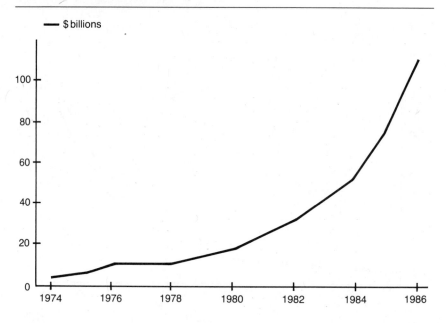

contracts are standardized agreements arranged on an organized exchange in which parties commit to purchase or sell securities for delivery at a future date. Forward transactions are agreements arranged in the over-the-counter market in which securities are purchased (sold) for delivery after five business days from the date of the transaction for government securities (Treasury bills, notes, and bonds) or after 30 days for mortgage-backed agency issues. Although the futures transactions are not markets in government securities, per se, they are highly liquid instruments that trade with a direct correlation to the U.S. government securities. Chart 6 shows how this has greatly increased the number of participants in the total market, which has added considerably to the liquidity of the markets. The futures markets have provided a valuable adjunct to the cash market by providing a more efficient means of matching the speculator with the hedger. This adds a considerable dimension to the overall efficiency and liquidity of the government market.

MARKET OPERATION

The U.S. government issues its marketable debt primarily by public auction via sealed bids. Any individual or institution may bid for the

CHART 6   Futures and Forward Transactions

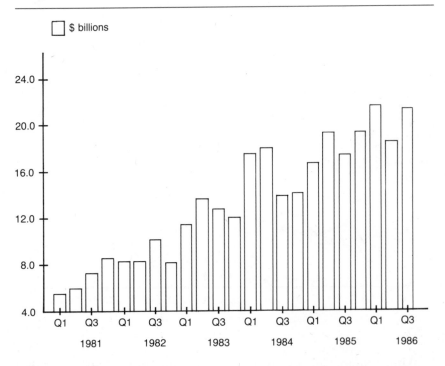

securities, but the securities are primarily underwritten by a group of dealers known as primary dealers. As of December 1986, there were 40 primary dealers. For the most part, the primary dealers are commercial banks or investment banks in the United States. Thirty-two of the dealers are controlled by U.S. interests, and eight are represented by foreign ownerships. The eight represent five different countries: Japan, Britain, Canada, Hong Kong, and Australia. This reflects the increased international character of the market and increased importance of foreign investors as holders of dollar-denominated assets in general and U.S. government securities in particular. This also gives further testimony to the breadth of the market for U.S. government securities.

Designation as a primary dealer in these securities is highly sought because only primary dealers are authorized to conduct business directly with the New York Federal Reserve Bank. The Open Market Desk of the New York Federal Reserve Bank is the conduit through which the Open Market Committee of the Federal Reserve Bank conducts monetary policy initiatives. When the Open Market Desk buys government securities, it injects reserves into the U.S. commercial

CHART 7   Repos and Reverses

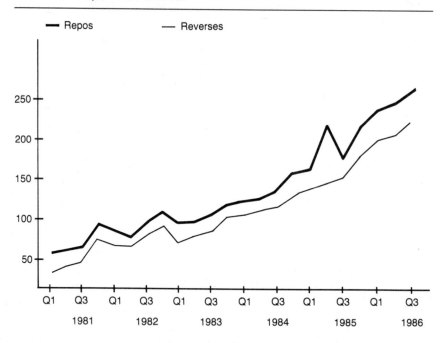

banking system. Conversely, when the Open Market Desk sells government securities, it absorbs (or withdraws) reserves from the commercial banking system. This action can be conducted either through the outright purchase (or sale) of securities or through temporary injection (or withdrawal) of reserves via repurchase agreements (or reverse repurchase agreements).

A repurchase agreement is a purchase and matched sale at a later date of the same securities by the Open Market Desk at the Fed. A reverse repurchase agreement is a sale with a matched purchase at a later date. Dealers bid competitively for the securities with other dealers when the Open Market Desk is selling and conversely offer securities at competitive prices to the Open Market Desk when the desk is buying. They are always in competition with the other dealers. The primary dealers increase their ability to make good bids (or offers) by virtue of the network they have established with major investors in government securities. This function, shown in Chart 7, is important in creating an efficient market.

The primary dealers must continuously and consistently be a major participant in the U.S. government over-the-counter market. They report their activity and their inventory positions daily to the Open

CHART 8   Dealer Positions

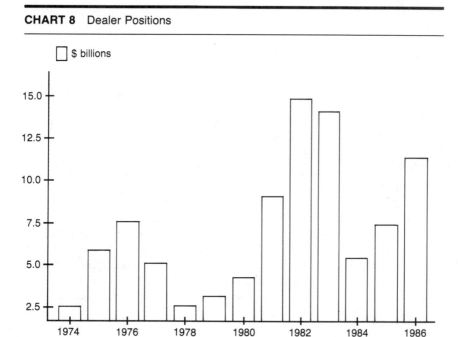

Market Desk of the Federal Reserve Bank of New York. Chart 8 ranks dealer positions.

   In this way, the Federal Reserve Bank is able to monitor the activity conducted by the primary dealers. Additionally, the primary dealers provide the Open Market Desk considerable intelligence on the monetary condition of the financial markets. In addition to the 40 primary dealers, there are numerous dealers who make markets as principal; that is, the dealers will provide bids and make offers in the U.S. securities market. These dealers are sometimes called secondary dealers. That is a misnomer. Many of the dealers are actively involved in the initial issuance of U.S. government debt issues which is a primary market function. Most major domestic and international, commercial, and investment banks are active as principal market makers in U.S. government securities.

UNITED STATES GOVERNMENT SECURITIES

U.S. government securities are issued under the Second Liberty Bond Act enacted in September 1917. At the end of the 1920s, the federal debt was $16 billion and had grown to approximately $48 billion by the end of 1939. Financing World War II and the reconstruction period following enlarged the federal debt to $271 billion by the end of 1946. The federal debt grew modestly to $341 billion by the end of 1967. Since 1967 continuous federal deficits have fueled the growth in the federal debt to in excess of $2 trillion in 1986. U.S. debt is tallied from several viewpoints in the following four charts.

The marketable U.S. government debt is primarily composed of U.S. Treasury bills, U.S. Treasury notes, and U.S. Treasury bonds. As of June 30, 1986, there were $397 billion U.S. Treasury bills outstanding, $869 billion U.S. Treasury notes outstanding, and $232 billion U.S. Treasury bonds outstanding. The three types of issues comprise 73 percent of total public debt outstanding as of June 30, 1986. Additional statistics are given in Chart 11.

In 1985 the average maturity of the marketable interest-bearing U.S. government debt held by private investors was five years. The explosion of the federal deficit beginning in 1968 was primarily financed by the issuance of short and intermediate maturity debt. In 1967 the average maturity was five years and one month and dropped to a low of two years and seven months in 1976. Since 1976 the U.S. Treasury has prudently endeavored to extend the average maturity of the debt and its success is shown in Chart 12.

CHART 9A   U.S. Government Debt

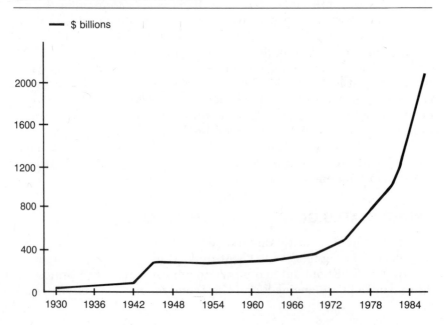

CHART 9B Real U.S. Government Debt per Capita

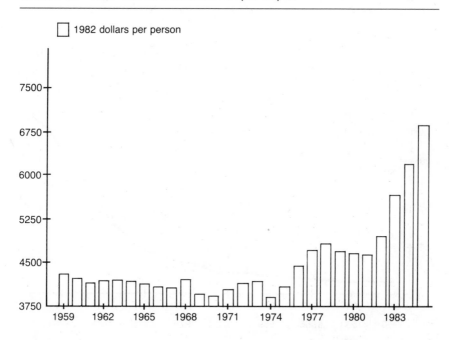

☐ 1982 dollars per person

CHART 9C U.S. Government Debt to GNP

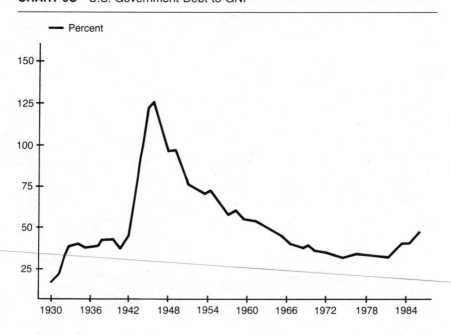

— Percent

CHART 10   Interest Paid on the Federal Debt

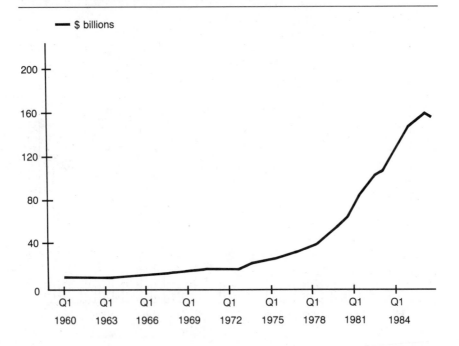

CHART 11   Composition of Marketable Securities

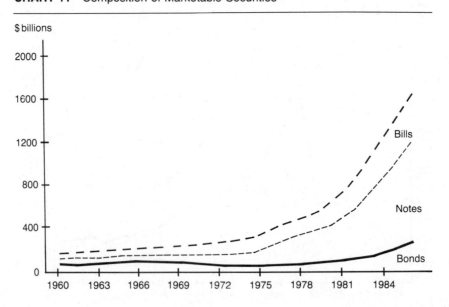

CHART 12   Average Maturity of Marketable Debt

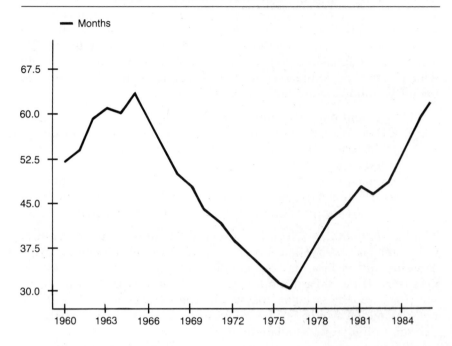

U.S. TREASURY BILLS

U.S. Treasury bills are issued at a discount from par with a maximum maturity of one year. The interest earned on securities is the difference between the purchase price and the matured par value. The Treasury bills are issued through auction. Every week there is an auction of a new 26-week bill and an auction of an addition to the 13-week bill, which had originally been issued as a 26-week bill or 52-week bill. The Treasury auctions a 52-week bill monthly and from time to time sells short-term Treasury bills known as cash management bills and tax anticipation bills. These normally have a very short maturity and are sold to finance the Treasury over a short period. The cash management and tax anticipation bills are normally issued in large amounts (up to $10-million minimum denominations). The Treasury bills are sold on a discount basis through competitive bids entered as a dollar price representing the price the bidding dealers or investors will pay for the issue. The dollar price is a function of the yield to maturity the investor is striving to obtain.

Treasury bills are traded on a discount basis per actual number of days over a 360-day year. Since the bills are traded on a discount, the yield is greater than the nominal discount basis. The longer a bill has to maturity, the greater the differences between the discount rate and the yield. Since the bills do not have interest coupons, no interest is received until the bill matures or has been sold. Treasury bills have three major intricacies relative to interest: (1) discount rate, (2) CD (certificate of deposit) equivalent yield, and (3) bond equivalent yield which is further delineated by shorter or longer than six months to maturity. Following are definitions of these factors.

1. Discount rate—the quoted interest rate.
2. CD equivalent yield—the discount rate converted to per annum yield based on the discounted dollars invested and also compiled on a 360-day per annum basis.
3. Bond equivalent yield—conversion of the CD equivalent yield to an actual day per annum basis (usually 365 days) from a 360-day basis to reflect the actual days of the investment.

The lack of cash flow by virtue of receiving interest only at maturity rather than a six-month coupon is taken into consideration. If the Treasury bill is less than six months to maturity, no adjustment is necessary. If the Treasury bill is greater than six months to maturity, it is presumed the cash flow that would have been generated had there been a coupon would not be reinvested (this results in a slight reduction in the yield calculation).

Following is the formula used to compute the discount:

$$A = \frac{B}{360} \times D$$

$$P = \$100 - A$$

where

$$D = \text{Number of days to maturity}$$
$$B = \text{Discount basis}$$
$$A = \text{Amount of discount}$$
$$P = \text{Dollar price}$$

Find the price of a Treasury bill due in 91 days on a 5.35% discount basis:

$$A = \frac{B}{360} \times D$$
$$= \frac{5.35}{360} \times 91$$
$$= 1.3523611 \text{ full discount}$$

$$P = 100 - A$$
$$= 100 - \$1.3523611$$
$$= \$98.65 \text{ dollar price for } 5.35\% \text{ discount basis for 91-day maturity}$$

CD equivalent yield:

$$CDy = \frac{360 \times \dfrac{B}{100}}{360 - \dfrac{(B \times D)}{100}}$$

$$CDy = \frac{360 \times .0535}{360 - (.0535 \times 91)}$$

$$CDy = 5.423\%$$

Bond equivalent yield:

$$BEy = CDy \times \frac{365}{360}$$

$$BEy = 5.423\% \times \frac{365}{360}$$

$$BEy = 5.499\%$$

The following formulas may be used to compute special figures desired when Treasury bills are sold prior to maturity:

I. Effective yield for the time a bill is held:

$$\frac{\text{Gain or loss}}{\text{in yield}} = \frac{\text{Days to maturity at date of sale}}{\text{Days held}} \times \frac{\text{(Purchase yield} -}{\text{Sale yield)}}$$

Assume a 91-day bill purchased at 5.35% is held for 30 days and sold at 5.40%. What is the yield for the time held?

$$\text{Gain or loss in yield} = \frac{61 \times (5.35 - 5.40)}{30}$$

$$= \frac{61 \times (-.05)}{30}$$

$$= -.10$$

Purchase yield 5.35
Gain or loss in yield .... -0.10
Rate of return for time held .. 5.25%

II. To find the number of days a bill must be held to break even in yield:

$$\text{Days to maturity at date of sale} = \frac{\text{Days to maturity at date of purchase}}{\text{Sale yield}} \times \text{Purchase yield}$$

Assume a 91-day bill is bought at 5.35%. How long must it be held to avoid a loss if it is sold at 5.60%?

$$\text{Days to maturity at date of sale} = \frac{91 \times 5.35}{5.60} = 90$$

Days to maturity at purchase 91
Days to maturity at sale 87
Break-even period .... 4 days

III. To determine the yield at which a bill may be sold to avoid a loss after holding for a specified period of time:

$$\text{Sale yield} = \frac{\text{Days to maturity at purchase}}{\text{Days to maturity at sale}} \times \text{Purchase yield}$$

Assume a 91-day bill is bought at 5.35% and held for 30 days. At what yield can it be sold to break even?

$$\text{Sale yield} = \frac{91 \times 5.35}{61} = 7.98$$

Sale yield required to break even is 7.98%.

TREASURY NOTES AND BONDS

Treasury notes and bonds are coupon-bearing instruments which have a minimum maturity of one year. Treasury bonds have no maximum maturity but do have a limit on the interest rate that can be paid. Treasury notes have no limitation on the amount of interest that can be paid but do have a maximum maturity of 10 years. However, Congress from time to time authorizes the issuance of bonds without a maximum interest ceiling in order to facilitate the management of the huge government debt.

The U.S. Treasury has used a variety of techniques in selling (or issuing) its bonds and notes, but currently the popular method is to accept the bids on a yield basis with the interest coupon to be determined by the results of the auction. The coupon selected will be up to an eighth of a percentage point less than the average yield with a result that the securities are issued at a slight discount from par. In most cases, the Treasury permits private bidders to bid for a small amount (up to $500,000) on a noncompetitive basis. The Treasury also allows U.S. government agencies, trust funds, and foreign governments to purchase unlimited amounts on a noncompetitive basis. The bidder will be awarded the securities at the average rate of all the securities issued. This helps to insure access by small investors to the market.

THE MARKETS FOR TREASURY SECURITIES

As mentioned previously, the U.S. government securities market is an over-the-counter market. The action occurs across the telephone lines that link the trading rooms of brokers, dealers, and bankers around the globe, rather than in a specific location. The normal trading hours in the United States are 9:00 A.M. to 3:30 P.M. (Eastern Standard Time) each business day. There is trading before and after these hours and with the advent of global markets, trading is conducted every hour somewhere in the world.

The normal terms of the trade are for delivery the next business day. If it is agreed on by both parties, delivery and payment may be on the same day (cash trade) or may be for a later delivery than the next day (deferred delivery). Payment for the securities should always be made simultaneously against the delivery of the securities to the investor or his agent. Payment for the securities is always in federal funds.

BOOK ENTRY

As the U.S. government securities market grew, the physical handling of securities became too cumbersome. The Federal Reserve Board and the U.S. Treasury created a system called book entry. Book entry is a computerized safekeeping system in which the physical securities themselves no longer exist, but instead are represented by computer entry in the Federal Reserve system. The book entry system has eliminated many of the risks involved with the physical transfer of securities and money, and the safekeeping of the securities.

U.S. TREASURY SECURITIES YIELD CURVE

Since U.S. Treasury securities are basically free from credit risk and through the size and operation of the market enjoy practically no marketability risk, the remaining risk inherent in the securities is the interest rate risk. As a result, the yields on the various maturities of government securities create a base-yield curve from which all other fixed income investments are measured (see Chart 13). The yield curve is created by plotting the constant yields to maturity of all the government securities.

CHART 13 The Government Yield Curve

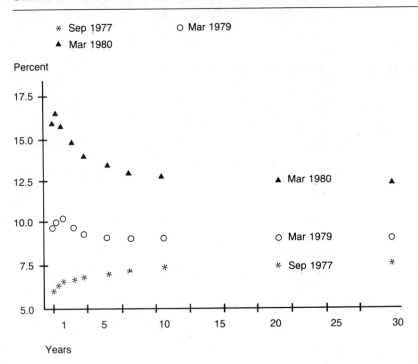

The plottings are connected to form a curve. An upward sloping (or positive) yield curve indicates higher rates for longer maturities. An inverted (or declining) yield curve will indicate lower rates for longer maturities. A flat yield curve indicates equal rates for all maturities. The three scenarios are depicted in Chart 13. Traditionally, an upward sloping (or positive) yield curve indicates the market is anticipating higher rates whereas a negative (or downward sloping) yield curve suggests that the market is expecting lower rates. Logically, in a period of normal rates, we would expect to see a slightly upward sloping yield curve to reflect the greater risk inherent in a longer maturity.

PRICE VOLATILITY

Even though these securities are virtually free from credit risk and have limited marketability risk, the securities are subject to considerable price volatility. Since the securities have a fixed maturity and a set interest-coupon rate, the yield is modified by changes in the

CHART 14   Maturity Duration*

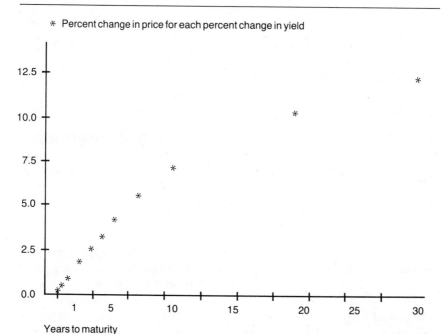

* Percent change in price for each percent change in yield

Years to maturity

*Based on the government yield curve for February 3, 1987.

price. However, the reducing of the various risks associated with fixed-income securities to interest rate risk does not lessen the price volatility. As interest rates vary, the price of the securities will vary inversely. Thus a period of volatile interest rates will be reflected in extreme price volatility of the securities. Additionally, the term to maturity will exacerbate the price volatility at any given change in interest rates. The longer the maturity, the greater the dollar price change per basis point change in yield. An example of maturity duration is shown in Chart 14.

Another volatile influence on bond and note investments is if the issue is trading at par, a premium, or a discount. This is additionally influenced if interest rates are perceived to be rising or falling. The bond equivalent yield may vary widely on securities that have different coupons but the same term to maturity. This is primarily due to the reinvestment assumption on the future stream of cash flow created by the security.

CHAPTER THIRTY-SIX

Instruments and Markets for Federal Agency Securities

Kenneth A. Bretthorst

Chairman
First St. Louis Securities

There are two types of U.S. government agencies: federally sponsored agencies and federal agencies. Federal agencies are actually part of the federal government, and some of their activities are included in the budget. The Government National Mortgage Association (GNMA) is the most well-known federal agency. Federally sponsored agencies are privately owned but are subject to federal regulation and supervision. These include the most well known "agency" securities, those of the Farm Credit System, the Federal Home Loan Banks (FHLB), and the Federal National Mortgage Association (FNMA). Most of the discussion in this chapter, with the exception of GNMA, will center on federally sponsored agencies.

U.S. government agencies were created by Congress to meet the special borrowing needs of specific segments of the economy and can be divided into three broad categories:

1. Agencies supporting agriculture:
   a. Farm Credit System.
2. Agencies supporting student loans:
   a. Student Loan Marketing Association.
3. Agencies supporting the housing market:
   a. Federal Home Loan Banks.
   b. Federal National Mortgage Association.
   c. Federal Home Loan Mortgage Corporation.
   d. Government National Mortgage Association.

There are several other small, highly specialized agencies, but the most popular ones are included in the list. Besides categorizing the agencies by purpose, it is also helpful to analyze them by the type of securities they issue. Here we find two very general and broad categories. They are agencies that issue debentures, notes, bonds, or discount notes, and those that issue mortgage-backed securities, primarily pass-throughs. Some agencies, such as FNMA, issue both types of securities depending on what purpose they are trying to satisfy.

We will discuss the more popular agencies first, those of the Farm Credit System (FCB), the Federal Home Loan Banks (FHLB), and the Federal National Mortgage Association (FNMA). Each of these agencies issues debentures, bonds, or notes to raise money to support the activities for which they were created. This is usually done through a nationwide selling group of dealers and dealer banks. Each agency has a fiscal agent who is responsible for assembling the selling group and making sure that its securities are sold. On the announcement date, the fiscal agent introduces the package it will bring to the market. This announcement will include the size of the issue and the maturity dates of the issue. The pricing date is usually one day after the announcement and at this time, after consultation with his selling group, the fiscal agent sets the interest rate on the securities. The following day is called the offering date and is the first time the whole package (that is, size, maturity, and interest rate to be earned) is offered into the market. Depending on the agency, the bonds may start trading on a "when-issued" basis on this day. On the settlement or dated date, the agencies are actually paid for. The intervening period between the offering date and the settlement date is usually a very active trading period for new issues because they can be traded before payment is made. They are trading when-issued. The announcement dates for the agencies are generally known well in advance so the market can anticipate with a fair degree of accuracy the timing of these issues.

All three of the most popular agencies also issue discount notes which are sold through much smaller selling groups and are usually offered daily whereas the bonds or debentures are usually issued monthly.

While the outstanding amount of bonds and debentures of these agencies has gone up during the past five years, the growth is not nearly as dramatic as the U.S. Treasury debt. In fact the Farm Credit System actually had less debt outstanding in June 1986 than it did in 1981. This decline was a reflection of what was happening in the agricultural segment of the economy as well as the Farm Credit System itself.

Through the years agencies have become popular with banks and are being widely used in bank portfolios. This reflects their acceptance in the marketplace as well as their perceived quality and certain pledging characteristics. The secondary market for agencies is very active, and holders of agency debt should experience little problem in disposing of these securities should the need arise. There are several factors, however, that the prospective purchaser of agency securities should be aware of: (1) the spread between the bid and asked prices of agency securities is usually larger than the spread on comparable government securities. This spread can range between ¼ to ½ point on some issues. This spread is a reflection of both creditworthiness and marketability. While the agencies are generally considered to be the next highest quality to governments, they do not carry a guarantee by the United States. In addition, individual issues of agencies may be comparatively small, and actual trading in any one issue may become limited. As activity becomes limited, the spread between bid and asked increases. When considering purchase of agency securities the portfolio manager is generally well advised to purchase more recently priced issues as opposed to older issues. (2) The rate spread between government and agencies can change based on a number of factors. When the Farm Credit System found itself experiencing credit problems during the mid-1980s, the rate spread between its securities and U.S. governments rose from approximately 20 to 25 basis points to as much as 85 to 100 basis points over comparable government issues. Holders of FNMA securities have experienced the same type of market changes when the housing market was having its problems. During periods of high interest rates and tight credit, the same type of spread distortion can take place. Direct governments and federal agencies have a much narrow rate spread during periods of low interest rates and easier credit. Knowing this, however, a portfolio manager can use it to his benefit by trading from agencies into governments or vice versa depending on the interest rate cycle. At any given time, one of the best measures of the secondary market for agencies can be determined by examining the spread between U.S. governments and comparable agencies. When this spread is narrow, the activity in agencies is usually more active than when it is wide. This measure can be used to judge the individual agencies and how they are perceived in the marketplace. It is also important to remember that these relationships change over time, so do not let history totally determine tomorrows purchase. Also, there can be short-term technical factors that can cause a temporary distortion in the market. Therefore it is always wise to follow spread relationships over a longer period of time.

The fastest growing segment of the agency market is mortgage-backed securities. The discussion here will focus primarily on pass-through securities issued by FNMA, FHLMC, and GNMA. The first factor that needs to be examined in the mortgage market is credit. Issues of GNMA carry the guarantee of the full faith and credit of the United States. Issues of the FHLMC and FNMA are guaranteed by the respective issuer. Because of the guarantee involved, GNMA is the most popular mortgage-backed security in the world. The growth of the mortgage-backed market can also be shown by the amount of securities outstanding with GNMA alone. In 1968 GNMA was formed; in 1986 it had over $200 billion in securities in the market. While there is an active secondary market in mortgage-backed securities (over $5 billion per day traded in 1986), there are numerous factors that make this market less attractive to most bank portfolio buyers. First, mortgage-backed securities have a much longer average life than most portfolio buyers prefer. By far the largest amount of pass-throughs outstanding are on single-family residences with 30-year maturities. Because these securities are pass-throughs, principal and interest are paid down monthly, increasing the amount of book work necessary to keep track of the payments. Also because of the monthly paydown, the "average life" of the pass-through may be longer or shorter than anticipated. This is true because the holder of the pass-through also receives any prepayments that may occur in his pool of mortgages. This brings us to the second feature of mortgage-backed securities that may prove troubling to banks. If a bank pays a premium for these securities and suddenly begins to receive large amounts of unscheduled principal paydowns, the actual yield can go down. The reverse is true also, because if rates go down the yield can increase. This means, however, that the average life also becomes longer on this particular pool of mortgages. A portfolio manager needs to be fully informed about this market before committing funds, not after the fact. Third, while pass-through securities are the most popular mortgage-backed securities, there are over 30 different related securities in the market. Some are adjustable rate, some have shorter maturities, and still others are a combination of both. Adjustable rate mortgages may float against a variety of indexes adding another twist to the marketplace. Even with all of these distractions, however, banks have tripled their holdings of mortgage-backed securities since 1975. The reason of course is yield.

Pass-through securities are usually evaluated relative to the U.S. Treasury securities yield curve. The spread changes based on a number of factors including supply and demand, credit, and general market conditions. This spread has varied between 24 basis points to as much as 190 basis points. The investor then is being "paid" by the marketplace for the inconvenience and limited marketability. The portfolio manager should remember that many of the mortgage-backed securities have limited market makers and participants. In periods of instability, the marketability of mortgage-backed securities could become limited. Because of this, the debentures, notes, and bonds of the Farm Credit System, FNMA, and the FHLB still remain the most popular agencies with bank portfolio managers.

FARM CREDIT SYSTEMS

The Farm Credit System is a cooperatively owned system of banks and associations that provide credit and other services to agricultural concerns and certain related businesses. This mission was given to the system by Congress in the Farm Credit Act of 1971 and amended by the Farm Credit Amendment Act of 1985. This multi-billion dollar system is owned entirely by its member borrowers. The Farm Credit System began with the creation of the Federal Land Bank in 1916, and by 1933 was structured much as it is today: twelve federal land banks, 13 banks for cooperatives, and 12 federal intermediate credit banks. These banks are located across the country and are regulated and supervised by the Farm Credit Administration in Washington, D.C.

Because the Farm Credit Banks and associations are not depository institutions, they must rely on the money and credit markets to raise funds to lend to perspective borrowers. This is accomplished through the Federal Farm Credit Banks Funding Corporation located in New York City. The funding corporation manages a selling group of approximately 145 dealers and dealer banks who offer farm credit securities. In the past each bank issued their own debt securities to the public, and the Federal Land Bank and the Federal Intermediate Credit Bank still have some bonds outstanding. As of June 1986, Federal Intermediate Credit Bank had $565 million outstanding and Federal Land Bank, $2.7 billion.

Federal Farm Credit Banks Consolidated Systemwide Bonds

In order to ensure an orderly and efficient acquisition of funds, the Farm Credit Bank introduced the Federal Farm Credit Bank Consolidated Systemwide Bonds in 1977. These bonds are the joint and several obligations of all 37 farm credit banks and as such are backed by the combined financial resources of the Federal Land Bank, the Federal Intermediate Credit Bank, and the Bank for Cooperative. The bonds are secured by collateral at least equal in value to the total amount of obligations outstanding. The collateral can consist of notes and other obligations representing loans made under the authority of the Farm Credit Act, obligations of the United States or any agency thereof, cash or other readily marketable securities approved by the Farm Credit Administration. Farm credit bank bonds are offered to the public approximately 16 times during the year with three- and six-month maturities offered every month. Longer maturities are offered periodically during the year. The bonds are issued in denominations of $1,000 for maturities of 13 months or longer and $5,000 for shorter maturities.

In January 1975 Federal Farm Credit Bank Consolidated System-wide Notes were first brought to the market. These notes are sold in multiples of $50,000 on a discount basis for periods of five to 365 days. They are used as an interim financing vehicle by the Farm Credit Bank and like the bonds are the secured joint and several obligations of the 37 banks.

The income derived from the consolidated bonds, systemwide bonds, and discount notes is exempt from state, municipal, and local taxation. However, it is not exempt from federal taxes.

Statutory limitations and restrictions that generally apply to the purchase of securities for a bank's own portfolio are not applicable with regard to the purchase of obligations of the Farm Credit System. In particular, the 10 percent limitation regarding the securities of any one obliger does not apply. This exemption is for national banks and state member banks of the Federal Reserve System.

Farm credit securities are lawful investments for all fiduciary and trust funds under the jurisdiction of the U.S. government. They are eligible as collateral for government deposits, and in many areas of the country can be used to secure state and local deposits as well. Federal credit union and savings and loan associations can also invest in farm credit securities. In addition, farm credit securities are used by the Federal Reserve System in its open market operations and may be accepted by the Fed as collateral for advances to depository institutions under Section 13 of the Federal Reserve Act. It must be remembered, however, that while the farm credit banks are a government-sponsored agency, no expressed liability is assumed by the U.S. government.

FEDERAL HOME LOAN BANK SYSTEM

The Federal Home Loan Bank System was created by an act of Congress in 1932. This act established the twelve Federal Home Loan Banks and the Federal Home Loan Bank Board. The purpose of the system is to serve as a central source of credit for its members and to support and ensure the availability of funds for home financing. The Federal Home Loan Bank System operates for savings associations and mutual savings banks in much the same way that the Federal Reserve Bank does for banks. The 12 district banks serve 12 geographical areas of the country and are wholly owned by their member institutions. The banks are regulated, however, by the Federal Home Loan Bank Board, which is an independent agency of the executive branch of the federal government. The 12 district banks make advances to their members to meet seasonal withdrawal needs, to meet unusual savings withdrawals, and to fund expansion of their mortgage lending program. There are other special purposes for which the district banks can lend funds but most advances are for the purposes previously described.

The bank board performs a number of supervisory and regulatory functions. It approves charters for new federal thrifts, supervises all federally chartered thrifts, and, in conjunction with state agencies, regulates state-chartered thrifts that are insured by the FSLIC. The bank board also oversees the operation of the FSLIC and the Federal Home Loan Mortgage Corporation. A more detailed discussion of the Federal Home Loan Mortgage Corporation will follow.

Since the Federal Home Loan Banks, like the banks in the Farm Credit System, do not accept deposits, they too must rely on the marketplace as a source of funds. These funds are derived from the sale of consolidated bonds and consolidated discount notes.

Federal Home Loan Banks Consolidated Obligations

To fund advances to its members, the system gets its money from capital (stock, reserves, and profits) and from liabilities, which include the consolidated obligations as well as member deposits. Membership is mandatory for thrifts chartered by the bank board, and other state-chartered thrifts are eligible to become members. To join, a qualified institution must purchase capital stock in its district bank for an amount equal to at least one percent of the aggregate of the outstanding principal of its mortgage loans. This base provides the support for the consolidated obligations.

Consolidated obligations (bonds and notes) are the joint and several obligations of all the banks and cannot be issued in amounts that exceed 12 times the total paid-in capital stock and reserves of all the Federal Home Loan Banks. In addition, the Federal Home Loan Banks are required to maintain assets free from any lien or pledge in a total amount at least equal to the amount of consolidated bonds outstanding. These assets can be cash, obligations of or fully guaranteed by the United States, secured advances, and guaranteed mortgages. Furthermore, the Secretary of the Treasury is authorized by the Bank Act to purchase up to $4 billion of the bank obligations. The consolidated bonds are not obligations of or guaranteed by the United States, but they are joint and several obligations of the Federal Home Loan Banks operating under federal charter with governmental supervision.

The income derived from the bonds and notes is subject to federal taxes but is exempt from local taxes. These obligations may be accepted as security for all fiduciary trust, and public funds under the authority or control of the United States. They are eligible as collateral at the discount window of the Federal Reserve Bank and for open market operations by the Federal Reserve System. National banks may invest in the Federal Home Loan Banks' obligations without regard to the statutory limitations and restrictions generally applicable to investment securities.

Bonds issued after October 1977 are available only in book-entry form, in a minimum amount of $10,000, and multiples of $5,000 thereafter. Primary distribution of the bonds is conducted by a group of more than a 100 banks and dealers on a monthly basis. As of March 1986, there were over $87.2 billion consolidated obligations outstanding (notes and bonds).

Federal Home Loan Banks Consolidated Discount Notes

First issued in 1974, consolidated obligations, issued on a discount basis to maturity with a maturity of one year or less, are called consolidated discount notes. They are used for cash management purposes by the Federal Home Loan Banks and are an important tool in achieving flexibility within the money markets. Discount notes are primarily distributed by a group of six securities dealers for a period of between 30 and 360 days. The maturity date is chosen by the buyer of the notes, and the rates are set daily and announced by the Federal Home Loan Bank System. Denominations of the notes are usually $100,000, $150,000 and $1,000,000. At year end 1985, there were over $13.1 billion notes outstanding. These notes carry the same credit and investment characteristics as the consolidated bonds.

FEDERAL NATIONAL MORTGAGE ASSOCIATION

The Federal National Mortgage Association (FNMA or Fannie Mae) is a federally chartered but stockholder-owned corporation. The original association was incorporated in 1938 under Title III of the National Housing Act. At that point it was a wholly owned government corporation that borrowed its funds from the United States Treasury. Title III was revised in 1954 and called the Federal National Mortgage Association Charter Act. At this point, Fannie Mae became a semiprivate and governmental agency of the United States. The Secretary of the Treasury held nonvoting preferred stock, and nonvoting common stock was issued to institutions from which Fannie Mae purchased its mortgages. In 1968 the Charter Act was amended again, and Fannie Mae was divided into two separate and distinct corporations. One, the Government National Mortgage Association (GNMA or Ginnie Mae) and the other FNMA. The Government National Mortgage Association became a wholly owned corporate instrument of the United States within the Department of Housing and Urban Development (HUD). FNMA became a federally chartered corporation that is 100 percent stockholder owned. However, there is still much government regulation of FNMA. The issuance of debt obligations by FNMA requires approval by the Secretary of the Treasury; the Secretary of HUD must approve issuance of stock. HUD can require FNMA to purchase mortgage loans that will help ensure housing for low- and moderate-income families. HUD can audit and examine the books of FNMA, and obligations of the corporation issued under Section 304b are subject to limitations imposed by the Charter Act. From its inception, the business of FNMA consisted primarily of purchasing and reselling mortgage loans insured by FHA and the Veterans Administration. The purpose was to institute a secondary market for these loans. FNMA would buy loans in times of tight money and sell them when there was an abundance of funds. Since 1970, under powers granted by the Emergency Home Finance Act, FNMA with the approval of HUD can purchase, service, lend on, and otherwise deal in conventional mortgages as well as FHA- and VA-insured loans. On June 30, 1986, FNMA held $29.3 billion of federally guaranteed or insured loans in its portfolio. Conventional mortgages totaled in excess of $67.7 billion. These included both fixed and adjustable-rate mortgages.

Federal National Mortgage Association Debentures

FNMA debentures are unsecured general obligations of the corporation issued under Section 304b of the FNMA Charter Act. The first debentures were issued to the public in 1956. They are sold by a nationwide group of securities dealers and dealer banks on a monthly basis. Debentures are available in denominations of $10,000, with $5,000 increments thereafter. They are issued in book-entry form only and are payable through any member of the Federal Reserve System. There are some debentures with special features (such as zero coupon debentures) that are offered by special underwritings. The total amount outstanding, however, is minimal. The debentures, along with other securities, are used to finance the mortgages purchased by FNMA. As of June 30, 1986, there were $78.4 billion of debentures outstanding.

Federal National Mortgage Association Short-Term Notes

FNMA short-term notes (Discount Notes) are issued for periods of up to 360 days by a group of 12 dealers and dealer banks. This operation began in 1960 and allows FNMA some flexibility in structuring its debt. FNMA discount notes are tailored to meet the short-term investing needs of corporate, institutional, and other investors. The rates are adjusted from time to time to provide a yield higher than Treasury bills with similar maturities.

Residential Financing Securities (RFS)

FNMA Residential financing securities are issued either in six-month or one-year debentures. Whereas regular debentures are marketed monthly, residential financing securities are offered every business day at rates announced by the corporation. They are sold through a select group of dealers and dealer banks in denominations of $10,000 and multiples of $5,000. They have all the same investment characteristics of other obligations issued by FNMA.

Federal National Mortgage Association Subordinated Capital Debentures

FNMA issues subordinated capital debentures from time to time as needs may arise. These debentures are unsecured obligations of the corporation, subordinated to other debts of the corporation. Some of the debentures are convertible to common stock, and some have been issued in zero coupon form. As of June 30, 1986, the amount of obligations senior in right of payment to the subordinated capital debentures was $90.5 billion.

While FNMA obligations are not obligations of the United States, the Secretary of the Treasury has discriminatory authority to purchase up to $2.25 billion of the corporate debt. Also, under current regulatory authority, the maximum amount of a corporation's general obligation outstanding at any time generally may not exceed 30 times the sum of stockholders equity, subordinated capital debentures, and reserves. All obligations issued by a corporation are acceptable as collateral for the deposit of public monies; able to be purchased by national banks without regard to the usual limitations imposed on investment securities; eligible for purchase by the Open Market Committee of the Federal Reserve Bank; legal investments for federal credit unions and federal savings and loan associations; and are eligible as security for advances to member banks by the Federal Reserve. Debt obligations of FNMA are subject to both federal and state taxes.

Federal National Mortgage Association Mortgage-Backed Securities

In 1981 FNMA began issuing mortgage-backed securities (MBS). These securities are guaranteed by FNMA mortgage pass-through certificates, which establish a beneficial interest by the holder in pools of mortgage-backed loans. The pools carry the corporation's guarantee of timely payment of scheduled principal and interest whether or not such payments are received from the mortgagor. MBS creates a source of free income for FNMA and enhances the secondary market for conventional loans by using the FNMA guarantee. On June 30, 1986, $72.3 billion MBS certificates were outstanding. These represent both fixed and variable rate certificates. Most MBSs are issued in "swap" transactions in which lenders swap pools of mortgages for MBS certificates, which they then either sell or hold. This program works much like the Guarantor Program of the Federal Home Loan Mortgage Corporation, and in fact these two programs compete with each other for the lenders' business. While the majority of Fannie Mae MBSs represent conventional fixed rate mortgages (30-year maturities), an increasing number of pools represent 15-year maturities (Dwarfs) and adjustable rate mortgages (ARMs).

STUDENT LOAN MARKETING ASSOCIATION

The Student Loan Marketing Association (Sallie Mae) is a stockholder corporation established by the Higher Education Act of 1965. The purpose of the corporation is to provide liquidity for the various types of student loans, just as FNMA and the FHLMC provide liquidity in the mortgage markets. Sallie Mae accomplishes this by both purchasing loans and warehousing advances. In addition, Sallie Mae also issues letters of credit to back their student loan revenue bond issues (municipals) and can assist in the financing of student loans where there is a shortage of funds available. From 1974 until 1982, Sallie Mae financed its activities primarily by issuing debt securities to the Federal Financing Bank (FFB). This was done at a set rate of .125 percent above the 91-day T-bill rate. In 1981 Sallie Mae began to tap the capital market through the revenue of nonguaranteed discount notes issued in minimum denominations of $100,000. In February 1984 Sallie Mae also began to issue short-term floating rate notes with maturities generally three years or longer. These notes were spread to the bond equivalent yield of the 91-day Treasury bill and had a floating rate. In addition to the floating rate notes and discount notes, Sallie Mae has a variety of other securities outstanding in smaller amounts and has also issued securities in the international capital market. The Secretary of the Treasury is authorized to purchase obligations of Sallie Mae up to an aggregate amount of $1 billion. Securities issued by Sallie Mae are lawful investments and may be accepted as security for all judiciary trust and public funds under control of the United States. They are eligible as collateral for the Federal Reserve Bank discount window and for Treasury tax and loan accounts. They are eligible for open market operations by the Federal Reserve, and national and state member banks may deal in, underwrite, and purchase Sallie Mae securities for their own account. Interest on obligations issued by Sallie Mae is subject to federal tax but is exempt from state, municipal, or local taxation. As of March 31, 1986, Sallie Mae had over $7 billion of securities outstanding. These securities are obligations of Sallie Mae and do not represent any guarantee by the United States government. Sallie Mae is an instrument of the government and subject to government regulations and restrictions.

FEDERAL HOME LOAN MORTGAGE CORPORATION

The Federal Home Loan Mortgage Corporation (FHLMC), also known as Freddie Mac, is a corporate instrument of the United States. The common stock of the corporation is owned entirely by the 12 Federal Home Loan Banks. Freddie Mac also has approximately 15 million shares of preferred stock outstanding. This stock was distributed to the Home Loan Banks who in turn distributed the stock to their member institutions. The board of the FHLMC is composed of the three members of the Federal Home Loan Bank Board; the chairman of the bank board is also chairman of the Board of Freddie Mac.

Freddie Mac was created pursuant to the Federal Home Loan Mortgage Corporation Act, Title III of the Emergency Home Finance Act of 1970, primarily for the purpose of increasing the availability of mortgage money for the financing of housing. It seeks to do this by providing an increased degree of liquidity for residential mortgage investments. This is accomplished by providing a secondary market for conventional mortgages. Prior to 1970 a viable secondary market existed only for FHA and VA mortgages. This market was supported by both the Federal National Mortgage Association (FNMA) and the Government National Mortgage Association (GNMA). However, at that point in time, no real secondary market existed for conventional mortgages, thus the need for Freddie Mac. Freddie Mac accomplishes these goals by purchasing a large volume of conventional mortgages in a nationwide market. It then sells mortgages by means of mortgage-related security instruments, primarily mortgage participation certificates.

Federal Home Loan Mortgage Corporation Mortgage-Participation Certificates

Federal Home Loan Mortgage Corporation mortgage-participation certificates (PCs) or Freddie Mac PC are the principle means by which Freddie Mac currently raises funds for its mortgage purchaser. In fact the principle purpose of Freddie Mac consists of the purchase of first lien, conventional, residential mortgages or participations therein and the resale of the mortgages in the form of guaranteed mortgage securities, primarily various types of PCs. So Freddie Mac PCs represent undivided interest in conventional (FHA/VA can also be used) mortgages purchased by Freddie Mac. Each certificate holder then receives a prorated share of all principal and interest payments, including any prepayments collected on the mortgages in the underlying pools. Freddie Mac guarantees the timely payment of interest and the ultimate collection of principal on the mortgages regardless of what happens to the underlying loans. In 1981 Freddie Mac initiated the Home Mortgage Guarantor Program. Under this program Freddie Mac purchases mortgages from sellers in exchange for PCs representing interest in the mortgage so purchased. In the Guarantor Program the mortgages are exchanged for PCs; under the cash program Freddie Mac buys the mortgages outright and then issues PCs. As of December 31, 1985, there were approximately $99.3 billion of Freddie Mac PCs outstanding, of which $68.5 billion were from the Guarantor Program. As of June 30, 1986, over $125 billion of PCs were outstanding. Conventional mortgages are pooled according to some standard, that is, 30-year mortgage pools, 15-year mortgage pools, adjustable rate mortgage pools (ARMS), and multifamily pools. The conventional 30-year mortgage pool has an approximate average life of 12 years and has been issued since the 1970s. In 1984, in response to the demand for shorter term mortgages, Freddie Mac began issuing 15-year mortgages known as GNOMES PCs. The securities, with an approximate average life of seven years, have been readily purchased by investors that traditionally would not purchase mortgage securities because of the longer maturities. Also in response to the marketplace Freddie Mac began issuing adjustable rate mortgage PCs or ARMS. While ARMs are only a small part of the program at this time, the popularity of the product should increase in periods when interest rates begin moving up.

FHLMC Collateralized Mortgage Obligations

From June 1983 to December 1985, Freddie Mac has issued nine series of collateralized mortgage obligations (CMOs) and has an aggregate amount of $5.8 billion outstanding. CMOs, which are guaranteed by Freddie Mac, have several different traunches, or maturity dates, with semiannual principal payments allocated to each class or traunche in the order of the stated maturity. This means that no principal payments are made to the holder of a class until all classes or traunches with an earlier maturity are retired. This enables Freddie

Mac to tap a market of very short-term buyers, including commercial banks. Very often the approximate average life of the first class is three years or less. Unlike the PCs, where the holder receives monthly paybacks of principal and interest, Freddie Mac CMOs pay only semiannually.

FHLMC Discount Notes and Debentures

Freddie Mac has a small amount of discount notes and debentures outstanding, which it began issuing in 1981. As of December 1985, there were only $1.47 billion of debentures and $3.5 billion discount notes outstanding. These are unsecured general obligations of Freddie Mac.

Other Programs

Freddie Mac has numerous programs under development and several that have been used in the past including guaranteed mortgage certificates (GMC) and graduated payment mortgages (GPMs). There are only small amounts of the securities outstanding at this time. Undoubtedly in the future, new products will come along to enhance the mortgage market and allow Freddie Mac to accomplish its goal of providing funds and a secondary market for conventional mortgages.

GOVERNMENT NATIONAL MORTGAGE ASSOCIATION

The Government National Mortgage Association (GNMA or Ginnie Mae) was created in 1968 when the Federal National Mortgage Association was portioned into two corporations. Under the power of the Housing and Urban Development Act of 1968, GNMA became a wholly owned corporate instrument of the U.S. government within the Department of Housing and Urban Development (HUD). GNMA's role is to support the government's housing objectives by establishing secondary markets for residential mortgages. By providing a vehicle for channeling funds from the securities markets into the mortgage markets, GNMA assures a supply of funds for housing. The act also authorizes GNMA to guarantee the timely payment of principal and interest on securities backed by VA, FmHA, and FHA and issued by approved institutions. It is this guarantee that makes GNMA securities unique in the mortgage market because the payments guaranteed by GNMA are backed by the "full faith and credit" of the U.S. government. Because of this guarantee, GNMA securities are the most widely held and actively traded mortgage-backed securities in the world. As of April 1986, GNMA had outstanding guaranteed mortgages in excess of $220 billion.

Mortgage-Backed Securities Program

Through the mortgage-backed securities program, GNMA guarantees privately issued securities that are backed by pools of mortgages issued by VA, FHA, of the FmHA. These securities are known as modified "pass-through" securities. This means the holder of the securities receives monthly payments of principal and interest from the issuer. That is, the issuer passes through to the holder of the pools any prepayments or other unscheduled recoveries of principal along with the scheduled paydown of principal and interest. The holder receives these payments whether or not such payments are made by the mortgagors. (They are called modified because of the guarantee as to timely payment of principal and interest by GNMA.) Ginnie Mae administers two mortgage-backed securities program, GNMA I and GNMA II. The GNMA I program was instated in 1970 and includes several programs not found in GNMA II. The GNMA II program was introduced in 1983 and includes the use of a central paying agent (as opposed to each individual issuer issuing checks) and the availability of larger geographically dispersed issuers as well as multifamily issuers. All underlying mortgages in a GNMA I pool have the same interest rate while mortgages in a GNMA II pool may have interest rates that vary within a one percentage point range. Each of these programs in turn have several subprograms. The subprograms are (1) single-family level payment mortgages, (2) prorated payment mortgages, (3) adjustable rate mortgages (GNMA II only), (4) growing equity mortgages, (5) manufactured home loans, (6) construction loans—multifamily (GNMA I only), (7) project loans (GNMA I only), (8) buydown loans (GNMA I only). By far the most popular program is the single-family mortgage program. Because each of these programs and the various subprograms have different characteristics they do trade differently in the secondary markets. Basically, the GNMA mortgage-backed securities program works as follows. A mortgage lender applies to GNMA for approval to become an issuer of GNMA mortgage-backed securities and for a commitment for this guarantee of a securities issuers. There are currently 1,400 approved issuers. The issuer then originates or acquires government insured or guaranteed mortgages and packages them into a pool. The pool of the underlying mortgages must be of the same type and have similar maturities. The interest rate structure is determined by whether the pool will be issued under the GNMA I or II program. The issuer submits pool mortgage documents to a private financial institution, which serves as document custodian. GNMA then reviews the documents and authorizes its transfer agent (Chemical Bank) to prepare and deliver the securities to the investors. Finally, the issuer is responsible for the marketing and administration of the securities. If it is a GNMA I program, the issuer also makes the monthly principal and interest payments. In a GNMA II program, the issuer remits its funds to GNMA's central paying agent, which in turn pays the holder. In both programs, the issuer continues to carry out the mortgage servicing on the loans.

FEDERAL FINANCING BANK

The Federal Financing Bank was established in 1973 to consolidate the government's cost of financing a variety of federal agencies and other borrowers whose obligations are guaranteed by the federal government. The Farm Credit System, the Federal Home Loan Bank, the Federal Home Loan Mortgage Corporation, the Federal National Mortgage Association and in most cases the Student Loan Marketing Association are not eligible participants in this program. However, a variety of government agencies including the United States Postal Service, General Services Administration, and the Tennessee Valley Authority do use the Federal Financing Bank as a conduit for easing debt. The agencies are charged a rate of ⅛ percent above the Treasury borrowing rate for comparable securities. The Federal Financing Bank can finance its operations by issuing obligations publicly, not to exceed $15 billion unless specifically outlined. It can also require the Secretary of the Treasury to purchase up to $5 billion of its obligations, but the Secretary can purchase any amount at his discretion. The Federal Financing Bank has usually financed itself by borrowing directly from the Treasury. Although the bank can purchase partially guaranteed obligations, it has followed a policy of purchasing only obligations fully guaranteed as to principal and interest by a federal agency.

UNITED STATES POSTAL SERVICE

The United States Postal Service was created as an independent establishment in the executive branch of the United States government. On July 1, 1971, the Postal Services took over the business of the Post Office Department. The service is authorized to borrow funds as necessary either through direct offerings to the public or to the Department of the Treasury at the discretion of the Secretary of the Treasury. Obligations of the Postal Service may be fully guaranteed as to timely payment of principal and interest by the United States government if the Postal Service so represents, and the Secretary of the Treasury determines that the guaranty is in the public interest. As of December 31, 1985, the Postal Service had $250 million in Series A Bonds, 6⅞ percent due February 1, 1997, outstanding. These bonds are not guaranteed by the United States government. In addition, the Postal Service had $1.69 billion in unsecured notes payable to the Federal Financing Bank and a small amount in mortgage notes secured by land and buildings payable to a variety of holders.

FARMERS HOME ADMINISTRATION

The Farmers Home Administration (FmHA) is an agency in the Department of Agriculture that extends loans in rural areas for farms, homes, and community facilities. The sale of certificates of beneficial ownership (CBOs) to the public were discontinued in March 1975. Since that time, the FmHA has financed its program through the Federal Financing Bank. As obligations secured by the full faith and credit of the U.S. government, CBOs are acceptable security for deposits of public money and can be used as collateral for borrowings at the Federal Reserve Bank. As of March 1986, approximately $1 billion CBOs were outstanding.

MARITIME ADMINISTRATION

Merchant Marine obligations are issued and guaranteed under provisions of the Merchant Marine Act of 1936, as amended under the auspices of the Maritime Administration. The Maritime Administration is housed in the Department of Transportation. Prior to the Ship Financing Act of 1972, ship mortgages were insured by the United States. After 1972 the concept changed. Instead of being insured, the obligations are directly guaranteed by the United States. The full faith and credit of the United States is pledged with respect to both principal and interest. Each issue of Merchant Marine bonds or notes is secured by a first preferred ship or fleet mortgage. Since 1958 various bonds and notes have been offered, and as of March 1986, $5.89 billion remain outstanding.

TENNESSEE VALLEY AUTHORITY

The Tennessee Valley Authority was created by Congress to assist in the development of the Tennessee River and adjacent areas. The notes and bonds are secured by a first charge on net power proceeds. Since 1974 TVA has sold long-term bonds only to the Federal Financing Bank. As of December 31, 1985, TVA had bonds and notes outstanding of $16.4 billion, of which $1.167 billion was payable to the public and the remaining amount was due to the Federal Financing Act.

OTHER AGENCIES

There are several small issues that still have some bonds outstanding to the public. These include (1) the Federal Housing Administration, which has FHA debentures outstanding amounting to $139.1 million as of December 31, 1985. These obligations are fully guaranteed to principal and interest by the United States; (2) the General Services Administration, which has several series of participation certificates outstanding which were issued prior to 1975. These in aggregate total less than $1 billion, and all subsequent issues have been sold to the Federal Financing Bank; (3) the Small Business Administration, which has about $1 billion in SBA guaranteed debentures outstanding. These debentures are secured by the full faith and credit of the United States. Currently, all sales of debentures are being made to the Federal Financing Bank.

CHAPTER THIRTY-SEVEN

Municipal Bonds:
A Decade of Change

Donald R. Lipkin

Assistant Vice President
The First Boston Corporation

INTRODUCTION

The Tax Reform Act of 1986 represents a turning point in commercial bank participation in the municipal credit markets. In the past, favorable tax treatment of banks' carrying costs for municipal bonds made tax exempt bonds an attractive investment vehicle. Commercial banks were net buyers of municipals in each year from 1976 to 1985 and by the latter year held $231.4 billion of such securities, 34 percent of all such debt outstanding. The tax act has abruptly changed banks' investment posture toward municipals. In 1986 they were net sellers of municipals, reducing their holdings by $28.5 billion.[1]

Yet banks will remain active participants in the municipal market. They will continue to be major underwriters of municipal bonds. In 1986, 13 of the top 50 leading underwriters of municipals were commercial banks. They also have active trading departments that deal in both the cash and futures markets. Banks will of course need to manage their current holdings of municipals and will continue to manage clients' portfolios through trust departments. Finally, commercial banks will likely be players in the new taxable municipals that have been spawned by tax reform. Clearly, commercial banks will need to stay current on the latest developments in the municipal market.

---

[1] *Flow of Funds Accounts, Financial Assets and Liabilities Year-End, 1962–85* (Washington, D.C.: Board of Governors of the Federal Reserve System), September 1986. *Flow of Funds Accounts, First Quarter 1987* (Washington, D.C.: Board of Governors of the Federal Reserve System), June 1987.

That market continues to change at a breakneck speed. In an earlier edition of the handbook, it was possible to define the categories of municipal bonds in terms of general obligation and revenue bonds, serial and term bonds. Today, investors must contemplate a panoply of credit and maturity structures that make investing in municipals more complex than ever before. There are traditional revenue bonds used to finance revenue generating facilities, but there are also bonds backed by mortgage or student loans, insurance companies, banks, and even other securities purchased with the bond proceeds themselves. There are still serial and term bonds, but there are also put option bonds, zero coupon bonds, and commercial paper. Even the hallmark of municipal bonds, their tax exempt status, is no longer a simple matter. There are minimum taxes on some municipal bonds, and other municipals are completely taxable.

The municipal bond market is at a major juncture for both the market in general and banks in particular. This chapter examines how the bonds themselves and the marketplace that supports them have developed. We will conclude with a discussion of the Tax Reform Act of 1986 (the Act) and the impact that it is having on this very important sector of the securities markets.

TYPES OF MUNICIPAL BONDS

The distinguishing feature of a municipal security has traditionally been that it is a debt issuance by a public entity for a public purpose, the interest on which is free from federal income taxation. Beyond this generic definition, municipal securities offer a multiplicity of variations. Issuers of municipal securities include states, local governments, special districts, and a vast array of public agencies, many of which have been established for the sole purpose of issuing debt. Public purposes range from building schools, roads, and sewer systems to making loans to college students and private corporations.

Under the doctrine of reciprocal immunity, the interest on most municipals is free from federal income tax. Interest earnings are usually free from state and local income taxes when the holder of a bond is a resident of the issuer's state. A resident of New York City who buys a bond issued by the city of Rochester will pay no city, state, or federal income taxes on the interest income on that bond. The tax exempt status of municipal securities has been under assault over the last several years. Starting in 1984, recipients of social security must include their tax exempt interest in calculating total income, which could make certain social security payments subject to income tax. A more serious incursion on this tax exempt status is contained in the Act, which we will discuss later.

Credit Features

The purpose of a municipal bond and the sources of security backing that bond are normally interrelated. The two basic types of bonds are the general obligation bond (GO) and the revenue bond. The general obligation bond pledges the full faith and credit of the issuer to pay principal and interest. GO bonds are normally issued for nonrevenue-producing projects such as schools, roads, and public buildings, but it is not unusual for them to be issued for revenue-producing projects such as water and sewer systems. States that issue general obligation bonds normally pledge the unrestricted revenues of their general fund, which is the main operating fund. Since localities have less revenue flexibility than states and they rely on the property tax as a major source of revenue, they often back the general obligation pledge with a promise to raise property taxes in an amount sufficient to pay debt service on the bonds. When the pledge to raise taxes is unrestricted as to the rate or dollar amount at which the property tax may be levied to pay debt service, the bond is said to be an unlimited tax general obligation. Localities, however, often have property tax limits set by state or local law; in this case, the bond is a limited tax general obligation. All tax bonds, however, are not general obligations. Sales tax bonds pledge as security and source of payment of debt service all or a portion of the sales tax collected in a particular state or locality. Highway bonds may be secured by a pledge of gasoline taxes. Special assessment bonds are payable from a tax on properties that directly benefit from the project being financed. One often sees this type of bond for local road or sewer line projects, the benefits of which are easily allocated among the affected parties.

Revenue bonds pledge the revenue from the project or system being financed. More traditional types of revenue bonds are issued for capital programs for municipal services such as water and sewer systems, toll roads, electric power plants, and airports. The revenue bond issuer covenants to raise rates, charges, or fees in an amount sufficient, after paying all other expenses, to cover debt service by a specified margin. A 1.5 times rate covenant would require an issuer of toll road bonds to raise tolls to a level sufficient to cover debt service 1.5 times after providing for the costs of operating and maintaining the road system. As additional security, there are also restrictions on the amount of additional bonds that can be issued to prevent diluting the revenue stream supporting debt service on the existing bonds. Another security feature would be a reserve fund established to pay debt service should there be a temporary interruption of revenues from the project.

General obligation and municipal service revenue bonds have long been the workhorse of municipal finance. There is widespread agreement that they finance proper government functions. The issuing entity raises the money through a debt issuance, builds the project, and then operates the facility. The financing vehicle is therefore only one leg of the government's role in carrying out its responsibilities. There is another type of revenue bond in which the issuing authority is only nominally involved in the transaction. In so-called conduit financing, the public body lends its name to the bond issue but really only acts as a conduit through which the money flows, linking the buyer of the bond and the user of the project being financed. Hospital bonds are a good example of this type of financing where an issuing entity (local government or special authority) floats a bond issue and then lends the proceeds to a private nonprofit hospital. The bond-holder can then only look to the hospital to pay debt service on the bonds. Another example of conduit financing is the industrial development bond which is issued to provide loans to a private corporation, inducing it to relocate or expand its facilities in the issuing authority's jurisdiction. Again, the bond is a "special obligation" of the issuer, meaning that the issuer is only required to pass through the loan payments paid by the company and is not itself directly or indirectly responsible for debt service.

In the revenue bonds described, the projects being financed were part of systems that had revenue flexibility: the hospital can raise rates, the corporation can raise prices. In structured financings like single- and multifamily housing bonds and student loan bonds, the proceeds of the bond issues are used to purchase specific revenue generating assets, the narrow cash flow from which is used to pay off the bonds. In a single-family housing bond, the bond proceeds are used to purchase home mortgage loans that pay interest at a specified rate. The issue is structured so that the mortgage payments of principal and interest more than cover debt service on the bonds. To guard against an unscheduled interruption of mortgage payments, there is normally a reserve fund, often funded from bond proceeds. To provide an added level of comfort to bondholders, the mortgages are usually insured to protect against nonpayment of the underlying mortgage loans.

An interesting form of security is the prerefunded bond. Most municipal debt has historically enjoyed 10 years of call protection. When an issuer wishes to retire its general obligation or revenue debt before the call date, either because interest rates have dropped or because it wishes to break certain restrictive covenants imposed by that debt, it will refund the issue. The issuer floats a new bond issue, uses the proceeds of the new issue to buy Treasuries, and then irrevocably pledges the interest and principal payments of the Treasuries to pay debt service on the old bond. This defeases the issuer's obligation on the old debt. For the investor, the defeasance can have the positive effect of substituting securities guaranteed by the U.S. government for a much weaker credit. Many of these prerefunded issues have been upgraded to triple A by the rating agencies.

Credit Enhancement

There has been a growing market for lower quality bond issues which have a second layer of credit support beyond the underlying revenue or general obligation structure. The most well known and widely used form of such credit enhancement is municipal bond insurance, in which an insurer guarantees timely payment of principal and interest on the bond to maturity.

With bond insurance, the claims paying ability of the insurer is substituted for the credit quality of the insurer. The rating on the bond is therefore tied to the rating on the insurer. The four major bond insurers are AMBAC Indemnity Corporation, Financial Guaranty Insurance Company (FGIC), Municipal Bond Investors Assurance Corporation (MBIA), and Bond Investors Guaranty (BIG), all of which are rated triple A by both Standard & Poor's and Moody's Investors Service. Bond insurers insure new issues of municipals and will also insure outstanding issues trading in the secondary market.

A major growth area for marketing insured bond issues has been with the individual investor, who may not have the level of sophistication or resources of the institutional investor to analyze underlying credits. The bond insurance in effect makes the bond issue a more generic product for the unsophisticated investor. There has been some debate as to whether bond insurance or any other form of external credit support can substitute for or merely enhances the underlying credit of the issuer. More conservative investors demand that they be satisfied with the creditworthiness of the underlying credit before they buy an insured bond issue.

Banks have also become important participants in the market for credit enhancement vehicles and will likely continue to play a major role. Letters of credit (LOCs) are provided for many issues and function in much the same way as bond insurance. They may be direct pay LOCs, where the bank makes debt service payments directly to the investor with the issuer reimbursing the bank for its payment, or they may be standby instruments, only used where the issuer fails to make a payment. As with insurance, the credit rating of the issue is dependent on the credit rating of the bank. Because of their high ratings and aggressive fee structures, Japanese and European banks have increasingly become dominant in writing LOCs in the municipal market.

Credit Risk

The two major rating agencies for municipal credits are Moody's and Standard & Poor's. In their ratings they try to capture the relative risk of default on an issuer's obligation to make timely payments of principal and interest. The risk of default has been a serious one. By the end of the 1930s, municipal bond defaults peaked at approximately 10 percent of bonds outstanding. Between 1945 and 1970, $450 million in principal amount of bonds defaulted or 0.4 percent of bonds outstanding in 1970.[2] In 1975 New York City sent shock waves through the municipal market by defaulting on its general obligation notes. In 1978 the New York State Urban Development Corporation defaulted on $130 million in short-term debt. Both of these defaults were subsequently made good by the issuers. The default by the Washington Public Power Supply System on its $2.25 billion in debt in 1983 for Projects 4 and 5 has not had such a positive resolution. Holders of that debt have little chance of fully recovering their principal.

While the risk of default is real, the vast majority of municipal issuers will likely make good on their debts. Beyond the question of pay-no pay, however, there is the very real and often costly question of credit volatility. The risk of a rating downgrade carries a financial penalty; when an issue is downgraded, the value of that issue will decline in the marketplace. In 1985, Moody's downgraded 295 municipal issues and Standard & Poor's downgraded 394. It is therefore incumbent on the investor to monitor his portfolio for developing credit situations. This has become even more critical as bond insurers and banks have substituted their credit ratings for those of many individual issues. This risk was realized on December 23, 1985 when Standard & Poor's downgraded the claims-paying rating of Industrial Indemnity Company from AAA to AA. As a result, 267 insured bond issues totaling $5.2 billion were downgraded to AA. In another case, Ticor Mortgage Insurance Company, which insures at least part of the mortgage portfolios in over $1.4 billion housing bonds, had its claims paying ability downgraded by Moody's from A2 to B1 and by Standard & Poor's from AA to CCC. Some of these housing bonds were subsequently downgraded depending on the degree to which they rely on the Ticor mortgage insurance. Many downgrades have also oc-

---

[2]James E. Spiotto, "Analysis of Defaults and Remedies," *Current Municipal Defaults and Bankruptcy 1983*, Course Handbook Series No. 238, (New York: Practicing Law Institute), pp. 29–32.

curred in recent years when the ratings on banks that provide letters of credit to various issuers have been downgraded.

It is clearly incumbent on buyers of municipals to monitor their holdings. When an issue first comes to market, an official statement is distributed by the issuer which outlines the various security features and discusses the financial and economic condition of the issuer. After issuance, the ability of the buyer to remain informed becomes more difficult but is nonetheless possible if sufficient resources can be devoted to monitoring the municipal portfolio.

Bond Structures

Most municipals are structured with 10-year call protection. It is important to note, however, that investors should pay close attention to the specific call provisions of their bonds. Many issues allow bond calls at par at any time. This is true with industrial development bonds should the company default on its payments, the project shut down, or the bonds be declared taxable. It is especially true with housing bonds, where calls are usually permitted or even mandated if the bond proceeds are unable to be loaned out or the single-family homeowner or multifamily project developer prepays his mortgage loan. Such call risk can seriously affect the trading value of outstanding bonds.

A large portion of the municipal bond market is still structured as fixed rate serial and term bonds. A bond issue will typically have a strip of serial bonds, each with a different specified interest rate, and one or more term bonds. The term bonds have mandatory sinking fund payments in the years prior to their maturity, avoiding the burden of having large balloon payments coming due in later years. For a general obligation bond, this spreads the tax burden more fairly over the life of the issue, and for a revenue bond issue it more closely approximates the expected stream of revenues.

When interest rates spiked upward in the early 1980s, issuers increasingly turned to innovative structures to lower their borrowing costs. One way to do this was to tap the short-term market to take advantage of the lower end of the yield curve. Traditionally, issuers had borrowed short term using revenue or tax anticipation notes for cash flow purposes so they could tap state or federal aid or tax revenues prior to their receipt. They would also use bond anticipation notes as a source of interim financing to establish final cost before a project was permanently bonded out. More recently, variable rate tender option bonds were developed. Tender option bonds enable an issuer to sell long term bonds which carry a short-term interest rate by allowing the bondholder to demand redemption on a specified tender date. The ability of the bondholder to put or tender a 30-year bond back to the issuer in, say, five years would allow the bond issue to be marketed at a rate closer to the five-year effective maturity rather than the 30-year stated maturity. To provide liquidity, the bond issue will normally be structured with a credit facility with one or more commercial banks to insure that, should the bondholders put their bonds back to the bond trustee and the issuer is not able to raise sufficient funds, there is a mechanism for the bondholder to be paid on a timely basis. Another innovative development has been the short-term variable rate demand bond. The demand feature of this bond allows the investor to demand payment of principal on a long-term bond over very short intervals, usually on seven days' notice. This allows the issuer to tap very short-term rates. These rates are periodically adjusted so that the noteholder is always paid the going market rate and suffers almost no principal risk on his investment.

Another innovation in structuring municipal bond issues is the zero coupon, or capital appreciation, bond. This has been especially prevalent in housing bonds. The investor buys these at a deep discount to the maturity value and is paid all principal and interest at maturity. There is also a modified form of zero coupon bond which pays no interest for a specified period and then converts to a current coupon bond until maturity. In both cases, the accreted value of the bond is treated by the Internal Revenue Service as tax exempt interest for tax purposes, allowing the investor to avoid paying federal income taxes thereon.

THE MARKET FOR MUNICIPAL BONDS

The Distribution System

The primary market for municipals has shown explosive growth in recent years. Between 1977 and 1981, total bond issuance fluctuated around $45 billion annually. In 1984, $101.9 billion was issued. In 1985 and 1986, $204 billion and $142.5 billion bonds, respectively, came to market with much of the increase engendered by the specter of tax reform. And while volume grew, the composition of the new issue market also changed dramatically.

In 1978, hospital, housing, industrial, and pollution control bonds comprised approximately 16 percent of the new issue market; by 1985 they captured almost 42 percent of the market (see Table 1). Issuers were clearly using their ability to tap the tax exempt market for an expanding array of purposes. They were in effect passing on the interest cost savings that they enjoyed for such clearly public projects as schools and highways to purposes less clearly tied to the common-

TABLE 1   Bond Issuance by Purpose ($ billions)

	1978	1982	1984	1985	1986
Schools	$ 6.2	$ 6.6	$ 9.8	$ 24.2	$ 17.3
Water and sewer	4.5	4.6	5.9	13.0	15.5
Transportation	1.9	1.1	8.8	13.3	12.9
Gas and electric	6.0	9.5	11.2	27.9	21.9
Hospital	3.1	9.7	10.2	30.2	9.3
Housing finance	—	15.7	20.5	37.5	8.7
Industrial & pollution control	4.1	10.1	19.2	17.5	8.3
Other	20.4	20.0	16.3	40.4	48.7
Total	$46.2	$77.2	$101.9	$204.0	$142.5

SOURCE: *The Bond Buyer 1987 Yearbook,* (New York: The Bond Buyer). Copyright © 1987 by The Bond Buyer.

weal. Congress had tried several times to contain the growth in the use of tax exempt bonds for nontraditional purposes. The Act went much further in this regard.

New issues of municipals are brought to market in either negotiated or competitive sales. In Table 2, the negotiated form of sale has become dominant, comprising 75.4 percent of the market in 1986. In a negotiated sale, underwriters compete for the opportunity to represent the issuer. Once an underwriter has been selected, it then structures the bond issue, prepares an official statement describing the financing and the credit behind it, forms an underwriting group, conducts a premarketing survey to help determine an appropriate interest rate in the present environment, and then negotiates the purchase price of the bond issue with the issuer. There is a particular incentive to come as a negotiated sale when a bond issue has a complex or unusual structure, is very large, or the credit supporting the issue is less than sterling. It is also not coincidental that negotiated sales became preponderant in a market that was increasingly dominated by revenue bonds. Issuers of revenue bonds often are free from the legal restrictions that force issuers of general obligation bonds to come through competitive bidding. In a competitive bond sale, the issuer will advertise the time of sale and the conditions of the bid. It then prepares and distributes the obligatory official statement. The underwriters, after polling prospective buyers, enter a sealed bid with the award going to the group whose bid produces the lowest interest cost for the issuer.

The dominance of the revenue bond has worked to the disadvantage of commercial banks. Because of restrictions under the Glass-Steagall Act of 1933, banks are precluded from underwriting most

TABLE 2   Composition of the Municipal Market (percent of total market)

	1976	1980	1986
Negotiated	42.3	58.7	75.4
Competitive	57.7	41.3	24.6
Revenue	50.0	65.3	61.9
General obligation	50.0	34.7	38.1

SOURCE: *The Bond Buyer 1985 Municipal Statbook* (New York: The Bond Buyer). Copyright © 1985 by The Bond Buyer. *The Bond Buyer 1987 Yearbook* (New York: The Bond Buyer). Copyright © 1987 by The Bond Buyer.

types of revenue bonds. This has prevented them from garnering any of the top spots in the underwriting leagues. Yet banks are becoming increasingly aggressive in pushing for expanded underwriting powers. Should they prove successful, we can expect them to compete vigorously for a larger share of the market.

Buyers of Municipal Bonds

Over the last 10 years, commercial banks, property and casualty insurance companies, and households have been the major buyers of municipal bonds. In 1986 these three sectors accounted for 97 percent of the total market. As Table 3 illustrates, what was once a market dominated by banks has been increasingly supported by the household sector.

Municipal bonds are attractive to investors when their yields are competitive compared to other types of securities in the investment universe. Buyers will acquire tax exempt securities when their yields are competitive with those on taxable securities on an after-tax basis. The concept of the taxable equivalent yield is useful in evaluating the relative attractiveness of tax exempts. The taxable equivalent yield on a municipal bond is that rate which would have to be earned on the security that would make it equally attractive to the investor if it were taxable. That determination is controlled by the investor's marginal tax rate. We calculate the taxable equivalent yield (TEY) by dividing the tax exempt yield (Y) by one minus the marginal tax rate, or in the case of an individual investor in the 50 percent marginal tax bracket in 1986: $TEY = Y/(1 - .50)$. As marginal tax rates go up or down, tax exempt yields must also rise or fall to remain as attractive to investors, all other factors being equal. Of course, all other factors are rarely equal, so municipal yields will not necessarily move in lockstep with changes in marginal tax rates.

TABLE 3 Holders of Municipal Bonds ($ billions)

	1974	1978	1982	1985	1986
Households & mutual funds	$ 61.9	$ 73.9	$145.0	$325.5	$399.7
Commercial banks	101.1	126.2	158.5	231.4	202.9
Insurance companies	34.4	69.3	96.0	97.3	99.5
Other	10.2	20.3	18.4	20.2	21.9
Total	$207.7	$289.7	$417.9	$674.4	$723.9

SOURCE: *Flow of Funds Accounts, Financial Assets and Liabilities Year-End, 1962–85* (Washington D.D.: Board of Governors of the Federal Reserve System, September 1986). *Flow of Funds Accounts, First Quarter 1987*, (Washington, D.C.: Board of Governors of the Federal Reserve System, June 1987).

The Individual Investor   The dominance of the individual investor in the municipal market has been caused by various factors that have made municipals more attractive to them and less attractive to other major buying segments. In 1978 households held 26 percent of all outstanding municipal bonds. By 1986 that figure rose to 55 percent of the total. Their willingness to absorb the burgeoning supply of municipals was in part caused by the high rates of inflation in the late 1970s and early 1980s. As wages and salaries were propelled upward, people were pushed into higher tax brackets. This "bracket creep" pushed up taxable equivalent yields, making municipals more attractive to a larger segment of the public. In addition, the advent of the tax exempt open-end mutual fund and unit investment trust made investing in municipals more approachable for more people. Mutual fund holdings of tax exempts went from $9.3 billion in 1981 to $76.3 billion in 1985, a 69 percent compound annual growth rate. In 1986, mutual fund holdings jumped 78% to $135.6 billion. It is safe to assume that, given the changes wrought by the Act, specifically those affecting banks' appetite for municipals, the individual investor will remain the dominant buyer of tax exempts.

Commercial Banks   Commercial banks held more municipals in the 1970s than any other segment of buyers. Banks found municipals attractive because, unlike other buyers, they have been able to invest deposited funds in tax exempts and deduct a portion of the interest paid on those funds as an expense for income tax purposes. This is the so-called TEFRA deduction. Other investors are not permitted to deduct the carrying costs of debt incurred to buy tax exempts. Banks' ability to deduct such interest costs was made less generous in the 1980s; for bonds acquired after December 31, 1982, banks can deduct only 80 percent of the interest cost incurred to carry such bonds. Tax exempts acquired before that date continue to benefit from the more generous deduction.

The less generous interest deduction worked to dampen banks appetite for municipals as a way to shelter profits, but the erosion in bank demand had really started much earlier. Where in the 1960s banks had increased their participation in the municipal market, the 1970s and early 1980s saw that participation weaken. In 1970 commercial banks held 48.6 percent of all municipals outstanding; by 1980 that had declined to 42.6 percent and by 1986 to 28.0 percent. Measured another way, municipals as a percent of banks total assets declined from 13.6 percent in 1970 to 7.8 percent in 1986. In the 1970s banks involvement in leasing increased dramatically and competed with municipals as a way to shelter profits. In the late 1970s and early 1980s, a slowdown in profit growth, increased loan loss provisions, the corporate tax rate decline from 48 percent to 46 percent, and an increase in banks cost of funds combined with the less generous TEFRA deduction to reduce bank demand for municipals.[3]

In 1985 banks were faced with impending tax reform which promised to end the TEFRA deduction for newly acquired tax exempts. To lock in existing TEFRA benefits, banks went on a buying spree and increased their net holdings of municipals by more than $57 billion, more net purchases than they had made over the previous six years combined. With the Act, banks are no longer able to deduct their interest costs on most newly acquired municipals.

Insurance Companies   The other major group to buy municipals are the property and casualty insurers. Such insurers increased their market share of municipals to 22.5 percent of outstanding bonds, but in the first half of the 1980s their market share dropped as their net purchases increased only marginally. As property-casualty insurers return to profitability, they can be expected to become a more important force in the market.

MUNICIPAL BONDS AFTER TAX REFORM

The Act distinguishes between private activity bonds and governmental bonds. Private activity bonds are those used for a private trade or business or to make private loans. These bonds are taxable unless they fall into one of six categories and comply with various new restrictions. The six categories are exempt facility bonds (such as for airports, multifamily housing, and water facilities), single-family mortgage bonds, small issue bonds (traditional industrial revenue bonds), student loan bonds, redevelopment bonds, and 501(C)(3) bonds (for hospitals and higher edu-

---

[3]Allen J. Proctor and Kathleene K. Donahoo, "Commercial Bank Investment in Municipal Securities," *Federal Reserve Bank of New York Quarterly Review,* Winter 1983–84, pp. 26–37.

cation). This greatly narrows the purposes for which tax exempts may be issued as compared to previous law.

In addition to restricting the purposes which may be funded with tax exempt money, total tax exempt issuance is also restricted. The Act imposes a state volume limitation on most private activity bonds equal to the greater of $75 per capita or $250 million per year. After 1987 this drops down to $50 per capita and $150 million. The Public Securities Association has estimated that the volume limit in conjunction with the restrictions on the kinds of bonds which can be issued will sharply restrict the amount of bonds which might have otherwise been issued. They project that 41 percent of all tax exempt bonds issued in 1984 would not be able to be issued on a tax exempt basis by 1991.[4]

The factors discussed so far affect an issuer's ability to come to market. Several provisions in the Act will affect municipal bonds' marketability. The alternative minimum tax (AMT) will now be applicable to tax-exempts. Tax exempt interest on most new private activity bonds will be included as a preference item in calculating the AMT for individuals and corporations. Since the Act was passed by Congress, newly issued private activity bonds subject to the AMT have been penalized by being priced 25 to 50 basis points above non-AMT bonds. In another provision, all tax exempt interest will be included as an item to be considered in the so-called book income alternative minimum tax for corporations. Of course, neither of these provisions hurts corporations or individuals whose preference items are not large enough to trigger the AMT.

Several provisions affect particular types of buyers. Banks will generally no longer be able to deduct the interest expense incurred to carry tax exempts. They will, however, be able to continue to deduct 80 percent of the interest expense for certain governmental and 501 (C)(3) bonds. The issuer of these bonds must not expect to issue more than a total of $10 million bonds in each calendar year. Banks will likely take advantage of this provision and remain active in buying the bonds of small issuers.

In a section of the Act that improves the marketability of tax exempts, it is now permissible to strip the interest payments off an existing tax exempt bond and sell the interest and principal payments as separate zero coupon bonds in the same way that U.S. Treasuries have been stripped. This may prove useful for certain commercial banks. If a bank is not currently profitable but expects to return to

---

[4]*The Impact of Provisions on Tax-Exempt Bonds in the Tax Reform Bill: A Statistical Analysis Regarding Volume and Increased Borrowing Costs* (New York: Public Securities Association, October 2, 1986), p. 1.

profitability in the future, it may be possible to sell off the near-term interest payments on their tax exempt holdings. By retaining the principal portion of the bond, the bank may retain the TEFRA exemption on that bond. In the meantime, the bank could replace higher yielding taxable income for the tax exempt income it does not currently need.

TAXABLE MUNICIPAL BONDS

One outgrowth of the Act will be the growth of taxable municipal debt. The trade papers estimate the potential yearly new issue market for the taxable municipals from between $10 and $40 billion. The volume limitations, arbitrage restrictions, and narrowing of permissible types of projects will drive many issuers into the taxable market to carry on the public purpose as they perceive it. To date, much of the volume in the taxable municipal market has been for arbitrage deals in which an issuer raises money to invest in higher yielding investment contracts with insurance companies. While these arbitrage deals have gotten most of the media attention, there will likely develop a bona fide taxable municipal market that attempts to meet the needs of government to carry out its public purpose. Indeed, with the severe restrictions now imposed on tax exempt debt, it would be surprising if such a market did not develop.

CONCLUSION

The taxable municipal bond will be an area in which banks will likely be a significant player. While the municipal market as a whole will probably not reach the size it did in 1985 for quite some time, it will remain a significant market. Various participants have estimated that tax exempt volume alone will be in the neighborhood of $80 to $100 billion per year over the next several years. Given their role as underwriters, dealers, and buyers of municipals, given their large trust departments, and given the $200-plus billion existing portfolio of municipals, the commercial banker will remain very interested in the progress of this changing product—the municipal bond.

CHAPTER THIRTY-EIGHT

Managing the Investments Portfolio of the Bank

John Ward Logan

Executive Vice President
First American Corporation

The bank's securities portfolio is necessarily a dependent variable in the structure of the bank's balance sheet. It is expected to be a primary store of liquidity enabling the bank to meet future contingencies. It is the balancing item by which banks can most readily alter their interest rate sensitivity. In addition, the portfolio must be of high overall credit quality and include no significant credit risks.

Despite these constraints, the securities portfolio can be a major contributor to the bank's earnings. Unlike the customer service oriented functions of the bank, the portfolio exists primarily for the benefit of the bank and for its shareholders. The well-managed portfolio increases the bank's returns, stabilizes the interest margin, and mitigates volatility in the earnings stream.

Successful portfolio management is not easy. Besides those constraints which necessitate a heavy concentration of relatively high-quality liquid assets in the portfolio, there is another—the relatively high cost of each dollar of a bank's investable funds—that sharply differentiates the goals of portfolio management in a bank from those of many other investors in the same markets and instruments. The result is a compelling need for the banker to be particularly astute in evaluating risk/return trade-offs when making investment decisions.

THE CONSTRAINTS ON PORTFOLIO MANAGEMENT

The portfolio manager must operate within limitations imposed by consideration of the bank's overall liquidity and interest rate sensitivity, and by the need for the bank to avoid undue concentrations of credit risk. Other factors influencing portfolio structure relate to the bank's capital adequacy, tax position, and degree of access to marginal funding sources.

Liquidity Considerations

Liquidity Measurement and Monitoring. There are different and equally valid ways of measuring liquidity within the bank. The ratio approach compares key variables such as liquid assets to total assets, purchased (nonretail) funds to total assets, and liquid assets to purchased funds. Another approach is to measure historic deposit and loan volatility, assume worst case scenarios in both variables, add an additional safety margin, and set minimum liquid asset levels based on the results of these calculations. The former approach would seem to be the more appropriate for banks with significant amounts of volatile purchased funds, the latter in banks with a high percentage of core deposits. Regardless of the approach, monitoring liquidity must be an ongoing process designed to detect trends toward improving or deteriorating liquidity at an early stage. Minimum liquidity standards should be approved by the board of directors and results of the liquidity monitoring process reported to them regularly.

There can be no universal standards regarding bank liquidity since each bank is unique. It is, however, extremely useful to seek out peer group banks that are willing to exchange data on liquidity measurements and standards.

The Portfolio as a Primary Store of Liquidity. Aside from cash, the bank's primary store of liquid assets is typically in the investment portfolio. Liquid assets are those that can readily be converted to cash. High-grade securities maturing within a short period of time are obvious liquid assets. In addition to these, securities meeting some combination of the following requirements can, to a greater or lesser degree, be considered to be liquid assets:

1. Securities for which there exists an exceptionally broad secondary market such as Treasury notes, Federal agency securities, or certificates of deposit of major domestic banks.
2. Securities which exhibit a high level of cash flow to the holder such as high coupon mortgage-backed securities (to the degree that the cash flow is assured in all likely interest rate environments).
3. Securities which can be liquidated without capital impairment; that is, whose current market value exceeds the bank's carrying (or book) cost.

4. Securities with exceptionally stable market value such as floating rate notes.
5. Securities which bear no appreciable default risk.

It should be evident that the liquidity inherent in a particular security holding is a matter of degree.

The Cost of Liquidity.   The more liquid a potential security holding, the lower the rate of return to the prospective buyer. There is a cost associated with liquidity, measurable in terms of the lower yield available on a more liquid investment compared to that of a less liquid alternative. Investor preference for short maturity investments is a major contributor to an upward sloping yield curve. The bank portfolio manager must walk a narrow path between underestimating his liquidity needs to the impairment of the bank's safety and overestimating those requirements to the shareholders' detriment.

Minimizing Liquidity Costs.   There is no such thing as *the* yield curve. At any point in time there are different yield curves for different types of securities. The yield curves for agencies, municipals, corporates, and bank certificates of deposit are nearly always steeper than the yield curve for Treasury securities. The primary way of minimizing liquidity costs is to meet liquid asset needs by investing in short-term Treasuries while investing those funds not required for liquidity purposes in intermediate and longer securities which offer relatively higher yields.

Interest Rate Sensitivity Considerations

Sources of Interest Rate Sensitivity.   Imbalances in interest rate sensitivity on a bank's balance sheet arise from the very nature of the business of banking: intermediation between the financial needs of savers and borrowers. Customer preferences for specific deposit structures will often fail to coincide with customer requests for similar loan structures. In serving his customer base and meeting the terms of a competitive marketplace, the banker must accept some interest rate risk if the bank is to grow and prosper.

Measurement of Interest Rate Sensitivity.   Before bankers can consider portfolio alternatives designed to minimize interest rate risk on the bank's balance sheet, they must know the extent of any imbalances and where they will exist in the future. How to define and measure interest sensitivity gaps is explained extensively in other parts of this book. For this purpose it is important to note that a snapshot picture of interest rate sensitivity must be complemented by reasonable estimates of how the sensitivity gaps might be affected by abrupt changes in the interest rate climate.

When rates fall, loans are prepaid (especially mortgages), and bonds are called. The result is often an unexpected shortfall of high yielding assets of a particular maturity. When rates rise, asset cashflows diminish, and deposits are withdrawn (in spite of bank penalties). The result can be a stock of relatively low yielding assets that are unintentionally shortfunded. Often "what if" analysis will point out a particular vulnerability within the bank's balance sheet to movement in the general level of interest rates in one direction or another. With this knowledge, the banker can take action to guard against what is perceived to be a significant risk to the bank's earnings. Such action more often than not will involve adoption of a particular portfolio strategy.

Portfolio Structure and Interest Rate Sensitivity.   There are several techniques by which the portfolio can be used to redress present or future imbalances in interest rate sensitivity. In the simplest case, a bank with cash on hand and an asset deficiency in a given maturity range purchases a security of that maturity to fill the gap. Without the luxury of investable funds, a bank faced with the same problem might sell a short-term security, or use it as collateral to borrow in the repo market and use the proceeds to purchase a longer term security. A more complicated technique with the same effect is to purchase a longer term Treasury or agency security, and finance it in the repo market or pledge it to secure a deposit of public funds so that the inherent negative interest sensitivity gap created by these transactions offsets a preexisting positive gap. Other tactics involve positioning holdings in two or more different securities, or combining a position in real ("cash") securities with futures contracts to create a "synthetic" security which will behave in the desired way regarding interest rate sensitivity. Security holdings can also be combined with positions in put and call options on the same securities to alter the degree of price risk inherent in the security itself.

Credit Quality Considerations

The Portfolio as a Source of Credit Risk Diversification.   Often the selection of portfolio assets can be aimed at diluting the credit risk inherent in the bank's loan portfolio. A bank with a great deal already at stake in the viability of its regional economy can avoid local issue municipal and corporate bond holdings. A bank with little real estate credit exposure in the loan portfolio might specifically favor residential or commercial mortgage-backed securities as portfolio assets. With the tremendous variety of securities to choose from, it is relatively easy for the banker to use the securities portfolio to diversify the credit risk profile of the bank.

Credit Spreads.   Given two municipal or corporate bonds of similar maturity, one rated Aaa and the other Baa, the higher yield available on the latter must be looked on as a credit spread. Credit spreads vary widely over time and are typically widest when interest rates are unusually high and narrowest when rates have been falling for a protracted period of time.

Credit Risk in Bonds and Loans.   Arguably, the holder of a corporation's senior bonded debt is in a position superior to that of a bank with a loan to the same borrower. This may be true whether or not there is a pledge of specific collateral or revenues securing the bond or loan. This opinion has in recent years led bank portfolio managers to look more favorably on corporate bonds for inclusion in the bank's securities portfolio.

Other Constraints

Leverage.   The size of the bank's portfolio is often heavily influenced by the bank's capital position. In some banks, leverage considerations can be a spur to add securities and thereby improve return on equity. In other banks, capital is already stretched to the limit, and securities portfolio growth must be restrained. A common strategy is to manage the bank to a desired leverage multiple with the portfolio as the dependent variable.

Tax Position.   The bank's tax position will greatly influence the *composition* of the portfolio. It is extremely helpful to the portfolio manager when the bank is able to make a projection of future tax liability. The decision to invest in selected municipal securities will most often depend on the bank's estimated future tax liability.

Access to Marginal Funding.   Portfolio decisions often depend on the bank's marginal funding sources. Treasury and agency securities can be financed in the repo market. Other securities can be used as collateral for securing deposits of public funds or borrowings from the federal government (in a Treasury tax and loan account). Mortgage-backed securities can be financed with the proceeds derived from issuance of longer term certificates of deposit. Short-term securities of all types can be financed with purchases of federal funds.

THE OBJECTIVE OF PORTFOLIO MANAGEMENT

The portfolio manager has one simply stated objective: acting within constraints to obtain the highest possible yield per unit of risk assumed. This is of course an oversimplification. The constraints, already discussed, are formidable. The concept of highest possible yield is ambiguous enough to require elucidation. The quantification of risk is only partially subject to mathematical formulation and even then deals somewhat with probabilities, not certainties. Finally, market conditions are not always amenable to the immediate accomplishment of the portfolio manager's goal necessitating, on occasion, either anticipatory action or deliberate delay in execution.

Concepts of Yield

Yield to Maturity.   Yield to maturity is the most commonly used measure of yield for a fixed income security. It incorporates the cash flows from the security's coupons, the income expected on reinvestment of those cash flows, and the accretion of any discount from par or the amortization of any premium paid for the bond over the life of the security. In the commonly used formula the reinvestment rate on the interim cash flows is conventionally assumed to be the yield to maturity itself. When comparing alternative securities, sophisticated portfolio managers often alter the formula by substituting other reinvestment rates on the interim cash flows in order to determine how the yield of each security is affected in alternative interest rate scenarios. This is particularly useful when evaluating the yield of longer term securities at times when the yield curve is unusually steep.

Total Rate of Return.   This measure refines the concept of yield by including consideration of interim change in the market value of the security. It is therefore a better measure of comparison when the concern is to determine the performance of a security over a time horizon shorter than that of the bond's final maturity. Under present accounting regulations, unrealized portfolio appreciation or depreciation (the current market value of the portfolio less the bank's book cost of the securities) is only a footnote in the bank's financial statements. Nevertheless professional portfolio managers consider a bank portfolio's total rate of return over a series of equal time periods to be a much better measure of performance than the portfolio's average yield to maturity.

Net Yield.   Both yield to maturity and total rate of return are subject to further refinement by adding consideration of the cost of the funds used to finance ("carry") the security. This is particularly appropriate for bank portfolio managers in that banks must pay a market rate of interest (plus the costs associated with reserve requirements and deposit insurance) for a high percentage of their investable funds. Bankers also must attempt to manage their bank's net interest margin to a return on assets objective. Therefore *net yield, not gross yield,* is the more important consideration for the bank portfolio manager.

For a bank the federal funds rate is the best measure of its marginal cost of funds. All else being equal, the purchase of any security necessarily entails an increase in federal funds purchased or a decrease in federal funds sold. It is always a useful exercise to attempt to estimate ("guess" would perhaps be a more accurate term) what the federal funds rate might average over the life of any prospective security purchase. With such an estimate, the portfolio manager can better evaluate the net return, whether measured in terms of net yield or in dollars, of a prospective security purchase. Often, when viewed in this light, the relative value of the security will become more readily apparent.

Portfolio Yield Objectives. Investing with view only toward *net yield to maturity* is appropriate when there is an exact match between the maturity of the security and the maturity of the underlying investable funds. A good example is the investment of the proceeds of a particular block of six-month money market certificates into a high grade Eurodollar deposit of a major money market bank. The portfolio manager in this case is not overly concerned if the market value of his investment rises or falls over its life. He has "locked in" a spread over his deposit costs and has no further interest rate risk. This was his goal, and he has accomplished it regardless of whether market rates rise or fall during the ensuing six months.

When dealing with longer term investments, especially when exact asset/liability matches are not possible or desirable, the portfolio manager cannot ignore the greater potential price volatility of longer securities. Unrealized losses in the portfolio can significantly erode a bank's "real" net worth. Further, they are a clear signal to current and prospective shareholders that the bank's portfolio is not yielding a "current" rate of return. The manager must therefore carefully consider acquisition of securities which exhibit a high degree of potential price volatility.

On the other hand, investing with a primary view toward capital appreciation in the portfolio is usually inappropriate. The bank's dealer or trading account is the proper place to house such risks. In fact the goal of managing a trading account, namely to take advantage of short-term price movements in a given security or securities, is fundamentally different from that of a portfolio manager who should aim to *minimize* exposure to price volatility in his security holdings.

Therefore the yield goal best suited for bank portfolio management is one that emphasizes maximizing *net yield to maturity* while minimizing the risk of potential future depreciation. In order to accomplish this goal, the manager must have a framework for evaluating risk.

Measurement of Risk

Duration Measures. Traders, arbitrageurs, and portfolio managers have long used the concept of the yield value of a 32nd, that is, how much the yield to maturity of a bond varies given a price change of one thirty-second of one point, as a measure of the relative price risk of that bond. The yield value of a 32nd, a property of the duration of the security, is readily ascertainable from a standard quote sheet or by simulating the price change on a desktop bond yield calculator. A 32nd on a two-year 6 percent Treasury note, trading at par, is worth 1.7 basis points (hundredths of a percentage point in yield); that of a 6.5 percent four-year note, also at par, 0.9 basis points. (At higher or lower coupon rates, or at prices other than par, the duration of the bond, and therefore the yield value of a 32nd, changes.) The arbitrageur, looking to profit from a narrowing in the yield relationship between two-year and four-year Treasury notes, will sell the two-year note short and purchase the four-year note. To create a "hedged" position to insure from the risk of rising or falling prices throughout the Treasury yield curve, the arbitrageur will sell approximately $1.9 million of the shorter security for every million of the longer security that is purchased. (The equation is $X = 1.7/0.9 = 1.9$. The arbitrageur would achieve the same answer if the ratio of the actual durations of the two notes, 1.86 years and 3.47 years, is used, but actual durations are more difficult to determine than the yield value of a 32nd.)

Duration-based comparative risk analysis can be extraordinarily useful to the bank portfolio manager in selecting the optimum area along the yield curve in terms of expected net yield versus the amount of risk assumed. It is also useful in risk-weighting interest sensitivity gaps in the bank's balance sheet. Finally it enables the manager to decide on remedial portfolio actions to either reduce a particular gap or to create an offsetting sensitivity imbalance in another time period equal (on a risk-weighted basis) to the first.

As a practical example, suppose one is concerned with a $10 million negative gap (excess of fixed-rate liabilities over fixed-rate assets) in the four-year maturity area. Assume federal funds have been trading at 5 percent recently and the bank portfolio manager has a "neutral" view of the federal funds market, that is he has no opinion as to whether the federal funds rate is more likely to rise or fall on average over the next several years. If two- and four-year Treasury notes are yielding 6 percent and 6 1/2 percent as in the above example, the manager can expect the bank to earn 100 and 150 basis points on each investment. Based on their respective durations, the manager may well decide to purchase $19 million two-year Treasury notes earning the bank $190,000 per annum (if the interest-rate forecast is correct), rather than $10 million four-year notes earning only $150,000 per annum for the bank. A yet more sophisticated portfolio manager will also consider the yields available on one- and three-year Treasury securities in order to determine whether over the coming one-year period the yield curve for Treasury securities is steeper between one- and two-year maturities or between three- and four-year maturities. In general the manager will be inclined to concentrate purchases in the maturity area just beyond where the curve is the steepest, adjusting the amounts to be purchased by "risk-weighting" alternatives by their respective durations.

Options Risk Analysis.   Many debt instruments involve imbedded options granting the issuer the right to call (or the holder to put) the securities whenever market conditions have changed sufficiently to warrant such action. Banks grant such options, willingly or not, when they make mortgages or set unrealistically low prepayment penalties on fixed-rate loans and withdrawal penalties on fixed-rate deposits. In the debt securities markets, callable bonds and mortgage-backed securities are classic types of instruments with imbedded call options.

Options pricing models, based on probability theory, seek to determine the theoretically "fair" price for such securities, such price being often expressed as a yield-to-maturity spread over a similar noncallable security. A useful example is the attempt to quantify what additional yield over that available on noncallable Treasury bonds a prospective purchaser of a pool of government-guaranteed mortgage-backed securities should receive in view of the mortgagor's par prepayment option. Options theory explains why it is that in light of the higher probability of early prepayments a pool of 10 percent mortgage-backed securities should reward a prospective buyer with a higher initial yield than a pool of 8 percent mortgages. It attempts to quantify what yield spread should exist between two 10-year corporate notes, one callable at par in seven years, the other noncallable. In all of these cases, the buyer of the callable security is deemed to have granted the issuer an option to prepay debt, an option for which the buyer should expect to be paid. "Payment" in these cases is in the form of a yield spread advantage over similar securities without such imbedded options.

The rapid development and diffusion of options pricing theory has led bank portfolio managers to examine their existing portfolios for imbedded options in various holdings and to reevaluate alternative prospective security purchases. Options theory has also induced bankers to seriously reconsider prepayment penalty provisions on fixed-rate loans and early withdrawal penalties on fixed-rate deposits.

Maximizing Returns.   The portfolio manager, armed with the ability to evaluate the net expected return on each of alternative equal-risk weighted investments, and with a sense of how investments bearing imbedded prepayment options will behave in alternative interest rate environments, is prepared to make the types of decisions that will lead to better returns. If, for example, the interest rate sensitivity analysis of the balance sheet shows a negative gap of $10 million in the four-year maturity area, the manager might consider several possibilities. Purchase of $10 million four-year Treasury notes is an obvious candidate. Based on credit spreads available in the federal agency or corporate markets, four-year notes in one of these types of securities may also be attractive.

Based on duration risk weighting, the manager may opt instead for purchase of $19 million two-year Treasury notes as already discussed. Of course this alternative is open only if the bank has capital sufficient to accommodate the increased leverage and if the addition of $9 million to the securities portfolio can be comfortably financed.

Another alternative may be an asset-backed security such as a collateralized mortgage obligation (CMO) having an expected average maturity of four years but with significantly higher current yield than that of a four-year Treasury note. In this case the portfolio manager must consider how this security will behave in terms of prepayments and price appreciation or depreciation if the general level of interest rates rise or fall significantly. By assigning putative probabilities to these alternative interest rate forecasts, the manager can judge whether the higher yield on the CMO is worth the additional risk.

Anticipation and Delay.   If portfolio buy and sell decisions were simply a matter of plugging the right variables into the appropriate mathematical formulae, banks would not need portfolio managers. Market analysis, however, like much of credit analysis, is as much art as science. It happens more often than not that the timing of portfolio transactions plays a significant role in the degree to which the objective of maximizing returns is realized. Even a poor initial choice among alternatives will often work out if it is purchased just before a major increase in prices in general. On the other hand, the best thought out portfolio move will appear in retrospect to have been less than optimal if the timing was wrong.

The portfolio manager can learn to improve the timing of portfolio moves by giving heed to various market analyses. *Fundamental analysis* attempts to discern value from consideration of economic trends and governmental policy. *Technical analysis* purports to derive future price trends from past trading patterns. *Historical analysis* considers price and yield spread relationships over long periods of time. The more the manager assimilates from these disparate sources, the finer will be his sense of "feel" for the market.

Having anticipated a future need by early purchase of a security because the market seemed undervalued, or conversely delayed a planned purchase in expectation of lower prices in the near future, the manager must have some criterion by which to judge these decisions, and some course of remedial action (a back door) if the timing was wrong. The first is simple: Subsequent market price action will prove beyond doubt whether the manager was right or wrong in the decision to anticipate or delay. If wrong (and no one is always right), the self discipline to admit one's error and cut losses before they become unmanageable is the single most important character trait of the successful portfolio manager.

PORTFOLIO MANAGEMENT POLICIES

Three commonly discussed issues in portfolio management involve establishment of proper portfolio policies, active versus passive portfolio management, and the taking of profits and losses on sale of securities.

Portfolio Policies

Investment Policy. An overall investment policy in writing, approved by the Board, and promulgated to all investment personnel, is a necessity in all but perhaps the very smallest banks. It should address the following:

1. Types and maturities of approved investments.
2. Approved counterparties for trading, and controls relating to delivery of and payment for securities.
3. Controls relating to the safekeeping and accounting for securities and security income.
4. Transaction size limits for individual personnel.
5. Division of responsibilities (for example, sending, receiving, and matching of trade confirmations ought not be done by personnel executing transactions).

6. Lines of responsibility for reporting on the current status of the portfolio and on all portfolio activity.
7. Nature and extent of credit reviews of all portfolio assets.
8. Controls relating to the relationship between the portfolio and any bank dealer or trading activity.

Other Policies.   Depending on the level of activity in various markets, other written and approved policies may be necessary. These include policies on:

1. Use of futures and options.
2. Repurchase and resale agreements.
3. Forward purchases and sales.
4. Interest rate swaps.
5. Securities borrowing and lending.

Active versus Passive Portfolio Management

General Comment.   The portfolio is not a trading account. A high degree of activity designed solely to take advantage of short-term market fluctuations is uncalled for. This does not rule out designation of some modest portion of the entire portfolio for maximization of total rate of return. Nor does it prohibit prudent swapping of bonds in order to take advantage of anomalies of market pricing from time to time. Finally, it certainly does not rule out portfolio moves dictated by changes in the bank's liquidity or interest rate sensitivity.

Portfolio Swaps.   Other than outright purchases and sales of securities undertaken in a context of managing the bank's balance sheet as a whole, the most significant and justifiable additional activity in the portfolio should be in the form of security swaps. A swap involves the sale of one security holding and the simultaneous purchase of another. The purpose is to take advantage of market pricing anomalies which are often the result of temporary imbalances of supply and demand for a security of a certain type. For example, when a large new issue of securities is initially marketed, price concessions can develop which make it advantageous for the astute portfolio manager to sell a somewhat similar holding and buy the cheaper (higher-yielding) security.
    Portfolio swaps can involve nearly identical securities as when a Treasury note maturing next November 15 is sold and a Treasury note maturing 15 days later is purchased at a yield higher than the sale yield of the slightly shorter term security. More often, portfolio swaps will involve securities with somewhat greater dissimilarities. Trea-

suries for agencies, certificates of deposit for Eurodollar deposits, agencies for corporates, and municipals for other municipals are examples of common swaps. Occasionally swaps become quite complex, perhaps involving sales of two-year and four-year Treasuries and purchase of a three-year agency security.

In all swapping the principal involved is to evaluate the expected after-tax return of the prospective security or securities to be acquired and compare it to the return of the current holding or holdings *as valued at the expected sale price*. It is common practice in evaluating swaps to assume reinvestment of the total proceeds of the sale of the current holding.

Profits and Losses on Sale of Portfolio Securities

Portfolio Profits and Losses. When a profit or loss is incurred on sale of a portfolio security holding, there is an immediate effect on the bank's reported earnings for the current period. There is also an effect on the bank's tax liability which somewhat diminishes the earnings effect. Typically, though, it is the earnings effect which can be a source of controversy within the bank.

Sometimes an ill-conceived purchase should be sold in order to prevent losses from deepening, and yet the sale is deferred due to a desire not to reduce the bank's short-term earnings results. Occasionally gains on the sale of securities are realized solely to bolster short-term results. Both courses of action are quite rightly regarded as behavioral aberrations by professionally minded portfolio managers and occasionally by current or prospective shareholders as well.

Nevertheless, banks generally regarded as among the best managed routinely realize both profits and losses on sale of securities in the normal course of adjusting their portfolios to changes in market conditions and to structural changes within the bank. The difference in these banks is that the realization of a profit or a loss is *incidental* to the accomplishment of the goal of maximizing portfolio returns over a long period of time. In particular, the realization of losses, due to the fact that tax liability is thereby reduced, is a common practice among many of the most successful banks.

CONCLUSION

Bank security portfolio management has greatly increased in complexity in the deregulated era. There has been an enormous proliferation of available bank-eligible securities and a corresponding increase in levels of sophistication among bank portfolio managers.

Banks are relying more than ever before on their security portfolios to make material positive contributions to the bank's earnings.

The essentials, however, have not changed. Good credit and market analysis coupled with thorough knowledge of the bank and its needs enables the portfolio manager to make wise decisions. Above all a strong sense of what is to be gained (the net return to the bank) versus the potential downside (the risk element) enables the manager to maximize returns within prudent constraints and in spite of highly volatile securities markets.

PART SEVEN

Special Systems in Banking

CHAPTER THIRTY-NINE

Architecture: An Enabling Process for Bankers

Richard E. Dooley

President
The Dooley Group

A GRAPHIC FRAMEWORK FOR ARCHITECTURE

If no vision for information systems exists, the data processing function tends to evolve in a fragmented, nonstandardized, or nonintegrated way, as diagramed here.

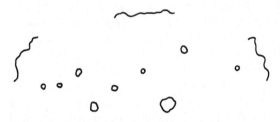

Each circle represents some system in a set with no unifying plan or framework (as represented by the disconnected "umbrella"). Many banks have this condition as a result of mergers or inattention to their data processing/information systems direction or just plain lack of enlightened execution by their technical staff.

If there is a strong vision or clear long-range strategy for technology, its symbolic schematic might look like this.

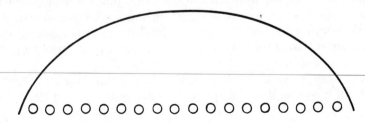

The umbrella represents the unifying plan or management direction, and the neat row of small circles represents multiple properly designed and implemented systems. Unfortunately, no one has or will ever likely have such a set of systems, or MIS, that looks like this handbook illustration.

But by aiming at this "ideal," by linking the technical vision to the long-range "business" strategy or the corporation's overall vision, and by understanding that this linking process is an ongoing responsibility, we can achieve a data processing/information systems status which *approximates* this figure. The "real" system will probably have some gaps in philosophy and involve imperfect execution.

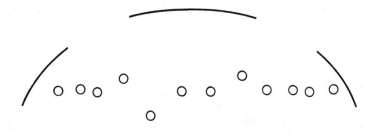

Realistically speaking, there are some inconsistencies and inadequacies in the execution of any long-range plan or architecture. Substandard systems are not connected properly to the network or to the appropriate data, but considerable progress can be made toward achieving the ideal system when banks aim at a near perfect one. There are banks which are achieving this "compromise state," or level of evolving architecture. It is quite possible in the late 1980s to do so.

Some bank managers avoid information systems planning. They contend that its theory has never been put to practical use or that implementation will take too long and cost too much.

Actually, the process involved in creating a condition like the first illustration takes longer and costs more when viewed from an investment position of total dollars, energy, and lost opportunities. It's just as difficult and costly to do it wrong.

The truth is there is no such thing as a perfect information system architecture. It is just an idea—a dream. But it is an idea or dream to aim for, and in trying to reach it the general efficiency of production systems and the connective support for more effective management will be improved. That's the payoff. Real progress is made in steps, or by projects along the way to this "never achieved" goal of a perfect MIS architecture.

The compromises implicit in the third figure simply reflect the reality of business life; for example, some systems must be done on a crash program basis (and will show it later) while other systems can and should stand alone.

The reason why overall architecture has been so difficult to define, justify, and understand is that it is conceptual. What does exist—models, workstations, computers, programs, terminals, systems, networks, and so on—individually may or may not always reflect the vision. Once management and the technically oriented staff agree on an evolving vision or direction, they can slowly improve the pieces of and connections between production systems and the management processes, providing an evolving set of information systems that moves toward the ultimate idea of architecture.

WHAT IS ARCHITECTURE?

Architecture is one of the "content free expressions" referred to in Chapter 14. Its meaning seems to change with speaker and context, but these four definitions cover its most common uses.

1. Overall design for the use of information technology in the bank.
2. A planned array of banking functions and technical facilities.
3. A set of rules/assumptions (for the overall technical design).
4. A bunch of documents kept up to date and communicated.

Each definition has its own merit.

The first is very broad, positioning architecture as an "umbrella" (like in the previous diagrams) that covers the entire business processes and its technical workings. In this sense, architecture is today's form of systems planning, adapted from previous methodologies and applied more completely to the total business organization and environment.

The second statement implies an orderly display of multiple and related units or activities—the way the work gets done and what people do—all mapped against a similar set of computer- or electronic-based capabilities. This is a matched pair so to speak.

As a third expression, architecture may be thought of as a number of interrelated guidelines or standards and the assumed rationale behind those rules.

Lastly, architecture is most familiar as schematics often seen on a conference room or office wall. These diagrams are often out-of-date and represent a blueprint or type of engineering drawing of some aspect of the overall design, or of the planned array, or list of the rules/assumptions. These are considerably more detailed than the schematics show in these chapters, and a number of examples exist in banks today.

Of course, there are other definitions, and not one is all-inclusive. It's a little like the story of five blind men describing an elephant, each with their hands on a different body part. People perceive architecture from their position, needs, or past training.

Thus, it's important to determine who the audience is and shape the description accordingly. There are "levels" in architecture which are very important for communication, contracting work, ensuring integration, and providing a view that can "hook" an audience or designer and carry them to the next level.

LEVELS OF ARCHITECTURE

The five levels of architecture are:

- Level 1—Bank description (BD)
- Level 2—Bank functions flow(BFF)
- Level 3—Technical facilities model(TFM)
- Level 4—Implementation plan—(IP)
- Level 5—Configuration schematic (CS)

First, at the highest most conceptual level, we describe the basic business and its thrust, that is, the bank's charter or long-range strategy. This involves (1) a few simple statements often visionary and then put into schematic form, (2) noncomplex and communicative to the market, employee, and shareholder populations, and (3) the enterprise view.

Next we diagram the various clusters of activity that make up the enterprise, often represented organizationally by divisions or groups (that is, retail, commercial, trust, and so on). These organizations are often understood well by only a few professionals, so to diagram them in detail is a real education. Flow diagrams will help those not deeply involved or knowledgeable, but experience helps the most. People will often identify themselves by the business function they belong to or have worked in for a long time.

Getting to the third level of architecture may involve a jump. The connection isn't obvious and often hasn't been made even in banks with a long history of automation. Different skills and working patterns are required to connect levels two and three. This should be the province of the information systems management. Bridging between levels 2 and 3 has been the subject of many seminars and much literature lately.

The fourth level is action. No longer conceptual, it's specific in nature, implies cost, and use of resources and assigned personnel. It's going on whether or not it's been planned.

Finally, we have detailed architectural representations that include machine numbers, vendor names, capacity or speed, plus directions of flow or options in operation. Some might argue this level is not architecture but current reality.

Few banks have or need all five levels, but most usually have "like" representations. Increasingly, organizations are attempting to update or create similar representations of architecture that are interrelated and can be used to plan, control, communicate, and improve the use of technology.

ELEMENTS OF ARCHITECTURE

Technology today is made up of many pieces. The expression "option shock" perhaps best conveys the problem. To understand architecture, it is relevant to list its main categories.

1. Functional applications (SYS)—All the systems, usually relatively large, that have been installed or are under development.
2. Processors (HW)—Includes *all* computers connected or standalone.
3. Operating software and utilities (SW)—The extensive machine instruction sets or programs often supplied by vendors for operating computer hardware.
4. Data (D)—Refer to Chapter 14.
5. Telecommunications (NW)—The network of lines, phones, cables and other "carriers" recently developed by both public and private vendors.
6. Terminals/workstations (EUC)—All the "nodes" or connections between networks and the software used by professionals, often referred to as "users" (end user computing is the buzz word).

Some banks use different labels or have regrouped their elements for their own communication/planning purposes. However, this generic set of six is practical enough for the discussion in this chapter.

Aligning these six elements along several axes together with the organization structure, we can form a conceptual "cube" that will define the architecture of any organization (Chart 1).

Such a model is similar to the Rubic's cube, a popular toy a few years ago. It can be changed around endlessly and may take a long time or be very difficult to solve. But the cube image can help specify where a bank systems plan might be applied most effectively, where the greatest need for technical interface is, or how best to sequence the approach to architecture (Chart 2).

For example, the retail division of a large bank holding company at its senior executive level, that is, its leadership, might focus on the systems needed to provide uniform service at all teller stations and see this as part of the current and future technological plan (Chart 3).

CHART 1   Three Dimensions—Levels, Elements, and Organization

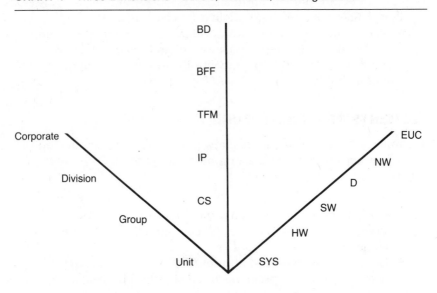

CHART 2   Conceptual Cube for Architectural Communication—Stage I

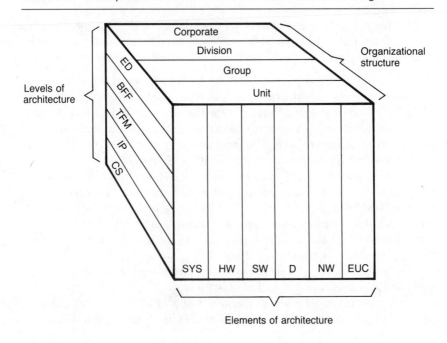

CHART 3   Conceptual Cube for Architectural Communication—Stage II

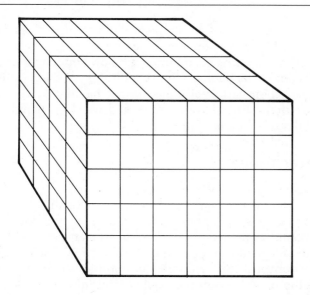

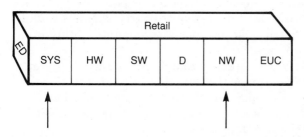

ATTRIBUTES OF ARCHITECTURE

When viewed this way, architecture helps bank organizations select the right place to apply resources.

Also the notions of integration and separation as organizational or management style issues are highlighted and can be examined for both their benefits or detriments.

Architecture is never finished—it's always yet to be fully achieved. We do a piece at a time. We accomplish certain projects and configurations, but as we do, the strategies shift and new areas come to the forefront. Thus architecture facilitates the changing nature of banking today by helping banks to reach new markets or support the new skills of the professional staff. Anyone who believes they have completed their architecture doesn't perceive it through this model. The elusiveness of the architectural goal is its strength. It demands continual flexibility.

Finally architecture helps accommodate the change of staff roles in the late 1980s. There are now highly technical people working in business areas ("niche gurus"), and there are now competent bankers (business managers) in technology. Both conditions are true to a degree that didn't exist when earlier editions of this handbook were published. Organizational lines have blurred, and we need people with both sets of skills in all parts of the cube.

WHY ARCHITECTURE?

A number of secular trends best say why.

For a number of years technology has been practically a consumer good. The microprocessor phenomenon surged ahead with huge leaps each Christmas, and many nontechnically trained managers and hordes of young professionals absorbed enough "tinker toy" technology to begin solving their business or intellectual problems and put to rest any doubts of the usefulness of personal computing. Technology became part of the public domain, no longer just a responsibility of some few trained technicians. Nearly all employees and customers wanted to be technically "in touch," and the personal computer "tiny iron" was everywhere.

During these same years, large computer technology ("big iron") became widespread. Departmental computing became a tactic if not a strategy so that what was once found only in a centralized and environmentally controlled area was now almost as available as the telephone and even thought of in the same way.

In addition, the breakup of the Bell System prior to divestiture provoked a new concern about telecommunication in banking. Cost, reliability, control, and flexibility were (are!) issues of great business and technical concern.

The explosion of technical options at an unprecedented rate (new announcements, new vendors, new products, enhanced older ones, and the like) seemed to suggest that anything currently installed or used was obsolete! How does one decide what to use or discard when there are so many choices?

Further, the continual pressure to reduce operating budgets, to limit staff growth or to cut its size, to develop better ways to do things, or to identify things not to do, stimulated an interest in automation in every sector of bank operations and management.

Over time most banks had developed a set of functional systems that might best be described as a "New England rock fence." They had just been built without consistent focus on their ultimate place in any architecture. Thus data were often not readily available, nor were the existing terminals able to access all systems, nor were all the needed functions automated or connected. What developed might be seen as a "pile of rocks" or even "boulders." The drawing below illustrates this development.

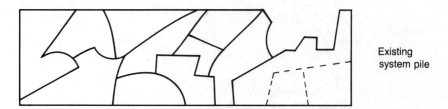

Existing
system pile

Further, customer requirements and management needs seemed to force integration of systems (or data) that had not been designed for compatibility. Any change in one system seemed to "shoulder bump" changes into several others. Additions to any one file had multiple impacts that showed up unexpectedly in other seemingly unrelated dimensions (response time at the terminal).

Also, mergers, acquisitions, and restructuring became a business routine. Banks with one technical maturity or protocol were combined with other banks with substantially different systems (or they were considering such action mergers). Pictorially this might be represented like:

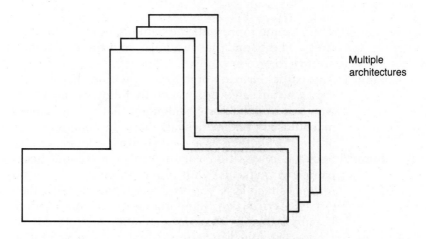

Multiple
architectures

Finally, a focus on technology as a competitive help in various markets perhaps has changed forever the image of DP/IS as a back-office ("backwater"!) function. Consideration and execution of electronic linkage to customers, suppliers, and allied businesses have highlighted a more global view of technology. Again to use a previous diagram, we want to connect multiple inverted Ts.

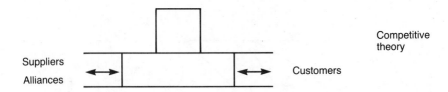

Nine secular trends (public domain, distributed, divestiture, option shock, cost pressure, old systems, integration, mergermania, and competitive theory) have caused bankers to begin viewing their future technological state proactively rather than passively. In the last few years, managers in some banks have begun to structure their technical plans and their information systems implementation to reflect a subjective vision of this future. Their intent is to shape it rather than suffer it.

Architecture is the conceptual vehicle for this process.

AN OVERALL CONCEPTUAL FRAMEWORK FOR ARCHITECTURE

Architecture may be best described by the following chart of 10 columns. The flow moves in either direction, but to explain it we'll start on the left.

Column 0   This column represents the banking industry in its entirety. The boundaries are open, and the descriptions are macro.

Column 1   Any particular bank organization within that industry strives to succeed (or survive) by following a strategy, which is usually a brief statement that doesn't change much in short time periods. Perhaps the composite view of the stockholders is a good shorthand label.

Column 2   Such an organization usually is made up of units (companies or divisions) with different, perhaps even unrelated, direction or objective statements. Usually there is a disparity in size or importance (profit contribution). Usually there is a process for generating such objectives.

Column 3   Underneath these more formally stated, larger, unit objectives, there are always a limited set of achievements that must be accomplished in the short term in order to reach the formal objectives. Priority is given to the critical few as opposed to the trivial many (the 80/20 rule). These shift more often either by year or by leader.

Column 4 At this level managers or banking professionals carry out their job responsibilities (or tasks) to ensure that the few crucial objectives (Column 3) within their unit's larger plan (Column 2) are accomplished in a way that will result in the whole organization (Column 1) being successful (profitable) enough to continue over time in that industry (Column 0). People can talk in detail about this column, especially about their problems. Preceding columns are often too general or removed, but this column represents who they are.

Column 5 This column represents what people in Column 4 need to know. This includes information that is required to perform the job as well as any other useful or helpful information. The information in this column isn't written down (though it's often searched for). It's simple know-how. Many people are not in the habit of thinking about it much, they just do (not just make do). It's nearly impossible to communicate the abstract nature of what we need to know (refer to Chapter 14).

Column 6 The column is easier to understand (and to get mad about). Most information comes from data. Not all, but most of what is useful in our jobs, is in data form somewhere. It is helpful to visualize this column as the "in-box," or the library, or research function. It's usually visable and physical. It can be studied, categorized, and changed. It gets more attention from managers and technicians because it's easier to analyze. There's a lot of it (maybe too much as we covered in Chapter 14).

Column 7 Most data comes from systems. Some systems are natural, and others are manual. Computers are the source of most data in today's business environment. However, the systems may not have been designed to provide data easily or even to be connected to various people with information needs.

Column 8 This column represents the integration of systems—all six elements of architecture. This column is the bottom level of architecture called configuration. It also has a future state that encompasses what we want it to be (target architecture).

Column 9 The last columns represent the connections increasingly made to other businesses as suppliers, customers,

CHART 4 An Architectural Framework for Linking All the Planning Processes and for Working the Critical

Column 0	*Column 1*	*Column 2*	*Column 3*	*Column 4*	*Column 5*	*Column 6*	*Column 7*	*Column 8*	*Column 9*
Environment	Ultimate organizational objective	Lower level strategies or organizational objectives	Profit criteria, key variables, or critical success factors	Manager recommended tasks, manager duties, or job description	Information requirements	Present data flow	Present manual and automated systems	MIS (IMS) the future overall technical architecture	Vendors Other networks
						Overall technical architecture			
Industry macro-econ	*Corporate direction*	*Formal objectives*	*Operating plans*	*Personal responsibility*	*Information*	*Data*	*Technical present*	*Technical future*	
Global	Long-range plan or charter	Market Function Geographic	"Get it done or else"	Any decision maker or professional	Need to know	"In Box"	Existing systems	Telecommunication network	
Open-ended					"Feel" Hear	Screens			Open-ended
						Reports Manuals Drawings	Data processing		
				Teams Taskforces					
Use					Value	Delivery or transaction processing			
Business or management competitive strategies Continual change, faster cycles, a return to business basics					Pressure Confusion	Information systems strategies and technical tactics Continual change, planning, and role evolution			

or allies in some joint venture. The various Bell operating companies are a part of both these last two columns.

Such an overall perspective isn't easy to come by. Most bankers today can comfortably only relate to a subset. We usually need teams to help provide all the ideas or visions we need for the future. Ideally we want more bankers who are comfortable with, aware of, and able to communicate about the financial services industry, their own organization, their position in and potential impact on the industry, and the elements of technology that bring improvement. Architecture enables that process.

A PARTIAL COOKBOOK FOR WORKING THE OVERALL ARCHITECTURE VIEW

This view is a process large enough in scope with a sufficient number of parts, and it requires so much attention over extended time, by both management and technicians alike, that some comments about execution are necessary. Suggestions about what to do, what not to do, and how and when, follow.

Mentality Shift.   First of all, a shift in mentality may be required—from a default response to change or opportunities made possible by technology, to a proactive or aggressive stance that seeks the right changes and the right technology. Such a development must take place over several layers of management and through multiple organizations.

Business Case.   The main focus should not be on how to use new technology but on its business relevance. Thus the business case predominates. Architecture is hardly ever sold for itself or its own benefits. That requires an unrealistic faith in the face of continual economic pressure. The application of technology must be tied to the basic business needs. The allegation in some recent literature that information systems provide competitive advantage is slightly misleading. More appropriately worded, business actions which provide competitive advantage today usually involve some base of technology. It's simply a change in orientation, and it implies that all bankers need a sufficient level of comfort, awareness, and communicative ability regarding technology.

Justification by Regulation.   The justification process also shifts from past tradition. It's done more on the initiative of line or client management. To be sure, it still must be a partnership with technical leadership, but a clearer responsibility must be assumed by the business people involved. More often this justification process rests primarily on the reputation or authority of the banking leader. Many believe that extensive cost-benefit analysis or feasibility studies should be reserved for only a few massive efforts. Many projects, especially those driven by market conditions, are best done with the focus on getting done, rather than long studying of the approach. This controversy (careful definition and long economic analysis versus fast implementation of a committed bank manager's need) will probably continue to rage, but competitive thought and the architectural view have changed the way management approval gets obtained. That is, it's more from the client side and rests more on the personality than statistical support.

Internal and Existing.   There has been a lot of hype in the literature for several years regarding competitive systems. These are real business gains to be realized, but the overexposure of these ideas have led some banks to look only outside themselves and to look only at new areas. There is real leverage to be gained internally from existing situations, that is, data already stored but perhaps not available, systems already in place but not fully understood or not fully used, and people on staff who are not properly motivated or assigned.

Constant.   Sometimes management attention is available but not lasting due to other pressures. To be most effective this view requires a constancy over many years. Consistency is more important than intensity.

Already Going On.   In some banks much of what is required is already going on, but there is no cohesive expression of it so that this fact is clear. No framework for understanding has been provided. The workers wonder why their leadership doesn't appreciate what has been done, and the leadership wishes more results were available. It's a communication problem.

"Comfort" Education.   There still exists a need for executive understanding which is based less on technical knowledge or personal skill and more on comfort or confidence about what's going on and who's doing it. This may be more emotional or psychological than digital in nature, but it's real and requires an ongoing program in most banks. This need for more credibility will probably continue for several years.

Basic Planning Disciplines.   Where a formalized planning process exists, input forms requiring explicit statements of both existing and future technical support required are important documents for all bank profit centers. Conversely, a documented connection of all technical work to business objectives is also a useful planning discipline or "cross-barred" planning forms so to speak.

Steering Committee. These might better have been labeled navigation committees. Let the steering be done by responsible managers. Even though the implication of the word committee is troublesome, a group that reviews all resource allocations (that is, the regular capital appropriation process), not just technical resource allocation, is better. So is a set of leaders who guide, not decide, and whose vision is very broad.

"Build Then Rethink"—Use versus Function. Many of the disciplines or methodologies learned in data processing over the last 30 years are still applicable. Sometimes it's best to build a transaction processing computer-based system with those old precepts and, when it's finished, step back for a rethinking of how it can be used. The use can be different from its function, especially when these uses are developed by professionals from other organizations (for example, marketing and customer service) who were not involved in the design or the implementation.

"Brainstorming". To get the insights or innovative use of either existing or new technology, it's best to have some process that encourages group creativity. Many are available. It is helpful to have an outside facilitator, to use chunk time (from half days to two days), to be prepared ahead of time (with "starter kit" ideas) generated by interviews or small study assignment, and to be explicit upfront about the ground rules. Some structure (matrixes, diagrams, or agenda) is required but not so much as to smother the creativity sought. The timing and pace of such efforts is crucial. The selection of attendees is most important (beware of too many boss-subordinate relationships; get some people who do the work; provide some commonality but get multiple views). This process must be repeated until it's the norm. It takes special handling and has a lot of visibility. In its best form, it's simply the way people communicate.

People Handling Suggestions. To a greater extent than in the past, cycling careers through line and staff (bank functions and technology support) helps provide the best individual background for generating the ideas and commitment required.

Sometimes changing the physical working location of the staff involved (often closer to where the work is performed) helps. Changing the organizational reporting structure may help also. Both need to be carefully considered. There are pros and cons, of course, but conditions often warrant either.

New employee orientation should include extensive introductions to the available and appropriate elements of architecture for their new assignments, and to the volunteer training that is provided.

The Way of the Future.   Institutionalizing a creative process of communicating about the use of technology to support business needs within a broad framework of strategies or directions, is absolutely fundamental to enable banks to reach their goals. The more random or unguided processes (represented by the initial diagram in this chapter) can no longer be counted on in today's financial services industry. This enabling function is the most precious benefit of an overall architectural effort.

Information Requirement (Column 5) Focus.   Remembering how central information is to all management processes, it is an effective beginning point for any group exercise in innovation. The ideas may lead to product, service, structure, or resources, but the information requirements are the anchor. That's the "peep hole" to human interaction in the never-ending struggle to understand and find out what bankers need to know and what they have to have in order to carry out their jobs to reach the bank's objectives.

Who Does This?   The claim has been made that most DP/IS professionals were neither skilled enough nor articulate enough, nor oriented enough to the bottom line, to help in accomplishing an effective overall architectural process. This is less true today. And with the right leadership and motivation need no longer be a problem.

Impact of "Charge Back" Philosophies.   How costs are absorbed by various accounting systems and their attached policies will determine the number of useful innovations. The argument becomes who gets charged how much rather than what must be done.

A "Mosaic" of Efforts.   No single program, individual leader, or simple process alone gets this done. A customized set of meetings, projects, managers, courses, assignments may lead to success, but there is no "cookie cutter" approach. Each effort is made up of an evolving number of pieces like those in a stained glass window.

CHAPTER FORTY

Technical Systems to Deliver Consumer Services

R. C. Letson
IBM

For over a decade, financial institutions have striven to install, operate, and market self-service delivery systems as part of their retail strategy. To date, these systems have primarily focused on automated teller machines (ATMs)—systems to deliver cash withdrawals, inquiries, deposits, and limited payments 24 hours a day. What drove this investment?

In the early 1970s the primary driving force for providers (financial institutions) was the belief that improved convenience for present and future retail customers would lead to greater marketing opportunity within their area. In each part of the country, especially high-density areas, one and sometimes two institutions led the way for installation of ATMs. By the late 1970s the institutions who were not part of the pioneering efforts installed ATMs as a defensive move; that is, they installed ATMs to maintain competitiveness in their retail delivery systems.

A secondary force that drove the installation of ATMs during the 1970s was the belief, or at least the hope, that financial transactions performed at the externally located ATMs would reduce the number of transactions within the lobbies of the financial institutions and therefore offer some form of cost offset or cost justification. The evaluation of success against this objective is arguable. On one hand, some financial institutions credit ATMs with allowing them to avoid increasing the number of tellers in the face of an increase in the total number of transactions handled per year. On the other hand, some financial institutions will argue that ATMs, in and of themselves, caused an increase in the total number of transactions performed per year. Whatever the case, we are currently in an ATM era; ATMs are part of the fiber of our retail delivery systems. They are taken for granted not only by those financial institutions in the retail business but by consumers as well. Given that these machines are part of our financial culture, both as a benefit to the consumer and an accepted expense for the provider, the industry is currently focusing on ways of increasing transaction volume on the currently installed ATMs as well as attempting to understand how, when and in what form, future self-service offerings will evolve.

This chapter will discuss a potential evolutionary path for self-service financial transaction delivery systems. In the course of this development, we will also consider problems generated by today's ATM development as well as several of the problems of ATM deployment from both a consumer and provider viewpoint.

HISTORICAL PERSPECTIVE

Early ATM installations had three fairly common characteristics: They were installed by large institutions, they were proprietary machines, and they were installed through-the-walls of existing central/branch locations. All three of these characteristics were logical given the nature of the original objectives.

One could conclude that large financial institutions entered the ATM era first since they tended to be more focused on marketing or had more of a financial capacity to make the heavy investments required for an ATM network. However, the large financial institutions also installed the early ATMs because the ATM concept matched their geographic presence better than smaller institutions. That is, if the consumers' image of ATMs was convenience, this dictated not only time convenience but location convenience as well. The larger institutions with the larger branch networks could by definition offer more ATM locations and therefore more location convenience. This factor also dictated that institutions in branching or limited branching states moved into ATMs earlier than those in unit bank states.

Most ATMs in the 1970s as well as the early 1980s were also proprietary; that is, they were available for use only by the retail customers of the owning installation. The rationale was clear in that the objective was to lure additional retail customers based on a higher level of convenience. Institutions drove this point home with some very creative names for their ATMs, most of them attempting not only to highlight them as a new and special service but to give their ATMs an almost human personality. During this era, however, the point most often stressed was time convenience, that is, 24-hour banking. The other part of convenience (location) was of course present to the extent an institution had a large number of branches.

The third characteristic of early ATM networks was that most of the machines were placed in a through-the-wall (TTW) configuration at financial institution locations. This configuration not only supported the objectives of time convenience and location but more importantly provided the "lowest cost" operating expense configuration—lowest cost in terms of servicing, security, and maintenance.

From a servicing standpoint, an on-premise employee could provide for cash replenishment, supply replenishment, deposit stripping and reconciliation without the expense of travel, armored car transport, and the physical security of a less protected location.

The connections of ATM security systems in a branch or central location offered the advantage of using the existing online security system for that location. This, of course, eliminated the need for additional communication cost that would be incurred in off-premise locations. Additionally, there was the tangible or intangible feeling that security risks were lower at a financial institution's location as opposed to an off-site or nonfinancial location.

While the frequency of maintenance required on an off-premise machine should on the average be equivalent to an on-premise machine, the cost of that maintenance is not. The expense differential is due primarily to the fact that ATM vendors would not service a machine without the presence of an employee of the owning institution. The employee of the institution would be required to open the machine, remove and replace the cash, and resecure the machine after the maintenance was complete. The expense of travel as well as delays incurred in coordinating the arrival time of employee and maintenance personnel made off-site locations more expensive to maintain.

Thus a decade into the ATM era, the industry reflected a predominantly proprietary, on-site TTW environment, heavily installed within the larger institutions and more sparsely installed down through the medium, even to some of the smaller, institutions. Many smaller to medium-sized institutions, however, did not install ATMs because they could not provide sufficient location convenience to their retail customers. This was not due to lack of desire but lack of locations. This was the environment prior to the emergence of sharing.

SHARED ATM NETWORKS

The second phase of ATMs began in the early 1980s, a phase highlighted by the emergence of shared networks, both regional and national. Shared ATM networks were perhaps a natural evolution of an ATM environment characterized by large institution domination, on-site TTW configurations, an industry looking to enhance ATM appeal and therefore consumer participation, and the emergence of a new entrepreneural perspective of ATMs as not only a means to provide improved service but also perhaps a means to produce revenue. Couple these factors with the existence of financial institutions that had not or could not participate in the ATM era, and the time was right for shared networks.

While shared networks were perhaps a natural evolution and provided benefit to all, the agreements required to make these networks a reality did not always come easily. The factor most difficult to overcome was the acknowledgement that the ATM networks, so fervently installed and marketed as a proprietary service, would now become part of a community pool of convenience ATMs and the acknowledgement that someone, probably the consumer, would be required on occasion to pay for this previously no-cost service.

The larger institutions tended to view sharing as a competitive leveler in a negative sense, while smaller institutions (with or without ATMs) viewed this evolution as a competitive leveler in a positive sense. In fact, except for the existence of foreign transaction pricing, comprehensive regional ATM networks could be viewed as a community utility with equal access by all providers and all consumers. ATMs would no longer be viewed in a marketing sense by financial institutions. The machines existed; they were part of virtually everyone's retail delivery system and were generally accepted by at least a part of the customer sector. From this emerged a more financially oriented view of ATMs, either in a cost justification or a revenue and profit manner.

The environment then progressed toward one in which virtually all financial institutions could offer their retail customers a plastic card that would allow them access to their financial accounts 24 hours a day at locations throughout their area, state, or nation. This second phase is still in process, but we will continue to see a leveling off of ATM competitiveness. One difference is already obvious—consumers will pay more or less for these financial transactions depending on which financial institutions hold their accounts and depending on their ATM needs by locality.

LESSONS LEARNED

While this second phase of ATMs is still in process, what are the lessons learned so far? We have learned at least the following:

1. Self-service delivery systems originate as marketing programs and evolve to cost justified programs.
2. These systems are initially installed, located, and positioned as proprietary devices for the exclusive use of the owner's customers.
3. These systems are initially driven by the larger providers, leaving many of the smaller providers unable to participate.

4. Providers initially position these devices for their benefit not the consumer.
5. Providers reach a point where additional service and benefits are contemplated to drive usage up and costs down.
6. As more providers install these systems, they become less of a competitive advantage.

CURRENT ASSESSMENT—WHERE ARE WE?

It is generally accepted that, as an industry, we have reached a certain maturity level with ATMs. Accepting this as fact, it is proper that we evaluate where we are, how satisfied we are with that status, and where we are going. Let's focus first on where we are.

ATMs are first and foremost consumer devices even though the initial impetus for these devices came from the financial institutions and not the consumers. Therefore it is appropriate to step back and view our current ATM status with respect to consumers.

Consumer market research has shown that there are two major consumer characteristics relative to financial services, especially ATMs. These characteristics are age of householder and income of household. Figure 1 is a graph of the household population of the United States according to these characteristics. Using market research figures, we can divide this demographic data into three distinctive groups by financial characteristics—the credit adverse, the credit user, and the set patterns.

Credit adverse households can be defined by household income, usually below $16,000 annually. This household segment shows the following traits:

- Like to pay cash for everything.
- Sometimes pay a bill in person.
- Sometimes get caught short of cash.
- Occasionally pay bill on or after due date.
- Do not carry credit cards around.
- Do not feel comfortable banking by mail.
- Do not like to charge things.

The credit user group has householders between 19 and 54 who have incomes greater than $16,000 annually. The credit users are characterized by the following traits:

- Carry all credit cards around and like to charge purchases.
- Cash checks at different locations.
- Like to take care of banking transactions by phone.
- Prefer an ATM to a teller.
- Do not pay bills at the same time every month.
- Do not pay cash for everything.

FIGURE 1   Household Population Pattern

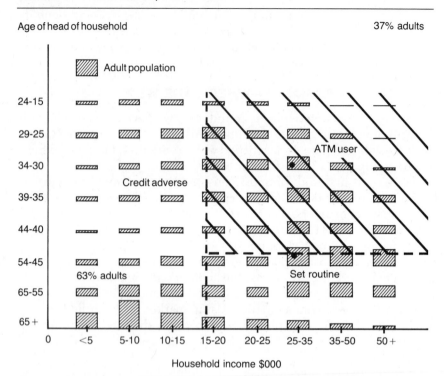

The third group, set patterns, is defined primarily by age of house-holder and generally includes those people 55 years of age or older. This population segment is characterized by the following traits:

- Prefer to deal with teller, not ATMs.
- Pay bills at same time each month, before due date.
- Set aside money monthly for savings.
- Pay monthly credit balances in full.
- Do not conduct banking transactions by phone.

It should be pointed out that there is overlap and exceptions to the characterizations of these groups. However, for the purpose of this discussion, we will view these groups as defined.

ATM users are usually in the credit user group, which represents approximately 37 percent of the U.S. adult population. Both the credit adverse and the set patterns population tend not to use ATMs. In probing these latter two groups, one discovers that the credit adverse group simply has little or no need for convenience cash.

The set patterns group represents those people who have adopted a lifestyle that precludes a need for ATMs. This group has traditionally obtained their cash or made their deposits either in the lobby of a financial institution or by some alternative method. This method, whatever it happens to be, was established long before ATMs were available, and research shows it would be most difficult to break or modify their current methods.

It is important to note that the key phrase relative to ATM usage is "convenience cash." While virtually everyone needs a source of cash, not everyone requires the service of convenience cash. For example, the credit adverse segment frequently obtains its cash requirement as a result of a weekly, in-person cash back deposit. The set pattern group typically obtains cash through an in-person lobby visit or by cashing a check at a nonfinancial institution.

Having established these three demographic groups and their respective traits and propensities, we could redefine the scope and the meaning of the much discussed "33 percent wall"[1] in ATM usage. Indeed, one could argue that the industry is not at a 33 percent wall but rather at a 90–95 percent wall with respect to satisfying the need for convenience cash with currently installed ATMs at currently defined function levels. One could further argue that the industry is not faced with a marketing problem, but rather a need problem. That is, ATM card acceptance might be increased through intensive marketing, but usage by the credit adverse and set pattern groups are generally impervious to marketing efforts.

The good news to those in the industry struggling to increase ATM consumer usage is that there is no general animosity toward automation or self-service. That is, there is no technology acceptance barrier, but rather there is a current saturation in satisfying need.

Have we really saturated the need for convenience ATMs within the United States? If we estimate from 55,000 to 60,000 convenience ATMs within the country, we have one ATM for approximately every 4,000 people. Given that at least 25 percent of the population is 18 years old or younger, we have one ATM for every 3,000 adults. If 60 percent of this population have cards and 50 percent of the card holders are users, we have one ATM for every 900 users. Multiply this by the average number of transactions per user per month, and one determines the average transaction volume per ATM.

Are we at the end of self-service automation in retail banking? Absolutely not. In the industry, we are simply digesting phase one.

---

[1]Refers to a much-used industry term which reflects that only one third of potential customers currently use ATMs and the fact that, as an industry, we have been unable to penetrate that wall.

THE FUTURE

As the financial services industry embarks on phase two of self-service delivery systems, it behooves us to restate the objectives of the provider and of the consumer. By understanding our objectives and drawing on our experiences and lessons learned from phase one, we can then understand the barriers that must be eliminated or lowered before realizing these objectives.

We must approach this analysis in a practical and methodical manner. Our attempts to expand self-service will not only be more successful, but will establish our success criteria, our "measuring stick", against which we can evaluate our progress. For without such criteria, how do we gain confidence to push forward, or change directions, or retreat? How do we make those decisions without waiting another decade and then a postmortem?

As an example, does the financial industry view our current level of ATM systems as a success or failure? If one reads the press or listens to conference speakers, the answer is argumentative. However, had the industry set its success criteria with respect to our current level of understanding regarding potential, our current ATM status would be an unqualified success. Those in the industry who continue to adhere to the 1975 criteria would reflect disappointment.

Accordingly, we must examine our current objectives and barriers in a more methodical manner.

The self-service delivery objectives of the financial services industry are straightforward.

1. Perform those transactions inherent in the relationships of a deposit holding institution and its retail customers in the most efficient and cost-effective manner.
2. Provide consistent, current, and accurate information regarding products and services in an efficient and cost-effective manner to maximize the purchase of these products and services by the retail customer.

The objectives of the retail customers are quite similar.

1. Perform their financial transactions in an economical, fast, private, and convenient manner.
2. Access current, consistent, accurate, and understandable information regarding products and services in an economical fast, private, and convenient manner.

Clearly these objectives, at least on paper, are similar.

OUR CUSTOMER—THE CONSUMER

As we enter the second phase of retail banking self-service delivery offerings, we must first and foremost accept that our collective customer (consumer) set is not homogeneous. This consumer set is not equal in product and service need, in willingness to participate, in personal priorities or concerns, and certainly not in receptivity. To complicate this scenario, this opportunity inequality within the consumer population is not a constant: It is a continuously changing environment. How does one approach the evaluation of a specific future offering in such a complex environment?

As a start, one must identify a self-service offering that a financial institution believes it can and wants to do. Once identified, an analysis must be made to assess whether there is sufficient rationale for the offering on the part of the financial institution. Is it a positive move which, if successful, would yield the marketing or cost benefits? Then one must assess whether particular segments of the customer base would be predisposed to participate. The segmentation of the customer base can be simple or complex depending on the demographics of a particular institution, area, or branch.

The following methodology is a rather gross technique to make this assessment. Its true value, however, is to force the providers not only to be objective about their own motivation and benefits, but more importantly, to be objective about the other participant's motivation and benefits.

In a rather hindsight manner and after living through years of ATM growth and slowdown, there appears to be a need for an algorithm, a technique for preassessing the probability of success for a new self-service offering. Figure 2 is an attempt at not only quantifying the probability of success but also a method that could be used to enhance an existing self-service program.

Typically, a financial institution would use this questionnaire for each of the participating parties in a new offering. For example, in a TTW convenience ATM, one would, as objectively as possible, attempt to answer the questionnaire separately for the consumer and the owning institution. If the result is positive, one could be optimistic. If the result is negative, one must review the (−) column to determine what action or procedure could be implemented to change that item to a (+) and what the cost or implication of that action or procedure would be. For example, the reader should answer this questionnaire objectively from the view of the credit user, credit adverse, and set pattern demographic groups. The result will, after the fact, "predict" what we have experienced as history in the convenience ATM era.

FIGURE 2 Criteria for Self-Service Acceptance (answer for each participating party in transaction)

1. Is there a need for this transaction at this location?	Yes	No
2. Is there a payback (benefit)? —Less expensive —Improved/better/more service —Additional or new benefit —Faster —More convenient (location/time) —Higher confidence		
3. Is there a payout (loss of benefit)? —More expensive —Worse and/or less service —Loss of benefit —Slower —Less convenient —Less confidence	No	Yes
4. Can they adapt easily? —Is this a repetitive transaction —Do they have tools/knowledge to use —Does it not have impact on lifestyle/habit —Do they have similar experience	Yes	No
5. Are they willing? —Evaluation of the above	Plus	Minus

This methodology could also be applied to other financial self-service offerings, including EFT at POS. (Remember, in POS, one must answer for the consumer, the retailer, the financial institution, and perhaps the switch, if independent.)

From this technique, one can quickly become convinced that the industry must evaluate future self-service offerings on a more specific, consumer-targeted basis. That is, any given retail banking offering at a particular location may be quite attractive for consumer segment A, but not segment B or segment C. Therefore our expectation level should be set accordingly, and our analysis of marketing value or cost justification must also reflect this "best case" level of expectation. Again, the fact that all consumers need a product or service does not translate into an equivalent need for the specific offering, as delivered and where delivered. Using convenience ATMs as an example, all consumers need cash. However, not all consumers need or desire convenience cash.

If this premise is valid, one could get very pessimistic contemplating different self-service devices at different locations performing specific functions for specific people. The cost of this hypothetical delivery system would be enormous and consumer acceptance at any given location lower than desired (for example, a consumer would tire of going to location A for function A, location B for function B, and so on). These two factors, resulting from a consumer targeted self-service delivery system are in fact the major barriers to overcome.

THE BARRIERS

The two major barriers to installing a successful self-service delivery system are cost to the provider and consumer usage. The cost to provide a proprietary service over dedicated communication lines to dedicated devices at dedicated locations can be enormous. From a consumer view, the major barrier is perceived usefulness—expected utility and benefit to existing life style. And yet, in spite of these barriers, there exist service providers who desire to deliver their products and services in an efficient and inexpensive electronic manner. On the other hand, we have an adult population that is presently carrying approximately 700 to 800 million magnetically encoded cards, and a population that is willing to use this medium in a self-service environment, given a perceived benefit to do so. In this environment, how does the industry entice more consumers to use their existing plastic cards more often? Entice nonparticipating consumers to obtain them? And how do we build the synergistic use of plastic cards as the access vehicle to a wider and more attractive self-service offering? Additionally, how do providers deliver this service in an economically justified manner?

PROPOSED SOLUTION

A similar problem was solved by the retail store industry with the emergence of shopping malls. Why not a "transaction mall" for retail banking delivery? Why not a transaction mall placed where the consumers are? Why not a consumer transaction mall that offers more than retail banking transactions/services? (Few successful shopping malls offer only clothes or only appliances or only financial institutions or only books!) Why not a transaction mall that is shared by all providers who offer products and services that can be delivered remotely and can be delivered reasonably, privately, and securely to a consumer on the insertion of a magnetically encoded card?

A major attraction of self-service, electronic delivery of product is convenience to the consumer. Convenience, however, is a very intangible benefit; what is convenient for one might not be convenient for another. What is convenient to the provider (for example, the ATM of a branch) might not be convenient for the user who might prefer to have it near the home or workplace. One thing is tangible, however.

If your target consumer population resides in a metropolitan area of 1 million people, a provider must install sufficient locations to provide convenience. Driving across town for a "convenience" offering is not convenient. And yet, if only 15 percent of this population are your customers (your target consumers), your delivery points will probably not yield the desired usage. The good news is that your four or five major competitors who have the remaining 85 percent of the population have a similar and perhaps worse problem. Why not share your delivery locations? Shopping malls share their delivery locations!

On this same theme, why couldn't these locations also deliver other self-service products and services of value to consumers such as value documents (airline tickets, entertainment tickets, commuter tickets, traveler's checks, food stamps, and the like), or a payment mechanism (utility bills, retail credit card payments, T&E card payments, or any payment that is frequent and repetitive), or information related to these other services (such as account statements, schedules, rates, balances, and so on)? How much more attractive this would be to the consumer. The credit adverse segment who does not use convenience ATMs might well find the utility bill payment feature very attractive. If these people get into a habit (or lifestyle) of using self-service devices, they might start obtaining that convenience cash through a machine even though the frequency of the need is slight. And if someone picks up an airline ticket on the way home from work, they might also get that convenience cash since they're at the transaction mall anyway.

If providers are sharing a transaction mall to offer a more attractive full-service package, why wouldn't the providers also share the cost of the delivery system, if you will, a transaction utility that allows a sharing of cost (usage based) for the delivery systems? Why not share the networks, the locations, and the devices? The same logic holds for other industries. We do not have four power companies installing poles and lines on your street, each competing to obtain you as a customer. Why? The capital investment in the delivery system forbids it. The local telephone company today offers you a voice delivery system to and from each of your customers. But it's not your proprietary system!

Let's compare the scenario with home banking. Home banking will probably never survive as an entity, it will be offered as a part of a total home video delivery system—a "video mall" that consists of banking, retail purchasing, news, information, entertainment, and so on. It will not, if successful, offer home banking for only one specific institution. The owner of the delivery system cannot afford a proprietary service that is not available to all of the target market, all households in the area.

Where would these transaction malls be located? Assuming all of the providers shared in the cost of the delivery system, one could anticipate that these transaction malls could be placed where the consumers are (convenience) such as work locations, home locations, entertainment and travel locations, schools, hospitals and similar settings.

This concept begs many questions. Is this really a utility? Wouldn't this blunt the competitiveness of financial institutions? Would consumers use the malls? Who pays for what? Would the economics be attractive to an operator? Who would operate such a system? What transactions would be offered? Would this be a local, state, or national system? Let's discuss these questions.

Is the future self-service delivery system a utility? In terms of being regulated, no! In terms of affordable delivery and wide consumer acceptance, perhaps! The realization of such a system will require a major commitment to satisfy the needs of the consumer, the user. There is no competitive edge nor cost justified self-service delivery system without consumer acceptance and usage. Given this, we must position the magnetic card access to products and services so that it becomes a part of the consumer lifestyle. This means allowing the consumer to use the technique every day, not only to access cash twice a week, but to pay bills, obtain other value documents, and access information.

Would such a facility blunt the competitiveness of financial institutions? Not likely. Today, branches of competitive institutions reside side by side, at the same intersections, in the same malls, or may share the same building. Financial institutions also share delivery systems today—in newspapers, magazines, mail, radio, television, and phone. Competitiveness lies in the product(s) not the delivery system!

Would such a facility be more attractive to consumers? Probably. If a self-service location can satisfy more of the consumers' daily or weekly transaction and information needs, they will have a greater propensity to use it and will use it more often. If this facility is placed conveniently near the consumer, this also will increase consumer propensity. Out of the transaction information menu, virtually every consumer would need to use several that are of use and value.

Who pays for what? This is a complex question, but the objective would be to assure that the consumer does not pay, at least not directly. This system does not need barriers to consumer participation. The economies of scale brought to bear with this system suggest that the cost of delivery of the products and information through the transaction malls would be less expensive than current or alternative proprietary delivery costs of the provider. Therefore the cost of this system is borne by the providers.

Would the economics of such a system be attractive to an operator? Likely. Switching systems are or can be "profitable" if loaded with transactions. Self-service devices can be profitable if used enough. Both switches and self-service devices are similar to an airport runway. There is a fixed capacity to fill and to sell. Runways have a fixed number of travel arrival and departure slots to sell. As an airport operator, my objective is to sell the slots. As a switch operator, my objective is to sell the message capacity from a transmission as well as a processor standpoint. As a self-service device operator, my objective is to sell the "footprint slot" in front of the device. In each case, as an operator, there is an expense associated with the slot—if empty, the operator is losing nonrecoverable revenue (perishable slots).

A self-service device generally used 12 hours per day over a 30-day month offers an operator 21,600 one-minute slots to sell per month. Over a year, this represents more than 250,000 one-minute slots. If a transaction value is 25 cents per slot, each machine has the potential of approximately $60,000 per year—if the slots are used!

Who would operate such a system? A difficult question. Existing ATM regional switches are clearly in a good position to do so. They have existing facilities, an organization, experience and probably, unused capacity. Other potential operators could be communication companies, other existing large network owners such as airlines or card processors, or any entrepreneur!

What transactions would be offered? This chapter has mentioned several. The right transaction and information products are those with value. The core offerings should be those that will never be delivered to the home such as value documents, transactions, and information that require printed output. Given a set of core offerings, other "softer" offerings could be made available. The key to choosing transactions would be to understand the population segments and attempt to offer several products and services aimed at the predisposition of each segment. Another facet of selection would be to sell the slots to the higher revenue offerings (that is, sell the last landing slot to a Boeing 747, not a Piper Cub).

Would this be a local, state, or national system? The basic success criteria would be local (for example, a metropolitian area such as an MSA or CMSA). Local systems would suffice for the consumer. For the provider, depending on the market area, state or national levels might be attractive but probably not a basic requirement. State and/or national availability would be a bonus for the consumer, but lacking this would not be a barrier to participation.

SUMMARY

As an industry, financial service is headed for increased automation, electronic delivery, and self-service delivery. Having experienced the evolution of our first self-service offering, it is an opportune time to reflect on our successes and failures, triumphs and mistakes, and future goals and challenges. There is no doubt that the financial services industry will continue to be a leader on the road to more efficient, effective delivery systems for its customers—the consumer. It is only a question of speed, specific direction, cost to get there, and degree of success. This chapter describes one of the potential roads on which we might choose collectively—a road designed to accommodate the user, not the provider.

CHAPTER FORTY-ONE

Payment Systems and Deposit Accounting

Virgil M. Dissmeyer
D/R Management Services, Inc.

This topic could also have been titled "Check Processing" since the scope of the comments covers a bank's receipt, internal handling, bookkeeping and finally, statement rendering. Since the passage of the Monetary Control Act of 1980, the processing of checks has undergone dramatic change. It appears the deposit accounting segment of processing is ready for even more change as you will see when that segment is discussed.

Historically, each decade has seen some major shift in emphasis. For example,

- 1950s—era of manual distribution of checks on multipocket proof machines followed by dual and single posting of on-us checks to paper ledgers.
- 1960s—adoption of MICR check encoding and use of electronic reader/sorters for distribution and sorting.
- 1970s—introduction of electronic check substitutes through ATMs and the ACH networks plus online tellers within banks. Very high speed reader/sorters became standard.
- 1980s—so far we have seen interest-paying demand and time transaction accounts, regional banking consolidation and expansion, plus an explosion of automation hardware.

The highlights of the changes so far in the 1980s and the outlook for the future will be covered in the comments to follow. This diagram illustrates the parameters of our topic.

CHART 1   Discussion Preview

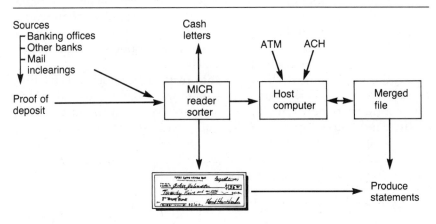

STATISTICAL MEASUREMENTS

The Bank Administration Institute made an extensive analysis of the check system in 1979 which was the last study of such a scope. Titled "Description of the Check Collection System: Part I. Checking Account Usage in the United States: A Research and Literature Survey," it identified check writer and receiver patterns. They estimated that 86 percent of all households maintained a checking account and that 32 billion checks were written on accounts at commercial banks. They estimated that 55 percent of those checks were written by individuals and 40 percent by businesses with about 5 percent by government bodies.

Since 1979, we have seen broad expansions of interest-bearing transaction accounts (demand and time) offered by banks, savings and loans, and credit unions. A total of 40 billion checks are estimated to have been processed in 1984. In addition about 400 million electronic ACH and 3.75 billion ATM transactions were posted to the same accounts. The 1979 Fed study had projected 40.1 billion checks for 1989. Trans Data Corp. now projects 46 to 48 billion checks by 1990. This represents a lot of transactions to be processed and reflected on the accounts of all financial institutions.

Costs of handling these transactions are very difficult to quantify. A couple of isolated citations will give an idea of the dollar magnitude associated with the transactions. The FDIC financial summary for all banks in 1982 showed noninterest expenses of $61,562 million. A cost study conducted by the author at Norwest Bank Minneapolis in 1982 revealed that all operational support for *all* services accounted for 41 percent of their noninterest expenses. The costs for check collection, deposit accounting, and account maintenance of transaction accounts accounted for 48 percent of these operational support expenditures or 19 percent of their total noninterest expenses.

The Bank Administration Institute in its 1985 study, "Data Processing Cost and Performance in Community Banks" reveals some interesting costs per item. These costs are based on the last quarter of 1984 and banks using some type of outside service bureau.

Unit application costs	Group Average
Demand deposit	
Cost/acct./month	$.647
Cost/transaction	.027
Time deposit	
Cost/acct./month	.215
Cost/transaction	.214
Proof and transit	
Cost/item	.028

The same BAI study shows how and where banks process these transactions. The data show

- 25 percent use in-house data processing systems (50 percent of banks under $50 million in assets use this alternative)
- 75 percent use some type of service bureau as follows:
  39 percent rely on a correspondent bank servicer
  31 percent are supported by a holding company affiliate
  28 percent use an independent service bureau

Banks, which use a service bureau, rely on couriers to move their items to the service bureau in 66 percent of the cases and the rest use online remote entry proof or reader/sorters.

PROOF OF DEPOSIT

The receipt by a bank of the customer's deposit requires that the amount be proved against the accompanying checks. This is a labor-intensive task; it requires physically reading the check and keying in the amount so the electronic equipment can handle the subsequent processing via MICR characters. This task has not changed—but the hardware to assist the clerical operator has seen major improvements. One major bank equipment vendor attempted in the late 1970s to develop a device that would read a customers handwriting by optical techniques and convert the amount to MICR characters. The readability rate was so low that no new efforts have been developed to automate the human element of encoding at the bank of first deposit.

Three types of proof equipment are generally used. They are illustrated on Exhibit 1 along with the key features. In all three approaches an operator must encode the documents with MICR characters and balance the checks to the deposit, then independently or through other equipment sort the checks for distribution and electronically capture the MICR numeric data for account updating. This is illustrated in Chart 2. The major vendors of this type equipment are IBM, Unisys, NCR, and Banctec.

This new proof equipment, which can be connected by communication lines to a computer, gives a financial institution a wide variety of options on where the proofing function should be performed. This is usually determined by location and volume. The four locations are:

1. The local bank or branch.
2. A regional processing center.
3. A centralized processing site.
4. A service bureau.

Two other banking functions are performed on the proof machine or reader/sorter equipment. Each item must be endorsed as it is processed and microfilmed for records retention and customer service. The microfilming is crucial if the checks are transported by a courier to the reader/sorter location and if a truncation service (check safekeeping versus return with the statement) is offered.

CHECK DISTRIBUTION

Significant improvements have been made since the 1970s in high-speed computer-controlled reader/sorters. These devices read the MICR numeric data on the bottom of the check or deposit slips, electronically capture the information for computer master file updating, sort the items into computer-controlled pockets for physical distribution, and may endorse and microfilm at high speed. These functions can take place at speeds of 750 to 2,400 items per minute and sort into 12 to 40 different pockets. It is these devices that allow financial institutions to economically process the billions of checks written each year. The electronic check alternatives have not grown at the pace anticipated in 1979 due to the efficiency of the present paper-based systems.

The major vendors of this equipment are Unisys, IBM, NCR, Lundy, Banctec, and Recognition Equipment. Illustrations and features of the

EXHIBIT 1 Types of Proof Machines

Single-pocket unit
- All 3 types require manual entry of numeric data through a keyboard
- Encodes and balances only
- Checks must be physically moved to reader/sorter location
(Unisys S690 is pictured; other models include NCR.)

Multipocket offline unit
- Encodes, balances, and sorts
- Endorses and may microfilm
- Multiple-pocket options and pocket listers
- About 20 dpm encoding mode, 180 dpm inclearings entry, and 400 dpm sorting mode
- May capture information on disks for transmission
(NCR 7770 is shown; other models include Unisys and Banctec.)

Online proof unit
- Encodes, balances, sorts, and transmits data for computer file updating
- Endorses and microfilms
- Accepts transmission from host computer for report printing
- Multiple-pocket options
(IBM 3694 is shown; other models include NCR, Unisys, Lundy, and Banctec.)

CHART 2 Type of Proof Machine

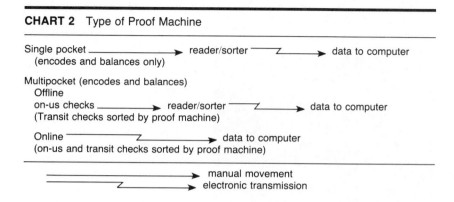

Single pocket ⎯⎯⎯⎯⎯⎯⎯⎯→ reader/sorter ⎯⎯⎯⎯→ data to computer
(encodes and balances only)

Multipocket (encodes and balances)
  Offline
  on-us checks ⎯⎯⎯⎯→ reader/sorter ⎯⎯⎯⎯→ data to computer
  (Transit checks sorted by proof machine)

  Online ⎯⎯⎯⎯⎯⎯⎯⎯→ data to computer
  (on-us and transit checks sorted by proof machine)

⎯⎯⎯⎯⎯⎯⎯⎯⎯⎯→ manual movement
⎯⎯⎯⎯⎯⎯⎯⎯⎯⎯→ electronic transmission

hardware are shown on Exhibit 2. However, the equipment cannot capture the MICR industry standard characters unless the reader/sorters are controlled by computer software programs. These programs have become very sophisticated as they calculate float based on time of day and drawee bank, accumulate totals for cash management services, transmit data to remote computers, and record control information. Each vendor has a name for the software which can be recognized as DOScheck, mini VIPS, Super MICR, Check Processing Control System, and so on. Although these programs have become sophisticated, the evolution has stabilized. There is only so much that can be done at speeds of 2,400 per minute. The big software changes will be discussed next.

DEPOSIT ACCOUNTING

The comments to this point on check processing of the payments system has concentrated on the hardware changes which impact the manual handling of the checks. The deposit accounting phase of this topic will concentrate on the electronic handling of the account and transaction information. This is done by software programs which are a set of instructions to the computer. The software solutions are more varied even than the hardware options, statistics are more difficult to accumulate, and the rate of change will make most data obsolete very quickly.

The Monetary Control Act of 1980 triggered a boom in deposit accounting application software. This was due to the ability of banks to offer new products, the necessity to treat a customer as a relationship rather than an account, and the need to improve service as new competitors entered the market and to process the electronic alternatives which are growing in acceptance. About 13.1 percent of the overall

EXHIBIT 2 Types of Reader/Sorters

Small-volume systems
• Generally 6 to 12 pocket models
• 750 to 1,000 documents per
  minute
• Endorses checks as entered
• Normally requires separate
  microfilm step
(Lundy MRS-90 is pictured. Other
models include IBM and Banctec.)

Large-volume systems
• 12 to 40 pocket units
• 1,400 to 2,400 dpm
• Endorses and microfilms
• Programmable offline outsort
  features
(NCR 6780 is pictured; other
  models include IBM 3890, Unisys
  91XX, Banctec CRIP, and
  Recognition Equipment TRACE.)

U.S. automation market was purchased by the 18,269 banks and thrifts for 1985. Table 1 shows the type of products.

Packaged software is not the only source for new application programs. Table 2 will present an idea of the source of new programs for 1985 based on the experience of larger banks. Other major software vendors would include Kirchman, Cullinet, SEI, plus various vendor-controlled software from NCR, Unisys, IBM, EDS, and others. Some of the major developments in deposit accounting software will be commented on later by vendor.

Three categories of deposit accounting application software are in use. The original and oldest batch processing dates from the intro-

TABLE 1   U.S. Automation Product Market

Product Category	1985 U.S. Revenue (billions)
Computers (except personal computers)	$26.5
Peripherals (printers and the like)	22.3
Terminals (bank, general purpose, and so on)	9.4
Packaged software	8.4
Personal computers	5.8
Total	$72.4

SOURCE: "Computers in Banking's Automation Report" *Computers in Banking,* August 1986, statistics by A.D. Little.

duction of computers. Each application is developed as an independent set of accounting programs. Transactions are accumulated and processed as a batch against the account master files at the end of the day.

The next category developed by banks is interfaced applications. This is an attempt to link separate batch applications so entries can be passed back and forth, in some cases to a common CIF, Customer Information File, to summarize general ledger entries and to facilitate multibank updating by service centers.

The advent of online terminals for inquiry and input has caused many banks to "memo post" certain transactions to a file during the day. These memorandum entries are later included with the day's transactions and reposted as the official master file is updated. Examples would be placing stops or holds on accounts, late ACH direct deposit amounts, or new accounts.

Financial institutions want even more communication between systems than the interfaced category allows. Many are seeking true integration, which has become a buzzword, to increase online flexibility. The goal is to make changes to services or relationships that are reflected throughout all systems as they occur. There are four levels of integration:

1. Interfaced software, described as the second category.
2. A common customer relationship view on a terminal screen.
3. Common systems architecture.
4. A common database of information used by all systems.

Another goal of true integrated packages is "real time" updating. That is, the official master file of accounts and applications is updated throughout the day as transactions occur rather than at the end of the day in one updating process. This does not preclude some applications from being online or updated in a batch mode or from using memo-post techniques.

TABLE 2   Software Sources 1985 (banks over $1 billion assets)

Software source	Number	Percent
Write their own	185	46%
Buy vendor packages—		
Hogan Systems, Inc.	95	23
Software Alliance Corp.	45	11
Systematics Corp.	45	11
Uccel Corp.	25	6
Others	10	3
Total	405	100%

SOURCE: "Profile Hogan Systems, the Leader in Bank Software, Draws Cautious Response from Users After Deal with IBM," *American Banker*, July 24, 1986, statistics by Donaldson, Lufkin & Jenrette.

Many bankers will be discussing these three categories or concepts with their technicians during the balance of the 1980s. Exhibit 3 illustrates some of the key differences in an attempt to simplify a very technical subject.

SOFTWARE VENDOR BRIEFS

There are many vendors of software. Some of them, however, should be mentioned individually to present the ramifications of the deposit accounting application changes which appear to be on the horizon. According to the research done by Trans Data Corp. reported in the July 17, 1986, *American Banker*, 24 percent of banks over $4 billion plan to buy deposit accounting software, 17 to 21 percent of midsize banks plan to buy, and the percent decreases to the smallest banks where only 4 percent plan to buy new software. Smaller institutions plan to buy from NCR, 20 percent, and Unisys, 12 percent. Midsize banks favor Systematics, Florida Software, Software Alliance Corp., Uccel Corp., and others. The top range of deposit banks plan to use Hogan and M&I (Marketed by Software Alliance Corp.).

No reference material can encompass every vendor, software product, or target market since these are constantly changing. New vendors and new products are announced constantly in response to marketplace demand. The brief comments on some of the major vendors cited in this chapter, are included only as an indication of the type of products, announced development emphasis, and markets they target. The reader is given these briefs to highlight the current industry status and variety.

Hogan Systems was one of the first to promote integrated deposit systems and installed the first system in 1981. They now have 140

EXHIBIT 3 Categories of Deposit Systems Design

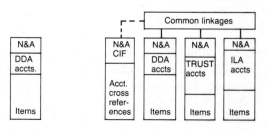

Batch	Interfaced	Integrated
• Stand-alone design	• Separate applications	• Common design
• Special purpose data	• Duplicate databases	• Use single
• No linkages	• Covert program to link	database
• Common data	• Common entries	• Automatic linkages
reentered	passed	• All data available
• Software unique	• Software interpreter	• Common software
• Application driven	• Account driven	• Transaction driven

customers and claim 23 percent of the total value of the banking software market. Hogan achieves integration using "middleware" software, or an umbrella module, which acts as a buffer between the application programs and the computer environment consisting of the operating system, databases, and communications network. It can be used as a stand-alone system or integrated with companion integrated loans (which took three years to develop), online collections, online delivery, or the customer information system called Prophet. It is by far the most complex system on the market today.

Software Alliance Corp. markets the Marsh & Ilsley Bank of Wisconsin system. It was developed for the M&I use, originally based on an integrated module concept. Again Trans Data Corp. (TDC) research estimates it is used by 10 percent of the banks with deposits of $2 to $4 billion and to a lesser degree by larger institutions.

Uccel Corp. markets a integrated system of 20 applications for banks called Infopoint. More significantly, Uccel in 1983 announced a $20 million three-year project called LEAP to create a new generation of banking applications. TDC estimates 70 percent of Uccel's current business is with institutions of $400 million to $2 billion asset size. A new integrated loans package and ACH were supposed to be available in 1986 followed by CIF, a transaction management system and profitability analysis.

Cullinet Software now offers a series of banking applications based on its popular IDMS database operating system. They targeted a new integrated banking system for early 1987. It will cover all functions on the asset and liability side of the statement plus an electronic banking module and customer information file. TDC indicates the current systems are used by the larger thrifts and banks $750 million to $2 billion in asset.

Unisys Corp. markets a system called Global Financial System which was introduced in 1985. It covers total banking, branch information, and thrift management. TDC indicates it is most popular in mid- to large-size thrifts and smaller banks.

NCR's Banker 80 system is installed in 10 percent of all institutions surveyed by TDC. It is targeted for both banks and thrifts with loan, savings, customer information, and demand deposit applications. A Universal Financial System is being developed for larger banks.

Systematics, Inc., not only offers deposit accounting software but 50 data centers throughout the country. It has over 700 customers which are most frequently in the top 500 banks and thrifts.

Florida Software, a Kirchman company, offers both software and data center services. Its applications are interfaced through a central information file. Its primary use is in institutions under $4 billion.

OTHER DEPOSIT ACCOUNTING INITIATIVES

Several joint ventures or development contracts were announced in late 1986 which indicate the emphasis deposit accounting is receiving by major vendors and institutions. The size of these programs parallels the growth in interstate banking expansions and liberalized branching laws in a number of states. Extracts from the various American Banker announcements clearly indicate a concentration on the large systems is needed to meet the needs of growing financial institutions. Four ventures are cited below to illustrate the magnitude and variety of options becoming available. The examples are not intended to be all-inclusive but to alert the reader to the type of development underway at this time.

Hogan Systems, Inc. announced in May 1986 that IBM would become the exclusive marketing agent for its products in the United States, Canada, and Puerto Rico. Hogan will retain marketing rights in some foreign countries and responsibility for its existing customer base. This matches the huge hardware base of IBM with the software technology of Hogan. Implications of this venture are yet to be seen.

Electronic Data Systems Corp. (EDS and now a subsidiary of General Motors) announced in October 1986 two related events. First, they will develop a fully integrated system for Banc One Corp. of Columbus, Ohio, a major regional bank holding company. Banc One Corp. has $11 billion assets and 400 branches. Second, EDS purchased the rights to Anacomp Inc.'s Continuous Integrated System which was intiated in 1980 at the same time Hogan's effort began. Financial difficulties have prompted Anacomp to phase out of the banking software field. EDS will deliver segments of the new system over the next three to four years. It will use the basic structure of Anacomp's CIS and include customer information, deposit, loan, and delivery modules. It will be built around the customer record rather than function so it should be easier to alter as conditions change. EDS already services 4,200 financial institutions. These include 700 medium-sized banks, 50 thrifts, and 3,500 credit unions.

Software Alliance Inc. announced that it has been contracted to install and run an integrated system for the nine banks of Louisiana Bancshares Inc. of Baton Rouge. The $4.8 billion-asset bank holding company was formed in January 1985. The integrated M&I modules will be installed over the next year and a half and supplemented by an advanced account analysis system and a computer-based training technique.

Hogan Systems, Inc. signed a contract in midyear to install a mega-bank system for Midland Bank PLC, which is Britain's third largest bank. Midland has $93 billion assets and global network of 2,188 branches.

Similar ventures will probably be announced by the time this reference guide is published. Since each of the vendors plan to market the final products to other banks, the progress of these efforts may influence the design of systems for smaller institutions.

NEW ALTERNATIVES

Personal computer-based systems for the very small institution have become a viable solution as the power of PCs has increased. One system provides demand deposit accounting, certificates, savings, general ledger, safe deposit, and loans on an IBM personal computer/AT. Another system controls a slow speed reader/sorter with a PC. The new third generation PCs based on the Itel 80386 processor will put more power at the disposal of the small institution.

Bulk filing eliminates the manual filing of checks by customer in account sequence. Under bulk filing, exception items (closed accounts, insufficient funds, or stop payments) are extracted by a separate pass through the high-speed reader/sorter. Physcial review for dates, alterations, signatures, and endorsements is normally limited to selected items, generally based on random sampling and dollar value of the item. Nonexception items are sorted into cycles and held until cycle date in the same order as originally processed. On cycle date, the items are fine sorted and, where volume warrants, can be matched with the appropriate statement by automated inserters, weighed and sorted by zip code for mailing. A great many of today's checks can be handled completely electronically after the initial manual proof encoding step.

Backup processing for contingency planning used to be ignored or relied on internal redundant capabilities. Electronic technology has presented other cost-effective alternatives. MICR reader/sorters can be operated at great remote distances by small front-end processors connected to a communication line to the processing center. These sorters may be in regional centers, or service bureaus operated specifically for that purpose (First Express in Memphis or Travelers Express in Minneapolis are two examples). Host computers required to update the master files can now be leased on a stand-by basis from a variety of hot site disaster backup centers (examples are Comdisco and Sungaard). Switching communication lines from a primary site, which is inoperable, to one or both of these backup alternatives protects a bank so this high-volume customer-sensitive deposit application can be operated without interruption.

Banks traditionally returned each paid check to the depositor as proof of payment. As the volume has grown and costs of mailing increased, many banks have looked at the alternative of not returning paid checks with the statements. The thrifts and credit unions generally followed this approach when they were granted transaction account authority by the MCA of 1980. The truncation system usually stores the paid check for a limited period of 90 days, and from that point on relies on microfilm to respond to customer inquiries.

Today four alternatives to truncation are followed:

1. No truncation—paid checks returned with the statement.
2. Truncation at payor bank—microfilm and destory after a limited period.
3. Truncation at bank of first deposit—the check is truncated at the point it enters the banking system, and only electronic data or images are sent to the payor bank. The ABA Check Safekeeping Task Force conducted a pilot of this system in 1981. Due to nonstandard interinstitutional requirements, legal issues, and the technical problem of image transmission, expansion of the pilot ceased. Less than one percent of all checks were being truncated in this manner in 1986.
4. Electronic elimination—ATM's, ACH, Point of Sale and telephone bill paying/transfer are four alternatives to the check. Electronic items are currently a small fraction of the paper transactions, but the combined potential of the alternatives is growing.

Image processing is the technology to capture video images of checks, digitize the information, and store or transmit the image for subsequent processing. It is limited today to a few lockbox and credit card applications. Conceivably, image processing could replace microfilm with optical disk storage and checks at the bank of first deposit with full or partial images displayed on the customer's statement. It is technically feasible today, but the transmission speeds, communications costs, and systems/hardware investments limit the current application.

THE FUTURE

The payments system in this country and deposit accounting application in the individual financial institutions are still undergoing major change. The exact direction or speed cannot be predicted, but this chapter alerts us to the potential.

The study "Displacing the Check" by the Federal Reserve Bank of Atlanta, August 1983, is a good way to end this analysis. They projected that the rate of acceptance of electronic alternative to the check would reduce the total volume of paper items by 10 percent in 1994 from its peak in 1989. A transformation of the way American households pay for things could evolve so that 51 percent of disbursements by individuals could be electronically by 1994. Even then this would not be a checkless society since over 40 billion checks would still have to be processed with the systems.

CHAPTER FORTY-TWO

Programs to Assist Individual Managers in Information Management and Decision Making

Thomas A. Farin

President
Farin, Parliment & Associates, Inc.

INTRODUCTION

No single technology has had a greater effect on the way managers perform their tasks than computers. The mainframe computer organizes and controls vast amounts of data bankwide, and data are the lifeblood of a modern commercial bank. The mainframe's benefits extend throughout the organization, allowing individuals to quickly locate key pieces of information essential to the flow of banking transactions. It can generate an astounding array of reports, ranging from customer statements, to daily departmental reports, to management reporting.

But the mainframe's mind boggling size and complexity are also its Achilles heel. It is too large and intricate for most managers to use effectively for the individual analyses that makes up a major portion of their daily work. The mainframe's complexity requires specialized teams of management employees with the skills necessary to tap its vast resources. Only a few years ago, in spite of the awesome capabilities of the mainframe computer, most managers went about their tasks using virtually the same techniques they had used for generations.

But bank managers, overlooked by computer technology for the first two decades of computing, are restructuring the way they work and think. Led by two young pioneers from Apple and validated by the endorsement of IBM, microcomputer technology is becoming a mandatory tool for every bank manager. In this chapter we will explore the role technology is playing in restructuring the way we think and perform our tasks. We will look at an individual case study of such a change and evaluate how microcomputer technology is influencing a number of crucial areas of bank management.

GENERAL ROLE OF MODELING/PLANNING SOFTWARE

Productivity Enhancement

There is no question that the microcomputer offers the potential for significant improvements in management productivity. In the pre-microcomputer era, bankers involved in the credit analysis, and finance and control functions found that in excess of 75 percent of their time was spent crunching numbers and preparing reports. The basic skills required for those tasks were learned in primary and secondary school. This left less than 25 percent of their time to exercising the analytical skills and making the recommendations that justified their salaries.

The purchase of a microcomputer, an electronic spreadsheet, and a word processing package caused an almost immediate turnaround in those two ratios. Managers found that within months only 25 percent of their time was spent on number crunching and report preparation and 75 percent was spent on analysis and recommendations. In terms of their true productivity (percentage of time spent on management-level tasks), a $5,000 investment in hardware and software could triple the productivity of a $30,000-a-year manager.

More Sophisticated Management Techniques

In addition to the productivity improvements gained from automating manual tasks, two additional benefits from microcomputer technology have become apparent. In eliminating the high management cost associated with evaluating alternative solutions to a problem, managers find that they no longer dread their manager looking at their analysis and questioning one of the underlying assumptions. Completing a revised analysis with a modified set of assumptions now takes minutes rather than hours. As a result, banks have been making more decisions based on "hard facts" and less based on a "seat of the pants" feel.

And the microcomputer has opened the potential of using more sophisticated analytical techniques than were feasible in a manual environment. Often these sophisticated analytical techniques provide answers that lead to a less complex and easier to understand decision-making process. Let's take a look at a real life example that illustrates this seemingly paradoxical statement.

INTEREST RATE RISK MANAGEMENT—A CASE STUDY

Overview

As we discuss elsewhere in this book, one of the key management tasks in a commercial bank is effectively balancing the objective of maximizing profitability against the necessity of effectively controlling risk. Interest rate risk is one of the most crucial risk management areas. While a number of techniques exist for evaluating interest rate risk, gap analysis is the method most commonly employed. Gap analysis is an example of a management analysis tool that was developed in the premicrocomputer era. It has the advantage of requiring only a pencil, accountant's worksheet, and a calculator. A gap analysis for Sample Bank is shown in Exhibit 1.

Gap Management—The Traditional Tool

The most commonly used guideline for measuring the extent of interest rate risk is the ratio of the gap between rate sensitive assets and liabilities to total assets. A frequent policy employed by institutions attempting to control interest rate risk is to keep the gap/asset ratio within the range of +/− 10 percent. Six-month and one-year gap/asset ratios, shown in Exhibit 1, are outside those guidelines.

Although gap analysis has a number of shortcomings, we'll only review its most significant shortcoming in this example. While the gap/asset ratio attempts to measure the extent of imbalance between rate sensitive assets and liabilities, it doesn't tell us the effect of a potential increase or decrease in interest rates on an institution's income. Senior managers and board members have difficulty undertanding why our interest rate risk management policy is built around a ratio (gap/assets) that doesn't tell them what they really want to know.

This problem is compounded when we attempt to choose between two or more alternative approaches to an interest rate risk problem. The best solution is one that controls interest rate risk and maximizes profitability at the same time. But gap analysis' inability to measure the effect of an interest rate environment on income prevents the effective comparison of alternative strategies. Consequently, managers employing gap analysis must resort to the "seat of the pants" approach in choosing between alternative solutions.

Computer Simulation—Micro-Based Alternative

Computer simulation, an alternative to basic gap analysis, is being employed by many innovative institutions as it overcomes many lim-

EXHIBIT 1 Gap Analysis (balances broken down by next scheduled repricing point)

Sample Bank Gap Analysis	Months until Next Scheduled Repricing			
	0–6	6–12	Over 12	Total
Rate sensitive assets (RSA)	200	400	400	1,000
Rate sensitive liabilities (RSL)	400	400	200	1,000
Gap (RSA-RSL)	−200	0	200	
Cumulative gap	−200	−200	0	
Gap/assets	−20%	0%	20%	
Cumulative gap/assets	−20%	−20%	0%	

itations of gap analysis. Exhibit 2 outlines the basic data requirements and output of a typical asset-liability (A–L) simulation model. The model requires a current data starting point along with assumptions about both the interest rate environment and the performance of the institution in that environment.

Let's say we wanted to evaluate the effect of a proposed solution to Sample Bank's interest rate sensitivity. The manager running this strategy tells the A–L model the amount and timing of the proposed solution and which specific instruments are affected. He then instructs the computer to simulate the effect of the transaction on Sample Bank in a variety of interest rate environments. For each rate environment, the A–L model would forecast a statement of condition and a statement of income and analytical reports allowing us to evaluate changes in gap, and other key management ratios.

For each additional proposed solution to Sample Bank's interest rate risk management problem, the manager describes the strategy to the computer and simulates the effect on the financial performance of the bank.

Two significant benefits are gained from computer simulation of alternative strategies. First, rather than use the gap/asset ratio as its primary policy setting tool for interest rate risk management, an institution's policy could be based on an acceptable level of variance in net income. For example, Sample's policy might be:

> It is the policy of Sample Bank to manage interest rate risk in such a way as to maximize profitability while at the same time controlling fluctuations in net income due to interest rate risk to within +/− 10 percent of net income.

Such a policy could be readily understood and approved by any board member.

EXHIBIT 2   Computer Simulation

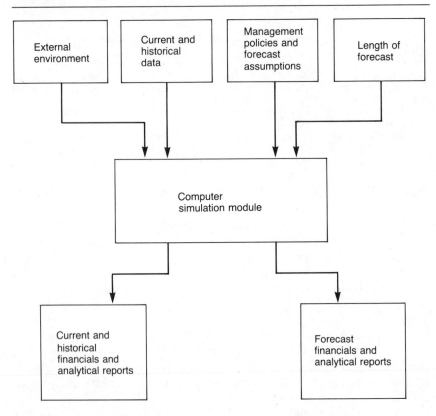

Second, alternative solutions to interest rate risk problems can be evaluated using a decision matrix similar to that in Exhibit 3. Net income for Model comparing its current management policy with two alternative solutions (asset sale/purchase and deposit shift) under all three rate environments is displayed in a simple table. Both the asset sale/purchase and deposit shift strategies bring net income fluctuations under the three interest rate environments chosen to within 10 percent of net income. But the asset sale/purchase strategy is superior in that it results in a higher net income under all three rate environments. It would be easy to explain to any management level bank employee or board member why it is inappropriate to continue using the bank's current management policy and why the asset sale strategy was being recommended.

In summary, the microcomputer both increases the sophistication of the analysis being performed as part of the decision-making process and at the same time leads to a more meaningful and easy to under-

EXHIBIT 3   Interest Rate Risk: Sample Bank Decision Matrix

Net Income - Different Scenarios

Proposed Management Policies

Interest Rate Trend	Management Policy Limits	Present Policy	Asset Sale/ Purchase	Deposit Shift
Increasing	+/− 10%	$ 75	$ 96	$92
Expected	Maximum	$101	$ 98	$93
Decreasing	+/− 10%	$127	$100	$94

Policy Rejected: Net Income varies by more than 10%.

Policies Accepted: Net Income varies by less than 10%. Asset Sale Strategy is recommended as it yields a higher net income under all three rate environments.

stand interest rate risk management policy. Finally, it provides the manager making a policy recommendation with a report (the decision matrix) that supports his position.

Of course, movement from a paper-based technique (gap analysis) to a more sophisticated microcomputer-based technique (simulation) is not without its costs. First, there is the cost of the investment in hardware. Second, the institution must purchase or develop an A–L simulation model that meets its needs. Third, while the decision matrix leads to an easier decision-making process, the management employee responsible for asset-liability management needs to be aware of new technology. But most institutions who have seen the benefit of computer simulation would be extremely reluctant to go back to their premicrocomputer methods.

APPLICATION AREAS

Overview

In much the same way as in the interest rate risk management example we just discussed, computer models are being used by managers to increase their productivity and enhance the decision-making process in all areas of commercial banking. Let's take a quick look at a few of these areas.

Finance and Control

In addition to employing A–L simulation models in automating interest rate risk management, innovative bankers are using strategic planning models to prepare a strong quantitative analysis to support the qualitative anlysis developed as part of their strategic plans. Microcomputers are also allowing managers to prepare budgets, update those budgets, and run year-end performance forecasts "on the fly" as the underlying assumptions driving their plans change.

Institutions realizing the importance of good cost data in a deregulated environment are using micros to perform functional cost analysis, and are using the resulting data in evaluating alternative strategies in pricing products and services. They are also using microcomputer technology to assess acquisitions, branch feasibility, and branch sales and purchases. Even the regulatory reporting process has been automated for some institutions with reports passing over phone lines electronically rather than on hard copy. And board members are finding that the computer-generated graphics prepared by the controller take much of the mystery out of financial institution reports.

Commercial Banking

Commercial banking has seen its own revolution. The microcomputer has taken commercial credit analysis from a static look at the historical trends of a commercial borrower, to a dynamic look at the potential effects of alternative loan packages on a borrower's cash flow, profitability, and long-term viability as an organization. It is not unusual for a commercial or agricultural borrower to work with his commercial banker in evaluating the effects of various financing packages on the financial performance of his farm or business.

Commercial bankers have used micros to automate loan processing and document preparation, and loan loss and collateral control. Small banks have even placed loan accounting on micros. Larger banks are offering micro-based cash management services to their customers. And banks of all sizes are using the micro to assess the profitability of commercial customer relationships so they might effectively price the relationship.

Retail Banking

Retail banking officers are expanding their productivity with microcomputers by automating the new account setup and document preparation processes. Micro-based officer call and sales tracking systems are helping bankers become more sales oriented. Cross-selling tools help in the sale of traditional banking products and services by performing IRA projections and account comparisons. Micros are also assisting in the marketing of more sophisticated products and services like financial planning, and insurance and discount brokerage.

Trust and Investments

The areas of trust and investments have seen the development of a number of very powerful micro-based systems. Providers of investment analysis and trading services have used microcomputer power to greatly enhance the analysis and information capabilities of their services. Investment managers have powerful information tools to assist in bond swap analysis and portfolio management. Banks offering discount brokerage services are offering online trading services to their customers. And microcomputer-based tools are handling the heavier analytical tasks in the areas of tax and estate planning.

SUMMARY

Throughout the bank, managers are using the micro to improve productivity, gain better access to essential data, automate previously manual tasks, and assist in the analysis and report preparation process. The result is more informed, more productive managers who are making better decisions.

Where We're Headed

The role of the microcomputer in the management process over the last seven years has evolved from an experimental tool, seen only in the most innovative institutions, to the essential tool in the modern bank manager's arsenal. But as the popular song goes, "We've only just begun." A number of trends point to the increasingly important role micro technology will play in management.

As the cost of managers continues to rise, the ratio of microcomputer price to performance will continue to fall. As a result, more micro-based applications will become cost effective. Capabilities of interfacing mainframes and microcomputers will evolve, making uploading and downloading of data easier. This factor will accelerate the development of microcomputer-based planning and analysis systems.

Graphics capabilities of microcomputers will continue to become more sophisticated. In combination with color laser printers, the computer will increasingly be used by managers to create easier to understand management reports.

The microcomputer's greatest effect on management, artificial intelligence applications, is already being employed at an experimental level. This evolution will gain momentum as the micro's capabilities continue to grow. Larger financial institutions are already employing artificial intelligence in the credit analysis function. The micro is no longer just a tool for quickly reporting key trends in financial ratios for corporate borrowing customers. The computer now goes beyond the number crunching and applies the skills of an experienced credit analyst in evaluating the trends in those ratios and making recommendations on credit structure and credit authorization.

This "experienced credit analyst in a micro" is a potential boon to all institutions. Larger institutions will be able to replace entry-level credit analysts with computer-based analysis at a much lower cost. Smaller institutions that had previously been unable to justify a formal credit analysis function will justifiably be able to increase the sophistication of their credit review process.

Will the micro ever be able to replace the ability of a seasoned loan officer to "look the customer in the eye" and make value judgments based on a subjective evaluation? Probably not in the near future. And yet, there are many quantitative management tasks in the commercial loan department and throughout the bank that lend themselves to artificial intelligence. As microcomputer technology continues to evolve, its presence and importance throughout the bank will continue to grow.

From computer simulation to artificial intelligence, managers will be able to propose potential solutions and evaluate the results before attempting to implement them in the real world. With the help of the microcomputer, the days of making decisions by the seat of the pants should no longer be the norm.

PART EIGHT

Managing the Bank's Credit Services

CHAPTER FORTY-THREE

Establishing Overall Credit Policies

Preston T. Holmes

Formerly Executive Vice President, Credit Administration
United Virginia Bank (now CRESTAR Financial Corporation)

GENERAL OBSERVATIONS

The credit or loan policy: What is it? Why have it? These are legitimate questions that deserve better answers than just "to satisfy the examiners."

Loans are the largest asset in practically all banks. Therefore, the soundness of the loan portfolio in large measure determines the earnings of the bank and its overall soundness.

The credit policy is a statement of basic principles that governs the extension of credit. It provides a framework in which to conduct business, and it enables a bank to have a long-term business plan, operating proactively instead of constantly reacting to the policies of its competitors. It should take into account the economic makeup and needs of the trade area the bank serves. For example, is the community highly industrialized; if so, is it dominated by one big company or industry or is there good diversification?

The credit policy must be viewed in the larger context of a broad business policy. It determines the character, public acceptance, and success of the bank as a quasi-public institution and profit-making venture. It must be closely coordinated with and fit other bank policies, such as investments, asset and liability management, human resources, and marketing.

WRITTEN CREDIT POLICY

One of the basic objectives of a credit policy is to render the maximum credit service to the area served within the limits of prudence, safety, and liquidity. Therefore, a written credit policy is almost essential for uniform treatment of borrowing customers.

A written policy provides a framework of reference and standards so lending personnel can function with a feeling of confidence when extending credit within delegated lending authority.

The credit policy should be prepared by the senior credit officer of the institution, and approved by the chief executive officer and the board of directors. It should be subjected to a detailed review and update at least annually.

It is important that the policy state what to do (not how to do it— too many credit policies become operating manuals) and that exceptions stand out clearly. The policy should be flexible but deal with major issues so it is not subject to frequent change.

BASIC ELEMENTS OF CREDIT POLICY

The following areas should be covered in a comprehensive statement of credit policy:

1. Legal considerations—The bank's legal lending limit should be clearly set forth to avoid any violation of banking regulations.
2. Maximum size of loan portfolio—The maximum size of the loan portfolio should be stated in relation to deposits, capital, or some other clearly distinguishable benchmark.
3. Loan portfolio mix—One of the most important elements of a loan policy is the type of loans the bank will and will not make and the amount of each type of acceptable loan it wants in its total portfolio.
4. Delegation of authority—Each individual with lending authority should know exactly how much credit he or she can commit and under what circumstances. The authority granted should also cover overdrafts in the borrower's deposit accounts because an overdraft is really an extension of credit. The delegations should be reviewed by senior management and approved by the board of directors at least annually.
5. Pricing—The price charged for the credit extended must compensate the bank for its cost of funds, cost of extending and administering the credit, and credit and time risk. To minimize customer dissatisfaction, it is desirable to maintain a high degree of uniformity for the same type risk in the same market. The interest sensitivity desired in the loan portfolio is an important policy consideration because it determines the aggregate amount of credit the bank will extend on a fixed basis and on variable rates. This subject will be dealt with in detail in the assets and liability management section.
6. Market area—Delineation of the primary area to be served is directly affected by the amount of the bank's capital, the nature

of the geographic area in which it is head-quartered, the age of the organization, and the size and ability of its staff.

7. Credit quality standards—The bank needs to determine the qualitative standards for acceptable credits. Does it want a very high quality, low rate, low charge-off portfolio or a higher risk, higher rate, more rapid growth orientation? How much influence will it let competition have on its quality standards?

8. Liquidity—Credit policy needs to address the quality issue, and the liquidity of the portfolio. Many factors affect the degree of liquidity needed in the loan portfolio, but foremost are the deposit mix and the liquidity of other bank assets. The volatility and seasonal fluctuation of the deposit base, the amount of purchased funds, and the composition of investment portfolio directly affect the setting of this portion of the credit policy.

9. Credit administration—Regardless of its name or designation within the organization, a good administrative setup is essential to see that policy is enforced and that proper procedures are in place and are adhered to. Otherwise, it is very difficult for policies and standards to be achieved, and management is vulnerable to big surprises.

LOAN PORTFOLIO MIX

After management has determined the desired maximum size of the loan portfolio in relation to its capital, loan loss reserves, and whatever other criteria it chooses, it must then subdivide the portfolio into the amount of each type of loan it wants to achieve its overall goal. Some major categories may include:

1. Real estate loans.

   Single-family residential.
   Apartments (condominiums).
   Office buildings.
   Shopping centers.
   Office warehouse.
   Resort properties.
   Hotels-Motels.
   Special purpose (restaurants, fast food, banks, manufacturing).
   Land development.
   Time sharing.
   Construction.

All of these types of real estate and financing vehicles have unique features that bear on the credit quality. The bank must have experienced qualified lending personnel in these specialized areas. Also, the bank must have a firm policy on the type of documentation and collateral it will require. For example, will take-out commitments be required on construction loans? Will the bank advance interest for several years during the rent-up period on commercial projects? Will "mini-perms" be made (converting a construction loan to permanent status with a long-term amortization schedule and an intermediate term call provision or balloon balance)?

Which appraisal methods or approaches will be acceptable—cost, replacement cost, or market value? How much does the bank want to lend in relation to the appraised value?

The bank must also decide if it wants to handle conventional loans or only government-insured loans. Selling and servicing mortgages is a good source of fee income that doesn't tie up large amounts of capital.

All these matters need serious consideration in determining how much in real estate loans the bank wants in its portfolio and which types of real estate loans it wants.

2. Consumer loans.

> Installment loans.
> Revolving lines of credit.
> Credit cards.

The bank must determine the type of loans it will make on the closed-end installment loan program (i.e., automobiles, recreational vehicles, mobile homes, boats) and what the maximum maturities and loan to value will be. It also must decide if it wants to purchase paper from dealers or make loans directly to consumers.

Often when a bank develops a network of dealers who sell loans to it, it must offer them wholesale or floor-plan facilities secured by the assets in the dealer's inventory. This type of lending requires close supervision with periodic on-site inventory checks and adequate insurance for fire, theft, and so on. A carefully prepared dealer agreement should be executed, spelling out the details of the arrangement with the dealer. The agreement should clearly state the percent of credit advanced in relation to dealer cost, the repayment schedule on inventory not sold, and the maximum amount of credit available.

Revolving lines of credit can be secured (many are on second mortgages) or unsecured and are usually granted to those in upper-income levels with good credit histories.

Bank credit cards are high-volume, low-ticket-size items, resulting in expensive handling. Also the charge-off rate is usually substantially higher than other consumer lending.

Some of these types of loans may fit a larger bank's portfolio, but smaller banks may have trouble justifying the cost in relation to the expected volume.

The bank must decide if it wants to use a credit scoring system for consumer loans. A scoring system gives greater uniformity to the approval process, but does not remove the judgment factor on marginal credits. If a credit scoring system is installed, the credit criteria used should be very carefully selected and reviewed periodically for effectiveness. Usually length of time on the job, length of time at present residence, income level, debt-paying history, and total payments on existing debt are major ingredients in a credit scoring system.

A collection policy must be clearly enunciated if past-due paper and charge-offs are to be maintained at acceptable levels.

3. Commercial loans—In addressing the policy issues in the extension of commercial credit, it is easier to spell out the types of loans that will not be handled than to list the acceptable types of credit. The policy must cover limitations on loans by class, such as loans to any one industry or loans against any one commodity or any one security. The policy must also cover the purpose of the loan, such as for short-term working capital (which is self-liquidating in nature) or the purchase of long-term assets, usually financed by a term loan or revolving credit and payable primarily from earnings rather than asset conversion in the normal course of business.

The policy needs to state the bank's position on loans for the purchase of a business, particularly leveraged buyouts and hostile takeover attempts.

An international loan policy is necessary for most larger banks. It should set out country limits and whether the loans will be short-term or long-term, backed by a U.S. government agency, or insured. Whether the bank will make loans in the private sector or only to sovereign risks is another important policy consideration.

Regardless of the types of loans included in the policy, financial statements should be required on all secured and unsecured business loans unless the security is government bonds or an adequate margin of listed collateral. These statements should be complete—including at least balance sheet, earnings statement, and net worth reconciliation. And they should cover a series of years because the trends in a business are very important in determining the creditworthiness of a potential borrower. It is highly desirable for the financial statements to be annual audits prepared by CPAs and bearing unqualified opinions. The footnotes to financial statements are very important in giving the lender a better understanding of the basis used for valuing assets, particularly inventory.

Interim statements may be helpful in some business loans where there are substantial changes that take place in the borrower's financial position during the 12-month cycle.

LENDING AUTHORITY

After the bank has decided the maximum size of the loan portfolio and the types of loans (and limits) it wants in its portfolio, it must determine how to implement the policy through delegation of lending authority. The delegation of lending authority is an integral part of loan policy and usually exists in some form in all banks even though there may not be a written credit policy.

There are a number of factors that must be considered in determining how much loan authority will be delegated and to whom.

Perhaps the most critical element in the delegation process is the number of people in the bank qualified to evaluate credit risks, make sure of proper documentation, and collect the loans in a timely manner. Specialized types of lending and loans to certain industries require personnel with special skills and training. For example, certain types of lending may require an engineering or geological background to properly evaluate the risks involved.

Even the smallest bank usually delegates some lending authority to one or more of its officers since the directors do not meet frequently enough to give timely responses to the credit requests of the bank's borrowing customers. The extent of delegation of lending authority by bank boards of directors as well as the organization of the credit function within banks varies widely.

The variations are caused by a number of factors, such as size, branch network or unit bank, type of loans being sought, experience and capability of staff, needs of the area served, and whether the major emphasis is on growth or quality.

Well-qualified bankers differ greatly in their philosophies about the amount of lending authority to be delegated. Basically, it is a matter of preference for maximum individual responsibility and accountability or collective judgment and decision making.

The various systems fall into three broad categories: (1) individual authorities, (2) groups or combinations of individuals, and (3) formal committees. Naturally, some combination of these can be, and often is, used.

Outside- or director-dominated loan committees are usually very influential in small banks; they meet regularly and approve sizable credits before they are made. In large banks, directors or a directors' committee review loans after the fact and have very little real say in the extension of credit.

Where the emphasis is on individual authority, the bank may delegate authority based on the experience and performance of each loan person or it may delegate authority by title in the bank.

An example of lending authority by title:

	Unsecured	Secured
Vice presidents	$50,000	$100,000
Assistant vice presidents	25,000	50,000
Loan officer	10,000	25,000

Proponents of individual authority feel that committees or groups tend toward a perfunctory action with no one member feeling the accountability strong enough. The advocates of group or committee delegation believe the judgment and experience of several people who bring their individual knowledge and expertise to bear on a credit results in better decision making and a sounder loan portfolio.

While there can be many modifications to fit a particular bank's needs and accommodate its management style, a typical description of the areas to be covered in the loan approval process in a medium-size bank might be as follows:

1. A definition of "secured" and "unsecured" lending for loan approval purposes (a loan secured by marketable securities has entirely different risk considerations than one secured by receivables or inventory).
2. A definition of "borrower's total liability" to the bank to protect the bank against maximum extensions of credit in all forms to various affiliates, subsidiaries, principals, and related interests, all dependent on one basic enterprise and subject to lending authority delegated to an officer or group.
3. The establishment of officer's loan committees, naming members (by position, not name), the chairman and secretary, quorum, voting procedures, and the maximum amount of each type of credit the committee may approve.
4. The listing of individual loan limits by name and amount and the establishment of combination authorities whereby certain individuals jointly or with others may approve loans up to specified amounts.

PRICING POLICY

In order to provide guidance for lending personnel and a reasonable degree of uniformity for customers, a written loan policy must include guidelines for pricing different types of credit.

Interest rate policies can range from general statements to very specific schedules. The general type lists broad ranges for certain categories of loans, allowing more latitude to the individual loan officer than would be true under the more rigid schedules.

The bank needs to consider the following major points when pricing a loan:

1. Risk exposure.
2. Cost of funds.
3. Term of loan (liquidity).
4. Account balances and other relationships.
5. Competition (can't be allowed to set your rates but can't be ignored).

CREDIT ADMINISTRATION

A good loan policy should provide for proper followup and check points on loans by a credit administration function. Credit administration is the system by which credit policy is enforced. It is aimed at making sure exceptions are recognized and that they receive special attention promptly.

A method or system of followup should make sure:

1. All loans are classified by industry type.
2. There is an application sheet for every loan or line of credit.
3. Every loan has a specified repayment program agreed on with the borrower at the time the loan was made.
4. Adequate information is in the credit file in the form of properly prepared financial statements and memorandums by the lending officer containing pertinent information on the borrower.
5. Loans are reviewed periodically to try to anticipate deterioration in credit quality.

A written loan policy should also contain guidelines for handling problem loans and collecting credits that have developed a need for special attention. Some banks believe loan officers should be required to work out their own problem loans since they are more familiar with the borrower than anyone else in the bank and also for training purposes. Others believe workout loans require too much time, and the loan officer should be relieved of the responsibility so he or she has time to service other customers properly. Also it is argued that the loan officer may lose his objectivity due to his closeness to the situation, and an independent qualified workout specialist or department should be assigned the credit.

Whichever method is used, too many problem loans indicate (1) poor policy, (2) poor personnel (bad judgment), (3) poor administration, or (4) a sudden change in the industry or economic environment.

Credit administration should have a major role in the training of future loan and credit people. An investment in people who are properly trained, using internal and external resources, is absolutely essential if a bank is to grow and develop a meaningful credit culture that will support its overall goals and objectives.

CONCLUSION

There is a basic need for a well-conceived, clear, concise credit policy in banks today. It should be stressed that the bank's primary obligation is to its depositors, not the borrowers. Also a credit policy should be tailor-made to suit the goals of that particular bank and its community.

Even the best thought out policy will have exceptions to it, but the exceptions should be clearly recognized as such when they are made.

Also, it must be recognized that the best credit policies and procedures are of little value unless properly implemented by qualified personnel. There is no substitute for sound judgment in the extension of quality credit.

CHAPTER FORTY-FOUR

The Expanded Role of Credit Administration Policy

Sanford F. Sadler

Senior Vice President
First Interstate Bank of Nevada

INTRODUCTION

Changes in the banking industry in the last five years have caused the role of credit administration to become much more involved in functions other than loan approval. The underlying causes of this functional expansion are the business dynamics of the industry (declining profit margins, higher risk loans) and competition (more providers of more services). In order for a bank to survive in the future, the credit administrator must interface substantially with marketing, pricing, and training, with the ultimate goal of helping line officers extend credits on a sound and constructive basis while meeting the various goals established by the bank's management. How and to what extent that involvement should take place is discussed in this chapter.

LOAN QUALITY

Although the industry has changed dramatically in the 1980s, one of the most important requirements of a bank is still the maintenance of a high-quality loan portfolio that generates positive cash flow regardless of the prevailing economic climate. In the vast majority of banks, the loan portfolio is the largest earning asset and therefore significantly affects the profitability and long-run survival of the institution.

The preservation of a quality loan portfolio originates with the implementation of a loan policy that is consistent with the bank's long-run objectives, formal to the point of providing good, general guidelines, flexible enough to give all credit requests appropriate consideration, and reasonable enough to take into account the bank's marketing area and personnel. Furthermore, loan officers must listen to all requests and attempt to structure a conforming loan out of one that may appear to be "out of policy" on the surface. For example, a bank may reconsider a policy of expanding its national account portfolio if it is located in a rural area predominately dependent on the agricultural sector. In addition, a bank should not lend to a specialized industry if it does not have qualified personnel to analyze and monitor those credits (agricultural, oil and gas, mining, etc.).

Adhering to loan policy, however, is not enough to ensure the continuance of a quality loan portfolio. Too frequently a false sense of security is created by the mere fact that a loan has been booked and conforms to policy. Once the loan is extended it is essential that the account officer practice consistent loan management in order to detect changes in the borrower's operations or financial condition. This should be done to discern not only deterioration but also opportunities to expand the bank's relationship with the customer. Furthermore, through proper loan/account management and periodic discussions with loan officers, the credit administrator can formulate a more solid opinion of the quality of the portfolio in addition to reviewing classified loan lists, past due liability reports, and so forth.

Regardless of the type of loan extended (real estate, commercial, consumer) the credit administrator must make sure that the credits are underwritten using the sound credit standards of bona fide purpose, primary source of repayment within a reasonable time frame, and sources and timing of secondary repayment. One of the most common errors made by lending personnel is not fully understanding each of the areas just mentioned. Then if repayment does not occur at maturity, a "red flag" is raised. This could have been avoided had the loan been initially structured with a different repayment schedule. Conversely, a loan may be repaid at maturity but from a different source than originally planned. If the loan officer is not aware of that fact, he or she may be lulled into extending a second loan on the basis that the first one was "paid as agreed." Thus, a full understanding of the proper source of repayment, timing, and secondary support is the principal element in maintaining a quality loan portfolio and will be discussed in more detail under Training.

The last item discussed under loan portfolio quality is degree of concentration to any one industry. Most local and regional banks are subject to some concentration due to their local economic/market area, but abnormal dependency on one or two business segments should be avoided if possible. Undue concentration in the loan portfolio may also occur during periods of economic growth when lenders have the opportunity to expand quickly, and very profitably, their loans to those industries enjoying the growth. However, when the economic climate no longer favors those industries and repayment is slowed, the quality of the bank's loan portfolio may deteriorate. Furthermore, in practically every instance there is an underlying ripple effect that results in other areas of the portfolio deteriorating in quality. For example, real estate and consumer lending portfolios normally deteriorate following a downturn in the major industries that support the local geographic area.

LOAN PRICING

The act of pricing a credit has changed more in banking the last five years than perhaps any other function. The process has evolved from drawing a 90-day note at a fixed rate, to a rate with compensating balances, to a floating rate with or without balances, to a combination of any of the above, with or without fees. In fact, the word *rate* is outdated; bankers today need to determine yield as a function of loan pricing, interest rate being only one component. The problem of determining yield for a loan becomes more difficult when the element of credit risk is considered. This is one reason why the credit administrator of today must be involved in loan pricing, both on a day-to-day and long-range planning basis. There are two principal reasons for this degree of involvement. First, the process of "credit administrating" provides the only clearinghouse or central point through which all loans in the bank are eventually exposed to one individual or group of individuals functioning in the same department. This common exposure is necessary for the bank to extend uniform pricing to the various types of loans in its portfolio. For example, risk is applied to an industry and the individual business operating within that industry. To compensate for the increased risk, a bank's highest pricing is usually imposed upon a high risk borrower (poor financial condition, questionable management skills,) operating in a high risk industry (agribusiness, energy, etc.). Conversely, a borrower that is well managed and financially strong may be operating in an industry considered less risky than those previously mentioned. In that case, the bank's lowest pricing would be levied due to the comparatively lower risk. These two cases make it relatively simple to decide the pricing category—the challenge to the loan officer and credit administrator is in pricing a credit in which there are mixed components of high-risk industry and very capable borrower or the reverse. This problem is further complicated if the bank is quite large and/or operates over a large geographical area. In both situations, there are probably more layers of management involved, which tends to dilute the discipline of equal pricing for similar risk.

The long-range planning process undertaken by senior management in the bank should include the credit policy and administration personnel. Credit policy input is required to provide a balance to marketing and loan production forecasts, which at times may be too aggressive considering the bank's loan quality objectives, penetration, and changing markets. All institutions, including segments within the same industry, are constantly changing and moving from relatively safe to high-risk to safe again (e.g., the utility industry). This constant flux must be kept in mind when projecting loan growth as it relates to market penetration and loan quality. The profit margins obtained from lending to industries during a boom period cannot be sustained when the credit markets become saturated or those industries enter into a depressed section of the economic cycle. It is the credit administrator's function to see that loan growth projections are in concert with economic forecasts so that loan quality does not deteriorate.

PORTFOLIO RAMIFICATIONS

Historically, credit administrators were principally concerned about the loan portfolio having too much concentration in any one type credit (commercial, consumer, real estate) and industry risk considerations. However, with the advent of frequent, and sometimes substantial, movements in interest rates, the loan portfolio is now subject to shrinking values causing an adverse effect on the bank's net interest margin. For example, until the mid- to late 1970s most commercial notes were written for 90 days with a fixed rate of interest. If the note were renewed at the end of the 90-day period, the interest rate may or may not have changed, but in any event, it would have been fixed for a subsequent 90-day term. During a stable interest rate environment, this frequency of repricing the asset was satisfactory since any negative impact on the net interest margin would be negligible.

Compounding the problem of rate sensitivity is the issue of the loan portfolio maintaining a degree of liquidity. In the last 20 years, there has been a steady trend of banks shifting earning assets out of the investment portfolio and into the credit portfolio. While this movement has generally increased net interest margin, it has caused banks' liquidity to deteriorate somewhat (despite the banks' ability to buy liquidity by purchasing large CDs, Fed fund borrowings, etc.). As a consequence, in today's environment a bank should always be aware of the liquidity feature of its portfolio in case it needs to sell or participate out a portion of its portfolio to raise cash.

As a closing statement, credit administrators are primarily concerned with the quality of the loan portfolio, but they must also be aware of the mix of the loans in regard to secondary liquidity requirements.

CREDIT TRAINING

In most banks credit training takes place in the credit department, which operates under the credit administration/policy division of the bank. Usually, credit training consists of formalized discussions and classes, credit analysis, and the understanding of various financial ratios. At times, the formalized training is augmented with preparing written reports on existing customers and prospects. This training period may last several months to several years and when it is concluded, the individual is assigned to a lending unit as a "bona fide lending officer." The fallacy in this training progression is that even a thorough understanding of credit analysis does not qualify an individual to become a loan officer. In fact, a person becomes a loan officer only after he or she attains the ability to understand the principal functions of a business and how the business performs those functions. It is only then that the individual fully understands the balance sheet, income statement, cash flow statements, and financial ratios and can adequately assess the financial condition of the applicant and the resultant risk to the bank.

Training of today's lending officers must not stop at credit analysis but must be expanded in scope and the "title" changed to business analysis. This second phase of credit training must be provided by individuals in the bank who have had good, solid lending experience—usually department managers or credit administrators. Individuals with this experience know "what the numbers mean," understand how to assess risk and to structure credits in such a manner that poses no more than undue risk to the bank while fulfilling the credit needs of the borrower. In turn, this knowledge can be passed on to the person undergoing credit training.

Unfortunately, the business analysis part of one's credit training takes time and can be learned only through exposure to real situations as opposed to a classroom/textbook environment. Frequently a bank's demands for line people do not permit time for this phase of credit training, but even three to four months would be extremely beneficial and worthwhile to the bank.

TURNAROUND TIME

Two of the most frequent complaints against banks are the constant reassignment of lending officers and the slow response time to a customer's credit request. Due to competitive pressures, the industry has improved its performance in this area during the last five years. Some banks have recognized this shortcoming and have turned it into a marketing tool by using quick response as a means of differentiating the product of money. If performed properly, the quick response feature can be utilized not only as a marketing tool, but also as a method to enhance and cement present customer relationships. If executed incorrectly, the bank is exposed to more credit risk as a result of acting on incomplete or unclear information.

In order to improve turnaround time in the normal course of customer credit approval procedures, two conditions must exist. First, as discussed earlier, the lending officers must have in-depth knowledge of the customer's business and method of operations. Such knowledge enables the loan officer to anticipate problems or opportunities, arrive quickly at credit decisions, and recommend those decisions to a higher level of approval if required. The second element that must exist is the early involvement of the credit administrator in the credit discussions. Usually, credit administrators are not informed or perhaps even aware of the credit until it is presented for approval in a written format. Normally, the credit administrator or the loan committee will have questions on items that need to be clarified, and, if those issues have not been satisfactorily covered in the written presentation, the package may need to be resubmitted. At times, the request may be out of policy for the bank, priced too low, have inferior credit quality, or entail other major items that would cause the loan to be declined. In any event, if the loan officer has to obtain additional information from the customer at this stage of the approval process or the loan is declined because of policy/structure considerations, the bank has taken too long to reach a decision and convey it to the customer. Such problems can be avoided by holding discussions with the credit administrator on a regular basis to discuss loans under consideration, new developments in existing requests, and so forth. If conducted effectively these meetings will save invaluable time for the loan officer since the basic questions of policy, structure, and pricing will surface. In many cases the credit administrator or loan officer may meet on two, three, or more occasions prior to submission of the written request. Thus, approval of the written credit request should be only a formality. By including the credit administrator periodically in the loan consideration process, problems, common differences of opinion, issues, and so forth, can be discussed and resolved earlier, and a decision conveyed to the customer sooner.

CONCLUSION

The business dynamics of banking have changed so radically in the last decade that the credit administrator now has a myriad of issues to consider in addition to the borrower's creditworthiness. The loan must be priced in such a manner that the bank's profit objectives are met, yet remain competitive. In order to maintain loan quality and to assist the line officer in detecting problems and opportunities, the credit administrator must continually function as an instructor and teach loan officers "what the numbers really mean." Over a longer-term basis, the credit administrator must be aware of the loan portfolio mix relative to concentration and liquidity in case cash reserves need to be raised in a short time span. However, the most noticeable change in the credit administrator's role is the need to become involved in the credit decision process much earlier than the point at which the loan officer's formal written request is read. In addition to reducing turnaround time to the customers, these types of meetings provide a forum in which the credit administrator can discuss the different facets of credit with loan officers in a learning environment.

CHAPTER FORTY-FIVE

Credit Administration: Organization and Management Issues for the Future

Edward T. O'Leary

Senior Vice President and Manager, Special Asset Group
Liberty National Bank

Imagine for a moment rewriting the story of Rip Van Winkle. Make him a mid-career chief executive officer of a large community bank in the late 1960s. At the time he falls asleep, he is successful, prosperous, and presiding over his stable bank in stable economic times. When he awakens 20 years later, his environment has become so different that his experience is probably obsolete. The skills and knowledge that brought him to the top 20 years ago are probably not the sort that will sustain him there today.

The simple explanation for this banking revolution of sorts is deregulation and all that the term implies. Perhaps the better way to understand what has happened is to ask, What has propelled deregulation? How do these forces continue to affect banking today? What are the implications for managing risk in the coming years?

When considered in that fashion one can note the changes in uses of funds and the shift of earning assets from the relatively large holdings of United States Treasury securities following World War II to the predominance of the loan portfolio which we are accustomed to today. On the sources side of the balance sheet, competition for lendable funds to maintain commercial banking's traditional share of the lending market resulted in intense rate competition. And it was rate competition that ultimately made Regulation Q obsolete. Enormous technological changes have broken down the traditional constraints of "trade area" for both loan and deposit business. Bankers must now cope with interest rate risk, shifting market measurements of bank performance, geographic spans of control, and penalties resulting from insufficient training and development of lending staff. Finally, as the traditional obstacles to branching eroded, the resulting growth in size and geographical outreach of banks have produced a remarkably different banking industry in terms of sources and uses of funds, market definition, risk/reward relationships, and capital adequacy perceptions.

Recognizing by the mid-1970s that banking was becoming a different kind of business, the Office of the Comptroller of the Currency with consulting assistance from the national accounting firm of Haskins and Sells (now DeLoitte Haskins and Sells) radically changed its manner of supervising banks. It is useful to recall that the OCC has responsibility for monitoring national banks, which comprise approximately one-third of the commercial banks, which in turn control approximately two-thirds of the commercial banking system's assets. This means that with a few exceptions, the OCC supervises the activities of considerably larger banks than do the 50 state banking departments, the Federal Deposit Insurance Corporation, or any of the 12 Federal Reserve Banks. It should not be surprising, therefore, that the implementation of new methods was originated by the Comptroller of the Currency.

Previously, the traditional supervisory approach to credit asset quality involved an audit of a certain dollar percentage of loans. A lending audit is a test of a bank's lending practices and includes more "due diligence" than simply an evaluation of quality. For example, examiners historically were no less interested in documentation sufficiency and devoted nearly as much manpower to reviewing collateral files as credit files. By the mid-1970s, however, it was evident that there were insufficient resources available to the Comptroller to continue supervisory practices in the former fashion. Emphasis began to change to a "systems" approach. If a bank has an auditable system, properly documented with written policy and procedural statements, it became possible to verify the effectiveness of the system rather than rely on an item-by-item review of the individual components. By systematizing credit quality control, the effectiveness of the managerial and supervisory processes can be measurably improved.

From this simple but significant change in emphasis and thinking was born the need for formal, written lending policies. This is not to say that many banks, particularly the larger ones, were not already well along in the process of formalization. Many were not, however, and for the next several years, the Comptroller's examining staff placed considerable emphasis on the formalization of a bank's lending policies. *Written* lending policies therefore became the documentation of a bank's credit standards.

The written standard can be supported by systems and subsystems to assure policy compliance both when the loan is made (or renewed) and on a periodic basis thereafter until repaid. For example, a bank's lending policy might state that the advance ratio on New York Stock Exchange collateral may not exceed 70 percent. Examiners, auditors, or internal loan review staff can then review a bank's procedures for assurance that the loan did not exceed the standard when made and has been tested periodically for compliance thereafter. Less supervisory effort is now spent on the physical verification of assets such as cash and securities, while increasing emphasis in all areas of bank examination is devoted to written statements of policy which in turn must be supported by systems and procedures. Following the Comptroller's lead, the other supervisory agencies now insist on similar formalization.

As banks gradually came into compliance with the new requirements, the loan review function became prominent throughout the industry. While loan review is not necessarily a formal function at all banks, its installation at mid-sized or large banks is now virtually complete. Ideally, loan review is an independent assessment of credit quality of a bank's portfolio. The methodology is very similar if not identical to that of outside examiners. At a minimum, portfolio loan review would be expected to produce a problem loan list. More comprehensive, elaborate systems are capable of generating much more management information. This might include measuring relative quality of so-called good loans, the information from which may then be used for liquidity management, loan officer evaluation, management by objective systems, and the like.

This evolution of emphasis from individual credit review to lending policy to sufficiently formalized loan review systems has resulted in a systematized manner of organizing the "credit back office" at most banks. In this context and against this background, the credit administration function has grown in size and importance in recent years. Our modern day Rip Van Winkle would hardly recognize the function at first, but he could soon break it down into its key managerial components.

To administer something is to "manage or supervise its execution or conduct." Credit administration at some banks means simply the grouping or collection into one place or under one head of the traditional credit staff support functions to line lending officers. Increasingly, however, it is coming to mean the organization charged with the responsibility to monitor and enhance quality of the credit portfolio as a whole. It is perhaps laboring the obvious to say that in the current-day sense, credit administration needs to be supportive of those activities that assure quality on a "systemic" basis rather than the individual extension of credit on a customer-by-customer basis. The use of the word systemic is important: Credit administration is part of a system of quality control and not a standalone function. It provides several services including vital credit information in support of the overall administration of the credit assets.

In considering how to specifically organize the credit risk management (or the credit administration) function of a bank, it is important to understand how a particular bank may articulate its credit standards. A money center or super-regional institution must consider how it communicates with those officers having credit authority at perhaps thousands of locations in hundreds of markets dealing with a wide range of customer requirements related to size, special industry needs, and the like. Contrast this with the manner in which the credit standards of a small community bank with few or no branch offices are communicated. The institutional responses are necessarily different but the results must be necessarily similar: Uniform, appropriate credit quality for the institution.

There is probably no more important point of departure for any intelligent consideration of organizational and systems issues in credit administration than that of bank size. Size will affect perceptions, formality, the ability to develop systems to measure results, and the ability to attract, motivate and properly compensate the necessary staff to accomplish the workload. The size issue contains elements of both a qualitative and quantitative nature. The qualitative aspects relate mainly to perceptions of what needs to be done and the nuances of how that is to be communicated, while the quantitative aspects relate to the volume of loans, geographic customer dispersion, numbers of people required to accomplish a desired work output, and the like. Since the larger banks have substantially implemented a credit administration system, the comments that follow are directed more to those institutions which may not yet have completely formalized the process or are upgrading the process in response to size, markets or shifting credit quality within the portfolio.

Credit administration must be an integral part of the management process. Management may be considered to have four elements: planning, organizing, directing, and controlling. The functions accomplished or participated in by credit administration within the *planning* process can include loan policy formulation, loan prospect identification, competitive assessment, and participation in developing the corporation's mission statement. Typically included under *organizing* are loan approval mechanisms, job descriptions, staffing, and so forth. Those functions related to the *directing* aspects of management include functional credit training, development of written credit procedures, and the development of interpersonal skills that relate to lending such as negotiating and listening. The *controlling* function may include loan review, some form of problem loan administration, participation in the loan approval process, corrective action or monitoring tools such as watch lists, exception lists, past due lists, budget reviews and performance appraisals. In a very real and direct way then, credit administration includes each of the management functions in support of portfolio quality control.

Whether it is a small bank organizing a credit administration function for the first time or a larger bank reorganizing a credit administration function to have it perform its role more effectively, there are several important organizational issues. The manner in which each of these is addressed is largely a matter of individual and institutional preference and it would be inappropriate to say that there is necessarily a right way or a wrong way to do it. However, there are some pitfalls that others have encountered and it would be well to recite them here.

Where should the function report? It is a superficial generalization to say that in smaller banks the function tends to report relatively high up in the organization chart while in larger banks the function may report "below the summit." The management issue here is how much "clout" the function needs to have. If you choose to consign it to limbo, be sure that it reports into the middle of the organization structure and that there are several reporting tiers between its manager and the bank's chief executive or a responsible board oversight committee. Choose an incumbent who is not particularly experienced in banking and, of course, award him or her with a junior title. On the other hand, if you're really serious about positioning credit administration for a positive contribution in achieving institutional goals relating to return on equity, return on assets, and a minimal level of criticized credits, then the function must be staffed and report no less prominently than any other *key* organizational component.

What are credit administration's appropriate subfunctions? The current consensus is that credit administration should sensibly include loan operations (the discount function and perhaps related loan ledger accounting), loan review for administrative reporting purposes, functional credit training, credit operations (such as maintenance of credit and collateral files and credit inquiry) and perhaps a recovery effort. There seems to be less industry consensus, however, about whether problem loan collection and recovery belong within credit administration, although there are a number of banks that have organized in this fashion successfully. Many bankers feel that there is an inherent conflict where loan review and loan workout share a common reporting relationship, particularly should the reporting channel also include the flow of delegated lending authority. This is another facet of the possible reporting conflict between loan review and the lending line.

There are a variety of reasonable responses and it is sufficient here to state that executive management and board sensitivity to this issue are essential.

What are the personality characteristics and professional experiences required of the credit administration manager? Are maturity and experience enough? Do you want an experienced "lender" or an experienced "examiner?" Does the size of your bank or the personalities of its senior officers tend to predetermine the answers to these questions? If they do, should they? Is the job of the manager of credit administration considered to be the final step on the career ladder, or is it one of many jobs that similarly qualified individuals could occupy? Is there career planning within the organization to assure a reasonably low level of turnover either through careful career pathing or salary compatibility within the organization? Can someone be transferred or promoted out of the function into something else? Are your staffing decisions resulting in a form of stereotyping (or could they)?

Is a credit administration job considered primarily "staff" or "line?" Is this purely a staff job or are there some line elements to it? For example, does the credit administration manager sit on the bank's loan committee? Does he have a vote or a veto? Is a veto really a form of line authority?

Is executive management sensitive to the environmental factors that could enhance or inhibit the effectiveness of credit administration? For example, is the credit administration staff capable of keeping up with the rapid growth of the bank or the market place? Are its systems adequate to assimilate, process, digest, and report on an escalating volume of loan business? If your bank significantly changes direction due to new ownership or a rapid change in the marketplace (e.g., the emergence of high tech and the decline of low tech), can the staff keep up?

What assumptions have you made about the impact of credit administration on the bank's credit culture? The credit administration function must reflect the current credit standards and the desired characteristics of good credit and lending habits. Here, however, is perhaps the greatest organizational trap of all. Is it reasonable to expect a largely staff-type function to significantly alter the credit culture of the bank? If you think it can change the culture, you are probably mistaken and you may ultimately be risking the viability of the institution. On the other hand, a strong, properly staffed and well motivated credit administration function can certainly reinforce a desired credit culture. But to expect it to *change* the culture on its own, particularly in the face of indifference or worse by executive management, will likely assure failure. An additional point to remember is that consistently high financial performance banks also have strong, highly developed credit cultures.

Assume that we have successfully addressed the urgent institutional questions, threaded through the traps and pitfalls of the organizational issues, and installed well-qualified individuals who can command the respect of peers, seniors, and subordinates. Then what is left to do? The most tempting response is to rely simply on the management principle of "control." But this may overlook some significant subtleties.

Let's go back to the cornerstone of the process. Is the lending policy sufficiently formal and sufficiently clear to properly document the credit standards of your bank? Does it bridge size, market, and industry differences within the customer base? Are your bank's lending managers reasonably sure that the credit standards of the institution are more or less uniformly understood and observed from one end of the building to the other or from one end of the state to the other? Does the loan review policy and its implementing procedures mirror the loan policy? Are these *reciprocal* kinds of policy statements? Are the proper things being looked at given current institutional priorities? Is information reported in a simple, concise, comprehensive, and timely manner to those various line managers who have ultimate accountability for credit quality either individually or collectively?

Probably the final test of effectiveness of the credit administration function is that of user satisfaction. "User" in this context includes the various banking constituencies such as supervisory authorities, directors, management, and individual lenders. Does the process identify credit weakness on a timely basis? Do the various systems support the line officer in an efficient and satisfactory manner? Is the filing of credit and collateral information done promptly and accurately? Is there integrity and sophistication in the credit analyses to support new credit extensions or ongoing monitoring of outstandings? Is the directorate supported in its responsibility of assuring proper credit quality and the viability of the bank? Is each of the above constituencies supported in the accomplishment of its objectives?

A senior officer from a large regional banking system observed recently that in his experience, approximately 20 percent of all loan problems were a result of faulty underwriting when the credit was originally made, while 80 percent appear to have arisen later and were the result of a combination of inattention by the lender, deteriorating environmental conditions, or mismanagement by the borrower. If your own experience validates these relative proportions, then what does that tell you about how to address the various components of the credit administration function? Do you need to put more emphasis on frequently monitoring collateral values such as inventory or receivables agings? Should you shift analytical emphasis from analyzing new credit to assisting the line officer to monitor outstanding loans and commitments?

Credit administration departments are an established and generally effective response to credit quality control problems confronting the banking industry today. On an industry-wide basis, what remains to be done falls into two areas: The first is to complete the formalization of the process into banks of increasingly smaller size. As previously noted, this process, which is well underway, appears to be a prime supervisory objective. The second task is to fully integrate the credit administration function into the strategic planning process of the bank.

Probably the fundamental controlling document of strategic planning is (or should be) the loan policy. The loan policy must define the specific credit standards in light of changing markets and environments. But increasingly, it must consider the forward allocation of lendable funds, identify areas requiring timely information for effective risk control, and identify and recite in qualitative terms the necessary support systems such as credit training, loan review, loan scoring, and so forth, to support and sustain satisfactory credit quality.

In other words, loan policies and loan review systems must become anticipatory. Consider, for example, how the concept of liquidity has changed since our Rip Van Winkle banker fell asleep. How simple it used to be to rely on a few ratios such as the loan to deposit ratio or the percentage of investment securities to loans or total assets.

Imagine instead a loan review system capable of grading credits at the higher end of the quality spectrum with an eye to participating loans in response to a sudden need for lendable funds. Concentrations of credit are another management concern of an anticipatory nature. How much is enough and when does enough become too much? What might a dynamic, real-time type of loan policy say on this subject? How can loan review generate and report the data to support the need?

To conceptualize or implement a credit administration function with anything less than a strategic perspective in mind is taking unnecessary risks. As banking regulation recedes, at least as we have traditionally understood it, the response for the future viability of the industry is essentially a managerial one. In the simplest form, this means a systemic approach to risk management through a credit administration function integrated into the management process of the corporation.

Peter Drucker has observed that one can quickly tell whether a company is well run or not. The well-run factory is a bore; it runs like clockwork. The poorly managed factory is a drama of crises. The analogy to the crises aspects of a poorly administrated credit function is painfully authentic today. Yet it doesn't have to be this way. Proper organization for success is possible and indeed essential for reasonable bank financial performance in the years to come.

CHAPTER FORTY-SIX

Financial Analysis for Credit Decisions

Charles S. Dickerson

President
Crossing Financial Consultants

INTRODUCTION

The commercial credit decision is the result of an extensive process. It represents the product of interviews, independent investigation, factual verification and analysis of all the material relevant to an applicant's creditworthiness. It is not a science; it is an art. It is an imperfect process because human beings are imperfect. And human beings are involved both as sources and analysts of data.

Much of the decision-making activity is based on assumption and interpretation. If one were to draw a model of that process as it develops within the commercial lender's mind, it might resemble a set of scales on which a number of factors are classified as either benefits or detriments to the borrower while its management will be using the bank's funds. In addition to the basic classification of benefit or detriment, the lender will attempt to determine the relative importance of each factor to the applicant company's success.

The anticipated result of this process is that the decision maker will understand the applicant company, its management, and its industry as fully as possible. The nearer he or she can come to achieving this goal, the more accurately the applicant's ability to repay the loan as agreed can be estimated. The principal objectives of the gathering and analysis of information should be fourfold:

- Determining the *strong points* about the applicant's situation.
- Recognizing the *weaknesses* in the application.
- Learning about the operating *peculiarities* of the company and its industry.
- Determining which particular factors are *crucial* to the proposed borrower's continuing success.

Continuing our analogy to the use of scales in the loan decision process and assuming that no policy restriction exists that would automatically eliminate the applicant from further consideration, the lender places the strengths and weaknesses on his or her mental scales and determines which way the scales tilt. No application is perfect; negative factors always become apparent during an extensive investigation of an applicant's operations. However, even if the scale tips heavily toward approval, every effort should be made to obviate any serious weaknesses through careful loan structuring.

Make no mistake about it. The lender's success is directly tied to the success of his or her borrower. The keystone of a profitable banker/borrower relationship is the *orderly* repayment of loans from funds generated in the ordinary course of the borrower's operations.

Banking is a low profit margin business. Many lay people don't think of it as such, but it is. There is not much room for judgmental error or for the incurring of unforseen additional expenses in servicing loans. Collecting the full amount of loan principal through liquidation of collateral will undoubtedly result in an unprofitable relationship because the expense of outside accountants, attorneys, appraisers, and auctioneers (to say nothing of the considerable time consumed by bank personnel) will probably offset most, if not all, of the interest income arising from the transaction. This is why the thrust of the lender's thinking must be on the applicant's ability to generate cash according to the proposed repayment schedule from its ordinary business activities.

The aim of commercial loan analysis, then, is to determine whether the prospective borrower can repay the requested loans (1) in a timely manner, (2) from the stated source of funds, and (3) without undue financial or operational difficulty.

Sources of Repayment

There are four sources of funds the borrower can look to in order to repay loans:

- Additional capital invested in the business
- Refunding of the debt with another lender
- Conversion of assets
- Earnings

The first two options, *additional capital* and *debt refunding*, are usually dismissed in loan decision-making activities because they depend on arbitrary decisions made by third parties with which the borrower often carries little or no influence. Ordinarily, they are relied on by lenders only in a very few situations when legally binding commitments have been made by the third parties and their financial capacity to carry out these commitments is unquestioned.

Therefore, the analysis of an applicant's ability to repay usually is limited to the *conversion of assets* and *earnings*. Each has its place in the borrowing needs of a business.

Asset conversion is the way funds are generated to repay short-term loans. Examples of such accommodations might be to fund the seasonal needs of a clothing store, a nursery, or a toy store. Stock must be purchased in advance of the season (i.e., back-to-school, planting, Christmas), and payment is often due before the inventory is sold. When sales take place, a significant portion (often a majority) of the sales are on credit, and actual cash availability must wait for those receivables to be collected. The source of repayment for these loans, then, is the conversion of assets from inventory to receivables to cash.

On the other hand, long-term loans are usually made to acquire something the borrower does not intend to resell to pay the debt (i.e., equipment, a product line, another company). In cases such as this, loan payments are expected to come from the additional earnings the purchased items will produce as well as from the borrower's previously demonstrated ability to operate profitably.

SOURCES OF INFORMATION

As stated before, good commercial loan decision-making is the result of (1) gathering as many facts about the applicant as possible, (2) determining which of the information is important and relevant to the loan decision, and (3) analyzing and interpreting the meaning of that information.

There are a great number of information sources. Among the most commonly used are:

- The applicant
- Financial statements and projections
- Credit information agencies
- Accountants*
- Trade associations
- Competitors†
- Suppliers
- Employees†
- Applicant's legal counsel*
- Plant visitations
- Customers†
- Banking history
- Public records

- Appraisers
- Applicant's insurance agent*

There is no single place where the lender can obtain a complete picture of an applicant's financial condition, method of operation, management policies, future plans, product quality, and so forth. Most of the sources listed above would likely only supply information about a few of these aspects. Some of them can supply hard data; others more subjective impressions. Getting the "complete story" is usually a matter of acquiring random pieces of information from many sources and trying to piece them together into a comprehensive understanding of the company's situation.

The most complete set of factual data comes from the financial statement. While credit decisions are not ordinarily made solely on the basis of the figures supplied, a succession of financial statements is likely to be the most useful single tool the analyst will have to interpret the applicant's present financial condition, determine how it reached this point, and suggest which material might need further clarification or amplification.

Methods used to analyze these financial statements will be covered later in this section. Before that, however, it is necessary to discuss the financial statements themselves with principal emphasis on what information they contain and how much they can be relied on.

THE COMPLETE AUDIT

There are two preliminary questions an analyst must address before beginning an examination of the applicant's statements. They are:

1. Has the applicant supplied all the information contained in the auditor's report?
2. How accurate and dependable are these financial statements?

The statement that "you get what you pay for" applies to the accounting field as much as any other. During preliminary discussions between CPA and client, the terms of an engagement are agreed on. The work to be done is specifically defined and bears a direct relationship to what the audit report will be used for. As an example, a closely held firm might not require nearly the amount of reporting detail a publicly held concern would. It also bears a relationship to the amount of funding needed. Corporate management is not inclined to pay for intense auditing activities and detailed supporting schedules

---

*With applicant's prior consent

†Excellent sources, but must be explored with great subtlety and diplomacy in order not to disclose applicant's plans during discussion.

if the company's anticipated maximum borrowings are not expected to exceed $100,000; on the other hand, if bank financing averages $10 million, creditors normally require much more information.

However, the borrower who informs his or her bank that a "complete audit" has been performed, certainly has received the following reports:

1. Balance sheet.
2. Statement of operations.
3. Earned surplus reconcilement.
4. Statement of sources and uses of funds.
5. Footnotes.
6. Auditor's certificate.

In addition, the following items might have been included:

7. Management letter.
8. Cash flow statement.

Balance Sheet

The basic accounting equation is Assets = Liabilities + Capital. This is to say that the funds used to acquire a company's assets came from one of two sources—*capital* invested by its owners or *debt* owed to creditors. The balance sheet is a numerical representation of this equation. It lists all the assets owned on a specific date at the lower of cost or market values and groups the sources of funds used to acquire these assets into debt and equity accounts.

Statement of Operations

This report lists all sources of income during a specific time period ending on the balance sheet date and groups the expenses incurred during the same period according to purpose (cost of goods sold, selling and delivery, general and administrative, income taxes, etc.).

Earned Surplus Reconcilement

This calculation mathematically ties together (1) the current balance sheet, (2) the prior balance sheet, and (3) the statement of operations. Such a schedule accounts for all changes that occurred in the earned surplus account since the previous balance sheet was compiled. As an example, assume that the earned surplus on December 31, 19×7 and 19×8 were $853,000 and $892,000 respectively, and that aftertax profit during calendar 19×8 was $66,000. A difference exists that must be accounted for if the reconcilement is to be useful to the reader:

Earned surplus, 12/31/×7	$853,000
Net profit, 19×8	66,000
Unexplained adjustment	(27,000)
Earned surplus, 12/31/×8	$892,000

The difference could be due to something as simple as declaration of a dividend or as complex as payment of additional taxes applicable to prior years' income resulting from an IRS audit. Regardless of the *size* of the difference, an earned surplus reconcilement is needed to supply answers about the *causes*.

Statement of Sources and Uses of Funds

Current assets are, by definition, those that will be converted to cash within one year in the normal course of operations. Current liabilities are those debts that must be paid during the same period. Working capital (defined as current assets less current liabilities) is the lifeblood of a business. It is the "cushion" that temporarily blunts the effect of timing differences between cash generation and creditor payment demands. The amount of working capital is not affected by any transaction in which both bookkeeping entries are made to a current account (for instance, paying off a bank 90-day note). It does change, however, if one of the entries is to a noncurrent asset, noncurrent liability, or capital account. Examples of this type of transaction might be making regular payments on term loans, investing in fixed assets, or selling common stock. A statement of sources and uses explains the factors that changed the level of working capital between balance sheet dates. Operating earnings (or losses) and noncash expenses are used to balance to the actual change. A sample of this type of statement follows:

Sources

Net profit, year ended 12/31×8	$ 66,000
Depreciation for year	18,000
Collection of receivables from affiliate	14,000
Sale of capital stock	29,000
	$127,000

Uses

Term loan payments	$ 37,000
Purchase of fixed assets	23,000
Dividends paid	27,000
	$ 87,000
Net increase in working capital	$ 40,000

Sometimes the accountant will choose to continue the analysis process by listing the changes in individual current asset and liability accounts and reconciling to a change in cash. This is a matter of individual preference and may be subject to change in the future.

Footnotes

Frequently the numerical representations on the financial statements or of the transactions that created them are insufficient to give the reader a clear picture of what has taken place. Expository material is needed to anticipate some of the questions an analyst might have. Footnotes perform this function. Typical of the kind of information contained in footnotes are:

1. Accounting methods used (to calculate depreciation, inventory, taxes, reserves, etc.).
2. Contingent liabilities, such as pending litigation, lease obligations, or guarantees of the debts of others.
3. Explanatory detail (schedules of term debt, fixed assets).
4. Material developments which took place between the date of the financial statement and completion of the audit.

Any entry further explained by a footnote contains reference to that footnote in the body of the financial statement. The footnotes are not an addendum to the statements, they are an integral part. Any analyst receiving statements with reference to footnotes is entitled to them. If the accountant considered the footnotes necessary for full comprehension of the statement, the reader obviously needs them for the same reason.

Certificate

The certified public accounting firm is an independent entity that examines financial statements prepared by the client and renders an informed opinion as to whether they fairly present the client's financial condition. Since the accountant's opinion is relied on by a wide variety of interested parties, he or she can incur professional liability. Thus, the accountant must be quite careful concerning any comments accompanying the financial statements. The standard auditor's certificate, written in letter form and addressed to the board of directors of the examined company, is composed of two sections, ordinarily contained in separate paragraphs:

1. An indication of the *scope* of the audit work performed.
2. A professional *opinion* as to whether the financial statements fairly represent the client's condition.

Corporate managers usually hope to receive an *unqualified* certificate as a result of the CPA's review of their statements. That is to say that the auditing firm states it has performed all the tests necessary to perform a complete examination and has found nothing material in the presentation to which it takes exception. This is sometimes called a *clean* certificate. An example of an unqualified certificate follows. (This, as well as the remainder of the sample opinions, are provided courtesy of James J. Kelly, CPA, Havertown, PA.)

To the Board of Directors and Stockholders of GHI Incorporated

We have examined the balance sheet of GHI Incorporated (an Arkansas corporation) as of December 31, 1990, and the related statements of income, retained earnings, and changes in financial position for the year then ended. Our examination was made in accordance with generally accepted auditing standards and, accordingly, included such tests of the accounting records and such other auditing procedures as we considered necessary in the circumstances.

In our opinion, the financial statements referred to above present fairly the financial position of GHI Incorporated as of December 31, 1990, and the results of its operations and the changes in its financial position for the year then ended, in conformity with generally accepted accounting principles applied on a basis consistent with that of the preceding year.

If the auditor has reservations about a particular aspect of the client's financial statements, he or she may issue a *qualified* certificate. This has the effect of alerting the reader to some irregularity in the scope of the examination or the method of presentation and serves to modify the accountant's professional liability concerning that item. The certificate is altered in two ways:

1. A separate paragraph is included explaining the item(s) to which the auditor takes exception.
2. The opinion paragraph is modified by a phrase beginning with "subject to" or "except for," depending on the type of reservation involved.

A typical qualified certificate follows:

To the Board of Directors and Stockholders of GHI Incorporated

We have examined the balance sheet of GHI Incorporated (an Arkansas corporation) as of December 31, 1990, and the related statements of income, retained earnings, and changes in financial position for the year then ended. Except as explained in the following paragraph, our examination was made in accordance with generally accepted auditing standards and, accordingly, included such tests of the accounting records and such other auditing procedures as we considered necessary in the circumstances.

The 1990 financial statements of GHI Incorporated include a 40 percent investment in TUV Corporation that is accounted for by the equity method of accounting. The 1990 financial statements of TUV Corporation have not been audited and we were unable to apply alternative procedures to substantiate the carrying value of the investment in TUV Corporation as of December 31, 1990, and the equity in its net earnings for the year then ended.

In our opinion, except for the effect of such adjustments, if any, as might have been determined to be necessary had we been able to obtain sufficient evidential matter regarding the investment in TUV Corporation, the financial statements referred to in the first paragraph present fairly the financial position of GHI Incorporated as of December 31, 1990, and the results of its operations and the changes in its financial position for the year then ended, in conformity with generally accepted accounting principles applied on a basis consistent with that of the preceding year.

There are occasions when the terms of the engagement do not permit a sufficient examination to satisfy the minimum requirements of "generally accepted accounting principles," or when the CPA believes that management's financial statements do not present the company's condition fairly. In this case the accountant will issue a *disclaimer* letter indicating the objections he or she has to the presentation and removing all professional responsibility to any reader who might take action based on the statements in question. Below is a sample of this type of opinion letter:

To the Board of Directors and Stockholders of GHI Incorporated

We have examined the balance sheet of GHI Incorporated (an Arkansas corporation) as of December 31, 1990, and the related statements of income, retained earnings, and changes in financial position for the year then ended. Except as explained in the following paragraph, our examination was made in accordance with generally accepted auditing standards and, accordingly, included such tests of the accounting records and such other auditing procedures as we considered necessary in the circumstances.

The company did not take a physical inventory of merchandise, stated at $985,006 in the accompanying financial statements as of December 31, 1989, and at $1,197,534 as of December 31, 1990. Also evidence supporting the cost of property and equipment acquired prior to December 31, 1989, is no longer available. We were unable to apply adequate alternative procedures regarding the inventories and the cost of property and equipment.

Since the company did not take physical inventories and we were unable to apply adequate alternative procedures regarding inventories and the cost of property and equipment, as discussed in the preceding paragraph, the scope of our work was not sufficient to enable us to express, and we do not express, an opinion on the financial statements referred to in the first paragraph.

In many cases in the past, notably with smaller firms, management has requested that its accountant merely assemble an unaudited financial statement in the proper format for presentation to creditors or other interested parties. This practice was not without its hazards, however. Creditors frequently assumed that some auditing had been done since the statement was submitted on the accountant's stationery.

To remove much of the uncertainty accompanying such statements, the American Institute of Certified Public Accountants in December 1978 approved two additional types of certificates. One is called a *compilation* letter. In this case, the accountant states that his or her only responsibility was to prepare the statements in an acceptable format from the client's books and records but that no outside verification was done. This is what such a statement looks like:

> The accompanying balance sheet of GHI, Incorporated as of December 31, 1990, and the related statements of income, retained earnings, and changes in financial position for the year then ended have been compiled by us.
>
> A compilation is limited to presenting in the form of financial statements information that is the representation of management (owners). We have not audited or reviewed the accompanying financial statements and, accordingly, do not express an opinion or any other form of assurance on them.

If the accountant should follow up on any irregularities that become apparent during a casual examination of the supporting data and try to resolve them while preparing the statements, a *review* letter accompanies the finished product (note that once again the CPA plainly states that no formal auditing procedures were performed):

> We have reviewed the accompanying balance sheet of GHI Incorporated as of December 31, 1990, and the related statements of income, retained earnings and changes in financial position for the year then ended, in accordance with standards established by the American Institute of Certified Public Accountants. All information included in these financial statements is the representation of the management (owners) of GHI Incorporated.
>
> A review consists principally of inquiries of company personnel and analytical procedures applied to financial data. It is substantially less in scope than an examination in accordance with generally accepted auditing standards, the objective of which is the expression of an opinion regarding the financial statements taken as a whole. Accordingly, we do not express such an opinion.
>
> Based on our review, we are not aware of any material modifications that should be made to the accompanying financial statements in order for them to be in conformity with generally accepted accounting principles.

Possible Additional Material

The terms of some engagements between CPA and client anticipate submission of a *management letter*. This is a communication above and beyond the opinion letter that accompanies the statements. In this document, the accountant is free to mention any strengths or weaknesses noted during the examination and offer suggestions for change. There are no limitations on its contents—it might address issues of accounting, security, insurance, safety, or any other matters the CPA believes worthy of management's attention. The contents are not always critical; an exceptional accounting staff might be complimented, for instance.

It is still an unusual occurrence when a management letter is submitted. However, if one were prepared, a careful review might offer the analyst additional insights into the borrower's operations.

Within the past decade, a trend has developed among commercial bankers and others to augment accrual statements with a *cash flow analysis*. The impetus behind this development has been the financial embarrassment of some firms with a historical record of acceptable accrual results. A number of interested parties (trade associations, etc.) have petitioned the AICPA to include a cash flow statement as part of the standard audit package.

The construction of a cash flow report is essentially accomplished through modification of the accrual-based operating statement by changes in balance sheet items and through reversal of noncash entries. The purposes of such a report are to:

1. Determine more exactly the principal sources and expenditures of cash.
2. Determine whether the subject company is able to generate sufficient funds from internal resources to finance its operations.
3. Determine the sources of funds used for debt service.

At the time of this writing, no decision has been reached on whether such a statement should be prepared, let alone a format for its presentation.

FINANCIAL STATEMENT ANALYSIS

The statements presented to support a credit request are numerical representations of all the transactions that have taken place in the business up to the statement date as well as an indication of its present financial condition. Analysis of these statements takes two forms, *internal* and *external*. Internal analysis is the comparison of various items on the financial statement against one another as well as an examination of trends noted over a period of years. External analysis is a comparison of the applicant's performance against others of similar size in the same industry.

Spreadsheets

For ease in credit analysis, statement data should be placed on a "spreadsheet" (see Exhibit 1, a spreadsheet copyrighted by the Robert Morris Associates, for example). It is common practice to round off and display each entry as a whole number representing thousands or millions of dollars. Ordinarily fiscal and interim statements are spread on separate sheets. The reasons for performing this exercise are:

1. It forces the analyst to consider the origin, actual values, and importance of each entry as part of the spreading process.
2. It presents similar items side by side for ease in spotting trends.
3. It facilitates discussion with others regarding the credit request.
4. The end product is useful in making presentations to loan committees, boards of directors, loan review personnel, or bank examiners.

Internal Analysis

Internal analysis is often called "ratio analysis." It is accomplished by mathematical calculations that measure the relationships among various entries on the balance sheet and operating statement. The number of comparisons is limited only by the analyst's imagination; however, this chapter will cover 11 of the most commonly used ratios.

As mentioned previously, both assets and liabilities are divided into current and noncurrent categories. Current assets are defined as those that will be converted into cash within one year of the statement date in the normal course of business. Current liabilities are indebtedness that must be paid within one year. Since these items are grouped together and totaled as part of the accountant's construction of the balance sheet, it is logical for the lender to examine the relationship between them. The formula for calculating this *current ratio* is:

$$\frac{\text{Current assets}}{\text{Current liabilities}}$$

The resulting ratio indicates whether the applicant can anticipate generating sufficient cash to meet its debts in an orderly manner during the coming fiscal year. The higher the ratio, the greater the likelihood this will happen. However, this calculation will only provide

EXHIBIT 1 Spreadsheet for Credit Analysis

NAME _____   BUSINESS _____

ADDRESS _____   SIC # _____ ROUNDED TO _____

_____   CPA _____

	ANALYST TYPE								
	ASSETS DATE		%		%		%		%		%
1	Cash & Equivalents								
2	Marketable Securities								
3	Trade Receivables–(Net)								
4									
5	Inventories								
6									
7	All Other Current								
8	TOTAL CURRENT ASSETS								
9	Fixed Assets–(Net)								
10									
11	Investments								
12	Intangibles								
13	All Other Noncurrent								
14	TOTAL NONCURRENT ASSETS								
15	TOTAL ASSETS								
	LIABILITIES								
16	Notes Payable-Short Term								
17	Current Maturities of L.T. Debt								
18	Trade Payables								
19	Income Taxes Payable								
20	Accrued Expenses								
21									
22									
23									
24	TOTAL CURRENT LIABILITIES								
25	Long-term Debt								
26	All Other Noncurrent								
27	Subordinated Debt								
28	Deferred Taxes								
29									
30	TOTAL LIABILITIES								
31	Capital-Preferred Stock								
32	Capital-Common Stock								
33	Paid-in Capital								
34	Retained Earnings								
35	Treasury Stock								
36	NET WORTH/OWNER'S EQUITY								
37	TOTAL LIABILITIES & NET WORTH								
38	WORKING CAPITAL (8-24)								
39	CAPITAL FUNDS (27+36)								
40	Ratios: Current								
41	Quick								
42	Sales/Receivables (Days)								
43	Cost of Gds. Sold/Inventory (Days)								
44	Cost of Gds. Sold/Payables (Days)								
45	Sales/Working Capital								
46	EBIT/Interest								
47	Cash Flow/Curr. Mat. LTD								
48	Fixed Assets/Net Worth								
49	Debt/Worth								
50	% Profit Before Tax/Tang. Net Worth								
51	% Profit Before Tax/Total Assets								
52	Sales/Fixed Assets								
53	Sales/Total Assets								
54									
55	Contingent Liabilities								

rma © 1985 Robert Morris Associates · Form C-112 A
5 Column Spread Sheet for use with Financial Statement Forms C-110H or C-110T
Order from Bankers Systems, Inc., St. Cloud, MN, 56301

These forms are intended for use in commercial lending transactions. Where any other use
is contemplated, it is suggested that a careful review be made to ensure compliance with applicable laws and regulations.

EXHIBIT 1 *(concluded)*

	INCOME STATEMENT		%		%		%		%		%
101	NET SALES										
102	COST OF GOODS SOLD										
103	GROSS PROFIT										
104	Selling Expense										
105	General & Administrative Expense										
106	Depr., Deple., Amort. Expense										
107	Lease & Rental Expense										
108	Officers' Compensation										
109											
110	TOTAL OPERATING EXPENSES										
111	OPERATING PROFIT										
112	Other Income										
113	Other Expense										
114											
115	EBIT										
116	Interest Expense										
117	PROFIT BEFORE TAX										
118	Income Tax										
119	PROFIT AFTER TAX										
120	Extraordinary Items										
121	NET INCOME										
	MISCELLANEOUS RATIOS										
122	% Depr., Deple., Amort./Sales										
123	% Lease & Rental Exp./Sales										
124	% Officers' Comp./Sales										
125											
	RECONCILIATION of RETAINED EARN.										
126	Retained Earnings – Beginning										
127	Add Net Income or Subtract Net Loss										
128	Less Dividends										
129	Other Additions (Deductions)										
130											
131	Retained Earnings – Ending										
	CASH GENERATION STATEMENT										
132	PROFIT AFTER TAX										
133	Depr., Deple., Amort.										
134	Incr (Decr) Deferred Items										
135	GROSS CASH FLOW										
136	(Incr) Decr Receivables–(Net)										
137	(Incr) Decr Inventories										
138	(Incr) Decr Other Current Assets										
139	Incr (Decr) Trade Payables										
140	Incr (Decr) Accruals										
141	Incr (Decr) Other Curr. Liabilities										
142	CASH FLOW FROM OPERATIONS										
143	Incr (Decr) Notes Payable										
144	Incr (Decr) Noncurrent Liabilities										
145	Incr (Decr) Equity										
146	Dividends										
147											
148	SUBTOTAL, FINANCING										
149	Net Capital Expenditures										
150	(Incr) Decr Investments										
151	(Incr) Decr Other Noncurrent Assets										
152											
153	SUBTOTAL, DISCRETIONARY										
154	Incr (Decr) Cash & Mkt. Sec.										
155	Beginning Cash & Mkt. Sec.										
156	ENDING CASH & MKT. SEC.										

© 1985 Robert Morris Associates

a very general indication of the applicant's liquidity. This ratio does not address two very basic questions:

1. *The timing of cash generation versus maturation of the liabilities.* It is possible to have an excess of current assets over current liabilities but be in a situation where those liabilities come due before the receivables or inventory are converted to cash.

2. *The quality of the assets expected to be converted into cash.* Receivables are shown on the balance sheet at invoice value less a reserve for bad debts. Inventory is ordinarily shown on a cost basis. But if the accounts are receivable from poor credit risks and the potential losses far exceed the reserve, their ultimate collectible value could well be far below the amount shown on the balance sheet. Similarly, a significant portion of inventory might turn out to be unsalable for some reason and its liquidation value could turn out to be considerably less than the balance sheet amount.

Inventory is the asset on the balance sheet that is most difficult to evaluate and liquidate. Bankers who are forced to dispose of inventory in order to retire their loans are in for a grueling experience. Therefore, the banker who has examined an applicant's current position might wish to refine the analysis by calculating the *quick ratio.* "Quick assets" can be defined as current assets less inventory. The formula for computing the quick ratio is:

$$\frac{\text{Quick assets}}{\text{Current liabilities}}$$

The purpose behind this calculation is to determine how much reliance there is on inventory liquidation to meet debts payable within the coming year. The higher the resultant ratio, the lesser the degree of inventory reliance. A ratio of greater than 1:1 indicates that there are sufficient quick assets (cash, marketable securities, receivables, etc.) to cover current debt. As was described when discussing the current ratio, there is no guarantee that receivables will be collected at balance sheet carrying value or that collection timing will be perfect.

The next computation to be discussed is the *debt/worth* ratio. This is a very important relationship to the lender because of the lender's position in situations where a borrower's business is liquidated. We have mentioned that the funds a business uses to acquire assets come from two sources—creditors and investors. The owner's portion (usually called "equity" or "net worth") is represented by the original and subsequent investments in capital stock as well as lifetime accumulated earnings of the business less any distributions in the form of dividends or withdrawals. In case of liquidation, the assets of the business are sold and all creditors are paid out first; the investors divide up any remainder. The owners' equity, therefore, is the lender's protective cushion. The higher the percentage of assets purchased with investor's funds, the greater the degree of protection afforded the creditor. Thus, a lower ratio is more desirable to the lender. The formula for calculating this ratio is:

$$\frac{\text{Total liabilities}}{\text{Net worth}}$$

Many financial institutions choose to modify this formula by substituting "tangible net worth" in the denominator. The purpose is to recognize that some assets have little liquidation value. Many of these assets of questionable value are classified on the financial statement as "intangible assets" (goodwill, patents, copyrights, etc.). The balance sheet value of these assets is subtracted from the net worth total when computing the ratio.

Three particular entries on the balance sheet are subject to a considerable degree to management actions. These are accounts receivable, inventory, and accounts payable. Corporate management has some control over when it pays its bills, how much pressure it applies to collect its receivables, and how much inventory it keeps on hand. The level of these three items has a great effect on the availability of cash to meet the balance of a corporation's obligations.

The general quality test for accounts receivable is the *receivables collection period*. This measurement device reports the average number of days that pass between the sale of goods or services and collection of the invoice. The formula for computing this time period when analyzing an annual statement (the answer is not a ratio but rather a number of days) is:

$$\frac{\text{Accounts receivable} \times 360}{\text{Total sales}}$$

The resultant number of days that receivables *on average* remain outstanding should be compared to the applicant's trade terms to determine if creditors are paying as anticipated. Remember that the number in the numerator of this fraction (as well as the two that follow) must be changed when analyzing an interim statement. As an example, if the statement of operations only covers a three-month period, use 90 in the formula.

The same sort of approach applies in reverse to accounts payable. Just as sales create receivables, so purchases create payables. To compute the average *trade payment period*, use this formula:

$$\frac{\text{Accounts payable} \times 360}{\text{Purchases}}$$

The resultant number of days represents the average time period that transpires between purchasing goods and paying for them. Usually the cost of goods sold portion of the operating statement will be broken out into its constituent parts; thus, the purchases figure is readily available. If this is not the case, most analysts have found the cost of goods sold total to be an acceptable substitute.

The amount of inventory on hand is crucial to effective management. Too little inventory could lead to production interruptions. Too much represents a diversion of cash from more productive uses and can result in inventory on hand being subject to all sorts of risks such as corrosion, breakage, obsolescence, or going out of style. Inventory levels are measured in terms of the number of days on hand at historic consumption levels. The formula for calculating *days inventory on hand* is:

$$\frac{\text{Inventory} \times 360}{\text{Cost of goods sold}}$$

All three of the above computations should be analyzed in respect to the degree of seasonality in the industry. Ordinarily, annual statements reflect a point in time during the year when the reporting company's financial condition is relatively strong. The more highly seasonal a business might be, the more necessary it becomes to insist on receiving regular interim statements. It is important to the analyst to determine how strained the company's resources are at the peak of its season.

One of the measurements of management effectiveness has to do with how efficiently corporate assets are employed. One way to measure efficiency is in terms of sales volume—how many dollars of sales are generated by each dollar invested in corporate assets. The *asset efficiency* ratio is calculated in this manner:

$$\frac{\text{Sales}}{\text{Total assets}}$$

While what constitutes a normal ratio varies widely by industry, a relatively low result might indicate that management has an inefficient plant, is not concentrating on collecting its receivables, might not be monitoring inventory levels as well as it should, or is in some other way squandering corporate assets.

Another approach to measuring management efficiency is in terms of the stockholder's return on his or her investment. This is, in many ways, the ultimate criterion of management efficiency. Individuals ordinarily invest in a business with the anticipation that the yield the investment generates will exceed other options open to them. The *net profit/worth* ratio computation is:

$$\frac{\text{Net profit after income taxes}}{\text{Net worth}}$$

There are two principal contributors to efficient and profitable operations—proper pricing and expense control. Simple techniques permit the analyst to determine which aspect may be the principal cause of above- or below-average results. One method is to calculate the *before-tax profit margin*. This ratio tells the analyst how many cents of each year's income dollar is retained in the business after paying all operating costs except income taxes. The calculation is:

$$\frac{\text{Net profit before income taxes}}{\text{Net sales}}$$

However, the most important element in determining the ultimate level of profitability is the *gross profit margin*. In a retail situation, this might be generally related to the "markup." This is a comparison of the income derived from the sale of goods against the costs of acquiring the merchandise sold. The acquisition costs could be merely purchases in the case of a wholesaler or retailer. If the company were a manufacturer, it would include all costs of producing the goods such as raw materials, labor, overhead, and equipment depreciation. The formula for this calculation is:

$$\frac{\text{Gross profits}}{\text{Net sales}}$$

The resultant ratio indicates how many cents of each sales dollar remain with the company after allowing for the largest single expense category on the operating statement—the cost of acquiring the merchandise that was sold. The relative performance of this ratio can be attributed to two factors—the ability to price the product profitably and the ability to manufacture (or purchase) the goods at a competitive cost.

Going one step further, if a firm's before-tax profit margin were below industry standards and the gross profit margin were low, the identification of the company's operating weakness probably has been reduced to poor pricing practices or manufacturing inefficiency. The analyst would then need to investigate each one in detail to better determine the specific causes of unsatisfactory results.

The difference between gross and before-tax margins is the inclusion of the remainder of the company's operating costs. Thus, if the firm's net profit results were comparatively weak but the gross profit margin were acceptable, the principal culprit would probably be expense control (i.e., selling, delivery, general, administrative, or interest costs).

Earlier in this chapter, the principal sources of loan repayment were identified and one conclusion reached was that term loans were expected to be repaid from earnings. This is an extremely important point because the alternative to repayment from earnings is to use the company's daily operating funds (working capital) for this purpose, thus reducing its liquidity. The term *debt coverage ratio* addresses that problem by trying to determine if earnings have been sufficient on an historical basis to meet annual payments on longer-term obligations.

An important concept must be discussed, however, before this ratio can be explained fully. It relates to noncash expenses. Certain expense charges are merely bookkeeping entries employed to change the value of assets on the balance sheet. Depreciation, depletion, and amortization are the most common. There are others, but they do not appear on many financial statements. They are labeled as noncash expenses because they are not paid by reducing the company's deposit account. A company's *cash flow*, then, would be larger than merely its net profit after taxes; the noncash expenses would have to be added back to profits. (The term *cash flow* has more than one interpretation, and we will discuss others later in this chapter. For the present, however, we will use the above definition.) The formula for calculating the term debt coverage ratio is as follows:

$$\frac{\text{Cash flow (Aftertax profit + Noncash charges)}}{\text{Current portion of long-term debt}}$$

The higher this ratio, the more adequately the applicant has demonstrated a capacity to pay its required term debt installments from earnings.

The analyst can learn a considerable amount from a review of the absolute numerical results of these financial tests. However, even more information can be obtained from a *trend analysis* in which these ratios are computed for a number of accounting periods and compared to determine which are improving or deteriorating. Remember that two accounting periods do not constitute a trend; at least three are needed, and many analysts prefer to obtain at least five years of history when appraising a loan request.

No loan should be made solely on the basis of ratio analysis. We will shortly mention a number of other issues that must be addressed. Not every ratio tells the analyst something important and conclusive. Ratios should be used to help pinpoint areas needing further investigation. The fact that receivables are slowing down is not the important discovery—the crucial part is determining *why* this development has taken place. It might be due to:

- Selling to financially weaker customers
- Resignation of the accounts receivable clerk
- Economic conditions
- Lack of current detailed reports for collection purposes

The greatest value of ratio analysis to the lender lies in the area of flagging unusual developments for further examination.

EXTERNAL ANALYSIS

We have defined internal analysis as the comparison of various entries on an applicant's financial statement against one another and against prior years. However, there is a second approach to ratio appraisal of financial statements called "external analysis." This refers to the comparison of the applicant's statement against those of other firms in the same industry of approximately similar size.

The analyst might be able to attempt a comparison between the applicant and its peers without outside help if there are similar borrowers already in the bank's portfolio. But there is no way to ascertain whether other customers' statements are indeed representative of the condition of their industry.

Fortunately there are sources of industry-wide data available to the credit analyst. Appropriate trade associations, the federal government, and credit rating agencies, such as Dun & Bradstreet, often provide this information. The most comprehensive bank-originated source of such information is prepared by Robert Morris Associates, the national trade association of bank commercial lending officers. Each year the bank members of RMA submit information taken from financial statements of their borrowing customers, identifying the statements only by use of an SIC code designation. If a statistically significant sampling is available, an industry financial profile, sometimes called a "common-size" statement, is prepared. (In its most recent annual publication, RMA published and copyrighted industry information on almost 350 different industry groups based on more than 86,000 individual statements received from its members.) In the preparation of each industry profile, the data from individual submissions is combined to create one composite statement.[1] The result is a balance sheet in which each entry is represented not in terms of dollars but rather as a percentage of total assets (see Exhibit 2). By converting the applicant's balance sheet entries to a percentage of total assets, the analyst can now directly compare it to the rest of the industry to determine if the company is as financially strong as its peers and where the proportions differ markedly from its competition. The same approach is used in analyzing the operating statement except that all the entries in the RMA sample are expressed as a percentage of net sales.

Ratios are displayed using a different format. They are calculated individually for each statement submitted and then arrayed within the computer from most to least favorable. Note the bottom section of Exhibit 2, which displays the ratio results. In each case there are three numerical representations. The middle figure represents the median point in the array. The top figure for each ratio is at the first quartile point, and the bottom one is at the third quartile. This three-point ratio presentation allows the analyst to obtain a better idea of where the applicant stands in relation to its peers.

External analysis provides another method to help determine the financial strength of a commercial loan applicant. As with internal financial analysis, no decision should be made solely on the basis of common-size comparison against others of similar size in its industry. However, it can provide more material to be measured on the scales as part of the decision-making process.

NONFINANCIAL CONSIDERATIONS

We have already stated that the most accurate credit decisions are logically those based on the most complete information. It has also been pointed out that there is no *single* source of all the information that the credit grantor requires. Despite their importance in the analytical process, financial statements have two noticeable shortcomings—(1) they are sterile (providing no sense of how an applicant's operations are carried out) and (2) they are reports of *past* performance.

---

[1]RMA cautions that the studies be regarded only as a general guideline and not as an absolute industry norm. This is due to limited samples within categories, the categorization of companies by their primary Standard Industrial Classification (SIC) number only, and different methods of operations by companies within the same industry. For these reasons, RMA recommends that the figures be used only as general guidelines in addition to other methods of financial analysis.

EXHIBIT 2   Composite Balance Sheet for External Analysis

WHOLESALERS - COFFEE, TEA & SPICES SIC# 5149

Type of Statement

Current Data					Type of Statement	Comparative Historical Data	
	23	16	2	41	Unqualified	38	41
		1		1	Qualified	3	1
5	16			21	Reviewed	DATA NOT AVAILABLE 27	21
14	10			24	Compiled	35	24
13	6	3		22	Other	20	22
59(6/30-9/30/85)			50(10/1/85-3/31/86)				

| | | | | | | 6/30/81-3/31/82 | 6/30/82-3/31/83 | 6/30/83-3/31/84 | 6/30/84-3/31/85 | 6/30/85-3/31/86 |

0-1MM	1-10MM	10-50MM	50-100MM	ALL	**ASSET SIZE**	ALL	ALL	ALL	ALL	ALL
32	56	19	2	109	**NUMBER OF STATEMENTS**	100	96	81	123	109
%	%	%	%	%	**ASSETS**	%	%	%	%	%
7.4	5.9	3.1		6.1	Cash & Equivalents	9.1	8.3	6.8	6.2	6.1
31.8	29.0	26.7		29.1	Trade Receivables - (net)	31.1	33.7	32.6	30.8	29.1
30.9	31.7	44.3		34.0	Inventory	34.2	30.3	33.5	34.4	34.0
1.7	1.8	1.8		1.7	All Other Current	3.1	2.3	2.9	1.9	1.7
71.9	68.4	75.9		71.0	Total Current	77.5	74.6	75.8	73.4	71.0
22.5	22.3	16.5		21.0	Fixed Assets (net)	15.7	16.9	15.7	19.2	21.0
1.7	.8	.8		1.1	Intangibles (net)	.6	.9	.3	1.1	1.1
4.0	8.5	6.9		7.0	All Other Non-Current	6.3	7.6	8.1	6.4	7.0
100.0	100.0	100.0		100.0	Total	100.0	100.0	100.0	100.0	100.0
					LIABILITIES					
14.3	22.1	24.3		20.4	Notes Payable-Short Term	16.7	15.5	17.3	17.4	20.4
5.0	2.4	3.9		3.4	Cur. Mat.-L/T/D	2.0	2.6	2.6	2.4	3.4
21.1	20.0	27.7		21.5	Trade Payables	19.8	21.4	24.7	24.2	21.5
1.2	.5	1.3		.9	Income Taxes Payable	–	–	–	.8	.9
4.8	5.9	3.7		5.3	All Other Current	11.3	10.0	10.4	7.8	5.3
46.4	50.9	61.0		51.5	Total Current	49.8	49.4	55.0	52.6	51.5
14.8	11.8	10.9		12.3	Long Term Debt	8.6	9.5	8.8	9.8	12.3
2.2	.7	1.4		1.2	Deferred Taxes	–	–	–	.3	1.2
.5	1.6	.7		1.1	All Other Non-Current	3.7	2.6	2.0	2.9	1.1
36.1	35.1	26.0		33.9	Net Worth	38.0	38.5	34.2	34.4	33.9
100.0	100.0	100.0		100.0	Total Liabilities & Net Worth	100.0	100.0	100.0	100.0	100.0
					INCOME DATA					
100.0	100.0	100.0		100.0	Net Sales	100.0	100.0	100.0	100.0	100.0
26.0	21.1	15.3		21.4	Gross Profit	22.3	22.6	20.4	21.3	21.4
22.2	19.0	12.6		18.6	Operating Expenses	18.6	20.2	17.6	18.6	18.6
3.7	2.1	2.7		2.7	Operating Profit	3.7	2.4	2.8	2.7	2.7
.7	.3	1.3		.6	All Other Expenses (net)	.9	.6	.7	.6	.6
3.0	1.7	1.4		2.2	Profit Before Taxes	2.8	1.8	2.1	2.1	2.2
					RATIOS					
2.5	2.1	1.6		2.1	Current	2.2	2.3	1.8	2.0	2.1
1.7	1.3	1.3		1.4		1.5	1.4	1.3	1.4	1.4
1.0	1.1	1.1		1.1		1.2	1.2	1.1	1.1	1.1
1.5	1.0	.7		1.1	Quick	1.1	1.2	.9	1.1	1.1
1.0	.7	.4		.7		.8	.8	.7	.7	.7
.5	.5	.3		.4		.6	.6	.5	.5	.4
21 17.2	19 19.1	19 19.7		19 19.1	Sales/Receivables	17 21.0	20 18.2	20 17.9	20 18.5	19 19.1
32 11.4	24 15.2	25 14.6		25 14.6		28 13.2	26 13.8	26 14.0	26 14.2	25 14.6
37 9.9	32 11.5	33 11.1		34 10.7		39 9.4	37 9.8	35 10.3	35 10.3	34 10.7
16 22.6	21 17.0	29 12.4		23 16.0	Cost of Sales/Inventory	18 20.1	17 21.8	24 15.0	20 18.2	23 16.0
33 11.2	37 9.9	52 7.0		38 9.7		39 9.4	31 11.6	37 10.0	36 10.2	38 9.7
79 4.6	51 7.1	74 4.9		65 5.6		62 5.9	58 6.3	65 5.6	70 5.2	65 5.6
13 27.3	8 44.0	25 14.8		13 27.9	Cost of Sales/Payables	9 39.9	10 35.0	12 31.2	14 26.7	13 27.9
23 16.0	21 17.5	33 10.9		24 15.0		18 20.6	21 17.1	25 14.6	24 15.4	24 15.0
43 8.4	35 10.5	43 8.5		38 9.6		38 9.6	35 10.3	42 8.7	41 8.9	38 9.6
8.4	12.6	13.1		11.4	Sales/Working Capital	9.1	7.1	9.2	10.7	11.4
17.8	27.0	24.7		22.1		17.3	17.8	22.3	22.6	22.1
-98.1	135.6	38.4		118.1		38.9	50.4	52.3	128.3	118.1
9.0	5.0	2.0		6.3	EBIT/Interest	6.7	7.6	5.9	6.0	6.3
(28) 5.9	(50) 2.3	(14) 1.5		(93) 2.2		(82) 2.9	(87) 2.5	(70) 2.5	(106) 2.7	(93) 2.2
2.0	1.1	1.1		1.3		1.4	1.3	1.2	1.5	1.3
4.1	4.9	4.3		4.4	Net Profit + Depr., Dep., Amort./Cur. Mat. L/T/D	7.6	5.7	8.4	6.4	4.4
(10) 2.1	(29) 3.0	(11) 1.5		(50) 2.4		(45) 3.5	(43) 4.0	(40) 2.9	(65) 3.3	(50) 2.4
1.2	1.6	1.1		1.4		1.6	1.3	.6	1.7	1.4
.1	.2	.0		.2	Fixed/Worth	.1	.1	.1	.2	.2
.5	.5	.7		.5		.3	.3	.3	.5	.5
2.3	1.3	1.4		1.4		.8	.7	.8	1.4	1.4
.8	.9	1.6		.9	Debt/Worth	.9	.8	1.0	.9	.9
1.8	2.3	3.2		2.2		1.7	1.6	2.3	2.3	2.2
7.2	4.2	11.5		5.6		3.8	3.3	4.2	4.8	5.6
39.0	25.1	26.8		28.5	% Profit Before Taxes/Tangible Net Worth	37.6	33.0	31.0	35.0	28.5
(26) 17.4	(54) 16.4	(18) 15.2		(100) 16.1		(95) 23.8	(92) 17.5	(77) 17.8	(115) 17.1	(100) 16.1
12.2	4.9	3.6		7.5		11.0	5.5	4.1	8.6	7.5
15.2	11.2	5.5		11.4	% Profit Before Taxes/Total Assets	15.5	13.1	12.5	10.2	11.4
8.3	6.2	2.5		5.3		8.5	5.9	5.0	5.7	5.3
3.9	1.1	1.0		1.5		3.3	1.5	.5	2.5	1.5
63.9	42.0	924.8		63.1	Sales/Net Fixed Assets	197.8	124.3	141.3	78.2	63.1
21.6	19.4	30.6		22.1		33.8	30.6	35.9	29.2	22.1
9.7	8.8	8.8		9.5		12.0	13.3	12.3	11.0	9.5
5.8	5.4	4.8		5.4	Sales/Total Assets	5.8	5.7	5.4	5.9	5.4
3.7	4.0	3.1		3.6		3.9	4.1	3.9	3.7	3.6
2.3	2.7	2.3		2.4		2.7	2.5	2.7	2.6	2.4
.8	.5	.0		.6	% Depr., Dep., Amort./Sales	.2	.4	.3	.5	.6
(26) 1.3	(51) 1.2	(15) 1.1		(93) 1.2		(93) .9	(86) .9	(75) .9	(107) 1.1	(93) 1.2
4.3	1.8	1.4		1.8		1.5	1.4	1.6	2.2	1.8
1.9	1.0			1.1	% Officers' Comp/Sales	.9	1.1	.9	.7	1.1
(15) 3.4	(19) 1.2			(37) 1.9		(37) 2.5	(34) 2.4	(27) 2.1	(45) 1.7	(37) 1.9
7.8	2.7			3.6		4.1	4.3	3.2	4.0	3.6
67130M	869986M	1461688M	242241M	2641045M	Net Sales ($)	2636040M	2303838M	2180522M	2743952M	2641045M
15992M	195260M	368547M	187231M	767030M	Total Assets ($)	570328M	615936M	545771M	791188M	767030M

©Robert Morris Associates 1986

M = $thousand   MM = $million

See Pages 1 through 13 for Explanation of Ratios and Data

But past performance is only useful as a guideline to the extent that the conditions under which the company operated in prior years resemble anticipated future conditions. Loans made today will be repaid in the future, so an important aspect of financial analysis is predicting what will happen while the loan under consideration is outstanding. We will discuss forecasting later in this chapter. Needless to say, in his area the analyst will not be dealing with hard facts but instead with the evaluation of some very "soft" information (opinions, estimates, predictions, etc.).

Occasionally, an application must be rejected without extensive consideration because it contains one or more elements which, if the loan were approved, would represent a violation of bank policy. A rather simple example of such a situation might be receipt of an application from a company located outside the bank's stated trade area. However, this is not the case with most applications. In these situations, a rather complete consideration of the company's operations is necessary in order to evaluate as accurately as possible its ability to repay the requested loans in a timely manner. A representative list of subject matter that might be addressed follows.

Management

1. Do the individuals have a reputation for honesty and integrity?
2. Are they open in discussing the company with their banker? Are they prompt in supplying requested information?
3. What is their collective attitude toward risk? Fiscal responsibility?
4. What is the background and experience level of each individual member of management? What operational area is each responsible for supervising?
5. Have plans been made for management succession? Is a competent level of junior management on hand?
6. Do the managers have an investment interest in the company or is it under absentee ownership?

The Operating Environment

1. How much competition does the applicant face? Is this competition based on price or product quality? Are its competitors stronger financially or do they have an advantage in product recognition?
2. What is the present and anticipated future state of the economy? How will it affect the applicant's ability to repay its proposed debt according to schedule?

3. Does the company operate in a regulated environment? Is it subject to pollution controls? Is it protected by tariff regulation? Is this protection likely to continue?

Labor Relations

1. Are workers unionized? What has been the history of the applicant's labor relations? When does the current contract expire? Are present wage scales in line with the local labor market?
2. Is there an ample supply of workers?
3. Are most of the workers highly skilled, semiskilled, or unskilled?

Raw Materials

1. Is there an abundant supply of whatever raw materials the applicant consumes in the manufacturing process?
2. Is there competition among suppliers?
3. Are price levels subject to market conditions or are they regulated by a governmental agency?
4. Do the raw materials have qualities which make shipment, storage or disposal a hazardous undertaking? Is insurance coverage available?

Products

1. Does the product line include consumer or manufacturer's goods? If it is composed of consumer goods, are these luxury or necessity items?
2. Is the product line growing in size? Are the items complementary (can they be sold by the same representatives to the same customers)?
3. Do any products in the line seem to be losing money? Why are they being carried?
4. If a manufacturer, does the manufacturing process require close tolerances? How does the company ensure that these tolerances are met?

Fixed Assets

1. What is the age of the plant and equipment? What are annual maintenance costs? Are replacement parts available?
2. If the plant is leased, when does the lease expire? Does the lease provide for automatic renewal? Is alternate space available? What would it cost to move the business?

3. Is there room for expansion in the present plant?
4. What are the projected annual fixed asset expenditures over the life of the proposed loan?
5. What is the insured value?

Customers

1. Does the customer list contain a number of long established relationships?
2. Do they represent strong credit risks?
3. Are returns and allowances in line with the industry?
4. Is the customer list growing? Stable? Declining?

Selling and Distribution

1. Are sales representatives paid on a salary or commission basis?
2. Are changes planned in the marketing effort?
3. What is the procedure for approving trade credit?
4. How are products delivered to the customer? Is the system reliable?

The Future

1. Is there a formal planning process?
2. Have plans been reduced to written form and distributed to the proper members of management?
3. Do plans involve new products, new territories, new clientele, additional personnel? How well have these changes been researched? What will they cost?

PROJECTIONS

It is common for a lending officer to suggest that the commercial loan applicant submit an operating projection covering the time period when the loan will be outstanding. Many corporate managers automatically include such material as part of the "package" that accompanies the request.

No applicant has yet submitted a projection that demonstrates an inability to repay the loan on a timely basis. This would run counter to human nature as well as the reason for its preparation. With this in mind, the credit analyst is obligated to scrutinize the applicant's projections to determine independently if they are realistic and attainable. The key to success with this type of analysis is obtaining management's *assumptions*, which form the basis for the projections, and conducting a subsequent discussion to determine whether the reasoning behind the assumption data seems valid. The focal points of such an examination should be:

- Sales growth
- Receivables collection period
- Days inventory on hand
- Trade payment period
- Fixed asset expenditures
- Depreciation calculations
- Gross profit margin
- Operating expenses
- Interest rates
- Tax rates
- Dividend policy

Each factor listed above should be examined for reasonableness in every year of the projection. If the assumptions seem unattainable or invalid for some reason, the analyst should prepare his or her own forecast using more realistic values for those assumptions. An entire balance sheet, operating statement, and earned surplus reconcilement can be constructed from the 11 factors on the preceding list. Any smaller item found on the statement could safely be made to fluctuate in relation to sales volume.

CASH FLOW

This subject was discussed to some degree earlier in the chapter. The key to making loan payments when due is the regular and continual generation of cash from internal operations. Financial statements are ordinarily prepared on an accrual basis. This method of preparation, while perhaps a more accurate approach to presenting a complete picture of the operations of a business, can be misleading from the standpoint of determining the sources, uses, and availability of cash to meet loan payments.

Accrual reports can be converted to a cash flow basis through a process that restructures the operating statement. The procedure involves making three important changes:

1. Reversal of any noncash transactions recorded during the accounting period (depreciation, depletion, amortization, write-down of assets, assumption of former contingent liabilities, changes in valuation reserves, etc.).
2. Modification of accrual operating statements using changes in related balance sheet entries (i.e., cash generated from accrual

sales is modified by changes in accounts receivable levels from year to year).

3. Rearrangement of the order of presentation to determine how much cash is generated from internal operations versus the amount coming from external sources (loans and investments).

The end product of a cash flow statement could be remarkably different from an accrual report for the same company. Firms reporting accrual profits may be consuming large quantities of cash, and vice versa. Understanding the sources and uses of cash will increase the lender's overall knowledge of an applicant's operations and constitutes a valuable additional analytical tool.

CONCLUSION

Credit analysis is only one aspect of the entire loan administration field. It is not an end unto itself: its purpose is to supplement and facilitate the rest of the commercial loan functions described in this handbook. It is an important facet of the lending process, however, because it has application throughout the life of a loan. It is essential to making proper initial loan decisions, to periodic surveillance of statements for signs of improvement or deterioration, and to the conduct of useful loan reviews. The keys to effective credit analysis are (1) gathering of relevant data from a wide variety of sources, (2) determining which of the data so obtained is important to the loan decision, and (3) learning the strengths, weaknesses, and operating peculiarities of the applicant and its industry.

CHAPTER FORTY-SEVEN

Handling Problem Loans

Willard Alexander
Vice Chairman
The Citizens & Southern Corporation

Gerald R. Downey, Jr.
Executive Vice President
Citizens & Southern Florida Corporation

Lending provides a major source of income for commercial banks. It is inevitable, however, that even with the soundest of loan policies some loan losses will occur if community needs are to be served. Since loans to businesses expose a bank to substantially higher losses than any other type of credit, it is important to keep losses on these credits within relatively small margins in order to realize a profit.

It has been said that a bank "never" makes a bad loan—a loan goes bad only after it has been made. This may be true in part, but surveillance of the borrower's operations after a loan has been made is a necessary part of lending. A banker with a watchful eye can often help a business customer steer clear of financial difficulty before it begins, thus holding problem loans to a minimum. Successful recognition of a potential problem can allow sufficient time to get paid out of a relationship if the banker takes appropriate action. In today's competitive banking environment good loan relationships are difficult to develop and retain. Therefore, many times bankers try and salvage a relationship when they see signals of a problem loan rather than dissolving the relationship completely.

A bank has a problem loan on its hands when one of its commercial credits is at or close to insolvency. The real bottom line result is a cash crisis where cash is not available to meet operating needs and maturing obligations. To be classified as a true problem loan, the credit must be significantly large in relation to the size of the bank; this excludes installment or charge card debt to an individual.

Problem loans are costly for a bank; some costs that go far beyond the loan charge-off and directly affect the bottom line. Because of time

657

spent in a workout situation, profit opportunities are missed, and less time is available to call on good clients or to seek out potential customers. Many dollars are spent for the legal and professional fees necessary to handle the credit properly. The demoralizing effect that handling a loan of this type has on the officers involved can take its toll in terms of self-confidence or willingness to take reasonable risks on future credits. A bank's reputation can be adversely affected by excessive loan problems, which can hurt the bank in the marketplace for deposits and capital.

How do problem loans come into being? Many things cause a problem loan to develop, but several events frequently trigger a problem situation. Timing is crucial. Identifying a problem early and taking action increases the chances of recovering all principal. The alert loan officer watches for these events and can often anticipate a problem before it occurs or gets out of hand.

1. Major problems can develop in a business when a change in management occurs. The account officer should be on the lookout for difficulty when there is loss of the top executive, key man, or head sales representative. The company's operations will most likely change somewhat, reflecting the new personality that has entered, and often the change can be for the worse.

2. The lender should also be aware of significant changes in the personal habits of current management. Although unrelated to the business at first, health problems, divorce, death of a close friend or relative, and so on can cause top executives to change habits rapidly in a short period of time. Close and early surveillance of the credit can help an officer gain insight into senior management's normal patterns so that later changes can be more easily detected.

3. Changes in industry trends may directly affect a thriving business so that it can no longer compete profitably. For example, a carpet manufacturer producing woven carpeting may not be prepared for the entrance and gradual acceptance of tufted carpeting. When the consumer buying trend moves almost exclusively to tufting, demand for the woven variety plunges, causing the company's sales to do likewise. Therefore, the lender should keep informed about the environment of each industry in which his customers operate.

4. New competition in a growth industry can eventually cause reduced sales and margins for a loan customer. Competition will steadily increase until sales growth and profitability slows considerably or disappears. During the "shake-out" period companies in the industry will usually experience considerable operating problems.

5. Deterioration in the overall economy can turn a good loan into a weak one. During unusual inflation or recession, many companies experience difficulties. During such times the lending officer will usually need to pay extra attention to marginal credits.
6. Rapid expansion in a business often leads to problems. When sales are booming, management often becomes overly ambitious, eager to increase the size of the plant. However, in trying to do too much too fast, management may be unable to cope with the added staff and equipment, and problems set in. It is a responsibility of the account officer to understand what the borrower is doing and help him set a prudent plan for expansion that will allow the company to control growth.
7. Government regulation can cause significant problems for weaker competitors in an industry. Airline deregulation in the late 1970s is placing extreme earnings pressures on major airlines trying to compete for the same routes without price supports or price regulation. New low-cost airlines added additional price competition, lowering sales and margins further. As a result there has been a "shake-out" in the industry.

As much as possible, a lender needs to keep an arm's length from the borrower's management so that he may realistically appraise the company and identify potential problems. This is usually harder to do in a small town since the borrower and lender probably know each other socially. However, once an account officer becomes involved with management on a personal basis, there may be a tendency for the officer to see what he thinks he knows rather than the facts as they really are.

EARLY WARNING SIGNS

Several early warning signs can alert an account officer to problems already in existence.

1. The first of these may be a company's delay in furnishing financial information. When statements do not arrive promptly and the borrower gives repeated excuses and the statements still are not available, problems are probably on their way.
2. From the beginning of the banking relationship, the account officer should know who the company's major trade suppliers are. Should the officer discover that a major supplier is contemplating reducing credit to the customer or cutting it off entirely, this could be a sign that the borrowing company is facing serious financial difficulties. In medium to larger banks, if the credit department handles credit inquiries from trade

suppliers, the account officer may be unaware that such inquiries have been made. The account officer should keep close
contact with the credit department to stay informed.

3. Rather than holding all meetings in the bank, regular visits to
the customer's place of business can be valuable. It usually
takes an experienced observer to determine precisely how things
are going, and the lender will have to work at determining if
conditions are slipping. He should observe the general state or
repair and maintenance of the plant and equipment, morale of
junior officers and employees, and, of course, the inventory.
Since overstated inventory is one way of inflating financial
statements, the lender should study the statements to be familiar with the inventory's dollar value and the main categories
(either raw material or finished goods). While visiting it is also
a good idea to inspect the larger inventory items as well.

4. Any significant change in the level of balances a company is
keeping should alert the lender to a potential problem. While
it is not necessary to pry unduly into a company's activities, it
is the lender's right and responsibility to keep posted on the
borrower's finances by inspecting the deposit account. There
may be a satisfactory reason why the account is not being maintained as called for in the loan agreement, but if so, the account
officer should be aware of it.

5. A lender should obtain annual credit reports on each commercial customer. Suits or judgments on file against borrowers may
be discovered through such reports. Also, the lending officer
needs to be aware of all court proceedings involving the customers, as well as how they pay the trade, and so on. The credit
department should send such information to the lending officer
as a matter of routine.

6. A borrower may change accountants because the accountant
has strongly recommended changes in systems and controls that
the borrower does not agree with. Explanations for accountant
changes should be looked at closely.

7. Financial changes from the norm should always be noted. Performance compared to plans, trends and the industry should
be investigated. Explanation of differences should be evaluated.

FACT FINDING AND REEVALUATION

If a credit shows any one or a combination of these warning signals
the account officer should quickly begin an in-bank investigation to
determine whether a substantial problem exists. In gathering this information the officer should be extremely careful not to alert the bor-

rower, outside creditors, suppliers, other banks, and so on to his or her suspicions but should collect all the data possible from internal sources.

The lender may have reviewed the company's financial data many times before, but should do so again in light of whatever information led him to suspect a problem. Any internal action that might in some way reveal new data about the company's position should be taken at this point.

If the investigation shows that a company indeed has a serious problem, the next step should be to contact the bank's attorney. It is possible for the lender to reduce legal fees involved by making certain he has conducted a thorough internal investigation and has a good grasp of the situation. The lender can then present the lawyer with a concise comprehensive written summary of the existing situation, along with a list of the questions to be answered. In addition, all loan documentation should be reviewed with the attorney for accuracy and completeness. The lender's first priority is to protect the bank's interest. If the loan documentation appears faulty, it should be corrected at once if possible. This is essential if the loan is collateralized. Courthouse records should also be checked to make certain liens are properly recorded.

Having completed the background preparation, the account officer should reevaluate the credit in light of the new information and prepare a written report assessing the present situation. At this point, another lending officer, usually senior to the one handling the account, should be called on to review the facts and discuss the different strategies of action for developing a game plan. If the bank proceeds one way, how will the borrower react? In what position will the bank be? If another route is taken, what will the company management's reaction be?

All the foregoing should be done and the bank's plan of action set before the borrower is approached with the problem. Unpleasant as it may be, the situation must be faced squarely and as objectively as possible so that the best course of action can be taken for the good of both the bank and the business.

It may be prudent to move the account from the originating loan officer to another who is not as close to the borrower or to a "problem loan unit," which may be less reluctant to take any unpleasant steps necessary to protect the bank. Since the originating loan officer should have better insight into the company and its management's capabilities and attitude, this is a difficult decision. Also, the originator will emerge as a better loan officer if he is able to work through the problem himself. Here the old saying applies: "Good judgment comes from experience—usually an experience that was a result of bad judgment."

Therefore, if the loan officer has not identified too strongly with the borrower and has been able to prepare a fresh review of the situation as it truly exists, it may be a good idea to let him remain with the account. In any event, a problem loan should have close supervision by a senior officer through the workout period.

CONTINUATION OF THE BUSINESS

At the appropriate time the decision must be made whether to try to keep the company in business or to permit it to liquidate. Based on what the bank knows of the existing management, product, and competition, it may be that the situation is temporary and can be overcome in time with the bank's assistance. Perhaps restructuring of debt could ease the strain over the long term. There are, however, certain external factors that may be beyond management's control—for instance, the economy—and these must certainly be considered when deciding whether to continue or liquidate the business. Management evaluation is critical in deciding to continue a business. Management must be strong enough to effectively operate the business through the difficult times. Integrity of management has to be absolutely there to continue the business.

Even if the problems appear too far gone to remedy, the decision might be to continue the business on an interim basis in order to better establish the bank's position. If there are documentation gaps, and a need to refile in court, it might be wise to keep the company going for at least 90 days in an attempt to avoid actions against the bank for securing unfair preference.

It should be noted that if the bank decided to advance funds to keep the company in operation temporarily, legal advice is needed before doing so. If a bank advances funds for payroll purposes without advancing sufficient funds to pay the accompanying withholding taxes, the bank may assume the liability of paying the taxes at a later date if the company has not done so. This liability could also be created for the bank if it handles payroll checks by creating an overdraft on the company's account and the company does not subsequently pay the withholding taxes. Obviously, for protection of the bank, sound legal counsel is advisable.

Liquidation may be inevitable. However, if it were possible to delay complete liquidation and scale the business down in order to reduce assets, the debt would be lowered and both the bank and the company could well be in better positions.

Whether it is too highly leveraged or unable to show a profit, a business that has been experiencing difficulty may have already begun a course of action that will deplete some of its assets. If it hasn't and the decision has been made to keep the business going, temporarily or otherwise, several steps can be taken in an attempt to improve the picture. Financial analysis is needed to evaluate the resources with which management has to work to affect a turnaround. Projections of pro formas and cash budgets are needed to guide the customer through the tough times.

An attempt should be made to reduce every expense possible. Begin at the top. The lender, company president, and adviser should examine the company's expenses line by line to determine which are absolutely essential. The principals should decide how much of their salaries and personal expenses charged to the company they are willing to cut. It should then be made clear to the rest of the staff that all expenses must be kept to a minimum. Naturally, any dividend payments should be stopped at once.

Next, inventory should be reduced and accounts receivable should be analyzed carefully. Methods of handling customer claims for returned and damaged merchandise should be studied. Although receivables generally shrink in liquidation, if credits and claims have not been handled properly, the receivables may have been substantially overstated to begin with.

Also, problems may occur if accounts receivable have concentrations. Even if these customers are financially strong, they frequently claim rather large credits due them. For this reason, no more than 20 to 25 percent of a company's sales volume should be to a single customer, and even this is a high percentage.

Next, any idle equipment or plants not essential to current operations should be disposed of. Production techniques should be examined to see if there are any steps which would improve the product or the profit margins.

To improve the cash flow, the company's payments should be analyzed to determine which are not required by contract and could be deferred. Perhaps some of the accounts payable can be postponed. If debt of current maturity can be extended and/or subordinated to bank debt, this also could be helpful.

Bankers should be careful not to exercise control over the operation, and they should not be placed in a position of appearing to force changes that could have detrimental effects. Bankers can be successfully sued for lender liability if placed in this situation.

Finally, the lending officer should discuss with management the possibility of obtaining new equity capital from officers or other sources.

Keeping a financially fragile company in business requires not only diligent effort on the part of lending officers, but often creativity and ingenuity as well. Although generally tried and true guidelines can be applied in most situations, each credit is different, and the workout plan must be tailormade to obtain the best results possible for all parties involved.

In most situations, lenders prefer to keep borrowers out of bankruptcy. Notwithstanding the emotional distress of the proceedings, they involve actions in federal courts and are expensive for everyone. Therefore, if the borrower and his or her creditors can cooperate in solving the problem, all parties will benefit. However, any time the lender feels that the borrower is trying to defraud the bank, conceal assets, or carry assets away, it would be wise to take legal action regardless of the outstanding debt that might otherwise be salvaged.

LIQUIDATION OF THE BUSINESS

If liquidation appears to be the only course open to the bank, there are several alternative ways to proceed. The lender may be able to obtain the complete cooperation of the borrower in trying to liquidate quietly. This approach is usually best. Inventory and equipment can usually be sold at closer to market values. A borrower would have to temporarily continue with the purpose of quietly liquidating. Before the lender can act in this regard, however, the borrower must be in default on some part of the bank debt instrument or the note must be due.

If liquidation is decided on, the bank should immediately bring in those professional resources, such as attorneys and accountants, needed to help protect its position.

Next, the lender should be certain he has all the collateral on the business he can possibly obtain. Remember, however, that although banks can take any security available for debt previously contracted, the effect that taking it can have on other creditors must be considered. For example, obtaining an inventory lien may scare trade suppliers into cutting off the source of supplies the company must have to continue functioning.

It may be worth additional dollars to the bank to purchase senior liens from other creditors. The lender should also keep in mind that the right of offset may be applicable in liquidation; however, advice should be sought from the bank's attorney before applying it.

In some circumstances, the lender may agree to compromise the bank's debt. For example, a company may owe the bank $100,000. Complete liquidation of the assets may yield $75,000. If the officers are willing to sell personal assets yielding another $10,000, the bank may decide to accept the $85,000 as sufficient payment of the obligation and dismiss the remaining $15,000 owed. This should be done if there appears to be a lengthy expensive litigation ahead and collateral values would probably erode during the process.

A borrower who is financially embarrassed may decide to call a meeting of creditors to inform them of the existing situation. Often these meetings are hastily arranged and not carefully thought out, and little is accomplished. If a lender learns that the borrower is close to calling a meeting of creditors, he should immediately attempt to meet with the borrower, along with the attorneys from each side. Assuming the borrower will cooperate, the banker can then assist in planning a concrete, viable plan of action to present to creditors.

It may be that liquidation will take the form of an informal settlement between the company and its creditors. The assets will be sold and the proceeds distributed among the creditors based on an agreement approved by all parties involved. Liquidation can also be accomplished through a formal assignment of assets to a third party responsible for liquidating them and distributing the proceeds. The advantages to these methods, formal or informal, are speed, efficiency, and lower costs.

ELECTION OF BANKRUPTCY

The borrower, however, may not wish to follow any of these paths and may elect instead to file for voluntary bankruptcy or reorganization. If either of these paths is chosen, the situation should be followed closely by the bank's legal counsel.

In many problem loan situations, the company is not willing to voluntarily file a petition under the Bankruptcy Code; therefore, the creditors may wish to petition the court to force the company to take this step. In situations where there are 12 or more creditors of the company, the petition must be filed by at least three creditors holding claims aggregating at least $5,000 more than the value of any lien held by them. In the event there are fewer than 12 creditors, then one or more of such creditors holding in the aggregate of at least $5,000 of such claims may file the petition.

When creditors attempt to force the company into bankruptcy, the company has the right to contest the petition at a hearing held before the bankruptcy judge. The bankruptcy judge will order that the case proceed in bankruptcy only if the creditors can establish (1) the debtor is generally not paying such debtor's debts as they come due (unless such debts are the subject of a bona fide dispute), or (2) within 120 days before the date of the filing of the bankruptcy petition by the creditors, a custodian, other than a trustee, receiver, or agent appointed or authorized to take charge of less than substantially all the property of the debtor for the purpose of enforcing the lien against such property, was appointed or took possession.

If the bankruptcy judge determines that the petitioning creditors have not met their burden of proof, the court can award a judgment against those petitioning creditors and in favor of the debtor for the cost of the litigation as well as reasonable attorneys' fees. In the event that the court finds that the petitioning creditors filed the involuntary bankruptcy in bad faith, the court can award the debtor any actual or punitive damages suffered by it. For this reason creditors should consult very carefully with their legal counsel prior to deciding whether to commence an involuntary bankruptcy case against the debtor.

Whatever path is chosen to work out the company's debt problem, the lender must be careful to carry all steps to a logical conclusion. Loose ends can generate further losses or the possibility of legal action against the bank.

SUMMARY

Clearly, bankruptcy in any form is not a pleasant experience for the debtor or the lender. Many bankruptcies could be avoided or their impact reduced, however, if bank lending officers followed a few guidelines in dealing with their commercial customers.

By knowing and frequently servicing the borrower, potential problems can be recognized early. Regular plant visits keep the account officer in touch with the company so that he or she can observe how it is actually operating. Complete and careful analysis of the business and its principals can help him learn the facts about all aspects of the business and its management. Diligence in obtaining and perfecting security agreements is important when the loan is made as well as later if inadequacies in documentation are discovered. Proper use of attorneys and accountants can minimize legal problems throughout the entire relationship. And, if a problem develops and persists regardless of the lender's close attention, the courage to take unpopular actions with the debtor may reduce the ultimate damage to all parties involved.

PART NINE

Special Credit Areas

CHAPTER FORTY-EIGHT

Traditional Seasonal Lending and Revolvers

George J. McClaran

President
Pittsburgh National Bank

WHAT IS TRADITIONAL SEASONAL LENDING?

Historically, banks have traditionally been short-term lenders. This is in part caused by the short-term nature of our funding sources. Also, this type of lending is generally much safer than long-term lending. However, today banks are doing many different types of long-term lending.

The seasonal loan is the traditional commercial bank short-term, "self-liquidating" loan. The temporary increase in inventory and subsequent receivables are, in turn, liquidated in the normal course of business. Out of this classic self-liquidating loan pattern has grown the traditional commercial banking requirement for an annual cleanup of short-term borrowings under lines of credit. The customer should have sufficient capital to finance basic operations in the off or dormant seasons. He should be out of bank debt at that time. The bank finances only his seasonal bulge.

But since the traditional bank loan is only a small percentage of commercial bank loans today, a test of the borrower's financial capacity by a cleanup or rest period cannot be strictly followed. The true purpose of the loan and the sources of repayment must be thoroughly examined.

REASONS FOR BORROWINGS

Often, a small company customer will call his banker and request a seasonal or short-term loan without really understanding why he needs to borrow. He may think that the loan is needed to pay taxes, to buy inventory, etc., and that he can repay quickly. However, the underlying cause of the borrowing need often goes much deeper, and repayment may not come so easily. Perhaps sales growth has caused cash to be tied up in current assets. Perhaps a fixed asset purchase was not funded through long-term debt. Perhaps consistent losses have drained cash from the company.

Any one of the following stated reasons for borrowing could conceivably be matched or partially matched with one of the following underlying causes.

Stated Reasons For Borrowing	*Underlying Cause*
Pay bills or taxes	Poor short-term asset and liability management
Take discounts on bills	
Pay on-time unexpected expenses	Seasonality
Refinance debt	Temporary fluctuations in inventory or receivable levels
Support receivables	
Buy inventory	Sales growth or business expansion
Purchase fixed assets	Fixed asset purchases
Repurchase equity	Insufficient equity investment
	Funding losses

By correctly assessing the underlying cause of the borrowing need, the lender may also determine the expected duration, the source of repayment, the size of loan needed, and the appropriate structure.

Example—Seasonal Borrowing

Consider a children's clothing store just before school starts. Since many children will need new clothes, the store always brings in extra merchandise at this time of year. Will the store need to make much of a profit over the next few months to repay that loan? No—the reduction of inventory back to normal levels frees up enough cash to repay the principal. Of course, the bank would want the store to charge enough for the clothing to cover interest expense too. But breaking even would be enough. It is not necessary to make a profit to repay this type of loan.

On the other hand, assume the owners of this same clothing store decided to expand into additional space opening up next door. They wished to borrow to purchase inventory to stock this area with shoes. Will the store need to make a profit to repay this loan? Yes—they are borrowing to support a basic level of inventory needed to be on hand at all times, not to support temporary fluctuations in the inventory level. Will they be able to repay the loan in the short-term? Probably not—unless their profits are extremely high.

Example—Temporary Borrowing

Consider a company that manufactures motor oil. It may need to buy an entire barge full of oil at a time in order to obtain the most economical price from its supplier. Accordingly, it borrows from the bank to purchase this large amount of supply. As its supply is used, it repays the bank. By the time the supply is mostly used up and the merchandise partially sold and paid for, the bank is repaid. But then the company must borrow again to bring in another barge full of oil.

Differences from Long-Term Borrowing

Long-term borrowing is usually more risky than seasonal or temporary borrowing inasmuch as the bank must look to the earnings and cash flow of the business for repayment rather a normal fluctuation in short-term asset levels. We should expect that cash flow (net income adjusted by nonrecurring items plus depreciation plus other noncash items) after dividends cover not only debt maturities but also increases in working capital needs due to sales growth and at least a down payment on fixed asset purchases. Although a rough analysis of a company's ability to repay long-term debt can be done by evaluating cash flow, it is more accurate (and also more time consuming) to evaluate income statement and balance sheet projections. Only then are we forced to estimate and examine at once all possible uses of the available cash flow.

The most traditional cause of long-term borrowing is for the purchase of fixed assets. Since the company will reap the benefits of these assets over a period of years, it is reasonable to permit repayment of the loan over a period of years.

BORROWING CAUSED BY SALES GROWTH

In businesses that require high levels of receivables and inventory, rapid sales growth sometimes causes a deterioration in the cash position and thus a need to borrow. This is particularly true if profit margins are low. Although caused by growth in short-term assets, this borrowing need is NOT TEMPORARY. It will continue until sales growth declines, receivable and inventory levels decline, or profitability improves.

This phenomenon occurs because receivable and inventory levels grow naturally as sales grow. The company needs to maintain sufficient inventory to service its customers, generally maintaining about the same number of days' supply as before. Clearly, receivables outstanding at the end of the month will grow in relation to the sales made during that month. Although payables and accrued expenses also grow as sales do, their magnitude is generally not as high and cannot counteract the effect of the short-term asset growth. Often, retained profits over the period cannot cover growth in net short-term assets, causing the need to borrow.

Small business owners often do not understand this phenomenon. They frequently see sales growth as a sign of success in and of itself. Bankers should help them concentrate on product line profitability and short-term asset management instead.

It is possible for a business to experience borrowing needs due to both seasonal and long-term sales growth at the same time. Consider a growing manufacturer of swimming pools. At the end of the normal borrowing season, the company may be able to repay part of its loan due to normal reductions in inventory and receivable levels at that time of year. However, part of that loan could remain outstanding due to sales growth. In this situation, often both the borrower and the loan officer are surprised.

Depending on the type of credit arrangement utilized, borrowing to support sales growth may be categorized as either short-term or long-term on the balance sheet. Regardless of categorization, it is important to realize that although the debt is supporting short-term assets, it probably cannot be repaid in the short term and it is not immediately clear how and when it can be repaid in the long term. Thus, it is a fairly risky situation to finance. Frequently, the undercapitalized rapid growth company (which cannot repay its borrowings in full) is a candidate for secured asset-based lending. With this borrowing arrangement, receivables and inventory may be taken as collateral and monitored regularly. Needless to say, quality of receivables as measured by quality, concentration, and payment practices of our borrower's customers is important. Also, quality of inventory as measured by composition and salability is important.

BORROWING RELATED TO SHORT-TERM ASSET AND LIABILITY MANAGEMENT

Borrowing related to short-term asset and short-term liability management could be either temporary or long-term in nature. It is necessary to examine the exact cause of the borrowing need in order to determine its extent and duration as well as the borrower's ability to repay. It may not be obvious as to whether the borrowing need is seasonal or temporary or whether the borrowing need will be longer is spite of being related to short-term assets or short-term liabilities.

ACCOUNTS PAYABLE MANAGEMENT

Slowing payment to suppliers can be a source of cash to a business. However, this benefit must be weighed against the potential damage this practice can have on the company's supplier relationships. Payment terms and practices are often influenced by the relative strengths of the supplier and company. In situations where the sources or availability of supplies are limited, the company must face both stricter terms and stricter adherence to those terms. On the other hand, large and powerful companies can dictate payment policies to its suppliers.

Payment terms vary from one industry to another. You may have seen the symbols 1%/10/net30, or 1/10/30. They mean that the purchaser is given a 1 percent discount off the amount of the invoice if it pays within 10 days. If not, the purchaser must pay for the full amount of the invoice in 30 days. Businesses offer this discount to encourage prompt payment, since the seller who receives prompt payment of invoices will have to borrow less frequently from outside sources and, therefore, will not have the expense of paying interest on loans.

If no discounts are offered, the terms are just written net 30, net 60, etc. These simply mean that payment must be made within 30 days and 60 days, respectively.

Depending on payment terms, it may be beneficial to a company to borrow to pay its bills early. Considering the example above, the company would get a 1 percent discount by paying its bills 20 days early (in 10 instead of 30 days). That is equivalent to an annual discount rate of 18.25 percent [(365 days divided by 20 days) times 1 percent.] Theoretically, if the company could borrow from the bank at less than 18.25 percent, it could save money by doing so. In reality, that depends on whether or not the company would actually have paid its bills in 30 days if it did not discount them. For instance, if the company could let the time slip to 40 days before paying its bills, its effective discount rate if it discounted its bills (paid in 10 days) would be only 12.17 percent [(365 divided by 30) times 1 percent].

When late payables seem to be a matter of concern, it is prudent to request a payables aging list. It is important for the lender to understand the status of a potential borrower's payables before making a loan. The lender does not want to find out that the company needs more money for payables, after he has already loaned out for another purpose the full amount that he feels the company can repay and, if appropriate, collateralize. At that point, the bank's decision-making process about making an additional loan to the company to satisfy angry suppliers may be influenced by the need to keep it in business to collect the original loan.

TABLE 1 Sample Portion of Accounts Receivable Aging

BURNS EQUIPMENT CO.
Period Ending 6/31/X4

Customer	Total	Current	Over 30	Over 60	Over 90
ABC Chevrolet 1282 Franklin Rd. Pittsburgh, PA	23,132.00	23,132.00	—	—	—
Narrows Protection Co. 440 William Rd. Philadelphia, PA	5,500.00	—	4,000.00	1,500.00	—
Municipal County County Courthouse Room 100 Anytown, PA	11,314.14	189.50	—	—	11,124.64
National Bridge Division Big Steel Corp. Gary, Indiana	42,884.26	42,884.26	—	—	—
Burns Sales Co. 300 N. Fair St. Belmont, PA	143,526.19	1,977.60	1,155.15	21.75	140,371.69
• • •	• • •	• • •	• • •	• • •	• • •
Wilson Ford Sales 113 Fairmont Ave. Chestnut, WV 27877	11,799.86	(156.14)	11,956.00	—	—
Total	723,222.91	325,401.09	179,296.57	11,687.25	206,838.00

ACCOUNTS RECEIVABLE MANAGEMENT

Prompt collection of accounts receivables and avoidance of bad debts can make a big difference in the cash level of business and its resultant borrowing needs. Slow collection of accounts receivable may result from a number of different factors, such as the following:

1) Lack of attention by management as its customers attempt to improve their cash position by slowing payment.
2) Generous credit terms granted to customers, perhaps for the purpose of boosting sales.
3) Important major customers dictating payment terms or ignoring company's terms.
4) Credit sales to financially weak companies.
5) Customer dissatisfaction.
6) Disputes.

Payment terms for our borrower's receivables work in much the same way as its payment terms from its suppliers. To the extent that our borrower gives discounts, it may collect receivables faster, but in lesser amounts. Of course, our borrower can try to raise prices to make up for discounts given or the expense of borrowing to support slow receivables.

The quick way of measuring accounts receivable quality is the computation of the company's collection period (receivable days). However, when receivables collection or quality seems a serious matter of concern or receivables are being taken as collateral, the receivable days' figure yields insufficient information. In those cases, the banker should request a receivables aging. From an aging, an analysis of overdue accounts, concentration accounts, and credit quality of customers can be made. The aging will include a detailed list of account names and addresses with unpaid balances broken down into categories indicating how long their invoices have been outstanding. Table 1 illustrates a portion of an accounts receivable aging.

It is important to understand what the categories on an aging mean. The number of days shown sometimes refers to the number of days old and sometimes refers to the number of days past due. If 30-day terms are given, the category of "current" will include receivables from 0 to 30 days old (not yet due). In the Burns Equipment Aging, the number of days refers to number of days old, not number of days past due. If the number of days referred to number of days past due, you would see both a "current" category and a "1–30" category.

In the aging shown for Burns Equipment, you might first look at the summary aging for total accounts receivable:

Total	Current (0–30 Days Old)	Over 30 (31–60 Days Old)	Over 60 (61–90 Days Old)	Over 90 (90+ Days Old)
723,223	325,401	179,297	11,687	206,838
100%	45%	25%	2%	29%

Obviously, there is a very large amount in the over 90 days category. Upon further examination, note that a large part of the problem is caused by Burns Sales Co., a subsidiary of Burns Equipment Co. Either one of the facts—(1) that it is from a related company or (2) that such a large percent is overdue—would disqualify it as collateral. Furthermore, from an analsis point of view, we should remove it from trade receivables and classify it as a receivable from affiliate. Affiliated receivables should be studied separately. A separate analysis of the affiliate and probably a request for combined statements is in order.

Adjusting the receivables balances to reflect only receivables due from outside companies, the following results are obtained:

Total	Current	31–60 Days Old	61–90 Days Old	90+ Days Old
579,697	323,423	178,142	11,665	66,466
100%	56%	31%	2%	12%

The adjusted percentages make the situation look much better. Still, the amounts over 90 days old are worth investigating.

It is also important to look at concentrations in the analysis of receivables. A concentration is a customer that represents a large portion of a company's sales, perhaps over 10 to 20 percent. Loss of such a customer could severely hamper the company's operating efficiency and perhaps put it into a loss position. Furthermore, such a company could be in a position to dictate terms and prices.

The method of analyzing concentrations consists of studying the aging, listing the 10 largest customers by receivables outstanding, computing the percentage of each customer to the total, and computing the summed percentage of all 10 customers. Note that the 10 largest receivables at any one date may not really represent the 10 largest customers in terms of sales for the entire year. Generally, it is a reasonable estimate. However, it is necessary to be careful that results are not distorted by a company with either (1) large amounts of old receivables or (2) no receivables in a particular month but large receivable amounts in other months.

In addition, both the payment practices and the credit quality of each concentration account are studied. The first step in evaluating the credit quality of a customer is to look at its credit agency report. Large accounts with poor credit ratings or poor payment practices deserve further analysis. In serious situations, it may even become necessary to have our borrower request statements from its customer.

INVENTORY MANAGEMENT

Evaluation of inventory management depends a great deal on the industry and business strategy. Clearly, one would be far less concerned about a buildup in lumber or brick inventory than about a buildup in a product with rapid technological changes. It is also possible for a company to trade off the cost of carrying additional inventory for the competitive advantage of being able to supply product quickly. Nevertheless, an exceedingly high level of inventory will tie up cash unnecessarily.

It is far more technically difficult to judge the quality of inventory and the quality of inventory mangement than to judge the quality of accounts receivable and their management. One reason for this is that accounts receivable are closer to cash. Another is that specific terms for receivable collection usually exist and can be compared to actual performance. Credit ratings for specific customers can be looked up in a credit agency reference book. On the other hand, a loan officer may not be able to easily determine the value of inventory, especially with a highly technical product.

One source of information could be to check with customers and potential customers as to their satisfaction with the product and its comparison to competitive products. Other sources include industry trade associations, trade journals, business periodicals, and the Robert Morris Associates Statement Studies.

INVENTORY DAYS

The inventory account is of interest both in terms of the value of the material or merchandise involved and of its size in relation to other funds needs and the sales volume it supports. An exact appraisal of the true value of the inventories usually is not possible short of a detailed count and verification. The lender can make some judgments via a ratio analysis, however, by calculating inventory days based on cost of goods sold.

The inventory-days figure is supposed to represent the number of days worth of inventory on hand at the balance sheet date. Presumably, the lower the days, the better the performance by the firm. This, in turn, may indicate that the inventory must be relatively current and useful and contains little unusable stock. On the other hand, a low number of days could mean inventory shortages and incomplete satisfaction of customer desires. A large number of inventory days could indicate poor liquidity, possible overstocking, obsolescence, or, in contrast to these negative interpretations, a planned inventory buildup in the case of material shortages. A problem with this ratio is that it compares one day's inventory to cost of goods sold and does not take seasonal fluctuations into account.

SEASONAL INVENTORY LEVELS

The level of inventory and the inventory-days figure can fluctuate significantly in seasonal industries. For example, a toy manufacturing company will often build up high levels of inventory in the summer before its heavy selling season in the fall. A toy wholesaler tends to have its heavy inventory period slightly later in the year and a retailer a little later yet. Banks can finance a seasonal inventory buildup with a traditional line of credit, which will be paid off after the receivables are collected at the end of the busy selling season.

LONG-TERM INVENTORY FINANCING NEEDS

Sometimes a company's inventory financing needs do not fluctuate during the year but instead remain constant or increase over time. This could be due to any number of reasons such as excessive inventory levels, effect of rapid sales growth on inventory, inventory buildup in the face of an unexpected sales decline, obsolete inventory, insufficient profitability, or insufficient capitalization. In cases where lines cannot be repaid yearly, bankers often take collateral on their loans.

INVENTORY AS COLLATERAL

From the viewpoint of secured lending, the best inventory collateral is one that can be sold easily to a variety of buyers. It is best if the bank does not have to buy the skills to complete the manufacture of the product. Therefore, banks often advance loans against raw materials and finished goods collateral, but not work-in-process inventory collateral. Bear in mind that, depending on the company, its raw materials may be another company's finished goods. In reality, those items would be work-in-process of a truly veritcally integrated company and probably not appropriate to advance loans against as collateral. In secured lending, banks often use the services of either in-house auditors or outside professional appraisers to evaluate inventory collateral. Ideally, these people have prior experience in appraising and liquidating that type of inventory.

LENDING ARRANGEMENTS

Banks typically use a number of lending facilities and different terminology for seasonal lending and revolving credits.

Line of Credit

A line of credit is an agreement between the bank and a customer whereby the bank agrees to lend the customer funds, usually at the lending officer's discretion, up to a previously agreed maximum amount, usually effective for one year or less. Each loan is evidenced by a note that normally has a maturity of 30, 60, or 90 days. The amount outstanding may fluctuate up or down as the customer's needs dictate, as long as the total outstanding under the line at any one time does not exceed the maximum credit. Banks usually require payout for a reasonable period of each year.

Interest is payable on the borrowed portion only. It is typical for banks to require compensating balances and/or equivalent fees. Borrowings are usually in the form of 90-day notes, which may be renewed.

The line of credit is usually confirmed in writing. The facility is considered discretionary if the phrase "officers are authorized at their discretion" is included in a confirmation letter. While availability is at the discretion of the loan officer, the accommodation represents at least a strong moral commitment to lend.

Guidance Line

A guidance line is similar to a line of credit except that the borrower is neither notified by letter nor verbally. The amount is for internal purposes only to relieve the loan officer of the necessity of obtaining individual approval for each transaction and to facilitate quick reaction to sound credit requests.

Revolving Credit

Revolving credits are formal contractual obligations in which the bank agrees to provide a stated amount of credit during a specified future period, usually for a period of from 12 months to three years. Each loan is evidenced by a note that normally has a maturity of 90 days. The amount outstanding may fluctuate up or down as the customer's needs dictate, as long as the total outstanding at any one time does not exceed the maximum credit. Because of the relatively long time period, revolving credits are supported by signed loan agreements.

One normal use of revolving credits is to finance working capital requirements, much as some companies use lines of credit. These more formal arrangements provide greater assurance that the funds will be there when needed and have a longer period of availability.

Revolving Credit/Term Loan

Many revolving credit agreements contain an option allowing the company to convert the credit into a term loan at maturity. Although there are exceptions, seven years seems to be a frequent maximum time for these arrangements, with various combinations of revolving credits and term loans allowed, such as two and five years or three and four years. Although funds might be provided for up to seven years, a repayment schedule does begin when the term loan option begins. In addition, the bank's term loan commitment is usually limited to the amount converted at the maturity of the revolving credit, even if it is less than the initial commitment.

This type of arrangement might be used for seasonal borrowing, but it is more appropriately used for longer-term needs. For instance, if a firm has a need for intermediate-term financing to finance a series of equipment purchases but is unsure as to the timing and/or the amount of funds required, this arrangement provides a helpful service. The company borrows the funds when and as needed over the period of the revolving credit. At the end of this period, it then converts the needed amount into a term loan.

Loan Agreement

For revolvers, the bank(s) and borrower negotiate to establish the terms and conditions under which the borrower obtains funds. The document(s) used to establish these terms and conditions is a loan agreement. Essential to the creation of effective loan agreements are the affirmative and negative covenants, which specify what the borrower must and must not do to comply with the agreement. Covenants may require regular submission of financial statements, maintenance of certain financial ratios, net worth and working capital minimums, limits on total borrowings, payment of dividends, capital expenditures, etc. In the event of default the bank, at its option, may (1) waive either temporarily or permanently, the condition that has been violated or (2) accelerate the maturity of the loan and demand payment.

CONCLUSION

In conclusion, when a company requests a seasonal loan or line of credit, the skilled lender thoroughly analyzes the company's financials, industry, and management to determine the underlying cause or causes of the borrowing need. Based on the stated reason, the customer may think that he can repay the loan quickly. However, other factors, such as sales growth, poor short-term asset management, or low profitability, could delay repayment.

It is wise for the banker to determine the full amount of the company's borrowing needs at the outset. Then the banker should loan the company either (1) the full amount that it needs with an attainable repayment schedule or (2) nothing.

CHAPTER FORTY-NINE

Asset Based Lending

John B. Logan

Senior Vice President
Barnett Bank

The purpose of this chapter is threefold. First, we will discuss the fundamental differences between asset based lending and more traditional forms of secured commercial lending. Second, we will discuss the various credit administration and monitoring techniques used by asset based lenders. Third, we will discuss various considerations used in the analysis of accounts receivable and inventory as a basis for collateralizing loans.

For the purpose of discussion, we will confine the scope of asset based lending to its more traditional use—namely, providing working capital lines of credit secured by current assets. Additional services that normally come under the umbrella of asset based lending, such as leasing, leveraged buyouts, and secured term lending, are discussed in other chapters.

FUNDAMENTAL DIFFERENCE

One of the easiest ways to illustrate the fundamental differences between asset based lending and conventional commercial lending is reviewing the sources of loan repayment.

In conventional commercial lending the primary source of loan repayment is earnings; conversion of collateral is a secondary source. The determination of the earnings capacity is measured using various analysis techniques based on a company's past performance. If we applied the same analysis to an asset based customer, the conclusion would demonstrate an inability to repay a loan based on earnings. The lender then shifts his focus on asset conversion as the primary source of repayment and earnings as a secondary source. This reversal of repayment source does not imply that asset based lenders are lenders of last resort, accommodating companies that have declining trends or are not "bankable." What it does suggest is that asset based lending provides a vehicle to address that spectrum of the middle market that falls below conventional standards. Emerging undercapitalized companies with insufficient track records, high-growth companies that have outstripped their capacity to fund their growth internally and have thus leveraged their balance sheets, and, of course, the current phenomenon of leveraged buyouts are all ideal candidates for asset based lending.

METHODS OF MONITORING COLLATERAL

If we then focus on the collateral, namely accounts receivable and inventory, we are faced with financing the most volatile collateral on a company's balance sheet. These assets by nature are designated to turn and earn for the company and, as a result, are constantly changing in both nature and substance. In order to maintain proper collateral to loan values, lenders must have monitoring tools available that will evaluate these ever-changing assets. To accomplish this, several methods are used.

Initial Exams

First is the use of initial exams. These are onsight reviews of a prospective borrower's books and records as well as physical inspections of a company's facilities. Included in the exams are such areas as financial analysis, cash flow analysis, internal controls, taxes and insurance, and, of course, collateral analysis. The main objective at this point is to learn as much as possible about a company and its operations, as well as collateral values, to determine if the loan is feasible and to structure the accommodation in the best possible way. It is here that collateral eligibility and prudent advance percentages are determined. Basically, the lender is determining whether the loan will work and if the bank should go ahead with funding.

If the loan is funded, additional monitoring tools are employed as a means of gauging the collateral value and overall health of the company on an ongoing basis. Reporting formats include the submission of monthly financial statements, agings of accounts receivable and accounts payable, inventory certifications, or other information that the lender may deem necessary. Other more frequent reporting formats are those used when requesting draws or paydowns on the line. Included in these reports might be copies of invoices, bills of lading, or other evidences of sale and shipment that would assist the lender in determining value.

Periodic Exams

Another monitoring tool employed is the use of periodic exams. These are on-site reviews of a customer's books, records, and physical facilities to ensure that what has been reported to the lender is being recorded in like fashion on the customer's books. In addition, other items such as taxes, insurance, receipts, disbursements, loans, and notes are also reviewed to give an indication of the company's health on an ongoing basis. Granted, the lender is receiving financial statements from the borrower on a regular basis, but the periodic audit attempts to get behind the numbers to ensure that collateral values are being maintained and that no material adverse conditions have occurred that might jeopardize the lender's position.

Cash Collateral or Agency Accounts

Another monitoring tool is the use of cash collateral or agency accounts, which are depository accounts set up to receive the proceeds of the accounts receivable. These proceeds are used to reduce the loan in total. Not only does the cash collateral account help ensure the repayment of the loan, it also by nature produces a pure revolving line. As sales increase, so does the line. As payments are received, the line is automatically reduced.

Confirmation Requests

Another monitoring tool is the use of confirmation requests. These can be either positive or negative in nature and are sent out randomly to have debtors confirm account receivable balances. Confirmation requests provide the lender with arm's-length independent verification of accounts receivable beyond the direct customer-bank relationship.

Documents

A final form of monitoring or control is found in the documents executed for the loan. The use of the Uniform Commercial Code, as well as loan and security agreements, give the lender a broad range of remedies should a default occur.

ACCOUNTS RECEIVABLE FINANCING

When analyzing accounts receivable as a source of collateral two considerations must constantly be evaluated—the willingness and ability of account debtors to pay. If these two considerations are positive, the probability of accounts receivable converting to cash remains high. If either or both considerations deteriorate, the probability diminishes rapidly.

In conjunction with these considerations, the lender must analyze three additional areas. These three areas—receivable management practices, establishing proper advance rates, and determination of eligible collateral—support the lender in maintaining a positive willingness and ability of the account debtors to pay.

Receivable Management Practices

As was previously mentioned, current assets, because of their ever-changing nature, are some of the most volatile collateral on a company's balance sheet. In many respects, effective receivable management practices affect the overall quality of accounts receivable and thus the willingness and ability to pay. Although no two companies are alike, lenders must feel comfortable in the quality of credit investigation procedures utilized by borrowers when evaluating new customers. Second, an analysis of collection procedures for normal past-due accounts and problem accounts must establish a comfort level that a company is maintaining firm control over its receivables. Third, a review of a company's internal controls should reveal adequate accounting controls and management information in the handling of accounts receivable.

Advance Rates

Advance rates must serve two functions. They must provide for adequate cash flow for the borrower and provide adequate protection for the lender. One aspect of protecting the lender is providing for downside costs of collection, which is a consideration in any secured loan transaction. Another aspect is to provide absorption for dilution in the receivables on a continual basis.

Virtually no company receives 100 percent of each sales dollar back in the form of cash. Lenders however, when financing accounts receivable, are asked to advance a certain percentage of sales without knowing whether the amount advanced (i.e., 80 percent) will convert to enough cash to retire the original advance. In order to understand the quality of a receivables portfolio, one must understand the amounts and causes for portfolio dilution. Only then can a proper advance rate be selected for a particular borrower. Some causes for portfolio dilution are positive in nature, such as prepayments, various allowances and industry practices, and the offering of discounts. Other causes are negative in nature, such as bad debts, returned merchandise, product liability, or warranty claims. An abundance of negative causes, such as bad debts, might indicate poor receivables management practices.

Whatever the causes, the lender must know how dilution is occurring in a given portfolio and be able to measure it on a continual basis to ensure that the advance rate selected and ultimate loan are protected by a receivables base that will convert to a like amount of cash.

Determination of Eligible Accounts Receivable

Once an advance rate has been selected, the lender must analyze the final ingredient for a successful receivables loan. We need to know which receivables, if any, we are not going to lend against. Certain types of receivables by their very nature carry a higher degree of risk relative to the willingness and ability of account debtors to pay. Some of the more common high-risk receivables are as follows:

Contra-accounts.   Contra-accounts usually arise in situations where the borrower both sells to and purchases from the account debtor. The possibility of direct offset against these accounts always exists.

Affiliate Accounts.   Unlike contra-accounts, affiliate accounts exist when a borrower sells to an account debtor, both of whom are linked by common ownership. Forgiveness of debt on behalf of the affiliate can always affect the conversion of the receivable.

Margin Accounts.   These are accounts with more than 50 percent of the total balance past due. Collectability could be doubtful.

Foreign Accounts.   Many foreign countries do not recognize the Uniform Commercial Code (UCC), and, as a result, a lender's security interest could be in jeopardy should a dispute arise.

Concentration Accounts.   Such accounts involve a situation in which a high and usually unhealthy percentage of a concern's total sales are made to a single customer. Too many sales, even to a good creditworthy customer, could ultimately spell disaster should disputes arise on product or contract.

Bonded Accounts.   In cases where accounts receivable are covered by a payment and performance bond, the right of a surety, in cases of dispute, could preempt the rights of secured parties covered under a UCC filing.

Past-Due Accounts.   Collection could be doubtful.

Bill and Hold Sales.   This occurs when merchandise ordered by a buyer is ready for shipment and actually billed but is held by the seller pending shipping instructions by the buyer. Bill and hold sales are not fully executed transactions. Without evidence of acceptance on behalf of the buyer, a secured party's claim could be of little value.

Progress Billings.   Progress billings involve invoices issued after partial completion of a contract, usually on a percentage basis. Progress billing is common in the construction business and other industries where long-term contracts are used. Failure to complete a contract could jeopardize the value of progress receivables.

Guaranteed Sales.   Usually associated with seasonal product lines with automatic buy-back provisions, these types of sales generally have high levels of returned merchandise.

Government Accounts.   Under the Assignment of the Claims Act of 1940, assignments of government accounts, which are accounts receivable owing by the United States or any of its departments, will not be recognized by the government unless the secured party gives written notice as specified in the act.

INVENTORY FINANCING

If the watchwords of receivables financing are willingness and ability to pay, the watchwords of inventory financing are marketability and accessibility.

As a general rule, inventory financing is more difficult than receivables financing, and, as a result, it carries lower advance rates. By its nature, receivables information is transmitted outside the confines of a borrower's place of business; as a result, it can be monitored via long distance. Additionally, accounts receivable generally have a higher predictability of value over inventory.

When evaluating inventory, having a firm understanding of marketability in all the various inventory stages is the key to a successful inventory loan.

The more commodity-like raw materials appear, the broader the marketability as a separately financed collateral component. Conversely, the more proprietary-like raw materials appear, the more marketability diminishes, and so does the ability to sell the goods beyond a very narrow user base.

Although we have all heard that work in process is a component of inventory that should not be financed, lenders generally end up financing this component unknowingly when financing raw materials inventory. What is extremely important to understand in the total inventory make up is the length of time and cost of taking work in process inventory to its finished goods state. From the point of view of marketability, we may not have a buyer for 12,000 shirts with one sleeve, but we may have multiple buyers for the finished product.

Knowing the work-in-process conversion time and cost provides great insight in the cost of administering inventory as collateral and thus assists in establishing a prudent advance rate.

Some additional factors affecting marketability and thus advance rates are:

- *Obsolescence*—which could mean not only merchandise no longer in demand but also an oversupply.
- *Seasonal goods*—knowing the seasonal peaks and valleys and costs associated with these *seasonal variations.*
- *Style products*—goods of this nature represent greater volatility in terms of potential obsolescence.

Two other areas a lender must analyze is the ease or difficulty, in terms of costs, of liquidating inventory in multiple locations. Coupled with location is the cost of maintaining certain inventory in a salable state, such as food stuffs that require refrigeration. These again are costs that should affect what a lender is willing to advance.

Assessing marketability of inventory based on the above criteria is an exercise that must be addressed constantly. From the day a loan is made, a lender must have a plan of extricating himself and should review the plan based on general economic conditions, general industry conditions, and the actual state of the inventory collateral supporting the loan.

The other side of the inventory lending equation is accessibility. If we cannot access our collateral, then all the liquidation plans become meaningless. In conjunction with accessibility, the lender must maintain a vigilance against those types of actions that can preempt a lenders security interest and thus eliminate any potential value that may exist in the inventory collateral. The more common actions come under the following headings:

- *Possessory liens*—Landlord liens are a common example of possessory liens and call for the issuance of landlord waivers if possible.

- *Nonpossessory liens*—This type of lien is best illustrated by purchase money security interest usually filed by trade suppliers against their customers.
- *Secret liens*—Tax liens are examples of secret liens. If a borrower develops financial problems, periodic lien searches should be performed to ensure that a loss of collateral does not occur.

CONCLUSION

Asset based lending, although a specialized form of commercial lending, derives its nature from the market served and not the collateral loaned against. It is an area of lending that recognizes traditional risks and mitigates those risks using a series of monitoring techniques. The collateral supporting asset based loans is the same found in any conventional commercial loan and in many respects should receive the same analysis no matter which environment a loan is housed in. What needs to be remembered in the select area of current asset financing is the volatility of the collateral coupled with its ever-changing nature. If the lender depends on the collateral for payment, then vigilance in maintaining collateral to loan ratios is constant. The methods described in this chapter are only tools available to assist the lender in this process. It is obviously the worst-case scenario that the lender must ultimately guard against and plan for.

Longer Term Lending

Donald S. Redding

Senior Vice President
NCNB National Bank

Longer term lending by the banking industry continues to grow in importance. This chapter will concentrate on techniques for analyzing the ability of a borrower to repay long-term debt, use this analysis in the discussion of proper structuring and use of term loans, and then discuss the place of collateral, loan agreements, and pricing in term loan financing.

EVALUATING ABILITY TO REPAY LONG-TERM DEBT

Use of Formulas

The main source of funds to repay longer term financing is an increase in equity of a borrower primarily through aftertax earnings. If equity does not increase, the debt will be shifted elsewhere on the liability side of the balance sheet, and no net reduction will occur in liabilities unless assets are liquidated which, in a growing company, would need replacement later. Many formula methods are available for viewing ability to repay, and each has different components that contribute to its usefulness, but for repayment of longer term debt the most important component is contribution to equity through earnings.

Several different formula approaches are discussed below, and the appendix illustrates their use in more details.

Some of the methods for evaluating the funds available to service term loans involve:

1. The bankers cash flow concept referred to in this chapter as FATSATL—funds available to service additional term loans.
2. CASHFLOW statement and source and uses of funds analysis.

689

3. The years' coverage concept.
4. Other indices.

Whereas all of these methods are somewhat different, they do have much in common, and any indices should lead to similar conclusions if they are appropriate indications of the ability of a borrower to repay debt.

Depreciation is important in analyzing the ability of a borrower to repay term loans. Little argument will be generated by the statement that "depreciation is a source of funds"; differences of opinion come from interpretation of this concept as providing funds to repay term debt. Assuming a borrower is profitable, the noncash charges that usually include primarily depreciation may be used as available to pay term debt, but often we view the depreciation as an offset to relatively small fixed asset expenditures during the period.

In actuality depreciation may not be a source of funds as much as it is a saving of cash flow. For example, renting a building at $1,000 a month uses cash for the rental payment and provides the renter with a tax deduction. If the company owned the building, then depreciation charges of $1,000 per month would result in no cash paid out but would provide the same $1,000 tax deduction. Most businesses do not own depreciable buildings outright and must make payments on a loan. To do this, part of the cash "saved" from depreciation is used to make part or all of the payment.

In analyzing ability to earn and repay, assumptions and projections are made based on information provided by customers or developed by credit officers, analysts, or loan officers. Any analysis is no better than the quality of the information or the experience levels of the loan and credit officer using the figures. Any projections, especially those reflecting a dramatic improvement, must be closely examined to determine their reasonability.

FATSATL Approach. The FATSATL approach takes into consideration funds generated through earnings and available for servicing a number of demands on those funds including repayment of *additional* term debt.

The formula is as follows:

Aftertax earnings (ATX)
+   Noncash charges (amortization, depreciation, and change in deferred taxes) (NCC)
=   Cash flow from operations (ATX + NCC)

Less: Dividends (if dividends normally have been paid by the borrower) (D)

Less: Fixed capital expenditures (usually small equipment purchases—large purchases would be a subject of financing by itself) (FX)

Less: Current maturities of long-term debt already on the books (CMLTD − AOB)

Less: Interest on the new loan (after-tax effect) (Δ INT)

Less: Increases in working capital (i.e., in the permanent level of trading assets or the net difference between current assets and current liabilities) (Δ WC)

= Funds available to service additional term loan (FATSATL)

The formula:

$$FATSATL = (ATX + NCC) - D = FX = CMLTD = INT = WC$$

In using the FATSATL approach, the selection of the aftertax earnings beginning figure is critical as with any indices. Many insurance companies use an average for the past five years, some banks use an average of the last three years, others use the current year, and some use the trend for the future. No one approach is always correct; the best approach depends on the circumstances, the economy, and the industry. Nevertheless, trends from past years can give support to projections based on reasonable assumptions.

The FATSATL formula is structured as if the current year's figures are being used—that is, the interest on the new debt is deducted as an aftertax effect. (An alternative approach is to project earnings, take into account the new interest expense, and deduct it from the before-tax earnings, and present that figure as the ATX earnings figure.)

The formula takes into account items from both the income statement and the balance sheet. From the income statement comes aftertax earnings, depreciation, amortization, dividends, and new interest. From the balance sheet comes the change in deferred tax charges, capital expenditures, and working capital (which in itself is a net presentation of sources and uses of accounts). Understanding the FATSATL approach and formula is essential in using more sophisticated analysis techniques.

Cashflow Statement and Analysis. Another method of evaluating the ability of a borrower to repay longer term debt is through the use of computer programs and a resulting CASHFLOW statement. Whereas in the previous approach the credit officer determines the amount of credit before using the formula or ratios, the computer program itself helps to develop the needs. For example, the financing for a new permanent level of trading assets is the result of establishing levels for what receivables one wants the borrower to have and then observing the resulting debt level based on assumptions for other changes in the financial statement. By continuing the projection for several years based on several variables such as sales, trading asset turnover, and payable levels, an estimate can be given as to what will happen to the level of debt for the company. The level of debt service in a rapidly expanding company may not permit reduction in long-term debts although earnings appear to be extremely strong. In short, the use of the computer CASHFLOW statement program and analysis of it provides information needed to project borrowing needs as well as repayment ability. It provides a measure, based on either historical trends or projected relationships, of the ability of a customer to generate funds needed to operate the business and to repay its debts—both short- and long-term in nature.

An explanation of each of the lines in the CASHFLOW statement is included in the example in the exhibits. A significant point is that the statement reflects the cash generated or used without consideration of the accrual concept of accounting. Depreciation is not specifically listed, rather the expenses which contain it are less by the amount of any depreciation included in them—that is, cost of goods sold is net of depreciation reported in the income statement. A resulting measure of the financing needs or surplus of the company is given based on either historical figures or projected figures, depending on which is being considered. The line below it reflects how the financing was or will be met.

This method is more sophisticated than the FATSATL approach, yet both make use of the same concept. The CASHFLOW statement has the advantage of making sure each significant item in the income statement and balance sheet are considered, whereas the FATSATL approach, which uses many of the same factors, concentrates more on the evaluation of a particular loan proposed after the structure is determined.

CASHFLOW is one in-house developed program. There are a number of similar programs available from software companies and the American Bankers Association. Any computer program such as CASHFLOW can provide the opportunity to quickly view the effects of changes in assumptions and the resulting financing needs. Lending officers often depend on credit departments to prepare computer projections, but many lending officers find that learning to use the computer is both timesaving and rewarding.

Years' Coverage Concept.   A third approach takes into account the total long-term debt of a borrower, adds to it the proposed financing, and divides the resulting figure by some measure of cash flow. The resulting figure gives an indication of the number of years necessary to repay the debt. If the years' coverage is within a normal bankable range (whatever that might be, but assuming five- to seven-year payback), then one could conclude that the company could find financing from a bank whether it is from the bank considering the request or another one—in either case, it is a "bankable" loan. If the years' coverage concept resulted in a payback period of 5.2 years, for example, then one would conclude that bank financing could be used appropriately for financing not only the new loan but loans already on the borrower's books.

One unique aspect of this approach is the inclusion of the current amount of interest projected for the first year into all years under consideration—going back approximately five years and going forward five. If one uses the same interest carry for earnings several years ago and makes adjustments based on the tax rates, and the coverage is improving to where in more recent years it is within normal bank financing terms, a banker could conclude that the borrower does have sufficient staying power to finance the debt. Also, future earnings include the same amount of interest giving even more of a trend for evaluation.

Another characteristic of this approach is that in the coverage table cash dividends and capital expenditures after the initial year are considered to be discretionary and are not included in the coverage ratios, although the worksheet for developing the financing needs would take such outflows into consideration in structuring the amount of loan needed.

WHY BANKERS NOW WANT LONGER TERM LOANS

A Historical Perspective

Initially, bank financing was limited to short loans—less than a year—because of the bank's liabilities to depositors. If depositors withdrew their money the banks would be able to get their money out of loans if they had loaned on a relatively short-term basis.

The Depression emphasized the possibility of depositors wanting their money, but the Federal Deposit Insurance Corporation and insurance of deposits alleviated much of that fear.

Banks and Expertise in Term Lending

Banks accustomed to lending short-term did not develop much expertise in long-term financing prior to World War II, and many "long-term" loans were based on the approach used for home financing. Such loans were placed on a demand basis—that is, the bank could demand repayment at any time.

Before World War II consumer finance companies successfully financed individual loans on a long-term basis. Business borrowers usually borrowed from banks for short-term purposes, borrowed from relatives for longer term uses, depended on equity capital, or issued longer term bonds. After the war pent-up demand for consumer products increased manufacturers' demands for traditional loans and for long-term financing to acquire capital assets to meet production needs. Nevertheless, even into the early 1960s, a long-term loan at a bank was considered two to three years.

In the last 20 years several things happened to encourage banks to make longer term loans. Several have been mentioned already—proof that consumers would repay, the built-up demands for longer term financing. But other forces also existed. Banks began to attract more savings deposits as interest rates were allowed to increase, and it seemed appropriate to put those supposedly long-term deposits into longer term assets as the savings and loan industry had been doing for years. It was felt that such deposits would be with a bank for a much longer period of time. As banks continued to compete and paid more for savings and time deposits, they were forced to offer financing instruments that would give a higher rate of return and such was possible with long-term financing. Competition contributed to the desire to service customers and to meet what other banks were offering.

Growth of Commercial Paper Market and Effect on Term Lending

As a more sophisticated market developed, larger companies found that the traditional short-term or seasonal loans from a bank could be obtained more cheaply through the commercial paper market, and by the early 70s, that market was an active source of funds. General Motors had extra money it found it could lend to General Electric on a relatively short-term basis. Assuming the prime rate was x percent,

General Motors would lend the money at x − 1 percent which would be a higher rate for General Electric than the x − 2 percent it could obtain from the bank through a certificate of deposit. General Electric would get the money at x − 1 percent, which would probably be less than the bank rate. As the short-term borrowing needs of larger borrowers moved to the commercial paper market, banks in the major metropolitan centers initially began moving to longer term financing and searched for other customers outside their normal banking areas. Such searching forced local banks to be more aggressive in structuring and pricing credits for their borrowers in order to compete with regional or New York banks.

The result of these trends has been the increased emphasis in commercial banks on making term loans, on making them long, and at times on making them without proper structure or analysis.

THE PLACE OF LONG-TERM LENDING IN THE PROPER STRUCTURING OF CREDIT

Proper long-term lending depends on several factors including the use of projections and pro forma statements, understanding the principles of structuring of credits, and the evaluation of ability to repay.

Pro Formas and Projections

Pro forma and projection figures are needed whether a computer is used or a lending officer does the analysis manually. Usually a pro forma statement takes the debt at a current date and adds to it changes in assets leaving a figure that reflects the amount of debt necessary. One of the problems with such an approach is that it reflects changes to a balance sheet that is several months old.

Projections take the same approach but attempt to build into the balance sheet dynamic changes that have occurred since the balance sheet date and add changes proposed in the financing. Additional projections reflect the condition at the end of future years. Both pro formas and projections help determine the level of financing a company needs.

Assets and liabilities are projected based on a number of assumptions made by the lending officer or based on information given to an officer by the borrower and subsequently modified in the credit analysis process. Certain assumptions must be made about several key ingredients in the trading cycle including the turnover of receivables, inventory, and accounts payable, since such projections are extremely important to the overall projection of needs.

Seasonal or Short-Term Debt

Much bank lending is short-term—less than a year. Historically such loans were based on a yearly cycle such as agriculture, which resulted in customers borrowing to build up inventory and receivables during a part of the year and then paying down the loan by the conversion of those assets into cash. Professor Williams at the Harvard Business School refers to this concept as a short-term self-liquidating loan.

One of the distinguishing characteristics of seasonal or short-term borrowings is that it is not necessary for a profit to be made in the cycle for funds to be available to repay the debt. For example, money can be borrowed to buy inventory, money spent to develop the inventory into work in process and later into finished inventory, the inventory sold and receivables created, and cash collected from the receivables. If it were a completely breakeven process the same amount of money would be available to pay the borrowings. The essential part of repaying a seasonal loan is the expansion of the trading assets, which gives rise to the need for the financing, and the subsequent contraction of those trading assets providing cash to repay financing. Therefore in evaluating the ability of a borrower to repay a short-term loan, the proper focus is not necessarily on profitability but on the turnover of the trading assets. However, this discussion is more theoretical than realistic because no lender wants to do business long with a customer who is not earning profits to support its growth and operation.

Longer Term Debt

On the other hand, repayment of longer term debt must come from an increase in equity or there is no net reduction in the level of term debt. Certainly over a short period of time reductions can be made. But long-run reductions are not possible unless the company is growing. There are several ways of providing equity for repayment of term debt—issuing stock, for example—but earnings are the normal method for generating increases in equity and reduction in debts.

Structuring Principle

In structuring credits, an important principle often overlooked even by experienced lending officers is that the use of the funds should indicate the repayment schedule. Too often "creative" financing encourages lenders to ignore this principle, especially if the borrower is financially strong or a good customer. Ignoring the principle often leads to unnecessary reworks of loans as well as workouts.

USES OF LONG-TERM LOANS

Long-term financing is appropriate for:

1. A permanent increase in the trading assets of receivables and inventory (or an increase in working capital, which is technically the difference between current assets and liabilities).
2. Equipment.
3. Building.
4. Acquisition of another business.
5. Restructuring of short-term debt into long-term debt or rework of long-term debt.
6. Purchase of treasury stock.

Permanent Increase in Trading Assets

For financing temporary expansions of receivables and inventory (trading assets) if the needs are seasonal, loans should be short-term. If the increase in level of trading assets is not temporary, a form of permanent capital is needed. Lending institutions are willing to provide levels of permanent capital on a temporary basis if there is the ability to repay within a five- to seven-year time period. In other words, if an initial expansion raises a permanent level of trading assets, lending institutions have elected to finance that permanent increase as long as the replacement capital over a reasonable period of time provides the funds for repaying the loan.

Therefore, the purpose of the loan for increasing the level of trading assets is more long-term in nature than a seasonal loan, its benefits will accrue over a longer period of time, and such loans should be repaid over the period being benefited.

Occasionally, it will not be clear whether the needs for expansion of trading assets or other assets are of a permanent or temporary nature. An expanding business with a need to carry trading assets might have some seasonal fluctuations, but each succeeding year there is an increase in the permanent level of trading assets. Under such conditions, a loan that does not have to be repaid on a definite basis but gives the borrower the flexibility to borrow and repay is desirable—a revolving credit. Needless to say, some senior executives refer to revolving credits as a "lazy loan officer's tool" in that the hard work of structuring the credit is not done and the decision to lend money is based more on the other reasons under consideration.

When a company does not have the earnings ability to service term debt and seasonality does not exist, yet it needs to carry a substantial level of inventory and receivables, asset based lending is used. Asset based lending relies on a borrowing base, control over the collateral, policing of collateral, and frequent audits and results in debt that fluctuates based on sales/inventory production level. Such lending, while long-term in nature, is not the subject of this chapter.

Equipment and Buildings

Other long-term assets acquired by financing include equipment and buildings. Financing equipment, again following the theory that its purpose in life should dictate the term of the loan, usually argues for a term of five to seven years, which is the normal range of financing for banks.

For financing buildings, a new set of conditions exists. Obviously the building will generate funds and provide benefit to a business for a long period of time; therefore, it is appropriate to consider financing over a long period of time. Although many buildings last 50 to 100 years, the Internal Revenue Service limits the writedown of the asset through depreciation. Correct financing suggests that the building either should be supported by equity or paid for with a term loan that would be repaid by the generation of equity over the life of the asset. Therefore, in order to structure credit effectively, a bank should be in a position to offer 20- to 30-year financing for buildings. Or, if it is felt that such financing does not meet the bank's liquidity requirements, as is usually the case, the bank should have the ability to place the loans with other traditional long-term financiers. The temptation is to finance a building in normal bank terms of less than 10 years. But, while cash flow estimates indicate ability of a borrower to pay back the loan, such financing strips a business of its ability to handle its affairs in an efficient manner and to provide for growth in trading and other assets. Also, it leads to the eventual need to refinance the building or other assets of the building over a longer period of time or additional time. Some banks are more inclined to finance long-term, and depending on the portfolio and mix of its liabilities some financing is appropriate. Nevertheless, although it might be the best structuring job for a loan officer to do in agreeing to a long-term loan, the nature of the banking business is that regulatory and policy matters limit 30-year financing.

Most surveys of policies by banks for maturity of term loans indicate a five- to seven-year range preference. There is nothing magic about this range. It appears to be the result of a middle ground between providing liquidity for the bank and meeting customers' needs for longer term financing. Thus banks are forced into a middle ground between extremely long-term loans and the historically short-term ones they previously handled.

Balloon balances often are used by some lending officers to keep the final maturity of a loan within bank terms. For example if a customer needs a 25-year loan and the bank's policy is a maximum of 10 years, the account officer might decide to make a loan with a 20- to 25-year amortization schedule with a balloon payment due at the end of the 10th year. The advantages of this technique is that it enables the bank to renegotiate the transaction based on the customer's relationship with the lender at the time. The disadvantage is that the customer is unsure if the financing will be continued.

Acquisition of Another Business

This use of funds has characteristics of all of the uses described above. Often the increased debt will strain the earnings ability of the acquiring company and require analysis of future trends. When earnings do not appear to be available yet the company does have a desirable financial condition, asset based lending provides an appropriate source of financing for a portion of the acquisition. Some bankers use the more conservative approach that the acquiring company should be able to finance the acquisition without relying on the company acquired. While this test is conservative, it is a good starting point in an overall evaluation.

Restructure

At times short-term loans must be reworked into longer term loans either because of incorrect initial analysis or changes in condition. At other times longer term loans must be reworked. Either situation requires the same analysis as a new long-term loan.

Purchase of Treasury Stock

Because of the availability of its own stock from shareholders, companies at times are in a position to repurchase it. Conditions vary as to why such stock is available—from a drop in its market value at a time when the company has or can arrange funds for its purchase to acquiring the interest of a deceased principal in a business. At such times, if long-term financing is needed, the structuring entails the same analysis as for other long-term uses. Pro formas and projections are especially important to reflect the increase in debt, decrease in equity, and resulting heavier financial condition. Also if the stock of a deceased principal is being acquired, the effect on the business of the absence of the principal must be considered.

Other Purposes and Structuring with the Use of Revolving Credits

Revolving credits are long-term financing tools that have become more popular in recent years. As mentioned above secured asset based revolving credits are useful when a borrower has little seasonality or limited ability to service term loans through profits. Another type of revolving credit is used in financing stronger companies often worthy of unsecured credit. This revolving credit facility often is provided to expanding companies with good earnings until the extent of short-term and long-term needs are established. Often analysis of the credit request indicates the proper structuring of such a credit into short-term and long-term categories, but the company is willing to pay extra to make sure funds are available to be used when needed.

Such a revolving credit normally is approved for a two- or three-year period with either a funding requirement at the end of the revolving period or a provision that the full amount of the credit be paid. The provisions of the revolving credit often provide that the credit continue to revolve during the two- to three-year period unless provisions of the loan agreement are violated. A fee is usually charged by the bank in the 1/4 to 1/2 percent range on the unused portion of the revolver. Often borrowers choose to increase their loan during the revolving period and to extend the final maturity or beginning amortization period, giving the facilities a permanent nature. While such revolving credit facilities have been criticized because of this permanent nature, they can be viewed the same as a regular term loan if the borrower has the ability to amortize the debt over the period of time covered by the revolving term as well as the amortization period. If a bank normally makes term loans in the seven-year category, then it might choose to offer a revolving credit facility of three years followed by an amortization period of four. Assuming the borrower does have the underlying financial earning ability to service the debt with a normal growth in its operations, such financing can be appropriate even if rolled over or extended each year. The critical factor here, however, is whether the borrower has the earnings ability to support the payout in a less expansive period.

The danger with using such a facility is that the structuring of the credit is often analyzed improperly and a determination is not made as to whether the borrower can service the facility over a reasonable payback period. Often revolving credits are provided by banks because the borrower is financially strong enough to demand it, competition will provide it, or the lending bank feels the risk is acceptable.

Nevertheless, such structuring of revolving credits can lead to difficulties if the underlying earnings power is not present.

PRICING OF TERM LOANS

Deciding how to price a loan for a borrower is both an art and a science. Whereas banks know what overall return they desire, accomplishing that return can be an art. Pricing can be the result of a combination of borrowings, deposit balances maintained, other services sold to the customer, the cost of the delivery system to the customer, and other tangible and intangible aspects of the relationship. One method of determining pricing is to take into account as many aspects of a relationship as possible, cost and price them, and evaluate the return on capital or assets.

Assumptions must be made based on discussions with the borrower and with the historical trends in arriving at conclusions about what the future will hold. For example, a company that historically maintained high balances and anticipated doing so in the future would be entitled to obtain a lower rate from the bank. On the other hand, a company with extremely low balances might be able to convince a lender that a low rate was appropriate in its situation based on potential for new business, the financial strength of the borrower, or related business. Tying all of these assumptions together is an art although we try—through science, with computers, and other methods—to help us in evaluations.

Usually term loans are priced at a higher rate than short-term loans. Prior to the advent of floating rate loans, such pricing on a fixed basis was to compensate for the additional interest risk of uncertainty in the future. As tremendous swings occurred in prime rate over the last 20 years, bankers became increasingly reluctant on term loans to offer fixed-rate financing. They did not feel capable of projecting with any certainty over a five- to seven-year period what would happen to interest rates. For relatively shorter periods of time, one to three years, many bankers felt comfortable in pricing fixed-rate loans, but because of the unique demands of the banking industry such pricing at fixed rates for longer loans was not desirable.

Another reason for higher rates on longer term financing is that a lender does not have control over the use of its funds even though a loan agreement may be drawn. With seasonal borrowings, the lender has several opportunities during a year to discuss changes with a borrower. With long-term loans, if the loan agreement is not breached, changes can occur in a borrower's business over which the lender has no control.

Most loans continue to be priced based on the prime rate despite repeated forecasts of its disappearance from use. Primarily because of legal action involving prime rate definitions and borrowers, the current definition used most is "the rate established by the bank as its prime rate." Definitions used in the past, which include "best rate" or "lowest rate," have caused the banking industry problems when it was shown that the prime rate was not the lowest rate paid by customers (because of fixed-rate loans where prime subsequently increased, rates limited by state statutes, etc.). Most of the difficulties developed with borrowers paying prime plus x percent instead of straight prime borrowers.

Nevertheless, because it is well known, the prime rate is used in pricing many larger term loans.

Whereas a rate to the best seasonal borrower might be at the prime rate, a rate to the same borrower for a longer term loan could be at least prime plus 1/4 to 1/2—not much of a spread to compensate for the difference in nature of the lending instrument.

Part of the theory for charging a higher rate on long-term financing is, of course, the uncertainty mentioned earlier but also the effort of a bank to set up, evaluate, and structure long-term financing which is more difficult than short-term. Even if an ironclad loan agreement is drawn, the trauma and difficulties that develop if a borrower defaults cannot be compensated for by the higher rate charged in terms of effort and collection activity.

One of the difficulties with prime plus a fixed amount pricing is that such pricing does not charge the same relative amount for a loan when rates are higher and lower. For example, assuming a prime rate of 6 percent and a prime plus 1/2 percent rate gives a rate above prime of 8.3 percent. Whereas the same rate with a prime of 10 percent results in an additional amount above prime of only 5 percent. To compensate for this, some banks used financing such as 105 percent of prime. A 105 percent of prime rate when the prime rate is 6 percent gives a 6.3 percent, resulting in a 5 percent higher rate than prime whereas at 10 percent the same formula would give a rate of 10.5 percent, which is, of course, the exact amount of the difference when prime was 6 percent.

Other types of pricing even on long-term financing give customers the ability to price at a rate tied to LIBOR, the CD rate, the Treasury bill rate, or some other external force. Some pricing gives the borrower the option of selecting for a coming period of several months which method of pricing is desirable.

USE OF COLLATERAL AND GUARANTEES IN TERM FINANCING

Collateral and guarantees can serve an important function in term lending, but primarily as a "fall back" position if earnings and cash flow are not available to support repayment. Term loans should be structured without repayment depending on the liquidation of collateral, but such structuring should not cause laxity in perfecting any collateral pledged.

Depending on laws in different states, the presence of collateral can slow the ability of a lender to collect in a distressed situation—for example, if a court rules that the building pledged to a loan must first be foreclosed and sold before a claim can be made on other assets of the business. A defense can be raised by the borrower that the property was not sold at a fair price, even if appraisals of the seller support the price, and the courts may disallow the sale or any deficiency against the borrowers. In other secured situations, improper filing or documentation can hurt the ability of the lender to pursue legal remedies. Many other examples are well known to lenders, and it is essential when structuring credits that term lending look to the ability of the borrower to repay from earnings generated in the normal course of business. Collateral can be valuable in term lending, but relying on it as the main support for a loan can have discouraging results, especially if any collateral pleged is not properly recorded, filed, and documented.

Historical performance in earnings is helpful in viewing the ability of the borrower to service future term debt, and when such information is available it is critical and helpful in coming to conclusions about the borrower's ability to repay. On the other hand, many situations involve either startup or companies with no history to indicate what their future earnings power will be other than projections. Assuming that other matters including evaluation of management are satisfactory, the fallback position of collateral becomes even more important in evaluating the start-up loan.

Often in lending, the guarantees of principals are requested for relatively small loans, but as the size of the credit increases, this request often disappears. Lending officers have learned that a guarantee is good psychological help but does not automatically ensure that the guarantor will immediately repay a debt or that the lender will have access to the assets of the guarantor without strong legal action.

In short, lending against collateral or with guarantees can help strengthen a credit, but when lenders have to use these avenues to collect their loans, many difficulties can arise.

TERM LOAN AGREEMENTS

To help give control over the borrower's use of the lender's money and to let the borrower know specifically what is expected of him in exchange, loan agreements with specific terms have been developed. Surveys of bankers indicate that most term loan agreements are used in most cases today whereas 20 years ago a term loan was subject only to the conditions of the note.

Content of Agreements

Unfortunately, many loan agreements have turned into extremely long and legalistic documents that appear to hide the essential purpose of a loan agreement. Usually there are a handful of provisions a banker is concerned about covering and much of the rest of the verbiage in loan agreements is boiler plate and applicable to many loan agreements. Usually bankers are primarily interested in establishing financial ratios, an understanding of what types of financial statements will be provided to the banks, that the management or business will not be sold or changed dramatically, and that a certification is given that all aspects of the loan agreement are in compliance. Loan agreements frequently are double spaced, which adds to their intimidating look, or are crowded into small print on a minimum number of pages. Business term loan agreements still continue to be worded more legalistically than colloquially in contrast to consumer instruments, which are often written in everyday language.

While an understanding of the various provisions in a loan agreement is important to the banker, this chapter will not discuss the subject in more detail than to refer to Exhibit 5, which is a sample of provisions in loan agreements by borrowing customer sorted with the strongest customer listed first. As one would expect, the number and restrictiveness of provisions increase as the credit rating drops. Although this summary was prepared several years ago, it can be an extremely valuable reference when drafting specialized loan agreements.

Negotiating and Drafting Agreements

Several approaches exist for negotiating and discussing term loan agreements with bank customers, ranging from a printed form to a completely customized agreement. Usually preprinted agreements are used with relatively small and uncomplicated loans, and they provide coverage of many necessary items without the time requirement of negotiating needed protection. A sample of a simple loan agreement is included at the end of this chapter. For more complicated credits, a checklist or outline of the agreement is given to the customer and discussed with him prior to formally drafting the documents.

While lending officers should negotiate and determine provisions desirable to the bank, attorneys should be used in drafting the final agreement. Some banks have in-house staff lawyers to help with agreements, but most bankers rely on outside attorneys at the customer's expense. Many account officers, however, draw their own agreement based on their expertise and experience.

Ensuring Compliance with Agreements

Following up on compliance with loan agreements is important but often neglected in some banks. Alternative methods for followup include:

1. By account officers.
2. By credit department.
3. By loan review.
4. By other methods.

No matter what system is used, a checklist of items to review for compliance is helpful. Such a checklist eliminates the need to completely reread the loan agreement each time a statement is received. For example, the minimum financial ratios may be added to the checklist when it is drafted and the actual ratios added beside the figures as they become available. In ensuring compliance with the loan agreement, one of the most effective devices is to include a provision in the agreement in which the company's auditors will certify that the company is in agreement with the provisions. To be able to give this certification, the CPAs will encourage management to take any necessary action to ensure compliance. Otherwise, the CPA will be obligated in many cases to move the term loan into a current category because a default exists that makes the term loan callable on demand. To prevent this scenario, management of the borrower often is more inclined to take the necessary required action. Often, to correct a provision that is not in agreement, the bank will be asked to waive or modify it; at least the system is working effectively in notifying the bank when its provisions are not being followed.

CONCLUSIONS AND SUMMARY

Term lending has grown in importance in the banking industry for many reasons. With its growth has come the need to closely analyze the ability of a borrower to generate an increase in equity through earnings as a repayment source for the term loans. Different analytical techniques are available for analyzing the ability to repay from the basic bankers' cash flow analysis to computer-prepared scenarios. But all of them depend on the borrower's ability to operate profitably and the ability of the analyst to project such earnings. Collateral, guarantees, and term loan agreements can help make a good loan better, but they are no substitute for proper structuring.

APPENDIX
ILLUSTRATIONS OF FORMULA APPROACHES

EXHIBIT 1 FATSATL Example

In this example, a borrower needs $700,000 and has a cash flow of $342,000. The formula below takes into account other sources of funds and uses determined by analysis or conversation with the company. The company already had a $1 million term loan.

$ Million

A		B
	Before interest earnings	450
	New interest (10% × 700M)	− 70
450	Before-tax earnings	380
−148	Taxes @ 33%	−125
302	ATX earnings [ATX]	255
+ 40	Noncash charges [NCC]	+ 40
342	Cash flow	295
− 10	Dividends [D]	− 10
− 47	New interest (10% × $700M × aftertax rate reciprocal) [Δ INT ×]	
− 45	CMLTD AOB (on LTD of $1MM) [CMLTD]	− 45
− 30	Fixed capital expenditures [FX]	− 30
− 55	Increase working capital [Δ WC]	− 55
187	Total "uses"	140
155	FATSATL	155

"A" represents actual figures—before new financing. It deducts the new interest before cash flow at the aftertax equivalent.

"B" is the same as "A" except that the new interest is deducted before reaching the taxable earnings.

In the example, one could conclude that a loan could be made because FATSATL of $155,000 would service a five-year of $775,000 ($155,000 × 5) or seven years of $1,085,000 ($155,000 × 7).

This analysis, as any, depends on the quality of the information and reasonableness of projections.

EXHIBIT 2 "CASHFLOW" Statement Computer Analysis

In this example, expansion of fixed assets, receivables, inventory and other assets are planned to support rapid sales growth over the next few years. Based on the projections of sales levels and turnover ratios, the resulting debt levels increased rapidly with bank financing—short- and long-term increasing—supported by expansion of trade debt.

Needless to say, a credit officer analyzing the company's needs would closely evaluate the reliability of the sixfold increase in sales in five years. The advantage of this or any other computer-prepared projections is the ability to vary assumptions easily.

BASE CASE

NCNB CREDIT DEPARTMENT

FIGURES IN THOUSANDS
CURRENCY: DOLLARS

PFT CTR: 00261
ANALYST:

FINANCIAL STATEMENTS	1984 31-Dec UNAUDR	1985 31-Dec UNAUDR	1986 31-Dec PROJECT	1987 31-Dec PROJECT	1988 31-Dec PROJECT	1989 31-Dec PROJECT	1990 31-Dec PROJECT
NO. MONTHS IN FISCAL PERIOD:	12	12	12	12	12	12	12
>>MASTER<<							
>>CASHFLOW STATEMENT<<							
NET SALES	16381.6	22202.9	29973.9	41963.5	58748.9	82248.5	115147.9
CSH EFF FROM CHANGE IN REC	−3.4	−7.5	−0.4	−6.0	−8.4	−11.7	−16.4
CASH RECEIPTS	16378.2	22195.4	29973.5	41957.5	58740.5	82236.8	115131.5
CASH COST OF GOODS SOLD	−11873.4	−15897.6	−21635.6	−30289.8	−42405.7	−59368.1	−83115.3
CSH EFF FROM CHANGE IN INV	−134.0	−220.6	−540.5	−574.6	−804.4	−1126.2	−1576.6
CSH EFF FROM CHANGE IN A/P	508.3	185.0	305.5	569.1	796.6	1115.4	1561.4
CASH PRODUCTION COSTS	−11499.1	−15933.2	−21870.6	−30295.3	−42413.5	−59378.9	−83130.5
GROSS CASH PROFITS	4879.1	6262.2	8102.9	11662.2	16327.0	22857.9	32001.0

EXHIBIT 2 *(continued)*

NCNB CREDIT DEPARTMENT

BASE CASE

FIGURES IN THOUSANDS
CURRENCY: DOLLARS

PFT CTR: 00261
ANALYST:

FINANCIAL STATEMENTS

	1984 31-Dec UNAUDR	1985 31-Dec UNAUDR	1986 31-Dec PROJECT	1987 31-Dec PROJECT	1988 31-Dec PROJECT	1989 31-Dec PROJECT	1990 31-Dec PROJECT
NO. MONTHS IN FISCAL PERIOD:	12	12	12	12	12	12	12
》MASTER《							
》CASHFLOW STATEMENT《							
CASH G & A EXPENSE	-3964.3	-5430.1	-7243.5	-10190.9	-14337.2	-20162.1	-28337.0
CHANGE IN DEFERRED CHARGES	6.4	-16.3	0.0	0.0	0.0	0.0	0.0
CHANGE IN OPERATING ACCRUALS	88.4	187.1	0.0	0.0	0.0	0.0	0.0
CASH OPERATING EXPENSE	-3869.5	-5259.3	-7243.5	-10190.9	-14337.2	-20162.1	-28337.0
CASH AFTER OPERATIONS	1009.6	1002.9	859.4	1471.3	1989.8	2695.8	3664.0
OTHER INCOME/EXPENSE	-13.2	44.4	0.0	0.0	0.0	0.0	0.0
NET OTHER CURRENT B.S. CHANGES	-59.8	0.0	0.0	0.0	0.0	0.0	0.0
NET OTHER DEFERRED B.S. CHANGES	1.5	0.0	0.0	0.0	0.0	0.0	0.0
NET CASH AFTER OPERATIONS	938.1	1047.3	859.4	1471.3	1989.8	2695.8	3664.0
INCOME TAX EXPENSE	-13.5	-35.9	-26.9	-36.8	-51.8	-75.8	-112.2
CHANGE IN DEFERRED TAXES	12.7	9.3	0.0	0.0	0.0	0.0	0.0
CHANGE IN ACCRUED INCOME TAX	0.8	15.9	0.0	0.0	0.0	0.0	0.0
INCOME TAXES PAID	0.0	-10.7	-26.9	-36.8	-51.8	-75.8	-112.2

INTEREST EXPENSE	-127.2	-108.7	-135.3	-211.8	-289.1	-318.6	-284.7
CASH DIVIDENDS	-100.0	-300.0	-341.3	-298.9	-420.8	-615.6	-911.6
CASH FINANCING COSTS	-227.2	-408.7	-476.6	-510.7	-709.9	-934.2	-1196.3
NET CASH INCOME	710.9	627.9	355.9	923.8	1228.1	1685.8	2355.5
CURRENT PORTION LTD/CAP. LEASES	-97.0	-160.4	-210.2	-143.0	-143.0	-143.0	-143.0
CASH AFTER DEBT AMORTIZATION	613.9	467.5	145.7	780.8	1085.1	1542.8	2212.5
NET CAPITAL EXPENDITURES	-396.2	-751.3	-1200.0	-1600.0	-1600.0	-1600.0	-1600.0
CHANGE IN DUE FROM/DUE TO AFFILATES	0.0	0.0	0.0	0.0	0.0	0.0	0.0
CHANGE IN INTANGIBLES	-1.4	0.8	0.0	0.6	0.0	0.0	0.0
CHANGE IN DUE FROM/TO OFF., STKHLDR	0.0	0.0	0.0	0.0	0.0	0.0	0.0
NON-CASH ADJUSTMENT (SURPLUS)	0.0	0.0	0.0	0.0	0.0	0.0	0.0
FINANCING SURPLUS/(REQUIREMENTS)	216.3	-283.0	-1054.3	-818.6	-514.9	-57.2	612.5
CHANGE IN SHORT TERM DEBT	96.8	357.8	436.9	818.6	514.9	57.2	-612.5
CHANGE IN LONG TERM DEBT	-203.0	55.5	655.3	0.0	0.0	0.0	0.0
CHANGE IN EQUITY	0.0	-142.8	0.0	0.0	0.0	0.0	0.0
TOTAL EXTERNAL FINANCING	-106.2	270.5	1092.2	818.6	514.9	57.2	-612.5
CASH AFTER FINANCING	110.1	-12.5	37.9	0.0	0.0	0.0	0.0
CHANGE IN CASH AND MKT. SECURITIES	110.1	-12.5	37.9	0.0	0.0	0.0	0.0
COVERAGE RATIOS							
NCAO/INT EXP	7.4	9.6	6.4	6.9	6.9	8.5	12.9
NCAO/INT EXP + PY CM	4.2	3.9	2.5	4.1	4.6	5.8	8.6
LTD/NET CASH INCOME	0.9	0.9	2.8	0.9	0.6	0.3	0.2
LTD/NCI − NET CAP EXP	2.1	-4.5	-1.2	-1.3	-1.9	6.7	0.6

EXHIBIT 2 *(concluded)*

CASHFLOW STATEMENT – EXPLANATION

1. Net Sales — —Corresponds to Net Sales
2. Csh Eff From Chg In Rec. — —Corresponds to changes in accounts receivable (year end to year end)
3.   CASH RECEIPTS — —Lines 1 + 2

4. Cash Cost of Gds Sold — —Corresponds to cost of goods sold (Net of any depreciation in COGS reported in the income statement.)

5. Csh Eff Fr Chg In Inv — —Corresponds to changes in inventory (year end to year end)
6. Csh Eff Fr Chg In A/P — —Corresponds to changes in accounts payable(year end to year end)
7.   CASH PROD COSTS — —Lines 4 + 5 + 6
8.   GROSS CASH PROFITS — —Lines 3 + 7

9. Cash G & A Expense — —Corresponds to total expenses (Net of any depreciation in G & A reported in the income statement).

10. Change In Def Charges — —Corresponds to changes in deferred charges (year end to year end)
11. Chg In Oper Accruals — —Corresponds to changes in operating accruals (year end to year end)
12.   CASH OPERATING EXP — —Lines 9 + 10 + 11
13.   CASH AFTER OPER — —Lines 8 + 12

14. Other Income/Expense — —Corresponds to net other income and extraordinary income on the income statement.
15. Net Oth Curr B/S Chgs — —Corresponds to chgs in oth liquid assets, marketable securities, curr asset optns, other curr liabilities, and sthe curr liab optn (yr end to yr end)
16. Net Oth Def B/S Chgs — —Corresponds to changes in non-curr asset options, other deferred assets, and the non-curr liab option (yr end to yr end)
17.   NET CASH AFT OPER — —Lines 14 + 15 + 16

18. Income Tax Expense — —Corresponds to income tax expense
19. Chg in Deferred Taxes — —Corresponds to changes in deferred taxes (yr end to yr end)
20. Chg in Accrued Inc Tx — —Corresponds to changes in accrued taxes (yr end to yr end)
21.   INCOME TAXES PAID — —Lines 18 + 19 + 20

22. Interest Expense — —Corresponds to interest expense on the income statement

23.	Cash dividends	—Corresponds to preferred and common dividends
24.	CASH FINAN COSTS	—Lines 22 + 23
25.	NET CASH INCOME	—Lines 21 + 24
26.	Curr Portion LTD/CL	—Corresponds to the prior year current portions of LTD and cap leases
27.	CASH AFT DEBT AMOR	—Lines 25 + 27
28.	Net Capital Expend	—Prior year net fixed assets-depreciation expense-current year net fixed assets
29.	Chg in Due Fr/To Affl	—Corresponds to changes in due from and due to affiliates
30.	Cash Chg in Intangible	—Corresponds to cash changes (net of amortization) in intangibles and net leasehold improvements.
31.	Chg Due Fr/To Off/Stk	—Corresponds to changes in due from and to officers, stockholders (yr end to yr end).
32.	Non-Cash Adjustment	—Adjusts the cashflow for any non-cash surplus adj. and other non-cash equity adj. (ex. for currency translation adj.)
33.	FINANCING SURP/(REQ)	—Measures the remaining cash (or deficit) from internally generated sources after covering all uses
34.	Chg in short-term debt	—Corresponds to changes in short term notes payable (yr end to yr end).
35.	Chg in long-term debt	—Corresponds to chgs in LT debt, LT Port Cap Leases, Debt Sub to NCNB, and LTD Option (yr end to yr end); and the curr yr's CMLTD/CL
36.	Change in Equity	—Corresponds to chgs in pfd stock, comm stock, pd in cap eqty options (cash), treasury stock, and min int (yr end to yr end).
37.	TOTAL EXTERNAL FIN	—Lines 34 + 35 + 36
38.	Cash After Financing	—Lines 33 + 37
39.	Chg in Cash	—Corresponds to changes in cash (yr end to yr end).

COVERAGE RATIOS

NCAO/Int Exp	—Measures the coverage of interest expense by Line 17
NCAO/Int Exp + DIV + PYCM	—Measures the coverage of interest expense, dividends (adjusted to pretax dollars), and current maturities of LTD and Cap Leases (adjusted to pretax dollars).
LTD/Net Cash Income	—Measures the coverage of long-term debt by line 25.
LTD/NCI less cap. exp.	—Measures the coverage of long-term debt by line 25 less line 28.

*All numbers with a (–) sign represent a use of cash, without the sign the number is a source of cash.

711

EXHIBIT 3   Years' Coverage Concept Example

In this example, through analysis of a source and uses worksheet, it was determined that the borrower's needs included $1,650,000 for building expansion, $470,000 for receivables and inventory permanent expansion, $200,000 for dividends, $1,000,000 for refinancing a seasonal loan that did not pay out during the year, rolling a present term lown of $1,900,000 into the new loan, and a payment of $348,000 for a stock purchase.

The resulting coverage table suggests adjusted cash flow in column 9 (with depreciation included as a source of funds) and column 10 (without depreciation included as a source of funds) that in 1982 the proposed new debt and interest could have been paid in 5.7 years with adjusted net income (column 10) and 3.6 years (column 9) if depreciation is considered—well within the bankable 5- to 7-year range. Of more

Company
      Southern Packaging Corporation

COVERAGE TABLE (000's)

Fiscal Periods		(1) Net Sales	Oper. Profits Before: Deprec., Amort. & Interest Expenses		(4) Depreciation & Amortization	(5) Interest Expense
			(2) $ Amount	(3) As a % of Sales		
Yr's End. 12-31:						
Projected	1985	$44605	$5539	12.4%	$807	$750
	1984	38787	5116	13.2	810	751
	1983	33728	4538	13.5	736	726
Actual	1982	30296	3389	11.2	592	632
	1981	28155	3049	10.8	588	496
	1980	22826	2384	10.4	560	358
	1979	18921	2081	11.0	503	353
	1978	16479	1764	10.7	480	218

(A) *Note (A):* Definition of "Adjusted Net Income"
   (EBIT—Maximum Pro Forma Interest Expense) 1 − x applicable tax rate = Adjusted Net Income (important: if EBIT less Maximum Pro Forma Interest Expense is a negative figure, do not apply a tax credit. Show the full amount of the (pre tax) loss in brackets).
(B) *Note (B):* Selected Items Used In Calculation of Coverage Figures
   Total amount of "Pro Forma, Non-seasonal, Borrowed Money Debt (including CMLTD & Capitalized leases).....................(D)............................. $ 5690
   Assumed (blended) interest rate to be in effect on Pro Forma, Non-seasonal, Borrowed Money Debt during first year..... Assume.................... × 11.50%
      Maximum interest expense on Pro Forma, Non-seasonal Borrowed
   Money Debt.. $ 654
      Est interest expense on seasonal debt during first year (Include only if significant)
                                                                    $ 143
   Maximum Pro Forma Interest Expense ....(C)....................... $ 797
   Income tax rate used in calculation of Adjusted Net Income....... Assume .   50%

EXHIBIT 3 *(continued)*

significance, however, is that the same debt and interest could have been covered over the previous few years also (5.1 years, for example, with adjusted cash flow in 1980) and that the coverage for the future projected years is adequate based on the projected trends.

The conclusion is that the proposed financing appears reasonable and that the company has the ability to service the proposed financing in a reasonable number of years. Granted, not enough facts are available for a reader to fully analyze these figures, but it is hoped that enough are available to illustrate the concept of the year's coverage concept.

		Coverages				
			Years Required to Pay Off Pro Forma Nonseasonal Debt (D)			
(6) Income Taxes	(7) Net Income	(8) Adjusted Net Income (A)	(9) Adjusted Cash Flow	(10) Adjusted Net Income	(11) Cash Dividends	(12) Capital Expends
$1911	$2071	$1968	2.1 yrs	2.9 yrs	$300	$ 800
1717	1838	1569	1.4	3.6	250	600
1473	1603	1502	2.5	3.6	200	1650
1082	1083	1000	3.6	5.7	200	640
982	983	832	4.0	6.8	200	942
732	733	563	5.1	10.1	150	700
548	677	390	6.4	14.6	150	912
456	610	243	7.9	23.4	150	1000

HINTS

$$\frac{D}{(8)+(4)} = (9); \quad \frac{D}{(8)} = (10)$$

$(2) - (4) = \text{EBIT} = \text{Earnings Before Interest \& Taxes}$

$[\text{EBIT} - (C)] \times 50\% = (8)$

(8) is Adjusted Net Income

	Prepared By	Date Prepared

EXHIBIT 3 (continued)

PAYBACK TABLE

FISCAL PERIOD	(1) NET SALES	(2) OPERATING PROFITS BEFORE DEPRECIATION AMORTIZATION AND INTEREST $	(3) % OF SALES	(4) DEPRECIATION AND AMORTIZATION	(5) INTEREST EXPENSE	BEFORE INCOME TAXES	TAX RATE	(6) INCOME TAXES	(7) NET INCOME
1985	44605	5539	12.4%	807	750	3982	48.0%	1911	2071
1984	38787	5116	13.2%	810	751	3555	48.3%	1717	1838
1983	33728	4538	13.5%	736	726	3076	47.9%	1473	1603
1982	30296	3389	11.2%	592	632	2165	50.0%	1083	1083
1981	28155	3049	10.8%	588	496	1965	50.0%	983	983
1980	22826	2384	10.4%	560	358	1466	49.9%	732	734
1979	18921	2081	11.0%	503	353	1225	44.7%	548	677
1978	16479	1764	10.7%	480	218	1066	42.8%	456	610

( ) OPERATING PROFITS BEF DEPREC AMORZ AND INTEREST $	( ) DEPRECIATION AND AMORTIZATION	( ) OPERATING PROFITS AFTER DEPRC AND AMORTIZATION	( ) MAXIMUM SUBSTITUTE PROFORMA INTEREST EXPENSE	( ) ADJUSTED PRETAX INCOME	( ) TAX RATE	( ) income taxes	(8) AFTER TAX ADJUSTED NET INCOME	( ) DEPRECIATION AND AMORTIZATION	(7) ADJUSTED CASH FLOW
5539	807	4732	797	3935	50.0%	1968	1968	807	2775
5116	810	4306	797	3509	50.0%	1755	1755	810	2565
4538	736	3802	797	3005	50.0%	1503	1503	736	2239
3389	592	2797	797	2000	50.0%	1000	1000	592	1592
3049	588	2461	797	1664	50.0%	832	832	588	1420
2384	560	1824	797	1027	50.0%	514	514	560	1074
2081	503	1578	797	781	50.0%	391	391	503	894
1764	480	1284	797	487	50.0%	244	244	480	724

( ) ADJUSTED NET INCOME	( ) ADJUSTED CASH FLOW	(11) CASH DIVIDENDS	(12) CAPITAL EXPENDITURES	( ) TOTAL DIVIDENDS AND CAPITAL EXPENDITURES	( ) AFTER DIVIDENDS AND CAPITAL EXPENDITURES ADJUSTED NET INCOME	( ) AFTER DIVIDENDS AND CAPITAL EXPENDITURES ADJUSTED CASH FLOW	FISCAL PERIOD
1968	2775	300	800	1100	868	1675	1985
1755	2565	250	600	850	905	1715	1984
1503	2239	200	1650	1850	−348	389	1983
1000	1592	200	640	840	160	752	1982
832	1420	200	942	1142	−310	278	1981
514	1074	150	700	850	−337	224	1980
391	894	150	912	1062	−672	−169	1979
244	724	150	1000		−907	−427	1978

YRS TO PAY BACK PRINCIPAL

(10) OF FROM ADJUSTED NET INCOME	(9) 5690 FROM ADJUSTED CASH FLOW
2.9	2.1
3.2	2.2
3.8	2.5
5.7	3.6
6.8	4.0
11.1	5.3
14.6	6.4
23.4	7.9

( ) AFTER DIVIDENDS AND CAPITAL EXPENDITURES YRS TO PAY BACK PRINCIPAL

( ) OF FROM ADJUSTED NET INCOME	( ) 5690 FROM ADJUSTED CASH FLOW	FISCAL PERIOD
6.6	3.4	1985
6.3	3.3	1984
−16.4	14.6	1983
−35.6	7.6	1982
−18.4	20.5	1981
−16.9	25.5	1980
−8.5	−33.8	1979
−6.3	−13.3	1978

EXHIBIT 3 *(continued)*

Southern Packaging Case—Back-up calculations of Notes A & B

Note (A) Back-up Calculations:

	EBIT	−	Max Proforma Interest Expense	=	Adj. Pretax Income	X	1-tax Rate	=	Adj. Net Income	+	Dep. & Amount	=	Adj. Cash Flow
1985	$4732	−	$797	=	$3935	X	.50	=	$1968	+	$807	=	$2775
1984	4306	−	797	=	3138	X	.50	=	1569	+	810	=	2379
1983	3802	−	797	=	3005	X	.50	=	1502	+	736	=	2238
1982	2797	−	797	=	2000	X	.50	=	1000	+	592	=	1592
1981	2461	−	797	=	1664	X	.50	=	832	+	588	=	1420
1980	1824	−	797	=	1027	X	.50	=	563	+	560	=	1123
1979	1578	−	797	=	781	X	.50	=	390	+	503	=	893
1978	1284	−	797	=	487	X	.50	=	243	+	480	=	723

Note (B) Back-up Calculations):

Loan	Initial Prin. Bal.	Interest Rate	Max Int. Ear.
Mortgage Loan	$ 838	X .11	$ 92
Stock Redempt. Note	852	X .12	102
Proposed Term Loan	4,000	X .1150*	460
Proforma BMP	$5,690	Max. Proforma Int.	$654

(*Assumed 1983 avg. prime = 11%; Loan is priced as prime plus 1/2)

$$\frac{654}{5690} = 11.49\% \text{ Blended interest rate on total proforma non-seasonal borrowed money debt.}$$

Southern Packaging Corporation

Uses of Cash Worksheet
(in thousands)

	ACTUAL				PROJECTED		
1980	1981	1982	Years ended 12–31:	1983		
$22,826	$28,155	$30,296	Sales	$33,728		
17,221	21,510	22,752	Cost of Sales	24,945		
3,003	3,431	3,997	Accounts Receivable	4,438		
7.6	8.2	7.6	Acc/Rec Turnover	7.6x		
			Increase in Acc/Rec	441		
2,870	3,282	4,506	Inventory	4,535		
6.0	6.6	5.0	Inventory Turnover	5.5x		
			Increase in Inventory	29		
			Capital Expenditures	1,650		
			*Principal Payments Warehouse Mtg. Loan	38		
			Stock Redempt	348		
			Prin. bal. on existing term loan from one bank	1,900		
			Prin. bal. on S.T. notes pay. under line	1,000		
			Cash Dividends	200		
			Income Taxes	1,473		

*Include in this section the 12/31/82 (total) balances on any loans to be retired out of the proceeds of the proposed new term loan (listed separately and principal payments on any existing term loans that are to remain outstanding and the initial cash payment or the stock redemption, but do *not* include principal payments to be required on your proposed new term loan.

EXHIBIT 3 *(concluded)*

Southern Packaging Corporation

Sources and Uses of Cash Worksheet
(in thousands)

I Schedule of (Internal) Sources and Uses of Funds	1983
Internal sources of Funds:	
Pretax Income	$3076
Depreciation & Amortization	736
Accounts Payable—Increase	188
Total Internal Sources of Funds	$4000
Uses of Funds:	
Accounts Receivable—Increase	441
Inventory—Increase	29
Capital Expenditures	1650
Income Tax Payments	1473
Cash Dividends	200
Principal Payments on Debt (1)	3286
Uses of Funds	$7079
II Calculation of Required Amount of New Term Loan	
(A) Difference Between Internal Sources and Uses of Funds (2)	(3079)
(B) Principal Payments to be Required on new Loan (3)	770
Total "Outside" Funds Required (B plus or Minus A)	3849
Amount of New Term Loan (4)	$4000
III Summary Recap of (Total) Sources and Uses of Funds	
Beginning Cash	$ 332 (5)
Total Sources (including Proceeds of New Loan)	8000
Total Uses (including Prin. Payments on New Loan)	7849
Ending Cash	$ 483 (6)

Note (1): This figure will be the sum of principal payments listed in the "Uses of Funds" worksheet. It excludes required principal payments on your proposed new term loan.

Note (2): Excluding principal payments to be required on new loan.

Note (3): At this point you have to leave the form, go to a scratch pad and "back in" to these principal payment figures. Whatever amounts you settle on will, of course, be a "use of cash" and will serve to increase the amount of loan needed. You are free to select the term of the loan you choose to make (5 year, 6, 8, whatever). Also, the principal payments need not be equal in each year of the loan. It's tricky.

Note (4): This figure will equal the (rounded off) "Total 'outside' Funds Required" in 1983.

Note (5): At 12-31-82.

Note (6): at 12-31-83.

EXHIBIT 4 Comparative Analysis of Affirmative Covenants for 9 Term Loan Cases

	RATED Aaa BY MOODYS	RATED Aa BY MOODYS			RATED A BY MOODYS				
	TERM LOAN CASE NUMBER								
	1	2	3	4	5	6	7	8	9
Furnish annual aud. financial statements		120 days		90 days	x	120 days	120 days	120 days	120 days
Furnish quarterly interim fin. statements				45 days		60 days	60 days	60 days	60 days
Furnish semi-annual interim fin. statements									
Furnish monthly interim fin. statements									
Furnish projections once each year									
Furnish quarterly non default certificate				x		x		x	x
Furnish annual non default certificate									
Furnish monthly non default certificate									
Furnish compliance certificate									
Furnish detailed reports prepared by CPA in connection with audit	x								
Furnish information sent to stockholders and/or SEC			x			x		x	x
Furnish information reasonably requested		x	x	x		x	x	x	x
Maintain system of accounting according to accepted accounting principles							x		

	Col 1	Col 2	Col 3	Col 4	Col 5	Col 6
Permit banks to have access to books & records						
Permit bank to inspect properties						
Give notice of any default:		10 days		X	X	
Give notice of environmental or labor dispute	X					
Give notice of any law suit						
Give notice of material adverse change in condition						
Give notice of reportable event under ERISA						
Give notice of Gov't. to acquire more than 5% of net worth.						
Comply with terms of another loan agreement	X		X	X		
Maintain corporate existence	X				X	X
Maintain properties in good repair						X
Preserve franchises						X
Pay liabilities when due						
Pay taxes when due	X					
Maintain insurance						X
Comply with all laws						
Engage only in present business						
Use proceeds loan for general corporate purposes or other specific purpose						
Set aside adequate reserves						X
Maintain an office in a particular state						
Discontinue one aspect of business						
Furnish Copy of Annual ERISA Report						

EXHIBIT 4 *(continued)*

	RATED Aaa BY MOODYS		RATED Aa BY MOODYS			RATED A BY MOODYS			
				TERM LOAN CASE NUMBER					
	1	2	3	4	5	6	7	8	9
Minimum working capital				30.2%	53.8%	55.9%	50.5%		
Minimum current ratio							33.3%		x*
Minimum tangible net worth									
Negative Pledge		x	x	x	x	x	x	x	x
Limit on idebtedness									
Limit on funded indebtedness				x			x	x	x
Limit on short term borrowings								x	
Limit on subordinated debt									
Limit on guarantees				x					
Limit on guarantees of funded debt							x		
Limit on rentals									
Limit on sale and leasebacks		x		x		x			x
Limit on investments									
Limit on loans or advances									
Limit on mergers and consolidations		x			x	x			x
Limit on acquisition of all or substantial part assets of others		x							

Limit on sale of all or substantial part of assets				x	x
Limit on sale or discount of receivables			x		
Limit on dividends					x
Limit on capital expenditures					
Not prepay other debt					
Not prepay subordinated debt					
Not speculate in commodities or margin securities		x			
Not dissolve business					
Not engage in business with controlling stockholders					x
Limit on transactions with affiliates					
Limit on sale of stock and/or debts of subsidiaries	x			x	
Limit on sale of assets of a subsidiary	x			x	
Various specific negative convenants (one of those above) relating to one or more subsidiaries	x			x	
Limit on Bankers Acceptances					
Limit on Conditional Sales Financings					
Not Amend other Agreements					
Not Enter into any Agreement restricting the Payment of dividends by subs.					
Not Discontinue its relationship as a supplier to a specific company					
Not sell any fixed assets for less than fair market value					

EXHIBIT 4 (continued)

	RATED Aaa BY MOODYS		RATED Aa BY MOODYS			RATED A BY MOODYS			
	TERM LOAN CASE NUMBER								
	1	2	3	4	5	6	7	8	9
Non payment of principal	x	x	x	x	x	x	10 days	x	10 days
Non payment of interest	10 days	x	10 days	10 days	x	x	10 days	10 days	x
Misrepresentation		x	x	x		x		x	x
Non performance of affirmative convenants			30 days				30 days		30 days
Non performance of all or certain negative covenants			30 days	x		x	30 days		30 days
Non performance of any other terms of loan agreement		10 days	30 days	30 days		30 days	30 days	30 days	
Working Capital falls below a prescribed level					*				
Change in Ownership of borrower									

Event of Default	1	2	3	4	5	6	7	8
Cross Acceleration	x							
Voluntary bankruptcy	x	x	x	x	x	x	x	x
Involuntary bankruptcy	x	x	x	x	x	x	x	x
Bankruptcy of a guarantor	x	x	x	x	x	x	x	x
Final judgement	30 days							
Trustee appointed and not discharged	30 days	60 days	60 days	60 days	60 days	30 days	60 days	60 days
Condemnation of assets								
Termination of defined benefit plan under ERISA or a reportable event								
Loan Agreement declared null & void								
Writ or warrant or attachment issued								
An order for dissolution of borrower								
Any involuntary lien on 5% of borrower net worth								
Default under security agreement								

NOTE: An X indicates that the loan agreement for that case contains an event of default equivalent to the default described opposite the X. In cases where a period of time is noted (10 days, 30 days, etc.), this also indicates that the loan agreement for that case contains the described default but the default provision contains a grace period before which the default can be effective.

EXHIBIT 4 *(continued)*

	RATED Aaa BY MOODYS	RATED Aa BY MOODYS			RATED A BY MOODYS		RATED A BY MOODYS		
					TERM LOAN CASE NUMBER				
	1	2	3	4	5	6	7	8	9
Prior to First Borrowing									
Legal Opinion From:									
Independent counsel for borrower	x								
House counsel for borrower		x	x	x		x	x	x	x
Special counsel for banks				x		x		x	
All legal details are to be satisfactory to special counsel for banks									x
Certificate of signature and incumbency		x	x		x			x	
Certified resolutions		x	x		x			x	
Certified copy of by-laws									
Certified copy of charter									
Good standing certificate									
Non default certificate						x	x		x
All other corporate proceedings acceptable to banks or receive such other papers as banks reasonably require		x				x	x		x

724

Consent from other lenders							
Consent from stockholders							
Federal Reserve Form U-1	x						
Copy of other Loan Agreements							
Collateral							
Prior to Each Borrowing Non default certificate			x				x
Consummation of borrowing constitutes representation that:							
No default	x				x		
Representations are true and correct	x		x		x		
Borrowing not contravene law					x		
Net Worth of Borrower must exceed a minimum level							
No law suit pending							
All legal details to be satisfactory to counsel for banks							
Certificate that Representations and warranties correct							

Note: An X indicates that the loan agreement for that case contains a condition of lending equivalent to the condition of lending described opposite the notation of the X. The requirement to furnish a note evidencing the borrowing has not been included above in the analysis.

*All conditions must be fulfilled prior to each borrowing.

EXHIBIT 4 *(concluded)*

	RATED Aaa BY MOODYS	RATED Aa BY MOODYS				RATED A BY MOODYS			
					TERM LOAN CASE NUMBER				
	1	2	3	4	5	6	7	8	9
Duly incorporated and/or organized		x	x	x	x	x	x	x	x
Due authorization		x	x	x	x	x	x	x	x
Enforceability of documents		x	x	x	x	x	x	x	x
No pending law suits		x	x	x		x	x	x	x
Loan doesn't breach other agreements		x	x	x	x		x	x	x
Financial statements correct		x		x	x	x	x	x	x
Borrower not engaged in extending credit for carrying margin securities									x
Concerning purpose of loan							x		x
No governmental action required			x			x			x
All tax returns filed and no taxes past due									
Title to property and no liens on property									
List of subsidiaries									

726

Representation and Warranty						
Stock ownership of subsidiaries						
Various other specific warranties (of those listed herein) concerning subsidiaries						
List of other credit agreements						X
No burdensome contracts						
Ownership of patents and trademarks						
Compliance with ERISA						
No defaults						
Loan constitutes senior debt under another agreement						X
No material adverse change in financial condition	X		X		X	
Borrower not an Investment Company under Investment Company Act of 1940				X	X	
Representations by Guarantor						
A true copy of another loan agree, furnished to banks						
Borrower entered into separate identical agreemtns with other banks						
As to true list of all outstanding debt						

NOTE: An X indicates that the loan agreement for the case contains a representation and warranty equivalent to the representation and warranty described opposite the notation of the X.

EXHIBIT 5 Loan Agreement

Date ____________________

NCNB National Bank of ____________________, ____________________, ____________________

RE: ____ ("Borrower")

In consideration of NCNB National Bank ("Bank") making a loan of $ ____________________ to Borrower (the "loan"), as

evidenced by a promissory note dated ____________________, 19 ______ (the "note"), Borrower agrees as follows:

1. **Representations and Warranties.** To induce the Bank to make the loan, Borrower makes the following representations and warranties, which shall survive the execution and delivery of the note:

(a) The financial information furnished to Bank in connection with its application for the loan and in the financial statements submitted to Bank is complete and accurate and Borrower has no undisclosed direct or contingent liabilities.

(b) If a corporation, Borrower is duly organized, existing and in good standing under the laws of the State of ____________________, has corporate power to carry on the business in which it is engaged, and the obtaining and performance of the loan have been duly authorized by all necessary action of the board of directors and shareholders of the corporation under applicable law, and do not and will not (i), violate any provision of law or any of its organizational or other organic documents, or (ii) result in a breach of, constitute a default under, require any consent under, or result in the creation of any lien, charge, or encumbrance upon any property of Borrower pursuant to any instrument, order, or other agreement to which Borrower is a party or by which Borrower, any of its officers as such, or any of its property is bound.

(c) There are no judgments, liens, encumbrances, or other security interests outstanding against Borrower or any of its property other than those disclosed to Bank in connection with its request for the loan.

(d) Borrower has not incurred any debts, liabilities, or obligations and has not committed itself to incur any debts, liabilities, or obligations other than those disclosed to Bank in connection with its request for the loan or shown on the financial statements submitted to Bank.

2. **Use of Loan Proceeds.** The proceeds of the loan will be used only for the purpose or purposes of ____________________.

3. **Affirmative Covenants.** Borrower will:

(a) Reserve and keep in force all licenses, permits, and franchises necessary for the proper conduct of its business and duly pay and discharge all taxes, assessments, and governmental charges upon Borrower or against Borrower's property before the date on which penalties attach thereto, unless and to the extent only that the same shall be contested in good faith and by appropriate proceedings.

(b) Furnish to Bank (i) within ninety days after the close of each fiscal year a detailed report of audit of Borrower bearing an opinion acceptable to Bank prepared by independent certified public accountants who are satisfactory to Bank; (ii) within thirty days after the close of the first, second and third quarters of each fiscal year of Borrower, a balance sheet and profit and loss statement on Borrower certified by Borrower to be correct and accurate; and (iii) such other information respecting the financial condition and operations of Borrower as Bank may from time to time reasonably request. At or before the time of furnishing the annual report of audit and each quarterly report, Borrower shall provide to Bank a certificate of an executive officer of Borrower to the effect that Borrower has complied with the provisions of this Agreement, or stating the respect in which it has failed to do so.

(c) Maintain with financially sound and reputable insurance companies insurance of the kinds, covering the risks, and in the amounts usually carried by companies engaged in businesses similar to that of Borrower. Borrower will also exhibit or deliver such policies of insurance to Bank upon request by Bank and provide appropriate loss payable or mortgagee clauses in the insurance policies in favor of Bank, as its interest may appear, when requested by Bank. Bank shall have the right to settle and compromise any and all claims under any policy required to be maintained by Borrower hereunder and Borrower hereby appoints Bank as its attorney-in-fact, with power to demand, receive, and receipt for all monies payable thereunder, to execute in the name of Borrower or Bank or both any proof of loss, notice, draft, or other instruments in connection with such policies or any loss thereunder and generally to do and perform any and all acts as Borrower but for this appointment, might or could perform.

(d) Upon request by Bank, execute and deliver to Bank financing statements in form and substance satisfactory to Bank to perfect or continue any and all security interests of Bank in any collateral securing the loan.

(e) Maintain executive personnel and management reasonably satisfactory to Bank.

(f) Permit any representative or agent of Bank to examine and audit any or all of Borrower's books and records when requested by Bank.

(g) Inform Bank immediately of any material adverse change in the financial condition of Borrower. Borrower will also promptly inform Bank of any litigation or threatened litigation which might substantially affect Borrower's financial condition.

(h) Maintain Borrower's property and equipment in a state of good repair.

(i) Maintain Borrower's net working capital in an amount not less than $ _____ and a current ratio of not less than _____ to one at all times during the term of this Agreement. For the purposes of this Agreement, "net working capital" shall mean the excess of Borrower's current assets over current liabilities, which shall be determined in accordance with generally accepted accounting principles as consistently applied in the preparation of Borrower's previous financial statements, and "current ratio" shall mean the quotient of current assets divided by current liabilities.

(j) Maintain Borrower's tangible net worth in an amount not less than $ _____ at all times during the term of this Agreement. For the purposes of this Agreement "tangible net worth" shall mean (i) the aggregate amount of assets shown on the balance sheet of Borrower at any particular date (but excluding from such assets capitalized organization and development costs, capitalized interest, debt discount and expense, goodwill, patents, trademarks, copyrights, franchises, licenses, amounts due from officers, directors, stockholders and affiliates, and such other assets as are properly classified "intangible assets" under generally accepted accounting principles) less (ii) liabilities at such date, all computed in accordance with generally accepted accounting principles applied on a consistent basis.

(k) No employee benefit plan established or maintained, or to which contributions have been made, by Borrower which is subject to Part 3 of Subtitle 1 of Title I of the Employee Retirement Income Security Act of 1974, as amended ("ERISA"), had an "accumulated funding deficiency" (as such term is defined in Section 302 of ERISA) as of the last day of the most recent fiscal year of such plan ended prior to the date hereof, or would have had such an accumulated funding deficiency on such day if such year were the first year of such plan to which such Part 3 applied; and no material liability to the Pension Benefit Guaranty Corporation has been incurred with respect to any such plan by Borrower.

EXHIBIT 5 *(continued)*

(l) Furnish to bank life insurance in amounts satisfactory to bank on the life (lives) of _____ .

(m) Other affirmative covenants:

4. **Negative Covenants.** Borrower will not, without prior written consent of Bank:

(a) Incur any additional indebtedness for borrowed money, any additional contingent liability, or assign, mortgage, pledge, encumber, grant any security interest in, or transfer any of Borrower's assets, whether now owned or hereafter acquired, except in the ordinary course of Borrower's business. For the purposes hereof, the sale or assignment of accounts receivable and the execution of leases or rental agreements shall constitute incurring indebtedness for borrowed money, and the execution of any guaranty agreement or letter of credit agreement shall constitute the incurrence of a contingent liability.

(b) If Borrower is a corporation, pay any dividends on any of its capital stock (other than stock dividends) or purchase, redeem or retire any of its capital stock.

(c) Guarantee, endorse, or otherwise become surety for or upon the obligation of any person, firm, or corporation.

(d) Lend money or credit to or make or permit to be outstanding loans or advances to any person, firm, or corporation.

(e) Enter into any merger or consolidation, or sell, lease, transfer, or otherwise dispose of all or any substantial part of its assets (except in the ordinary course of business), whether now owned or hereafter acquired; or change its name or any name in which it does business; or move its principal place of business without giving written notice thereof to Bank at least thirty (30) days prior thereto.

(f) Make any distribution of cash or property to its shareholders or owners or permit the withdrawal of any assets from Borrower's business.

(g) Increase the compensation of any officer of Borrower, as shown on financial statements submitted with Borrower's application for loan, by more than _____% per year during the term of the loan.

(h) Purchase fixed assets costing more than the accumulated depreciation on fixed assets for the previous four consecutive fiscal quarters in any fiscal year of Borrower while the loan is outstanding.

(i) Permit the ratio of total liabilities to tangible net worth to be greater than _____ to one.

(j) Other negative covenants:

5. **Security For Loan.** As security for the loan and any other indebtedness of the Borrower, Borrower hereby grants a security interest in and will deliver to Bank or will execute appropriate security agreements in form satisfactory to Bank the following collateral:

Borrower represents and warrants that it is absolute owner of the above collateral and that the collateral is owned free and clear of all liens, encumbrances, and security interest of any kind.

6. **Events of Default.** The Bank shall have the option to declare the entire unpaid amount of the loan and accrued interest immediately due and payable, without presentment, demand, or notice of any kind, if any of the following events occurs before the loan is fully repaid:

(a) Any payment of principal or interest on the loan is not made when due.

(b) Any provision of this Agreement is breached or proves to be untrue or misleading in any material respect.

(c) Any warranty, representation, or statement made or furnished the Bank by Borrower in connection with the loan and this Agreement (including any warranty, representation, or statement in the Borrower's financial statements) or to induce the Bank to make the loan, is untrue or misleading in any material respect.

(d) Any default occurs under any agreement with another financial institution, which default is not corrected within the cure period provided in such agreement, if any.

(e) Any voluntary or involuntary bankruptcy, reorganization, insolvency, arrangement, receivership, or similar proceeding is commenced by or against Borrower under any federal or state law, or Borrower makes any assignment for the benefit of creditors.

(f) Any substantial part of the inventory, equipment, or other property of the Borrower, real or personal, tangible or intangible, is damaged or destroyed and the damage or destruction is not covered by collectible insurance.

(g) Borrower defaults in the payment of any principal or interest on any obligation to Bank or any other creditor.

(h) Borrowers suffers or permits any lien, encumbrance, or security interest to arise or attach to any of the Borrowers' property, or any judgment is entered against Borrower that is not satisfied or appealed within thirty days.

It shall also constitute an event of default and Bank shall also have the option to declare the entire unpaid amount of the loan and accrued interest immediately due and payable, without presentment, demand, or notice of any kind, if Bank reasonably deems itself insecure or its prospects for payment of the loan impaired.

7. **Remedies Upon default.** Upon the occurrence, or the discovery by Bank of the occurrence, of any of the foregoing events, circumstances, or conditions of default, Bank shall have, in addition to its option to declare the entire unpaid amount of the loan and accrued interest thereon immediately due and payable, all of the rights and remedies of a secured party under applicable State law. Without in any way limiting the generality of the foregoing, Bank shall also have the following specific rights and remedies:

(a) To take immediate possession of all equipment, inventory, fixtures, and any or all other collateral securing this loan, whether now owned or hereafter acquired, without notice, demand, presentment, or resort to legal process, and, for those purposes, to enter any premises where any of the collateral is located and remove the collateral therefrom or render it unusable.

(b) To require Borrower to assemble and make the collateral available to Bank at a place to be designated by Bank which is also reasonably convenient to Borrower.

(c) To retain the collateral in satisfaction of any unpaid principal or interest on the loan or sell the collateral at public or private sale after giving at least five days' notice of the time and place of the sale and with or without having the collateral physically present at the place of the sale.

(d) To make any repairs to the collateral which bank deems necessary or desirable for the purposes of sale.

(e) To exercise any and all rights of set-off which Bank may have against any account, fund, or property of any kind, tangible or intangible, belonging to Borrower which shall be in Bank's possession or under its control.

(f) To cure such defaults, with the result that all costs and expenses incurred or paid by Bank in effecting such cure shall be additional charges on the Loan which bear interest at the interest rate of the Loan and are payable upon demand.

EXHIBIT 5 *(concluded)*

The proceeds from any disposition of the collateral for the loan shall be used to satisfy the following items in the order they are listed:

(a) The expenses of taking, removing, storing, repairing, holding, and selling the collateral, including any legal costs and attorneys' fees. If the note is referred to an attorney for collection, Borrower and all others liable for the loan jointly and severally agree to pay reasonable attorneys' fees not to exceed 15% of the amount of the outstanding balance of the note at the time it is referred to the attorney.

(b) The expense of liquidating or satisfying any liens, security interests, or encumbrances on the collateral which may be prior to the security interest of Bank.

(c) Any unpaid fees, accrued interest, and then the unpaid principal amount of the loan.

(d) Any other indebtedness of Borrower to Bank.

If the proceeds realized from the disposition of the collateral shall fail to satisfy any of the foregoing items, Borrower and all others liable for the loan shall forthwith pay any deficiency to Bank upon demand.

8. **Waiver.** No failure or delay on the part of Bank in exercising any power or right hereunder, and no failure of Bank to give Borrower notice of a default hereunder, shall operate as a waiver thereof, nor shall any single or partial exercise of any such right or power preclude any other or further exercise thereof or the exercise of any other right or power hereunder. No modification or waiver of any provision of this Agreement or any instrument executed pursuant hereto or consent to any departure by Borrower from this Agreement or such instrument shall in any event be effective unless the same shall be in writing, and such waiver or consent shall be effective only in the specific instance and for the particular purpose for which given.

9. **Benefit.** This Agreement shall be binding upon and shall inure to the benefit of Borrower and Bank and their respective successors and assigns. Bank may assign this Agreement in whole or in part with any assignment of the loan. Borrower may not assign this Agreement or its obligations under the loan without Bank's written consent.

10. **Additional Provisions.** Borrower also agrees to the following provisions:

11. **Construction.** This agreement shall be governed and construed in accordance with the laws of the State of _____, and any litigatin arising out of or relating to this Agreement or the loan shall be commenced and conducted in the courts of that State or in the federal courts of that State.

(SEAL)

ATTEST:

_____

Secretary of Borrower (if Corporation)

WITNESS:

Corporation, Partnership, etc.

_____

By: _____

Title: _____

_____ (SEAL)

Individual

_____ (SEAL)

Individual

ACCEPTED:
NCNB National Bank of _____

BY: _____

Title: _____

733

EXHIBIT 6 Steps in Structuring Credits Including Long-Term Financing

---

While any one-two-three step approach is subject to considerable variation when applied in actuality, the following steps are appropriate in evaluating the ability of a borrower to repay long term debt:

1. "Normal" evaluation of the financial strength and history of the borrower.
2. Review of its financial statements.
3. Projection of a pro forma or projected balance sheet in the future reflecting the current needs under consideration, funds needed to bring the borrower's trade debt within desirable terms, assumptions about inventory and receivable turnover, and other unusual characteristics of the borrower's situation.
4. Evaluation of funds available to service the new additional term loan.
5. Structuring of repayment schedule to reflect unusual/nonrecurring demands on the borrower.
6. Discussions with the customer pertaining to loan structure and loan agreement.
7. Drafting outline of loan agreement.
8. Fully documenting the term loan agreement.
9. Execution of the term loan agreement and related documents.
10. Followup for compliance.

CHAPTER FIFTY-ONE

Financing Leveraged Buyouts

Steven J. Beck

Vice President
Huntington National Bank of Indiana

Buying and financing a business is a great deal like raising a child; you must spend a lot of time on the basics to ensure it will grow into something you are proud of.

In order to make good loans for the purpose of financing leveraged buyouts, you first must understand the process of buying and selling businesses. By having a thorough understanding of the process, you can better allocate your time to the loans that have a higher potential of closing.

You must first understand what kinds of situations your bank is interested in and capable of handling. Are they only interested in "gold-plated" deals where there is very little risk, or are they interested in "true" leveraged buyouts? The amount of time, effort, and knowledge dedicated to each varies greatly, depending on your bank's desires.

UNDERSTANDING THE PLAYERS

In order to participate in the leveraged buyout field you must fully understand the different types of "players" who are involved in the purchase of a business. You must realize that even though a firm, individual, or group of individuals are considered to be very astute businesspeople, it is unlikely that they have been through the process of buying a business before. They therefore do not have the skills or knowledge to do it alone and must look to you for a great deal of assistance.

Corporations—they are normally purchasing companies that complement their existing business and usually have a great deal of expertise regarding the technical aspects of the company they are purchasing. Yet, however technically astute the company, unless it has been through the acquisition of a company, it is still in for a lot of surprises.

Individuals—these people are normally highly motivated, self-starting individuals with a great deal of knowledge in one or more of the basic skills of running a business—finance, marketing, and production. They have a strong desire to compete and be the masters of their own destiny. Their main reason for wanting to own their own business is that they want to create a dynasty. Even with all of these strong traits they are normally very naive about what it takes to own their business and even more so about what is involved in buying a business.

Individuals buying a job—these individuals may also be highly motivated, self-starting, and have a great deal of knowledge in their areas of interest. Their main reason for wanting to purchase a business is to have a stable job. There is nothing wrong with this goal if the purchaser has the desire and stamina to stick with it.

Groups of individuals—these are normally the same types of individuals as described above, except that they have decided for various reasons that they have a higher chance for success if they join forces with others who have the same motivation but different skills.

Investment group—this group is probably the most sophisticated of the potential purchasers you might deal with. Such groups are normally composed of highly trained professional investors who buy businesses that appear to be underpriced, with the idea of increasing their value and then selling them for a profit.

Regardless of which group is the potential buyer of a business, you will have to spend a lot of time and effort to ensure that the transaction is handled properly.

SELLERS

Large corporations—for most corporations the sale of a division or subsidiary is an economic transaction. For one reason or another the company no longer feels the assets being sold provide the necessary return, no longer fit in with the company's long-term goals, or any of numerous other reasons. The key reason for the sale is economic, and there is very little emotion involved in the decision. Receiving book value is the normal goal of most large corporations when they divest a subsidiary; they do not want to show a loss on the sale of an asset on their financial statements. Occasionally, they will be flexible on the selling terms and seller financing in order to accomplish their goal. Once a corporation has decided to sell a subsidiary, the transaction normally progresses quickly.

Closely held business—these transactions, when compared to large corporations, can be very emotional. This is because the seller has probably spent many years building the business, which has become as important as family.

Most of these types of sellers are very unrealistic about the value of their companies. They feel that due to the many years of "sweat equity" they have invested in the company, they should receive a highly inflated price at the time of sale. The transaction will probably proceed very slowly, and the potential buyer should proceed very patiently. In many cases later bidders have a better chance for success because the seller has become more realistic regarding price and terms of the sale.

ADVISERS

As in most transactions where the parties lack a great deal of knowledge, it is imperative that they be assisted by the best advisers available. These advisers can mean the difference between a good deal and an exceptional deal. They can ensure that all the bases are covered and can be a great deal of help to the lender.

Attorney—The buyer's attorney is a very important player in the purchase of a business. The attorney's main duty is the preparation of the Letter of Intent and the detailed Purchase Agreement. The whole success of the transaction can be made or lost based on these documents. It is important that the buyer engage the services of a top attorney with past experience in mergers. Hopefully the attorney who is used is also a CPA. A large part of the transaction's planning is based on the tax laws, and a good tax attorney can see both the legal and tax side of the transaction.

Accountant—A good accountant is a must. In any leverage buyout, the purchaser has to do a great deal of financial analysis to determine whether the proposed transaction is economically sound. It is very important that a reputable accountant with some knowledge in acquisition financing be part of the buyer's team. Besides providing a great deal of knowledge in the analysis of the data, they must also play an important role in (1) verification of the information (due diligence) that is provided by the seller, (2) act as an independent third party on which the lender can place trust, and (3) act as a sounding board for the purchaser in determining how to structure the transaction.

Investment banker—depending on the size of the purchase, it might be necessary for an investment banker to become involved in the transaction. The investment banker helps (1) structure the deal, (2) raise equity if necessary, and (3) find a financing source. Most investment banking firms are normally interested in deals above $10 million.

DETERMINING WHAT A BUSINESS IS WORTH

Determining the value of a business is critical to ensure that you are spending your time on deals that have a good potential to close. Deals that are unreasonably priced are normally "killed" before they can be closed.

Methods of Valuation

1. Adjusted Balance Sheet Value.   One of the most commonly used methods of valuing a business is to determine the net worth. However, the accountant's definition of net worth usually greatly differs from the "true economic net worth." The balance sheet method of valuation adjusts the asset to show the true tangible net worth at market.

In computing the tangible net worth, all intangible assets, such as goodwill, patents, deferred financing costs, etc., are deducted from net worth. Some intangibles, such as patents and franchise rights, could have potential value and should be evaluated carefully.

Some tangible assets, due to tax and other regulations, have an actual value in excess of the stated book value and must be taken into consideration. The two most common areas of undervaluation are inventory and plant and equipment.

In some cases, it may be necessary to further adjust net worth to eliminate assets that, while tangible, are extraneous to the company's main business (for example, an investment in an affiliate not related to the company's business).

An example of adjusted balance sheet value for Your Company, Inc., looks like this:

Reported net worth	$1,000,000
Plus: Inventory undervaluation	300,000
Plant and equipment undervaluation	100,000
Less: Intangibles	(60,000)
Adjusted net worth	$1,340,000

The above example is used only to illustrate how the adjustments affect the true value of the business but do not include all the potential adjustments that could be made. Several other likely adjustments could include: bad debt reserve, low interest debt securities, investment in affiliates, loans to shareholders or officers.

2. Price-Earnings Value.   The most commonly used method of valuing a publicly held company is the price-earnings ratio (P/E), which is simply the price of a company's share of common stock in the public market divided by its earnings per share (after preferred stock dividends).

For example, if a company has 100,000 shares of common stock outstanding and net income of $100,000, the earnings per share would be $1. If the stock were selling for $10 per share in the market, the P/E (multiple) would be $10 divided by 1, or 10.

Since the company has 100,000 shares of common stock outstanding, the valuation of the entire company would be 100,000 shares times $10 per share, or $1 million.

As a result, valuing a closely held business by the P/E method involves simply multiplying its net income by an appropriate multiple, which can be determined by examining the multiples for similar publicly traded companies.

The primary advantage of the P/E method is its simplicity. However, serious drawbacks exist with the derivation of the proper multiple. These drawbacks can be summarized as follows:

a. First and most important, the stock of a private company is not publicly traded. It is illiquid and may actually be restricted from sale (i.e., not registered with the Securities and Exchange Commission). Thus, by definition, any P/E multiple usually must be subjective and lower than the multiple commanded by comparable publicly traded stocks.

b. The stated net income of a private company may not truly reflect its actual earning power. To avoid or defer paying taxes, most businessowners prefer to keep pretax income down. In addition, the closely held business may be "overspending" on fringe benefits instituted primarily for the owner's benefit.

c. Common stock that is bought and sold in the public market normally reflects only a small portion of the total ownership of the business. The sale of a large, controlling block of stock (typical of closely held businesses) demands a premium.

d. It is very difficult to find a truly comparable publicly held company, even in the same industry. Growth rates, competition, payments of dividends, and financial profiles are rarely the same.

Notwithstanding these drawbacks, a comparison can still be valuable—but only as a benchmark. For example, in today's market, comparing typical smaller companies may disclose that their average P/E ratio is about 8. However, back in the mid-1960s, at the end of the bull market on publicly traded common stocks, the average P/E was about double this level. Thus, it is important to note that the P/E gives an indication of value—but only within the context of current market conditions.

The calculation of Your Company, Inc., value, using the P/E method, would look like this (assuming a P/E of 8):

Adjusting Net Income	
Reported pretax income	$150,000
Plus: Inventory undervaluation	25,000*
Excess compensation	15,000†
Excess fringes	10,000†
Adjusted pretax income	200,000
Less: Taxes (50%)	(100,000)
Net income	$100,000
Value	
Adjusted net income	$100,000
Times P/E	8
Price-earnings value	$800,000

*Assumes $125,000 excess inventory was accumulated over prior five years and thus only $25,000 applicable this year.

†$15,000 of owners salary and $10,000 of fringe benefits are added back to pretax income.

The P/E and the Capitalization Rate. One more thing has to be said about the P/E multiple. Note that the reciprocal of the P/E ratio is the earning-price ratio—which is, in effect, the capitalization rate or rate of return.

For example, assume the following:

Net income	$100,000
Shares outstanding	100,000
Earnings per share	$1
Market value per share	$8

Based on the above data, the P/E is 8 ($8 divided by earnings per share of $1); when expressed as a capitalization rate, it's 1 divided by 8, or 12.5 percent.

In other words, at a valuation of $800,000, the company yields a rate of return of 12.5 percent—net income of $100,000 divided by $800,000.

3. Discounted Future Earnings Value. Fact: When you discount future earnings, you apply a present value factor to those earnings to determine their value today.

Why?

A dollar earned five years from now is not worth a dollar today.

Example: Using a present value factor of 15 percent, $200,000 of earnings five years from now is worth only $99,400 today—0.497 fifth-year present value factor times $200,000. (Note: Present value factors can be found in financial handbooks. Also, most hand-held calculators can compute them.)

The balance sheet and P/E methods of valuation principally tell you the value as of today, based on what you've accomplished in the past.

Discounting future earnings looks to the future. There are four steps:

1. Project future earnings for five years
2. Discount those future earnings at a certain discount (present value) rate to determine the value of the earnings today.
3. Apply a multitude to the fifth-year earnings to place a value on the stream of earnings after five years.
4. Discount the fifth-year value in 3 using the same present value rate used in 2.

Using the projected annual growth rate of 20 percent for Your Company results in the total value shown in the table below; i.e., $1,393,751.

Two observations: (1) The adjusted net income of $100,000 was assumed to grow at 20 percent for five years; i.e., $120,000 in 1987, $144,000 in 1988, and so forth, and (2) a present value of 15 percent was used.

Value of Your Company, Inc.

Year	Net income	Present Value ×Factor (15%)	=	Value Today
1987	$120,000	.870		$ 104,400
1988	144,000	.756		108,864
1989	172,800	.658		113,702
1990	207,360	.572		118,610
1991	248,832	.497		123,670
Value of 1987/1991 net income				$ 569,246

Value of 1992 and thereafter

Net income (1991)	$ 248,832
Times multiplier (1 ÷ 15%)	6.667
	1,658,963
Apply present value of .497 (5th year)	× 0.497
Value 1992 and thereafter	$ 824,505

Total Value

First five years (1987–1991)	$ 569,246
1992 and thereafter	824,505
Total value	$1,393,751

There were three principal assumptions used above:

1. The growth rate of earnings.
2. The discount or present value rate.
3. The P/E multiple applied to the fifth-year net income.

Change any of the assumptions and you change the final result. For example, if we assume a 10 percent annual growth in net income, a discount rate of 20 percent, and a multiplier of five, then the final value would be $762,258, 45 percent less than the value above.

Weighted Value of Three Methods

As shown above (and in the table below), each method produces a different value. The range was $645,000 (adjusted balance sheet method) to $1,393,751 (discounted earnings method).

You now can apply a weight to each value to determine a final value for Your Company. We applied the highest weight (50 percent) to the balance sheet method—which was adjusted to fair market value since this was known. The other two methods were weighted 25 percent each.

The logic behind the above "weighting factors" is to apply higher weights (percentages) to more known results.

The weighted values are computed as follows:

Weighted Value			
Valuation Method	Value	Weight	Weighted value
Adjusted balance sheet value	$ 645,000	50%	$322,500
Price-earnings value	800,000	25%	200,000
Discounted future earnings value	1,393,751	25%	348,438
Weighted value			$870,938*

*The Business Owner, Special Report 4.

After you have computed the value on several businesses you will find that you can determine which deals have the best probability of closing and you will improve your productivity.

Determining the True Cost of the Business

It is very important to thoroughly examine the purchase agreement to fully understand the true cost of the company being purchased. While the debt financing may be one number, the full cost might be significantly higher due to (1) noncompete agreement payments, (2) royalty payments, (3) consulting agreement payments, and (4) seller financing.

You must fully understand how the various components of the agreement affect the company's ability to repay not only your debt but all obligations. A typical example follows:

Cost of asset purchase	$1,000,000
Noncompete @ $50,000 per year for five years	250,000
Consulting fee @ $10,000 per year for five years	50,000
Total price	$1,300,000

The noncompete and consulting fees add an additional $60,000 to the annual cost of the purchase and could be the difference between the deal being financed.

CREDIT ANALYSIS

In analyzing a request for financing of the purchase of a business, the basic five Cs still hold true. The only difference is in their order of importance. Below is a list of the traditional five Cs followed by the five Cs in the order of priority for an acquisition.

Traditional	Acquisition
1. Character.	1. Character.
2. Capital.	2. Cash flow.
3. Cash flow.	3. Collateral.
4. Collateral.	4. Capital.
5. Conditions.	5. Conditions.

Below is a discussion of the key elements of the five Cs of credit as they apply in acquisition financing and in the structuring of a loan.

1. The Management Team

The single most important factor in the success of any acquisition is the quality of the management team. The management team plays a much more important role in a leverage buyout than in an existing business because of the small margin for error in the leveraged buyout.

Does the management team have experience in the key functional areas of marketing, production, finance, and engineering? Determine management's level of experience in the industry of the business in which they are buying. Have the purchasers determined who will be president, head of sales and marketing, head of production, and head of finance and accounting?

Determining the commitment level of the management team is very important. How much of their own funds have they invested? The dollar amount invested is not as important as the percentage of the available funds invested. If the management team has invested only $100,000 in a $4 million purchase, but that is every dollar they have, you have a higher commitment level than if the $100,000 was only 25 percent of their available funds. How willing are they to personally guarantee the debt? Lack of willingness to guarantee is a sure sign of their uncertainty about their potential success.

Checking references of the management team in a leveraged buyout is probably more important than in any other type of lending transaction. In a leveraged buyout you don't have the luxury of reviewing the financial statements of their existing company and making the assumption that they probably will be able to continue the company's trend. In a buyout, it is important that you check references to determine the character of the individuals you are dealing with. Granted, they will give you only the names of individuals they are sure will give you good references. However, you can normally get the names of several individuals from their references. By checking with these additional references you will normally get a less biased opinion. A word of caution—you must be very discreet in checking references that the buyer has not provided to ensure that you do not divulge any information on the transaction that could injure the buyer.

2. Cash Flow

The success of most leveraged buyouts depends a great deal on the quality of the cash flow forecasts provided by the purchaser. A great deal of time must be spent on a thorough analysis of the cash flows, both past and future, to ensure that there will be adequate funds to service all debt (both bank and any other outside debt). It is normally a good practice to have the purchaser provide you a net cash flow forecast, provided by an outside CPA, for at least the next three years. These forecasts should be monthly for at least one year and quarterly for remaining years. They should be compared to the same months for the prior year, if monthly statements are available, to determine any discrepancies in the annual pattern of cash flow. If possible you should have the borrower's accountant restate the prior two years' income statements to show what the income and cash flow would look like if the company had been structured as they are proposing. This normally gives you a good idea of what you can expect in the future. Such a process is not simple, but with the advent of the computer spreadsheet it has become much less difficult. A good minimum cash flow coverage is 1.4:1. This will provide you with an adequate cushion to ensure that if the buyers' forecast is incorrect, they will still be able to meet the necessary debt service.

In addition to the cash flow forecast it is absolutely necessary that you require the borrower to provide you with a forecasted income statement and balance sheet for the same time frame and format as the cash flow forecast. You should also require a pro forma balance sheet as of the opening day of the company so you can determine the structure of the assets and liabilities, what collateral will be available, and what the balance sheet ratios will be.

All of the normal ratios should be figured on the forecasted statements and compared to industry or RMA averages to ensure there are no major discrepancies.

3. Collateral

Collateral, as we are all aware, is considered by most bankers as their secondary source of repayment. In a leveraged buyout, however, since you will be leveraging the use of these assets to a much higher degree, it is much more important that you know a great deal about the quality of the collateral.

Accounts Receivable.   To thoroughly understand the quality of the accounts receivable you will be using as collateral, you must examine the following: (1) aging, (2) selling terms, (3) credit policy, (4) bad debt experience, (5) normal credits on returned goods, (6) composition of A/R, (7) concentration of A/R, and (8) relative strength of the customer base. It is only after you have satisfied all your questions that you can determine the possible advance rate on accounts receivable.

Inventory.   Like accounts receivable, before you can determine what you can lend on a borrower's inventory you will have to make a thorough examination of all facets of their inventory. Things that you should take into consideration are: (1) composition of raw materials, work in process, and finished goods; (2) turnover, (3) year-end adjustments, (4) physical condition, (5) number of items, (6) commodity market value, (7) obsolescence, (8) gross profit margins, (9) product return experience, (10) warranty policy, and (11) valuation method (LIFO,FIFO). Again, only after you have answered all your questions can you make a determination of what type of advance can be made on the inventory.

Fixed Assets.   In many leveraged buyouts the value of the fixed assets is the deciding factor in the deal being financeable. One key factor is that often the fixed assets have considerably more value than is indicated on the financial statements. To ensure that an adequate value is given, it is important that a thorough analysis of the fixed assets be made. The only real way to determine the collateral value on fixed assets is to have a market value appraisal of land and buildings and a liquidation appraisal of machinery and equipment. These appraisals should come from independent third parties who are not involved directly in the industry other than as appraisers and auctioneers.

In addition to the loan value of the fixed assets it is important to consider the following: (1) physical condition and maintenance, (2) operational efficiency, (3) capacity utilization, (4) OSHA problems, and (5) future fixed asset requirements.

Other Assets.   While the assets listed above are the normal source of collateral, another group of assets should not be forgotten. They are:

a. Patents.
b. Copyrights.
c. Trademarks.

Though such intangibles may not have specific value, they can be critical to the business being financed. Control of these assets could therefore be critical to the future of the business.

4. Capital

The most typical sources of equity are: buyer's investment, seller financing, and third-party investors.

The buyer's investment is always the best because it carries the lowest cost and has the most flexible terms. Unfortunately, in most purchases the buyers do not have adequate funds to ensure the transaction will close, so seller financing or third-party investors become necessary.

In most types of acquisitions there is a strong likelihood that the seller will have to provide some type of financing. This financing can be in the form of debt, noncompete agreement, management contract, or various other types. The debt portion of seller financing is normally on some type of subordinated basis and can be considered as equity. Most other types of seller financing, while repaid over a period of time, are not usually subordinated. While subordinated debt is important in helping to reduce the debt-to-worth ratio of the purchasing company, it is very important that enough cash equity be invested in the new company. One of the main reasons for this importance is that if the new company should incur a loss and this causes the company to have a negative equity, the courts and creditors could charge that there has been a fraudulent conveyance of assets, and this could jeopardize your collateral position.

Whenever buyer and seller financing is not adequate, it becomes necessary for third-party investors to provide the equity to fill the gap between the amount of money provided by both buyer and seller and the amount of money provided by banks. Third-party financing is the most expensive and comes in the following types:

1. Small business investment companies (SBIC)—these private venture capital firms are registered by the U.S. Small Business Administration and invest their funds in small companies.
2. Bank, insurance, and private venture funds—these are firms that invest their own or managed funds in small or growing firms with the hopes of later selling their investment for a significantly higher value. Many of these funds also make investments in leveraged buyouts that have the potential for growth and will provide them with a higher return than could be expected in the money market. The normal annual expected return on this type of transaction is 25 to 30 percent.
3. Private placement by investment bankers—depending on the size of the transaction, it has become very common for investment bankers to sell debentures (junk bonds) to provide the necessary equity.
4. Private investors—in most locales there are groups of private wealthy investors who are looking for investments in the $25,000 to $50,000 range. If the sum of money needed is not too large, these types of investors might be a desirable source of equity.

Regardless of which type of investor might be needed to help close the transaction, it should be noted that it will require considerably more time to close the deal.

5. Conditions

One area of great importance, and one often neglected, is a thorough evaluation of the condition of the industry and economic conditions at the time of the acquisition. Several key factors that should be considered are: (1) historical sale patterns of the industry, (2) size of the market, (3) industry outlook, (4) industry cycle, (5) market evolution, and (6) product life cycle.

In addition to industry conditions the following company information should be reviewed: (1) position of the company within the market, (2) relations with the labor force (union or nonunion), (3) uniqueness of product offering, (4) patent, copyright protection, (5) long-term contracts or commitments, and (6) pending litigation.

Hopefully, all of the information you need to evaluate the company will be provided in a detailed business plan. A good business plan should answer five key questions: Where is the company today? Where does the company want to go (goals)? How is the company going to get there (strategies)? What resources (people, assets, money) are going to be needed? Where are the resources going to come from? If the purchaser has not thought these questions through, you should require that they do so.

FINANCIAL STRUCTURE OF THE LOAN

The actual structure of the financing package varies with each individual acquisition. There are, however, some general guidelines that can be used in structuring a leveraged buyout.

General Advance Rates on Collateral

One of the keys to properly structuring a leveraged buyout, is the use of proper advance rates on the various types of collateral. Again, they vary with each situation. Below are the generally accepted advance rates.

Accounts Receivable.   The normal advance rate for clean receivable is 70 percent to 90 percent of A/R less than 90 days old, with a 10 percent to 25 percent taint rule. The percentage of advance varies depending on the quality of the customers and the size of the typical invoice, which are indicated in your analysis of the accounts receivable aging. The better the customer base and the larger the invoice, the higher the percentage of advance. The lower the quality of the customer and the smaller the invoice, normally the lower the advance rate. The "taint rule" basically is a mechanism that eliminates any accounts that could possibly become a problem. The percentage refers to that percent of the entire A/R of any one account over 90 days old. As an example, if you were using a 20 percent taint rule and any of your customer accounts had 20 percent or more of their receivables over 90 days, the entire receivable would be eliminated from the borrowing base. By adjusting the advance rate and taint rule to each individual case you have a better chance of collecting the account if you were forced into liquidation.

Inventory

Again, as in accounts receivable, the advance rate varies with the individual situation. Below are the typical advance rates on inventory.

1. Raw Material 0 to 70 percent. The advance rates normally are determined by the commodity value of the inventory. If the inventory is a material, such as steel of normal size and lengths, then it would have a much higher advance rate than if the material were of odd sizes. The rationale is, if you were forced to dispose of the inventory in a liquidation, you would probably receive a higher value for the standard size than you would for the odd size. Remember, the higher the commodity value, the higher the potential value. The lower the commodity value, the lower the potential value.

A second important consideration that must be evaluated in determining the advance rate is number of potential purchasers of the material if it must be sold. If there are a large number of potential purchasers the chance of selling the material at a decent price is better than if there are a limited number of potential buyers. This analysis must be done at the time of the credit decision to ensure that you have the best chance of being paid out if the customer must be liquidated.

2. Work in Process 0 to 30 percent. As you would imagine, the normal advance rate for WIP is the scrap value of the material. The rationale is this: If you are forced to liquidate the inventory, who is going to buy a half completed widget? While there may in fact be a buyer who would buy the WIP, it is improbable. The rare exception is if your customer is a single-source supplier to some major company. Then a point could be made that the buyer could not go without the product and would make some attempt to ensure continuation of the operation. A very careful analysis of the situation must be made.

3. Finished Goods 0 to 70 percent. The value of the finished product is determined by: (*a*) the number of potential buyers of the finished product (the higher the potential number of buyers, the higher the advance rate), (*b*) the amount of customization of the product (the most customized the product is for the end purchaser, the lower the value), (*c*) scrap value.

4. Machinery and Equipment: 80 to 90 percent of Appraised Value.
Two keys determine the advance rate on M & E:

Types of Appraisal. There are three types of appraisals: fair market value, in-place value, and forced liquidation. Fair market value is basically the value of the equipment if it were to be replaced today with new equipment. It is basically used for insurance purposes. In-place value is the value of the equipment if it were sold in place as a going concern. Forced liquidation is the value of the equipment if it were sold at auction. Conservative lenders usually use liquidation value as their basis for determining advance rates. Less conservative lenders use in-place value.

Confidence in Your Appraiser's Ability.   Confidence in your appraiser's ability will also affect the advance rate and type of appraisal you use. If you are using an appraiser you have used before or one who has an excellent reputation in your market for providing accurate appraisals, you might be inclined to use a higher advance rate. Conversely if his accuracy is suspect you might choose to reduce your advance rate or change the method of appraisal you use. (The accuracy of an appraisal can only be determined when you are forced to liquidate a company and you sell the assets. If the values the appraiser established hold up in the liquidation, his accuracy is validated.)

5. Land and Building—25 to 80 percent of Appraised Market Value.   As with machinery and equipment the quality of your appraiser plays a major role in determining the advance rate you will use. The better the appraiser the higher the potential advance rate; the lower the quality, the lower the advance rate. A good way to determine the appraiser's ability is to determine if they have either a MIA or SRA certificate. These indicate that they have passed the requirements established by the real estate industry to do commercial appraisals.

Locale and market conditions also play a major factor in determining the value of the real estate. Real estate located in a well-developed industrial park will almost always bring a higher value than an identical building in a rural setting. You must also determine what the economic conditions are in the area where the real estate is located. Good market conditions will increase the value and poor market conditions will reduce the value of the real estate.

General Loan Structure

Any revolving lines of credit should be matched to the values of the accounts receivable and the inventories. Term debt should be matched to the values of the fixed assets and the cash flow.

Alternative Financing Structure

If you choose to lend outside the normal formals discussed above, you should keep three things in mind:

    a.   The company you are lending to should have a strong earnings history.

    b.   The coverage ratio should be strong.

    c.   The term of the overadvance should be short—from six months to two years.

SUMMARY

Experience in leveraged buyout financing, as in everything else, is the best teacher. If there are people in your organization who have done a leveraged buyout, ask for their assistance. If not, find someone in your locale or someone at another organization in another city with whom you can discuss your pending deal. You will be glad you did.

CHAPTER FIFTY-TWO

Equipment Leasing

Milton M. Harris

Chairman
Maryland National Leasing Corporation

EQUIPMENT LEASING

Since there are many types of leases and many types of lessors, the total amount of all of the equipment leasing written to date or in any one year is unknown. However, the best estimate of 1985 volume was $75 billion worth of equipment. The best estimate of the total amount of equipment under lease at the end of 1985 was over $300 billion. Bank participation in equipment leasing probably exceeds $100 billion.

Proposed tax changes designed to take place during 1986 and beyond raise some questions about the future of equipment leasing. However, corporations will continue to require the financing of equipment and, though the types of equipment leases may change, equipment leasing in some form should continue to flourish. This is especially true since it is extremely doubtful if the new tax structure will long remain unchanged.

HISTORY

It is interesting to note that Congress first established a 7 percent investment tax credit for industrial corporations and a 4 percent investment tax credit for utilities in 1962. These benefits were suspended in 1966, reinstated in 1967, repealed in 1969, and enacted again in 1971, this time with both industrials and utilities receiving a 10 percent credit. Thus, it is doubtful that the third suspension in 1986 is final.

The Economic Recovery Tax Act of 1981 (ERTA) greatly enhanced the attraction of equipment leasing until its provisions were repealed in 1982 and 1983. ERTA, through Safe Harbor Leasing, allowed corporations to sell their tax benefits through the medium of equipment leasing. By allowing almost completely free transferability of tax benefits from lessees to nominal lessors, ERTA greatly increased the number of corporations, both leasing and acting as lessors. The attraction was so great, however, that Congress became concerned about the loss of revenue, and in the Tax Equity and Fiscal Responsibility Act of 1982 (TEFRA), Safe Harbor was repealed except for certain specific exemptions. The 1984 Deficit Reduction Act tightened the requirements even further so far as lessors enjoying tax benefits were concerned. Present legislation calling for repeal of the investment tax credit and a minimum tax for corporations will further limit the attraction of tax-motivated leasing to all lessors.

DEFINITION

An equipment lease is a contract that enables an equipment user (the lessee) to secure the use of equipment by making specified payments (rentals) to the owner (the lessor).

Such leases may include a variety of terms relating to maintenance, insurance, payment of personal property taxes, early termination, end use of the equipment, use of depreciation, and treatment of the investment tax credit.

TYPES OF EQUIPMENT LEASES

In general, equipment leases fall into two broad categories, nonpayout and full payout. In a nonpayout lease the lessor receives a guarantee of rentals in the initial lease insufficient to pay for the entire cost of the equipment. The lessor must secure a series of new lessees to obtain full return. Often such a lessor will provide various services as part of the lease; thus the name "service lease" or "full service lease" is often applied to such an arrangement. Usually the lessor pays for maintenance, insurance, and personal property taxes.

The Federal Reserve Board does not allow national banks to participate in such leases yet such banks are allowed to consider a residual value of the equipment up to 20 percent of the original cost in computing return. As a practical matter, most banks are not in a position to readily perform the services that are usually offered by a manufacturer, nor are they so knowledgeable about equipment that they might want to speculate in future equipment values. Most independent lessors who have had financial problems have been nonpayout lessors who incorrectly estimated their ability to re-lease or sell equipment. A notable example is the group of equipment leasing companies who wrote short-term (often as little as one year) leases on IBM-360 computers. Every company so engaged had serious problems when the residual value of the equipment did not meet expectations.

The focus of this chapter will, therefore, be the full payout equipment lease. This is the type of lease most written by all financial institutions. These leases are categorized by their structures and accounting treatment.

The finance lease, now called the "capital lease" by the Financial Accounting Standards Board (FASB), is an equipment lease in which the user of the equipment (the lessee) enjoys the advantages of ownership of the leased equipment. This means that the lessee obtains the benefits, if any are available, of accelerated depreciation and the investment tax credit (ITC), and has the right to acquire the equipment at a predetermined price when the original lease term ends. Such a lease will probably be treated by the lessee and lessor as a loan for accounting and income tax purposes.

Such a capital lease usually meets one or more of the following criteria: (1) Transfers title to the equipment to the lessee at the end of the lease term for a predetermined price; (2) contains a bargain purchase option; (3) has a lease term equal to 75 percent or more of the equipment's useful life; (4) has an estimated residual value at the end of the lease term of less than 25 percent of the equipment's original cost; and (5) the equipment is special purpose to the lessee, and so will have little economic value at the lease's termination to anyone other than the original lessee.

The true lease is now called the operating lease by the FASB. The term *operating* has led to some confusion since operating lease has been used to refer to a lease in which the lessor provided services, such as a manufacturer leasing his own product, usually a nonpayout transaction. In this type of lease, the lessor enjoys the advantages of ownership, in that he looks to the residual value for part of his return.

The FASB Exposure Draft of August 26, 1975, was modified by the Revision Exposure Draft of July 22, 1976. A final Statement of Financial Accounting Standards No. 13, dated November 1976, was issued. Under the terms of this statement, a lessee must classify all leases as either capital or operating. A capital lease is one which meets one or more of the following conditions:

1. The lease transfers ownership of the property to the lessee by the end of the lease term.
2. The lease contains a bargain purchase option.
3. The lease term is equal to 75 percent or more of the estimated economic life of the leased property.
4. The present value of the minimum lease payments less certain costs of lessor equals or exceeds 90 percent of the original

equipment cost (less any investment tax credit retained by lessor).

All other leases are classified as operating leases.

From the standpoint of the lessor, if a lease meets any one of the preceding criteria and both of the following criteria, it shall be classified as a sales type lease (by a vendor) or a direct financing lease (by a financial institution):

1. Collectibility is reasonably predictable.
2. There are no important unknown unreimbursable costs.

Any lease that does not meet the above standards is classified as an operating lease.

The percentages of residual value and lease term duration do not equal FASB definitions. They do meet the guidelines set forth in the Internal Revenue's Revenue Procedure 75–21 dated April 11, 1975. The tax implications are of greater import to most lessors than FASB proposed accounting treatment. Most lessors treat such leases as operating for tax purposes, to obtain maximum tax benefits, but as capital for accounting purposes to enable them to obtain maximum reported earnings by using the finance method of accounting rather than the operating method. If a lessor were forced to report lease income for book on the same basis as tax, his book would show the losses taken for tax purposes. Most lessors would not find this acceptable since continued leasing would continue to show increasing losses.

Under FASB Statement No. 13, even though a lease is accounted for by the lessee as an operating lease, the lessor may account for it as a capital lease, and the reverse as well. In addition, the accounting and tax treatments need not be the same by lessor or lessee.

THE LEVERAGED LEASE

This type of lease is a true or operating lease with something added. In a leveraged lease, the lessor, instead of supplying all of the funds necessary to purchase the equipment to be leased, forms a trust and supplies only a part of the purchase price. The remaining funds necessary are borrowed by the trust from an institutional lender. It is this borrowing of leverage that causes the lease to be called "leveraged," or "with debt." The debt is secured by the equipment being leased, and the underlying credit of the lessee. Neither the lessee nor the equity participant, however, guarantees the debt, which is solely the obligation of the borrowing trust.

Although the lessee has the sole obligation of paying rentals to the trust, and the trust is obligated to the equity participant and to the lenders, the equity participant and lenders look beyond the trust, to the credit of the lessee in making their credit decision.

For tax purposes, a minimum of 20 percent equity is necessary in such a leveraged lease, but 30 to 40 percent equity is not uncommon. The equity participant, since he obtains 100 percent of the tax benefits of accelerated depreciation and often the investment tax credit, as well as 100 percent of the equipment's residual value, is able to provide the lessee with a lease rate often substantially below the debt rate of the trust.

In the cash flow figure, the residual of $200,000 less an offset of $100,000 salvage, results in a $50,000 net tax due.

In evaluating leveraged leases, it is necessary not only to see a printout, but to know how the computer program is structured, what it indicates, and what it combines or eliminates.

Under the present method of accounting for leveraged leases, the full economic benefits to the lessor are not translated directly into book earnings. One reason is that the treatment of the investment tax credit may be such that it is spread over the lease term rather than "flowed through" directly to first-year earnings, which would reflect the economic benefits actually received.

In addition, the funds earned by the pool for future taxes are not reflected in book earnings, although the lessor receives the economic benefit of such funds.

For example:

Total equipment cost	$1,000,000
Equity provided by bank	300,000
Debt provided by insurance company	700,000
Term	15 years
Depreciation	10 years to 10% salvage
Residual	20% of original cost
Lease rate	6.5%
Debt rate	10.0%
Investment tax credit	$ 100,000
Estimated residual	200,000
Total rentals	1,595,295
Total principal repaid	700,000
Total interest paid	680,474
Total debt service	1,380,474
Rentals less debt service	214,821
Yield to lessor	26.97%
Tax Rate	50.0%

In addition, the lessor gains the value of accelerated depreciation in the beginning of the lease (see Exhibit 1 for the analysis of this transaction) and receives the benefits of funds earned by the pool set up for payment of future taxes. This pool or fund for future taxes is considered to earn a return on investment (ROI), or pool rate. In this analysis the ROI is a 3.5 percent annual after-tax rate.

All of the above leases—capital, operating, and leveraged—are usually net leases, with the lessee responsible for maintenance, personal property taxes, and insurance, as well as all other expenses connected with operation of the equipment, except the lessor's state and federal income taxes.

ATTRACTIONS TO LESSORS AND LESSEES

Banks find it attractive to act as equipment lessors because:

1. The return or yields on equipment leasing will generally exceed the yields obtained from loans to the same company.
2. When a bank writes true leases, and obtains the equipment's value at the lease termination, it gradually builds up a considerable hedge against inflation by its ownership of varied types of equipment, at least some of which should appreciate beyond original estimates.
3. Equipment leases can be written for short payback periods when so desired, or written for long "lock-in" periods when rates are attractive. Rentals may be fixed rate or fluctuating. Thus a bank can create a portfolio suitable to its particular requirements.
4. Many banks feel that if their present customers want to lease, they must be able to provide such service or lose prestige and perhaps the account relationship as well.
5. Equipment leasing may be used as a competitive tool to enlarge the banks list of customers and prestige, both locally and nationally.

Corporations lease equipment instead of borrowing in order to:

1. Avoid the use of cash and conserve working capital—usually not even a down payment is required.
2. Avoid the use of short-term bank lines, conserving borrowing capacity for financing inventory, accounts receivable, and other short-term assets.
3. Provide intermediate term financing, longer than most bank lines, but shorter than most insurance loans.
4. Provide a new source of funds, enlarging the pool of capital available to the lessee. During periods of expansion, or tight money, this added source of funds may be invaluable.
5. Allow the delay of permanent financing when long-term rates are unattractive.

EXHIBIT 1 Leveraged Lease

Year	Rents	Principal Amortization	Interest	Depreciation
1	$ 106,353	$ 22,032	$ 70,000	$100,000
2	$ 106,353	24,235	67,797	180,000
3	$ 106,353	26,658	65,373	155,294
4	$ 106,353	29,324	62,708	136,471
5	$ 106,353	32,257	59,775	117,647
6	$ 106,353	35,482	56,549	98,824
7	$ 106,353	39,030	53,001	80,000
8	$ 106,353	42,934	49,098	31,764
9	$ 106,353	47,227	44,805	
10	$ 106,353	51,950	40,082	
11	$ 106,353	57,145	34,887	
12	$ 106,353	62,859	29,173	
13	$ 106,353	69,145	22,887	
14	$ 106,353	76,059	15,972	
15	106,353	83,665	8,366	
Total	$1,595,295	$700,002	$680,473	$900,000

The following takes place for income tax purposes in year 1:
+ Rentals	$106,353
− Depreciation.	100,000
− Interest	70,000
Net loss for taxes	− 63,647
Taxes saved.	$ 31,824

The cash flow is as follows:
+ Rentals	$106,353
+ ITC (investment tax credit)	100,000
+ Taxes saved.	31,834
Total in.	238,177
− Interest	70,000
− Principal	22,032
Net in.	$146,145

In year 15 for taxes the printout shows:
+ Rentals	$106,353
− Depreciation.	0

6. Allow the delay of equity financing when the terms would be unacceptable due to market conditions.
7. Provide flexible financing, structured to specific circumstances, available in odd amounts, and on short notice.
8. Avoid the restrictions common to loan agreements.
9. Allow the lessee to trade the value of the investment tax credit (if any) and depreciation, which cannot be used in a timely manner, for lower rentals.
10. Provide a lower cost for intermediate term financing rather than for short-term borrowing when all factors are considered.

Exhibit 1   *(concluded)*

	Taxes Saved/ Paid	Cash Flow	Tax Fund	After-Tax Cash Flow
1	$ 31,824	$ 146,145	0	$146,145
2	70,722	85,043	0	85,043
3	57,157	71,478	0	71,478
4	46,413	60,734	0	60,734
5	35,535	49,856	$45,392	4,463
6	24,510	38,831	38,831	0
7	13,324	27,645	27,645	0
8	−12,745	1,576	1,576	0
9	−30,774	−16,453		0
10	−33,135	−18,814		0
11	−35,733	−21,412		0
12	−38,590	−24,269		0
13	−41,733	−27,412		0
14	−45,190	−30,869		0
15	−48,993	115,328		115,328
Total	$− 7,408	$ 457,407		$483,191

− Interest	8,366
Net profit for taxes	97,987
Taxes paid	$ 48,993

(This is exclusive of the residual value.)

The cash flow is as follows:

+ Rentals	$106,353	
+ ITC.	0	
+ Taxes saved.	0	
+ Residual	200,000	
Total in.	306,353	
− Interest	8,366	
− Principal	83,665	
− Taxes paid	48,993	(Exclusive of residual)
− Taxes paid	50,000	(On net residual value)
	$115,329	

For example: Assuming a 10 percent prime rate, a borrower maintaining 10 percent balances when the line is not in use, incurs a true cost of 12.90 percent assuming 100 percent usage. If the line is only 90 percent used, the true cost is 13.05 percent. A 30-day period "out of the banks" raises the cost to 13.19 percent. Equipment leasing at 12.5 percent would be lower as well as longer term.

11. Be used to obtain equipment not foreseen in capital budget planning.

12. Free funds for ownership of such appreciating assets as land.

13. Allow the equipment to pay for itself out of earnings rather than capital investment.
14. Allow repayment in depreciated dollars, lowering true cost compared to purchase for cash.
15. Improve return on assets and equity ratios.

Any or all of these reasons may be valid in a particular situation. The specific reasons are many and varied. In general, large corporations lease because of leasing's ease and convenience. Smaller corporations lease not only because of ease and convenience, but because equipment leasing is often more available than alternative methods of finance, particularly in times of "tight money" when debt money may be virtually impossible to obtain.

ALTERNATIVES OPEN TO A BANK WHICH WISHES TO PARTICIPATE IN THE EQUIPMENT LEASING

Financing equipment leasing companies is the easiest, perhaps the riskiest, and certainly the least profitable method for a bank wishing to participate in equipment leasing. It is the easiest method because there are many lessors, from national to local in scope, all requiring as much money as they can obtain. It is the riskiest because the bank is usually unable to evaluate the true worth of the borrower or his receivables. Generally accepted accounting practices allow such latitude in book accounting that a company on the verge of receivership may appear to be quite profitable. Earnings are front-loaded and residuals are booked in year one, although actual cash may be obtained only after the lease's termination, if ever. Often the underlying portfolio is composed of substandard credit risks, borrowing at high rates, with minimum credit evaluation, documentation, and collateral. These are often credits the bank would not accept at any rate.

This is often the least profitable business since the banks usually lend at low rates, competing (at the same time) with their own commercial loan department and thus really add nothing to net loans.

If a bank does lend to a leasing company, the following minimum safeguards should be taken:

1. Earnings statements should be developed indicating profit net of any estimated results.
2. Cash flow statements, excluding estimated residuals, should be developed.
3. The equipment leasing companies documentation package, credit evaluation procedure, UCC filing procedures and insurance coverage (of leased assets) should be analyzed for quality and accuracy.

Another way for a bank to participate in equipment leasing is to appoint an individual in the bank to evaluate, structure, and complete various types of equipment leases for the bank's customers. This procedure has the advantage of low cost. Its disadvantages are that the person so designated may be poorly qualified, and since most leasing is sold rather than bought, the volume of business will probably be minimal. This method is most common to smaller banks.

The next step for a bank is to set up a group of individuals to handle equipment leasing in the bank. Many large banks use such a group to meet the needs of bank customers, or potential bank customers, rather than mount a large-scale solicitation program to develop equipment leasing activity. Establishing a group may permit a greater degree of expertise to be developed, and allows the handling of a larger volume. This method is being used by a number of medium to large banks.

The same format as above, only changing the equipment leasing group from a bank operation to a bank subsidiary, has been used by some banks. This allows a different compensation plan, some insulation from liability, and makes out-of-state operations easier from a taxation viewpoint.

In most larger bankholding companies, the equipment leasing group is a subsidiary of the holding company.

A negative aspect of this structure is that the subsidiary may not borrow from its associated bank. Thus the low cost of funds enjoyed by other structures is forbidden. The benefits include financing outside of the bank structure, some bank insulation from liability, a more autonomous organization, improved state income tax position, and the potential for a national identity.

In evaluating which of the above methods of participating in equipment leasing is best for a particular bank, the following questions should be asked:

1. How much money does the institution wish to invest in equipment leasing?
2. What type of lease will be most beneficial?
3. What are the bank's objectives?
   a. Cash income?
   b. Tax shelter? What is the bank's taxable income for this year? The next five years?
   c. A hedge against inflation?
   d. Obtain new bank business? Local? National?
   e. Satisfy present customers?
   Perhaps all of these, or perhaps none of these, may be a given bank's objective.

4. What is the bank's present level of experience? Is it enough to gain its objectives? If not, how much assistance is required? Where will it come from? What will it cost?
5. How long will it take to show profits? What is the ultimate goal?
6. Is the bank willing and able to make the necessary long-term commitment? Many of these questions are complex. However, failure to answer them has caused many banks to enter the equipment leasing business for the wrong reasons. Often the banks have given up leasing based on equally poor planning.

CREDIT EVALUATION

In general, the same credit evaluation used for granting term loans of equal duration should be used for granting equipment leases. In addition, the following should be considered:

1. When doing 100 percent financing, the lessor will often find that the equipment's value in a distress situation will be insufficient to meet the lessee's obligation. The secured nature of the lease must not obscure this important fact.
2. A lease does not allow the lessor to demand payment in full except when in default, or when the lessee is in receivership or bankruptcy. This control is considerably less than in the usual loan arrangement.
3. Because of the above, the lessee's credit should be better than required for a comparable term loan, not poorer. Many leasing novices lose sight of this, and lease equipment to marginal credits based on the value of the equipment.
4. It is possible to obtain down payments, security deposits, advance payments, additional collateral, and personal guaranties, depending on the individual situation. Thus a borderline lease may be developed into a secure one.
5. When lesser credits are being considered, the maximum term should be five years unless there is a substantial front-end deposit of some nature. For better credits, terms to 10 years and beyond are customary.
6. In the case of an operating or leveraged lease, an early default can cause a loss of all of the tax benefits through sale of the equipment. In such a case, tax credits previously taken may be lost, increasing your exposure. Most lessors restrict such leases to better credits.

YIELD EVALUATION

"Capital" or "Finance" Lease.   Since such a lease has the economic impact of a loan, with no tax implications, its evaluation is very similar to a term loan. Economic benefits derive from:

  a. The difference between funds disbursed and rentals received, synonymous with interest for a loan.
  b. Any rentals received in advance (will increase yield).
  c. Any security deposits received at the lease's origination (will increase yield).
  d. Any termination fees, charges paid at the end of the lease (will increase yield). Lessors writing this type of lease usually use a standard reference book of tables, showing yields for various combinations of rentals and fees.

"Operating" or "True" Lease.   Analysis becomes more complex, since the value of accelerated depreciation, the estimated residual value of the leased equipment, and perhaps the investment tax credit, must all be added to the value of the rentals received. Economic benefits derive from:

  a. The difference between the funds disbursed and rental received, comparable with interest for a loan or the rentals from a capital lease.
  b. The value of accelerated depreciation, the use of funds which would have been used to pay federal and/or state income taxes. Since money has a "time" value, the funds obtained from delaying taxes can be quite valuable.
  c. If the lessor elects to use the investment tax credit, this results in an immediate tax savings that, unlike the value of accelerated depreciation, is not offset by future liability.
  d. At the end of the lease, the equipment may be leased at "fair market rental" or sold for "fair market value" either to the present lessee or a third party. In either case the lessor may obtain substantial economic advantage.

Lessors writing this type of lease usually compute their yield with the aid of a computer program.

The most difficult part of the yield analysis is the estimation of residual values.

  a. The lessee and lessor represent to the Internal Revenue Service that such residuals are at least 20 percent of the original cost of the equipment.

b. The impacts of inflation, technological change, changes in law or customs, and wear are all unknown.

c. Equipment of little value in an open sale may be of considerable value to an existing lessee who will wish to continue rentals almost indefinitely if a reduction from the original rentals is offered.

Probably the best approach is to evaluate each transaction three ways: With no residual, with your best estimate, and with 20 percent of original cost. If the yield meets your minimum yield standards without any residual, it is obviously a sound transaction. It is also well to consider all of the residuals in your portfolio as a "pool." Thus, if your average residual ranges between nothing (very unlikely) and 50 percent, it is quite easy to substantiate a 20 percent figure for IRS and your own accountants.

The leveraged lease yield evaluation becomes even more complex. Since, in addition to the factors affecting yield for an operating lease, repayment of debt, interest, and the establishment of a "pool" for further taxes, with ROI on the pool, all affect yield. Also, the tax benefits and residual benefits are magnified by the borrowing. The economic benefits are as follows:

a. The difference between funds disbursed, and rentals received, comparable to other types of leases. This difference may be quite small due to the increased benefits from other sources.

b. The value of accelerated depreciation. This value is an increased benefit (as compared to an unleveraged lease) since it is greater in proportion to funds invested.

c. The investment tax credit, if taken by lessor, also has a greater value than in an unleveraged lease, since it is greater in relation to funds invested.

d. The equipment's residual value at the end of the lease is also magnified.

A simplified comparison of the three main types of leasing is shown in Exhibit 2.

Note that the effect of receiving a $100,000 investment tax credit for the operating lease is equal to 10 percent of funds invested, and a $100,000 investment tax credit is 40 percent of funds invested in the leveraged lease.

Obviously the return on investment for the operating lease is higher than for the financial lease, and higher for the leveraged lease than either.

EXHIBIT 2 Yield Evaluation of Different Types of Leases

	Capital Lease	Operating Lease	Leveraged Lease
Amount	$1,000,000	$1,000,000	$1,000,000
Funds invested	All	All	250,000
Term.	10 years	10 years	10 years
Annual rental	$ 159,345	$ 159,345	$ 159,345
Total rental	$1,593,450	$1,593,450	$1,593,450
Residual	0	$ 50,000	$ 50,000
Termination fee	$ 50,000	0	0
Total received.	$1,643,450	$1,643,450	$1,643,450
Nonrecourse interest	0	0	$ 450,000
Net profit exclusive of tax benefits	$ 643,450	$ 643,450	$ 193,450
As a percentage of investment	64.345%	64.345%	77.380%
Additional benefits:			
Accelerated depreciation	No	Yes	Yes
Investment tax credit (if applicable).	No	$ 100,000	$ 100,000

BOOK EARNINGS, CASH EARNINGS, AND TAXABLE EARNINGS

In dealing with a capital lease, the book earnings from rentals equal the cash earnings and taxable earnings. Any termination fees or bargain purchase options cause book to exceed cash or taxable earnings until termination.

For example:

Assumptions—Capital Lease

Lease amount $1,000,000
Lease rate 10%
Tax rate. 51.64%
Term. . . . . .10 years
Annual rentals $159,345
Termination fee . . . .$ 50,000
Total receivable . . . .$159,345 × 10 = $1,593,450 Rentals
                                                                                     50,000 Residual
  Total benefits $1,643,450

Year One

	Book Earnings	Cash Earnings	Tax Earnings
From rental.	$159,345.00	$159,345.00	$159,345.00
From residual.	9,090.91	—	—

Total income....................	168,435.91	159,345.00	159,345.00
Less amortization	61,000.00	—	61,000.00
Net:			
Before taxes................	107,435.91	159,345.00	98,345.00
After taxes	55,866.67	112,139.40	51,139.40

In the following years, book earnings decline as the residual adds less and less to income. Cash earnings continue level until the last year when the residual is realized. Taxable earnings decline as the amortization factor increases, but increases in the last year as the residual is realized.

Year Ten

	Book Earnings	Cash Earnings	Tax Earnings
From rental.........................	$159,345.00	$159,345.00	$159,345.00
From residual.......................	909.91	50,000.00	50,000.00
Total income........................	160,254.91	209,345.00	209,345.00
Less amorization....................	150,000.00	—	150,000.00
Net:			
Before taxes.......................	10,254.91	209,345.00	59,345.00
After taxes	5,332.55	180,859.40	30,859.40

In an operating lease the differences are even greater. For example:

Assumptions—Operating Lease		Terms of Lease
Lease amount $1,000,000		10% salvage
Rate......................................10%		5% residual
Term......................................10 years		48% income tax
Depreciation............................. 8 years		rate
Annual rentals 159,345		
Investment tax credit ....None (to lessee)		

Year One

	Book Earnings	Cash Earnings	Tax Earnings
From rental..............	$159,345.00	$159,345.00	$159,345.00
From residual.............	9,090.91	—	—
Total income.............	168,435.91	159,345.00	159,345.00
Less amortization			
depreciation	61,000.00		125,000.00
			(½ year depreciation)

Net:			
Before taxes............	107,435.91	159,345.00	34,345.00
After taxes	55,866.67	142,859.40	17,859.40

Book earnings show $107,435.91 B/T, A/T $55,866.67, but cash earnings are $159,345 B/T of which only $34,348 is taxable. After tax is paid $142,859.40 is after-tax cash earnings.

Year Two

	Book Earnings	Cash Earnings	Tax Earnings
From rental..............	$159,345.00	$159,345.00	$159,345.00
From residual............	8,181.82	—	—
Total income.............	167,526.82	159,345.00	159,345.00
Less amortization	68,000.00	—	218,750.00
Net:			
Before taxes...........	99,526.82	159,345.00 B/T	(59,405.00)(loss)
After taxes	51,753.95	187,859.40	28,514.40 (tax saved)

As the lease progresses, tax shelter turns into tax liabilities.

Year Ten

	Book Earnings	Cash Earnings	Tax Earnings
From rentals.............	$159,345.00	$159,345.00	$159,345.00
From residual............	909.41	50,000.00	50,000.00
Total income.............	160,254.91	209,345.00	209,345.00
Less amortization	150,000.00	—	100,000.00(salvage)
Net:			
Before taxes...........	10,254.91	209,345.00	109,345.00
After taxes	5,332.55	156,859.40	56,859.40

If the investment tax credit is taken by the lessor, the difference between book, cash, and tax incomes during the first year is further accentuated.

For leveraged leasing the picture is complicated by the introduction of debt, with its principal repayment a cash outlay but not a tax deduction, and interest, with its cash outlay and tax deduction. Often book earnings are small, since the economic justification is primarily cash flows realized from tax avoidance (ITC) and tax deferral (accelerated depreciation).

A simplified example using the same situation as used above in the operating lease example, with the addition of a ten-year loan of $700,000 bearing interest at 8 percent and annual repayments of $101,976 to cover principal and interest is shown in Exhibit 3.

EXHIBIT 3   Use of 10-Year Debt to Partially Fund Operating Lease

	Book Earnings	Cash Earnings	Tax Earnings
Year One			
From rentals	$159,345.00	$159,345.00	$159,345.00
From residuals	9,090.91	—	—
Total income	168,435.91	159,345.00	159,345.00
Less amortization depreciation	61,000.00	47,600.00	125,000.00
Interest.........................	54,376.00	54,376.00	54,376.00
Net:			
Before taxes	53,059.91	47,369.00	(20,031.00) (before taxes loss)
After taxes....................	27,591.15	56,983.88 (Including tax saved)	9,614.88 (taxes saved)
Year Ten			
From rentals	$159,345.00	$159,345.00	$159,345.00
From residuals	909.41	50,000.00	50,000.00
Total income	160,254.91	209,345.00	209,345.00
Less amortization depreciation	150,000.00	97,300.00	100,000.00 (salvage)
Less interest...................	4,676.00	4,676.00	4,676.00
Net:			
Before taxes	5,578.41	107,369.00	104,669.00
After taxes....................	2,900.77	57,127.88	54,427.88

There is considerable discussion about recording the book earnings. Being considered are a number of ways designed to record earnings more in tune with the actual cash flows, which are high during the first years of the lease, decline, and then increase with the realization of a residual. In general, conservative opinion indicates spreading income over the entire lease period. Some banks have been spreading income over the shorter payback period.

The treatment of residuals has also been open to considerable discussion. Generally accepted accounting principles allow residuals to be booked on the basis of "sum-of-the-years' digits," starting with the first year, even though the equipment may not be sold for many years. In the meanwhile the residual is an estimate, optimistic or pessimistic, as only time will tell.

A further consideration is the effect of the tax savings generated by the equipment leasing group upon the parent's tax picture. Since an equipment leasing effort which is writing tax-motivated equipment leases will usually not only shelter its own income, but develop excess tax deductions, the parent's tax picture is quite important in gauging how much of such excess shelter should be developed. The parent's income tax bill and potential income tax bills are the final limiting factor upon the amount of operating and leveraged leases which can be written by its leasing group.

There are several ways by which the parent corporation may compensate the equipment leasing group for the tax benefits obtained: (a) The parent may make a cash payment to the leasing group, equal to the tax payments permanently avoided through the ITC; (b) the parent may make a cash payment to the leasing group equal to the tax payment permanently avoided through the ITC, and for taxes deferred by accelerating depreciation, on the grounds that as a practical matter, sure tax-deferral benefits will continue indefinitely; (c) the parent may set up a reserve on the books of the leasing group to reduce borrowings, thus giving the effect of a cash payment, without going through the profit and loss statement. The reserve will equal the total amount of taxes avoided and deferred, and has the effect of a loan of equity, or perhaps subordinated debt.

There are two methods of showing the effect of the investment tax credit, as in ownership, flow-through, and spreading.

OBTAINING BUSINESS

There are numerous ways in which a bank equipment leasing company may obtain business. Each has its own advantages and disadvantages.

1. A bank may obtain equipment leasing prospects through its own commercial and retail loan division. Advantage—no added cost. Disadvantage—competing with your own company, only a little added business.

2. Local vendors of various types of equipment are constantly seeking financing. Such dealers are a good source of leads. Disadvantages—constant pressure for undue speed in credit approval and compromise of credit standards. Failure of vendor to provide service may be a problem. Advantage—a constant stream of varied credits.

3. Prospecting requires a trained sales force. Its main advantage is a steady stream of varied business. Its disadvantage is the cost of maintaining the sales force.

4. Brokers vary from prestigious investment bankers to local freelancers working out of a phone booth. Advantage—a wide variety of types of credits and equipment. Disadvantages—the broker has a conflict of interest in trying to sell the lease at its lowest rate and trying to obtain the highest return to the lessor. Sometimes the broker does not give the lessor all of the pertinent facts. The lessor has little direct contact with the lessee and must continue to pay fees if any added business is written.

Some banks are participating their leases with other banks and are probably better sources than most brokers since they, unlike the brokers, are investing their own funds.

COMPETITION

A bank equipment leasing company faces competition from many sources. Among these are the bank's commercial department, other local banks and their leasing companies, the equipment leasing operations of many major money center banks, the major finance companies, numerous investment bankers, many large brokers, and a multitude of small brokers and equipment leasing companies.

Facing all of this competition, it is only because of the constant demand for financing that so many equipment lessors have been successful. Most of the top 1,000 companies are contacted on a routine basis by 20 or more lessors. It is among the smaller companies below the top 1,000 in size, that the best opportunities abound for the bank lessor.

Since rates are quite competitive on all levels, and competitive almost to the point of profitlessness for some larger transactions, the bank-lessor will also find better profit margins available from smaller companies.

SUMMARY

Although the rewards can be substantial, a potential bank lessor should research leasing and its desirability in depth before making a commitment. A realistic assessment of the possible benefits, costs, and the bank's chances of accomplishing its objectives, can be most useful in preventing a premature entry into, and even more hasty exit from, unchartered waters.

CHAPTER FIFTY-THREE _____

Agricultural Lending

David R. Christenson
President
Farmers State Bank

INTRODUCTION

The evolution that has taken place in agriculture over the last five years has had a significant impact on all participants in that industry. Farm businessmen and their lenders are facing challenges that have not existed since the 1930s. The need for careful analysis and evaluation of agricultural loans is more evident now than ever before. Both the lender and farm businessman must possess the information and abilities to accommodate and resolve those needs and resulting challenges.

Commercial banks, the Farm Credit System, insurance companies, captive finance companies, and various government agencies extend credit in excess of $200 billion for agriculture. Banks have typically been the primary supplier of short- and intermediate-term credit, specifically granting operating lines and extensions of credit for the acquisition of medium-term assets including machinery and equipment, storage facilities, and, in some cases, carryover of previous years operating lines that by their nature have become intermediate-term debts.

In the 1970s, agriculture expanded as never before. Farmers were encouraged to increase production, while record levels of inflation drove prices for land and machinery to heights that began to destroy the economic base for profitability. Toward the end of the decade, commodity prices coupled with government support payments began to decrease, contributing further to the problem. As the rate of inflation began its decline, the cost of capital assets acquired between 1975 and 1981 could not be supported by existing cash flow levels. These negative factors were compounded by a decline in the volume of exports of agricultural products, which further depressed prices, creating circumstances in which the farm businessman with a debt/worth ratio greater than 1:1 had an extremely difficult time servicing debt.

Agricultural management can no longer thrive only on the ability to understand soil conditions, crop varieties, and marketing conditions. Today's farm businessman is required to be an astute financial manager as well. At the same time the agricultural banker must be aware of and sensitive to significant financial implications involved in a variety of agricultural scenarios. Discussions with the customer must involve production plans, financial statement and cash flow analysis, current and future market conditions, and customer marketing plans.

Farm businessmen today must possess the necessary skills to effectively manage a variety of financial functions, including a detailed knowledge of their financial condition, projected cash flows, and debt service requirements. Finally, farm businessmen must be able to address the implications of a fluctuating economic environment.

The agricultural lender today must have a similar set of talents. The success of the agricultural bank depends heavily on experienced lending officers who have a good understanding of banking practices and an in-depth knowledge of agricultural production. They should be able to review the farm businessman's strategic plan and the tactical implementation of that plan. This review must take into consideration the costs of production, anticipated revenues, timing of these costs/revenues, cash flow considerations, and balance sheet dynamics of these activities.

The fluctuations of farm inventory volumes and capital assets also suggest that the agricultural lender have the data necessary to properly judge the value of those assets as collateral. It is not possible to accurately predict the future value of farm assets, thereby requiring the lender to design a lending transaction that will insulate the bank against unplanned variances. This ensures adequate protection by collateral.

Hedging may provide some opportunities for the borrower; however, both lender and borrower must be careful to ensure that they understand the implications of hedging and have access to a responsible commodity broker for advice and execution.

To accomplish this the agricultural lender should expect to spend significant time with the borrower to understand both the operation and the credit request. The lender must also determine how the borrowed funds will fit within the framework of the farm businessman's plan. Risk management is the key word in the agricultural lender's dictionary. Identifying the risks that exist in a transaction and effectively managing an acceptable level of risk will be the measure of a successful agricultural lender.

The remainder of this chapter will examine the sequential process for a new agricultural credit request, including the analysis/evaluation steps that are necessary to properly identify and manage the risk.

THE CREDIT REQUEST

A request for credit should initially take the form of an interview with the prospective borrower. At the beginning of the interview, the lender will want to inquire about any existing relationship with the bank that may have an impact on the request. It is important at this time to establish a positive rapport with the customer so that questions are freely asked and answered, thus ensuring a candid and successful interview. The lender should obtain information reflecting the type of operation, past experience, family situation (if appropriate), corporate structure (if applicable), or other form of ownership. The nature and amount of the request should be discussed in detail. At that point the lender should discuss with the customer the bank's policy considerations as they relate to the request. If the request fits within the policy framework of the bank and if the guidelines of the bank will accommodate the needs of the borrower, the process can continue. If an impasse occurs, the interview can be ended without difficulty or misunderstanding from either party. If lender and customer are willing to proceed, the loan application can be completed.

Agricultural loan applications can have many different forms; however, there is some basic information that should be covered in all forms:

1. Date.
2. Name and address.
3. Personal history.
4. Financial statement.
5. Experience.
6. Education.
7. Amount of loan requested.
8. Purpose.
9. Repayment terms.
10. Secondary source of repayment.
11. Collateral offered, if any.
12. Description of operation; including land owned, land leased, crop production schedule, livestock (production versus feeding), other capital assets, including machinery and equipment, facilities, etc.

Using the information provided with the application the lender will be able to make some tentative judgments regarding present situation analysis, financial stability of the customer, and reasonableness of the request. The next step should be an on-site visit or inspection. The value of this inspection is twofold. First, the accuracy of the balance sheet and various schedules may be verified. Second, the agricultural lender will have the opportunity to view firsthand the layout of the farm, the quality of maintenance and upkeep, and the adequacy of the equipment line and facilities.

The next process should be a character evaluation of the prospective borrower. Previous lenders should be traced and checked, as should relationships with suppliers and other trade creditors and third-party lenders, (i.e., Federal Land Bank, insurance company, contract holder, or captive finance company).

Lien searches along with other contacts and verifications are also recommended to ensure the accuracy of indicated liabilities.

ANALYSIS OF THE REQUEST

In order to properly prepare for the analysis of a credit request, the agricultural lending officer must require the submission of a variety of financial data reflecting past operations and current financial position. The primary purpose of the analysis is to make a judgment on the potential success or failure of the farming operation. The data required is as follows:

1. Current financial statement (within 90 days).
2. Financial statements from the last two years (calendar or fiscal).
3. Profit and loss statements (including schedule F from the borrower's tax return).
4. Total farm budgets.
5. Comparison of previous years' operation to budget.

Once the information requested has been delivered to the lending officer it can be assembled into a form that best fits the bank's standard analysis format. There are many types of analysis formats available, including those for personal computers.

The analysis should begin with a comparison of the financial statements provided. Special note should be taken of changes from year to year. This will suggest to the analyst the manner in which various assets are valued and the nature of financing used, if any, to acquire assets. The financial statement of a commercial customer is generally divided into two categories. For an agricultural financial statement it is preferable to catagorize both assets and liabilities into three areas: current, intermediate, and long-term.

Using the division of assets and liabilities indicated above, current assets are defined as cash or other assets that can be converted to cash within the current year. Conversely, current liabilities are those with a current-year maturity or payable in full within the current year, including the portion of any intermediate- or long-term liabilities due within the same time frame.

Intermediate assets are generally considered to be those that support production (machinery and equipment), and have a useful life of

1 to 10 years. This category also includes any assets with a maturity or convertible to cash within the same time frame. Intermediate liabilities are notes, contracts, and other amounts payable in 1 to 10 years. As the financial statement is reviewed one should remember that current amounts due under intermediate liabilites have been included in current liabilities above.

Long-term assets include real estate owned, and structures or other permanent fixtures attached to the real estate. Long-term liabilities are those used to support long-term assets or those with maturities of over 10 years. Payments on liabilities due within the current year are also included in current liabilities.

The manner in which assets are valued should be examined very closely to ensure that the analyst can identify if they are valued on a cost or market value basis. Cost basis valuation gives bankers a better picture of the relationship between the assets and the corresponding liabilities used as a funding source for acquisition. Care should be taken to remember that market value can differ significantly from cost value, particularly in deflationary times. When the lender performs the analysis, one of the factors to be determined is the availability of collateral and the ease of converting the collateral to cash in sufficient amounts to cover the obligations. Therefore, the most important path to follow is the one that provides the most realistic value of assets.

The agricultural lender should also stress the need for consistency in valuations and the form for presentation of financial statements. An important analytical function to be performed is one of determining the state of financial progress. Without a consistent presentation and form, it is very difficult to examine that progress.

Bank policy may dictate that a particular form of analysis be used (financial progress, future income, cash flow, etc.). However, all analyses must begin with the same information presented in a uniform fashion with realistic values.

Figures 1 and 2 demonstrate a comparative financial statement spread, as well as the trend analysis that can be used to identify the direction in which the operation is headed and areas of exposure that may exist. While many ratios are used in the analysis process, the following appears to present the best opportunity to effectively measure the trend of the operation:

1. Net Worth (Total Assets − Total Liabilities)

This will demonstrate how much the operation is in debt and the volume of assets owned by the borrower and his creditors. The extent to which leverage has been utilized (increased debt) indicates that an increased level of efficiency and profitability is needed to meet debt service payments. A rising interest rate environment necessitates in-

FIGURE 1 Statement Spread

	9/30/87	9/30/86	9/30/85	9/30/84	9/30/83
Current assets					
Cash savings	$ 62.2	$ 14.5	$ 45.3	$ −10.0	$ −85.0
Crop-inventory	820.0	653.3	672.8	778.6	561.3
Receivables	27.8	28.7	29.4	35.9	40.1
Livestock for sales	0.0	0.0	0.0	0.0	0.0
Grain and feed	0.0	0.0	0.0	0.0	0.0
Market secur	360.3	300.3	250.2	225.2	225.3
Prepaid expense	0.0	0.0	0.0	0.0	0.0
Other current	326.7	305.6	281.3	261.3	257.8
Subtotal	1597.0	1302.4	1279.0	1291.0	999.5
Intermediate assets					
Breeding livestock	0.0	0.0	0.0	0.0	0.0
Autos and trucks	0.0	0.0	0.0	0.0	0.0
Machinery and equipment . . .	829.5	811.0	775.4	657.7	608.0
Nonmarket sec	25.0	25.0	25.0	32.0	19.0
Subtotal	854.5	836.0	800.4	689.7	627.0
Fixed Assets					
Farm land (M)	2912.0	3120.0	3120.0	3120.0	3120.0
Farm improve	153.0	153.0	150.0	150.1	3.0
Subtotal	3065.0	3273.0	3270.0	3270.1	3123.0
Total assets	$5516.5	$5411.4	$5349.4	$5250.8	$4749.5

Current liabilities					
Notes pay. bank	$ 325.0	$ 401.5	$ 395.5	$ 108.8	$ 235.0
Notes pay other	0.0	0.0	7.1	26.2	15.6
Accts. payable	0.0	0.0	0.0	0.0	0.0
Current matur.	0.0	0.0	0.0	0.0	0.0
Accrued expense	0.0	0.0	0.0	0.0	0.0
Other current.	0.0	0.0	0.0	0.0	0.0
Subtotal	325.0	401.5	402.6	135.0	250.6
Intermediate liabilities					
Other inter	0.0	0.0	0.0	0.0	0.0
Subtotal	0.0	0.0	0.0	0.0	0.0
Long-term liabilities					
Farm mortgages	518.5	559.5	600.0	637.3	685.4
Land contracts	0.0	0.0	0.0	0.0	0.0
Other long-term	0.0	0.0	0.0	0.0	0.0
Subtotal	518.5	559.5	600.0	637.3	685.4
Total liabilities	843.5	961.0	1002.6	772.3	936.0
Total net worth (M)	4673.0	4450.4	4346.8	4478.5	3813.5
Total net worth (C)	3737.0	3306.4	3202.8	3334.5	2669.5
Total liabilities and net worth (M)	$5516.5	$5411.4	$5349.4	$5250.8	$4749.5

FIGURE 2 Trend Analysis

Statement Dates	9/30/87	9/30/86	9/30/85	9/30/84	9/30/83
Current ratio .... #	4.9	3.2	3.2	9.6	4.0
Adjusted current ratio .... #	4.9	3.2	3.2	9.6	4.0
Acid test .... #	2.4	1.6	1.5	3.8	1.7
Current margin.............. $	1272.0	900.9	876.4	1156.0	748.9
Adjusted current margin....... $	1272.0	900.9	876.4	1156.0	748.9
Intermediate assets/intermediate liabilities.................. #	0.0	0.0	0.0	0.0	0.0
Adjusted intermediate assets/ intermediate liabilities .... #	0.0	0.0	0.0	0.0	0.0
Intermediate asset equity...... $	854.5	836.0	800.4	689.7	627.0
Adjusted intermediate asset equity.................... $	854.5	836.0	800.4	689.7	627.0
Farm land equity (M)......... $	2393.5	2560.5	2520.0	2482.7	2434.6
Refinancing capacity (M) ...... $	1795.1	1920.4	1890.0	1862.0	1826.0
Debt/worth ratio (C)........... #	0.2	0.3	0.3	0.2	0.4
Debt/worth ratio (M) .... #	0.2	0.2	0.2	0.2	0.2
Change in net worth (C)....... $	430.6	103.6	−131.7	665.0	
Change in net worth (M) ...... $	222.6	103.6	−131.7	665.0	

creased cash flow and profitability just to stay even. Considering the volatility of the economy today, a "normal" standard of leverage is not an operative term. Cash flow, profitability, and balance sheet structure need to be reviewed in tandem with each other to determine an acceptable ratio of total assets to total liabilities (net worth).

2. Current Ratio (Current Assets − Current Liabilities)

This ratio indicates within a current time frame the solvency of the operation. The amount by which current assets exceed current liabilities also provides the level of working capital owned and the comfort with which the lender can consider short-term advances to the applicant.

3. Intermediate Ratio (Intermediate Assets − Intermediate Liabilities)

A measure of the level of funding in the intermediate range and equity owned in those assets.

4. Long-Term Ratio (Long-Term Assets − Long-Term Liabilities)

Shows base financial strength and refinance capacity for a potential secondary source of repayment for short-term debt.

5. Change in Net Worth (Current Net Worth — Previous Net Worth)

Shows profitability and the ability of the operation to retain earnings. Depending on the consistency of presentation, the level of earned increase in worth will be demonstrated.

Using the format suggested in Figures 1 and 2, the comparison of ratios currently in existence with those of previous periods helps in the analysis of changes from period to pereiod. The agricultural lender should recognize that these ratios may provide an indication of the financial strength and liquidity of the operation, but until these ratios are reviewed along with profitability, cash flow, and future prospects, a final determination cannot be made.

PROFIT AND LOSS

Profitability repays debit! Therefore the agricultural lender must be prepared on a consistent basis to measure the true profitability of the customer. Both the financial statement along with a properly prepared income and expense statement (including final adjustments for inventory changes) deliver the necessary information to make this determination.

Figure 3 illustrates an example of a profit and loss statement that takes into consideration all operating aspects of the borrowers operation, including a simplified calculation for sources and uses of funds, which can be related back to the financial statement thereby verifying the accuracy of information.

Several calculations are critical to the agricultural lender in analyzing the proposed transaction and the past performance of the farming operation:

$$\text{Asset turnover} = \frac{\text{Gross receipts}}{\text{Total farm assets}}$$

This calculation provides the analyst with the opportunity to examine the efficiency of the operation; that is, how many dollars of assets are required to generate a dollar of sales (gross receipts). The higher the ratio, the more effective the assets are being employed. This measure also helps the lender in evaluating requests for funds needed for expansion. If the farm operator has shown consistency in this measure, the lender can easily project this ratio on the basis of the request and make a judgment relative to future total assets, funding needs, and receipts.

FIGURE 3   Profit and Loss Statement

Farm operating receipts........................	$788.7	
Less: Farm operating expenses.................	405.1	
Net farm income		$383.6
Adjustments:		
Livestock inventory change....................	0.0	
Crop and feed inventory change	10.0	
Prepaid expenses change.....................	0.0	
Accounts payable change.....................	0.0	
Accounts receivable change..................	2.2	
Total adjustments		12.2
Less: Depreciation		80.0
Net farm earnings............................		315.8
Nonfarm income	0.0	
Less: Living expenses	36.0	
Income tax................................	12.0	
Social security............................	0.0	
Nonfarm expenses........................	0.0	
Net nonfarm contribution.....................		−48.0
Total net profit		267.8
Sources of funds:		
Total net profit	267.8	
Depreciation..............................	80.0	
Sale of capital	0.0	
Additional term debt.......................	0.0	
Total sources		347.8
Uses of funds:		
Term debt payments........................	30.0	
Machinery and equipment...................	30.0	
Land purchases............................	0.0	
Building and improvements..................	0.0	
Breeding livestock purchases................	0.0	
Total uses.............................		60.0
Change in current position.		287.8

$$\text{Return on investment} = \frac{\text{Profit}}{\text{Average total assets}}$$

This measure assists the lender as well as the farmer in determining how the return to the farmer compares with other investments as well as other farm operations.

$$\text{Net profit margin} = \frac{\text{Profit}}{\text{Gross receipts}}$$

These profitability measures assist in explaining why the farmer's return may be either high or low. Declining asset turnover combined with decreased profitability suggests inefficient production, excessive overhead, or poor marketing conditions. These considerations may be an indicator of needed changes in financing methods, production schedules, capital expenditures, etc.

The analytical procedures discussed relative to the financial statement as well as the profit and loss statement should generally be viewed in light of economic and other conditions that existed during the affected period. Comparisons to previous years provide insight into the method of operation in the past; in particular, whether the data suggests either positive changes or those that present an area of exposure to both the farm businessman and lender.

CASH FLOW

The cash flow statement is the most important of the documents used in the analysis of an agricultural credit request. The capacity to repay debt is determined through the use of a budget, which provides the ability to project cash flow for the period under review. The cash flow analysis, financial statement, and profitability data create the opportunity for the agricultural lender to gauge the ability of the operation to properly service its debt. Figure 4 is an example of a cash flow statement that provides the necessary data to make an evaluation relative to debt servicing capacity.

A cash flow statement consists of two basic parts: cash inflows and outflows. To prepare the cash inflows, the analyst must carefully examine the operations projected for the period under review; that is, the type and volume of production, projected sales, prices, government payments, and other sources of cash available to the borrower. Determining the value of projected sales must be as accurate as possible. An overly optimistic projection will distort the volume of cash inflows and invalidate the final results. A livestock operation requires the analyst to take into consideration the need to provide feed needs out of production.

Cash outflows should be prepared with the same care as inflows. All uses of cash projected for the period under review must be entered on the form including, but not limited to, crop inputs, feed expense, capital expenditures, debt payments, living needs and other payments planned. The cash flow plan should be prepared on a quarterly basis at minimum, but will be more effective when prepared monthly. The beginning available cash together with the results of the cash flow analysis provides a realistic view of projected cash needs during the period. The cash flow statement indicates the high point of the operating loan needed as well as the ability of the operation to repay its debt. Combining the needs for credit indicated by the cash flow statement along with the beginning loan balance identifies the level of credit outstanding at the end of the period.

FIGURE 4   Cash Flow Statement

	Apr	May	Jun	Jul	Aug	Sep	TOTAL
Operating receipts							
Crop sales	111.5	0.0	61.8	103.9	0.0	0.0	758.7
Livestock sales	0.0	0.0	0.0	0.0	0.0	0.0	0.0
Dairy products	0.0	0.0	0.0	0.0	0.0	0.0	0.0
Custom work	0.0	0.0	0.0	0.0	0.0	0.0	0.0
Gov't payments	0.0	0.0	0.0	0.0	0.0	15.0	30.0
Other farm inc.	0.0	0.0	0.0	0.0	0.0	0.0	0.0
Nonfarm income	0.0	0.0	0.0	0.0	0.0	0.0	0.0
Divids. and int.	0.0	0.0	0.0	0.0	0.0	0.0	0.0
Total oper. rec.	111.5	0.0	61.8	103.9	0.0	15.0	788.7
Operating expenses							
Fert-chem-seed	55.0	57.6	0.0	0.0	0.0	0.0	112.6
Hired labor	3.0	3.0	10.0	10.0	5.0	5.0	65.0
Machinery hire	0.0	0.0	0.0	0.0	0.0	0.0	0.0
Rent-leases	0.0	0.0	0.0	0.0	0.0	7.3	14.5
Repairs	4.0	4.0	4.0	4.0	4.0	4.0	48.0
Supplies	0.5	0.5	0.5	0.5	0.5	0.5	6.0
Livestock misc.	0.0	0.0	0.0	0.0	0.0	0.0	0.0
Fuel	9.0	0.0	9.0	0.0	9.0	0.0	46.0
Irrigation	0.0	0.0	0.0	0.0	0.0	0.0	0.0
Storage and dry	0.0	0.0	0.0	0.0	0.0	0.0	0.0
Property taxes	0.0	8.0	0.0	0.0	0.0	0.0	16.0
Insurance	0.0	0.0	0.0	0.0	0.0	10.0	10.0
Utilities	0.5	0.3	0.3	0.3	0.3	0.3	6.9
Interest exp.	0.0	0.0	29.0	0.0	0.0	2.2	72.8
Other (farm)	0.6	0.6	0.6	0.6	0.6	0.6	7.2
Livestock purch.	0.0	0.0	0.0	0.0	0.0	0.0	0.0
Feed purchases	0.0	0.0	0.0	0.0	0.0	0.0	0.0
Nonfarm exp.	0.0	0.0	0.0	0.0	0.0	0.0	0.0
Total oper. exp.	72.6	74.0	53.4	15.4	19.4	29.9	405.1
Net oper. inc.	38.9	−74.0	8.4	88.5	−19.4	−14.9	383.6
Other expenses							
Family living	3.0	3.0	3.0	3.0	3.0	3.0	36.0
Income tax	0.0	0.0	0.0	0.0	0.0	0.0	12.0
Social security	0.0	0.0	0.0	0.0	0.0	0.0	0.0
Term debt pymts.	0.0	0.0	15.0	0.0	0.0	0.0	30.0
Total oper. inc.	35.9	−77.0	−9.6	85.5	−22.4	−17.9	305.6
Capital receipts	0.0	0.0	0.0	0.0	0.0	0.0	0.0
Capital expenses	0.0	0.0	0.0	0.0	0.0	15.0	30.0
Net cash change	35.9	−77.0	−9.6	85.5	−22.4	−32.9	275.6
Cash bal B-O-M	15.0	22.0	15.0	15.0	20.9	15.0	
Req. cash balance	15.0	15.0	15.0	15.0	15.0	15.0	
Cash exc./def.	35.9	−70.0	−9.6	85.5	−16.5	−32.9	
Payments	28.9	0.0	0.0	79.6	0.0	0.0	
Short-term debt	0.0	70.0	79.6	0.0	16.5	49.4	

The proper analysis of cash flow data along with calculated changes in inventories on hand and changes in loan balances assists in projecting the financial and profitability results of the operation. To make the best use of the cash flow data, the farm businessman should maintain an actual cash flow record during the period. This is critical for identification of variations from projections, where adjustments can be considered and executed promptly.

DECISION

Using the information discussed in the preceding paragraphs, the agricultural lender is in a position to make judgments regarding the loan application. The function of the lending officer is to make an evaluation of the risk inherent in the proposed transaction. As a result of the analysis, the lender will have a good picture of the profitability, financial strength, liquidity, and repayment capacity of the agricultural operation. The use of the cash flow statement will help determine the timing of loan advances and repayments, beginning and ending loan balances, and peak credit needs. The borrower's marketing plan is the driving force behind projected cash inflows and thereby allows the agricultural lender to make observations relative to the practicality of those plans.

The analysis may suggest weaknesses in the operation, whereby a longer term evaluation may be necessary. A reallocation of resources and/or a different configuration of the operation in terms of expansion or contraction may result in a strengthening of the business.

COLLATERAL

As described above, the risk evaluation indicates the need, if any, for collateral to secure the obligation. Legal considerations relative to properly securing a loan vary among jurisdictions. Sound advice is necessary to properly protect the lender's position in the collateral. The agricultural lender must be familiar with the process required to perfect any security interest. The type of collateral taken will vary according to the terms of the credit extension as well as the financial position of the borrower. If collateral is taken it is well to remember the importance of requiring a primary and secondary source of repayment and to cover both in any security interests taken.

The on-site inspection provides the opportunity for the lender to make a "barnyard" appraisal of assets available for collateral. To the extent that the lending transaction depends on collateral for risk management, it may be advisable to obtain professional appraisals of those assets. Careful attention should be directed to the difference, if any, between implementation and market value of farm assets so that adequate protection is provided at all times. Up-to-date data should be maintained on all collateral taken, including valuations, insurance coverage, and documentation validating the bank's lien position.

DOCUMENTATION AND LOAN MAINTENANCE

For any lending transaction the credit file is the combination of all source documents with the exception of the promissory note. The number of documents indicated in this discussion can best be displayed in a six-sided credit file. The following is a suggested configuration for credit file maintenance:

1. Comments, which should include a discussion of financial trends, operating plan, collateral assessment, security position, etc.
2. Financial statements, profit and loss statements, cash flow statement.
3. Collateral documents, lien searches, appraisals.
4. Borrowing resolutions, guarantees.
5. Insurance coverage.
6. Correspondence.

Each lending institution should have its own procedures for file maintenance. However, a checklist similar to the one shown in Figure 5 helps make sure that each credit transaction is documented properly and in accordance with bank policies and procedures as well as prevailing laws and regulations.

All lines of credit should be reviewed at least annually and in some cases more frequently. The financial documents should be updated to ensure that the operation is progressing according to plan. The review will also provide the lender with the opportunity to observe changes and make suggestions or adjustments in the handling of the transaction as required. On-site inspections can be a very helpful tool in monitoring the loan and developing a close working relationship with the borrower.

A line of credit appropriate to the needs of the farm businessman can be facilitated by the use of the budget and cash flow, demonstrating peak needs as well as the amount and timing of repayments. The commitment to lend can also be based on these documents. Advances and repayments should be noted in the credit file along with the correlation of those money transactions to the cash flow statement.

Large and more complex credit transactions may require the use of a formal loan agreement that spells out the rights and obligations of both lender and borrower. The use of legal counsel in drafting such

FIGURE 5 Loan Documentation Checklist, Date Completed

	Requirement	Date Received
Balance sheet	_____	_____
Trend sheet	_____	_____
Tax forms	_____	_____
Cash flow	_____	_____
Profit and loss	_____	_____
Risk rating	_____	_____
Loan review comments	_____	_____
Trend	_____	_____
P&L	_____	_____
Program and purpose	_____	_____
Collateral assessment	_____	_____
Recommendation and service plan	_____	_____
Chattel search	_____	_____
Security agreement	_____	_____
Blanket	_____	_____
Crop mortgage/legal		
description/fee holder	_____	_____
Insurance—loss payee	_____	_____
Vehicle titles	_____	_____
Financing statement	_____	_____
R.E. mortgage	_____	_____
Update abstract	_____	_____
Preliminary title	_____	_____
Opinion	_____	_____
Mortgage	_____	_____
Final opinion	_____	_____
Note	_____	_____
Line of credit agree	_____	_____
Other	_____	_____
_____	_____	_____
_____	_____	_____
_____	_____	_____
_____	_____	_____

an agreement is recommended. The value of legal assistance quickly becomes evident in the event of liquidation or default.

The agricultural lender must be in contact with and record information received from suppliers and other lenders. The borrower who has numerous outside debts with a variety of lenders or suppliers should be examined carefully. This generally suggests poor management and presents significant additional risk for the operating lender. When debt other than that for capital asset acquisition is in the hands of many lenders, control is lost as well as accountability on the part of the borrower. It presents many problems in creating a structure that will provide for appropriate monitoring and risk management.

LIQUIDATION

Until the last three or four years, this term has not held much significance for the agricultural lender. Current conditions suggest, however, an increasing probability that the lender must consider liquidation to protect the bank from additional loss.

Once the lender has determined that problems exist with an agricultural line of credit, it is imperative that the borrower be contacted to discuss the situation. Hopefully, a restructuring of the transaction, the sale of unneeded assets, or other income sources will provide the necessary cash flow to put the credit arrangement back on schedule. However, if this is not possible, alternative plans must be made. This can include the conversion of operating debt to a longer term or the process of negotiating with the borrower for a voluntary, partial, or complete liquidation of assets. The agricultural lender may also consider a combination of asset sales and partial forgiveness of debt.

If these types of arrangements fail to mediate the problem, liquidation of the bank's position may be necessary. The first order of business should involve the bank's legal counsel. A careful review of the collateral documentation should be made. Notification to the borrower must be made relative to the position of the bank. The correct process of conversion of collateral to the possession of the bank will differ from state to state; however, the involvement of the bank's counsel will ensure the use of appropriate liquidation methods.

Considering flat or declining capital asset values and the volatility that exists in commodity prices, one will generally find that the first loss is the least expensive. This is not to suggest that efforts should not be made to work out a reasonable solution to the financial problems that face the farm businessman. Once liquidation becomes the only outcome, prompt action of the agricultural lender will ensure the best result for the bank. Legal counsel that is competent to deal with and conversant with the Uniform Commercial Code, as well as all relative chapters of the Bankruptcy Act, is essential to minimize the bank's exposure during the liquidation process.

CONCLUSION

A significant portion of commercial bank lending to agriculture is provided by relatively small rural banks. Methods of delivering agricultural financing vary among providers. The objective, however, remains constant throughout; that is, to provide extensions of credit that address the needs of the borrower while allowing the bank to identify and manage its risk. A properly structured agricultural loan can be mutually profitable for both lender and farm businessman. Diligent use and understanding of the credit analysis tools and process will ensure the desired results.

CHAPTER FIFTY-FOUR

Residential Mortgage Lending and Mortgage Loan Warehousing

H. Richard Noon

President
Bankers Mortgage and Investment Group, Inc.

Residential mortgage lending is that type of financing that provides the funds for the purchase of a dwelling to be used as a residence. Residential mortgage lending is commonly limited to buildings that are from one to four units in size. Loans that are originated for buildings that have more than four units are commonly called multifamily loans. The mortgage finance industry and especially the secondary mortgage market have traditionally acknowledged the distinction between residential mortgage lending and multifamily mortgage lending at five units in a single building.

Prior to a discussion on residential mortgage lending, some brief comments on the various types of home ownership are warranted. Traditionally we have always thought of residential mortgage lending as encompassing only the single family detached residence with fee simple title. There are other forms of home ownership, however, that are significant and deserve mention here since they are commonplace in the market today. For example, the condominium form of ownership is quite common today. A condominium residence may be a single apartment-type unit within the framework of a large building structure or a single building structure dependent on other similar building structures for some common services and amenities. Basically a condominium unit is a legally independent, easily defined dwelling unit that shares certain areas of common ownership with all the other units in the building or project. These common areas can be social in nature, or they can be such other types of common facilities that are important and necessary to the use of the building—for example, green areas versus elevators.

The cooperative is another type of ownership where a corporation is formed and stock is issued to the members of the corporation. The purchase of the stock enables the individual to purchase his individual housing unit within the complex. Cooperative ownership is common in areas where there is high rise construction and apartment-type dwelling units. In these instances, the cooperative corporation is the mortgagor and there is one mortgage on all the dwelling units. The owner of the shares in the cooperative thereby owns a certain portion of the corporation and the buildings, which is translated into his unit. His payments to the corporations or cooperative are used to satisfy the mortgage indebtedness, the upkeep of the facilities, etc. With this form of ownership, the stockholder does not hold title to the real estate, but does hold title to his shares of stock in the corporation. The cooperative corporation holds title to the real estate.

In addition, it should be noted that there is another form of ownership closely related to the condominium. This is the planned unit development (PUD). The PUD is used to a great extent today to obtain better usage of the land. With PUD, the owners of the dwelling units have common ownership in the grounds, streets, and amenities. By establishing a PUD, developers are able to, in some cases, work with smaller lot sizes, narrower streets, and more common types of amenity packages. In this form of home ownership, home associations are formed to control and maintain such things as streets, green areas, exterior maintenance of the residential units, etc. Architectural control is also exhibited. This form of home ownership is very common at this time, due to the rising costs of land and the real estate developer's ability to increase his density with PUD. Since the common areas are policed and maintained by homeowners associations, there are mandatory assessments to maintain the property and the neighborhood. These association dues and assessments are charged to the individual homeowner and therefore need to be considered in residential mortgage lending. They are also a necessary part of maintaining the quality and soundness of the project and thereby the individual units.

THE LENDING PHILOSOPHY

The lending philosophy will take one of two directions determined by management. If the philosophy is to originate residential mortgage loans for the portfolio, then management will set any criteria that it determines is in the best interest of the institution relative to the underwriting of the residential mortgage loan. If, however, management determines that it will originate residential mortgage loans either for sale into the secondary mortgage market at this time, or at some later date, its lending criteria will be determined by the secondary mortgage market. Management should consider carefully the advantages and disadvantages of each course of action. A word of caution here, however, is warranted. It is much easier to structure the residential mortgage loan according to accepted secondary mortgage guidelines at the time of origination with supporting documentation, than it is at some later date to go back and determine that the loans previously originated should now be sold. The marketplace, if in fact there is a market for these loans, will penalize the seller due to the lack of documentation that is in acceptable form.

UNDERWRITING THE RESIDENTIAL LOAN

Underwriting the residential mortgage loan is a two-part process. The loan amount must be warranted by the property, the collateral. Also the borrower or mortgagor must have the capacity, creditworthiness, and character to repay the loan. A good residential mortgage loan will be properly underwritten in both areas. In order for the bank to make a proper evaluation of the risk involved with this loan, it must estimate the value of the security for the loan—that is, the residential unit— and the borrower or mortgagor's ability to repay the loan over an extended period of time. Consideration, therefore, should be given to the anticipated future economic life of the collateral and to the anticipated future economic abilities of the borrower. Of the two elements to be considered, the most important is probably the collateral value, which is determined by an appraisal of the real estate.

THE APPRAISAL

The appraisal of real estate, if properly done, uses techniques that result in a reliable value decision. This, of course, assumes that the appraiser is well qualified and is experienced in the area.

The real estate profession has determined that value can be obtained on residential property by using three approaches to its value. The first approach that is used is the cost approach. The rationalization for using this approach is that nothing is worth more now than it would cost reproduced. As a result, the appraiser determines the cost of the structure new, adds to it the cost of the land, and improvements to the land, and then depreciates the existing improvements to establish current value. This depreciation is divided into three categories: physical, functional, and economic. Physical depreciation is depreciation that results from use—for example, sidewalks in need of repair, etc.

Functional depreciation is depreciation that results from those factors inherent in the property because of the design. For example, poor access to a bathroom would limit its use and thereby possibly restrict the value of that facility and the overall value of the unit. The third area of depreciation is economic depreciation. This form of depreciation occurs from factors outside the residence itself. For example, a properly maintained residence surrounded by other residences in need of repair could cause economic depreciation. These forms of depreciation are not found in all cases, but when they are found by the appraiser in evaluating the residence, they do provide a limitation on value.

The second approach to value that the appraiser considers is the market approach. The appraiser evaluates recent sales of similar properties and makes adjustments of either a positive or negative nature to establish the value of the residence that he is appraising as compared to the other recent sales. These recent sales are called "comparables." The appraiser is particularly interested in such items as the date of sales, the location of the property, the number of rooms, overall condition, quality of construction, parking, etc. All these factors are compared to the residence being appraised, and the appraiser determines his value by comparing the property being appraised to the comparables and making the necessary adjustments.

The third approach to value that the residential home appraiser makes is the income approach. In this approach, he compares the rental rates being obtained by similar properties and uses them as a multiplier to determine the value of the residential unit being appraised. This method, in most cases, is not nearly as reliable. In fact the market approach is deemed to be the most reliable in most instances.

After the appraiser has determined the value of the three various approaches, he correlates his data and establishes a final value as of a given date. As mentioned above, in most instances the most reliable data and the approach that receives the most merit from the appraiser is the market approach.

Unless the lender has a specific form that he desires to use for his appraisal, the recognized appraiser will probably use the Fannie Mae or Freddie Mac form 1004. This very comprehensive form provides the lender with a detailed review of the property and of the comparable properties. When completed, it will have a supply of photos, a location map, etc., and provide the lender with a good, reliable, noteworthy profile of the real estate that will be used as collateral. This appraisal form is the only form that is recognized universally as an acceptable appraisal report form; therefore, if the lender intends now or in the future to sell the loan, the appraisal should be done on this form by a qualified appraiser.

THE BORROWER

The borrower must have not only the capacity to repay the loan, but also the character and the willingness to do so. In underwriting the capability of the borrower, the lender should review his current employment status, both from the viewpoint of current and future earnings and the stability of the income stream. The same process should exist for co-borrowers. To determine the above, an applicant should execute an employment verification that allows the lender to contact the applicant's employer directly and determine his conditions of employment. This should be done for borrowers and co-borrowers alike. To determine the employment stability of a borrower/applicant, employment verifications should be completed for at least two years.

In addition to an evaluation of the borrower's income from employment sources, his other sources of income should also be verified. These include rental income, income from stock and bonds, etc.

In order to determine the borrower's capability of repaying the loan, a careful evaluation of the applicant's other outstanding obligations is warranted. A borrower who is laden with consumer debt may not be capable of assuming a house payment that is significantly higher than his current rental obligations, especially when coupled with the other costs of home ownership. A factual data credit report helps the underwriter to determine the borrower's obligations and his payment history. If it is necessary for the borrower/applicant to originate a loan for the downpayment of the home in order to qualify for the mortgage loan, this should be so noted and should be a matter of concern. As a result, if the borrower/applicant indicates that he has the necessary downpayment on hand or on deposit in an institution, it should be confirmed in writing directly with the institution by use of a verification of deposit form. There is a generally accepted form for this purpose.

To properly evaluate the borrower's capability and capacity to repay this loan, the lender should in his initial interview have the borrower complete a residential mortgage loan application form. If the lender has determined that he will originate this loan for the portfolio, then of course he can use his own loan application. If, however, he intends to sell the loan in the secondary market now or ever, he should complete the nationally accepted residential mortgage application known as Fannie Mae/Freddie Mac form 1003. The completion of this form provides a complete and accurate profile of the borrower/applicant. When the statements that are made on the application are confirmed, through verifications and a credit report used to supplement the application, the lender should have a clear, accurate profile on the borrower/applicant.

With the aforementioned appraisal, the application, and supporting documentation in hand, the lender will be in a position to make an intelligent decision based on the information that he has on the borrower's capability of repaying this loan. If the lender intends to sell the loan at some later date, there are nationally accepted ratios of income-to-housing expense and ratios showing all the applicant's total debt payments to his income. If the loan is to be sold, these ratios should be adhered to. While they are benchmarks, and not necessarily rules, time has proven that they deserve merit and should be respected. Further considerations, of course, should be given to the amount of downpayment, and the stability of the borrower's income and possibility for future advancements.

TYPES OF LOANS

There are three major types of residential mortgage loans. They are the FHA loan, the VA loan, and the conventional mortgage loan. The FHA loan is a first mortgage loan insured by the Federal Housing Administration. The VA loan is a first mortgage loan guaranteed by the Veterans' Administration. The conventional mortgage loan can include private mortgage insurance that provides insurance coverage on the top portion of the loan, in case of foreclosure and loss by the lender, or there can be a downpayment in excess of 20 percent of sale price on the conventional mortgage loan with a 15- or 20-year amortization. Underwriters use the same process as mentioned above, but some of the forms differ when dealing with the VA or FHA.

FHA-INSURED LOANS

Federal Housing Administration (FHA), which had its beginning in the early 1930s, insures residential mortgage loans with high ratios of loan to value. It generally uses its own appraisers, does its own credit analysis, and makes its own loan approvals. In recent years, lenders have been able to secure from the FHA the designation of "direct underwriter." With this designation, a lender can do all the processing that was previously done by the FHA and issue an FHA firm commitment to insure the loan. This is done by the lender on behalf of FHA. The responsibility of the direct underwriter is significant, and the privilege is not granted to a specific lender until he has demonstrated that he has the capability of handling it with prudence. Most originators of FHA loans today are direct underwriters.

The FHA-insured loan has traditionally been a high ratio of loan to value and, when originated, has been very marketable to national investors. Most FHA and VA loans today are originated to be put into

GNMA mortgage backed pools and sold to institutional investors. Very few FHA-insured home loans are sold to investors on an individual basis. Because the FHA insures the loan, there is a fee to be paid and it essentially provides the underwriting criteria for the loan. It also determines the amount of downpayment. Downpayments are set at minimums and from time to time change, as do the interest rates on the loan. The interest rates on FHA loans are determined by money market conditions. The charges to the borrower are controlled by regulation. The loan maturities, as in conventional mortgage lending, are determined by the economic life of the real estate.

VA LOANS

The Veterans' Administration at the end of WW II, in an effort to support housing for veterans, established a housing policy. This housing policy and the VA loan program allowed a borrower to purchase a home within the veterans' guidelines and obtain a 100 percent mortgage with no down payment. The Veterans' Administration guaranteed the repayment of the upper portion of a loan. From time to time, the Veterans' Administration's guarantee has fluctuated as housing prices and mortgages have increased. The Veterans' Administration reserves the option of purchasing the foreclosed real estate from the mortgagee at the mortgage balance and providing the total reimbursement for the outstanding principal and interest, or of making a payment in lieu of total payment and paying only the guaranteed portion of the loan. In recent times, some lenders have received this guaranteed portion in repayment and have suffered losses due to the eventual sale of the property not covering the entire mortgage balance.

Like the FHA, the VA sets the maximum interest rates for the loans it guarantees, limits the term of the loan, and establishes the borrower's guidelines. The VA loans that have been originated are also placed in GNMA mortgage backed pools and sold to investors. This process works like the FHA loans. The loans are placed in the same GNMA pools and offered as mortgage-backed securities.

CONVENTIONAL LOANS

The conventional mortgage loan is underwritten entirely by the lender and does not require approval of any other entity, except in cases where private mortgage insurance will insure the top portion of the loan. In those instances, the private mortgage insurance companies determine the acceptability of their risk and, for a premium, guarantee repayment of the top portion of the loan in case of default. Their underwriting standards are similar to those established in the secondary mortgage market. They do, however, reflect certain economic changes that exist in geographical sections of the United States. The private mortgage insurance company does make its own underwriting decisions.

The traditional conventional mortgage loan requires a down payment of at least 20 percent and usually has a term of not greater than 30 years. In recent years, the popularity of a 30-year fixed-rate conventional mortgage has dropped, and in its place is a more popular 15-year amortization. The payment difference in the two loans is not as significant as thought to be with the difference in amortization period. The traditional conventional loan, when underwritten according to the standards already mentioned, is usually a safe investment for the mortgage lender.

In recent years, several other types of conventional mortgage loans have become popular. These include the adjustable rate mortgage (ARM) and the graduated payment mortgage (GPM). Both of these loans require, in addition to the normal underwriting standards, additional due diligence. The adjustable rate mortgage provides for rate increases and decreases over the life of the loan. As a result, the assumption is made that the interest rate adjustments will follow general market conditions; therefore, the borrower will be able to make the additional payments necessary if the interest rate goes up and the lending institution will be able to sustain a drop in the interest collected when rates go down. When properly underwritten, the adjustable rate mortgage can be a good investment for the lender and a beneficial tool for the borrower.

The graduated payment mortgage provides for payment increases over the initial life of the mortgage loan. The initial rate of interest on the loan is artificially low to enable the borrower to qualify for the loan. As the loan matures, the rate increases. The assumption is that the borrower's income will also increase. Again, this loan requires a significant amount of underwriting because of the variables mentioned above. When underwriting conventional mortgage loans, whether they be fixed rate long-term self-amortizing, adjustable rate mortgages, or graduated payment mortgages, with or without private mortgage insurance, significant attention should be paid to the dictates of the secondary mortgage market if these loans are to be sold. The structure of the loans, the indexes in cases where an adjustable rate mortgage or graduated payment mortgage is being originated, and other factors need to be considered if a loan is to be sold. Both national secondary mortgage market agencies, Federal National Mortgage Association and Federal Home Loan Mortgage Corporation, purchase conventional loans of all types. They do, however, have their own underwriting standards. When the loans are to be sold, these underwriting standards should be complied with at the time of origination.

SECONDARY MORTGAGE MARKET—TRADING MORTGAGES FOR CASH

Throughout this chapter, reference has been made to the secondary mortgage market. As a result, some explanation of this market and how it works is warranted.

Commercial banks, thrifts, and mortgage bankers all originate residential mortgage loans. Some sell their loan to federal agencies, such as Fannie Mae and Freddie Mac, to state and local housing finance agencies, or to private conduits. Still others package their loans creating GNMA pools or conventional mortgage-backed securities and sell them to brokers/dealers. These securities then are sold by security dealers for cash. The cash is returned to the thrift or commercial bank or mortgage banker who starts the process again. This process enables the commercial bank to exchange the mortgage that has been created for cash. It enables the commercial bank to originate another home loan for a customer, and the process starts all over again. In this process, the commercial bank retains the ability to service the loan and the customer contact. In many cases, there is a significant deposit account, either in the form of an escrow account or customer relationship accounts. The loans generated by this activity provide a base for other banking services. The secondary market enables a commercial bank to expand its service throughout its community, without depleting its own lending funds. It also provides an excellent source of lending discipline that guides the institution and assist its lending officers in the creation and production of good high-quality mortgage loans. Commercial banks that are interested in selling their loans into the secondary mortgage market should establish a primary relationship with the Federal Home Loan Mortgage Corporation (Freddie Mac), the Federal National Mortgage Association (Fannie Mae), and the Government National Mortgage Association (GNMA). These quasi-government-sponsored secondary market lenders exist for the purpose of providing mortgage funds to the primary lenders in exchange of the mortgages. This service is certainly appropriate in times of short money supply. The discipline required to work these secondary lenders is certainly warranted if liquidity in the mortgage loan portfolio is desired.

MORTGAGE LOAN WAREHOUSING

This type of loan is a real estate related loan; however, it is truly a commercial loan and is most likely to be handled on the commercial loan side of the bank. Usually the loan request is handled as a line of credit, secured by real estate mortgages and/or deeds of trust. The primary customers for this type of loan are mortgage banking companies, although savings and loans, credit unions, and commercial banks that sell their loans into the secondary market have a need at times for lines of credit to temporarily fund residential mortgage loans until they are sold and purchased in the secondary mortgage market.

There are several methods of establishing a warehouse line at a commercial bank. The terms of these loans vary, depending on the relationship that is established.

Generally speaking, first mortgage loans secured by either mortgages or deeds of trust are originated by the primary lender. The primary lender exchanges, at his loan closing, his funds for a first mortgage or deed of trust on the property. The primary lender has already made a decision to either retain this loan in his portfolio of loans or to sell the paper in the secondary mortgage market. If the primary lender is doing a volume of business for sale into the secondary market, then he probably has need for a warehouse line of credit. This line of credit is necessary since, in many instances, rather than selling individual loans into the secondary market, he is forming mortgage pools or loan packages for sale. It is time-consuming, economically unfeasible, and practically impossible to sell individual loans into the secondary market. Therefore, loan packaging or pooling of large groups of loans into one sale or purchase is desirable and, in fact, is almost a mandatory requirement of the marketplace. Therefore, a line of credit is necessary.

There are several different types of warehouse line loans. The format and terms of the various types of lines depends primarily on the eventual disposition of the residential mortgage loans held within the framework of the line. Some of the more common types of warehouse line loans are as follows:

Revolving Line Loan.   This is a line of credit fixed at a certain maximum where the outstanding loan balances vary depending on the number and the amount of individual residential mortgage loans that have been funded through this line. As these individual mortgage loans are removed from the line and passed to an investor in the secondary market, the line balance is reduced. With this type of line of credit, there is usually continuous activity of "new" loans being funded through the line and "old" loans being paid off by funding through their purchase by a secondary mortgage market investor. This line could contain either presold loans or loans being held in inventory for purchase at a later date by an investor currently unknown. This type of revolving line usually contains a requirement that would "mark to market" the value of the residential loans used as collateral. The value of the loans within the line can vary from time to time depending on the current pricing in the secondary market. While the mortgage interest rate does not change on the residential loans, the pricing within the secondary market may change, and therefore the underlying collateral within the line may be worth substantially more or less at any given time. As a result, a monitoring system is necessary that prohibits a loan from not being marketable in the secondary mortgage market due to its interest rate.

Nonrevolving Line Loan.   This type of line of credit is usually for a fixed amount and is established when the mortgage banker desires to assemble a group of loans for sale to a specific investor. It usually has a fixed expiration date. The expiration date corresponds with the loan deliveries to the secondary investor. This type of line of credit is quite useful and desirable when loans are being gathered for the creation of a pool, particularly when mortgage bankers are creating pools of FHA and VA mortgage loans. It is also used for the segregation of loans that are being sold to specific conventional investors.

There are several other types of warehouse line loans used in specific cases. For example, some commercial banks require that they close residential mortgage loans in their name for their mortgage banking customer and that the mortgage banking company then purchase them and sell them to the investor against a preauthorized commitment. This is not a common practice; however, it does exist in some instances. Additionally, some commercial banks have and use what is called a "deferred line." This is a line of credit similar to a nonrevolving line, but for a longer period of time. Such a line of credit exists at times so that loans that are presold and waiting for a delivery date in the future can be held within the line. The need for a deferred line exists sometimes because the documentation of the individual mortgage loans must be approved by the investor, the documentation must be recorded in his name. The use of deferred lines causes an additional word of caution in that price fluctuations in the secondary market can cause a definite weakening in the value of the collateral package within the framework of this line. The longer the deferred line of credit, the more potential for a deterioration of the collateral value due to price fluctuation.

In warehouse line loans, almost universally the underlying mortgages or deeds of trust on the residential individual loans are assigned to the warehousing lender. In fact, the warehouse lender usually receives a complete documentation file, including such items as certified copies of the mortgage note, evidence of acceptable title, either a report or a title policy (if it is already available), credit reports, appraisal, and all the documentation that enables the warehouse lender to sell the loan should he deem it necessary. The original mortgage is held, and it is assigned to the warehousing bank as security. This mortgage can be reassigned to the permanent investor when the loan is sold. There are some variations in the above practices, but it behooves the warehouse lender to have as complete a package as possible.

Loans presented to the warehouse lender for funding are either presold or not sold. Presold loans—loans committed to purchase by a secondary market investor—are the most desirable and, comparatively speaking, the most free of risk. Such loans are usually in the warehouse line for a rather short period of time, usually just until the package of loans is put together and funding is obtained from the investor. Some investors require complete documentation prior to the purchase of the residential mortgage loans; others allow the mortgage banker to ship the loans for purchase to the investor without complete documentation, with the understanding that he will repurchase the loans should the documentation not be satisfactory and not be obtained within a reasonable amount of time.

In warehousing loans that are not presold there is a significant amount of risk, as previously discussed. In establishing lines of credit for loans that are not sold, the commercial bank should be sensitive to the capital structure and the capability of the mortgage banking customer. The mortgage banking customer should have the capability of repurchasing these loans when necessary. The mortgage banking customer should also have the capability of funding the necessary discount, if warranted, in order to sell these loans in the secondary market. A safeguard that is commonly used to prevent a buildup of unsold stagnant residential mortgage loans is to establish a terminal date for the loans' funding within the warehouse line. For example, the establishment of a 120-day or 180-day maximum time for any one loan within the warehousing line prevents huge fluctuations in the pricing of these loans by secondary mortgage market investors. Even within a period of 120 days, there can be wide variances in the prices paid by secondary mortgage market investors. A warehouse lender needs to be very sensitive to a line of credit loan supported by non-presold loans. The individual residential mortgage loan is only worth what a secondary market investor will pay for it at a given time. Otherwise, its value is its interest rate on the note or mortgage when viewed in relationship to its term. For example, a mortgage loan with an interest rate of 9 percent may be an acceptable investment today, but when viewed with a term of 30 years, it may not be an acceptable investment. The value of presold loans is determined by the investor's willingness to pay the price. With loans that are not presold, general market conditions determine the eventual price paid for the loan.

As a result, in order to monitor a warehouse line of loans that are not presold, it is necessary to have continuous knowledge of prices being paid by investors for the type of product being held within the line. Individual residential mortgage loans should not be funded through the line of credit for more than their current value in the marketplace, even though it appears the individual loans will have greater value after some seasoning. The current value can, and in fact does, fluctuate up or down as general market conditions warrant. These comments on the value of the loan being affected by interest rates apply to both government-insured and/or guaranteed loans, as well as conventional loans. Any increase in the overall interest rates in the general marketplace will lower the value of loans already in the warehousing line. When this occurs, loans in the warehouse portfolio can be held until the general market conditions improve, or discounts can be paid to bring the yields on the loans up to current market conditions. A word of caution is warranted here; sometimes it can be a very long wait for general market conditions to return to a level that eliminates the necessity for paying a discount. In many instances, it's best to pay the discount and clear the line.

Most warehousing lenders provide separate lines for government-insured and government-guaranteed loans, and conventional loans. That is, most lenders have a warehouse line that they use for the funding of FHA and VA loans, and a separate line for conventional mortgage loan funding. The FHA and VA loans are universally accepted by the marketplace. They are generally pooled and funded by the issuance of GNMA mortgage-backed securities. Conventional loans are usually sold in packages to private investors, such as Fannie Mae or Freddie Mac, or to various conduits for the eventual formation of conventional mortgage-backed securities.

When properly handled and with effective controls, this can be profitable lending for the commercial bank. The bank retains an adequate interest return on the secured collateral and usually insists on and is able to obtain compensating balances and fees. This type of business is actively sought by commercial banks, and therefore the interest rates, as well as the fees and the compensating balances, are always subject to negotiation. Compensating balances usually run from 10 to 20 percent of the line in use but again are subject to negotiations. In this type of lending, the individual mortgages often require escrow accounts, and therefore the compensating balances are available. Some lenders have been able to charge a fee on a per individual loan basis. However, these fees and the interest rates charged on the line are certainly negotiable. In recent years, as mentioned above, this has become a sought-after business, particularly due to the compensating balances usually placed in noninterest bearing accounts.

The monitoring of warehouse lines does require more than the average amount of supervision. The computer can, of course, be used to monitor the loans once they are on the books of the bank and within the line. But the detail and supervision necessary to monitor the initial documentation to ensure that it is proper, present, and acceptable to the permanent investor is significant. This requires a trained individual. There is also a significant amount of work required when loans are delivered to the permanent investor. Documents must be assembled, transmittal letters must be forwarded, and followup must exist to ensure the accurate transmittal of collateral and the repayment of the loan. This type of business can be profitable, but as indicated above, it requires a significant amount of loan management in order to maintain an acceptable level of risk.

CHAPTER FIFTY-FIVE _____

Lending on Income Property

Charles G. Reavis, Jr.

Senior Vice President
Wachovia Bank and Trust Company, N.A.

Income property can be defined as a property created or acquired for the purpose of generating income sufficient to provide the owner a net return adequate to induce his investment.

Each bank decides to what extent and on what basis if any it will participate in lending on income-producing real estate. Regardless of the position taken, every bank should be aware of the opportunities and risks involved in this type of lending as a basis of taking their position.

We are all aware that income properties are essential in the conduct of business in our nation and present opportunities for all segments of our lending community. If we choose to participate in financing this tremendously important segment of our business world, we have the obligation to our community and shareholders to do it prudently.

If our banks are to have an enduring program for lending on income properties, we need personnel who have the training, experience, expertise, and divine guidance necessary to identify successful projects and structure sound loans. In the following few pages we will attempt to touch on elements of this type real estate lending, which we believe to be important. Subjects to be addressed will include banks as mortgage bankers, banks as direct mortgage lenders, property types, underwriting policies and procedures, applications, appraisals, and servicing.

BANKS AS MORTGAGE BANKERS

Originating mortgage loans for other investors in the capacity of a mortgage banker can be a means of involvement in income property lending. This accomplishes the following: it allows your bank to compete for these type loans without using bank funds; (2) it allows you

801

to compete on terms and conditions that might be contrary to your bank's lending objectives; and (3) it provides a source of fee income for originating these loans. Servicing fees are also available from many lenders.

If you choose to operate as a mortgage banker, some of the areas of responsibility would include:

a. Soliciting business.
b. Loan packaging and submission.
c. Negotiating loan terms and conditions.
d. Loan closing.
e. Loan servicing.

While there are certain advantages and benefits to originating these type loans, there are some disadvantages: (1) The loan must be underwritten and documented to meet the criteria of the particular lending institution for which you are originating, (2) No special considerations can be given as to loan terms and conditions to "good customers" of your bank, (3) It can be difficult to retain qualified loan production people because of competition from independent mortgage banking companies, (4) A conflict of interest can develop if your bank's investment objectives become similar to that of your investors, (5) You must represent the interests of both your investor and your borrower.

BANKS AS MORTGAGE LENDERS

Banks as mortgage lenders usually grant two types of real estate loans: loans *on* real estate and loans *with* real estate.

Many loans are granted where real estate is pledged as collateral, although this security might not have sufficient value and produce sufficient net income to properly collateralize and pay the indebtedness on reasonable terms and conditions. Other credit considerations and sources of repayment are the primary factors in granting these loans, making this a loan with real estate.

Loans on real estate should have sufficient collateral value and net income from the pledged real estate security to have a properly margined loan that can be paid from the net income generated within a reasonable term. In today's market, it is quite common for loans on real estate to be amortized on a longer basis (20 to 30 years) and have a balloon payment at the end of a shorter period (5, 7, or 10 years).

Since many additional credit considerations are usually involved where loans with real estate are made (these type considerations are covered in other parts of this handbook), this chapter will be devoted primarily to income property loans on real estate.

PROPERTY TYPES

For purposes of this chapter we will place properties in two broad categories: general purpose properties and special purpose properties.

General Purpose

General purpose properties, such as office buildings, warehouses, retail stores, general commercial and industrial plus apartments, have a broad base of potential users.

From the viewpoint of the income property lender, there is ordinarily much less risk in granting credit secured by this type property. The number of potential users is usually quite broad and increases the likelihood of attracting a user if the facility is well located and well conceived. This is important in the event a new tenant is needed or a sale of the property is desired. The type of property alone, however, does not assure a trouble-free income property portfolio. Feasibility, sponsorship, physical facility, and *location* are essential elements that affect the most important consideration, which is "quantity, quality, and duration of net income." We will address these elements later in the chapter.

Most real estate lenders with long, successful track records have established lending criteria directed toward lending on general purpose real estate only.

While most of us as bankers do not have the luxury of making loans on general purpose properties only, we need to be keenly aware of our risk position and analyze our exposure accordingly.

Special Purpose

Special purpose properties include single or limited purpose properties and both have a very narrow base of potential uses. In most cases, single purpose properties accommodate only a duplicate of the original user, such as a steel mill or oil refinery.

Limited purpose properties include for example, service stations, funeral homes, theaters, and fast-food restaurants. Alternative uses of these properties are extremely limited, and most uses that are different from the original will not support the original investment in the property.

Loans on either of these type properties depend on the successful operation of a specific business, and failure of this business will make recovery of your loan very doubtful. Strong credit and greater margin of protection are necessary ingredients to justify such loans. These loans should be structured to be more akin to loans with real estate than loans on real estate.

UNDERWRITING POLICIES AND PROCEDURES

We as bankers should develop broad underwriting rules and regulations for our mortgage lending activity. These broad guidelines are likely to be influenced by our prior lending experience, current economic conditions, current loan position of our bank, demand for these properties in our community, and profit potential, just to name a few.

Underwriting a real estate loan can be defined as: (1) weighing all factors or considerations involved and deciding the basis on which you are willing to grant the loan (both risk and return are considered); or (2) the process of evaluating the risk to be incurred and the return to be expected and arriving at a balance between the two that you consider to be reasonable.

Lending guidelines should be established for the following areas:

1. Property types—general purpose, special purpose.
2. Loan to value ratios.
3. Debt coverage ratios.
4. Pricing (fixed rates, variable rates and fees).
5. Terms (length and structure).
6. Leasing requirements.
   a. Prior to funding (floor funding).
   b. Holdback until requirements are met.
   c. Holdback for tenant improvements.
7. Sponsorship—financial strength, experience, integrity.
8. Liability (personal, corporate, joint and several).
9. Documentation.
10. Due on sale clause and control of secondary financing.
11. Prepayment provisions.
12. Escrow deposits.

Property Types. Many lenders restrict their lending activity to general purpose properties unless there is sufficient credit strength outside the real estate security to make them comfortable. Liability from financially strong sponsorship or strong tenants on a lease of satisfactory terms and conditions is most commonly used to overcome concerns about special purpose real estate.

Loan to Value Ratio. The current market value of the security in relation to your loan amount is an important margin of protection the collateral gives. A reliable value estimate is essential, and, since values change with time and economic conditions, this makes a continuing awareness of changing property values necessary.

We most often think equity dollars give the best margin of protection when lending on real estate, and this is usually true. However, these equity dollars may not produce a current market value sufficient to protect us.

With many lenders 75 percent loan to value is a common standard that is adhered to.

Debt Coverage Ratios. Debt coverage ratios are oftentimes a better measure of protection to a lender than a loan to value ratio. In using a debt coverage ratio, it is essential that the income and expenses used in arriving at net income available for debt service be realistically related to market conditions. The margin of protection to the lender is the extent to which the income available for debt service covers the debt service of the loan being considered plus an additional amount to give a margin of safety. The margin required often varies with property type, economic conditions, and interest rate level, just to mention a few. In today's market, minimum coverage ratios for various type properties would probably be: office buildings 1.20:1; apartments 1.25:1; warehouses 1.20:1; and motels 1.35:1.

A conservative use of loan to value and debt coverage ratio measures is to apply both and limit your loan amount to the lesser of the two.

Pricing. Pricing on real estate loans needs to be greater than corporate lending not only because of term and risk but because of the cost of originating, documenting, and servicing this type loan. In addition to the interest on the loan, an up-front fee to cover origination expenses is justified if competition will allow.

Terms. Although making loans with long-term fixed rates might not be compatible with many banks' investment policies today, this type loan is desired by most income property developers and owners. Since the source of repayment for most of these loans is a fairly stable income stream generated by the security property and since the maximum available loan amount is usually sought by the borrower, the flexibility of income available for debt service is limited. Variable-rate loans with fixed payment rates are acceptable to some developers, but not to most.

Most owners need an amortization period ranging from 25 to 30 years but are willing to accept a shorter maturity of 5 to 7 or possibly 10 years with the unamortized loan balance due at that time. An alternative pricing arrangement is a variable priced loan with a fixed payment schedule or variable payment schedule.

Leasing Requirements.   All of us as lenders prefer to have properties 100 percent leased at the time loans are granted; however, this is not always possible. When the supply of a certain category of space is greater than demand, we are likely to require substantial preleasing with longer term leases that have some relationship to the term of our loan. We are likely to be more liberal in this regard when the supply of space is short and demand is strong. When all leasing is not in place, common practice with many lenders is to allow closing of the loan when leasing income reaches a break-even point; that is, sufficient rent is generated by the tenants in occupancy to pay expenses plus debt service on a 1-to-1 basis. A portion of the loan proceeds is often withheld by the lender until additional leasing sufficient to reach stabilized occupancy is in place. This is known as an economic holdback.

If the unleased space lacks tenant improvements (or upfitting), there is ordinarily a tenant finish holdback as well. This is generally related to estimated cost of tenant finish plus a margin for error, say 125 percent of such estimated cost.

For many property types, it is quite common for lenders to require a minimum amount of space to be leased by financially strong or "credit" tenants. In a strip shopping center, for example, many lenders require a minimum of 50 to 65 percent of the space to be leased to credit tenants with lease terms ranging from 15 to 20 years, allowing the remainder of space to be rented to "local," less proven tenants with shorter term leases. For purposes of lease analysis, a form should be used as a guide to ensure that essential items in the lease are not overlooked. An example of such a form is attached as Exhibit 1.

As we know, the credit tenants can usually obtain space at a lower rent because of their financial strength and their ability to attract customers. The local tenants generally pay a higher per square foot rental because they usually have less financial strength and drawing power. From the owners' perspective, a balance between both categories of tenants is desirable to bring stability and profitability to the project.

Sponsorship.   Financial strength, experience, and integrity are essential elements of sponsorship and cannot be taken lightly.

   a. Financial stability of a sponsor is a concern even though you might be willing to look to the real estate alone and not require personal liability. The borrower has the responsibility for performance of the duties required in the loan documents, and an insolvent sponsor is not likely to care for the property to the lender's best interest.

   b. A sponsor of any major income property you might consider financing should have successfully owned and managed several similar properties as evidence of his proven capability. If experienced personnel are not members of the sponsoring group, then outside expertise should be engaged.

c. Unless the individuals involved in the sponsorship are persons of integrity, financial strength and experience are meaningless, and you should not consider making a loan to them under any circumstances.

Liability. Income property developers and buyers, particularly on projects of $5 million and greater, most often insist that liability on loans for completed and leased general purpose properties be limited to the real estate only. To be competitive in the long-term market, the willingness to make this type loan is usually necessary. On smaller loans, interim or construction loans, loans on special purpose property, or loans with real estate of any sort, liability of creditworthy sponsors should be required.

Documentation. Documentation for income property loans is subject to extremely close scrutiny in the event litigation is required in collection of monies owed. The importance of complete and correct documentation cannot be overemphasized because of the inherent complexity of real estate law. A well qualified real estate attorney should represent the lender in all significant transactions.

Due on Sale Clause and Control of Secondary Financing. Such elements should be incorporated in all income property documentation. If you choose to allow a second mortgage or loan assumption, it should be based on the circumstances existing at the time of request but should always be your option because either happening can jeopardize your position.

Prepayment Restrictions. Such restrictions should be imposed where longer term fixed rate loans are granted. These provisions are needed for protection when rates fall; otherwise, refinancing with you or a competitor is almost certain.

Escrow Deposits. Escrow deposits should be required where possible to assure funds will be available when tax or insurance payments are due. This is an excellent source of deposits for your bank as well.

APPLICATION

The mortgage loan application used by your bank will probably be slightly different from those used by other banks; however, certain basic information should be included in order for you to have adequate

EXHIBIT 1 Lease Analysis and Approval Form

Article/Paragraph
Number

_____ 1. TENANT: _____

_____ 2. LEASE GUARANTEED BY: _____

_____ 3. LEASE DATE: _____, 19____; Amended _____, 19____; (Signed) (Unsigned).

Lease commencement date _____, 19____. Is the lease recorded _____. If YES, what is book _____

and page _____ number and date _____ of recordation. Will the lease be recorded: _____

_____ 4. LEASE TERM: _____ years; From: _____, 19____ To: _____, 19____

Number of Renewal Periods: _____ For _____ Years each

_____ 5. LEASED PREMISES: Address: _____

_____ Land Area: _____ sq. ft.; Building Area: _____ sq. ft.

Does Lease cover any property outside mortgage: _____.

_____ Are there any conditions that must be complied with (other than completion) prior to commencement of lease term (if YES, explain): _____

_____

_____. Is there a Cross

_____ Operating and Easement Agreement: _____; Is one proposed _____ (Inlcude as attachment). Indicate any action relative to

leased property outside of mortgage (i.e. Condemnation, Restrictions on Landlord, etc.) that result in termination of lease: _____

_____.

6. RENT: Annual Fixed: $ _____ ; Per sq. ft.: $ _____ ; Rent as percentage of sales: _____

% of sales above $ _____ gross/net sales per year/month.

Minimum Rent: $ _____ ; What is rent during renewal periods: $ _____ ; Is there a

charge for C.A.M.: _____

7. PARKING REQUIREMENT: Required spaces on leased premises: _____ ; Spaces on non-leased premises: _____ ;

Spaces outside of mortgage _____ ; Are parking spaces exclusively for this tenant: _____ ; Is there any

provision or need for cross-parking easements: _____ ; Does lease specify a ratio of parking spaces to rental area:

_____

8. CONDEMNATION: Is lease terminated by total taking: _____ ; By temporary taking: _____ ;

By partial taking: _____ . If YES, on _____ % of floor area and/or _____ % of land area and/

or _____ number of parking spaces. Does tenant have right to share in award: _____ ; recover leasehold interest value: _____

. Are these tenant rights subordinated to mortgagee: _____ . Is Landlord obligated to use total award for repair or rebuilding: _____

. Is Landlord obligated to restore in event of partial taking: _____ ; Total taking _____ .

9. PURCHASE OPTION: When exercisable: _____ ; at what price: $ _____ .

Is option subordinated to mortgage: _____ . Will purchaser recognize any outstanding mortgage lien: _____ .

. Can prepayment clause be circumvented: _____ .

10. ADDITIONAL SPACE: Must it be furnished by Landlord: _____ . If YES, under what conditions: _____

_____ . How

much space: _____ ; additional rent: $ _____ . Any extension of

term relating to this lease due to expansion: _____ . If additional space would need to be constructed in

future, will it be built on land secured by our mortgage: _____ .

EXHIBIT 1 *(concluded)*

INSERT PROPER ARTICLE/PARAGRAPH NUMBER UNDER APPROPRIATE ANSWER FOR SECTIONS 11 THROUGH 14.

11.

	YES	NO
LESSOR may cure LESSEE'S default and add to rent:		
LESSEE may cure LESSOR's default and deduct from rent:		
LESSEE granted exclusive operation:		
LESSEE can assign or sublet with/without LESSOR'S consent:		
LESSEE released from obligation by subletting or assignment:		
LESSEE can cancel if premises not available by _____, 19___ :		
LESSEE to notify MORTGAGEE of LESSOR'S default:		
LEASE is/can be subordinated to mortgage:		
MORTGAGEE needs to give LESSEE "non-disturbance" assurance:		
MORTGAGEE needs to obtain attornment agreement from LESSEE:		
Lease provides for payment of BROKER'S COMMISSION:		
Other:_____ :		

12. TAXES & INSURANCE:

	Paid By	
	Lessee	Lessor
Real Estate Taxes:		
Tax Stop After _____, 19___ :		
Hazard Insurance:		
Liability Insurance:		
Insurance Stop After _____, 19___ :		

13. UTILITIES:

Paid By

	Lessee	Lessor
ALL:		
A/C:		
HEAT:		
ELEC.:		
WATER:		
OTHER:		

14. MAINTENANCE:

Paid By

	Lessee	Lessor
INTERIOR:		
EXTERIOR:		
CLEANING:		
STRUCTURAL:		
ROOF:		
GLASS:		
OTHER:		

15. Comment on any areas of lease that are unsatisfactory or objectionable: _____

_____

16. With the exception of any items noted in #15 above, this lease is approved for consideration of the loan request as follows:

BORROWER: _____

LOAN AMOUNT: _____

TERM: _____

RATE: _____

_____
Loan Officer

_____
Date

811

details for the request you are considering. An example of desirable information is:

1. Information on the borrower.
   a. Who the borrower is—individual, general partnership, limited partnership, corporation.
   b. Individuals who are actively involved in ownership and their background experience.
   c. Financial information and references.
2. Information on the real estate.
   a. Property type, size, location, age, condition, parking (plot plan and survey are desirable plus plans and specifications).
   b. Operating figures (income and expenses) for current period and previous three to five years.
   c. Purchase price or cost of construction.
   d. Tax value and rate plus insurance information.
   e. Tenant information to include copies of leases and financial statements.
   f. Proforma operating figures.
   g. Engineering and soils reports.
3. Loan request.
   a. Amount.
   b. Term—amortization period, balloon.
   c. Rate—fixed, floating (absolute cap—average cap, floor).
   d. Due on sale or assumable under certain conditions.
   e. Prepayment restrictions.
4. Bank relationship with borrower or principals.
   a. Present indebtedness.
   b. Indirect liabilities.
   c. Deposit relationship.
5. Loan analysis.
   a. Loan to total value.
   b. Debt coverage ratio.
   c. Loan per square foot.
   d. Loan per unit (apartment, hotel room, etc.).
   e. Income/expense analysis.

APPRAISALS

The appraisal process is a subject too broad to cover in our allotted space; however, because of the importance of the value of security in our income property lending activity, we must focus on this critical area briefly.

Because the appraisal of real estate is not an exact science, but rather a subjective concept that some have even described as an "art form," we are very dependent on the person who performs this function for its reliability. However elementary it might seem, we must recognize that an appraisal is an *opinion* of value supported with data from the market. This data must be documented, and, while not necessary, an appraisal should usually be in writing.

Since we are so dependent on the estimate of value of our security as mortgage lenders, we need to be very careful about the characteristics of the people performing this appraisal function. They should have unimpeachable judgment, skill, competency, objectivity, and intellectual honesty. Without the honest application of these characteristics, the estimate of value produced can be misleading and cause mortgage lenders to make serious mistakes.

These skills of appraisal may be developed within your own organization, or you may choose to work with professionals outside your bank. If you work with outside professionals you still must be knowledgeable about appraisals and the appraisal process to be able to determine the abilities of such appraisers and how realistic their estimates of value are.

As mortgage lenders, a reliable estimate of market value of our security is quite often the best protection we have against loss. We have focused briefly on the necessary qualifications of the appraiser. Now we need to take a brief look at some of the essential elements of an appraisal.

Related to real estate, what is *market value*?

> The most probable price in cash, terms equivalent to cash, or in other precisely revealed terms, for which the appraised property will sell in a competitive market under all conditions requisite to fair sale, with the buyer and seller each acting prudently, knowledgeably, and for self-interest, and assuming that neither is under undue duress.[1]

The following are fundamental assumptions and conditions presumed in this definition.

1. Buyer and seller are motivated by self-interest.
2. Buyer and seller are well informed and are acting prudently.
3. The property is exposed for a reasonable time to the open market.
4. Payment is made in cash, its equivalent, or in specified financial terms.

---

[1]The Dictionary of Real Estate Appraisal (Chicago: American Institute of Real Estate Appraisers, 1984).

5. Specified financing, if any, may be the financing actually in place or on terms generally available for the property type in its locale on the effective appraisal date.

6. The effect, if any, on the amount of market value of atypical financing, services, or fees shall be clearly and precisely revealed in the appraisal report.

What procedures or steps does an appraiser need to complete in order to estimate market value?

1. Define the problem.
   a. Identify property to be appraised, date of appraisal, property rights involved, purpose of appraisal, define value.
2. Preliminary survey and appraisal plan.
   a. Determine the character, scope, and amount of work to solve the appraisal problem.
3. Collect data.
   a. City, neighborhood, specific information on subject property.
4. Data collection analysis.
   a. Cost approach.
   b. Income approach.
   c. Market approach.
5. Reconciliation.
   a. Bring together facts from each approach to form picture of appraisal problem.
6. Make value estimate.

From a mortgage lender's point of view, we often do not focus on project feasibility to the extent we should. What is the demand for the project? How much rent will a user pay? What is the likelihood of continued demand and at what rental? Will economic rent support the cost or purchase price?

Related to income property loans, as stated previously in this chapter, the quantity, quality, and duration of net income is the most important factor. The old saying that the three most important factors affecting residential real estate are location, location, location is also very important to income properties, from the point of view that location affects the production of income. Economic rent is estimated in several ways:

1. Out of the marketplace—from comparative properties.
2. Operating history of the subject property.
3. Estimating future rents based on expected future economic conditions as they may affect the subject property.

The estimating of income losses resulting from vacancies is a very important consideration and must be arrived at by the appraiser after surveying and analyzing competitive real estate and making a judgment based on future expectations. Gross income minus a vacancy allowance is "effective gross income."

After estimating effective gross income, we must focus on expenses necessary for operating the property. There are three categories of expenses to consider:

1. Fixed charges.
2. Variable operating charges.
3. Reserve for replacement.

Here again an estimate must be made for expenses and this can be done in several ways:

1. Surveying and analyzing comparable real estate.
2. History of the subject property.
3. Market standards.
4. Examine leases for expense responsibilities.

After deducting expenses from effective gross income, we arrive at the net income, which is the figure dear to a lender's heart.

This process of estimating net income appears simple on the surface; however the real challenge, which is all-important, is obtaining truly comparable data and properly evaluating and analyzing this data. This is indeed a subjective process, and the abilities of the personnel involved in this process cannot be overemphasized.

SERVICING

There is no substitute for a mortgage loan being "properly made" as the best aid to future servicing. The loan servicer must know the terms and conditions of the loan documents. He must be certain that the borrower fully understands all details of the transaction and what is expected and will be required.

The five areas of loan servicing include:

1. Payments, collections, and foreclosures.
2. Property taxes.
3. Insurance.
4. Annual operating statements.
5. Inspections of the property.

PAYMENTS, COLLECTIONS, AND FORECLOSURES

On a very cordial but businesslike basis, the borrower must be made to understand the amount of his payment, when it is due, and what the consequences will be if the payment is not made on a timely basis. Details should include:

1. When a penalty will be charged and how much.
2. A time beyond which a late payment will not be tolerated.
3. The necessity for the borrower to keep the lender informed on any unusual or unexpected happenings.

The prudent lender (servicer) must:

1. Follow any delinquency on a timely basis.
2. Be alert to any danger signal (returned checks, etc.).
3. Make immediate contact with investor or borrower when appropriate (telephone call is usually better).
4. In absence of response, take appropriate action.

If the borrower has problems beyond his control and you determine that he is doing the best job possible under the circumstances, then working with him to solve the problems will often be the best alternative. To make the borrower understand the necessity of keeping the lender informed is essential.

PROPERTY TAXES AND INSURANCE

Early detection by the lender of any increase in taxes and insurance and notification of the borrower of increasing escrow requirements as early as possible before the increase takes place is very important.

ANNUAL OPERATING STATEMENTS

A reminder of annual operating statements due on the property should be sent at year's end for the property. A followup must be made if not received on a timely basis. This should be made by telephone. If not received within a reasonable time thereafter, a personal visit could be necessary.

A careful review of all statements must be made to be certain any contingent interest is paid or other required conditions are met. This close review should also reveal possible future collection problems based on earning trends, etc.; in addition, a meeting with the borrower to address these difficulties and seek solutions might avoid servicing problems later.

INSPECTION OF PROPERTY

Periodic inspections of the properties securing your loans could reveal situations that might signal loan problems in the future. If the property is not being maintained properly or if vacancies are noted, this gives the bank an opportunity to address possible solutions at an early date.

CHAPTER FIFTY-SIX

International Credits

Donald R. Mandich

Chairman and Chief Executive Officer
Comerica, Inc.

International credit in the three decades since 1955 has moved from a *nominal level* characterized by caution to one of *development* to *expansion* to *overexpansion* with problems and again to a status of caution. Before describing the types of international lending and the techniques, it would be well to review briefly the historical development of international lending since World War II and the current conditions in the industry so as to give the reader a mind-set for the present environment.

POST WORLD WAR II BACKGROUND

The historical role of international bankers has been heavily geared to the importing and exporting of goods and the resulting clearing of exchange transactions. Hard currency loans were also made to foreign governments, foreign companies, and companies doing business in foreign countries. Prior to World War II, British bankers with sterling loans were the major international lenders, followed at a distance by lenders in a handful of European countries. However, the aggregate of all the types of activities was only a small fraction of the proportions achieved in recent decades. Of singular importance after 1945 was the emergence of the U.S. dollar as a unit of settlement for international transactions—a currency of a large country and a currency deemed "hard," as the United States was a major industrial nation that had been a major victor in World War II.

Table 1 depicts the growth of international lending in the U.S. banks after World War II. The total in 1955 was little more than the previous high in the 1920s and was geared mainly to trade financing. It might be wondered why dollar lending did not accelerate more rapidly in the decade from 1945 to 1955 with the dollar being so

TABLE 1   Total Foreign Claims of U.S. Banks ($ millions)

December 31,	1955	$ 1,892
	1960	4,391
	1965	10,953
	1970	40,867
	1975	185,648
	1980	415,200
	1985	391,900
September 30,	1986	391,400

SOURCE: Federal Reserve Bank of Chicago.

needed by countries seeking to rebuild from the ashes of the war; the reasons for modest growth seem to have been several:

1. U.S. bankers were preoccupied with banking activities primarily geared to the reconstruction of the U.S. economy.
2. U.S. banks had minimal experience in international lending and lacked experienced and receptive ears to process loan requests.
3. The recovery of foreign economies had not progressed sufficiently to warrant serious consideration of loan requests.

The Eurodollar market emerged after 1945 as a natural consequence of the widespread use of the dollar for international transactions and, although regarded in the early 60s with suspicion and concern that it might only be a temporary phenomenon, it steadily gained in size and importance. In 1965 the U.S. government placed a lid on foreign lending with its Voluntary Foreign Credit Restraint Program, which encouraged the maintenance of offshore dollar holdings. It also accelerated the formation of London branches by numerous American and later foreign banks. Interest rate ceilings in the United States in 1969 caused an exodus of deposits from the domestic offices of American banks that caused their London branches to "repatriate" large sums of Eurodollars. In 1970 when the U.S. economy cooled and the regulated ceilings were lifted on large certificates of deposit up to 90 days, the issue subsided. However, the Euros were in hand and rather than being repaid were dealt into international loans to offset declining earnings on the banks' domestic businesses.

The experience with international lending for a decade into the early 1970s had been excellent—better than domestic lending—and the profits were very handsome. Spreads of 4 percent over the cost of money were common and even ranged up to 8 percent. It began to be accepted that foreign governments do not fail like commercial businesses and foreign governments would not permit their major banks or businesses to fail or renege on debt obligations.

Beginning with the first jump in oil prices in 1974, large quantities of dollar holdings were shifted into Middle Eastern hands. Initially, this was perceived by leading international banks as an opportunity to act as an intermediary by accepting the flow of oil dollars as deposits and recycling them to oil-short countries. By gradual immersion, short-term opportunities became short-term problems, and short-term problems became long-term problems as initially creditworthy borrowers began to accumulate heavy debt burdens. Paralleling the accumulation of such debts was the rapid rise in interest rates (Chart 1) in the United States in the period from 1977 to 1981, which became very costly to foreign borrowers and finally culminated in the rescheduling of the indebtedness in over 45 countries up to the time of this writing.[1]

As can be seen in Table 1,[2] the sharp growth of international lending has leveled off, and the near term future will be one of working with individual countries until appropriate adjustments can be made in their economies and growth can proceed again. However, lending will undoubtedly be at a slower pace with more caution being exercised by both borrowers and lenders.

The American piece of the international credit total is significant. However, there are very substantial involvements by other countries as shown in Table 2. The various data sources show foreign claims to vary in total from roughly $2.5 trillion to $3.75 trillion.[3]

---

[1]Countries that have rescheduled their indebtedness in whole or part since 1971 include Argentina, Bolivia, Brazil, Chile, Cambodia, Costa Rica, Central African Republic, Cuba, Dominican Republic, Ecuador, Ghana, Guyana, Honduras, India, Ivory Coast, Jamaica, Jordan, Liberia, Madagascar, Malawi, Mexico, Morocco, Mozambique, Mauritania, Nicaragua, Niger, Nigeria, Pakistan, Peru, Poland, Philippines, Panama, Romania, Sierra Leone, Sudan, Senegal, Somalia, Turkey, Togo, Uganda, Uruguay, Vietnam, Venezuela, Yugoslavia, Zaire, Zambia. (Source: International Monetary Fund)

[2]Table I and this chapter focus only on bank lending. During the last two decades, the Eurobond market has reached a husky size with placements reported of over $183 billion in 1986 compared to $133 billion in 1985.

[3]Various global series on international credit outstandings are published by the Bank for International Settlements, World Bank, International Monetary Fund, and jointly by the Organization for Economic Cooperation and

CHART 1 Three-Month Eurodollar (annual average rates)

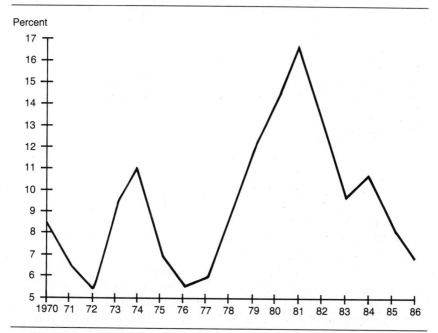

Percent

SOURCE: Chart provided by Data Resources, New York, N.Y.

TABLE 2 Foreign Claims of Banks by Nationality of Bank Ownership ($ millions)

Country of Parent Bank	Total Foreign Claims
Japan	$1,019
United States	601
France	264
Germany, Federal Republic	250
United Kingdom	213
Switzerland	145
Italy	121
Canada	90
Netherlands	89
Belgium	66
Austria	56
Other developed countries	173
Eastern Europe, Latin America, Middle East, and others	98
Consortium banks	44
Total	$3,229

SOURCE: Bank for International Settlements Interbank Series, September 30, 1986.

TABLE 3   Cross-Border Outstandings of the Largest U.S. Banks, December 31, 1986 (millions of U.S. dollar equivalents)

Citicorp	$ 48,000
Bank of America	27,574
Chase Manhattan	27,014
J.P. Morgan	17,120
Manufacturers Hanover	18,955
Security Pacific	6,829
Chemical	11,976
Bankers Trust	10,437
First Interstate	4,664
First Chicago	5,774
	$178,343

SOURCES: Annual reports.

Very impressive in Table 2 is the Japanese total of over $1 trillion—a country that struggled to maintain foreign reserves of roughly $2 billion in the 1960s. Japan is truly a phoenix that rose from the ashes of World War II.

The other European countries and Canada listed in Table 2 undoubtedly have heavy mixtures of trade-related debt in their totals. Into the late 1960s and early 1970s, these countries were yet preoccupied with post World War II reconstruction and development. However, in the 1970s excess dollar holdings were being accumulated which found their way into cross-border lending for profit.

Within the United States the major international banks, as might be expected, are among the largest banks shown in Table 3. However, the total is less than half of the total for all U.S. banks, reflecting the fairly widespread involvement among larger U.S. banks.

THE LENDING PROCESS

Essentially, the basic business processes throughout the world are pursued by mankind in similar ways, such as rendering services, extracting raw materials, converting materials to another form, or buying and selling goods. A lender might assist any of these processes if the likelihood of repayment seems reasonable and the risk of involvement does not appear to be excessive.

Development and the Bank for International Settlements. Statistics for the United States are prepared by the U.S. Treasury and the Federal Reserve Bank (in the FRB bulletin) and Federal Financial Institutions Examination Council which prepares a Country Exposure Report. The October 1986 Federal Reserve Bulletin contains a comprehensive discussion of the various global and U.S. series and their differences.

Within his or her own country a lender operates with a feeling of relative comfort in regard to the legal framework, the business customs, the accounting conventions, and the many pressures that bear on a business by the country's economic trends and political manifestations.

Once a lender ventures across national borders, he is well advised to exercise extreme caution in assuming that any of the environmental elements of the business process are similar. However, these differences should *not* be extrapolated to arrive at the conclusion that *everything is different*. The basic business processes are much the same, and the *fundamentals* of credit analysis remain unchanged; if the lender can maintain his focus on these, he may avoid losing track of the essential risk-repayment analyses and in turn avoid problems.

Other sections of this book cover the fundamental concepts of all credit extension. They should be considered the basic building blocks for any material contained in this chapter, most of which will not be repeated. This chapter will dwell primarily on special, additional aspects of international lending. The focus throughout will be directed toward the aspects of lending across national borders, such as from the United States to any foreign country, or from London (or Nassau) to other foreign countries. Local loans in foreign countries made by the local branches of U.S. banks in local currency are primarily "domestic" type loans and will not be covered in this chapter.

TYPES OF INTERNATIONAL LOANS

International lending can be basically divided into two types—government loans and loans to the private sector.

Government loans have a variety of purposes—general borrowings for the Treasury, loans to finance imports or projects in the private sector, loans to develop roads, ports or irrigation systems, and loans for the many other reasons that governments need funds. Actually, the purpose of a government loan is primarily one of interest to the extent that it will provide more insight to that country's future balance of payments; for example, does the loan produce foreign exchange or will it save foreign exchange for the country in the future? In the simplest term, *all foreign government loans are undertaken to increase or replenish that country's holdings of foreign exchange*, regardless of the project purpose that is attached to it. Foreign currencies (e.g., dollars) are not needed for local projects except to the extent that such projects include foreign goods or services.

Loans to the private sector generally fall into two classes—loans to finance the movement of goods (i.e., imports or exports) and loans to finance the multitude of other projects in which businesses get involved. Loans for imports provide the importer (and the country) with the foreign exchange to pay for the import. Loans to finance exports give the exporter (and his or her country) the foreign exchange proceeds a little faster than they would receive them in the normal course. Loans to finance other projects such as the construction of a new plant or the expansion of inventory are simply loans to increase the foreign country's holdings of hard currencies, except to the extent that the proceeds are used to purchase foreign goods or services for the project. The borrower is unconcerned with this truism and simply knows that if he can borrow dollars he can exchange them for local currency (indirectly released by the central bank), which he can use for any business purpose.

Loans to the private sector may be to purely local companies or to subsidiaries of U.S. companies—with or without the suppport of the parent. Occasionally, loans are made to individuals for personal or investment purposes. Private sector loans also include loans directly to foreign commercial banks for a variety of purposes. Depending on the country, these might appear either as a loan to the bank or as a deposit.

Leasing has become common as an international financing device. This is probably one of the more complex types of international trans-actions because it takes careful legal and tax planning to build a good transaction wherein the lessor may be domiciled in a different tax environment than its parent, in a different country than the source of funds, in a different country than the lessee, and possibly the leased item may be in a fifth country.

Loans for the movement of goods comprise a substantial amount of total international lending. Such loans have developed complex practices and terminology and include devices such as letters of credit and banker's acceptances. The subject of letters of credit itself would fill a book. However, a short explanation may be useful.

An export from the United States could arise from a purchase order in dollars from a company in, say, Italy. If the exporter is comfortable with the credit standing of the buyer and the likelihood that the buyer can obtain dollars in Italy to pay on the due date, he will ship the goods and await payment. On the other hand, he may be unsure of the credit standing of the buyer and ask that the buyer have his bank write the exporter a letter saying that the bank will guarantee payment. Hence, a *letter of credit* arises, which in usage has become very for-malized and is surrounded with an extensive list of traditional prac-tices and an extensive legal framework. The cost of the guarantee of payment is paid by the importer but is part of the total transaction cost and is allocated between buyer and seller somewhere in the trans-action negotiation. A further variation is a case where the exporter might not feel comfortable even with a letter from the Italian bank and insist that the letter be sent to his local American bank, which in turn will add its confirmation (guarantee) at a fee to be paid by the importer.

Usually, the American exporter will want his money when the goods are shipped and will draft upon his American bank (in the case described immediately above). However, the importer may desire time to receive the goods before paying and ask for a delay of 90 days or more. If a 90-day delay is agreeable to all parties, a 90-day time draft will be presented by the exporter to his American bank after the goods are shipped. The American bank will affix its guarantee to the draft by marking it "accepted" with the bank's name and an authorized signature. The bank has now created a *banker's acceptance*, which in essence has become an IOU of the bank. The exporter can hold the draft until the maturity date, can sell it in the market through a broker anytime before the maturity date, or can sell it to the accepting bank at the market rate of discount; the bank can then either hold it as an investment or sell it in the market. The interest cost of discounting the acceptance is usually borne by the exporter, but if the term of acceptance is longer than his usual practice for domestic sales, he may adjust the price of the goods to compensate.

In handling the above transactions, the American bank will probably establish lines of credit (or at least internal limits) for the foreign banks for which it confirms letters of credit or creates acceptances. Obviously, the U.S. bank will have to perform the usual credit analyses on the banks, as well as analyses of risks of the countries in which the banks are domiciled.

In the case of an import by a U.S. company, a U.S. bank may be asked to present a letter of credit to a foreign exporter (directly or through a foreign bank), and the entire process is reversed. However, if acceptance financing is desired to finance the goods while enroute and the transaction is denominated in dollars, the U.S. bank will provide it. In that event, as far as the American bank is concerned, all of the credit risk in the case of an import lies with the local importer.

The foregoing is a thumbnail sketch of handling transactions involving the movement of goods. If a bank should undertake this business, it is well advised to have on its staff a person competent in letters of credit. The need to analyze foreign banks and countries cannot be overemphasized. Some familiarity with the import practices in foreign countries is also necessary for exporters, as some countries require letters of credit to be issued by a local bank before *any* import can legally be undertaken or else the necessary foreign exchange will not be made available to pay for the import. However, such a letter of credit is not an ironclad guarantee that the exchange will be available;

it is more an expression of intent. Analysis of the country must also be performed in advance to determine the likelihood of exchange availability.

TRANSLATION AND ANALYSIS OF FOREIGN STATEMENTS

The basic objectives in analyzing foreign financial statements are the same as in domestic lending. The lender wishes to understand the nature of the customer's business activity so that he or she can determine that future cash flows will likely provide the funds to repay either short- or long-term loans. In addition, the lender wishes to understand the figures well enough to appraise the trends of the borrower, the character of the assets, and the actual or potential claims on the assets, so that a judgment as to risks can be made.

Statement translations involve both the selection of appropriate English words to describe the account captions as well as the conversion of the foreign currency to dollars. Differences in practice exist in converting foreign currency values to dollars. Some banks feel that the figures should simply be left in the foreign currency. Others spread both the foreign currency and the equivalent dollar value at the date of the statement. Still others (especially those using a computer facility) convert all the figures to dollars at the rate existing on the date of the latest statement, including a recasting of historical information at the latest rate. Each lender will have to select an approach that suits his or her tastes.

The process of translating account captions from foreign statements is an area which warrants serious attention. Many commercial terms translate easily from one language to another, but the accounting conventions, legal significances, and underlying business practices vary substantially from one country to another, so no assumptions should be made. In all cases, comprehensive analyses of the anticipated cash flows must be performed to ensure that repayments of any loans will be forthcoming.

The global expansion of the large American accounting firms (the so-called Big Eight) has had a good influence on accounting conventions and practices in many countries. Several of the Big Eight firms publish worthwhile material explaining the translation of business financial statements in various foreign countries together with information on the local taxation and unusual business practices.

The translation and analysis of foreign *central* bank statements is probably a useful exercise. However, since the central bank of a country is a government entity and its obligations are thereby directly or indirectly government obligations, the real analysis that must be pursued is that of the country's holdings of gold and foreign exchange and the trends of such holdings. Most central bank statements can be manipulated with "mirrors"—capital can be raised at will with the infusion of local government bonds, and bad assets can be switched to budget appropriations for other government entities, leaving the central bank in an apparently strong condition. Thorough understanding of a central bank's figures may provide some interesting information on the bank, the government, and the monetary process but, as indicated above, repayment of foreign loans comes only from hard currencies.

In many foreign countries, it is common for companies to have numerous subsidiaries which are not consolidated on the published financial statements. International lenders should insist on the details, the same as expected from U.S. borrowers.

A problem can arise when a foreign bank asks an American bank to lend to a foreign company with the guarantee of the foreign bank. Frequently, the information supplied about the borrower is meager, and the American bank may be reluctant to insist on more detail. If the foreign bank is large and apparently sophisticated in its lending, the lack of detail might be excused. On the other hand, if the guarantor is less sophisticated, the American bank probably should study the credit fully and not hand the guarantor a bad piece of paper if the American bank ultimately has to look to the guarantee.

Finally, it should be noted that while the analysis of the financial data of a foreign borrower requires special techniques and efforts, this exercise is not an end in itself. The financial information is also to be used to give the lender greater insight in appraising the people with whom he or she is dealing and their managerial abilities.

COUNTRY RISK

Loans to a government or one of its official entities are essentially a country risk.[4] Loans to the private sector also contain varying elements of country risk. Few companies can operate completely independently of their environment, unless the borrower is a multinational concern with the ability to repay from external sources.

Analysis of country risk is usually classified as a combination of analysis of (a) economic risk and (b) political risk. However, because of its unique importance, the analysis of the country's international liquidity should be given the status of a separate category.

---

[4]Loans to a government or one of its official entities involve a special legal risk, sometimes referred to as "sovereign risk." Invariably, it is difficult or impossible to sue a government without its permission. Therefore, analyses of country risks are equally important for public and private sector loans.

Caution should be exercised in analyzing individual countries and arriving at final judgments on the acceptability of the composite of economic and political risk. Economic averages can be misleading as indicators of ability to repay. Norms for individual economic indicators cannot be applied to all countries. Each country analysis is a somewhat unique exercise to determine whether the economy seems to be functioning reasonably well, that the political mechanism seems to be in control, and that the trends suggest a continuance of reasonable performance and stability at least throughout the life of any proposed loans.

ECONOMIC RISK

Any approach to analyzing a foreign country should be done with the warning firmly in mind that the statistical raw material is of varying quality and reliability. The development of statistics can be costly and budget priorities vary from country to country. Furthermore, definitions and statistical techniques are subject to varying opinions, and it cannot be assumed that an economic indicator used in one country is comparable to those in others. Perhaps the best source of information for that which it publishes is the International Monetary Fund (IMF). Regular visits by calling officers to borrowing countries should be used to corroborate the analysis of the country and to obtain additional data, if necessary, from government and (possibly) private sources.

Aside from the reliability of the statistical data, another concern of the country analyst is the fact that one country cannot be compared directly to others. For example, the economy of a developing country cannot be compared directly to the United States. In the United States most of the residents participate in the economy in varying ways, whereas perhaps one third of the population of a developing country does not participate at all in its measured economy, and the gradual absorption of that one third into some sector of the economy over a period of years will present a continually changing picture which can be a challenge to any analyst.

While retaining the caveats mentioned above in the forefront of all analytical thought, it would seem that the following economic indicators would be the minimum to be observed for a period of at least five years:

1. Gross national product.
   a. Annual total of GNP.
   b. Annual percentage change of actual GNP.
   c. Annual percentage change of real GNP, that is, adjusted for inflation.
   d. Real GNP per capita.

2. Industrial production.
   a. Index of level of industrial production.
   b. Annual percentage change of industrial production index.
3. Population.
   a. Total population.
   b. Rate of growth.
   c. Age distribution.
4. Employment.
   a. Unemployment percentage.
   b. A comparison of agricultural and industrial employment to total population.
   c. Employment total vs. eligible work force.
5. Wages.
   a. Index of wage level.
   b. Annual percentage change of wage index.
6. Money supply.
   a. Actual money supply.
   b. Rate of growth each year.
7. Inflation indices.
   a. Consumer price index.
   b. Annual percentage change in consumer price index.
   c. Wholesale price index.
   d. Annual percentage change in wholesale price index.
8. In addition to the above indicators, others that are special to a given economy should be monitored closely; for example, energy self-sufficiency, tourism, or mining production and world prices of the commodities mined, or production of agricultural items such as cocoa and its world price.
9. Overlying all of the foregoing are the human and cultural resources which will determine the country's ability to produce, to adjust to change, and the likelihood of the ability of the people to govern themselves reasonably. Insights into the human and cultural resources can be obtained from studying the country's history.

The economic analysis should result in a basic indication of economic trends and potential pressures that might develop, particularly from excessive inflation. Economic developments can strongly affect political developments in a country.

INTERNATIONAL LIQUIDITY

The analysis of international liquidity is undoubtedly part of the economic analysis of any country, but as mentioned above, it is of such importance that special emphasis is warranted. Indeed a country might be quite stagnant in its economic growth, or have severe inflation, and yet manage its international liquidity so as to meet all external obligations quite readily.

Essentially, a country's international liquidity is its holdings of gold and hard foreign currencies. This can be augmented by its holdings of Special Drawing Rights of the International Monetary Fund and its Reserve Position in the Fund. Changes in the total holdings are created by (a) surpluses or deficits in the country's balance on current account (i.e., the difference between its imports and exports of goods and services), and (b) the net of all capital flows.

Considerable attention to all components of the balance of payments is warranted. Are imports increasing faster than exports? Is the country vulnerable to losing an important part of its exports in the world markets? Is tourism increasing or decreasing? Is the local political posture encouraging or discouraging tourism? Is the official rate of exchange for the country's currency encouraging imports and discouraging tourism or vice versa?

A country might suffer a continuing deficit in its balance of trade and make up the difference in capital flows; that is, borrowings abroad and investments within the country by foreigners. This pattern might persist over some period of time. However, it is worth considering as a philosophical concept that *over a long period of time a country's balance of trade will be its balance of payments;* in other words, borrowings must be repaid or stabilized and investments must eventually create a reverse cash flow of repatriated earnings.

In viewing a country's international liquidity, the primary question is: How much is enough? Unfortunately, countries do not publish balance sheets with a scheduling of all external debt maturities (public and private). Therefore, this analysis must be approached by viewing past history coupled with any available information on the debt structure that the analyst can accumulate from various published sources. Along with the review of historical data, it is imperative that the analyst obtain sufficient information to make forecasts of liquidity.

In viewing the historical data two ratios are usually used: (a) the number of months of reserves of gold and hard currencies in relation to annual imports, and (b) the debt service ratio, that is, the annual requirements for debt amortization (principal and interest) of the public sector in relation to earnings from exports of goods and services. In viewing either ratio, the trend is perhaps as important as the absolute level.

In the case of the number of months of reserves versus imports, a period of at least three to four months is desirable. However, individual countries seem to operate satisfactorily on lesser amounts. Some study of the actual nature of a country's reserves is useful in viewing this ratio, as its gold may be the backing for its currency, or there may be other restrictions on the allocation of foreign reserves.

The debt service ratio has no absolute level that is safe or bad for all countries. As a rule of thumb, 20 to 25 percent or more can be considered serious. However, each country must be analyzed as to its trends and its capacity for adjustment: Does it have access to temporary outside borrowings and can it control imports if necessary? Unfortunately, the details of the indebtedness of the private sector may be unknown, and any conclusions should be tempered by this lack of information.

POLITICAL RISK

While serious efforts are made by most international lenders to analyze the available economic data for a country, the analysis of political risk is more difficult as fewer quantitative indicators are available. Presumably, if a lender places funds in a country, he or she is satisfied with the government, its attitude toward debt, and its likely future administration of the country, whether it be a dictatorship or a government elected by the people. If it is a country with an elected government, trends in elections may point to a forthcoming change in leadership. However, most election trends are difficult to analyze, if a trend should exist at all, and usually the information for lesser offices and off-year elections takes considerable effort to develop from outside the country. Additionally, the exact temperaments and goals of individual political parties and their leaders are often difficult for an outsider to appraise; the analysis of cultural and religious influences in politics can also be challenging.

The geography of a country can explain and often forecast political tensions. Internally, a country with people well segregated by mountainous terrain might reflect the basic lack of national cohesion. Historically unfriendly neighbors might have continuing pressures on a country's politics, and modern weaponry in the 1980s has radically altered the balance of power between countries that counted their strength in population size.

In countries where dictatorships prevail and control is dependent on the army or police force, the question of succession is apt to be quite uncertain. Direct questioning about future control in such countries usually elicits the comment that the military is in firm control and undoubtedly will remain so—suggesting that little if any change can be expected. However, an examination of history would reveal that unexpected successions can occur, often very rapidly.

Political risk can be wide ranging and indirect, such as legislation or regulations that simply reduce profits or profit opportunities. However, the biggest danger of political change for a lender is the fear of mismanagement of the economic affairs of a country with the subsequent inability to pay its external indebtedness—or worse yet, the fear that a new government might be militant and unfriendly to the free world and expropriate externally owned assets and repudiate external indebtedness, such as Russia did in 1917 and Cuba in 1960.

As indicated above, close information on the political situations in foreign countries is difficult to develop. The news media, furthermore, tend to be shallow and sensational in their reporting, if they choose to report certain events at all. The only recourse that a lender has is to make serious efforts to obtain information within the country itself and to hope that unexpected internal and external pressures do not develop to cause an unpredictable and undesirable series of events.

LEGAL PROBLEMS

Domestic lenders operate within a framework of laws that are a part of their daily routine, and with which they usually feel fairly comfortable. When loans are made across national borders, none of the legal framework of the foreign country can be taken for granted. Each foreign country has its own system of laws with its own roots, such as the English law, the Napoleonic Code, and so forth. In translating any lending documents from one language to another it might be difficult or impossible to give exact translations. Words, commercial terms, and phrases may have unique and different legal significances in each country. At times it can seem nearly impossible to achieve a clear understanding of the legal circumstances surrounding an international loan. A lawsuit against a foreign company in an American court may produce nothing if the borrower's assets are in the foreign country.

Part of the solution to these legal impediments is to obtain competent legal counsel in both countries and to satisfy both with all documents, and to have borrower and lender be aware of their rights and any potential problems. A second part of the solution is to deal only with borrowers of satisfactory reputation and credit standing. Like casualty insurance, it is desirable to have good legal counsel, but it is better not to have to rely on it.

Having accepted the underlying problem of the confusion of alien laws, a foreign lender is further confronted with two specific categories of legal problems: (a) laws imposed on American lenders by foreign countries, and (b) laws imposed on American lenders by their own country.

Foreign laws affecting American lenders are best identified with the assistance of local legal counsel. They may include the need to register to determine tax status and the need for borrowers to record the indebtedness with the government to ensure that the dollars will be made available for repayment.

FOREIGN CURRENCY LOANS

At times U.S. banks might make a loan in a currency different from the currency used to fund the loan; for example, a Deutsche mark loan funded with U.S. dollars. If a bank should exchange dollars for a foreign currency and use the foreign currency to make a loan, it has the option of selling in the foreign exchange future market the proceeds it expects to receive from collection of the loan. In the case of a Deutsche mark loan funded with dollars, the interest rate for Deutsche marks would be lower (than the U.S. interest rate) in today's markets, and the bank would probably sell the marks forward to increase its yield from the spread between the current market/dollar exchange rate and that rate in the forward market.

The reverse exercise of borrowing marks at a lower interest rate and converting to dollars to lend at a higher rate would create an artificially higher spread between the cost of funds and the rate on the loan.

In the cases described above there are elements of interest earned as well as a foreign exchange earning or cost. It is strongly suggested that all loan operations run a balanced position with the loans and the funding in the same currency. If they are not, it is suggested that the loan department obtain an internal foreign exchange contract with its own foreign exchange desk at arm's length rates. This will sort out the true interest earned on the loan from the foreign exchange income or expense. It will also put the foreign currency exposure on the records of the exchange trading department where it can be carried without a cover, or hedged, depending on its trading authorities. Of importance is the consideration that the foreign exchange dealers will monitor any open positions constantly and be in a better position to take protective action than if the exposure is filed away somewhere in the loan records.

At times foreign currency loans are offered at rates that are unattractive if the foreign exchange aspects are properly evaluated. The system of internal contracts suggested above should help to avoid improper pricing on this type of loan.

SYNDICATED LOANS AND BROKER PAPER

As the international lending business expanded significantly in the last two decades, individual credits grew in size, and borrowers sought to obtain larger individual loans rather than a number of small accommodations. Banks were also looking for more fee income. The syndication of loans provided that vehicle.

As the spreads on international loans have narrowed, the compensation for participants in many syndicates has at times been too thin. This has caused a withdrawal by many participants. At the same time, syndicators are being driven to sell even more of their transactions to generate fee income to offset the low spreads on their retained portions. The inevitable outcome may result in wider spreads or a realignment of the major lenders if some lenders, such as the Japanese banks, continue to remain satisfied with relatively low returns.

Closely aligned to the banks that syndicate loans are the nonbank brokers which may be large, established underwriting firms or small operations. As banks have become more and more active internationally, the list of nonbank brokers has diminished, but a number of active ones remains on the scene and seems to fill a needed role.

A caveat in dealing with brokers is that the buyer of any notes must know in advance the payee to whom the notes have been originally issued and who the endorsers were or will be. In the United States even a nonrecourse endorsement carries the guarantee that the note is genuine and that the parties executing it have the capacity to do so. If a broker should appear as the last endorser, the buyer of the paper would be well advised to check the credit standing and the amount of capital of the broker. If the capital is not sizable, it would be better to have the notes reissued and delivered directly to the buying bank. This may make it difficult for the broker to obtain the desired commission, if he or she expected to obtain a profit from the lowering of the effective interest rate at the time of resale. Therefore, the verification of the signatures on the note by a commercial bank may be offered. If an error should be made in such verifications, however, the responsibility of the verifying bank is questionable. A further alternative would be to confirm the existence of the note with the obligor.

MATURITIES OF LOANS

Until the mid-1960s international lending was primarily short-term, up to six months or a year, and primarily for the movement of goods. Occasionally, a lender might grant an outright loan for as long as five years, but only as an exception and for good compensation. Grace periods were typically a year or 18 months at the most. The term of financing was tied to traditional reasoning; for example, if the borrower was importing trucks, the loan would not be for more than three or four years, the useful life of the equipment on the foreign roads. Competition, and possibly a reach for earnings, caused maturities to lengthen during the early 1970s to as long as 12 years with grace periods as long as 6 years. (Certainly this reflected a departure from domestic lending standards where term loans of 8 to 10 years were the outside limit.) The lengthening of terms tended to ignore the underlying use of the funds and to look more at the country's overall balance of payments data, the merits of which can be supported by some good arguments when loans are to government entities.

The principal justification for long-term loans seemed to be because interest rates were typically adjusted every six months, and therefore there was no rate risk. Obviously, this ignores the question of credit risk and the question of the role of a commercial bank and the need for liquidity in its assets. The long-term bond market for international borrowings has developed to good size and sophistication, but has not yet achieved the relative size and niche for long-term borrowings such as exists in the U.S. securities market. Consequently, borrowers seeking longer maturities have regularly found themselves dealing with banks and often inviting them to bid against each other for transactions. Bidding arrangements do not develop the close relationships that are of mutual interest to the lender and the borrower. It is obvious that customer loyalty cannot be purchased with the longest loan maturities, nor can the loyalty of lenders be gained by paying the lowest tolerable interest rates.

FUNDING

The funding of international loans can come from domestic or foreign sources, such as Eurodollars. Until 1965, when the United States placed restrictions on lending abroad, most foreign loans were financed with domestic funds. After 1965, the volume of offshore financing (mainly in Eurodollars) increased rapidly and has provided a very substantial portion of the funding.

In the 1960s, particularly the early part of the decade, there was concern that the Eurodollar market was too new and uncertain to guarantee funding for longer term loans. It was then used as a source for shorter loans mainly, and foreign banks obtained standby commitments from American banks to insure availability of dollars over longer periods to back the funding for their longer term loans. Today it is fully accepted that the Eurodollar market is "here to stay." It has great size, efficiency and apparent stability.

INTEREST RATES

In the 1950s and 1960s most international loans were made at fixed rates. During the 1970s the industry changed from fixed interest rates with wide spreads to floating rates (tied to the U.S. prime rate or the cost of Eurodollars with changes no less often than each six months) with more narrow spreads. In the mid-1960s spreads over the cost of money were typically a minimum of 2 percent for short- or long-term loans, and spreads of 4 percent or higher were very common.

In the late 1960s spreads moved down to as low as 0.625 percent to 0.75 percent, and more than a few term loans were booked as low as 0.375 percent and even 0.125 percent without any supplemental benefits. The minimum rate on banker's acceptances was 1½ percent per annum in the 1960s and rates up to 3 percent per annum were not uncommon. In the 1980s the confirmation rate had slipped to as low as 8 to 10 points. The rationale for the lower rates was the pressure of competition. However, during the same period many banks increased their loans and deposits by increasing their ratios of assets to capital and also introducing capital notes on their balance sheets. The question that goes begging is whether the common shareholders reap the rewards of leverage for their added risks or whether the benefits flow to the borrowers.

For American banks engaging in international lending, interest rates of ⅝ or ¾ or 1 percent are simply unacceptable as total compensation if the bank wishes to earn ¾ percent or more on its assets after expenses and taxes. Also, in a growing portfolio to which is attached a loan loss reserve of 1 percent or more, such loans obviously produce a loss in the first year. With more attention in recent years to understanding costs and returns on individual bank products and services, many banks, including money center banks, are grossly aware of the substandard returns on international lending. A further complication is the increasing pressure by regulators for American banks to strengthen their capital bases. All of this forecasts some rethinking and likely realignment of the types of returns that will be requested for international loans, and/or who will be doing this type of lending in the future.

COUNTRY LIMITS

With the emergence of concern for bank capital adequacy in the last decade, the related question of concentrations of international loans and country limits has become topical. The questions basically are: Should there be a portfolio limit for a given country related to a percentage of a bank's capital (including or excluding capital notes)? Should there be sublimits within the country limit for loans to the public and private sector? And should there be limits on the amount of term lending? Although it theoretically might be desirable, an American bank ordinarily does not concern itself with a country limit for the United States, since a majority of its assets *and* liabilities are domestic.

The optimum size of any country limit is a matter of judgment and is difficult to quantify. Decisions of the management of one bank might leave another totally uncomfortable. Despite the difficulties, however, every bank should have specific, documented country limits approved by a designated member of management, or better yet by an executive committee or an asset-liability management committee. A bank management really cannot claim that limits are too complex to be set in exact terms; in such a case the policy is obviously one of having no limits. If the bank has any significant involvement in international lending, it can expect the bank examiners to review its decision-making process on country limits.

Thus far no rule of thumb exists as to whether a bank should commit an amount equal to 10, 50, or 100 percent or more of its capital in a single foreign country. A practical consideration is whether, after tax considerations, a bank would care to lose as much as a year's earnings or more if unexpected developments should occur too quickly in a foreign country to reduce the total exposure significantly. Even in a highly developed country which appears to be quite stable, it is often very difficult to detect gradual changes in the economic or political structure that would prompt a reduction in country exposure. For example, in the 1950s the strength of the U.S. dollar was undoubted—"paper gold" it was called. Yet by the end of the following decade it was under severe pressure and would soon devalue. In retrospect, the signs of deterioration were quite obvious.

The good is often the familiar, and as we do business in countries over a period of time we are apt to gain confidence and possibly cease to probe deeply enough for weaknesses; and if indeed weaknesses are detected and diagnosed as severe, when is the time to have the courage of one's convictions and begin the withdrawal process? Experience has shown that, if a lender waits until the moment of crisis to seek a reduction in loans, it is usually impossible to achieve reductions in significant amounts. On the other hand, there is the risk that the problems are apt to be temporary with substantial correction forthcoming, and suspension of business in that country might later be regretted.

Each bank management should meet the problem of establishing specific country guidelines in dollars and should do so in writing; this exercise is probably the real value of having guidelines, even though universal, quantitative formulas cannot be developed. Guidelines should be reviewed at least annually for the more stable countries and perhaps more often for problem areas or for areas where the bank has a sizable commitment. As to the size of guidelines, the only answer appears to be the size that makes a bank's management feel comfortable and the size that seems prudent for that bank. The total guideline for each country should include amounts for short- and long-term accommodations and specific strategies, such as perhaps letting term loans run off in a country that seems headed for problems.

THE FUTURE

In looking to the future, it might be concluded without much hesitation that international lending is today a broad-based business. Despite the fact that some banks have cut back on their international activities, it will likely continue on a large scale, barring an event of chaos such as widespread armed conflict. Whereas information was sketchy and often nonexistent in the early days of the expansion, it is now accepted by both lenders and borrowers that information, projections, and commitments to performance will be given and received.

Heavy debt burdens are saddled on some countries and their bankers conversely feel the burdens of heavy risks to those countries. Nevertheless, despite the reams of sensationalism that have been published on this issue, meaningful restructurings have been put into place with serious plans for economic adjustments in debtor countries. Good progress has been made by major debtors such as Mexico and Brazil. There will undoubtedly be further debt restructurings, likely by many of the same borrowers, but it is grossly in the interest of debtor and lender to exercise patience until it is clear that the economic affairs of the debtor country are under control and it can resume borrowing for its reasonable needs and growth. No one can realistically expect that any country will fully repay all of its debt, anymore than one could expect the U.S. government to completely retire all of its outstanding indebtedness. No country wishes to experience a total default in its indebtedness and perhaps lose access to the credit markets for a generation or more, and its bankers likewise do not wish to suffer the chargeoff.

The likelihood of resolution of existing workouts is much higher in the 1980s than it would have been ten or twenty years ago as the borrower/lender relationship is quite generally on a much higher plane. As indicated above, the exchange of information and the willingness to make commitments is at a much higher and more meaningful level. No one can predict interest rates with certainty, but at this writing we do seem to be in an era of conservatism after having weathered the high inflation and high interest rates of a few years ago which caused pain and/or fright to many elected officials and political parties. This should auger well for debt-laden countries. However, there is no guarantee that oil prices will not stiffen again as existing wells are exhausted while exploration activities are at low levels. Energy-rich and energy-poor countries may well gain or lose from a resurgence of oil prices despite some progress on conservation and substitution.

The question of who will be the principal "players" in the international lending arena in the next decade is not obvious at this moment. Regulators in the United States are pushing for more capital in U.S. banks which will make it difficult for them to compete with foreign banks that are thinly capitalized. Similarly, it is difficult for traditional business lenders to obtain satisfactory spreads—risks vs. rewards—when others, such as the Japanese, seem driven to simply place their abundance of dollars at *some increment* over interbank rates. And finally, it lies in the hands of the borrowers to decide as a strategic objective whether they will seek the cheapest deal or try to build meaningful long-term relationships with bankers whom they feel have long-term objectives that are compatible with their needs.

PART TEN

Retail Banking

CHAPTER FIFTY-SEVEN

Retail Banking in a Bank's Overall Strategy

Dr. Frederick S. Hammer

Chairman and Chief Executive Officer
Meritor Financial Group

David C. Melnicoff

Senior Adjunct Professor of Finance
Temple University

"The bank is dead, long live the Financial Service Institution" is the apocryphal toast often quoted during the 1980s.[1] It is commonplace these days—and, in this handbook, probably redundant—to call attention to the changing environment in which commercial banks and other depository institutions find themselves. Yet no discussion of business strategy can begin without pointing out that the line-of-business definitions of a few years ago have changed. New players, some of them very large, have entered banking's formerly exclusive domain. Everyone knows that the answer to the classic strategic question, "What business are we in?" has changed from "commercial banking"—or "savings banking," for that matter—to "financial services."

The main outline of banking's long-standing organizational, legal, and regulatory framework remains in place. This gives rise in the new era to many anomalous and inappropriate constraints; but banking, its culture, and its collective memory are identifiable and have considerable momentum. Many financial interests seek bank status or wish to buy banks. Banks make money. Their functions are vital to a successful integrated financial services enterprise. This article, therefore,

---

[1] See, for instance, Martin Mayer, "The Money Bazaars: Understanding the Banking Revolution Around Us" (New York: Truman Valley Books, 1984).

is written from the viewpoint of the traditional banker faced with new marketing and competitive challenges. He is well aware that he cannot permit his institution to drift or to take the short-run path of least resistance. He knows that he must plan a deliberate response to the developments of the financial revolution. However, new strategies do not fall from the sky. They must be carefully thought through; and the banker begins the process with the resources, knowledge, and organizational support that he has.

THE NEW BUSINESS OUTLOOK

That said, the banker had better free himself from old stereotypes and worn-out categorizations. The legal definitions of and limitations on banking—for instance, the court's delineation of banking functions in connection with the Girard-Philadelphia National merger in 1963[2] and the definition of banking in the 1970 amendments to the Bank Holding Company Act[3]—never should have been accepted as fixed limitations on strategic thinking. Certainly they were not absolute constraints for the big financial services winners—like Citibank, for instance. In any case, they have now been rendered virtually obsolete by deregulation and technology and by the financial crisis of important segments of the financial system.

Beyond this (and beyond the concerns of the banker's legal counsel), the banker's own perceptions of the services he provides must be reexamined and, in some instances, restructured. For example:

- Consumer lending was traditionally the whole bundle of functions involved in making the loan, funding the loan, servicing the loan, and collecting the repayment. The growth of "securitization" clearly suggests that these functions be analyzed separately, that strategic thinking accept the option of originating *and/or* servicing loans that are sold to others who may wish to fund them and take the risk of losses.
- Providing fee-based transactions services can be thought of as independent of deposit gathering. That is the way many nonbank providers look at it, and, increasingly, in a nonceiling liability market, some banks are looking at it this way, too, providing sweep accounts for customers and checking or credit card administration capabilities for nonbanks or for other depositories.

---

[2]*U.S.* v. *The Philadelphia National Bank, et al.*, 374 U.S. 321.

[3]Generally, a commercial bank is defined as an institution that makes commercial loans and accepts demand deposits.

- Running a regional switch for a computerized payments network has been a good source of earnings for those who saw the opportunity early on.

Not all such options will be considered attractive in the long run—or they may be viewed as nothing more than extensions of the correspondent bank business. Competitive pressures demand, however, that these "unbundled" functions be viewed as options and understood in the context of advancing technology as an important part of the anatomy of present-day financial services. Given, then, the changing nature of the banking industry in its new "financial services" context, the banker can put the key questions raised in this chapter into perspective:

- What is the scope of "retail banking?"
- What role does it play in the overall strategy of a bank?

THE SCOPE OF RETAILING

There is a tendency in some quarters to define the retail business in terms of particular products and services. This is useful after the strategy is formed. At the outset it begs the question of what the retail market needs, and sometimes it leads to ambiguities in organization as well as execution on an ongoing basis. Better to look at the market, gauge its needs, then formulate a retail program that fits both the market and the bank.

The retail market, most bankers would agree, consists of households, nonprofits, and small businesses:

- Who require and demand convenience;
- Who require a relatively high level of information and accounting services;
- Whose market information is incomplete; and
- Whose access to financial service alternatives is limited.

The size of that retail market is a key piece of strategic information. Unless the banker has a good idea of the number of potential customers he can reach, the kinds and sizes of borrowings in place, the amount of deposits and other financial assets held, he is hard put to assess the profit potential of retail business for his institution. As a practical matter, measuring the size of that market, or some segment of it, has to be done by proxy—by analyzing family income, education level, gross sales, and other indicators, properly calibrated—for some geographical area. Much market information is easily available, and standard research techniques can develop additional specifics where necessary.

RETAILING'S ROLE

How much retail business should the banker seek? What kind of asset mix and liability mix does he want? Should he dedicate less of his resources to the wholesale, big business market? There is, of course, a very wide range of appropriate emphasis on retail business, depending on the bank's size, the economics and demographics of its geographic market, its traditional role in the community, and the competitive situation. However, these days—in the latter part of the 1980s— the retail business should receive especially strong consideration. There are four key reasons for this:

1. The Traditional Bank Has an Edge over Impersonal Financial Conglomerates in Consumer Contact.   In the face of huge investments in nationwide financial services marketing by giant firms, there is still a reasonable presumption that local institutions—and most banks are still that—have a net advantage in a business that is inherently local. Selling at retail on a national scale provides many opportunities and economies, but it is unable to customize products and promotions for local markets. (If you were a Texan, how much would you trust the Brooklyn accent at the other end of the 1-800 number—or vice versa?) Most importantly, if the banker can bond the retail customer to his bank and expand his lending to him, he will likely make his institution more profitable.

2. Retail Lending Produces Higher Spreads.   Spreads in wholesale lending have deteriorated in recent years as some large investors have gained easy access to credit data bases and have chosen to bypass commercial banks. The rise in commercial paper issuance attests to this. Wholesale banks often provide backup lines of credit for commercial paper; but this is small comfort in the face of intense pressure on spreads across the board as the result of this new type of disintermediation. Returns on equity are generally higher these days for banks with relatively heavy consumer loan portfolios. The ratio of such consumer-oriented banks' stock prices to their book value is likely to be higher than for those without a large consumer business.

3. Retail Deposits Are More Stable and Less Costly.   To be sure, consumer loan spreads will fluctuate and eventually may be placed under pressure by securitization, but the other side of the retail banking balance sheet is also productive. Recent financial results show that the return on assets is higher for banks with a high proportion of "consumer-type" deposits than for those whose funding comes predominantly from the money market. The smaller banks and the regional banks, to which household and smaller businesses bring their funds, usually have a better ROA than the big money center banks, which depend on their ability to buy liquidity in large Eurodollar chunks and repeated note issues.[4]

4. Retailing Is Productive of Fee Income.   Fee income arising out of activities that are not "asset intensive"—off-balance sheet sources of earnings—which are usually associated with wholesale and merchant banking, are also available in retail banking. Depending on the strategy adopted, the retail banker may look forward to origination or servicing fees on consumer loans and mortgages that have been sold, with income arising out of insurance and mutual funds sales, brokerage fees, and other services. With rising supervisory demands for higher capital ratios, such fee-for-service income will be crucial for a satisfactory return on equity. Moreover, the more services that can be sold through the branch, the less the "overhead" cost that must be attached to each branch function.

THE ELEMENTS OF A RETAIL BANKING STRATEGY

Virtually all banks carry on some aspects of the retail business. Generally, the smaller the bank and its community, the more likely that retailing dominates banking activity. Occasionally, a smaller bank in a large metropolitan area may be a wholesale banking specialist with only a smattering of retail business. More often, larger banks in highly developed regions may discourage retail customers.

If the banker is comfortable with his wholesale-retail mix, he still has to raise several questions:

- Am I serving my retail constituency in such a way that I can keep it loyal to my bank?
- Can I improve my profit performance in the long run by seeking a bigger share of the retail market?
- Is it feasible and profitable to obtain a heavier retail balance for my predominantly wholesale banking business?

Some help in finding the answers to these questions lies in a careful appraisal of all the elements of a retail banking strategy.

---

[4]Reports and analysis of bank earnings have been made by Federal Reserve sources such as Dauler and McLaughlin's article in the November, 1984 *Federal Reserve Bulletin* and in a paper appearing in the Federal Reserve Bank of New York's *Quarterly Review* for Summer 1986.

EXHIBIT 1 Elements of a Retail Banking Strategy

	Demographics and Economics of the Market	
	Elements	
Internal Influences	1. Services/Products	**External Influences**
	2. Distribution	
Customer Profile	3. Pricing & Promotion	Competition
Tradition	4. Human Resources	Public
Current Market Shape	& Organization	Attitudes
resource constraints		Reregulation
	Technology and Communications	

The diagram in Exhibit 1 sets forth the core elements of a retail strategy, the influences that impinge on them from both inside and outside the bank, and an indication that all of these forces are conditioned by the social and economic parameters of the market environment.

With respect to the last, although there is constant movement, some of it is predictable, especially on a nationwide basis. The baby boom and its aftermath, for instance, have had profound and well catalogued effects on business and banking. It is less well noticed, however, that the number of school-age children in the nation is again beginning to rise, in part the result of higher than expected birth rates for women in their 30s. If this is also a characteristic of a bank's local market, some reappraisal of old business plans might be called for.

More important than little surprises like the second baby boom is the impact of industrial restructuring, which has brought about painful downward readjustment in some communities and heady expansion in others. Large segments of the labor force have seen their status and their income levels change—which means that their needs and preferences for financial services may also change. How permanent is this change? The answer to this question is a strategic consideration. It could lead to important decisions concerning the appropriateness of the geographical scope and the population segments targeted by the retail strategy.

FUNDAMENTAL STRATEGIC QUESTIONS

Planning manuals all contain the basic questions that form the framework for creating an effective strategy:

- Where are we now?
- Where do we want to go?
- What are our strengths and weaknesses and the threats to us from competition, regulation, and technology?
- How do we get to where we want to be?

BEYOND THE MISSION STATEMENT

All too often the planning exercise stops with the creation of a mission statement and some departmental objectives. This will not suffice. The basic questions must be asked about each of the core elements, taking into account internal influences, external threats, and the changing state of the art. For the transaction services the bank provides, for instance, what is the share of market the bank holds? Is it increasing or decreasing? Who are the bank's transaction account customers? Do their characteristics—the customer profile—presage declines or gains? Is the bank's transaction technology consistent with customer needs? Is it prepared to move ahead as the state of the art changes—at least as rapidly as its competitors? If not, how does the bank get prepared? Can promotion bridge the gap between the present product and a better product?

If the transaction product is superior, is there an opportunity to piggyback a savings product—say, a self-directed IRA—on it to help build stable deposit balances? Is the tradition and culture of the bank such that an active cross-selling program will be embraced with enthusiasm? If not, how does the bank get to that point from here? What kind of training, what kind of incentives will be necessary? How do the costs and rewards of getting from here to there compare with alternative opportunities? Will the IRA opportunity, if successfully executed, make the kind of contribution to ROA—by providing stable funding and a flow of fee income—that is suggested by the superior "consumer bank" averages?

This succession of questions suggests a process that builds elaborate "decision trees"—reaching well into bank operations matters—for many possible services and products as well as for distribution and other core element issues. There is no neat software package that will grind out optimizations for decision networks. The process is one of trial and error, iteration and reiteration, and a large measure of judgment. However, several broader issues cut across the particulars. One has to do with the breadth of the retail program, contrasting a niche strategy—specialization in one or two products—with the concept of full retail service.

FULL SERVICE VERSUS NICHE

The niche strategy is typified by concentration in mortgage lending by some of the larger thrifts, or by revolving credits secured by second mortgages or other specialties. It often seeks impersonal, high-technology, low-cost coverage of a particular product area. The 1-800 telephone number and high-volume direct mail distribution are part of this strategy. In contrast, the "full service" approach seeks to capture a consumer constituency and meet most of its financial service needs. Insurance and brokerage services are provided, for instance, along with the full range of more conventional products, utilizing relationship pricing designed to encourage multiproduct use. This approach tends to require more one-on-one service, less high technology, and is pointed toward the development of a stable source of deposit funds from traditional savings vehicles.

The speciality strategy, whichever particular niche it seeks to fill, is inherently risky. It can be very successful under favorable circumstances. In time, however, the profit structure of the product may be eroded by competition, new technology, or cyclical business developments. Adverse public or regulatory opinion can occasionally zero in on the product with devastating effect. In contrast, the diversity and personal input of a full service strategy provides flexibility. It does create human resource problems in that it is much harder to train and sustain a work force capable of handling customized products than it is to provide assembly line technicians. In addition, a proliferation of new systems for multiproduct presentation may be difficult to handle. This approach is likely, nevertheless, to provide a better fit for most banks' overall strategic plans. If the bank's resources are limited, it is probably better to circumscribe the target market segment than to present a truncated product line.

"Full service" need not mean the presentation of every product in the book, of course. Not all markets require a long list. However, "full service" must mean more than the lip service often paid to it in the old institutional "Full Service Bank" ads. A viable strategy must provide an ample bundle of related financial products at an appropriate level of service for the particular market if it is to capture the customer. A hit or miss product line or one that is not sufficiently broad for the targeted market will not enable the bank to provide the convenience necessary to compete with televised specialty product purveyors and the nonbank giants.

BUY OR MAKE

Limitations on the product line are often forced by a lack of systems expertise or computer capacity or by insufficient training facilities. Before such limitations are accepted, before introduction of products is stretched out ineffectively, and certainly before a vital new service is introduced without adequate backup, the retail banker should explore the possibilities of buying expertise, software, and training from outside sources. This course of action goes down hard with the many banking industry victims of N.I.H. syndrome—the malady that casts doubt on anything that was Not Invented Here. There are many excellent suppliers of complete product systems who can not only offer economical installation, but also provide maintenance and enhancement on a more timely basis than the bank's own hard-pressed staff. Discount brokerage setups and mortgage origination and servicing systems are examples of "store-bought" packages that do an excellent job.

Few of the standardized packages are a perfect fit, but often it is far better to adapt one's operations to them than to undertake what amounts to the reinvention of the wheel. Banks are accustomed to using correspondent services for backroom operations. Purchased product systems and training should be evaluated on the same cost-benefit basis. The analysis should include, however, the cost of the time lost and the competitive risk of stumbling into operation because the bank unnecessarily started from scratch or tried to customize excessively.

DEFINING THE MARKET

Defining the market and measuring the bank's share in it is probably the most basic task of the retail strategy exercise. It is at this juncture that the banker can seek some synergy with his wholesale business—for instance, a payroll deposit plan may open the door to a customer base—and it is here that the bank's resources and its existing strengths and weaknesses can be reconciled with opportunities. Market definition has both geographic and qualitative aspects, ranging from nationwide to "this side of town," and from banking-for-everyone to a tea-in-the-afternoon private banking mode. For instance, the geographic scope of the medium size bank that intends to stay regional may well be determined by its television perimeter. Depending on the density and diversity of the household population in that area, however, the market can be segmented, and the retail effort may emphasize a particular segment. More leading questions:

- Does the bank have a tradition and current market share that makes the age 55 and over segment a logical target?
- Is the competition neglecting the over-55 market or bombarding it with direct mail applications that are difficult to understand and trust?
- This segment is growing nationally. Does the region mirror this trend?

- How many potential customers does the bank expect to reach? Too many in the area? Perhaps the target market should be segmented further—to some income class, say, or some culturally identifiable group.[5]

Cutting the market segments too fine probably does not pay, as some of the recently created "Women's Banks" have learned. But a clear sense of who it is the bank is trying to reach is essential. It is the market that dictates what kind of pricing and promotion policies should be adopted and what level of service should be provided. Institutional advertising should not portray the bank as a 21st century phenomenon, if its primary target is an older group. Nor should it attempt to position itself as the region's stripped-down, low price, do-it-yourself financial supermarket. Nor does it want to risk public alarm by testing the regulatory authorities tolerance with state-of-the-art services of questionable legality. Tried and true, safe and sound is probably the image the bank wants to project to a middle-age, middle-class market. That would be the wrong image, to be sure, for a predominantly younger market of upwardly mobile folks who know all about personal computers and who view home banking facilities as a mark of progress, if not a useful real world tool. Above all, make sure that the bank's customers and its employees know what the bank is about and what it is striving to accomplish.

DISTRIBUTION FACILITIES: THE TECHNOLOGY IS THE PRODUCT

In recent years, technology and communications have drastically changed the channels of distribution for financial services. As indicated above, with the aid and stimulus of television, the telephone-hooked-into-the-computer and highly sophisticated, computer-assisted direct mail techniques have been used more and more to deliver financial services and products. It is probably fair to say that nonbank financial institutions took the lead in this, possibly because the banks and the thrifts had a large vested interest in their branch networks.

Beyond the telephone and the mail, however (which are, after all, merely transformations of face-to-face selling), the financial system now has in widespread use a technology that is distributing services at the same time that it is a product in its own right. The plastic card

---

[5]Some retail activity can today be developed on a scale much greater than capital resources formerly would have allowed. The liquidity that has been characteristic of the secondary mortgage market for many years is growing now for consumer loans through "securitization."

for credits and debits and its supporting electronic networks and switches have revolutionized the payments mechanism. The plastic card technology is a distribution system, and that system is the product—a transactions service that also gives access to credit in various forms. The card is getting "smarter" all the time and is delivering more services. What does this mean for the banks' traditional distribution mechanism—the tellers' window at the branch?

Some look at the new technology and bemoan the obsolescence of branch offices. Many large mutual fund distributors get along without offices, as do some of the discount stock brokers.[6] Some insurance companies contact the customer on TV and then let the postman and row upon row of hourly-paid part-time employees with telephone headsets do the rest. Has the branch office become a brick and mortar white elephant? Not likely. No doubt the branch now has a different function to perform and must be reconfigured. No doubt the branch must be supplemented in some degree by remote ATMs and by mail and telemarketing. But the appropriate distribution mix depends on the retail strategy. The discount brokers have theirs, the funds have theirs, and the banks should have something quite different, reflecting the versatility and breadth of their capabilities. The banker who has targeted the 55-and-older customers will be able to use the branch to create a product with a clear difference from that of the mass marketers. His low-tech one-on-one approach may give him an advantage, and his per capita distribution costs for a line of products need not be higher, provided his strategy is well-founded and consistent. (An obvious horrible example of lack of consistency: Buying television time that delivers 250,000 household viewers, when the banker is trying to reach a 25,000 household market.)

EXECUTION: THE PEOPLE PROBLEM

Many dollars have been wasted on new product promotions and on well-conceived retail strategies that the sales staff could not execute. This happens because the people on the line in the branches and in the backrooms are not sufficiently schooled in the strategy and in the techniques it demands. It can also happen because front-line people are being called on to do jobs that do not appear to contribute to their advancement or their compensation. It can happen because one part of the bank's organization is at cross purposes, competing with another part. The need for training and understanding of retail programs is

---

[6]Some of the large no-load funds have, however, begun to establish downtown offices in large cities to "establish a presence."

fairly obvious. What is not so clear is that many banks have a limited number of employees who can absorb the training and do the job. A new kind of employee may be needed for some tasks—not latter-day Leonardo da Vincis, but somewhat more broadly educated people than the bank may now have face-to-face with the public—people who are somewhat more outgoing and aggressive than was suitable for the highly structured and regulated banking world of 10 years ago. The people problem is likely to be a bottleneck that can be broken only gradually and, in some cases, painfully. It is, however, dangerous to ignore it.

There is an organizational problem, too, that is often ignored. Failure to give managers the proper scope of authority or failure to give them the proper incentives can frustrate the best-laid plans.

- Is the branch manager's bonus dependent on minimizing employee hours per deposit dollar? If so, he is not likely to take kindly to the urgings of a product manager to help sell insurance policies or make mortgages—particularly if the product manager reports to some distant corporate staff department head.
- Are the managers of the bank's various "lines of business" given narrow incentives pertaining to their own activities only? If so, many of the hoped for "synergies" arising out of new product introductions (and out of acquisitions and mergers) may not occur, and the retail effort may be inefficient. Line-of-business managers may be allowed to "suboptimize" in terms of the retail strategy's goals. It is not uncommon to see spin-offs of businesses that banks or other financial institutions acquired only a few years before. This is often attributed to a "clash of cultures." This phrase might also read "inappropriate organizational structure and incentive systems."

CONCLUSION: USE A BLACKBOARD

One might, in conclusion, propose another toast like the one with which this chapter began: "The retail strategy is dead! Long live the new retail strategy!"

There is nothing about retail banking strategy that is sure and permanent these days. The planning horizon is necessarily three to five years, but the banker must expect to make many changes and adjustments along the way. The basic market environment shifts slowly (unless one switches to new markets) and internal influences are fairly stable, but external influences on the core elements are volatile and powerful. Reregulation, technology, and competition are forcing constant reappraisal and revision. The forward-looking banker should not carve his retail strategy in stone or engrave it on the brass plates of which bankers are so fond. He should write it on a blackboard—and keep an eraser handy. The new financial service industry hasn't jelled yet. The retail customer will always be seeking the best deal. It's doubtful that it's been invented yet.

CHAPTER FIFTY-EIGHT

Providing Retail Services for the Upscale Customer

Marilyn MacGruder Barnewall

President
The MacGruder Agency, Inc.

INTRODUCTION

The banking industry will remember the 1980s as the decade of change brought about by deregulation: a change in competition and a change in core retail banking products that banks are permitted to offer the consuming public.

The 1990s are likely to be the decade of determination. During that time span it will likely be determined which banks have made change their friend by learning to manage it and which banks have made change their foe, letting it manage them. Banks in the former category are likely to prosper; those in the latter are not.

Whether deregulation is impacting the airlines or banks, it always increases competition. When competition broadens and becomes more intense, it becomes necessary to become a specialist at certain things—to do a limited number of things better and more effectively than anyone else. Only by doing so can a market niche be created. And only by creating a special niche can bankers offer their consumers the thing they are demanding—value added.

At a time when the increasingly competitive marketplace requires bankers to become more specialized, more and more bankers appear to want to be more and more generalist in their approaches to the marketplace. If you want to compete effectively for the most potentially profitable customers—the upscale—you must understand them, rather than demand they understand you. Specialists develop a knowledge base that allow them to understand the customer; generalists are usually kept so busy trying to be all things to all people, they require the customer to understand them.

Many bankers avoid target marketing the upscale because they feel an obligation to serve the needs of the mass market. It is not necessary to stop serving the needs of nonupscale customers in order to target the upscale. The largest percentage of retail banking customers, the mass market, does not have need of a broad range of financial service products. Thus, targeting as the primary market those customers who do have such needs doesn't take anything away from the mass market. It merely gives to the upscale the broad range of financial services products they need.

Implementing a business development strategy based on customer segmentation, then, does not mean taking anything away or withholding any services from any segment of the general public. It does mean, though, making the right products available to the right customers.

In today's banking environment, the most successful marketing program does not attract the highest percentage of available marketshare. *The most successful marketing program attracts the highest percentage of profitable customers.* Understanding this difference is the key to profitability in the current financial services competitive marketplace.

The 80/20 statistic has long been accepted as accurate: 20 percent of a bank's customers account for 80 percent of its retail deposits. However, another statistic critically important to the banker interested in enhanced retail banking profits has emerged: 10 percent of a bank's customers are responsible for 90 percent of retail banking profits. The objective, then, is to effectively expand your marketshare of the 10 percent while not pursuing (but not avoiding) the 90 percent.

Fortunately, intelligent retail banking market segmentation strategies do not force us to eliminate volume, they merely require separation of quantity from quality. In other words, there is no suggestion here that bankers ignore one market segment in favor of another. The suggestion is to give certain market segments the quality of service and product opportunities their profit contributions to the bank warrant. To achieve that, it is necessary to define the most potentially profitable segments, identify them, identify their buying motivations and product needs, provide them with product packages that appeal to them, physically house them in an area where volume does not prevent quality product and service delivery, and provide personnel trained to handle the specific (and special) needs of the targeted group.

RETAIL BANKING'S MOST PROFITABLE SEGMENTS

Before discussing how to provide retail banking services for upscale customers, it is first necessary to define the group of people for whom we are developing the marketing strategy.

One of the biggest problems in banking today is the lack of an industry standard that defines all of the various market segments indigenous to retail banking. Webster's, by the way, defines indigenous as "native; inborn; inherent; innate."

When discussing how to provide retail services for upscale customers, it is necessary to discuss individuals who need certain retail products, as opposed to discussing retail banking products that bank marketers want to sell to upscale customers.

Affluent passive investors are usually handled by trust bankers. They have a strong need for personal and investment trust products. However, they also have strong retail product/service needs. So, while this material discusses retail services for the upscale, mention of these trust customers must be made. In my experience, about 85 percent of the private banking areas designed to appeal to affluent passive investors report to trust, 15 percent report to retail banking.

Of the private banking departments designed to handle the needs of affluent active investors, I estimate that about 50 percent of them report to the retail bank, 30 percent report to commercial banking, and 20 percent to trust.

All middle market segments discussed here traditionally report to retail banking.

Thus, the first confusion regarding upscale customers is brought to the surface. Bank organizational structure does not fit their needs, although bankers tend to view it from a different perspective, feeling that customer needs should fit bank organizational structure. It should not surprise anyone that upscale customers react negatively to such an expectation.

As people progress "up the scale" economically, their bank product and service needs broaden. Upscale customer product and service needs are not fragmented. Traditional bank organizational structure is fragmented when trying to serve the needs of the upscale customer. The banker who accepts this thesis will be far ahead in developing a sales philosophy that appeals to the upscale.

Upscale customers need personal and investment trust products and services, commercial banking business purpose loans based for repayment on personal assets outside the loan's purpose, and access to all other products developed for individuals—from checking accounts to asset management, to money market accounts, to discount brokerage.

Bank structure, then, prevents bankers from serving the needs of upscale customers on a relationship management basis. Since the number one thing affluent customers say they want from their bankers is one person to handle their total banking relationship, there is no doubt that this is a critical issue. Banks that deal most successfully with the incompatibilites between bank structure and customer need are those banks willing to encourage a "hybrid" banking relationship that does not confront political and territorial lines within the bank but, instead, avoids them.

Following are definitions of the most profitable upscale market segments.

DEFINING UPSCALE

As the person who coined the word "upscale," I used to claim the right to define it. However, since common usage of the word upscale within the banking industry has changed the meaning I attached to the word when I coined it, I now accede to industry wisdom. Perhaps you might be interested in where the word originated, why I started using it in the first place. In the purest sense, the word "upscale" refers to an active investor who continually and rapidly moves "up the scale" of affluence—the Howard Hughes of the world. People who inherit, instead of earn, their wealth do not move "up the scale" of affluence; they merely arrive at some point or another of affluence as a result of the reading of someone's last will and testament or by being designated as a beneficiary on an insurance policy.

The word has been overused. Today, an upscale person is defined by the banking industry as almost anyone who has achieved a level of financial strength that makes him or her a profitable bank customer. "Upscale" is used to define any profitable market segment not a part of the mass market. It is from this common usage perspective that the following definitions derive.

It is important to remember that there are several upscale segments, each as different from the other as all of them are different from the mass market. They have different buying motivations, different product needs, and different ways of contributing to bank profits. To try to treat the entire upscale market as a homogeneous group is as big a mistake as to treat the entire retail mass market as a homogeneous group.

Upscale customers fall into four different categories:

CATEGORY 1

Private Banking/Trust Customers (Affluent Passive Investors)

Those individuals who:

- Come by their wealth through passive means; that is, they inherit (or marry) it;

- Earn their own wealth in their own lifetimes, but do so by risking the capital of other people (corporate executives with little or no equity in the companies they run, for example) instead of risking their own capital; and
- Regardless of whether they inherit or earn their wealth, have a stronger need for that security than tolerance for risk.

Minimum Net Worth and Income Requirements— Passive Affluent

To be considered a passive affluent bank customer, the individual must have a *minimum* $1 million net worth and an annual household income in excess of $100,000.

CATEGORY 2

Private Banking Active Investor Customers

Those individuals who:

- Actively earn their own wealth in their own lifetimes;
- Risk their own capital in the sources from which their fortunes flow; and,
- Have a higher tolerance for risk than need for security.

Minimum Net Worth and Income Requirements

There are three different economic categories of active investors: junior-, middle-, and senior-level customers.

JUNIOR LEVEL CUSTOMERS (ACTIVE INVESTOR)

To be considered an active investor who qualifies for private banking, the *junior* level customer must have a *minimum, individual* (not family) net worth of $150,000 (*exclusive of primary residence equity and all other consumer possessions*) and an annual, *individual, declared income* in excess of $40,000. Remember, a declared income is after taxes, and this is a tax shelter-sensitive customer. Their minimum individual annual *gross* incomes are probably closer to $75,000.

This sounds like a very small net worth for qualification as a private banking customer. But bear in mind that in calculating the net worths of active investors, all consumer goods (including home equity) are deducted from the total. Thus, the actual amount is much more substantial than it appears to be. It is also well to remember that these people are on a fast to very fast track, and their net worths and incomes increase at very rapid rates once they are over 30 years of age. The average age of junior level private banking customers is 35.

Junior level active investor customers are almost totally credit-driven and have little interest in bank products outside of creative credit, which they use for personal business investments to achieve wealth objectives. If you do not develop these customers during this phase of their professional and banking lives, their response to you when you do approach them is: "Where were you when I needed you?" When that occurs, it is difficult (if not impossible) to establish a relationship based on bank loyalty to the customer and customer loyalty to the bank. In other words, they never quite forgive the bank for overlooking their potential when their need for a creative banker was greatest.

Middle Level Customer (Active Investor)

The middle level active investor private banking upscale customer has an individual (not family) net worth of at least $350,000 but less than $1 million (exclusive of primary residence equity and all other consumer possessions) and an annual, *individual, declared* income in excess of $50,000. Again, the declared income is after taxes, and the gross income much higher. Remember, this person is tax shelter-sensitive (a fact that tax reform is not likely to change). The middle level active investor is both wealth achievement and wealth maintenance motivated. Thus, this customer is both credit and investment driven.

This is the most profitable of all affluent market segments. The average size loan is $100,000, and they have not yet reached such a substantial level of affluence that they are not willing to pay either a good loan rate or, instead, a good loan fee. They can be leveraged into keeping good, low-cost deposits; usually they do not as yet have money managers outside of themselves.

Senior Level Customers (Active Investor)

The senior level active investor private banking upscale customer has an individual (not family) net worth *of at least* $1 million (exclusive of the primary residence equity and all other consumer possessions) and an annual, $100,000 declared, individual (not household) income (after taxes). The greater is the person's financial achievement, the more the person is motivated toward wealth maintenance rather than wealth achievement.

Though the credit drive remains (they never truly become passive—like Howard Hughes on the day he died, they want to accrue more wealth), as the main device utilized to implement investment strategies, the senior level active investor customer is more investment-driven than credit-driven. They never evolve with age into passive investors (a mistaken assumption on the part of many), but they do begin to delegate more to others—outside financial advisors and managers—as they age.

CATEGORY 3

Young Upwardly Mobile Professionals in Economic Stress (Yumpies)

From which the word "yuppie" was taken, this is the third category of upscale customers.

Yumpies are active investors and will, as a result, move "up the scale" quickly; yuppies are passive investors and will move "up the scale," but will do so more slowly because they will not take the same investment risks as their yumpies counterparts. As the title suggests, these individuals are recent college graduates who do not, as yet, have the economic qualifications of either a passive affluent or a junior level active investor private banking customer.

Frequently, certain categories of yumpies are solicited as junior level private banking customers right out of school. Surgeons, for example, tend to earn very large sums of money and acquire the minimum net worth requirement within two or three years after starting their practices. If you wait until they've "made it," your competition for them as bank customers will be intense.

Or yumpies may be entrepreneurs who did not graduate from college (it is good to remember that more than 75 percent of all new millionaires each year are noncollege graduates), who spent their late teens and early 20s learning and earning. However, if the bank does not identify them and market effectively to them at the point in time when they truly *need* a bank, it is very difficult to establish a relationship based on any kind of loyalty. And, if not identified and provided special service of some kind before they achieve economic status, they will be (1) lost in the branch network and serviced along with the rest of the mass market and (2) susceptible to competitors who lure them to their active investor private banking groups as junior level customers and away from your bank.

Thus, future profits from them are lost unless they are identified early. They have no economic qualifications as such, but are for the most part employed in professions where they have substantial opportunity to earn high incomes and accumulate the minimum junior level net worth very quickly. They are easily identified, for example, independent attorneys (as opposed to lawyers with large firms), surgeons (young nonsurgeons are usually passive yuppies), small business owners who start (rather than inherit) the business, and independent CPAs (as opposed to Big 8 professionals).

CATEGORY 4

Personal Banking Upscale Customers

Personal banking customers are the final upscale category. These customers are frequently confused with private banking customers because they often have a substantial *household* income. Income alone does not qualify a customer for private banking. That status requires *both income and net worth.* However, a person does not have to be a private banking customer to be considered as upscale. Personal banking customers fall into three different segments:

Senior Middle Market Upscale Personal Banking Customers

Senior personal banking customers are those individuals who have achieved substantial incomes and assets, but they are passive investors who do not have the minimum net worth requirements ($1 million) with which to qualify for the passive affluent private banking customer designation. Senior upscale middle market customers have inherited smaller fortunes, or are members of senior and executive management for small to large companies.

The larger the company, the more likely it is for top executive managers to achieve the minimum million dollar net worth to qualify as a passive affluent private banking customer. The smaller the company, the less likely. In other words, the size of the company that employs the member of senior or executive manager will tell the bank marketer a great deal about which market segment the individual qualifies for: senior middle market or passive affluent private banking.

Lee Iacocca from Chrysler is, by the definition given above, passive affluent; John Smith, president of ABC Print Shop, is more likely to be a senior middle market upscale customer. Categorizing the entrepreneurial Lee Iacocca as a passive investor may surprise some. Aren't all entrepreneurs active investors? *Only if their own capital is at risk in their entrepreneurial endeavors.* While Mr. Iacocca will score higher as a having more active investor traits than other, more conservative executive managers at major corporations when using the guidelines given here, he is still, by my definition, a passive investor. It is not his capital at risk at Chrysler Corporation.

Senior middle market customers are mostly empty (or soon-to-be-empty) nesters, preretirees, and retirees. They have annual *family* incomes in excess of $75,000. Both spouses frequently work during the younger years. Their tastes favor symbols of wealth established by others (passive investor private banking customers establish wealth symbols that are then imitated by others—currently it is the BMW, an investment property second home in a warm winter location, etc.). Thus, they are people who imitate the wealthy and sometimes appear more wealthy than they really are. They are joiners of country clubs, civic organizations, and political groups.

Many widows and widowers fall into this category. The average age of this group is 59.5. Bear in mind, this is a passive, not an active, investor group. Thus, they have a lower tolerance to risk and a greater need (over 50 percent) for security. Their main motivation is the retention of assets on which they can earn a reasonable return. When properly banked, they will maintain up to $50,000 in a single deposit account.

They are very interest rate-sensitive. These people did not hesitate to take their deposits out of their family banks and put them into money market funds with a substantially higher rate of return when these accounts first became available from bank competitors. They are very fee-sensitive. As security-driven passive investors, they do not risk their own capital in accumulating their asset base. They are usually single-income families in their later years. Emphasis on bank products centers on deposit accounts, advisory services, planning assistance, and investment services. They have little need for credit products (the older the passive investor upscale customer, the lower the credit drive), and when a borrowing need arises, traditional retail banking consumer loans can handle the need.

Mid-Level Upscale Middle Market Personal Banking Customers

Mid-level upscale middle market personal banking customers represent those families with household incomes in excess of $50,000. They are in the early stages of gaining a substantial net worth. At this point in their lives, their net worths average about $150,000, if the primary residence and all consumer goods are included. Their average age is 39.5. They are nesters who are passive investors (their need for security outweighs their tolerance for risk). They, too, enjoy purchasing the symbols of wealth and follow the lead set by senior middle market customers (who are following affluent private banking customers) in that endeavor. They are members of middle management at medium to large companies, or they own their own small successful business— the mom and pop dry cleaning shop.

They join athletic clubs and, as soon as the budget allows, the country club. They are traditionalists. While they are still very asset acquisition oriented, they are also beginning to be sensitive to the need to maintain assets. They are, more often than not, double-income families, though frequently the wife stops working until the children are school age. A large percentage of these customers will, with age and success, become the new senior level personal banking middle market segment. At that point, they usually become single-income families.

They are very interest rate-sensitive. However, because their financial resources are not as great as those of the senior middle market customer, they did not strip all of their deposit dollars out of banks when money market funds became available, but split them with some funds going to a broker money market account, some staying in the bank (a reflection of their security drive and FDIC availability). When properly banked, they will maintain in excess of $10,000 in deposit balances, though seldom in a single account.

While these customers still have strong borrowing needs, they also place strong emphasis on investment and deposit products. They are extremely good target customers for services like financial planning because they are the hardest hit by taxation and inflation, yet are seldom the primary segment targeted for this service.

Junior Middle Market Personal Banking Customers

Junior middle market personal banking customers fall into two categories: yuppies (young urban professional passive investors in economic stress); and, older, double-income blue-collar families/older single-income white-collar families.

Yuppies are upwardly mobile in that almost all of them will move up to qualify as the new mid-middle market, and a large percentage of them will go on to the senior level designation. These are young CPAs (at Big 8 firms), lawyers (with large law firms), health care professionals (nonsurgeons), and business majors at the beginning of their corporate careers. Average age of this group is 29. They have not just graduated from college, but have had a few years of professional experience. They are just getting to the point where they have strong incomes.

The main thing that segregates them from middle level upscale customers discussed in the previous category is their lack of net worth, which is minimal. Immediately after graduation, their economic resources are used to get started—a new car, professional attire, furniture, appliances, the down payment on a home, etc. They are nesters and prenesters. They are frequently double-income professional families—a lawyer wife and a doctor husband, etc. Their credit needs are strong. These are very status-oriented people, but tend to set their own trends rather than imitate the wealth symbol preferences of other groups. If banks want to sell nontraditional bank products like life, health, and disability insurance, this is the best target market.

Their balances (between $1,000 and $10,000 on average) make them profitable customers to the bank, but their real strength is the future potential they offer and their need for credit to fund their lifestyle. They are very active people with high energy levels. The word "passive investor" should not be confused with "wimp." A passive investor merely gains economic resources in a more passive way than do active investors.

Double-Income Blue-Collar/Single-Income White-Collar Families

Double-income blue-collar families also fall into the category of junior level middle market personal banking customers, not because of their ages (they are, on average, 49.5 years and can hardly be called "junior" on that basis), but because of their junior level financial qualifications. So do older single-income white-collar families where the earner has not progressed beyond the levels of middle management to higher incomes.

They frequently maintain stronger deposit relationships than yuppies (from $10,000 to $20,000), but do not have their potential rise to the top of their corporate or professional worlds. Blue-collar workers most frequently rise up through the ranks of labor. They will not become junior middle market customers until they reach their 40s, and after that will not move further "up the scale." However, their profit contribution cannot be ignored, and they need to be singled out as preferred bank customers because of it.

This group is the most security-motivated of any of the upscale markets. This is logical in that they, of all the targeted groups, can least afford to lose what they have accumulated. This is the worker who either has or will soon walk away from his blue-collar job with a substantial amount of retirement benefits. This family has accumulated a net worth of about $100,000 (including the primary residence), and the family's average earnings before retirement are between $35,000 and $55,000. The family income may consist of a policeman's and a secretary's salary; or, a cab driver's and a teacher's, a plumber's and a bus driver's.

Because of their strong security drives, these people never did take their money out of banks and put it in uninsured broker money market accounts (prior to deregulation and the time bankers could offer competitive rates). Their loyalties are strong, and they are the most likely of all profitable market segments to establish a total relationship with a single financial institution. Their need for financial planning services (the largest percentage of them are preretirement) is high. They trust their bankers more than they do bank competitors.

They have used credit only when necessary, during the consumer goods accumulation period of their 20s and 30s, and the closer they get to retirement, the less and less attractive credit products are to them. Such needs, when they do occur, center on purchasing recreational vehicles, home improvement loans, student loans for their children, etc. They do not join clubs, but do join organizations—Elks, bowling leagues, churches, PTA, and other professional, social, and civic organizations.

Psychographics and Buying Motivations of Each Segment

There are only two psychographic (buying motivation) traits with which bankers need to be concerned in determining financial services product needs of upscale customers: They must understand which customers are active investors and which are passive investors. Once this has been determined, bank marketers can utilize demographics, a strategy with which they are more familiar, to complete the business development plan.

As stated above, active investors have a higher tolerance for risk than they have need for security; a passive investor is the flip side of the same coin, having higher security needs than risk tolerance levels. This sounds easy, but it is extremely complex. Once understood, it is so logical that it becomes quite simple to include in the strategic planning process.

Chart 1 identifies the various levels of risk tolerance levels and security drives that identify affluent passive and active investors. When reading Chart 1, the reader should keep the following in mind:

1. All people, wealthy or not, have risk tolerance levels and security needs that resemble those shown on this chart. However, only affluent people have investment portfolios compatible to the explanations given. A person with a $20,000 a year income may be a 30 percent active and 70 percent passive investor, but his or her investment portfolio will not contain the mix of products shown on Chart 1 because it applies only to the affluent market.

2. The largest numbers of and the most traditionally profitable upscale retail banking customers have a 30 percent tolerance for risk and a 70 percent need for security. The security of banks has always held strong appeal for security-motivated people. It is important to understand before reading further that unless your bank has a private banking area specifically developed to serve the unique needs of active investors, you do not have active investors banking with you in a profitable way.

The banking needs of active investors are so specialized, they will not establish a profitable relationship with your bank unless you have the substantial and necessary expertise to serve the needs of these customers. They may be banking with you, but chances are their "relationship" consists of a checking account with a $1.98 balance. They are not profitable customers until they are provided the unique credit products they require. Then, they become the most profitable of all bank customers. Thus, as you read Chart 1, understand that passive investors are the banking industry's traditional customers, and active investors represent nontraditional customers—they are your marketing opportunity, not success story.

3. If the reader is a banker, chances are the reader is a passive investor. Bankers are risk analysts, not risk takers. That is as it should be. But it does somewhat limit your perceptions of who active investors are because your psychological makeup is precisely the opposite of theirs. Further, your best traditional customers are the opposites of active investor nontraditional bank customers, too. Everyone tends to judge others by their own standards, their own universe. Once the reader has finished reading Chart 1, continue on and read Chart 2. This data explains the different personality traits of the two segments. And active and passive investors are not just a little different from one another—they are opposite personality types with totally different buying motivations.

Chart 1, then, will identify the different levels of risk tolerance versus security needs and explain how that data translates into sample personal customer financial statements. When a person's risk tolerance level exceeds 50 percent, that person is an active investor.

No one is a 100 percent active or 100 percent passive investor. The person who is 55 percent active and 45 percent passive is less of an active investor than the person who is 90 percent active and 10 percent passive, but both are active investors, nonetheless. When a person's security need exceeds 50 percent, that person is a passive investor. The person who is 10 percent active and 90 percent passive is substantially different from the person who is 45 percent active and 55 percent passive, but both are passive investors, nonetheless.

Chart 2 explains the personality traits of those people whose risk tolerance levels exceed 50 percent (active investors) and the personality traits of those people whose security needs exceed 50 percent (passive investors). Retail bank product packaging can then be based on these personality traits, which make up the buying motivations of the segment target marketed.

For example, most banks target marketed their traditionally profitable high deposit customers—passive investors—for discount bro-

CHART 1 Guidelines for Identifying Affluent Active and Passive Investors

[The left portion of the figure represents the customer's level of risk tolerance.]

[The right portion of the figure represents the customer's need for security.]

Left	Right
0%	100%
10%	90%
20%	80%
30%	70%
40%	60%
50%	50%
60%	40%
70%	30%
80%	20%
90%	10%
100%	0%

0% Since it is impossible to live without some form of risk, individuals without any tolerance for risk are probably frightened, complex ridden people.

10% People with this level of risk tolerance invest money into insured accounts, such as certificates of deposit (CDs).

20% People with this level of risk tolerance invest in products that have ensured returns, such as CDs, money market accounts, and life insurance products. A small part of their portfolios may be invested in blue chip stocks. These people also consider their primary residence as an investment. The smallest portion of their portfolios will be invested in the highest quality of municipal bonds and mutual funds. They dislike borrowing or being leveraged in any way.

30% Affluent people with this level of risk tolerance are traditional trust banking customers. They invest heavily in blue chip stocks. They use their primary residence as an investment and their secondary residence in other locales for depreciation. Until tax law proposals changed the tax benefits, these individuals were heavy investors in limited partnerships in real estate syndications. Their other investments include commercial paper, mutual funds, and municipal bonds. These people borrow with the 30 percent of their asset bases they are comfortable in leveraging. The 30 percent they are willing to leverage will not include items needed to enhance their consumer lifestyle. For example, primary residence home equity will never be leveraged for loan collateral. The 30 percent to be leveraged is that portion of the asset base not associated with lifestyle security. And, as long as only 30 percent of their asset bases and cash flows that do not involve lifestyle security are at risk, these people will borrow money to make fairly aggressive investments—but only with that 30 percent not involved in lifestyle security

40% The total portfolio for people with this level of risk tolerance will strongly resemble the 30 percent customer described above. The major difference is that 40 percent of the asset base not associated with lifestyle security is comfortably put at risk. Historically, the 40 percent risk tolerance group has invested more heavily into real estate than the 30 percent group. However, as tax laws change tax advantages, real estate will be used less as the primary investment for these passive investors. Acceptable replacements for traditional real estate investments include more aggressive mutual funds (international funds, for example), most stocks (except calls, puts, options, and commodities), and new, high-quality, over-the-counter stock issues.

50% Half of the portfolio for people with this level of risk tolerance will resemble that of individuals at the 30 percent level. Again, the major difference is that 50 percent instead of 30 percent of the asset base not associated with lifestyle security is comfortably put at risk. The risk portion of the portfolio will be invested in self-directed real estate investments (for example, the purchase of an apartment building and control of its conversion into condominiums), agricultural investments, such as water rights, and all forms of stock with a small percentage in calls, puts, and options. At this level, the biggest behavioral change is the investor's need for personal involvement in the investment product. As risk tolerance levels and investor's need increase, the investor gathers more information and becomes more personally involved in controlling the outcome of the investment. Active investors believe knowledge, involvement, and control of investment products reduce the risk. The nonrisk portion of the portfolio will resemble that of other passive investors with higher security needs.

60% At least 40 percent of the investment portfolio for people with this level of risk tolerance will be in products offering a high level of security. The remainder of the portfolio will be invested in such ventures as oil and gas limited partnerships, water rights, hopper cars, cable television, and equipment leasing. These people will make limited investments into precious metals. They will also invest in private offerings of new business start-ups but want to be involved in controlling them. As a result, they frequently own their own businesses. At the very least, they will be active members of the board of directors. The levels of risk involved in their businesses will be lower than the levels of risk in businesses started by people with higher tolerance for risk. (For example, they will start a small computer store rather than an oil and gas drilling company.)

70% People at this level of risk tolerance are mostly independent business people who do not work for large companies, whether they are a major corporation or a Big Eight CPA firm. (Of all corporate executives, 80 percent fall between the 30 percent and 40 percent level of risk tolerance; most of the rest fall between 50 percent and 60 percent.) For those people with a 70 percent level of risk tolerance, 30 percent of their portfolios will still reflect a high level of secure investments. Because these people have substantial amounts of secure assets available for collateral, they are the ideal customers for creative credit and, thus, private banking. They usually invest the remaining 70 percent of their portfolios in such things as oil and gas, water rights, hopper cars, cable television, equipment leasing, precious metals, and thoroughbreds. These people are extremely tax-shelter sensitive and profit motivated, they have strong ego and control needs. However, even though they are often personally unhappy in such a setting, they are still able to work for large corporations without causing disruptions.

80% People with this level of risk tolerance are often disruptive to a large company due to their strong need for personal control and ego gratification, and their high-risk orientation. These people are often not team players and are very internalized. They may not be terribly concerned with what the president of their large company thinks of them but are concerned with self-approval. They primarily invest into self-controlled small companies that usually have a fairly high level of risk (for example, a shipping company in the Caribbean, a new robotics company, or a new cable television station).

90% At 90 percent, the customer's risk tolerance is becoming too risky for bank borrowing, unless the bank has special expertise in tracking tax-sheltered income that is difficult to find and monitor (for example, thoroughbred depreciation). The personal financial statements of these customers are usually highly leveraged, again having a negative credit implication. Like people with an 80 percent level of risk tolerance, these people usually invest in companies that they own which have aggressive purposes. However, these people are 10 percent more aggressive than those in the 80 percent category. They view as "secure" investments into precious metals, water rights, and cable television. They are very egocentric, control oriented, and profit motivated. They gather tremendous amounts of information about investments in order to "beat the odds."

100% It is difficult to perceive of people who are willing to risk their total asset bases with periodic regularity. Obviously, these people would view their assets as something with which to gamble. Because of the amount of information they gather in order to have better control over their investments, their gambles often pay off. However, like the people who are unwilling to take any risks, these people are not psychologically healthy. Their quality of life depends on the state of their balance sheets and their ego drives prevent the development of close interpersonal relationships.

Chart reprinted from pages xi and xii of *Profitable Private Banking: The Complete Blueprint* by Marilyn MacGruder Barnewall, published by the American Bankers Association, Washington, D.C., in 1986.

CHART 2 Active/Passive Personality Traits

Passive Affluent

Income-motivated
Security-oriented
Deposit interest rate-driven
Utilizes income to purchase consumer
  lifestyle
Motivated to gain power over others; the
  greater the level of affluence, the
  greater the drive to gain power (impacts
  through others)
Strong team ego
Likes bankers

Trusts bankers
Always has strong net worth ($1 million
  minimum) as long as personal
  possessions are included (because of
  the quality of life-drive that motivates
  consumer buying)
Always shows large declared family
  income
Traditional taxpayer
User of consumer goods

Active Investor

Profit-motivated
Risk-oriented
Credit-driven
Utilizes profit for more investments, more
  wealth
Motivated to gain control over own
  destiny, financial as well as other
  categories involving lifestyle (impacts
  through self)
Strong individual ego
Thinks bankers had last creative thought
  at least 25 years ago
Considers bankers adversaries
Always has minimum net worth of
  $150,000 (excluding all personal
  possessions, especially the primary
  residence)

Always shows lowest individual, declared,
  annual income
Nontraditional taxpayer
Provider of consumer goods

Chart reprinted with permission from "Understanding the Psychographics of the Affluent Market," by Marilyn MacGruder Barnewall, *ABA Journal of Personal Financial Services* 2, no. 2 (Winter 1986), p. 13.

kerage services. Passive investors are security-driven people. They are the least likely segment to make stock sale and purchase decisions without the advice and counsel of an advisor—something bankers are frequently prevented by regulation from doing. Does it, therefore, make sense to target such a service for the market segment whose buying motivations spotlight the banking industry weakness of non-advisory capabilites? Or does the discount brokerage service have more appeal to active investors who like to control their own financial destinies, make their own investment decisions, and want to do business with facilitators, not advisors?

Financial planning services are best directed at the passive investor who wants advice and will delegate control, not the active investor who does not want investment advice and will not delegate control. Travel agencies will find more fast track travelers in active investors than they will with passive investors.

The following rules are good guidelines when matching the right products with the right customer segments:

1. Determine whether the customer is an active or a passive investor.

2. Evaluate product purpose(s) to determine whether it features security or risk, and advisory or facilitation. Product positioning can often make what normally has little buying appeal, appealing. For example, nonsecurity motivated active investors have little interest in security-oriented trust products like wills and estate planning. However, when the private banker informs the active investor how, by having a will, the bank considers him or her a better borrowing customer, having a will suddenly becomes important to the active investor. Bear in mind that access to creatively structured credit is the active investor's hot button. To product position in this way is not difficult. It requires only that the banker understand the customer's buying motivations so the banker can make a statement such as "Mr. Active Investor, I notice you don't have a will. Frankly, having one would make me view you as a stronger borrower. If something happens to you during the term of the loan, I don't want to wait three years for probate to settle your estate and pay my loan." To offer a will to someone on the basis of the peace of mind and family security, when the person is not motivated by those things, is a waste of energy.

3. Evaluate the product process to determine if the customer is in control (active) or the banker making the product available is in control (passive). Credit products, for example, can be positioned to fill either need. The affluent passive investor is likely to borrow to fund a limited partnership (where others are in control), while the affluent active investor is likely to borrow to buy a small apartment building, working directly with a contractor to turn them into condominiums (where the investor is in control).

The above definitions of a retail bank's most profitable upscale customers, and the explanations regarding the psychographics (buying motivations), include only those segments of primary importance to the banker wanting to take advantage of the substantial cost-efficiencies inherent in market segmentation. It only makes sense to market specific products to customers attracted by those products, especially when you can select the most potentially profitable customers to whom they appeal.

The mass market has little need of large, creative credits for speculative investment purposes, or for meaningful financial planning, discount brokerage, or estate planning. They don't have sufficient assets to maintain the minimum balances required for most cash management accounts or the assets available that make asset management accounts appealing. The financial services products that appeal to people with money have little appeal to those without money. However, in order to avoid the mistake most commonly made by bankers when attempting to market to the affluent, remember that the products that appeal to active investors have little appeal to passive investors, and vice versa. Certain product incompatibilities can be overcome by positioning. Most cannot.

The soon-to-retire affluent corporate executive (80 percent of corporate executives are passive investors) has totally different financial services needs than the surgeon (90 percent of surgeons are active investors) who lives next door. One is a more aggressive investor because his or her risk tolerance level is higher. One has more conservative investment habits because he or she is more security motivated. When bankers approach passive investors with aggressive products, or active investors with conservative products, they lose credibility. The customer walks away from the sales session believing the banker to be unsophisticated and unknowledgeable. Credibility suffers. And credibility is the most important sales tool available to bankers in a marketplace where competition is increasing, not decreasing.

Once it has been determined whether the customer (or customer segment) is an active or a passive investor, the process of offering the right product to the right customer (or group of customers) can be refined even further with only two pieces of data: occupation and age.

A small business owner is more likely to invest in pension and profit-sharing plans than the person who works for a large corporation where retirement benefit packages are provided. The same is true of professional people who own and manage their own practices rather than working for a large firm, such as lawyers and CPAs who own and run their own practices. They offer different sales opportunites than do those who are employed by large firms. The independent businessperson will have pension and profit sharing, IRA and/or Keough plan needs, whereas the corporate executive may not. Age determines the customer segments' current and future lifestyle cycles. Several guidelines are helpful in developing product packages on this basis:

1. The younger the customer, the stronger the need for consumer credit, the less the need for deposit services (other than checking), asset management, financial and estate planning, etc. From age 25 to 35, the motivation is to acquire consumer goods and secure lifestyle. Bank credit products are utilized to achieve this goal. They want car loans and credit cards. (Those who inherit wealth are frequent exceptions to this rule.)

2. The older the customer, the stronger the need for advisory, saving, investment, trust, and asset management services, the less the need for credit products. From age 45 through 65, the customer can be considered preretirement. The motivation begins at about age 45, and it becomes more and more important with age to maximize assets and income for retirement. Borrowing needs still exist with this group

but are usually directed at maximizing assets and income for retirement. Or they borrow as a matter of necessity—to send their children to college or for home improvement loans (get the home ready for the retirement years). While it cannot be said with any degree of certainty about the mass market that the older the customer the greater the level of economic achievement, it can be said about upscale market segments. Age is closely tied to the financial achievements of upscale customers.

3. Customers in their middle years are usually nesting, and all products that assist in that process have appeal. Credit needs are still very strong, and the need to put down financial roots that help establish family security is just beginning to emerge. All products that can help this 35- to 45-year-old market segment achieve family security should be developed and offered.

4. The more profitable the customer potential, the less likely it is bank credit scoring systems will fill their needs.

   a. The recently-graduated CPA, lawyer or health care professional who applies for a loan will be denied due to lack of employment history. It is not likely that the bank will have an opportunity to serve future needs (when the customer's assets and income are substantial) if it does not serve needs when customers most need the bank.

   b. The higher customers' incomes, the more likely the customer is to have loan requests too large to be handled by credit scoring systems. The lower the consumer's income, the more likely it is that credit scoring will fill consumer borrowing needs. Since the lower the income the higher the credit risk, banks that depend too strongly on credit scoring systems to handle all consumer borrowing needs will probably attract customers who are the highest credit risks. The customer who wants to buy a boat, an airplane, a recreational vehicle, etc., and has the financial resources to do so, may not be well handled through credit scoring. Thus, mass market customers, not upscale customers, will be handled by this credit scoring service.

HOW TO IDENTIFY EXISTING PROFITABLE RETAIL CUSTOMER SEGMENTS

Chart 3 clearly explains how to identify existing bank customers who fall into the targeted market segments explained above. Only a few words of explanation are needed here to expand on the information contained in Chart 3.

CHART 3   Research Methods to Identify Personal and Consumer Banking
              Customers and Those Who Are Affluent Passive and Active Investors

Research Technique Bank Profile: 20% of the Bank's Retail Customers Are Responsible for 80% of Its Retail Deposits	Purpose	Percentage of the 20% Who Maintain 80% of All Retail Deposits	Method to Determine Whether an Individual Customer Is a Personal or Consumer Banking Customer, or an Affluent Passive or Active Investor
Research all customers who have an average minimum balance over $10,000 in either a single savings or demand deposit account.	To identify personal banking customers	25% by dollar volume 30% by number of customers	If the customer's net worth exceeds $150,000 but is less than $1 million and the customer's age is over 50, this is a personal banking customer.
Research all customers who have an average minimum balance between $1,000 and $9,999 in either a single savings or demand deposit account.	To identify consumer banking customers	15% by dollar volume 50% to 60% by number of customers	If the customer's net worth exceeds $50,000 but is less than $150,000 and the customer's age is over 50, this is a consumer banking customer.
Research all demand deposit accounts with an average minimum balance of less than $1,000 to determine depositors who make demand deposits in excess of $5,000 each account cycle for three consecutive cycles.*	To identify affluent active investors	0%	If the customer's net worth exceeds $150,000 (excluding residence and personal possessions), taxable income exceeds $40,000, and the age criteria are met, this customer is likely to be an active investor.
Research all savings accounts to find those with a balance over $50,000	To identify affluent passive investors	60% by dollar volume 10% to 20% by number of customers	Determine the level of risk contained in the customer's investment assets. This information will indicate whether the customer is an affluent passive or active investor.
Research all retail accounts to find those customers with such titles as "Doctor" "PC" (Professional	To identify affluent passive and active investors and potential	Percentage unknown. If they are high depositors, they will be found in the categories of consumer or	Same as the previous method.

CHART 3   (concluded)

Research Technique Bank Profile: 20% of the Bank's Retail Customers Are Responsible for 80% of Its Retail Deposits	Purpose	Precentage of the 20% Who Maintain 80% of All Retail Deposits	Method to Determine Whether an Individual Customer Is a Personal or Consumer Banking Customer, or an Affluent Passive or Active Investor
Corporation), "CPA", and "Attorney-at-Law."	wealth accumulators	personal banking customers, or affluent passive investors; if they are not high depositors, they are not among the 20% maintaining 80% of retail deposits.	

*Each marketplace must be individually evaluated to determine the appropriate flow-through amount. New York is different from Denver; Denver is different from Des Moines.

Chart reprinted from pages 25 and 26 of *Profitable Private Banking: The Complete Blueprint* by Marilyn MacGruder Barnewall, published by the American Bankers Association, Washington, D.C., in 1986.

Bear in mind that active investors cannot be identified by deposit balances. Their money is actively invested in items where, though there is no FDIC insurance, the risk-oriented active investor is likely to realize a 30 or 40 percent return if the investment pays off, not a 7 or 8 percent return on a CD. Your reaction may be "Yes, but look how many investment deals fail. They are taking big risks to get that return." Actually, that's not quite accurate.

Active investors like to maintain control of their investments. Thus, they were not the ones who took losses on real estate syndication deals when tax reform made them unappealing. Syndication deals are controlled by others and, therefore, have little appeal to active investors. Quite the contrary, it was the less risk-oriented passive investor, willing to let someone else manage his or her investments, who took this investment loss.

The point is, though active investors are willing to take risks in order to gain higher rates of return than deposit accounts at any organization offer, they minimize risk by maintaining control of the investment. They are willing to devote the time and energy necessary to keep risk of loss at a minimum. And, because of these investments, they do not often have excess capital available to maintain large bank balances.

What they do have, though, is substantial amounts of cash flowing through their deposit accounts each month. Thus, to find active investors, look for low deposit account balances with substantial amounts flowing through them each month. The marketplace in which the bank is located will largely determine how "substantial" is defined. In Des Moines, an account with a low balance and over $5,000 per month flowing through it each month for three months will indicate an active investor. In Denver, $7,500 will probably be more accurate. In New York, it is probably closer to $10,000 or $15,000 (or more) in flow through. The one exception to this is yumpies. And, since they neither maintain large balances nor run large amounts through the account, they are very difficult to find other than by occupation (this will be explained at the end of this material).

Passive investors can be identified by deposit account balances:

1. Affluent passive investor private banking customers will usually maintain in excess of $50,000 in a single account balance.
2. Yuppies (personal banking customers) will maintain between $1,000 and $5,000 in average balances in a single account.
3. Other personal banking customers will maintain from $5,000 to $10,000 average balances in a single account. "Other" personal banking customers usually represent older blue- or white-collar families. They may have several $5,000 CDs maturing on different dates. Don't try to get them to consolidate them into one large CD because they usually won't.

For guidance on how to operationally identify your existing profitable upscale customers in order to develop and provide special retail banking services for them, see Chart 3.

HOW TO IDENTIFY PROFITABLE NONCUSTOMER SEGMENTS

Knowing an upscale customer's occupation is the key to achieving this.

Substantial research has validated the belief that by knowing targeted customers' occupations, you can largely determine whether that person is an active or a passive investor. Look once again at Chart 2, which explains the personality trait differences (and buying motivations) between active and passive investors. Those same personality traits attract a person to particular occupations/professsions.

The active investor's need to control will frequently prevent that person from achieving at high levels in a large corporation. Their risk tolerance means they are not necessarily attracted to jobs that, though they offer substantial security, restrict creative freedom. Thus, not many of them work for large companies—at least not for long. Active investor personality traits were, in my opinion, what caused H. Ross Perot to walk away from IBM to start Electronic Data Systems (EDS).

On the other hand, the security-motivated passive investor is usually attracted to the sick leave, retirement, profit sharing, and other security-oriented benefits packages made available by larger companies. The results, then, should not surprise anyone. Of corporate executives, 80 percent are passive investors.

Active investors are independent attorneys, independent CPAs, surgeons, small business owners who risk their own capital and start their own companies (as opposed to inheriting or buying them), entrepreneurs, etc.

Passive investors are attorneys and CPAs who work for large firms, corporate executives, physicians other than surgeons, those who inherit wealth and, in general, those who are employed by large companies.

Chart 4 identifies the percentages of each occupation that are active or passive investors. Thus, an effective marketing campaign designed to offer active investor products and services to the active investors to whom they appeal, and to offer passive investor products and services to the passive investors to whom they appeal, can be designed for the cost of a copy of the Yellow Pages and a good direct mail communications piece.

Professional associations can offer much assistance to bankers who understand the benefits of market segmentation that targets the three professions most likely to produce profitable bank customers: local Bar, CPA, and Medical Associations have much useful information available. For example, in addition to having access to a membership list of health care professionals indicating whether the practitioner is a surgeon (active investor) or a nonsurgeon (passive investor), membership lists also give the length of time in practice. Thus, passive investor yuppies and active investor yumpies can be segmented from older practitioners.

CONCLUSION

The above material puts into very broad, general terms and conceptual overviews what is truly a complex concept. Increasing bank profits through cost-efficient market segmentation strategies designed to market retail banking products to upscale customers is not a simple task. Nor is it a gimmick. Increased profits usually do not come easily. Things that are meaningful seldom do. This is not a "quick-fix" philosophy, nor will it appeal to those looking for easy ways to solve problems.

To implement the strategies explained here requires a new look at bank organizational structure. It requires a look at how customer problems are handled for personal banking customers. It requires a

CHART 4   How to Determine the Number of Passive Affluent and Active
Investors in Local Marketplace (figures apply only to passive
affluent people with minimum $1 million personal net worth and
active investors with minimum $150,000 net worth exclusive of all
consumer goods)

Occupation Profession	Total Number	Number of Active Investors	Number of Passive Investors	Market-share of Active Investors
Corporate executives	2,500	500	2,000	250
Small business owners	16,160	8,080	8,080	4,040
Surgical physicians	1,000	900	100	450
Nonsurgical physicians	1,500	300	1,200	150
Surgical dentists	700	630	70	315
Nonsurgical dentists	1,600	320	1,280	160
CPAs (independent)	1,200	1,080	120	540
CPAs (big 8)	500	100	400	50
Lawyers (independent)	1,200	1,080	120	540
Lawyers (large firms)	350	70	280	35
Entrepreneurs	3,000	3,000	–0–	1,500

Note: The above figures are not an accurate representation of any marketplace but are
provided only to give examples as to how many customers fall into targeted market segments
by occupation and profession. Column on far right explains the percentage of marketshare
a bank that is implementing the first active investor private banking program in its marketplace
can expect to achieve.

Chart reprinted with permission from "Understanding the Psychographics of the Affluent
Market," by Marilyn MacGruder Barnewall, *ABA Journal of Personal Financial Services* 2,
no. 2 (Winter 1986), p. 20.

look at traditional loan policies that do not fill the needs of active
investors who are aggressive investors and borrowers. It requires a
new look at the parameters of trust banker account management res-
ponsiblities and personnel skills: If the passive affluent are to be
banked by trust bankers (where these customers are traditionally handled), then the trust banker must be able to serve the entire relationship need, from personal and investment trust needs to deposits and
loans.

Is it worth the time, effort, and capital required to segment existing
customers into groups that have specific product needs? Is it worth it
to have a special area within the retail bank to serve the needs of

prospective new upscale customers and to develop marketing strategies and organizational structures and specially trained personnel required for the effort?

With regard to active investor private banking programs, those banks that have taken a cold, hard, honest look at the ways in which they were not serving the needs of these customers and made adjustments to be able to do so should have a net bottom line profit contribution that answers the question: "Is it worth it?"

At the end of three years, active investor private banking groups usually have a 150 percent deposit-to-loan ratio, a cost of funds of at least 2 percent less than that of the rest of retail banking, a loan loss ratio of less than .03 percent, and an average return on assets that exceeds 5 percent.[1] These are actual, average statistics taken from a group of banks of all sizes located in different regions of the country. These active investor private banking areas broke into the black within five to nine months and recovered costs in less than 18 months. Their answer to the question "Is it worth it?" is a resounding yes!

Prior to resigning her senior vice presidency at Bankers Trust in New York, private banking manager G. Lynn Shostack was quoted as saying "It takes 10,000 mass market customers to replace the profit contribution of one really good, well-banked upscale customer."

Which do you think is least expensive? Attracting and serving the banking needs of 10,000 mass market customers? Or attracting and serving the banking needs of one really good, well-banked upscale customer?

Such a statistic probably makes sense only in a population center like New York City where large bank customer bases number in the millions. However, if the same philosophy were applied in Denver, Colorado, where the population is about 1/15th that of New York City, it means that it takes 667 mass market customers to achieve the profits available from one good upscale customer. Put into that perspective, Ms. Shostacks's quote is quite realistic.

---

[1]These results come only when a specifically designed, proven, active investor private banker program is implemented.

CHAPTER FIFTY-NINE

Managing Retail Deposit Services

Leslie H. London

Senior Vice President
First National Bank of Louisville

James B. Schmitt

Vice President—Retail Banking
Norwest Corporation

The retail deposit acquisition function, more than any other facet of banking, exemplifies the significant change occurring in our industry. The incremental cost of utilizing retail deposits as a funding source has increased dramatically with our ability to pay market rates for these deposits. In 1983 alone, with the advent of the money market deposit and super NOW accounts, the additional interest cost exceeded $10 billion for the banking industry.

The genesis of change began in 1980 with the passage of the Depository Institution Deregulation and Monetary Control Act. The legislation mandated the orderly phase out of Regulation Q by 1986. While the structured deregulation is complete (final phase—January 1986), the adaptation has just begun. Rate deregulation combined with other ongoing change agents—de novo competitors, electronic delivery, new consumer preferences—force retail deposit managers to carefully assess our past as the first step to positioning the bank for the future. Such an assessment of the past is likely to reach the conclusions that:

- Interest expense has inextricably increased.
- Delivery has been dependent on brick and mortar—high cost.
- Delivery has been labor intensive—high cost.
- Products have been structured by the government—minimal differentiation.
- Product pricing has been constrained by regulation.
- Systems have been designed to meet government regulations, not market demand.

- Financial customers have had minimal product or institutional choice.

The magnitude of this change should not be underestimated. The good news is that other industries have preceded us down the deregulation path and have been quite successful. The bad news is that there are an ample number of examples of those who have not been able to make the transition. Those who have succeeded have taken the time to reevaluate their position and develop a focused plan for the future.

STRATEGIC ANALYSIS

The first step to manage retail deposits effectively in the future is to fully acknowledge the change that is occurring. The management function for the new environment will demand a high level of active commitment. Mistakes in product positioning or pricing will prove to be costly even though the competitive differences may be minimal.

The process should begin by incorporating a program for the acquisition of deposits as an integral part of the bank's long-term strategic planning effort. Management must reevaluate the role of consumer deposits. The combined interest and noninterest expense of retail deposits is likely to be higher than purchased funds. Conversely, retail deposits will be more stable, but new competition seeking market share could force interest expense even higher. To assess properly the contrasting dynamics, retail deposit gathering should be viewed as a separate and unique business distinguished by its own customer base. Within this context, all facets of the business need to be examined.

The following schematic is a suggested process for retail deposit strategic analysis:

1. *Methodology*
   a. Identify major components of the business and evaluate current position along with trends for the past three years. Include product, deliver/distribution, human resources, systems.
   b. Rate component performance as inferior, at par, or superior when compared to the competition.
   c. Focus comparison on the *three largest local competitors* across industry lines; that is, banks, savings and loans, credit unions, and quasi-financials.
2. *Elements to be reviewed*
   a. Competitive market share position. Cite current deposit market share (both dollars and number of accounts) of the three largest competitors and trends for the past three years.

   b. Product lines—segregate into three categories:
   (1) Primary—transaction, open time, certificates.
   (2) Secondary—related fee producing services such as travelers checks, money orders, balance inquire, reconcilement.
   (3) Attendant services—discount brokerage, insurance, mutual funds, safe deposit, financial planning.

Evaluate trends in terms of relative product quality in comparison to identified competitors.

- Product cost: Assess from the perspective of total cost—interest and noninterest expense. Even though sophisticated costing systems may not be in place, one can make reasonable estimates based on prudent assumptions; for example, a branch may primarily serve as a deposit facility and consequently should be allocated to deposit cost.
- Product pricing: Utilizing the component performance ratings, complete a comparison with the top three competitors.
- Distribution delivery: Complete critical review of both place and time comvenience in terms of both the competition and the anticipated market development. How are we located with respect to the type of customers we intend to serve? Is there a need to provide additional off-premise capability (expanded time convenience)?
- Human resources: In the past, deposit services could be managed with relative impunity because of the strong constraints of both rate regulation and locational barriers to entry. Today, careful attention must be given to determining whether or not we have the necessary talent to: (*a*) sell our services against strong market drive competitors, and (*b*) manage our environment, including targeting the right consumer base, paying the proper interest rate, positioning our liabilities to match loan demand at the right spread and being able to enhance products to meet competitive offerings.
- Systems: Our past environment gave us the equivalent of a Maginot Line and systems expense represented a relatively small percentage of total cost. Investment in systems was only sufficient to meet limited competitive change and regulatory demands. The future, however, will be driven by competitor initiated change. We must examine our system capabilities as these relate to enhancements such as relationship reporting, relationship pricing, tiered rate pricing, discount certificates, tax and IRA reporting, external funds transfer, and EFT transaction pricing.

3. *Future driving forces*

Develop a list of the five most critical factors likely to impact the deposit gathering business within the banker's trade area during the next five years.

a. External forces: Evaluate outside events likely to occur that are beyond our control, such as:

(1) Consumer household base will (a) decline, (b) remain stable, (c) increase by an undetermined percentage within the next five years.

(2) More banks and savings and loan failures but stronger, more focused competition.

(3) Lower cost competitors will utilize predatory pricing to gain local market share.

(4) "Truth in Deposit" legislation regarding rates paid, accrual, and compounding methods will be mandated.

b. Internal forces: Assess changes that would be beneficial to the bank in remaining competitive and within our control, such as:

(1) Organizational structure changing from functional to fully integrated in order to achieve cost/market control.

(2) Funds management must develop internal pricing process for retail deposits to provide an incentive for attracting dollars matched to asset needs and at the proper margins.

(3) System being upgraded to accommodate relationship pricing, management reporting, and cost assessment.

(4) Distribution network being revamped to eliminate costly nongrowth branches and incorporate new growth locations and EFT delivery points.

4. *Mission*

To develop a clear purpose statement for retail deposit gathering within the overall context of the bank's total mission. Include:

a. Who we intend to serve; that is, all consumers, targeted audiences.

b. What we intend to offer; that is, full product line, limited product line.

c. How we intend to offer services; for example, distinctive quality, average quality but low price; through physical presence; through EFT.

d. Where our retail markets will be, our defined and redefined market area.

e. Why retail services; i.e., to fund commercial asset base, retail asset base, leveraged investment, generate fee income, maintain stability.

5. *Objectives*

Statements—both financial and nonfinancial, which represent our broad direction, such as:

a. Regain profit contribution consistent with ROA goals.

b. Sustain number one depository competitive ranking.

c. Achieve and sustain lowest cost of major competition.

6. *Goals*

The quantified measurable targets we expect to achieve within the terms of our strategic plan, including,

a. Hold deposit noninterest expense at inflation rate annually.

b. Grow depository fee income by 10 percent annually throughout next three years.

c. Manage interest paid within 15 basis points of local competition by product category.

7. *Key programs*

List the tactics that will be employed to meet the goals set. Estimate the cost to implement, including:

a. Establish a weekly funds management price setting process for retail deposits, incorporate competitive analysis, alternative costing, gap parameters, and transfer pricing mechanism. Complete within six months; implement—ongoing.

b. Revamp compensation system to incorporate a 10 percent incentive base component. Complete by year end; implement by January, following year.

c. Consolidate all operating functions at one location and provide dedicated staff for check processing, input, and statement preparation within 18 months.

d. Review depository fee components and establish "perceived value" pricing within major product categories. Complete primary services within 12 months, secondary services within 18 months, and attendant services within 24 months.

The discipline required to conduct a meaningful strategic audit and create an intelligent strategic plan should not be underestimated. Historically, long-term plans have either not been developed for retail deposits or the effort has been to satisfy directors rather than to serve as a blueprint for the business. In light of the competitive environment the task is more than warranted—it is mandatory if we are to sustain our institutions as viable banks. The plan should be pragmatic and realistic, and it must be acted on.

PRODUCT ANALYSIS AND MANAGEMENT

An integral part of managing deposit services is understanding our products. Each deposit product has a life cycle. The life cycle of a product can be divided into five phases. These phases include intro- duction, growth, maturity, decline, and termination. It is important to understand the product life cycle to properly position and price prod- ucts and services.

Each phase of the life cycle presents different opportunities and challenges for customer acceptance, profitability, and volume of ac- tivities. New products in the introductory stage are often accepted by innovators and early adopters. The growth stage of a product life cycle produces the maximum volume and the maximum profit potential. Products that reach the decline stage in their life cycle should be repositioned, modified, or enhanced, which will, in turn, change the life cycle and produce additional benefits. If a product cannot be modified or enhanced and is in the decline stage of the life cycle, then the product should be eliminated.

It is extremely important to know the attributes of the product, identify the product's strengths and weaknesses, and determine what the customer wants. Product differentiation is important. Products must be positioned so that the customer perceives a value difference be- tween your deposit product and that of the competition. If a product is not differentiated, then price becomes a dominant buying factor.

A product is deemed successful if there is sufficient market de- mand, which means a sufficient number of customers who are able and willing to pay for the product or service. The ability to identify market segments, including the use of market research, increases the potential effectiveness of individual products and services. Thus, tar- get marketing produces a more intelligent use of advertising dollars and provides more effective results.

CUSTOMER CHARACTERISTICS

Historically, banks have positioned themselves within the constricted regulatory framework as primary providers of financial transaction, savings, secure investments, recordkeeping, and safekeeping services. The principal differentiation has been "place" convenience. Beyond "place" convenience, consumer options have been limited.

Today, two important differences may be noted: (a)consumer life- styles have changed significantly—there are more highly educated and two-income households, and (b)many more financial options are avail- able to them—savings and loans, discount brokerage, and financial planning firms, to name a few.

To sustain or win customer allegiance requires a serious analysis of the current motivating factors for selecting and maintaining a bank relationship. Each bank should segment its own consumer market to make that determination. While segmentation can take many forms—

geographical, level of income, age, or psychographic—a relatively recent approach by Dr. Leonard Berry perhaps best illustrates the process. Berry describes three basic consumer behavior patterns:[1]

"Get My Money's Worth." Today's consumer is seeking the best value for the price paid. Customers are aware of the new options available to them and will seek out institutions that offer distinguishable choices they can control. Basically, they want the choice to pump their own gasoline (EFT Delivery) or have full service (teller interaction). They are quite willing to pay a differential but want the ability to make the selection on their own terms.

"Time Conscious." As referenced earlier, the consumer today is most likely to be actively employed. Time is a finite quantity our customers are forced to allocate as a scarce resource. The consumer will seek immediate feedback and quick decisions at their own convenience, not that of banks. The implications for us are to provide more, not fewer, access points, but electronically rather than labor-driven. Instant response will become pivotal.

"Individualist." Higher education leads to great affluence. Our customers have more complex financial needs. They expect personalized service and are quite willing to pay for that service when they feel it is warranted. Consequently, for specific services, quality and availability become the determining factors.

The differences in expectations is an issue which, of course, must be addressed, but its complexity will oftentimes be mitigated by the local market served. Of prime importance is the necessity of determining the basic values of our community in order to assess our ability to meet those needs.

DISTRIBUTION

Before addressing product mix, the next major factor to reassess is our distribution network. Until deregulation, the best method to achieve deposit market share was to develop an extensive branching system. In other words, providing convenience was paramount. The proposition is true today but the definition of convenience has changed fundamentally from an emphasis of place to an emphasis of time. The implications are substantial. Our customer base, for reasons cited in the previous section, will place pressure on the financial institution to offer delivery options. Our new competition, not saddled with high

---

[1]Based upon presentation by Dr. Berry at the Stonier Graduate School of Banking, June 1986.

brick and mortar investment, will be in a better position to satisfy these options at a lower cost.

Essentially, the consumer described earlier is more likely to have a composite of the characteristics mentioned than an absolute predisposition to any one way of taking delivery. As an example, we as consumers are quite willing to shop through a catalog sales outlet, a large discount house, a boutique, or a major department store depending on what our value needs are at a particular time. If the quality is known (name brand) and the price is an issue, the catalog may be our choice. If quality is known but time is important, we tend to use the discount. On the other hand, if we need product knowledge, or are concerned about aftersale performance, we will choose a quality department store or boutique. The challenge for banking institutions is to recognize that the same customer will want as many options as possible. We must decide the implications of being truly "full service" or specializing in a particular category.

To the extent that we can provide the distribution point options, we are more likely to be the bank of account. A preferred distribution network will include telephone access and ACH for routine functions, electronic off-premise terminals for cash needs, point of sale transfer, and traditional brick and mortar for personal banker consultation.

PRODUCT

First and foremost, we as bankers need to recognize that what we are offering the consumer is not a retail good but a retail service. Our consumers are not buying tangible items. They are purchasing a flow of activity that can be under constant scrutiny and reevaluation if they so choose. The service—product—we provide can be terminated at any time. It represents a full integration of knowledgeable staff, comprehensive reporting, negotiability, pricing—both rate and fee, delivery options, locations, and perceived quality. Emphasis placed on product without sufficient analysis of the components listed above is likely to result in disappointing results. Understanding the specific features with the most appeal is a function of placing the proper emphasis on known customer values.

The second important aspect is to clearly define the services we provide. Our past environment has prompted us to provide attendant services without determining value. Since deposits were artificially maintained at a minimum interest expense, we attempted to distinguish ourselves by packaging additional services—free—such as no charge checking, free checks, no fee for balance inquiry, statement reconciliation, travelers checks, and more. The practice was quite appropriate in a constrained rate environment. Today, however, it bears thoughtful reexamination.

DELIVERY

Today's consumer is demonstrating a preference for both high-tech—electronic, and high-touch—personalized service. In each case, quality defined in terms of expertise, accuracy, and timeliness will be a critical differentiating factor. The emphasis will be on fulfilling the customer's needs on their terms, and providing a continuum of choice.

At the same time, technologically advanced competition without the burden of a high cost distribution network will seek to exploit these advantages by featuring price incentives. Bankers are confronted with the task of providing better service at a lower cost.

The implications for our production function are indeed substantial. Serious consideration needs to be directed to the following issues:

1. Which technological methods should be employed? Investment decisions should be made with a strong bias to customer acceptance, not internal performance.

2. Pragmatically, will the technology contribute to lower cost? Assess both purchase and ongoing operational expense. Paraphonics, as an example, may be an appropriate answer for balance inquiry, but should we pay the price for automated loan payment, telephone activated statement reconciliation, etc.?

3. What are the trade-offs between interim needs and long-term requirements? When do we stop upgrading our transaction, savings, and certificate applications and direct our investment commitment to fully integrated systems.

4. Should we buy or build? Internal systems enhancement may be excessively expensive to build and operate. Given the rapid changes in applied product technology, is there a reasonable opportunity to purchase and operate through a vendor?

5. What management regulatory reporting requirements must be anticipated? With the likelihood of lower margins and more frequent rate changes, we need the capacity to assess impact and respond quickly. The ability to report rate modifications to management, our customers, and regulatory agencies will increase in importance.

PRODUCT ENHANCEMENT/DEVELOPMENT

Impetus for change can be expected to increase in a market driven environment. New product development (discount brokerage, money market deposit accounts) and existing product enhancement (draft access to savings, new minimum balance requirements, relationship pricing) will require resources dedicated to reaching correct decisions and implementing change effectively.

The paramount needs are to establish the process and assign accountable resources to the tasks. The cost implications for inappropriate product development or poorly executed introduction can be quite negative. The following section outlines one method to address objectively the product enhancement/development issues:

Phase 1—Product Proposal—Evaluation

Tasks	Sources
Research	Research Department Secondary Research
Cost/Revenue Implications	Federal Reserve Functional Cost Information
Rate/Index and Development	Primary/Secondary Research Conclusions
NonInterest Expense	Financial Accounting
Systems/Operational Requirements	Systems Department Operations Department Audit
Legal Requirements	Legal Department Outside Legal Counsel
Strategic Plan Validation	Senior Management
Market Plan • Positioning • Advertising • Training • Public Relations	Marketing Department Advertising Agency Human Resources
Review	Line/Branch Management

Phase 1 will be consolidated within an overall action plan specifically assigning individual accountability and time frames. Key qualifying criteria for proceeding or terminating the process should also be incorporated within the plan.

Phase 2—Executing the Action Plan

Once the necessary steps have been outlined and key accountability has been established, a project manager should be given the responsibility for managing the entire effort and making the initial recommendations. A suggested outline for the recommendation is listed below:

   a. Situational Analysis.
   b. Strategic Objectives.
   c. Financial Considerations.
      Cost.
      Revenue.
      Goals.
   d. New Product/Enhanced Product Description.
   e. Pricing Parameters/Rationale.
   f. Training/Implementation.
   g. Systems Requirements.
   h. Operational Requirements.
   i. Collateral Issues (Legal/Audit).
   j. Introduction Requirements.
   k. Overall Recommendation.

Phase 3

Present the recommendation for approval to senior management.

Phase 4

Assign implementation team.

Phase 5

Execute pilot test or full implementation.

Phase 6

Monitor results and make the appropriate adjustments.

Phase 7

Transfer to product management.

PRODUCT COST ANALYSIS

The basic objective of developing cost data is to supply significant information to management. The knowledge of cost and the various cost concepts are essential elements in the efficient management of deposit services.

The cost of a deposit product or service is not a single, precisely calculable figure. Costs are a composite of numerous elements consisting of direct, indirect, fixed, and variable factors. Thus, the word cost has a slippery connotation. It is used indiscriminately with several different meanings.

Available cost data are typically in two forms: direct cost and fully allocated cost. Direct and fully allocated costs are appropriate approximations for incremental costs at some institutions in specific circumstances. There are other institutions for which neither direct nor fully allocated costs are reasonable approximations for incremental costs. Introducing a new type of deposit account is an example where incremental costs are greater than direct costs, especially if incremental costs include a full allocation of overhead. Management must understand the appropriate cost data in order to determine the proper revenues and costs for each product or service.

Concepts of Cost

The concept of absorption costing is used by many financial institutions. It is defined as the assignment of all fixed and variable costs to goods and services produced. The price of every product must cover not only its variable costs, but also its fair share of the company's fixed costs, leaving enough margin to provide an adequate return on capital investment. All of the expenses of a bank, fixed and variable, direct and indirect, are allocated or assigned in some manner to various services under full absorption costing. The size of the bank will determine the extent to which expenses should be broken down by department or cost centers.

The concept of standard costing is also a cost tool used by financial institutions. A standard cost is a predetermined cost or an explicit statement of what cost should be under the most efficient methods of operations that can be obtained and sustained. Standard cost provides a financial institution with the means of comparing the actual cost of a service with what the cost should be under efficient operating conditions and good utilization of capacity.

Opportunity costing is another cost management tool. It is an abstract concept and is the sacrifice involved in accepting the alternative under consideration rather than the next best opportunity. An analysis of new products and services may be an appropriate use of opportunity cost.

Cost Factors

There are four major cost factors involved with deposit products and services. These cost factors include sales, operations and delivery of service, administrative support, and interest. Operations and the delivery of service to the customer contribute the majority of noninterest costs for deposit products and services. These include the total processing of deposits, withdrawals, and statement communications. This area of deposit costs is very capital and labor intensive. The relative magnitude of operations and delivery costs means that this is one area with potential for cost reduction. The sales and customer service expense for deposit products and services is the second largest noninterest expense category. This area includes the acquisition of new accounts and the servicing of existing accounts. General administrative costs are costs incurred to support and administer the organization. Examples of these costs are advertising and general management expenses.

The largest expense factor for deposit products is interest cost. The payment of interest on deposit accounts has evolved from stable fixed rates to include variable money market factors. The increased interest sensitivity for bank deposits has increased the need for better cost information and more effective pricing of deposit products and services. Identifying the most effective methods and delivery systems, combined with establishing the most appropriate and effective rates paid for deposits, is a challenge bankers must constantly meet.

PRICING DEPOSIT PRODUCTS

Pricing Philosophy

In recent years with deregulation and increased competition, pricing of deposit products has become a major concern of most banks. Today, pricing deposit products and services is a key consideration in overall bank profitability. For years the business world has regularly reviewed profit objectives and repriced products and services to support those objectives. Banks must quickly learn to emulate their nonregulated business counterparts.

Since banks had not been compelled to develop a pricing philosophy that drives profit objectives, they often by default operated on the premise of lowering the price to gain volume. This philosophy usually results in additional, but not profitable, volume. Many customers maintain low balances, use only one or two bank services, and require a disproportionate amount of time and expense from the operating and customer service areas. Today's consumers are more likely to question price, but they will also relate price to value. Establishing value differentiation is the first step in developing a reasonable pricing structure.

Pricing involves more than arriving at a dollar and cents figure for a single product or service. To manage the pricing function, a bank must develop detailed objectives, a monitoring system with mathematical models, and a discipline process to manage the pricing function. Many components must be integrated and managed as a unit if a bank is to quickly capitalize on its pricing opportunities. Historically, financial institutions have subscribed to a cost orientation in pricing, making the decision that cost leads to price. However, the purpose of price is not necessarily to recover cost but, more importantly, to capture the value of the product in the mind of the consumer.

One of the most difficult of all areas in decisionmaking for deposit services is establishing price. Yet, this is the key decision in determining product profitabililty. Pricing deposit services is probably the area of management in which there is the least agreement as to theory and the least consistency in practice.

Pricing Objectives

The pricing of deposit services must take into consideration management objectives, competition, cost, and price sensitivity. In order to measure performance an institution must first establish its pricing objectives and these pricing objectives must coincide with management's philosophy and objectives for the bank.

There are various objectives that management can establish in the pricing of deposit services. Management's objective can be cost disbursement, market share movement, or revenue generation. If management's objective is increased market share, then price sensitivity is extremely important. If the market is not price sensitive, then reducing the price will not increase market share. If costs decline with volume, then market share penetration is a valid objective.

For many banks the objective in pricing is to meet the price of competition. The bank that bases its pricing strategy on the competitor's price may be giving the competitor too much credit for knowing what is going on. The two banks may not have the same pricing criteria, even though they are competing in the same market. The only time one institution has to meet the competition is when the customer perceives no difference in the products or services of the two competitors. The lack of perceived differences indicates that either the marketing program is faulty or perhaps there is no justification for being in that market.

Profitability is a basic objective for most banks because this objective implies marking up on cost to achieve a target rate of return. Most banks are working with present cost, rather than future cost, or on standard cost data based on assumed volumes that may or may not be generated. Thus, they are looking at profit in a unit transaction rather than in the total. Essentially, profitability is really a way of measuring performance objectives, not necessarily an objective by itself.

Competitive Pricing

Competition is an important determinant of price. Few banks are in a position to set price without regard to the possible reactions of competitors. While the degree of competition may vary from market to market, no bank is completely immune from the effects of competition. In establishing a price, a bank must consider the aggressiveness of competition, any differences that may exist in the competitor's operating costs, and the likelihood that the competitor will follow any price change initiated. In most banks the possible reactions of customers and competitors probably have more influence in determining price than does cost. This is not to minimize the importance of cost data; it merely emphasizes that pricing cannot be accomplished in a vacuum. A bank must evaluate the capabilities of competition in order to develop a proper price or an effective pricing strategy.

A thorough knowledge of the competition, their objectives, and their pricing strategy are important in developing a price for deposit services. It is important to know how competition will respond to modifications in service or price changes. A competitor's reaction may be a function of price. If a product or service is enhanced or modified and has a low price, then competition may be encouraged to stay out of the market. Conversely, a high price for the service may encourage competition to enter the market at a lower price.

It is important to evaluate the competitive environment based on the strengths and weaknesses of each major competitor in the marketplace. Factors used in assessing strengths and weaknesses are number and location of branches, convenience, managerial depth, past performance, stability, size, reputation, and quality of service. After the strengths and weaknesses or significant buying influences have been identified, a competitive profile can be developed. This profile is a subjective exercise based on the experience and knowledge of how the customer perceives the banking environment in the community and should reflect estimated potential market share for that area. These judgments based upon a thorough knowledge of competition are important factors in developing a bank's pricing strategy.

Price Sensitivity

Price sensitivity, which is sometimes referred to as price elasticity of demand, is a very important concept of pricing. It is one key to determining whether a particular increase or decrease in price is a good strategy. In a competitive situation, it is assumed that as a competitor raises or lowers prices, customers will react by changing where they do business. If a contemplated increase in price produces greater incremental revenue from those customers who remain than it loses from those customers who leave, then it is usually considered a good pricing decision. This inelastic demand curve is created when customers are relatively insensitive to price changes.

There are a number of factors which influence the price sensitivity of deposit products and services. The two most important factors are the availability of a substitute service and the importance of the price. If equally convenient competitors offer the same products or services, the products or services tend to be price sensitive. If the price is rather unimportant relative to the consumer's total expenditures, the service tends to be relatively price insensitive.

It is difficult to determine the precise degree of price sensitivity for deposit products and services in each market. Each bank product has a specific and different combination of factors influencing its own price sensitivity. These factors include convenience, population turnover, product differentiation, market segmentation, income levels, and image of the institution. Therefore, the strengths/weaknesses profile is a subjective tool which is important in analyzing the factors that influence price sensitivity.

Pricing Strategies

A pricing strategy for deposit services should be based on the financial goals of the institution, price sensitivity, and marketing strategies for the product. Financial goals of the institution may favor growth as compared to earnings. Some banks will choose to sacrifice short-term profits for improvements in market share. The larger financial institutions usually place priority on profits rather than market share. Some examples of pricing strategies are:

Penetration Pricing. Penetration pricing is a strategy where an undifferentiated service is offered to as many people as possible. The price usually reflects a small mark-up over cost when it is the desire of the institution to sell as many accounts as possible. The initial price is set low with the objective of obtaining a large share of the market. A large volume will spread fixed costs broadly and provide better cross selling opportunities. Loss leader pricing is an example of penetration pricing. Some banks use the checking account as a loss leader hoping to cross sell additional services.

Skimming Pricing. Skimming pricing is a concept designed to describe a higher mark-up pricing strategy. It is usually used in an environment of rapid technological change characterized by a high degree of product differentiation or market segmentation. Skimming pricing is most advantageous in extracting maximum short-term profits. The disadvantage of skimming pricing is that it encourages competition and discourages the volume necessary to spread fixed costs.

Follow the Leader Pricing.   Follow the leader pricing is a concept which establishes price at the going market rate, often following the price leader. This type of pricing strategy is used when there is little differentiation of services and price reduction will not stimulate demand. The disadvantage of follow the leader pricing is that the service may be priced unprofitably.

Target ROI Pricing.   Target ROI pricing is a concept designed to produce a target rate of return on investment normally using standard costs based on standard volume. This type of pricing strategy is designed for planned profits and should be used primarily with new services rather than mature services.

CONCLUSION

The key to managing retail deposit services is an understanding that deposit gathering is a distinct business. The financial marketplace has become extremely competitive and competition is increasing from many different sources. The spiralling cost of doing business and increased pressure on earnings in a time of inconsistent loan demand have prompted many bankers to focus more attention on pricing and managing deposit services. Deregulation, combined with changing consumer lifestyles, continues to challenge retail banking. Product analysis and proper planning are critically important functions for retail managers. The successful banker will identify the need to properly manage deposit services and will adapt to the changing demands of the future.

CHAPTER SIXTY

Credit Services for the Retail Customer

Paul R. Beares

Vice President
The First National Bank of Maryland

Credit services available to retail customers have undergone a steady evolutionary process in recent decades. Change has manifested itself in the form of a growing number of credit products tailored for consumers and in more variety in the features of basic loan products. The most dynamic changes have occurred in the open-end/revolving credit product line, in which wide scale introduction of home equity line of credit products, combined with the much wider availability and very aggressive marketing of other open-end products—particularly credit card and unsecured line of credit plans—have led to a significant shift in the way many consumers borrow. Traditional closed-end lines have been expanded to include variable rate pricing schedules, wider use of the simple interest method of income recognition, periodic use of interest subsidy programs, affinity group and other specifically tailored loan programs, and the selective offering of balloon payment options.

The consumer credit market reached a pivotal point in 1980. Double-digit growth rates, which were common in the 1970s, gave way to an almost stagnant market from 1980 through 1982. A very strong rebound began in 1983 and has continued throughout 1986, as shown in the selected market share data shown in Table 1.

Stagnation in the market occurred for a number of reasons. First, the high rate environment of 1980, with its accompanying erratic rate patterns, was greeted by the customary consumer reaction—reduced borrowing. Consumers curtailed discretionary borrowing and postponed many purchases in anticipation of lower rates. Too, the share of the consumer's income committed to debt service reached historically high levels at the end of 1979 (Exhibit 1), a characteristic nor-

TABLE 1   Consumer Credit Outstanding ($ millions, seasonally adjusted, end of period)

Period	Total Market	Annual Percent Change	Commercial Banks	Annual Percent Change	Commercial Bank Market Share
12/79	$296,483	13.2%	$152,747	12.7%	51.5%
12/80	295,763	− 0.2	145,556	(4.7)	49.2
12/81	310,965	5.1	146,030	0.3	47.0
12/82	325,136	4.6	149,057	2.0%	45.8
12/83	373,048	14.7	169,339	13.6	45.4
12/84	446,183	19.6	209,158	23.5	46.9
12/85	522,805	17.2	240,796	15.1	46.0
12/86	577,784	10.5	261,612	8.6	45.3

SOURCE: Federal Reserve Board G.19 Statistical Release.

EXHIBIT 1

Installment Debt as a Percentage of Disposable Personal Income*

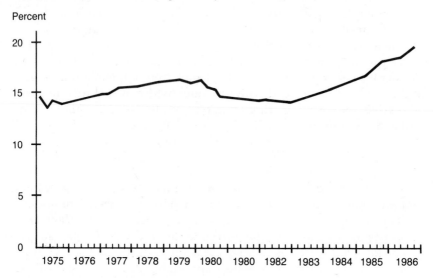

*Seasonally adjusted annual data.
SOURCE: Board of Governors of Federal Reserve System.

mally followed by reduced borrowing activity. Second, many financial institutions, caught in the squeeze between the high cost of funds and fixed rate consumer credit portfolio yields, reduced the availability of funds for consumer loans. Third, many state lending laws limited profit opportunities by imposing unrealistic rate limitations and restricting the types of loan products and product features which could be offered to retail customers.

The trauma within the market in 1980 was made all the more dramatic as a result of the Carter Administration's Consumer Credit Restraint Program. While this legislation was targeted toward dampening the demand for unsecured and nonpurchase money consumer credit, it combined with erratic cost of funds to force major shifts in the level of commercial bank activity in the market. Many banks responded by curtailing promotional activities, raising credit underwriting requirements, purging their indirect dealer bases of marginal dealers, and beginning the process of relocating portions of their consumer credit operations to states with more responsive lending laws. The effect of all of these factors can be clearly seen in the virtually stagnant total market gain of .4 percent and the 4.7 percent decline in commercial bank outstandings in 1980.

The combination of events which produced the market stagnation led to essential structural change within the consumer credit market. The stage was set for changes which altered the complexion of the market and moved it in new and challenging directions.

Motivation for change was driven primarily by the consumer. Increasingly sophisticated consumers were still demanding the basics— convenience in obtaining and using credit, fair loan rates, and manageable monthly payments—but they wanted more. They wanted control over their use of credit. They wanted products which offered greater value, such as higher credit limits, increased access to convenient credit, and attractive pricing alternatives.

Legislators responded to the needs of consumers and financial institutions by enacting significant changes in consumer credit laws in many states. Chief among the changes were the elimination or raising of interest rate caps, provisions allowing greater flexibility in designing loan products, permitting some additional fees, and permitting variable rate loans on many consumer loan products. These legislative changes were essential to allowing the market to be responsive to the consumer's credit needs and to enabling financial institutions to adopt consistent strategies in the market.

Many financial institutions had fought proactively for legislative change and they were strong supporters of the movement for change. They also quickly implemented new programs to meet the changing wants and needs of the consumer as new legislation came into being. And, many lenders were more careful in targeting their desired market segments after 1980. They abandoned the theme of "being all things to all people" in favor of providing higher value products and quality service to carefully selected segments of the market.

The early 1980s experience served to reshuffle the competitive market and shift market share trends. Commercial banks saw their market share peak at 51.5 percent at the end of 1979, and fall steadily to 43.3 percent by September 1986. Retailers and credit unions also experienced market share declines during the period. Market share gains were achieved by finance companies and thrifts. Finance companies, lead by the captive automobile firms, increased their share of the market from 19.2 percent at the end of 1979, to 24.7 percent by September 1986. This gain may be attributed to the withdrawal of many commercial banks from indirect lending markets in 1980–1982, the broadening of captive finance company product lines to include other types of consumer credit products, and the frequent use of factory-supported interest rate subsidy programs. Thrift institutions achieved the largest gain in market share, increasing their share from a meager 3.8 percent in 1979, to 10.5 percent in September 1986. This gain is attributable to the deregulation movement which allowed thrifts to increase the size of their consumer credit portfolios, and to the fact that many thrifts were attracted to the benefits which the market offered—shorter maturity structures, higher portfolio yields, diversification of risk, and the opportunity to build on existing retail customer relationships.

EMERGING CONSUMER CREDIT PRODUCT LINE

Consumer credit demand emerged from the doldrums in 1983. Aided by new products and product features, which were permitted by recently enacted changes to lending laws, and by pent-up consumer demand, the market resumed double-digit growth rates.

The shift which had taken place in the consumer credit product line at a typical bank is demonstrated in Exhibit 2.

This exhibit, while certainly not meant to be all inclusive or representative of the situation in all states, can help to focus on some of the key areas of change.

Traditional closed-end products have evolved slowly, with changes reflecting a desire to make the products more acceptable to consumers while at the same time allowing lenders to earn a fair return on their investment. Consumer oriented changes such as the use of simple language documents and the elimination of the confusing and controversial rule of 78ths method of income recognition in favor of simple interest, are the direct result of focusing more on the consumer. The availability of variable rates and some fees, on the other hand, are a direct response to the 1980 experience and the need which financial institutions have to protect themselves from interest rate risk and earn a fair return on their investments. The addition of variable rate features

EXHIBIT 2   Sample Consumer Credit Product Line

Product Category	Characteristic	1970	1986
Closed-end loans	Rates	Fixed	Fixed and
Direct loans			variable
Indirect loans	Fees	Late charges	Application
			Late charges
	Documents	Legal language	Simple language
	Income	Rule of 78ths	Simple interest
	recognition	actuarial	
	Maturities: new	36 months	60 months
	car		
	Distribution	Branches	Branches
			Direct mail
Open-end credit			
Unsecured lines	Check overdraft	Available	Available
	Stand alone	Rare	Available
Credit cards	Regular card	Available	Available
	Premium card	Not available	Available
Secured lines	Equity line	Not available	Available
	Access devices	Regular and	Same plus
		special checks	ATMs
	Rates	Fixed	Variable and
			fixed
	Minimum	5% of average	3% of ADB,
	payments	daily balance	Interest only
			option on
			secured lines
Leasing		Rare	Available

to the product line will enable lenders to be more consistent in their strategies regarding credit availability, since it will help to preserve profit margins throughout swings in the interest rate cycle. Traditionally, lenders have reduced credit availability to retail customers during high cost of fund stages, since they were unable to preserve profit margins.

The pressure for ever-lengthening maturities is well known to consumer lenders. The typical maturity for a new car loan has lengthened by two years since 1970. This increase is representative of the pressure on maturities for all types of closed-end loans. This pressure is due to the fact that the cost of the average new car increased from $3200 to $12,500 over the same period, and even though incomes also rose, consumers and lenders attempted to preserve a balanced monthly debt payment to income ratio. Generally speaking, maturities on all types of closed-end loans have increased and are likely to continue increasing in the future.

Another significant change occurred in the manner in which lenders distributed closed-end loan products. These products were traditionally distributed only on a direct basis from branch offices or from associated dealers. The distribution network widened to include loan by mail programs and other indirect approaches which broadened the market area and provided a higher level of convenience for selected consumer market segments. Special programs were developed for affinity groups, companies, college students, and other target market segments. While target marketing and tailored programs were certainly in use in 1970, their use had been greatly expanded by 1986.

As previously noted, the most dramatic changes to the consumer credit product line occurred in the revolving credit products. The typical 1970 product line was confined to offering one major credit card and a check overdraft program. Both products offered relatively low credit limits—under $1000—which significantly restricted their value as a source of credit to meet major borrowing needs. By 1986, the line had been expanded to include stand-alone unsecured lines of credit, many offering credit limits as high as $100,000, and, most recently, the home equity line of credit. Credit card product lines were expanded by adding premium cards which added both tangible and intangible benefits for the consumer.

The newer open-end credit products were generally on a variable rate basis, and provided for a variety of transaction or "event" type fees—such as late charges and over-limit fees—which were designed to achieve both profitability and positioning objectives. Annual fees helped to compensate lenders for the costs associated with convenience users, while "event" fees helped compensate lenders for additional costs incurred in handling certain accounts.

Another important addition to the consumer credit product line which grew rapidly during the past fifteen years is leasing. Many consumers demonstrated a preference for leasing rather than owning their automobiles. In response, leasing products were made available by a variety of financial institutions. Leasing became a direct competitor to traditional consumer credit programs, and it offered the consumer benefits such as lower monthly payments, minimal up-front down payment requirements, and in some cases, tax advantages. As leasing programs have expanded in terms of availability and consumer acceptance, many lenders have developed closed-end credit products which are structured in the same manner as a lease. These new "balloon payment" plans are an example of the way in which financial institutions are responding to the demands of the retail consumer.

TABLE 2   Consumer Credit Outstandings by Type of Loan ($ millions, seasonally adjusted, End of Period)

	Outstandings		
Type of Loan	1975	1985	Percent Increase
Automobile	$56,989	$206,482	362%
Revolving	14,507	118,296	815
Mobile home	15,388	25,461	166
Other	80,159	184,859	231

SOURCE: Federal Reserve Board G.19 Statistical Release.

We will now begin to examine in greater depth the changes which have been taking place within the consumer credit product line. Our discussion will include an overview of how these changes have affected the consumer and the financial institutions serving this market.

OPEN-END/REVOLVING CREDIT PRODUCTS

The most dramatic increase in consumer credit outstandings has come in revolving credit products. The other forms of credit grew at a much slower rate between 1975 and 1985. See Table 2.

The increase in revolving credit was led initially by credit card programs, and more recently, by home equity based lines of credit. Unsecured open-end credit products round out this part of the portfolio, and they have been an important part of the overall growth at some financial institutions.

HOME EQUITY LINES OF CREDIT

Home equity based lines of credit are a new product for most financial institutions. They did not become widely available until the mid-1980s and to this point have not been tested through a full economic cycle. Nevertheless, home equity lines are the most exciting consumer credit product since credit cards hit the mass markets in the late 1960s. For qualified customers, an equity line account can replace virtually all other credit products, while for financial institutions they create a strong lending relationship and a sound basis for building a large retail loan portfolio.

Equity lines of credit offer many benefits to the consumer. These include:

• Access to large amounts of credit which can be used to meet virtually any borrowing need;

- Access to credit for any purpose which the borrower deems appropriate;
- Control over when, where, and how much they borrow (subject to the maximum credit limit);
- Access to credit via checks, ATMs, and other convenient access devices;
- Simplified financial management by eliminating the need for other types of loans, eliminating the need to reapply each time credit is desired, and concentrating borrowing in one easily managed account;
- Access to lower rates than are available on many other types of loans.

Many of the benefits described above can be applied to all open-end credit products. Indeed, these loan products shift a great deal of the control of credit usage from the financial institution to the consumer. They also add different dimensions to the definition of convenience, since once the credit line is established, it remains available to the consumer indefinitely. The major differences between equity line and unsecured line of credit products are the size of the line, the lower monthly payment requirements, and access to lower rates. Banks are able to offer these benefits because they are in a well-secured position and because the equity line product attracts a very strong base of retail customers. At this point we will examine some of the features of various equity line programs and discuss their effect on the consumer. See Exhibit 3.

This example helps to focus on some of the issues to be considered in designing equity line products.

The loan to value ratio directly affects the collateral risk on the loan and the size of the line which can be offered to customers. A conservative approach (Bank A) will strengthen the collateral position, but will exclude consumers with lower equity from the program and limit the size of the credit lines available to all consumers.

The minimum monthly payment can be a powerful marketing tool if properly promoted. Interest only options represent the most aggressive position. This feature gives the consumer substantial control over loan repayment and gives rise to the possibility of "evergreen" loans, that is, loans with no curtailment of principal. This means higher interest income, but also potentially higher credit risk. Further, if the customer fully utilizes the line, but never repays any of the principal, the line loses its value as a source of credit, and simply becomes a debt burden. From the customer's perspective, the interest only option (Bank A) results in a significantly lower minimum monthly payment

---

EXHIBIT 3   Sample Equity Line Programs

Feature	Bank A	Bank B
Maximum credit line	Equity based on loan to value ratio, minus the first mortgage balance	Same
Loan to value ratio	70% of appraisal	80% of appraisal
Debt to income ratio	35% of gross income	38% of gross income
Rate	2% over prime	4% over 90 day T-bills
Minimum monthly payment	Interest only, or any term up to 30 years	1.63% of the average daily balance
Fees	Closing costs include appraisal, title search, title insurance, and recording fee	Same, plus late charge overlimit, and annual fees
Access devices	Checks, ATM, branch withdrawal	Same, plus credit card (VISA or MasterCard)

Now let's assume that a creditworthy consumer with the following characteristics applies for an equity line account at each bank.

Gross income	$ 60,000
Appraised value of home	100,000
First mortgage balance	22,000 ($500 per month)

Combining the product feature information with the customer characteristics yields the following:

	Bank A	Bank B
Appraised value	$100,000	$100,000
Loan to value ratio	.70	.80
	70,000	80,000
First mortgage balance	-22,000	-22,000
Maximum credit line	48,000	58,000
Gross monthly income	5,000	5,000
Debt to income ratio	.35	.38
Maximum debt service per month	1,750	1,900
Minimum monthly payment (assuming 9.5% APR and $10,000 average daily balance)	$83	$163

---

and gives him more control over the amount of money applied to the loan each month.

Other monthly payment factors affect not only the amount of the payment, but also the size of the credit line. For example, if the customer wanted to obtain a line from Bank B, but had other debts outstanding, it might be necessary to pay off some of the existing loans or reduce the size of the credit line in order to qualify the request to meet the bank's debt to income ratio requirement.

Maximum debt service per month	$1900	
First mortgage payment	500	
Minimum payment on $58,000 line	945	($58,000 × .0163)
Payment on other loans	600	
Total monthly payments	$2045	

In this case, the lender may require the customer to pay off existing loans from the equity line account in order to reduce the debt service to an acceptable level, or the lender could reduce the size of the equity line to $43,000—the maximum line available with a $700 monthly payment level necessary to bring the request within the underwriting guidelines.

Interest rates on equity line accounts tend to be virtually identical within a given market area. However, many banks have used low introductory rates to attract equity line prospects. Offers such as: "7.5 percent fixed rate for the first six months," and "5.9 percent fixed rate until April 1st," appeared in many markets. This kind of penetration pricing, a strategy designed to build market share rapidly, has been used because market share is a major concern on equity line accounts. Since the customer can only have one equity line account at a time, many banks felt it was desirable to build their account base as rapidly as possible, even at the expense of short-term profits, in order to optimize earnings in the long run.

The attractiveness of equity line accounts from the consumer's perspective received two major boosts. First, 1986 federal tax reform legislation retained the tax deductability of interest paid on these accounts and traditional second mortgage loans, while phasing out similar deductions for all other types of consumer credit loans. Second, lenders seeking to maximize equity line activity adopted aggressive pricing strategies, including low introductory rates and the elimination of closing costs.

The tax reform legislation brought public policy firmly in support of home equity based consumer credit. While the role which the tax deductability feature has on borrowing decisions can be debated, it seems likely that favorable tax treatment will encourage many borrowers to use equity line products as an alternative to other types of loans. Thus, instead of financing his next car through the dealer, or charging a major purchase on his VISA card, the customer may write a check on his equity line account in order to be able to deduct the interest on the loan for tax purposes.

It took the tax reform effort to get many lenders excited about equity line programs, and it set up a rush of marketing activity. Aggressive promotional campaigns quickly merged with aggressive pricing strategies designed to capture market share in the newly booming equity line market. Low introductory rates were made even more attractive when competitors began to absorb the closing costs associated with establishing these accounts. Closing costs, which typically ranged from $250 to $500, had been a major barrier to many consumers in establishing these accounts. Without this barrier, the consumer was more likely to consider opening an equity line account, whether or not he had an immediate borrowing need. This practice also eliminated a major barrier to switching one's equity line account from one bank to another, an important consideration for a product which is limited to one per customer.

Home equity lines of credit emerged as the consumer credit product of the 1980s. However, this new product also presented new challenges for portfolio managers. Lenders now needed to sharpen their skills and develop the tools required to monitor a growing base of open-end credit accounts. It was now necessary and desirable to build on-going account monitoring systems which could monitor the consumer and help to control the credit and collateral risk of each account over time. Monitoring systems can control risk by identifying potential credit and collateral problems before they reach a serious stage. To accomplish this level of control, new account monitoring and line reconfirmation programs have been established, which identify deteriorating collateral value and spot problems with the customer's creditworthiness, such as newly delinquent credit obligations, increases in debt load, and declining income or ability to pay. These programs not only help to reduce credit risk by facilitating early identification of problems and initiation of corrective action, but also provide a marketing tool by encouraging good customers to increase the size of their credit line or use their line more fully.

UNSECURED LINES OF CREDIT

The expansion of unsecured line of credit programs beyond the early check overdraft plans has been another response to the consumer's desire for more control over his use of credit. Check overdraft plans fulfilled basic needs, protection from inadvertent overdrafts and the flexibility to meet short-term cash flow requirements in a convenient and relatively inexpensive manner. However, the relatively small size of the credit limits—typically $1000 or less—and the requirement for a checking account relationship, restricted the value of these plans as an alternative loan source and limited the potential customer base. Thus, stand alone, unsecured loan programs began to emerge.

Unsecured line of credit programs opened up a much larger potential retail market. These products can readily be marketed to creditworthy consumers without regard to state boundaries or account relationship requirements. Prescreened and preapproved direct mail programs, copied from earlier credit card promotional campaigns, became widely used by banks and other financial institutions. Many offerings were targeted at retail customers far outside the lender's traditional market area. Private banking customers often are a primary target for these loan products. These high net worth, high income customers have proven to be attracted by the convenience and flexibility of these credit products, and many people in this category have also been identified as heavy users of consumer credit.

There is relatively little difference among unsecured line of credit programs and they are relatively simple in terms of operation. The biggest change has been in the availability of such lines and the size of the credit lines which are available. Given aggressive marketing in the mid-1980s, it is not unusual to find many consumers with multiple unsecured credit lines at their disposal, with the majority of the lines having credit limits between $2,000 and $5,000. The aggregate credit available to a given customer can quickly reach a significant level and be quickly and easily accessed by the consumer.

Open-end, unsecured lines of credit are perhaps the riskiest type of consumer credit. As a result, credit underwriting requirements tend to be most stringent for these products. Also, lenders have attempted to limit risk on existing accounts by refining their account monitoring programs in order to identify potential problems and limt risk exposure before problems reach a serious stage. However, it is apparent that the industry needs to further refine its credit and account behavioral analysis skills in order to continue to improve the control over all forms of open-end products.

CREDIT CARDS

Credit cards are viewed by consumers as both a credit service and a transaction device. The consumer, at his discretion, can use the account and the related credit line to finance purchases or may simply use the account as an alternative to cash. The fact that consumers have clearly accepted credit cards is demonstrated by the fact that at the end of 1985, over 92 million people carried VISA cards, and over 68 million carried MasterCards. To this can be added countless millions of credit cards issued by retailers and other financial institutions.

TABLE 3 Selected Domestic Bank Card Statistics, VISA and MasterCard (1983 – 1985)

Item		MasterCard	VISA
Cardholders	1983	53,740,000	70,040,000
	1985	68,070,000	92,860,000
Volume	1983	$32,948	$47,204
(millions)	1985	51,125	75,232
Outstandings	1983	$16,509	$22,195
(millions)	1985	29,085	40,744
Percent of	1983	71.0%	72.8%
accounts with	1985	74.0%	73.2%
a balance			

SOURCE: American Bankers Association, 1986 Retail Bank Credit Report.

The credit card market has been segmented by the introduction of premier cards, which offer added features and which often have different rates and repayment terms than the regular cards. Premier cards typically require higher annual fees, though these are often offset by lower interest rates and higher credit limits. Such cards compete with well-known travel and entertainment cards such as American Express Gold Cards and Diner's Club for the upscale segment of the consumer market.

The major bank card market went through some significant changes from 1980–1982. During that period, many banks relocated their card operations from states with restrictive laws to states with favorable laws, primarily Delaware and South Dakota. Those states became havens for credit card issuers seeking to reverse losing operations and provide a sound basis for future growth.

Realignment of the credit card market had a definite impact on the consumer. New laws allowed lenders to significantly increase rates and to impose a variety of fees on these accounts. Despite the higher cost to the consumer, it is clear that these accounts were highly valued. Credit card volume remained very strong, outstandings grew at a faster pace than other forms of consumer credit, and the number of cardholders continued to grow rapidly, even after these pricing increases. See Table 3.

As credit cards have reached the mature stage of the product life cycle, there is evidence of renewed interest rate competition and product enhancements. Several variations have emerged in the pricing strategies used on bank cards. Some banks have introduced variable rate pricing programs, while other lenders have implemented tiered pricing schedules. The latter approach offers consumers with higher balances a lower rate as illustrated on the next page:

Average Daily Balance	Rate
Under $2,500	18.0%
$2,501 and higher	16.0%

This approach may also encourage cardholders to use the issuing bank's card instead of a competitor's card. This is an important consideration for all open-end products. Only lines in use will generate finance charge income. Thus, it is important to encourage account holders to use their accounts. Another approach used to encourage card usage is the provision of rebates when card volume reaches a certain level, as shown on the schedule below:

Annual Purchase Volume	Rebate Percent
Less than $600	0.5%
$600 to $1500	1.0%
$1500 and over	1.5%

The rebate is generally credited to the customer's account at the end of the year. This and other incentives designed to stimulate account usage are likely to continue as banks seek to induce consumers to use their accounts rather than a competitor's loan service.

CLOSED-END LOAN PRODUCTS

The major changes to traditional closed-end consumer loan products in recent years have been the implementation of variable rate pricing options and the use of interest subvention programs by automobile manufacturers as a means of stimulating auto sales. We will look first at the very large automobile consumer loan market and then at variable rate pricing plans.

AUTOMOBILE LOANS

Consumer credit secured by automobiles is the largest single loan type, accounting for over 40.4 percent of the total consumer credit market at the end of September 1986. The share of this market held by commercial banks has declined from 49.2 percent at the end of 1983 to 40.4 percent as of September 1986.

Many factors have combined to account for the market share shifts in the automobile portfolio. Two primary factors have been the wide-scale use of domestic automobile manufacturer interest subvention programs and the increasing use of vehicle leasing programs as an alternative to traditional finance programs. Subvention programs, in which the manufacturer subsidizes the lender in order to offer below market rates to the consumer, first appeared on a broad scale during the high rate environment of 1980. These plans continued to be offered to stimulate sluggish car sales through 1986, with some programs offering rates as low as 3.9 percent and even 0 percent.

Consumers responded to these programs and eventually seem to have changed their buying behavior to hold off purchases in anticipation of the next incentive campaign. The exclusive nature of later incentive programs forced a shift in domestic auto loans toward the captive manufacturer finance subsidiaries. Some banks attempted to compete against the programs by offering longer maturities and the related lower monthly payments, while others chose simply to divert their efforts to other segments of the consumer credit market which offered greater profit potential.

Leasing programs have also become an important factor in the automobile market since 1970. Leasing programs offer consumers benefits such as lower monthly payments, reduced down payment requirements, and in some cases, tax advantages. In addition, image conscious consumers discovered they could drive a high priced, prestige car on lease for the same monthly payment they would pay to finance a less prestigious model. This psychological benefit was emphasized by dealer sales personnel and bank leasing specialists.

To compete against subvention programs and leasing, some banks marketed a closed-end program with a final balloon payment feature. This product, sometimes referred to as residual value financing, offered the consumer many of the same benefits available through leasing programs. Monthly payments and down payments were kept at levels below traditional financing options by establishing a large balloon payment, representing the residual value of the collateral at the end of the loan term. The customer could pay the residual by selling the vehicle and paying off the balance due, or by financing the balance for an additional term.

Balloon payment plans, which have also been used for boat and other types of consumer loans, produce higher interest income for the bank, since the unpaid balance reduces more slowly than on traditional loans on which the entire balance is liquidated during the term of the loan. However, they also increase the credit risk on the loan, since the customer never establishes an equity position in the collateral. This factor is taken into consideration when establishing the underwriting criteria for such products.

VARIABLE-RATE LOANS

The experience of 1980 catapulted the attention given to managing interest rate risk from a back office staff concern to a critical issue for all levels of management. Many consumer credit managers found themselves in the position of having to react to the circumstances thrust upon them rather than being in a proactive position. They responded to vanishing profit margins by seeking the regulatory freedom to offer variable rate products and then by attempting to market these loans to consumers.

The problem with having a loan portfolio filled with fixed rate assets is demonstrated in Exhibit 4. While variable rates help to preserve gross margins, they also eliminate the opportunity to widen spreads during some stages of the interest rate cycle.

Managers seeking to optimize profits over the long term often attempt to achieve a balance of fixed and variable rates within their portfolio, while achieving the desired matching of assets and liabilities within the bank. The dangers of being locked into a portfolio filled with fixed-rate receivables was amply demonstrated in 1980, while the disadvantages of having a portfolio full of variable-rate loans was demonstrated during the low rate environment of 1986. However, no one portfolio mix is right for all institutions, and achieving the desired mix will be strongly affected by shifts in consumer demand.

The initial concerns about consumer acceptance of variable rates proved largely unwarranted. Many consumers displayed a willingness to choose a variable-rate loan over a fixed-rate loan under certain conditions, while more traditional and conservative segments of the consumer market could not be moved away from fixed-rate products. Perhaps the most visible proof of this situation is the level of activity on adjustable residential mortgage loans made in 1983, just a few years after their introduction to the market. While this usage was affected by the limited availability of fixed rate options, it also proved that variable-rate products can be structured in a manner which will be acceptable to the consumer and still meet the bank's needs.

Consumers who are receptive to variable-rate loans seem to consider the spread between the fixed and variable rate and the difference between the monthly payment on the two options. When the rate spread is large enough to be regarded as significant by the customer, he will at least consider the variable rate. Bias towards the variable-rate option will be enhanced when the consumer also feels that the interest rates may fall over the term of the loan. On the other hand, when prevailing fixed rates reach relatively low levels, as they did in 1986, consumers evidenced a clear bias for locking in low fixed rates whenever possible. This bias also led to a rash of refinancing of both fixed- and variable-rate loans at the low end of the interest rate cycle.

EXHIBIT 4 Consumer Credit Portfolio Yield Behavior Patterns

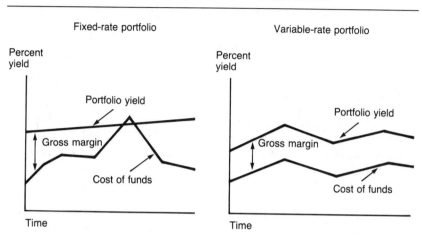

Variable-rate loans have been offered with both fixed- and variable-payment options. The fixed-payment option allows the consumer to manage his family budget without the risk of being squeezed in a rising rate environment, while the lender may view this as a way to avoid increased credit risk brought about by unexpected increases in monthly debt burdens. Fixed payments do not appear to represent a major concern on loans with maturities up to 60 months; however, they do present significant concerns on longer term loans. Negative amortization, increased collateral risk, and the resulting potential for customer ill will present major issues for lenders offering the fixed-payment feature on long-term variable rate loans.

Variable payment options raise other issues for consumers and lenders. Variable payments are the norm for open-end credit accounts, and variable rates are used on most equity line and stand alone, unsecured credit programs. The level of payment on these accounts varies with the balance on the account and the method in which the minimum payments are calculated. Thus, the consumer can control the monthly payment by electing to use, or not use, the account. It should also be noted that there has been a general trend toward reducing the required minimum monthly payment on these accounts in order to make them more attractive to consumers. Closed-end products present a different problem. The customer has no control over the amount of these payments. Significant increases can cause problems for the customer's cash flow, which may then be reflected in increased delinquencies and losses. Payment variability should therefore be factored into the underwriting process in order to reduce this risk.

SUMMARY

The credit services available to retail customers have evolved in recent years in a manner which has given the consumer more control over his use of credit. Increased product availability and the expanding open-end credit product line give consumers access to large amounts of credit, which they may use for any purpose they deem appropriate, and which they may access simply by writing a check or going to an ATM.

Expansion of the consumer credit product line was positively affected by legislative changes which followed the pivotal year of 1980. The deregulation and reregulation movements combined to produce liberalized rate caps and greater flexibility in designing and implementing products to meet the wants and needs of the consumer and the financial institutions which served the market.

Banks now have considerable freedom in tailoring credit products designed to attract target market segments. They are also free to market credit services beyond their traditional market areas. At the same time, new skills will be needed to properly evaluate and manage the risk within the portfolio. Managers must control their portfolios to insure that the level of credit, collateral, and interest rate risk is consistent with the objectives of their particular institution.

CHAPTER SIXTY-ONE

Special Issues Related to Credit Cards in Retail Banking

Richard S. Braddock

Sector Executive
Citicorp/Citibank

Axel M. Neubohn

Vice President
Citicorp

INTRODUCTION

Over the past two decades, except for cash, bankcards have become the most widely used consumer payment means for goods and services in the United States. In 1986 Visa and MasterCard, the two bankcard systems, had issued through their members 185 million cards in this country, with card sales of $119 billion. In the last five years, the bankcard business has become highly profitable. It is fair to state that bankcard service is the most successful product innovation ever launched and rolled out cooperatively by American commercial banks.

The two bankcard associations, Visa and MasterCard, have been crucial for this success. They were established to perform those functions that banks alone could not fulfill: To assure universal point-of-sale acceptance of bankcards by promoting common service marks and by facilitating the exchange of bankcard transactions between banks (interchange). The associations have performed well in this task, extending bankcard acceptance worldwide as well.

Both associations offer essentially the same service, although perception of service quality by member banks is not always the same. Both Visa cards and MasterCards may be issued by the same banks, and both types of cards are generally accepted for payment in the same places.

The two organizations compete for new business, not only with one another but also with their nonbank rivals—American Express in particular. At the same time, Visa and MasterCard cooperate in efforts to cut operating costs, reduce credit losses, and expand the market for bankcards generally. Some observers think that in the interests of efficiency and standardization, the two organizations eventually will merge into one giant entity, servicing a single card that will be accepted anywhere. Others welcome the competition and expect the U.S. Department of Justice to prevent a merger, should it ever be proposed.

As the bankcard business has grown and evolved over the years, several issues have emerged that continue to command attention and debate. From the very beginning, there has been the issue of control and membership restriction of the bankcard associations. Within the associations, the key economic issue has been the setting of the interchange fee, the internal pricing mechanism for transactions between member banks. The bankcard business was a money-loser for banks for almost 15 years, only recently turning around to profitability. Banks paid for bankcard growth with substantial credit losses, and had to learn credit risk management in the process. Bankcard services typically have been provided by banks on a stand-alone basis, and are not well integrated into traditional retail bank services. As yet another issue, the bankcard associations have been casting about for some time for an expanded charter, with mixed success so far.

The list of issues discussed here is not complete. Other issues will emerge as the bankcard industry continues to look for further growth and new opportunities.

Control and Membership of the Bankcard Associations

The two bankcard associations, the principal sponsors of the Visa and MasterCard payment systems in the United States, are creatures of the commercial banks. Over the first two decades of their history, the question of restrictions and limitations on association membership has been a much debated issue, pitting the founders' interest in membership exclusivity against the outsiders' advocacy of universally open membership. Over the course of the years, this debate has resulted in broad membership of commercial banks in both bankcard associations, and has given nonbanks de facto membership. It has not led to a merger of both bankcard associations, but has produced two healthy payment systems, competing with each other as well as with other card and noncard payment systems.

The Bank of America (now BankAmerica) was the first bank to develop a payment card for universal use. Its BankAmericard, initially tested in Fresno, California, in 1956, was backed by a prenegotiated line of credit and quickly gained acceptance as a convenient way of purchasing goods and services. Success on the regional level convinced the Bank of America that the program could be extended nationwide through its network of correspondent banks. In 1966 it began to license the card program to other banks and to establish procedures for operating it. The licensees received franchises, in effect, paying a fee to the service corporation in return for the right to use the BankAmericard name and the packaged program.

The nationwide expansion of the BankAmericard program was not accomplished without experiencing difficulties in administration and coordination. The growing pains, especially severe in the 1968–70 period, included problems in exchanging sales drafts from one bank to another, processing authorizations, and controlling fraud. The licensee banks first formed committees to devise solutions for these problems, then decided to form a new central body to operate the card system. In 1970, the Bank of America agreed to transfer control of the card system to a newly created National BankAmericard, Inc. (NBI), thus relinquishing its dominant position and becoming one of the many members of NBI. The break with BankAmericard's origins was completed with the phasing in of Visa, starting in 1977, as the new name of the card. At the same time, the name of NBI was changed to Visa U.S.A. Inc. The name change was of immense importance. By eliminating the last association of the card with a particular bank from a particular geographic area, the new name smoothed the way for the card's entry into all markets, not only in the United States but also abroad.

As the Bank of America was starting to go national with Bank-Americard, other groups of banks began to join together to offer competitive card programs. In 1966, Interbank Card, Inc. was formed to administer a card program for 14 New York banks. That same year, four California banks also banded together to create the Western States Bankcard Association; as the name of their card, they adopted Master Charge. Within a year, the East and West Coast groups decided to combine forces in order to compete nationally with the Bank of America. The New York administrative unit, now called Interbank Card Association (ICA), became the governing body of the new national organization. The name Master Charge survived the merger and was used on the cards of most ICA members until 1979, when it was superseded by the present name, MasterCard.

Both bankcard associations had from inception adopted by-laws that prohibited a bank member from joining the competing bankcard association. This membership restriction became known as the principle of exclusivity. It caused the commercial bank community in the United States to break into camps across the country, with strong and aggressive banks in each, and both associations competing fiercely with each other. The Bank of America, Chase Manhattan, and the First of Chicago were the leaders of the Visa camp; Citibank, Wells Fargo, and Continental Illinois led the other side. Nobody but commercial banks needed to apply.

All of this changed drastically as a result of what, in the beginning, seemed like an innocuous protest of a small regional bank in 1971. The Worthen Bank and Trust Company of Little Rock, Arkansas, already an issuer of BankAmericard, wanted to issue Master Charge cards on behalf of its correspondent banks, and joined ICA for this purpose. When NBI refused to admit this exception to its policy against dual membership, the Worthen Bank went to court, contending that the organization's prohibition was a "per se violation of Federal antitrust laws and horizontal restraint of trade." Worthen and NBI reached a settlement in 1974, whereby Worthen agreed to drop its suit pending a review by the Department of Justice of NBI's ban against dual membership. The Department ruling, issued in early 1976, held that a bank could offer both cards without necessarily violating the antitrust law. With this, NBI removed its ban against dual membership and, within one year, banks around the country began offering both cards to individuals and to merchants.

While it had been feared by some that duality would lead to a weakening of bankcard competition, it apparently had the opposite effect. The ability of banks to provide both national cards led to rapid growth in new accounts and card credit volume. The large bankcard issuers began soliciting cardholders outside of their regional market areas, building a national customer base. It was no surprise therefore that financial service competitors other than the commercial banks, mainly thrifts and nonbanks, began to eye bankcards as an opportunity in which they wanted to participate.

In the course of deregulation of interest rates on consumer deposits, which culminated in the Depository Institutions Deregulatory and Monetary Control Act of 1980, thrifts and credit unions had been given enlarged powers so that they could compete with commercial banks by offering a broader range of financial services, including issuance of bankcards. Equally interested in issuing bankcards were other financial organizations, such as brokerage houses, insurance companies, and retailers, also referred to as nonbanks. Since they were not members of either Visa or MasterCard, both thrifts and nonbanks contracted with banks that would sponsor them as quasi-issuers of cards. For example, in 1978, BancOne, of Columbus, Ohio, began issuing Visa cards on behalf of Merrill Lynch. Technically, the card remained a bankcard, but the distinction was not apparent to Merrill Lynch's customers, as it was the name of the brokerage house on the card, not that of the bank. A Visa card thus became an important element of a financial services package—including asset management, check writing, money fund investments, and lines of credit—that enable Merrill Lynch to function almost as though it is a bank, even though it is not regulated as one.

With passage of the 1980 act giving thrifts broader powers, both associations began to admit thrifts to membership, albeit very reluctantly. No such concession was made to the nonbanks. But this proved to be a losing battle. Technically, association membership was limited to financial institutions whose deposits are insured by the federal government, which includes commercial banks, industrial banks, mutual savings banks, savings and loans, and credit unions. However, nondepository institutions could become de facto members of the Visa and MasterCard associations by acquiring or creating institutions that are eligible for membership in them. There had been much furor in banking circles when J. C. Penney Co. was permitted to acquire Visa sales drafts at its stores as though it were a member. Visa promptly retreated, declaring that Penney's status would be considered unique and not be repeated. However, in 1985, Penney incorporated the J. C. Penney National Bank in Delaware, and began issuing Visa cards and MasterCards through this subsidiary, thus rendering immaterial any question about its membership status. Other nonbanks did the same. Merrill Lynch has been issuing its own Visa cards since 1984 through the Merrill Lynch Bank & Trust Co. of Princeton, New Jersey; John Hancock Life Insurance Co., through its First Signature Bank of New Hampshire; and Beneficial Finance Co., through its Beneficial National Bank, Delaware.

While nonbanks have gained de facto access, control of the associations to date has remained firmly with the largest card issuers and most powerful members, all of them commercial banks. Since 1984, the debate within the associations has begun to shift from membership restrictions on nonbanks to the question of desirable and necessary collaboration between the two associations.

The opportunity to explore synergy between the associations had been around since the shift from exclusivity to duality in 1976 resulted in identical membership lists for both associations. It was not until the mid-80s, however, that internal cost pressures and fear of other card competitors—notably American Express and Sears with its just launched, proprietary Discover card—led to the first attempts to explore how both associations could work together. Members of the boards of the two organizations spent some 18 months in 1984 and 1985 discussing the possibility of combining their back-office computer and communications systems. While a merger did not materialize, they did agree to allow electronic transactions to be transmitted freely between each other's network—a significant departure for once bitter rivals.

The two organizations also agreed on technical standards to make their operations more compatible. This has enabled Visa and MasterCard to issue joint warning bulletins for retail merchants, listing restricted or "hot cards." And staffs of the two organizations began a joint advertising and public relations program in 1986 to persuade leading upscale department stores to accept bankcards. They targeted 30 top department stores that did not accept bankcards and managed to sign 11 of them by the end of 1986, among them several prestigious retailers (Bloomingdale's, Brooks Brothers, Neiman Marcus).

Finally, Visa and MasterCard embarked on a much-heralded joint venture in 1986, the Entree debit card. Both organizations had failed previously in attempts to establish debit cards on their own.

The Interchange Fee

The interchange fee has been a crucial issue for the bankcard industry from the beginning. The fee is paid from bank to bank for each card transaction that passes hands; the bank which has acquired a card transaction from a merchant pays the interchange fee to the bank which issued the card used in the transaction. In turn, the issuing bank pays the acquiring bank the face value of the transaction.

The effect of the interchange fee on bankcard profitability of individual banks and, hence, on strategic direction of the bankcard business, has been pervasive. The fee is a cost to acquiring banks and governs their profitability; the fee is also a revenue to issuing banks and affects their profitability as well. If issuers and acquirers cannot agree on the economic justification of the fee, it will be perceived as a subsidy by the acquirer to the issuer, or vice versa. Furthermore, merchants who pay a discount per transaction to the acquiring bank might well argue that they are indirectly subsidizing the card issuer and the cardholder. As a result of the multiparty relationships involved, the interchange fee debate has been continuous and shows no sign of abating.

The concept of an interchange fee paid by the acquirer to the issuer dates to 1966 when the Bank of America began licensing the BankAmericard—the future Visa—nationally. Both bankcard associations, as they were to be called, adopted interchange fees based on similar, if not identical, principles. The merchant was willing to pay a discount for the acquirer to receive the benefit of making incremental sales without financial risk of payment. The acquirer, after covering operating costs—transaction authorization, data capture and transmission, and other items—and after making a profit, was asked to pass the remaining revenue as interchange fee to the card-issuing bank. The issuer, providing bankcards to its bank customers without a fee, received the interchange fee to cover costs of billing and collecting from its customers.

During the first 10 years of bankcard use in the U.S., retailer discounts were high, ranging over 3 percent of the transaction value, as high-margin merchants were glad to make additional sales for which payment was guaranteed.

Interchange fees were high as well, ranging over 2 percent, leaving the acquirer with a good margin, but not large enough to make a profit, since operating costs were high. The issuer received a solid interchange fee, but was equally struggling with high operating expenses at low processing volumes and not breaking even either. In fact, in those years, the interchange fee served not to allocate profits between acquirers and issuers, but rather to allocate losses, of which there were plenty in both bankcard systems.

Up to the mid-70s, the interchange fee was not a burning issue to the bankcard member banks, since most operated simultaneously and equally as acquirers and issuers, thus compensating perceived interchange inequities in-house.

As the bankcard business grew, both merchant discounts and interchange fees declined. The shrinkage in discounts was due to increased competition among banks (particularly after duality was established in 1976, allowing banks to offer both Visa and Master-Card). At the same time, processing costs declined, as facilities for transmitting and handling data became more automated. In turn, the increasing degree of automation led to greater competition as major money-center banks, with large processing capabilities, began to extend their reach and competed nationally with local banks on the local level.

In another development, these large national bankcard issuers did not build equally strong acquirer activities, and became predominantly net interchange fee recipients.

The pivotal role of the interchange fee in distributing bankcard profits had caused the Justice Department to review this subject in the context of examining the duality issue in 1975 and 1976. The Justice Department recommended to the associations that they define the derivation of interchange fee levels in more precise terms. Each association commissioned studies on how this could be done, and began setting interchange fees in 1977 according to complex formulas designed to take into account such factors as the cost of funds to issuer, credit losses, fraud losses, and basic operating costs. However, the exact weighting given to each factor is not a matter of public knowledge.

Both Visa and MasterCard adjust their interchange fees periodically, not at regular intervals, and also have them reviewed periodically by outside consultants. The fees of the two associations are never quite the same at the same time and, considering the antitrust implications of uniform fees, this is almost certainly not a matter of choice. During the most recent years, with lower cost of funds but higher cardholder credit losses, the interchange fee has declined to a range around 1.5 percent.

The interchange fee has also been used since the early 1980s as a tool to encourage electronic automation of transactions. Visa spearheaded this effort, introducing a two-tier fee system, with a lower fee for electronically authorized transactions. Both associations have clearly asserted that the lower fee for electronic transactions reflects credit and fraud loss, as well as operating cost avoidance resulting from faster and lower cost authorization. There is general agreement in the bankcard industry that the two-tier system has accelerated conversion to fully electronic authorization, by giving the acquirer concrete incentives to do so.

Bankcard Profitability

The bankcard business became, in the mid-1980s, one of the most profitable sectors of consumer banking in the United States. Aftertax return on assets is exceeding 2 percent and return on equity capital employed is often over 30 percent. This was not always so. In fact, from the start-up of this business in the mid-1960s until about 1981, most banks had racked up an unprecedented string of consecutive operating losses while growing the business at break-neck speed. By the end of the 1970s some banks, with cost of funds spiraling, looked at the bankcards business as a neverending and ever growing disaster; others continued to believe that they were financing one of the most courageous business investments American banks had ever made. Bankcard profitability was certainly then and is still today an important issue, if not the most important financial issue in many retail banks.

Bankcard profitability has been buffeted, squeezed, and lifted in its history by many factors. It has been a story of living with interest rate fluctuations through economic cycles and inflation, of outwitting government's attempt to regulate bankcard revenues from consumers, of merciless bank-to-bank price competition for merchant business, of unforeseen and close-to-ruinous credit loss surges as a result of too rapid business expansion, and of continuing efforts to increase productivity by using new technology.

The major bankcard revenue sources are interest revenues and fee revenues from cardholders, accounting for about 80 percent of total revenue today, and discount revenue from merchants accounting for the remainder. The largest expense category is cost of funds, currently about 35 percent of total expense, followed by operating expenses with a 30 percent share, and credit and fraud losses accounting for about 15 to 20 percent.

It is obvious that composition and size of revenues and expenses have been subject to fluctuations, some under the control of the banks but others not at all. The historic dynamics of profit behavior can be characterized as follows: Cardholder revenues, both interest and fees, used to be controlled by regulation. The banks struggled free of this constraint, and today competition is the main factor governing cardholder prices. Revenues from merchants always were subject to market pricing, and have been forced by competition from initially high to currently bare-bones levels. Cost of funds used to be considered not controllable, since banks funded bankcard receivables with short-term deposits. Longer term funding has taken its place, with a higher degree of cost predictability over the medium term. Credit losses are the key growth-cost category, largely under the control of card issuers unless they overcommit for growth. Operating expenses are the best controlled expense category, on a steady downtrend as the result of consistently applied cost management.

The rates that banks could charge on revolving credit accounts and other loans were traditionally governed by state usury laws. The permissible limits varied from state to state, with some having no ceilings at all. Banks typically charged interest to cardholders at the permissible limit of their home state, and charged no annual fee, generally because they thought this was necessary to attract new cardholders, and often because state usury law prohibited fees.

The usury laws did not pose severe problems for card issuers until 1976 when the cost of funds began rising sharply. Spreads decreased, losses mounted, and banks, in the midst of a costly growth period after introduction of duality, were upset. They responded to this situation in predictable ways. Those in states with low interest ceilings began to issue cards only to the very best credit risks. Some left the card business entirely, selling their receivables to other banks. Others began to increase their minimum repayment schedules, to institute annual fees, where permitted by law, and to reduce the number of grace days allowed before interest is charged to cardholders.

The most significant long-term result of the profit margin squeeze of the late 1970s, however, was the successful attempt by banks to export bankcard pricing from unregulated states to heavily regulated states, thus effectively dismantling state regulation of cardholder pricing. A court test occurred in 1976, when the Marquette National Bank of Minneapolis, which was permitted by Minnesota law to charge no more than 12 percent on credit card loans and an annual card fee of $15, sued the First National Bank of Omaha, which was marketing cards in Minnesota while charging the 18 percent annual interest rate and a $10 fee permitted by its home state, Nebraska. The case eventually reached the Supreme Court of the United States, which decided unanimously in 1978 that a national bank could export the rates permitted by its home state to customers in other states.

The Marquette decision left unanswered whether a national bank also can export annual fees, late charges, or variable interest rates. Nevertheless national banks, in need of new revenues and with home state leeway for pricing bankcards freely, began to extend their card programs to other states. In order that state-chartered banks and other financial institutions not be placed at a competitive disadvantage, the principle of exportation was included in the Depository Institutions Deregulatory and Monetary Control Act of 1980.

Thus, bankcard pricing was deregulated. Taking full advantage of the new clarification of regulatory law, Citicorp established a new bank in South Dakota to serve as its bankcard base and South Dakota, in turn, deregulated bankcard pricing. Other banks and nonbanks followed this strategy, with South Dakota and Delaware becoming the most used rate-exporting states. A major breakthrough had been accomplished by the bankcard industry. When cost of funds returned to lower levels in the early 1980s, banks remained free to price their cardholder services at rates the market would allow, insuring for the first time a period of prosperity for the bankcard business.

The bankcard business is a heavy user of funds. Traditionally, banks have considered the cost of funds for their bankcard loans to be their opportunity cost of attracting bank deposits. Interest paid on deposits was low as long as interest on deposits was regulated; when interest on deposits was deregulated by 1980, banks used short-term money market rates as their cost of funds. It has been argued, however, that bankcard businesses should fund their receivables not with short-term funds, but at maturities that are in step with their ability, or their necessity, to reprice cardholder service should interest rates fluctuate. Just as large finance companies, such as GMAC, borrow at maturities matching their outstanding loans, some bankcard businesses have been trying to borrow longer term to match the de facto maturity of their revolving loan portfolio. There are no simple answers here. Banks have become much more attentive to this issue after the last great cost-of-funds crisis in the late 1970s.

Credit losses are seen by banks as a cost of acquiring new customers and establishing a firm relationship with them. Over the lifetime of a bankcard account, credit-loss propensity is the highest during the first two years of the account life, accounting for more than half the potential life credit loss over the life of an account. This obviously is a result of relatively imperfect customer screening, a task that is made difficult given regulatory constraints on investigating new customers, the cost of new customer investigation, and the rush to gain cardholder market share that has been common during most of the bankcards 20-year growth history. It is by now a bitterly learned lesson among banks that bankcard expansion must be paced to spread acquisition-caused credit losses, and that skillful attention must be given to new customer screening. As the industry approaches market saturation, credit losses for new customer acquisition will mount. The industry is currently operating at an all-time high of credit losses per outstanding loans.

Operating expenses of bankcard businesses have a less dramatic effect on profit dynamics, but have presented the industry with the opportunity to accomplish long-term improvements of productivity and cost structure. As major inputs to operating expenses, the costs of data processing equipment and of telecommunications have been declining substantially during the last decade. Two other important inputs, human resource cost and postal costs, have been rising, but generally within the bounds of inflation. Most importantly, the bankcard business has used economies of scale and new data-processing technologies to improve productivity gradually and substantially. Annual productivity gains of 5 to 10 percent have not been unusual in the bankcard industry, giving an indication that many competitors have been successful in putting low cost bankcard operations into place.

For the last two years, bankcard profitability has been under criticism in the public arena, with various legislative attempts to reintroduce price regulation to reduce profit margins. It is quite possible that in the future a challenge to profit margins will come from a different direction, be it yet another interest-cost rise, higher credit losses to establish market position, or price competition for cardholders.

Credit Risk Management

Since they began marketing bankcards in the late 1960s, banks have cast ever-wider nets for new credit card accounts, building over 20 years a loan portfolio that currently has reached $81 billion. Credit losses have also grown substantially, both in absolute terms and as a percentage of total credit card debt. The challenge for bankcard credit managers, then, is to attract new customers who are also good customers, while not raising credit standards to a level that chokes off growth.

When banks began instituting card plans in the 1950s, credit controls were relatively tight and losses small. Cards were offered only to known customers of the banks. Starting in 1969, banks began distributing "take-one" applications. The credit-granting process no longer depended on a personal interview, but on an analysis of the customer's application, supported by information from a credit bureau, and, perhaps, telephone contact.

Tremendous growth in credit applications was accompanied by similar changes in the credit bureau business. During the 1970s the nation's many small urban credit bureaus, numbering about 400, gradually were consolidated into the five national credit bureaus, which today serve as fully automated clearing houses for consumer credit information. Simultaneously the banks, which had previously been members of local credit bureau cooperatives, began leaving this field.

The activities of the credit bureaus are governed by the Fair Credit Reporting Act of 1971. This law was designed "to insure that consumer reporting agencies exercise their grave responsibilities with fairness, impartiality, and a respect for the consumer's right to privacy." Bureau files can be made available only to those with a legally permissible purpose for obtaining the information. A bank must become a member of a credit bureau, and be assigned a special access code, in order to gain information from its files. In its turn, the bank will supply the bureau with monthly updates of information about its debtors.

The electronic automation of the national credit bureaus makes it possible to screen large lists of names very quickly and this, in turn, led to a new form of bankcard marketing—the use of direct mail. Citicorp pioneered this concept in 1976–77, using credit bureaus to prescreen lists of people scheduled to receive direct mail offers. This approach was quickly adopted by other banks. By the late 1970s, direct mailings to prescreened lists had become the most important method of acquiring new bankcard customers.

Another important development for credit management in the bankcard industry has been the introduction of credit scoring systems in the early 1970s, which have become instrumental in making credit decisions about prospective and current cardholders. Credit scoring systems are developed statistically from historical credit experience with a large number of customers, rating credit risk on the basis of diverse information obtained about an individual. They make it possible to combine in one score negative and positive characteristics or variables. Once proven and validated, scores can rate consumer information from "take-one" applications, from credit bureau reports, and even from bankcard transaction records.

Credit scoring made it easier to process vast amounts of information in support of credit decisionmaking. It allowed credit managers to institute credit policies and to predict their financial effect fairly precisely. Credit scoring also introduced a sense of objectivity in the decision process, which consumers probably did not appreciate but nevertheless came to rely upon. Credit scoring systems significantly aided banks in constructing preapproved direct mail lists that produced predictable credit performance, and thus contributed substantially to the rapid growth of the bankcard business.

While credit decisionmaking in bankcards matured as a managerial discipline, this did not mean that credit losses of the industry were low. It had been well recognized that signing up new customers, even under strict credit scoring control, led to surges in credit losses. Credit loss ratios for bankcards, which hovered around 2 percent during times of slower growth, typically accelerated to levels of 4 percent and above, when strong account growth had occurred. It is generally accepted in the industry that the probability of credit losses is concentrated in the first two years of an account life, and that more than 50 percent of all credit losses occur at that early stage. The phenomenon has become more pronounced as the United States liberalized its personal bankruptcy laws in the early 1980s, and as fewer consumers without bankcards remain as growth targets.

The large credit risk-taking of banks for the purpose of bankcard expansion has led to another innovation; that is, the development of highly automated telephone collection systems. While communications with customers about account delinquency is still conducted by bank service personnel, collection systems direct this process by selecting accounts that warrant attention with the help of scoring systems, by queuing phone calls to be made by priority and most promising contact time, and by managing the phone call followup.

Credit losses usually account for about 90 percent of total gross charge-offs in the bankcard business. The remaining losses are caused by fraud such as misuse of lost and stolen cards, cardholder collusion, merchant fraud, and counterfeiting. The latter, almost unheard of previously, suddenly jumped to more than 2 percent of total losses in the early 1980s, with the advent of high-quality duplicating equipment. Counterfeiting of cards became a federal crime in 1984, and losses of this type began dropping almost immediately. This was also due in part to improvements in card technology, including hard-to-copy holograms and new terminals that help merchants detect counterfeit cards at the point of purchase. Both Visa and MasterCard are experimenting with the so-called "smart card," which contains a computer chip that holds information about the cardholder and requires the bearer to furnish a personal identification number (PIN) at the point of sale.

Bankers generally agree that credit risk management of bankcards today is more professional, statistically sound, and managerially more mature than ever, and is qualitatively equal, if not superior, to credit risk management in other sectors of retail banking. There are divided opinions, however, on whether the bankcard industry can afford, over the longer term, to carry on at credit loss ratios that are substantially above those for secured loans and even for other unsecured personal loans. There is a strong view that bankcard credit losses are a growth cost that needs to be managed with discipline and circumspection. There is another view that considers credit loss rates of over 2 to 3 percent per year as socially corrosive and not sustainable over the long run.

Integration into Traditional Bank Retail Services

Banks have integrated their bankcard services only to a very limited degree into their traditional bank retail services. The lack of integration has puzzled many observers, not the least perceptive bank customers who have wondered why their bankcards have become a stand-alone service at most banks.

Lack of integration has been conspicious in two main aspects: The lack of integrating bankcards into branch services and the lack of integrating bankcards with checking and other payment products. Today, bankcard customer service is offered from a central location by phone. Customer service at branch locations is often cumbersome and usually discouraged. Cash withdrawal, bill payment, and customer service for bankcards at branch-based automatic teller machines (ATMs) is the exception, not an expectation. Replacement cards are sent by mail from a central location, not offered for pick-up at branches. Deposit of bankcard sales slips by merchants at branches is discouraged; direct deposit by mail is encouraged.

Bankcard and checking account statements are rendered separately, not integrated in the form of one monthly payment record. Automatic bankcard bill paying from a checking account is not widely available. Bankcards cannot be used to guaranty checks. Very few banks offer integrated customer service for cards, checking, and other payment services. Bankcards cannot be used as check bouncing back-up.

It has been somewhat embarrassing to commercial banks that the most visible attempt for integrating a bankcard into a broader financial service have come from Merrill Lynch, a nonbank, which used a BancOne-sponsored Visa card as the key access device for its very successful Cash Management Account.

While the issue can be debated as a failure of the commercial banks, as it often has been, it is more useful to examine the conditions and incentives that generally caused banks to pursue a stand-alone strategy for bankcards. Three main reasons appear to be most important: (1) The inability to service bankcard customers effectively within an existing retail bank infrastructure; (2) to avoid burdening bankcard activities with distribution overhead of traditional branch distribution; (3) the reluctance to promote the Visa and MasterCard marks, both shared brand names, in the environment of a proprietary bank distribution system.

The introduction of bankcard services by commercial banks in the late 1960s required appropriate processing and service systems. As a rule, banks chose to develop these systems from ground up outside of their conventional processing systems for deposit accounts and personal loans. Existing systems were not equipped to handle the new service, which functionally looked like a combination of a checking account and revolving loan. So banks began building new systems, leap-frogging technically existing bank systems, and departing for the next 20 years on a course unconstrained by other bank systems.

Typically, bankcard operations were established in suburban facilities, away from inner city operations centers; account information needed to be made accessible on-line to service personnel for authorization, customer service, and collection, all of whom primarily used the telephone to communicate with cardholders and merchants. Soon, bankcard systems were operating independently from the rest of the bank. Branches were seen as secondary service points, with branch personnel either not service-trained or incapable of accessing the information needed to give service. Smaller banks, which were not capable of building dedicated bankcard facilities, often joined regional processing organizations, such as the Western States Bankcard Association, Eastern States Bankcard Association, Southwestern States Bankcard Association, and the Midwest States Bankcard Association. The latter, which later became First Data Resources, was acquired by American Express and is today among the largest bankcard processors.

The course of operational independence taken by bankcard operations has greatly discouraged integration with other bank services. It has made implementation of integration efforts more difficult, but by no means impossible. But there was another obstacle: The reluctance of banks to burden their bankcard operations with branch distribution costs in the absence of a clear need of branch support for bankcard service.

Bank customers caught on fairly quickly that they hardly needed branch service to use their bankcards effectively. As a sure sign of this, an increasing share of customers began to maintain a bankcard account at a bank other than the one providing their checking service. These so-called "deserters" accounted for close to 50 percent of all checking customers in the late 1970s; "deserter" share is currently estimated to be between 60 and 70 percent. Most often, their bankcard bank is out of region with no branch offices close to the customer. In this environment, it became increasingly plausible to banks to ignore for their bankcard business not only branch distribution costs but also branch distribution capabilities. While the bankcard businesses saw themselves as a "no bricks and mortar" bank financial service, opportunities to integrate with branch-based services were few, if any.

Yet another factor inhibited the traditional branch-based retail bank organizations to embrace bankcards as their own product. Bankcards promoted their own brand marks, Visa and MasterCard. All bankcard issuers, in effect, shared these brand identifiers, with little opportunity for the individual issuer to assert its own brand identity. Banks were, therefore, reluctant to make bankcards the access vehicle for their checking accounts; they preferred a proprietary debit card for this purpose. The conflict has not been easy to solve. The bankcard associations traditionally insisted on strong Visa and MasterCard brand identifiers, even to the detriment of their members' wishes. The larger banks over the years persuaded a majority of member banks to relax card-face uniformity, thus reducing the card-face presence for Visa and MasterCard from close to 100 percent in 1976 to only 33 percent today. As a result, the significance of this issue has declined, but it certainly has not disappeared.

Extending the Bankcard Association Charters

Extending the charter of the associations has been a much-debated issue at every occasion within the bankcard constituency. Smaller banks have often encouraged a larger role for the associations, since their own resources are limited and they naturally look for cooperative solutions to their limited geographic reach and resources. The managements of the associations most often spearheaded attempts to expand their own activities, since it would give them more importance and increased influence. The larger banks, since they command substantial resources and have remained suspicious of granting the associations more powers have, for the most part, discouraged a larger role for the associations.

There have been major attempts to enlarge the role of Visa and MasterCard in three areas: (1) traveler checks, (2) debit cards, and (3) cash distribution (ATMs). In 1975, MasterCard led an effort to sponsor a MasterCard traveler check to be issued by association members and interchanged by MasterCard. At that time American Express, a nonbank competitor, already commanded a lion's share of the traveler checks market, with the largest money-center banks competing in a second tier. The smaller and medium-size members of MasterCard, with a majority on the association board, favored the move, which they felt was directed primarily against American Express and less so against their co-members who issued traveler checks and sold this service to other banks. Nevertheless, Citicorp, the number-two traveler check issuer, took exception and sued MasterCard—but without success, except for delaying MasterCard's plans. By 1977, both associations began implementing traveler check programs but licensed the service to individual, large association members. The programs, a success for both associations, are still in operation today, but they have not been able to challenge American Express' market leadership.

There has been an even deeper and more extended debate about whether and how the associations should sponsor a universally accepted debit card. Member banks began in the mid-1970s to issue proprietary cards for their customers to access their checking accounts via automated teller machines (ATMs). The opportunity existed to extend access of these so-called debit cards to the point of sale of goods and services, where bankcards were already accepted. Both Visa and MasterCard made a number of attempts to introduce debit cards, with authorization and settlement interchange provided by the associations.

Visa introduced Entree in 1975, a debit card that looked like a Visa card. Its transactions were processed in the same manner as bankcards, with Visa providing interchange, but they were posted at the card-issuing bank to the cardholder's checking account. MasterCard followed with Signet, which was a different card, not a lookalike. Signet transactions were to be authorized by a new and separate authorization system, and then processed through MasterCard interchange. Neither attempt succeeded. Visa then changed its strategy and sponsored a Visa debit card, undistinguishable from a bankcard at the point of sale, but also without success. In 1981, Visa put forward a new concept, the Electron debit card, that would have required fully electronic authorization and settlement processing between the point of sale and the card issuer. This initiative also met with limited interest.

In the meantime, regional bank groups in a number of states had been more successful in launching locally accepted debit cards. Most notably, the large California banks established Interlink in 1984 and have made a promising start. Interlink decided to use Visa software to operate its interchange switch, and most recently has asked Visa to operate the system. In yet another development, Visa and MasterCard agreed in 1986 to pool their resources to sponsor a common debit card, using the revived Entree name, designed for use only at point-of-sale terminals.

The 10-year struggle for a universal debit card has been without success for the following key reasons: There is generally consumer resistance to the use of debit cards at the point of sale, particularly since a very convenient and widely distributed alternative, the bankcard, is available. Retailers, the operators of the point of sale, have been skeptical, expecting lower discount rates for debit card transactions but not getting them. Banks, as bankcard issuers, have been half-hearted in supporting point-of-sale debit cards because they fear cannibalizing their highly profitable bankcard business. And real-time, electronic authorization and settlement—a next-to-indispensable requirement for debit card transactions—has been slow in arriving at the point of sale.

In a related field, Visa and MasterCard have attempted to operate, under their service mark, ATM cash distribution networks. Both associations were latecomers to ATM interchanges, however. By the time they launched their programs in the early 1980s, a number of regional switches had already been established to enable cardholders from one bank to use ATMs of another. Furthermore, dissension within both association boards caused powerful association members to walk away and establish independent national ATM networks: A group of MasterCard banks founded Cirrus, and a group of Visa banks formed the Plus System. By 1987, Cirrus and Plus were the largest among eight national ATM networks, with MasterTeller (MasterCard) and Visa's Electronic Money in lesser positions. Negotiations for agreements are underway to merge Plus into Visa should MasterCard acquire Cirrus. The competitive situation is fluid, and the longer term market structure for national ATM cash distribution remains unsettled.

CHAPTER SIXTY-TWO

Opportunities in Nondeposit Retail Services

Donald M. Douglas

Senior Vice President
Sovran Investment Corporation

James M. LaVier III

First Vice President
Sovran Investment Corporation

In response to deregulation, increased competition and other marketplace developments, banks have now placed greater emphasis on retail fee services, such as the sale of nondeposit retail services, as their traditional lines of business have become less profitable. In addition to allowing banks to diversify their sources of income, these retail fee services may be "off the balance sheet," permitting banks to book fee income without a balance sheet entry and thereby inflating the return on assets measure.

Because today's customer base is often more sophisticated than it was in the 1970s, selling nondeposit retail services can be a difficult exercise. Banks must now operate with less loyalty and greater competition, making it imperative that they have a proper understanding of what their customers want and when they want it. However, once a bank reaches a certain size, this task becomes difficult-to-impossible. This chapter is included to give emphasis to the importance of these retail fee services and to aid the nonuser bank in their decisions relating to the introduction of these services. This is not intended to be a complete study of these activities but rather a compilation of thoughts from the hands-on experience of the writers.

BACKGROUND

The shift in emphasis toward retail fee services might well have had its beginning in the May 1, 1975, Securities and Exchange Commis-

933

sion (SEC) decision to deregulate stockbroker commissions. Major changes in the pricing of brokered products followed, creating a favorable environment for bank entry. In 1982, Bank of America received approval by the Federal Reserve Board to buy Charles Schwab & Company, the nation's largest discount brokerage, becoming the first bank to enter the brokerage business.

Prior to this 1982 approval by the Federal Reserve Bank, banks were in the unfortunate position of having to operate in a high interest rate environment. Regulation Q imposed ceilings on the rates they could pay customers on their deposits, resulting in a disintermediation of funds to nonbank competitors, for example, mutual funds. Banks responded with a varied menu of new deposit products to circumvent the rate restrictions. In 1981, the "retail repo" became a tool for banks to use in avoiding the limitations of Regulation Q. In December of 1982 the introduction of the money market deposit account led to a ferocious rate war, targeted to fight the mutual funds but resulting in one bank against another.

To some extent and from the banks' own promotional efforts, customers (and prospects) had a much greater awareness of alternatives to checking and savings accounts. The deluge of ads that promoted the retail repo accounts was a contributor, as was the heavy promotion of IRAs in 1982 and thereafter. Money market funds heavily promoted their yields in successfully attracting bank depositors. As brokers, S&Ls, credit unions, mutual funds, and other direct vendors of financial services products all began heavily competing for the same investment dollars in the mid-1980s, the consumer awareness level climbed to new heights. Often confused but seldom without reminders, investing consumers began to ask questions that made the banker somewhat uncomfortable. Perhaps more importantly, the banker discovered that investing consumers were not only asking questions but doing their serious investing elsewhere. The "maturity phenomenon" occurred whereby customers were forced to rethink and remake their new investment decision as their investment matured into high interest rate levels. Driven by this realization, banks moved as a group to establish personal or private banking efforts in one form or another and looked for fee-generating products to supplement their lending and deposit-gathering activities.

Banks almost made use of nondeposit fee services in 1981 when they considered offering sweep accounts linked to money market mutual funds—some having asset management accounts—packaged for banks by brokerage competitors. As a group, banks turned away from these products, favoring the redesign of their own deposits, such as the money market demand accounts. However, as stated above, high interest rates in 1980, 1981, and 1982 continued to plague the banking business and, as market rates approached 15 percent levels in 1982, banks become convinced that a solution "away from the balance sheet" was needed.

AFFECTING THE BOTTOM LINE

Simply stated, banks turned toward nondeposit retail income sources because rate competition was squeezing their profit margins. Competitive pressures impacted bank operations several ways. First, spreads on assets were narrowed forcing a closer examination of the return on those assets and, thus, a concern over the use of the balance sheet. Second, deposits were being lost to competitor institutions which were willing to pay higher rates. Third, nonbanks entered the picture by offering attractive alternatives to deposit and bank-product investors. And finally, government and agency instruments at times drew funds from commercial banks. In sum, banks were running the risk of losing their advantage, particularly that of being the focal point for their customers' overall financial needs. Until this time, products not offered by banks were often "extras" that were purchased with funds housed primarily at the banks. As nonbank competitors expanded their product lines, banks ran the risk of becoming the "extra."

STOPPING THE OUTWARD FLOW OF FUNDS

A move by banks to offer fee-generating investment products is often made, along with development of personal banking strategy, to stop the outward flow of funds. To accomplish this task, management should approach their customers in one of three modes: defensive, offensive, or anticipatory. The key to success is the proper selection of one of these modes for each customer. **Defensive** means taking steps to protect existing deposits where the customer's awareness has triggered an inclination to seek a more attractive home elsewhere for the funds. If money market funds are growing nationally, this growth is most likely happening at the expense of bank deposits. Most banks having accurate information find that their customers' funds are moving into brokerage products or that a significant amount is already there. An educational effort must be made to convince customers that investment shopping can be done at one place: *the bank.*

The second mode is **offensive,** the selective targeting of customers, or prospects who have known investments at competitor institutions. By selectively offering nondeposit fee-based services, the bank does not risk cannibalizing deposits but rather goes after additional business that has heretofore been lost.

The third mode is **anticipatory**, a critical concept yet most difficult to successfully engage. In this mode, the banker must determine the level of customer sophistication and offer only the appropriate products for each customer. The difficulty in utilizing this mode clearly lies in the **selective** offering (i.e., making only specific products available to specific customers) and the accurate assessments of customer sophistication levels. The difficulties are more readily overcome in a personal banking environment where each banker is held accountable for a designated customer list. Before one feels uncomfortable with this strategy, however, recall that it exists wherever a bank still has passbook savings customers while market rates are at higher levels. Anticipating requires an awareness of the customer's upward movement, stepping forward to fulfill his or her needs just prior to the customer's dissatisfaction. Overall the D.O.A. acronym aptly describes the customer base that is not properly managed.

AVAILABLE PRODUCTS

Any "products available" list will be quickly outdated as old products mature and new ones are introduced. One generally thinks first of discount brokerage services within the context of retail of nontraditional bank investment services and products to their customers. The next section contains what we think are the most common fee-producing investment products offered by banks.

Discount Brokerage

Discount brokerage is best defined as a service that offers the investor discounted commission charges for the execution of stock, registered options, and corporate bond transactions. Lower transaction commissions are offered in large part because the high cost of providing investment advice is eliminated (discounters do not provide stock advice) and because traders are generally not on a commissioned sales program. Thus, discount brokerage services are best suited for customers who do not require or need advice when making investment decisions.

Banks offering discount brokerage services usually charge commissions that parallel those of nonbank discount brokers. Banks contemplating offering a discount brokerage service should consider the following:

1.   Fully Disclosed versus Omnibus.   Banks wishing to have their employees handle customer discount brokerage transactions may choose one of two clearing arrangements. Under the fully disclosed option, all clearing and recordkeeping is performed by an outside clearing, broker/dealer firm. While the bank's employees take the trade and settle with the customer at the prescribed time, all other aspects of the transaction, including the execution of the order, are handled by the outside broker/dealer.

The omnibus relationship, on the other hand, allows the bank to handle customer trades and perform all customer recordkeeping, avoiding divulging customer names to the clearing broker/dealer. The clearing broker/dealer is responsible for the market execution function. This arrangement usually is more costly than the fully disclosed arrangement and is generally chosen by institutions that have substantial daily transaction activity. Given the substantial volume, the omnibus discount brokerage unit can benefit by negotiating lower execution charges and by having more control over their customers.

2. Bank versus Affiliate Delivery Approach. Banks may offer discount brokerage services through the bank entity itself or through a subsidiary organization created specifically for the purpose of providing stock and bond transaction services. Until the advent of the Securities and Exchange Commission's (SEC) Rule 3b-9, which maintained that banks offering brokerage services must either register themselves as a broker/dealer or set up a broker/dealer subsidiary, a majority of banks offered brokerage services directly through the bank. Following the ruling, banks largely opted for the affiliate arrangement. Under this arrangement, only the affiliate offering the service is subject to the new regulatory requirements. While Rule 3b-9 is currently under appeal, banks may still find the affiliate option more attractive in the long term as certain activities prohibited under banking laws may be permissible by a broker/dealer affiliate.

3. The Correspondent/Vendor Networking Alternative. Banks not wishing to make the financial commitment to fully staff a discount brokerage operation may find a networking arrangement with a broker/dealer of another bank attractive. This option allows the user bank to offer tailored discount brokerage services to its customers through a toll-free number. Registered brokers at the member firm handle transactions and give out market information to customers of the subscribing user bank. The user bank, in turn, receives a share of all commissions generated, varying from 15 to 40 percent of gross commissions charged.

Fixed-Income Securities and Money Market Instruments

For many years, banks have offered customers access to government bonds and some other fixed-income investments. The basic fixed-income products line includes U.S. Treasury bills, notes, and bonds; U.S. agency issues; and tax-free notes and bonds. Other instruments offered are money market securities including "jumbo" certificates of deposit, taxable and tax-free variable rate (master) notes, commercial paper, mortgage-backed securities, and repurchase agreements.

The typical financial institution, when offering government agency and municipal securities, performs two primary functions for its retail customers. Customers interested in participating in the regular auctions of these securities may subscribe to these issues through the bank. If, prior to a scheduled auction, the customer wishes to invest funds in these instruments, the bank can purchase these securities from a government dealer for the customer's benefit. Larger banking institutions may actually purchase for their own inventory blocks of attractive issues for resale to their customers in this "secondary" market. A transaction fee generally is charged on any purchase of a government issue through the auction market. Purchases in the secondary market are normally done at a net basis—no fee is charged but a spread is made on the transaction.

Financial institutions may also offer to their customers the bank's own instruments. These include a variety of deposit issues as well as short-term instruments such as commercial paper and master notes of the holding company. In addition, repurchase agreements on the bank's government investments may be offered to the public. With the brokerage industry's increased emphasis on principal-safe money market funds over the past decade, banks have seen significant savings assets move to other institutions. This, in part, prompted some banking institutions to offer alternatives to these higher yielding money market funds. Taxable and tax-free master note products, having very short maturities and high levels of safety, have been created. These products have allowed banking institutions to offer their customers similar products of a more localized nature and a high level of safety to their more sophisticated investors.

Mutual Funds and Unit Investment Trusts

Two recent additions to the growing portfolio of fee-based investment products are mutual funds and unit investment trusts. Mutual funds available to bank customers include both load and no-load products. The loaded product contains a sales charge to the customers generally ranging from 3 to 9 percent. No-load funds have no sales charge but may offer the bank, through what is known as a 12b-1 arrangement with the fund, a small percentage of the total value of the fund being utilized by the bank's customers. Typically, this percentage is 20 to 30 basis points. A wide range of funds with varying investment objectives and mixes is available for banks interested in offering such services to their customers.

Banks also have access to the unit investment trust (UIT) product. Unlike mutual funds, which are professionally managed investment portfolios under continual asset restructure, UITs are portfolios of fixed-income securities of set maturities. As the securities in the trust mature, principal from the maturing issues is paid back to the unit trust holder. Unit trusts may contain either taxable or tax-free fixed-income instruments. Sales charges generally range between 3 and 4.9 percent depending on the average maturity of the trust portfolio.

Precious Metals

The introduction of the new American Eagle gold and silver coins has sparked a renewed interest in precious metals as investments. This could bode well for those banking institutions willing to develop a precious metals program for customers. Similar to offering discount brokerage, banks can either start their own metals department or negotiate an arrangement whereby another institution provides a trained staff of professionals to handle metals transactions.

Banks can generally give customers three options when setting up a precious metals account. Customers can set up a safekeeping account, have a metals account relationship, or have the purchased metals delivered to them. A safekeeping account allows the customer to safekeep coins, wafers, and bars at the United States Depository. By setting up a metals account, the customer has metals left "on account," providing liquidity and allowing most transactions to be executed by phone. One reason for offering a metals program is the positioning of metals against a brokerage program that depends on a good equities market. As a possible hedge and for little additional cost (through a correspondent program), the bank can enjoy the better margins and be prepared for its popularity, such as occurred with the American Eagle introduction. Metals also nicely complement a personal banking program.

Cash Management Account

Several major "full-service" brokerage houses offer control asset or cash management accounts—CMAs—which conveniently places a customer's liquid funds not currently invested in stocks or other securities in an interest-bearing cash management fund. The customer receives a consolidated statement reflecting all security positions, including assets invested in a CMA.

Some banking institutions have ventured into this area with what appears to be mixed results. At present, it appears some money center banks are committed to offering a CMA-type service. While customers favor having all of their assets fully invested, the cost of developing a CMA is very high. In addition, monies that may have been otherwise placed in checking or savings accounts may be diverted to more costly, higher yielding liquid assets (money market) deposit accounts. CMAs may become attractive when banks are able to offer deposit accounts with a consolidated statement. At present, it is not clear whether a central asset account can contribute to an institution's bottom line.

Self-Directed IRA

At the inception of individual retirement accounts (IRAs), a major portion of these funds were placed in traditional bank deposit instruments, such as investment certificates. With interest rates ranging upwards to 15 percent, investment certificates offered customers a safe, high-yielding product. However, an ensuing decline in interest rates combined with a rising stock market encouraged the investor to look toward other investments for the IRA. Higher yielding, income-oriented mutual funds and individual stocks became attractive alternatives. Many banks responded by offering the self-directed IRA, where the bank acts as custodian for the IRA and the customer makes his or her own investment decisions. An annual maintenance fee is generally charged to help pay administrative costs. In addition, an initial "opening" fee may be charged. Typically, the customer's funds are first placed in an IRA money market account until an actual transaction takes place. The customer has the flexibility to tailor a portfolio to meet his or her needs; choices range from individual stocks and bonds to mutual funds and taxable unit investment trusts. In addition, the American Eagle coin is now eligible for purchase in an IRA. The self-directed IRA continues to increase in popularity, and this trend is likely to continue into the future.

Insurance Products

Insurance sales represent a fee-producing, low-risk, noncapital-intensive service that fits well within existing bank product lines. The income potential, lack of credit or interest rate risk, and minimal fixed asset and funding requirements have prompted many banks to list insurance sales as a very attractive business to pursue.

A major issue confronting banks is one of maintaining a large, costly delivery system. The insurance industry is struggling with inefficient and limited methods of delivering its products. Cooperative and innovative solutions such as joint ventures, leased space agreements, reinsurance of credit life portfolios, and agency ownership are developing, providing banks increased fee income in exchange for opening their delivery channels to insurance providers.

At present, regulations restrict the ability of banks to participate in insurance activities. However, the attractiveness and fit of insurance sales and banking will continue to foster new and creative ways to incorporate insurance products in banks offerings.

OPPORTUNITIES AND BENEFITS

Offering retail fee services can positively impact a bank's operation in a number of ways. Explicit profits may be gained through fees paid by investors, fees received from vendors, or spreads made on principal transactions. Implicit profits can be gained through lower cost of funding as funding products are positioned with other products (e.g., a master note for the holding company) or from the retention of deposits and customers that would otherwise be gone (and possibly funded through a higher rate instrument). While explicit revenues can be easily tracked and reported against some cost allocation, cost savings from funding and deposit retention will be more difficult to measure. One solution is to perform the measuring through proxy values (e.g., comparing new funding costs against a market measurement) or sampling (e.g., statistical sampling of the deposit impact of discount brokerage). These products can generate and retain deposits when properly offered by the bank.

Beyond the explicit and implicit profit generation are additional benefits of control, coordination, image, and completeness. Control suggests that the bank chooses to control its direction and strategy, and only by assessing the value of these products can that control be exercised. By having the product offering capability, the bank can consider and determine which product it chooses to offer for which category of customer. Internal control should also be considered so that the proper grouping of expertise takes place and so that pieces are not merely offered by various departments on a conflicting basis.

Synergism and efficiency will come from the coordination of the product offerings. Handled properly, this leads to an image benefit which entices or solidifies customer relationships. Completeness is the full extent of being a retail bank with the accompanying range of product. This is not to say that every bank should offer every product, but rather that an informed decision should be made. More on internal factors will be covered later in this chapter.

COSTS, RISKS, AND DRAWBACKS

As with every decision, the decision to offer any or all of these products depends on many factors, including the risk and cost-versus-reward trade-offs. Being able to offer these products will require some cost, even if it is not significant. The answer is to make the money well worth spending.

Research, legal opinions, people costs, supplies, training, and many other related costs might have to be overcome to make offering these services worthwhile. The word "might" is used because of the quick alternative of turning customers over to a correspondent. For many banks this "quick fix" is also a distasteful one, so that they will choose to at least be involved in much of the customer contact or in assuming credit for offering the service.

The greater a bank's involvement, the greater the people costs, both in numbers and in specialized hiring or training. Retail contact personnel may consider these products merely something else to learn and sell. Initially, you must sell senior management and then your staff, before selling the customer. Training will be required, the extent of which will depend on the bank's involvement (vis-a-vis the correspondent or vendor relationship).

Cannibalization

Cannibalization of customer retail deposits can be either a real or perceived risk when discussing the offering of alternative investment products to bank customers. Any introduction of new investment products should be initiated only after careful consideration has been given to the effect such new products would have on both traditional deposit balances and accompanying bottom line income. It is also important to recognize that in today's more sophisticated retail banking environment, alternative investment vehicles may be necessary to avoid losing a banking relationship. Even though more income may be generated by having the customer keep retirement funds in a low-interest savings account, it is certainly preferable to make him aware of other in-bank investment alternatives as opposed to losing the entire relationship to a competitive financial institution.

Regulatory Costs

The addition of many nondeposit financial products may require substantial cost outlays due to regulatory requirements relating to these products. Depending on the products offered and the manner in which they are offered, a bank can be subject to scrutiny by the Comptroller of the Currency, the Federal Reserve Bank, the Securities and Exchange Commission, and the National Association of Securities Dealers. Proper guidance in this area is a required expense since the cost of not complying may be even greater. Additional staffing costs, registration expenses, and more costly accounting procedures can be significant.

CONSIDERATIONS/DECISIONS

With many decisions to be made, the first and foremost may be whether to employ the services of a correspondent institution. If these products are to be new to the bank, the experience of a correspondent certainly bears consideration. The extent to which the bank chooses to be involved can then be determined after considering the following factors:

Pricing and Positioning Strategy.   The style and type of bank and its customer base will be important. The dependence on funding, access to various types of customers, visibility and promotion style, size and experience of staff, economy and wealth of marketplace, profitability, and a weighing of its other strengths and weaknesses also come into play. Explicit charging of fees for services may be new for a bank; unbundling its charges may lead to an overall review of prices.

Physical Facilities.   Having the amount and type of space needed will be a consideration as will the cost of meeting these requirements.

Sales Stimulation.   If the product or products are a part of an offensive, aggressive strategy, then incentives should be considered, even though they may be new to the culture and therefore threatening to some areas. Both internal and external incentives are possible. Internal includes awards to employees for referrals as well as direct incentives to those producing sales. Much can be gained from the experience of other banks of similar size and style. Vendors or correspondents should be able to provide support on this. Keep in mind that any incentive program must have the open support of senior management. In fact, having management firmly behind the product introduction and promotion will sometimes be sufficient. The link with all contact areas must be strong and supportive enough to gain the most from the effort.

Recruiting and Training.   To have the appropriate expertise to match the product might mean acquiring or training. The level of involvement, timing, and availability of resources will have a bearing. Training will be required both from outside sources (to tap the experts) and eventually from inside staff. At least someone must become a designated expert through whom all pertinent information is funneled. Brochures and other training material must be gathered and maintained, to the extent that the bank is involved. Procedures are important whatever the involvement, perhaps even more so when only one person holds the total responsibility.

Legal/Regulatory.   While most of the steps to be taken can actually be listed and clearly defined, the most elusive and clouded are the legal considerations. Partly because of its ever-changing nature and partly because opinions and situations vary, outside counsel must be sought for most of the fee-based products that will be introduced. Seeking counsel that is experienced in these matters can be well worth the price even if that price is higher than the price of local counsel without the experience.

Briefly and with great qualification, in order to sell municipal securities, the Municipal Securities Rulemaking Board's (MSRB) rules must be considered, which includes following the MSRB's registration requirements. For discount brokerage activities, the NASD's rules must be considered, and registration requirements exist if staff is involved. The SEC may also be involved with brokerage activity, and the Federal Reserve Bank must be considered for activity that involves a holding company affiliate. Also the bank's other regulators (e.g., FDIC) should be consulted if in question. A checklist of who must be seen for which service can best be obtained from a correspondent.

Since the status of the SEC's 3b-9 rule, which requires that banks having 1,000 trades per year in brokerage activities register that activity in a broker/dealer affiliate, is presently under review, there is too much uncertainty to make a definite statement for this chapter. We are able to discuss only those steps required at this time.

Until the SEC's 3b-9 Rule, banks involved in securities sales needed only to register their dealer operation under the MSRB. Salespeople were registered through a filing and successful passing of the Series 52 exam. One or more principals registered and completed the Series 53 exam. As the SEC entered the picture, the NASD became the primary regulatory agency, bringing its own exams and registration requirements. Although several alternatives were available, the standard approach was to use the Series 7 for all salespeople, the Series 24 for principals, and the Series 27 for the operations principal. All had to meet state registration requirements, which often were satisfied through the successful completion of the Series 63 exam. In short, these requirements resulted in many new exams and filings for registration.

Marketing. To determine what to do and how to do it means that marketing research is needed. Much research on consumer desires and practices are available for purchase or from public studies. The library at any Federal Reserve bank may be a good source for information. Gathering specific data on each bank's particular customer base and market area will be crucial. Much of this information may best be formed by gathering input from contact officers or by using a customer survey to gather information. The marketing function can help assimilate and analyze the data critical to decisions regarding what products to offer and how to offer them.

After the initial offering of these services, marketing's help with advertising and producing marketing collateral will be needed. Printing related stationary, brochures, branch collateral, and confirmations must be done if the bank is to be actively involved. Marketing will likely be involved in the product and service introduction to effectively coordinate public awareness with the internal preparation and awareness. Newspaper and radio advertising may be used along with statement stuffers, notices, and direct mail to the bank's customer base and/or its targeted prospect list.

The key to success at this point is the readiness the bank has for its responses, such as being properly prepared in the branches for customer inquiries. What the products are and who is to be called are minimums. It is essential to have specialized personnel available, if the bank is to handle this step, along with adequate telephone lines or meeting time and space. Capturing customer data in the beginning can also be of great benefit both in learning more about who does business and in building information for cross-selling other products and services. Using a microcomputer to build a data base on inquiries, prospects, leads, referrals, along with customer typing by net worth, income, product holdings, other relationships, and branch nearest to them are only some of the possibilities. After all is said and done the basic tenet, "Know Your Customers," will be the most important point to remember—from protection and opportunity standpoints. Finally, to the extent that the bank is heavily involved, a sales force for these products must be recruited, trained, and readied—a major task of its own.

ALTERNATIVES IN ORGANIZATIONAL STRUCTURE

Some surveys of existing bank operations involving discount brokerage and related financial services sales show that the most popular areas to house these activities are either the money market investment area or the retail side of the bank. Certainly the size of the bank and the availability of existing resources go a long way toward determining the best location. Other possibilities include the Trust Department and even the Marketing Department. If the SEC's Rule 3b-9 remains enforced, all banks with the 1,000 trade level effort will likely operate most of their activity out of a broker/dealer affiliate. Banks below that level will attempt to consolidate as much activity as possible, working with a correspondent for much of the support.

Retail

An argument for retail's involvement is that it is retail's customer base that will most likely be involved in these services and their branch personnel who will be actively involved in responding and selling. Further, retail customer lists will be prime opportunities for sales. In fact, all of this will come together particularly well in a personal banking environment. Because of the necessary involvement of retail, the support and backing of retail's senior management is ever so critical. Without this support, sales cannot reach their optimum levels. While each bank will have different strengths, to effectively carry out its involvement, retail must have the experience, product knowledge, and capacity to meet regulatory requirements. For banks of a certain size where investment expertise is gathered in one area, these three ingredients will not likely be found in retail. For smaller banks, the selling capability of retail combined with the expertise provided by a correspondent may make this the appropriate area for some aspects of the program.

Trust Department

In some banks, the discount brokerage function falls in the trust area. Banks may attempt to combine the order execution expertise of trust investments with the discount brokerage order execution to gain efficiencies and volume. While the execution and volume benefits can be real, the trust involvement must not take the activity away from the bank's normal customer flow. Whether in or out of trust, orders for trust agency accounts can give volume benefit to the brokerage department. Whether the benefit of increased volume for brokerage will offset any loss of soft-dollar trust benefit (e.g., research) must be answered by management.

Investments

For most banks, the investment area offers product expertise that most closely aligns with these nondeposit fee-based products. The key to the alignment of a particular bank may be the size of the investment staff and the scope of their responsibility. An existing dealer operation should have no difficulty taking on additional responsibilities relating to the products we have discussed. In fact, regulatory reasons may dictate that the assignment be given to the investment area, particularly if a broker/dealer affiliate exists. Smaller banks, however, may have only one or a few dedicated to the investment needs of the bank and not have a marketing emphasis with this effort. The absence of marketing thinking and coordination with the bank's contact officers might make the fit inappropriate.

Product Management

Taking on one or more of the products discussed requires a great deal of research and ongoing support. While the day-to-day managing of the product will likely be handled in one of the areas immediately above, the support may best come from the bank's marketing area or its product management area, if one exists. Training, product enhancements and updates, product profitability, promotion, introductions, and referral tracking can all come together in a product management view.

As mentioned, no one area is right for every bank. Moreover, many areas may be involved in optimizing the effort. It is important to define each area's responsibility from the top so that confusion and conflict do not grow. The time to do this is when the product is first considered or while the effort is still small. As products, markets, and organizations evolve, change may be needed and responsibilities can then be redefined. Procedures, job descriptions, and responsibility definitions should be addressed up front.

CONCLUSION

Traditional sources of revenue must be supplemented by nondeposit, retail-oriented services for today's bank to survive and prosper. Competition from other financial companies, including those in the insurance and brokerage industries, coupled with an increasingly sophisticated customer base, make it apparent that this gradual shift toward other investment products will continue in the future.

For the large banking institution, the cost of hiring and maintaining a staff of investment professionals in-house should be exceeded by income received from sales of additional investment products. The offering of such products by the "supermarket" bank will enable the institution to maintain and possibly increase the percentage of customer assets placed therein. The high cost of in-house investment specialists makes it difficult, however, for many smaller to medium-sized banks to compete in today's more demanding financial environment. A thorough examination of these costs is necessary before entering many of these nontraditional markets. Serious consideration of networking arrangements through third-party vendors with highly trained investment professionals should be given.

Today, many financial institutions enjoy arrangements of offering brokerage services to their customers. Several vendors who offer these services to banks share marketing costs in addition to attractive commission splits. Start-up costs are minimal, as labor and equipment expenses are borne by the broker/dealer vendor supplying the services. It is possible to offer mutual funds, fixed-income, and precious metals services along with stock execution services. The selection of a broker/dealer to service the user bank's customer base should not be taken lightly. It is critical that any organization considered have a thorough understanding of the importance of giving its user bank customers a high level of personal service. Insensitivity to the customer can damage a lot more than a brokerage account and all other relationships at the subscribing bank can be placed at jeopardy as well. It is also important that all parties agree that the broker/dealer servicing the bank's customer base cannot solicit these clients for its own purposes.

Today's banking institution has seen dramatic changes since the mid-1970s. The novelty of banks offering discount brokerage services to their customer base has been replaced with a certainty that banks today and in the future will become total financial supermarkets, offering the investor the gamut of investment products and services. The challenges facing today's banking institutions are many, but so are the potential rewards.

PART ELEVEN

Wholesale Banking

CHAPTER SIXTY-THREE

Organizing and Managing the Wholesale Banking Function

Richard H. Snelsire

Group Vice President
First Wachovia Corporate Services

INTRODUCTION

The financial needs of corporate businesses vary dramatically. A large multinational company may require many sophisticated banking services, while a small local company may need only a single checking account. Few banks can adequately provide the complete banking needs for every corporation located within their particular trade areas. However, the basic principles for managing the wholesale banking business are similar, and a properly organized and managed wholesale business function will be a significant profit contributor to a bank of any size. In recent years increased competition, sophistication of corporate clients, and overall profit pressures resulting from deregulation have forced banks to become more professional in managing the wholesale banking segment of their customer base. These customers include any business or nonprofit institution—foreign or domestic—that requires one or more financial services offered by the banking industry. Banks have had to reevaluate methods they use to obtain and service these accounts as well as how they manage staff, markets, and products.

In the 1970s, interest rates rose to extremely high levels, causing the implicit costs of banking services to increase dramatically. As these costs rose, a heavier emphasis was placed on employing cash management techniques to ensure the maximum benefits from the companies' natural cash flow cycles. These techniques were employed first by large businesses and later by middle-sized businesses. With more money available from a more closely managed cash management system, companies began to hire more sophisticated individuals to work within their treasury functions to maximize the efficiency of their cash management programs. This caused a negative profit impact on the banking industry.

As banks began to look for ways to expand relationships to offset profit declines, they realized that they would need a different set of skills in their corporate banking officers. Previously, the ability to analyze financial risk was not only the predominant criterion but often was the only evaluation banks used when hiring corporate banking officers. Training included extensive time working through credit risk analysis in a credit department before being given a commercial banking assignment. Banks now are realizing the need to balance this important skill with other skills such as the individual's ability to perform needs analysis on more financial services and to sell services in a more competitive market. Because of the change in the market and the skills level needed to service the market, the need for professional management of the wholesale banking function has increased.

Unlike the consumer market where an adequate branch system, effective advertising, and good product line usually can create enough market demand to provide an adequate profit, accountability for each individual customer and prospect is the keystone to effectively managing the wholesale banking function. Individual account assignments may be accomplished through different organizational structures, which usually are determined based on the bank's size and its particular market. However, accountability remains a constant and key factor.

The remainder of this chapter will address how to assign accountability within various organizational structures and how accountability relates to the managing of the wholesale banking function through human resource management, market management, and product management.

ORGANIZATIONAL STRUCTURES

Most banks organize the wholesale banking function in one of the following ways. Corporate accounts may be assigned based on geographic location. For example, a corporate accounts officer would be assigned a specific geographic area, and the customer and prospect base would include all businesses located within that particular area. These geographic areas could be as large as states, when the bank has a national marketing effort, or small geographic areas within the communities where the bank is located. An advantage of assigning accounts on a geographic basis is that the area can be clearly defined and accountability easily communicated throughout all departments of the bank. The disadvantage is that a given geographic area will have businesses of all sizes and industry classifications, requiring the corporate officer to have the ability to service the banking needs of a very broad range of customers. Banks often use a geographic organization to service customers outside their immediate market and another organizational structure to service companies within markets where the bank has a physical presence.

Many larger commercial banks use specific industry groupings to assign customers and prospects to a corporate account officer. This approach allows the account officer to develop an expertise on a particular industry, its needs and its inherent risks, which makes it possible to serve both the industry and the bank better. One drawback to this structure is the substantially higher selling and administrative cost that results from the geographical dispersion of the industry specialist's clients. In addition, banks with limited corporate staff must assign the corporate officer too many industries, a move that can substantially dilute the officer's expertise in any one industry.

Banks often assign clients to account officers based upon the sales or asset size of the customer or prospect. This method of organizing is particularly effective in large metropolitan areas. The bank can assign individual accounts by size and train account officers based on the financial needs of companies within that size category.

The number of banks that assign corporate accounts by product line rather than corporate relationship is growing. This type of account assignment is often prevalent in smaller banks where a commercial account officer administers the credit needs of a corporate client while noncredit needs are assigned to other bank officers. Product line account management gives the product specialist a better understanding of particular products, how to install the products, and the nature of the competition. Product specialists sell directly to the company with some coordination with other product specialists. Potential problems arise if the communication and coordination efforts break down. Often the corporate client is besieged by many people from a single bank, each attempting to sell a particular line of services. Frequently the overall relationship suffers. Some banks have minimized this problem by assigning a team to each corporate client. Individual accounts are assigned to a group of product specialists with a lead coordinator, usually the commercial loan officer, to coordinate the relationship. This method can be very effective, but it is more expensive to implement.

Each of the organizational structures outlined have strengths and weaknesses but the primary consideration when organizing a wholesale banking function is to determine which structure best fits a bank's corporate culture, management style, and market potential. Once an organizational structure has been established, refinements can be achieved through human resource management, market management, and product management.

HUMAN RESOURCE MANAGEMENT

The quality of corporate account officers is key to any corporate business function. Five general issues—recruiting, training, measurement systems, compensation, and career path development—should be addressed in order to have an effective corporate human resource program. Recruiting quality individuals to serve as corporate banking officers is critical. Recruiting programs should be planned and proactive rather than reactive. Corporate bank management should identify the technical and interpersonal skills it requires and communicate the criteria to the individuals responsible for hiring. Commercial account officers should be hired directly for a corporate assignment rather than being selected from a general pool of new employees. The two best sources for corporate account officers are: first, an aggressive recruiting program specifically for corporate trainees who come from colleges and universities within the bank's market area. The bank needs to communicate to college placement officers and faculties the criteria it requires for new corporate employees, and it needs to gain their confidence that the bank will be a good place of employment for their graduates. A second source is from within the bank itself. Candidates might have been hired for other jobs and been successful in those jobs, but demonstrate the skills needed to make them an effective corporate account officer. These individuals' career progress should be monitored and, when appropriate, they should be transferred into the corporate function.

Once potential corporate account officers have been identified, training becomes the next issue. The training should be based on the organizational structure and on the goals and objectives established by management for the calling officers. For example, if the account officer is being held responsible exclusively for marketing and monitoring commercial loans, it is only necessary to provide credit training. However, if responsibility is for selling and servicing the full product line of the bank, the training should be on all products being offered to the commercial market. Training can be either internal or external, depending on which approach is most cost effective. Many large banks have internal training programs that address the full needs of a corporate banker and often are willing to provide training to other bankers on a fee basis. In addition, trade associations offer excellent training seminars on a wide range of financial subjects. Banks should identify the specific skills they want account officers to have and then develop a training program that blends internal and external sources.

Information and measurement systems are also important elements in human resource management in wholesale banking. Central information systems can monitor and measure the overall profitability of a corporate account and the effectiveness of the account officer assigned to that account. Usually these systems consolidate and report data on all relevant demand deposit, time deposit, and trust accounts, as well as commercial loans and commitments. The system should have detailed account information for the current month and the year to date for comparative purposes. Such a system assists the account officer in properly managing assigned accounts and aids the manager in evaluating the account officer's success in expanding relationships and developing new ones.

For many years, commercial account officers have been compensated primarily through salary. In recent years, some banks have installed incentive compensation programs. Banks have used incentive compensation programs to develop new business on both a product line and total relationship basis. Properly administered incentive compensation programs can be effective; however, history has proven that incentive compensation will not replace good management and that it can create inordinately high risks if not established with adequate controls.

Career path counseling is important in the overall human resource management of commercial account officers. Proper counseling and motivation can keep account officers motivated, productive, and satisfied and can reduce the incidence of turnover. Corporate clients do not like frequent changes in the account officers assigned to service their accounts. Turnover has been cited in many market research surveys as a primary reason for dissatisfaction with a bank's corporate banking effort. Therefore, the manager of a wholesale business function must continually communicate to account officers the existence of future opportunities within the department and the overall corporate banking organization.

In summary, the primary goal in human resource management for the wholesale banking manager is to hire, train, and retain qualified individuals. Once the manager achieves this goal, the market and product management aspects of the wholesale business can be addressed.

MARKET MANAGEMENT

A corporate banking manager should have a general understanding of all wholesale banking markets and the needs of companies in those markets. Size is a major factor in an individual bank's ability to service each market effectively, but an understanding of the market dynamics for each market is important in managing the wholesale banking function. The three major wholesale market segments are the large corporate market, including companies with sales in excess of $250 million; the middle market, companies with sales between $20 million and $250 million; and the commercial market, companies with sales up to $20 million. Market dynamics for each of these segments differ to some degree.

The large corporate market includes the major multinational companies that have many banking relationships and often require complex banking services. These companies employ financial professionals who are sensitive to both price and product differential when selecting banking services. In recent years, the number of banks servicing this market has been declining as companies have consolidated their banking relationships with fewer banks. This makes it essential for a bank servicing this market to become more adept at cross-selling its full line of services, to accept greater commitments of credit, and to provide a fuller range of noncredit services. Otherwise, the bank will be eliminated from the company's bank picture. Since this market is redistributing and consolidating its banking services, it is an extremely difficult market for a new bank to penetrate.

The middle market is an attractive market for expanded banking services. Instead of consolidating relationships, companies in this market have been adding banks, often because their growth has created a need for expertise in service areas not available from their current banks. In addition, credit services are relatively more important to this market than to the large corporate market. And, since interest margins have not eroded to the same degree, credit services generally are among the more profitable services offered. Often banks offer imaginative credit or noncredit services as a means of differentiating themselves to obtain increased market share. Many large banks are beginning to focus on the middle market to offset market share losses they are incurring in the large corporate market. Because of this, competition is becoming more intense, and this market is being exposed continuously to a wide range of services by banks located outside the company's traditional market.

The commercial market's larger companies ($10 million to $20 million in sales) can be characterized as companies where the primary financial officer has a strong accounting background and possibly is an individual from an outside accounting firm. In the smaller companies ($10 million or less in sales), the owner/manager makes the banking decisions. For the most part, the commercial market is more credit-driven than larger markets and does not use a broad range of financial services. These companies usually have one primary bank and are not as receptive to changing banking relationships as are larger companies.

Banks usually manage their approach to these broad markets through an organizational structure that either segments business acquisition from account management or emphasizes total relationship or transaction management. In order to address market management, these structures need to be examined. First, management should determine if it is desirable to separate its business development effort from its account management effort. Many banks have been successful in assigning individuals exclusively to business development. These individuals have good sales skills and often have little interest in account maintenance. One value of business development officers is to ensure that the business development function receives proper attention within the financial institution. When the business development officer obtains a new account, it is usually assigned to an account manager who services the account. These individuals should be well-rounded bankers who are carefully directed to solicit the types of business that the financial institution wants to have and can service when it's in the bank.

Many banks differentiate between relationship management and transaction management when servicing accounts. Relationship management is a concept in which account responsibility is assigned to one officer who has the authority and responsibility to make decisions regarding that relationship within the policies and regulations of the bank. In carrying out this role, the relationship manager operates as the focal point to orchestrate the entire development and maintenance of a commercial relationship. Specific responsibilities include:

1. Monitoring the status of each account.
   a. Reviewing corporate information reports.
   b. Knowing the total account relationship.
   c. Reviewing credit risk and usage.
   d. Noting changes in services used.
   e. Reviewing the industry and company's position within that industry.
2. Maintaining each relationship and ensuring its profitability and worth.
   a. Developing rapport with key company officers.
   b. Introducing other officers into the relationship for technical assistance.
   c. Ensuring that the customer receives proper service.
   d. Functioning as the primary lending officer.
3. Developing and expanding each relationship.
   a. Identifying company needs and establishing and implementing a marketing plan to satisfy those needs.

    b. Keeping current on the financial institution's full line of services and presenting them effectively to the company.

    c. Coordinating and monitoring the solicitation and servicing efforts of the product managers.

The value of the relationship management concept is that accountability for the profitable maintenance and expansion of each relationship is clearly assigned. Everyone within the bank knows who to contact concerning any issue that develops with the company. Relationship management is an extremely effective method of organization if the relationship manager is properly trained in the skills and service lines to perform the job effectively and if account officer turnover can be kept to a minimum. Inadequate training or high turnover can debilitate a relationship management program.

Transaction management is a concept in which individuals have accountability for individual product lines and in which client profitability is measured on the profit margin of individual transactions. More than one contact officer services the same company, each with a particular expertise to offer the company. The advantages of such a system are that it allows customer contact personnel to specialize and become expert in a few products and to ensure that each individual transaction is profitable to the bank. However, if not properly coordinated transaction management often creates problems with a customer who questions whether it is his long-term benefit or the bank's individual transactions profitability that is at the base of the bank's solicitation.

Whichever market management system is used, many banks are installing a business development concept called targeted market selection. This concept, while rather simplistic, is very effective at managing the corporate account officer and properly directing efforts toward companies that best meet the financial institution's standards for soundness, profitability, and growth. Targeted market selection includes identifying specific companies the financial institution wishes to do business with and determining how the bank can obtain that business. It begins by establishing a list of companies located within the specific market (geographic, industry, market size, etc.) and qualifying them for potential business risk and profitability. After qualifying is completed, the companies are classified as to their potential as a client. This classification process focuses on the needs of the company, its industry, and its current banking relationships. It requires the corporate account officer to determine which services will satisfy the company's explicit and implicit needs. Once classifications are established, an account plan is developed indicating what business the bank wishes to obtain, whether any bank currently has the business, and how the account officer plans to obtain the business. The individual account plan is an excellent document to measure against call reports to ensure that the account officer is effectively implementing the plan. This systematic approach allows the manager and the account officers to focus on companies that have been preselected to meet the bank's standards as desirable customers.

In summary, market management requires the corporate banking manager first to determine the unique market dynamics of the markets to be serviced and then to structure a marketing effort that most effectively penetrates these markets. This can be done through organizational structures like relationship management or transaction management, and a systematic approach to targeting specific companies to solicit within each market.

PRODUCT MANAGEMENT

The final issue in organizing and managing the wholesale banking function is the development of effective product management. The assignment of accountability and responsibility for the development, maintenance, and enhancement of each product offered by the financial institution is important in any effective wholesale banking organization. In large banks, products can be assigned to individual product managers whose full-time job includes these responsibilities; in smaller banks, the accountability can be one task assigned to an individual with broader responsibilities. In either case, product responsibility is assigned to one officer who coordinates the production and marketing of assigned products, monitors service quality and pricing, and collects and evaluates competitive information. The officer's primary objective is to increase volumes, market share, and product profitability of the products that are assigned. In carrying out these responsibilities, the product manager should:

1. Prepare and monitor the implementation of annual product plans.
2. Recommend pricing action and monitor competitive pricing.
3. Monitor sales advertising and other promotional efforts of the product line.
4. Resolve any service delivery or quality problems of the services assigned.
5. Serve as a focal point for all product information on the assigned products.
6. Assist the account officers in selling and servicing products as needed.

Product development within any effective wholesale banking function does not always begin with the product manager. In most cases, the corporate account officers first will identify needs of corporate customers and submit those needs to the product manager for review and evaluation. The product manager must decide if the multitude of corporate needs identified by the account officer can be converted into profitable services. The product manager then coordinates the development of those services that can satisfy corporate customer needs at a profit to the bank.

SUMMARY

As competition in banking intensifies, proper organization and management of the wholesale banking business become imperative to the financial institution that plans to effectively serve this market. Initially a bank should determine which segments of the market it can best serve and install the organizational structure that best fits the markets, its corporate culture, and its management style. Once the organizational structure has been completed, the key elements in an effective wholesale banking program are an effective human resource management program, market management program, and product management program.

CHAPTER SIXTY-FOUR

New Products in Financial Services

Andre A. Cappon

Partner,
Oliver, Wyman & Co.

Walter A. Diaz

Principal,
Booz Allen & Hamilton, Inc.

In recent years, the financial services industry has undergone dramatic change. The most obvious indicator of this change is the flood of new products it has generated. Consider the following illustrative list of prominent products, which, as of this writing, can be considered new or recent.

New Products Examples

Retail products	Wholesale products
CMA type account	Interest rate swaps
Money market funds/accounts	Financial futures/options
ATMs/debit cards	Floating rate notes
Adjustable rate mortgages	Financial guarantees
Home-equity secured credit lines	Zero-coupon bonds
Premium credit cards	Collateralized mortgage
Discount brokerage	obligations (CMO's)
New types of mutual funds	Bond portfolio immunization
(tax-exempt bond funds,	Multicurrency securities
GNMA funds, international funds)	Index funds
IRAs/Keoghs/401K	

While many industries are characterized by an abundance of new products, it is the magnitude of their impact that is surprising in the financial services. Many of the above products have replaced the very

961

core of traditional banking products (money market accounts, adjustable rate mortgages, etc.). All generate significant revenues and are associated with substantial changes in their relevant marketplaces—that is, changes in the process of intermediation of capital. Customers have come to expect all of these products, and it would be difficult to imagine financial institutions that did not offer all of them.

The importance of these new products in the financial services industry is thus clear, and it is equally evident that each significant competitor in the industry must pay active attention to the process of developing and introducing new products in order to maintain its competitive position and customer relationships.

The innovation and new product development process in financial services is very different from that in most other industries because of the specific characteristics of financial services:

Financial Services Are Highly Affected by Changes in Government Regulation, Tax, and Accounting Rules. Regulation has traditionally shaped and defined most financial products and often constrained their pricing. Accordingly, much if not most significant financial innovation is driven by regulatory changes. Examples are the money market accounts, discount brokerage offered by banks, and so on.

Beyond government's regulation, changes in tax and accounting are important drivers of innovation in financial products, especially on the wholesale side. Examples are leasing, industrial revenue bonds, etc.

The implication is that innovation is often driven by exogenous forces that affect the entire industry simultaneously. While these innovations can be tailored to an institution's unique marketing strategy and positioning, the fundamental direction of change is often beyond the control of individual competitors.

Financial Services Industries Are Highly Dependent on Macroeconomic Trends, Particularly Interest Rates. While this is an obvious fact, it is worth noting the large number of financial innovations that were spawned by the volatile interest rates and inflation trends in the late 70s early 80s: swaps, money market accounts, FRNs, zero-coupon bonds, adjustable-rate mortgages, etc. Economic trends such as interest rates, credit conditions, and overall growth will continue to drive the development of new financial products.

Again, the fundamental drivers of innovation are beyond the control of individual financial services competitors. While unique new product strategies can be developed to capitalize on economic change, they are by necessity reactive, not proactive.

The Financial Services Industry Is a Mature Industry. Financial services—commercial and investment banking and related businesses—

have been around for centuries in a form not too different from today. The fundamental financial needs of individuals and organizations have been well understood, and the ways to serve these needs have been devised gradually over time.

This implies that innovations in financial services have tended to be more evolutionary than revolutionary. It also implies that many new products will result from resegmentation or redefinition of existing markets. For example, premium T&E and credit cards are fundamentally the same financial product as ordinary cards except that they are designed and tailored for an upscale clientele. Similarly, the various new types of mutual funds that have come into existence lately are attempts to address specific customer groups with homogeneous investment preferences.

Financial Products Are Easily Imitated.   There is little in the way of proprietary products or proprietary technology in financial services. Once a product has been launched, there is generally sufficient public information for competitors to develop a similar product. For new products where a particular knowledge base is the differentiating factor, the expertise can be hired away or developed (e.g., many investment banking products). Even new technology in financial services, which generally means systems technology, can be (relatively) easily obtained by competitors.

This implies that the diffusion of innovation is relatively rapid in financial services and that, while new products will usually provide some competitive advantage and superior returns to the pioneers, this advantage is unlikely to last.

The Introduction of New Financial Products Is Often Expensive and Risky.   The introduction of new products in any industry obviously entails significant costs: In financial services, some of these costs are greater than expected:

- The need to *"reeducate"* customers. There is often considerable inertia in customer behavior regarding financial matters.
- The need to *reeducate the sales force.* The sale of financial products is generally a complex, consultative type of sale that often requires unique skills and experience.

At the same time new product introductions in financial services involve unique risks:

- The *risk of perceived financial instability.* Customers rely on their financial institutions for stability and security first, high returns and value second. Failed new product offerings, particularly those due to unplanned credit or capital losses, can significantly damage this critical perception.

- The *risk of losing valuable customer relationships due to service disruptions.* New product offerings in financial services often involve the disruption of existing operations and existing customer relationships. Customer relationships that are typically long-lived in financial services are perhaps the most valuable asset of financial institutions, and the risk of disrupting them in any way should be evaluated carefully.

These significant costs and risks of product introduction in financial services strongly suggest that only the largest competitors can afford to innovate or pioneer new products.

The Financial Services Industry Is Highly Fragmented. The degree of fragmentation is very high in most financial businesses—there are some 14,000 banks, 4,000 thrifts, and 250 broker dealers in the United States. In each of these markets, there are typically a small number of large competitors and a large number of small and medium-sized firms.

Most of the time, only the largest firms can afford and absorb the costs and risks of significant new product development and introduction. This implies that for most of the other industry participants, "new product development" often means the adoption and introduction of new product concepts developed elsewhere. While the "imitation" strategy may be the only choice for many financial institutions, it can be quite profitable when effectively implemented—as perhaps the example of Japanese manufacturing firms illustrates. The challenge is to be a quick and effective imitator.

New product development in financial industries is therefore quite different from new product development in most other industries. Table 1 summarizes these differences.

There are therefore two valid strategic postures any institution can adopt with respect to new product development: to be an innovator/pioneer or to be an imitator. For either strategy, *the key to successful new product innovation is relative pace.* The importance of rapidity in financial services is very high for the following reasons:

- *Gaining market share in financial services businesses is difficult.* Customers in financial services businesses show considerable "inertia" in their behavior. Relationships are typically long-lived, and customers tend to stay with their lead financial institutions for a long time if the financial institutions provide reasonable service at competitive prices. Other things being equal, gaining market share is tough.

TABLE 1   New Product Development in Financial Services

Industry Characteristic	Impact on New Product Development
Importance of regulation, taxation, and accounting	Innovation often driven by exogeneous forces that affect the entire industry simultaneously. Beyond the control of individual competitors.
Importance of macroeconomic trends	Unique new product strategies are often reactive not proactive. The fundamental direction of innovation is beyond the control of individual competitors.
Mature industry	Most new products are evolutionary rather than revolutionary. Market resegmentation or redefinition is often a key source of new products.
Innovation easily imitated	Rapid diffusion of new products. Competitive advantage and superior returns due to pioneering new products are relatively ephemeral.
High cost/risk of innovation	Only the largest competitors can afford to *innovate* or *pioneer* new products.
Fragmented industry	Most other competitors can capitalize on new product opportunities with a strategy of quick *imitation*.

- *New products offer innovator/pioneers opportunities to gain share with reduced cost and risk.* New products are one of the few opportunities to gain market share without sacrificing price or compromising the risk profile of a financial institution. The value of preempting competitors can be enormous as is evidenced by Merrill Lynch's success with the CMA account. Figure 1 illustrates the substantial penetration advantage (normalized on a "per broker" basis) gained by Merrill. Beyond the specific new product, products innovators offer the perfect excuse to call on new customers and entice them to begin a complete new financial relationship in order to gain access to the new product.
- *Rapid imitation also offers effective imitators substantial share gains.* As noted earlier, new products in financial services can be quickly imitated over time, and their strategic value in gaining share tends to erode. Herein lies the importance of introducing new products early, rather than adopting them late and defensively. Figure 1 again suggests the importance of rapidity in product innovations; Dean Witter's quicker imitation strategy provided it with significant gains over slower imitators.

FIGURE 1   Penetration of CMA-Type Accounts

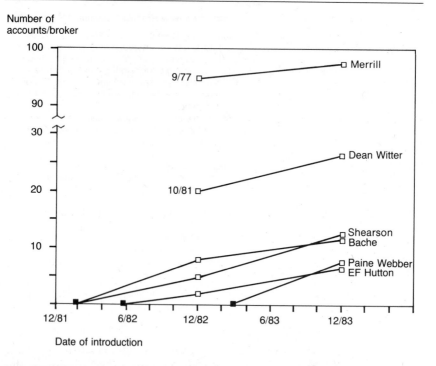

Number of
accounts/broker

NEW PRODUCT DEVELOPMENT PROCESS

Successful new product strategies that achieve rapid innovation with
reasonable cost and risk require the implementation of a structured
new product process. For institutions that wish to be innovators, the
process needs to include a significant emphasis on "basic R&D" to
generate new product concepts. For insititutions that wish to be only
rapid imitators, a simplified verson of the process is usually sufficient.
The diagram in Figure 2 illustrates this process.

Basic R&D

The objective of the R&D process is to generate new product concepts.
There are three types of activities that support this process.

Monitor/Influence Environmental Sources of Change.   As noted above,
most of the time the sources of product innovation in financial services
are beyond the control of any particular competitor. However, each

FIGURE 2   Financial Services: New Product Development Process

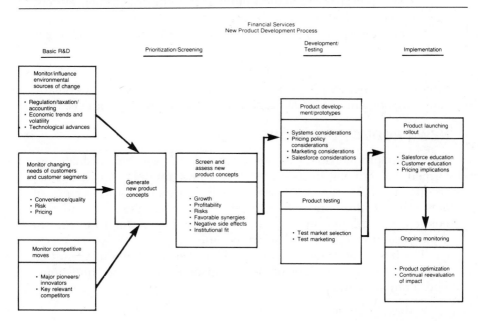

institution *can* and should monitor its environment on a systematic basis to detect early signs of impending changes. The larger and more aggressive players also can attempt to *influence* the process of regulatory, tax, and accounting rule changes.

In addition, larger pioneers/innovators can influence the direction of particular technological innovations that generate new products (e.g., ATMs, service convenience, bundled products, and integrated financial statements; customer information processing for resegmentation).

Monitor Customer Needs.   This is perhaps the single most important step in generating new product ideas. Shifts in customer behavior or needs and redefinition of those needs are a key source of innovation in financial products. Furthermore, monitoring these needs and acting on them is one of the few proactive steps that financial institutions can take.

Several types of activities aid this process:

- *Market research* is often a useful tool for understanding what customers need, how they behave, and how their behavior is likely to change.

- *Customer analysis* ranges from simply listening to customers to systematic analyses of their purchasing patterns, use of products, overall profitability, and resegmentation.
- *Sales force input* is also extremely valuable in gauging changes in customer needs and behavior.

Monitor Competitive Moves. This activity includes the systematic watching of competitors' strategies in the area of new products.

NEW PRODUCT DECISIONS

Once new product ideas are generated, it is necessary to make informed and rational decisions to select new products for actual development. This step is key, since there is usually an abundance of new product ideas but only a tiny minority make practical and economic sense. Identifying the latter early on is important in order to avoid wasted resources and scattered efforts.

The best way to screen new product ideas is to submit them to a rigorous test against a set of preestablished criteria and questions. These might include:

- Market size for the new product.
- Market growth.
- Potential market share that may be captured.
- Profit potential of new product.
- Credit, capital, or institutional risks of new product.
- Resource commitments required for development of new product.
- Favorable synergies between the new product and the existing business.
- Possible negative impacts—for example, cannibalization of existing business.
- Congruence with management style and preferences.
- Customer expectations.
- Impact on institutions image and prestige.

DEVELOPMENT/TESTING

Once the new product concept has been accepted, the phase of actual development and testing begins. The key consideration in the development and testing stage of the product innovation process is to assure rigor and practical reality concerning all of the key considerations related to the product—that is, from detailed systems design considerations to realistic market testing.

PRODUCT DEVELOPMENT/PROTOTYPING

Systems Considerations

Many new products in financial services have significant systems implications. The modifications in computer software that are often needed to support the new products or occasionally the new systems required are a major constraint and problem in implementing new products. Systems development requires long lead times, is expensive, and, more often than not, is beset by unforeseen complications and delays. Devoting attention to the systems issues early in the product prototyping process pays off handsomely.

Pricing new products is a delicate task, particularly in financial services where customers have repeatedly demonstrated their high price sensitivity. Indeed, one must balance several considerations.

- The price must be high enough to make the product profitable and help defray the investment made in developing the product.
- At the same time, the price must be low enough to discourage competitors and to attract early users of the product.

Product innovators often commit an error in pricing by pricing too high in the early phases of the product lifecycle and creating a so-called "price umbrella." With a price umbrella, the new product looks extremely profitable, which practically invites competition. Competitors usually rush in, and soon a situation of overcapacity appears, leading to depressed prices and profits in the later phases of the product lifecycle. In sum, pricing can and should be used as a tool to gain and maintain (early) market share.

Pricing decisions should enter early into the product development/testing process since they will be key drivers of customer acceptance and systems volume requirements. In addition, pricing is a key parameter in determining the ultimate marketing position of the product (e.g., higher price/quality versus lower price/quality).

MARKETING CONSIDERATIONS

As discussed earlier, the fundamental drivers of product innovation are often beyond the control of individual competitors. In addition, the diffusion of fundamentally new products concepts is rapid. This suggests the importance of an institution's efforts to tailor new product introductions to their market positioning strategies. While difficult, any method of differentiating your institution's product should be integrated in the final new product concept and incorporated in product prototypes/market testing.

SALES FORCE IMPLICATIONS

Each sales force has its unique mix of expertise, cultural styles, and experience. New product development efforts must consider these parameters when designing, testing, and implementing new products. New product characteristics must match the unique capacities of each institutions' sales force for effective implementation.

Product Testing

No "laboratory" work can substitute actual live product testing in (as much as possible) controlled conditions. Testing is vital to verify that the product lives up to expectations and to obtain the early feedback necessary to modify it and ensure its success. Test market prototypes should realistically integrate all key considerations noted above. In addition, test markets should ideally be realistic representations of the total customer base but isolated from remaining customers to limit the impact of unsuccessful tests. Lastly, duration of test marketing should be sufficient to measure all favorable and unfavorable side effects of the new product introductions.

IMPLEMENTATION

Product Launching/Roll Out

Launching a new financial product requires thorough preparation of the customer base and the sales force.

Customers have to be educated about the benefits and the use of the new product. The sales force has to be similarly educated about the new product and how to sell it.

Ongoing Monitoring

No matter how well planned, all new product introductions generate unplanned and unforeseen contingencies. Such occurrences should be viewed as opportunities to optimize the final product. If handled appropriately, what may seem like problems can be converted into yet more examples of responsive service.

Finally, it is critical that all new product introductions be continually reevaluated. Growth, profitability, risk, institutional synergies, and side effects must be monitored as the product is rolled out and matures. No new product, no matter how well conceived, should be beyond withdrawal if these screening criteria are not eventually achieved.

ORGANIZATIONAL CONSIDERATIONS

The new product development process described above is fairly generic and applicable to most financial institutions, whether they adopt a strategic posture of innovation or one of rapid imitation. The innovators should devote more systematic effort to the R&D phase of the process, whereas the imitators can rely more on watching the competition.

The organizational structure necessary to support the new product development process should be responsive to the strategic posture. In addition, it should integrate all the critical functional groups necessary for offering the final product successfully to customers—that is, systems, operations, marketing, sales force.

Aggressive, larger, innovative firms generally benefit from having a distinct new product function, responsible for the entire product development process. Since the new products of these institutions are by definition new ideas to the institution, it is often useful for this group to be headed by an individual who is highly integrated in the organization. As a champion of the new product concept his/her skills must be oriented toward effectively selling it first within the organization—often a difficult task within many financial services institutions.

Smaller firms—rapid imitators—can more efficiently respond with a more informal arrangement whereby some individual, often the head of marketing, is assigned part-time responsibility for new products. For imitators, the need for the new product is often quite clear, and the need for an effective internal salesman/champion is reduced.

The organizational arrangements are important, but in the final analysis what matters most is the firm's commitment to respond quickly and effectively to customer needs and the mechanisms and incentives it sets up to achieve this end.

CHAPTER SIXTY-FIVE

Cash Management Services for Business Customers

J. William Murray

Senior Vice President
First National Bank of Maryland

INTRODUCTION

More and more companies are using cash management services in order to maximize the use of their cash resources and to establish control over their banking systems. While larger companies were traditionally the primary users of these services, middle market companies, small businesses, governmental entities, and not-for-profit organizations are now employing them as well. As a result, the importance of cash management services as part of banks' marketing programs has increased significantly.

Larger banks have cash management groups and actively market these services to customers and prospects. Over the years, banks have used them to solidify relationships. Today, cash management services are an important way of generating fee income. Each bank needs to determine the cash management services it will offer with the primary factor being the markets it serves. For smaller and middle market companies credit continues to be the driving force in selecting a bank, with cash management more of a differentiating factor. However, for the Fortune 500 companies, cash management services play a more important role. In fact, if a bank wants to successfully establish a relationship with larger companies, cash management is a must.

CONCEPT OF CASH MANAGEMENT

Cash managment consists of the following functions:

1. Collecting money from customers.
2. Disbursing funds to suppliers, employees, shareholders, etc.

3. Concentrating funds from depository accounts.
4. Monitoring bank relationships.
5. Forecasting cash requirements.
6. Investing surplus funds.
7. Borrowing funds to meet short-term needs.
8. Participating in the management of the Cash Management Time Line (the complete accounting processes of buying, selling, and paying for goods and services).

A variety of banking services are available to assist companies in accomplishing these tasks.

ENVIRONMENT FOR CASH MANAGEMENT SERVICES

While cash management's importance has increased in recent years, its roots can be traced to the mid-1940s. Since this time, it has evolved continually. Important times in the development process are:

- Mid 1940s—wholesale lockbox
- Early 1970s—automated concentration systems
- Early 1970s—automated balance reporting systems
- Mid 1970s—controlled disbursement
- Mid 1980s—treasury workstations
- Mid 1980s—new and expanded ACH services

Cash management needs continue to evolve. Likewise, the services offered by banks will continue to change. Companies want to reduce administrative expenses in the treasury and accounting functions. Technological advances in banks' processing systems and the advent of the microcomputer are redefining cash management services. Changes in Federal Reserve policies and procedures have had major impacts on cash management services. These factors have been largely responsible for the following trends.

1. *Cash management is moving from an emphasis on float management to an emphasis on information management.* Traditionally, most cash management activities have dealt with float management, that is, reducing collection float and increasing disbursement float. While this is still the predominant activity, managing information related to cash is becoming equally important. Consequently, cash management services must provide the corporate cash manager with the necessary information to control and monitor banking activity.

2. *More use of electronic banking services is occurring.* While the check will continue to be the main payment instrument for years to come, innovative services using the Automated Clearinghouse (ACH)

are being developed and utilized. Data transmission of all types of information is on the increase between companies and their banks.

3. *Companies are automating their treasury operations to boost productivity by reducing the manual processing in their offices.* The microcomputer has become a key tool. Its use will increase. Microcomputers will likely become the key communications device between companies and banks and will be used to initiate a variety of transactions with banks. Banks will make their internal data bases accessible to companies via microcomputers.

4. *Companies will continue the movement toward paying for bank services with fees rather than compensating balances.* Banks must accurately cost services, include adequate profit margins in service fees, and charge for all services provided. Additionally, banks must improve their billing and collection procedures.

5. *Companies will decrease demand deposits and move more funds to interest bearing accounts.* Excess balances will decrease. Automatic investment accounts will become an important part of a cash management program.

6. Instead of expanding the number of banking relationships as occurred in the 1960s and 1970s, *companies will consolidate their banking networks and establish "more meaningful" relationships with key banks.* It will be more difficult for banks to establish new relationships with companies.

7. *Institutions other than banks will provide certain cash management services.* More and different players will exist.

8. For many years, the risks associated with cash management services were virtually ignored. Banks were willing to provide services for companies to which they would not lend money. This situation is changing. There are risks associated with providing certain cash managment services. Banks should clearly understand these risks. *Certain services have credit and processing risks that must be evaluated.* It is quite possible that a bank will not provide certain services to a company with a weak credit rating. In addition to prudent management dictating that the risks be considered, various bank regulators are insisting that banks do a better job in this area.

Every bank has a number of cash management services it can offer. The following sections explore the major ones from which a bank can determine what it needs to fulfill the needs of its customers.

COLLECTION SERVICES

The key objective of collection services is to accelerate the funds flow from the customer to the company. Additionally, appropriate information for updating accounts receivable must be provided. The most common collection services are lockbox, pre-authorized payments, and handling over-the counter deposits.

Lockbox.   Lockbox has long been the most important cash management service. With a lockbox, a company directs its customers to send payments to a post office box that is serviced by a bank or another institution. The bank picks up the mail, processes the remittances, deposits the checks, and sends information to the company for posting to accounts receivable.

There are two types of lockboxes—wholesale and retail. A wholesale lockbox is for company-to-company payments. The typical wholesale lockbox has relatively few payments for large dollars, most often in excess of $1,000. A retail lockbox is for individual-to-company payments. It consists of a large number of small dollar payments. To aid in processing, most times the individual is mailed an OCR (Optical Character Recognition) scannable document that is returned with the check payment.

The purpose of a lockbox is to increase a company's working cash by accelerating the collection process. This is done by reducing mail float (the time a check is in the mail), processing float (the time it takes to deposit a check), and availability float (the time it takes to be credited with funds that can be used).

Companies often establish more than one lockbox in different cities to minimize collection time. Lockbox studies are conducted to determine the best locations and to quantify the additional working cash that will be generated from these additional lockbox locations. Sophisticated computer models have been developed for this purpose.

The lockbox business is very competitive. Banks who are major providers have made significant investments in order to differentiate themselves. Major lockbox banks have unique ZIP codes to accelerate mail receipt, process remittances around-the-clock seven days a week, have developed sophisticated capabilities to capture and transmit data, and employ extensive direct send programs to improve their availability schedules.

While much work has been done to automate wholesale lockbox processing, it is still labor intensive. Nevertheless, in the future, more capital investments will be required by banks to remain competitive.

A substantial investment is also required to be competitive in retail lockbox processing. This business is price competitive and banks must automate in order to provide the necessary services in a cost-effective manner. For this reason, few banks have chosen to be active in providing this type of lockbox processing.

Capturing and data transmitting information that can be used to automatically update a company's accounts receivable has become an integral part of lockbox processing. For wholesale lockboxes, the primary information is the MICR line on the check and selected information from accompanying remittance documents such as invoice numbers and amounts. For retail lockboxes, the information is contained in the OCR scan line of the return documents. Lockbox automation has made capturing data easier. The incidence of data capture will increase in the future.

An innovation of the 1980s is the lockbox network. Its premise is to enable a company to achieve the benefits of having multiple lockbox locations and at the same time deal only with a single bank. A single bank coordinates all of the activities of opening accounts, concentrating funds, and providing customer service. There are five types of lockbox networks:

1. Consortium of independent banks—a group of banks provide lockbox services for each others' customers.
2. Multistate processing center—a single bank uses its own processing centers in various cities. Mail is picked up in each city, processed, and checks are deposited into a local correspondent bank.
3. Mail intercept program—mail is picked up at multiple locations and is transported to the bank's main operations center for processing and deposit.
4. Joint venture—a bank contracts with another company to provide lockbox processing in different cities.
5. Multistate holding company—because of its affiliated banks in different cities and states, a holding company is able to offer multiple lockbox points.

Each option has its pros and cons. The acceptance of lockbox networks by companies is still a question.

Preauthorized Collections. Life insurance companies have used preauthorized drafts to collect premiums from policyholders for years. Preauthorized collections may be either a check (preauthorized draft) or an electronic debit (preauthorized debits) through the Automated Clearinghouse (ACH). The trend is toward the use of the ACH. This collection tool is ideal for regular fixed payments from consumers. Such payments as mortgage, car loans, cable TV, insurance premiums, and utility bills are possible applications. Some corporate to corporate applications are slowly beginning to find acceptance.

To utilize this service, the company furnishes its bank with a file containing the information needed to create checks or ACH debits. Typically, the bank requires the file one or two days in advance of settlement date. From this tape, the bank will send debits through the ACH or will create checks and deposit them to the company's account. On settlement date, the company receives funds and the consumers' accounts are debited.

While the trend is toward using ACH entries, not all financial institutions are members of an ACH. Consequently, it is unlikely that 100 percent of the items will be electronic and some checks will need to be printed. A few banks have the capability to receive a single file, automatically determine which items will be ACH debits or checks, and prepare the appropriate instrument. This service is often known as a "switch" product.

Over-the-Counter Deposits.   The nature of some companies' business necessitates physical deposits to a bank. In many ways, this is the simplest form of a deposit, but it can become quite complicated if a bank decides to perform cashier-like functions. Also, high volume of checks and coin and currency being deposited may require that special processing capabilities be developed.

For companies that are able to encode the dollar amounts on checks prior to deposit, banks may want to establish pricing differentials or later deadlines for making deposits. Table top encoders are making it easier for more companies to encode checks. Additionally, some companies are able to sort checks by various drawee banks. Further price breaks may be warranted for this effort.

Some banks provide extensive coin and currency handling functions in conjunction with accepting deposits. Often, they are serving as the company's cashier. They also furnish coin and currency. Some banks contract these services to third parties, usually a company associated with an armored courier. Computerized vault management systems have been developed to aid banks in providing these services. The level of service offered is highly dependent on a bank's market and customer base. Not every bank will want to make the investments needed to be an active provider in this product category.

Availability.   Critical to all depository services is the availability a bank gives on checks deposited with it. Availability is the time after which a company can use its deposits. This typcially is zero to two business days. Most banks publish a schedule detailing what availability they will grant on each check deposited. A small number of banks assign a fixed float factor to all deposits.

Banks compete vigorously with the availability they offer. Rather than clearing all checks through the Federal Reserve system, they implement direct send programs using correspondent banks designed to clear checks faster. This enables them to offer better availability to customers.

DISBURSEMENT SERVICES

A major disbursement objective is to control accounts so that funding occurs as checks are presented to banks for payment. Companies that fund their disbursement accounts early are likely to have excess balances in them. Late funding may result in overdrafts. Additionally, forecasting when checks will clear is a difficult process. The possibility of extending or maximizing disbursement float is also a consideration. A variety of banking techniques are used to meet these disbursement objectives. Depending on whether a company has a decentralized or centralized disbursement system, different combinations of services will be used.

Controlled Disbursement.   The most difficult task in managing disbursement accounts is determining when checks will be charged to an account. While elaborate cash forecasting programs can be developed, they are all less than prefect. Controlled disbursing is a technique that allows a company to fund its disbursement account as checks clear against its bank.

   With controlled disbursing, a bank is able to notify its customers in the morning (usually by 10 A.M. of the total dollar amount of checks that will be presented against the account that day. Thus, the forecasting problem is significantly reduced, and idle funds are eliminated. The dollar totals are made available for access through a bank's information system or are reported by telephone to the company. The company then funds the controlled disbursement account by wire transfer or through some other arrangement made with its bank. Some banks allow their customers to fund accounts with depository transfer checks or through the ACH. Others have established lines of credit. Special caution needs to be taken with any of these latter techniques since they create risk for the disbursing bank.

   The typical controlled disbursement point is a bank, processing center of a bank, or bank branch that can be isolated so that it receives its checks presented for payment early in the morning. Most often this is a RCPC or country routing transit number. For many years, a bank's controlled point received only one presentation of checks early in the morning. However, because Federal Reserve programs designed to accelerate the collection of checks, most banks that offer controlled disbursement now receive a second presentation mid-morning. While most of the checks are still in the first presentation, a second notification to customers is now required for these controlled disbursing points. Banks compete vigorously to have the earliest reporting times. The Federal Reserve has developed payor bank services that banks may choose to use in developing totals for customer notification.

Controlled disbursement is most often used for general payable accounts. While some companies use it for payroll applications, others are very concerned that their employees may have a difficult time cashing these checks and, consequently, will not use it. There does not seem to be a clear concensus one way or another.

Some companies try to extend disbursement float by selecting disbursing locations where the checks take longer to clear. Computer models have been developed to determine the most effective disbursing locations for a company given its suppliers' depository banks. The Federal Reserve has looked with disfavor on the practice of using remote disbursing locations.

Zero Balance Accounts (ZBA). ZBAs are used by companies to minimize idle funds in a bank. A ZBA system is within one bank and consists of a master account and a number of subaccounts. Daily, after all debits and credits have been posted to an account, funds are automatically transferred to or from the master account to bring the subaccounts back to a zero balance. Better control over accounts is established. Funding of accounts can be made easier. A cash manager needs only to monitor the balances in the master account.

Payable Through Drafts (PTDs). Payable Through Drafts are payment instruments drawn on a company rather than a bank. The bank acts as a clearing agent, receiving the drafts and presenting them to the company for review and payment. Typically, banks present PTDs the morning after they have received them. However, some banks can present PTDs the same day as received. Depending on when a company receives the drafts, it will have from a few hours to 24 hours to complete the verification process and return to the bank any items it does not wish to pay.

The usage of PTDs has declined. The most common user of them is a company that has a large number of authorized signers in many locations and wants to review the items before they are paid. Insurance companies are good examples. In most cases, there is no advantage for a company to use PTDs over checks.

Account Reconciliation Program (ARP). ARP services are designed to aid companies in reconciling their checking accounts. They are based on having the check number in the MICR line. The most common services are as follows:

1. Sort only—checks are sorted in numerical order.
2. Partial reconciliation—bank provides a listing of all checks paid in numerical order. This information may also be provided on

a magnetic tape for direct entry into a company's reconciliation system.

3. Full reconciliation—bank provides a listing of all checks paid and a listing of check number and amounts issued but still outstanding both in numerical order. The company provides the bank with all the checks issued usually via magnetic tape.

Which service is the best for a company is highly dependent on the number of checks it writes.

ACH SERVICES

A variety of collection and disbursement services using the ACH payment mechanism are offered by banks. While ACH volume is only a small percentage of check volume, it is increasing. Companies are becoming more aware of how using the ACH can improve their cash management systems.

Three forces are driving this movement. First, there is a desire to reduce a company's administrative expenses. The ACH offers numerous opportunities to reduce expenses related to payroll, accounts payable, accounts receivable, general accounting functions, and even inventory control. Second, with the value of disbursement float decreasing, a major objection to the use of the ACH is becoming less important. Certainly, no company wants to give away its float advantages. However, by negotiating settlement dates, float becomes a moot point. Third, as bank prices for cash management services continue to increase, companies are looking for lower cost alternatives. The ACH provides opportunities to reduce banking expenses.

Direct Deposit Service.   The most common ACH disbursement service is direct deposit of payroll. With this service, a company sends/transmits information in the ACH format to its bank, usually two or three days before the payday. Contained on the file are the banks, bank accounts, and amounts to be credited for the employees participating in the program. The originating bank distributes this information through the ACH network. Employee accounts are credited on payday, and the company's account is debited on the same day.

Direct deposit has been used most heavily by the salaried and white-collar employees in a company. Usage by more diverse groups is on the increase. The United States Treasury has been an important force in increasing this activity with its social security direct deposit programs. Companies are also beginning to use direct deposit for disbursing pensions, annuities, commissions, and even dividends.

All of these programs require a sales program to generate participation. Since it is unlikely that all eligible people will participate in the program, a company will need both a check and direct deposit payment option. Some banks offer retail banking packages to employees in order to increase participation and generate new retail business.

Corporate to Corporate Payments. A key feature with corporate to corporate ACH services is the information component. The ability to pass increasing amounts of data concerning a payment opens up the possibility for banks to develop innovative services which meet specific company needs. For example, companies generally do not want their accounts to be directly debited by a vendor or service provider. However, a company might be willing to let its account be debited provided it has proper financial incentives, timely notification from its bank concerning the amount of the debt, who is making it and its purposes, and adequate time to review payments for acceptability. Banks have developed this service—Electronic Controlled Disbursement—to overcome the objections, and are successfully marketing it.

Similarly on the receipt side, banks must be able to notify their customers of ACH receipts on a same day basis. Since these funds are immediately available, a company loses one day of funds availability if it is not notified until the day after the transaction has posted. This is not acceptable in the corporate market.

Some companies have implemented successful corporate to corporate direct debit programs. According to payment terms, ACH debits are used to collect payments from customers. These systems work best when the customer is in a captive or semicaptive environment such as distributors, franchisees, or dealers.

Given the concern about direct debiting of accounts, services are being developed that place the control of the debit back into the customer's hands. On due date, the customer makes a telephone call or inputs information through a terminal or personal computer indicating the amount to be paid and the invoices being paid. At the end of the day, the information is gathered and ACH debits are originated to draw down the funds. The accounts receivable information is data transmitted to the company for direct application to the accounts receivable file. In effect, this is an electronic lockbox.

Some companies want to use the ACH to make payments but are not able to make the necessary changes to their accounts payable systems. In order to allow this, ACH programs that run on personal computers are being developed. A company can enter all the necessary information and then transmit it to the bank for processing. These systems are good for low volumes. They allow companies the opportunity to benefit from ACH use. More and more banks will offer this type of product in the future.

It is important for a company to determine whether it will be an originator or receiver of ACH transactions. For most companies, it is easier to be a receiver than an originator. To be an originator, companies must make changes to accounts payable systems in order to generate ACH formatted tapes. This could be a major project. As far as being a receiver is concerned, a bank should be able to receive the ACH transactions and convert them to a format for direct input into a company's accounts receivable systems. From a bank's perspective, it is much easier to provide services for a company that is an originator rather than a receiver. Banks need to develop more capabilities to be effective receivers of ACH transactions.

ACH Standard Entry Classes.   When one considers ACH products it is important to have an understanding of the various standard entry classes used for ACH payments. These classes determine the rules and regulations governing ACH payments. For corporate services, the most commonly used classes are as follows:

- PPD—Prearranged Payments and Deposits
- CCD—Cash Concentration and Disbursement
- CTP—Corporate Trade Payment
- CTX—Corporate Trade Exchange

PPD transactions are those between an individual and a corporation. They are governed by Regulation E of the Federal Reserve System. The most common examples of these transactions are direct deposit of payroll and preauthorized debits for insurance payments.

CCD, CTP, and CTX are the transaction classes used for corporate to corporate payments. They are governed by the National Automated Clearinghouse Association (NACHA) corporate to corporate payment rules. Cash concentration and various collection and disbursement services use these classes. Each of these classes has a format that allows information concerning the payment to be passed along with the payment. Which class is used depends on the application and the information requirements of the companies involved.

All ACH participating banks must accept PPD and CCD transactions. Not all banks have the capability to accept CTPs and CTXs. Consequently, the growth of services using these formats has been limited. In the future, it is likely that more banks will develop the necessary capabilities because of the information transfer possibilities they offer.

In summary, ACH services will continue to evolve. They will be used to solve companies' cash management problems. Innovative thinkers in banks and companies will continually look for new product offerings. The ACH is rapidly becoming a viable and accepted payment system alternative.

CONCENTRATION SERVICES

Concentration services are used by companies to move funds from depository accounts to centralized accounts. A good concentration system is essential to an effective cash management system. With it, control over a banking system is enhanced, excess balances in outlying accounts are reduced, and a pool of funds is made available for corporate use.

There are basically two types of banking networks for which concentration services are used: field banking and lockbox banking. Field banking networks consist of a number of local depository accounts into which company personnel make deposits. Lockbox banking networks are associated with lockbox processing. Each network requires different mixtures of concentration services. The most commonly used methods are Depository Transfer Checks (DTCs), Electronic Depository Transfer (EDTs), Wire Transfers, and Deposit Reconciliation Programs (DRPs)—also known as Branch Consolidation Services.

Depository Transfer Check (DTC). A DTC is a check with a restricted payee and requires no signature. It is used in two ways. The person making the local deposit fills in the dollar amount of the deposit and mails it to the concentration bank, which deposits it. The check clears back through the banking system and is debited against the depository account. The second and more commonly used method is for the person making the deposit to notify the concentration bank of the amount via telephone or data terminal. The concentration bank creates a DTC, deposits it, and clears the check. In both cases, available funds are granted according to a bank's availability schedule. Systems are structured so that most DTCs become available in one day or less.

There are several ways in which the concentration bank can be notified: (1) calls may be made to one of several firms that specialize in gathering information from depository units; (2) calls may be made directly to a company's headquarters; (3) a company's internal Point of Sale (POS) system may be used to gather the information; (4) calls are made directly to a concentration bank. In each case, the depository amounts are gathered, consolidated, and relayed to the concentration bank.

Electronic Depository Transfers (EDTs). EDTs are the electronic equivalent of a DTC. These transactions are cleared through the ACH network. Information for originating EDTs is gathered in the same fashion as with DTCs. The concentration bank prepares an ACH tape and sends the entries to the ACH for clearing. All EDTs become available funds one day after origination. Companies are switching from DTCs to EDTs because they are less expensive and they are all available in one day.

Wire Transfers. With a wire transfer, an authorized individual gives a bank instructions to transfer funds from a depository account to a concentration account. At times, there is a standing order for a transfer giving the depository bank instructions to automatically transfer funds to the concentration bank based on some formula.

Wire transfers are the fastest method of moving funds. However, they are more expensive than other means of concentrating funds. Consequently, they tend to be used for moving large amounts of money that need to be transferred on a same day basis. This method of concentration requires significant monitoring and action on the part of the cash manager. Nevertheless, its use is an important part of any concentration system.

Deposit Reconciliation Program (DRP). Deposit Reconciliation or Branch Consolidation Services are very effective concentration techniques in those states with extensive branch banking networks. With this service, it is necessary for a company's units to use branches of the same bank. While a single account is used, the different depository units are identified by a numerical code contained in the MICR line of the deposit tickets. Each unit must use only deposit tickets containing its unique code for this service to be effective. Deposits are automatically consolidated in a single account. A variety of reports is prepared showing deposits by unit. This information can be provided to a company on magnetic tape allowing them to perform an automatic reconciliation of deposits. Typically, a cash manager would use a wire transfer to move funds from this account to the main concentration account.

Automated Loan/Investment Services. Some companies do not want to actively forecast cash requirements and monitor balance levels. They would like to have their cash management systems do the work for them. In order to meet this need, automated loan and investment services have been designed. Since overdraft banking is not permitted, various types of sweep accounts have been developed. Typically, they work as follows. A target balance is established. Each day, any funds over the target are swept into a predetermined investment. If the account balance is below the target, a loan is made to bring the balance back to the target. Some of these arrangements are investment only sweeps, others loan only sweeps, and still others work both ways.

These accounts save time and ensure that no excess balances exist in the account. From the company's perspective, interest income can be maximized and interest expense minimized. From a bank's perspective, these services are a two-edged sword. While popular with companies, they expose banks to reductions in both account balances and loan balances. Consequently, cautious positioning by banks for these services is required. Nevertheless, these accounts are cash management services of the future and banks must learn to live with and adjust to them.

INFORMATION SERVICES

The corporate cash manager needs information about a variety of banking activities to monitor a cash management system effectively. Information on these activities is often as important as the transactions themselves. A bank active in cash management services must have an extensive array of information services.

Information Types.   Information is needed for daily cash management purposes. These data consist of previous day's information such as balances, individual debits and credits to accounts, lockbox deposits, concentration activity, loan and investment transactions, and international activity. More and more current day information is being requested by cash managers. The most typical items are controlled disbursement totals, availability reports on lockbox deposits, ACH debits and credits to be posted to the accounts that day, and wire transfer activity.

Information is required for accounting and planning purposes. Updating the appropriate accounting journals and forecasting cash requirements are major objectives. Since most of this information is internal to a company, a bank can offer few services in this area.

Management information for decision making is the third category. The most important activities are balance monitoring and maintaining records of banking relationships. The account analysis is a key tool.

The cash manager also needs information for managing borrowings and investments. Making borrowing/investing decisions is the culmination of the cash manager's activities. To do this properly, rate information, summaries of debt and investment activities, and information on debt and investment portfolios must be available.

Delivery Systems.   Most banks' information reporting systems are part of a package developed by an outside company and are also linked with a timesharing system. Some large banks have developed their own systems. More banks are bringing the functions in-house in order to eliminate the time sharing costs.

Information on a company's accounts is taken from a bank's systems and transmitted to the information reporting system for direct access by a company. The cash manager can access the information by telephone, "dumb" terminal, or microcomputer. Because of the capabilities of microcomputers, their use has increased significantly. They will become the primary communications vehicle between a company and its bank.

Many banks, as part of their information reporting package, allow companies to initiate certain transactions through a terminal or microcomputer. The most common services provided are wire transfer and concentration activity (DTCs and EDTs). Terminal-based products to initiate all types of ACH credits and debits, communicate letter of credit instructions, place stop payments, and make investments are also available. More such products are likely to become available.

Treasury Workstations. The development of treasury workstations has had a significant impact on cash management information processing. These microcomputer-based systems have enabled the cash manager to automate a number of functions and become more productive. Another objective of these systems is to enable companies to integrate their cash management systems with accounting systems. This has proven to be more difficult than many companies anticipated. Nevertheless, this integration will continue to be an objective for companies.

A company may design and build its own treasury management systems, purchase pieces of it, or buy a complete software package from a bank or another provider. Because of the unique needs of each company, it has been difficult to develop a system which can be used by large numbers of companies without customization. Flexibility is the key in any offering. An important component in providing this flexibility is a good spreadsheet interface. Spreadsheet programs are very important parts of the treasury workstation concept.

While banks have made significant investments in developing and marketing treasury workstations, the sales have been disappointing. With low corporate demand, the number of institutions marketing them has declined. This trend will continue.

Nevertheless, cash managers use microcomputers heavily in their cash management systems. Banks must be prepared to interface with a microcomputer and to provide data in a form that can be used and manipulated by cash managers using microcomputers. While treasury workstations are not substitutes for good cash management systems, they have been forces in pushing the development of new cash management services.

Account Analysis. To be effective, a cash management system must have a process for actively monitoring account balances. Daily balance reports serve as the short-term mechanism. The account analysis is the longer term mechanism. Produced monthly by the bank, it contains information showing average account balances (ledger and collected), services used, and whether or not there were sufficient balances to pay for services provided and credit availability. In effect, it is the bank's invoice. As companies reduce balances and compensate with fees, it takes on added importance.

Companies' biggest complaints about the account analysis are the length of time it takes for banks to generate them and the difficulty of comparing different banks' analyses. Differences in terminology, methodology, and pricing concepts cause problems. Companies would like to see a standardized account analysis. Cash managers are actively pursuing this.

Banks need to improve these systems. Any bank desiring to provide extensive cash management services must have a strong account analysis system.

CONSULTING SERVICES

A number of banks offer cash management consulting services. These services are designed to aid the cash manager in structuring an effective cash management system. The most common is a lockbox study followed by disbursement optimization studies. The third most common study is a cash management systems analysis in which all aspects of a company's cash management practices and procedures are reviewed. While some banks have separate consulting groups, other banks' consultants are also their sales people. Other banks have chosen not to offer consulting services or to provide minimal lockbox and disbursement analysis.

Lockbox Studies. These studies are used to determine the best location for lockboxes, the number of lockboxes needed, and the increase in working cash that results from various lockbox combinations. Sophisticated computer models are used. These models optimize solutions on a combination of mail times and availability. A considerable amount of information is generated. Interpreting the data properly requires an expertise which few banks have.

Disbursement Studies. By optimizing on check clearing times, these studies determine the best places for a company to use as disbursing points. They also calculate the disbursement float associated with each location. Computer models are used once again. Interpreting the data is much easier than with a lockbox study. However, data input into the models is complicated and expensive.

Cash Management Systems Studies.   These reviews involve all aspects of a cash management system. Particular attention is paid to all activities along the collection time line from invoicing through posting of accounts receivable and the disbursement time line from receipt of an invoice requesting payment to funding an account when the check clears. Other activities reviewed are such things as concentration systems, account balance monitoring, bank charges, cash forecasting, and investment policies. Few banks have the personnel to undertake these activities.

In order to assure that they obtain unbiased results, more cash managers are using banks for consulting work which have separate consulting groups. They also compensate for consulting services with fees. A number of them are indicating that banks performing the reviews will not be permitted to bid on the company's transaction business. Consequently, consulting services must be priced to generate a profit and not be used as a business development tool.

CONCLUSION

Banks have a great deal of latitude in the extent of cash management services they can offer. Since most companies and organizations need some of these services, banks need to decide what their strategies will be. Cash management services can be profitable, but will require ongoing attention and investment. These services will continue to evolve and are likely to become more complex as the information requirements increase. For those of us involved in the cash management services business, it is an exciting place to be and from all indications, it will continue to be a challenging area.

CHAPTER SIXTY-SIX

Financial Services to Other Financial Institutions

William J. Stallkamp

Executive Vice President
Mellon Bank, N.A.

BANK TO BANK—A HISTORICAL SYNOPSIS

The origin of banks offering financial services to financial institutions started before the organization of the Federal Reserve System. Correspondent banking has always been a part of commercial banking. Correspondent relationships were first established as a means of redeeming bank notes outside of a bank's own geographic territory. Historically, commercial banks maintained a deposit account with another bank in return for services rendered. The bank extending the service is generally known as the correspondent, and the one utilizing the service is known as the respondent. Normally, the correspondent is a major city bank and the respondent is a community or country bank. Originally, balances required for specific services were not clearly defined. During the 1960s, as more products were offered and computers became available for recordkeeping, more explicit pricing evolved for each product offered.

Correspondent relationships developed on a regional basis for the most part because many of the services, such as check clearing, required geographic proximity to be effectively performed. However, aggressive calling efforts by money center banks developed significant relationships for these New York and Chicago banks. At its height of correspondent banking activity, Manufacturers Hanover reportedly had the largest number of correspondent relationships and balances.

Calling on respondent banks was a major part of most young officers' careers at Manufacturers Hanover. As the 1970s progressed, however, the money center banks modified their strategies for a number of reasons and curtailed their aggressive marketing efforts. Although these money center banks still have significant correspondent relationships, they play a less significant role than in the 1960s and 1970s. One subtle benefit realized by the money center banks results from their early dominance of corporate trust functions. Because these banks issue millions and millions of dividend checks for corporate customers, which end up in the hands of shareholders all over the country, money center banks have always had vast numbers of on-us checks coming in for collection. This offers an advantage to any bank in the check collection business since it has a virtual monopoly on setting price and availability on these items. Certain products that were dominated almost exclusively by the money center banks are being offered by more regional banks. This includes functions such as corporate paying (dividend disbursement) and custodial and securities safekeeping.

As the number of banks continued to expand to just under 15,000, there was a growing need for correspondent services. The vast majority of these banks had under $100 million in assets and needed assistance from larger banks in performing functions they were too small to do for themselves. Suppliers of product fell into one of two basic categories—those that limited their offerings to a few basic services they already did for themselves and those that offered a full range of products and services. The former group of suppliers made no effort to develop products and usually called on the respondent banks with representatives from the operating area(s) where the service was performed.

Full service banks, on the other hand, had relationship managers who called on the smaller banks regularly and presented them with a broad base of products. By focusing on a few natural comparative advantages, some of the smaller regional suppliers became quite competent at their limited offerings. This is why smaller respondent banks frequently carried as many as 6, 8, or in some cases, 10 or more correspondent relationships.

Loan participations have always been an important way that correspondent relationships have been valuable. Traditionally, this developed because the smaller bank had a corporate customer whose borrowing needs outgrew its lending limit. Thus, the correspondent would take an "over line" from the respondent bank. In recent years, however, many smaller banks have found themselves with highly liquid positions and an appetite to buy participations. Large banks have responded by developing syndication programs. Securitization, the packaging and marketing of debt, seems to be an activity that will play a growing role among banks in the years ahead.

As the 1970s ended, correspondent banking was characterized by many suppliers with varying degrees of product development and many buyers, a greater thrust by the larger regionals for this business, and a leveling off, if not actual curtailment, of activities by most of the money center banks.

FINANCIAL SERVICES TO OTHER BANKS

The Deregulation Act of 1980 and other developments have imparted the services offered by larger banks to other banks. First, the Federal Reserve has become a major competitor with the private sector for some products and services such as check clearing and wire transfer. Thus, a number of money center and regional check clearing banks have become less active, and those that have remained in the arena have been struggling to maintain volumes. Some Federal Reserve banks have been more aggressive than others. Although the Federal Reserve feels they have been operating within legal guidelines, the pricing and availabilities being offered have made it very difficult for many private sector banks to continue to view check clearing as a profitable endeavor. In some Federal Reserve districts, aggressive pricing and changing availability schedules have caused the major players to merely shift customers among themselves as they compete for transit volume. One observer has referred to this as merely "pushing soap around in a bathtub," where no supplier ever really has an advantage.

A second change that occurred in the early 1980s was the emergence of state branching and interstate banking laws in the various states. Although anticipated by some as the instantaneous demise of correspondent banking, merger activities have created new opportunities for banks that choose to pursue this market actively. For example, it has created a need for merger and acquisition borrowing by a number of banks and bank holding companies.

Capital notes to increase capital levels have also presented lending opportunities for some banks. Furthermore, a merger does not immediately reduce a bank's need for products from a correspondent. Until our nation has only a handful of major banks or holding companies, smaller institutions will always need certain products from other banks. Thus, sellers that develop products intelligently should find the bank market attractive for some years ahead.

The third result of deregulation was that many of the major banks accelerated their learning curve in developing a number of ways to hedge against interest rate risk. Not until the late 1980s will a number of these products really achieve a practical level for use by smaller respondent banks. For example, a few smaller banks are now beginning to use interest rate swaps to assure themselves of a fixed-rate funding source to match their fixed-rate loan products. More swaps and other rate risk management tools will be sold by larger banks to smaller banks in the years ahead.

The past 20 years have witnessed a much wider range of products being developed beyond the traditional transit, safekeeping, and coin and currency offerings. In the early 1970s a number of major banks doing data processing made a decision to get out of this business. The remaining bank affiliated processors such as M & I, M-TECH, and Mellon Bank have found data processing companies to be fierce competition. Successful processors must stay on the front edge of technology and develop state-of-the-art products to support the ever-growing needs of the larger community banks that must compete in their respective marketplaces.

Remote job entry involves a relatively inexpensive data capture computer and operating center at the smaller banks which, in turn, transmits the data to a larger CPU for processing and updating. This has become a rather standard operating mode for bank data processing in the 1980s. Further, the capability to handle ATMs in an on-line mode has become rather standard for today's data processors. Additionally, the need to switch ATMs between networks has created the requirement for another data processing capability, and processors are offering this capability to other banks in the form of network membership or as a switch for other private label networks. The traditional operating services such as check clearing, coupon collection, coin and currency, and safekeeping still remain regional in nature. Check clearing, as mentioned earlier, has become extremely competitive, primarily as a result of actions by the Federal Reserve Bank.

For years, safekeeping or institutional custody, particularly for trust securities of regional banks, was a product offered almost exclusively by the large New York banks. Recently, a few regional banks such as Mellon Bank have upgraded their institutional custody capabilities and aggressively marketed this product. It has been a very successful endeavor and serves as another example of how regional respondent banks are looking carefully to find low-cost quality producers for needed products. Securities lending has been an offspring of safekeeping and institutional custody, and it offers the opportunity for banks with idle security in storage to transform it to earning assets through the clearinghouse and recordkeeping activities of the correspondent bank.

Corporate Trust Services such as trusteeships and the ability to perform shareholder recordkeeping with the associated accounting and legal reporting has been needed by many small banks and has offered an opportunity for larger correspondent banks to share their expertise and services. With the merger and acquisition activities that have taken place, many banks and bank holding companies have found it necessary to find a more sophisticated processor to handle their shareholder records and associated activities. Some correspondents have even made this service available to the corporate customers of the respondent banks: The dividend checks that are produced are drawn on the respondent bank.

Banks with large credit card operations normally are willing to offer their card services to smaller banks. Essentially, this service takes one of two forms: (1) The provision of backroom processing when the receivables are maintained and owned by the smaller bank; (2) the paper created by the holders of the cards issued by the smaller bank is owned by the larger processing bank. In either case, the handling of the local merchant is the responsibility of the smaller respondent bank. Some banks have developed a corporate card program which does special subsidiary accounting for MasterCard or VISA cards that are used for expense accounts. The corporate card is offered to the corporate customers of the smaller respondent bank and to the respondent bank itself to use for its own officers' expense accounts. The corporate card program is designed to break down expenses on the charge card by individual for each unit of the organization. It is excellent for controlling expense accounts, tracking individual expenses, and analyzing expenses for tax purposes.

A number of major banks that have developed their own on-premise capabilities for producing the plastic cards also offered this as a service and share these capabilities with their respondent banks. This includes the production of plastic cards for both credit and debit cards. The handling of debit card accounting is more normally tied in with the ATM switching program and the data processing operation of each individual bank so that most banks in the data processing business include these products as part of their total processing package.

Some of the more recent developments in cash management services offered by correspondent banks to their respondents include electronic account information retrieval. This normally involves a terminal at the respondent's location through which information on account balances and activity can be quickly retrieved by the respondent bank. The automatic investment in Fed funds of all balances over a set amount is offered by some correspondent banks.

Wire transfer continues to be a major means by which funds are moved between banks in this country. Operations, procedures, and controls have been significantly upgraded by most major transferring banks. A few major banks, including some Federal Reserve banks, have given their respondent banks terminals which permit them to make direct wire transfer originations. Going forward, we will see continued emphasis on daylight overdraft controls of wire transfer activity. Essentially, a daylight overdraft occurs when a customer generates a debit wire going out before the credit wire coming in has arrived or been located in the system, thus creating a temporary over-draft condition.

Because of the growing market for daylight funds and the risk associated with temporary overdrafts, the Federal Reserve has felt it necessary to implement controls on daylight overdrafts. Smaller banks who use their correspondent banks for a number of activities have the propensity to appear in a daylight overdraft situation because they have a number of debits and credits going through their demand de-posit account and through the wire transfer system on any given day. As more controls are placed on daylight overdrafts, it is possible that banks will actually charge other banks for allocations of daylight over-draft capacity.

Cooperation in offering other cash management services to the corporate customers of the smaller respondent bank can serve the corporate customer well and benefit both banking institutions. Through the use of the lockbox and possibly funds concentration for the cor-porate customer, funds can be garnered at the correspondent bank with balances maintained to cover the operating services. Excess amounts can be moved to the local bank for the company to handle its daily cash needs for payroll and other necessary operating accounts. By working together, all three parties can benefit, and the local re-spondent bank can remain very much a part of the local business' banking picture. Such relationships can also foster loan participation arrangements by the banks for the company.

Since deregulation investment advisory services, including asset liability management consulting, have been required by many re-spondent banks and have been offered by a number of correspondent banks, management assistance and counseling have always been avail-able to respondent banks who maintain good balances.

Both this type of assistance as well as general consulting services are undergoing some changes in the 1980s. First, because of tighter balance positions being maintained by respondent banks, these ser-vices of today are more frequently offered on a fee basis. Second, the degree of specialization and the rate at which these needs are changing differ dramatically from earlier years. For example, with many banks and bank holding companies recently completing their mergers, there is an immediate need to recognize efficiencies and productivity as a result of the merger. This type of integration consulting is a popular area that may be served by correspondent banking relationships in the latter part of the 1980s.

Finally, because most banks will at one time or another have a corporate customer with some kind of international need, this will always remain an area where a larger bank will be able to assist its smaller respondent. This could be nothing more than advice on country risk, but could involve foreign exchange needs and very well may result in foreign trade services such as letters of credit.

In summary then, the 1980s have seen some dramatic changes in the traditional "correspondent banking" business. The needs have changed and those correspondent banks wanting to stay in this business have had to be aware of the changing needs and to develop products and services to meet those needs. Simply because three $200 million banks join to form a $600 million holding company, it does not mean that all the products and services they needed from their correspondent bank will now no longer be needed.

As a matter of fact, not so much changes immediately as one might think. Check clearing, for example, is still a function of geographic proximity to the clearing bank and transportation routes; so very little change will happen there. Trying to consolidate into one location is frequently less efficient and results in greater loss of availability than if the entities kept their own clearing arrangements.

Coin and currency is another service that is a function of geographic proximity and transportation availability, so very little change should be expected. However, three banks who join together to form a larger institution may be able to combine their volumes for certain products in order to negotiate better contracts for these services. The correspondent, on the other hand, may prefer dealing with the larger combined volumes for certain services and would be willing to offer better prices based on the volumes from all three entities. This might be true, for example, if the trust departments were to combine safekeeping or institutional custody services; or it might be that the charge card volumes of the three institutions would allow for more attractive processing prices. Pricings or possibly more ATMs would make the combined entity far more attractive for an ATM network than as individual banks. Thus, over the next five years, those correspondent banks that offered a broad range of quality services and products should find that an attractive market for these services and products will remain.

Obviously, over time, if our industry evolves into only 100 fewer major banks or holding companies in the whole country, most of the services and products offered by a correspondent to a respondent will eventually be consolidated and integrated into the respective holding companies. Even when this happens, we can see in particular geographies that there will always be some independent community banks with the same needs for service and products from a correspondent relationship that had always existed.

The fact that merger and acquisition activity could possibly cause a correspondent bank to be a major competitor of many of the respondent banks that it now services, does not necessarily have to deter a correspondent bank from continuing in this business. If the correspondent bank offers a broad base of quality products and treats the relationship with integrity and confidentiality, a competitor/customer situation does not necessarily present a problem. We even had a situation once where a credit request was sent into our credit department through our community banking department and the same request came to the credit department from the correspondent bank to his relationship officer. The credit analyst discovered that he had the same credit request from two areas or institutions. We came out of loan committee with the same pricing, same terms, and same conditions for this single credit. Our community banking department representative made its proposal with the company. As a matter of fact, the respondent bank even offered a slightly lower rate on his portion of the participation, and the blended rate through the correspondent participation proposal was slightly less than Mellon's own direct quote. The sequel of the story is that we both lost the business to a foreign bank. The point is, however, that we were able to look at the credit objectively and to respond promptly and fairly to both requests.

In the years ahead, offering services to other banks is not an area for new entrants. The number of buyers will be shrinking, but so will the number of sellers. The players that do not have updated products and services will not be players for long. However, those that have relationship banking and a broad base of quality services and products to offer should continue to find opportunities for growth in profits in offering products to other banks.

THE FINANCIAL INSTITUTIONS CONCEPT

As many major banks recognized that their correspondent banking business had reached a mature market position, they were aware that the distinctions between banks and other financial institutions were narrowing. Thus, in the late 1970s and early 1980s, some correspondents organized a financial institutions structure that included not only the traditional correspondent banking functions, but encompassed other related industries. Although banks have differed somewhat in the industries they include as financial institutions, the most commonly identified are thrift institutions, insurance companies, securities brokers and dealers, finance companies, mortgage companies, mutual funds, private investment companies, and equity syndicators. It is perceived that many of the same relationship management disciplines and product offerings necessary for correspondent banking will be equally applicable for other financial institutions.

Some banks already had developed industry specialization and have made no change in their organizational approach to these businesses. Others, however, for the first time are taking an industry specialization view of these financial institutions. It is still too early to tell if these financial institutions' approach will be perpetuated and the degree of success. We do know, however, that as a general rule banks that develop industry specialization are far more successful in those industries with both credit and operating products than those without specialization. Some broad observations on specific financial institutions are noted below.

Thrifts

With the Deregulation Act of 1980 savings and loans, for all practical purposes, were given the same powers—and in some respects, broader powers—than commercial banks. Those who allowed this expansion of powers, which would automatically make some 4,000 savings and loan institutions become candidates for the identical products offered commercial, have been surprised. Few of the leopards have been quick to change spots. Many of these thrifts have been slow to change from mortgage originators, and those with a desire to sell into the secondary market had services other than correspondent banks (many of which did not develop this product for respondent banks anyway) to get to the secondary market. Thrifts moving into commercial lending have done so slowly and continuously except for a few very large institutions on the west coast. The number of S&Ls experiencing their new trust powers could probably be counted on one hand. A number had already introduced some form of demand account prior to the Deregulation Act and systems and procedures for handling these accounts had been developed.

Banks performing data processing for commercial banks have not found their processing packages readily transferrable to the thrift market. Thrifts had systems that were designed before they had demand accounts or paper volumes. Thus, with only a monthly mortgage payment and a savings deposit to post for each customer once a month, the S&Ls were accustomed to systems that posted on a true real-time basis. Commercial banks, on the other hand, automated to overcome paper volume from demand deposit accounts.

Thus, their systems were designed to do posting on an overnight basis. Upon reviewing the commercial bank processing systems, many thrifts felt they would be taking a step backward to go from real time to overnight posting. As time progresses, the economics of the market will adjust these differences. Meanwhile, it has been an inhibitor in the signing of thrifts to correspondent bank's data processing systems.

Direct lending to S&Ls has been slow to develop because commercial banks were concerned about the low capital ratios in this industry and the generally low earnings. Further, Federal Home Loan Bank members could borrow far more cheaply from the FHCB than commercial banks were willing to lend. Larger, more sophisticated thrifts have used rate management products such as swaps to cover their large portfolios of fixed-rate assets.

Some correspondents have developed tailored products for thrifts such as pass-through data capture from transit runs of thrifts and demand deposit transactions, but this has not developed into a universally offered product. On a broader basis, thrifts have turned to correspondent banks to sell excess funds into the Fed funds market, to use wire transfer, safekeeping, ATMs, and other more conventional products as needed. Thrifts moving from a mutual to stockholder charter have found correspondent banks that were willing to handle the shareholder recordkeeping and dividend disbursements for them.

In summary, then, the Deregulation Act of 1980 did not cause a ground swell of thrift institutions moving to correspondent banks for services as many had anticipated. Because of the smaller number of institutions and the variety of strategies employed by these thrifts, this market is not as attractive to correspondent banks as commercial banks.

Finance Companies

Much like the commercial banking industry, the broad spectrum of sizes in this industry makes it difficult to generalize about opportunities to do business with these institutions. While finance companies cannot participate in the payment system like commercial banks, there are many ways finance companies have worked with banks over the years. Because of the rates, finance companies have been permitted to change, and banks that have been able to develop lending skills in this industry have found good lending opportunities with attractive spreads. One must really view this industry as two types of businesses— those in the personal finance business and those in the commercial finance business. Because of their single purpose type of business, the personal finance companies run with comparatively low staff and overhead expenses.

A variety of strategies seems to be emerging. A number of small, personal finance companies seem content to maintain business as usual. There has been evidence of smaller closely held companies merging with larger companies which may offer merger and acquisition opportunities to interested commercial banks. Larger companies running chains or branches present cash management opportunities to commercial banks, particularly where tight centralized control is desired by management. Commercial Credit Corporation seems to be developing a number of strategies.

Commercial Credit is an institution with a strong commercial credit background that also has personal financial products. It appears to be moving toward consolidating these retail outlets into a commercial banking entity.

At the extreme end of the spectrum are the very large commercial finance companies, most of which were originally organized as captives to finance the products sold by the parent. Most do far more than this today and offer lending, capital markets, and cash management opportunities for larger commercial banks with sophisticated products in these areas. Although technically these companies would be identified as "captive," they are large enough to handle their own banking relationships and, except for controlling credit exposure internally, do not necessarily need the relationship handled by the same individual(s) handling the parent.

Insurance Companies

Broad classifications for analyzing a commercial bank's potential relationship to this industry would include life underwriters, property and casualty underwriters and brokers, or agencies. Insurance companies have moved closer to the retail customers with the development of many products which are service or investment oriented rather than pure insurance. Thus, consumers and small businesses are attracted to insurance companies, which extend universal life and other similar products that are invested in a manner to take advantage of new tax shelter provisions. From this perspective, life companies in a sense cooperate with consumer deposit products offered by commercial banks.

Many observers feel that the delivery system, which banks have developed, provides a natural opportunity for selling insurance products to consumers. Already, a few banks are experimenting with insurance companies by leasing space in their facilities to sell insurance products. For years, banks have sold, or in some cases, actually underwritten, credit life insurance for their own borrowers. Banks making installment loans require property and casualty insurance on the vehicle, or other assets purchased; and this presents another marketing opportunity for insurance. Both banks and insurance companies continue to flirt with ways to circumvent existing legislative restrictions to combine products and delivery systems. Ultimately, how far these two industries will be permitted to go in combining their efforts to deliver a full financial services package to consumers will be a legislative issue. Both industries are regulated and any legislative approval will have to deal with a myriad of regulations from both industries, something that could prove fatal to change.

Meanwhile, banks that have developed industry expertise have found opportunities to do business with these financial institutions. Because insurance companies, for the most part, are self-funding through their flow of premiums, they have not required large amounts of credit. Some insurance companies use bank lines to take advantage of portfolio investment opportunities that occur before liquidity occurs from scheduled maturities. Merger and acquisition have been the primary need for term debt. Insurance companies prefer long-term, fixed-rate investments, and historically banks have coordinated with them to structure loans for borrowers which permitted the banks to have floating, shorter term debt and the insurance companies to have the longer, fixed-rate debt.

In recent years, banks that have developed private placement capabilities have used insurance companies as a primary source of placement. As securitization of debt by banks continues to develop, insurance companies will be obvious buyers. They already have found mortgage-backed securities frequently meet their long term, fixed-rate needs.

There appears to be a trend toward consolidation in the broker, or agency, end of this industry. Buyout contracts are frequently structured with a portion of the price up front and the remainder paid based on future earnings. Banks familiar with this business have found reasonable risk lending opportunities for mergers and acquisitions.

Insurance companies also represent cash management opportunities starting with premium collections and including concentration of funds. These institutions are also candidates for short-term investment products offered by bank's capital markets. Although long-term investment policies with rather simplistic terms and rate requirements do not make these companies good candidates for interest rate management products, opportunities for these capital market products should not be ruled out.

Broker/Dealers

Broker/Dealers, or investment bankers, have been the most important single force in stripping the large commercial loan volumes from the commercial banks. Working capital lines of banks have been replaced to a great extent by commercial paper. The medium-term investment notes in both domestic and international markets, which is a product of the investment, has replaced much commercial bank term debt.

Commercial banks, in fact, distribute their own CDs and other liability products through the broker/dealer network. These investment bankers have a distribution network and a marketing mentality that stimulates creative product development for large users of credit. Many of these products developed by investment bankers involve lending opportunities for commercial banks such as leveraged buyouts, or RUFs and MIFs in the Euronote market. Thus, large commercial lending banks must maintain communications with investment bankers to be involved at an early level with these lending opportunities. Here again, there will have to be legislative change to permit commercial banking and investment banking either more or less competitive positions.

Broker/dealers move large amounts of cash through the commercial banking system and represent cash management opportunities. Brokers have a need for overnight loans and in some cases, day loans which are supplied by commercial banks. Broker loans have always offered volume opportunities for banks but have narrow margins, which have not made them as attractive to banks seeking to improve ROA ratios. Funding needs of the major brokers, for the most part, are handled by the major commercial banks. Because of their thin margins, these loans are frequently syndicated to other banks. Smaller, regional broker/dealer borrowing needs are, for the most part, handled by regional banks domiciled in proximity to the broker.

Equity Syndicators

There are an estimated 9000 syndicators operating in the U.S. today. This astounding number ranges from the "Big Six" syndicators—Integrated Resources, American Express, JMB Realty, Equitec Financial, Consolidated Financial, and McNeil Securities Corporation—to your next door neighbor. Anyone can be a syndicator. There are no educational or licensing requirements. This industry is reported to have grown 1,000 percent in just 10 years. However, the sudden change in tax laws brought this business to its peak at the end of 1986. Going forward, it is expected that the new tax laws will change the business significantly but not completely do away with it. Deals will have to be structured on their pure economic merit without tax shelter considerations. Certainly, this can be done, but it is expected to reduce the number of syndications for a period of time.

Although equity syndicators are thought of as primarily being in real estate based transactions, syndications can be established for virtually any asset with depreciable value. Computers, bank ATMs, oil

and gas loans, and race horses are examples of other assets for which
syndications can be established. Limited partnerships are the most
common and the preferred legal entity for syndications because unlike
other forms, investor liability is limited to the extent the investor is
obligated or financially committed.

Equity syndicators are users of bank credit. Basically, these credits
take the form of one of the following structures. Gap or bridge loans
under a guaranteed line of credit are short-term loans made for acquisitions and cover that period prior to syndication which may include construction, rehabilitation, or "packaging time" to prepare the
syndication memo for market. A second form of loan is the secured
revolving credit or term loan to finance investor notes, and the third
structure is a general purpose revolving credit which is extended to
diversified real estate companies and is normally seasoned. The larger
syndicators have need for bank cash management products and may
be candidates for capital market risk rate management products.

MUTUAL FUNDS

Mutual funds are mentioned here because of their tremendous growth
since the 1970s. This growth was the result of high interest rates and
improved technologies. The ability to do unit share accounting on an
asset portfolio that is widely diversified, to reprice these assets regularly, and to produce timely reports and statements, was perfected
by computer software. The mid-1970s was a time when mutual funds
became a favored investment for individuals and institutions. These
funds compete directly with banks' retail and commercial savings and
investment products. They offer a great deal of diversification of risk
with both taxable and tax-free earnings options.

For life insurance companies, these funds are virtually self-funding
through clients investment payments. Credit opportunities are limited
to lines for liquidity purposes in the portfolio. Because of their rapid
growth, mutual funds are generating significant volumes for the commercial bank payment systems, which are still controlled by banks.

Disbursement and payment services appear to be the most significant products commercial banks can offer this growing industry
today. Those few banks that have developed the technology to perform
mutual fund accounting have found business is booming.

CUSTOMER, COMPETITOR, OR COHABITOR

The 1980s in banking are viewed as an adjustment period to deregulation. But, we've really had only limited deregulation since there
are many products offered by the financial institutions described in

this study, which banks still are not permitted to offer. This, then, creates a period of time when the commercial bank looks on many of those other financial institutions with mixed feelings. These institutions present customers with opportunities to develop business and increase earnings. These same institutions are frequently competitors who are competing aggressively for the same deposits and loans that have traditionally been our bread and butter. Banks also think of total deregulation, and envision how effectively they could combine efforts with many of these same financial institutions to develop a complete package of financial services to a multitude of markets through a shared delivery system. As bankers think ahead toward the time when a totally integrated financial services industry might exist, we must continue to view these financial institutions as valued customers. It is simply an added benefit that we have the opportunity to learn more about these customers as competitors and as potential future partners.

PART TWELVE

Trust Services

CHAPTER SIXTY-SEVEN

The Role and Management of Trust Services

Robert F. Clodfelter

Lecturer in Law
School of Law
Wake Forest University

When the first of our early ancestors found it necessary to seek a loan from another of our early ancestors, this must have been the beginning of banking or something very close to it—particularly, when the lending ancestor hit on the idea of borrowing other people's money at a low rate, and thereafter lending it out at a higher rate. Thus, traditional banking was born. Trust banking also had its beginnings early on. As those first bank customers prospered and accumulated wealth, they were faced with the problems of its management, application, and distribution. Questions must have occurred to them, such as, how should I leave my property when I die? In such event, who should I name to see that my desired distribution plan is carried out? If I become incapacitated who will attend to my property and see to the needs of myself and my dependents? Our early ancestors wanted to know who indeed they could trust to render these services on their behalf. This must have been the beginning of trust banking or something very close to it.

Our forbearers quickly and correctly surmised that the character and attributes they sought in their bankers they also sought in the persons they named to serve as their executors, trustees, and those in similar capacities. Indeed history has shown us that a family's personal banker was often named individually to serve as executor and trustee of his banking customers' estates and trusts. Even today in numerous small towns throughout our country, when the local bankers play their traditional roles they find themselves asked to render these trust services in their individual capacities. The essential quality society looks for in its banks and bankers is trustworthiness. This is also the number one attribute of a trustee. Trust in the bank or banker's honesty and integrity causes people to place their savings in their bank or banker's hands. Similarly many of these same people for the same reason name their bank or banker as their executor or trustee.

Banking services and trust services were made for each other. Their marriage was inevitable. No longer did banks think of themselves in terms of saving depositories and money lenders only, but more as financial managers. Banks would begin to offer a wide range of financial management services along with their money lending. This transition has been a continuing evolution within the banking industry. More and more financial management services are now made available by banks to better serve their customers.

Trust services are a group of interrelated and mutually dependent financial services. They are grouped together because of their fiduciary character and the similarity of administration needs required to render such services. The management unit within a bank set up to carry out and promote this function is usually called the "trust department." It takes its name from that ancient common law property ownership and management arrangement called a "trust." However, the standard definition of the word "trust," namely, "To rely upon or to commit to one's care or keeping," does indeed set the tone for the type of services rendered by trust departments.

Historically the corporate form of trust business in this country was initiated by a life insurance company. This was in the early 1800s. The transition from life insurance companies to banks as the major movers in corporate trust business occurred relatively quickly. Around 1850, banks began to enter the trust business. In 1913, national banks were authorized to render trust services. Now the majority of corporations offering trust services are banks, both state and national.

The authority of a bank to do trust business is generally referred to as the bank's "trust powers." A state bank's charter containing its "trust powers" is granted by the state's legislature or an administration agency of the legislature. In a given state, a national bank's authority to engage in trust business is circumscribed by the right of state banks in that state to do trust business. However, application is made to the office of the Comptroller of the Currency for its trust powers.

From its beginning, "trust services" added a new dimension to banking. The bank as debtor to its depositors and "arm's-length" lender to its borrowing customers was accustomed to its honest, aggressive, self-interest role. The concept of rendering fiduciary services is in many ways opposite the traditional self-interest role of banking. Beneficiaries' interests in trust accounts are paramount to that of the bank. Fiduciary account assets are not assets of the bank. Gains or losses in their management belong to the account beneficiaries, not the bank.

A bank earns fee or commission income as compensation from rendering trust services, not interest income as from its own assets. This basic and fundamental difference between traditional banking and trust banking (rendering of trust services) posed obvious management and administration problems.

Bank managers traditionally separated banking (depositor and lender functions) from the trust banking (delivery of fiduciaries services). This separation has been singularly significant in the banks' management of trust departments from their very beginnings. It is to prevent unauthorized and perhaps illegal use of confidential information derived from either side. It enhances and encourages trust personnel to make fiduciary objectives their primary obligation. This separation of banking and trust functions within the organizational structure of a bank has been referred to as the "Chinese Wall." A trust department head is usually answerable directly to the CEO, keeping the administration of the trust department separate and apart from that of the banking department. The very natures of the work, responsibility, and obligations of traditional banking versus trust banking have demanded their functional separation for management and administration purposes.

The ever-continuing process of seeking improved management through organizational changes is evident in the trust industry. A variety of management approaches are in vogue with respect to the delivery of trust services. Some banks have spun off their trust divisions into separate solely owned subsidiary corporations in an attempt to have the "trust departments" operate independently, separate and apart from traditional banking. This arrangement may have many pluses but it also has some serious drawbacks. Perhaps the biggest criticism of this approach is that you lose most of the marketing edge achieved when the trust department is operated as an integral part of the traditional bank. On the other hand, some hold that a trust department as a free-standing entity gives it a better opportunity to create a new more acceptable image. In other words, it frees trust banking from perhaps the more conservative inflexible commercial bank image. There does not seem to have been any great exodus to this particular subsidiary approach.

Another organizational move by some banks has been to more closely align the trust functions with the traditional bank functions. This would be the opposite of the subsidiary approach. Such integration could be so structured, for example, so a "personal banker" would serve as both contact person for the trust customer and the traditional bank customer. Pluses could possibly be: Better promotes cross-selling; ties trust and banking customers closer to the bank; gives trust department better access to desirable markets; and reduces personnel cost. Criticisms could be: Such integration would lead to regulatory authority action for lack of separation (chinese wall problem); the trust department would lose its identification as a strong fiduciary to that of a simple service center; and the integration could lead to a de-emphasis of profitable trust fee income business.

The standard organizational approach is to have the trust department as one of the several departments or divisions within the banking corporation. Traditionally this is the more acceptable organizational arrangement. It allows for emphasis on fiduciary administrative management within the departmental organization while keeping open the best of cross-selling opportunities with other banking department customers. Whatever one's opinion may be as to the more beneficial organizational arrangement this is the more prevalent one, namely the trust department as one of the several departments of the bank.

Trust services, sometimes referred to as fiduciary services, are further distinguished as "institutional" and "personal." Institutional trust services are those rendered to the nonperson customers such as corporations; the public sector (governmental units of city, county, and state); and public charities and other nonprofit groups. Personal trust services are those rendered to individuals and include estate settlement, trust administration, and agency services. These two major categories of trust services are significantly different. As a consequence a trust department organized along product lines (services) would have as its first subdivision, a personal trust group and an institutional trust group. Larger trust departments oriented along product lines further subdivide; for example, institutional trust into employee benefit section; charitable trust section; stock transfer and bond trustee sections, etc. Examples of such further subdivision under personal trust could be estates settlement section; trust administration section; agency service section, etc.

Also, trust departments are in part organized along functional (activity oriented) lines. Basic support functions within a trust department needed to facilitate the service delivery capability are usually organized this way. These support functions are broadly described as "operations," "systems," and "investments." Sometimes these groupings may include "tax," "real estate," and perhaps others. However, "tax" is usually a separate unit within the personal trust group. It is utilized principally as a support function limited to that group. Real estate, if a separate unit, would again be under personal trust administration or perhaps under an investment unit.

Operations would be charged with the accounting, receipt and delivery, and disbursement activities of the trust department. Such activities are common to both institutional and personal trusts. Operations is a people intensive activity. The key to its success is timeliness and accuracy. It is transaction oriented, handling purchases and sales of securities for the investment unit. It is responsible for security movement and control in, out, and through the trust system; the accounting; asset income control and recordkeeping; and physical safekeeping and vault operations.

Systems is responsible for the acquisition, maintenance, and operation of the trust department electronic data processing capability. This may be under the control of the trust department or may be under the bank's overall electronic data processing effort. It would include all the EDP for the trust department. In many banks this is on the bank's main frame. In others it is handled by outside vendors who supply the software and processing capability. Still other banks use minicomputers within the trust department.

Investments (the investment unit) is usually the heart of any trust department. Success or failure of a trust department so often hinges on the successful operation of this unit. In terms of individual accounts needs, the investment product will vary widely. For example, compare personal trust with its typical trust customer and institutional trust with its charitable trust customer. Their investment needs are different. One may be very sensitive to income tax, while the other does not pay income tax; consequently investments would differ. Employee benefit plans call for highly individualized investment management usually leaning toward capital growth. On the other hand a personal trust may be looking for high income yields. Assessing the risk element against the investment need is the required skill of this unit. Investment alternatives traditionally available to trust accounts are common stocks, fixed income investments, collecting funds (common trust funds), in some instances real estate, and short-term fixed income investments.

A typical organizational plan for a trust department would show the head of the department answerable directly to the chief executive officer of the bank. This preserves the Chinese Wall. Under the trust department head usually come the section heads of the personal trust, institutional trust, investment, operations, and systems. Under personal trust would be tax, accounting, real estate, and various account administration units for estate settlement, trust administration, and agency services. The account administration units contain the customer contact personnel charged with account administration. These are a key to the trust department's successful operation.

On the institutional side, there would also be administrative units for employee benefits accounts, charitable accounts, and the public sector accounts. Investment is similarly organized with certain of its personnel assigned as portfolio managers to the various personal and institutional trust accounts. Others, as specialists in investment alternatives, provide research analysis and recommendations as to investments. Obviously any given trust department will have its own particular organizational plan dictated by its own needs and circumstances. The comments here are intended as a brief overview of a typical trust organization.

Much has been written about the value of a trust department to the overall bank. Management has long debated the merits of a trust department as a profit center or as a necessary accoutrement to the bank's commercial success. Large bank trust departments are usually substantial profit makers for their banks both in generating fee income and bank balances. Indeed in many instances the trust department's reputation substantially carries the bank. Mostly the question of maintaining a trust department or terminating a trust department arises in banks with small or medium size trust departments or banks considering starting one. Banks' CEOs often have second thoughts concerning the high risk involved in rendering trust services as compared with the fees and commissions produced. For the small or marginal department this question is one that should be carefully investigated. An assessment of the need for such services, that is the market potential and the cost of their delivery in terms of quality and quantity, is essential.

It is still possible to start a trust department by arrangement with a correspondent bank to render some of the support function activities. This sort of piggyback arrangement has been beneficial in the start-up of trust departments in banks where none previously existed. Likewise the larger trust department providing such support functions has discovered this as a new source of revenue. It would seem that all banks with trust powers desiring to provide such services to their customers could reasonably expect to do so by such an arrangement as suggested. If "no trust department" is a bank's decision, then perhaps an arrangement could be made with a friendly correspondent for that correspondent to offer such services to the nontrust department bank's customers. Perhaps such a correspondent would give some assurance that the resulting trust business bank accounts would be maintained in the nontrust department bank.

Medium-size trust departments operating within their banks probably have the greatest number of management problems. The separation of trust accounts and their confidential nature from the commercial banking activities is made more difficult by virtue of the very size of the trust department and the bank. Often the trust officer and banking officer are so close it is difficult, if not impossible, to maintain the so-called Chinese Wall. Usually there is more pressure on the trust operation for profits and the attendant difficulty of increasing output with limited facilities. Management under such circumstances must carefully assess its trust markets and make every effort to take what the market gives.

For example, a medium-size trust department may have a real competitive edge in going after small employee benefit accounts (say one to one hundred employees) as opposed to trying to compete for a large corporation's account called on by a giant trust department. Likewise, in the personal trust area the local trust department should develop any special expertise needed for its area, such as farm operation and management, timber operation, small business operation, and real estate managements. So often it is this special quality or expertise that will land the trust account for the smaller trust department rather than its larger competition. The competitor, more often than not, is not a competing trust company but a layman serving in a trust capacity.

Trust management in recent years has taken to a much more aggressive posture in marketing trust business. Trust new business is always an integral part of any successful trust department. Traditionally, the new business person endeavored to have prosperous individuals appoint the bank as executor and testamentary trustee under their wills. The classic approach was to provide estate-planning services to customers and, in the process, to sell the bank as corporate executor and trustee. Trust departments built up and maintained substantial "will banks" (confidential files of wills wherein it was named to serve). As these will appointments became active, the trust department had an estate to settle and perhaps a trust to administer. Of course, the new business person also busied himself to acquire for his trust department as much active immediate fee business as he could. This would be living trusts, agencies, or investment management accounts. Salespersons on the institutional trust side were always "immediate fee" producers because all accounts there are immediate fee accounts. But as suggested, the traditional personal trust new business approach has changed. Now there is a more aggressive move for personal immediate fee trust business. Management's push for more profitable trust departments has caused trust managers to reassess what it is they have to sell.

In the past decade, this reassessment of trust services has the trust department breaking down in service rendering activities in order to determine if there is a market for any of these. This has been termed "unbundling." Many trust departments looking at these unbundled services have developed new profitable immediate fee areas. As a result we see trust department investment divisions selling their investment counsel to smaller trust departments; their closely held business appraisal ability as a marketable service to lay fiduciaries and other unbundled services in a like manner. The tax unit of the trust department through unbundling may sell its expertise in filing fiduciary returns. Personal trust through unbundling offers its services to lay fiduciaries to do part of their work such as accounting and record-keeping, securities transactions, custody services, etc.

Trust departments' aggressiveness is not limited to new business. There is a whole new attitude, a new vitalized thought process related to trust banking. The leaders in the banking industry no longer consider the trust department as a token community service, but rightfully place it in the forefront with all other banking activities. Given all its inherent differences and indeed its peculiarities as compared to the traditional side of banking, a trust department should be a vital part of its bank and not its stepchild. Trust management is expected to produce a fair share of the bank's profits. A bank CEO is expected to provide a fair share of management expertise in order to accomplish this.

CHAPTER SIXTY-EIGHT

Trust Services for Corporate Customers

George W. Cowles

Senior Vice President
Bankers Trust Company

Trust services for corporate customers are as many and varied as the banks that provide them. They range from the extraordinarily sophisticated and complex services provided by the largest banks, to the fairly simple services provided by the smaller banks as an accommodation to their good commercial customers. Often the organizational structure of the bank will dictate the variety and combinations of trust services provided to corporate customers, but they can be broken down into four general categories:

1. Employee benefit services.
2. Investment management services.
3. Corporate trust and agency services.
4. Custody services.

A given institution may provide some or all of these services, varying the organizational responsibilities as it mixes and matches the services in various combinations. In this chapter, however, an outline of trust services generally available to corporations will be described without attempting to address organizational or other groupings of the services throughout the banking industry.

EMPLOYEE BENEFIT SERVICES

Generally speaking, this group of services or products will be designed to satisfy the needs of corporations as sponsors of employee benefit plans, both defined benefit and defined contribution plans. The services required by a plan sponsor will vary based on the type of plan,

1015

the particular corporation's in-house capabilities, etc. Banks can and do provide a variety of services in this area.

Every employee benefit plan must have a trustee and frequently the plan sponsor appoints a bank to serve in that capacity. The services provided by the bank, as trustee, include safekeeping of securities, collection of income, settling securities purchase and sale transactions, and the rendering of reports to the plan sponsor. The trustee is a "fiduciary" as that term is defined in the Employee Retirement Income Security Act of 1974 (ERISA) and, as such, assumes fiduciary responsibility for those responsibilities allocated to it.

A bank's trustee services range in complexity. It may, for instance, trustee the assets of a single employee benefit fund managed by a single investment manager (either the bank itself or some other investment manager); or it may act as master trustee for a very complex employee benefit set-up for a plan sponsor. When the bank acts as both trustee and investment manager of a portfolio, the bank is referred to as a *discretionary* trustee; when the bank acts as trustee only and some other entity has investment discretion over the assets, the bank is referred to as a *directed* trustee.

Providing services to a master trust is the most recent development and, indeed, the most complex product line in the employee benefit area. A master trust, simply stated, is a single trust which funds multiple employee benefit plans sponsored by a single corporation, or group of related employers, the assets of which are managed by multiple investment managers. While the basic trustee services remain essentially the same, the client reporting requirements increase geometrically. The master trustee must be prepared to report to the sponsor by individual portfolio, groups of combined portfolios, and the entire master trust. In addition, the trustee may be called upon to render reports at the plan level—that is to say, the master trust assets as they are allocated among the participating plans.

Participant Recordkeeping

A second major product line for employee benefit plan sponsors is participant recordkeeping. This service is required for profit sharing, thrift/savings, 401(k) (cash or deferred arrangements), and Employee Stock Ownership (ESOP) Plans. Someone—either the plan sponsor itself, an outside service provider, or the trustee—must maintain a record of each individual participant's share in the plan. Like most employee benefit services, participant recordkeeping for defined contribution plans can be relatively simple and straightforward, such as tracking each individual's account in a single fund, non-contributory, profit sharing arrangement, or it can be extremely complex, such as the participant recordkeeping in a thrift plan with a 401(k) feature where there can be pre-tax and post-tax employee contributions, an employer matching contribution, and multiple investment funds among which each participant may allocate and re-allocate his plan balance. The Tax Reform Act of 1986 added several other layers of complexity to all participant recordkeeping, particularly in the case of 401(k) plans.

The frequency of updating participating records in a defined contribution plan also varies. Some profit sharing and Employee Stock Ownership Plans (ESOPs) require valuation and record updating only at the time of the annual contribution. Thrift and 401(k) plan records generally require at least quarterly record updating while most require monthly updating, and the trend is toward weekly, or even daily processing. Part of any participant recordkeeper's duties will be to prepare individual participant statements, generally annually or quarterly, depending on the type of plan.

Each bank acting as trustee of defined contribution plans must decide whether or not to provide recordkeeping services. Many potential corporate clients prefer that the same institution be both trustee and recordkeeper, and there are clear advantages to this arrangement. If a bank decides to provide these services, it can do so either by designing its own system and providing the service totally in-house or by joint venturing the service with an outside vendor. In the latter situation, some banks make the joint venture transparent to the plan sponsor while others prefer to have the plan sponsor deal directly with the joint venturer on recordkeeping issues.

There are clear advantages for a bank to provide recordkeeping services, either in-house or through some sort of joint venture. However, many banks prefer not to get involved in this sometimes complex product line because of the varying requirements of plans and corporate clients.

Benefit Payment Services

The purpose of all employee benefit plans is to deliver benefit payments to plan participants and beneficiaries. Another service required for these customers, then, is benefit disbursement. Defined benefit plans usually provide monthly payments for the life of the retiree (or the joint life of a retiree and his or her spouse), while defined contribution plans provide for a variety of payment options: Lump sums, installments, in-service withdrawals, and the like. While the Tax Reform Act of 1986 will undoubtedly change the volume, frequency, and types of distribution options provided by plans, the disbursement service will still provide a product opportunity for bank trustees.

The disbursement of monthly pension checks is normally considered to be a function of the trustee at the direction of the plan sponsor. The disbursement of benefits from defined contribution plans, on the other hand, is generally done by the participant recordkeeper. The service, however, involves somewhat more work than would at first seem evident. In addition to the preparation and distribution of benefit checks, the service provider is also responsible for the preparation and distribution of tax information. There is also considerable contact with the recipients of payments.

Consulting

Since the trustee, particularly the master trustee, sits on the data base of security holdings and transactions, it is logical that the plan sponsor will look in that direction for data manipulation. As a result, many banks provide investment performance measurement products. These frequently include not only calculation of investment performance periodically, that is, quarterly, annually, three years, five years, and the like, but often broken down by asset class as well as on the total employee benefit fund. In addition, there are performance attribution products that allow the plan sponsor to determine what contributed to good (or bad) performance; whether, in fact, an investment manager is doing what he was hired to do; and other similar analytical information. Many of these types of products will require a consultant from the trustee to help the plan sponsor interpret the data.

Other potential consulting products for employee benefit trustees include asset and liability modeling, asset mix consulting, and investment manager evaluation. They can even go so far as investment manager selection, although that has been rare.

Ancillary Products

Ancillary products for employee benefit clients (which can also apply to corporate custody clients as will be discussed later in this chapter) include securities lending and global custody products.

Securities Lending

From time to time, the brokerage community needs to borrow securities to cover short securities positions, make timely deliveries, or for various other reasons. They obviously look to large holders of such securities as potential lenders; therefore banks, as trustee of employee benefit accounts or as custodian of corporate and other assets, have the opportunity to be the lender. In these cases, the borrower collateralizes the loan with cash, securities, or a letter of credit, and the lender—that is, the employee benefit trust or custody account—receives either a fee or the spread between what the invested cash earns and the interest on the cash collateral he pays the borrower. Frequently, the profit on a loan is shared by the bank and the lending entity. While this service is relatively complex and sophisticated, and generally attractive only to holders of large securities positions, it does provide an opportunity to enhance portfolio returns for the lender and add to the product line of the lending institution.

Global Custody

Global custody services are rapidly expanding among employee benefit and custody accounts. And as more and more investment portfolios are diversified internationally, the need to safekeep, collect income, and report on global portfolios will continue to increase. A bank can use its own worldwide branch system, create its own subcustodian network, or engage a single subcustodian with its own network to fulfill this need.

Central depositories are virtually unknown outside of the United States so that physical custody capabilities are necessary

In addition to the basic custody services, safekeeping, income collection, and transaction settlement, an adequate global custody product will generally include a multi-currency reporting capability, performance measurement capability (including a break-out of the performance impact of currency fluctuations), and a capability to combine reports on global and domestic portfolios.

While all of the employee benefit services discussed so far are designed for corporations many, if not all, are also appropriate for noncorporate clients, such as endowment funds, foundations, unions, and municipal employee benefit funds. In addition, several of the services are appropriate as ancillary products for corporate or other customers utilizing a bank's custody services.

INVESTMENT MANAGEMENT SERVICES

The primary market for investment management services to corporations is managing the assets underlying employee benefit plans. There are, of course, other opportunities, such as management of corporate assets themselves. Opportunities also extend beyond the corporate market to foundations, endowments, states, municipalities, and labor unions.

The range of investment management services is as broad as the imagination of the bank's investment professionals. Strategies are most easily categorized along the risk spectrum from low-risk cash equivalent products through very aggressive equity products using small capitalization equities or venture capital. Banks are also able to create pooled funds to facilitate the efficient investment of relatively small portfolios. Pooled funds may also be offered as specialty products. Another arena is computer techniques that enable a bank to provide a range of passively managed products, such as index funds and dedicated portfolios.

To fulfill the investment objectives of the client, any bank providing investment services would provide an overall investment product with an optimal mix of fixed income, equity securities, and cash, determined by the bank. Generally speaking, the balanced portfolio product client will have a single portfolio being managed by a single institution, usually plans at the small end of the market.

Of course, once a bank has developed this product line it is positioned to offer each of the component products independently (i.e., fixed income management, equity security management, and cash management). This enables the bank to compete in the larger end of the market, where usually the corporation will hire banks and others to manage one portfolio among the several comprising the pool of assets to be managed. Frequently in these cases, the corporation will hire investment managers for specific tasks, such as managing an equity portfolio or a fixed-income portfolio. In these situations, the corporation itself decides the asset mix—that is, how much of the entire pool will be invested in the various asset classes.

As a bank extends its investment products, it may choose from a number of options. With equity products, for instance, a bank can provide a basic core equity approach, or equity products designed to produce above average growth or income or any number of other variations. The same types of options are generally available to both fixed-income and cash management products.

Pooled Funds

Pooled funds also can be used imaginatively to meet the needs of the marketplace. Generally, banks use pooled funds (where multiple investment portfolios own units) to provide efficient, well-diversified investment opportunities. Participating accounts are generally portfolios too small to be so invested on their own. Pooled funds may also be used as a convenient way to participate among multiple portfolios, mortgage and real estate investments, venture capital, small capitalization equity securities, foreign securities, and the like, where there may be a desire for a relatively small investment as a part of an overall portfolio strategy. The potential use of pooled funds is virtually infinite.

Passive Management

All of the investment management techniques discussed up to this point employ active management, where an individual portfolio manager makes buy and sell decisions with respect to the individual securities comprising the portfolio. In recent years a whole new product line has developed which banks may decide to offer—passively managed portfolios.

The classic passively managed portfolio is designed to replicate the investment performance of a specified equity or fixed income index (i.e. the S&P 500). Here, too, a bank may provide these passive products on either an individual portfolio or pooled fund basis. The passive management technique has a vast number of potential applications since, by computer simulation, a manager can replicate the performance of virtually any group of securities or class of assets.

Cash Management

Cash management is a necessary part of any bank's array of investment products. Many of the larger banks provide a pooled fund comprised of short-term cash equivalent instruments into which the cash in all investment portfolios is swept for investment on a daily basis. Other banks choose to invest portfolio cash balances in its money market account, while still others make arrangements for the investment of cash balances in mutual funds. Any bank which provides investment management services to corporations or other entities will need to establish some mechanism to manage the uninvested cash in its portfolios efficiently.

Specialty Investment Products

As we have said, the range of a bank's investment products is as wide as the imagination of its investment professionals. That imagination has led to a vast array of specialty products. Examples include dedicated fixed income products, where a strategy is designed to produce a specified cash flow to fund a known series of liabilities; immunized fixed income portfolios, whereby a bond portfolio is structured and rebalanced to generate a target rate of return independent of interest rate and bond price changes; portfolio insurance, an investment strategy that provides the assurance of a minimum rate of return, regardless of market fluctuations, and the opportunity to enjoy a significant percentage of the positive return in a rising market.

Global Investment Management

Finally, as the securities markets become truly global, worldwide investment management is becoming increasingly popular. Banks may provide global investment portfolios, either pooled or individually managed, actively managed or using indexing techniques. These products can be country-specific such as a Japanese index fund, or can be literally global with securities holdings in many countries, including or excluding the United States. The potential for global investment management, too, is limitless.

CORPORATE TRUST AND AGENCY SERVICES

Corporations and other entities need trust services that support their issuance of securities and other financial transactions. This group of loosely related trust services is frequently provided by local or regional banks, although some of the more complex services are usually provided only by larger banks.

Whenever a domestic or foreign corporation borrows money from the general public in the United States through the issuance of bonds, notes, or debentures, the Federal Trust Indenture Act of 1939 requires that a trust company (or a bank with trust powers) be designated as trustee of the issue. A bank accepting such an appointment acts in a fiduciary capacity on behalf of the debtholders. A trustee's duties and responsibilities are specifically defined in the indenture, the legal document under which the securities are issued, which is an agreement between the issuer and the trustee.

Key aspects of the trustee's initial functions are the negotiation of indenture provisions and the trustee's responsibilities, duties and indemnifications, and the issuance of the bonds at closing. Ongoing functions, which usually accompany a trusteeship, include the registrar and paying agency capacities. These relate to the maintenance of registered bond holder records, transfers of ownership, and the payment of interest and principal. In agreeing to serve as a trustee for a public debt issue, the bank assures the debt holders that it will make sure the covenants and all other indenture provisions are performed in the agreed manner and ensure, for a secured debt issue, that there is a proper lien on the trust estate and that the trust estate is maintained.

Private Placements

Bank services as trustee, registrar, and paying agent are also sometimes used with respect to private placements. A private placement is an offering of a corporation's securities to a limited number of sophisticated institutional investors. A trustee is not ordinarily required for private placements since they are not publicly traded and are exempt from the registration provisions of the Securities Act of 1939. If a transaction is secured or is unusually complex, however, investors may require a trustee.

Stock Transfers

The payment of periodic dividends and the recordkeeping relating to the transfer of ownership from one holder to another require the services of a transfer agent. Banks offer this service, which may also include administering the Dividend Reinvestment Plan (if any), proxy mailing and tabulation (vote counting for the corporation's annual meeting), and serving as registrar.

The stock transfer agent's functions are fairly complicated and are expected to run smoothly. A stock transfer agent, therefore, becomes visible to the corporation only when the agent fails to resolve problems quickly. Such mishaps as lost checks or certificates and incorrect dividend amounts can lead unhappy shareholders to contact the company. Prompt turnaround and quality service are critical components of stock transfer service.

Commercial Paper

Many corporations and other entities that issue commercial paper utilize a bank's services in connection with this activity. Commercial paper is short-term, bearer, promissory notes that finance interim funding, and the bank's functions include receiving issuance detail on notes sold from the client (or dealer), completion and same day delivery versus payment of the notes, reconcilement and payment at maturity, and various reporting and accounting services.

Recent years have seen rapid growth in the number and variety of commercial paper issuers whose paper is selling under special credit-enhanced structures. The credit of these programs is secured by underlying letters of credit, insurance policies, or collateral requiring fiduciary handling. Credit enhancement opens access to the commercial paper market for otherwise nonrateable issuers, and offers marginal issuers improved rating and more attractive interest rates and distribution. These arrangements require a depository trustee to perform certain functions over and above the issuance/payment activity. The depository trustee will hold the letter of credit and/or collateral, monitor the issuance and redemption of all commercial paper daily (or whenever it occurs), insure that the covenants or the credit support agreements are being met, draw down on the letter of credit if required, and execute all of the funds transfer and payment activity.

Eurobonds

An ever-growing market that banks may choose to service involves Eurobond issues. The Eurodollar market for medium-term debt gives U.S. corporations an alternative to marketing a public issue domestically. Eurobonds offer the advantage of selling an issue when rates are attractive literally overnight, without regulatory constraint. Currently, most issues are entirely in bearer form in small denominations, though registered securities are sometimes provided for. These issues require the services of a trustee or fiscal agent, plus paying agents in European cities where the bulk of Eurobonds are deposited. The trustee functions in Euro issue indentures are basically similar to those of a debt issue sold publicly in the United States.

Pass-Through Securities

During the late 1970s, private sector institutions began packaging mortgage originations and selling interests to investors. As mortgage-related securities became more accepted in the secondary market, a variety of vehicles were created that provide these institutions with an outlet to the capital markets. This development, in turn, gave impetus to the securitization of other receivables, such as pass-through securities, mortgage-backed bonds, and pass-through bonds. All of these issues require a trustee to handle and monitor the collateral along with the standard fiduciary duties, and thus have opened yet another product line for banks. More recently, as an outgrowth of mortgage securitization, investment bankers have begun to develop and offer publicly auto loan, computer lease, and similar credit-backed, pay-through issues. These, too, will provide opportunities for banks to provide trustee services.

Mergers and Acquisitions

The current flurry of activity in corporate mergers and acquisitions, along with leveraged buyouts, also provides a service opportunity for banks. A bank can act either as depository or exchange agent for stock and bonds of companies involved in mergers, acquisitions, or leveraged buyouts. In these situations the bank will handle cash purchases, redemptions, and tender offers.

CUSTODY SERVICES

Some banks provide custody services as part of their trust activities; others banks, including those not providing a full range of trust services, provide custody only as a service to their commercial clients.

The basic custody service is that of safekeeping and servicing of a client's security holdings. In servicing a custody account, the bank collects interest and dividend income and acts as agent in the execution of corporate actions, and it will settle the client's buy and sell orders to receive or deliver book entry or physical securities.

The bank also maintains records of the account holdings and renders periodic statements of the holdings in the account; provides timely notification to the account holder of exchange offer, tenders, conversion privileges, stock purchase rights, and warrants or other options, and other developments such as mergers, reorganizations, stock splits, stock dividends, and any other matter which may require the client's action. In addition, a custodian must automatically present called and matured securities for payment. Since the client or any designee must decide how its assets are to be invested, the custodian will usually provide timely notice with respect to receipt of income, maturities, and the like to facilitate efficient cash management. The custodian will also forward proxies, proxy statements, and annual reports to its clients.

Escrow Agent

Other services sometimes provided by a bank's custody area include acting as escrow agent. Used in a variety of financing arrangements, a bank's custody area acts as an escrow agent to accept deposits of cash, securities, or documents in the interest of one or several parties. It does not permit any party to utilize such assets for any purpose not clearly defined in the escrow agreement. The escrow agent's responsibilities often include investment collection, disbursement, or valuation of assets. Satisfied by the evidence that certain conditions have been met, the agent releases the cash, securities, or documents.

Bank custodians may consider offering global custody services to their custody clients, although global services and reporting requirements can be very complex. Securities lending services, as earlier explained, can also be offered to custody clients.

Clearly, not all banks are equipped to offer a full range of trust services for corporations, nor will they necessarily choose to do so. This chapter has merely outlined a reasonably full range of trust services for corporations. Each bank will need to determine the appropriateness of a given product for its marketplace as well as its own capacities.

CHAPTER SIXTY-NINE

Trust Services for Individual Customers

Richard W. Heiss

Senior Vice President and Senior Trust Officer
Manufacturers National Bank of Detroit

PURPOSE OF A PERSONAL TRUST ACTIVITY

The purpose for which a bank establishes a personal trust department may have one of two broad objectives, either defensive or aggressive in nature.

- *Defensive*—to provide an ancillary service to its best customers to preclude the customer from having to obtain the service from another financial institution and eventually lose the banking relationship to that competitor.
- *Aggressive*—to establish a business segment which offers a financial service that will contribute profits to the banking organization.

When deciding to develop a trust department, most community bank type organizations do it as a defensive measure. They may have experienced the loss of some valuable customer relationships to a competitor because a wealthy client died and another bank, or possibly attorney director of another bank, was named as the personal representative of the estate. The bank accounts soon were closed and moved to the competitor bank.

As a trust activity grows, the potential for profitability is seen by bank management as a contributor to the "bottom line." Once the profitability motive becomes the objective, the pricing of the trust product becomes significantly different than that which existed when "taking care" of the good customer was primary. The trust product is then no longer a loss leader and cannot be priced comparably to the competitor institution which still may treat the trust product as an ancillary service to the good bank customer.

TYPES OF ACCOUNTS FOR INDIVIDUALS

The hierarchy of account types typically found in a trust department for individuals is as follows:

- Custody or safekeeping accounts.
- Investment agency accounts.
- Revocable living trusts.
- Irrevocable trusts.
- Guardianships or conservatorships.
- Decedent estates.

The complexity and degree of specialization required to service the customer ascends the hierarchy in the order as listed above.

The services provided by the trust department for each type of account are summarized below:

Custody or Safekeeping Account

- Safekeeping of securities (stocks and bonds).
- Collection of dividends and interest.
- Remittance of income collected, usually on periodic basis, monthly or quarterly.
- Processing the purchase and sale of securities as directed by the customer.
- Notification of capital changes issued by corporations affecting stockholders.
- Notification of maturities or called bonds.
- Preparation and issuance of periodic statements of cash transactions and inventory of assets.
- Summarizing of information relative to income tax return preparation.

Investment Agency Account

- The customer is provided with information on specific securities, and purchase and sale recommendations are made if the customer reserves the right to approve changes in the portfolio; *or*
- The investment portfolio is managed with the exercise of discretion in accordance with investment objectives established with the customer where the customer has not reserved the right to approve the changes to the portfolio.

Periodic statements are issued detailing transactions in the portfolio, as well as an inventory of assets usually reflecting the tax/cost basis and current market value of each security.

The custodial and safekeeping services listed above are also normally provided with an Investment Agency Account.

Revocable Living Trust

By definition, a "Living Trust" is a trust created by a person (referred to as the settlor or grantor) during his or her lifetime, thus making it a "living" trust. When the settlor transfers assets to the trust, it becomes a "funded" trust. If revocable, the creator reserves the right to change or revoke the trust. A trust may be designated irrevocable from the date of its execution or remain revocable until the death of the settlor. The living trust has become a primary instrument for the administration and distribution of family assets and often functions as a "will substitute," in which case the will serves as a conduit for transfer of probate assets to the trust.

Advantages of a living trust over a will by itself include the following:

- If funded during lifetime, it provides a vehicle to manage a disabled person's property without the expense and publicity of a court-supervised guardianship.
- It provides the settlor an opportunity to observe how the trustee performs while the settlor is living and able to make a change if the advertising was better than the performance.
- It reduces, if not eliminates, the probate expense at the time of settlor's death.
- It provides more privacy for the settlor and the beneficiaries since no information need be filed which is open for public scrutiny as are the records of a probate proceeding.
- In general, it is a more flexible estate planning tool.

Funded Trusts (with assets requiring supervision)

- Funded trust accounts require the same services as investment agency or safekeeping accounts—the collection of income and processing of investment transactions with or without the approval of the customer depending on the trust agreement.
- A major benefit of the living trust is to avoid the probate proceedings upon the death of the settlor for the assets which are in the trust.
- The bank, serving in the capacity of trustee or cotrustee after the death of the settlor, immediately begins to administer the

trust assets for the benefit of the beneficiaries designated in the trust agreement in accordance with the directions outlined by the settlor. Typically, income is distributed periodically to the surviving spouse or to the children until specified ages are reached, at which time the assets or a portion thereof are distributed to the persons or, in some cases, charities so designated.

- For income tax purposes the settlor of a revocable living trust is treated as the owner of the assets. The bank must provide accurate information for reporting on the settlor's federal income tax and estate tax returns.
- For inheritance and estate tax purposes, the settlor is also considered the owner of the trust assets. Consequently, revocable trusts should not be sold to the customer on the premise of tax savings to the settlor.
- Any tax savings through the use of revocable trusts will result following the death of the settlor and will depend on how the trust is set up for distribution to the beneficiaries. Services provided by banks in preparing for tax savings are usually done during the estate or financial planning process.

An Individual Retirement Account (IRA) Rollover is a form of revocable trust whereby the grantor transfers the proceeds of a qualified employee benefit plan distribution to the bank as trustee (custodian) to defer taxation until a later date. The bank may manage the investments or merely act as custodian of accounts in which the grantor directs the investments. If the grantor revokes the IRA and withdraws the assets prior to attaining age 59 ½, the bank is required to report the withdrawal to the Internal Revenue Service as the grantor will be subject to a penalty tax. Amounts withdrawn after age 59 ½ are also subject to reporting requirements as they are taxable as ordinary income in the year withdrawn.

Unfunded Trust

- Unfunded trusts are commonly designated as the beneficiary of life insurance policies or employee benefit plans.
- The bank executes the trust agreement, as trustee or successor trustee, at the time the settlor signs the agreement but does not undertake any responsibility until the assets are deposited, which is usually after the death of the settlor. The bank retains a copy of the trust document in its future business file.
- In some cases the settlor is designated as the initial trustee and the bank as successor trustee, in which case the bank will assume its duties when the initial trustee resigns or is unable to serve because of death or incapacity.

- Following the receipt of the assets, the duties of the bank as trustee are the same as outlined above for the funded trust.

Irrevocable Trusts

Funding with Assets during Lifetime of Settlor

- The purpose of establishing and funding an irrevocable trust during the settlor's lifetime is usually to shift taxable income to another person whom the settlor wishes to benefit during his/her lifetime or a period of years, following which the remaining assets in the trust are distributed to persons or charities designated in the trust agreement.
- The bank may serve as trustee or cotrustee to carry out the specific directions of the settlor as outlined in the trust agreement.
- Once the trust document is executed, the irrevocable provisions cannot be changed by the settlor even if subsequent events may occur which are not expected and cause the settlor to desire a different course of action. Consequently, the bank, prior to accepting the trust, must be assured that it can fulfill the duties as outlined in the trust document.
- The trustee has the responsibility of investing the assets of the trust, in accordance with the terms of the trust agreement and in accordance with the laws of the state which has jurisdiction over the trust. (See subsequent section on the Prudent Man Rule.)
- The trustee has the responsibility of collecting and distributing the income earned on the investments in accordance with the terms of the trust provisions.
- The trustee has the responsibility of preparing and filing tax returns with the various governmental agencies and accounting for its actions to the beneficiaries and other parties having an interest in the trust. Typically, a statement of transactions and an inventory of assets is provided on a quarterly basis; in some cases, annually is sufficient.
- The 1986 Tax Reform Act removed many of the income tax shifting advantages which were available by the use of the Clifford Trust (10-year trust) and the Spousal Remainder Trust. Both of these special purpose trusts allowed the shifting of taxable income for a period of time to persons, usually children or elderly dependents, whose federal tax bracket was considerably lower than the settlor's. The tax law change, generally effective for any transfers to these trusts after March 1, 1986, eliminates the tax benefit in most cases by taxing the income of the trust to the settlor rather than to the beneficiary.

Unfunded Irrevocable Insurance Trusts

- An irrevocable insurance trust is designed to avoid federal estate tax on the proceeds of group term life insurance which is usually provided the settlor as part of an employer's employee benefit package.
- The provisions of the trust are designed to deal specifically with the proceeds of the life insurance policies, the ownership rights of which are assigned to the trustee. Immediately thereafter the trustee must execute a change of beneficiary form designating the trust as the beneficiary of the life insurance assigned to the trust. Other assets from the settlor's estate may also be added to the trust. In order to gain the desired benefit of excluding the insurance proceeds from the federal estate tax, the settlor must give up *all* rights of ownership and must survive three years after the date of assignment of the insurance policies.

As in the case of funded irrevocable trusts, once the assets are assigned and delivered to the trustee, no amendments can be made changing the provisions of the trust document. Occasionally family circumstances change which prompt the settlor to desire a change of the beneficiaries. An unhappy customer may result when the bank, as trustee, informs the settlor that amendments are not allowed. Careful drafting of the trust document can anticipate some potential changes, such as a divorce, by providing that the income beneficiary is the spouse at the time of the death of the settlor.

All trust documents should be thoroughly reviewed by competent personnel before they become irrevocable before the bank accepts the responsibility of trustee. Some banks have all irrevocable documents approved by their outside legal counsel before signing the document as trustee.

Testamentary Trusts.   Another form of irrevocable trust is the testamentary trust which is part of a Last Will and Testament. This type of trust can be changed by any means that a will can be legally revoked or amended.

The testamentary trust becomes operative only after death, at which time the trust becomes irrevocable. The court which has jurisdiction over the probate of the will usually has continuing supervision over the trust. In many cases the bank, named in the will as trustee, will not have knowledge of the appointment until after the death. Because the provisions are unilaterally established without the bank's concurrence, the trust may not be acceptable, in which case the bank may decline to accept the appointment, requiring the court to appoint an alternate trustee.

Once the testamentary trustee receives the assets from the probate estate, the duties of trust administration are essentially the same as for an irrevocable trust funded during the settlor's lifetime.

Guardianships or Conservatorships

Minor Children. All states have a designated age at which time a child reaches his or her majority and is legally able to make binding contracts or receipt for property. In some states the legal age is 18, in others 21. Prior to reaching the legal age, it is often necessary for a guardian or conservator to be appointed by the appropriate court to receipt for and manage the property for the minor until the age of majority is reached. The bank may serve in this fiduciary capacity, in which case the duties are similar to that of a trustee and are usually spelled out in the statutes of the state in which the child resides.

Accounting reports reflecting all cash and security transactions are required to be filed periodically with the court having jurisdiction until the minor reaches the age of majority, at which time the child receipts for the property and the guardianship terminates.

During the guardianship, the assets must be invested as authorized by the law of the state or as permitted by the court. Funds may be dispersed for the care and well-being of the child after approval by the court.

Mentally Incompetent Persons. When a person has been adjudicated mentally incompetent to handle his or her own affairs, an independent party is usually sought to manage the property of the incompetent person. Banks qualify as independent and are often selected by the court to serve, especially when there are no close relatives who are deemed capable of objectively managing the property for the ward of the court.

During the term of the guardianship, which normally lasts until the death of the ward or until all the property is distributed, the assets must be managed as provided by state statute or as directed by the court.

Disbursements for the care and well-being of the ward are made pursuant to authorization received from the court.

Accountings of all transactions are filed with the court as required, usually annually, until the death of the ward or until the ward is proven competent in the eyes of the court.

During the guardianship, the guardian or conservator is responsible for filing all income tax returns on behalf of the ward.

Decedent's Estate

By definition, "probate" refers to the process of disposing of a person's property at death. A will must be filed with the probate court when a person dies, and the title to his or her property is transferred to the personal representative (executor) of the probate estate. When administration of the probate estate is completed, the property remaining after payment of debts, taxes, and expenses is distributed to those recipients named in the will or to the heirs at law if there is no will.

The role of the fiduciary who administers the probate estate of a decedent may be referred to as administrator, executor, or personal representative, depending on the state in which the decedent was domiciled at the time of death and whether the fiduciary was named in the Last Will and Testament or appointed by the court in a situation where there was no will (intestate). When a bank serves in any of these capacities, its responsibilities are essentially the same, including the following duties:

- Locates will and arranges for its filing with probate court.
- Assists family, where desired, with funeral and burial arrangements.
- Arranges for clearance of safe deposit boxes with government tax officials where necessary.
- Gathers and collects all the property which belonged solely to the decedent.
- Investigates status of life insurance, veteran's benefits, social security, pension plans, and collects proceeds to which estate is entitled.
- Establishes living allowance for surviving family in accordance with terms of will and local law.
- Prepares an inventory of the assets which is filed with the court having jurisdiction over the probate proceeding.
- Establishes current values of the assets on which estate and inheritance taxes are determined, hiring appraisers if necessary.
- Upon approval of the court, investigates and pays all valid claims for the debts of the decedent.
- Prepares or contracts for the preparation of all tax returns, including all decedent's final income tax returns and the federal and state estate and inheritance tax returns. Because the fiduciary normally has personal liability for payment of the taxes owed by a decedent's estate, caution must be taken to assure that a qualified tax procedure exists in the bank. Many banks have their own tax departments and prepare the various tax returns for their trust accounts. Others farm the tax work out to

lawyers or tax accountants. The responsibility for timely filing of the returns and payment of any tax liability rests with the bank, as fiduciary.

During the administration of the estate, the assets must be managed in order to preserve the principal of the estate for the beneficiaries. Cash must be invested to earn a reasonable return. It cannot be left idle in a bank account pending distribution to the beneficiaries or payment of taxes and expenses. Failure to maintain the estate assets fully invested may subject the bank to surcharge liability. If a bank holds itself out to be a fiduciary, it is expected to have the expertise to fulfill its responsibility as a professional.

Special assets require special attention in the administration of an estate. Normally a bank cannot afford to have on its staff specialists required to manage all types of assets. Commercial real estate, oil and gas properties, and closely-held businesses are examples of assets requiring special knowledge. The bank, as fiduciary, cannot allow these unique assets to go unmanaged during the administration of an estate without risking substantial liability for losses which might occur. The value of a closely held business may depreciate in value if continuing management is not present to provide the managerial knowledge required, especially in situations in which the decedent was the driving force of the business prior to death.

When a decedent's estate matures, it is too late for estate planning. The fiduciary must assess the status of assets and corresponding beneficiaries. The estate must be administered in accordance with the precise instructions set forth in the decedent's will or state law.

Post-death tax planning is critical to the successful administration of an estate. What fiscal year should be established for tax purposes? What assets should be sold to raise cash? Should assets be sold or distributed? These decisions are examples of post-death planning which, if performed properly, will usually more than offset the expense of administration by a professional fiduciary.

If a bank, in the exercise of its trust powers, undertakes the administration of decedent estates, it must make a commitment to staff the trust department with competent, experienced trust administrators or risk being surcharged by the court for substandard performance.

DEVELOPMENT OF BUSINESS

The emphasis of a personal trust business development activity may be either future business or current fee business.

Current Fee Business

Obviously, the desired business development approach would be to sell new account relationships which are income-producing immediately. However, in order to achieve that desired result the personal trust activity must have a product or group of products which the prospective customer is willing to buy from the bank. Does the bank have a product or service to offer that is better or at least as good as the customer can obtain elsewhere at a competitive price? If not, it will be a difficult task to make sufficient sales of current fee business to pay for the expense of marketing these average-at-best services.

Ordinarily before a strong current fee marketing objective can be implemented, the bank must establish itself with an image among its customer base that it has an above-average investment management capability. This is a difficult task to accomplish in a short span of time because banks generally do not enjoy an image as top investment advisors. Secondly, it is difficult because current federal regulations preclude banks from advertising the performance of their common trust funds even when their record is superior to that of the recognized indices or popular mutual funds.

Future Business

Until a personal trust activity has an established performance record, the usual business development approach is to generate future business by being named a fiduciary in wills and trusts which become effective following the death of the prospective customers. This approach normally is a two-pronged marketing effort.

- One marketing target includes the lawyers in the community who draft the Wills and trusts for their clients. If a corporate fiduciary is to be named as a trustee or personal representative, the lawyer usually has a strong influence on which financial institution is recommended. A successful business development representative usually cultivates a core of lawyers. Of course, the bank must deliver satisfactory service to the lawyer and the survivors in the administration of the decedent's estate and family trusts to expect repeat business.
- Another marketing target for future business is within the bank's customer base. This approach is normally conducted by offering an estate planning service to individuals identified by other bank departments or through advertising. Estate planning seminars are often conducted for specific market segments pointing out the tax benefits to be derived by proper estate planning.

The difficulty with the future business marketing approach is the length of time it takes to generate sufficient fee income to offset the expense of developing the business. Only after years of developing future appointments do the documents begin to mature, as customers die, which provide a flow of fee revenues to support the trust activity. One trust department attempted to attract potential will appointments by renting space on a billboard which read, "A tisket, a tasket: We'll see you in your casket." Records are not available to know the success of that marketing campaign.

THE PRUDENT MAN RULE

The standard to which a trustee is held is known throughout the nation as the "Prudent Man Rule." The precept was laid down in writing by Justice Putnam in 1830 in an opinion concerning the court case, *Harvard College* v. *Amory*.[1] His precedent-setting statement reads as follows:

> All that can be required of a trustee to invest, is, that he shall conduct himself faithfully and exercise a sound discretion. He is to observe how men of prudence, discretion and intelligence manage their own affairs, not in regard to speculation, but in regard to the permanent disposition of their funds, considering the probable income, as well as the probable safety, of the capital to be invested.

As of this writing, the Prudent Man Rule has not been overruled by subsequent case law or statute with respect to the conduct of a trustee in personal trust investments.

Although the rule is applicable to both individual and corporate fiduciaries, there appears to exist a differentiation relative to the degree of skills applied when administering trust funds. Noted author on trust matters, Austin W. Scott, recites a statement from a 1947 case:

> It would seem also that where the trustee has secured his appointment as trustee by representing that he has a certain amount of skill, he may incur a liability if he fails to exercise the skill which he represented that he had. In a number of cases the court has expressed the opinion that a corporate trustee, a bank or trust company, may be held to a higher standard of care and skill than that which is required of individual trustees.[2]

---

[1] *Harvard College* v. *Amory*, 9 Pec 446, p. 461.

[2] Austin Wakeman Scott, *The Law of Trusts*, vol. II (Boston: Little Brown, 1956), pp. 1628–29.

PUNCTILIO OF AN HONOR

"The standards of a fiduciary are not the morals of the marketplace but the punctilio of an honor the most sensitive." This quotation by the late New York Justice Benjamin Cardoza, often seen in trust literature, so clearly expresses the high standards of performance required of a trustee.

Certainly one of the most important responsibilities of a trustee is the investment of the property held in the trust estate. Consequently, the success or failure of the trustee in the perception of the grantor or beneficiaries is often measured by how the trustee performed in relation to the investment expectations of the parties having an income or remainder interest in the trust.

If the bank being considered as trustee is not looked upon by the grantor or the draftsman of the trust document as having investment expertise, the parties may decide that it would be advisable to allow one or more of the beneficiaries to select a third party to advise or manage the investments. In some cases an investment counselor, insurance agent, or financial planner may be a part of the estate planning process and have more than a passing interest in having a provision in the trust document which will provide for the appointment of an independent investment advisor to the trustee.

Where provisions for an independent investment advisor exist, normally exculpatory language will be included in the trust agreement which will appear to absolve the trustee from any liability for following the directions of the independent investment adviser. The issue here becomes whether or not the trustee has any responsibility for protecting the interests of the beneficiaries from speculative investments made by an investment adviser who is in an agent capacity and not a trustee. Does the exculpatory clause clearly protect the trustee from any potential liability if, in fact, imprudent investment judgment is exercised and the trust principal goes down the drain?

Case law and textbooks on trusts do not provide comfort to a bank trust officer who is faced with this dilemma. Austin W. Scott, noted author in his book, *The Law of Trusts*, states:

> Even though the trustee commits a breach of trust which is of a kind for which by the terms of the trust he is relieved from liability, the provision is ineffective to protect him if it is against public policy to give him such protection. No matter how broad the provision may be, the trustee is liable if he commits a breach of trust in bad faith or intentionally or with reckless indifference to the interests of the beneficiaries, or if he has personally profited through a breach of trust, it is arguable that a provision in the trust instrument relieving the trustee from liability even for ordinary negligence is against public policy. There has been of late years a growing feeling that it is improper for a professional trustee at

least, who professes to give careful and skillful service, to escape liability for failure to afford such service.[3]

In the case of *Chase National Bank* v. *Reinecke,* 287 N.Y. Supp. 937 (1937), the trustee declined to follow the obvious imprudent direction of the advisor and went to court for instructions, wherein the court held for the trustee. A trustee cannot sit idly by, relying on the trust exculpatory provision as a shield, where the trust estate is endangered by the conduct of an agent providing investment advice.

It is the opinion of the author that to provide a power which will be activated at some time in the future to one who is not a trustee or to appoint an unknown investment advisor with total uncontested authority is too broad and provides an unjustifiable degree of risk, both to the safety of the trust estate and to the liability of the corporate trustee, who is deemed to have the skill to protect the beneficiaries.

It would seem appropriate for the bank, as trustee, to demand at least a power to veto the investments directed by an independent advisor if they are deemed to be too speculative.

CONCLUSION

If a banking organization desires to offer a range of financial services to protect and expand the highly profitable segment of the individual market, trust and investment services are a natural choice to include in the package. When providing trust services, it is imperative that the staff assigned the responsibility have the competence and experience to manage the trust accounts in order to meet the standards of prudence required by law and the degree of performance expected by the affluent customer sought to be served.

---

[3]Ibid.

PART THIRTEEN

Business Development and Marketing Bank Services

CHAPTER SEVENTY

Integrating Strategic Planning and Marketing Planning

Jerry Goldstein

Senior Vice President
Mercantile Bank

During the 1980s, formalized strategic planning was both adopted and adapted by most bank holding companies with assets over $1 billion, and by many with assets well below that magic mark. The top 20 BHCs had previously adopted strategic planning perhaps a decade earlier, utilizing the existing planning concepts proven at General Electric, IBM, and Xerox.

Early in the 80s the bank consultants such as Booz-Allen, McKinsey, The Boston Consultant Group, and Golembe were all actively teaching bank CEOs and their staffs the basics of strategic planning and strategic business units (SBUs). No one knew what all this cost, but over a hundred banks probably spent at least $½ million each, which would suggest a minimum industry expense in excess of $50 million. Numerous articles in the American Banker, Forbes, Fortune, etc., all emphasized the need for more strategic thinking throughout the banking industry, which served a very positive purpose.

As a result, most large banks set up planning departments and via trial and error learned to develop strategic plans, usually of three- to five- year duration. Gradually the concepts of strategic thinking permeated these organizations, often fueled by the efforts of bright, well-paid new MBAs who fortunately began populating banks in the same time frame. Banks became more aggressive entities fighting for market share expansion, eliminating unprofitable business units, simultaneously opening and closing branches, entering new businesses such as discount brokerage, leasing, mortgage banking, investment banking, operating large D.P. networks, and a host of other new ventures. Had all this not occurred, the banking industry might have declined in importance as deregulation spread, instead of growing through adaptation and change.

Through this period of the 80s, the five key strategic issues were:

1. Restructuring and repositioning.
2. Interstate expansion.
3. Credit type and quality changes.
4. Asset and liability improvement.
5. Market segmentation.

THE STRATEGIC PLAN

Interestingly, the tools developed to manage this process closely parallel the strategic planning mechanism developed a decade earlier in U.S. industry, and remain equally valuable today. The universality of these concepts are such that all banks gravitate to approaches, with only minor variations in timing, style, content, and level of detail.

Most strategic plans are built around five major concepts, each of which becomes a portion of an integrated planning document:

1. Mission.
2. Objectives.
3. Situational analysis.
4. Strategies and action plans.
5. Financial projections.

The *mission* defines the bank's overall reason for being, its role, and often its style. Typically this is a one- to three-paragraph statement shared with all employees. More recently, the emphasis upon corporate culture frequently is displayed within the mission statement as it answers two questions: Who are we? and Why are we here?

The *objectives* are quantitative statements of goals or targets which in turn become the measures of future success. Objectives answer the question, Where do we want to be?

Situational analysis consists of measuring and defining the present reality to determine the starting point. Before embanking upon a journey (of change) it is imperative to know where one is. Usually very statistical, this section normally includes competitive analysis, market share, and strengths and weaknesses. The latter is critically important, as any organization must build upon its strengths and either overcome weakness, or devise a means to by-pass those weaknesses. Situational analysis answers the question, Where are we?

The *strategies* then naturally evolve as a means to reach the objectives by altering the present situation. These are the specific plans of action the organization will take during the next three to five years.

Strategies answer the question, "How will we get there?" Often the strategies are detailed to another level of *action plans*, thereby becoming more specific so as to answer the questions, Who will do what? By When? and To What Extent?

The last concept in this section consists of *financial projections*, typically a P & L and balance sheet for three to five future years, with the current year as the base line. Here organizations differ in level of detail, and many include ratios, rate analyses, personnel projections, facility plans, and/or capital plans. The question answered by this section is, what will we look like when we get there?

THE CHALLENGE

Having a written strategic plan, signed off by senior management, is only half of the solution to improved performance for the shareholders. The other half, and by far the most difficult portion, is accomplishing the plan and achievement of the target results.

William Shakespeare's famous quote, "Many a slip exists betwixt cup and lip," is unfortunately all too well known to most bank CEOs. Banks have faltered, with Continental-Illinois, Bank of America, and Crocker among the more obvious. Timely and successful execution of strategic plans is the real challenge to all levels of bank management.

One area of particular difficulty is the integration of the strategic plan with market planning—or the bank's marketing in general.

MARKET PLANNING

So much has already been written on banks' previous failures to become market-driven and their prior orientation toward "order taking," that any additional comments would be trite. Instead, the positive aspect is that in the 1980s our industry is aggressively embracing all aspects of marketing—media advertising, direct mail, incentive compensation, market segmentation, marketing research, and relationship management.

Perhaps the largest single reason that strategic plans fall short of their objectives concerns problems in marketing. Successfully integrating the strategic plan with the marketing plan (or plans) has been the hallmark of high performance bank holding companies in the 1980s.

Effective market plans are built around the "Four Ps" of marketing, which were originally denoted by the product managers at Procter & Gamble in the 1930s:

- Product
- Price

- Promotion
- Place (Proximity)

While evolving from the soap and packaged goods segments of our economy, the same four principles are equally germane to bankers' marketing programs. While competitors are not one of the four Ps, they are part of each of the four.

Product must be needed, have value, and ideally provide a competitive advantage. Witness all the recent enhancements to credit card accounts as attempts to provide competitive advantage. While many bank products are viewed as "like commodities," there is a continual product enhancement process on-going to strengthen product differentiation.

Bankers who doubt that such mundane services as DDAs can be instilled with unique product differentiation features ought to look to Charmin toilet paper's success—it's squeezable! Which leads one to wonder if bankers are huggable?

Price is probably the one aspect that bankers have always felt most comfortable dealing with, especially interest rates. While free DDAs and no-closing-cost home-equity loans are examples of down-pricing, many private banking units have enjoyed success by up-pricing and providing a quality image. Competitive pressure from nonbank financial competitors will exacerbate price competition, keeping this P very much in the forefront.

Promotion, particularly sales promotion, various forms of advertising, and incentive compensation for banking officers all reflect the increased emphasis upon aggressive marketing programs.

Place is also called proximity, location, or in current banking vernacular—delivery systems. All banks are reconfiguring at the local branch, stateside, and often on the interstate and international levels. While most of the dreams concerning cashless societies, bank-at-home, and gas-station ATMs have not (profitably) come to pass, other steps are underway including sale of branches, ATM sharing, rep offices, interstate mergers, supermarket minibranches, and ACH transfers.

The key then is to not only develop a strategic plan and a marketing plan, but to integrate implementation of both in order to succeed in the 1990s—which are just around the corner.

The bottom line is that if you're not developing an integrated program to increase earnings 15 percent annually and to dominate your marketplace—someone at another financial institution is. And if your bank does not implement well enough to achieve that objective, someone at a competitive financial institution will. And, if your bank can't achieve all this fairly soon, the name over the door will change— as will the occupant of your chair!

CHAPTER SEVENTY-ONE

Establishing Policies for Pricing Bank Services

Jere J. Brommer
Senior Vice President
Valley National Bank of Arizona

INTRODUCTION

The focus of this chapter on pricing is to present readers with banking industry pricing practices adaptable to their own institutions. The practices have been culled from other more experienced industries and hundreds of banks from across the country. The basic concepts presented have been used for ten years by the author's own company, The Valley National Bank of Arizona, a $10 billion-plus statewide branch banking organization. The total pricing program used at Valley National was codeveloped by the author and William D. Wilsted, Ph.D., director, Graduate School of Banking, and professor of business strategy, Graduate School of Business Administration, University of Colorado. The concept, known as Proximate Value Pricing©* and its techniques have been taught in graduate schools of banking across the country and in marketing seminars for savings and loans and credit unions as well as commercial banks.

A HISTORICAL PERSPECTIVE

Historically, in the financial services industry and commercial banking in particular, the pricing function was a very static activity. This was the result of legislation and regulation providing a franchise to commercial banking covering products, prices, and markets. Beginning in the early seventies inroads were carved into this exclusive arrangement with the birth and successful promotion of money market mutual

---

*©Copyright 1978 by William D. Wilsted, used by permission.

funds. These funds, targeting on time-deposit customers of banks and savings and loans, introduced a new form of dis-intermediation to deposit-taking financial institutions. Money market funds took on the appearance of time deposits but paid an unregulated market rate of interest superior to rates that could be paid by regulated banks and savings and loans. Thus began deregulation and the demise of commercial banking's product franchise. Today not only security brokers but insurance companies, savings and loans, finance companies, retailers, and others offer products and services formerly offered exclusively by banks. To accommodate commercial banking's need to compete with these new suppliers of financial services, government at the federal and state levels, and regulators enacted laws and modified regulations to deregulate interest rate pricing on deposits and loans. They also moved to eliminate geographic boundaries with enactment of branching and interstate banking legislation and eased the chartering of new banks and new offices. The financial results of deregulation have been increased competition with increased pressure on the net interest margin and increasing noninterest expense.

In response to narrower funds margins and increased operating expenses, it is critical that banks pay more attention to noninterest income and the pricing of noninterest products—the focus of this chapter.

Pricing is one of the traditional four elements of marketing along with product, promotion, and place (or distribution). Such sophisticated pricing has been practiced by other industries for many years. Pricing, however, is relatively new to banking, taking its early form of today's practices in the mid-seventies. If we are to compete effectively with our new competitors, who are offering similar products and are experienced pricers and marketers, we have a lot of catching up to do.

The concepts discussed in this chapter were studied and extracted from other industries' practices, then modified to fit the financial services industry. They have also been molded into a format and process which parallels banking processes, identifiable as being similar to functions operating within the reader's own bank. Examples of such similarities are: programmed instruction through the completion of specific forms; a documentation and approval process which flows in a manner similar to lending in a bank; and budgeting/financial planning and fixed accountability for this profit-producing function of pricing.

OTHER INDUSTRIES' PRICING PRACTICES

Over the years a variety of pricing strategies, developed in other industries, have proven successful for businesses who know their costs. Some examples of these strategies follow.

Follow the Leader Pricing is a strategy in which prices are set at or close to the going market rate, often following the price leader. This strategy is pursued primarily by producers or retailers who sell undifferentiated products, such as staples. An example is a supermarket's sale of bread or milk. Although employed by banks as well as other types of businesses, this strategy places profit control in the hands of a competitor and at times can totally destroy the profitability of a needed and useful customer service. This is particularly true where neither the price setter nor its followers have identified the cost of production and delivery.

Pricing to Achieve Market Share is a strategy used to maintain or increase market share. A business acts deliberately to reduce unit costs and increase profit through increased volume at the expense of its competitors. The risk in this strategy is that competitors meet the reduced price quickly, thereby lowering revenues and profit for all suppliers with no increase of volume and market share for the initiator. An example in the banking industry is the introduction of the automatic teller machine. The originator of this service had an excellent opportunity to charge for a value added service—valuable to that market segment who needed or desired 24-hour-a-day, seven-days-a-week banking. Although expensive to produce and deliver, most market originators of ATM service chose not to charge for the service, and so hoped to increase market share. Most frequently the end result, after a competitor's quick response with a similar product at the same zero price, was no improvement in market share but a more costly operation. This pricing strategy also tended to establish a value for the service in the customer's mind, based on what the bank apparently thought the service was worth: Nothing. This trend in the banking industry in general could be the explanation of why it took so long and so much money to convince bank customers that ATMs are a valuable service. The obvious risk in a strategy of pricing to achieve market share is that in a competitive climate a new lower price structure is established, profitability is reduced, and in some cases a customer-satisfying product is discontinued.

Penetration Pricing is a strategy in which a relatively low price is set with the objective of capturing a larger share of a market. The airline industry is an example of the application of this strategy in a period of deregulation. In this case, a number of carriers introduced low fares and expanded networks to stimulate more air travel by the public. Those carriers who did so had the dual objectives of increasing the industry's volume of business overall and increasing their own market share of the airline business. As in earlier discussed strategies, there is a risk involved. When a major supplier of a service cuts its price, there is a high likelihood that competitors will follow. This situation has been readily apparent in the airline industry in recent years.

Market Skimming is a pricing strategy in which the price is set relatively high to tap that segment of buyers to whom the product has a high present value. Mercedes-Benz and some other foreign car manufacturers have been users of this strategy. To set themselves apart from the mass market automotive suppliers, they target a limited group who are the willing-and-able-to-pay-for market segment of auto buyers. The profit objective is satisfied through deeper margins on limited sales volumes. The customer appeal is based on price as an indicator of value. There is risk in this strategy, particularly for a service organization like banking. By projecting an image of exclusivity, the banks hamper their objective of serving a substantial segment of their market. For money center banks or niche banks who have chosen to specialize in a business segment or upscale individual banking, the strategy does have merit.

There are additional pricing strategies that have been practiced by other industries over the years. These few have been cited to acquaint the reader on how pricing has been used to accomplish specific objectives in other businesses. To a substantial degree, all of the strategies cited require that users know their costs—otherwise, profits may suffer. Even when volume objectives are successfully achieved, if a price is set below the cost to produce and deliver, "the battle is won but the war is lost." As of this writing, the nation's 20,000 plus vendors of financial services do not have a good handle on product costs. The likelihood is that this situation will prevail for some period of time, probably 5 to 10 years—the life cycle of this handbook. The reason for the industry's limited knowledge on costs and the absence of cost standards is justified by the number and diversity of producers and deliverers of financial services. It is further justified by the variety of services produced and delivered by each financial institution in its operations, customer services offices, and branches. Much of the product-allocated cost represents a subjective judgment on the part of the cost analyst.

The lack of solid cost figures is further aggravated by no provable economies of scale among the larger institutions in the industry. Many instances exist of smaller banks producing products at lower unit cost than large scale producers of same or similar products.

If a cost-plus approach or strategies dependent on accurate cost figures are not available or good for banking, the question becomes, What is appropriate?

TECHNIQUES FOR EVALUATING PRICE POTENTIAL

The Profit Formula that applies to banking is the standard formula: Profit equals the volume of services sold times the profit on each service sold, or—

$$[\text{Profit} = \text{Volume} \times (\text{Unit price} - \text{Unit cost})]$$

The obvious objective in pricing is to increase profit. This can be accomplished in one of two ways: Either by increasing the volume of a service sold or by increasing the margin of profit. A third way is a combination of both increasing volume and profit margin. As commercial banking responds to the profit pressures of deregulation, it is critical that the profit formula be made a part of the pricing process. Concentrating efforts on regularly increasing prices without adequate consideration for volume and margin changes can result in a reduced rather than an enhanced bottom line. A further negative result can be the loss of customer relationships earned over a period of years with expensive marketing efforts. This crucial formula and the pricing techniques that follow are a part of the pricing process that is described in this chapter.

The Concept of Proximate Value Pricing© states that products or services should be priced and promoted on the basis of their value or worth, from a customer's perspective. Inherent in the value concept are the further thoughts that a service should *not* be priced on the basis of cost or whatever the traffic will bear. There are four elements to value pricing, namely, product utility, customer alternatives, customer perception, and buyer capacity.

Product utility is defined as the usefulness of a service in its ability to satisfy customer needs. A checking account satisfies multiple needs such as a safe place to store money until needed, the ability to exchange money value with another party without carrying cash, an automatic receipt of the exchange, guaranteed safe delivery of value, etc. Generally speaking, the functional usefulness or customer benefits of bank services have been both unrecognized and undercommunicated by bankers.

Customer alternatives represent the availability of alternative products or services which will provide similar customer usefulness or benefits. Alternatives are supplied by our competitors. The service pricing of our competitors and the positioning of their products, delivery systems, and institution have a bearing on what we charge. The reverse is also true. How we positively differentiate our bank, products, and forms of service delivery, and how we communicate this to the market will impact the prices we can charge.

Customer perceptions of a product's ability to supply need-fulfillment or benefit are not always accurate or uniform. When perceptions differ on the utility of a service or product, the value or worth will be influenced. Customers' perceptions of an institution or of a product are not always based on facts. Certain financial institutions have superior reputations while others have average or inferior reputations. The superior institution can get a higher price for basically the same checking account service as that produced by an institution with an average or inferior reputation. The objective is to position ourselves as positively as possible in the markets we serve.

Customer capacity represents the desire and ability of customers to pay for a service. In order for a service to be profitably produced, sold, and delivered, there must be a market of a certain size. Without an adequate number of people willing to pay for a service, volume will be insufficient to cover costs and required profit margins.

The four elements of product utility, customer alternatives, customer perceptions, and customer capacity when used together represent a sound basis on which to price banking services. The reader may be concerned that cost has not been included among the value pricing elements which all tend to be marketplace-customer related. As indicated in the opening of this chapter, costs are not consistently and accurately measured in the banking industry, nor are they a consideration on which customers determine their willingness to pay. Costs, however, are a part of the element of customer capacity and will be considered in the pricing process when price sensitivity is measured.

All of the elements of Proximate Value Pricing© are embodied in the pricing methodology as presented later in this chapter.

Strength-Weaknesses Evaluation

In determining the range of product pricing alternatives, consideration should be given to the strength and weaknesses of the offering institution and the strength and weaknesses of the need-filling characteristics of the product being priced. Customers will justify to themselves the different prices for similar products offered by a variety of service providers. This justification is based on both perceived and real differences in the offering institutions and in the service being sold. In retailing, customers shopping at upscale specialty stores recognize that their prices will be higher than a purchase of similar merchandise at Sears, Penney's, or Kmart. Customers will also justify the price they pay for a service based on real differences such as convenience, quality of service, product feature differences, and the like. Identifying the limited but primary customer considerations is the first step in determining the strengths or weaknesses in an institution's product offering. The second and equally important step is to measure the institution's strengths and weaknesses against those of its competitors. This type of objective evaluation will help to determine the available flexibility in pricing.

Determining Price Elasticity of Demand

Customer price sensitiveness determines elasticity of demand. If customers are very sensitive to price changes, up or down, elasticity of demand is said to be high. If customers are relatively insensitive to price changes, elasticity is said to be low. The price of grocery staples such as milk, bread, and eggs are examples of elastic or sensitive pricing. Customers will be attracted to low prices and avoid high prices by seeking other sources for the products. There are a number of techniques for evaluating product price elasticity, such as market research, price experimentation, and probabilistic estimating. The pricing process proposed here uses probabilistic estimating. This option was selected because it favors the newness of pricing in the financial services industry, whereas the other alternatives each have weaknesses. The market research approach is strong on products with a pricing history but falls short on industries and products which have limited history on which to predict customer behavior. Price experimentation which provides empirical behavioral results has its shortcomings because of time required to gather and analyze results and the fact that pricing "errors" tend to be irreversible. Once a price is set and well communicated to a marketplace of customers and prospects, it is very difficult, particularly in banking, to adjust the price if the implementation did not meet desired results. With potentially 100-plus bank products, using price experimentation in changing prices every one or two years is not feasible.

In probabilistic estimating, a variety of prices and results can be tested against an acceptable range of results. This is accomplished by asking selected, experienced customer service employees to estimate the best, worst, and most likely customer behavior to specific price changes up or down. Using a matrix of four to six changes, with three possible outcomes for each, will provide a set of scenarios from which a specific price action can be selected for implementation.

External Environment Considerations

Totally beyond the control of management but with impact on pricing flexibility are external conditions such as legislation, regulation, political and social trends, technological changes, and the economy. These, too, must be considered, particularly when repricing services in a commercial bank. Time and space will not permit an elaboration on each of these items which must be considered in both the short- and long-term outlook and their likely impact on the market served and on the institution offering the service.

All of the foregoing considerations and techniques are covered in the pricing process proposed in the concluding pages of this chapter. They are brought together in a form of programmed instruction which provides for a step-by-step evaluation of pricing alternatives and selection which best fits a specific institution in its market.

STRUCTURING A PRICING PROGRAM

A well-structured pricing program will have accountable people, a pricing philosophy, a goal, a pricing methodology, and a monitoring system for tracking results.

The assignment of a person or persons to be accountable for the pricing function is as critical to its success as the designation of staff to the functions of credit, operations, or financial management. Similarly, in large organizations where these functions are sponsored by chief financial officers, chief operations officers, and chief credit officers, it is important to have a chief pricing officer. If management deems noninterest income vital to the well-being of the institution, it deserves to have a senior executive who can garner resources and sufficient visibility to make it an ongoing part of the organization. The loss of "free deposits" and the payment of market rate interest for time deposits have dictated structural changes in banking organizations.

A pricing philosophy statement serves as a road map to members of executive and senior management, as well as to those staff members who are carrying out the pricing function. Just as there are policies and guidelines, written or unwritten, for credit and operations so, too, it is important to have explicit guidelines for pricing.

A set objective or goal can enhance the effectiveness of the pricing function by causing the institution to focus on a future visible achievement. The goal can be both short- and long-term. It can be based on an annual growth percentage or dollar amount, a fixed percentage coverage of noninterest expense by noninterest income, or a percentage of average daily assets. Noninterest income goal setting is inherently a part of strategic as well as business planning. The goal provides both a challenge and a target for the development of noninterest income as well as a standard by which success can be measured.

A pricing methodology or process is as critical to the development of profitable noninterest income as is the credit process to the production of net interest income, or operating processes to delivery of quality services.

The credit process in most banks involves a loan officer who compiles a history on a prospective borrower, analyzes the borrower's financial performance, prepares a pro forma statement and presents a recommendation to appropriate approving officers or committees. This same approach is recommended for pricing. Therefore, history compiling and analysis of product performance are built into the pricing process proposed.

On investigation, most bank operations are found to be activated by the completion of certain forms or computer screen formats. This represents a form of programmed instruction which, if followed, will produce the desired operating results. This concept is also built into the proposed pricing process. The set of forms which complete this chapter, along with the accompanying instructions, represent a programmed instruction approach to pricing which can be used in a credit-like approval process to secure sound pricing decisions. Before introducing the pricing process, the following thoughts on monitoring should be read to complete the overall description of structuring a pricing program.

A pricing monitoring system needs to be both micro and macro in scope. "Micro" means tracking each product's performance against plan as to units sold and revenues collected. "Macro" is the tracking of growth in noninterest income revenues against established goals monthly, annually, and long-term. The monitoring should also provide strategic direction for the growth of noninterest income as various product and functional sources ebb and grow in our constantly changing markets. To meet these requirements, a product performance report citing the growth or shrinkage of each fee-producing service, and amount of service charge collected, should be prepared periodically. For reasonable use and comparisons, these reports should be prepared no less frequently than quarterly. Where price changes have been made, more frequent reporting is desirable.

A PRICING METHODOLOGY

The pricing process that is presented in this section has been used by The Valley National Bank of Arizona for over ten years. In addition, the use of the methodology has been spread by Dr. Wilsted, its codeveloper, while consulting with over 100 banks and savings and loans both nationally and internationally. The methodology has been taught by Dr. Wilsted and the author of this chapter at graduate schools of banking throughout the country. The conclusion to be drawn is that many banks, using all or some of the process, have determined that it conceptually and practically fills the needs for service pricing.

The methodology is comprised of three parts: An inventory of pricing opportunities, a process for analyzing pricing opportunities, and a decision mechanism.

The inventorying of pricing opportunities leads the methodology. The inventorying logically follows the determination that an institution needs to formalize its pricing function. It starts by assigning accountability to a senior management member and his designates. This staff recommends a pricing philosophy and a goal, and performs the inventorying of pricing opportunities. An inventory form with instructions appears on page 1058.

In keeping with the concept of value pricing, it is recommended that products inventoried be viewed both unbundled as well as bundled. Since service is what we sell, it is also useful to inventory services being provided for which a charge is not currently made. In compiling an inventory, most banks discover that they have more priceable opportunities than they ever realized—usually over 100.

The analytical process of the methodology, beginning on page 1056, consists of Pricing Analysis Instructions, the Pricing Analysis Worksheets, and the Product Pricing Review. The Pricing Analysis Worksheets with accompanying instructions incorporate the concept of Proximate Value Pricing© and all of the other pricing techniques discussed in this chapter.

The Product Pricing Review form acts as a decision-making tool, encapsulating all of the information analyzed in the Pricing Analysis Worksheets. The Review form is designed in a credit review format, useful in that it "feels familiar" to senior management decision makers involved in the credit review process.

The third part of the methodology is a decision-making process which somewhat parallels the credit approval process as it exists in medium to large banks. The decision process, as well as all other parts of the methodology, needs to be tailored to the nature and size of the organization using it.

MANAGING THE PRICING PROGRAM

In order to properly manage a pricing program, you need to know your market, maintain reports that accurately and frequently monitor performance and tailor your pricing program to match your organization's changing needs.

Knowing your market means keeping abreast of changing customer needs, your competitors—their products and their prices—and the environmental changes affecting the total market, including your customers. In these days of deregulation with new nonbank competitors and interstate banking, it does not seem likely that we can generalize and superimpose pricing schemes developed in one community or state on another market located in another state. Costs, competition, regulation, and other factors, do vary from one market to another, thereby requiring customized approaches to managing, marketing, and pricing. We would do well to watch and learn from members of the retailing industry who have operated in a nonregulated environment for many years.

Reports to measure performance against plan are as valuable to the marketing and pricing function as are net interest margin, loan loss, and nonperforming reports to the credit function. To ensure success, a member of senior management must review the reports and take action when necessary.

No matter how effective in one organization, a pricing program cannot be superimposed on a different organization and be expected to work as effectively. The most successful programs are built from within the institution. Outside resources, including consultants, are used to bring concepts, policies, and practices to the attention of the accountable people for adaptation to their organization. Resource commitment will vary from one organization to another. In a community bank, one member of senior management may represent the entire pricing program. In an international money center bank, it could be many people in numerous committees—but all using similar principles and concepts.

SUMMARY AND CONCLUSIONS

The commercial banking industry is undergoing unprecedented changes as it moves from a fixed price, rigidly regulated industry to a deregulated, market priced, market driven industry facing new giant, nationwide, nonbank competitors. Many of these new competitors are experienced at operating in a free environment without regulatory restraints on their marketing activities, including the pricing of their products. As an industry, banking is being challenged as never before to meet the expectations of its consumers in the maintenance of sound financial competitive institutions while producing acceptable returns for its shareholders. The proper pricing of deposits, loans, and services is critical to our meeting the expectations of consumers and shareholders and the competitive threats of our new nonbank competitors. While the pricing of deposits and loans carries the greatest impact on our profit and loss statement, noninterest revenues as determined by profitable pricing will be a substantial factor in separating the high performing institutions from their industry peers. Noninterest revenues will provide the "frosting on the cake" for high performance banks.

It is the author's hope that the policies and practices proposed here will serve as one stepping stone to help members or the industry reach higher levels of sophistication in pricing and marketing to match and even beat those of our new nonbank competitors.

The Pricing Process*

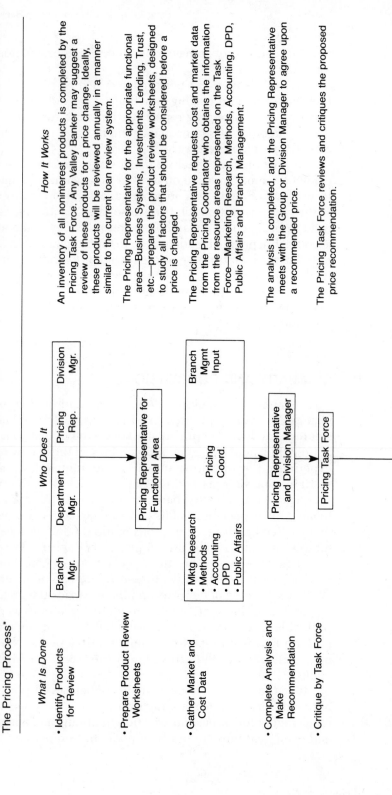

Who Does It

| Branch Mgr. | Department Mgr. | Pricing Rep. | Division Mgr. |

What Is Done | **How It Works**

• Identify Products for Review

An inventory of all noninterest products is completed by the Pricing Task Force. Any Valley Banker may suggest a review of these products for a price change. Ideally, these products will be reviewed annually in a manner similar to the current loan review system.

• Prepare Product Review Worksheets

Pricing Representative for Functional Area

The Pricing Representative for the appropriate functional area—Business Systems, Investments, Lending, Trust, etc.—prepares the product review worksheets, designed to study all factors that should be considered before a price is changed.

• Gather Market and Cost Data

Pricing Coord.

• Mktg Research
• Methods
• Accounting
• DPD
• Public Affairs

Branch Mgmt Input

The Pricing Representative requests cost and market data from the Pricing Coordinator who obtains the information from the resource areas represented on the Task Force—Marketing Research, Methods, Accounting, DPD, Public Affairs and Branch Management.

• Complete Analysis and Make Recommendation

Pricing Representative and Division Manager

The analysis is completed, and the Pricing Representative meets with the Group or Division Manager to agree upon a recommended price.

• Critique by Task Force

Pricing Task Force

The Pricing Task Force reviews and critiques the proposed price recommendation.

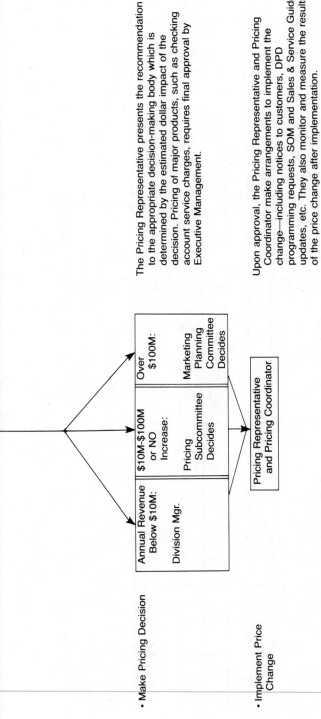

- Make Pricing Decision

Annual Revenue Below $10M:	$10M-$100M or NO Increase:	Over $100M:
Division Mgr.	Pricing Subcommittee Decides	Marketing Planning Committee Decides

Pricing Representative and Pricing Coordinator

The Pricing Representative presents the recommendation to the appropriate decision-making body which is determined by the estimated dollar impact of the decision. Pricing of major products, such as checking account service charges, requires final approval by Executive Management.

- Implement Price Change

Upon approval, the Pricing Representative and Pricing Coordinator make arrangements to implement the change—including notices to customers, DPD programming requests, SOM and Sales & Service Guide updates, etc. They also monitor and measure the results of the price change after implementation.

*Structure for a large bank where total organization input is critical.

Noninterest Income Product Inventory (instructions on back)

Accountable Group and Division/Department _____

Date _____   Prepared By _____

Product	Current Price	12 - 24 Month Schedule	Last Review		Business Plan			Total Anticipated Gain/Loss	
			Date	Total Annual $ Gain	Review Date	Recommen- dation	Implem. Date	$	# Cust.

Instructions

Product— List of all current noninterest income products or services in division or department. Break down major products, such as business analysis checking, into all "priceable" components, even if all parts would normally be handled in one review.

Current Price—The current price of the product or service. If the price depends on variables such as number of items deposited or dollar amounts of drafts, enter "see schedule attached" in this space and attach schedule to sheet.

12-24 Month Schedule—The frequency with which the particular product should be reviewed. No product should be reviewed less than once every two years. Products with substantial annual revenues should be reviewed every 12 to 18 months.

Last Review—(a) Date—The month and year of last price change implementation or of last review if no price change made. (b) Total Annual $ Gain— The total annual amount of increased revenue brought in as a result of the last price change. If at the time of the last review, no price change was made or more customers than anticipated were lost resulting in lost income, note this here, i.e., "no change" or "loss."

Business Plan—All products of an area should be scheduled for review in the business plans of that area. This section can be completed using your business plans. (a) Review Date—The month and year this product is scheduled to be reviewed again. (b) Recommendation—An indication of what you feel the recommendation will be for this product at the next review, i.e., raise, lower, or no change in price, discontinue the product, enhance it, or replace it. (c) Implementation Date—If applicable, when the next price change would go into effect or when the product would be discontinued, enhanced, or replaced, if approved. (d) Total Anticipated Gain/Loss—(If applicable) $—The total annual amount of increased or decreased revenue anticipated as a result of the price change, discontinuance of the product, or other change to the product, if approved. # Customers—The total increase or decrease in number of customers anticipated as a result of the price change, discontinuance of the product, or other change to the product, if approved.

1059

PRICING ANALYSIS INSTRUCTIONS

The Pricing Analysis packet has been designed to provide a systematic approach to analyzing noninterest products for possible price changes. This approach has been selected to provide a standard means of reviewing and presenting product pricing information to management. The purpose of using such a standardized approach is to familiarize management with a format just as they have become familiar with the credit review form to review loans. A Pricing Analysis is to be completed on every noninterest product being reviewed. Products are to be reviewed annually on an ongoing basis. New products should also be analyzed using this format.

The Pricing Analysis packet consists of nine sections: (A) Proximate Value, (B) Market Conditions, (C) Competitive Analysis, (D) Cost Profile, (E) Product History, (F) Price Volume Relationship Estimates, (G) Pro Forma, (H) Monitoring Method, and (I) Conclusion.

Section A. Proximate Value (Product Utility/Customer Perceptions)

Proximate value is defined as the worth of a product as seen by the customer. It is *not* the cost of producing that product. However, the cost does set the floor below which the price *ideally* would not drop. And the highest price that the customer is willing to pay sets a ceiling. The difference between this floor and ceiling then is the range of possible prices, with the most profitable one being closest to the perceived value.

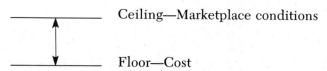

Ceiling—Marketplace conditions

Floor—Cost

1. Describe the product as perceived by that customer—*not* as perceived by you, the banker. Try to determine what the product really does for the customer.
2. Since it is the customer who defines the product and sets the ceiling price, it is important to know who that customer is and what segment(s) of the market he/she represents.
3. Taking into consideration who the customer is, what the product does for the customer, and how it differs from similar products of VNB and other institutions, comment why the customer may or may not be willing to pay a higher price for the product.
4. One goal in pricing is to differentiate products, using the customer's perception as the basis for that differentiation. Keeping

this in mind, note the difference between this product and similar Valley Bank products *and/or* similar products of other institutions, remembering that these differences may provide the basis (justification) for a higher price *in the eyes of the customer.*

Section B. Market Conditions (External Environment)

Since price is determined in the marketplace, it is important to examine the factors in our external environment that can influence price. These include:

1. *Regional/National Economic Trends*—consider current trends. Our economic environment is really a set of regional economies that together form a national economy. Since VNB is a regional bank, the economic situation of the region within which we operate will influence our pricing. But since our region is just part of the total picture, the state of the entire national economy also is relevant.

   This factor as well as all others should be looked at both in terms of the present condition and the future condition one to five years down the road. The anticipated impact of this—either present or future—should be noted. If it is felt that a particular factor does not significantly impact a decision to change price, make a statement to that effect. *Do not leave any section blank.*

2. *Legislative/Political/Social*—from time to time, regulatory changes, or anticipated ones, or social changes can influence the direction of a decision or change in price. Note any possibility of such a legislative, political, or social influence in this section.

3. *Technological*—Technological changes often mean lower costs and product improvement. They can also mean that some products may become obsolete or of less value to the customer in the future. If any such technological changes are currently underway or anticipated that will impact on the product being reviewed, this should be indicated.

Section C. Competitive Analysis

This section provides an opportunity to compare Valley Bank's current prices and products with those of the major competitors.

1. Current product prices for VNB and the other local banks can be obtained from the Pricing Coordinator who will contact Marketing Research for this information. In some cases, this data

may already be available or will be of a nature such that the information could be more easily gathered by someone in the Price Reviewer's functional area. You, as a Price Reviewer, can probably best determine this. Also, check banks nationally and/ or S&L's, CUs, trust companies, mortgage companies, finance companies, etc., if appropriate, and enter your choices in each column.

Do not attempt to make any agreement nor discuss with a competitor any proposed rates, fees, or service charges. Such actions may be perceived as price fixing, which is illegal. This does not restrict the availability of such information, as it can be monitored and gathered through marketing shopper techniques.

2. *a.* The Customer Alternatives section is a tool designed to identify the competitive position of the product and the financial institution. This competitive position must be known before a pricing strategy can be developed. Enter your choice of major competitors under the heading "competition." Your competition, in addition to banks, can be S&Ls, Credit Unions, Trust Companies, etc.

   b. Next, list the relevant customer needs and institutional features of the product in the first column. Among those customer needs to consider are product features such as safety, convenience, price, interest rate, etc. Institutional features include such items as number and location of offices, past performance, size, reputation, quality of service etc.

   c. After the customer needs and significant institutional features have been identified, a rank or weight of one, two, or three should be assigned to each (three being the highest) and entered under the importance column.

   d. Next, review each institution separately, and on a one–five scale, rate the quality provided by that institution for each of the factors listed. Enter this rating in column A under the respective institution.

   e. *For each institution,* multiply the weight of each factor as noted in the importance column by the rating given that factor for the institution, and enter the answer under column B. Total column B for each institution to obtain the results of this evaluation. The highest total indicates the institution with the greatest strengths and opportunities for the particular product. To easily recognize significant factors affecting these totals, circle the highest number and "box-in" the lowest number in *each* row. This should enable you to identify and work toward promoting or correcting important features of VNB's product and see from which of the competitors' strengths or weaknesses we can learn. Remember that not completing this section may be comparable to saying that there is a low price sensitivity for the product, and that the customer did not select Valley Bank because of the strengths of this product.

3. and 4.

The nature and timing of competitive reactions to price changes can be significant. It can be important to know who is most likely to react, when they are most likely to react, and how they are most likely to react. Probably the best indicator of this is a record of past reactions to price changes.

Section D. Cost Profile

Although pricing is not strictly a financial exercise, it is important to examine the costs associated with producing and delivering a product.

There are three levels of cost incurred in performing any function or service. The first is *variable* costs which are those costs which vary with the volume, such as postage, materials and supplies, energy, part-time labor, etc. It can also be said that variable costs are those costs that you should incur if you were to produce one more element of service tomorrow, or likewise, the cost that you would avoid if you were to do one less service tomorrow.

The next level of costs are *fixed* costs. Fixed costs represent the major assets and resources which the bank finds necessary to put in place to perform the service or services in question and as a general rule do not vary with volume over short periods of time, but can vary with volume over extended periods of time. Examples of fixed costs are buildings, land, equipment, full-time staff, associated asset carrying costs, and allocated service center expenses.

The sum of variable and fixed costs is the *direct* cost of providing the service or product.

The last level of costs are *G&A* costs. These are costs which are incurred to support and administer the organization and are generally regarded as costs incurred in relation to the function or service performed in the organization. Examples of these costs are advertising, liability insurance, stockholder expense, bond interest, Board of Directors expenses, and administrative salaries and expenses. The sum of all three levels of cost combined—variable, fixed, and G&A (General and Adm.)—is the *full* cost of offering the product or service.

Please try to provide as much information as possible here to assist the Methods Department in computing the data and avoid duplication of effort in gathering data.

Section E. Product History

Historical information is one of the elements identified as being important in any pricing decision.

1. In this section, indicate the date the product was initially introduced, date of the most recent price change, and the reason for the change.
2. A five-year history of the product is requested in this section covering (1) cost, (2) price, (3) volume, (4) collected revenue, (5) overhead contribution, (6) market share, and (7) stage in life cycle, all of which taken together indicate significant historical trends.

The two items, market share and stage in life cycle, may be of particular interest in that these may give an indication as to what pricing strategy to employ—perhaps based on achieving what may be considered the optimal market share or to take advantage of the favorable aspects of the current stage in the product life cycle.

The three major stages in the product life cycle represent the sales history of the product—early, mature, and decline. In the early growth stage of a product, sales start slow and then accelerate rapidly if demand persists. There are few, if any, competitors during this stage. As the mature stage is reached, sales are very good and, because of this, many competitors enter the market. Finally, if demand falls off, fewer sales are made, and the declining stage is reached. At this stage, decisions must be made whether to continue the product as is, change it, or find new markets. Sometimes it is desirable to price high in an early stage of the product life cycle. In a later stage, product diversification or expansion may be considered. Diversification involves creating new products for new customers so that the new product is in an early stage while the older product is in a later and perhaps less profitable stage. Expanding involves finding new uses for current products to perhaps appeal to another market segment. There are many options—the importance lies in identifying these stages and trends to take advantage of what they tell us.

Again, attempt to complete as much of this section as possible. Some portions—such as cost, collected revenue, market share, etc.— may require research by Methods, Accounting, and/or Marketing Research. If this is the case, notify the Pricing Coordinator who will request assistance from the appropriate areas.

Section F. Price-Volume Relationship (Customer Capacity)

Customer capacity is really a measure of price sensitivity. A product is price sensitive if, when you raise the price, volume will drop at an accelerating rate. On the other hand, when the product is price insensitive, volume changes vary little in relation to the price change. Thus, when customer demand is insensitive, it may be wise to raise the price; when it is sensitive, you may want to lower the price to increase volume.

Price sensitivity is affected by these factors:

1. *Availability of substitutes.* The issue here is: What other product is available that will do the same thing? If there are many substitutes, there could be high sensitivity to price increases. The idea is to differentiate (as mentioned earlier) to create a gap so that the customer no longer sees the substitutes. When there are limited substitutes, it may be wise to come in at a high price to generate profits and growth. Over time, substitutes may appear; so when this happens, price can be lowered to keep profits and possibly gain market share.

2. *Frequency of purchase.* The more often a product is purchased, the more price sensitive it usually is.

3. *Budget impact.* The lower the percent of income spent by the customer (individual *or* company), the less price sensitive the product is. So for a customer who spends a very small percent of his/her income on banking services, prices (theoretically) could be raised significantly without losing the customer.

4. *Economic conditions.* When the economy is on the upswing, and conditions are favorable, demand will generally tend to be less sensitive in comparison to times of unfavorable economic conditions when people are limiting spending and concentrating on savings, causing a situation of price sensitivity.

The exercise in this section is to assist you in determining the impact on product demand of several proposed prices. When estimating the price-volume relationships at various prices, keep in mind that the 25% and 50% figures may be changed to lower or higher percentages or to dollar amounts to fit the purpose of the particular review. After completing this exercise, select the "best" price. This will be your recommended price.

Section G. Pro Forma

This section provides an opportunity to project impact of a price change—in dollars, volume, competitive reaction, and possible loss of customer and market share.

1. The break-even analysis (optional) is a device for determining the point at which sales will cover total costs. The equation for this is

$$Q_{BE} = \frac{FC}{P - VC}$$

Q_{BE} = quantity at breakeven
FC = total fixed costs + G&A
P = unit price
VC = variable unit cost

Note that it is only reliable at one point in time at each specified price, and changes as any one of its components changes over time.

2. This section provides an opportunity to estimate volume, gross revenue, full cost, and gross margin at the price level chosen in the price-volume relationship section under circumstances rated as "optimistic," "most likely," and "pessimistic."

3. Anticipate the likely competitive reaction to the proposed new price. Consider whether or not the increase would be followed, and if so, who might be likely to follow and when; Or if the competitors would maintain their current prices and attempt to use them to their advantage and our disadvantage.

4. Based upon that anticipated reaction, estimate the impact on VNB in terms of loss of profitable business, loss of unprofitable business, or any other significant effects.

5. If the impact is such that VNB could lose volume and/or market share, consider whether or not it would be acceptable to experience a decline.

6. Consider timing in making changes and notifying customers.

Section H. Monitoring Method

In order to determine if a price change has been effective and has produced the desired results, a method of monitoring and measuring must be developed. Since this will vary from product to product, this will need to be considered in each analysis to decide the best method of measuring results of a price change on a particular product.

Section I. Conclusion

Based on the analysis, summarize the recommendation, volume and revenue to be realized if the decision is approved.

* * * * * *

Pricing Analysis Worksheets

Product: _____ Prepared By: _____ Date: _____

****

A. Proximate Value (Product Utility/Customer Perceptions)

1. Describe product. (What does the product do for the customer?) _____
   _____
   _____

2. Describe market segment. (Who is the customer?) _____
   _____

3. Would customers be willing to pay VNB a higher price for this product? Why or why not? _____
   _____
   _____
   _____

4. In the eyes of the customer, how is this product different from other similar products of VNB and other institutions? _____
   _____
   _____

5. What could be done to further differentiate, enhance or expand the product to: (1) increase sales, or (2) justify a higher price? _____
   _____
   _____

****

B. Market Conditions (External Environment)

Comment on the effect of each of the external environment factors listed below on present and future sales of this product. If not applicable, indicate "NA."

Factor	Present Condition	Future Condition (1,2,5 Years)	Anticipated Impact
Regional/National Economic Trends			
Legislative/Political/Social Trends			
Technological Trends			

C. Competitive Analysis

1. Current Price Status

Local:	National:	Other: (S&Ls, CUs, etc.)
VNB _____	_____	_____
FNB _____	_____	_____
TAB _____	_____	_____
UB _____	_____	_____
CONT _____	_____	_____
GWB _____	_____	_____

2. Customer Alternatives/Strength-Weaknesses Profile—Identify the main customer needs and institutional features (such as safety, interest, convenience, size of bank, reputation, quality of service, etc.) related to the sale of each product and rate them by institution, i.e., bank, S&L, CU, trust co., etc.

Customer Needs/ Institutional Features	Impor- tance	Valley Bank		Competition									
		A	B	A	B	A	B	A	B	A	B	A	B
Totals													

3. What have past reactions by competitors been to price changes in the marketplace?
_____
_____
_____

4. What is the anticipated competitive situation in the future? _____
_____
_____

****

D. Cost Profile

Variable Cost:	_____	Monthly Volume: _____
Fixed Cost:	_____	Annual Volume: _____
Direct Cost:	_____	
G & A Cost:	_____	
Full Cost:	_____	

E. Product History
1. Date of introduction _____ Date of last change _____
   Reason for change: _____
   _____

2. VNB five-year history

Factor	19 ___	19 ___	19 ___	19 ___	19 ___
Direct Cost (Unit)					
Price (Unit)					
Volume					
Collected Revenue					
Overhead Contribution					
Market Share					
Stage in Life Cycle					

****

F. Price-Volume Relationships (Customer Capacity)
Estimate increases (or decreases) in sales if price is increased or decreased 25-50% (or other suggested percentages). Look at this from an optimistic, most likely, and pessimistic point of view.

	Price	Optimistic	Most likely	Pessimistic
+ 50% or + ___ %				
+ 25% or + ___ %				
Present price				
− 25% or − ___ %				
− 50% or − ___ %				

Conclusion: Based on the above estimates, demand for this product appears to be
<u>price sensitive/price insensitive.</u>
(circle one)

Comments: _____
_____
_____
_____

G. Pro Forma

1. Break-even analysis (optional)
   Recommended price   _____
   Fixed costs + G&A   _____
   Variable costs   _____
   Estimated break-even
      volume   _____
2. At recommended price of _____ :

	Optimistic	Most likely	Pessimistic
Estimated Volume			
Estimated Gross Rev.			
Estimated Total Cost			
Estimated Gross Margin			

3. Anticipated competitive reaction to suggested price: _____
   _____

4. Impact of anticipated competitive reaction to suggested price: _____
   _____

5. Are we willing to accept possible decline in volume? If so, how much? _____
   _____

6. Is there any problem with timing of anticipated price change or notification of customers?
   _____
   _____
   _____

****

H. Monitoring Method

What type of follow-up will be required, and how should we monitor and measure the
results of this price change? _____
_____
_____

****

I. Conclusion—Based on the above analysis:

1. Recommendation is: _____
2. Estimated volume is: _____
3. Increased additional revenue is: _____

PRODUCT PRICING REVIEW FORM INSTRUCTIONS

The Product Pricing Review is a one-page summary of the Pricing
Analysis Worksheets. It is to be used to review both new and existing
products. The purpose of this form is to present the vital pricing information in concise form to the Pricing Committee for their review
and decision.

All information (with the exception of the "Action Plan" section)
is taken directly from the Pricing Analysis Worksheets.

Product Pricing Review

Product: _____   Prepared By: _____
Division: _____   Date: _____

☐ New product   ☐ Annual Review   ☐ Special Review

Recommendation: _____
_____
_____

Reason & Objective: _____
_____
_____

Recom-mended Price	Percent of Change	Date of Recom. Change	Date of Last Change	Annualized Revenue		
				Present	Potential	Difference

Number of lost customers anticipated: _____

Proximate Value: _____
_____

Price Sensitivity: _____

Market Conditions—External Environment (economic, legislative/political/social, tech.) ____
_____
_____

Five-Year History:	19 __	19 __	19 __	19 __	19 __	% of Change
Direct Cost						
Unit Price						
Collected Revenue						
Overhead Contribution						
Market Share						
Volume						

Competitive Analysis: Current Price Status

Local:	VNB	_____	CONT	_____
	FNB	_____	UB	_____
	TAB	_____	GWB	_____

Competitive Analysis (Con't.):

National: _____   Other: (S&Ls, CUs, etc.) _____
                 _____   _____
                 _____   _____

Past reactions to price changes by competition: _____
_____
_____

Cost Profile: Variable cost: _____   Monthly volume: _____
             Fixed cost: _____   Annual volume: _____
             Direct cost: _____
             G & A cost: _____
             Full cost: _____

Pro Forma:
     Estimated break-even volume:_____   Estimated gross revenue: _____
     Recommended price: _____   Estimated total cost: _____
     Estimated volume: _____   Estimated gross margin: _____

Other:
1. Is there any problem with timing of price change or announcement of increase? Explain.
_____
_____
_____

2. Can product be differentiated, enhanced or expanded to increase sales or justify higher
    price? Explain. _____
_____
_____
_____

Action Plan:
    Method of implementation: _____
_____

    Hours: _____   Estimated expense: _____

    Computer Programming _____   Supplement   _____
    SOM/Circular Letter _____   Stuffer   _____
    Sales & Services Guide _____   Brochure   _____
    Audio Tapes/Letter   _____   Other   _____

    Method to monitor & measure results: _____
_____
_____

    Other comments: _____
_____
_____

Next scheduled review (month/year): _____
Approved by: _____   Date: _____

Rev. 9/80

CHAPTER SEVENTY-TWO

Keys to Successful Corporate Business Development Programs

Thomas V. Moriarty II

Senior Vice President
Shawmut Bank, N.A.

DEALING WITH THE CULTURE

The words "business development program" automatically bring to mind the vision of a CEO or division head who has just announced, "Hey, we haven't been getting any new accounts lately, what we need is a new business development program!" What that means to the commercial lenders is, "Oh boy, here we go again," and is usually followed by a great deal of scurrying about, normally involving a trip to the marketing department for a "list." Calls are made and call reports are submitted. For the first few weeks the big guy who ordered the troops into battle reviews every call report and shows a great deal of interest in "the program." A few more weeks pass, the number of calls begins to go down, a credit problem comes up, the audit committee wants to know what's going on in the mortgage area, the big guy gets distracted—and eventually the "new business development program" dies of its own weight. The commercial lenders look at it as a necessary evil, a distraction from their routine. But they have patience, and as sure as the sun rises and sets, all new business development programs have a defined beginning, and a *very* predictable end. This phenomena, as silly as it sounds, is enacted every day in commercial banks around the country. It is the product of a hundred years of commercial banking culture and isn't about to be turned around by some quick and easy fix. No, it's more about bankers committing to a gradual but steady change in this culture through the development of some rather traditional managerial disciplines which have long been practiced in consumer and industrial organizations.

Those disciplines include the following:

1. Organizing—around markets and people, not the bank;
2. Planning—setting goals, objective and the plans which will achieve them;
3. Implementing and Directing—working with and through people to execute those plans;
4. Controlling—developing feedback mechanisms to measure progress; and
5. Reviewing—deciding what's working and what needs to be changed.

Cast solely in the light of business development, what we are talking about is traditional sales management. When was the last time you were in a bank which had a commercial lender who was designated as the "sales manager?" We need to think hard about the way we define the role of the commercial lender. Banking is the only profession I am aware of which asks one individual to perform so many functions: Sales, engineering, customer service, quality control and collections! In many cases he or she is expected to manage others at the same time. So the first place we need to look is at the organization. We need to decide what roles people will play. Who will sell, who will service, and who will manage. Many organizations are restructuring the roles of their people around their defined strengths. Lenders who are strong business developers end up with a heavier sales component and less servicing. Others who are stronger at servicing existing accounts find themselves with larger customer portfolios, and less selling responsibility.

SOME THOUGHTS ON ORGANIZATION

OK, now that we have assessed the roles people will play we now need to look at the organization hierarchy. There can be no managing without managers. You can have sales people, but they will *never* be effective without a sales manager. Here's where we run pell mell into the culture. "Ah ha," says the senior lender, "now you're stepping on *my* feet. I'm the head honcho around here!" Here, the culture has dictated that the senior credit guy has all of the lenders reporting to him—for credit *and* sales. Can you think of another industry in which the quality control manager is also in charge of the sales force? Banking has done just that, placing a higher cultural value on credit skills than selling skills, and then implying that superior credit skills have something to do with the ability to manage salespeople. Besides which, isn't that a classic conflict of interest? Sales volume and credit quality under the same guy? One answer is to separate the functions. Charge the sales manager with the development of acceptable new business, and the senior lender with the job of quality control. "Sure," says the senior lender, "what you want to do is put the animals in charge of the zoo. All I'll see is a series of mushroom shaped clouds!"

The key operant word is "acceptable" business. Somewhere, somehow, the organization must have faith in its system of quality control, its credit policy, approval, administration, and review processes. Otherwise, the problem isn't sales or sales management, it's something much more serious and the reader should stop here and go back to the chapter on credit administration.

OK, there's room to disagree. I've seen organizations who separated the functions and placed the lenders under the sales manager for volume objectives and the senior lender for credit quality objectives, and I've seen banks who have kept both roles with the individual who was the senior lender. In the latter case, those banks emphasized the duality of the roles, and measured the individual on each equally. The issue is, in order for sales management to take place, there must be someone with his hand in the air saying "that's my responsibility." Establishing clear accountability for the sales management role is by far more important than how it is accomplished organizationally. It establishes the basis for responsibility, reward or punishment. Accountability is the management holy water that changes the culture. It says it's real, it's permanent, it's how we do business—not just a passing program.

NEW BUSINESS VERSUS SERVING CURRENT CUSTOMERS

Current Customers = Profitability
New Business Development = Destiny

These were the words used by mentor and friend Neal Finnegan in speaking to graduating commercial banking trainees. The message is clear and succinct and addresses the question as to where the Commercial Lender should be spending his or her time. The truth is that we generally lose money during the first year of a new relationship due to the rather high cost of acquisition. What follows, however, is an annuity stream of profitability that is likely to last for years and years. The secret, then, is growing our portfolio of relationships at a rate necessary to build our profitability at the desired rate, while replacing accounts which leave, are asked to leave, or are stolen by the competition. This, of course, assumes that we have the capacity to turn the dials, to control the volume and rate of new business which we see.

THE VALUE OF A CUSTOMER

There is nothing more sacred or valuable to a commercial lending officer than a good customer. Why? That annuity stream of income is there and will continue without a tremendous amount of effort. Just serve the customer well, meet his needs, and in general he will stay. Greenwich Research Associates work tends to give credence to the postulate that you have to do something pretty egregious to have the average middle market customer up and leave. Customers take quite a beating before they will seriously consider moving to another bank. Why? Trust, credibility, knowledge of their business which they have built up over the prior years represent their investment in their bank. To leave would simply mean starting all over with a new bridegroom— very painful. To the banker, on the other hand, the issue is, "What will I have to do to replace this customer?" The customer is a known quantity with known profitability and creditworthiness. He must be replaced with another company with just as good creditworthiness and profit potential. But how do banks compete? In general, on price. Therefore, I need to go find another company equally unhappy with its current bank, just as creditworthy, but with even *more* profit potential than the one I just lost. Needless to say, there aren't too many like that out there, and what price will I have to pay to rip that customer from the arms of my competitor? Yes, current customers are like gold and should be lovingly cared for.

TARGET MARKETS

Targeting the corporate markets which best suit your bank's strengths, capacity to serve and ability to compete is, by itself, at least a chapter, if not a full book. The idea begins with the assumptions that you can't effectively serve the whole market, and that there are certain segments of the market which have the highest profit potential for your particular bank. If you haven't been through this thought process, you are operating randomly at best. If you are successful, terrific; but don't raise your hand for the credit. Chances are that the market is "happening to you," and your ability to control business flow is strictly reactionary. You can slow it down, shut it off, or let it run, but there's very little you can do proactively to *increase* the flow when the natural momentum of the market slows. During high times when credit is tight and loan demand is high, this isn't a problem, but what do you do when the going gets tough? If you don't know exactly where to go to find the best possible profit potential and if you don't have an efficient system in place to pinpoint it, you're shooting in the dark. Sad as it may seem, this random game of corporate pin-the-tail-on-the-donkey is practiced far and wide in commercial banks around the country. "Hey, but we're getting new loans," says the commercial lender. But can he answer the right questions:

1. Are they the "right" new loans?
2. Are they the most profitable loans available?
3. Are they from the most important market segments?
4. Are they the best new loans available?

Without properly defined target markets, it's impossible to answer these questions. The real question is whether or not the guy who is flying the airplane knows where he is going and how to get there. Would you buy a ticket on a plane who's only flight plan was to take off and then land?

Targeting your market, then, is the first step in developing a capacity to control your destiny, but there's targeting, and there's TARGETING. I recall working in a former incarnation for a traditional old line banking organization where the following was standard practice. A "credit trainee"—let's call him Biff—might spend from two to four or even five years in the credit analysis area engaged in the singularly stimulating process of spreading credits—in effect doing the number crunching on behalf of some commercial lender (a culturally imperative component of the rights of passage into the analytical science of commercial lending). Today, of course, the advent of the P. C. has reduced the crunching component which would get Biff to the analytical level quicker—but that's not the point. One fine day the senior lender would walk in, place his hands on Biff's shoulder and say, "Son, we think you're ready. You are now a commercial lender. Here are three accounts to get you going. Your territory is from the Charles River north. Good luck, we know you'll do a fine job for us."

Terrific! Here's someone who has no sales training, no marketing background, who's main claim to fame is that he can spread a company's statement in under an hour—turned loose to do the good job that we all know he can. He has a group head, but this individual has over two hundred good customers of his own and hasn't been across the Charles River since his days at Elliot House.

What kind of a chance does Biff have of finding "the right loan," the most profitable loan, from the best market segment? It's dart board time. The poor guy has to reinvent the wheel, find out what companies are in his territory, their sizes, industries, who their current banks are and how happy they are with their current banking relationships. Sounds like about ten years worth of research. Good luck, Biff.

So when we talk about targeting the right market, that includes focusing in on the detail, developing the research and the data base. Probably the biggest sin that goes on in a traditional commercial lending operation is the wasting of account intelligence. Because there's no formal data base to capture information on customers and prospects, lenders typically rely on "lists." The fact is that someone may have called on the ABC Company, Inc. three times in the last two years, the final time learning that they were in Chapter 11. However, Biff doesn't know this and wastes two phone calls, a letter and three personal calls on this same company. It's what we used to call "doing it twice." It's not Biff's fault, it's management's fault for not providing him with the tools that would enable him to efficiently ply his trade. Today's P. C. technology makes the development and use of a data base simple and easy. Once captured, company data can be manipulated and changed. The use of a data base which accurately reflects the target market is critical in helping commercial lenders increase their efficiency and profitability.

THE DATA BASE ISN'T ENOUGH

Simply having a data base is a major step forward, but it will be useless unless it's used for something more than "just a list." First and foremost, it needs to be constantly updated. Bankers expect accounting accuracy. If Biff calls on a company which is supposed to have $115 million in sales and finds that, no, it really has $15 million, he'll immediately assume that *all* of the sales data is inaccurate. And if the sales data is wrong, he'll wonder what other little sources of embarrassment await him in that wonderful data base. He'll reject it and go out and find himself his own "list," and the bank will be back to square one, "doing it twice."

How should the data base be updated? There are several parts to the answer. First, all of Biff's current intelligence needs to be loaded in. After all, if we expect Biff to use it, he has to own the quality of the information. In addition, there are many sources including directories, D & B, and other list compilers, which can be regularly screened to add new data and new companies over the years. The next part of the question is *who* should do the actual updating. My experience in establishing data bases in several banks tells me that although Biff should be required to provide updating information, Biff should *not* be asked to do the actual input. First, we are not paying Biff to be an input clerk. He probably won't want to do it in the first place. Moriarty's first law of success in dealing with lenders is "first you gotta wanna." They have to *believe* in the ideas you are asking them to accept, and they have to "buy in".to the whole process. If they don't believe or buy in, you may get a hand salute, but they'll resist and find ways to do it their own way, despite how "intelligent" your approach may be. This law applies across all bankers, and all humans for that matter. So if Biff doesn't really want to do the input, guess what happens? Either it doesn't get done right, or it doesn't get done at all. OK, what happens if Biff decides that he really does want to do the input? Again, you get one of two fairly predictable results:

A. Biff spends 70 percent of his work week planted bug-eyed in front of a CRT and decides that he REALLY LIKES to manipulate his data base. Remember, we are dealing with analytical types, and its a proven fact that personal computer technology can have a narcotic effect on that type of mind set. Getting the information displayed in different sorts by size, industry, credit rating, geography and playing "what-if" games becomes *much* more fun than making sales calls. Biff ends up with the best doggone data base you have ever seen. Unfortunately, he has very little time to spend on sales calls; or:

B. Biff does the input for a few weeks or months, and *then* decides that he really doesn't wanna. There's no one else to worry about it and his data base gets stale very quickly. He loses confidence in its accuracy, and pretty soon he's back in the marketing department looking for a new "list."

The best approach seems to be to provide an administrative type who touches base with Biff at least once per month to get his updates. This individual can also be the one who runs the special sorts that Biff may ask for.

CALLING CAPACITY

The other major use for the data base is as the primary tool to control and allocate the most valuable (and often wasted) resource possessed by the commercial lender, his time. You only get one shot at using your available time—and then it's gone, and you can't get it back. It's a *limited* resource and given the complex nature of the commercial lender's role, the amount available for face to face selling is *severely* limited.

An interesting exercise is to ask your commercial lenders to break down how they spend their time over a typical work week. The first thing that leaps out of this analysis is that you really can't compare lenders to a typical industrial or consumer products salesman. The analytical and service components of their job leaves significantly less time for selling. Exhibit 1 shows the results of how over 150 lenders answered that question. On the average they spent about one third of their time in credit, one third in loan administration, and finally have only about one third of their time left for sales.

The next logical question is, What is the average number of calls that a commercial lender with this type of time constraint can make

EXHIBIT 1 How 150 Commercial Lenders Analyzed Their Time

in a year? When I first started to ask that question I always heard that it would be a stretch, but a good commercial lender could make about 100 calls in a year. Now I've said that sales time is limited—but not *THAT* limited. So the next step is an analysis of the time to get the job done. Exhibit 2 shows what happened when we looked at those same 150 lenders and how much time they really had. We start with a 365-day year, and then backed out weekends, holidays, vacation, and sick time to get to the number of work days available. In this example there were 225 available work days. We then apply the time allocation arrived at in Exhibit 1, and find that there are about 75 days available for credit work, 75 days for loan administration, and finally 75 days for sales calls. If the lender made one good call in the morning and one good call in the afternoon, the minimum "calling capacity" equals 150 calls or more than one third more than the lenders had *said* they could make. Just look what happens when they take a third client to lunch! Voila, their calling capacity goes all the way to 225!

Obviously, this exercise doesn't fit every lender and every bank, but the method of reasoning does. I would invite you to fill in your

EXHIBIT 2   An Analysis of the Time to Get the Job Done

365	days in the year				
	Less weekends	@ 104	=	261	
	Less vacations	@ 20	=	241	
	Less holidays	@ 12	=	229	
	Less sick/personal	@ 4	=	225	
225	workdays available				
	less 75 for administration		=	150	
	less 75 for credit		=	75	
75	days for selling				
	× 2 good calls/day		=	150	calls
	+ 1 lunch call		=	225	calls

own assumptions in the formula, and calculate your own lenders' capacity. It won't be perfect, but it is better than stomach muscles.

But whether it's 100 calls or 225, that's all there is, and if your target market is large you've got to be very selective about how you spend those calls. The data base can be an effective tool in helping to develop a strategy for sales call allocation. Remember, you've got to cover your customers out of that fixed number of calls—as well as develop new customers.

SALES CALL ALLOCATION

How much time should I spend on my customers? It's a good question and one that can have many answers. However, the culture recognizes the worth of a "good and valued customer," and in many instances the status of "customer" is somehow mixed up with the assumption of "valuable customer." It is not unusual to hear Biff say, "I call on each and every one of my customers twice a year." What you don't hear is, "Whether or not I'm making any money on them." This presumed equality among all customers can be attributed to the universal lack of good relationship profitability systems in the industry. It is only in the last few years that the technology and software have become available to develop and maintain reasonable Corporate Central Information Files which gather all of the data about a customer and their many potential relationships with the bank, allocate costs, and develop customer profitability information. Instead, banks and bankers tended to rely on relative size of loans or deposits as a surrogate. Anyone who has been involved in customer analysis will agree that volumes are a lousy substitute and can hide a multitude of sins.

Obviously all customers aren't equally profitable, so why do they get an equal share of Biff's time? It would seem to make more sense to allocate more time to those customers who are going to produce more profitability. The data base can be used to help accomplish that objective. One approach is to do a hand version of the profitability analysis (if you don't have a system) and segment your customers into profitability tiers. Too many tiers aren't going to be useful and when we did this we found a very clear living example of the 80/20 rule: 20 percent of our customers were providing 80 percent of the profitability. We labeled each of these customers "C1," connoting our most profitable customers. We then analyzed the rest of them to isolate those who had the potential to grow into C1s, and labeled them "C2." Those customers who were problematic we labeled "C4," and the rest were labeled "C3." We now had a hierarchy of importance in the customer base to begin to decide who gets allocated calls and how many. Well, if that works on customers, how about prospects? A prospect was defined as a company we had called on or knew enough about to assign an intelligent rating. Here again, there are a hundred ways to assign ratings. The one we chose was an attempt to describe the relative attractiveness of the prospect along with how we felt about the timing and probability of closing a sale with them. Here's how that system worked:

- P1—best quality prospect with near-term chance of doing business;
- P2—still best quality prospect, but for whatever reason represents a longer term sell (over a year);
- P3—good quality prospect (maybe even one of the best-known names in the market) but there is something wrong which makes the likelihood of selling this prospect not good;
- P4—something's wrong, not an attractive prospect.

But what about the rest of the world, companies we didn't know anything about? Those we called suspects, and the objective there would be to develop enough information to classify them as a prospect.

MBOs, SETTING THE EXPECTATIONS

Now we had a data base which identified the most critical companies and could be used in planning the allocation of a limited number of sales calls. The next step in the process was to list all of the companies by rating, showing how much business we already had, how much we were forecasting that we could get over the next year, and the number of personal sales calls that we thought we would need to invest to do the planned level of business. When you added up the columns you had a summary of your current portfolio, your business plan forecast for the coming year, *and* your calling plan. That's when the reality check occurs. Biff and his sales manager would sit down and review that plan together. Is there enough volume to achieve the unit's budget? Is there enough reach, or is Biff setting his fence too low? How has Biff allocated his time? If he has concluded that he needs to make 735 calls, most likely there's a problem. Once the sales manager and the lender agree that the plan makes sense, they have a preagreed set of goals and objectives that can become Biff's MBO. They can review it quarterly, make adjustments if necessary, and Biff always knows where he stands. He and his manager have agreed on the definition of success. If Biff is having a problem meeting his goals his manager can work with him to help—before it's too late. Too often in banking we see managers getting judgmental after the year is over, rather than managerial during the year, when something can be done about it *before* the game is over.

MANAGING THE SALES CALLING EFFORT

OK, Biff has a plan and a set of MBOs. Shall we assume that enough has been done, and now it's up to Biff? Nope! This is where planning stops and sales management starts.

The calling plan is never taken as cast in cement. After all, no one can create the perfect plan. Contingencies come up, a problem needs to be worked on, a referral from a company that isn't on the plan comes in. The commercial calling officer needs some flexibility to deviate intelligently from the plan. Most of the sales managers with whom I have been associated required that at least 80 percent of the calls made by their staff come from the plan. This assures that the plan is taken seriously, but there is room left for fire drills and unexpected opportunities.

The sales manager should then work with Biff to break that annual plan down into digestible manageable chunks. The first step is to create a breakdown of calls by quarter, and from there do a "month-in-advance." This is a good way to ensure that sales calls are pre-planned and the "month-in-advance" can be used as an appointment scheduling tool. I've seen some sales managers use the quarterly plan as a check off to record call reports and help the lender track progress against his plan. He can tell very quickly when someone is in a rut, perhaps calling on the same comfortable customer many times, or is trying the "shopping center method" of making his monthly calling quota in one day.

Joint calling is a critical component of the sales manager's job. How else will Biff come up the learning curve other than through the school of hard knocks? This is a good reason why the sales manager should *not* have a heavy portfolio of his own to manage. He should be imparting his experience and wisdom through curbside coaching sessions, helping Biff to develop his selling skills. He should also be using his presence as part of the negotiating team, strategizing ahead of time what role he will play. Very often a commercial lender will feel that he is being judged or upstaged by having a senior officer along. I know several sales managers who carry cards without titles for just that reason. They can be introduced as "my associate" if the situation calls for it, or pull out their regular cards and be introduced as "senior management" if the flag needs to be waved.

SUMMARY

Business development "programs" don't work unless the classic management disciplines of organization, planning, control, and review are in place and a part of the culture. Bankers should look carefully at their organizations to ensure that they are positioning people toward their strengths and not asking them to do too many functions. The bank also has the responsibility of providing the tools and talent to do intelligent planning and goal setting so that performance objectives can be established up front and monitored during the year. The critical functions of sales management provide a definition of success for the commercial lender along with the regular coaching, strategizing and reviewing that can build expertise and react to problems before it's too late. This is a function which is new to the banking industry and often runs smack into the old cultures which are a product of an era in which regulators told banks what their prices could be, what products could be sold, and protected the banks from competition. Deregulation has changed the face of competition forever, and banks that survive will have to deal with changing their culture. They will develop the disciplines which have been proven successful across American industry, modifying and improving them as they go. There are no "perfect" business development systems or programs. There are many intelligent approaches and I hope that I've succeeded in stimulating some ideas that you might find useful.

CHAPTER SEVENTY-THREE

Organizing and Managing Programs to Market Retail Services

Dee Hamilton

Vice President
Hancock Bank

Red lights are flashing all across the board. The banking industry is locked in a struggle for its very existence. It is threatened and under heavy siege.

Make no mistake about that. Mergers, acquisitions, hostile takeovers, failures, deregulation, technological explosion, and today's consumer, who is much better versed than ever before in what he wants and needs, are forging a totally different financial environment. Bankers who understand this reality early on can use these drastic changes to advantage with a calculated and visionary approach. Do not be so preoccupied with the swirling cauldron of competition and confusion that you lose your sense of urgency for a new strategic outlook. The very presence of the multifaceted competitive environment we find ourselves in is a signal from the consumer announcing that, while challenges are much greater for our industry, our opportunities as problem solvers to improve and expand our products and services, to respond to the market and the potential harvest of a continuing successful, rewarding industry, are legion.

Time is a luxury that we do not have. We must act with a realistic sense of urgency. The banker says: "I'm not concerned. It always gets done." But who does it?

CEOs, managers and leaders, it is YOUR responsibility. "It" will not happen if you do not initiate "it," nurture, and harvest "it."

What is "It?" "It" is a successful, productive, and ongoing sales culture. You will continue to hear such admonitions as "You must convert your bank to market-driven and consumer-driven." We hear that such expressions of intent and achievement as "service-driven," or "production-driven," are passe and no longer desirable. This looks like semantics (buzz-words) to me. Boil it down any way you like to say it, but the bottom line will continue to be "giving customers what they need and want—at a profit." This salesmanship, marketing, or strategy is not really so new. For more than thirty years, banks have felt the competition keenly enough to be concerned about this "sales culture," market-driven necessity. Some banks are in a better position of preparedness to expand sales, service, strategy, and style than others. Banks must be INVOLVED and COMMITTED!

From here on, the changes will be so substantial and rapid in our banking environment that the margin of error will become more and more narrow, and the price (punishment) for not making the correct strategic plans and tactics will increase.

We still have a prime shot at it, but the status quo will not redeem your bank. Do you believe that things are no longer, nor will they ever be, what they were? Our problem must be solved now. We must begin at once, with "first aid" and, if necessary, "major surgery." Everything will not "come out all right" if we do not accept the challenge and immediately plan and proceed to ensure that our banks, along with the banking industry, will rise to the opportunity to continue to be the leader in providing the best of financial services to our retail customers and prospects.

THE ENVIRONMENTAL MORASS

Do not feel helpless and intimidated by the flood of consultants, books, audio cassettes, video tapes, and the like warning you that, in some esoteric manner, your bank must achieve an almost mystical metamorphosis to attain the new buzz words, "a sales culture."

What IS a culture? Let's really simplify this NEW thought process. Isn't culture what you are now? Of course, we banks have to shift gears to get up to speed—to "sales" speed, that is. By now, most banks have been shocked as we discover again and again the new environment we now operate in. That's a fairly natural reaction to the loss of a franchise and the flood by new competitors—not only new, but different—and with many unfair advantages brought about by legislation and deregulation. But do not forget that the rich heritage enjoyed by successful banks is what the attraction of all the new players is about.

Banking has been changing for decades and now seems to have accelerated to laser speeds, and it is not likely to slow down, settle down, or to "shake-out" in the foreseeable future. We must "gear up" and we must not fail to plan, or we might as well *plan to fail*. Does all this mean we must work harder and longer, push ourselves to the limit? Perhaps it does to some extent, but what it most certainly means is that we must operate "smarter;" that is, be better prepared, better equipped, better informed, and definitely better committed.

Banks at this writing are still the mainstay and the benchmark of commercial financial institutions. But we can become the dinosaurs of the industry in time if we do not change our philosophy to become more and more "sales-minded." Does that term "sales-minded" sound familiar to you? Are you more comfortable with the terminology and thought process of sales consciousness? Sales culture, sales-minded, sales consciousness are all one and the same. Pursue them successfully by any name and you can survive and prosper. So, join the experts and pursue sales culture, and achieve sales culture. It will not be easy or cheap, and it will not happen overnight. Not all banks, and certainly not all bankers, are going to change gracefully into viable sales forces because of several generations of value programming and franchise protection. But the protection is gone and it is now "bank eat bank" in a hostile environment, electrically charged with all the relatively new entities in the financial services industry, such as the nonbanks, the financial supermarkets, the massive retailers, the investment "bankers," and the real estate firms. Of course, we still have our traditional competitors, such as other banks, savings and loans, credit unions, insurance companies, to name but a few. These so-called traditional opponents groping for our customers will come in the side door and take our customers if we forget about them while we are being consumed with anxiety over all the new players.

Interstate banking (nationwide branching) will probably come in the near future. However, this drastic change may have become academic by the proliferation of the so-called nonbanks as they are on the move with a recent favorable supreme court ruling. One way or another, we will have the equivalent of interstate banking.

As brokers, mutual funds, and insurance companies position themselves to become "one stop shopping centers," banks will complete the deregulation cycle when they can offer additional services. It seems apparent our financial shakeout will never be complete, but rather, change will become the constant that does not change.

Make sure that your strategic training and tactics plan supports and reflects your strategic marketing plan as well as your "culture statement." Otherwise, your strategic marketing plan is worthless. You can have a great advertising program and a great strategic marketing plan, but you must communicate these plans and strategy to your staff, and you must position your institution with well-trained, highly motivated sales people to make anything good happen. If your strategic marketing plan is for three or five years, then your strategic tactics—training—sales plan must be for three or five years also.

Many customers have changed their opinions about the importance of such things as whether your bank is part of a much larger organization with central headquarters in some remote place. The customer seems to be more interested in such matters as access and cost (ATMs, branches, location, rates, etc.).

Smile, offer to help, say thank you! Show respect for the individual. Say to yourself, "I'm going to give the best service in the world." Emphasis on quality and excellence will pay rich dividends in a world where customers expect, "Prices up—service down."

Two radical new changes have already changed the future of financial services and the way we handle our money:

1. Financial deregulation: Will change all the accepted and comfortable ways of how and where we save and invest our money.
2. High technology: Now we have megacomputers that will create scores of new financial services and present them to mass markets of personal services.

In all this monetary morass, there are still some constants: Research and development, education and training, strategy and tactics, measurements, results, rewards, and those two magical and mandated ingredients: Attitude and communications.

From the thousands of letters this writer has received, the central question is always, "How can I motivate my staff to get up and get out of the bank and sell something?"

We are inundated in new products, services, technology, concepts and presentations, but starved to the point of panic (or apathy) for an understanding of what all this means to us.

HOW TO GO ABOUT IT

It is time to change our culture statement: "We are going to cause and to nurture certain high principles and ideals that quickly become a way of life for our bank, principles and ideals adhered to by every member of the staff, from check filers to the chairman of the board, and to establish an attitude commitment which will at once be apparent to all who interface with the bank, internally and externally." These principles will become infectious and contagious to everyone. This bedrock posture must be taken in everything from personal contacts and telephone conversations to printed materials and written correspondence. If you can achieve this, then you will be building a sales culture with two magic ingredients: ATTITUDE and COMMUNICATIONS. You can call it sales culture, advertising, public relations, or sales awareness. Just make sure that you are not merely trying to sell a product, but instead are forming a matrix for the solution of specific financial problems. You cannot force your product on the consumer just because you want to sell that particular product. You cannot pick an old service off the shelf, dust it off, and expect the public to grab it up. Your customer does not care what you CALL a product as long as they like it. You must do your homework through market research (personal interviews, opinion polls, market testing, and other methods) of your consumers' needs and wants—and for which they are willing to pay a reasonable price.

The name of the new game is quality service. With our current retail environment, our market has been, is, and will be, offered every conceivable financial service. Our banks have an opportunity to keep our customers as well as attract new ones. The very fact that we are "banks" can enable us to meet and beat our competitors by improving our products and concern for our market in a convincing way, if we follow up on our advantage (we got there first).

Almost any bank is ahead of all the new entries into the financial services industry. It matters not that they are the so-called "near banks," the financial supermarkets, the aggressive brokerage houses, or even giant retail merchandisers. It matters not that deregulation has opened the floodgates so that these institutions can offer financial services which banks cannot, and that they can open "offices" ANYWHERE and ANYTIME they want to. It matters not that "technology" has advanced; it matters not that our customers are infinitely more knowledgeable and sophisticated as to how they handle their financial affairs.

What does matter is that we, as banks, are able to maintain the aura and perception that the general public traditionally has of us, and to build on this foundation of trust, integrity, past acceptance, and experience, as a launching pad for new and exciting products.

Let's look at some prime target areas in organizing and managing programs to market retail services.

FEW ROLE MODELS

There are precious few financial institutions that could serve the industry as role models in successfully transforming traditional banking systems into dynamic, customer-oriented, high-performance sales forces (cultures).

It is a very tough transition and few bank leaders can even convince themselves that it is a possibility. But because the concept is so alien to commercial banking, it is clear that a radical change in your bank must be your top priority.

The principal facet of a sales culture (i.e., positive attitude of selling) only can come from a firm COMMITMENT, clearly communicated from sales management (CEO, management team, a savvy director of marketing, or other person or persons in a strong leadership posture in the bank). Almost all banks are "talking" about these disciplines to create a sales culture, but few have had success at this point in turning their unprepared organizations into dynamic sales forces. With customer-centered products and services, we must have effective sales management training before we can engage in sales training.

Now, we must learn from the present, rather than the past, to plan for the future. It has been observed that there has been more change in the banking industry in the past five years than in the last 50 years. Will you predict the financial environment in the next ten years? Well, you have to try!

RESEARCH

It is important to know where we have been, where we are now, and where we want to go. Depending on the type of banking structure and environment you are operating within, you may want to use a well-recommended professional service for your research, or, depending on your size and capability, you may perform this market research in-house with your existing resources. Or, quite possibly, you will find the need for a combination of both approaches.

It is essential to know certain things about your bank, as well as about your competitors, and you need this information from an objective perspective. The last thing you need to hear is what you want to hear, as opposed to how your institution and its services are really perceived by your market.

Determine what share of your market that you presently hold, as well as how the rest of the pie is divided among competitors. This information will assist you in your strategy in pursuit of additional business, and it can help define those segments of your existing business which are most profitable, as well as what market areas you will want to concentrate on. Your objective should be to provide the people with what they need and want in financial services—and at a profit. Just because you currently offer a service does not necessarily mean the customer wants or needs it.

IMAGE

What is your bank's image?
How is your bank thought of in your community or trade area?
Are you perceived to be concerned and progressive, competent, safe, and service minded?

Of course you want to have positive answers to all of these questions, but do you? Can you be sure? You probably never can, but you can gather enough data in your market to get a much more objective and realistic idea of your image. The very good, as well as the very bad things you are doing and the products and services you are offering, or not offering, should register fairly strong in effective market research.

Are your bank's hours for business convenient and generally satisfactory to the public? If there is strong negative reaction to them, you need to make changes quickly. Are your officers, tellers, receptionists, and staff perceived to be friendly and helpful? You may be the last to hear if there is dissatisfaction here. Do not wait to find out through closed accounts. Seriously consider having your bank "shopped." While you are at it, consider shopping your competition, too. It is quite cricket for they are probably shopping you. By "shopping," of course, we mean to have open-minded, objective and, I might add, intelligent individuals pose as customers and/or prospective customers (and they may well be customers). And have these "shoppers" report the treatment and reaction they have received from all segments of your system where staff is interfacing with the public. This research is equally as important with the people who handle your incoming and outgoing telephone calls.

When you do get some reliable data that can be reviewed and digested, be prepared for a shock. You will get some good news and some bad news, and some of the bad news may astound you! But, you first have to know yourself. You need to know your strengths in order to expand and capitalize on them. You need to know your weaknesses so you can include in your strategy the steps to take to quickly correct them, replace them, and shore them up with strong points. You must know what you are presently doing that pleases the public, and what you are doing that is displeasing or leaves the public apathetic to your products and services. You must do your homework and have a good feel for what the public (your market) needs, wants, and will pay for.

MARKETING PLAN

Do you need one? Do you need several?
Should it always be in writing?
How broad should it be?

Let's examine this most mystical of bank concepts. I suspect that nowhere will you find a viable, active bank that has produced a written strategic marketing plan that is for the bank in total. No banker has yet put together a written plan that at once encompasses all of the organization's plans for each and every product and service or activity that the bank offers at present, or plans to offer. If such an effort were attempted, it would only occur one time. It would be a useless, obsolete, and incredibly unwieldly exercise in futility, because it would become an anachronism before you attempted to make it tactical.

You do need to put down in writing your goals and how you plan to achieve them. Each goal should be given its priority. For example, when bringing a new product on line, how does it fit into the strategic plan? Has it been researched? Market tested? Does it have features that beat competitors, or is it just another "copy cat" offering because "everyone else is doing it?"

This is not to suggest that you do not need to put in writing, perhaps in broad terms, the standards and general purpose of your organization. An example: Just as we have the three Cs of credit, we can consider the three Cs of a brief, broad, written description of how we want to operate our bank.

- *C-1: Our Creed:* The principles and beliefs that we feel are relevant and ethical to be successful.
- *C-2: Our Culture:* What we are now, and our short-and long-term goals in serving our customers with excellence.
- *C-3: Our Commitment:* A statement of the depth of our dedication to give our customers what they need and want, and at a profit.

That format will serve as a broad, general, overall conceptual plan for your bank.

Now, for the nitty-gritty. You put in writing your "plans" for individual and specific procedures to achieve your corporate goals with the properly thought out and researched steps. Richard Rosenberg, Vice Chairman of Bank of America, says he often writes "subplans" to his specific marketing plan, to spread out the facts and the approach to follow.

In writing your specific strategic marketing plans for your retail program, management and marketing should clearly identify the final desired objectives. There can be many ways of doing this, but flexibility must always be provided for. The necessary research will provide criteria for measurement. You must know where you were when you started so you can measure the extent of your success in achieving your goal.

A written plan will be very helpful in achieving desired results, such as increasing your market share in home improvement loans or auto loans, increased activity in the use of ATMs, or the introduction of a Senior Citizen Program or a Young Adult Program. Before you offer any new product or service, scrutinize it thoroughly with this question in mind: Does this product enhance customer access and convenience, and does it provide economy of scale (cost efficient) for your bank?

Again, remember your programs all must be understood internally to be successfully transmitted externally.

As the financial environment becomes more and more complex, you will need to determine the segments of your market on which you should concentrate. You will probably need to specialize more and more in months and years to come.

SERVICES/PRODUCTS OFFERED

In the fast-changing environment in which we find ourselves, we must bring new, helpful, and often exciting products on line in our banks. Just like the necessity of a satisfactory cash flow, we must have a sound, attractive products flow. We must remain flexible enough to start and stop a product when appropriate. In each and every case we must strive relentlessly for "economy of scale." New products and existing products must stand the test of being cost efficient. In relation to the size and structure of your organization, this must be one of your primary disciplines. The very small ratio of profit to total assets—(that banks work with)—requires that each new product be evaluated with the economics of scale foremost in one's strategy. On the other hand, sitting on the products you have and doing nothing can be the most expensive decision of all in the long run.

Presentation is still a major determinant of the success or failure of a service. Therefore, we must "package" and "price" our products and services so they will receive consideration even before they are accepted. Price, like most everything else, is something of a quid pro quo. Price must be reasonable from the standpoint of the consumer and similar services offered by competitors. At the same time, the profit received must contribute appropriately to the bank's objectives.

Let's consider strategy before getting down to the specific issues with reference to actual products. You cannot spend all of your time planning to get ready or your bank will be a casualty. But you must be very thoughtful and as thorough as possible when you revamp and tune your institution in products and services after perhaps years of performing in a certain way. You may very well need "first aid" as well as "major surgery" as you position your bank in retail services for the present and for the near future.

First, the "first aid." Begin at once to proceed with your own personal analysis of the current retail products and services in your bank. After taking the time to do deeper research in your market, analyze the data and plan and develop new products and services with the necessary training for your staff to assume a more positive sales posture.

Your bank very likely needs some "first aid" in the customer service area. You must do what you can today and in the days ahead to hold your customers, with all the cheerful and well-planned service staff members can muster, while you gird up to broader goals to retain and expand your existing customer retail services. This is so critical that only those who *can* and *will* should perform and be given public contact positions.

As for the "major surgery," many banks may need this badly, and we should be ready to reevaluate our plans for long-term strategy. In the present environment, long term is six months to a year, and will probably continue to be so in the foreseeable future. There is a deluge of literature, video, cassettes, consultants, and seminars that have sprung up in a very short time. Each offers ideas on new bank products and services, and a judicious appraisal of these aids can be helpful. Banks of all sizes are caught up in the pressure of our changed environment and must continually monitor their ability to adapt products and services to these changes.

That posture can present an opportunity for banks to chart a course with integrity, intelligence, and flexibility. If you are a small bank you may fear that the technological revolution that is affecting the delivery of retail banking services will be more than your budget and imagination can match. This is one major concern that probably should not burden you unduly, but rather be in your favor. No matter what the state-of-the-art is now or what it becomes in the so-called high tech area, you can probably purchase or lease these capabilities from a myriad of suppliers. There will be enough high tech in the market to make it a reasonable expense for your institution.

SPECIAL SERVICES

Regardless of the size, structure, and environment of your bank, you will necessarily devote a great deal of time and effort to retaining and attracting the so-called up-scale customer. Your retail marketing efforts should emphasize the needs for this special group, as well as all segments of your market. We know that our up-scale customers and prospects are very important to the bank, and to the community. These are people with the money! These are the people with high balances, high net worth, and high income. They make up about 20 percent of your customers, and they control about 80 percent of your deposits. You pay for their banking business, but if you handle this key group properly, their business will be profitable. They can also be costly, if you are not able to achieve a reasonable "economy of scale" in how you serve them. Their largest balances, more often than not, are time deposits and you are paying top dollar to retain them. This group may not use your credit cards, installment loans, or the like. When they make a loan, it is generally of a single payment type, and with substantive deposit balances (that you are paying for) they expect and usually get a consideration in the interest rate they are charged. They do not usually pay charges for a number of other services, notary fees, traveler's checks, and investment and trust advice. Your marketing programs for these customers must be carefully integrated with essential managerial ingredients. Interest rates paid and charged must be monitored as a certain number of these customers will "run close" on you, and you may need to monitor certain of them by profitability studies. Be careful not to run them off, however, until you are certain they will continue to be a losing situation for your bank. After all, the number of up-scale customers is limited.

But, how about "all the rest?" Let's consider the other 80 percent of your customer base. It is obvious that the next two 10 percent segments, those within the top 30 percent or the top 40 percent, are desirable, too; in fact, most of your customer base can be very profitable and provide valued relationships. Special services to any of these groups must be planned for their needs and priced appropriately.

Banks all over the nation are plotting and planning on how to get their fee income up for new services until it matches their expenses for added retail products. Operating a successful bank on the thin spread between the cost of funds and the cost of operations is a thing of the past, for core demand deposits no longer provide the basis for bank profitability. Although the consumer, regardless of income bracket, is much more knowledgeable and concerned about what financial services are costing, customers are willing to pay a reasonable price for useful and appealing additional retail services geared to their needs. Make sure that you know what services your market segments need and want, and price those services wisely. Sounds like a simple formula, doesn't it? Actually, it's as complex a formula as can be found in any industry today. But we must cope with these issues and present them to our market in the most effective way as we strive for an "economy of scale." A bank can operate in, say, a blue collar area and enjoy perhaps as profitable a return on assets as a bank of similar size in a more posh environment, if the services are tailored to needs—and properly priced.

Although it is loan demand that currently drives most bank earnings, banks must concentrate on getting noninterest income up to noninterest expense. That ratio is only at about 60 percent at the very best banks at this time. There are a number of "hot ticket" banking products being offered to the middle income family market. Many of these services are new and innovative. This middle income market represents a third of American families whose incomes are reported to be in excess of $20,000 and expected to be in excess of $40,000 before the end of the century. This is a strong market now, and will greatly improve in the next few years. This group deserves a prominent place in a bank's long range retail marketing strategy, as does the other end of the customer scale.

Senior citizen programs are on many planning boards, for this "grey power" is a force to be reckoned with. Do not miss this opportunity. As a nation we are living longer and growing older. The number of people between 15 and 27 is declining, while the number over 27 is rapidly increasing. This is also true for over 40, over 50, over 60, and over 70.

In addition to providing services for the "senior market," the bank can practice on the "mature market." During the remainder of the 1980s and the 1990s, more than 65 percent of the purchasing power will be with the 35 to 50 group, which in ten years will be by far the largest population group in the country. As producers, this mature, better educated generation will serve to stabilize and increase productivity in the manufacturing and service sectors, and as better equipped consumers they will be looking closely for the retail banking products and services with the most value. They will be expecting banks to provide better products and services and will patronize the financial institution that do, and reject the others.

Perhaps the key group that is demanding excellence in the late 1980s and 1990s is the rapidly increasing two-worker families. These are new American mores, not just a response to the major inflationary cycles. It is a new approach to family life that has been steadily increasing since the mid-1960s. From 1965 to 1980 more than 25 million women joined the work force, accounting for about 65 percent of its total growth. This dynamic demographic change must be given specific attention in your strategic marketing plans.

ACCESS TO SERVICES

Let's refer back to what motivates customers to stay with an institution or to move from one institution to another. Access and costs are the two most important determinants. We have talked about costs to some extent. People have shown that access to their money (bank) is a primary concern and that branch banking greatly heightens one's access to financial transactions.

Since most states now allow branch banking, and before long almost all states will have branch banking of some type, branching is moving the bank closer to the people. This close personal relationship is still the best salesmanship. No matter how large and imposing a banking system is, it breaks right down to empathy with customers—

taking products and services to them, near their homes, their offices, and their shopping areas. While addressing "access" to funds and services for our customers, the banks must consider the ever rapidly developing electronic funds transfer services. ATMs (automated teller machines) have already become more popular with practically all segments of the market, including all age groups, than previously imagined.

Because of the popularity of ATMs, there is a growing number of bankers who feel that the days of "brick and mortar" full-service branches are over. They may be right. More and more banks are opting for the convenient branches which offer services used on a daily or weekly basis, such as making deposits and cash withdrawals, while directing customers to central bank locations for specialty services that are used only two or three times a year.

The increasing complexity of handling some types of loans makes it virtually impossible to have an expert in all aspects of lending at every branch location. The solution—pull your experts into a central location where they can serve a greater number of customers faster and more efficiently.

As more customers accept ATMs as a means of handling a majority of their banking transactions at supermarkets, shopping malls, or free-standing units in their neighborhoods, this will reduce the need for a standard branch office. With the difference in cost of building a full-service branch versus the installation of an ATM, a bank can add several conveniently located ATMs to serve its customers better, and at the same time extend banking services to twenty-four hours a day with a reduction in capital outlay and salary expenses. And, with the growing number of banks participating in nationwise ATM networks, the bank can provide customer services in every major city in the nation.

ELECTRONIC BANKING

Electronic banking has brought about many of the changes in retail banking and the way customer services are marketed. Those changes will continue into the 1990s. Consumers have generally accepted this new style of convenience banking, but these developments challenge the bank's programs to market its retail services. Most ATMs are tied into a network of shared machines by telephone lines and customers may access their accounts through these "shared" machines. This gives the bank's retail customers access to their account in many cities away from the home bank. Many mid-size and large banks report excellent success in customer ATM acceptance, thus reducing the demand for more branches, more tellers, and higher volume paper items. ATMs are being installed inside branches, through bank external walls, and in drive-up lanes. More popular recently are ATMs as "stand-alone" facilities in shopping malls and at retail outlets. Access to an ATM is with a plastic card and a "personal identification number" (PIN); a secret number known only to the cardholder.

A further development of electronic banking is the "point of sale" terminals (POS). These terminals are small cash register-type machines in retail stores tied in to the same "shared networks" as ATMs. Retail customers will be able to use their ATM cards to make a retail purchase. The terminal will link to their own bank's computer and the transactions will be charged directly to the customer's account. The advantage to the retail merchant is the elimination of check clearance delay and the immediate authorization of the available funds.

There are other developments in retail banking such as automatic clearing houses and a variety of programs to deliver banking services through personal computers. How does the bank effectively market these retail services?

Electronic banking is widely accepted by consumers because of the excellent conveniences of time and ease in conducting one's banking. As it becomes more and more accepted by the public, banks will benefit with reduced congestion in their lobbies.

On the other side of the coin, bankers are losing important opportunities for retail cross-sales. You cannot cross-sell easily to people who do not come into your lobbies. As a result of this, quality time for sales and service must be extended to every customer during those few times they come into the bank—especially during the account opening process.

Consumers will open accounts! If we have not established a quality relationship in the short time span during account opening, what is to guarantee they will come back into our bank for the next product they need? They may be happy with the ATM. That is great—but will they lose a sense of that personal belonging associated with face to face contact with human bankers?

Thus, the advantages of electronic delivery services are many, but extensive use of these systems reduces the opportunities to market retail products. These conflicting trends provide an unusual challenge to the bank's retail marketing programs.

THE ROLE OF ADVERTISING IN THE RETAIL MARKETING PROGRAM

Your bank might have the best services, the lowest loan rates, the highest deposit rates, the friendliest and most efficient tellers, officers and staff in the world, but if you keep it a secret, how is the public to know? Today's consumer has neither the time nor inclination to visit every financial services institution in town to find out what services are offered. If you believe that customers will stay with you forever because their fathers and grandmothers banked with you, you fool only yourself. For the bank to reach the greatest number of potential customers, advertising is a necessary tool. It is an essential part of the bank's program to get and keep retail banking customers.

Exactly what is advertising? "Advertising is the dissemination of openly signed or sponsored messages through purchased space, time, or other media for purposes of identification, information or persuasion." It is an instrument of communication for the bank to say how it can satisfy personal wants (solving financial services problems), a *sales* tool for moving products and services, and an economic force for opening new markets. Unless you tell the banking public about yourself and your products and services, you do not exist.

Advertising involves a solid commitment by the management of the bank to determine the needs and wants of your customers; to create products and services to satisfy those needs at a profit; and to communicate with your customers through an honest, effective, informative advertising program. "But advertising costs money," you say. Of course it does. What is worthwhile that doesn't? That's where the commitment comes in. Make the research investment, and budget the money necessary if you hope to expand your retail customer base or even to sustain existing customer loyalty.

The next thing that must be determined is the bank's philosophy. Are you trying to provide many services to everyone? Do you want only retail consumer customers? Are you going after high balance commercial accounts, the corporate community, or the upscale community? Or, perhaps you want a community institution dedicated to the service of all whom you can persuade to come through the front doors.

Once you have made your commitment to advertising, there are a number of ways to set up an advertising program. You can, of course, find yourself a good advertising agency, tell them what you want to do and how much you want to spend, then sit back and wait for the results, which can find you long on expenses and short on returns.

This approach could spread your budget too thinly over fees, production and space charges, and miscellaneous expenses. If your budget is too small to hire an agency, consider using an advertising consultant on a part-time basis. You can also opt for an in-house advertising department, often a one-person operation charged with the duty of translating management's mandate into salable services. An effective advertising program demands clear and open lines of communication between management and the person charged with the advertising function. Anything less will inevitably lead to chaos and frustration on the part of everyone involved—from the board room to the basement.

As you ready yourself to leap into the advertising arena, be aware of an undisputed truism: "Everybody has opinions, theories, and advice concerning advertising and advertising tactics." For starters, consider the intrinsic dichotomy facing advertising strategists: 1) Consistent advertising is most effective because, when followed through on a regular basis, week-in and week-out, you are able to keep your name and products constantly exposed to the public; and 2) flight advertising, the practice of concentrating on short-term (four- to six-week) media-intensive campaigns promoting a particular retail product or service that demands the public's immediate attention.

Perhaps the correct answer lies somewhere within these alternatives. Continuity is necessary in order to maintain positive corporate and product identification, but therein also lurks the demon, boredom. (In defense of working each ad to the fullest, a very wise and successful advertising account executive often offered this caveat: "When you get tired of reading your own ads or listening to your radio commercials, the general public is only beginning to take notice of them.") Flight advertising, on the other hand, offers the impact and excitement of a highly visible campaign and the pride of apparent media dominance. But, without adequate back-up and support, the seeds of your brilliant campaign and sales effort could fall on unproductive ground.

One of the most helpful and rewarding things that the person responsible for advertising can do is to contact and make friends with key people in the media. You will discover these professionals are a storehouse of ideas, information, and know-how who are eager to help you and they have considerable knowledge of the retail markets.

Not every advertising program you launch will necessarily lend itself—in concept, presentation, or affordability—to media. For example, it may not be feasible to use television's broad coverage and costliness to promote a service which is available only in one locale or to one group of customers. If the same service were available over a large geographic area served by an extensive branch network, then television could conceivably be the most economical medium. Using the local, daily, or weekly newspaper (as well as the local radio station, if its program format is compatible with your service) to promote this service will let you pinpoint your target retail customers with a considerable degree of accuracy at reduced expense.

So how do you determine which media to use? It is necessary to identify your market first. If your service area is made up of average-income families, a full media campaign promoting sophisticated investment consulting services would probably be a waste of advertising dollars. On the other hand, a direct-mail approach, centered around a well-written, attractive brochure included with a no-nonsense letter from the president of the bank to a carefully screened mailing list of individuals who would most likely be candidates for this particular service, could be relatively inexpensive and successful. Even if you were not able to sell the service to every client on your mailing list, you have made valuable inroads by getting your name and message into the hands and (ideally) receptive minds of potential customers.

What is needed, then, is a well-rounded, attention-getting, informative, and most importantly, an honest program that gets the attention of potential retail customers for your bank. If advertising is not honest and truthful, it is nothing but a needless expense which can completely negate any gain you worked long and hard to achieve.

Often overlooked as a necessary adjunct to effective advertising are the bank's physical appearance, facilities, and personnel. When constructing a new building, for example, early in the design stage, plan for the installation of signs or other means of corporate identification on the building. Because the architect usually treats such projects as very personal artistic expressions, to clutter his masterpiece with signs is immediately abhorrent. But he would rather design a display to complement his structure than to have "something" attached to the side of the building by an outdoor sign building crew as an afterthought. By all means, install adequate signs and logos at street level which quickly and easily identify your building to your old, new, and potential customers. The customer lobby and teller areas should be kept clean, neat, and presentable, devoid of shabby, outdated interest rate notices or other banking-related graffiti taped to the counters. To many of your customers, the lobby and the tellers ARE the bank, and very possibly the only part of the bank with which they ever come in contact. When they come into the bank's lobby, impress them positively.

And so, while advertising is considered by some bankers to be a necessary evil, others recognize it for what it is—a means to communicate with and influence the public's buying decisions. Use it to promote your product and it can become an invaluable marketing tool. But treat it as a giveaway program and it becomes a valueless expense and drain on profits.

SELLING THE RETAIL SERVICES

Nothing happens until a sale is made. That's what keeps the doors open, pays the salaries and dividends. Sales is the reason for being in business and no one will argue the point for long that all else is dependent on the sale. Yet, gearing up for organizing and controlling a successful sales effort can be among the most elusive, most misunderstood, and most difficult of the major aspects of a financial institution. A consensus of our industry would probably reflect that the overriding, the absolutely most important aspect of a retail sales program is to have all related sales activities administered by one unit.

Fortunately, for 10,000 banks this will not present a major hurdle—10,000 of our 15,000 banks are still of the size that all retail sales often come under one administrative unit. But this is also important for larger banks.

At least half of the expense of research and development in many organizations is attributable to sales training for personnel, from entry level employees to seasoned staff. While the cost for personnel is the second, or maybe even largest expense, there is no denying that your staff is your key asset. Look closely at your staff and build the best sales force that you can from this source. If your seasoned employees, however, obviously will not or cannot "get on with it," then it is time for some "fresh blood." As a matter of long-term strategy, when you recruit and hire for all positions in your bank, screen each applicant closely at the outset and choose prospective new employees with a conviction that they are open-minded and likely to contribute to your sales culture.

Leadership is basic, and is the ability to persuade—to motivate people and be capable of transmitting ideas both verbally and in writing. Employees must listen to the customer, and be quick to react. People usually want to tell any and all what we think and what we know. But we generally do not want to hear anybody else out. Emphasize the importance of being a good listener.

It will take time for the new employee to become acclimated to your work. He or she will not be familiar with your products, services, and bank philosophy. It will take time for them to learn the names of officers, department heads, and branch managers. And even then the new employee may not get up to speed for a year or more.

Since you have an enormous investment in your current staff and a vast amount of knowledge and experience, by all means take advantage of what you already have. With research and development and education and training, you can make it work. Obviously training is expensive and time consuming, so it is not to the bank's advantage to train an individual merely for the sake of training. The new employee is not a likely candidate for the same sales training that you would provide to a seasoned employee. A word of warning on your sales callers. They really must have training, direction, and motivation. But do not get them programmed like robots striving for an inflexible spiel. Under such circumstances if they are interrupted by the customer or prospect (heaven forbid), they could panic as they lose their "place" in their delivery, and end up with a complete disaster.

A calling officer must empathize with his client to gain any confidence from him or her. You certainly must be prepared, but not robotically programmed; it will give you away and do you in every time.

WHAT'S IMPORTANT TO CUSTOMERS

A customer's idea of service may be about 180 degrees away from a banker's idea of service. A customer will not be even slightly impressed with all of your latest high technology, fancy computers, and brilliant machines that make your task so much easier. He really doesn't care if it is short and easy, or tough and long for you. What your client does care about is what is in it for him or her. They are interested in access and costs. They no longer care that your institution has been operating uninterrupted for 175 years and neat old things like that.

A recent poll of customers showed their interest lay in such as the following: Are you safe, quick, and caring? They also want you to "be courteous" and "do the right thing." Asked for three things that would make their bank better, they responded with: Shortened waiting time, fewer mistakes, and cashed checks with no hassles. Where does your super computer fit in there?

Many banks have initiated sales training programs but, through oversight or lack of awareness, have not provided the sales management tools to the managers. Sales management is the glue that holds the sales program—sales culture—in place. Do not presume that your managers know how to manage—especially in the sales process. They could be at a tremendous disadvantage if they do not receive this type of training.

HIGH TECH AND HIGH TOUCH

At the vortex of the frenzy in the financial services business is the myriad of vehicles delivering the products that our market needs and wants. As technology pushes these delivery systems to state-of-the-art expertise, and as these financial systems spread and expand geographically, we will necessarily be required to balance the high tech with the so-called high touch techniques. More and more, we are seeing "personal banker" programs handling the complete financial affairs of a family. This approach has been tried before but seems to be gaining momentum with a number of banks. Wachovia Bank and Trust Company, N.A., in Winston-Salem, North Carolina is a splendid example of how it can work quite well for the institution and for its clients. Basically the concept is that each family, or individual, is assigned to a particular banker who becomes familiar with the customer and is responsible for delivering crisp, efficient, full bank service assistance to his or her customers. The premise is that the "personal banker" is a one-stop service for all the financial needs of a family, vis-a-vis a customer "running all over the bank" using first one service and then another. There is one vital dimension of high touch that will endure as long as there are people: One-on-one personal contact with our customer. There can be no substitute for personal communications and personal service.

At my bank, Hancock Bank in Gulfport, Mississippi, we call it "Outreach," and fortunately for us we have been practicing this eyeball-to-eyeball personal contact OUTSIDE the bank as well as inside. For a number of years, we have operated an officer sales call program which has proven to be a success for staying close to our clients and their needs. This approach has made our bank sales culture conscious, even before the banking industry decided on what to call it! We require all of our officers to make a "quality call" each week on a customer or prospect.

What is our definition of a "quality call?" We think it is the BEST call an officer can make on one of the "quality" customers or prospects of his or her choosing. Put another way, we encourage our staff to prepare themselves with the necessary information to ensure an intelligent and persuasive contact outside the bank with an individual and/or business firm which can result in a meaningful, or a MORE meaningful, relationship with our bank. This means we MUST do our homework (research) so that we are not wasting our client's time, nor our own.

Since we allow our staff to call on customers and prospects of their own selection, we do require that the selection process start at the high end of each officer's calling list. Obviously, we want our most profitable clients called upon first. This may or may not be all upscale clients with high net worth, high income or high balances. It does take into account the total relationship. We can all have a very profitable client and serve them well, but he may not meet any of the above characteristics. If our products are "problem solvers," and if they are reasonable to the clients and are generally in line with the competition, and if they are PRICED correctly, then here can be a fertile market of the so-called nonupscale clients, who can return a satisfactory profit for your institution.

We also encourage our key nonofficer personnel to make sales calls in a fashion very similar to our officers. The nonofficer group, however, does not have a mandatory program. This group is made up solely of volunteers. Many of them have used the "above and beyond" participation in selling the services of the bank to advance to the officer level.

Adopting a strategy to train, motivate, measure, and reward every staff member from the janitor to the CEO, we put in place yet a third phase of this tactical operation called "The Together We Grow Club." It really does not matter what you call it, but it works for Hancock Bank. This program is also for nonofficers. Sales performers are rewarded with cash when they successfully solicit new deposits and sell additional bank services that would not have been realized except for their extra sales effort. These sales contacts can be made both inside and outside the bank.

These three sales programs can be summed up in three words: The President's Club. All of our sales effort can and do produce real perks for the performing individual. Big ticket career items such as bonuses, promotions, and salary increases, as well as presidential and management "approval," are just some of the rewards.

These are rewards that can affect our staff's quality of life and fulfillment—and also job security. Yes, we are all required to sell the services of the bank every day of the year. This program has made Hancock Bank people see the "big picture," rather than just their individual areas of activity within the bank. Equally important, the program has produced major deposit growth and expanded services for the bank. This program is a result of the vision of our CEO, Leo Seal, some eighteen years ago. And we did not know then that it would later be called a "sales culture."

This sales culture will not just happen and there are no shortcuts to the desired results. We, too, are embroiled in this all-enveloping hostile atmosphere to keep the competitive edge we have hacked out. And we must constantly hone the cutting edge of our strategies. We must all work towards fee-based income, demand deposits notwithstanding, until fee-based income matches and then surpasses our expenses. Maybe then we will not be quite so vulnerable to a one-quarter percent differential from a competitor, be it bank or nonbank, moving our clients back and forth as CDs and money market funds mature.

So for us, as for you, we must continually forge our sales and retail marketing plan and constantly reshape our sales training and tactics strategy to meet each new challenge. Through effective leadership a bank can maintain a cadre of service-minded, smiling, helpful, tactful, sincere, aggressive, creative, and entrepreneurial people—people who know what you want of them and who are properly trained and motivated for the assignment; people who know that when this chemical reaction takes place they will be appropriately recognized and rewarded. Communications between management, staff, customers, and prospects is vital for success.

Banks must keep their competitive edge in retail markets against the "new entries," near-banks, and the like, and we must put as much distance between "them" and "us" as we can. We must do this with all haste and intelligence as the picture of the financial industry continues to blur.

And remember what those two very wise guys said: Theodore Roosevelt said "Nine-tenths of wisdom is being wise in time." Mark Twain said, "Always do right, this will gratify some of the people, and astonish the rest."

CHAPTER SEVENTY-FOUR

Marketing Research in the Bank's Marketing Programs

James C. Montague

Chairman
Financial Information Products, Inc.

INTRODUCTION TO MARKETING RESEARCH

It used to be that "marketing research" was something that only larger banks needed and could afford.

Time and marketplace events—such as deregulation, intense competition, and new products—have combined to make marketing research an essential ingredient of success for banks of all sizes and shapes. However, outside of most of the larger institutions, few banks have marketing research departments and/or staffs. This introductory chapter on marketing research is intended for bankers who are interested in acquiring a basic level of "working" marketing research knowledge.

Many are intimidated by "marketing research"—the last thing you want is someone asking you to explain "what the 95 percent confidence interval level" means or, "how many surveys should we conduct?" Consultants, research firms, college professors, and the like seem to have a way of making marketing research more complicated than it really is—many use technical jargon and fancy names for what are actually quite simple concepts and ideas. Of course, all of these "outsiders" have a vested interest—they want you to hire them to do your bank's marketing research work. It doesn't have to be that way. Once you develop a basic understanding of marketing research, you'll find that most research projects require more *energy and attention to detail* than technical expertise.

The focus of this chapter is to help you to become better equipped to handle your bank's need for marketing research. It is not designed to make you a research "expert." As a result of the time you invest in reading this chapter, you should be able to address most of your bank's marketing research needs on your own. And, for those marketing research needs that require outside assistance, you should be able to deal with outside resources on your terms, not theirs.

THE ROLE OF MARKETING RESEARCH

The science and art of making a bank successful is judgment and decision making. The purpose of marketing research is to provide *information* on products, markets and competitors that can be used to reduce the inherent risk in marketing decisionmaking. Research doesn't replace management. It won't make decisions for you, but it can assist you in making better decisions.

You cannot practice the marketing concept discussed earlier in this book without marketing research. You can't identify the needs and wants of target markets without marketing research (in fact, you can't choose target markets without research). You need information to plan successful product, pricing, distribution, or communication strategies. And, you cannot measure how well you are satisfying the needs and wants of the market without marketing research. If you try to make important marketing decisions without research, you better hope that your competition is asleep at the switch. However, given the risks involved in today's competitive market, more and more competitors are "doing their homework" (i.e., conducting marketing research) before making important decisions.

As can be seen below, marketing research can play an important role in the success of your bank:

Success Factors for Being in Business

1. *Know the marketplace better than your competition.*
   a. Research shows that 33 percent of what the typical financial marketer believes about the marketplace is incorrect.
   b. Don't market by assumption; you'll make better decisions if you're better informed.
   c. Know what influences consumers (versus what they say is important).
   d. Know your strengths and weaknesses.
   e. Know your competitors' vulnerabilities.
2. *Have what consumers want to buy.*
   a. What dictates your product decisions—what the bank wants to sell or what the consumer wants to buy?
   b. Strategies should change as markets mature. Marketing strategy depends on a product's life cycle. In a mature market

you need depth; you grow primarily by getting business from first-time users and taking business from competitors. In a market which has not yet reached maturity, the greatest opportunity often lies in qualified nonusers.

3. *Develop successful new products.*
   a. Successful new products are the lifeblood of any company.
   b. Set a goal for the percent of revenue from new products each year.
   c. Set up a "corporate culture" where only probable winners make it through development.

4. *Improve sales of problem products and business units.*
   a. Know the success factors for individual products, services, and business units.
   b. Measure the performance of problem products and business units against standards to determine how to improve sales performance (or whether to discard them).

5. *Track customer satisfaction.*
   a. A customer is hard to get but easy to lose.
   b. Only customers can tell you how satisfied or dissatisfied they are—customer dissatisfactions are early warning signs to bigger problems.
   c. Most companies don't know why they lose business.

6. *Have a company for which people want to work.*
   a. What do your employees think of your company as a place to work? What do prospective employees think of your company as a place to work? Personnel surveys usually concentrate solely on what management wants to know. Remember that a key part of corporate reputation is what prospective employees think of the company as a place to work.
   b. Learn what both management and employees have on their minds. Quantify how people feel about various issues.

Marketing research is an integral part of the bank's *marketing planning process.* (See Figure 1.)

How Much Should You Spend on Marketing Research?

Many banks like to say that they are "customer-driven." Actions, however, speak louder than words and, based upon actions, most banks are more "process-driven" than customer-driven. In this environment, and with the current emphasis on cost containment, it is difficult to convince bank management to invest in marketing research.

FIGURE 1   Marketing Planning

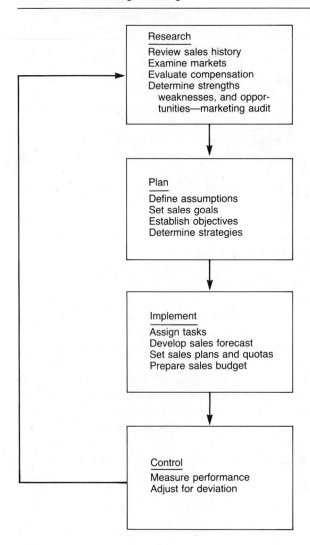

When to Call upon Marketing Research

When does your bank need to research something? Your bank should look to marketing research when it has the following needs:

1. Diagnostic need—when you need to determine why something works or doesn't work.

2. Exploratory need—when you're trying to find out about things you don't know much about.
3. Evaluation need—when you're trying to decide which option to choose.
4. Prediction need—when you are trying to predict the likely outcome of something.
5. Documentation need—when you are attempting to determine the degree to which something exists.

Before embarking upon a marketing research project, you should ask yourself the following "litmus test" questions:

1. Is the issue substantive? Only proceed if the answer is "yes."
2. If a decision or action is required, can it wait until completion of research? If the answer is "no," don't do the research.
3. Is management willing to be guided by the results? If the answer is "no," don't do the research.

There are many times when it is not in the best interest of the bank to proceed with a marketing research project. Conducting marketing research should be avoided in the following situations:

1. When the cost of research would exceed its value.
2. When there is an insufficient budget to do a technically adequate job.
3. When time is an enemy.
4. When the conduct of research would tip your hand to a competitor.
5. When research findings would not be actionable.
6. When you honestly know what you want to do without research.
7. When the problem is not clear and the objectives are not well defined.
8. When the research would be technically inadequate.
9. When a test does not represent later reality.
10. When what is to be measured changes slowly.
11. When the information already exists.
12. When the research is politically motivated.

What to Look for in a Market Researcher

Marketing researchers come in all sizes and shapes. Successful marketing researchers have a number of attributes in common:

- Good listening skills.
- Ability to put self in client's or research user's position.
- Curiosity and enthusiasm.

- Imagination and creativity.
- Problem-solving orientation.
- Good organization and planning skills.
- Good presentation skills.
- Tolerance of pressure from deadlines, demanding clients, and multiple assignments (all of which had to be done yesterday!).
- Knowledgeable about and comfortable with data, numbers, and statistics.
- Understanding of basic research techniques.
- Leaning towards terseness (long reports are a no-no).
- Ability to make dispassionate and emotion-free judgments.
- Thick skin/high threshold of pain.

SETTING UP FOR MARKETING RESEARCH

Organize to Gather and Provide Information

Where should you start? If you haven't already, you'll need to get organized to gather and provide information. A good place to start is to acquire a basic marketing research reference library containing the following:

- *Bank Directory* (Polks, McFadden, or McNally).
- *Bank Marketing Association Directory.*
- Census publications for your area.
- *Statistical Abstract of the United States.*
- *State and Metropolitan Area Data Book.*
- *Sales and Marketing Management* Magazine's *Annual Survey of Buying Power.*
- Standard Industrial Classification (SIC) Manual.
- A good textbook on marketing research (e.g., Robert Ferber, *Handbook of Marketing Research*).
- A good dictionary.

The *Bank Marketing Association Directory* will put you in touch with individuals in other banks who share your responsibilities. Despite the intensified competition of recent years, banking is still a very courteous and sociable industry. With the possible exception of the bankers directly across the street, most bankers will be happy to help you if you ask for it.

Develop an "Information Center"

Many bankers could easily spend 20 hours a week just reading the printed matter that crosses their desks. Figuring out how to organize it for later use could consume another 20 hours, so most simply pile it up somewhere in the vain hope that they will actually read it all. Take a moment to look at your desk and office area. Do you have piles on or behind your desk, in your briefcase, or at home? Do you find yourself saying, "When I have the time, I'm going to read it and then organize it?"

If you answered "yes," you are not alone. While your arms may be getting stronger because of all the paper you lug around, the bank's information needs often go unfulfilled because information should be organized into files, not piles. You need to establish an information center for your bank. Your life will become much easier. No more guilt trips, no more wringing of your hands because you've "not had time" to read the *American Banker*—by organizing an information center for your bank, you'll be in control!

How do you do it? Very simply—it does not require a librarian's degree or a mainframe computer. Most paper-based marketing research material (i.e., your reading material) will fit into eight files:

1. Research report file.
2. Subject file.
3. Competitor file.
4. Supplier file.
5. Books file.
6. Periodicals file.
7. Data file.
8. Miscellaneous file.

The *research report file* contains copies of every marketing research report produced/purchased for your bank. These reports should be numbered in chronological order and indexed by title, author, date and subject.

Most banks subscribe to many magazines and periodicals. But unless you organize for it, it's difficult to retrieve articles that address issues of importance to the bank. Most people are not inclined to browse through 22 back issues of the *ABA Banking Journal* to find that article on home equity loans. This is where the subject file can help. While it is the largest and most troublesome of all files, it is worth the effort when you can provide material on almost any topic immediately (which, by the way, is when it's usually needed). After periodicals have circulated through the bank, literally tear them apart and file the articles by subject—don't read them, just scan them and put them in a file. How do you categorize the subjects? The challenge is to limit the number of subjects, but there is help available. Bank Marketing Association's Information Center maintains a ready-made list of broad topics and subheadings ("Thesaurus of Financial Services

Marketing Terms"). This will provide you with a logical hierarchy of topics and the ideas for subjects not currently covered.

The *competitor file* should contain information from a variety of sources about your bank's competition. It is nearly impossible to keep up with the flow of information on competition in the financial services industry. You will need to develop a network of sources who will channel information on the bank's competition to you. In most banks, several departments will have valuable information on competitors that will reflect each department's particular interest. Ask your colleagues to share it with you so that your bank will have valuable clues as to your competitor's marketing strategy.

Suppliers of services to financial institutions do an admirable job of keeping banks informed of their offerings—the sagging amount of mail in your "in-box" is testimony to the job they're doing. A *supplier's file* allows you to keep information on those companies and services that are of interest to your bank. Bank purchasing decisions can be made a lot quicker and easier if this file is maintained. What should you do with materials received that aren't of interest to the bank? Continue to use the adjunct to the supplier's file—the circular one.

Your *books file* will probably be just a book shelf—a catalog of books is easy to maintain, especially if you have a PC. The key is to try to keep all of the bank's books in one location—you'll be surprised at how many multiple copies of the same book are floating around the bank.

Establish a *subscription periodicals file* to manage the bank's list of periodicals. List each periodical received, the renewal date (remember, publishers send out October renewal notices in February!), who in the bank is the primary recipient and maintain a record of who has a special interest in similar topics. You'll be surprised at the duplicate subscriptions received (and, the savings they represent to your bank). Before automatically renewing a subscription, get the opinions of those who receive it.

The *data file* should contain all paper-based raw data materials the bank has that have marketing implications, plus the physical sources of machine-readable data (e.g., diskettes); for instance, copies of FDIC Call Report data, information on competitive interest rates, etc.

The *miscellaneous file* is just that—it's for anything that doesn't fit into one of the others. The same principles apply—you need to index by title, author, date, and subject (if appropriate).

To make the *information center* work for the bank, you need to do three things: 1) index the information; 2) continuously evaluate it; and 3) use it.

The PC has vastly simplified the task of indexing and cataloging an information center. Many of the off-the-shelf data base software allow you to easily establish and maintain an information source, such as an information center. Continuously evaluating the material is a hard job, mainly because it requires some discipline. Most of us are "rat packs" who hate to throw away material we might need in the future. However, if you never throw anything away, you will defeat the purpose of your information center. So, at least once a year, you should review the material in your information center for its continuing usefulness. Try it—you'll like it! Throw it out—it will become a religious experience!

A marketing information center should be the main gear of a market-driven bank and there are at least three things you can do to promote the use of marketing research information in your bank. First, package the information for use—don't make users scrounge around your "information center" for the information they need. Find out what they want, retrieve and put it in a binder or folder—remember, professionalism sells. Second, take an active role in channeling market information to those in the bank who need it most (i.e., let them know you have things that are of interest to them). And, third, make it your responsibility to know about and retrieve marketing information for anyone in your organization—you'll find that you will become an indispensable resource within the bank.

What are the benefits to you personally of establishing and maintaining an information center? The next time someone in the bank needs something, you'll be able to respond quickly; you'll become a key player in the bank and, probably most important, you'll have a cleaner desk and office!

Learn the Sources of Information

There are three types of sources of information available to your bank: 1) Internal secondary sources within the bank; 2) external secondary sources, such as publications; and 3) primary sources, such as your bank's customers.

Internal Secondary Sources.   Your customer files are a rich source of marketing information, if you can easily access it and analyze it. Until recently, for most banks, that was a big "if." Thanks to advances in computer technology and the spawning of outside suppliers, many banks have been able to develop *customer information files* or, CIFs). CIFs allow you to examine "total" customer relationships rather than just the pieces (i.e., accounts). A CIF takes separate account files (e.g., DDA, credit card, CDs, etc.) and groups them by household or, on the commercial side of the bank, by company.

If your bank's own computer capabilities are not sophisticated enough to handle the "household" matching required, don't despair. Several outside companies offer this service. With these companies, you give them a copy of all account files at a given point in time and they use their sophisticated matching technology to produce a "static" CIF for your bank. Although the service is not cheap ($10,000 and up), if used properly, you will find it to be one of the best marketing investments your bank will ever make. Since these outside companies give you a "point-in-time" picture of your customer files, you should contract with them to update it at least annually.

A CIF opens up a number of sales and marketing opportunities for the bank. Among them are:

- *Cross-selling analysis:* How many services does a household have with you? What use characteristics suggest that you could sell additional, specific products and services to specific households? How does Branch A compare with Branch B?
- *Direct response marketing:* You can develop lists of the best prospects for specific products and services, and avoid the duplication that so often occurs in sending solicitation pieces to customers.
- *Customer profitability analysis:* Which are your most profitable customer households and companies? Which ones deserve special attention? Which ones are marginal or unprofitable?
- *Relationship banking:* What services or products does Mr. John Q. Public have with you? What happens if you reprice one of the accounts that he has with the bank—are you vulnerable?
- *Sales management:* Specific sales goals can be assigned and measured on a branch-by-branch and person-by-person basis.

The bank's personnel can also be a valuable source of information. Branch staff, commercial calling officers, and others can tell you a great deal about customers, their problems, and expectations. The bank's personnel can help you measure the success of new products or promotions. Use them.

External Secondary Sources.   There's one good thing about the burden of federal and state regulatory reporting required of banks: It provides researchers with a rich mine of information on their competitors. In addition, banking is served by a number of affinity groups— like American Bankers Association—all of which pump out useful information about their particular view of the industry. You should learn of these sources. Here are some that you should become familiar with:

- Census of Population and Housing.
- Economic Censuses covering.
  - Retail trade.
  - Wholesale trade.
  - Manufacturing.

- Construction.
- Agriculture.
- Service industries.
- Government.
- County Business Patterns (annual).
- Bureau of Labor Statistics.
- Internal Revenue Service.
- FDIC/FSLIC/Federal Reserve Banks/State Regulatory Agencies.
- Local Boards of Realtors/Home Builders Association.
- State/Local Government Data Center/Planning groups.
- Federal Depository Library.

The information centers of the *American Bankers Association* and *Bank Marketing Association* have outstanding professional staffs to help you.

You should become familiar with a number of periodicals published for the banking industry, even if you cannot afford to subscribe to each one. Included in this list are:

- General Business.
    Wall Street Journal.
    Fortune/Forbes.
    Business Week.
    Local business publications.
- General Banking.
    American Banker.
    Bank Letter.
    The Banker's Magazine.
    ABA Banking Journal.
    ABA Bankers Weekly.
    U.S. Banker.
    Federal Reserve Bulletins.
    Banker's Monthly.
    State banking publications.
- General Marketing.
    Advertising Age.
    Marketing News.
    Journal of Marketing.
    Journal of Marketing Research.
    Sales and Marketing Management Magazine.
- Bank Marketing.
    BMA Bank Marketing Magazine.
    Bank Advertising News.
    BMA Ad Trends.
    Financial Advertising Review.
    Journal of Retail Banking.

Primary Sources.   When a source of information does not exist for your needs, you need to specifically develop the information. You need to go to the "primary source" itself. In most cases, the primary source for your information needs will be the bank's customers and prospects.

There are two ways to obtain the needed information from the primary source: You can observe them or you can ask them. Gathering primary information requires an intelligent research plan, controlled methods in data collection, and energy and imagination in the analysis and reporting of results. All of these will be discussed in greater detail later on in the chapter.

Inexpensive Sources of Information

Customized research—research that is conducted by you to address specific needs that your bank has—is usually expensive. For many banks, it's all but out of their reach budget-wise. Don't stop reading this chapter if you find yourself in that boat. There are several sources of information available to you for free or at minimal cost.

Getting this "low cost" information requires some effort on your behalf and a "do-it-myself" attitude. What you may lack in budget funds can be made up with energy. When you have a need, don't hesitate to use your acquaintances and correspondent banks—develop a network if you don't already have one. Join BMA National and BMA Local—you'll meet people who have already done a lot of the legwork and who are willing to share it with you.

The top consultants in the banking industry regularly appear at a seemingly endless round of conferences and seminars. While you may not be able to attend as many as you would like, many of the presentations are published, recorded for sale, or are available for the price of a telephone call. So, they may ask to come and see you—big deal, it's worth a little to get a lot free.

Many national studies that are done are published. While we all feel our market is "different" than the national averages, if you make some "seat of the pants" judgments about how it is different and apply them to the free national data, you'll have valuable information that can help you address some marketing issue (e.g., how to market to senior citizens, etc.).

Here is a list of inexpensive information sources, all available to you for $0 to $500:

- Bank Customers/Prospects.
    Customers files/product records/CIF.
    Past marketing research studies.
    Other bankers/your network.

- Competitive Environment.
    Regulatory agencies (FDIC, FSLIC, etc.) or companies such
        as Carner & Associates (Bancpen), Sheshunoff, etc. that re-
        port competitive data.
    Call reports (published or exchanged).
    Newspapers/trade journals/"clipping" file/business publica-
        tions/professional journals.
    Trade associations (BMA, ABA, etc.).
    "Keyword" data sources (The Source, CompuServe, BMA's
        FINIS, etc.).
    Traders' groups/peer groups data exchange/network.
    Applications to regulatory authorities/court records.
    Annual reports.
    Industry directories.
- The Market.
    Census and/or service bureaus/census update companies/geo-
        demographic companies, such as NDS, Claritas, CACI, etc.
    Trade association libraries (ABA/BMA).
    Trade association reports and studies.
    Industry conferences and seminars (or, tapes and transcripts
        of them).
    Magazine-sponsored studies.
    Newspaper/media market profiles (use to sell advertising).
    Reports produced by utilities/economic development groups
        (usually contains market projections).
    Ph.D. dissertations and banking school theses.
    Syndicated research proposals.
    Syndicated research (Unidex, Conference Board, PSI, Uni-
        versity of Michigan, etc.).
    Special purpose publications ("Survey of Buying Power," etc.).
    Dun and Bradstreet.

Keep your eyes and ears open, get on mailing lists, send away for
everything, and never hesitate to ask others for help. Invest some
"sweat equity"—a good researcher must have the energy to sift through
haystacks of information, looking for the straws that will be useful.

HOW TO APPROACH YOUR BANK'S MARKETING RESEARCH NEEDS

In this section, we will consider the steps you should follow in undertaking a *primary marketing research project*. A primary marketing
research project is one that involves gathering data from a group in

which you have an interest—for example, small business owners, trust customers, etc.—and creating information that no one else has or is not available to you.

Once you have set yourself up to handle your bank's marketing research needs, you will need to develop a systematic approach for handling individual requests. What do you do if someone asks why the discount brokerage operation hasn't been more successful? How do you respond when you're asked how the bank should position itself in the new market area? To be as efficient and as effective as possible, there are a series of related tasks that you should perform for each research request that you receive. By doing so, you will be able to handle more than one project at a time and you'll ensure that each request is done to some standard.

You should develop a system that is *process oriented*—that is, you take the same steps each time. Here are the steps you'll need to take:

1. Specify what information is needed.
2. Always begin with what already exists.
3. Decide if you should do it yourself or go outside.
4. Select data collection method(s).
5. Design sampling plan.
6. Design questionnaire/data collection instrument.
7. Manage the project.
8. Analyze and report the results.

All of the above are, of course, useless unless you use the results of the research.

Specify Information Needs

Research of any kind should begin with a clear understanding of the issues to be addressed or the problem to be solved. Failure to do so can lead to wasted time and money, and a lot of finger-pointing.

You will find that most people who come to you are not research specialists. This causes most to state the symptoms of their problem rather than the problem itself. A good researcher never takes someone else's statement of the problem for granted because people are people. It's only natural to frame problems in terms of our assumptions and biases. To overcome this, you should always do the following:

1. Probe for the source of concern that brought them to you in the first place. What do they *really* want to know? What will they do with it when they have it? Ask questions.
2. Define the problem/issue to be addressed and get the user's agreement.

3. Write it down. It's a good idea not to start a marketing research project until you have prepared a written proposal. A good format to use is:
   a. Background—a brief review of the situation that led to the need for research.
   b. Specific objectives—be precise.
   c. Research method—briefly describe how the research will be conducted.
   d. Deliverable—what the user will receive.
   e. Timetable and costs—how long will it take, when will the user receive the results, and how much will it cost.

Always Begin with What Already Exists

The use of secondary sources of information—both inside the bank and outside—has been previously discussed. The key thing here is to "not reinvent the wheel." With a little effort, you can often find existing information that can be used to address the bank's marketing research needs or, at the least, narrow the scope (and, limit the expense) of the effort. With the proliferation of outside resources over the past few years, there is virtually no subject that has not been researched to a degree. It's usually out there; it just takes a little effort to find. Don't waste the bank's money or your time—always see if the information you need already exists before conducting primary research on your own.

Doing It Yourself versus Going Outside

When should you attempt to conduct a primary research project yourself and when should you go outside? There is no one answer to that question. Very few bankers have highly developed marketing research skills, yet it can often cost quite a bit to employ outside expertise.

In making this decision for your bank, you will need to take into consideration your own marketing research expertise, your staff resources and skills, and the time you have available to devote to the marketing research project. What do you gain by going outside? What do you give up?

You Gain:	You Give Up:
Objectivity	Some control
Special skills and knowledge	Generally will cost more and may take longer
Anonymity and security (especially important if you do not want to alert your competition)	Involves individuals not as close to actual situation

Doesn't require as many staff
  resources
Often results in more ready acceptance
  of results (i.e., you're not a prophet
  in your own backyard)

What types of outside help are available?

- *Full-service marketing research firms,* that have all of their capabilities "under one roof," are one option. These firms usually have interviewing (data collection), data processing (data entry, cleaning, and tabulation), and analysis (statisticians, technicians and other professionals) capabilities.
- *Field/data processing firms/other specialists* are another option. These firms specialize in one of the activities associated with conducting a marketing research project—for instance, interviewing—usually subcontract the other services (e.g., data processing) and do not get involved in the analysis.
- *Consultants/freelancers/other intermediaries* are a third option. These are individuals and/or firms that have a special expertise/knowledge, such as electronic banking. Generally, they subcontract the interviewing and data processing parts of the project.
- *Academics* are another option. Many college professors "moonlight" outside of the university environment. Generally, these individuals subcontract all facets of a marketing research assignment.

How do you find suppliers? There are a number of good sources available.

1. *Bank Marketing Association Directory.*
2. *Marketing Research Association Directory.*
3. *American Marketing Association Research Directory.*
4. Your network.

The main thing, though, is not to worry because they'll usually find you.

What should you consider in selecting a research supplier? A number of things should be taken into consideration. These include:

1. The scope and relevance of their expertise and experience.
2. Their technical and administrative skills.
3. Personnel.
4. Quality control measures.
5. Thoroughness.
6. Professionalism.
7. Their reputation and references.

8. The quality of their proposal.
   a. Specific assumptions used.
   b. Level of detail.
   c. Organization/writing style.
   d. Appropriateness of method/candor.
   e. Realistic time scheduling.
   f. Reasonableness of price/what it includes.
9. Chemistry—do you like them? Do you think you could work with them?
10. Proximity to you.

A good rule of thumb to use in making the "buy or make it yourself" decision is to assess the risks involved with doing it yourself versus going outside. If the research is being done for an important reason (i.e., risks are high) and: a) acceptance of the results will be higher if an objective third party is involved and/or b) you do not feel comfortable undertaking the project, look to the outside. On the other hand, if you feel comfortable with your abilities and technical skills, and the risks of you doing it are limited (little or no impact on the acceptance of the results), then do it yourself.

SELECTING THE RIGHT METHODOLOGY

Now that you have established the objectives of your marketing research project and have decided who is going to do it, you are ready to select the proper data collection methodology. As noted earlier, there are essentially two primary data collection methodologies: *Observation,* where you view someone or how something occurs, is an unobtrusive method that involves collection of data without the subject being aware of it and *questioning,* where you ask people—called respondents—about topics of interest to the bank.

Qualitative versus Quantitative

Most marketing research projects involve the questioning method, usually referred to as the "primary research" method. There are two types of primary research that you can use: You can do *qualitative research* or *quantitative research.* Qualitative research methods are more oriented to *exploring feelings and attitudes,* while quantitative methods are more geared to *determining how many,* or numbers. Depending upon your bank's needs, this will be the first data collection methodology decision you'll have to make (qualitative vs. quantitative). Here are the various methodologies that are widely used:

Qualitative Methods	Quantitative Methods
Focus Groups	Mail Interviewing
Indepth Interviews	Telephone Interviewing
	Personal Interviewing
	Intercept Interviewing
	Shopping Research

Each of these methods has various strengths and weaknesses. Which one you select for your project will depend on a number of factors, including:

- Your study objectives.
- The type of information needed (feelings versus numbers).
- Your timeframe.
- Your budget.
- Your need for exactness.
- The ease/difficulty of reaching respondents.
- Your need for control over the interviewing process.
- Your need to observe respondents.
- Your need to sequence questions.
- Your need to use certain techniques (e.g., visuals).

Advantages and Disadvantages of Primary Research Methodologies

To help you choose the methodology which is right for your bank's various marketing research projects, a discussion of each of the primary research methods follows.

Focus Groups.   A typical focus group involves recruiting 8 to 12 individuals together for an indepth discussion of a certain topic. A moderator—yourself or someone you hire—"leads" the group participants through a discussion of topics that are of interest to the bank. Most focus groups last approximately one and one half hours and are audio tape recorded. Some are video taped. This research methodology is usually used as a prelude to further quantitative study. For example, new product concepts are most often first tested in focus groups. Usually two or more groups are conducted in order to avoid the misleading results of one bad group. And these do happen, for one must rely on the dynamics of the group working together—sharing opinions and insights unabashedly.

Advantages	Disadvantages
Opportunity for indepth coverage of subjects and "richer" responses	Not quantifiable or projectable
Preliminary insights into solutions to marketing problems (hypothesis generation)	Rarely definitive
	Usefulness overly dependent on skill and experience of moderator
	Often difficult to analyze
Aid to development of questions	Often subject to misinterpretation and /or misuse of results
Determination of consumer preferences (e.g., colors, language to use, etc.)	Recruiting can sometimes be a problem
Relatively low cost	
Flexible and permits observation/direct participation	
Group dynamics and interaction	
Discovery-oriented	

Focus groups cost approximately $2,500 per group and more, if a "big name" moderator is used. For groups involving "upscale" individuals, professionals (e.g., doctors) or business people, the per group cost can be $1,000 to $1,500 higher. Most focus group projects can be completed within four to six weeks.

Focus groups are excellent when you don't know much about the topic at hand, and want to explore or screen ideas and concepts. The following are the steps you should take in doing focus group research:

Preliminary Steps

Develop proposal/objectives.
Determine recruiting and screening criteria.
Obtain a location.
Obtain a host or hostess for the groups.
Recruit.
Mail confirmation/reminders to respondents.
Design topic guide.
Prepare questionnaires or demonstration materials.
Obtain necessary equipment (tape recorder, tapes, etc.).
Arrange for refreshments.
Arrange for observers (limit them).

Doing the Groups

Have a "warm-up" with easy questions.
Don't lead respondents.
Always ask "why?"
Be flexible with your topic guide.
Be polite but firm with "dominators."
Draw out the shy ones.
Don't be afraid of silence.
Repeat for the tape if necessary.

Post-group Analysis
Immediately write down or record your thoughts.
Vis-a-vis objectives.
Listen to your tapes and take notes or transcribe.
Type verbatims, organize by subject, and retype.
Write your report.

Indepth Interviews. Indepth interviews are similar to focus groups in that both use a questioning guide to gather information rather than a tightly structured questionnaire (i.e., the interviewer is allowed leeway to probe and explore) and both concentrate on only one or two topics. The skills of indepth interviewers are comparable to those of a focus group moderator. Indepth interviews can be conducted in-person or by telephone. Usually, telephone indepth interviews should not exceed 30 minutes, while in-person indepth interviews can go considerably longer. In many instances, indepth interviews can be a productive and cost effective alternative to focus groups. Also, to a limited degree, done in enough quantity, indepth interviews can provide some projectability.

Advantages	Disadvantages
Has exploratory benefits of focus groups	Expensive
Can be more cost effective than focus groups because of quantitative qualities	Difficult to find competent indepth interviewers
Sensitive to detecting slight differences (e.g., bank images)	Results are often difficult to analyze
Can be easily discontinued when learning ceases	While some projectability may exist, often this is abused

---

Indepth interviews are expensive, ranging from $75 to over $200 per interview, depending upon the difficulty of reaching respondents. Turnaround time on indepth interviews projects is usually a fairly quick two to four weeks.

Indepth interviews are most useful when you already know something about the topic in question and you want to be able to "focus" the attention of designated respondents on it. In particular, indepth interviews are useful when studying imprecise topics like bank images. Also, they can be used in place of focus groups when the designated respondents are geographically dispersed and it would not be economically feasible to bring them together (e.g., treasurers of Fortune 500 companies).

Mail Interviewing.   Mail surveys, while the least expensive of possible data collection alternatives, must be used with caution. Unless certain steps are taken (which add significantly to your budget), response rates for mail surveys can be low (5–10 percent) and, since who responds is sometimes a matter of chance and always out of your control, respondents aren't always representative of the population they supposedly represent. Nevertheless, mail surveys are appropriate at times, especially if respondents have some affinity with you and/or are prerecruited for their willingness to participate. Basically, a mail survey involves sending a questionnaire through the mail to be self-administered. Response rates under 15–20 percent are poor (and, suspect), those in the 20–40 percent range are acceptable and response rates exceeding 40 percent are excellent.

Advantages	*Disadvantages*
Least costly of research methods	Often not projectable because of low response rates
Efficient for trend studies or replications of studies	Known variance from certain population parameters
Pre-identification of certain demographic characteristics or other useful criteria for sample preselection	Time required for execution of study
	Limitations in questionnaire design and forms of investigation
More appropriate for certain topics (e.g., privacy, lengthy lists/questions, etc.)	Possible nonindependence of response
More complete dispersion of sample than other methods	Costs of improving response rates makes less attractive than some other methods

Mail interviewing is typically the lowest cost method of collecting data, ranging from under $5 an interview to more than $20, depending upon response rates and what you have to do to get them up. The only out-of-pocket costs are: printing of questionnaire, outbound envelope, letter, inbound envelope and outbound/inbound postage. Of course, as with the other methodologies, there are additional costs for data tabulation and, if you have someone do it for you, analysis. Since you cannot control when respondents return the questionnaires, mail interviewing projects generally take longer than some of the other methodologies (typically, 8-12 weeks).

Mail surveys work well in those situations where the group you want to respond have some affinity with you (e.g., members of an association) or when they have a vested interest in the topic under study (e.g., customer satisfaction). Mail surveys also work well as an adjunct to another primary research methodology—for instance, many researchers will follow up a telephone survey with a mail survey to obtain additional information. Mail surveys do not work well in those situations where quantification (i.e., number counting) is the primary concern nor in those situations where probing and exploration is important.

Can you do mail surveys yourself? Of course you can, but be careful. If you haven't done mail surveys before, hire someone to do your first one or contact your network. Go to school on these others and you'll find that mail surveys are valuable ways of keeping in touch with the bank's customers and employees.

Personal Interviews. In-person interviewing is generally the most expensive data collection method. However, it is also the most flexible in that you can use sophisticated techniques (e.g., visual aids, cue cards, etc.) and longer questionnaires can be employed (upwards to 60 minutes). Personal interviews are conducted at the respondent's home and/or place of business (for commercial studies). Personal interviewing is not used as frequently as it once was because of: a) the cost factor—it's expensive; b) the control factor—it's difficult to supervise interviewer quality; and c) the timing factor—turnaround time is lengthy.

Advantages	*Disadvantages*
General benefits of controlled interview (sequence control) probing opportunities	Costly
Most flexible research medium, in terms of . . .	Possibly troublesome for experimental designs requiring closely matched subsamples
Interview length	Danger of interviewer bias/cheating
Use of visual aids, cue cards, self-administered material	Lengthy turnaround time
Most suitable for attitude rating scales	Difficulty of reaching certain types of respondents
Best medium for probing open-end responses	
Opportunity for acquisition of data through observation	

In-person interviewing is expensive, ranging from $50 an interview to more than $100, depending upon the difficulty of contacting respondents, the length of the questionnaire, the number of callbacks, the degree of quality control employed, etc. And, personal interview studies take a long time to accomplish, typically running from 10-15 weeks. If done properly, the data collected through this method is usually the most reliable of all methods. However, to conduct in-person interviews properly is an expensive proposition. You should consider personal interviewing when you need either a large quantity of data from the same respondent and/or a variety of data requiring special data collection techniques. A key question to always ask when contemplating using in-person interviewing is: "Will another less costly data collection method meet my needs?" If the answer is "yes," use the other method.

Telephone Interviewing.   Telephone interviewing has become the most prevalent data collection methodology. Telephone interviewing shares many of the pluses associated with in-person interviewing and generally costs much less. There are two types of telephone interviewing: central-location and field. In a central-location environment—all of the interviewers are in the same location—a high degree of quality is achieved because of on-site/on-line supervision (i.e., supervisors can observe the interviewer and can listen in on the interview). In a field environment—the interviewers conduct the interview from their home—costs are generally lower, but so is data quality (generally) because there is no direct supervision.

Advantages	Disadvantages
Can collect data from respondents located in widely dispersed areas	Bias against nontelephone households
Short turnaround time	Must take steps to reach nonpublished households
Cost per respondent reasonably low	Questions must be short and to the point
Nonresponse is generally low	Interview length must be limited
Provides access to difficult to reach respondents	Respondent can easily refuse or terminate interview
Allows for questionnaire flexibility	Certain techniques cannot be used
Often can secure more candid responses	
Results can be projected	

The cost of this type methodology varies greatly with the length of the interview and the degree of difficulty associated with reaching respondents (referred to as "incidence rate"). Telephone interviewing can range from $15-$50 for consumer interviews to $25-$75 for business interviews. Unless you have a very large sample (more than 500), most telephone interviewing projects can be turned around quickly (less than four weeks). Most research conducted by banks can employ telephone interviewing as the data collection medium. Dollar-for-dollar, telephone interviewing has become the best buy among the quantitative techniques.

Intercept Interviews.   Another form of in-person interviewing becoming more popular is intercept interviews. These interviews get their name from the process used—an interviewer stops, or "inter-cepts" a potential respondent, screens him/her to make sure he/she is qualified for the survey and then administers the survey. These typically take place in a shopping mall but can be done at other places as well (e.g., in front of a branch, in an office building, etc.). Intercept interviews are desirable when respondents must be shown certain visual aids (as in, for example, a copy test) or when you need to know something about subjects who are in a certain area.

Advantages	Disadvantages
General advantages of any personal interview . . .	Noncoverage (or inefficient coverage) of certain segments
Probing opportunities	Poor sample dispersion
Sequence control	Possible overuse of respondents
Use of visual aids, self-administered material, other stimulus material	Subject to interviewer recruitment bias
Flexibility in questioning techniques	
Much less costly than area sampling	
Only method available for certain kinds of studies	
Fairly efficient for locating low incidence samples	
Controlled or consistent response environment	

The cost of intercept interviews varies greatly with the length of interviews and the qualifications for a respondent. Generally, intercept interviews run from $20-$25 per interview. Timing is also a function of how difficult it is to locate and recruit qualified respondents, but most intercept interviewing projects take four to six weeks to complete. In many ways, intercept interviewing has become a substitute for the much more expensive personal interviewing method. With the exception of the dispersion of the sample (intercept interview samples are limited to the geographic area in which the interviewing takes place), intercept interviews are best used in those situations similar to personal interviewing.

Shopping Surveys.   In recent years, because of the emphasis on sales and quality of service in banking, shopping surveys have become more popular. Shopping surveys are a form of in-person interviewing. Interviewers are trained to simulate certain customer-frontline bank employee situations. Using a defined schedule, the interviewer goes to the designated office of a bank, engages the designated employee and then records (through observation and subsequent completion of a questionnaire) how well the employee handled the situation (e.g., opening/closing an account, following up on a lead, resolving a problem, etc.). Many banks use shopping surveys to spot areas in which training is needed and to ensure that employee presentations are consistent across all branches. While most shopping surveys are administered on the retail side of the bank, they can also be valuable evaluation tools for monitoring trust and commercial presentations as well.

Advantages	*Disadvantages*
Combines observation and questioning	Difficult to control process
Gives management a window into the customer/employee interaction environment	Results sometimes lead to misuses (e.g., firing of employee)
Can spot gaps/deficiencies in training programs	Very interviewer-dependent
Can be used to evaluate consistency of sales presentations	Logistics difficult to control

Shopping surveys are not inexpensive. A significant amount of budget should be devoted to the interviewer selection and training process to ensure that bank employees don't catch on and modify their behavior. Shopping surveys generally cost $50-$100 per shop, depending upon the geographic dispersion factor and the specific bank employee who needs to be shopped. Also, shopping surveys take a long time to accomplish, anywhere from four to eight weeks. Because of the potential for abuse—both from the interviewer side and the user side—shopping surveys should be almost always conducted by professionals.

WHICH METHODOLOGY SHOULD YOU USE?

It is important to realize that the methodologies just discussed are not mutually exclusive nor are they truly exhaustive. On the first point, oftentimes a complete research plan will begin with a focus group (for direction), proceed through copy testing (using intercept interviews) and conclude with an awareness study (via a telephone survey). These decisions depend upon the precise objectives of the marketing decisions to be made. As for the second point, there are other research procedures. Mail surveys can be used in conjunction with telephone surveys to attach a particular issue (e.g., image), or respondents can be recruited to a central location for in-person interviewing (e.g., to study reactions to a new product). Test marketing a new product may involve such things as simulated computer models.

FIGURE 2   Which Methodology Should You Use?

	Qualitative	Quantitative
Orientation:	Feelings	Numerations
Based on:	Words	Numbers
Who:	Select group	Sample
Questions:	Unstructured	Structured
Goal:	Understanding	Measurement

FIGURE 3   Research Methodology Comparison

	Quality	*Reliability*	*Control*	*Speed*	*Costs*
Focus Groups	Medium	Low	High	Fast	Low
Indepths	Medium	Low	High	Fast	Low
Mail	Low	Medium	Low	Slow	Low
Personal	High	High	Medium	Medium	High
Telephone	High	High	High	Fast	Medium
Intercepts	High	Low	Medium	Fast	Medium
Shopping	Medium	Medium	Low	Slow	Medium

Remember, your first methodology decision is whether to use a *qualitative* or *quantitative* primary data collection method—see Figure 2 for input regarding this decision. Once you have made your "feelings vs. numbers" decision, you next must decide which particular methodology is right for you. To aid that decision, refer to Figure 3, which compares the various primary research methodologies. You should consider using the following:

- *Focus Groups* when . . .
  Indepth attitudes and behaviors are needed.
  Not quantifiable, just directional data needed.
  Quantitative research to follow.
  Showing/using visual aids is required.
  Interaction between respondents is desirable.
  You want to observe.
  You don't know much about the topic in question.
- *Indepth Interviews* when . . .
  Indepth attitudes and behaviors are needed.
  Not quantifiable, just directional data needed.

You want to fully explore an issue/probing is needed.
Bringing respondents together is not feasible.
You already have some knowledge of the topic in question.
Interaction between respondents not necessary.
- *Mail Surveys* when . . .
 Respondents can be targeted via mail.
 Respondents have some reason to reply (affinity or vested interest).
 Responders won't be significantly different from non-responders.
 Questionnaire layout can be made simple.
 Your budget is limited.
 You don't need number counting per se.
 Time is not critical.
- *In-person Interviews* when . . .
 Projectable data is needed.
 A large amount of data needs to be collected from each respondent/long questionnaire is used.
 Sophisticated questioning techniques need to be employed.
 Showing/using visual aids is required.
 Your budget is not limited.
 Time is not critical.
- *Telephone Interviewing* when . . .
 Projectable data is needed.
 Respondents are geographically dispersed.
 Time is critical.
 Unlisted/no telephone number will not bias results.
 Showing/using visual aids is not required.
 Questions are brief and understandable.
- *Intercept Interviews* when . . .
 You cannot afford in-person interviewing.
 Showing/using visual aids is required.
 You need some degree of both qualitative and quantitative data.
 Time is critical.
 The location of the interviewing will not bias results.
 Sophisticated questioning techniques need to be employed.

Shopping surveys are basically a single-purpose type of research: Your goal is to evaluate how the bank's employees interact with its customers.

The methodologies that have been discussed are designed to give you some understanding of how one can research a given issue. Below is a list of research issues and the methodology(ies) best suited for it:

Research Issue	Methodology to Use
Awareness	Telephone
Attitudes/Image Perceptions	Focus Groups/Indepth Interviews followed by Telephone/Personal Interviews
Product Usage/Behavior	Telephone
Ad Copy Testing	Focus Groups/Intercept Interviews
Feasibility Study	Telephone/Indepth Interviews
Concept Testing	Focus Groups/Intercept Interviews
Site Location	Secondary/Telephone/Mail
Market Potential	Secondary/Focus Groups/Personal Interviewing
Awareness/Ad Tracking	Telephone
Employee Performance	Shopping
Employee Satisfaction	Depth Interviews/Self-Administered
Customer Satisfaction	Telephone/Mail

In the final analysis, your decision about which methodology to use should be driven by:

- Your information needs.
- Your time constraints.
- Your budgetary constraints.
- Ease of respondent access/understanding.
- Research tools/skills/expertise required.

And, most importantly, choose what you and your colleagues are comfortable with—if you don't think it can be done using a certain methodology, you'll never be comfortable with the results.

DEVELOPING THE RIGHT SAMPLE PLAN

Now that you have determined HOW you are going to collect the data, you must determine how many respondents you need to interview—you must design your *sample plan*. And, as a result, you are about to enter marketing research's equivalent of the "Twilight Zone" (or, so it will appear).

A sampling plan must answer three questions:

1. Who is to be surveyed?
2. How will they be selected?
3. How many should you survey?

The "Who" is a function of the target audience for your marketing problem/issue—are you interested in the entire retail customer base or only selected groups (e.g., seniors, newcomers, etc.). This question is usually fairly easy to answer. The "hard" part (which, for a professional, isn't usually difficult) is to translate the "who" into how do we select them. Respondent selection is accomplished with screening questions, which are used by the interviewers to make sure that only qualified individuals are interviewed. For instance, if you wanted to interview households with incomes of $35,000 or more, you might have a screening question like the following: "We're interviewing households that, in 1986, had before-tax income of at least $35,000. Would your household's total 1986 income fall into that category?"

Depending upon how the respondent answered the screening question, they would continue with the survey or be terminated by the interviewer.

The most difficult sampling question to answer is *how many should you interview*? Of course, this only applies to quantitative methodologies because qualitative methods do not produce projectable results anyway. The key to answering this question is for you to make a decision about the level of imprecision with which you can live. Just remember, most marketing research is a series of tradeoffs. Because you don't have enough time, you use focus groups instead of in-person interviewing. Because you don't have enough budget, you conduct a 10-minute questionnaire rather than an 18-minute questionnaire. Well, the "how many" issue is often dealt with in the same manner. That is, tradeoffs are made—you trade precision (your ability to say that the sample represents the universe of target individuals in which you have an interest) for time/budget saving.

So that you will know what you are giving up when you cut back on sample, let's examine what goes into determining the "ideal" sample size, given your need. *Sample size is determined by*:

- The confidence level—or, the odds of being right—that you require.
- Sample error that you can live with—usually expressed as ± percent.
- Anticipated response rate—since this is the very reason you are often doing the research in the first place (i.e., you don't know what it is), most researchers use the "worst case" scenario of 50 percent; in other words, in your survey, 50 percent of the respondents answered a certain way.

Confused? Starting to reach for your old statistics book? Do you want to see the "formula" that statisticians use to calculate sample size? Is that a big "NO" you say? Well, don't worry, our statistician friends have figured it all out for us and have provided us with reliable charts that we can use to determine what sample size to use. (See Figure 4.)

FIGURE 4 Confidence Interval Table (95% confidence level)

Percentage Analyzed

Base	5% or 95%	10% or 90%	15% or 85%	20% or 80%	25% or 75%	30% or 70%	35% or 65%	40% or 60%	45% or 55%	50%
50	6.16	8.49	10.10	11.31	12.25	12.96	13.49	13.86	14.07	14.14
100	4.36	6.00	7.14	8.00	8.66	9.17	9.54	9.80	9.95	10.00
150	3.56	4.90	5.83	6.53	7.07	7.48	7.79	8.00	8.12	8.16
200	3.08	4.24	5.05	5.66	6.12	6.48	6.75	6.83	7.04	7.07
250	2.76	3.79	4.52	5.06	5.48	5.80	6.03	6.20	6.29	6.32
300	2.52	3.46	4.12	5.62	5.00	5.29	5.51	5.66	5.74	5.77
350	2.33	3.21	3.82	4.28	4.63	4.90	5.10	5.24	5.32	5.35
400	2.18	3.00	3.57	4.00	4.33	4.58	4.77	4.90	4.97	5.00
450	2.05	2.83	3.37	3.77	4.08	4.32	4.50	4.62	4.66	4.71
500	1.95	2.68	3.19	3.58	3.87	4.10	4.27	4.38	4.45	4.47
550	1.86	2.56	3.05	3.41	3.69	3.91	4.07	4.18	4.24	4.26
600	1.78	2.45	2.92	3.27	2.54	3.74	3.89	4.00	4.06	4.08

Sample size										
650	1.71	2.35	2.80	3.14	3.40	3.59	3.74	3.84	3.90	3.92
700	1.65	2.27	2.67	3.02	3.27	3.46	3.61	3.70	3.76	3.78
750	1.59	2.19	2.61	2.92	3.16	3.35	3.48	3.58	3.63	3.65
800	1.54	2.12	2.52	2.83	3.06	3.24	3.37	3.46	3.52	3.54
850	1.50	2.06	2.45	2.74	2.97	3.14	3.27	3.36	3.41	3.43
900	1.45	2.00	2.38	2.67	2.89	3.06	3.18	3.27	3.32	3.33
950	1.41	1.95	2.32	2.60	2.81	2.97	3.09	3.18	3.23	3.24
1,000	1.38	1.90	2.26	2.53	2.74	2.90	3.02	3.10	3.15	3.16
1,050	1.35	1.85	2.20	2.47	2.67	2.83	2.94	3.02	3.07	3.09
1,100	1.31	1.81	2.15	2.41	2.61	2.76	2.88	2.95	3.00	3.02
1,150	1.29	1.77	2.11	2.36	2.56	2.70	2.81	2.89	2.93	2.95
1,200	1.26	1.73	2.06	2.31	2.50	2.65	2.75	2.83	2.87	2.89
1,250	1.23	1.70	2.02	2.26	2.45	2.59	2.70	2.77	2.81	2.83
1,300	1.21	1.66	1.98	2.22	2.40	2.54	2.65	2.72	2.76	2.77
1,350	1.19	1.63	1.94	2.18	2.36	2.49	2.60	2.67	2.71	2.72
1,400	1.16	1.60	1.91	2.14	2.31	2.45	2.55	2.62	2.66	2.67
1,450	1.14	1.58	1.88	2.10	2.27	2.41	2.51	2.57	2.61	2.63
1,500	1.13	1.55	1.84	2.07	2.24	2.37	2.46	2.53	2.57	2.58
1,550	1.11	1.52	1.81	2.03	2.20	2.33	2.42	2.49	2.53	2.54
1,600	1.09	1.50	1.79	2.00	2.17	2.29	2.38	2.45	2.49	2.50

Note: For sample sizes exceeding 1,600, the maximum plus or minus variation which can be expected related to any percentage shown will be less than 2.50%.

Sampling is as much "art" as it is "science." Statisticians have tried to take something very complex and make it so that most lay people can use the concepts. One final word of advice: When in doubt, check with a professional.

DESIGNING QUESTIONNAIRES THAT WORK

The number one cause of poor marketing research is improperly designed questionnaires. Questionnaires are a lot like advertising copy or direct mail pieces: Everyone thinks they are an expert, including the CEO! Generally, questionnaire design is better left to experts who have had experience in finding out what works and what doesn't.

If you hire someone else to design a questionnaire and you have some concerns about questions, always ask: "Have you used that before? How did it work? What were the responses?" If you decide to try it yourself, a simple rule of thumb to use is to put yourself in the respondent's shoes and ask yourself: "Would I understand that? Would I know how to answer that? Would I be able to concentrate long enough to listen to that question?" etc. Questionnaire design should follow the KISS philosophy—the shorter and clearer you can make it, the more likely it will achieve what you are after.

If you have followed your marketing research process, designing the questionnaire should go quickly because you will have already done most of the homework. Here are the steps you'll need to take:

1. Outline specific information needed.
2. Prepare questions to obtain information.
3. Sequence the questions.
4. Prepare a first draft.
5. Pretest and revise; retest if necessary.
6. Secure user's approval.

As noted above, keeping things simple makes life simple. Here are some rules of questionnaire design that you should follow:

- Keep it simple—use as few words as possible.
- Make it easy for the interviewer to follow and give clear instructions.
- Leave ample space for open-ended responses.
- Make it readable and attractive.
- Precode for computer data format.
- Use respondent's language—not jargon.
- Discuss one subject at a time.
- Start with introduction and screening questions.
- Start with simple, nonthreatening questions.

- Vary the pace, don't ask many questions of the same form in sequence—it causes respondent fatigue.
- Ask demographics and other sensitive questions last.

Some types of questions work better than other types. There are certain questions that should be avoided, either because they produce misleading results and/or because they heighten the possibility that the respondent will terminate the interview. Among the types of questions to avoid are:

- Direct account balance questions—use ranges instead.
- Direct demographic questions.
- Third party/hypothetical questions.
- Long detailed questions.
- Dead giveaways regarding sponsorship.
- "What should your bank be doing."
- "How much should a service cost," or "How much would you pay for it?"

Lastly, to give you some ideas, here is a list of topics which usually find their way onto many bank marketing research questionnaires:

- Activities, interests and opinions (AIOs, or self-perceptions).
- Perception/importance values.
- Image/satisfaction perceptions.
- Behavior patterns.
- Ontographics: Ownership/holdings/related activities.
- Financial goals/attitudes.
- Concept reactions/special topics.
- Trade-offs/tolerances.
- Demographic/financial classification data.

A good questionnaire is one that works; a poor questionnaire is one that causes problems. As with sampling, when in doubt, get a professional to do it.

MANAGING THE PROJECT AND REPORTING RESULTS

Managing the Research Project

Once the questionnaire has been designed, you need to turn your attention to managing the marketing research project, particularly if you have hired professionals to assist you. Essentially, there are three "management" tasks that will require your attention: 1) field control; 2) editing and coding; and 3) data processing and analysis.

"Field Control"

Field control means setting up standards and procedures to ensure that the interviewing (the "field") is executed as planned. This means living up to the standards that you establish and on time. It also means providing your interviewing source with a) supervisor instructions; b) interviewer instructions and c) shipping instructions. All of these should lay out the "whats," "wheres" and "how to handles"—they should let the support staff know how you want things handled. For instance, the supervisor should know that you want half of the interviews to be completed with female respondents and the other half with male. Interviewers need to know what to do if someone responds with something that is not precoded on the questionnaire. All of these should be part of your "field control" instructions. By the way, this could (and, perhaps, should) include on-site visits by you during the project—there's nothing quite like eyeball supervision.

Editing and Coding

Editing and coding is what happens to a questionnaire after it has been completed. The editing staff goes through each questionnaire, question-by-question, to make sure each one was properly recorded and that all skip patterns were followed. A "skip pattern" is followed when a person's response to one question disqualifies him/her from another question(s). Depending upon the data collection methodology used, editing may also include some validation of each interviewer's work to ensure that the questionnaires were done as presented. "Validation" means the respondent is recontacted and asked to verify that the interview actually took place. All "open-ended" questions need to be coded for data tabulation purposes. The coding staff will go through the first 50-150 questionnaires and handtab the results of the open-ended responses. From this, they will develop a coding scheme and assign response codes to each open-ended response for later data processing.

Data Processing

Data processing includes data entry (keypunching), data cleaning, data tabulation and, if necessary, statistical analysis. After a questionnaire has been edited and coded, a keypuncher enters the data into the computer. Always insist upon 100 percent verification of the keypunching work (this is basically keypunching the work twice)—this will save you some headaches later when things don't add up. Data cleaning is usually done by computer, where the program searches for inconsistency in response patterns and identifies the number of the questionnaire so that the staff can look up the correct response. If you use your own software package—either on your PC or your bank's mainframe—you'll probably have to write your own crosstab scheme. Or, you can simply tell a programmer what you want and they'll do it for you.

Reporting the Research Results

Once the marketing research project is through the data processing stage, you are ready to report on what was found. As you prepare to write your report, remember a few tips:

A. *Writing a Report*
   1. Try to establish a report format and stick to it so that others in the bank will know what to expect in the future. A good format to follow is something like this:
      a. Executive summary of results, conclusions and recommended courses of action
      b. Background/introduction—the whys, whats and hows of what you did
      c. Findings—a brief discussion and presentation of the key findings
      d. Assessment and recommendations
      e. Copy of questionnaire, if appropriate
   2. Remember, there is absolutely no virtue to thick reports—do you like to read them? Don't make them read through the whole to find out what you want them to know. Get them (the user/decisionmaker) upfront in the report. Be brief.
   3. Packaging is a key—remember, others will need to "buy" your ideas and thoughts. Put the report in a clean, nice cover, use a laser printer if you have one, get some letterhead that states "Marketing Research Report," etc.—you'll be surprised at the reaction (professionalism).
B. *Presenting the Results*
   1. Be organized and rehearse if you can. Focus on the key issues in your oral presentation. Let them read about the other issues. Anticipate what questions might be asked and be prepared to handle them. Bankers sometimes can be like Romans—they kill the messenger, so be prepared. Quickly cover how the research was conducted—the objective is to not gloss over the methodology, but to get it behind you early because it may sap the effectiveness of the remainder of your presentation.

2. Most people think better with their eyes—take advantage of this. Use visuals—slides, overheads, easel, handouts, and so forth—to get the participants focusing on the key results.
3. Don't wear out your welcome—brevity is important. Try to have your presentation take no longer than 30 minutes. This will leave ample time for discussion and allow the "ants in the pants" crowd to depart without having it distract from the overall presentation.

This is an area where planning and preparation pay off. "Winging it" more often than not produces the wrong reaction. Participants will focus more on the presentation "form" and less on the substance.

The marketing researcher's greatest challenge comes after the research has been completed. Getting the bank to follow through with the recommendations will take adherence to the salesperson's credo: followup, followup, followup.

SOME FINAL THOUGHTS

If you have read through this part of the "Marketing Research" chapter, you should have at least a basic understanding of many marketing research concepts and techniques. To be sure, to be a marketing research expert will require a lot more reading, asking questions, and doing, than is presented here, but you should be on your way.

As you apply what you have learned in this book to your bank's marketing research needs, please keep in mind the following *success factors*:

- *Ask the right questions*—specific questions you want the research to answer.
- *Ask the questions right*—for example, ask people what they have done rather than what they intend to do.
- *Ask the right people*—qualify people as much as is practical and affordable.
- *Focus on the responses of the right people*—you can't get all the business in a market. So, focus on the business of those you want.
- *Know what the answers mean*—you always need benchmarks to make responses relative; focus on what people mean rather than what they say; and, beware of the obvious answer.
- *Compare the answers to what you believe*—do this in a disciplined manner to reveal information gaps (i.e., differences between what the bank thinks about itself and what the market thinks about the bank); try to minimize marketing by assumption.

- *Demand "user friendly" results*—people can't use what they don't understand. Reserch should be communicated from the standpoint of the user, not the researcher. As the world becomes more complicated, marketers who make their offerings easy to understand will be the winners.
- *Believe the research*—commit to believing ALL of the research or none of it, not selected parts that parallel preconceived notions.
- *Implement the research*—if the first eight steps have been followed, action is clearly indicated. Get the best talent you have or can afford involved in the implementation.

Lastly, there are some conditions and situations you will want to avoid as you undertake the bank's marketing research needs. Most are functions of lack of marketing research knowledge and understanding of the process. Try to avoid the following:

- Prejudging results before market information is collected, thereby influencing subsequent interpretation.
- Projecting or generalizing from an insufficient amount of data.
- Knowingly using research procedures that are generally considered unacceptable for a particular type of study.
- Collecting data from nonrepresentative sources and presetting them as characteristic of the actual situation.
- Suppressing some facts and emphasizing others in order to produce a desired effect.
- Presenting findings and interpretations of a study without qualifying them by a statement of the limitations and assumptions inherent in the research procedure.
- Making extravagant claims for the use of marketing research.
- Being swayed by management pressure or political considerations.

To avoid becoming a victim of the above, as noted earlier, a good rule of thumb to use is: When in doubt, go to a professional or turn to your network for help. In the long run, you'll be better off.

CHAPTER SEVENTY-FIVE

Bank Advertising—Principles and Guidelines

M. Carl Sneeden

Senior Vice President
Third National Bank
A SunTrust Bank

For many years most people in banking did not understand advertising—nor did they try. Too often, advertising was considered a luxury, and not a necessity. If advertising had been termed "sales calls" or "officer calls," it would have been understood immediately, simply because there is no other way to make the required number of contacts at an affordable price and get the appropriate message across in an effective way. In other words, something had to be done to reduce the cost of sales/calls and at the same time increase the penetration of the marketplace. Advertising was, and still is, the best way.

As the marketplace grows increasingly complex and the relationship of the consumer and banker becomes less personal and contacts less frequent, advertising must be an increasingly important aspect of the bank's business development.

As advertising has progressed from the luxury status to the status of an essential element in banking, management requires that the function must be held accountable in terms of measurable achievement just as any other department or function is held accountable. The advertising program must be a part of the total marketing plan.

We have witnessed several changes in attitude in advertising over the past few decades. In the 50s, it seemed that the only thing needed was a better mousetrap and money to promote it. However, in the late 50s, technology started to make itself heard and it was more difficult to establish that unique selling proposition. Toward the end of the "product" era, there was an avalanche of "me too" products that descended on the marketplace. Whenever anyone completed or introduced their better mousetrap, two or more just like it quickly followed and all claimed to be better than the first one.

In the 60s, most companies found that their reputation or their image was more important in selling a product than any specific product feature. But again, just as the "me too" products killed the product era in the 50s, the "me too" companies killed the image era.

Today most companies feel the need to create a position in the prospect's mind. Most writers have called this era the "positioning" era, which means what advertising does to affect how the prospect thinks about the product. In other words, some advertisers use advertising to position a product, and not to communicate its features. When you have positioned the product, you then have placed it in a certain way in the consumer's mind. After making that all-important decision of consumer mind positioning, you must then have a strategy to get you there. The marketing strategy is the master plan.

A creative strategy must also be determined and should cover at least five points: (1) Have an objective stating what the advertising should do, (2) have a target audience determining who the consumer will be, (3) have key consumer benefits determining why the consumer would want to purchase your product or service, (4) have support—a real reason for the consumer to believe in the benefit of your service, and (5) have personality—a statement of the product's tone and manner.

PLANNING

It is very important to plan in advance to stretch the advertising budget. Plan ads that can be repeated; this will save money on production and leave more money to pay for space insertions. Plan the campaign as a unit and not piecemeal. This enables an individual to utilize the same art, photography, headlines, and so on for such things as ads, direct mail pieces, and in-bank displays. It also sets a style and avoids wandering off the track—going off in all directions and not getting anywhere.

Plan printing so several pieces can be run at one time. This will give several colors at the price of one. It will save money both on presswork by printing several mailers simultaneously on a large sheet, and on paper through quantity purchasing. Plan space advertising to take full advantage of frequency discounts by discriminate use of rate holders which can cut drastically the cost of some larger insertions.

Plan the timing of news releases to coordinate with and hopefully reinforce advertising mileage. There are hundreds of good media for advertising and no single bank can, nor would it want to, use them all. It is up to the advertising manager to determine which media can best reach the target audience and then allocate the resources accordingly. Generally, a medium should be chosen with three things in mind:

1. The character of the market—how many people do you want to reach? What kind? Where do they live?
2. The nature of the product—and its appeal.
3. The selling approach—a slogan identification, long copy story, or a short spot.

Have the right story for the right medium (don't particularly advertise "we're a woman's bank" on television during the World Series), and stay in the medium in which you can compete and look strong. Always consider the reputation and appearance of the medium selected. Remember, your image is very important during the positioning era.

The pros and cons of the various media and how each should be used most effectively should be considered:

1. Press Media.   The press is the first of the media to be considered. The business press is the most efficient and economical means devised to reach the tens of thousands of hidden buying influences throughout the market.[1] The word "press" covers newspapers and magazines. Although this medium is very powerful and comparatively low in cost, the ad must appear in the right publication in order to reach the prime prospects.

Magazines are the most selective of all media. They have the advantage of good graphic quality and selectivity of audience. Magazines have long lives because they are circulated over an extended period of time. They also have the confidence of their audience. (Remember to tailor the ad to the audience.)

A disadvantage of magazines is that their circulation may cover too large a territory. The bank may not wish to advertise to an entire region of the country. Also, magazine copy is sometimes long in preparation time.

The newspaper is probably one of the favorite media for bankers. Newspapers can completely saturate the local market area. Newspapers also have the advantage of a broad and diversified appeal. The bank can reach all kinds of people. Scheduling is satisfactory and the rates are usually good.

A disadvantage is that a small-space advertisement can get lost in the paper—it may wind up as inconspicuous filler. Also, color quality

---

[1]Richard H. Stansfield, *Advertising Manager's Handbook* (Chicago: Dartnell Corporation, 1969), p. 1068.

is generally poor. There are some pointers for using the newspaper: Use enough space to be seen; don't be subtle, the reader is in a hurry; and remember to use specific sections of the paper, depending on which market the bank wants to attract.

There are several ways to be effective in print advertising. It is very important that the message be in the headline, for the headline is used to flag the prospect. Always offer a benefit in the headline and very definitely inject news in the headline. Sometimes long headlines can be more effective than short ones, but always avoid a negative within the headline. Be sure to look for story appeal in the illustration. Photographs are almost always better than drawings. Be sure to use simple layouts and put a caption under the photograph. Do not print body copy in reverse type. It looks good but it generally reduces the readership of the ad.

2. Broadcast Media—Radio and Television. Both of these media have network, regional and local advertising time available. Banks are usually concerned with local advertising.

There are several things to consider in deciding whether to use a broadcast medium. Costs can be quite high and the advertisement is at the mercy of the show's rating. Commitments, particularly with TV, can be long indeed, from 13 to 52 weeks. Generally, a simple message is better for the broadcast medium. Think in terms of saying all that should be said in 10 or 30 seconds. TV has the advantage of being able to attract visually. A demonstration of one's product or service is effective. The picture should do most of the work. It is also important that the format of the program be considered in deciding where an advertising spot is placed. A program format can be totally unfavorable to an ad.

Radio has the disadvantage in product advertising simply for lack of visuals. However, it has been suggested that since radio is in fact the theatre of the mind, be creative!

In both broadcast media, make sure the advertisements are done professionally or they will suffer in comparison to the network ads. It is well to ask for responses from the audience to judge just how effectively the ad is reaching the market.

There are more radios than people in the United States today— millions of sets in homes, cars, boats, or on the beaches. Since almost everyone has a radio, people tend to listen alone and they choose exactly the kind of programming they want to hear. Because they do, that audience segmentation is a great advantage for bank advertisers. Radio permits one to select the audience. There are several points to remember in trying to achieve a better radio commercial. First, be sure to stretch the listener's imagination. What will make the ad memorable? Always present one idea. Be sure to mention the bank's name and its promise early. Don't overlook the use of music because it can help. However, it must be kept simple. Have enough commercials for the bank's campaigns. You need more radio commercials than television commercials. Humorous commercials fare the worst with repetition.

It is important to remember that prime time for radio is 6 A.M. to 10 A.M. Sometimes, it is a good idea to hear your radio commercials spliced into a tape of several minutes of actual program content. Select your audience by station, time of day, and season of the year. Rely on the flexibility of radio to keep your message current and again, above all—be *sure* to stretch the listener's imagination.

In producing a television commercial, be sure that the advertisement is effective and that the best dramatic technique was used for the product and the strategy. In producing a television commercial, look at a storyboard of your commercial. There is only one simple rule for looking at a storyboard—look at the pictures first. Ask yourself if they are telling the story of your commercial—then look at the words. From this point, you are able to decide if the storyboard will make an effective commercial. The pictures must tell the story. Look for the key visual and grab the viewer's attention within the first few seconds. Be direct—a good commercial is always uncomplicated. Be sure to register the name of the bank's service visually. Always have a payoff by showing the advantages of the service. The tone of the advertising must also reflect your product's personality. Avoid too many words in the commercial and keep in the back of your mind that you are building a campaign and not just individual commercials.

It is sometimes important that the commercial be entertaining as well as hard sell. However, if you can remove the sales message from the commercial and still have a commercial, the entertainment portion of your message is getting in the way. Use humor when it can contribute to the sale, music when it can reinforce the message of your service, emotion to involve the viewer, and any unusual film techniques to drive home the message to the consumer.

3. Direct Mail. Direct mail is also a selective medium. It is possible to choose people for the mailing list that you already know a great deal about. There are also definite disadvantages to direct mailing. Rising postage cost is a major one. Mailing lists can be very expensive, and they are very difficult and time-consuming to keep up-to-date.

If direct mail is used, it should be worthwhile and interesting. People receive a great deal of "junk" mail and your ad must stand out. Have the advertisement fit the job to be done. If you wish to reach small loan prospects, a brightly colored folder might do the trick. A more subdued ad might work for the person who would use your trust department.

Personalize the mail. By all means, use a name and *spell it correctly*. Hand-addressed mail will catch the attention quickly, but it is not practical in most cases. Make it easy for the prospect to act. Give the bank's address and phone number. You may wish to include the name of a person (i.e., personal banker) who could give special help. Most of all, direct mail is an accountable medium. It is very easy to figure its costs and your results.

4. In-bank Displays. In-bank displays are effective if you wish to have your present customers expand their use of the bank's services. The ad should be located at the point of heaviest traffic. The ad should be uncomplicated. It is best to feature one service at a time. Change the display often or the customers will stop noticing it. Keep the display in good condition or it will be to your disadvantage if the customers do notice it. In this day of the drive-in window, consider displays there. Many customers use only the drive-in window.

5. Transit and Outdoor Advertising. Car cards, bus posters, station ads, and billboards are overlooked much of the time. However, there are advantages to using such media. People see the ads under good reading conditions. People riding the bus or passengers in cars may have little to do other than read ads. There is also little competition in some of these media. Short messages and strong artwork are necessary for this type of ad. A disadvantage is that the same people are exposed to the ad. The signs also deteriorate rapidly and must constantly be maintained.

Another advantage of outdoor advertising is the ability to zero in on your target. It is usually the most localized of all the media and you can select an audience with precision, reaching the consumer outside of his or her home, often on the way to buy. Look for a big idea. Keep it simple—always use bold lettering; use art for impact, and color for readability. Use the locations to your advantage. Look for something that is memorable. Announce new products with an extra bang. Remind people about the bank's television campaign by tying in your outdoor boards. And always be sure to "ride" the boards. You cannot always tell by sitting in your office, or even by looking at one board which has been posted for your approval, what works and what is not working until you get out and drive around to personally view your boards.

In transit advertising, there are four points to consider in dealing with copy. Think about your audience, buy special routes, and use transit to deliver a coupon. "Take-ones" are sometimes useful; be imaginative.

6. Novelty Items.   Finally, novelty items are used frequently to advertise. Calendars, personal diaries, or other often-used items are appreciated and repeat your message many times. The cost of the item must always be weighed against the results.

HOW TO CREATE MEDIA PLANS

The average consumer is bombarded with over 1,500 different advertisements per day. As an extension of the total marketing strategy, simply put your money where your business is—or where you want it to be. By specifying your objectives, you then build around the answers to the questions: Why? When? Where? How often? and In what way?

First, you must decide whom you want to reach. Your target audience must be defined by their demographics including age, sex, income, education, occupation, buying habits, or family status. And if you know their lifestyles or attitudes, you should describe those to your media planner.

You must then decide when you want to reach your target audience. For instance, if you were selling Individual Retirement Accounts (IRAs), it would make a lot more sense to concentrate your efforts toward the latter part of the year showing the benefits of the tax shelter factor with an IRA.

Then, where is your consumer? Most commercial bankers know where their consumers live; however, on a national scope such as corporate headquarters in one state and city and an affiliate company in another, utmost importance must be given in determining effective means of targeting in on specific areas. Also, market segments within your own localized area must be considered in finding where and how dollars are spent.

Next, you must decide how often you want to reach them. This involves the concepts of reach, frequency, and impact. For instance, if you are trying to reach 60 percent of the homes to make them aware of your new service or product, then it cannot be done if your reach is less than 60 percent, and as the reach goes up, the frequency comes down. It has been said that people forget 60 percent of what they learn within a half-day, so the more repetition, the better the retention.

Finally, you must consider in what way you want to reach your target audience. You must consider the best environment for the copy. For example, it would be totally useless to advertise in a local newspaper for correspondent banking relationships.

In obtaining better media plans, always be sure to establish marketing objectives and strategies. Allow the right timetable for developing that plan and be sure to include your media planner in meetings with your copy people concerning the overall campaign.

RESEARCH: PRETESTING AND POSTTESTING

Research for advertising differs from market and product research in that it concentrates mainly on testing copy and other advertising elements in terms of readership and results. Most current pretesting concentrates on the bank's promotional strategy and with the analysis of whether the intended messages via specific advertisements are communicable to the target audience. Within the overall framework of pretesting, the elements most often under evaluation are: (1) Message recall, (2) narrative playback, (3) sponsor identification, (4) presence of any deleterious elements, and (5) presence of any confusing elements. The purpose for this research is to correct problem areas so the bank can maximize the probability of communicating the intended message to its target audience and maximizing the probability that the target audience will realize just *which bank* is communicating the message.

If ads are pretested one against the other, or if several slogans, themes, headlines, copy approaches, product features, and user benefits are pretested, the most effective one may be used. Specific objectives make development of survey questions and interpretations of results both easier and considerably more valid. And by having specific objectives, it is then possible for the advertising manager to measure accurately and precisely the effectiveness of an advertising campaign.

Some marketers feel that posttesting is unnecessary because it is asked to tell you what you already know. To make things even more confusing, the market environment may change drastically since the spot was first placed. There are critical factors adversely affecting the validity of information to be derived from a followup. It is difficult to rely on a respondent's memory on the television spot alone, since it was supported by other media. If testing is to be done, it should focus on those particular areas which can assist you in determining what to do next.

Posttesting should concentrate on the impact of the bank's overall strategies, as well as an assessment of the current and/or projected state of the marketplace environment. Within this framework, posttesting should concentrate on the following factors for both your bank and your competitors: (1) Consumer awareness of the marketing effort, (2) consumer attitudinal shifts which relate to image and intended use of product, and (3) consumer behavioral shifts—for example, "Did they change banks or buy your services?"

In short, pretesting should focus on the question, Will it communicate? while posttesting research should focus on, Did it sell?

ADVERTISING AGENCIES

Of all marketing expenditures, advertising is usually the largest single expenditure. In most instances, these expenditures are channeled through an advertising agency. There are three ways of utilizing an agency: (1) For specific, one-time needs with the bank's own advertising department doing most of the work, (2) in conjunction with the advertising manager (here the manager may be the only person directly employed by the bank in the advertising field and he may direct the agency's efforts), and (3) complete utilization of the agency for the agency's full services.

There are definite advantages in using an agency. Advertising is not a business to be conducted on the basis of guesswork. If it is worth doing, it is worth doing well. It should be handled by those who have made it their full-time business. They know the pitfalls, problems, and opportunities associated with advertising.

An agency will devote its time to preparing, producing, placing, and checking advertisements, as well as supervising the entire operation. The bank that uses an agency must be involved in the overall planning strategies of the total marketing plan. Agencies also do research in market areas, and can be of great assistance to those banks that lack research departments.

Few banks use a "half and half" plan anymore. The staggering cost of photography and art equipment, plus specialty personnel, make the cost of this approach prohibitive. Banks should not be in the art and photography business. Another reason for using an agency is that new ideas are secured. Agencies must produce or they lose accounts. Agency personnel are also in a position to keep up with marketing trends. Many media representatives actually prefer working with agency personnel because of their skills and their experience with the media.

A good recommendation for an agency is membership in AAAA— American Association of Advertising Agencies. Requirements for membership are high. Other considerations are (1) output for other clients, (2) length of time in business, (3) growth record, (4) physical appearance of office and employees, (5) persons who would work on your account and how many other accounts they would handle, (6) experience in the banking field, and (7) size. Is the agency large enough to handle the bank's needs—or are they too large?

The client and agency relationship should be a partnership. A strong bond of trust should develop between the two partners. By keeping secrets from each other, the advertising will most certainly suffer. The bank can get the most out of an agency by always being very explicit in its instructions—letting them know exactly what it wants them to do and how it will check on them to be sure the goal is accomplished. By giving the agency specific, realistic, attainable objectives, you accomplish your number one priority in being a productive advertising manager.

The cost of an agency depends on how much and what kind of services it renders. However, the cost should be considered in terms of return on investment.

It has been said that all people have a feeling of expertise in the following areas: (1) building fires, (2) making the world's greatest martini, and (3) writing advertising copy. And an advertising director can receive more advice and opinions in one day than the average person receives in a year.

Help from within the bank is most vital. Specialists in various phases of banking services must be called upon in planning and executing ads pertaining to their particular field of expertise. Also, a complete review of final copy is a must to ensure accuracy. They should not, however, expect to inject creative approach in either copy or art work.

Conclusion

An advertising manager must deal with many difficult problems, but his greatest responsibility is to keep his bank "on target" and to justify his existence by providing contributions to the bottom line. He must constantly be aware of new products affecting his area, and competitors' advertising, both locally and regionally.

There are too many banks these days that do not know specifically where they are or where they are going—but they are getting there very fast. The reason for this is that they are not willing to take time, energy, patience, and provide funds to create a realistic marketing plan. Without that written plan, many a bank becomes an "unguided missile."

A written plan is one of the greatest benefits ever devised for the advertising director. It provides him with guidelines for daily, weekly, and monthly activities. It also helps in monitoring results.

THE BUDGETING PROCESS

As each bank approaches the overall advertising effort, it must have a budget—a plan for allocating resources for expected expenditures. Most structured companies of any size or stability operate from a rather precise budget which is broken down into individual departmental budgets. Two areas are of concern: (1) How the bank determines the portion of the resources that will be allocated to advertising (the department and/or function), and (2) how the manager of the advertising department decides to break down the allocated resources—by media, process, and so on.

Many of the corporate budgeting methods were derived from attitudes toward the function of advertising, and just as attitudes have changed considerably, so have the budgeting methods.

Budgeting Methods

There are two basic approaches to budgeting for advertising. The first approach is a passive one. Some of the formulas used in this approach are (1) percentage of sales; (2) competitive parity; (3) "what's left over;" and (4) arbitrary allocation. The second approach is active. Typically, in this approach marketing objectives are stated, needs are analyzed, and funds are allocated on a need basis.

1. Percentage of Sales. The first method we will examine is the percentage of sales method. The advertising-sales ratio (A/S) can be either a determinant or an analytical tool. In terms of analysis, it is used like other ratios—a convenient summary figure enabling executives and analysts to compare advertising expenditures and associated sales. These ratios may have to do with advertising in different markets, advertising in successive time periods, advertising under varying expenditure strategies, and advertising by the company versus that of its competitors.

The entire basis for this method hinges on an expected market response from a given expenditure. A tool for predicting what the allocation should be is the "demand schedule" for "response curve." This is merely a graphic representation of the A/S ratio experienced in the past with applications of varying amounts of advertising. (See Exhibit 1.)

Budgeting by this method is in the form of "what's needed to obtain the desired revenue volume." Experience may indicate that a particular percentage of gross sales or income spent on advertising will maintain a certain positive volume of sales. The basis for the ratio may be either past revenues or projected future revenues. At any rate, the total amount allocated on the percentage basis is then divided among all sales expenses.

The limitations of the A/S method (or any other ratio method) are numerous. If the ratio is used year after year without a newfound basis, the cause and effect relationship between advertising and mar-

EXHIBIT 1 The Marketing Response Curve: Revenue as a Function of Advertising

Sales revenue ($000)

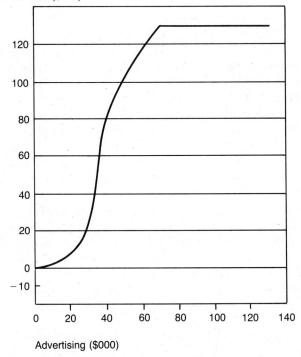

Advertising ($000)

Three factors define the shape of the response curve:

1. An exponential sales decay constant—the rate at which sales fall off in the absence of advertising (because of product obsolescence, competing advertising, and so on).

2. The saturation level, which can be defined as the practical limit of sales that can be generated, depending on the product or service being promoted and also on the advertising medium being used.

3. The response constant—the sales generated per advertising dollar when sales = zero. For example, if a company had no sales and decided to spend $5,000 per month on advertising, and sales went from $0 per month to $10,000 per month as a result of the advertising, the sales response constant would be $10,000/$5,000 or 2. These factors are parameters that remain constant from one calculation to another until new assumptions are made or new values are discovered.

Three variables also affect the curve:

1. The rate of sales/revenue at a given time.
2. The increase in rate of sales at a given time.
3. The rate of advertising expenditure.

SOURCE: Adapted from: David L. Hurwood and James K. Brown, *Some Guidelines for Advertising Budgeting* (New York: The Conference Board, 1972), p. 61.

ket response is reversed. The advertising budget should be controlled for the purpose of accomplishing something—a sales objective. The sales should not control the advertising allocation.

Also, the A/S method may fail to recognize changed conditions. Using the same percentage year after year implies that (1) there was a logical basis for it to begin with, and (2) nothing has happened since to alter the amount of advertising needed. Even if the percentage were logical at the outset, the fluidity of the market and new management objectives could render the percentage obsolete. It also implies that no change has occurred in the rate of market response to the level of advertising investment.

Lastly, the A/S method gives the advertising department unique treatment. Other departments tend to determine budgets more logically. It implies that advertising is a luxury and, therefore, expendable. The ratio method can be used, but if it is used, it should be treated as a starting point to be adjusted with needs.

2. Competitive Analysis. The method of tracking competitive advertising (competitive analysis) is considered normal and essential. Also, comparing your bank to the industry norm can be revealing. The information can be available in (1) enabling a comparison of the company's expenditures and results with those of important competitors or the industry norm, and (2) permitting the marking of various computations involving share of the market, share of industry advertising, or both.

In comparing company similarities in expenditures, it is well to compare with selected competitors. (See Exhibits 2 and 3.) If sharp differences are found, it would be wise to look for reasons. It has been shown that overall marketers selling comparable services or goods to similar markets under similar conditions tend to have similar marketing-cost ratios. This is because a fixed market responds the same way to the same approaches from each seller. Studying competitors does not mean that you should duplicate them. It only means that you wish to know where your organization is outperforming others and, likewise, where your organization does not perform as well.

The objection to using the company parity budgeting method is that it is not wise to match competitors in spending without weighing all the facts and consequences. It may well be that the data available on a competitor is insufficient for comparison with your company. The data may cover more than one service when you only need data on one service. Suppliers of services are not as fortunate as product producers in that there is not as much data available. Even if you could determine the exact amount a competitor allocated for advertising one

EXHIBIT 2 Average Marketing Expenditure by Service Type and Asset Size (all reporting banks—1985)

Service Type	Asset Size in Millions of Dollars								
	Under 10	10–25	25–50	50–100	100–250	250–500	500–1,000	1,000–5,000	5,000 or More
Retail Services (individuals)	7.7	12.0	19.9	36.6	77.3	155.5	436.1	825.2	2842.8
Commercial/Corporate (business)	4.4	5.9	9.7	14.2	32.6	51.0	123.4	287.7	657.8
Trust	3.2	2.5	2.9	5.9	11.6	19.1	39.1	104.8	407.5
Institutional	6.1	5.9	8.9	16.1	38.8	69.0	128.8	256.2	1123.5
Other	1.1	2.6	5.4	8.5	17.0	27.2	54.8	195.1	1112.3

EXHIBIT 3 Percentage of Reporting Banks' Budgets Spent on Each Service by Asset Size

Service Type	Asset Size in Millions of Dollars								
	Under 10	10–25	25–50	50–100	100–250	250–500	500–1,000	1,000–5,000	5,000 or More
Retail Services (individuals)	73.4%	67.5%	63.1%	56.8%	56.4%	54.3%	60.5%	57.8%	57.8%
Commercial/Corporate (business)	16.4%	21.2%	22.0%	20.4%	18.9%	18.6%	16.0%	17.7%	10.6%
Trust	.2	1.7	1.4	3.3	5.3	4.8	4.4	4.4	6.1
Institutional	9.6	8.1	10.8	16.9	17.9	20.5	16.3	16.6	17.1
Other	.4	1.6	2.7	2.6	1.5	1.8	2.7	3.5	8.4
Total	100%	100%	100%	100%	100%	100%	100%	100%	100%

Share of Expenditures by Asset Group

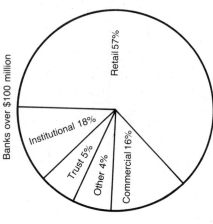

Banks over $100 million

Retail 57%
Institutional 18%
Trust 5%
Other 4%
Commercial 16%

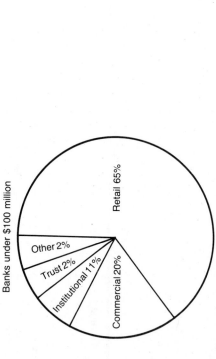

Banks under $100 million

Retail 65%
Other 2%
Trust 2%
Institutional 11%
Commercial 20%

Notes: Percentage figures do not total due to rounding.
SOURCE: Bank Marketing Association, *Analysis of 1985 Bank Marketing Expenditures*. (Reproduced with the permission of the Bank Marketing Association.)

service, you would also have to match his or her campaign medium for medium, market approach for market approach, to get the same results. The sheer magnitude of resources is not as important as the effectiveness of programs. Long-range plans of the competitor could make a vital difference in advertising allocations and should be considered. Finally, a strong competitor may be financially so powerful that it would be folly to try and match its spending. Effective original advertising will do more to beat competitors than will trying to outspend the competition.

3. Available Funds. The method of available funds concerns the financing of any marketing element with money left over, but it can hardly be termed "budgeting." This automatically treats advertising as a managerial activity that should be financed with little regard for needs, objectives, or opportunities. Even if media requirements of resources were modest as compared with sales force requirements, budgeting by this method might be too small to do even a modestly effective job. Budgeting by funds available might not support other marketing functions.

A certain level of promotional intensity is required before the promotion's presence can be felt in the market.

The available funds method benefits the company in that it assures that the company will make a satisfactory profit or break even in the short run. The need for profits cannot be questioned, but there must be a provision for long-term profits. It is shortsighted to achieve a good current profit picture by withholding funds from advertising, on which many future sales and profits depend.

Use of this method can result in one of two possible ends, neither of which is satisfactory:

1. Spend what the company can afford—the budget may be too small.
2. Spend all that the company can afford—the budget may be larger than necessary.

4. Need Determination. Heretofore, the budgeting methods that have been discussed have been passive and not much research or real analysis is necessary in these methods. In fact, one might say the passive methods allow external factors to set the budget. The active approach, on the other hand, allows the department to submit a budget recommendation based on need, and is commonly referred to as the task method or the objective method.

The object of the task method is to build a budget based on concrete estimates of the various jobs to be done. The expenditure patterns of the industry, the amount of resources available, past experience, and many other factors must necessarily be considered in the process of working out the advertising budget; but none of these factors can be allowed to dominate the decision on various segments of the budget or to offset a valid budget prepared under the task method.

The task method approaches budgeting systematically. The governing considerations are the marketplace objectives. The first step is to look at the marketing program as a whole. It may be that the advertising functions make up the marketing department to a large extent. Or it may be that advertising plays a smaller role in the entire marketing program. The objectives of the entire marketing program should be set forth in writing in terms of the company, service, campaigns, and/or markets.

After these objectives are defined, it must be determined what part advertising will play in achieving the total program. Then it is necessary to determine the cost of producing the advertisements and of disseminating the material through the various media. This, in effect, becomes the provisional advertising budget. It is recommended that a contingency fund be added to the budget after the known and expected costs are set forth.

This budget is called provisional because the approval must come from top management, who probably have had little to do with its determination up to this point. It is well to have management look not only at the figures of the budget, but also at the objectives that the figures represent. Have management assign priorities to the objectives so that if budget trimming is necessary, management will have already decided what objectives do not necessarily have to be accomplished.

One criticism of the task method is that it is pointless to set objectives since the company has no way of knowing for sure how much or what kind of advertising will be required to achieve the objectives. There is no doubt that this method requires much probing and research, and that experience can play an important part.

The broad applicability of the task method allows the company to expend resources for research which can be widely helpful in areas other than budgeting. The task method rests on data collected from both experience and research. The data then must be sifted and projected to the marketing problem (objective) under consideration. Inherent in this method are two requirements: (1) The systematic working out of objectives, and (2) the continuous gathering and analysis of marketing-response data.

An important step in this method is to measure both the value of the objective and whether or not it is worth the probable cost of obtaining it. In other words, what intensity of demand is an economically sound target? This simply means that objectives should be framed in the light of probable contribution to profits.

The neglect of this element in budget planning has contributed largely to the skepticism about the effectiveness of advertising. Many senior bank managers say they cannot see sound, analytical reasoning in advertising budgets. They desire return on investment and this emphasizes the advantages of the task method.

All the budgeting methods mentioned have advantages and drawbacks. All methods might be used, but used critically in light of their strong points. It seems best to approach budgeting from the active side, using research and experience and then tempering the results with knowledge derived from the more passive methods.

Marginal Analysis

Managers want to have proposals closely related to profits. They want to know what they will receive from advertising. It is also well to know the boundaries (the minimum and maximum amounts that should be spent) on advertising expenditures. Marginal analysis provides a framework for establishing advertising goals and budgeting funds necessary to accomplish them.

Marginal analysis says that in order to maximize profitability money should be spent on advertising (or on any productive resource), once the break-even point is passed, until the last dollar spent brings in one additional net dollar of revenue; or in economic terminology, until the marginal cost (MC) of advertising equals the marginal net revenue (MR) it produces.

An advertising budget of a smaller amount is not optimal, because before the point of equilibrium of marginal revenue and marginal cost, an additional dollar spent on advertising will yield more than an additional dollar of net revenue. And an advertising budget of greater amount is not optimal, because the last dollar spent on advertising will result in less than an extra dollar of net revenue. (See Exhibit 4.)

The closer the company gets to drawing its "market response to advertising curve," the closer it can pattern its advertising budget in accordance with the principles of marginal analysis. In applying this economic principle, one must also be constantly aware of the ever-changing marketplace.

In the sample that will follow (Exhibit 4), three simplifying assumptions are made:

1. Advertising is the only element of the marketing mix under consideration.

EXHIBIT 4 Schedule of Expenditure Levels with Associated Sales Revenue and Profit

---

A. Schedule of Expenditure Levels

Total Advertising Expenditure	(1) Marginal Advertising Expenditure	(2) Total Sales Revenue	(3) Marginal Sales Revenue	(4) Total Profit Col.3 – Col.1	(5) Marginal Profit Col.4 – Col.2
0..........	—	0	—	0	0
10..........	10	0	0	(10)	(10)
20..........	10	5	5	(15)	(5)
30..........	10	30	25	0	15
40..........	10	80	50	40	40
50..........	10	110	30	60	20
60..........	10	122	12	62	2
70..........	10	130	8	60	(2)
80..........	10	130	0	50	(10)

B. Total Revenue and Total Profit as Functions of Advertising Expenditures

Revenue/profit ($000)

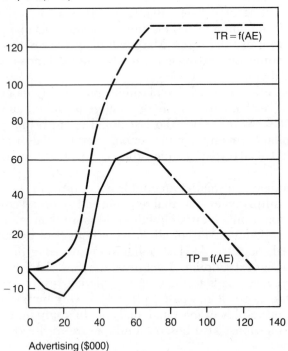

Advertising ($000)

SOURCE: David L. Hurwood and James K. Brown, *Some Guidelines for Advertising Budgeting* (New York: The Conference Board, 1972), pp 16–17.

2. Sales revenue is defined as sales revenue net of nonadvertising costs. (Revenue left after deducting all costs except the advertising.)
3. Advertising must be purchased in increments of $10,000.

How much should be spent on advertising? Inspection of the schedule tells the answer—$60,000. With this input, total profit is greatest—$62,000. If another $10,000 were spent on advertising, bringing the total to $70,000, the marginal revenue would be only $8,000, and hence total profits would drop to $60,000.

The principle is also subject to modification if there is a significant time lag between expenditure and related revenue. Generally, revenue produced by advertising is not generated immediately or in one sum, but is a stream of income over a period of time. This income should be discounted to its present value by a suitable rate of interest, usually, the company's opportunity cost or cost of capital. The same should be done with successive advertising expenditures in a campaign.

This approach has wide appeal to managers. It is mathematically demonstrable; also, it imposes discipline on those responsible for devising advertising campaigns, in that they must be able to justify their recommendations in terms of expenditure.

Some firms have found that this model can be applied successfully even in the absence of information about how revenues vary with advertising and sales promotion. The advertising achievements to look for are improvements in consumer knowledge, attitude, preference, and intention to use the service of the company. The market response related to advertising can be determined by analyzing the changes recorded in the respondent's attitudes in successive interviews or by a sampling of new customers (why did you decide to try our bank?). Advertising can be made accountable.

This is not to say that applying marginal analysis is easy. Those who can apply it rather well are retailers and mail-order houses. They generally enjoy uncomplicated marketing programs, and the impact of their advertising is quickly reflected in revenues.

Another problem is that it is difficult to predict the impact of advertising. It is also hard to know what the lingering effect has been (during the period of a present advertising campaign) of previous company advertising. For how long will the new campaign have an effect? When will it begin to register an effect? The activities of competitors can also influence market response considerably. There are many variables from one time period to the next.

Some of these problems can be overcome, or at least estimated, from an analysis of past advertising campaigns and also through market tests of new campaigns. Few advocates of marginal analysis contend that it provides easy answers, but it is very necessary in establishing the optimal advertising budget and useful in budget justification.

Framework for Budgeting Decisions and Research

Now that budgeting methods and the importance of analytical budgeting have been covered, we must discuss when—in what time frame—budgeting decisions should take place.

The requirements for matching advertising budget to advertising need constitute a sturdy framework for budgeting decisions on a cyclical basis.

They are as follows:

1. Formulate the marketing objectives for the budget period—marketing objectives that are compatible with the long- and short-term objectives of the company.
2. Agree on the tasks that advertising (along with other components of the marketing mix) is to accomplish if these marketing objectives are to be reached.
3. Assemble and analyze data necessary for developing the scale and specifications of an advertising campaign likely to carry out these tasks.

The first two requirements have to do with goal setting. It is important to note that these goals should be related in two ways to the entire company (not just the marketing program): (1) They should tie in and support both the long-range and the short-range plans of the company, and (2) the goals should maximize overall company profit. This is where marginal analysis can be of great value.

The goal-setting steps are somewhat contingent on the third step if a valid budget is to be made. If assembly and analysis of data on markets and market response to advertising is bypassed, budgeting by task or objectives is only good in theory, not in actual practice. Undoubtedly, this research and analysis is the most difficult part of the entire budgeting process.

Some companies find it helpful to develop diagrams or flowcharts for showing how various budgeting activities are related and how they fit into a time sequence. (See Exhibit 5.) This provides a visual framework for planning and analysis, and helps to account for all essential factors. At any one time, a company may be involved in several of these cycles, each cycle representing separate services or campaigns; an the company may be at a different stage in each cycle.

In looking closely at the advertising cycle, it is readily apparent that research and analysis are like strands interweaving all the cyclical elements—planning, campaign, execution, and evaluation. Research also helps make advertising more efficient in media analysis and test-

---

EXHIBIT 5   Flowchart for Planning and Evaluating the Advertising Budget

---

```
                    ┌─────────────────────────────────────┐
                    │ Formulate marketing objectives for   │
                    │ the budget period subject to         │
                    │ management constraints and agree on  │
                    │ the tasks of marketing components in │
                    │ achieving these objectives.          │
                    └─────────────────────────────────────┘
                                      │
┌──────────────┐    ┌─────────────────────────────────────┐    ┌──────────────┐
│ Ensure       │    │ In the light of these objectives and │    │ If feasible, │
│ satisfactory │    │ tasks, assemble and analyze relevant │    │ employ       │
│ advertising  │◄───│ data on:                             │    │ strategy-    │
│ copy content,│    │ 1. Markets and their susceptibility  │    │ planning aids│
│ for example, │    │    to advertising approaches         │◄───│ such as      │
│ by copy      │    │ 2. Results of previous comparable    │    │ simulation,  │
│ testing.     │    │    campaigns                         │    │ gaming, and  │
└──────────────┘    │ 3. Results of previous marketing     │    │ decision     │
                    │    tests and experiments             │    │ theory.      │
                    │ 4. Media under consideration and     │    └──────────────┘
                    │ 5. Competition and other             │
                    │    environmental factors             │
                    └─────────────────────────────────────┘
                                      │
                    ┌─────────────────────────────────────┐
                    │ Refine objectives. Devise advertising│
                    │ campaign with supporting detailed    │
                    │ budget to cover it. Consider:        │
                    │ 1. Campaign proper                   │
                    │ 2. Experimental campaigns            │
                    │ 3. Contingency reserve               │
                    │ 4. Tracking of results               │
                    └─────────────────────────────────────┘
                                      │
                    ┌─────────────────────────────────────┐
                    │ Submit proposals to top management   │
                    │ for review. Revise objective,        │
                    │ campaign, and/or budget as required  │
                    │ by any additional constraints.       │
                    └─────────────────────────────────────┘
                                      │
                    ┌─────────────────────────────────────┐
                    │ 1. Conduct the campaign proper and   │
                    │    any experimental campaigns.       │
                    │ 2. Use contingency reserve to        │
                    │    capitalize on unforeseen          │
                    │    opportunities and cope with       │
                    │    unexpected difficulties.          │
                    │ 3. Track the results.                │
                    └─────────────────────────────────────┘
                                      │
                    ┌─────────────────────────────────────┐
                    │             Repeat cycle             │
                    └─────────────────────────────────────┘
```

SOURCE: David L. Hurwood and James K. Brown, *Some Guidelines for Advertising Budgeting* (New York: The Conference Board, 1972), pp 16–17.

ing, copy research, tracking and evaluating advertising results, and conducting experimental campaigns.

Methods of Setting Forth the Allocation of Budgeted Funds

If the task method has been used in the determinations of the allocated funds, there will already be a breakdown of the budget according to objectives. If the task method has not been used up to this point, the advertising manager must decide how he will show his department's allotment of funds in a detailed manner. Even if the task method has been used, there could be a need or interest in analyzing the departmental budget in a different manner other than objective. There are a number of ways to show allocations for the advertising department in a budget format.

1. Services.   One approach is the service approach, which lists all the services (products) that the bank wants to sell through advertising and shows the allocation for each. The first step is to list the services to be advertised (checking, savings, automated teller machine, and so on). Then list the general market to which each service has the most appeal. List the media by which each group can be reached most effectively. List the months when each service should ideally receive major emphasis. From the information gathered, draw up a tentative "control calendar" for the projected program.

2. Corporate Advertising.   A more general way to break down allocated resources is between corporate and services advertising. Corporate advertising sells an intangible idea—a positive idea of the company. The company sells its own capabilities—quality of service, friendly staff, dominance of market. A favorable public opinion constitutes a valuable business asset. Not only can corporate advertising exert a great influence on future sales, it can also determine the company's ability to attract employees, particularly high-caliber executives.

There are two ways of communicating a corporate image to the public: (1) Through publicity—news releases, newspaper, TV, radio, for which no money need be expended, and (2) by regular advertising. Companies are leaning more heavily on corporate image today than ever before. There is no doubt that it can be an important element.

3. Processes.   Another way to show the allocation of resources is the process plan. There is a process for developing every ad that is used: The theme must be developed, the medium for delivery must be chosen, copy must be written, and the layout or format must be designed.

It is quite possible to break a budget down into costs for each of these items, allocating percentages of the money to each process, depending on which process is deemed the most important. For example, if theme development were considered highly critical to the effectiveness of the advertising program, a manager might allocate 25 percent of the resources available to theme development.

Because media choices and markets are changing constantly, a wise advertising plan and budget are more crucial than ever. With the bulk of a bank's marketing budget going to advertising (63 percent of reporting banks budgets),[2] it is a critical, yet vital, investment in future profits and growth.

---

[2]Bank Marketing Association, *Analysis of 1985 Bank Marketing Expenditures.*

CHAPTER SEVENTY-SIX

Community and Corporate Affairs for Banks

Willis Johnson

Vice President
SunTrust Banks, Inc.

Banks and the communities they serve tend, in a very real way, to be a reflection of each other. It would be almost impossible to identify a healthy, growing community which is not served by one or more strong, progressive banks. Any bank, whether locally owned, member of a holding company group, or part of a branch network, is one of the key economic cornerstones of its community. As such, the bank should have a stated and understood commitment to dedicate a generous share of leadership and support to local endeavors which are not directly related to its basic business of providing financial services.

Good banks and good communities seem to grow and prosper hand in hand, nurturing each other. Every bank, no matter how large or small, has a stake in the economic and social well being of the geographic markets in which it has a franchise to operate. This interdependence between the bank and its community, and the responsibilities and opportunities this presents, is the subject of this chapter.

COMMUNITY LEADERSHIP

In the eyes of the general public, banks epitomize financial strength and integrity. Banks and bankers are generally held in high esteem within their communities. Bankers are perceived as representing significant local control of money and credit, occupying a power base that must be exercised carefully, fairly, and judiciously.

Communities usually have high expectations of the role their banks should play in civic affairs. In most communities, it is common to find local bankers fulfilling leadership capacities in every imaginable civic endeavor. The interest and willingness of bankers to make themselves, their organization, and a portion of their resources available for community service is the foundation of a successful community relations program.

EASIER SAID THAN DONE

It's easy enough to make the broad, general statement that banks have a moral obligation and duty to be good corporate citizens, and to invest a generous portion of their human and financial resources to worthwhile community activities. The tough part comes in developing sound policies and practices, and implementing these in a consistent, effective, and meaningful manner.

The bank enjoys innumerable direct and indirect benefits when it can operate in a healthy community environment. It is from the community that the bank draws its customers and its employees. In its position of corporate citizen, the bank has certain obligations and duties which must be shared by all concerned citizens.

Senior management has a serious, on-going responsibility to assure that the bank's relationships with the community are handled in a well conceived and constructive manner. While it should not be the bank's only motivation, good community relations generally produce favorable response and generate good feelings toward the institution. Good community relations, while almost impossible to quantify in terms of direct or immediate returns, over time somehow find their way to the bottom line. A well planned and well executed approach to community affairs becomes a matter of enlightened self-interest. It's simply a matter of good stewardship, good citizenship, and good business.

PREREQUISITE: ADEQUATE SERVICE

The first prerequisite for good community relations is to be sure that the bank is providing necessary financial services to all segments of its market at fair prices. Any bank whose services are inadequate or poorly delivered can hardly hope to build good community relations.

If the bank does not properly serve the public, does not earn satisfactory profits, and is not reasonably successful, the institution is severely limited in what it can do in the community.

MORE THAN GIVING AWAY MONEY

Banks should be at least as prudent in how they give away their money as they are in how they lend it. It is unlikely that a business day goes by at any bank when somebody doesn't make a request for a donation for some community cause. But merely doling out dollars to this almost endless line of those who approach the bank with their hands out could become a very wasteful, unproductive, and losing proposition.

Many such requests have absolutely commendable and worthy purposes and may unquestionably merit some degree of financial support. Many other requests may be for dubious reasons and occasionally are pure "con" jobs. Sometimes it takes courage and fortitude to say "no," especially when a request comes from a customer or an influential source. But the bank should be more concerned with how the funds are to be used than by giving in to the intimidating approaches sometimes encountered.

There seems to be a proliferation of fund-raising dinners for causes of every description, usually "honoring" some well-known local person. This is becoming a burdensome problem in many communities, and banks would be well advised to weigh carefully the degree to which they participate in these affairs.

In general, it is unwise ever to make any commitment to unknown persons soliciting donations, "advertisements," or selling tickets by telephone. These frequently come in the guise of an emotional appeal to help orphaned or underprivileged children, or widows and families of policemen and firemen. It's a good idea to ask that requests be made in writing. Without guidelines and controls, a lot of money can be thrown away for no useful purpose. The Better Business Bureau can be a valuable source of helpful information about the legitimacy of groups or individuals soliciting funds.

WHAT TO CALL IT?

Each bank has its own distinctive organizational structure. Various terms are used to define or label the functional areas which deal with the community: Community relations, corporate affairs, community affairs, urban affairs, public affairs, public relations, and so on. These terms can mean different things to different people, depending on how one chooses to define them. What the bank calls these functions is far less important than the underlying philosophy and the procedures used in organizing and carrying out the bank's relationships with its environment.

Much of the terminology used in community relations implies concerns for minority groups, consumer groups, educational and cultural activities, and other specialized areas. These are all potential elements of a total community relations program for most banks. However, it is important that the bank maintain a proper balance and perspective of the total picture, based on the special priorities and conditions within any given community.

TWO BASIC INGREDIENTS

Banks interact with their communities in two primary ways. One is the intelligent and creative application of its financial resources, including its credit policies. The other is the commitment of its human resources in roles of leadership and support of activities with which the bank wishes to be identified. Management should be concerned about the danger that either or both of these basic aspects of community involvement could become unrealistically imbalanced without adequate planning and a system for monitoring its levels of participation.

RESPONSIBILITY

The board of directors should regard the bank's community relations as part of its overall responsibility in overseeing the management of the institution. From time to time, it would be appropriate for the board to ask for a review and accounting of the bank's activities which involve outside community affairs. Bank directors are generally in the forefront of community leadership and can be the source of constructive ideas and guidance in evaluating areas which warrant special emphasis by the bank.

The chief executive officer of the bank must assume the primary responsibility for the institution's performance in its community relations. In addition to exercising this basic management function, the chief executive can also play an important role in setting an example for the entire organization through personal leadership and participation in appropriate activities. The organization will sense the spirit of genuine commitment and enthusiasm the chief executive exhibits in his own work in the community. The CEO can also encourage members of the staff to become involved in community programs and projects on a voluntary or sometimes assigned basis. It must be recognized that many of these activities will require time away from the bank during normal work hours, and provisions must be made for this.

Because of high visibility and position, the chief executive will often be called on to give a great deal of personal time to key community undertakings. It takes judgment and selectivity to avoid becoming committed to more than one person could be reasonably expected to do. The chief executive must always see the proper management of the bank as the highest priority.

In a small bank, the senior officer may find it necessary to accept virtually all of the bank's direct community involvement, if the staff is so limited that there are no others to whom these duties can be delegated. However, in larger banks, it is obvious that top management must delegate much of these responsibilities to insure that community work is properly handled without impairing the operation of the bank. In making such delegations, the chief executive should nevertheless have a systematic procedure to monitor the activities and commitments for the bank as a whole, both in terms of dollars and staff time involved.

STATEMENT OF POLICY

In the interest of uniformity and consistency, it is most desirable for the bank to establish a written statement of policy (Exhibit 1) as a guideline for the conduct of community affairs. By having such a definition of policy, it is much easier to make a determination of those things which are appropriate and those things which are inappropriate for the bank. The policy statement should set broad parameters within which decisions for action can be made. While nobody likes to hide behind, "That's not our policy," the fact that something is outside of policy provides support for a negative decision. The statement of policy should be a positive declaration of the bank's position. However, the community affairs officer may need backing from senior management when a controversial negative decision must be made, often in the face of heavy outside pressure.

EXHIBIT 1 Example of a Bank's Statement of Policy concerning Community Affairs

---

It is the policy of (Bank Name) to devote a generous portion of its financial and human resources to conduct and support worthwhile activities which benefit the community in which we operate. We intend to be a good corporate citizen in every way to ensure that we operate in the best possible environment and that our community will be a desirable place in which all people may live and work harmoniously, and enjoy the good things of life.

The management of this bank accepts its responsibilities to provide leadership and cooperation in constructive community endeavors, and we encourage the members of our staff to follow this example. Maintaining good relationships with our community is consistent with our primary mission of providing ample financial services to all segments of our market at fair prices and at a reasonable profit.

We are committed to an active role in the interests of social and economic improvement and to develop our most important resource—people. In addition to doing those things which produce high visibility for the bank in the community, we also recognize the need to work through other organizations and often without specific recognition to achieve desirable goals.

The Community Affairs Officer of the bank is charged with the day-to-day coordination and oversight of our relationships with the community, to serve as a channel of communication between management and the community, and to keep management advised of significant community needs and to recommend appropriate bank response.

ORGANIZATION

Larger banks generally find it most desirable to concentrate the administration and day-to-day responsibility for community relations in the hands of a designated officer. This person will usually report directly to the chief executive officer or at least a member of senior management. The precise organizational structure may vary widely from bank to bank, depending on the special needs of the institution and its particular corporate culture.

Where the community relations function is less than a full time job, this may well be an additional responsibility of the person charged with managing the bank's public relations. The size and composition of the staff needed to carry out a well-rounded community relations program must be determined by each individual bank. It is important that the bank's approach to its community relations be communicated throughout the organization. Every officer and employee should have an understanding of management's philosophy and attitudes regarding the fulfillment of community responsibilities.

It is highly desirable to have a written statement of policy which establishes internal guidelines for participation in community affairs, such as recruitment of staff members for external activities. Middle managers and supervisors should have reasonable criteria for allowing those under their supervision to use bank time in approved community matters. The coordination of staff participation should be one of the responsibilities of the community relations officer.

THE COMMUNITY AFFAIRS OFFICER

The individual selected to head up the community affairs area of the bank should have several important personal characteristics. In addition to being a good manager and administrator, it is desirable that this person possess an extroverted personality, able to communicate well and to deal with people in a positive manner. This officer should have a strong, personal interest in the community and a commitment to work enthusiastically on activities designed to make the community a better place for everyone.

There is no easily definable educational background which equips one for this function in the bank. Prior service with a nonprofit social agency could be helpful, but the main ingredients are on-the-job experience and a willingness to learn the requirements of the job. A typical job description is shown in Exhibit 2.

Since this is a specialized staff position, it is not necessary that this function be performed by someone with previous line experience in the bank. However, the person who has this job can perform more

---

EXHIBIT 2 Typical Job Description for a Bank Community Affairs Officer

---

The responsibilities of the Community Affairs Officer of this Bank include the following functions:

To coordinate various activities of the bank to ensure that the institution maintains its posture as a good corporate citizen.

To develop and recommend policies, plans, programs, and budgets associated with community activities.

To encourage members of the staff to be involved in worthwhile civic activities and to provide them with adequate support.

To stay abreast of and to evaluate community needs, and to maintain adequate files on community organizations and issues.

To process and take appropriate actions on all requests for donations, contributions, and other support of community activities.

To assist senior managment as necessary in representing the bank in outside activities, and to act as the bank spokesperson in various community organizations.

To keep the chief executive officer properly informed concerning the bank's community activities, including evaluations and recommendations.

---

effectively if he or she has been a resident of the community long enough to be sensitive to its needs and to have a good working knowledge of its social and political structure. Well established contacts in the community are an essential for effective coordination in relating the resources and interests of the bank to community needs. It should be an objective of the community affairs officer to develop and maintain good relationships and communication with peers in other banks and local businesses.

MATTERS OF STYLE

Management styles and philosophies vary widely from bank to bank. Some institutions project an aggressive and outgoing corporate personality, while others tend to take a very conservative and low key approach. Between these extremes are all degrees of variation. There is no reason why a bank's policies for dealing with community relations should represent a different style from its approach to all other matters. Perhaps the key point here is the need to establish absolute credibility and acceptability of the bank's posture in the community.

DIRECT OR INDIRECT INVOLVEMENT

A bank's community relations activities generally fall into one or two main categories. The first involves independent programs conceived and executed by the bank itself as the sole or leading sponsor or participant. The other relates to ways by which the bank joins in as a supporter of outside activities without necessarily occupying a dominant or leadership role. While the latter approach may produce less immediate and direct public relations benefits for the institution, the indirect involvement through cooperative ventures may provide a stronger avenue for long-range influence on community affairs.

In considering the potential public relations values of good community programs, there is absolutely nothing wrong with the bank getting adequate credit for those things it does in the interests of the community. But such recognition should always be the secondary consideration where genuine community concerns are involved. The primary question management must ask itself is not, "What can we do in the community that will get us a lot of good P.R.?," but should be, "What can we do that will truly benefit the community?"

A BANK FOUNDATION?

Many banks find it advantageous to establish a private, not-for-profit foundation as a vehicle for effectively coordinating and administering the funds it wishes to make available for community and charitable purposes. Within the foundation framework, it is possible to maximize the dollars which are available, using appropriate tax advantages, and to minimize the pressures which are often exerted by nonqualified sources seeking bank funding. There appears to be no shortage of "good causes" clamoring for the bank's financial support. Through the foundation approach, the bank can significantly tighten the criteria used to determine where funds may be properly applied.

A bank-sponsored foundation provides management with a useful degree of flexibility, allowing for greater funding in highly profitable years to serve as a cushion against possible lean years when bank earnings may not be so good.

Generally, the foundation will operate with a donations committee composed of senior officers. This committee will meet periodically to review requests for foundation grants and to consider creative and constructive uses to which the available funds may be contributed. It is customary that the community affairs officer should serve as a member of the donations committee, possibly as its secretary, with the chief executive officer in the role of chairman.

Through its foundation, the bank can take a more formalized approach to processing and responding to requests for grants. Those who wish to make such requests may be required to provide detailed operational and financial data which the donations committee can review to ensure that funds are allocated only to appropriate and deserving recipients.

A foundation also permits maximum objectivity and thoughtful analysis in making good decisions about the distribution of funds. Through its foundation, the bank can maintain a structure and process which keeps members of senior management involved and informed about who in the community is requesting financial support for what purposes. Through judicious and careful use of tax effects for various categories of contributions, donations, and grants, the bank may realize considerable extra mileage for the dollars which it is willing to commit to worthwhile, qualified community programs. Banks should take full advantage of current tax regulations to maximize the impact of the funds it sets aside in its foundation.

Nonprofit organizations which seek financial support from the bank or its foundation should be required to provide full information about themselves, the amount they are requesting, the purposes for which the grant would be used, and a list of other contributors. They should also be asked to submit budgets and a determination letter regarding tax status from the Internal Revenue Service whenever this is appropriate. In the interest of keeping this information in a concise and consistent manner, the bank or its foundation may wish to use a simple form (Exhibit 3).

Appropriate legal and tax counsel should be sought in setting up and operating a bank-sponsored foundation.

BUDGETING COMMUNITY AFFAIRS

On an annual basis, it is important for the bank to prepare a projected budget for its community affairs and related activities. If this is a bank-sponsored foundation, the donations committee should make a thorough review of the budget and give its approval. In the absence of a foundation, there should nevertheless be a management committee charged with the review of all requests for large grants and significant donations. The community affairs officer may be given discretion to act independently on requests below some stated dollar amount.

There are no hard and fast guidelines as to how much a bank should budget for its community affairs. Between 1972 and 1984, it is estimated by the Council for Financial Aid to Education that total charitable giving by all U.S. corporations rose from approximately $1 billion to about $3.8 billion.

The 1986 edition of the Annual Survey of Corporate Contributions compiled by The Conference Board indicates that for the banking industry, the median yearly contribution as a percent of pretax income is slightly more than 1.5 percent. The upper quartile median is 2.4 percent while the lower quartile median is just above 1.0 percent. This same survey shows the median percentages of bank charitable

EXHIBIT 3

Fact Sheet
for Grant Consideration

Name of organization _____

Address _____

| City | Zip | State |

Amount Requested _____
Name of individual making application _____
Position in organization _____
Board of Directors or Trustees:

Name	Business or Profession
_____	_____
_____	_____
_____	_____
	_____

Purpose for which grant will be used if made _____
_____
_____
_____
_____
_____

Other contributors _____
_____
_____
_____

Attached budget and IRS Determination Letter

giving in major categories as: 47.7 percent to health and human services, 19.5 percent to education, 14.3 percent to culture and art, 14.7 percent to civic and community, and the remainder to other undefined recipients.

Generally speaking, the bank's giving policy should be segregated into those contributions which recur each year, such as The United Way, and nonrecurring contributions such as capital funds campaigns and other donations which have a defined payment period.

ASPECTS OF COMMUNITY AFFAIRS

The more obvious areas in which banks may find it desirable and worthwhile to become involved in their communities include such matters as:

- Social and human service programs
- Charitable organizations

- Health-related activities
- Educational organizations
- Civic improvements
- Governmental matters
- The arts and cultural programs
- Parks and recreation
- Programs for older citizens
- Historic preservation
- Environmental activities
- Programs for the disabled
- Advocacy groups
- Mental health programs
- Work with schools and colleges
- Sports-related activities
- Youth activities
- Support of Public Broadcasting

GETTING MORE SPECIFIC

The major areas of community affairs outlined above can be defined more specifically as follows, with a few examples:

1. Community Services. This includes such organizations as The United Way, its member agencies, and all other nonprofit community agencies which provide services to meet human needs.

2. Education. Banks can find many ways to work with local elementary, secondary and high schools, as well as institutions of higher learning which may be in the community. The bank may elect to concentrate its financial support to private schools since they do not generally have access to public funding.

Banks may also find it worthwhile to sponsor informational and educational programs or seminars designed to help people of all ages understand more about various aspects of economics, banking, personal money management, financial planning, wills and estates, and other suitable topics. These programs can utilize bank personnel or special guest speakers who bring a particular expertise. Format for such programs may include luncheons or dinners, providing an opportunity for interaction with participants.

Many banks maintain an informal Speaker's Bureau with a list of staff members who are qualified and willing to talk to various types of groups about subjects on which they have some expertise. Speaking to civic clubs, school classes, and other organizations can be a worthwhile and productive effort.

Bank tour programs, usually aimed at young people, can help to strengthen the ties between the bank and the community.

Sponsorship of Junior Achievement groups is an excellent way for a bank to help young people learn more about business and the free enterprise system.

3. Culture and Art. There are virtually no limits as to what a bank might wish to do toward local cultural enrichment. This could include bank-sponsored arts and crafts exhibitions, concerts, theatrical performances, and other programs related to culture and art. Most communities have one or more local organizations with a cultural orientation and bank support and involvement is always welcomed.

4. Health and Recreation. Organizations which are dedicated to seeking cures or controls for diseases and the improvement of health provide a wide variety of opportunities for bank support. In addition to contributions of money, banks can sponsor blood drives, health fairs, "runs" to benefit the local heart association, and so on.

An example of a meaningful and lasting recreational contribution to the community would be donation of land and/or equipment for a public park or picnic area.

5. Religious. Interdenominational and joint religious councils provide an appropriate means for bank support of programs designed to help people in need of emergency assistance, food, and clothing. As a general rule, it would be unwise for a bank to become heavily identified with any one religious denomination.

6. Other. In special situations banks may justify community programs designed primarily to benefit specific local minority groups (blacks, American Indians, other ethnic and cultural groups). An example would be assistance in the publication of a Spanish language newspaper in a sector of the community heavily populated by non-English-speaking residents.

The only limitations on the potential range of community affairs and bank-sponsored programs are imagination and resources.

MATCHING GIFTS PROGRAM

Many banks find that they can extend the impact of the organization's total charitable giving by establishing a Matching Gifts Program with their employees. In such a plan, the bank agrees to match on a dollar-for-dollar basis (or some other formula) the contributions employees make to nonprofit institutions up to some stated maximum amount.

The bank should carefully define eligible recipients for matching gifts, excluding such organizations as churches, fraternal groups, and veterans organizations. A Matching Gifts Program also helps to raise the awareness and sensitivity of employees to the bank's concerns for the community.

PUBLIC VERSUS PRIVATE

In recent years, there has been a reduction in the amount of federal financial support for many social programs, placing greater demands on local government and the private sector. Bank policies should take into account the current and anticipated degree of governmental involvement in those activities of particular interest to the bank.

It may be entirely appropriate for a bank to provide supplemental financial support and local leadership to programs which are predominantly public in nature.

OTHER AREAS OF SERVICE

Many bankers find satisfaction in holding public office, placing them in positions of leadership in which they can exert significant influence on local public issues. It would be helpful for any bank to have a statement of policy on its position regarding officers and employees who wish to run for elective offices, such as the city council or the school board.

There are numerous public and private efforts underway to restore or rebuild downtown areas and neighborhoods. Banks can participate in such projects through direct contributions, special credit considerations, and personal leadership.

Banks are frequently in the forefront of community industrial and economic development organizations, producing not only broad benefits for the community in general but also opening up the possibilities for significant new banking relationships.

CRA AND MINORITY LOANS

Banks must be sensitive to the letter and spirit of the Community Reinvestment Act and the need to support and encourage minority enterprises. Credit policies must be administered fairly and equitably to all sectors of the community.

There are a large number of minority businesses which may not meet the bank's general credit standards. In such cases, the bank may provide educational and technical services for these marginal credits in an effort to help minority business entrepreneurs to become better

managers and financially self-sustaining. This can be a challenge to
the bank since the percentage of failures can be high. However, banks
which are concerned about the total business environment must do
their part in upgrading the quality and effectiveness of minority businessmen, and to bring them into the mainstream of the local economy.

MANAGING BANK PEOPLE-POWER

One of the functions of the community affairs officer is to coordinate
and monitor the participation of bank officers and employees in outside community activities, especially those which involve significant
time away from bank duties. Through personal knowledge, personnel
records, questionnaires, and other sources of information, the community affairs officer should maintain an inventory of the special interests and talents of individuals within the organization. Requests
from community organizations for bank personnel to serve on boards,
assist in fund-raising efforts, and related activities should be channeled through the community affairs officer.

While individual staff members should have the freedom and encouragement to become involved in those aspects of community life
in which they have a particular interest, there is always the possibility
that the bank can become overcommitted with too many persons involved in a single activity.

Centralized files should be maintained by the community affairs
officer as a record of what individual members of the staff are doing
in the way of outside work, both on bank time and personal time. A
simple form (Exhibit 4) can be used to take an annual audit of the
individual activities of staff members. This gives the community affairs
officer a reasonably current record of who is doing what with which
groups.

An annual audit of individual activities can be translated into the
total amount of hours the organization devotes to outside activities.
Many banks may find this is much more time than they realize. Asking
staff members to complete such a personal record each year also serves
as a reminder that the bank has ongoing concerns in encouraging its
people to take part in community activities. These records may also
prove to be helpful in making personnel evaluations.

MEASURING EFFECTIVENESS

At best, measuring the effectiveness of a bank's community affairs
program is difficult if not impossible. To the extent that specific goals
can be set for stated periods, the community affairs officer may be
able to measure and evaluate how well the bank is meeting its goals.

EXHIBIT 4   Inventory of Community Involvement

Your Name: _____

Your Company: _____

Department Name: _____

Center Code: _____

Organization	Your Role	Estimated Bank Hours for 1985	Estimated Personal Hours in 85

COMMUNITY ACTIVITIES (Example: United Way)

_____ _____ _____ _____
_____ _____ _____ _____
_____ _____ _____ _____
_____ _____ _____ _____
_____ _____ _____ _____
_____ _____ _____ _____
_____ _____ _____ _____

BUSINESS AND PROFESSIONAL GROUPS (Example: Bank Administration Institute)

_____ _____ _____ _____
_____ _____ _____ _____
_____ _____ _____ _____
_____ _____ _____ _____

SOCIAL CLUBS AND ORGANIZATIONS

_____ _____ _____ _____
_____ _____ _____ _____
_____ _____ _____ _____

OTHER (Such as church involvement)

_____ _____ _____ _____
_____ _____ _____ _____
_____ _____ _____ _____

SPEAKERS' BUREAU:

Would you be willing to speak to outside groups? _____

Subjects you like to speak about: _____

_____

Types of groups preferred: _____

Date: _____

Through the budgeting process, the bank can document its level of financial support in various areas of the community.

Surveys of community attitudes and awareness can be structured in such a way to provide insights into public knowledge and feelings about the bank and its community relations. In a large institution, such a survey might be a highly sophisticated study as part of an overall marketing project. For a small bank, this could be as simple as occasional meetings between bank management and community leaders in an informal setting over coffee or Cokes. Reports on local economic activity, often available from the chamber of commerce or other sources, can provide data reflecting the effects of certain types of bank community programs.

Any assumptions management may make on the effectiveness of its community programs are an inexact form of evaluation. However, most banks sense whether or not they are making adequate contributions to the community. The community affairs officer should use whatever means are available to assess whether or not various programs are accomplishing their purposes, whether such programs should be expanded or phased out, and whether or not the bank is carrying its fair share of responsibility toward maintaining and building a favorable community environment.

DEVELOPING LEADERSHIP

Beyond the more obvious direct and indirect benefits which accrue to the bank through a good community relations program, there are important side benefits to the bank and its people. Community activities offer an excellent vehicle for developing the leadership potential within the bank's staff. This can have significance not only for the community as a whole but also as part of the process of bringing along candidates for management succession. By working as "loaned executives" during a United Way campaign and in other community-oriented efforts, younger men and women find excellent opportunities to learn what they can do and to improve their skills as they move up the ladder toward positions of greater responsibility within the bank. Senior management can observe and evaluate the up and coming members of the staff in situations which reflect their ability to work with people and to assist in making meaningful contributions to the community outside the bank environment.

SOME PR CONSIDERATIONS

If the community affairs officer and the individual charged with responsibility for public relations are not one and the same person, there is an obvious need for these two officers to work together very closely. While there should be a clear delineation of responsibilities and duties, there is a grey area in which community affairs and public relations overlap. Small donations, purchase of tickets for fund-raising dinners, gifts of door prizes, flowers and gifts for special situations, and so on may be more public relations than community affairs. There's a thin line between community affairs and PR, and each bank will have to make its own determination.

Some of the more traditional bank public relations activities, which have a bearing on community affairs, would include the following:

- Providing bank facilities for community meetings. Many banks have rooms which are available for this purpose.
- Distribution of maps, brochures, and other literature related to community matters.
- Sponsorship of special events.
- Programs to recognize outstanding young people in various activities—such as Scouting and 4-H.
- Bank floats in local parades.
- Bank advertisements promoting community events, programs, and activities.
- Giveaway items for distribution at community gatherings.

SUMMARY

Every bank has the responsibility to provide leadership and support in outside activities which promote the general interests and welfare of the community and its people. Senior bank management should maintain some systematic, organized method to determine priorities and to take appropriate actions to ensure that the bank is properly serving the needs of its marketplace. Besides simply reacting to outside influences in the community, banks should also be proactive in applying creative, imaginative, and productive approaches to serve the needs of the community. Banks are uniquely positioned as a result of their people-power and financial resources to play a leading role in their community. In summary, effective involvement in community affairs is basically a matter of enlightened corporate self-interest.

PART FOURTEEN

Bank Supervision and Regulation

CHAPTER SEVENTY-SEVEN

The Role of Regulation and Supervision in the Global Banking System

Robert R. Bench*

Partner
Price Waterhouse

The purpose of this chapter is to briefly and generally provide an overview on the role of bank regulation and supervision.

Nearly every country in the world has established public policies for the regulation and supervision of banks, since banks are the depositories of the public's savings, allocators of capital in the economy, and managers of nations' payments systems. The policies vary depending on the history of each country's governance. For instance, authorities for bank regulation and supervision may be delegated to a concentrated point, such as the central bank, or the delegation may be disbursed among a number of parties, such as in the U.S., where the Federal Reserve, OCC, FDIC, SEC, congressional committees, and the public at large all participate in policy development as well as the direction of regulatory and supervisory activities. The history of governance also will determine the degree of regulation and supervision in particular areas such as market entry, degrees of competition, and the variety of product and asset powers banks may have. U.S. governance traditionally promotes a banking system comprised of thousands of banks with limited geographical and product powers. Governance in other countries permits banking systems comprised of relatively few, very large banks which can operate on a nationwide basis and in all areas of finance.

---

*Formerly Deputy Comptroller of the Currency, Office of the Comptroller of the Currency.

One aspect of governance common to all countries is that the regulatory and supervisory scheme support the lender of last resort, deposit insurance, and/or investor of last resort functions that governments may have to perform to maintain confidence in the financial system. During any government assistance effort, the central decision makers need current and accurate information to determine the level of assistance required. Without such information, the government may underreact or overreact to a problem, thus exascerbating it. While crisis assistance is never an exact science, the more decisionmakers know about a problem, the better assistance they can provide to restore confidence.

The regulatory and supervisory process in all countries usually covers three areas: corporate authorizations, risk assessment, and sanctions. The corporate process deals with new charters, geographical and product expansion, mergers and acquisition, and bank failure. The risk assessment function determines: the risks in individual bank operations, the condition of each bank in the system, and the condition of the entire banking system. Risk assessment traditionally has been a static, point-in-time analysis. Increasingly, supervisors are making this assessment process more dynamic, assessing risks prospectively by learning more about banks' future operations and strategies. Sanctions comprise the enforcement and compliance process which can include formal agreements, cease and desist orders, removal of bank management, civil penalties, and criminal penalties.

Supervisors' methodologies for assessing risks vary from country to country. A methodology common to all countries is assessment of banks' risk through the analysis of data that banks submit in prudential returns ("Call Reports"). This off-site assessment may be supplemented in some countries with on-site visitations by supervisors and/or bank audits by firms selected by the supervisors. In the U.S., regular on-site examinations by supervisory staff, supplemented by visitations and off-site computerized performance analysis, provide U.S. supervisors with continual flows of current and accurate information on the conditions of banks. A corp of trained professional examiners knowledgeable about bank operations can provide governments with immediate valuable assistance in sorting out a bank problem.

The assessment of capital adequacy is a fundamental aspect of bank supervision. Capital is required to start up a banking business as well as to make investments in fixed assets and subsidiaries. It also provides a disciplined measure of bank management performance. Capital can be used to absorb unexpected losses, match certain risks, and maintain market confidence, albeit market expectations for capital vary depending on changing perceptions about risks in the banking system. However, the determination of capital adequacy is difficult.

First, there is the problem of how to define capital, and second, how to measure capital adequacy. The definition of capital may vary depending on what are considered as components of capital, such as hidden reserves, inner reserves, or loan loss reserves.

A common measure of capital adequacy is the gearing ratio, such as capital/assets or capital/liabilities. However, this measure does not include off-balance sheet activities. The other common measure is the risk-weighted approach which tries to relate risks banks take on to their capital. However, financial liberalization is changing this traditional risk measurement, which generally concentrated on risks in types of assets banks held. While some of these risks remain, they may be reduced or eliminated through newly developed hedging techniques. In addition, open dealing positions, interest rate sensitivity, concentrations of credit, sovereign risks, and off-balance sheet risks are expanding and traditionally have not been included in risk-weighted capital adequacy schemes.

Bank supervisors in many countries, including the U.S., are revising their capital adequacy measurements to incorporate these changes arising from the new activities of banks. Active work is going on nationally as well as multilaterally, such as in the Basle Supervisors Committee. The main job here for all supervisors seems to be to: Forge ahead and provide leadership on the subject; achieve compatibility of definitional and measurement questions; establish a simple framework and methodology which addresses the obvious; and, implement the scheme with enough bite that bankers take it seriously.

Financial liberalization and innovation also mandate that supervisors review their traditional attitudes toward and measurement of liquidity. While supervisors should continue to insist on some survival stock of liquid assets, the marketization of finance also requires supervisors to view liquidity as a dynamic phenomenon in banks rather than as a static, point-in-time measurement. Supervision of bank liquidity needs to go beyond stock and flow concepts to dynamic considerations, such as: Overall balance sheet symmetry, variety and sensitivity of funding sources available, asset credit concentrations, assets that can be securitized, and the markets' perception of a bank's current and future asset quality, as well as present and future earning capacity. Overall, the supervision of banks' liquidity has become very complex and supervisors are revising their expectations about the adequacy of banks' internal controls, management reports, and contingency plans for managing liquidity.

The designs of bank regulation and supervision also are concentrating more on the quality of management and earnings capacity during this period of financial change. As the business of banking changes, new skills and knowledge are required of bank management. The changing business also leads to new sources of income. The quality of those earnings and the abilities of bank managements to plan, control, and respond to change are becoming more important considerations in the assessment of the conditions of banks.

In this regard, there *is* a private side to bank regulation and supervision in those countries where governance promotes private ownership of banks. It is first and foremost the responsibility of bank management and directors to establish the policies, practices, and procedures for the banks under their fiduciary stewardship. Second, communities of banks have responsibilities for establishing standards and controls for bank activities. Third, public disclosure and accuracy of financial statements are the responsibilities of public accountants. Fourth, financial innovation in banks' liability products, securitization of banks' assets, and expanded distributions of banks' capital instruments, have led to the development of "private supervisors" which increasingly rate or grade the financial assets distributed by banks. Greater disclosure by banks and the increase in rating services create market discipline as a supplement to official regulation and supervision of banking.

Finally, *bank* regulation and supervision increasingly need to be more internationally compatible, as well as more integrated, with *securities* regulation and supervision. While the liberalization of financial services is bringing mutual opportunities to the world, it may also raise mutual vulnerabilities. In response, financial authorities are developing broader and more dynamic forms of governance to ensure financial stability during this period of change.

CHAPTER SEVENTY-EIGHT

The Changing Face of Bank Supervision

Robert Herrmann

Senior Deputy Comptroller for Bank Supervision
Office of the Comptroller of the Currency

Bank supervision in the United States has changed substantially since its pre-Civil War beginnings in New York. On-site review and examination is no longer the only tool used to oversee the system. At the Office of the Comptroller of the Currency (OCC), it is not even the primary mechanism we use to fulfill our mission of promoting safety and soundness within the national banking system. Examinations are just one of a variety of tools we use to assess the condition of a bank.

The OCC believes that successful bank supervision is a matter of tailoring a strategy to fit the needs of each regulated institution. In this era of ever-changing bank activities, much of a regulator's success depends on flexibility and practical innovation. To cover the general question of the changing face of supervision, this article will focus on the OCC and the way it has adapted its approach to meet changing circumstances over the years.

The first part of the article traces the office's activities from its creation during the Civil War through the 1950s, emphasizing the changes brought about by the demands of the evolving American banking system. The second part covers the more dramatic changes of the 60s and 70s. The article ends with a section devoted to the OCC as it exists today, when it is coming to grips with how to deal with the ongoing needs of its regulatory charges — the national banks. This section will explain some of the changes that have occurred in the OCC and the reasoning behind internal decisions about its supervisory role which have been implemented in the last two years.

The author acknowledges the assistance of Susan K. Fetner, National Bank Examiner, and Charles L. Lambert, Executive Assistant, in the preparation of this chapter.

THE FIRST HUNDRED YEARS —
EXPERIENCE DICTATES CHANGE

The OCC and the national banking system were created on February 25, 1863, when President Lincoln signed the National Currency Act into law. This new system was established to fund the Union war effort by creating a captive market for government-issued bonds and to help overcome the problems associated with a market where thousands of different bank-issued currencies circulated at various discounts.

The need for a uniform currency was evident. President Lincoln, in providing relief for the situation, established a market for U.S. funding bonds (they backed national bank notes) and created the Office of the Comptroller of the Currency in the bargain.

Although the National Currency Act, later retitled the National Bank Act, explicitly provided for supervision of the institutions chartered by the agency, no law has ever defined the exact powers or responsibilities involved. What constitutes examination and supervision for national banks has been left to be defined by the individual who occupies the comptroller's office.

The first examinations of the condition of the banks were intended to ensure that the banks would be able to redeem notes when presented. After a decade or so, it became evident that supervision had to encompass more than ensuring currency redemption reliability. Henry W. Cannon, the third comptroller, established parameters within which examiners would operate. He formulated an examination that went beyond a mere inspection of the books of an institution; he emphasized the need for close scrutiny of the business of the bank, the responsibility and prudence of its management, and the total quality of its loan and investment portfolios.

Another comptroller, Lawrence Murray, appointed by Theodore Roosevelt, strongly urged boards of directors at national banks to create committees that would supplement the work of the federal examiners. When he found that many directors did not have the slightest idea of what constituted an effective examination, he issued a circular to all banks that outlined proper procedures.

From those beginnings, bank examination developed only slowly as the industry weathered the excesses of the 1920s, the discipline of the Banking Act of 1935, and the conservatism of the 1930s, 1940s, and 1950s.

THE NEW CENTURY/TIME OF TRANSITION

With the appointment of James J. Saxon in 1961, bank supervision became more dynamic. Comptroller Saxon added an economic staff, expanded the OCC legal staff, and went on record as a proponent of expanded charter and branch application initiatives. He appointed an advisory committee of bankers to recommend changes that would broaden the lending and investing powers of national banks and expand the scope of banks' activities. The comptroller believed there was more to bank supervision than just maintaining the "soundness" of individual commercial banks; he saw the diversification and services offered by nonbank intermediaries as a threat to the banks' competitive position and, therefore, as a supervisory issue.

To respond to that issue, Comptroller Saxon moved to increase banks' competitive strength by expanding their powers. He was convinced that, in the last third of this century, the problems created by unduly constraining banks would be greater than the systemic risk created by permitting banks to fail in a less constrained environment.

The supervisory legacy of Comptroller Saxon, although profound in its effect on the OCC, pales in comparison to the changes brought about by Comptroller James E. Smith in the mid-70s. Comptroller Smith commissioned an external study of the office's supervisory functions and related activities. The recommendations from that study provided the basis for sweeping changes designed to allow the OCC to achieve its supervisory objectives more effectively and more efficiently.

To operate within its manpower constraints and in the rapidly changing financial industry, the study recommended that the OCC rely more on the work performed by others. This was the biggest change to date in the way institutions were supervised. Individual examiners were asked to evaluate a bank's internal controls to determine the nature and extent of review and verification procedures they would perform. The extent to which they felt they could rely on work performed by others (bank staff and external auditors, etc.) was the basis for determining the scope of an examination.

This approach revolutionized examination at the OCC and supervision of the national banking system. It led to a revised format for reports of examination to identify more clearly matters of special concern to the OCC, factors that caused the problems, and remedial actions necessary.

The new policies and procedures were published in 1976 in the *Comptroller's Handbook for National Bank Examiners* and were furnished to all examining personnel and each national bank. This handbook has since been updated semiannually and is complemented by companion handbooks that deal with trust activities, consumer examination, and the specific laws and regulations that pertain to national banks.

The study commissioned by Comptroller Smith also recommended the implementation of a computer-based data collection and monitoring system called the National Bank Surveillance System

(NBSS). The system was intended to detect unusual or significantly changed circumstances in a bank or in the national banking system and evaluate the impact of such changes on bank soundness. A system of reports was established to collect certain data from the computer database for subsequent analysis by experienced examiners. This allowed the OCC to identify key indicators of changing or unusual circumstances that might indicate potential problems.

NBSS has evolved to allow retrieval of information from examinations as well as from Reports of Condition and Income. Today the National Bank Surveillance Video Display System (NBSVDS) lends itself to modeling and forecasting as well as analysis of past performance. Virtually every examiner has easy access to NBSVDS, and it is widely used to help plan the scope of examinations and compare examination-generated data.

THE CURRENT SUPERVISORY APPROACH — TAKING THOSE THINGS ADDED TO THE PROCESS SINCE 1863 AND MODIFYING THEM TO FIT TODAY'S BANKING WORLD

In the early 1980s the rapidly changing environment of commercial banking necessitated a rethinking of the OCC's supervisory philosophy. The nature of banking was changing dramatically; new products and services made possible by technological advances were producing a rapidly changing industry and increased competition. By 1987, banks could offer more diverse products and services, such as discount brokerage and electronic funds transfers and, because of more competition for deposits, they faced increased costs.

In addition, today many banks are affected by serious problems in limited sectors of the economy. Phenomena such as a declining energy industry, downward spiralling farm prices, and overambitious real estate development have taken their toll on banks in various regional markets. This has led to a significant increase in the number of banks that are under special supervision by the OCC.

The OCC has changed its focus of looking at the results of a bank's operations to looking at the policies and controls under which it operates. It has incorporated technological advances into supervision so that now the latest advances in microcomputers support its supervisory activities.

But even with those changes, the OCC can no longer rely solely on traditional on-site examination to satisfy supervisory responsibilities. Although examination is an important and irreplaceable supervisory technique, an intensive review of a given bank at a single point in time followed by a relatively long period of no contact no longer makes sense. It has become crucial to target supervision/examination specifically to areas posing the greatest risk to the banking system. And ongoing supervision is necessary.

The need to gather information about individual banks remains important as banks diversify in products and services. Such diversity demands that the supervisor develop a strategy unique to the needs and conditions of each individual bank. In the OCC, the growth of computer databases and the increased use of microcomputers have paved the way for such individualized, ongoing supervision.

In 1984 the OCC began to develop a supervisory approach using the new technology. Under the new approach, detailed information on every national bank is filed in the OCC's computer-based Supervisory Monitoring System (SMS). In 1985, definitive data on each bank was entered into the SMS and it has been updated regularly since then. Data received from banks, through call reports, progress reports, telephone calls or other methods, becomes part of a chronicle on each institution maintained and evaluated by the responsible examiner.

Data in this information system helps the OCC decide how to schedule the review time spent on each institution. Resources are allocated to institutions that need attention while not neglecting those not currently of regulatory concern. At one time the OCC spent 80 percent of its examining and regulatory time in banks which held only 20 percent of total bank assets. Although this meant that oversight of small institutions was good, from an overall regulatory point of view it was illogical; only 20 percent of regulatory time was available for supervising 80 percent of regulated assets.

The OCC's supervisory approach attempts to strike a balance and, after identifying the needs of each institution, makes resources available to those that need attention, regardless of size. Examiners are responsible for specific banks in the geographic area where they are stationed. Multinational, large regional, and problem banks are monitored out of the district offices or out of Washington. Review examiners at each level use the vast resources of the agency, including information ranging from past performance to the latest input from the institution, to determine the amount of time and the type of supervision each institution requires.

Not every case calls for on-site examination. Sometimes a phone call to the bank or request for periodic progress reports may be the most effective means of addressing a weakness. The examiner is the expert who determines how to address the needs of the banks assigned to him or her.

Review examiners use the tools available to them to determine when to conduct a limited, or perhaps extensive, on-site examination. A bank may be chosen for a routine on-site review from among those banks that offer similar risk to the system, or on-site activity may be prompted by an indication that a detrimental trend exists or that the bank has potential problems. In some cases, an examiner may decide a visit to the bank is warranted to get a better feel for the institution when available data are inconclusive.

When examiners are present in a bank, they have already had the benefit of considerable off-site preparatory analysis and review of the bank's operations. Through microcomputers, they plug into OCC's central database to get additional information or perform modeling exercises. Anything the examiner finds can be entered directly into the bank's supervisory profile in that database.

The OCC's revised supervisory approach establishes a hierarchy of risks within the national banking system. Resources are allocated to institutions based on where they fall within the hierarchy. The levels of the hierarchy are:

1. Systemic risk.   No institutions are assigned to this level. It simply reflects the OCC's assignment of resources to monitoring and tracking specific sectors or risks resulting from changing legal or regulatory situations, changes in the economy, etc. Analysts in the district offices and Washington scrutinize the national banking system's operations to identify areas of potential high risk. OCC's Economic and Policy Analysis Division continually reviews the financial health of major sectors of the economy to identify areas that pose a threat to the system.

It may be somewhat misleading to put this element at the head of the hierarchy since it runs through all the levels in varying degrees and affects where a given institution falls within the hierarchy. For example, a bank that would normally be a level eight bank may become a level six bank bacause it is subject to systemic risk.

2. Multinational companies.   This level includes the largest national banks and their respective holding companies, including their national bank subsidiaries. These companies are at the top of the hierarchy because of their size, volume of activity, and potential impact on the system.

3. Shared National Credits (SNC) and international loans subject to the Interagency Country Exposure Review Committee (ICERC).   This level, like level 1, reflects the OCC's commitment of resources to review factors that may cause a bank's position in the hierarchy to change. SNCs are loans or formal loan commitments in original amounts aggregating $20 million or more that are shared by two or more banks under a formal lending agreement or a portion of which is sold to one or more banks, with the purchasing bank(s) assuming its prorata share of the credit risk. ICERC is an interagency committee of federal bank supervisors that evaluates the country risk factors involved in international lending and establishes uniform classifications for such risk. These loans are near the top of the hierarchy because of their size, the potential problems of collection and special reserve requirements, and their potential system-wide effect.

4. Regional banking companies.   This level includes companies with at least one subsidiary national bank with total assets of more than $1 billion. These companies present risk because of their size, volume of activity, and potential impact on the system.

5. Community banks rated 4 and 5 and unstable 3-rated community banks.   This level includes banks with those composite examination ratings.[1] Banks with composite ratings of four and five have an immoderate volume of serious financial weaknesses that, if not corrected, could impair their future viability. Unstable three-rated banks have identified problems that have not been fully addressed or that have not yet improved as a result of actions taken.

6. Unstable 1- and 2-rated community banks.   This level includes banks with these composite ratings and indications of instability. These banks are known to be experiencing changes, such as changes in management, that may or may not have an adverse effect on their condition.

7. Stable 3-rated community banks.   This level includes banks with composite examination ratings of 3. These institutions have identified problems that are being properly addressed but have not been fully resolved.

8. Stable 1- and 2-rated community banks.   This level includes banks with these composite ratings. These institutions are sound and well-managed and show no signs that their condition will change in the near term.

The review examiner, in consultation with the appropriate supervisory office, develops an individual supervisory strategy for each bank, based in part on where it falls within the hierarchy of risk. Each strategy is a dynamic plan that includes on- and off-site analyses and

----

[1]Composite ratings are reviewed for each bank at the end of each supervisory activity. The composite rating of 1 to 5 is assigned based on the examiner's rating of 1 to 5 in the five "CAMEL" areas — capital, assets, management, earnings, and liquidity. For more information on the rating system refer to Office of the Comptroller of the Currency Examining Circular 159.

is tailored to address the OCC's supervisory concerns about the bank. Supervisory strategies are developed annually, but may be updated more frequently as circumstances change. Every strategy answers three questions: (1) What are OCC's concerns about the bank? (2) What needs to be done about those concerns? (3) How should the actions be carried out?

As the strategy for an institution is implemented, the OCC communicates with the institution according to the level and nature of regulatory concern. In addition to requests for information and reports and other contacts, the OCC reports to each bank on its supervisory oversight at least once a year. This report of supervisory activity normally answers these questions:

- What supervisory activities (on- or off-site) were performed?
- Why were those activities appropriate?
- What were the findings and conclusions?
- What actions should the bank take to respond to those findings?
- How will the OCC follow up to see whether identified concerns have been adequately addressed?

Under the new approach to supervision the OCC is changing the way it ensures compliance with law. In addition to attempting to identify noncompliance, it is also promoting compliance as a responsibility of bank management. Part of this program involves specialty examinations, including compliance procedures, for random selection of banks. The examinations will focus on trust and electronic data processing activities; compliance with consumer laws, the Bank Secrecy Act, and Municipal Securities Rulemaking Board requirements; accuracy of regulatory reports; and insider transactions. The randomly selected sample provides information about the entire population of banks that makes it possible for the OCC to extrapolate which problems may be systemwide. The OCC then issues guidelines and policies in those areas to all banks so that problems will be corrected without having to examine every national bank for compliance each year. The OCC will also work with bank managements to make sure they fully understand their compliance responsibilities.

That is the broad outline of the OCC's approach to bank supervision in the 1980s. It allocates resources to areas of highest risk and improves the OCC's ability to predict and plan for future problems. This supervisory approach and the associated information and technology enables the OCC to continuously monitor risks to the national banking system and take swift corrective action when problems are identified.

Bank supervision at the Office of the Comptroller of the Currency has evolved over the past 120 years from rudimentary examination for currency redemption into a highly sophisticated predictive system that looks at the safety and soundness of the industry and evaluates the level of risk in the national banking component. Much of the evolution was effected to keep abreast or ahead of the banking industry. The agency today is the culmination of all the best efforts of "pioneers" like McCulloch, Saxon, and Smith, who wanted to forge the best bank supervisory agency possible.

CHAPTER SEVENTY-NINE

Federal Deposit Insurance and the Changing Role of the Federal Deposit Insurance Corporation

William M. Isaac*

Managing Director and Chief Executive Officer
The Secura Group

Margaret L. Maguire

Managing Director
The Secura Group

INTRODUCTION

The stock market collapse of 1929 and the ensuing Great Depression produced a raft of legislation designed to involve the federal government to a far greater degree than ever before in managing the nation's economy. Among the most far-reaching of those laws was the Banking Act of 1933, enacted after the closing of nearly 10,000 banks between 1929 and 1933 had culminated in the declaration of a banking holiday. The act mandated the creation of a system of federal deposit insurance. While times have changed since the FDIC's inception, and the agency has evolved accordingly, the FDIC's mission has remained the same: to maintain stability in the nation's financial system by insuring bank depositors and reducing the economic disruptions caused by bank failures.

To carry out its mission, the FDIC insures depositors in virtually all 14,763 United States commercial banks, as well as 471 savings banks and 48 branches of foreign banks operating in this country. It acts as receiver for failed institutions and enforces standards of safe-and-sound banking through the examination and supervisory process.

---

*Formerly Chairman, Federal Deposit Insurance Corporation.

By any measure, the FDIC has been a resounding success. The challenge for the current and coming decades is to meet the unprecedented demands of the continued high level of bank failures and problem banks, while at the same time making needed adjustments to the deposit insurance system so that it remains a viable component of the safety net for our nation's financial system.

OPERATIONS OF THE FDIC

At year-end 1985, there were 14,487 insured banks with total deposits of over $2 trillion. Over three quarters of those deposits were insured, and the ratio of the deposit insurance fund to insured deposits was 1.19. Since 1980 the insurance limit has been $100,000 per depositor per bank. The insurance limit was raised from $40,000 to $100,000 in 1979. At the end of that year there were 14,688 insured banks with approximately $1.2 trillion in total and $800 billion in insured deposits. The ratio of the fund to insured deposits was 1.21 at year-end 1979.

During the FDIC's first 47 years it handled $9 billion worth of bank failures and suffered insurance losses of $500 million. In contrast, from 1981 through 1985, the agency handled over $35 billion in failures, excluding Continental Illinois, and its insurance losses averaged $1 billion per year. Despite record numbers of bank failures and the unprecedented losses due to those failures, the deposit insurance fund has grown and has never been stronger. The fund, which is invested in short-term United States Treasury obligations, has nearly tripled over the last decade. At the end of 1975, the fund was $6.7 billion; at year-end 1985, it stood at just under $18 billion. Gross income from assessments and interest exceeded $3 billion in 1985 and net income was approximately $1.5 billion.

The FDIC is an independent agency of the U.S. government, governed by a bipartisan board whose three members are appointed by the president, subject to Senate confirmation. Two board members—the chairman and the appointive director—are appointed to the board for six-year terms. By tradition, the chairman is of the same party as the president. The third board member is the Comptroller of the Currency.

Headquartered in Washington, D.C., the FDIC is organized both functionally and geographically. It has two principal operating divisions—Liquidation and Bank Supervision—and two main support divisions—Legal and Accounting and Corporate Services. In addition, there are nine support offices: Executive Secretary; Personnel Management; Corporate Audits and Internal Investigations; Legislative Affairs; Corporate Communications; Equal Employment Opportunity; Consumer Affairs; Corporate Budget and Planning; and Research and

Strategic Planning. These units for the most part are headed by the career professional staff of the agency.

Most of the FDIC's staff are located outside of Washington and are employed by the Divisions of Liquidation and Bank Supervision. Total employment at year-end 1985 was 7,125, up 2,049 from the end of 1984. Most of the increase was attributable to temporary employees hired by the Division of Liquidation to cope with the record number of bank closings during the year. That division accounted for nearly half (46 percent) of the FDIC's staff, while about a third (29 percent) are employed by the Division of Bank Supervision, principally field examiners.

Geographically, the FDIC operates six major regions, headquartered in New York, Atlanta, Chicago, Kansas City, Dallas, and San Francisco. Each of these regions is headed by regional directors for liquidation and for bank supervision. Historically, there had been a larger number of bank supervision regions, and the Division of Liquidation had not had a regional structure at all. Prompted by the increasing number of bank failures and the need to handle them more effectively, the FDIC Board of Directors in 1982 established a regional structure for the Division of Liquidation and began the process of consolidating the 12 bank supervision regions into six, so that the regional alignment of the two divisions would coincide. As of year-end 1986, in addition to the six principal regions, there are bank supervision regions headquartered in Boston, Memphis, and Columbus, Ohio, which are scheduled to be consolidated into the six major regions. The Division of Liquidation, in addition to its six regional offices, operates a number of consolidated liquidation sites and, for a short time after the bank's closing, local sites where banks have closed.

Although it is a government agency, the FDIC receives no appropriated monies and is funded exclusively by bank assessments and income on its portfolio of Treasury securities. Gross revenue for 1985 was $3.4 billion, including $1.6 billion attributable to investment income and $1.4 billion from premiums paid by insured banks.

Since 1950, the FDIC—unlike its sister agency, the FSLIC—has had in place a rebate system. Each year the agency's administrative expenses and losses on bank failures are deducted from gross assessment income, and 60 percent of the balance is rebated to insured banks. The effect of the rebate typically has been to reduce a bank's deposit insurance premium from the statutory rate of 1/12 of 1 percent of domestic deposits to an effective rate of about 1/25 of 1 percent. In 1981, the rebate was cut dramatically, to about 20 percent of what it had been the year before. In the three succeeding years, the rebate was also small by historical standards, and for 1985 there was no assessment rebate.

Despite sustaining expenses and losses for the year of $2 billion, the deposit insurance fund grew by about $1.5 billion during 1985 and at year-end stood at just under $18 billion. Moreover, the fund enjoys a high degree of liquidity and market appreciation. At year-end 1985, the investment portfolio's average maturity was just over two years—shortened from two years, four months the year before—and the market value of the portfolio increased over $2 billion, from $14.4 billion at year-end 1984 to $16.5 billion at the end of 1985.

CHANGING ROLE OF THE FDIC SINCE MID-70S

After the trauma of the Great Depression, a number of factors converged to keep risk in the banking system to a minimum. Laws restricting what products banks could offer, where they could offer them, and at what price severely limited the ability of banks' management to take on risk. The system of bank regulation and supervision assembled in large part through post-Depression legislation further curtailed banks' propensity to engage in too much risk-taking. Finally, bankers themselves, burned by their recent experience, were all too willing to avoid risk.

The economy also contributed by providing a hospitable environment for a stable, risk-controlled banking system to flourish. From the burst of growth caused by World War II through the expansionary period of the fifties to the Vietnam era of the sixties, the U.S. economy posed no threat to the vitality of the banking system. The result, for most of the FDIC's first forty years, was a very stable banking system, with few problems and isolated failures of small institutions.

The last dozen years have seen dramatic changes in the economic and banking environments, both of which have resulted in a greater degree of risk in the U.S. financial system than ever before. The United States' domination of the postwar world economy came to an abrupt end with the first oil shock in the early '70s. "Petrodollars" flowed into the U.S. banking system and were encouraged to be "recycled" in the form of loans in lesser developed countries, the soundness of many of which are now widely acknowledged to be questionable. Inflation that had been ignited by the "guns and butter" philosophy of the early Vietnam years ravaged this country during the late seventies and contributed to unfortunate economic decisions whose repercussions began to be felt in the late 1970s and are continuing to ripple throughout the banking system.

Severe disintermediation caused by unprecedented high interest rates caused depository institutions the loss of literally hundreds of billions to the unregulated money market funds. This was followed by two back-to-back recessions, the second one the most severe in 50 years, and severe price deflation in commodities. The net result of this harsh economic and competitive climate at the beginning of the decade of the 1980s was a banking system that reflected a far greater degree of risk than ever before, as measured by soaring numbers of problem and failed banks.

THE FDIC'S RESPONSE

As it approached its 50th anniversary, the FDIC faced what were to be the most challenging years since its inception. After nearly three decades during which the number of failed banks was 10 or fewer per year (the only two years between 1943 and the end of 1981 in which there were more than 10 were 1975 and 1976, with 14 and 17 failures respectively), in 1982 the number of failures quadrupled, to 42. Every year since has seen an increase, culminating with the record-setting 120 insured bank failures in 1985, and 138 in 1986. It is only because of the historically low bank failure rate that the recent numbers seem extraordinary. Compared to any other industry, the banking industry still enjoys a very low failure rate, with 120 institutions representing less than 1 percent of the universe of insured banks. Nevertheless, the dramatic increase has meant significant changes for the deposit insurance agency.

First, in the area of bank supervision, there has been a wholesale shift in emphasis, the purpose of which is to more effectively employ limited resources. In its supervisory role the FDIC historically had emphasized its function as the federal regulator of state-chartered banks that are not members of the Federal Reserve System. While those banks are largest in number—over 8,000 of the more than 14,000 insured banks—they are for the most part small institutions that in the aggregate control only 23 percent of the banking assets. These state nonmember banks used to be examined routinely every 18 months, and the FDIC refrained entirely from any oversight of or involvement with national banks or Fed-member state banks. As the number of problem banks—that is, those designated four or five on the "CAMEL" or uniform bank rating system—climbed and failures mounted, the role of the insurer in maintaining confidence in the banking system became more critical. The FDIC recognized the need to focus more of its attention on problem and larger institutions, irrespective of their charter, in order to allocate resources to those cases that posed the greatest risk to the system.

The rise in the number of problem and potential failure cases, combined with personnel shortages, also spurred the development of tools to supplement the traditional, on-site examination. The FDIC has invested millions in recent years to develop and implement off-site, computerized monitoring systems. These help allocate scarce human resources to where they are most needed and have enabled the agency to monitor the condition of banks between on-site examinations—a critical ability in today's fast-paced banking environment.

From an 18-month interval between regularly scheduled examinations of all banks just a few years ago, the FDIC has lengthened the interval to 36 months for well-rated, smaller banks and has shortened it to every six months for problem institutions. Cooperative examination programs with the Comptroller of the Currency, the Federal Home Loan Bank Board (the charterer of FDIC-insured federal savings banks), as well as state authorities and the Federal Reserve have also enhanced the FDIC's ability to stay on top of problems and control its exposure.

Forbearance, too, has been employed by the FDIC to cope with the rising tide of problems. While subject to minimum capital requirements, FDIC-insured savings banks were given extra time within which to comply when uniform capital requirements were adopted by the regulators in 1985. Early in 1986, the regulators adopted a program of capital forbearance for agricultural and energy banks, which permits qualified institutions to operate below minimum capital levels provided they do not pursue high-growth or high-risk business strategies.

Staffing and training have also become critical. The FDIC has recognized the need to hire additional examiners and ensure that they receive superior training in order to perform effectively in an ever more challenging environment.

An even greater challenge to the FDIC has come in the liquidation area. While many of the changes in bank supervision have been—at least on a relative basis—evolutionary, the liquidation activities of the FDIC have undergone a virtual revolution over the last five years, as the number of failures escalated rapidly from 10 in 1981, to 42 in 1982, to 48 in 1983, to 79 in 1984, to 1985's record-setting 120, which was broken in 1986 with 138 failures. At the end of 1981, the Liquidation Division was handling approximately 25,000 assets, with an aggregate book value of $1.8 billion; at the end of 1985 the number of assets was 170,000, with a book value of $11 billion.

Not only has the sheer volume of liquidation activities grown, but the methods of handling bank failures have evolved as well. The FDIC has essentially three ways of handling a bank failure. In two, a bank is closed by its chartering authority and the FDIC is appointed receiver. The FDIC then either sells the failed bank's liabilities and some portion of its assets to another bank in a purchase-and-assumption (P&A) transaction, or pays off the bank's insured depositors and liquidates the bank's assets. In a P&A, all creditors—not just insured depositors—are made whole, whereas in a payoff, insured depositors are made whole up to the insurance limit and uninsured depositors and other creditors share in the recoveries on the failed bank's assets as they are liquidated. The third way of handling a failure involves the FDIC stepping in before a bank is closed to provide financial support to avert the closing, either to facilitate the acquisition of the failing bank or to prop it up directly.

Until fairly recently, the FDIC has dealt exclusively with closed banks, tending to favor payoffs in the early years and P&A's in recent decades. With one exception, only small failed banks have been handled as payoffs. The exception was the 1982 failure of the approximately $500 million Penn Square Bank in Oklahoma City. Before Penn Square, the largest failed bank to have been paid off was under $100 million.

With Penn Square the FDIC Board believed that the case for a payoff, as against a P&A, was overwhelming and that the FDIC would lose all credibility if it effected a P&A for Penn Square. That would have given financial markets a signal that all deposits, at least in banks above a certain size, were for all practical purposes fully insured. Discipline in the markets would have been seriously eroded, with deleterious long-term ramifications. Moreover, the FDIC's statutory "cost test" for a P&A could not be satisfied due to the enormous volume of contingent liabilities for which the FDIC would become liable in a P&A transaction.

Paying off Penn Square had immediate repercussions. Uninsured depositors became more sensitive to the possibility of loss and could not assume that all but the smallest bank failures would be handled through purchase-and-assumption transactions. Some banks had difficulty rolling over large CDs. The business of money brokers, who divide up large deposits and participate them to several banks, was significantly boosted. Depositors generally became more selective in their choice of banks.

The P&A avoids the disruptions of a payoff and provides continuity of banking services to the closed bank's community. Nevertheless, a statutory cost test requires that the FDIC board make a finding that the cost of a P&A would be less than the cost of a payoff, so that the agency does not have unlimited discretion to do a P&A. All failures of large—over $500 million—banks have been handled through a P&A or open-bank assistance.

Although the authority for open-bank assistance was granted to the FDIC in 1950, it was not employed until 1971 and has been used sparingly since. The statute gives the FDIC broad authority to assist banks in order to prevent their closing. Assistance may be provided to the failing bank directly or to an acquirer to facilitate the acquisition.

While there have been relatively few instances of open-bank assistance over the years, the last five years have seen a significant number. Between 1950 and 1971 there were none, and between 1971 and 1980, there were only five. Between 1981 and now, though, the FDIC has provided open-bank assistance in more than two dozen cases. Most of those, however, involved mutual savings banks. Between 1981 and the end of 1985, 17 mutual savings banks were acquired, without being closed first, with assistance from the FDIC. Of the assisted commercial bank transactions since 1981, most involved acquisitions by other institutions.

The FDIC has been very reluctant to grant aid that might benefit existing management or shareholders. Thus the 1980 assistance package for First Pennsylvania required substantial changes in First Pennsylvania's board and dilution of shareholders through warrants issued to the FDIC. In the assisted mutual savings bank mergers of the early 1980s, the FDIC required the resignation of the top officers and board members as a condition of assistance. And, in the largest commercial bank rescue in history—Continental Illinois—the virtual elimination of the existing shareholders' interest, as well as the resignation of directors, was an essential part of the deal. Nevertheless, it is clear that the FDIC, faced with unprecedented demands on its resources, is expanding the use of open-bank assistance as it seeks innovative ways of dealing with the continuing high level of failing banks.

While the financial resources of the FDIC have been more than adequate to cope with the heightened demands on the FDIC, its human and technical resources have felt the strain. Over the last five years, the number of employees more than doubled from 3,394 at the end of 1981 to 7,185 at the end of 1985. Most of the increase has been attributable to temporary employees in the Division of Liquidation, but additional hiring has been required in most other divisions or offices to support the increased workload caused by so many bank failures and problem banks. In addition, the FDIC has had to invest millions of dollars to upgrade computer support systems and to train personnel.

There are limits to what the agency can do on its own, however, and legislation has been sought and adopted to give the FDIC additional tools to cope with its expanded workload. The so-called "Regulators' Bill," adopted as part of the 1982 Garn-St Germain law, provided for emergency interstate acquisitions of large failed banks, thus giving the FDIC a greater range of options to deal with a large failure. That law was originally enacted with a two-year sunset, and was extended three times before expiring in 1986 when the Congress adjourned without reenacting it. It was recently reenacted as part of the Competitive Equality Banking Act of 1987.

One of the difficulties the FDIC has encountered in dealing with large banks faced with insolvency is having enough time to put together a merger or acquisition of the institution before its value has diminished to the point where it is no longer an attractive target. The 1987 version of the "Regulators' Bill" included authority for the FDIC to establish so-called "bridge banks"—interim vehicles to facilitate the FDIC's disposition of large failing banks. The "bridge bank" authority gives the FDIC the power to step in and establish an interim organization, the purpose of which is to stabilize the deteriorating condition of the failing bank and buy time to arrange an orderly merger or acquisition. If the FDIC's use of the "bridge bank" authority is not carefully circumscribed, it will likely touch off a lively debate about government control and ownership of banks.

DEPOSIT INSURANCE REFORM ISSUES

It is not hyperbole to characterize the changes now taking place in the financial system as revolutionary. A structure put into place a half century ago, at the nadir of the Great Depression, is crumbling. In part this is occurring by design, but in larger part it is caused by the forces of economics and technology. The central question facing government today is not whether change will or should continue but, rather, how to insure that the financial structure that eventually results will best serve the public interest. No discussion of the country's financial structure would be complete without addressing the role of the insuring agencies.

Deposit insurance has been an integral part of the financial system for over a half century, responsible in considerable part for the depository institution structure that has evolved and the nature of supervision and regulation of depository institutions. But the system put in place more than fifty years ago needs to be streamlined to fit the needs of a vastly altered banking system. Opinions abound about how to reform the system.

At one end of the spectrum, some people advocate that we dismantle much of the governmental infrastructure and place virtually total reliance on market forces. At the other end, some espouse a greatly expanded role for the government, particularly at the federal level. Proponents of the first approach would turn the clock back to 1925 and pretend the financial collapse of 1929 did not occur. Proponents of the second approach would turn the clock back to the 1960s and pretend the past quarter of a century did not occur.

A balance between these extremes must be struck. The collapse of 1929 did occur, and it taught us a lesson we must never forget: the government has a vital role to play in maintaining financial stability.

At the same time, it must be recognized that in many respects there was an overreaction to the trauma of the Great Depression. Many things were "fixed" that did not need fixing. Efforts to stifle competition and innovation were far too zealous. The past couple of decades have made clear that the marketplace will not indefinitely tolerate unnecessary and inefficient restraints. Either the restraints themselves or the businesses subject to them will be eliminated.

Deposit interest rate controls are one example. The marketplace forced their elimination. If Congress had taken much longer to receive and act on the market's message, the damage to our nation's banks and thrifts would have been beyond repair.

There are other artificial barriers to competition that should be substantially reduced or abolished. They are weakening the regulated firms substantially and denying the public the fruits of a fully competitive and responsive financial system. Specifically, the restraints on interstate banking, the Glass-Steagall Act, and the Bank Holding Company Act should be reexamined in light of marketplace realities. Deregulation of financial services is good for banking, for consumers and for the nation.

Nevertheless, it is essential to recognize that deregulation—that is, the dismantling of artificial restraints on competition—necessarily requires that our supervision of banks be strengthened and our system of deposit insurance be reformed. To fail to do either is a prescription for disaster.

A deregulated environment is more complex and faster paced. It requires more skilled, better trained examiners and analysts. It also requires more reliable and sophisticated offsite monitoring systems to enable us to spot potential problems more quickly and better target scarce personnel resources. Once abuses or unsound practices are uncovered, enforcement actions should be swift and strong.

While these efforts to enhance supervision are critically important, they are not alone sufficient and total reliance should not be placed on them. Promulgating countless new regulations to govern every aspect of banking behavior, and hiring thousands of additional examiners to enforce them, would be prohibitively expensive, undercut the benefits sought through deregulation, favor the unregulated at the expense of the regulated and ultimately fail.

New ways must be sought, in the absence of rigid government controls on competition, to limit excessive risk-taking and abusive practices. The support of the marketplace must be enlisted to instill a greater degree of discipline in the system. To accomplish this, the deposit insurance system must be reformed.

The collapse of the banking system in the 1930s provided the impetus for the FDIC, even though the measure was opposed by

President Roosevelt and the American Bankers Association. They believed the system would be too costly and would subsidize marginal, high-risk institutions at the expense of the well-managed firms. A compromise was agreed upon to provide modest coverage of $2,500 per depositor. Larger, more sophisticated depositors remained at risk and were expected to supply the necessary discipline.

Most of the early bank failures were handled by the FDIC as payoffs of insured depositors only. Depositors over the insurance limit were exposed to loss. Eventually, the FDIC developed and employed more frequently the purchase and assumption transaction. Despite the advantages of a P&A—it is less disruptive than a payoff, and it tends to be less expensive to the FDIC because it preserves some of the franchise value of the failed bank—an unfortunate side effect is that all depositors and other general creditors are made whole, thereby undermining discipline. This flaw was of little concern in those relatively tranquil days when only a handful of very small banks failed each year.

The deposit insurance system was largely transformed, through the purchase and assumption technique, into a system of *de facto* 100 percent coverage. The perception of 100 percent coverage became particularly pronounced with respect to larger banks when the FDIC infused capital into Bank of the Commonwealth in 1972; arranged mergers for United States National Bank in San Diego, Franklin National Bank and a few other sizeable banks during the mid-to-late 1970s; and infused capital into First Pennsylvania in 1980 and Continental Illinois in 1984.

While *de facto* 100 percent coverage, or the perception of it might not have been cause for much concern in the 1960s, it is enormously troubling in the decontrolled rate environment of the 1980s. How, in a deregulated environment where most depositors do not believe they are at risk, do we insure that funds flow to the vast majority of banks that are prudently operated instead of to the high flyers that pay the highest rates? The answer is clear: an element of discipline needs to be restored to the system.

So one major objective of deposit insurance reform in a deregulated environment should be to achieve greater market discipline. This can be accomplished in any one or more of three ways: pull back from *de facto* 100 percent depositor coverage, find new ways to impose discipline through the capital accounts (in particular, subordinated creditors), and implement risk-related premiums.

A second major objective of deposit insurance reform should be to achieve greater fairness in the system. The fairness issue takes two forms. First, there is the question of how bank failures can be handled so as not to discriminate or give the appearance of discriminating against smaller banks. Second, there is the question of how to allocate the cost of the deposit insurance system in an equitable fashion. For example, is it fair that the best bank in the country pays the same price for deposit insurance as the worst bank? Is it fair to require well-run banks to pay for the extra cost of supervising problem banks?

Whatever reforms are adopted for banks, the rules must be applied equally to savings and loan associations. With the condition of the FSLIC increasingly precarious, merger of the deposit insurance funds becomes a more likely possibility. A merger of the FDIC and FSLIC would create a stronger insurance system with greater resources, a larger income stream, and a more diversified risk base. It would also facilitate interindustry takeovers of foundering institutions and unify the procedures for handling insurance claims. Because banks and thrifts should be required to abide by equivalent standards with respect to capital, accounting, and disclosure, any legislation to merge the funds should include a mandate to phase in common standards in these areas over a period of years. It makes little sense, and is patently unfair, to have depository institutions that compete head-to-head be subject to different regulatory treatment and disparate rules and supervision.

Many bankers are opposed to a merger of the funds because they fear their institutions will be assessed to cover the cost of handling S&L problems. S&L executives have expressed the same concern in the opposite direction. These objections can be overcome by calculating bank and S&L insurance rebates on a separate basis for each industry for a period of years until common standards on capital, disclosure, and accounting are fully phased in.

The challenge in the area of deposit insurance is for the FDIC, the banking industry, and the Congress to devise and implement needed reforms in the latter part of the 1980s so that the safety net for our financial system remains strong and resilient for the future. Deposit insurance reform issues will likely weigh heavily in the political debate about financial services for at least the next several years.

CHAPTER EIGHTY

The Role of the Federal Reserve System in Supervising and Regulating Banking and Other Financial Activities

Frederick M. Struble

Associate Director Division of Bank Supervision and Regulation
Board of Governors of the Federal Reserve System

Rhoger H. Pugh

Manager, Policy Development Section
Division of Bank Supervision and Regulation
Board of Governors of the Federal Reserve System

In addition to the uniquely important roles it performs in conducting monetary policy and serving as lender of last resort, the Federal Reserve, as the central bank of the United States, is responsible for supervising and regulating a wide range of financial activities. Principal among these activities are the supervision and regulation of the operations of a large number of banking organizations in the United States and of United States banking organizations abroad, and the regulation—under the Bank Holding Company Act of 1956, as amended, the Bank Merger Act of 1960, and the Change in Bank Control Act of 1978—of the structure of the banking system and the powers of banking organizations. As set out more fully below, responsibility for some of these activities is shared with other federal and state regulatory agencies.

The Federal Reserve is also responsible, under the Securities and Exchange Act of 1934, for regulating the amount of credit that can be used to purchase and carry market-traded securities. In addition, the Congress has assigned the Federal Reserve supervisory and regulatory responsibility for a number of consumer protection statutes that apply not only to banks but to others that extend credit to consumers. These statutes—such as the Truth in Lending Act, the Fair Credit Billing

Act, and the Equal Credit Opportunity Act—were enacted to insure that consumers are adequately informed and fairly treated in their credit transactions. The Federal Reserve, along with other federal agencies, is also responsible for monitoring banking organizations' adherence to the provisions of the Community Reinvestment Act and the Bank Secrecy Act.

The combination of functions performed by the Federal Reserve are complementary. Thus, the broad perspective essential to developing monetary policy heightens the Federal Reserve's awareness of, and appreciation for, the impact regulatory or supervisory decisions are likely to have on financial markets and on the economy as a whole. Likewise, the experience gained in regulating and supervising banking organizations helps impart a practical understanding of how monetary policy decisions will flow through, and interact with, the depository system (particularly banking organizations) and financial markets generally.

REGULATION AND SUPERVISION OF THE OPERATIONS OF BANKING ORGANIZATIONS

The Federal Reserve shares responsibility for supervising and regulating banking organizations with the Office of the Comptroller of the Currency (OCC) and the Federal Deposit Insurance Corporation (FDIC) at the federal level with the banking agencies of the various states, and, in the case of the international operations of United States banks and the operations of foreign banks in the United States, with foreign banking authorities. The banking organizations for which the Federal Reserve has primary responsibility at the federal level are the following:

1. *State chartered banks that are members of the Federal Reserve System.* The Federal Reserve shares with state banking agencies responsibilities for supervising and regulating these 1,087 banks with total assets of $501 billion.[1]

2. *All bank holding companies.* There are 6,250 of these companies in the United States, of which 4,700 own one bank and 1,550 own more than one bank. Holding companies altogether

---

[1]The OCC has primary responsibility for supervising and regulating national banks which it charters. By law, national banks, which number 4,916 and have total assets of $1.7 billion, must be members of the Federal Reserve System, and the Federal Reserve has residual supervisory responsibilities for these banks. The FDIC is responsible for supervising the 8,246 state-chartered banks that are not members of the Federal Reserve, with $610 billion in total assets.

own about 9,024 banks, controlling 90 percent of all commercial bank assets; 305 companies also have substantial nonbanking interests.

3. *All Edge Act and agreement corporations.* There are 89 Edge corporations with total assets of about $21 billion that conduct banking activities in the United States related to international transactions; there are also 47 Edge corporations that are essentially overseas investment companies holding assets of about $50 billion in foreign countries.

4. *U.S. branches and agencies of foreign banking organizations, if they are licensed by state governments and are not insured by the FDIC.* There are 369 such organizations with total assets of about $301 billion.[2]

5. *Foreign branches and subsidiaries of state chartered member banks and foreign subsidiaries of bank holding companies.* The Federal Reserve has regulatory authority over all foreign branches and subsidiaries of all member banks, both state- and nationally chartered, and of all foreign subsidiaries of bank holding companies. However, it has supervisory authority only over foreign branches and subsidiaries of state-member banks and of the foreign subsidiaries of bank holding companies, as well as the foreign subsidiaries of Edge Act corporations. The Federal Reserve directly supervises 130 foreign branches of state member banks with total assets of $106 billion.[3]

Governmental supervision and regulation of banking organizations are in place to help ensure that banks operate in a safe and sound manner and in conformity with all applicable federal and state laws and regulations. These two functions, regulation and supervision, are closely related but easily distinguished. Regulation entails the establishment of prudential rules and standards defining the scope and character of banking activities. Supervision, on the other hand, entails determining that banks are operating in conformity with regulatory standards and are otherwise in a safe and sound condition. It also involves the identification of problem situations—through the examination process or by the use of surveillance techniques—and the

---

[2]The OCC is responsible for the supervision and regulation of the 87 agencies and branches of foreign banks that it has licensed. These institutions have assets totalling $20.6 billion. The FDIC is responsible for the supervision and regulation of 32 state chartered insured branches of foreign banks with total assets of $7.7 billion.

[3]The OCC directly supervises 786 foreign branches of national banks with total assets of $223 billion.

correction of deficiencies. This approach, encompassing both the setting of operating standards (through the establishment of regulations) and oversight of regulated institutions (to determine both compliance and soundness), together with the institution of remedial action (by formal or informal means) is common, to a greater or lesser degree, to all regulatory authorities and to both domestic and international banking operations. Thus, the Federal Reserve employs this approach in supervising and regulating the U.S. operations of domestic and foreign banking institutions as well as the foreign operations of U.S. banking institutions.

Regulation

The Federal Reserve carries out its regulation-setting function by establishing prudential rules and standards consistent with legal authority, that present a time-tested, prudent operating framework within which banks can be expected to conduct their business in a safe and sound manner. These standards may be in the form of formal regulations, rules, policy guidelines, or supervisory interpretations and may be predicated upon specific provisions of law or may be established by bank supervisory agencies under more general authority contained in the banking statutes. These standards may be either restrictive—limiting the scope of a banking organization's activities—or permissive—authorizing banking organizations to engage in certain activities. Some regulations are imposed upon state member banks and bank holding companies as a result of laws enacted by the several states; other regulations are derived from requirements contained in federal law. Limitations on insider transactions, dividend guidelines, restrictions on certain kinds of investments, and capital adequacy standards are typical examples of such prudential standards. This last standard, capital adequacy, has received perhaps the closest scrutiny during the current decade in response to the declining levels of bank capital in the 1970s. As a result, the federal agencies have established minimum capital standards for banks and the Federal Reserve has set concomitant guidelines for bank holding companies.

The capital standards now in place seek to ensure that organizations will have capital adequate to cover unexpected losses, thereby helping to protect against failure and, in the event that such an undesirable development occurs, to avoid or minimize loss to the federal deposit insurance fund. Prior to the issuance of these standards, the banking agencies had sought to promote adequate capital in banking organizations on a case by case basis through the examination process. Despite these efforts, however, the capital ratios of many banks, particularly large banking organizations, drifted downward steadily, and it was concluded that regulations or guidelines were needed to help reverse this downtrend.

Experience gained with capital regulations and guidelines has made it increasingly clear that, while generally working to strengthen capital positions, such standards have also provided a disincentive to hold liquid assets. In addition, they do not take into account important off-balance sheet risk exposures, and make no differentiation between the riskiness of different types of on-balance sheet assets. With these shortcomings in mind and in the hope that U.S. capital standards can be coordinated with those devised by banking authorities in other major countries, the three U.S. banking agencies have begun to develop a risk-related capital standard. At this writing, those efforts appear to be moving toward a successful conclusion. Each agency has published for comment a common risk-based capital proposal to which the Bank of England has agreed in principle.

Supervision

Like other bank supervisory agencies, the Federal Reserve conducts ongoing activities that are concerned with determining whether individual banking organizations are operating in a safe and sound manner and in compliance with relevant regulations and laws. In addition, in cases where organizations are found not to be so operating, supervision involves taking appropriate steps to rectify problems as soon as practicable. The condition and operating results of banking organizations are assessed by both off-site surveillance and on-site examinations.

Off-Site Surveillance.   Off-site surveillance involves reviewing information on individual banking organizations that is obtained from a variety of sources. These sources include the results of prior examinations, newspaper reports and other market information, and, most importantly, the standard statistical reports filed by banks and bank holding companies, namely, the Reports of Condition and Income for banks and the Y-6 and Y-9 reports for holding companies which are discussed more fully below.

The Federal Reserve has long used off-site surveillance as an important tool in its ongoing oversight of banking organizations. In recent years, however, the banking agencies have developed standard procedures for reviewing reported information. These procedures involve the use of a computerized screening process that is designed to help identify developing problem situations at banking organizations. In addition, the process helps the Federal Reserve to track the progress (or lack thereof) that a troubled organization is making in correcting its problem situations. This activity helps signal the need for an immediate examination of an organization that seems to have developing problems; moreover, it helps in the establishment of examination and inspection schedules that will make most effective and timely use of the Federal Reserve's examiner resources.

Official Reports Filed by Banks and Bank Holding Companies. Reports of Condition and Income (the Call Reports) are filed quarterly by all insured commercial banks. The contents of these reports are determined by the Federal Financial Institutions Examination Council and are uniform for all three federal bank regulatory agencies. There are forms for banks that have domestic and foreign offices and for different size classes of banks that only have domestic offices. The reports designed for smaller banks contain less detail and other accommodations to reduce the reporting burden on these institutions. The reports may be submitted either on preprinted forms provided by the agencies or by computer prepared facsimiles that are substantially identical to the preprinted forms. Plans are currently underway to permit the filing of these reports electronically. Copies of the call reports submitted by individual banks are available to the public from the National Technical Information Service in Springfield, Virginia.

The reporting standards to which holding companies are subject, like the Federal Reserve System's inspection criteria, make a distinction between large and small institutions. Bank holding companies with consolidated assets of $150 million or more and multibank holding companies of all sizes submit quarterly standardized consolidated and parent-only financial statements. Holding companies with only one bank subsidiary and assets of less than $150 million submit a parent-only report semiannually. Bank holding companies must file an annual report with the Federal Reserve System and must also report on their changes in investments and certain financial data for nonbank subsidiaries. The largest bank holding companies, those with consolidated assets of $1 billion or more, and those that have significant nonbank activities must also file combined nonbank financial statements quarterly, and an annual report of the primary types of nonbanking business they engage in. Unless a holding company has requested and been granted confidential treatment for its reports to the Federal Reserve, copies may be obtained through any Federal Reserve Bank.

On-Site Examinations and Inspections. While off-site surveillance plays an important role in the Federal Reserve's supervisory activities, on-site examinations (of state member banks) and inspections (of bank holding companies and their nonbank subsidiaries) remain the major means by which the Federal Reserve carries out supervisory activities. The examinations of state member banks entail: (1) an appraisal of the soundness of the institution's assets; (2) an evaluation of internal operations, policies, and management; (3) an analysis of key financial factors such as capital, earnings, liquidity, and interest rate sensitivity; (4) a review for compliance with all banking laws and regulations; and (5) an overall determination of the institution's soundness and solvency.

Safety and soundness inspections of bank holding companies review these same general elements but also include a review of non-bank assets and funding activities, an evaluation of policies and procedures for managing the holding company and its subsidiaries, and a review for compliance with the Bank Holding Company Act and other relevant banking statutes. State member banks that are subsidiaries of holding companies are separately examined by the district Federal Reserve banks, in conjunction with state banking authorities if possible, or by the appropriate federal or state regulators if the subsidiary is a national bank or is not a Federal Reserve System member.

In addition to examinations and inspections focusing on the general safety and soundness of state member banks and bank holding companies, the Federal Reserve conducts special examinations in certain areas such as consumer affairs, trust activities, securities transfer agents, municipal securities dealers, and electronic data processing.

The Board of Governors of the Federal Reserve has recently reiterated and emphasized the importance it assigns to on-site examinations in the supervisory process. In response to the growing number of banking and other financial problems over the current decade, the Board decided to intensify the Federal Reserve's on-site examinations and inspection activities. The new schedule requires that each state member bank be examined at least once within each twelve-month period. In the case of all but the largest banks and problem banks, examinations conducted by state banking agencies, based on cooperative agreements they may have with the Federal Reserve System, will satisfy this requirement. Large banks, however, must be examined by the Federal Reserve Bank of the district in which they are located. It is the policy of the Federal Reserve System to cooperate fully with state supervisory authorities, to the extent possible and to the extent they are willing to do so. Such cooperation lessens the examination burden imposed upon state banks and minimizes the costs incurred by the Federal Reserve System and state supervisory authorities.

The new schedule approved by the Board also requires that all large holding companies and smaller ones with significant nonbank assets and those with severe problems be inspected annually. The remaining companies must be inspected at least once in every three years except for the very smallest holding companies without significant debt outstanding to the public, which can be inspected on a sample basis. Inspections are carried out by specially trained examiners and focus on the operations and activities of the parent holding company and its nonbanking subsidiaries.

Correcting Problems.   If in the process of an examination or inspection, or by any other means, the Federal Reserve determines that a bank or bank holding company has problems that are or have the potential for affecting safety and soundness, or is not in compliance with laws and regulations, it takes immediate steps to ensure that the organization takes corrective measures. The preferred approach is to communicate the findings of the examination or inspection to the management and directors of the banking organization in order to enlist their cooperation in resolving problems. This has traditionally been done by providing a written report setting forth the examiner's findings and conclusions. The Board, as part of its recent program to strengthen the system's supervisory activities, also has required that separate summary reports of examinations and inspections be provided to each director of any banking organization identified as having relatively serious problems. These summary reports highlight the bank's or holding company's problems in clear, succinct language and using nontechnical terms.

In addition to written reports, the Federal Reserve has generally followed the practice of making oral presentations on the findings of examinations and inspections to the directors and management of large organizations and relatively troubled organizations. Here, too, the Board, in its recent program to strengthen supervisory activities, has placed added emphasis on such communications, instructing that senior officials of Federal Reserve banks make presentations in cases where an organization has serious problems.

While the Federal Reserve prefers to rely on informal means for getting management and the directors of a bank to take appropriate actions to correct problem situations, it has, as do other agencies, the power to initiate more formal compulsory actions to achieve these ends. In cases where a banking organization's problems are not severe, informal memoranda of understanding are used. These memoranda spell out the general nature of the problems and the measures deemed necessary to correct them. In the cases of more severe problems, or when an organization fails to comply with the specifications of a memorandum of understanding, the Federal Reserve may use its legal powers to issue a cease and desist order against a member bank, a bank holding company, a nonbank subsidiary of a bank holding company, or any director, officer, employee, agent, or person participating in the conduct of the affairs of a member bank, bank holding company, or its nonbank subsidiaries. These actions may be initiated when there is a finding that an offender is engaging, has engaged, or may engage in unsafe and unsound practices in conducting the business of the institution. Such actions may also be deemed necessary due to a finding that the offender is violating, has violated, or may violate a law, rule, regulation, or any condition imposed in writing by the Federal Reserve in connection with the granting of any application or written agreement entered into with the Federal Reserve. The Federal Reserve may also issue temporary (emergency) cease and desist orders.

Regulation and Supervision of International Banking

In addition to those general regulatory and supervisory responsibilities discussed above which are broadly applicable to both the domestic and international operations of banking organizations, there are several specific aspects of the Federal Reserve's authority respecting the international operations of U.S. banking organizations and the U.S. activities of foreign banking organizations that warrant separate discussion.

International Operations of U.S. Banking Organizations.   The Federal Reserve has four principal statutory responsibilities with respect to the supervision and regulation of the international operations of U.S. banking organizations that are members of the Federal Reserve System. These responsibilities are: (1) authorizing the establishment of foreign branches of member banks and regulating the scope of their activities; (2) chartering and regulating the activities of Edge Act corporations; (3) authorizing overseas investments by member banks, Edge Act and agreement corporations, and bank holding companies, and regulating the activities of foreign firms acquired by such investments; and (4) establishing supervisory policies and practices with respect to the foreign lending of member banks.

Federal law provides that U.S. banks can conduct a wider range of activities abroad than they have usually been permitted to pursue in this country. The Board was given broad discretionary powers to regulate the overseas activities of member banks and bank holding companies to allow U.S. banks to be fully competitive with institutions of the host country in financing U.S. trade and investments overseas. In addition, through Edge Act and agreement corporations, banks may conduct a deposit and loan business in U.S. markets outside their home states, provided that the operation of these corporations are related to international transactions. The statutes and regulations relating to these corporations ensure that the foreign operations of member banks do not undermine the restrictions on the interstate banking activities of domestic banking organizations.

The International Lending Supervision Act of 1983 directed the Federal Reserve and other banking agencies to consult with the supervisory authorities of other countries with the aim of adopting effective and consistent supervisory policies and practices with respect to international lending. It also directed the banking agencies to take a number of steps to strengthen the international lending procedures of U.S. banks. The act provided for the maintenance of special reserves when the quality of an institution's assets has been impaired by a protracted inability of public or private borrowers in a foreign country to make payments on their external indebtedness, or when no definite prospect exists for the orderly restoration of debt service. The act also required federal banking agencies to establish minimum capital levels for banking institutions in order to strengthen both their domestic and international activities, and to establish regulations for accounting for fees on international loans and for the collection and disclosure of certain international lending data.

U.S. Activities of Foreign Banking Organizations.   The International Banking Act of 1978 provided for federal regulation of U.S. operations of foreign banks and granted important new responsibilities to the Federal Reserve for the supervision and regulation of such operations. Enactment of this legislation followed rapid growth in the activities of foreign banks in the United States and an increase in their competitive impact upon domestic markets.

The International Banking Act created a federal regulatory and supervisory structure for the U.S. branches and agencies of foreign banks similar to that applicable to U.S. banks. This policy of "national treatment" promotes competitive equity between domestic and foreign banking institutions in the United States by giving foreign banks operating in this country the same powers and subjecting them to the same restrictions and obligations that apply to U.S. banks. As part of the implementation of national treatment, the International Banking Act limited expansion of interstate deposit-taking and domestic nonbanking activities of foreign banks, provided the option of either state or federal licensing for agencies and branches of foreign banks, and required FDIC insurance for branches that engage in retail deposit-taking.

At the federal level, the International Banking Act apportioned primary supervisory responsibility for U.S. branches and agencies of foreign banks among the three federal banking agencies, according to the type of license and whether the banking office has federal deposit insurance. In addition, the Federal Reserve was given broad residual and oversight authority for the supervision of all federal and state-licensed branches and agencies of foreign banks operating in the United States. In fulfilling this responsibility, the Federal Reserve must assess the impact and condition of foreign banks operating across state lines. To carry out its responsibilities, the Federal Reserve has statutory authority to examine on-site the assets and liabilities of all branches and agencies; yet it generally relies upon examinations that state and other federal banking authorities conduct.

Under the Bank Holding Company Act and the International Banking Act, the Federal Reserve also has responsibility to approve, review, and monitor the U.S. nonbanking activities of foreign banking organizations.

FEDERAL RESERVE REGULATION OF BANKING STRUCTURE

The Federal Reserve System has statutory responsibility for the administration of the Bank Holding Company Act of 1956 as amended, the Bank Merger Act of 1960, and the Change in Bank Control Act of 1978. Under these acts, the Federal Reserve Board approves or denies the acquisition of banks and closely related nonbanking activities by bank holding companies and permits or rejects certain other changes of control and mergers of banks and bank holding companies.

Bank Holding Company Expansion

The Bank Holding Company Act of 1956 gave to the Federal Reserve the primary responsibility for supervising and regulating the activities of bank holding companies. This act, as amended in 1966 and 1970, was designed to achieve two basic objectives. The first was to control the expansion of bank holding companies to avoid the creation of monopoly or restraint of trade in banking. The second was to limit the expansion of bank holding companies to those nonbanking activities that are closely related to banking, thus maintaining a separation between banking and commerce.

Bank Acquisitions

Under the Bank Holding Company Act as amended in 1970, a bank holding company is defined as any company that: (1) directly or indirectly owns, controls, or has the power to vote 25 percent or more of any class of the voting shares of a bank; (2) controls in any manner the election of a majority of the directors or trustees of a bank; or (3) exercises a controlling influence over the management or policies of a bank. A company that seeks to become a bank holding company must obtain the prior approval of the Federal Reserve. Any company that qualifies as a bank holding company must register with the Federal

Reserve System and file reports. An existing bank holding company must obtain the approval of the Board before acquiring more than 5 percent of the shares either of additional banks or of permissible non-banking companies. To limit interstate banking operations by bank holding companies, the Douglas Amendment to the act, passed in 1966, provided that a bank holding company operating in one state may not acquire a bank in a second state unless that state authorizes the acquisition expressly by statute. In recent years, many states have authorized such acquisitions, generally on a reciprocal basis with other states. Bank holding companies can engage in nonbanking activities that are closely related to banking without geographic restriction.

In considering applications to acquire a bank or a bank holding company, the Board must take into account the likely effects of the acquisition on banking competition, the convenience and need for banking services of the community to be served, and the financial and managerial resources and prospects of the holding company and the bank.

NONBANKING ACQUISITIONS

In enacting the Bank Holding Company Act of 1956, the Congress indicated its intent to prevent, with few exceptions, holding companies from engaging in nonbanking activities or from acquiring non-banking companies. At the same time, the Congress recognized that a complete prohibition of holding company involvement in nonbanking activities might not be in the public interest. Consequently, it provided some exceptions to the prohibition against bank holding companies engaging in nonbanking activities, and the 1970 amendments to the act broadened the exceptions somewhat. The most important exception is that holding companies may undertake certain activities that the board determines to be so closely related to banking, or to managing or controlling banks, as to be a proper incident to banking which would result in benefits to the public. In making its determinations, the Board considers such factors as the risks of the activity, its effects on competition, the potential for an undue concentration of resources, and possible conflicts of interest. In approving nonbanking activities, the Board relies upon section 23A of the Federal Reserve Act that controls relations between banks and their nonbank affiliates. Section 23A is intended to prevent unsafe practices by limiting certain intercompany transactions and requiring collateral in other transactions.

As of early 1987, the Board has ruled that, subject to approval of individual proposals and with certain qualifications, a bank holding company might engage in 25 activities closely related to banking:

1. Making and servicing loans and other extensions of credit.
2. Operating as an industrial bank.
3. Performing trust activities.
4. Acting as an investment or financial advisor.
5. Leasing real or personal property on a full-payout basis.
6. Making equity and debt investments in corporations or projects designed primarily to promote community welfare.
7. Providing financially-related bookkeeping and data processing services.
8. Acting as an agent or broker for credit-related insurance and certain other limited forms of insurance.
9. Acting as an underwriter for credit life insurance and for credit accident and health insurance directly related to extensions of consumer credit by the bank holding company system.
10. Providing financially related courier services.
11. Providing management consulting advice to nonaffiliated bank and nonbank depository institutions.
12. Acting as agent or broker for the sale at retail of money orders having a face value of not more than $10,000, the sale of U.S. savings bonds, and the issuance and sale of travelers checks.
13. Performing real estate and personal property appraisals.
14. Arranging equity financing for commercial real estate.
15. Underwriting and dealing in government obligations.
16. Providing foreign exchange advisory and transaction services.
17. Acting as a futures commission merchant.
18. Providing discount securities brokerage services.
19. Investing in export trading companies (specifically authorized by the Congress in 1982).
20. Providing investment advice, including counsel, publications, written analyses and reports, as a futures commission merchant subject to certain limitations.
21. Providing consumer financial counseling.
22. Providing tax preparation services to individuals, businesses, and nonprofit organizations.
23. Providing check guaranty services.
24. Operating a collection agency.
25. Operating a credit bureau.

In addition, the Board of Governors has approved a limited number of other nonbanking activities for individual bank holding companies because these organizations demonstrated that their unique circumstances afforded net benefits to the public. Such approvals have included the acquisition of distressed thrift institutions.

Bank Mergers

Another major responsibility of the Federal Reserve is to act on proposed bank mergers when the surviving institution is to be a state member bank. During the 1950s, there was a sharp rise in the number of bank mergers, several of which involved large banks located in the same metropolitan area. Fearing that a continuation of this trend could seriously impair competition in banking and lead to an excessive concentration of financial power, the Congress passed the Bank Merger Act in 1960.

The act requires that all proposed bank mergers between insured banks receive prior approval from the federal bank regulatory agency under whose jurisdiction the surviving bank will fall. To foster uniform standards among the three federal bank supervisory agencies in assessing bank mergers, the act also requires the responsible authority to request reports on competitive factors from the two other banking agencies, and from the Department of Justice as well. Mergers of two bank holding companies come under the sole jurisdiction of the Federal Reserve.

The Bank Merger Act, as amended in 1966, requires the responsible agency to take into consideration in every case the financial and managerial resources and prospects of the existing and proposed institutions, and the convenience and banking needs of the community to be served. The responsible agency may not approve any merger that could substantially lessen competition or tend to create a monopoly, unless the agency finds that the probable beneficial effect on the convenience and needs of the community clearly outweighs the anticompetitive effects.

Other Changes in Bank Control

The Change in Bank Control Act of 1978 gives the federal bank supervisory agencies the authority to disapprove changes in control of insured banks and bank holding companies. The Federal Reserve Board is the responsible federal banking agency for changes in control of bank holding companies and state member banks, and the FDIC and the OCC are responsible for insured state nonmember and national banks, respectively. The act specifically exempts holding company acquisitions of banks and bank mergers because these transactions are already covered by the statutory and regulatory procedures for approval discussed above.

The act requires that the appropriate federal banking agency consider such factors as the financial condition, competence, experience, and integrity of the acquiring person or group of persons, and the effect of the transaction on competition. The Federal Reserve's objectives in its administration of the act are to enhance and maintain public confidence in the banking system by preventing serious adverse effects from anticompetitive combinations of interests, inadequate financial support, and unsuitable management.

OTHER REGULATORY RESPONSIBILITIES

Margin Regulations

In 1934, federal regulation of initial margin in securities markets was established in an effort to reduce speculative price volatility, to protect unsophisticated investors, and to diminish the level of credit used for speculative purposes. The Securities Exchange Act of 1934 authorizes the Board to regulate this type of lending. In fulfilling its responsibility under the act, the Board limits the amount of credit that may be provided by securities brokers and dealers (Regulation T), by banks (Regulation U), and by other lenders (Regulation G). These regulations apply to credit financed purchases of securities traded on securities exchanges and certain securities traded over-the-counter when the credit is collateralized by such securities. In addition, Regulation X prohibits U.S. persons from obtaining such credit overseas on terms more favorable than could be obtained from a domestic lender.

In general, compliance with the margin regulations is enforced by a number of federal regulatory agencies. In the case of banks, the three federal bank supervisory agencies examine for Regulation U compliance during examinations. Compliance with Regulation T is verified during examinations of broker/dealers by securities self-regulatory organizations under the general oversight of the Securities and Exchange Commission. Compliance with Regulation G is checked by the National Credit Union Administration (NCUA), the Farm Credit Administration, the Federal Home Loan Bank Board (FHLBB), or the Federal Reserve in the case of other lenders.

Consumer Laws

In recent years, the Federal Reserve has been authorized by the Congress to implement a number of statutes designed to ensure that consumers, including bank customers, have sufficient information and are treated fairly in credit and other financial transactions. To help carry out its responsibilities for consumer protection, the Board is advised by a Consumer Advisory Council, which is composed of representatives of consumers, creditors, and others concerned with these issues.

The Federal Reserve is responsible for writing and implementing regulations to carry out many of the major statutes protecting consumers in financial transactions. However, its responsibility for enforcing many of these laws and regulations generally extends only to state-chartered banks that are members of the Federal Reserve System. Other depository institutions are subject to examination for compliance with consumer laws and regulations by their primary federal supervisory agency—the FDIC, OCC, FHLBB, or the NCUA. However, the Federal Reserve will accept complaints about the policies or practices of any bank or thrift institution and refer them to the appropriate regulatory agency.

The Truth in Lending Act requires disclosure of the "finance charge," the "annual percentage rate," and certain other costs and terms of credit so that consumers can compare the prices of credit from different sources. This act also limits liability on lost or stolen credit cards.

The Fair Credit Billing Act sets up a procedure for the prompt correction of errors on a revolving credit account and prevents damage to credit ratings while a dispute is being settled.

The Equal Credit Opportunity Act prohibits discrimination in the granting of credit on the basis of sex, marital status, race, color, religion, national origin, age, receipt of public assistance, or the exercise of rights under the Consumer Credit Protection Act. The Federal Reserve regulation provides that notice of the reason for denial be given to applicants who have been denied credit. It also gives married individuals with jointly held credit accounts the right to have credit histories maintained in the names of both spouses.

The Fair Credit Reporting Act sets up a procedure for correcting mistakes on credit records and requires that the records be used only for legitimate business purposes.

The Consumer Leasing Act requires disclosure of information to help consumers compare the cost and terms of one lease of consumer goods with another, and the cost of leasing with that of buying on credit or for cash.

The Real Estate Settlement Procedures Act requires disclosure of information about the services and costs involved at "settlement," when real property is transferred from seller to buyer.

The Electronic Fund Transfer Act provides a basic framework regarding the rights, liabilities, and responsibilities of consumers who use electronic transfer services and of the financial institutions that offer the services.

The Federal Trade Commission Improvement Act authorizes the Board to identify unfair or deceptive acts or practices on the part of banks and to issue regulations to prohibit them.

Community Reinvestment and Development

Several laws address the issue of lending for housing-related purposes and for the development of communities served by financial institutions.

The Home Mortgage Disclosure Act requires depository institutions to disclose the geographic distribution of their mortgage and home improvement loans. The purpose of the act is to provide to depositors and others information that will enable them to make informed decisions about whether institutions in metropolitan areas are meeting the housing credit needs of their communities.

The Community Reinvestment Act encourages banks to help meet the credit needs of their communities for housing and other purposes, particularly in neighborhoods of families with low or moderate income, while maintaining safe and sound operations. An institution's performance under the act is assessed during the course of bank examinations and is taken into account, along with other factors, when the Federal Reserve considers certain applications for bank mergers and bank holding company formations, mergers, and acquisitions.

Bank Secrecy Act

The Bank Secrecy Act was enacted in 1970 and requires financial institutions doing business in the United States to report large currency transactions and retain certain records. It also prohibits the use of foreign bank accounts to launder illicit funds or avoid U.S. taxes and statutory restrictions. The Department of the Treasury has primary responsibility for the issuance of implementing regulations and enforcement of this statute; it has delegated responsibility for monitoring the compliance of banks to the federal bank regulatory agencies. Therefore, during the course of the examinations of state member banks and Edge Act corporations, Federal Reserve examiners verify compliance with the recordkeeping and reporting requirements of the act and related regulations.

CHAPTER EIGHTY-ONE

State Banking Departments

Dr. Lawrence E. Kreider
Executive Vice President and Economist
Conference of State Bank Supervisors

PURPOSE AND GOALS OF STATE BANKING DEPARTMENTS

Each state has a banking department headed by a state bank commissioner or official of comparable title. State banking departments are the primary chartering, examining, supervisory, and regulatory bodies for state-chartered commercial plus savings banks.

Traditionally, the primary goal of state banking departments has been to assure the safety and soundness of state-chartered banks. This goal is of singular socioeconomic importance to respective trade areas: If a bank fails, it has much greater impact on a community or trade area than if a filling station fails.

In like manner, the Office of the Comptroller of the Currency has worked to assure the soundness of national banks. The Office of the Comptroller and state banking departments generally have been successful in the past half century in their respective efforts. There were three exceptions to this good record—the early 1930s, mid-1970s, and 1980s. All three periods were in the aftermath of abnormal financial disruptions and other dislocations largely, but not entirely, beyond the control of state banking departments and the Office of the Comptroller.

Although strong state-chartered banks capable of sustained service to respective trade areas remain a primary goal of state banking departments, other goals have increased in importance. Competition between financial institutions, competitive equality between state and national banks, competitive equality between banks and other financial institutions, quality of financial services to individual bank customers, the cost of delivering financial services to consumers, business, and government, and effective, efficient examination of multistate, multiregulated, multibank holding companies have added new dimensions to the goals and roles of state banking departments.

Goals of State Bank Supervisors as a United Body

Although the goal of each state banking department is directed primarily toward each respective state, state bank supervisors nationwide are organized into a Conference of State Bank Supervisors (CSBS).

The Conference's goals are:

1. A state banking system which provides readily and equitably available banking services to all trade areas and all worthy potential customers.
2. A flexible state banking system which assures bank products and services best suited to each diverse state.
3. Capable state banking departments and safe and sound state banks with abilities to deliver without interruption needed banking services.

The United States is the only major industrial nation with a banking system which so fully achieves ready and equitable access for all areas and all types of customers of widely diverse services needed by highly diverse states. The U.S. banking structure can best be described as a "democratic financial system." And, a democratic *financial* system is highly supportive of a democratic *political* system—and vice versa.

To achieve equitable and readily available bank services for everyone, CSBS defends state and local control over the financial resource base in the form of bank deposits, particularly household deposits. This intermediate goal is based on the fundamental economic concept that most savings come from households, and on the fact that U.S. depository banking is the *sole remaining* financial entity to which all worthy potential customers have ready and equitable access to banking services well suited to diverse needs of each state.

In addition to providing ready availability of services to all worthy potential customers, the U.S. democratic banking system facilitates upstreaming and adequate concentrations of funds needed to serve large businesses and governments.

During the 1980s, major benefits from the U.S. decentralized banking system were threatened by rapid expansion of interstate ownership of full service banks. Potential losses, however, were largely avoided by the fact that the terms of interstate ownership were set by individual states and control over financial resource bases in the form of bank deposits was generally maintained, to the extent states so desired. The credibility of the McFadden Act and the Douglas Amendment to the Bank Holding Company Act was maintained.

In defending major benefits from state determination, state banking departments have joined ranks with state bankers and others who want a dual system of state/federal checks and balances, good banking services, capable state banking departments, and sound banks. These goals are in the public interest, and the joint effort of all in pursuit of common goals is more successful than if each was working separately.

Composition of State System

The state bank regulatory system includes 54 banking departments— 50 states plus the District of Columbia, Guam, Puerto Rico, and the Virgin Islands.

State banking departments are organized in a variety of ways. In 42 states and Puerto Rico, banking department heads are appointed by respective governors; in Virginia, South Carolina, and Texas, state bank commissioners are appointed by separate commissions; in Hawaii, Maryland, and Minnesota commissioners are selected by another senior state official; in the District of Columbia the superintendent is appointed by the mayor with the advice and consent of the D.C. Council; in Colorado the head serves under a State Civil Service statute; and in Florida, Guam, and the Virgin Islands banking department heads are elected.

The lengths of commissioners' terms vary. The majority serve at the will of each respective governor. Although the average length of tenure of state bank supervisors is considered by some to be too short for optimum effectiveness, positions generally have become more professional in nature with continuance from one administration to another more frequently preferred by incoming governors. Increasingly it is recognized as good practical politics to retain qualified supervisors from one administration to another, even when the incoming governor is of a different political party than his or her predecessor. This has had a positive effect on the stability and capability of state banking departments. As of January 1, 1987, the average tenure of state bank supervisors was over four years and was 27 percent longer than that of federal bank regulatory appointees.

In addition to 54 state bank supervisors, there are approximately 3,000 professional state bank examiners and support personnel, a significant increase over a decade ago. Like commissioners, the examiners and support personnel have become increasingly well-qualified through training programs and experience. By the late 1980s, approximately 1,300 state banking department personnel were trained annually in one or more of the CSBS Education Foundation-administered or supported schools.

In the past decade, state banking departments have increased significantly their abilities to take their rightful places in the bank regulatory structure of the nation.

PLACE IN REGULATORY STRUCTURE

State banking departments collectively are one of several state and federal government groups which regulate banks in one way or another. State banking departments, however, are the chartering and primary regulatory authorities for approximately 10,500 state-chartered commercial plus savings banks which hold nearly one-half of the bank assets of the nation.

The role of states in the examination, supervision, and regulation of state-chartered banks and bank holding companies changed significantly during the 1980s. Capabilities of state banking departments increased rather dramatically, the number of professional personnel rose significantly, training increased five-fold, applied research increased by a comparable amount, and the CSBS accreditation program both raised and revealed capabilities of state banking departments.

At the same time state banking department capabilities were rising, economic conditions forced the Federal Deposit Insurance Corporation and Federal Reserve System to allocate more personnel and financial resources to failing and failed banks and to withdraw from the examination and supervision of many state-chartered banks. Fortunately, states had become prepared to assume more responsibilities.

Beyond economic and troubled bank problems, the 1980s was a period of complex growth of multistate, multiregulated, multibank holding companies. Most of this structural change was controlled by individual states or by alliances of states. State bank supervisors participated in the change and worked effectively with federal regulators to achieve efficient examination and supervision for these expanded holding companies and their subsidiaries.

Reflecting increased state capabilities, serious bank problems, and banking structural changes, a new working relationship between state and federal bank regulators evolved in the 1980s. State banking departments, in part by design and in part by chance, became more nearly equal partners with federal agencies in the examination, supervision, and regulation of banks and bank holding companies. At the same time, the FDIC and FRS developed excellent capabilities to handle important matters other than examination and supervision of state banks.

One major benefit of this new relationship has been a reduction in the old traditional pattern of duplicatory oversight of state-chartered banks. Unnecessary duplication has been reduced by diverse forms of sharing of responsibilities between state banking departments and the FDIC and/or Fed. In numerous states, the withdrawal of the FDIC and Fed from the examination of significant proportions of state-chartered banks reduced the cost to banks and ultimately bank customers. Quality of examination and supervision, however, was maintained or increased.

As the few remaining state banking departments become fully capable of discharging chartering, examination, and regulatory responsibilities, they doubtless will have an opportunity to assume these responsibilities on a parity with the Office of the Comptroller of the Currency. Fortunately, the trend is in the direction of state responsibilities consistent with capabilities; and the accelerated training, applied research, and accreditation programs of the Conference of State Bank Supervisors hastens the elimination of unnecessary duplication. As is normal under such circumstances, however, there is a time lag between the ability of state banking departments to assume full responsibilities and the withdrawal of federal regulators from unnecessary duplicatory oversight.

State Leadership in New Techniques and Procedures

As state banking departments have become more capable, they have exercised more leadership in regulatory matters.

Beyond capabilities of performance, the nationwide system of decentralized state banking departments inherently fosters sound experimentation in regulatory techniques and procedures. States have diverse economic environments and banking department structures. These encourage experimentation. Also, state bank supervisors have diverse backgrounds. This infuses a flow of new concepts into the system. And each state, being relatively small and representing only a fraction of the whole, can experiment in a more manageable fashion and with a minimum of risk if experiments fail.

The decentralized state system has yielded many successful experiments. Several years ago, for example, the California Banking Department initiated what was called "top down" examination. The primary focal point of this experiment was an evaluation of bank management, policies, and procedures. This evaluation of the "top" reduced the amount and cost of subsequent examination and yielded better results. Reflecting the success of this experiment, other state and federal bank regulators now place increased emphasis on each bank's management, policies, and procedures while continuing to examine individual asset and liability items.

Other state experiments have included the selected "mini-exam" technique developed years ago by the Indiana Department of Financial Institutions. Through controlled experimentation and change, the mini-exam has evolved as a tool which saves time and money yet maintains basic goals of the examination exercise.

A variation of the mini-exam, called "Target Examination," was developed in the mid-1980s by the California Banking Department. CAMEL 1 and 2 rated banks were "targeted" to receive minimum on-site supervision. Less costly methods were developed to obtain certain data periodically and to signal a return to on-site examination if "red flags" appeared.

Time and money were saved by this procedure and more resources could then be employed in the on-site examination and supervision of problem or near-problem banks.

State banking departments have also been leaders in early warning statistical techniques. The Illinois Banking Department was among the first in the nation to experiment with such a system. With improvements based on experience, the system continued in use. However, as bank problems increased and banking organizations became more complex, the department returned to greater reliance on full scale on-site examinations. This ability to experiment and then change quickly as circumstances change further demonstrates why states can experiment so effectively.

With the more recent advent of multistate, multiregulated, multibank holding companies, state banking departments have again demonstrated their flexibility and ability to provide leadership for the examination and supervision of increasingly complex organizations. Experience as of this writing suggests that increasingly complex interstate organizations may now be examined and supervised with better coordination among regulators than were smaller and less complex intrastate holdings. By the mid-1980s at least four regions of state supervisors, along with federal counterparts, were well on their way toward good coordination in the examination and supervision of interstate holding companies. Apparently "interstate" triggered a sense of urgency for the need for more effective examination and supervision. Whatever the motivation, some of the larger multistate, multibank holding company managements in the late 1980s obtained better evaluations of their entire holding company operations than did smaller multibank holding companies in earlier years.

Finally, much of the early off-premises electronic funds transfer (EFT) experimentation was at the state level and was made possible by early EFT legislation by states.

The decentralized dual banking system is an excellent breeding ground for new techniques and procedures.

INHERENT STRENGTHS OF STATE BANKING DEPARTMENTS

State banking departments have certain inherent strengths:

1. Their offices generally are closer geographically to respective communities and bank trade areas. They are in a good position

to know each local environment, its economic problems, and its financial needs.

2. By virtue of relative proximity to the people of each community, the state regulatory system is inherently more responsive to the thinking of citizens of each bank's trade area. State banking departments reflect more accurately the will of the public of each trade area and state with less formal procedures; and reflecting relative proximity, state bank supervisors can more accurately evaluate consumer, business, and state or local government needs.

3. Reflecting the decentralized, less bureaucratic state structure, state banking departments have a higher proportion of their personnel in line functions. They get the job done well at less cost to banks and their customers.

4. The state system, also reflecting the proximity of banking departments to the public, has an inherent financial discipline. Although it is widely believed that some state banking departments are inadequately financed, proximity facilitiates good service per dollar spent.

5. On national as well as state issues, the highly democratic state banking system has an inherent quality of thoughtful deliberation reflecting the consolidated views of a relatively large number of people. As a consequence of collective judgments, the state system tends to be relatively free of major mistakes.

6. The state system can act with relative speed, responsiveness, and flexibility on matters affecting each community.

INHERENT WEAKNESSES OF STATE SYSTEM

Although the state banking department regulatory system has inherent strengths reflecting its decentralized and flexible structure, it also has certain tendencies for weakness reflecting somewhat those same characteristics.

The decentralized state system has to work harder to coordinate a nationwide effort, whether it be in educational or banking structure matters. When a course of action appears appropriate, for example, it is inherently more difficult to coordinate a decentralized 54-state banking department system than it is for one person in a centralized federal agency to issue an order directing all within that system to pursue a given course of action. Although this may be a weakness under some circumstances, it is a strength under others: Just as decentralization fosters democratic inputs and true consensus, it also fosters more enthusiastic participation.

Finally, financial strength is harder to achieve under a decentralized system. Adequate control over funds collected for examination and supervision historically has been perhaps the number one impediment to state banking departments' capabilities to serve the public interest. In some states, inflexibilities imposed by mid-level officials frustrate efforts by state bank supervisors to pay salaries needed to hire and retain qualified professionals who, in turn, are needed to assure safe and sound banks and protect interests of citizens—even though funds may come from bank assessments and fees.

Unfortunately, in the mid-1980s, comparable forces were imposed on federal bank regulatory agencies; and like the state problem, most of these pressures came from mid-level government personnel, not elected administrative or legislative officials. Reflecting practical political pressures, the FRS, FDIC, and OCC felt compelled to restrict their manpower capabilities to examine and supervise banks—and did so at a time when bank liquidations were reaching a peak.

Fortunately, however, at both federal and state legislative and elected executive branch levels, there has been a growing awareness of the public interest need for greater flexibility to permit federal and state bank regulatory agencies to use funds more effectively, for example, to pay competitive salaries and hire qualified personnel. On this score, state and federal bank regulators have a strong bond of agreement.

STATE AND NATIONAL SYSTEMS COMPLEMENT ONE ANOTHER

The dual banking system is most frequently praised for its reinforcement of state/federal checks and balances; and the system merits praise on this score. It is important to protect against monopoly power in bank regulation. But quite aside from this somewhat competitive quality, the two systems are highly complementary in many ways. Each spawns good, diverse ideas which are then frequently adopted by the other and each can motivate and get some things done better than the other.

As one example of this complementary quality of innovation and implementation, the earliest ideas, experimentation, and workable statutes on off-premises EFT facilities came from states. States were inherently in a better position to perform those early experimental roles. Then, in a complementary fashion, the national bank regulatory system, reflecting its centralized structure, was inherently better postured to provide a stimulant which motivated further study, experimentation, and a movement toward workable state and federal statutes. There are those who would argue that the national stimulant was overly dramatic and imperfect in its approach, but it also has been argued that in net it was mutually complementary with the state system. The national system did that which the states could not have done as expeditiously and vice versa. Consequently, the U.S. is gradually moving toward an efficient nationwide automated EFT system and doing so without an undue concentration of or control over our nation's financial resosurce base in the form of bank deposits.

Reflecting complementary factors and careful planning, regulators of state and national banks now enjoy a better working relationship than was considered feasible a decade or two ago.

EVOLVING PATTERNS OF STATE BANKING DEPARTMENTS

The ability of state banking departments to assure safety and soundness, protect the public interest, contribute to competition, and help shape the banking structure is being enhanced by several favorable patterns of events.

First, state banking departments have increased significantly their capabilities in the past decade. States have increased the number of banking department personnel, raised levels of training five-fold, reduced salary disparities vis-a-vis federal counterparts, selected supervisors of a higher stature, assumed stronger positions as individual departments in national affairs, and achieved a more effective voice collectively through CSBS in national affairs.

Some deficiencies, however, are being corrected only slowly. For example, a few state banking departments, for financial or other reasons, have not taken full advantage of training opportunities, even though education nationwide has increased sharply; some must labor under inadequate statutes, even though a great amount of recodification has taken place in the past two decades; a few still have frustrating political problems within their states, even though individual banking department policies are consistent with policies of respective state administrations; several states are handicapped by bank examiner pay scales below federal counterparts, even though nearly all state bank CEOs are more than willing to provide adequate funding; numerous state banking departments are weakened financially by counterproductive controls from outside the departments over their funds, even though state bankers want good state regulation and are willing to pay for it; and a few departments have concerns about handling troubled banks. However, they consistently have kept failures at levels lower than or equal to their federal counterparts over the past decade.

Notwithstanding only partial solutions to some problems, the overall pattern of state banking departments is one of an increasingly responsible role in an increasingly complex banking system and more nearly one of parity with that of the primary regulator of national banks. In most states, banking departments are now well qualified to charter, examine, and regulate banks and bank holding companies under state jurisdictions.

CHAPTER EIGHTY-TWO

The Securities and Exchange Commission

A. A. Sommer, Jr.

Morgan, Lewis & Bockius
Counselors at Law

INTRODUCTION

The Securities and Exchange Commission (the SEC or the Commission) was created by Congress in 1934 to administer the Securities Act of 1933 and the Securities Exchange Act of 1934, the statute which created the agency. The commission is an independent regulatory agency consisting of five commissioners appointed by the president and confirmed by the Senate for terms of five years, one of whom is appointed by the president as chairman to serve as such at the pleasure of the president. With respect to policy, quasi-adjudicatory and rule-making matters, each commissioner has one vote. The chairman is vested with certain administrative duties and powers.

The commission is the policymaking body which supervises a staff of approximately two thousand persons, approximately 800 of whom are attorneys, accountants, and financial analysts. About 1,300 of the employees are located at the commission's headquarters in Washington and the remainder are in nine regional offices.

The commission has the responsibility to administer and enforce seven statutes, the most notable of which—and the ones this discussion will center upon—are the Securities Act of 1933 (the 1933 act), the Securities Exchange Act of 1934 (the 1934 act), the Investment Company Act of 1940, and the Investment Advisers Act of 1940.

THE SECURITIES ACT OF 1933

The Securities Act of 1933 requires essentially that, unless a security is exempt or the transaction in which it is sold is exempt, it must be registered with the SEC before it may be sold. Ancillary to this basic requirement are limitations on offering activity before the registration statement is effective, requirements concerning the contents of prospectuses used in the offering and sale of the security, and a number of other provisions to facilitate the principal purpose of the act, the public dissemination of accurate and current information to the public in connection with the distribution of securities in interstate commerce.

Banks are exempt from the registration requirements of the 1933 act. However, *bank holding companies* are fully subject to the requirements of the act. Thus, unless the transaction in which it is offering and selling its securities is exempt, a bank holding company must: 1) refrain from offering the securities before the registration statement is filed with the SEC, 2) confine offering activities after filing but before effectiveness basically to oral solicitations and distribution of the prospectus included in the registration statement as filed, 3) refrain from selling the security until the registration statement is effective, 4) include in any prospectus used information required by commission rules, and 5) deliver a final prospectus to each purchaser.

The exemptions from registration are narrow and quite technical. The principal ones are:

The Private Offering Exemption.   This is an offering limited as to the number and characteristics of the offerees. Generally such an exemption is available if it is confined to limited numbers of "sophisticated investors," including so-called "accredited investors" (institutional investors and individuals meeting certain standards of income and net worth). A number of technical requirements with respect to disclosure, methods of offering, and the like must be met for this exemption to be available.

The Intrastate Offering Exemption.   This is an offering essentially confined to a single state: The issuer must be incorporated or organized in the state, it must do the most substantial part of its business in the state, all of the offerees must be residents of the state, and the bulk of the proceeds must be used in the state.

The Small Offering Exemption.   This exemption is available for (1) offerings of securities having an aggregate value of no more than $500,000, and (2) offerings of securities having an aggregate value of no more than $5,000,000 to an unlimited number of accredited investors and no more than 35 "nonaccredited" investors. In any case, a number of specific rules with respect to disclosure and other matters must be observed.

The registration statement of a bank holding company making its first registered offering is usually a lengthy and complex document. It includes the prospectus which is usually circulated publicly during the pre-effective offering period and which must be delivered in final form to each purchaser. This must include, among other things, information concerning the holding company's business and its property; the identity and backgrounds of its directors, executive officers, promoters, and persons in control of the company; the compensation of the principal executives; the security holdings of certain officers, directors and certain other persons; relationships and transactions between executive officers, directors, and large security holders and the company; and any material pending legal proceedings.

But the most important information in the prospectus, of course, is financial information. The prospectus must include balance sheets at the end of the two most recent fiscal years and income statements and statements of changes in financial position for the three most recent fiscal years. They should be prepared in accordance with generally accepted accounting standards and SEC regulation S-X and audited by independent accountants, and unaudited interim statements should be included if a specified period has elapsed since the end of the most recent fiscal year. Additional specified financial information for the most recent five fiscal years, plus interim period if appropriate, must also be included.

Beginning in 1976, largely as a consequence of concerns about the adequacy of disclosures by banks concerning municipal securities held by them and the collectibility of certain loans and obligations, the commission adopted a guide applicable to both 1933 and 1934 act filings concerning additional statistical disclosures by bank holding companies, which it has steadily expanded as new concerns about banks have emerged. This guide requires, among other things, the disclosure for two to five years, depending on the size of the company and the nature of the information, of extensive detail concerning the assets, liabilities, investment portfolio, maturities, and sensitivities of loans to changes in interest rates, nonaccrual, past due and restructured loans, potential loan problems, foreign loans, loan concentrations, loan experience, and return on assets.

After the initial one, 1933 act registration statements may be somewhat simpler if the holding company has been registered under the 1934 Act for three years (see below). Depending upon its size and the nature of the offering, the holding company registered under the 1934 act may register securities by incorporating certain information previously filed with the SEC into the registration statement by reference. It may also satisfy the prospectus delivery requirement by giving offerees and purchasers either its most recent annual report to shareholders plus supplementary material concerning recent events and details of the offering, or a brief document containing only such supplementary material.

There is a complex web of civil liabilities woven about the registration and prospectus provisions of the 1933 act. If the registration statement, at the time it becomes effective, contains a material misstatement or omits a statement required to be included or necessary to make the statements made not misleading, then:

- The issuer may be liable to anyone who purchased the registered security, and it has for practical purposes no defense.
- Each director, each person who has consented to become a director, and each officer who signs the registration statement (the principal executive, financial, and accounting officers) may be liable unless he can show that after a reasonable investigation he had reasonable grounds to believe, and did believe, that the nonexpertised portions of the registration statement did not include a material misstatement or omission.
- Each expert whose opinion with his consent is included in the registration statement or used in connection with it may be liable with respect to that opinion unless he can satisfy a due diligence standard similar to that applicable to directors and officers (accountants, of course, are those most commonly exposed to liability under this provision).
- Each underwriter of the registered securities may be liable unless it can satisfy a due diligence standard similar to that applicable to directors and officers.

As mentioned, *banks* are not subject to the registration provisions of the 1933 act. However, the regulatory agencies supervising banks have established procedures which banks must follow in offering their securities that in most cases bear close resemblance to those required for bank holding companies under the 1933 act.

THE SECURITIES EXCHANGE ACT OF 1934

The Securities Exchange Act of 1934 was intended to do a number of chores. First, it established a framework for continuous reporting, at first only for issuers with securities listed on registered exchanges, but from 1964 on also for issuers with a specified number of shareholders and amounts of assets. Second, it provided the foundation for the regulation of credit used in securities transactions. Third, it provided a foundation, at first for the regulation of proxy solicitations directed to shareholders of companies subject to continuous reporting requirements, and then in 1968 for the regulation of anyone making a tender offer for such a company. Fourth, it gave the SEC extensive regulatory power over the exchanges and the over-the-counter market and brokers/dealers. Fifth, it required reporting of their transactions by officers, directors, and holders of more than 10 percent of a class of equity securities of an issuer subject to continuous reporting and provided for recovery by the issuer of short-term profits realized by any of them. Sixth, it contained several antifraud and antimanipulation provisions. In 1975 the act was expanded to give power to the SEC to regulate the security clearing and settlement process and those engaged in it and to create the Municipal Securities Rulemaking Board which was empowered to regulate the trading of municipal securities.

Publicly held bank holding companies are subject to the full panoply of the 1934 act. That means:

1. Generally, they must register with the SEC under the 1934 act, which entails filing a registration statement with the SEC containing substantially the same information as that which must be included in an initial registration statement under the 1933 act.

2. They must file annual reports (Form 10–K) with the SEC which in effect update the original registration statement filed under the act.

3. They must file quarterly reports (Form 10–Q) which consist principally of unaudited balance sheets as of the end of the most recent quarter and the end of the previous fiscal year, income statements for the most recent quarter, for the period from the end of the previous fiscal year to the end of such quarter, and for the same periods of the preceding fiscal year, and statements of changes in financial position for the period from the end of the preceding fiscal year to the end of the most recent quarter and for the corresponding period of the previous year.

4. They must file periodic reports (Form 8–K) upon the occurrence of certain significant events, such as changes of auditor, changes in control, acquisitions, or dispositions of significant amounts of assets, bankruptcy, or receivership proceedings, and certain resignations of directors.

5. They must conform to the SEC's rules with respect to any proxy solicitations, or if action is taken without solicitation, then with the disclosure rules adopted under Section 14(c). This entails extensive disclosure with respect to matters submitted to shareholders and compliance with a number of other rules governing the solicitation of proxies, including furnishing to shareholders an annual report concerning specified information and audited financial statements. Holding companies must also obey the rules with respect to the inclusion of shareholder proposals in their proxy statements.

6. Anyone who accumulates more than 5 percent of a class of equity security of a holding company must make disclosure in accordance with section 13(d) of the act, and anyone proposing to make a tender offer for equity securities of the holding company which, if successful, would result in the ownership of more than 5 percent of a class of equity securities of the holding company must comply with that section and the rules thereunder, as well as other requirements. In addition, tender offers by issuers for their own securities are subject to regulation.

7. Officers, directors, and the beneficial owners of more than 10 percent of a class of equity securities of a holding company must report their ownership and any changes in it.

8. The holding company, either on its own initiative or upon that of a shareholder, may recover any profit realized by an officer, director, or 10 percent equity securityholder as the result of a purchase and sale, or sale and purchase, of equity securities of the company within a six-month period.

9. Moreover, as will be discussed below, any bank that acts as a transfer agent, clearing agency, or municipal securities dealer is subject to additional provisions of the 1934 act which were added by the 1975 amendments.

Unlike the 1933 act, *banks* were not exempted from the provisions of the 1934 act. However, the SEC soon after the act became effective adopted a "temporary" exemption until it could adopt a form for the registration of bank securities under the act. The form was never adopted. However, since very few bank stocks were traded on exchanges, and since until 1964 the main impacts of the 1934 act fell only on listed companies, the status of banks under the act was not of pressing importance.

In 1964, however, when Congress extended the 1934 act to embrace companies with more than 500 security holders and more than one million dollars of assets (now increased to five million) regardless of where their securities were traded, the absence of a formal exemption was no longer a matter of indifference, since many banks had securities traded over-the-counter. During the discussion leading to enactment of the amendments many associated with the banking industry expressed misgivings about becoming subject in any measure to regulation by yet another federal agency, the SEC. Recognizing this hesitancy, when the commission proposed legislation to subject issuers of over-the-counter securities to the 1934 act, it recommended that the registration and related provisions be administered as to banks by the federal bank regulatory authorities.

As enacted, the amendments provided that the powers, functions, and duties vested in the commission to administer and enforce sections 12 [the registration requirement], 13 [the continuous reporting requirements], 14(a) [proxy regulation], 14(c) [disclosure requirements when proxies are not solicited], 14(d) [tender offer regulation], 14(f) [disclosure upon certain changes of directors], and 16 [insider reporting and short-term trading] were vested as to national banks in the Comptroller of the Currency, as to all other members of the Federal Reserve System in the board of governors of the system, and as to all other insured banks in the Federal Deposit Insurance Corporation.

Thus the bank regulatory agencies had the power to adopt whatever rules and regulations they deemed necessary to administer the specified sections and to enforce compliance, including the securing of injunctions, the issuance of stop orders, the ordering of corrective filings, and the recommendation in appropriate cases of criminal proceedings.

Soon after the adoption of these amendments the Board of Governors of the Federal Reserve System and the Federal Deposit Insurance Corporation adopted forms and rules closely conforming to those of the SEC. The Comptroller of the Currency, however, pursued a significantly different course. In 1975 the Congress eliminated the potential for much of the diversity of approach when it adopted an amendment to section 12(i) of the 1934 act which provided,

> In carrying out their responsibilities under this subsection, the agencies named in the first sentence of this subsection shall issue substantially similar regulations to regulations and rules issued by the Commission under sections 12, 13, 14(a), 14(c), 14(d), 14(f), and 16, unless they find that implementation of substantially similar regulations with respect to insured banks and insured institutions are not necessary or appropriate in the public interest or for protection of investors.

As a consequence of all this, today the rules, regulations, forms, and practices of the banking agencies with respect to the sections enumerated are supposed to be virtually identical unless good reason is shown. For the most part they are. However, the banking regulatory agencies only require that financial statements filed and distributed under the 1934 act be "verified" by appropriate officers of the company; if an independent accountant does give an opinion on the financial statements, the independence standards are substantially the same as those of the SEC. Further, the SEC Guide requiring extensive detail concerning assets, liabilities, foreign lendings, and the like has not been adopted by the bank agencies, although they do require disclosure of much of the same information. Further, there are occasional lags by the banking agencies in conforming their requirements to changes adopted by the SEC; for instance, none of them has yet adopted the integrated disclosure system which the commission adopted several years ago, although they do have provisions for incorporating information in one filing into another.

Thus, banks are subject to the 1934 act and they must, subject to the manner in which the relevant regulation implements the act's provisions, do everything that is mandated for other issuers subject to the jurisdictional provisions of the act. While there may be a great deal of uniformity with respect to rules, forms, regulations, and the like, inevitably there will be, and there are, differences, in the manner in which and the vigor with which the requirements are enforced.

ANTIFRAUD PROVISIONS

Both the 1933 and 1934 acts contain provisions that may be characterized broadly as "antifraud." Banks, as well as governmental units and others, are specifically exempted from section 12(2) of the 1933 act, which provides a civil remedy for the use of material misstatements and omissions in the offer and sale of securities.

However, banks are subject to section 17(a)of the 1933 act and section 10(b) and rule 10b–5 under the 1934 act. Both of these prohibit in connection with the offer or sale of any security, and in the case of rule 10b–5, the purchase of a security, the employment of any device, scheme, or artifice to defraud; the use of any untrue statement of a material fact or any omission to state a material fact necessary in order to make the staetments made, in light of the circumstances under which they were made, not misleading; or engaging in any transaction, practice, or course of business which operates or would operate as a fraud or deceit upon the purchaser of the security.

While there remains uncertainty whether a private party can recover under section 17(a), there is no such uncertainty under rule 10b–5: Both defrauded buyers and sellers can recover under it. Of course, the SEC can proceed under either section, and criminal proceedings may be brought under both. Whether the grant of power in section 12(i) of the 1934 act to the federal banking agencies extends to enforcement action under sections 17 and 10(b) is uncertain.

REGULATION OF TRANSFER AGENTS, CLEARING AGENCIES, AND MUNICIPAL SECURITIES DEALERS

As a consequence of the turmoil which characterized the securities clearing and transfer process during the late 1960s and early 1970s and the charges which accompanied New York City's financial crisis during the 1970s, Congress in 1975 amended the 1934 act to establish a regulatory structure for clearing agents, transfer agents, and municipal securities dealers. This structure reflected the continuing uneasiness of banks with the prospect of SEC regulation of their affairs. In each instance, the agency designated to administer each new regulatory system with respect to a participant was the regulator of its primary business: That is, the Comptroller of the Currency was named as the "appropriate regulatory agency" with respect to transfer agents, clearing agencies, and municipal securities dealers which were national banks; the Board of Governors of the Federal Reserve System with respect to those that were state members of the Federal Reserve System and with respect to bank holding companies; the FDIC with respect to other banks insured by it; and the SEC with respect to the remaining participants which, of course, included members of the securities industry. The SEC had a primary role in each instance, but was required to cooperate with the other agencies.

REGULATION OF BROKERS AND DEALERS

Under the 1934 act, all brokers and dealers engaged in an interstate business are required to register with the SEC which is given broad power to regulate, either directly or through oversight of self-regulatory agencies, their affairs, including their capital sufficiency, their manner of keeping books and records, the safeguarding of customer securities, and a host of other matters. In fulfilling its responsibilities, the commission is given broad inspection and investigatory powers.

The definitions of both "broker" and "dealer" specifically exclude "banks," which in turn are defined as banking institutions which are members of the Federal Reserve System or which are supervised and examined by a state or federal authority having supervision over banks.

In the 1980s banks and other institutions entered the discount brokerage business. In many cases they did this through a separate subsidiary either of the bank itself or of a bank holding company. A subsidiary of a bank or of a bank holding company does not enjoy the bank exemption from the broker or dealer definition under the 1934 act, hence it must register with the commission and thus become subject to the SEC rules and regulations pertaining to brokers and dealers.

In 1985 the commission, acting on the basis of its belief in "functional regulation," that is, financial institutions engaged in similar activities should be subjected to the same scheme of regulation, adopted rule 3b–9 under the power given it in section 3(b) of the 1934 act "to define technical, trade, accounting, and other terms used in this title. . . ." Under the rule, the commission *excluded* from the term "bank," for purposes of the broker and dealer definitions, any bank engaged directly in a public brokerage business with certain exceptions. The commission's basic argument was that section 3, which contains the definitions of terms used in the 1934 act, is prefaced by the words "unless the context otherwise provides" and that the factual context in which Congress used the term in 1934 had changed, thus justifying an administrative redefinition of the term "bank" for purposes of the broker/dealer definitions.

The District Court for the District of Columbia sustained the commission; however, late in 1986 the Court of Appeals reversed and invalidated the rule. Thus, unless Congress intervenes or the Supreme Court reverses the Court of Appeals, the commission is without power to regulate the brokerage business in which banks engage directly rather than through a subsidiary.

INVESTMENT COMPANIES AND INVESTMENT ADVISERS

Banks, defined similarly to the manner in which they are defined in the other federal securities laws, are excluded from the definition of "investment company" and "investment adviser." As in the case of the exemption of banks from the definitions of broker and dealer, the exemption does not carry through to subsidiaries of banks or bank holding companies which do not have the characteristics of a bank identified in the exemption.

However, this simple statement masks a mass of complexity that continues to churn at an increasingly rapid rate. Extremely difficult questions arise when banks are in some fashion involved with the pooling of funds in various investment vehicles. Some such pools are expressly excluded from the definition of investment company, such as common trust funds "maintained by a bank exclusively for the collective investment and reinvestment of moneys contributed thereto by the bank in its capacity as a trustee, executor, administrator, or guardian," and collective trust funds used as receptacles for funds of employees' stock bonus, pension, or profit-sharing trusts. Similarly, the SEC has indicated that the pooling of funds contributed through banks under H.R. 10 or IRA plans (largely curtailed under the 1985 tax reform legislation) does not constitute an investment company.

However, other types of poolings, such as those resulting from the public solicitation of investors, whether done within the bank or through a subsidiary of either the bank or a holding company, may constitute an investment company and result in a need for registration under the Investment Company Act of 1940. In some cases the offering of interests in such pools of investments may entail the necessity of registering under the 1933 act.

As banks and bank holding companies venture into new areas, either directly or through subsidiaries, the statutory language of these acts, as well as the other federal securities laws, will be sorely tested.

* * * * * * *

The relationship of federal securities laws to banks is in a state of unprecedented flux. As banks are permitted to engage in activities thought heretofore denied them, the applicability of the federal securities law will change—sometimes through commission interpretation, sometimes through court decision, other times as the consequence of legislation. Hence, like the proverbial excursion ticket, the above discussion is "good for today and today only."

PART FIFTEEN

The Impact of Monetary and Fiscal Policies on the Banking System

CHAPTER EIGHTY-THREE

Special Relationships between Monetary Policy and the Banking System

Gary H. Stern*

President
Federal Reserve Bank of Minneapolis

We hear and read much these days about competition between banks and nonbank financial firms. These discussions are pervaded with such terms as *market share, level playing field,* and *fairness.* Undoubtedly, it is true that banks are relatively handicapped in such competition because they are more heavily regulated than most nonbank firms. It is also true that competitive equity is a worthy goal of public policy. However, bank regulation has multiple objectives, and one of the most fundamental is to facilitate the conduct of monetary policy by the Federal Reserve System. This fundamental objective, while not totally ignored in the current debate, has been given less than adequate attention. This chapter aims to partly redress the imbalance.

The conduct of monetary policy is closely related to the performance of the banking industry. Healthy banks make monetary policy easier to carry out and generally more effective. This is evident from a look at current monetary control procedures—procedures that both influence banking practices and are in turn influenced by those practices. This two-way relationship necessitates some form of regulation to ensure the safety of the banking system, and thereby preserve the means to effectively implement monetary policy. This is not to say that current regulatory practices are optimal, for they almost surely are not.

*The views expressed herein are those of the author and not necessarily those of the Federal Reserve Bank of Minneapolis or the Federal Reserve System. The author gratefully acknowledges John H. Boyd, V. V. Chari, Stanley L. Graham, and Michael J. Stutzer for their contributions to this chapter.

This chapter proceeds as follows: Section I discusses the objectives of monetary policy; then Section II briefly explains how monetary policy is actually implemented. Section III considers the effects of monetary policy on the banking system, while Section IV explains how the banking system, in turn, affects monetary policy by its responses to government policies. Section V discusses the relationship between bank regulation and monetary policy. And Section VI considers (and rejects) arguments that banks should not be regulated at all. Finally, Section VII summarizes and concludes the chapter.

I. THE OBJECTIVES OF MONETARY POLICY

As students of introductory economics quickly learn, macroeconomic policy in the United States comprises mainly fiscal policy and monetary policy. *Fiscal policy*, which is the responsibility of the administration and the Congress, deals with changes in federal government spending and taxation. *Monetary policy*, which is under the purview of the Federal Reserve System (Fed), pursues macroeconomic goals by influencing the cost and availability of money and credit in the economy.

The goals of U.S. macroeconomic policy and, by implication, of monetary policy, are embedded in the nation's laws. The Employment Act of 1946 and the Full Employment and Balanced Growth Act of 1978 (commonly known as the Humphrey-Hawkins Act) commit the government to promote high employment and price stability.

Whether or not monetary policy can in fact achieve both objectives is a matter of ongoing controversy. Policymakers have long been aware of a possible inconsistency between the goals of full employment and price stability. In other words, higher employment may be achieved, but at the cost of greater inflation; or lower inflation at the cost of higher unemployment. Beyond this inconsistency lies the question, How much can monetary policy actually influence employment and inflation?

The answer depends on whether we're looking at the economy from a long- or short-term perspective. There seems to be general agreement that in the long run, monetary policy has little or no influence over employment and production. Other factors—population growth and technological advances—are the main ingredients fueling the nation's long-term growth. For the short run, the controversy focuses on the stabilization of business cycles. What might be called the traditional view—encompassing both monetarists and Keynesians—holds that changes in the money supply influence real output. The two groups differ over the relative strength of monetary policy and over how changes in the money supply affect production. While the dominant view is that monetary policy has real effects, more recently some authors [for example, Prescott 1986] have denied that monetary policy actions have any significant effect on output and employment, even in the short run.

Moreover, even the conventional wisdom that monetary policy has a significant effect on inflation has also come under attack. Certain studies [Sargent and Wallace 1981, Smith 1984, Wallace 1981] emphasize that monetary policy simply cannot be analyzed without also considering fiscal policy because fiscal decisions imply a path for current and future deficits. Through open-market operations (explained below), the Fed determines the extent to which a federal deficit is *monetized*—that is, financed by the creation of money. Since the national debt cannot grow indefinitely at a rate higher than the economy's ability to grow, fiscal policy decisions that imply large, continuing deficits will force the Fed to monetize the debt. In this sense, it is appropriate to say that any resulting inflation is a consequence of fiscal, not monetary, policy decisions.

Despite these arguments and counterarguments about the effectiveness of monetary policy, the prevailing view is that "money matters" and that monetary policy is an important component of a macroeconomic policy directed at maintaining high employment and stable prices.

II. HOW MONETARY POLICY IS IMPLEMENTED: AN OVERVIEW

The Federal Reserve System is responsible for setting and implementing monetary policy. The arm of the Fed primarily responsible for policymaking is the Federal Open Market Committee (FOMC). At each FOMC meeting, held roughly every six weeks, the committee considers general economic conditions, evaluates the performance of monetary policy, and reviews long- and short-run targets for various measures of the money supply, called *monetary aggregates.*

Currently, targets are set for several monetary aggregates, and the target growth rate for each aggregate is specified as a range rather than a single value. Stipulating monetary targets as a range partly reflects controversy over the relative importance of stable interest rates versus stable monetary growth. A well-recognized principle in policymaking is that the Fed cannot simultaneously control both interest rates and the money supply. Attaching ranges to the monetary targets can be viewed as a strategy aimed at sacrificing some stability in money growth for more stability in interest rates, or vice versa.

The targets for the monetary aggregates are contained in a directive to the New York Fed, which is responsible for carrying out the

FOMC's instructions. The principal tool for implementing the FOMC's directive is *open-market operations,* the buying and selling of U.S. government securities by the New York Fed. When the Fed wants to increase the money supply, it purchases U.S. government securities; when it wants to decrease the supply, the Fed sells securities. (For an illustration of this process, see the box on page 1270.)

Although open market operations are the main tool for controlling the money supply, they are not the only one. Another tool, the *reserve requirement,* is the power to alter the required ratio of bank reserves to deposits. Increasing the reserve ratio reduces the excess reserves banks have available for making loans, and thus reduces the size of the *money multiplier* (the ratio of the change in the Fed's securities to the change in bank deposits). However, since changes in the money supply can be effectively obtained by open-market operations, reserve requirements have been changed infrequently in recent years.

Another means for controlling the money supply is the Fed's *discount window.* In fulfilling its role as lender of last resort to the banking system, the Fed is empowered to lend to banks. Technically, a Fed loan to a bank has the same impact on the money supply as an open market purchase of government securities; that is, such a loan increases the money supply.

The interest rate banks pay on Fed loans is called the *discount rate.* By changing the discount rate, the Fed influences the amount of bank borrowing at its discount window. Furthermore, some believe that the importance of the discount rate goes beyond influencing the amount of bank borrowing. In their opinion, the financial markets view changes in the discount rate as signals of the Fed's future monetary policy.

Credit controls are yet other means the Fed has for controlling money and credit. For example, during World War II the Fed required that downpayments on auto loans be increased and their terms be reduced. This action decreased auto purchases and thereby increased resources for the war effort. In the United States, credit controls such as these have been used sparingly.

III. HOW MONETARY POLICY AFFECTS THE BANKING SYSTEM

Given that the Fed has four main tools to implement monetary policy (open market operations, reserve requirements, the discount window, and credit controls), how does their use affect the banking industry? The question is answered for each of the policy tools in turn. This discussion is followed by an examination of some additional (indirect) effects of monetary policy on banks. We find that monetary policy influences both short- and long-term interest rates and, in the long run, is probably the most important determinant of the rate of inflation. These macroeconomic variables—interest rates and inflation—affect the banking industry in ways that are often not well understood by the public.

A. Effects of Open Market Operations

To review briefly, open market operations affect the composition and volume of the liabilities of the banking system. The volume of currency and reserves held by the banking industry and the public increases (or decreases) with an open-market purchase (or sale) by the Federal Reserve. The volume of deposits held by the banking industry also increases (or decreases) with such an operation. These changes in the money supply also induce changes in interest rates.

Consider the case of an open-market purchase. Assuming the government's fiscal decisions remain unchanged, when an open-market purchase is carried out the public ends up holding fewer government bonds and more currency than it did before. As a result, prices on government bonds rise and interest rates decline. A decline in interest rates, in turn, affects the opportunity cost (lost income) of holding assets in noninterest-bearing form. Thus, bank customers will be willing to hold more of their assets as currency, and banks may be willing to hold more excess reserves at the Fed. The point is that both banks and the public respond to open-market operations: They do not passively accept them. Moreover, their responses will tend to attenuate, though not eliminate, the growth of the money supply caused by the Fed's open-market purchase.

In a dynamic, ever-changing real world, of course, the effect of open-market operations is vastly more complicated than in the static analysis just presented. If the analysis has any validity, then it immediately follows that *anticipations* by banks and the public of future open-market operations may well affect interest rates *even before such operations occur.* Indeed, a number of investigators [Urich and Wachtel 1981, 1984; Roley 1983] have found that unanticipated increases in the money supply *raise* short-term interest rates—exactly the opposite of what static theory might predict. How can this phenomenon be explained? One explanation is that the Fed will respond to the unanticipated increase in the money supply by reducing the growth rate of the money supply in the future. The anticipation of higher interest rates in the future may well cause firms to speed up investment decisions and consumers to buy more durable goods now. The resulting increase in current economic activity will, in general, cause interest rates to rise.

There are two conclusions to be drawn from these considerations. First, the effects of the Fed's actions on the banking system depend on the private sector's expectations about the Fed's *future* actions. Second, the private sector's expectations about the Fed's future policy may in turn influence current policymaking.

B. Effects of Other Policy Tools

Changes in the *required reserves* a bank must hold against transaction accounts are infrequent. However, they are potentially even more important than open-market operations in determining the volume of the money supply. Increases in reserve requirements will, at least temporarily, cause banks to sell interest-bearing securities to increase their reserves at the Fed. If monetary policy remains otherwise unchanged, the net effect will be a reduction in the total money supply or, in other words, a substantially smaller volume of bank deposits.

When the Fed changes the *discount rate*, it changes how much banks must pay for funds from one source. A change in the discount rate can thus directly affect the industry as a whole. As in the case of open-market operations, discount rate changes affect both the level of interest rates as well as the composition and volume of the liabilities of the banking industry. When the Fed reduces the discount rate, banks borrow more from the Fed, thereby increasing the money supply.

Although the Fed can impose *credit controls* to curtail money growth, direct interventions intended to alter the asset side of the balance sheets of the banking industry have been relatively rare. (The most recent intervention occurred in the second quarter of 1980.) Such interventions generally take the form of ceilings on the interest rates that banks charge on new loans. If these ceilings are set below prevailing market rates, the resulting excess demand for loans must somehow be rationed. This will cause the banking industry to reduce the total volume of bank lending (possibly very sharply), thereby leading to a contraction in the money supply. The Fed has the authority to impose such controls at the president's request.

C. Interest Rates, Inflation, and Banks

There is a widespread public perception that bankers prefer high interest rates, or more precisely, that banks reap higher profits when market rates are high. This view, which seems to focus on banks as lenders (but not as borrowers), is not supported by the data. For example, one careful study [Flannery 1980, p. 21] concludes that "when market rates change, the responses of bank revenues and costs approximately cancel one another, leaving the level of commercial bank profits only slightly sensitive to market rates in most cases. The popular conception that the banking industry reaps unreasonably large profits during tight money times thus is not supported by the evidence."

A related issue is how bank profits are affected by changes in interest rates. That is, Are banks more profitable when interest rates are rising or falling? Or are they indifferent between the two? The answer may vary from bank to bank, since it depends on how a bank's balance sheet is structured. If, on the one hand, a bank's balance sheet has assets with relatively short maturities and liabilities with relatively long ones, the bank will benefit when interest rates rise. This is because interest rates on assets (which generate income) will adjust more quickly than interest rates on liabilities (which generate expenses). A bank with such a balance-sheet configuration is said to have *positive gap*.

If, on the other hand, a bank's assets are relatively long in maturity and its liabilities relatively short, the bank will profit when interest rates decline. This second sort of balance sheet configuration is referred to as *negative gap*. For many years, negative gap was an identifying characteristic of virtually all savings and loan associations (S&Ls) in this country. Their assets consisted primarily of fixed-rate mortgages of long maturity, and their liabilities of short maturity deposits. With the advantage of hindsight, it is not surprising that when interest rates rose rapidly in the late 1970s and early 1980s, this industry suffered enormous losses and many S&Ls even failed.

On average, commercial banks fared much better during this same period than did S&Ls, precisely because bank asset and liability maturities were more closely matched. Moreover, the data suggest that in recent years, the typical bank has maintained a gap fairly close to zero, so that its profits have not been terribly sensitive to interest rate movements. Of course, not all banks are average and as interest rates move, some experience gains and others losses [Flannery 1980].

Bank profits do appear to be significantly and positively related to the rate of inflation. Part of this relationship stems from the well-known fact that nominal rates of return (which include returns on bank assets and equity) adjust over time to offset the effect of changes in the price level. However, that fact cannot fully explain the correlation. Even after bank profits are adjusted for inflation, there is still a discernible positive association between real bank profits and the rate of inflation (see Figure 1). This relationship is not, however, a fluke; nor is there any reason to conclude that bankers prefer inflation. Rather, the association is primarily explained by the fact that rates of inflation are also correlated with levels of economic activity over the business cycle. As the economy expands, the rate of inflation tends to rise; as it contracts, the rate usually falls, only to rise again some time after

FIGURE 1   Real Bank Profits versus Inflation Rate

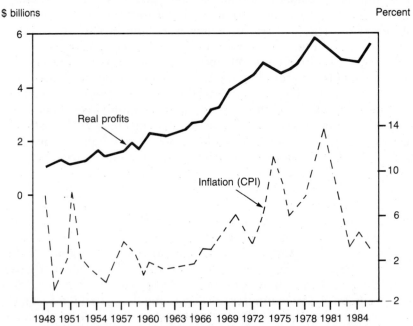

SOURCES: *Banking and Monetary Statistics, 1941–1970,* Board of Governors of the Federal Reserve System; Bureau of Labor Statistics; *Federal Reserve Bulletin,* vols. 66, 71, 72.

the next expansion begins. As is well documented, bank profits also tend to follow this sort of procyclical pattern [Federal Reserve Bank of New York 1986, pp. 73–88].

It is worth noting that during the 1980s, the rate of inflation has declined rapidly; at the same time, the rate of bank failures has increased enormously (see Figure 2). Some have interpreted these data as suggesting that disinflation is harmful to banks. A more precise interpretation, however, would be that whenever entire industries get into severe financial difficulty (for whatever reason), banks that lend to them also suffer. The recent hardships of industries such as agriculture, energy, and in some areas, real estate—all of which have largely suffered from unexpected price declines—have been felt by the banking industry as well.

IV. HOW THE BANKING INDUSTRY AFFECTS MONETARY POLICY

Thus far we have considered how Fed policies affect the banking industry. This emphasis might seem to imply that the monetary policy

FIGURE 2   Bank Failures versus Inflation Rate

Number of failures   Percent

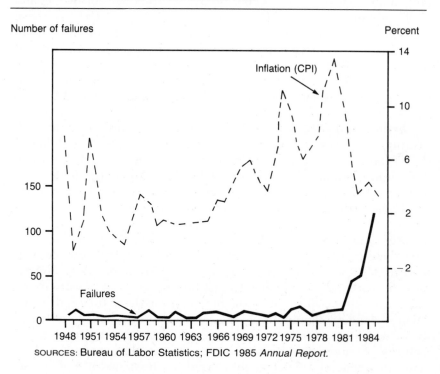

SOURCES: Bureau of Labor Statistics; FDIC 1985 *Annual Report.*

process flows in one direction only. But this is far from the truth. At an increasingly rapid pace, commercial banks have been developing new management strategies, inventing new financial instruments, and opening new financial markets. Many of these financial innovations have been *responses* to Federal Reserve policies. Although financial market innovations are generally healthy for the economy, they often do complicate the Fed's task in conducting monetary policy.

A. Financial Innovations and Monetary Policy: A Two-Way Street

Financial innovations can be classified into three general categories: (1) liability innovations, (2) asset innovations, and (3) off-balance-sheet innovations. Many of each kind have appeared in recent years. A few examples should suffice to show how such innovations occur and how they can complicate the conduct of monetary policy.

1. Liability Innovations.   In the 1960s, when interest rates on bank deposits were regulated and market rates often exceeded these limits, banks initiated several liability management innovations. These included large certificates of deposit (CDs), Eurodollar borrowing, and bank holding company (BHC) commercial paper. Essentially, these instruments were devices to circumvent deposit rate ceilings (and to avoid reserve requirements at the same time if possible). The Fed responded to these innovations by imposing reserve requirements on Eurodollar borrowing and BHC commercial paper. Rate ceilings were also imposed on some types of CDs [Eastburn and Hoskins 1978, pp. 1124–25].

In the mid-1970s, S&Ls and eventually banks introduced interest-bearing transaction accounts, such as negotiable order of withdrawal (NOW) and automatic transfer of savings (ATS) accounts. In response to such innovations, the Congress enacted the Monetary Control Act of 1980, which progressively reduced and eventually eliminated interest rate ceilings on most deposits over the next six years.

2. Asset Innovations.   Also in response to rising inflation and interest rates, banks and S&Ls initiated asset innovations. For instance, late in 1979, California S&Ls began issuing growing numbers of adjustable-rate mortgages as a hedge against interest rate risk. As discussed previously, the savings and loan industry was long troubled by its balance sheet configuration of long-term assets and short-term liabilities. The adjustable-rate mortgage was a device to reduce the effective maturity of mortgages. Responding to this needed change in asset maturities, federal regulators authorized the regulated use of adjustable-rate mortgages nationally in 1981. [Stutzer and Roberds 1985.]

3. Off-Balance-Sheet Innovations.   In the 1980s, banks have increasingly emphasized so-called off-balance-sheet sources of income. These sources generate fee-for-service income rather than interest on loans and investments, which have been the traditional sources of bank income. Examples of these innovations include loan guarantees, letters of credit, currency and interest rate swaps, and forward-rate agreements. These innovations have fostered an ongoing debate about the need for adjustments to monetary policy [see BIS 1986, pp. 1–8].

B. Financial Innovations Complicate the Conduct of Monetary Policy

There are three ways in which financial innovations have complicated the conduct of monetary policy. First, some innovations have made it more difficult for policymakers to define and control the monetary aggregates. Second, other innovations have changed how monetary policy affects different segments of the economy. Third, some innovations have made it necessary to consider regulatory changes to ensure the continued safety and soundness of the banking system. Each of these three complications is considered below.

1. Defining the Aggregates. Liability management innovations have complicated monetary policymaking by making it more difficult to define meaningful monetary aggregates. Historically, the money measures have been defined according to their function—either as a *medium of exchange* or as a temporary *store of value*. For example, demand deposits serve primarily as a medium of exchange, while savings accounts serve primarily as a store of value. Virtually all economists agree it is crucial to control the supply of the media of exchange, which are items the Fed includes in its M1 aggregate.

Before banks developed liability management innovations, the distinction between bank transaction accounts and store-of-value accounts was clear. The former were demand deposits and the latter were time and savings deposits. With the advent of certain financial innovations, however, the distinction between the two categories has blurred. Shifting funds from store-of-value accounts to transaction accounts has become virtually costless. Moreover, banks now offer interest-bearing deposit accounts (for example, NOW accounts) that combine both functions.

In response to these financial innovations, the Fed redefined M1 to include NOW and ATS accounts to obtain a better measure of the media of exchange. The Fed also redefined M2 (a measure of money as a store of value) to include overnight Eurodollars, repurchase agreements, and shares in money market mutual funds. Other redefinitions were necessary as well [see Duprey 1982, pp. 10–13].

2. Economic Effects of Monetary Policy. Financial innovations have also changed how monetary policy affects certain segments of the economy. For example, variable-rate mortgages have exposed millions of homeowners to a source of interest rate risk virtually nonexistent before 1980. That is, homeowners' monthly mortgage payments can change in response to movements in market interest rates. Most of these mortgages contain provisions limiting the amount that monthly payments can be adjusted in any one year and provisions setting a cap on the maximum payment that can ever be reached. Even so, at some future time it may become politically difficult to control inflation if anti-inflation policies are accompanied by sharply higher interest rates. One result of rising rates—higher mortgage payments—could force lenders to foreclose on some homeowners. And more generally, all variable-rate borrowers would be adversely affected.

3. Regulatory Changes. While some of the newer financial innovations could potentially reduce risk, they also have the potential to increase risk if used improperly. For example, hedging a fixed-rate mortgage position in the futures market may reduce interest rate risk. If, however, the hedge is made incorrectly, it could reinforce the interest rate risk a bank or S&L was attempting to eliminate in the first place.

V. THE INTERPLAY BETWEEN BANK REGULATION AND MONETARY POLICY

There are two main objectives of bank regulation in the United States: (a) to maintain the safety of the banking system and (b) to facilitate the conduct of monetary policy. Although the regulatory authorities have other goals, these two are the most important. Incidentally, they are the same goals pursued by most central banks worldwide. Both goals are closely interrelated: Maintaining a safe banking system— one essentially immune from bank runs and financial panics—is a necessary condition for the efficient conduct of monetary policy.

A. Maintaining a Safe Banking System

Although banks are less regulated today than they were just a few years ago, they are still rather heavily regulated compared with firms in most other industries.[1] These regulations are mainly intended to preserve bank safety. Among the most important are capital requirements, which specify minimum permissible ratios of equity to assets for banks and bank holding companies. Also restricted is the type of assets banks may hold, which in essence prohibits assets with highly volatile values. Banks are also required to diversify their loan portfolios; essentially, a bank is not allowed to loan more than ten percent of its equity capital to any one borrower. There are also entry restrictions in banking: Individuals wishing to enter the business must establish that they have adequate equity capital and expertise and that sufficient demand for bank services exists where they plan to locate. The rationale behind these entry restrictions is to limit the number of small, newly opened banks that fail.

---

[1]There are a number of different bank regulatory agencies, including the Comptroller of the Currency, the Federal Reserve System, the Federal Deposit Insurance Corporation, and the state banking commissions in each of the states. In some instances, specific regulations may differ among the agencies. However, these differences tend to be slight and in recent years lessening.

There are other forms of government intervention which, though not strictly considered as bank regulation, nevertheless have the objective of guaranteeing bank safety. For example, the Fed's discount window is intended to serve as a source of emergency borrowing for banks experiencing large, unexpected withdrawals. Also, the Federal Deposit Insurance Corporation (FDIC) was formed to guarantee the safety of bank deposits, at least up to a maximum amount. This removes any uncertainty about the security of deposits and reduces deposit-holders' incentive to participate in bank runs.

B. Facilitating the Conduct of Monetary Policy

Several forms of government intervention—reserve requirements and the discount window—are *directly* related to the conduct of monetary policy. In addition, there are regulations requiring banks to report detailed and timely information to the Fed—information necessary for measuring the monetary aggregates.[2] *Indirectly,* regulations aimed at preserving bank safety may also work to facilitate monetary policy conduct. That is, the Fed's effectiveness in achieving monetary policy objectives may depend on the health of the banking industry. Therefore, the distinction between the two main objectives of regulation is actually a bit hazy.

Since monetary policy works initially through the banking system, major disruptions in banking may substantially reduce the Fed's ability to conduct monetary policy. During the Great Depression, for example, economic activity fell at an alarming rate. The situation called for an expansionary monetary policy. Although the Fed did inject large amounts of reserves into the banking system, the money supply didn't respond as expected. This was partly because many banks increased their reserve holdings in excess of requirements. Students of the Depression believe this was in part due to the many bank failures (over 9,000 between 1930 and 1935) and the resulting caution of surviving banks. It has been argued [in Friedman and Schwartz 1963] that the Fed could have—and should have—intervened even more drastically by providing still more reserves. Even so, the evidence suggests that during the Depression, the conduct of monetary policy

---

[2]There are other forms of bank regulation, not discussed here, which are intended to promote competition in the markets for financial services. Primarily, these include various restrictions on mergers or acquisitions of one bank by another bank that operates in the same marketplace. Many forms of anticompetitive behavior are directly prohibited, too. These include cooperative rate-setting (collusive interest rate fixing between banks) and tied sales.

was complicated enormously by the problems of the banking industry. Economic relationships previously viewed as stable could no longer be relied on and, in particular, the relation between bank reserves and the money supply was dramatically altered.

More generally, whenever the Fed implements a significant change in monetary policy, it produces a shock to the banking system—particularly if that change is unanticipated. A large shock can cause problems for commercial banks and, naturally, some will be harder hit than others. If the banking industry is in weak financial condition, the Fed may feel considerable constraint in pursuing monetary policy objectives, since it is not eager to cause large numbers of bank failures.

VI. BANK REGULATION: SOME BROADER ISSUES

So far, we have discussed bank regulation only in the context of monetary policy and have concluded that, insofar as regulation promotes bank safety, monetary policy conduct is also likely to be facilitated. Next, we consider some additional issues in bank regulation, presenting arguments from both sides of the old and continuing debate over the need for regulation.

A. Arguments against Regulation

Some economists would argue that bank regulation is fundamentally undesirable. Their view [see, for instance, Fama 1980], basically, is that banks are no different from other firms and therefore need not be regulated any more or less than these others. For example, some scholars [Rolnick and Weber 1984] have reviewed the evidence from the Free Banking Era (a period when U. S. banks were minimally regulated) and have concluded that when banks were little regulated, the system actually worked quite well. Others have reviewed the same period, however, and concluded just the opposite.

Those who favor little or no regulation of banks argue that regulation is not only unnecessary, but genuinely harmful. It interferes with free market forces, confounds interest rates as allocators of investment, and restricts the mobility of capital. Undoubtedly, there is truth to their arguments, and estimates of the historical costs of bank regulation suggest that the costs have been substantial [Taggart 1978, Pyle 1974].

In recent years, a quite different argument against bank regulation has developed. Nonbank firms now supply many of the same services traditionally supplied by commercial banks, and these nonbank firms are generally much less regulated. It is argued, therefore, that nonbank firms have an unfair competitive advantage over banks. Although the data are mixed, some evidence supports the view that commercial banks are losing their share in some markets [Federal Reserve Bank of New York 1986]. As a result, the argument goes, bank regulations should be loosened so that banks can compete on an even playing field with their many nonbank competitors.

B. Arguments Supporting Regulation

In contrast, advocates of bank regulation argue that banks are essentially different from other firms and, consequently, some special regulations are warranted. Two basic arguments are given in support of their position. The first we have already considered; that is, banks play a special and unique role in the conduct of monetary policy. The second argument is that, unlike other firms, banks are inherently susceptible to liquidity problems and bank runs. This susceptibility, they argue, is due to the nature of bank liabilities, many of which have extremely short maturities—unavoidably so, since they are used for transaction purposes. As E. Gerald Corrigan [1982, p. 9], president of the New York Fed, explains

> ... the critical difference between banks and other classes of financial institutions rests with the capacity of banks to incur (and to create) liabilities that are payable on demand at par and that are readily transferable to third parties. The resulting mismatch of the maturities of assets and liabilities makes banks particularly vulnerable to sudden drains on deposits that can jeopardize their solvency.

Recent research [Diamond and Dybvig 1983, Chari and Jagannathan 1986] supports this view, showing that even when all agents in an economy are perfectly rational, bank runs are still likely. Moreover, bank runs may not be confined to a single institution. History indicates that for various reasons, bank runs can spread from one institution to another. Again, there are fundamental economic reasons why this may occur, even if all bank depositors are rational economic agents. For instance, banks lend to one another, so if one bank fails, losses may be transmitted to others. More generally, banks are in a relatively homogeneous line of business, and their profits and losses tend to be positively correlated. Thus, from the depositor's perspective, problems at one bank may signal problems at others. And since there is usually little cost to withdrawing transaction deposits, bank runs may be transmitted across institutions.

Such problems in the banking sector may complicate the Fed's task in carrying out monetary policy. They may also have other undesirable external effects on the economy. In particular, by making it difficult to execute payments, they may interfere with the normal conduct of commerce. This occurred during the Great Depression and, in a much more limited way, during the recent thrift crisis in Ohio [see Federal Reserve Bank of Cleveland 1985].

C. Solving One Problem Has Created Another

The point is that bank runs and failures, particularly the contagious kind, may have significant external costs for the economy, including, but not limited to, their effects on monetary policy conduct. In this country, the response to such problems has been to establish the Fed's discount window and the FDIC. These regulatory devices have largely solved the problem of bank runs by eliminating the incentive for depositors to withdraw funds. However, these devices have caused other fundamental problems, not well recognized until recently. The discount window and deposit insurance tend to defeat the free market mechanisms which normally constrain a bank's incentive to take risks. That is, if a bank's creditors are, by intent, protected by these devices, as a result they may not care much about their bank's taking undue risks. But if not protected by government, they surely would care.

Theoretically, the effect of the discount window and deposit insurance may even be stronger than this suggests, giving bank managers an actual *preference* for risk-seeking behavior. After all, bank managers are involved in a gamble in which "heads, we win; tails, the FDIC loses." This twisting of incentives, sometimes referred to as *moral hazard,* has been widely discussed in the academic literature on banking [Kareken and Wallace 1978, Merton 1977, Sharpe 1978].

The dilemma should now be clear. Even if bank regulation was unnecessary *before* the establishment of the discount window and deposit insurance, it appears to be necessary *after* these regulatory devices are in place. Otherwise—and this is hardly an exaggeration— government intervention has created an environment in which banks have the ability and incentive to gamble with the public's money. Of course, the discount window and deposit insurance could be eliminated. But then we would again be confronted with the real possibility of bank runs and banking instability.

There are other possible ways of dealing with instability in banking—ways that would not have such undesirable side effects. For instance, a system of 100 percent reserve banking has been proposed as early as 1935 [Hart 1935] and as recently as 1983 [Kareken 1983]. The idea, very simply, is to match all bank transaction liabilities with assets of equally short maturity and with no default risk. If banks were restricted to holding only such assets, depositors would have no reason to trigger bank runs, so deposit insurance and the discount window would be unnecessary. This sort of system is theoretically very appealing and is being actively debated by bankers, regulators, and economists. However, to implement such a 100 percent reserve system would require a radical change in our banking system. And, although this sort of system has been discussed for years, it's never been actually tried. As Corrigan [1982, p. 12] aptly observes,

> There have been, or are, schemes for conducting monetary policy and operating a payments mechanism that do not use bank reserves and the banking system in the way the U. S. system currently operates. However, it is also true that any of these alternative arrangements would entail major institutional changes and run the risk that they might not work as efficiently as the current framework or the possibility that they might not work at all. In short, to justify departure from the current arrangement the weight of evidence should be overwhelming that the current system is not working or that some alternative system would work decidedly better.

VII. SUMMARY

Ultimately, monetary policy affects all sectors of the economy, but it works through and has its initial effects upon the banking sector. Whenever the Fed changes monetary or regulatory policy, the banking industry may respond by creating new asset or liability instruments, opening new financial markets, or inventing new portfolio strategies. In recent years, such changes have occurred at an extremely rapid pace and through processes not easily predicted. Such financial innovations have profoundly changed the way monetary policy is conducted. Each new innovation temporarily complicates policymaking as monetary authorities take time to learn how interest rates, the monetary aggregates, and their interrelationships are affected. With so much financial innovation in recent years, policymakers have been hard pressed to keep up with the changes.

Recent years have also witnessed the heating up of an old debate: How much, if any, bank regulation is desirable? Increasingly, the debate has centered on equitable competition between bank and nonbank firms—the so-called *level playing-field* concept. While equitable competition among financial intermediaries is a worthy objective, so too is the effective conduct of monetary policy. Fundamentally, banks are regulated for two reasons: to maintain the safety of the banking system and to facilitate the conduct of monetary policy. The two objectives are not really distinct, however. An effective monetary policy may be difficult to conduct if many banks are in weak financial condition, and even more difficult if many banks are failing.

The regulatory system now in place in the United States has largely solved one major safety problem in banking—the problem of runs and panics—through deposit insurance and the discount window. These regulatory devices, however, have solved this problem only to create another one that has only been widely recognized in recent years. This is the problem of *moral hazard,* the disruption of natural market forces that constrain the risk-taking of banks. Even if bank regulation was unnecessary before these regulatory devices, it is necessary now that they are in place.

Of course, it may be possible to devise other mechanisms that solve the bank instability problem without resulting in moral hazard. One hundred percent reserve banking is a possible solution that is theoretically very appealing.

HOW AN OPEN-MARKET OPERATION INCREASES THE MONEY SUPPLY

The process by which a Fed purchase of securities increases the money supply is illustrated below. T accounts are used to show the relevant changes in the balance sheets of the Fed and the banks involved.

Transaction 1

In transaction (1), the Fed purchases $1,000 of Treasury bills by asking for bids from dealers in U. S. government securities. Suppose bank A offers the lowest price. Since bank A must keep its reserve account at the Fed, the bookkeeping entries are as follows: The Fed increases its securities portfolio (S) and bank A's reserve account (R_A) by $1,000. On its own books, bank A increases its reserve account at the Fed (R) and reduces its securities portfolio (S) by $1,000. Fed reserve requirements stipulate that banks maintain reserve balances at the Fed (plus currency in their vaults) no lower than a specified proportion of checkable deposits. If bank A held the required amount of reserves at the time of the Fed's open-market operation, the $1,000 added to its reserves would be excess reserves (XR) and thus would be available for making loans. (Simply because a bank has excess reserves does not necessarily mean those funds will be lent. The bank may choose to hold excess reserves even though the Fed does not pay interest on such balances. In this example, however, we assume bank A does not want to hold excess reserves.)

Transaction 2

In transaction (2), bank A uses its entire excess reserve balance to make a loan to a customer, and credits that borrower's checkable deposit account. The borrower immediately uses the proceeds to issue a check to a creditor, who is a deposit customer of bank B. Upon receipt of the check, bank B places it in the nation's check-clearing system, and in short order it is returned to bank A. The bookkeeping entries are as follows: Bank A increases its loans (L) and reduces its reserve balance at the Fed (R) by $1,000. Bank B increases its customer's checkable deposit balance (D) and its reserve balance at the Fed (R) by $1,000. The Fed increases bank B's reserve balance (R_B) and decreases bank A's reserve balance (R_A) by $1,000.

Suppose that the Fed's required reserve ratio for checkable deposits is 10 percent. Further assume that depositors do not exchange part of their increased deposits for currency. The increase of $1,000 in deposits at bank B means that its required reserves (RR) rise by $100, so that its excess reserves (XR) available for lending is $900 (the $1,000 increase in reserves minus the $100 increase in required reserves).

Transaction 3

Transaction (3) in the example follows the same pattern as transaction (2) assuming, of course, that bank B does not wish to hold excess reserves. The $900 increase in checkable deposits at bank C means that required reserves at bank C rise by $90, leaving $810 in excess reserves for making new loans.

The Money Multiplier

As this process continues from bank to bank, the amount of each new loan and deposit diminishes because each bank needs to hold additional reserves against new deposits. At the end of this process, the aggregate increase in deposits resulting from the initial open-market operation can be shown mathematically to be $\Delta D = \Delta S/r$, where ΔD = the change in deposits, ΔS = the change in the Fed's securities holdings, and r = the required reserve ratio. Substituting, we have $\Delta D = \$1,000/.10 = \$10,000$. This $10,000 is the increase in deposits caused by the Fed's initial $1,000 purchase of T bills from bank A.

The ratio of the change in the Fed's securities holdings to the change in bank deposits is called the *money multiplier.* In this example, therefore, the money multiplier is 10,000/1,000 = 10. Relaxing the assumptions used for this example increases the complexity of the process, but does not change the basic conclusion that the money supply increases by some multiple of the increase in the Fed's securities.

T-Account Illustration

	Federal Reserve				Bank A	
	Assets	Liabilities			Assets	Liabilities
(1)	(S) +1,000	(R$_A$) +1,000		(1)	(R) +1,000 (XR) +1,000 (S) −1,000	
(2)		(R$_B$) +1,000 (R$_A$) −1,000		(2)	(R) −1,000 (XR) −1,000 (L) +1,000	
(3)		(R$_C$) +900 (R$_B$) −900				

	Bank B				Bank C	
	Assets	Liabilities			Assets	Liabilities
(2)	(R) +1,000 (RR) +100 (XR) +900	(D) +1,000				
(3)	(L) +900 (R) −900 (XR) −900			(3)	(R) +900 (RR) +90 (XR) +810	(D) +900

REFERENCES

Bank for International Settlements (BIS). 1986. "Recent Innovations in International Banking." Report produced by a Study Group established by the Central Banks of the Group of Ten Countries. Reproduced by the Federal Reserve Bank of New York. April.

Chari, V. V., and R. Jagannathan. 1986. "Banking Panics, Information, and Rational Expectations." Discussion paper, Center for Mathematical Studies in Economics and Management Science, Northwestern University. June.

Corrigan, E. Gerald. 1982. "Are Banks Special?" In *Federal Reserve Bank of Minneapolis Annual Report 1982*, pp. 5–24.

Diamond, Douglas W., and Philip H. Dybvig. 1983. "Bank Runs, Deposit Insurance, and Liquidity." *Journal of Political Economy* 91 (June): 401–19.

Duprey, James N. 1982. "How the Fed Defines and Measures Money." *Federal Reserve Bank of Minneapolis Quarterly Review* 6 (Spring–Summer): 10–19.

Eastburn, David P., and W. Lee Hoskins. 1978. "Influence of Monetary Policy on Commercial Banking." In *The Bankers' Handbook,* ed. William H. Baughn and Charls E. Walker (Homewood, Illinois: Dow Jones-Irwin): 1116–35.

Fama, Eugene F. 1980. "Banking in the Theory of Finance." *Journal of Monetary Economics* 6 (January): 39–57.

Federal Reserve Bank of Cleveland. 1985. "Unfoldings in Ohio: 1985." In *Federal Reserve Bank of Cleveland Annual Report 1985*, pp. 5–24.

Federal Reserve Bank of New York. 1986. *Recent Trends in Commercial Bank Profitability: A Staff Study.*

Flannery, Mark J. 1980. "How Do Changes in Market Interest Rates Affect Bank Profits?" *Business Review* (September/October): 13–22. Federal Reserve Bank of Philadelphia.

Friedman, Milton, and Anna Jacobson Schwartz. 1963. *A Monetary History of the United States, 1867–1960.* A study by the National Bureau of Economic Research. Princeton: Princeton University Press.

Hart, Albert G. 1935. "The Chicago Plan of Banking Reform." *Review of Economic Studies* 2: 104–16.

Kareken, John H. 1983. "Deposit Insurance Reform or Deregulation is the Cart, Not the Horse." *Federal Reserve Bank of Minneapolis Quarterly Reveiw* 7 (Spring): 1–9.

Kareken, John H., and Neil Wallace. 1978. "Deposit Insurance and Bank Regulation: A Partial-Equilibrium Exposition." *Journal of Business* 51 (July): 413–38.

Merton, Robert C. 1977. "An Analytic Derivation of the Cost of Deposit Insurance and Loan Guarantees: An Application of Modern Option Pricing Theory." *Journal of Banking and Finance* 1 (June): 3–11.

Prescott, Edward C. 1986. "Theory Ahead of Business-Cycle Measurement." In *Real Business Cycles, Real Exchange Rates and Actual Policies,* ed. Karl Brunner and Allan H. Meltzer. Carnegie-Rochester Conference Series on Public Policy 25: 11–44. Also, reprinted in *Federal Reserve Bank of Minneapolis Quarterly Review* 10 (Fall 1986): 3–22.

Pyle, David H. 1974. "The Losses on Savings Deposits from Interest Rate Regulation." *Bell Journal of Economics and Management Science* (Autumn): 614–22.

Roley, V. Vance. 1983. "The Response of Short-term Interest Rates to Weekly Money Announcements: A Note." *Journal of Money, Credit, and Banking* 15 (August): 344–54.

Rolnick, Arthur J., and Warren E. Weber. 1984. "The Causes of Free Bank Failures: A Detailed Examination." *Journal of Monetary Economics* 14 (November): 267–91.

Sargent, Thomas J., and Neil Wallace. 1981. "Some Unpleasant Monetarist Arithmetic." *Federal Reserve Bank of Minneapolis Quarterly Review* 5 (Fall): 1–17.

Sharpe, William F. 1978. "Bank Capital Adequacy, Deposit Insurance and Security Values." *Journal of Financial and Quantitative Analysis* 13 (November): 701–18.

Smith, Bruce D. 1984. "Money and Inflation in Colonial Massachusetts." *Federal Reserve Bank of Minneapolis Quarterly Review* 8 (Winter): 1–14.

Stutzer, Michael J., and William Roberds. 1985. "Adjustable Rate Mortgages: Increasing Efficiency More Than Housing Activity." *Federal Reserve Bank of Minneapolis Quarterly Review* 9 (Summer): 10–20.

Taggart, Robert A., Jr. 1978. "Effects of Deposit Rate Ceilings: The Evidence from Massachusetts Savings Banks." *Journal of Money, Credit, and Banking* 10 (May): 139–57.

Urich, Thomas, and Paul Wachtel. 1981. "Market Response to the Weekly Money Supply Announcements in the 1970s." *Journal of Finance* 36 (December): 1063–72.

———. 1984. "The Effects of Inflation and Money Supply Announcements on Interest Rates." *Journal of Finance* 39 (September): 1177–88.

Wallace, Neil. 1981. "A Modigliani-Miller Theorem for Open-Market Operations." *American Economic Review* 71 (June): 267–74.

CHAPTER EIGHTY-FOUR

The Impact of Fiscal Policy and Debt Management on the Banking System

Stuart A. Schweitzer

Vice President
Morgan Guaranty Trust Company

The finances of the federal government affect commercial banks in many ways. The budget deficit and Treasury borrowing influence economic activity and interest rates and thus exert a significant impact on the demand for credit, bank funding costs, and loan changes. Federal financing is of concern to banks in their roles as underwriters of and investors in government securities. And swings in Treasury cash balances affect banks in their role as repositories of federal monies in Treasury tax and loan accounts.

EFFECTS ON FINANCIAL MARKETS

Federal borrowing influences financial markets by increasing the demand for credit, by altering inflation expectations of financial market participants, and by increasing the dependence of U.S. borrowers on inflows of funds from abroad.

Credit demand. Federal borrowing has accounted in recent years for roughly one-fourth of total credit demand. Thus, a significant change in the budget deficit can make a substantial difference to the economy's demand for credit—and, as a result, to the level of interest rates.

Rates have to gravitate to whatever level will equate the demand for funds by borrowers with the supply that is forthcoming from domestic savers and foreign investors. That supply, it must be stressed, is importantly determined by monetary policy.

Any increase in demand that is not matched by an increase in supply will force the equilibrating level of interest rates higher. Thus, if the budget deficit and Treasury borrowing increase, and there is not an offsetting reduction in private credit demand or an increase in credit supply, interest rates will be higher than they otherwise would be.

If the economy is operating below its potential, however, an increase in the nation's budgetary deficit ordinarily would not push up interest rates. Indeed, it is primarily in those circumstances that monetary policy would be accomodative and supportive of an expansionary budget.

Inflation Expectations.   Whether inflation accelerates following a rise in the budget deficit depends upon the cyclical state of the economy and, if that is one of full employment or resource strain, on the policies followed by the Federal Reserve. If expansive budget policies are accompanied by a generally accommodative monetary policy, economic activity is likely to be pushed intermittently above the level at which shortages of labor and productive capacity put upward pressure on inflation. If, on the other hand, the Federal Reserve constrains the growth of economic activity through monetary policy, then even a very large budget deficit need not be inflationary. That is illustrated by the decline in inflation in the first half of the 1980s, even though the federal deficit rose to record levels.

Inflows from Abroad.   In the circumstances of the 1980s, capital, worldwide, sought out assets in the U.S. because prospective returns here (adjusted for perceived currency risk) were higher than elsewhere. This, in turn, was partly the product of large federal deficits, which helped to keep interest rates in this country higher than they otherwise would have been. Budget deficits also encouraged capital inflows by boosting economic growth, adding to foreigners' perceptions that the U.S. was a comparatively high-performing economy— with correspondingly high prospective returns. Capital inflows helped to drive up the dollar, thus pricing American goods out of foreign markets. The result: An unprecedented trade deficit.

When, subsequently, the trade deficit became so large that it undermined U.S. production, interest rates naturally fell sharply and so did the dollar (since prospective dollar returns diminished). The federal budget deficit, meanwhile, was little changed.

CONGRESSIONAL BUDGET PROCESS

Financial markets keep a close watch on the budget process for signs of possible change in Treasury borrowing requirements. Ironically, however, for all the attention that Congress gives it, a budget is never enacted into law. Indeed, the budget results from the interaction of the economy with a myriad of separate laws governing taxes and spending. The process of budget decision making has changed considerably over the years, as Congress has searched for a way to discipline its decisions over the individual components of the budget.

Economist Arthur F. Burns once observed that "no major democracy that I know of has had a more deficient legislative budget process than the United States." Throughout most of U.S. history, Congress lacked an orderly approach for reviewing and modifying the president's budget proposals. Before enactment of the so-called Budget Control Act of 1974, neither Senate nor House deliberations involved any link between revenues and expenditures. Tax issues were resolved by committees that had no concern with expenditures, and expenditure issues were parceled out among a dozen or so appropriations subcommittees that carried on their work independently of one another and almost invariably finished their work at different times. The whole process was haphazard in the extreme. Budgets simply happened; they were never planned.

Growing impatience with those procedures—and with the bias they produced toward deficits because of the absence of any focal point of responsibility for results—finally produced in the mid-1970s the present structure of congresssional budget review committees that in theory is supposed to provide a coherent, disciplined approach to budget making. In fact, the deficiencies of the Congressional budget process are as egregious as ever—more so when measured by the succession of bloated deficits and the perpetual fiscal disarray that has characterized the 1980s.

Mounting congressional frustration with the budget situation led to the adoption in late 1985 of the Gramm-Rudman-Hollings apparatus for automatic, across-the-board spending cuts if Congress fails to meet specified deficit targets. In crude political terms, the chief attraction of G-R-H as enacted was that it seemingly provided a means of achieving deficit reduction without the need for recorded votes on individual programs enjoying strong constituency support. The courts, however, promptly struck down its arrangements for automaticity, forcing Congress to take responsibility for achieving (or not achieving) the deficit targets in G-R-H. And while Congress, in 1987, enacted new procedures designed to overcome constitutional objections, it also liberalized G-R-H's deficit targets.

Budget Calendar.   The annual cycle of budget decision-making begins with budget proposals by the President each January. The President's budget is reviewed by the House and Senate Budget Committees, with the aid of the Congressional Budget Office. The

Budget Committees' own budget plans are summarized in budget resolutions. The two houses of Congress are charged with passing a concurrent resolution by April 15.

A budget resolution is only a statement of Congressional intent and is passed without the concurrence of the president. After a resolution is passed, Congress must enact legislation to determine spending and taxes. About half of federal spending—including virtually all military spending, as well as outlays for such things as education and agriculture—is determined by appropriations laws, measures that provide "budget authority" to government departments. Other federal spending, including most entitlement programs, is governed not by annual appropriations but by laws that have to be changed if Congress wants to achieve some budgetary objective. Such budget-related spending changes, as well as budget-related changes in tax laws, generally are made through a so-called reconciliation bill, a measure whose name reflects the notion that it is supposed to reconcile Congress' legislative actions with its previously passed budget resolution. In reality, however, there often are major differences between Congress' plans and its implementing legislation.

All appropriations and reconciliation legislation are supposed to be enacted prior to the start of a fiscal year on October 1. As a practical matter, however, Congress often fails to complete the necessary legislation on time, and has to enact "continuing resolutions" to keep the government operating until the necessary appropriations legislation passes.

Debt Limit.   In addition to legislation governing spending and taxes, Congress also periodically sets a new limit on the amount of Treasury debt that can be outstanding. While Congress has no choice but to authorize an increase in the national debt once it has authorized spending in excess of likely tax collections, legislation concerning the debt limit typically is used as a vehicle for efforts in Congress to impose new constraints on spending. Indeed, after passing a budget resolution and all necessary appropriations and reconciliation legislation, Congress frequently will approve an increase in the debt limit sufficient to last only a few weeks or months rather than the full fiscal year. Typically, the intention in these situations is to force Congress to revisit budget issues before the fiscal year is out.

Gramm-Rudman-Hollings.   This law calls for the deficit to be reduced gradually to zero by 1993—either via Congressional action or through automatic spending cuts if Congress does not achieve preset annual targets (exceptions are allowed in the event of war or recession). Prior to each fiscal year, the Office of Management and Budget (OMB) calculates the prospective budget deficit, the expected savings from enacted budget cuts, and the additional spending cuts that would be necessary to achieve the target for the year. OMB takes account of similar calculations by the Congressional Budget Office (CBO), but the CBO analysis is not binding. If OMB determines that the deficit has not been reduced as much as required, the law requires that OMB formulate for the president's signature a schedule of across-the-board spending cuts to close the gap.

TREASURY BORROWING

The Treasury's responsibilities for debt management go beyond raising the funds to finance a given year's budget deficit. There is the continuous need to provide for the refunding of maturing debt—Treasury bills, with maturities of up to one year; notes, with maturities from 2 to 10 years; and bonds, with maturities of over 10 years.[1]

The public debt outstanding grew from $710 billion at the end of fiscal 1980 to $1.757 trillion at the end of fiscal 1986.[2] Four categories make up that 1986 debt total:

1. Some $86 billion was held by individuals in "nonmarketable" savings bonds (nonmarketable in the sense that a holder can sell his savings bonds only to the Treasury). Commercial banks are the principal agents for the Treasury in the sale of savings bonds to the public.
2. Some $107 billion of other nonmarketable funds were outstanding. Almost all were in the form of so-called SLUGs—securities issued to states and local governments—which serve as a temporary investment outlet for the proceeds of bond issues by states and localities.
3. Some $191 billion of marketable securities were held by the Federal Reserve System—debt that the Fed has acquired over

---

[1]Treasury debt managers also must plan to meet temporary seasonal cash needs, since large revenue inflows occur periodically during the year (in April, for example, when personal tax returns are due), while expenditures tend to be spaced fairly evenly throughout the year. For this reason, so-called cash-management bills, scheduled to mature when tax receipts are strongest, are offered occasionally by the Treasury.

[2]These figures exclude Treasury debt that is owed to federal entities such as the Social Security and Civil Service Retirement Trust Funds. Such intra-governmental debt—$366 billion at the end of fiscal 1986—is counted as part of the national debt for purposes of the statutory debt ceiling, but does not raise any funds to finance the federal deficit.

CHART 1 Average Maturity of Treasury Debt (privately held marketable securities)

Years

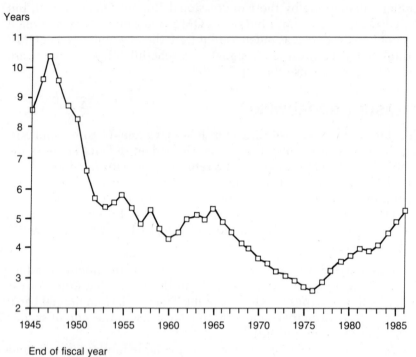

End of fiscal year

SOURCE: U.S. Treasury Department.

the years to expand the reserves of the banking system and facilitate the growth of the money stock.

4. The remainder—$1.374 trillion—represented the marketable debt held by other investors, including individuals, banks, corporations, pension funds, and international investors.

Maturity Distribution. Over the years, marked change has occurred in the maturity distribution of marketable borrowing and, thus, outstanding debt. The debt, as measured by its "average maturity," grew appreciably shorter from its post-World War II high until the mid-1970s, and has been lengthened somewhat since then (Chart 1). Indeed, while Treasury bills accounted for almost half of net marketable borrowing in 1975, their share dropped to roughly 12 percent by 1986 as the net issuance of notes and bonds increased sharply.

Securities are auctioned by the Treasury according to a fairly fixed schedule. Three- and six-month Treasury bills are auctioned each week, one-year bills every four weeks, and two-year notes every month. Most other notes and bonds are grouped into one of two sets of auctions—a mid-quarter "refunding," in which 3- and 10-year notes and 30-year bonds are sold early in the second month of each quarter, and an end-of-quarter "minirefunding," in which 4- and 7-year notes are auctioned late in the final month of each quarter. Also, five-year notes are offered once a quarter, late in the second month.

ROLE OF BANKS IN THE TREASURY MARKET

Commercial banks play major roles both as dealers and investors in treasury securities.

Banks as Dealers.   Treasury debt is sold through an over-the-counter market at the center of which are 40 "primary dealers" (including 17 affiliated with commercial banks) designated by the Federal Reserve Bank of New York. These dealers are the only ones eligible to trade with the open market desk at the New York Fed, which undertakes open market operations on behalf of the Federal Reserve System. Commercial banks of all sizes play a limited dealer role in the government securities market, submitting orders for new Treasury securities on behalf of their nonbank customers (both businesses and households), but the bulk of government-securities activity is undertaken by large banks.

To be designated a primary dealer, a government bond dealer must meet several criteria established by the Federal Reserve Bank of New York. A firm must make a secondary market in the full range of Treasury issues for a reasonably diverse group of customers, and must be committed to being a "market maker" over the long term. It must participate meaningfully as a buyer in Treasury auctions. It must have management depth and experience and good internal controls and report daily on its activity to the Federal Reserve Bank of New York. And it must have sufficient capital to support its activities and prudently manage its risk exposure.

The growth of the federal debt, together with increased volatility of interest rates since the late 1970s, has spurred a significant increase in government securities trading and hence the activities of government securities dealers. The dollar volume of transactions by government securities dealers has more than quadrupled since 1980.

Banks as Investors.   Commercial banks are major buyers of Treasury securities, having acquired over 10 percent of the net new debt issued

---

CHART 2 Bank Credit

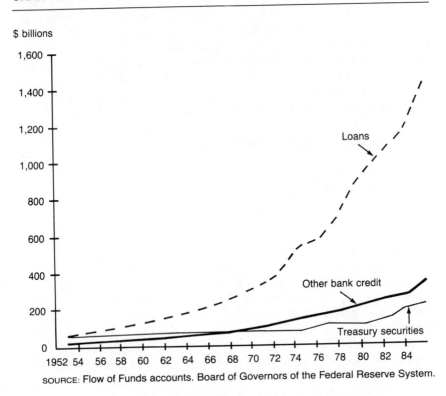

$ billions

SOURCE: Flow of Funds accounts. Board of Governors of the Federal Reserve System.

by the Treasury from 1980 through 1985. Treasury securities play numerous roles in bank portfolios: They provide liquidity, since Treasury securities can readily be used as collateral for short-term borrowings through the sale of Treasuries to short-term lenders under agreements to repurchase them. Treasury securities may also serve as collateral against borrowings at the Federal Reserve discount window, Treasury Tax and Loan accounts, and deposits from states and local governments. In addition, Treasury securities assist a bank in limiting the overall riskiness of its portfolio.

As important as Treasury securities are in bank portfolios, their importance is nothing like it was in the early 1950s, for example, when banks held as much in Treasury securities as loans (Chart 2). During World War II, when government financing needs were enormous, banks acquired a commensurate volume of government securities, and were sated with them for a long while afterwards. As economic activity gained steam in the postwar years, and bank loan demand picked up,

TABLE 1 Net Acquisition of Treasury Securities (annual averages)

	Dollar amounts (in billions)			
	1950s	1960s	1970s	1980–85
Federal Reserve	0.8	3.1	6.0	10.6
Commercial banking	−0.8	−0.4	4.3	16.5
Nonbank financial	0.5	−0.4	4.9	50.1
Households	0.3	2.5	9.0	40.5
Foreign	0.8	.0	10.9	15.7
Other	1.5	−0.6	2.8	23.0
Total	2.0	4.2	38.0	156.5

	Percent of total			
	1950s	1960s	1970s	1980–85
Federal Reserve	39.1	72.9	15.9	6.8
Commercial banking	−40.5	−9.4	11.4	10.6
Nonbank financial	−26.7	−8.6	12.9	32.0
Households	13.4	58.6	23.7	25.9
Foreign	40.8	1.1	28.6	10.0
Other	73.9	−14.6	7.5	14.7
Total	100.0	100.0	100.0	100.0

SOURCE: Flow of Funds Acocunts, Board of Governors of the Federal Reserve System.

banks reduced their Treasury portfolios slightly to help finance the addition to loans (Table 1). It was not until the mid-1970s that banks began to add again to their holdings of Treasuries, as they sought to balance the growth in their loans with expanded holdings of risk-free assets—and, of course, as the supply of Treasury securities itself began to increase substantially, with deficit finance becoming the norm of the federal government.

TREASURY TAX AND LOAN ACCOUNTS

On a day-to-day basis, the aspect of Treasury finances that is perhaps most important to banks is the fluctuation in Treasury cash balances. The Treasury's cash is maintained in two forms—as deposits with the Federal Reserve and as investments in Treasury Tax and Loan (TT&L) accounts at commercial banks. The government's cash balances fluctuate considerably—ranging in 1986, for instance, from a low of $4.6 billion to a high of $42.5 billion. Under an agreement with the Federal Reserve, the Treasury endeavors to maintain a relatively stable balance of $3 billion at the Fed. Thus, the amount of Treasury cash placed in bank TT&L accounts fluctuates considerably.

Deposit Accounts. The Treasury maintains two types of accounts with depository institutions—TT&L *deposit* accounts and TT&L *note* accounts. TT&L deposit accounts are noninterest bearing, demand accounts of the Treasury. Institutions designated as Tax and Loan Depositories may receive tax payments on behalf of the Treasury, crediting such payments to their TT&L deposit accounts. Such accounts are subject to reserve requirements. Under Treasury rules, a bank has the interest-free use of any (collected) funds in its TT&L deposit account until the business day following the crediting of tax deposits. In fact, during the interest-free period, the balances in TT&L deposit accounts are not even counted by the Treasury as part of its operating cash balance.

Note Accounts. On the next business day following the crediting of funds to a bank's TT&L deposit account, one of two events occurs: (1) The bank remits the funds to the Federal Reserve for the Treasury's account, or (2) if the bank is authorized as a TT&L note depository, it will transfer the previous day's tax deposits into its TT&L note account. TT&L note accounts are interest-bearing, fully collateralized[3] liabilities of depository institutions; they are not deposit accounts, and hence are not subject to reserve requirements. Banks are obligated to pay interest to the Treasury on TT&L note accounts at a rate equal to the weekly-average federal funds rate less one-quarter of a percentage point.

The amount of funds in the TT&L note account of an individual bank is affected not only by tax deposits received by the bank but also by "direct investments" of funds taken by Treasury from its Fed account and placed with depository institutions, and also by "calls" of funds back from such depositories and into Treasury's Fed account. Treasury classifies banks into three categories—A, B, and C, according to the size of each bank's deposits—and allocates direct investments and calls according to a bank's size.

---

[3]Depository institutions are required to pledge collateral to secure their tax and loan note account balances. Eligible collateral includes: Securities of the U.S. government and agencies, the World Bank, and student loan authorities, counted at face value; obligations of the States and Puerto Rico, and commercial and agricultural paper (i.e., loans) and banker's acceptances approved by the Federal Reserve, counted at 90 percent of face value; and obligations of counties, cities, and other local government bodies, counted at 80 percent of face value. As a result of TT&L collateral requirements, any increase in a depository institution's note balance absorbs a portion of the collateral that would otherwise be available to support window borrowings.

MAKING HARD CHOICES

Given the magnitude of the deficit problem, the congressional quest to reform budgetary procedures seems likely to continue. But deficiency of procedure is not the fundamental cause of the problem. Rather, it is lack of consensus as to the appropriate use of limited national resources.

The budget deficit has been reduced from more than 5 percent of gross national product in 1984–86 to around 3½ percent in fiscal 1987. While this represents a constructive start toward more responsible budgeting, there remains a wide gulf between spending and receipts. That gulf is not bridgeable by process or procedure, but by a new agreement on the economic policy goals that Washington should aim to achieve.

While considerable lip service is paid to the necessity of balancing the budget, action is slow in coming because the financial-market effects of sustained deficits have largely been masked by the availability of increased financing from abroad. The rapid accumulation of federal debt and the complementary rise in U.S. external indebtedness, however, has set in motion huge claims on future resouces. Sadly, a really determined effort to slow the rate of federal debt accumulation appears unlikely until the debt burden becomes so difficult to manage that action becomes unavoidable.

CHAPTER EIGHTY-FIVE

The Outlook for Banking in the Next Ten Years

Dr. Charles M. Williams

George Gund Professor of Commercial Banking, Emeritus
Harvard University

This author's assignment is to project major changes in commercial banking in the decade ahead. Before undertaking this challenging task, let me freely acknowledge that my crystal ball is no less murky than those of most prognosticators who have demonstrated the fragility of longer term forecasts in dynamic interactive environments. Remember the "checkless society," the $80 a barrel oil by 1988, and the "Club of Rome" predictions of eminent shortage of food and almost all natural resources—all eminently sponsored, well argued, widely accepted, and very wrong.

It is easy to accept the conventional view that major changes in the banking industry are underway and more are in prospect. Truly the industry is in transition from long established patterns—but transition to what? And at what pace? And what will separate the banking organizations that will make change their ally from the losers or also rans?

In trying to respond usefully to these daunting questions, I will focus on a few areas I see as especially significant. The risks of my overlooking or underestimating other developments that will prove important are reduced by the fact that the authors of most of the preceding chapters have been forward looking as they have addressed their specialities.

INCREASING DIVERSITY WITHIN THE "COMMERCIAL BANKING INDUSTRY"—WILL THE TREND CONTINUE?

My answer is a categorical "yes!" Recent years have been characterized by widening differences in pattern of operations, market focus and emphasis, and outlook between the major classes of commercial banks—money center or "global banks," regionals, and community oriented banks. Thus, Bankers Trust has progressively less and less in common with the First National Bank of Dodge City, Kansas. Moreover, the pursuit of increasingly divergent and distinctive strategies by banks in the same category has heightened the differences between the individual banks. Over time, the differences between, say, Morgan and Chemical, Citibank and Manufacturers Hanover, or Bankers Trust and Irving Trust, should widen further. The developing heterogeneity within the industry makes use of industry averages less useful and analyses of "*the* industry" or generalizations about changes in it conducive to oversimplification.

THE COMPETITIVE CLIMATE IN THE YEARS AHEAD: INTENSIFYING PRESSURES?

A key determinant of the rate and degree of change in the banking business is the sense of competitive pressure experienced by the leaders of the banks. Some banking leaders relish opportunities for new initiatives and major changes of direction or emphasis for their organizations. But, leading academic studies (and the author's observations) suggest that most leaders of reasonably successful businesses embrace the stresses and risks inherent in major new initiatives into unfamiliar areas reluctantly, indeed only when the hazards of carrying on in traditional fashion become painfully apparent and formidable. Fear of not measuring up can be an especially powerful stimulant to change for top managers in periods of corporate mobility; most find the role of the hunter decidedly preferable to that of the hunted.

Few banking leaders, I believe, will challenge a judgement that the competitive pressures on them and their banks have intensified in recent years. Examination of the sources of the more formidable competitive pressures leads inexorably, I believe, to the conclusion that these pressures will gain further force, not ease, in the decade ahead. Several factors have contributed to more intense intraindustry competition in both funding and asset use. A first is the growth of foreign-owned banks in the U.S. Despite the mediocre results of some foreign entrants (i.e., Midland and Crocker), the attractions of the U.S. market and the relative ease of entry by acquisition or by new branch offices have led many foreign banks to initiate or expand U.S. activities. An ability to operate on purchased dollars and with low overheads has encouraged the building of loan volumes through very aggressive pricing. Although some foreign banks that have built sizeable U.S. loan totals may become less aggressive in loan pricing, it is likely that the competitive impact of the foreign banks overall will continue to grow. Japanese banks, particularly, already a force in some U.S. markets, should expand their efforts and impact in the U.S. and other world markets.

The process of dismantling state barriers to geographical expansion, now well under way, should continue and indeed accelerate. Interbank competition can be expected to become more fluid and wide ranging.

An equal or more important source of competition for the corporate loan business of banks has been the increasing availability to larger business borrowers of capital market funding on favorable terms. The growth of the U.S. commercial paper market and of the short-term Eurofunds market and the market's receptivity to issues of high yield, noninvestment grade bonds, illustrate the enhanced opportunities for corporate borrowers to draw funds directly from the money and capital markets without bearing the expense of bank intermediation.

Moreover, the well publicized problems of several major U.S. banks and the related downgrading of the credit ratings of a number have increased the cost and reduced the reliability of market funding for large banks. Many of their especially valued loan customers can now draw funds from the market at rates equal or better than the banks themselves.

The competitive response of many banks to the loss of quality loan volume has been to shift their competitive focus to the middle and lower middle corporate borrowers who have less favorable or reliable access to the "arms length" markets. Naturally, this has increased competitive pressures on pricing and loan quality in this important loan market. Some have observed that "we bankers are now giving top quality terms and prices to third-rate borrowers."

Will corporate bypassing of the banks continue? In past tight money periods, the capital markets have turned unreceptive to lower quality corporate offerings. And a rash of defaults on major junk bond issues could cool the appetites of high yield bond fund managers and other once avid buyers of these securities. But the specialist investment bankers have been imaginative and ingenious in designing securities to fit changing investor needs or demands and in helping issuers adapt to shifting market conditions. Altogether, it is likely that direct market access borrowing will continue to grow, although perhaps at a slower rate, and continue to put pricing and volume pressure on bank corporate lending.

Competition for mortgage and consumer loans has also been vigorous, although perhaps less intense than in the corporate sector. The opportunities for passing along mortgage, and to a lesser degree, consumer installment credits to capital market buyers through securitization programs probably will be expanded, and exert further pressures on the pricing of these loans. Car manufacturers may well become "hooked on" discount financing as a powerful marketing tool and find it hard to cut back or abandon the practice. Altogether, it appears very likely that the competitive pressures banks face in acquiring loan assets will continue strong and will probably intensify.

THE COMPETITION FOR FUNDING

In recent years, banks generally, and big banks particularly, have developed new market funding options, instruments, and techniques on a global basis. These have helped solidify market access by banks generally despite the concerns noted earlier. They include, for example, sizeable quantities of funds from perpetual, adjustable rate preferred stock issues and from no-maturity floating rate notes that also have the merit of qualifying as primary capital.

Competition for corporate or individuals savings will deepen and broaden. Mutual funds have become active, often attractive, alternatives for affluent savers/investors and an increasingly well-informed general public. New funds to appeal to special interests or concerns of investors continue to proliferate—tax exempt money market and bond funds, ARP no-loan funds for corporations, and high yield bond funds are examples. Many offer convenience and responsivity to saver/investor needs equal to or exceeding that of bank alternatives. Life insurance companies have shown imagination and skill in developing new competitive products which combine tax sheltered investment with some liquidity and with death benefits. In raising funds from individuals banks still enjoy some shelter from full rate competition deriving from long standing relationships, habits, convenience, and the protections of federal deposit insurance. But consumer awareness of alternatives and sophistication in assessing them will surely grow and limit the capacity of banks to gather savings at rates much below those set by aggressive market competitors.

THE BOTTOM LINE—TRENDS IN INDUSTRY PROFITABILITY

Perhaps it is appropriate at this point to test our assertions of intensified competitive pressures against the recent record of bank earnings performance *and* against security market assessments of the quality and outlook for large bank's earnings as reflected in the price-earnings ratios assigned the bank earnings.

Table 1 depicts industry profitability in terms of return on assets (ROA) and return on equity (ROE). Each of these key ratios show striking declines in the four years through 1984, but a significant up-

TABLE 1 Profit Rates, All Insured Commercial Banks, 1981–85

	1981	1982	1983	1984	1985
Return on assets,* percent					
All banks	.76%	.71	.67	.64	.70
Less than $100 million	1.14	1.07	.96	.81	.70
$100 million to $1 billion	.91	.84	.84	.88	.84
$1 billion or more					
Money center banks	.53	.53	.54	.52	.45
Others	.66	.60	.54	.53	.77
Return on equity,† percent					
All banks	13.09%	12.10	11.24	10.60	11.33
Less than $100 million	13.39	12.45	11.12	9.49	8.10
$100 million to $1 billion	12.78	11.74	11.86	12.40	11.71
$1 billion or more					
Money center banks	13.57	13.27	12.57	11.42	9.61
Others	12.80	11.42	10.15	9.66	13.69

*Net income as a percent of fully consolidated net assets. Data are based on averages for call dates in December of the preceding year and in June and December of the current year. In 1984 data are based on averages for call dates at the begining and end of the year only.

†Net income as a percent of average equity capital. Data are based on averages for call dates in December of the preceding year and in June and December of the current year. In 1984 data are based on averages for call dates at the beginning and end of the year only.

SOURCE: Federal Reserve Bulletin, September 1986, p. 625.

turn in 1985, a year of falling interest rates and concomitant increases in bond values.

The breakdown of the profitability measures by size of bank shows that the 11,358 banks under $100 million in assets experienced a marked and continuing five-year decline in both ROA and ROE from levels much above the much better than industry average in the earlier years. Note that the money center banks were consistently low in ROA and, reflecting in part major additions to equity, showed a striking decline in ROE through the five years. Large regionals performed relatively well in 1985 and were largely responsible for the improvement in overall bank profitability that year.

More detailed profit and balance sheet data shows that surging provisions for loan losses to the highest levels in fifty years were a major factor in the sagging profit performance. We will examine the loan loss experience and the future outlook for loan losses at a later point.

How have bank stock investors and dealers evaluated bank earnings? The overall answer is, "with considerable caution." Throughout the years, 1981–86, investors regarded the prospects of the money

---

TABLE 2 All Insured Commercial Banks (in billions of dollars)

	1981	1982	1983	1984	1985
Loan loss provisions	5.1	8.4	10.6	13.7	17.0
Net income	14.7	14.8	15.0	15.4	17.9
Loss provision as percent of net income	35.0	57.0	71.0	89.0	95.0
Dividends paid	5.8	6.5	7.3	7.6	8.4
Loss provision as percent of dividends paid	88	129	145	180	202

SOURCE: Federal Reserve Bulletin, September 1986, pp. 618 and 624.

---

center banks particularly dimly assigning P/E multiples in the 5–7 range. The larger banks' holdings of troubled LDC debt was of continuing concern to investors. While the P/Es of particular regional banks varied widely, as a group the regionals enjoyed P/Es higher by some 50 percent than those of the money center banks.

Relative to the average P/E of the broadly based S & P 500, the P/Es of most money center banks were 50 percent of the S & P 500 average. Again regionals enjoyed greater favor, particularly in 1985–86, but even the more highly regarded regional banks have sold at PEs well below the S & P average.

Altogether, the earnings trends and market assessments support the view that the environment of the future will be one of intensive and increasingly severe competition and demanding pressures on top managements to very much more than traditional "business as usual."

BURGEONING LOAN LOSSES—TRANSITORY PHENOMENA OR CONTINUING CHALLENGE?

As noted earlier, bank provision for loan losses in 1985—the third year of an economic expansion—had surged to the highest levels in fifty years. (See Table 2.)

Over the years, net loan losses have tracked closely on a lagged basis the provision for loan losses. Net loan charge-offs in 1985 amounted to 0.86 percent of average loans. Yet the net charge-off totals do not reflect the full burden of troubled loans; interest deferrals or concessions, the special demands on officer time, and the legal expenses of collection efforts add materially to the burden of nonperforming credits. Moreover, many observers have insisted that the recognition of large potential losses in the large bank portfolios of LDC credits has as yet been inadequately reflected in their accounts.

What caused the upsurge in losses? A number of plausible explanations have emerged:

1. The numbers reflect growing portfolios of high rate credit card and other consumer loans. High loss rates are seen as a cost of doing this sort of business and will, it is hoped, be more than covered by the higher rates typically charged on these credits.
2. The loss experience reflects the competitive loss of higher quality corporate business to the money and capital markets that we discussed earlier.
3. Intense competition has led to lower credit standards and thresholds of risk acceptance.
4. Pressures on corporate borrowers toward greater use of leverage.
5. Greater inherent risks in business lending as borrowers have to contend with broader international competition, shorter product life cycles related to rapid technological change and shifts in buyer preferences, shifts from an inflationary to a relatively deflationary environment, and the related depressed conditions in such important sectors as oil and gas production and services, agriculture, mining, forest products, and real estate development.
6. Weak lending processes and controls.

An argument can be made that a coincident confluence of these negative factors caused the particularly painful 1985 and early 1986 peaks. But it must be noted that these occurred in a period of general, albeit slow, economic expansion. If, or more realistically, *when* we encounter a major economic recession, the pressures on loan quality surely will intensify. If the problem of loan quality is becoming unacceptably severe and/or chronic, what will banks do to better cope with the problem? So far no startling cures are in sight. Rather the more successful banks seem to be combining multifaceted remedial approaches. These include:

1. More intensive and sophisticated credit training that shifts the emphasis in credit analysis from the historical numbers to more demanding, forward looking industry and company competitive analysis.
2. Top management support for a strong "credit culture" that couples a rigorous credit policy and review process with top management direction that tempers loan growth and volume objectives to the realities of the market place.
3. Aggressive and well-staffed loan recovery management.
4. The avoidance of adventurism in lending, that is, leaps into unfamiliar lending areas (ala Seafirst and the oil patch) that were supported with stronger incentives for loan production than for prudence.

5. Well thought-through senior management targeting of those industries and loan types to stress or alternatively to be approached with special caution and restraint.

Until strengthened credit policies and processes produce demonstrable results, the Shakespearian advice, "In cases of defense 'tis best to weigh the enemy more mightily than he seems" seems appropriate. So we conclude that the task of maintaining loan quality will continue to be a very taxing and challenging one.

THE STRUCTURAL CHANGES AHEAD: SOME MANAGEMENT IMPLICATIONS

Sweeping changes in the structure of U.S. banking are underway. As noted earlier, *de facto* breaches in the legal barriers to interstate banking have brought a measure of interstate banking to the country for some years. Notable are the many loan production offices and Edge Act banks that have been located in other states, and the move across state lines of banks acquiring severely troubled banks and savings associations. In very recent years, regional compacts (most notably in the Southeast and in New England) have permitted acquisitions by banks in one state of banks in other states offering reciprocal privileges. By 1987, some eighteen states have provided for entry by banks from any reciprocating state. While rear guard actions may continue, it now seems highly likely that geographical restrictions will crumble in the relatively near future. How will banks generally respond? Any parallel to the Oklahoma Territory Land Rush seems remote. Banks wishing to penetrate an attractive market area will have an array of strategic options to acquisitions of strong local banks or *de novo* branching. Additional competition from early entrants into attractive areas may well dim the attractions for others. Nevertheless, it is no longer fanciful to think in terms of truly nationwide banks and banking before a decade is out.

A tide of deregulation seems in flood around the world. Important countries have joined a movement to lower barriers to entry by banks from other countries. In the U.S. and in many foreign countries, credit controls have been lifted and interest rate controls largely set aside. Remaining interest rate restrictions such as the U.S. prohibition of interest on demand deposits seem anomalous relics of the past that logically should disappear.

Recent years have also seen a major diminution in the *de jure* and *de facto* lines separating the powers and functions of commercial banks, savings banks, and savings and loan associations. Further breakdown in the distinctions between deposit-taking institutions is in prospect.

At the same time that the dismantling of legal barriers to geographical expansion has stimulated merger activities, the relaxation of once stringent, indeed unrealistic, antitrust constraints on merger activity has also encouraged major acquisition activity, such as the 1986 Wells Fargo acquisition of major rival Crocker. Those banks that have enjoyed investor regard and strong PEs are in a favored posture to acquire ("Them that has, gits" was never truer), since the favored banks have a valued currency for merger and can compete aggressively price-wise with less potential earnings dilution. Conversely, those banks with low market valuations are severely constrained in price competition for major acquisitions and indeed become vulnerable acquisition candidates. Thus, in early 1987, most money center banks have little economic incentive, given their low PEs, to pursue banks other than those that offer unusual strategic potential or where special circumstances afford interesting price/potential ratios. The Chemical-Texas Commerce deal of late 1986 may be such a case.

WILL MERGER MANIA DEVELOP?

Major mergers or acquisitions tend to stimulate further deal making. Obvious benefits to selling shareholders or other interest groups from a completed deal offer positive incentives or rationales for action by other potential players. And upset to old competitive balances (stature, share of market, etc.) encourages counter moves by managements to redress the balance. Further, the "merger game" can become a fascinating preoccupation of top management. And those highly "incentivated" merger midwives, the investment bankers, can be relied upon to produce the necessary quantitative rationale for top management's chosen moves. Combine these elements and a uniquely nonconcentrated industry, (in 1985, some three hundred banks had more than $1 billion each in assets) and one would appear to have the ingredients for a sustained burst of merger/acquisition activity, perhaps even "merger mania."

Yet there are basic constraints. The predominant evidence to date indicates that economies of scale in banking beyond a certain imprecise point are by no means automatic by-products of expansion. The premium that must be paid to accomplish most acquisition-mergers can be justified only if the acquiror can squeeze enough added benefits out of the acquired to match the premiums. These benefits usually are hard-won and achieved only by effective management action. True, the EPS burden of overpriced or underachieving small acquisitions can be buried in the acquiror's much larger totals. But many expensive small acquisitions that do not represent inherent opportunities for disproportionate earnings improvements under the new owner inevitably will prove a drag on per share earnings growth.

What will happen to the twelve thousand odd banks under $100 million in assets? To date, consolidation in this sector has been much slower than many had predicted. Several factors seem to explain the slower pace. First, the owners or managers of many smaller banks in attractive areas have believed they were in the favored bargaining position and could afford to be demanding in both their "social" and economic terms. And high prices paid in accomplished deals encourage holdout for even higher prices. At the same time, sensible acquirors have to question the economic wisdom of a higher assessment of the future value of the smaller potential acquisitions than that which the market affords their own entity. Further, it seems likely that enhanced competition and continued pressure on their earnings will put more managements of smaller banks (or their shareholders) in a mood to cash out rather than hold out. The consequent increase in the number of willing sellers and decrease in market prices could prove a major stimulant to greater acquisition activity and industry consolidation. At the same time, the past success of some strongly managed smaller banks in very competitive markets suggests that particularly well-run banks will continue to have independence as a viable alternative. But overall, pressures for consolidation on realistic terms should grow.

Perhaps more important are the legal limits on commercial bank functions, products, and activities. The largest commercial banks particularly have been chafed under Glass Steagall legislation, preventing them from competing on a broader basis with prospering investment banking counterparts. Spokesmen for these banks have urged that they be allowed to offer a full line of financial services to their corporate customers. And many other banks have expressed eagerness to broaden their offerings of financial services and to participate fully in the spate of new financial products and services. Drawing on the philosophical support for less government intervention and control, they have argued that "financial innovation and regulation make uneasy partners," and that banks were losing place to less constrained and hence, more innovative competitors.

On a practical basis, wider product scope would let the banks take fuller advantage of their computer-assisted capacity to handle large volumes of transactions efficiently and economically, of their reputation for responsibility and integrity, their FDIC-supported deposits and their unrivaled network of customer relationships.

Why then has major liberalization proceeded at such a slow and erratic pace? Reasonable explanations include the limited political appeal of liberalization. Many legislators and supervisors have not been convinced of any compelling public need or benefit to clearly outmatch possible risks of deregulation. In any case, many other issues have had higher legislative priority. Further, the growing diversity in the banking industry has made it harder for industry association leaders to muster broad industry support behind particular liberalizing proposals. For example, most of the members of the American Bankers Association have shown little support for full bank powers to underwrite corporate security issues since they see these powers as important only to a few of the largest banks. Equally or more important has been the vigorous lobbying effort by securities industry or other groups that fear the competitive entry of the banks into their preserves.

Opponents of wider bank powers, functions, and products have argued that liberalization would likely have more hazards than public policy benefits. They cite the widely reported troubles of some commercial banks as evidence that the industry has trouble enough coping within their traditional powers. Second, they suggest that the relatively high capital leverage of banks is ill-suited to bear the risks and uncertainties of new, inherently uncertain initiatives. Third, in answer to banker arguments that new powers would be carried out by nonbank subsidiaries within an overall company, they point out the demonstrated difficulties of insulating banks from customer concerns when other subsidiaries of the holding company get into trouble. Fourth, they hold that the existence of deposit-making powers and FDIC insurances gives the banks an unfair advantage over noninsured competitors in the financial services industries. Finally, they argue that new bank powers would give the banks undue economic influence and power. Without a high degree of confidence in my questimate, I project some liberalization over time but that progress will be labored, piecemeal, and painfully slow.

THE ONGOING TRANSITION FROM TRADITIONAL BANKING—KEY IMPLICATIONS FOR SENIOR/TOP MANAGEMENT

It is not at all clear that commercial banks will be able to secure the structural changes that will afford them the "level playing field" they have espoused. But surely the competitive playing field will be wider and the game faster.

An equally valid and basic observation is that the banking business is becoming more highly management intensive. That is, the effectiveness of top management in meeting the mounting demands on their leadership skills and judgment is increasingly critical to the competitive success of their banks. As one writer aptly captioned an article developing this general point, "Now Management Can Make or Break the Bank."

What particular skills of top management will prove of special importance in determining the banking winners, losers, or also rans in the environment we see ahead? A first critical area is that of coping effectively with the widening array of strategic options. The comfortable option of "business as usual" may be a viable option for some but not for many. Most banking leaders will have to choose among strategic options:

- That involve moves into the new and unfamiliar where their experience and instincts are not reliable guides to wise choice.
- That often are highly complex.
- Where the costs of mistakes are high.
- Where pressures to move with vigor and speed make cautious, "feeling your way" approaches infeasible.
- That should realistically take into account the distinctive competence and limitations of their organizations.
- That require well-considered and closely monitored programs of implementation.

The difficulties and disappointments many banks, including the largest, have had in their strategic planning efforts heighten the challenge as well as the importance of effective strategic choice.

A second critical area is that of managing innovation. Issues here include that of being a pacesetter in developing new products, services, pricing approaches, etc. versus that of an alert and discriminating follower, the pace of innovation, and the organization's capacity to implement the initiatives effectively.

Especially important will be senior management's skill in increasing the organizational agility and competitive intensity of their banks. Many, perhaps most, banks still project an image of bureaucratic ponderousness and inertia obviously ill-suited to fast-paced, hard-driving, and innovative competition. Greater effectiveness will encompass:

- Progress in customer—sensitive product design and marketing.
- Greater skill in mustering broad support within the organization for new initiatives that cut across organizational lines.
- Senior management support and skill in "making things happen" through their rewards/punishments systems.

A fourth and related testing area for management is that of adapting their traditional structures of rewards/punishments to the emerging competitive realities. Leading competitors, most notably (notoriously?) the investment bankers, have attracted and intensely motivated their key personnel with compensation schemes that are highly results-related. These directly and richly reward high performance; a bit less directly they penalize limited accomplishment. Surely competition will force the banks toward much greater use of results-oriented compensation and greater pressures on the low producers. But unless the new approaches are carefully and skillfully managed, counterproductive impacts are all too likely. These include the dissipation of strong two-way loyalties between banks and their people, unnecessary escalation of overall personnel costs, and damaged morale that will result from perceptions that the systems for measuring individual performance are capricious or unfair. Perhaps of even more concern in the potential damage to the bank's valuable reputation for creditability and fair dealing that can result from overaggressive, "hard-sell" pursuit of short-term results.

A fifth prerequisite for success is a sharpening of risk management skills. As we have noted this will be highly important in the familiar area of management of the loan portfolio. But it also encompasses the use of a variety of new techniques and approaches (options, hedges, swaps, etc.) to manage risks exposure in interest rate fluctuations, in foreign exchange, and in trading and marketmaking more broadly.

A final attribute of senior management that will prove an important determinant of success in an increasingly dynamic environment is attitudinal in nature. Earlier we have stressed the importance of strategic choices—of being deliberately and thoughtfully different in focus and direction of development. Top management must place its bets; since it takes years to fully implement a distinctive strategy, major changes in the chosen strategy are not to be made lightly. But the dynamics of an open competitive environment make it important that top management recognize the need to continually assess and reassess their strategic decisions. Mistakes are inevitable; false pride that delays needed adjustment can only court disaster. Top management's success in striking an effective balance between resolutely keeping on a strategic course and sensibly adapting to experience and an ever-changing environment will be critical to the success of their banks.

The next decade will be one of unusual opportunity and of unusual vulnerability that will challenge even the best bank managements.

GO bonds; *see* General obligation (GO) bonds
Gold, 830–31, 939–40
Government accounts, as collateral, 686
Government agency securities; *see* Federal agency securities
Governmental bonds, 529–30
Government lending agencies, 21–23
Government loans, 823
Government National Mortgage Association (GNMA), 22, 477, 500, 513–15
mortgage-backed securities, 477, 502–3, 513–15, 793, 795, 799
and secondary mortgage market, 795
Graduated-payment mortgage loans (GPMs), 513, 794
Gramm-Rudman-Hollings law, 1277–79
Great Depression
branching in, 90–91
and federal deposit insurance, 694, 1200, 1203, 1208–10
monetary policy in, 1265–66, 1268
Greenwich Research Associates, 1076
Gridley, Richard, 36
Gross national product, 828, 1285
Gross profit margin, 647–48, 655
Growing equity mortgages, 514
G-10 countries, 61
Guaranteed mortgage certificates (GMCs), 513
Guaranteed sales, 686
Guarantees of principals, 703
Guidance lines, 679
Guardianships, 1032

H
Haircut, 468
Hancock Bank, 1104–5
Hanweck, Gerald A., 198, 203
Harfield, Henry, 74
Hart, Albert G., 1268
Harvard College v. *Amory*, 1036
Haskins and Sells, 622
Haslem, John A., 199
Haug, Richard L., 400 n
Hay, Robert D., 162 n

Health, and community relations, 1178
Hedging, 304–5, 479, 539, 772
Higher Education Act of 1965, 510
High-touch banking, 1103–6
Highway bonds, 520
Historical analysis, 542
Hogan Systems, 588–91
Holt, Robert N., 202
Home banking, 576
Home equity lines of credit, 897, 902–7
Home Mortgage Disclosure Act, 1228
Home-office protection statutes, 91
Home ownership, forms of, 787–88
Horvitz, Paul M., 24 n
Hoskins, W. Lee, 1262
Hospital bonds, 521, 525, 529–30
Hot money, 199
Households, municipal bond investment by, 527–28
Housing and Urban Development Act of 1968, 513
Housing bonds, 521, 524–25, 529
Human resource management, 185–284; *see also* Management; Selection of employees; *and* Supervision of bank personnel
areas of, affected by change, 213–24
trends affecting, 209–15
for wholesale banking, 954–55
Human resources
for retail deposit services management, 882
and risk management, 441–42, 446
Humphrey, David B., 200
Humphrey-Hawkins Act, 1254

I
Iacocca, Lee, 863
Illinois Banking Department, 1234
Image of bank, 1090–91, 1166
Image processing, 593
Immunized fixed income portfolios, 1021
Implementing function, 1074
Import-Export Bank, 23–24
Imports, loans for, 824–25
In-bank displays, 1149
Incentive pay, 239, 241

Tax-exempt securities; *see also*
  Municipal bonds
  commercial paper, 475, 478
  Federal agency securities, 476
  municipal securities, 478
  and retail market, 937–38
  Treasury bills, 475–76
Tax liens, 688
Tax planning, 425–39; *see also*
  Taxation
  implementation of, 428–29
  by independent accountants, 422–
    23
  objectives of, 425–28
  and profitability, 202
  specific areas of, 430–37
Tax Reform Act of 1984, 283–84
Tax Reform Act of 1986, 202, 291,
  361
  and employee benefit services,
    1017
  and home equity lines of credit,
    906–7
  and irrevocable trusts, 1030
  and municipal bonds, 518–19,
    526, 529–31
  and tax planning, 425–37
Tax Reform Law of 1986, 202
Tax services, 422–23
Tax unit, of trust department, 1010,
  1013–14
Taylor, Frederick, 238–39
Technical analysis, 542
Technology; *see also* Computers
  and architecture, 553, 556–58
  and auditing, 407–8
  and capital planning, 333
  and deregulation, 130–31
  in economic unit model, 191–92
  electronic, and organizational
    structure, 122–23
  and financial product innovation,
    963, 969
  and human resource management,
    208, 212, 218–19
  information systems, 171, 181–83
  and marketing, 1088, 1103
  and pricing policy, 1051, 1061
  as productivity model variable,
    243–45, 248
  and profitability, 195–98, 200
  and retail banking, 852–53, 888
  and shared costs, 30

Technology—*Cont.*
  and strategy, 147–48, 155
  and supervision, 252
TEFRA deduction, 528–31
Telephone
  automated collection by, 927
  marketing research interviews by,
    1126, 1129, 1133
Television advertising, 1100, 1147–
  48, 1151
Tellers
  downgrading of, 40–41
  efficiency of, 30
  job of, 244–45
10K report; *see* Annual report
Tennessee Valley Authority (TVA),
  515–16
10Q report; *see* Quarterly report
Term bonds, 524
Term Federal funds, 294, 467
Term lending; *see* Long-term loans
Term repurchase agreements, 295
Term structure of interest rates; *see*
  Yield curve
Testamentary trusts, 1031–32
Third-party investors, as equity
  source, 746–47
Third-party liability, 443
Third World, competition from,
  212–13
33 percent wall, 571
Thrift institutions; *see* Savings and
  loan associations
Thrift plans, 1016–17
Ticor Mortgage Insurance Company,
  523
Time deposits, 15, 289–92
Timing differences, 427, 430–31,
  434
Toll road bonds, 520
Top down examinations, 1233
"Total Bank Productivity
  Measurement" (BAI), 236–37
Total rate of return, 537–38
Trademarks, 746
Trade payment period, 645–46, 655
Trading assets, and long-term
  lending, 697–98
Traditional seasonal lending; *see*
  Seasonal lending
Training, 207, 217–18, 232–34; *see*
  also Education
  credit, 618, 624–25